Physicians' Desk Reference

THIRD EDITION

PDR® 1982

For Nonprescription Drugs

Publisher • CHARLES E. BAKER, Jr.

Director of Production
JEROME M. LEVINE

Managing Editor
BARBARA B. HUFF

Medical Consultant
IRVING M. LEVITAS, M.D.

Manager of Production Services
ELIZABETH H. CARUSO

Index Editor
ADELE L. DOWD

Editorial Assistants
SUSAN CVELICH
F. EDYTHE PATERNITI

Contributing Editors
CHARLOTTE ISLER
HARLAND WADE

Business Manager
EDWARD R. BARNHART

Administrative Assistant
DIANE M. WARD

Director of Printing
RALPH G. PELUSO

Circulation Director
THOMAS S. KRAEMER

Fulfillment Manager
JAMES SCIURBA

Research Director
ALAN J. FLETCHER

Account Managers
GARY J. GYSS
JOHN R. MARMERO
DEBRA REYNOLDS

ADVISORY BOARD

Officers of Medical Economics Company Inc.: Chairman, Charles P. Daly; President, Carroll V. Dowden; Executive Vice Presidents: Thomas J. McGill, Bartlett R. Rhoades; Senior Vice President: Charles E. Baker, Jr.; Vice Presidents: Jack E. Angel, Robert T. Smith, Stephen J. Sorkenn, Kathleen A. Starke; Treasurer; Charles O. Bennewitz.

ISBN 0-87489-854-4

Foreword to the Third Edition

Responsible self-medication continues to evolve in importance in the American healthcare delivery system. Self-medication offers quick and inexpensive relief from common minor health discomforts. Additional impetus for self-medication comes from the U.S. Food and Drug Administration (FDA).

The FDA has now completed the advisory panel phase of the OTC Review—the exhaustive evaluation of the ingredients found in the more than 100,000 over-the-counter medicines (OTCs) available to the American consumer. Seventeen advisory panels have forwarded to the FDA their reports on some 73 therapeutic categories and the FDA is now studying them. Based on the reports, and on public comment offered in response to them, it will develop its own recommendations covering ingredients, dosages, combinations, and labeling.

Although it will be several years before the final phase of the OTC Review is complete, panel recommendations have been already implemented in many products. Higher dosages of some ingredients, and some ingredients formerly restricted to prescription sale are now available in OTCs. Much of the labeling also reflects recommendations of the review panels.

The prescription-to-OTC trend is expected to continue, through the OTC Review and other regulatory avenues.

PHYSICIANS' DESK REFERENCE For NONPRESCRIPTION DRUGS has been designed to satisfy the need for medical information concerning the large number of nonprescription or OTC drugs now available.

The PHYSICIANS' DESK REFERENCE For NONPRESCRIPTION DRUGS is published annually by Medical Economics Company Inc., with the cooperation of the manufacturers whose products are described in the Product Information Section. Its purpose is to make available essential information on nonprescription drugs.

The function of the Publisher is the compilation, organization, and distribution of this information. Each product description has been prepared by the manufacturer, and edited and approved by the manufacturer's medical department, medical director, and/or medical consultant. In organizing and presenting the material in PHYSICIANS' DESK REFERENCE For NONPRESCRIPTION DRUGS, the Publisher is providing all the information made available to PHYSICIANS' DESK REFERENCE For NONPRESCRIPTION DRUGS by manufacturers. Besides the information given here, additional information on any product may be obtained from the manufacturer. In making this material available it should be understood that the Publisher is not advocating the use of any product described herein.

CHARLES E. BAKER, JR.
Publisher

HOW TO USE PDR

If you want to find . . .	And you already know . . .	Here's where to look . . .
the brand name of a product	the manufacturer's name	White Section: Manufacturers' Index
	its generic name	Yellow Section: Active Ingredients Index*
the manufacturer's name	the product's brand name	Pink Section: Product Name Index*
	the product's generic name	Yellow Section: Active Ingredients Index*
essential product information, such as: active ingredients indications actions warnings drug interaction precautions symptoms & treatment of oral overdosage dosage & administration how supplied	the product's brand name	Pink Section: Product Name Index*
	the product's generic name	Yellow Section: Active ingredients Index*
a product with a particular chemical action	the chemical action	Yellow Section: Active Ingredients Index*
a product with a particular active ingredient	the active ingredient	Yellow Section: Active Ingredients Index*
a similar acting product	the product classification	Blue Section: Product Category Index*
generic name of a brand name product	the product's brand name	Pink Section: Product Name Index. Generic name will be found under "Active Ingredients" in Product Information Section.

*In the Pink, Blue and Yellow Sections, the page
numbers following the product name refer to the pages
in the Product Identification Section where the product
is pictured and the Product Information Section where
the drug is comprehensively described.*

Contents

INDEX SECTION

PRODUCT IDENTIFICATION SECTION

Capsules, tablets and packaging are shown in color as an aid to identification. Products are shown under company headings, and are not necessarily in alphabetical order since some manufacturers prefer to show their products in groups.

PRODUCT INFORMATION SECTION

An alphabetical arrangement, by manufacturer, of nonprescription drugs which are described as to action, uses, administration and dosage, precautions, the form in which supplied and other information concerning their use, including common names and chemical names.

EDUCATIONAL MATERIAL

Part 1—Books and brochures as well as other material made available by participating manufacturers.
Part 2—Organizations to contact for help with specific health problems.

Manufacturers' Index

The manufacturers whose names appear in this index have provided information concerning their products in either the Product Information or Product Identification Sections. It is through their patronage that PHYSICIANS' DESK REFERENCE For NONPRESCRIPTION DRUGS is made available to you.

Included in this index are the names and addresses of manufacturers, individuals or departments to whom you may address inquiries, a partial list of products as well as emergency telephone numbers wherever available.

The symbol ◆ indicates that the product is shown in the Product Identification Section.

PAGE

ABBOTT LABORATORIES   **403, 502**
Consumer Products Division
North Chicago, IL 60064
         (312) 937-7900
OTC Products Available
◆Clear Eyes Eye Drops
◆Ear Drops by Murine
  (See Murine Ear Wax Removal
  System/Murine Ear Drops)
◆Murine Ear Wax Removal
  System/Murine Ear Drops
◆Murine Plus Eye Drops
◆Murine Regular Formula Eye Drops
◆Selsun Blue Lotion
◆Tronolane Cream
◆Tronolane Suppositories

ABBOTT LABORATORIES—   **503**
ABBOTT PHARMACEUTICALS,
INC.
North Chicago, IL 60064
    Address inquiries to:
Medical Director   (312) 937-6100
    Distribution Centers
ATLANTA
  Stone Mountain, GA 30302
  P.O. Box 5049   (404) 491-7190
CHICAGO
  Abbott Park
  North Chicago, IL 60064
  P.O. Box 68   (312) 937-5153
DALLAS
  Dallas, TX 75265
  P.O. Box 225295   (214) 398-1350
DENVER
  Denver, CO 80217
  P.O. Box 5466   (303) 399-7576
HONOLULU
  Honolulu, HI 96819
  2815 Kilihau Street (808) 833-1691

PAGE

LOS ANGELES
  Los Angeles, CA 90060
  60162 Terminal Annex
          (213) 921-0321
MINNEAPOLIS
  Minneapolis, MN 55440
  P.O. Box 271   (612) 599-5666
PHILADELPHIA
  King of Prussia, PA 19406
  920 Eighth Ave., East
          (215) 265-9100
SEATTLE
  Seattle, WA 98124
  P.O. Box 24064   (206) 433-0164
    OTC Products Available
Optilets-500
Optilets-M-500
Surbex-750 with Iron
Surbex-750 with Zinc
Surbex-T

ADRIA LABORATORIES INC.   **504**
5000 Post Road
Dublin, OH 43017
(includes products formerly marketed
by Warren-Teed Laboratories)
    Mailing Address:
P.O. Box 16529
Columbus, OH 43216
    Address inquiries to:
Medical Department   (614) 764-8100
    OTC Products Available
Modane Bulk
Modane Plus
Modane Soft
Modane Tablets & Liquid
Myoflex Creme

PAGE

ALCON/bp   **403, 506**
Alcon Laboratories, Inc.
6201 South Freeway
P.O. Box 1959
Fort Worth, TX 76101
    OTC Products Available
◆Adapettes
◆BoilnSoak
 Clens
◆Flex-Care
◆Preflex
◆Soaclens

ALLERGAN   **403, 508**
PHARMACEUTICALS, INC.
2525 Dupont Drive
Irvine, CA 92713
    Address Inquiries to:
Customer Service   (714) 752-4500
   For Medical Emergencies Contact:
Medical Research Dept.
         (714) 752-4500
    OTC Products Available
◆Liquifilm Tears
◆Prefrin Liquifilm
◆Tears Plus

ALMAY HYPOALLERGENIC   **508**
COSMETICS & TOILETRIES
Almay Inc.
850 Third Avenue
New York, NY 10022
    Address inquiries to:
Professional Service Dept.
Apex, NC 27502   (919) 362-7422
    OTC Products Available
Balanced Makeup for
  Normal/Combination Skin
Blotting Powder for Oily Skin
Brush-On Blush

(◆ **Shown in Product Identification Section**)

Brush-On Eyeliner
Castile Shampoo
Cheq Antiperspirant/Deodorant
Cheq Extra-Dry
    Antiperspirant/Deodorant Spray
    (Aerosol)
Cheq Roll-On Antiperspirant/Deodorant
Cheq Soft Powder Extra Dry
    Antiperspirant Spray (Aerosol)
Chip Resistant Top Coat
Clean and Gentle Oil-Free Conditioner
Clear Nail Enamel
Cold Cream
Cold Cream Soap for Normal,
    Combination and Dry Skin
Conditioning Shampoo
Cover-up Stick - light, medium, dark
Cuticle Treatment Oil
Deep Mist Cleansing Cream
Deep Mist Cleansing Lotion
Deep Mist Eye Cream
Deep Mist Gentle Gel Mask
Deep Mist Moisture Cream
Deep Mist Moisture Lotion
Deep Mist Purifying Freshener
Deep Mist Purifying Toner
Deep Mist Ultralight Moisture Lotion
Deep Mist Ultralight Night Cream
Deep Mist Ultrarich Night Cream
Deep Pore Cleansing Mask
Enamel Quick Dry
Extra Cover Cream Makeup
Extra Hold Protein Conditioning Hair
    Spray (Aerosol)
Eyebrow and Liner Pencil
Eye Color Pencils
Fluffy Facial Cleanser
Gentle Cleansing Facial Soap for Dry
    Skin
Gentle Cleansing Facial Soap for
    Normal/Combination Skin
Gentle Cleansing Facial Soap for Oily
    Skin
High Gloss Nail Guard
Lengthening Mascara
Lip Color Pencils
Lip Liner Pencils
Long Wearing Eye Color
Long Wearing Eye Color Duo
Moisture Rich Lipstick (Cream &
    Frosted)
Moisture Stick
Moisturizing Eye Makeup Remover
    Pads
Moisturizing Make-Up for Dry Skin
Nail Enamel Remover
Natural Blush Cream Cheek Color
Non-Oily Eye Makeup Remover Pads
Oil Control Facial Cleanser
Oil Control Purifying Lotion
Oil-Free Make-Up
Oil-Free Moisture Lotion
Protective Base Coat
Protective Formula Nail Enamel
Protein Conditioning Hair Spray
Regular Hold Conditioning Hair Spray
Ridge Filling Pre-Coat
Skin Softening Lotion for Hands and
    Body
Thickening Mascara
Translucent Face Powder
Translucent Pressed Powder
Under Eye Cover Creme, Ivory, Natural
Waterproof Mascara

ALOE CREME   **403, 509**
LABORATORIES
a Division of ALO-SCHERER
HEALTHCARE, INC.
2313 N.W. 30th Place
Pompano Beach, FL 33060
    Address Inquiries to:
Valerie A. Thomas or Jack Girardi
P.O. Box 5847
Fort Lauderdale, FL 33310
                    (305 979-0300
    For Medical Emergencies Contact:
Mr. Jack Girardi   (305) 979-0300
    OTC Products Available
◆Alo-Lip-Shield
◆Alo-Ointment
◆Alo-Relief

◆Alo-Sun Fashion Tan SPF 15 Sun Block
    Lotion
Alo-Sun SPF 15 Sun Block Stick

ALTO PHARMACEUTICALS,   404, 509
INC.
P.O. Box 271369
Tampa, FL 33688
    Address Inquiries to:
John J. Cullaro   (813) 961-1010
    OTC Products Available
Akne Drying Lotion
◆Efed II Capsules
Zinc-220 Capsules

AMES DIVISION, Miles   404, 509
Laboratories, Inc.
P.O. Box 70
Elkhart, IN 46515
    Address Inquiries to:
Customer Services   (219) 264-8901
    For Medical Emergencies Contact:
Medical Department   (219) 264-8444
    After Hours   (219) 264-8111
    OTC Products Available
◆Microstix-Nitrite Kit

ANABOLIC LABORATORIES, INC.   510
17802 Gillette Avenue
Irvine, CA 92714
    Address inquiries to:
Georgiana Hennessy   (714) 546-8901
    OTC Products Available
Ana-Pro (protein products)
Aqua-A
Aved-Eze
Aved-Gest
Aved-M
B6-Plus
B12-Plus
CPA
Cal-M
Calpadon
Cholagest
Chromease
Dermagen
Digestaid
Diu-Erb
Enhance (Vitamin E Topicals)
Flexamide
Hy-C-3000
Hyper-E
I-O-Plexadine
Immunase
K-Orotate
Lax Special
Lipall-Plus
Lysamin-C
Nutra-Cal
O-A-Crine
Osatate
Pro-Enz
Prostana
Sedaphan
Selenace
Sofn
Tercopan
Tri-88
Tri-Adrenopan
Tri-B3
Tri-B-Plex
Tri-C-500
Tryptophan-250
Vasotate
Vitamin C Wafer
Zinotate

ARCO PHARMACEUTICALS, INC.   511
105 Orville Drive
Bohemia, NY 11716
    Address inquiries to:
Professional Service Dept.
                    (516) 567-9500
    OTC Products Available
Arco-Cee Tablets
Arco-Lase Tablets
Arcoret Tablets
Arcoret w/Iron Tablets
Arcotinic Tablets
Codexin Extra Strength Capsules
Co-Gel Tablets
Mega-B
Megadose

B. F. ASCHER & COMPANY, INC.   511
15501 West 109th Street
Lenexa, KS 66219
Mailing Address: P.O. Box 827
Kansas City, MO 64141
    Address inquiries to:
Joan Bowen Nash   (913) 888-1880
    For Medical Emergencies Contact:
Michael Adams, Pharm D.
                    (913) 888-1880
    OTC Products Available
Ayr Saline Nasal Drops
Ayr Saline Nasal Mist
Dalca Decongestant/Analgesic Tablets
Mobigesic Analgesic Tablets
Mobisyl Analgesic Creme
Soft 'N Soothe Anti-Itch Creme
Unilax Laxatives Tablets

ASTRA PHARMACEUTICAL   404, 513
PRODUCTS, INC.
7 Neponset Street
Worcester, MA 01606
    Address inquiries to:
Roy E. Hayward, Jr. (617) 852-6351
    For Medical Emergencies Contact:
Dr. Joseph C. Oakley (617) 852-6351
    OTC Products Available
◆Xylocaine Cream
◆Xylocaine Ointment 2.5%

AYERST LABORATORIES   404, 513
Division of American Home Products
Corp.
685 Third Ave.
New York, NY 10017
    For Medical Information
Business hours only (9:00 A.M. to
    5:00 P.M.), call   (212) 878-5900
    For Medical Emergency Information
After hours or on weekends, call
    (212) 986-1000; (212) 878-5000;
    or
    (212) 878-5900
    Regional Sales Offices
Burlingame, CA 94010
    Suite 100
    840 Hinckley Road (415) 692-4258
Chamblee, GA (Atlanta) 30341
    3600 American Drive
                    (404) 451-9578
Rockville, MD 20852
    6252 Montrose Rd. (301) 984-9140
Chicago, IL 60648
    7545 N. Natchez Ave.
                    (312) 647-8948
Lakewood, OH 44107
    Suite 795
    14701 Detroit Ave. (216) 226-4128
Los Angeles, CA 90061
    12833 S. Spring St.
                    (213) 321-5550/1/2
Mesquite, TX (Dallas) 75149
    3601 Executive Blvd.
                    (214) 285-8741
South Plainfield, NJ 07080
    4000 Hadley Rd.
                    (201) 754-6220(NJ)
                    (212) 964-3903(NY)
    Distribution Centers
Chamblee, GA 30341
    3600 American Dr. (404) 457-2518
Chicago, IL 60648
    7545 N. Natchez Ave.
                    (312) 763-0888 (Chicago)
    (312) 647-8840 or 8841 (Niles)
Cleveland, OH 44135
    15620 Industrial Pky.
                    (216) 267-9090
Lenexa, KS 66210
    10700 Pflumm Rd. (913) 888-4310
Los Angeles, CA 90061
    12833 S. Spring St.
                    (213) 321-5550/1/2
Mesquite, TX 75149
    3601 Executive Blvd.
                    (214) 285-8741
Seattle, WA 98188
    405 Baker Blvd., Andover Park
                    (206) 244-1921
South Plainfield, NJ 07080
4000 Hadley Rd.(201) 754-6220 (NJ)
                    (212) 964-3903 (NY)

(◆ Shown in Product Identification Section)

OTC Products Available
Beminal-500
Beminal Forte w/Vitamin C
Beminal Fortified w/Iron & Liver
Beminal Stress Plus
◆Beminal Stress Plus with Iron
◆Beminal Stress Plus with Zinc
Clusivol Capsules & Syrup
Clusivol 130 Tablets
Cytoferin Hematinic Tablets
◆Dermoplast
Enzactin Cream
◆Kerodex Cream 51 (for dry or oily work)
◆Kerodex Cream 71 (for wet work)
Larylgan Throat Spray
Riopan Antacid Chew Tablets
◆Riopan Antacid Suspension
◆Riopan Antacid Swallow Tablets
Riopan Plus Chew Tablets
◆Riopan Plus Suspension

BAKER/CUMMINS 514
Div. of Key Pharmaceuticals, Inc.
50 N.W. 176th Street
Miami, FL   (305) 652-2276
OTC Products Available
Acno Astringent
Acno Lotion
P&S Liquid
P&S Plus
P&S Shampoo
Panscol
Ultra Mide Moisturizer Lotion
Xseb Shampoo
Xseb-T Shampoo

BAUSCH & LOMB, INC.   404, 515
Personal Products Division
1400 N. Goodman St.
Rochester, NY 14692
Address Inquiries to:
Customer Service   (800) 828-9030
OTC Products Available
◆Bausch & Lomb Sterile Daily Cleaner
◆Bausch & Lomb Sterile Disinfecting Solution
◆Bausch & Lomb Sterile Lens Lubricant
◆Bausch & Lomb Sterile Preserved Saline Solution
◆Bausch & Lomb Sterile Saline Solution

BEACH PHARMACEUTICALS 516
Division of Beach Products, Inc.
Executive Office
5220 S. Manhattan Ave.
Tampa, FL 33611   (813) 839-6565
Manufacturing and Distribution
Main St. at Perimeter Rd.
Conestee, SC 29605
Toll Free 1-(800) 845-8210
Address inquiries to:
Raymond LaForge, Ph.D.
(803) 277-7282
Richard Stephen Jenkins
(813) 839-6565
OTC Products Available
Beelith Tablets
Fer-Bid Improved

BECTON DICKINSON CONSUMER 516
PRODUCTS
365 W. Passaic Street
Rochelle Park, NJ 07662
Address inquiries to:
Allen C. Foster   (201) 368-7324
For Medical Emergencies Contact:
Dr. T.J. Medrek   (201) 628-9600
OTC Products Available
Cankaid
Mercurochrome II

BEECHAM PRODUCTS 517
P.O. Box 1467
Pittsburgh, PA 15230
Address inquiries to:
Professional Services Dept.
(412) 928-1050
OTC Products Available
B.F.I. Antiseptic First-Aid Powder
Children's Hold
Cuprex

Eno Sparkling Antacid
Hold
Massengill Disposable Douche
Massengill Disposable Medicated Douche
Massengill Liquid Concentrate
Massengill Powder
S.T. 37
Scott's Emulsion
Sucrets (Regular, Mentholated & Children's Cherry)
Sucrets—Cold Decongestant Formula
Sucrets Cough Control Formula
Thermotabs

BEIERSDORF, INC.   405, 519
Duke Place
South Norwalk, CT 06854
Address Inquiries to:
Mr. Chauncey O. Johnstone
(203) 853-8008
For Medical Emergencies Contact:
Mr. Frank Madaio, R.Ph.
(203) 853-8008
Branch Offices
Bell, CA 90201
5651 Rickenbacker Rd.
(213) 264-7042
OTC Products Available
Aquaphor
Coverlet
Coverlet Eye Occlusor
Elastoplast
◆Eucerin Creme
◆Eucerin Lotion
Gelocast
◆Mediplast

BLAIR LABORATORIES, INC.   520
Affiliate, The Purdue Frederick Company
50 Washington Street
Norwalk, CT 06856 (203) 853-0123
OTC Products Available
Calamatum Lotion, Ointment, Spray
Isodine Antiseptic
Kerid Ear Drops

BLOCK DRUG COMPANY, INC.   521
257 Cornelison Avenue
Jersey City, NJ 07302
Address inquiries to:
Barbara Ripianzi   (201) 434-3000
For Medical Emergencies Contact:
T. Treitler   (201) 434-3000
OTC Products Available
Sensodyne Toothpaste
Tegrin for Psoriasis Lotion & Cream
Tegrin Medicated Shampoo

BOEHRINGER INGELHEIM   405, 521
LTD.
90 East Ridge
P.O. Box 368
Ridgefield, CT 06877
Address inquiries to:
Medical Services Dept.
(203) 438-0311
OTC Products Available
◆Dulcolax Suppositories
◆Dulcolax Tablets

BREON LABORATORIES   405, 522
INC.
90 Park Ave.
New York, NY 10016
Address inquiries to:
Medical Department (212) 972-6316
Main Office
90 Park Avenue
New York, NY 10016 (212) 972-4141
OTC Products Available
◆Breonesin Capsules
Fergon Capsules
Fergon Elixir
Fergon Tablets
Measurin Tablets

BRISTOL LABORATORIES   523
(Div. of Bristol-Myers Co.)
Thompson Rd. P.O. Box 657
Syracuse, NY 13201 (315) 432-2000
Address medical inquiries to:
Dept. of Medical Services
(315) 432-2838 or (315) 432-2000
Orders may be placed by calling the following toll free numbers:
Within New York State
1-(800) 962-7200
Continental U.S.   1-(800) 448-7700
Alaska - Hawaii   1-(800) 448-1100
Mail orders and all inquiries should be sent to:
Bristol Laboratories
Order Entry Department
P.O. Box 657
Syracuse, NY 13201
OTC Products Available
Naldecon-CX Suspension
Naldecon-DX Pediatric Syrup
Naldecon-EX Pediatric Drops

BRISTOL-MYERS PRODUCTS   405, 524
(Div. of Bristol-Myers Co.)
345 Park Avenue
New York, NY 10154
Address inquiries to:
Dr. Ruth M. Palmes   (212) 546-4744
OTC Products Available
Ammens Medicated Powder
◆Arthritis Strength Bufferin Analgesic
B.Q Cold Tablets
Ban Basic Antiperspirant
Ban Big Ball Antiperspirant
Ban Cream Antiperspirant
Ban Roll-on Antiperspirant
Ban Super Solid Antiperspirant
Body on Tap
◆Bufferin Analgesic
◆Comtrex Capsules
◆Comtrex Liquid
◆Comtrex Tablets
◆Congespirin Cold Tablets
Congespirin Cough Syrup
◆Congespirin Liquid Cold Medicine
◆Datril Acetaminophen Tablets
◆Datril 500 Acetaminophen Tablets
◆Excedrin Analgesic Capsules & Tablets
◆Excedrin P.M. Analgesic Tablets
◆Extra-Strength Bufferin Capsules & Tablets
◆4-Way Cold Tablets
◆4-Way Long Acting Mentholated Nasal Spray
◆4-Way Long Acting Nasal Spray
◆4-Way Mentholated Nasal Spray
◆4-Way Nasal Spray
Minit-Rub Analgesic Balm
Multi-Scrub Everyday Scrubbing Lotion with Particles
Multi-Scrub Medicated Cleansing Scrub
Mum Cream Deodorant
◆No Doz Keep Alert Tablets
Pazo Hemorrhoid Ointment/ Suppositories
Sal Hepatica Laxative
Score Hair Cream
Tickle Antiperspirant
Ultra Ban Roll-on
Ultra Ban Solid Antiperspirant
Ultra Ban II Antiperspirant
Vitalis Dry Control Hair Groom
Vitalis Dry Texture Hair Groom
Vitalis Hair Groom Liquid
Vitalis Hair Groom Tube
Vitalis Regular Hold Hair Spray
Vitalis Super Hold Hair Spray

BURROUGHS WELLCOME   406, 527
CO.
3030 Cornwallis Road
Research Triangle Park, NC 27709
Address Inquiries to:
Mr. C. A. Parish, Jr.   (919) 541-9090
Branch Offices
Burlingame, CA 94010
1760 Rollins Rd.   (415) 697-5630

(◆ Shown in Product Identification Section)

OTC Products Available
Borofax Ointment
◆Empirin
Marezine Tablets
◆Neosporin Ointment
Polysporin Ointment
◆Sudafed Cough Syrup
◆Sudafed Plus Tablets & Syrup
◆Sudafed S.A. Capsules
◆Sudafed Tablets and Syrup
◆Sudafed Tablets, Adult Strength
Wellcome Lanoline
◆Wellcortin Cream and Lotion
◆Wellcortin Ointment
Zincofax Skin Cream

CAMBRIDGE PLAN 407, 529
INTERNATIONAL
World Headquarters
Garden Road
Monterey, CA 93940
Address Inquiries to:
Jim Coover, Executive Vice President
(408) 646-9933
For Medical Emergencies Contact:
Vaughn Feather, President
(408) 646-1851
OTC Products Available
◆The Cambridge Diet Plan

CAMPBELL LABORATORIES, INC. 529
300 East 51st Street
New York, NY 10022 (212) 688-7684
Address Inquiries to:
Richard C. Zahn, President
P.O. Box 812, FDR Station
New York, NY 10150
OTC Products Available
Herpecin-L Cold Sore Lip Balm

CARNATION COMPANY 530
5045 Wilshire Blvd.
Los Angeles, CA 90036
Address inquiries to:
Ron Scott (213) 932-6535
OTC Products Available
Carnation Instant Breakfast
Carnation Instant Nonfat Dry Milk
Slender Diet Food For Weight Control
(Instant)
Slender Diet Meal Bars For Weight
Control
Slender Diet Meal For Weight Control
(Canned)

CARTER PRODUCTS 407, 531
Division of Carter-Wallace, Inc.
767 Fifth Avenue
New York, NY 10153 (212) 758-4500
OTC Products Available
◆Answer At-Home Early Pregnancy Test
Kit
◆Carter's Little Pills

CETYLITE INDUSTRIES, INC. 532
9051 River Road
Pennsauken, NJ 08110
Address inquiries to:
Mr. S. Wachman (609) 665-6111
OTC Products Available
Protexin Oral Rinse
Skin Screen

CHATTEM LABORATORIES 407, 532
Division of Chattem, Inc.
1715 West 38th Street
Chattanooga, TN 37409
Address Inquiries to:
Peter S. Iorio (615) 821-4571
OTC Products Available
Black-Draught Granulated
Black-Draught Syrup
Black-Draught Tablets
Blis-To-Sol Liquid
Blis-To-Sol Powder
◆Pamprin Capsules
◆Pamprin Tablets
Soltice Quick-Rub

CHESEBROUGH-POND'S 407, 534
INC.
33 Benedict Place
Greenwich, CT 06830

Address Inquiries to:
Paul B. Koehler, M.D.
(203) 377-7100
For Medical Emergencies Contact:
Paul B. Koehler, M.D.
(203) 377-7100
OTC Products Available
◆Vaseline Dermatology Formula Cream
◆Vaseline Dermatology Formula Lotion
◆Vaseline Pure Petroleum Jelly Skin
Protectant

CHURCH & DWIGHT CO., INC. 534
20 Kings Bridge Road
Piscataway, NJ 08854
Address Inquiries to:
Mr. Richard K. Lehne (201) 885-1220
Branch Offices
Arlington Hgts., IL 60005
121 S. Wilke Rd. (312) 398-2397
Dallas, TX 75234
4445 Alpha Rd. (214) 386-0053
Atlanta, GA 30329
2250 N. Druid Hills Rd., N.E.
(404) 633-8161
Memphis, TN 38132
2600 Nonconnah Blvd.
(901) 345-2640
Huntington Beach, CA 92649
15236 Transistor Lane
(714) 895-1088
OTC Products Available
Arm & Hammer Baking Soda

CIBA PHARMACEUTICAL 407, 534
COMPANY
Div. of CIBA-GEIGY Corporation
556 Morris Avenue
Summit, NJ 07901 (201) 277-5000
Shipping Branches
Eastern
14 Henderson Drive
West Caldwell, NJ 07006
(201) 575-6510
Central
7530 North Natchez Ave.
Niles, IL 60648 (312) 647-9332
Chicago, IL (312) 763-8700
Western
12850 Moore Street
Cerritos, CA 90701 (213) 404-2651
OTC Products Available
◆Nupercainal Cream & Ointment
◆Nupercainal Suppositories
◆Privine Nasal Solution
◆Privine Nasal Spray
Vioform Cream & Ointment

COLGATE-PALMOLIVE 407, 535
COMPANY
A Delaware Corporation
300 Park Avenue
New York, NY 10022
Address inquiries to:
Consumers:
Consumer Affairs
300 Park Avenue
New York, NY 10022
(212) 751-1200
Physicians:
Medical Director
909 River Road
Piscataway, NJ 08854
(201) 463-1212
For Medical Emergencies Contact:
9 AM to 5 PM (201) 463-1212
5 PM to 9 AM (201) 547-2500
OTC Products Available
Colgate Dental Cream
◆Colgate MFP Fluoride Gel
◆Colgate MFP Fluoride Toothpaste
Colgate Toothbrushes
Curad Bandages
Dermassage Dish Liquid
◆Dermassage Medicated Skin Lotion
◆Fluorigard Anti-Cavity Dental Rinse
Mersene Denture Cleanser
Ultra Brite Toothpaste

COMBE INCORPORATED 408, 536
1101 Westchester Avenue
White Plains, NY 10604

Address inquiries to:
Teresa C. Infantino (914) 694-5454
For Medical Emergencies Contact:
Mark K. Taylor (914) 694-5454
OTC Products Available
◆Gynecort Antipruritic 0.5%
Hydrocortisone Acetate Creme
Lanacane Medicated Creme
Lanacort Antipruritic Hydrocortisone
Acetate 0.5% Creme
◆Vagisil Feminine Itching Medication

CONSOLIDATED CHEMICAL, INC 537
Healthcare Products Division
3224 S. Kingshighway
St. Louis, MO 63139
Address Inquiries to:
J.A. Brereton, Pres. (314) 772-4610
For Medical Emergencies Contact:
Kiff Barnds, V-Pres. (314) 772-4610
OTC Products Available
CC-500 Body Wash and Shampoo
Concept Skin and Hair Cleanser
Consol Concentrate Skin Cleanser
Formula Magic Lubricating Body Talc
GCP Shampoo, Geriatric Shampoo
Loving Lather Professional Hand
Cleanser
New Consol "20" Skin Cleanser
Perineal/Ostomy Skin Cleanser
Satin Body Wash and Shampoo
Shower Team Body Wash and Shampoo
Skin Magic Lotion
Swirlsoft Whirlpool Moisturizer Additive

CREIGHTON PRODUCTS 409, 537
CORPORATION
a Sandoz Company
(see also Ex-Lax Pharmaceutical Co.,
Inc.)
605 Third Avenue
New York NY 10158
Address inquiries to:
M.H. Bedrick (212) 687-7575
OTC Products Available
◆BiCozene Creme
◆Derma+Soft Creme
◆Gas-X Tablets

DAYWELL LABORATORIES 538
CORPORATION
78 Unquowa Place
Fairfield, CT 06430
Address inquiries to:
Judge J. H. Norton (203) 255-3154
OTC Products Available
Vergo Cream

DERMA LABS, INC. 538
802 Easy Street
P.O. Box 40266
Garland, Texas 75042
Address Inquiries to:
Bill C. Coats, R.Ph. (214) 494-6565
OTC Products Available
Hydrostat Lotion

DERMIK LABORATORIES, INC. 538
1777 Walton Road, Dublin Hall
Blue Bell, PA 19422
Address inquiries to:
A.M. Packman, V.P. &
Technical Director (215) 752-1211
Distribution Centers
Hammond, IN 46320
2500 165th Street (219) 845-1677
Langhorne, PA 19047
P.O. Box 247 (215) 752-1211
San Leandro, CA 94577
1550 Factor Avenue
P.O. Box 1569 (415) 357-9741
Tucker, GA 30084
4660 Hammermill Road
(404) 934-3091
OTC Products Available
Fomac Foam
Hytone Cream & Ointment½%
Loroxide Acne Lotion (Flesh Tinted)
Shepard's Formulations for Dry Skin
Care
Shepard's Cream Lotion
Shepard's Dry Skin Cream
Shepard's Hand Cream
Shepard's Soap

(◆ **Shown in Product Identification Section**)

Vanoxide Acne Lotion
Vlemasque Acne Mask
Zetar Shampoo

DEWITT INTERNATIONAL CORPORATION
408, 539

5 N. Watson Road
Taylors, SC 29687
Address inquiries to:
Bud Templeton   (803) 244-8521
For Medical Emergencies Contact:
Ron Romano   (803) 244-8521
OTC Products Available
DeWitt's Absorbent Rub
DeWitt's Alertacaps
DeWitt's Antacid Powder
DeWitt's Aspirin
DeWitt's B Complex W/Vit. C Capsules
DeWitt's Baby Cough Syrup
DeWitt's Boric Acid Solution
DeWitt's Calamine Lotion
DeWitt's Camphor Liniment
DeWitt's Camphor Spirits
DeWitt's Carbolized Witch Hazel Salve
DeWitt's Castor Oil
DeWitt's Children's Aspirin
DeWitt's Cold Capsules
DeWitt's Cold Sore Lotion
DeWitt's Creosant Cough Syrup
DeWitt's Feet Treat
DeWitt's Flowaway Tablets
DeWitt's Glycerin
DeWitt's Glycerin & Rosewater
DeWitt's Gumzor
DeWitt's Iodine
DeWitt's Joggers Lotion
DeWitt's Merthiolate
DeWitt's Multi Vitamins
DeWitt's Multi Vit./Iron
DeWitt's Oil for Ear Use
DeWitt's Oil of Cloves
DeWitt's Oil of Wintergreen
DeWitt's Olive Oil
◆DeWitt's Pills for Backache & Joint Pains
DeWitt's Pyrinyl
DeWitt's Secta Sooth Ampules
DeWitt's Spirit of Peppermint
DeWitt's Sweet Oil
DeWitt's Teething Lotion
DeWitt's Terpin Hydrate w/D.M.
DeWitt's Thera-M Vitamins
DeWitt's Toothache Drops
DeWitt's Turpentine
DeWitt's Vit. C 250 mg. Chewable Tablets
DeWitt's Vit. C 250 mg. Tablets
DeWitt's Vit. C 500 mg. Tablets
DeWitt's Vit. E 200 I.U. Capsules
DeWitt's Vit. E 400 I.U. Capsules
DeWitt's Vit. E 1000 I.U. Capsules
DeWitt's Zoo Chews Vitamins
DeWitt's Zoo Chews w/Iron Vitamins
HTO Stainless Manzan Hemorrhoidal Tissue Ointment

THE E. E. DICKINSON CO.
408, 540

40-46 No. Main Street
Essex, CT 06426
Address Inquiries to:
Linda C. Patterson   (203) 767-8261
OTC Products Available
◆E. E. Dickinson's Witch Hazel
◆E. E. Dickinson's Witch Hazel Towelettes

DOAK PHARMACAL CO., INC.
408, 540

700 Shames Drive
Westbury, NY 11590
Address Inquiries to:
Director of Physician Services
     (516) 333-7222
Branch Offices
Vernon, CA 90058   (213) 583-8981
Obergfel Brothers
2660 East 37th Street
OTC Products Available
Doak Oil
Doak Oil Forte
◆Doak Tar Lotion
◆Doak Tar Shampoo
◆Formula 405 Skin Care Products

Enriched Cream
Eye Cream
Light Textured Moisturizer
Moisturizing Lotion
Moisturizing Soap
Skin Cleanser & Patented Buffing Mit
Solar Cream
Therapeutic Bath Oil
Lavatar Tar Bath
Tarpaste
◆Tersaseptic Hygienic Skin Cleanser

DORSEY LABORATORIES
408, 541

Division of Sandoz, Inc.
P.O. Box 83288
Lincoln, NE 68501
Address inquiries to:
Medical Affairs
Sandoz, Inc.
E. Hanover, N.J. 07936
     (201) 386-7500
OTC Products Available
◆Acid Mantle Creme & Lotion
◆Cama Inlay-Tabs
Chexit Tablets
◆Dorcol Pediatric Cough Syrup
Kanulase Tablets
◆Triaminic Expectorant
◆Triaminic Syrup
◆Triaminic-DM Cough Formula
◆Triaminic-12 Sustained Release Tablets
Triaminicin Chewables
◆Triaminicin Tablets
◆Triaminicol Decongestant Cough Syrup
Tussagesic Tablets & Suspension
Ursinus Inlay-Tabs

ENDO LABORATORIES, INC.
409, 543

Sub. of the DuPont Company
One Rodney Square
Wilmington, DE 19898
Address inquiries to:
Director, Professional Services
     (302) 773-3657
Emergency No.   (302) 773-3657
Branch Offices
Chicago, IL 60641
4956 W. Belmont Ave.
     (312) 282-0440
Los Angeles, CA 90064
11400 W. Olympic Blvd.
     (213) 272-7153
Garden City, NY 11530
1000 Stewart Ave.
     (516) 832-2210
OTC Products Available
◆Percogesic Tablets

EX-LAX PHARMACEUTICAL CO., INC.
409, 543

a Sandoz Company
(see also Creighton Products Corporation)
605 Third Avenue
New York, NY 10158
Address inquiries to:
M.H. Bedrick   (212) 687-7575
OTC Products Available
◆Ex-Lax Chocolated Laxative
◆Ex-Lax Pills, Unflavored

FLEETWOOD COMPANY
409, 544

1500 Brook Drive
Downers Grove, IL 60515
Address inquiries to:
Nelson J. McMahon   (312) 495-9300
or Donald R. Kloss   (312) 495-9300
OTC Products Available
Fayd Skin Cream
Fleetwood's Red Label Iron Tonic
◆Super Wate-On Emulsion
Super Wate-On Shake Mix
Super Wate-On Tablets
Tintz Cream Color Shampoo
Wate-Off Shake Mix
Wate-On Emulsion
◆Wate-On Tablets

FLEMING & COMPANY
544

1600 Fenpark Dr.
Fenton, MO 63026

Address inquiries to:
John J. Roth, M.D.   (314) 343-8200
OTC Products Available
Impregon Concentrate
Magonate Tablets
Marblen Suspension Peach/Apricot
Marblen Suspension Unflavored
Marblen Tablets
Nephrox Suspension
Nicotinex Elixir
Ocean Nasal Mist
Purge Concentrate

FOREVER LIVING PRODUCTS, INC.
409, 545

P.O. Box 20491
Phoenix, AZ 85038
OTC Products Available
Aloe Activator
Aloe Cleansing Lotion
Aloe Heat Lotion
Aloe Jojoba Shampoo
Aloe Lotion
Aloe Mask Powder
Aloe Moisturizing Lotion
Aloe Suntan Lotion
◆Aloe Vera Gelly
◆Aloe Vera Juice

FOX PHARMACAL, INC.
545

1750 W. McNab Road
Ft. Lauderdale, FL 33310
Address inquiries to:
Sandra Cook   (305) 971-4100
OTC Products Available
E-Z Trim
Odrinil
Super Odrinex

G & W LABORATORIES, INC.
545

111 Coolidge Street
South Plainfield, NJ 07080
Address inquiries to:
Customer Service Dept.
     (201) 753-2000
OTC Products Available
Acephen Acetaminophen Rectal Suppositories
Aspirin Suppositories
Bisacodyl Suppositories
Hemorrhoidal Rectal Ointment
Hemorrhoidal Suppositories
Hem-Prep Combo
Sani-Supp Foil Wrapped Glycerin Suppositories

GEIGY PHARMACEUTICALS
409, 546

Div. of CIBA-GEIGY Corporation
Ardsley, NY 10502   (201) 277-5000
OTC Products Available
◆Otrivin Nasal Spray & Nasal Drops
◆Otrivin Pediatric Nasal Drops
◆PBZ Cream

GERBER PRODUCTS COMPANY
546

Fremont, MI 49412   (616) 928-2000
Address inquiries to:
Professional Communications Dept.
OTC Products Available
Gerber Biscuits
Gerber Cereals
Barley Cereal
Cereals with Fruit
High Protein Cereal
Mixed Cereal
Oatmeal Cereal
Rice Cereal
Gerber High Meat Dinners (Strained & Junior)
Gerber Junior Cookies
Gerber Junior Foods
Gerber Junior Meats
Gerber Strained Egg Yolks
Gerber Strained Food
Gerber Strained Juices
Gerber Strained Meats
Gerber Toddler Meals
MBF (Meat Base Formula) Liquid

GLENBROOK LABORATORIES
409, 547

Division of Sterling Drug Inc.
90 Park Avenue
New York, NY 10016

(◆ Shown in Product Identification Section)

Address inquiries to:
Medical Director　　(212) 972-4141
OTC Products Available
◆Bayer Aspirin
◆Bayer Children's Chewable Aspirin
　Bayer Children's Cold Tablets
　Bayer Cough Syrup for Children
◆Bayer Timed-Release Aspirin
◆Diaparene Baby Powder
◆Diaparene Baby Wash Cloths
◆Midol
◆Phillip's Milk of Magnesia
　Vanquish

**GOODY'S MANUFACTURING　410, 548
CORPORATION**
436 Salt Street
Winston-Salem, NC 27108
Address inquiries to:
T.H. Chambers　　(919) 723-1831
OTC Products Available
Goody's Extra Strength Tablets
◆Goody's Headache Powders
Sayman Soaps & Salves

**HEALTH CARE INDUSTRIES,　410, 549
INC.**
Division of Accra Pac, Inc.
2825 Middlebury Street
Elkhart, IN 46515
Address inquiries to:
Walter Tuman, RPh. PhD. or
Roland C. Zagnoli, RPh.
　　　　　　(219) 295-0000
OTC Products Available
◆Allimin Filmcoated Tablets
◆Cosanyl Cough Syrup
◆Cosanyl-DM Cough Syrup
◆Oil-O-Sol Liquid

HERBERT LABORATORIES　410, 550
Dermatology Division of Allergan
Pharmaceuticals, Inc.
2525 DuPont Drive
Irvine, CA 92713　　(714) 752-4500
OTC Products Available
Aquacare Dry Skin Cream & Lotion
Aquacare/HP Dry Skin Cream & Lotion
Blueboro Powder Astringent Soaking
　Solution
Clear By Design Acne Gel
Danex Protein Enriched Dandruff
　Shampoo
Eclipse After Sun Lotion
Eclipse Sunscreen Lip & Face
　Protectant
Eclipse Sunscreen Lotion & Gel,
　Original
◆Eclipse Sunscreen Lotion, Total (Alcohol
　Base)
◆Eclipse Sunscreen Lotion, Total
　(Moisturizing Base)
Eclipse Suntan Lotion, Partial
Vanseb Cream & Lotion Dandruff
　Shampoo
Vanseb-T Cream & Lotion Dandruff
　Shampoo

**HOECHST-ROUSSEL　410, 550
PHARMACEUTICALS INC.**
Routes 202-206 North
Somerville, NJ 08876
Address inquiries to:
Manager, Scientific Services
　　　　　　(201) 231-2611
For Medical Emergencies Contact:
Medical Department　(201) 231-2000
OTC Products Available
◆Doxidan
◆Festal
◆Surfak

**HOLLAND-RANTOS COMPANY,　551
INC.**
Post Office Box 385
865 Centennial Avenue
Piscataway, NJ 08854
See YOUNGS DRUGS PRODUCTS
CORPORATION

**HYNSON, WESTCOTT　410, 551
& DUNNING**
Division of Becton Dickinson and Co.
Charles & Chase Streets
Baltimore, MD 21201(301) 837-0890
OTC Products Available
◆Lactinex Tablets & Granules
　Thantis Lozenges

**JOHNSON & JOHNSON　410, 551
BABY PRODUCTS
COMPANY**
Grandview Road
Skillman, NJ 08558
For Medical Emergencies Contact:
Z. Frann Krajeski, R.N., B.S.N.
　　　　　　(201) 874-1456
OTC Products Available
◆Johnson's Baby Bath
◆Sundown Sunscreen
　Moderate Protection
　Extra Protection
　Maximal Protection
　Ultra Protection

**JOHNSON & JOHNSON　410, 552
PRODUCTS,
INCORPORATED**
501 George Street
New Brunswick, NJ 08903
Address inquiries to:
Information Center
Call Toll Free 10AM-4PM EST Mon-Fri
In Cont. USA　　(800) 526-2459
In New Jersey　　(800) 352-4845
For Medical Emergencies Contact:
Dr. H.L. Dickstein
　　office hours: (201) 524-5125
　　after hours: (609) 799-3675
OTC Products Available
◆Johnson & Johnson First Aid Cream

KREMERS-URBAN COMPANY　552
P.O. Box 2038
Milwaukee, WI 53201
Address inquiries to:
Professional Service Dept.
　　　　　　(414) 354-4300
OTC Products Available
Kudrox Suspension (Double Strength)
Milkinol

THE LANNETT COMPANY, INC.　552
9000 State Road
Philadelphia, PA 19136
Address inquiries to:
Medical Service Dept. (215) 333-9000
OTC Products Available
Acetaminophen Tablets & Elixir
Acnederm Lotion & Soap
Alphamul
Anulan Suppositories
Bellafedrol AH Tablets
Castaderm
Cebralan MT Tablets
Decavitamin Tablets
Disanthrol Capsules
Disodan Capsules
Disolan Capsules
Disonate Capsules
Disoplex Capsules
Lanamins
Lanatuss Expectorant
Lycolan Elixir
Magnatril Suspension & Tablets
Prelan Tablets
S-A-C Tablets
Salagen Tablets

LEDERLE LABORATORIES　411, 552
Division of American Cyanamid Co.
Wayne, NJ 07470　　(201) 831-1234
*Address inquiries on
medical matters to:*
Professional Services Dept.
Lederle Laboratories
Pearl River, NY 10965
　　　　　　(914) 735-5000
Distribution Centers
ATLANTA
Bulk Address
Chamblee (Atlanta), GA 30341
　5180 Peachtree Industrial Blvd.

Mail Address
Atlanta, GA 30302
　P.O. Box 4272
　　(GA Only)　(800) 282-0399
　(All Other)　(800) 241-3043
　　　　　　(404) 455-0320
BOSTON
Westwood, MA 02090
　201 University Avenue
　　　　　　(617) 329-4300
　(MA Only)　(800) 532-9684
　(All Other)　(800) 225-6022
CHICAGO
Bulk Address
Rosemont, IL 60018
　10401 W. Touhy Ave.
Mail Address
Chicago, IL 60666
　P.O. Box 66189
　　(IL Only)　(800) 942-1493
　(All Other)　(800) 323-9744
　　　　　　(312) 827-8871
CINCINNATI
Bulk Address
Cincinnati, OH 45241
　10340 Evendale Drive
Mail Address
Cincinnati, OH 45241
　P.O. Box 41316
　　(OH Only)　(800) 582-4661
　(All Other)　(800) 543-4590
　　　　　　(513) 563-6200
DALLAS
Bulk Address
Dallas, TX 75247
　7611 Carpenter Freeway
Mail Address
Dallas, TX 75265
　P.O. Box 225731
　　(TX Only)　(800) 442-7510
　(All Other)　(800) 527-9770
　　　　　　(214) 631-2130
LOS ANGELES
Bulk Address
Los Angeles, CA 90040
　2300 S. Eastern Ave.
Mail Address
Los Angeles, CA 90051
　T.A. Box 2202
　　(CA Only)　(800) 372-6325
　(All Other)　(800) 423-4120
　　　　　　(213) 726-1016
PHILADELPHIA
Fort Washington, PA 19034
　185 Commerce Drive
　　(PA Only)　(800) 562-6924
　(NY-NJ-MD-DE)　(800) 523-6610
　(CT-VA-WV-DC)　(800) 523-6230
　(Phila. Only)　(215) 248-3900
　(All Other)　(215) 646-7000
OTC Products Available
Acetaminophen Capsules, Tablets, Elixir
Ascorbic Acid Tablets
Aureomycin Ointment 3%
Bisacodyl Tablets
◆Centrum
Dimenhydrinate Tablets
Docusate Sodium (DSS)
Docusate Sodium w/Casanthranol
◆Ferro-Sequels
Ferrous Fumarate
Ferrous Gluconate Iron Supplement
Ferrous Sulfate
Filibon Prenatal Vitamin Tablets
Gevrabon Liquid
Gevral Protein Powder
Gevral Tablets
Gevral T Tablets
Guaifenesin Syrup
Guaifenesin w/D-Methorphan
　Hydrobromide Syrup
Incremin w/Iron Syrup
Lederplex Capsules, Liquid & Tablets
Meclizine HCl
Neoloid Emulsified Castor Oil
Niacin
Peritinic Tablets
Pyridoxine HCl
◆Rhulicaine
◆Rhulicort Cream & Lotion
Rhulicream
◆Rhuligel
Rhulispray

(◆ **Shown in Product Identification Section)**

Stresscaps Capsules
◆Stresstabs 600 Tablets
◆Stresstabs 600 with Iron
◆Stresstabs 600 with Zinc
Thiamine HCl (Vitamin B-1) Tablets
Vi-Magna Capsules
Vitamin A, Natural
Vitamin C Chewable
Vitamin E, Natural, USP
Vitamin E, USP
Zincon Dandruff Shampoo

LEEMING DIVISION   **556**
Pfizer Inc.
100 Jefferson Rd.
Parsippany, NJ 07054
Address inquiries to:
Research and Development Dept.
    (201) 887-2100
OTC Products Available
Ben-Gay External Analgesic Products
Desitin Ointment
Nytilax Tablets
Rheaban Tablets & Liquid
Unisom Nighttime Sleep-Aid
Visine A.C. Eye Drops
Visine Eye Drops

LEHN & FINK PRODUCTS   **558**
COMPANY
Division of Sterling Drug Inc.
225 Summit Avenue
Montvale, NJ 07645
Address inquiries to:
John Winson   (201) 573-5622
For Medical Emergencies Contact:
Dr. Ernst Zander   (212) 972-4141
OTC Products Available
Medi-Quik
Stri-Dex B.P.
Stri-Dex Medicated Pads

LOMA LINDA FOODS   **558**
Address inquiries to:
Marketing Office
Riverside, CA 92515 (714) 687-7800
Branch Offices
Mount Vernon, OH 43050
  P.O. Box 388
  13246 Wooster Road
      (614) 397-7077
Riverside, CA 92515
  P.O. Box 8128
    11503 Pierce St. (714) 687-7800
OTC Products Available
I-Soyalac: Liquid Concentrate,
  Ready-to-Serve and Powder
Soyalac: Liquid Concentrate,
  Ready-to-Serve and Powder

LUYTIES PHARMACAL CO.   **559**
4200 Laclede
St. Louis, MO 63108
Address Inquiries to:
Customer Service   (314) 533-9600
OTC Products Available
Yellolax

MACSIL, INC.   **560**
1326 Frankford Avenue
Philadelphia, PA 19125
    (215) 423-5566
OTC Products Available
Balmex Baby Powder
Balmex Emollient Lotion
Balmex Ointment

MARION LABORATORIES,   **411, 560**
INC.
10236 Bunker Ridge Road
Kansas City, MO 64137
Address inquiries to:
Steve Wonderly   (816) 363-4900
For Medical Emergencies Contact:
Corporate Medical Director
    (816) 761-2500
OTC Products Available
◆Ambenyl-D Decongestant Cough
  Formula
◆Debrox Drops
  Fumasorb Tablets
◆Gaviscon Antacid Tablets
◆Gaviscon Liquid Antacid
◆Gaviscon-2 Antacid Tablets

◆Gly-Oxide Liquid
  Metasep Shampoo
  Os-Cal 500 Tablets
  Os-Cal Forte Tablets
  Os-Cal Plus Tablets
◆Os-Cal Tablets
  Os-Cal-Gesic Tablets
◆Pretts Tablets
◆Throat Discs Throat Lozenges

MAX FACTOR & CO.   **412, 562**
1655 N. McCadden Pl.
Hollywood, CA 90028
Address inquiries to:
Carol Walters   (213) 856-6000
For Medical Emergencies Contact:
Joe DiSomma (805) 499-4560 (home)
    (213) 856-6000 (work)
OTC Products Available
◆Maxi Extra-Long Thick Lash Mascara
  w/Sealer
◆Maxi-Lash 24-Hour Polymer Mascara
◆Maxi Stay-Fresh Crease Resistant Eye
  Shadow
◆Maxi-Thick Double-Lash Mascara
◆Maxi Unshine Oil Blotting Make-Up
◆Maxi Unshine Oil Free Liquid Make-Up
◆Maxi Unshine 100% Oil Free Blotting
  Powder
◆Maxi Unshine 100% Oil Free Blushing
  Gel
◆Maxi Unshine 100% Oil Free Blushing
  Powder
◆Sebb Dandruff Shampoo
◆Sebb Dandruff Treatment Lotion
◆Skin Principle Basic Clarifying Lotion
◆Skin Principle Daily Light Moisture
  Lotion
◆Skin Principle Daily Rich Moisture
  Lotion
◆Skin Principle Gentle Cleansing Bar
◆Skin Principle Purifying Cleansing
  Lotion
◆Skin Principle Serious Moisture
  Supplement
◆Tried & True Hair Thickener

MAYBELLINE   **565**
3030 Jackson Ave.
Memphis, TN 38151
Address inquiries to:
Consumer Relations   (901) 320-2386
For Medical Emergencies Contact:
Clinical Affairs Department
    (901) 320-2011
OTC Products Available
Moisture Whip Lip Balm
Moisture Whip Lipstick
Moisture Whip Liquid Make-up &
  Moisture Whip Cream Make-up
Moisture Whip Protective Facial
  Moisturizer

MAYRAND INC.   **565**
P.O. Box 8869
Four Dundas Circle
Greensboro, NC 27419-0869
Address Inquiries to:
Vice-President, Sales (919) 292-5347
For Medical Emergencies Contact:
Technical Director   (919) 292-5347
OTC Products Available
EnTab-650 Tablets
Glytuss Tablets
Nu-Iron 150 Caps
Nu-Iron Elixir

MCHENRY LABORATORIES,   **412, 565**
INC.
118 Wells - Lee Building
Edna, Texas 77957
Address inquiries to:
McHenry Lee   (512) 782-6714
OTC Products Available
◆Ora 5

McNEIL CONSUMER   **413, 566**
PRODUCTS CO.
McNEILAB, INC.
Fort Washington, PA 19034
Address inquiries to:
Professional Relations Department
Fort Washington, PA 19034

Manufacturing Divisions
Fort Washington, PA 19034
Southwest Manufacturing Plant
4001 N. I-35
Round Rock, TX 78664
Distribution Centers
Arlington, TX 76010
  3129 Pinewood Drive
      (817) 640-1167
Broadview, IL 60153
  2122 Roberts Drive(312) 343-1569
Doraville, GA 30360
  2801 Bankers Industrial Drive
      (404) 448-0200
Glendale, CA 91201
  512 Paula Avenue (213) 245-1491
Montgomeryville, PA 18936
  2 Progress Drive   (215) 699-7081
OTC Products Available
◆Children's Tylenol Acetaminophen
  Chewable Tablets, Elixir, & Drops
◆CoTylenol Children's Liquid Cold
  Formula
◆CoTylenol Cold Formula Tablets and
  Capsules
◆CoTylenol Liquid Cold Formula
◆Extra-Strength Tylenol acetaminophen
  Adult Liquid Pain Reliever
◆Extra-Strength Tylenol acetaminophen
  Tablets & Capsules
◆Infants' Tylenol Drops
◆Regular Strength Tylenol
  acetaminophen Tablets & Capsules
◆Sine-Aid Sinus Headache Tablets

MEAD JOHNSON NUTRITIONAL   **568**
DIVISION
Mead Johnson & Company
2404 W. Pennsylvania St.
Evansville, IN 47721 (812) 426-6000
Address inquiries to:
Scientific Information Section
  Medical Department
OTC Products Available
Casec
Ce-Vi-Sol
Criticare HN
Enfamil
Enfamil Nursette
Enfamil Ready-To-Use
Enfamil w/Iron
Enfamil w/Iron Ready-To-Use
Feminins
Fer-In-Sol
Isocal
Isocal HCN
Isocal Tube Feeding Set
Lofenalac
Lonalac
Lytren
MCT Oil
Nutramigen
Poly-Vi-Sol Vitamins, Chewable Tablets
  & Drops
Poly-Vi-Sol Vitamins w/Iron, Chewable
  Tablets & Drops
Portagen
Pregestimil
ProSobee
Sustacal
Sustacal HC
Sustagen
Tempra
Trind
Trind-DM
Tri-Vi-Sol Vitamins, Chewable Tablets &
  Drops
Tri-Vi-Sol Vitamin Drops w/Iron

MEAD JOHNSON   **413, 580**
PHARMACEUTICAL
DIVISION
Mead Johnson & Company
2404 W. Pennsylvania St.
Evansville, IN 47721 (812) 426-6000
Address Inquiries to:
Scientific Information Section
  Medical Department
OTC Products Available
◆Colace
Natalins
◆Peri-Colace

(◆ Shown in Product Identification Section)

MEDICONE COMPANY   581
225 Varick St.
New York, NY 10014
Address inquiries to:
Professional Service Dept.
          (212) 924-5166
OTC Products Available
Derma Medicone
DioMedicone Tablets
Medicone Dressing
Mediconet
Rectal Medicone Suppositories
Rectal Medicone Unguent

MEDIQUE PRODUCTS   582
8050 N. Lawndale
Skokie, IL 60076
Address inquiries to:
Robert E. Musick   (312) 674-4903
For Medical Emergencies Contact:
Robert E. Musick, BS R.PH.
          (312) 674-4903
OTC Products Available
Industrials & Prepacks
All Sugar-Free, Alcohol-Free
    Formulations
APAP Non-Aspirin Pain Relief Tablets
APAP-Plus Non-Aspirin Extra Strength
    Pain Relief Tablets
Alamag Fruit-Flavored Antacid Tablets
Alcalak Antacid Tablets
Aspirin
Aspirin, Buffered
CCP Tablets
Cosyrel Cold Symptom Relief Tablets
Di-Gon Diarrhea Relief Tablets
Femaids Menstrual Relief Capsules
Medidrops Eye Drops
Medikoff Sugar-Free Cough
    Expectorant/Supressant
Mediwash Eye Irrigant
Onset Forte Allergy Relief Tablets
Sep-A-Soothe Throat Lozenges
Seracaine Spray For Burns
Sudodrin Decongestant Tablets

MENLEY & JAMES   413, 582
LABORATORIES
a SmithKline Company
One Franklin Plaza
P.O. Box 8082
Philadelphia, PA 19101
Address inquiries to:
Medical Department (215) 751-5000
OTC Products Available
◆A.R.M. Allergy Relief Medicine Tablets
◆Acnomel Cream
◆Benzedrex Inhaler
◆C3 Cold Cough Capsules
◆Contac Capsules
◆Contac Jr. Childrens' Cold Medicine
◆Contac Severe Cold Formula
◆Dietac Diet Aid Capsules
◆Dietac Diet Aid Drops
◆Dietac Diet Aid Tablets
◆Dietac Once-A-Day Maximum Strength
    Diet Aid Capsules
◆Dietac Twice-A-Day Maximum Strength
    Diet Aid Capsules
◆Ecotrin Tablets
◆Feosol Elixir
◆Feosol Plus
◆Feosol Spansule Capsules
◆Feosol Tablets
◆Ornacol Capsules
◆Ornex Capsules
◆Pragmatar Ointment
◆Sine-Off Extra Strength No Drowsiness
    Formula
◆Sine-Off Extra Strength Sinus Medicine
    Non-Aspirin Capsules
◆Sine-Off Extra Strength Sinus Medicine
    Non-Aspirin Tablets
◆Sine-Off Sinus Medicine Tablets-Aspirin
    Formula
◆Teldrin Spansule Capsules
◆Troph-Iron Liquid & Tablets
◆Trophite Liquid & Tablets

THE MENTHOLATUM COMPANY   588
1360 Niagara Street
Buffalo, NY 14213

Address Inquiries to:
Diane R. Kaminsky   (716) 882-7660
OTC Products Available
Mentholatum Deep Heating Lotion
Mentholatum Deep Heating Rub
Mentholatum Lipbalm with Sunscreen
Mentholatum Ointment
Red Cross Toothache Kit
Resicort Cream
Resinol Cream
Resinol Ointment
Stop 'N Grow

MERICON INDUSTRIES, INC.   589
P.O. Box 5759
Peoria, IL 61601
Address inquiries to:
Thomas P. Morrissey (309) 676-0744
OTC Products Available
Delacort
Orazinc
Zinc Tabs

MERRELL DOW   589
PHARMACEUTICALS INC.
Subsidiary of The Dow Chemical
Company
9550 Zionsville Road
Indianapolis, IN 46268
Address inquiries to:
Nan Collinson   (317) 873-7550
For Medical Emergencies Contact:
Dr. Malcolm H. Fine   (513) 948-7086
For Price Information Contact:
William H. Hutchinson (800) 543-4692
Ohio Residents call   (513) 948-7071
OTC Products Available
Bacimycin Ointment
Cēpacol Anesthetic Troches
Cēpacol Mouthwash/Gargle
Cēpacol Throat Lozenges
Cēpastat Sore Throat Lozenges
Cēpastat Sore Throat
    Spray/Gargle/Mouthwash
Children's Cepastat Sore Throat
    Lozenges
Consotuss Antitussive Syrup
Cotussis Syrup
Decapryn Syrup
Delcid
Diothane Ointment
Ganatrex Elixir
Kolantyl Gel
Kolantyl Wafers
Mercodol Cough Syrup w/Decapryn
Novahistine Cough & Cold Formula
Novahistine Cough Formula
Novahistine DMX
Novahistine Elixir & Cold Tablets
Novahistine Sinus Tablets
Pyridoxine Hydrochloride Tablets
Resolve Cold Sore & Fever Blister
    Relief
Simron Capsules
Simron Plus Capsules
Terpin Hydrate & Codeine Elixir

MERRICK MEDICINE   415, 595
COMPANY
501-503 South 8th (76706)
P.O. Box 1489 (76703)
Waco, TX
Address inquiries to:
W.B. Clayton, President
          (817) 753-3461
OTC Products Available
◆Percy Medicine

MILES LABORATORIES, INC. 415, 596
1127 Myrtle Street
Elkhart, IN 46514
Address inquiries to:
Medical Department (219) 264-8955
For Medical Emergencies Contact:
Medical Department (219) 262-7886
OTC Products Available
◆Alka-Seltzer Effervescent Antacid
◆Alka-Seltzer Effervescent Pain Reliever
    & Antacid
◆Alka-Seltzer Plus Cold Medicine
◆Alka-2 Chewable Antacid Tablets

◆Bactine Antiseptic/Anesthetic First Aid
    Spray
◆Bactine Hydrocortisone Skin Care
    Cream
◆Bugs Bunny Multivitamin Supplement
◆Bugs Bunny Plus Iron Multivitamin
    Supplement
◆Bugs Bunny With Extra C Multivitamin
    Supplement
◆Flintstones Multivitamin Supplement
◆Flintstones Plus Iron Multivitamin
    Supplement
◆Flintstones With Extra C Multivitamin
    Supplement
◆Miles Nervine Nighttime Sleep-Aid
◆One-A-Day Core C 500 Multivitamin
    Supplement
◆One-A-Day Multivitamin Supplement
◆One-A-Day Multivitamin Supplement
    Plus Iron
◆One-A-Day Multivitamin Supplement
    Plus Minerals
◆One-A-Day Stressguard Vitamins

MILES PHARMACEUTICALS   599
Division of Miles Laboratories, Inc.
400 Morgan Lane
West Haven, CT 06516
Address Inquiries to:
Director, Medical Service
          (203) 934-9221
OTC Products Available
Acne-Dome Creme & Lotion
Acne-Dome Medicated Cleanser
Decholin Tablets
Domeboro Powder Packets &
    Effervescent Tablets
Dome-Paste Bandage (Unna's Boot)
Domol Bath & Shower Oil
Exzit Medicated Cleanser
Exzit Medicated Creme & Lotion

MOSS CHEMICAL   416, 599
COMPANY, INC.
183 St. Paul St.
Rochester, NY 14604
Address Inquiries to:
Moss Chemical Co., Inc.
          (716) 546-6187
For Medical Emergencies Contact:
Moss Chemical Co., Inc.
          (716) 546-6187
OTC Products Available
◆Mosco Corn & Callus Remover

MURO PHARMACEUTICAL, INC. 599
890 East Street
Tewksbury, MA 01876
Address inquiries to:
Professional Service Dept.
          1-(800) 225-0974
          (617) 851-5981
OTC Products Available
Duolube Ophthalmic Ointment
Murocel Ophthalmic Solution
Muro Tears
Salinex Nasal Mist

NATRA-BIO CO.   416, 599
1427½ Santa Monica Mall
Santa Monica, CA 90401
Address Inquiries to:
William Pinkerson/Terry Jacobs
1427½ Santa Monica Mall
Santa Monica, CA 90401
     (213) 393-2752 or 395-8450
OTC Products Available
◆501 Indigestion
502 Cough
503 Nervousness
504 Injuries
505 Fever
506 Neuralgic Pains
507 Sinus
508 Arthritis
509 Sore Throat
◆510 Menstrual
511 Nausea
512 Chest Cold
513 Head Cold
514 Earache
515 Headache and Pain
516 Prostate

(◆ Shown in Product Identification Section)

517 Menopause
518 Bedwetting
519 Cold and Hay Fever
520 Hemorrhoids
521 Laxative
522 Bladder Irritation
523 Insomnia
524 Diarrhea
◆525 Herpes
526 Acne
527 Flu
528 Exhaustion

NATURE'S BOUNTY, INC.   **600**
105 Orville Drive
Bohemia, NY 11716
   Address inquiries to:
Professional Service Dept.
            (516) 567-9500
            (800) 645-5412
   OTC Products Available
Acerola C (100 mg)
Acerola C (300 mg)
Acidophilus Capsules
Alfalfa Tablets
B-1 Tablets
B-2 Tablets
B-6 Tablets
B-12 Tablets
B-50 Tablets
B-100 Tablets
B-100 Time Release Tablets
B-125 Tablets
B Complex & B-12 Tablets
B Complex & C (Time Release)
   Capsules
B & C Liquid
Bee Pollen Tablets
Biotin Tablets
Bone Meal with Vitamin D Tablets
Brewer's Yeast Powder (Debittered)
Brewer's Yeast Tablets
C-250 with Rose Hips Tablets
C-300 with Rose Hips (Chewable)
   Tablets
C-500 with Rose Hips Tablets
C-1000 with Rose Hips Tablets
C-Complex Tablets
C-Liquid
C-Time 500 Tablets
C-Time-750 Time Release Tablets
C-Time-1500 Tablets
Calcium Ascorbate Tablets
Calcium Lactate Tablets
Chelated Calcium Tablets
Chelated Chromium Tablets
Chelated Copper Tablets
Chelated Magnesium Tablets
Chelated Manganese Tablets
Chelated Multi-Mineral Tablets
Chelated Potassium Tablets
Chelated Zinc Tablets
Chew-Iron Tablets
Children's Chewable Vitamins
Children's Chewable Vitamins with Iron
Choline Tablets
Chromium, GTF Tablets
Citrus Bioflavonoids Tablets
Claws
Cocoa Butter Soap
Dolomite Tablets
E-200 Capsules
E-200 (Natural Complex) Capsules
E-400 Capsules
E-400 (Natural Complex) Capsules
E-600 (Natural Complex) Capsules
E-1000 (Natural Complex) Capsules
Emulsified E-200 Capsules
Ferrous Sulfate Tablets
Folic Acid Tablets
Garlic Oil Capsules
Garlic & Parsley Capsules
Ginseng, Manchurian Capsules &
   Tablets
Glutamic Acid Tablets
l-Glutamine Tablets
Halibut Liver Oil Capsules
Herbal Laxative Tablets
Inositol Tablets
Iron Tablets
Jojoba Shampoo
KLB6 Capsules
KLB6 Complete Tablets

KLB6 Diet Mix
Kelp Tablets
Lecithin Capsules
Lecithin Chewable Tablets
Lecithin Granules
Lecithin with Vitamin D Capsules
Liver W/B-12 Tablets
l-Lysine Tablets
Magnesium Tablets
Manganese Tablets
Mega V & M Tablets
Mega-B with C Tablets
Multi-Mineral Tablets
Nature's Bounty Hair Booster Tablets
Nature's Bounty Slim
Niacin Tablets
Niacinamide Tablets
Oyster Calcium Tablets
PABA Tablets
Pantothenic Acid Tablets
Papaya Enzyme Tablets
Potassium Tablets
Potassium & B-6 Tablets
Protein For Body Building
Protein Tablets
RNA Tablets
RNA/DNA Tablets
Rutin Tablets
Selenium Tablets
Spirulina Tablets
Stress "1000" Tablets
Stress Formula "605" Tablets
Stress Formula "605" w/Iron Tablets
Stress Formula "605" w/Zinc Tablets
Superoxide Dismutase (SOD) Tablets
Tryptophan Tablets
Ultra "A" Capsules & Tablets
Ultra "A & D" Tablets
Ultra "D" Tablets
Ultra KLB6 Tablets
Ultra Vita-Time Tablets
Vitamin A Capsules & Tablets
Vitamin A & D Tablets
Vitamin C Crystals
Vitamin D Tablets
Vitamin K Tablets
Vita-Time Tablets
Water Pill Tablets
Water Pill w/Iron Tablets
Water Pill w/Potassium Capsules
Wheat Germ Oil Capsules
Yeast Plus Tablets
Zacne Tablets
Zinc Tablets

NICHOLAS LABORATORIES,   **416, 603**
INC.
P.O. Box 110
99 Morris Avenue
Springfield, NJ 07081
   Address Inquiries to:
Jo Anne Pipes   (201) 467-2140
   OTC Products Available
Ambi Body Moisture Lotion
Ambi Cocoa Butter Soap
Ambi Complexion Soap
Ambi Dual Purpose Deep Cleanser
Ambi Facial Moisturizer
◆Ambi Skin Cream, Dry Skin Formula
◆Ambi Skin Cream, Normal Skin Formula
◆Ambi Skin Cream, Oily Skin Formula
◆Ambi Skin Cream with Moisturizers

NORCLIFF THAYER INC.   **416, 603**
One Scarsdale Road
Tuckahoe, NY 10707 (914) 631-0033
   OTC Products Available
◆A-200 Pyrinate Liquid, Gel
Esotérica Medicated Fade Cream
◆Liquiprin Acetaminophen
◆Nature's Remedy Laxative
◆NoSalt Salt Alternative
◆Oxy-5 Lotion
◆Oxy-10 Lotion
◆Oxy-Scrub Abradant Cleanser
◆Oxy Wash Antibacterial Skin Wash
◆Tums Antacid Tablets

NORWICH-EATON   **417, 605**
PHARMACEUTICALS
Division of MortonNorwich Consumer
   Products Group
17 Eaton Avenue
Norwich, NY 13815

   Address inquiries to:
Medical Department (607) 335-2565
   Branch Offices
ATLANTA
  Avondale Estates, GA 30002
  P.O. Box 508   (404) 292-9298
DALLAS
  Dallas, TX 75265
  Box 225490   (214) 337-4794
ELK GROVE
  Elk Grove Village, IL 60007
  1350 Greenleaf Avenue
            (312) 593-0100
GREENVILLE
  Greenville, SC 29602
  P.O. Box 2468   (803) 277-7110
LOS ANGELES
  Los Angeles, CA 90051
  Terminal Annex
  P.O. Box 2171   (213) 726-0505
WINDSOR LOCKS
  Windsor Locks, CT
  101 Turnpike Road
  Suite #210   (203) 623-5331
   OTC Products Available
BPN Ointment
◆Chloraseptic Preparations
◆   Chloraseptic Aerosol Spray
◆   Children's Chloraseptic Lozenges
◆   Chloraseptic Lozenges
◆   Chloraseptic Liquid
◆   Chloraseptic Cough Control
     Lozenges
     Chloraseptic Gel
◆Encare Contraceptive Inserts
Morton Salt Substitute
NP-27 Cream, Liquid, Powder &
  Aerosol Powder
Necta Sweet Non-Caloric Sweetener
◆Norforms
◆Norwich Aspirin
Norwich Bacitracin Ointment
Norwich Glycerin Suppositories
◆Pepto-Bismol Liquid & Tablets
Unguentine Plus First Aid & Burn
  Cream
Zinc Oxide Ointment

OPTIMOX, INC.   **417, 608**
Suite 1, 801 Deep Valley Drive
Palos Verdes Peninsula, CA 90274
   Address Inquiries to:
Guy E. Abraham, M.D.(213) 541-3096
   For Medical Emergencies Contact:
Guy E. Abraham, M.D.(213) 541-3096
   OTC Products Available
◆Optivite for Women

ORTHO PHARMACEUTICAL   **417, 609**
CORPORATION
Consumer Products Division
Route #202
Raritan, NJ 08869 (201) 524-0400
   For Medical Emergencies Contact:
Dr. B. Malyk   (201) 524-2170
   OTC Products Available
◆Conceptrol Birth Control Cream
◆Conceptrol Disposable Gel
◆Conceptrol Shields Latex Prophylactics
◆Conceptrol Supreme Lubricated Thin
  Prophylactics
Daisy 2 Home Pregnancy Test
◆Delfen Contraceptive Foam
◆Gynol II Contraceptive Jelly
◆Intercept Contraceptive Inserts
◆Massé Breast Cream
◆Ortho Disposable Vaginal Applicators
◆Ortho Personal Lubricant
◆Ortho-Creme Contraceptive Cream
◆Ortho-Gynol Contraceptive Jelly

ORTHO PHARMACEUTICAL   **418, 611**
CORPORATION
Dermatological Division
Raritan, NJ 08869
            (201) 524-0400
   OTC Products Available
◆Purpose Brand Dry Skin Cream
◆Purpose Brand Shampoo
◆Purpose Brand Soap

(◆ **Shown in Product Identification Section)**

PARKE-DAVIS 418, 612
Division of Warner-Lambert Company
201 Tabor Road
Morris Plains, NJ 07950 USA
(201) 540-2000
Regional Sales Offices
Atlanta, GA 30328
1140 Hammond Drive
(404) 396-4080
Baltimore (Hunt Valley), MD 21031
11350 McCormick Road
(301) 666-7810/1
Chicago (Schaumberg), IL 60195
1111 Plaza Drive
(312) 884-6900
Dallas, TX 75234
12200 Ford Road
(214) 484-5566
Detroit, MI 48084
500 Stephenson Highway
(313) 589-3292/3
Los Angeles (Tustin), CA 92680
17822 East 17th Street
(714) 731-3441
Memphis, TN 38138
1355 Lynnfield Road
(901) 767-1921
New York (East Hartford, CT) 06108
111 Founders Plaza
(203) 528-9601
Pittsburgh, PA 15220
1910 Cochran Road
(412) 343-9855/6
Seattle (Bellevue), WA 98004
301 116th Avenue, SE
(206) 451-1119
OTC Products Available
Abdec Baby Vitamin Drops
Abdec Kapseals
Abdol with Minerals Capsules
Acetaminophen (Tapar)
Agoral
Agoral, Marshmallow Flavor
Agoral, Raspberry Flavor
Alcohol, Rubbing (Lavacol)
Alophen Pills
◆Anusol Hemorrhoidal Suppositories
◆Anusol Ointment
Aspirin Compound Tablets
Aspirin Tablets
◆Benadryl Antihistamine Cream
◆Benylin Cough Syrup
◆Benylin DM
◆Caladryl Cream, Lotion
Calcium Lactate Tablets
Capsolin Ointment
Cherry Syrup
Docusate Sodium Capsules (D-S-S Capsules)
Docusate Sodium with Casanthranol Capsules (D-S-S Plus Capsules)
Ferrous Sulfate Filmseals
◆Gelusil Liquid & Tablets
Gelusil-M Liquid & Tablets
Gelusil-II Liquid & Tablets
Geriplex Kapseals
Geriplex-FS Kapseals
Geriplex-FS Liquid
Hydrogen Peroxide Solution
Lavacol
Milk of Bismuth
◆Myadec
Natabec Kapseals
Natabec-FA Kapseals
Paladac
Paladac with Minerals Tablets
Peroxide, Hydrogen
Quinine Sulfate Capsules
Rubbing Alcohol (Lavacol)
Siblin Granules
Terpin Hydrate Elixir w/Codeine
Thera-Combex H-P Kapseals
Tucks Cream
Tucks Ointment
◆Tucks Premoistened Pads
Tucks Take-Alongs
Unibase
Vitamin B Complex, Kapseals
◆Ziradryl Lotion

PERSON & COVEY, INC. 419, 616
616 Allen Avenue
Glendale, CA 91201

Address inquiries to:
Lorne V. Person, President
(213) 240-1030
OTC Products Available
A.C.N.
DHS Conditioning Rinse
◆DHS Shampoo
◆DHS Tar Shampoo
◆DHS Zinc Dandruff Shampoo
Enisyl 334 mg and 500 mg Tablets
Solbar
Solbar Plus 15
Xerac

PFIPHARMECS DIVISION 419, 617
Pfizer Inc.
235 E. 42nd Street
New York, NY 10017
Address inquiries to:
Pfizer Inc. (212) 573-2323
Branch Offices
Clifton, NJ 07012
230 Brighton Rd. (201) 546-7702
Doraville, GA 30340
4360 Northeast Expressway
(404) 448-6666
Hoffman Estates, IL 60712
2400 W. Central Road
(312) 381-9500
Grand Prairie, TX 75050
502 Fountain Parkway
(817) 261-9131
Irvine, CA 92705
16700 Red Hill Ave.
(714) 540-9180
Portland, OR 97210
3333 N.W. Industrial St.
(503) 222-9281
OTC Products Available
Bacitracin
◆Bonine
Cortril ½% Cream
◆Coryban-D Capsules
◆Coryban-D Cough Syrup
◆Li-Ban Spray
Obron-6 Tablets
◆Rid
Roeribec Tablets
Terramycin Ointment
Viterra C
Viterra E
Viterra High Potency Tablets
Viterra Original Formula Tablets
◆Wart-Off

PHARMACRAFT DIVISION 618
Pennwalt Corporation
755 Jefferson Road
Rochester, NY 14623
Address inquiries to:
Professional Service Dept.
P.O. Box 1212
Rochester, NY 14603
(716) 475-9000
OTC Products Available
Allerest Tablets, Children's Chewable Tablets, Headache Strength Tablets & Timed-Release Capsules
CaldeCORT Hydrocortisone Cream, Spray & Ointment
Caldesene Medicated Ointment
Caldesene Medicated Powder
Cruex Antifungal Cream
Cruex Antifungal Powder
Desenex Foot & Sneaker Spray
Desenex Powders, Foam, Ointment, Liquid, & Soap
Sinarest Regular & Extra Strength Tablets

PHARMTECH RESEARCH 419, 620
INC.
1750 Montgomery St.
San Francisco, CA 94111
Address Inquiries to:
PharmTech Research Inc.
(415) 397-8116
For Medical Emergencies Contact:
PharmTech Research Inc.
(415) 397-8116
OTC Products Available
◆Herbitol

PLOUGH, INC. 419, 620
3030 Jackson Avenue
Memphis, TN 38151
Address inquiries to:
Consumer Relations Dept.
(901) 320-2386
For Medical Emergencies Contact:
Clinical Affairs Dept.
(901) 320-2011
OTC Products Available
◆Aftate for Athlete's Foot
◆Aftate for Jock Itch
◆Aspergum
◆Correctol Laxative Liquid
◆Correctol Laxative Tablets
◆Cushion Grip
◆Di-Gel
Duration Mentholated Nasal Spray
◆Duration Nasal Spray
◆Duration Nose Drops
◆Regutol
◆St. Joseph Aspirin for Children
◆St. Joseph Cold Tablets for Children
◆St. Joseph Cough Syrup for Children
◆Shade Plus
◆Shade Sunscreen Lotion (SPF-6)
◆Solarcaine
◆Super Shade

WM. P. POYTHRESS & CO., 420, 623
INC.
16 N. 22nd Street
P.O. Box 26946
Richmond, VA 23261 (804) 644-8591
Address inquiries to:
Special Services Department
OTC Products Available
Bensulfoid Lotion
◆Panalgesic

PROCTER & GAMBLE 623
P.O. Box 171
Cincinnati, OH 45201
Address inquiries to:
Arnold P. Austin (513) 977-5547
For Medical Emergencies Contact:
W.S. Lainhart, M.D.
(513) 763-6905
OTC Products Available
Head & Shoulders
Scope

THE PURDUE FREDERICK 420, 624
COMPANY
50 Washington Street
Norwalk, CT 06856 (203) 853-0123
Address inquiries to:
Medical Department
OTC Products Available
Arthropan Liquid
Betadine Aerosol Spray
◆Betadine Antiseptic Gauze Pad
Betadine Antiseptic Lubricating Gel
◆Betadine Douche
◆Betadine Douche Kit
Betadine Helafoam Solution
◆Betadine Medicated Douche
◆Betadine Mouthwash/Gargle
◆Betadine Ointment
Betadine Perineal Wash Concentrate
Betadine Shampoo
◆Betadine Skin Cleanser
Betadine Skin Cleanser Foam
◆Betadine Solution
Betadine Solution Swab Aid
Betadine Solution Swabsticks
Betadine Surgical Scrub
Betadine Surgi-Prep Sponge-Brush
◆Betadine Viscous Formula Antiseptic Gauze Pad
Betadine Whirlpool Concentrate
◆Fibermed
Parelixir Liquid
Probilagol Liquid
Senokap DSS Capsules
Senokot Suppositories
Senokot Syrup
◆Senokot Tablets/Granules
Senokot Tablets Unit Strip Pack
Senokot w/Psyllium Powder
◆Senokot-S Tablets
Sulfabid Tablets
Supertah Ointment

(◆ **Shown in Product Identification Section**)

REED & CARNRICK 625
1 New England Avenue
Piscataway, NJ 08854
Address Inquiries to:
Professional Service Dept.
(201) 981-0700
For Medical Emergencies Contact:
Medical Director (201) 981-0070
OTC Products Available
Alphosyl Lotion, Cream
Phazyme
Phazyme-95
ProctoFoam/non-steroid
Proxigel
R&C Spray
Trichotine Liquid, Vaginal Douche
Trichotine Powder, Vaginal Douche
Trichotine-D, Disposable Vaginal
Douche

REQUA MANUFACTURING 421, 626
COMPANY, INC.
1 Seneca Place
Greenwich, CT 06830
Address inquiries to:
John H. Geils (203) 869-2445
OTC Products Available
◆Charcocaps

A. H. ROBINS COMPANY, 421, 626
INC.
CONSUMER PRODUCTS
DIVISION
3800 Cutshaw Avenue
Richmond, VA 23230
Address inquiries to:
The Medical Department
(804) 257-2000
For Medical Emergencies Contact:
Medical Department (804) 257-2000
(day or night)
If no answer, call answering service
(804) 257-7788
OTC Products Available
◆Allbee C-800 Plus Iron Tablets
◆Allbee C-800 Tablets
◆Allbee with C Capsules
◆Chap Stick Lip Balm
◆Chap Stick Sunblock 15 Lip Balm
◆Dimacol Capsules
◆Dimetane Decongestant Elixir
◆Dimetane Decongestant Tablets
◆Dimetane Elixir
◆Dimetane Tablets
◆Robitussin
◆Robitussin-CF
◆Robitussin-DM
◆Robitussin-PE
◆Z-Bec Tablets

ROCHE LABORATORIES 422, 630
Division of Hoffmann-La Roche Inc.
340 Kingsland Street
Nutley, NJ 07110
For Medical Information
Write: Professional Services Dept.
Business hours only (8:30 a.m. to
5:00 p.m. EST), call
(201) 235-2355
For Medical Emergency Information
only after hours or on weekends,
call (201) 235-2355
Branch Warehouses
Belvidere, NJ 07823
Water Street (201) 475-5337
Dallas, TX 75229
2727 Northaven Rd.
(P.O. Box 29009) (214) 241-8573
Decatur, GA 30031
421 DeKalb Industrial Way
(404) 296-1241
Des Plaines, IL 60018
105 E. Oakton St. (312) 299-0021
(Chicago) (312) 775-0733
San Leandro, CA 94577
1599 Factor Ave. (415) 352-1660
OTC Products Available
◆Vi-Penta Infant Drops
◆Vi-Penta Multivitamin Drops

WILLIAM H. RORER, INC. 422, 630
500 Virginia Drive
Fort Washington, PA 19034
For Medical Emergencies Contact:
John F. A. Vance, M.D.
Medical Director (215) 628-6761
For Quality Matters Contact:
William E. Kinas, Vice President
Quality Assurance (215) 628-6420
For Product Information Contact:
Ronald A. Amey, Marketing
Services Manager (215) 628-6492
Branch Offices
Langhorne, PA 19047
2201 Cabot Blvd. West
(215) 752-8555
Oak Forest, IL 60452
P.O. Box 280
4325 Frontage Rd. (312) 687-7440
San Leandro, CA 94577
P.O. Box 1569
1550 Factor Ave. (415) 357-9741
Tucker, GA 30084
4660 Hammermill Rd.
(404) 934-3091
OTC Products Available
◆Ascriptin
◆Ascriptin A/D
◆Emetrol
◆Gemnisyn
◆Maalox Plus Suspension
◆Maalox Plus Tablets
◆Maalox Suspension
◆Maalox Tablets (No.1 & No.2)
◆Maalox TC (Therapeutic Concentrate)
◆Perdiem Granules

ROWELL LABORATORIES, INC. 633
210 West Main
Baudette, MN 56623
Address Inquiries to:
Professional Service Dept.
(218) 634-1866
For Medical Emergencies Contact:
V.P., Medical Affairs (218) 634-1866
OTC Products Available
Balneol
Hydrocil Instant

RYSTAN COMPANY, INC. 633
470 Mamaroneck Avenue
White Plains, NY 10605
Address inquiries to:
Professional Services Dept.
(914) 761-0044
Branch Office
Little Falls, NJ 07424
47 Center Avenue (201) 256-3737
OTC Products Available
Chloresium Dental Ointment
Chloresium Ointment & Solution
Chloresium Tooth Paste
Derifil Tablets & Powder
Prophyllin Ointment
Prophyllin Powder

SDA PHARMACEUTICALS, INC. 633
919 Third Avenue
New York, NY 10022
Address inquiries to:
Dr. Edward L. Steinberg
(212) 688-4420
OTC Products Available
Anorexin Capsules
Anorexin One-Span Capsules

S.S.S. COMPANY 634
71 University Avenue, SW
P.O. Box 4447
Atlanta, GA 30302
Address inquiries to:
Lamar Swift (404) 521-0857
For Medical Emergencies Contact:
Jerry McHan, PhD (404) 688-6291
OTC Products Available
Mothers Friend Cream
Mothers Friend Liquid
S.S.S. Tonic Liquid
S.S.S. Tonic Tablets
20/20 Contact Lens Wetting Solution
20/20 Eye Drops

SCHERER LABORATORIES, INC. 634
14335 Gillis Road
Dallas, Texas 75234
Address Inquiries to:
F. R. Stravs (214) 233-2800
For Medical Emergencies Contact:
F. R. Stravs (214) 233-2800
OTC Products Available
HuMist Saline Nasal Mist
Xero-Lube-Saliva Substitute

SCHERING CORPORATION 423, 634
Galloping Hill Road
Kenilworth, NJ 07033
Address inquiries to:
Professional Services Department
(201) 931-2000
Branch Offices
Southeast Branch
5884 Peachtree Rd., NE
Chamblee, GA 30341
(404) 457-6315
Midwest Branch
7500 N. Natchez Avenue
Niles, IL 60648 (312) 647-9363
Southwest Branch
1921 Gateway Drive
Irving, TX 75062 (214) 258-3545
West Coast Branch
14775 Wicks Blvd.
San Leandro, CA 94577
(415) 357-3125
OTC Products Available
A and D Cream
◆A and D Ointment
◆Afrin Menthol Nasal Spray 0.05%
◆Afrin Nasal Spray 0.05%, Nose Drops
0.05%, Pediatric Nose Drops
0.025%
◆Afrinol Repetabs Tablets
◆Chlor-Trimeton Allergy Syrup, Tablets &
Long-Acting Repetabs Tablets
◆Chlor-Trimeton Decongestant Tablets &
Long Acting Decongestant Repetabs
Tablets
Chlor-Trimeton Expectorant
◆Cod Liver Oil Concentrate Tablets,
Capsules
◆Cod Liver Oil Concentrate Tablets
w/Vitamin C
◆Coricidin Children's Cough Syrup
◆Coricidin Cough Syrup
◆Coricidin 'D' Decongestant Tablets
◆Coricidin Decongestant Nasal Mist
◆Coricidin Demilets Tablets for Children
◆Coricidin Extra Strength Sinus
Headache Tablets
◆Coricidin Medilets Tablets for Children
◆Coricidin Tablets
◆Demazin Decongestant-Antihistamine
Repetabs Tablets & Syrup
◆Dermolate Anal-Itch Ointment
◆Dermolate Anti-Itch Cream & Spray
◆Dermolate Scalp-Itch Lotion
◆Emko Because Contraceptor Vaginal
Contraceptive Foam
◆Emko Pre-Fil Vaginal Contraceptive
Foam
◆Emko Vaginal Contraceptive Foam
◆Mol-Iron Tablets, Liquid & Chronosule
Capsules
◆Mol-Iron Tablets w/Vitamin C
◆Sunril Premenstrual Capsules
◆Tinactin Aerosol Powder 1%
◆Tinactin Antifungal 1%, Cream,
Solution & Powder

SEARLE CONSUMER 425, 642
PRODUCTS
Division of Searle Pharmaceuticals Inc.
Box 5110
Chicago, IL 60680
Address inquiries to:
Medical Communications Department
G.D. Searle & Co. (312) 982-7000
For Medical Emergencies Contact:
Medical Department, G.D. Searle & Co.
(within IL) (312) 982-7000
(outside IL) (800) 323-4397
OTC Products Available
◆Dramamine Liquid
◆Dramamine Tablets
◆Icy Hot Balm

(◆ **Shown in Product Identification Section**)

◆Icy Hot Rub
◆Metamucil, Instant Mix
◆Metamucil, Instant Mix, Orange Flavor
◆Metamucil Powder
◆Metamucil Powder, Orange Flavor

E. R. SQUIBB & SONS, INC.   425, 644
General Offices
P.O. Box 4000
Princeton, NJ 08540 (609) 921-4000
Address Inquiries to:
Squibb Professional Services Dept.
Lawrenceville-Princeton Road
Princeton, NJ 08540 (609) 921-4006
Distribution Centers
ATLANTA, GEORGIA
P.O. Box 16503
Atlanta, GA 30321
State of GA Customers Call
                    (800) 282-9103
Customers in States of AL, FL, MS, NC,
SC, and TN Call   (800) 241-1744
All Others Call   (800) 241-5364
CHICAGO, ILLINOIS
P.O. Box 788
Arlington Heights, IL 60006
State of IL Customers Call
                    (800) 942-0674
All Others Call   (800) 323-0665
KANSAS CITY, KANSAS
Mail or telephone orders and customer
service inquiries should be directed to
Chicago, IL (see above)
State of IL Customers Call
                    (800) 942-0674
All Others Call   (800) 323-0665
LOS ANGELES, CALIFORNIA
P.O. Box 428
La Mirada, CA 90638
State of CA Customers Call
                    (800) 422-4254
State of HI Customers Call
                    (714) 521-7050
All Others Call   (800) 854-3050
SEATTLE, WASHINGTON
Mail or telephone orders and customer
service inquiries should be directed to
Los Angeles, CA (see above)
States of AK and MT Customers Call
                    (714) 521-7050
State of CA Customers Call
                    (800) 422-4254
All Others Call   (800) 854-3050
NEW YORK AREA
E.R. Squibb & Sons, Inc
P.O. Box 2013
New Brunswick, NJ 08903
N.Y. City Area Customers
Call   (212) 227-1371
State of NJ Customers Call
                    (800) 352-4865
States of ME and NC Customers Call
                    (201) 469-5400
All Others Call   (800) 631-5244
HOUSTON, TEXAS
P.O. Box 1510
Houston, TX 77001
State of NM Customers Call
                    (713) 622-4242
State of TX Customers Call
                    (800) 392-2030
All Others Call   (800) 231-3209
SQUIBB LABORATORIES
E.R. Squibb & Sons, Inc.
Georges Road
New Brunswick, NJ 08903
OTC Products Available
◆Spec-T Sore Throat Anesthetic
   Lozenges
◆Spec-T Sore Throat/Cough Suppressant
   Lozenges
◆Spec-T Sore Throat/Decongestant
   Lozenges
Theragran Liquid
Theragran Tablets
◆Theragran-M Tablets
◆Theragran-Z Tablets

**STELLAR PHARMACAL CORP.   645
DIV./STAR PHARMACEUTICALS
INC.**
P.O. Box 600354
N. Miami Beach, FL 33160

Address inquiries to:
Scott L. Davidson   (305) 949-1612
For Medical Emergencies Contact:
Scott L. Davidson   (305) 949-1612
OTC Products Available
Star-Otic 15 c.c.

**STUART   425, 645
PHARMACEUTICALS**
Div. of ICI Americas, Inc.
Wilmington, DE 19897
Address inquiries to:
Yvonne A. Graham, Manager
  Professional Services
                    (302) 575-2231
OTC Products Available
◆ALternaGEL Liquid
◆Dialose Capsules
◆Dialose Plus Capsules
◆Effersyllium Instant Mix
  Ferancee Chewable Tablets
◆Ferancee-HP Tablets
◆Hibiclens
  Hibistat
  Hibitane Tincture (Tinted & Non-Tinted)
◆Kasof Capsules
◆Mylanta Liquid
◆Mylanta Tablets
◆Mylanta-II Liquid
◆Mylanta-II Tablets
◆Mylicon (Tablets & Drops)
◆Mylicon-80 Tablets
  Orexin Softab Tablets
  Probec-T Tablets
◆The Stuart Formula Tablets
  Stuart Prenatal Tablets
◆Stuartinic Tablets

SUGARLO COMPANY   426, 649
600 Fire Road
P.O. Box 111
Pleasantville, NJ 08232-0111
Address inquiries to:
Alan E. Kligerman   (800) 257-8650
OTC Products Available
◆LactAid brand lactase enzyme

SYNTEX LABORATORIES, INC.   650
3401 Hillview Avenue
Palo Alto, CA 94304
Address inquiries to:
Medical Affairs   (415) 855-5545
OTC Products Available
Carmol 10, 10% Urea Lotion
Carmol 20, 20% Urea Cream
Topic Benzyl Alcohol Gel

**THOMPSON MEDICAL   426, 650
COMPANY, INC.**
919 Third Avenue
New York, NY 10022
Address inquiries to:
Dr. Edward L. Steinberg
                    (212) 688-4420
OTC Products Available
◆Appedrine, Maximum Strength
◆Aqua-Ban
◆Aspercreme
◆Control Capsules
◆Cortizone•5
◆Dexatrim
◆Dexatrim Extra Strength
◆Dexatrim Extra Strength, Caffeine-Free
◆Prolamine Capsules, Super Strength

THOUGHT TECHNOLOGY, LTD.   652
2180 Belgrave Avenue, Suite #47
Montreal, Quebec, Canada H4A 2L8
Address inquiries to:
Lawrence Klein, Vice President
                    (514) 489-8251
For Medical Emergencies Contact:
Dr. H.K. Myers   (514) 731-9195
OTC Products Available
GSR 2
GSR/Temp 2

ULMER PHARMACAL COMPANY   652
(Division of Physicians & Hospitals
Supply Co.)
2440 Fernbrook Lane
Minneapolis, MN 55441

Address Inquiries to:
Professional Services Dept.
                    (612) 559-3333
OTC Products Available
Aerosan
Andoin Ointment
Aspirin Tablets
Auto-Kler
Bacitracin Ointment
Bi-Amine
Bu-Lax Capsules
Bu-Lax Plus Capsules
Cal-Zo Ointment
Cardio-Gel
Chloral Methylol Ointment
Co-Gel Tablets
Col-Vi-Nol Ointment
Dextro-Tuss GG
Dibucaine Ointment
Gentle Shampoo
Hematovals
Hiscatabs
Kler-ro Liquid
Kler-ro Powder
Lobana Bath Oil
Lobana Body Lotion
Lobana Body Powder
Lobana Body Shampoo
Lobana Conditioning Shampoo
Lobana Derm-Ade Cream
Lobana Liquid Hand Soap
Lobana Peri-Gard
Lobana Perineal Cleanse
Milk of Magnesia
Mineral Oil
Pentazyme Tablets
Pheneen Sanitizer
Pheneen Solution
Pheneen Solution N.R.I.
Reagent Alcohol
Surgel Liquid
Ta-Poff
Ta-Poff Aerosol
Tokols Capsules
Ultar Cream
Ulvical SG
Vitamin A & D Ointment
Vleminckx' Solution
Zinc Oxide Ointment

THE UPJOHN COMPANY   427, 653
7000 Portage Road
Kalamazoo, MI 49001
Address inquiries to:
Medical Services   (616) 323-6615
*Pharmaceutical Sales Areas
and Distribution Centers*
Atlanta (Chamblee),
  GA 30341   (404) 451-4822
Boston (Needham Heights),
  MA 02194   (617) 449-0320
Buffalo (Cheektowaga),
  NY 14225   (716) 681-7160
Chicago (Oak Brook),
  IL 60521   (312) 654-3300
Cincinnati, OH 45214
               (513) 242-4573
Dallas, TX 75265   (214) 824-3027
Denver, CO 80217   (303) 399-3113
Honolulu, HI 96809   (808) 538-1181
Kalamazoo, MI 49001
               (616) 323-7222
Kansas City, MO 64141
               (816) 361-2286
Los Angeles, CA 90051
               (213) 463-8101
Memphis, TN 38122 (901) 761-4170
Miami, FL 33152   (305) 758-3317
Minneapolis, MN 55440
               (612) 588-2786
New York
  Long Island, NY 11514
               (516) 747-1970
Philadelphia (Wayne)
  PA 19087   (215) 265-2100
Pittsburgh (Bridgeville)
  PA 15017
               (412) 257-0200
Portland, OR 97208 (503) 232-2133
St. Louis, MO 63177
               (314) 872-8626
San Francisco (Palo Alto)
  CA 94304   (415) 493-8080

(◆ **Shown in Product Identification Section**)

Washington, DC 20013
(202) 882-6163
OTC Products Available
Alkets Tablets
Aspirin Tablets, USP
Baciguent Antibiotic Ointment
Calcium Gluconate Tablets, USP
Calcium Lactate Tablets, USP
Casyllium Granules
Cebefortis Tablets
Cebenase Tablets
Cebetinic Tablets
Cheracol Cough Syrup
Cheracol D Cough Syrup
Citrocarbonate Antacid
Clocream Skin Cream
◆Cortaid Cream
◆Cortaid Lotion
◆Cortaid Ointment
◆Cortef Feminine Itch Cream
◆Cortef Rectal Itch Ointment
Diostate D Tablets
Epinephricaine Rectal Ointment
Ergophene Skin Ointment
Ferrous Sulfate Tablets, USP
Gerizyme Liquid
Hydriodic Acid (Upjohn) Cough Syrup
Hydrolose Syrup
◆Kaopectate Anti-Diarrhea Medicine
◆Kaopectate Concentrate Anti-Diarrhea
Medicine
Lipomul Oral Liquid
Medicated Foot Powder
Mercresin Tincture
Myciguent Antibiotic Cream
Myciguent Antibiotic Ointment
◆Mycitracin Antibiotic Ointment
Orthoxicol Cough Syrup
P-A-C Compound Tablets
Pentacresol Instrument Disinfecting
Solution
Pentacresol Oral Solution
Phenolax Wafers
◆Pyrroxate Capsules
Salicresin Fluid
Sigtab Tablets
Super D Perles
Unicap Capsules & Tablets
Unicap Chewable Tablets
◆Unicap M Tablets
Unicap Plus Iron Tablets
Unicap Senior Tablets
◆Unicap T Tablets
Upjohn Vitamin C Tablets
Upjohn Vitamin E Capsules
Zinc Sulfide Compound Lotion,
Improved
Zymacap Capsules
Zymalixir Fluid
Zymasyrup Fluid

VICKS TOILETRY 427, 655
PRODUCTS DIVISION
Richardson-Vicks Inc.
10 Westport Road
Wilton, CT 06897
Address inquiries to:
Scientific & Regulatory Affairs
Vicks Toiletry Products Divn.
Vicks Divisions Research &
Development (203) 929-2500
For Medical Emergencies Contact
Medical Director
Vicks Divisions Research &
Development (203) 929-2500
OTC Products Available
Clearasil Antibacterial Soap
Clearasil Acne Treatment Stick
◆Clearasil 5% Benzoyl Peroxide Lotion
Acne Treatment
◆Clearasil Pore Deep Cleanser
◆Clearasil Super Strength Acne
Treatment Cream, Tinted
◆Clearasil Super Strength Acne
Treatment Cream, Vanishing
Demure Douche
Liquid
Packets
Lemon Jelvyn Beauty Cleanser
Lemon Jelvyn Beauty Freshener
◆Topex 10% Benzoyl Peroxide Lotion
Buffered Acne Medication

ORAL HEALTH PRODUCTS
Benzodent Analgesic Denture Ointment
Complete Denture Cleanser and
Toothpaste in One
Denquel Sensitive Teeth Toothpaste
Fasteeth Denture Adhesive Powder
Fixodent Denture Adhesive Cream
Kleenite Denture Cleanser
Lavoris Mouthwash and Gargle

VICKS HEALTH CARE 427, 656
DIVISION
Richardson-Vicks Inc.
10 Westport Road
Wilton, CT 06897
Address inquiries to:
Director of Scientific & Regulatory
Affairs
Vicks Divisions Research &
Development (914) 664-5000
For Medical Emergencies Contact
Medical Director
Vicks Divisions Research &
Development (914) 664-5000
OTC Products Available
◆Daycare Multi-Symptom Colds Medicine
Liquid & Capsules
Formula 44 Cough Control Discs
◆Formula 44 Cough Mixture
◆Formula 44D Decongestant Cough
Mixture
◆Headway Capsules and Tablets
◆Nyquil Nighttime Colds Medicine
Oracin Cherry Flavor Cooling Throat
Lozenges
Oracin Cooling Throat Lozenges
◆Sinex Decongestant Nasal Spray
◆Sinex Long-Acting Decongestant Nasal
Spray
Vaposteam
Vatronol Nose Drops
Vicks Blue Cough Drops
Vicks Cough Drops
Regular Flavor
Wild Cherry Flavor
Lemon Flavor
Blue Mint
Vicks Cough Silencers Cough Drops
Vicks Cough Syrup
Vicks Formula 44 Cough Control Discs
◆Vicks Formula 44 Cough Mixture
◆Vicks Formula 44D Decongestant
Cough Mixture
Vicks Inhaler
◆Vicks Nyquil Nighttime Colds Medicine
◆Vicks Sinex Decongestant Nasal Spray
◆Vicks Sinex Long-Acting Decongestant
Nasal Spray
Vicks Throat Lozenges
◆Vicks Vaporub
Vicks Vaposteam
Vicks Vatronol Nose Drops
Victors Menthol-Eucalyptus Vapor
Cough Drops
Regular
Cherry Flavor

WALKER, CORP & CO., INC. 660
20 E. Hampton Place
Syracuse, NY 13206
Address inquiries to:
P.O. Box 1320
Syracuse, NY 13201 (315) 463-4511
For Medical Emergencies Contact:
Robert G. Long (315) 638-4763
OTC Products Available
Evac-U-Gen

WALKER PHARMACAL CO. 660
4200 Laclede
St. Louis, MO 63108
Address inquiries to:
Customer Service (314) 533-9600
OTC Products Available
PRID Salve

WALLACE LABORATORIES 428, 660
Half Acre Road
Cranbury, NJ 08512
Address inquiries to:
Wallace Laboratories
Div. of Carter-Wallace, Inc.
P.O. Drawer #5
Cranbury, NJ 08512 (609) 655-6000

For Medical Emergencies:
(609) 799-1167
OTC Products Available
◆Maltsupex
◆Ryna
◆Ryna-C
◆Ryna-CX
◆Syllact

WARNER-LAMBERT 428, 662
COMPANY
201 Tabor Road
Morris Plains, NJ 07950

WARNER-LAMBERT INC. 428, 662
Santurce, PR 00911
Address Inquiries to:
Robert Kirpitch (201) 540-3204
For Medical Emergencies Contact:
Dr. Robert Gabrielson
(201) 540-2301
OTC Products Available
◆e.p.t. In-Home Early Pregnancy Test
◆Halls Mentho-Lyptus Cough Tablets
Halls Mentho-Lyptus Decongestant
Cough Formula
◆Listerine Antiseptic
◆Listermint Cinnamon Mouthwash &
Gargle
◆Listermint Mouthwash & Gargle
◆Lubath Bath Oil
Lubriderm Cream
◆Lubriderm Lotion
◆Sinutab Extra Strength Capsules
◆Sinutab Extra Strength Tablets
◆Sinutab Long-Lasting Decongestant
Nasal Spray
◆Sinutab Tablets
◆Sinutab II Tablets

WESTWOOD PHARMACEUTICALS 666
INC.
468 Dewitt St.
Buffalo, NY 14213
Address inquiries to:
Jerome Levy, M.D., Medical Director,
Dermatology
(716) 887-3400
OTC Products Available
Alpha Keri Bath Oil
Alpha Keri Soap
Alpha Keri Spray
Balnetar
Estar Tar Gel
Fostex 5% Benzoyl Peroxide Gel
Fostex Medicated Cleansing Bar
Fostex Medicated Cleansing Cream
Fostex Medicated Cover-Up
Fostril
Ice Mint
Keri Creme
Keri Facial Cleanser
Keri Facial Soap
Keri Lotion
Lowila Cake
Pernox Lotion
Pernox Scrub
Pernox Shampoo
PreSun 4 Lotion
PreSun 8 Lotion, Creamy Lotion & Gel
PreSun 15 Creamy Sunscreen Lotion
PreSun 15 Lotion
PreSun 15 Sunscreen Lip Protector
Sebucare
Sebulex and Sebulex Cream
Sebulex Conditioning Shampoo with
Protein
Sebutone & Sebutone Cream
Transact

WHITEHALL LABORATORIES 429, 670
Division of American Home Products
Corporation
685 Third Avenue
New York, NY 10017

Address inquiries to:
Medical Department (212) 878-5508
OTC Products Available
◆Anacin Analgesic Capsules
◆Anacin Analgesic Tablets

(◆ **Shown in Product Identification Section**)

Manufacturers' Index

◆Anacin Maximum Strength Analgesic
  Capsules
◆Anacin Maximum Strength Analgesic
  Tablets
◆Anacin-3 Analgesic Tablets & Capsules
◆Anbesol Gel Antiseptic Anesthetic
◆Anbesol Liquid Antiseptic Anesthetic
◆Arthritis Pain Formula by the Makers of
  Anacin Analgesic Tablets
◆Aspirin-Free Arthritis Pain Formula by
  the Makers of Anacin Analgesic
  Tablets
 Bisodol Antacid Powder
 Bisodol Antacid Tablets
 Bronitin Asthma Tablets
 Bronitin Mist
 Cleansing Pads by the Makers of
  Preparation H Hemorrhoidal
  Remedies
 Compound W Solution
 Denalan Denture Cleanser
◆Denorex Medicated Shampoo
◆Denorex Mountain Fresh Scent
  Medicated Shampoo
◆Denorex Shampoo & Conditioner
◆Diet Gard 14 Day Diet Plan
 Dristan Cough Formula
◆Dristan Decongestant/Antihistamine/
  Analgesic Capsules
◆Dristan Decongestant/Antihistamine/
  Analgesic Tablets
 Dristan 12-Hour Nasal Decongestant
  Capsules
 Dristan Inhaler
◆Dristan Long Lasting Menthol Nasal
  Mist
◆Dristan Long Lasting Nasal Mist
◆Dristan Menthol Nasal Mist
◆Dristan Nasal Mist
 Dristan Room Vaporizer
 Dristan-AF Decongestant/Antihistamine/
  Analgesic Tablets
 Dry and Clear Acne Medication
 Dry and Clear Double Strength Cream
 Dry and Clear Medicated Acne Cleanser
 Freezone Solution
 Heather Feminine Deodorant Spray
 Heet Analgesic Liniment
 Heet Spray Analgesic
 InfraRub Analgesic Cream
 Momentum Muscular Backache
  Formula
 Neet Aerosol Depilatory
 Neet Depilatory Cream
 Neet Depilatory Lotion
 Outgro Solution
 Oxipor VHC Lotion for Psoriasis
 Predictor In-Home Early Pregnancy
  Test
◆Preparation H Hemorrhoidal Ointment
◆Preparation H Hemorrhoidal
  Suppositories
◆Prepcort Hydrocortisone Cream 0.5%
◆Primatene Mist
 Primatene Mist Suspension
◆Primatene Tablets - M Formula
◆Primatene Tablets - P Formula
 Quiet World Analgesic/Sleeping Aid
 Semicid Vaginal Contraceptive
  Suppositories
 Sleep-Eze Tablets
 Sudden Action Breath Freshener
 Sudden Beauty Country Air Mask
 Sudden Beauty Hair Spray
 Trendar Premenstrual Tablets
 Viro-Med Liquid
 Viro-Med Tablets

THE J. B. WILLIAMS COMPANY, INC. 679
767 Fifth Avenue
New York, NY 10153
Address inquiries to:
R.E. Hansen   (212) 752-5700
Branch Offices
Cranford, NJ 07016 (201) 276-8000
OTC Products Available
Acu-Test In-Home Pregnancy Test
Deep-Down Pain Relief Rub
Femlron Tablets

FemIron Multi-Vitamins and Iron
Geritol Liquid-High Potency Iron &
  Vitamin Tonic
Geritol Mega Vitamins
Geritol Tablets - High Potency Iron &
  Vitamin Tablets
Serutan Concentrated Powder
Serutan Concentrated Powder - Fruit
  Flavored
Serutan Toasted Granules
Sominex Sleep Aid
Vivarin Stimulant Tablets

Consumer Products Division 681
WINTHROP LABORATORIES
Division of Sterling Drug Inc.
90 Park Avenue
New York, NY 10016
Address inquiries to:
Professional Services Dept.
                    (212) 907-2520
For Medical Emergencies Contact:
Medical Director   (212) 907-2525
OTC Products Available
Astring-o-Sol
Bronkaid Mist
Bronkaid Mist Suspension
Bronkaid Tablets
Campho-Phenique Liquid & Gel
Caroid Laxative
Caroid Tooth Powder
Creamalin Tablets
Haley's M-O, Regular & Flavored
Mucilose Flakes & Granules
NTZ Drops & Spray
Neocurtasal
Neo-Synephrine Jelly
Neo-Synephrine Nasal Sprays
Neo-Synephrine Nasal Sprays
  (Mentholated)
Neo-Synephrine Nose Drops
Neo-Synephrine II Long Acting Nasal
  Spray
Neo-Synephrine II Long Acting Nose
  Drops (Adult & Pediatric Strengths)
Neo-Synephrine II Long Acting Vapor
  Nasal Spray
Neo-Synephrine 12 Hour Nasal Spray
  (Adult & Children's Strengths)
Neo-Synephrine 12 Hour Nose Drops
Neo-Synephrine 12 Hour Vapor Nasal
  Spray
Neo-Synephrinol Day Relief Capsules
pHisoAc
pHisoDan
pHisoDerm
pHisoDerm-Fresh Scent
WinGel Liquid & Tablets

WYETH LABORATORIES 430, 685
Division of American Home Products
Corporation
P.O. Box 8299
Philadelphia, PA 19101
Address inquiries to:
Professional Service (215) 688-4400
For Medical Emergency Information
Day or night call   (215) 688-4400
Wyeth Distribution Centers
Andover, MA 01810
  P.O. Box 1776   (617) 475-9075
Atlanta, GA 30302
  P.O. Box 4365   (404) 873-1681
Baltimore, MD 21224
  101 Kane St.   (301) 633-4000
Boston Distribution Center
  see under Andover, MA
Buena Park, CA 90620
  P.O. Box 5000   (714) 523-5500
              (Los Angeles) (213) 627-5374
Chicago Distribution Center
  see under Evanston, IL
Cleveland, OH 44101
  P.O. Box 91549   (216) 238-9450

Dallas, TX 75235
  P.O. Box 35213   (214) 631-4360
Denver, CO 80201
  P.O. Box 2107   (303) 388-3635
Evanston, IL 60204
  P.O. Box 1659
              (Skokie) (312) 675-1400
              (Chicago) (312) 463-2400
Honolulu, HI 96814
  1013 Kawaiahao St.(808) 538-1988
Kansas City Distribution Center,
  see under North Kansas City, MO
Kent, WA 98031
  P.O. Box 5609   (206) 872-8790
Los Angeles Distribution Center,
  see under Buena Park, CA
Memphis, TN 38101
  P.O. Box 1698   (901) 353-4680
New York Distribution Center,
  see under Secaucus, NJ
North Kansas City, MO 64116
  P.O. Box 7588   (816) 842-0680
Philadelphia Distribution Center
Paoli, PA 19301
  P.O. Box 61   (215) 644-8000
              (Phila.) (215) 878-9500
St. Paul, MN 55164
  P.O. Box 43034   (612) 454-6270
Seattle Distribution Center, see under
  Kent, WA
Secaucus, NJ 07094
  P.O. Box 2306   (201) 867-0300
              (N.Y.C.) (212) 964-0041

OTC Products Available
◆Aludrox Oral Suspension & Tablets
◆Amphojel Suspension & Suspension
  without Flavor
◆Amphojel Tablets
◆Collyrium Eye Lotion
◆Collyrium with Ephedrine Eye Drops
 Nursoy Soy Protein Infant Formula
 SMA Iron Fortified Infant Formula
 SMA lo-iron
◆Simeco Suspension
 Wyanoid Ointment
◆Wyanoids Hemorrhoidal Suppositories

W. F. YOUNG, INC. 430, 686
111 Lyman Street
Springfield, MA 01103

Address Inquiries to:
Robert F. Ferrin   (413) 737-0201

For Medical Emergencies Contact:
Donald Smith   (413) 737-0201

OTC Products Available
Absorbine Arthritic Pain Lotion
Absorbine Athlete's Foot Powder
◆Absorbine Jr.

YOUNGS DRUG PRODUCTS CORPORATION 687
Post Office Box 385
865 Centennial Avenue
Piscataway, NJ 08854

Sole Distributors for products
manufactured by HOLLAND-RANTOS
COMPANY, INC.

Address Inquiries to:
Mr. Philip L. Frank or
Mr. Murray H. Glantz (201) 885-5777

OTC Products Available
Koromex Contraceptive Foam
Koromex" Contraceptive Cream
Koromex" Contraceptive Jelly
Koromex"-A Contraceptive Jelly
Nylmerate" Solution Concentrate
Transi-Lube

(◆ Shown in Product Identification Section)

Product Name Index

In this section products are listed in alphabetical sequence by brand name or (if described) generic name. Only described products have page numbers to assist you in locating additional information. For additional information on other products, you may wish to contact the manufacturer directly. The symbol ◆ indicates the product is shown in the Product Identification Section.

(◆ **Shown in Product Identification Section**)   (**Products without page numbers are not described**)

(◆ Shown in Product Identification Section)   (Products without page numbers are not described)

(◆ Shown in Product Identification Section)   (Products without page numbers are not described)

Product Category Index

Products described in the Product Information (White) Section are listed according to their classifications. The headings and sub-headings have been determined by the OTC Review process of the U.S. Food and Drug Administration. Classification of products have been determined by the Publisher with the cooperation of individual manufacturers. In cases where there were differences of opinion or where the manufacturer had no opinion, the Publisher made the final decision.

A

ACNE PRODUCTS
  (see under DERMATOLOGICALS)

AEROSOLS
  R&C Spray (Reed & Carnrick) p 625
  Tinactin Aerosol Powder 1% (Schering) p 425, 642

ALLERGY RELIEF PRODUCTS
  A.R.M. Allergy Relief Medicine Tablets (Menley & James) p 413, 582
  Afrinol Repetabs Tablets (Schering) p 423, 635
  Allerest Headache Strength Tablets (Pharmacraft) p 618
  Allerest Tablets & Capsules (Pharmacraft) p 618
  Caladryl Lotion & Cream (Parke-Davis) p 419, 613
  Chlor-Trimeton Allergy Syrup, Tablets & Long-Acting Repetabs Tablets (Schering) p 423, 635
  Chlor-Trimeton Decongestant Tablets & Long Acting Decongestant Repetabs Tablets (Schering) p 423, 636
  Chlor-Trimeton Expectorant (Schering) p 635
  Congespirin Liquid Cold Medicine (Bristol-Myers) p 405, 525
  Contac Capsules (Menley & James) p 413, 583
  Coricidin Decongestant Nasal Mist (Schering) p 424, 636
  Coricidin Medilets Tablets for Children (Schering) p 424, 637
  Delacort (Mericon) p 589
  Demazin Decongestant-Antihistamine Repetabs Tablets & Syrup (Schering) p 424, 638
  Dimetane Decongestant Elixir (Robins) p 422, 628
  Dimetane Decongestant Tablets (Robins) p 422, 628
  Dimetane Elixir (Robins) p 422, 627
  Dimetane Tablets (Robins) p 422, 627

  Dristan Decongestant/Antihistamine/Analgesic Capsules (Whitehall) p 430, 673
  Dristan Decongestant/Antihistamine/Analgesic Tablets (Whitehall) p 430, 673
  Dristan 12-Hour Nasal Decongestant Capsules (Whitehall) p 673
  Dristan Long Lasting Nasal Mist, Regular & Menthol (Whitehall) p 430, 674
  Dristan Nasal Mist, Regular & Menthol (Whitehall) p 429, 674
  Dristan-AF Decongestant/Antihistamine/Analgesic Tablets (Whitehall) p 674
  4-Way Long Acting Nasal Spray (Bristol-Myers) p 406, 526
  4-Way Nasal Spray (Bristol-Myers) p 406, 526
  Headway Capsules and Tablets (Vicks Health Care) p 428, 657
  Novahistine Cold Tablets (Merrell Dow) p 593
  Novahistine Elixir (Merrell Dow) p 593
  Pyrroxate Capsules (Upjohn) p 427, 654
  Sinarest Tablets (Pharmacraft) p 620
  Sinex Decongestant Nasal Spray (Vicks Health Care) p 428, 658
  Sinex Long-Acting Decongestant Nasal Spray (Vicks Health Care) p 428, 658
  Teldrin Spansule Capsules, 8 mg., 12 mg. (Menley & James) p 415, 587
  Topic Benzyl Alcohol Gel (Syntex) p 650
  Triaminic Syrup (Dorsey) p 408, 542
  Triaminicin Chewables (Dorsey) p 542
  Triaminicin Tablets (Dorsey) p 408, 542
  Vatronol Nose Drops (Vicks Health Care) p 659
  Vicks Sinex Decongestant Nasal Spray (Vicks Health Care) p 428, 658
  Vicks Sinex Long-Acting Decongestant Nasal Spray (Vicks Health Care) p 428, 658

  Vicks Vatronol Nose Drops (Vicks Health Care) p 659
  Visine A.C. Eye Drops (Leeming) p 557

ANALGESICS
  Internal
    Acetaminophen & Combinations
    Acephen Acetaminophen Rectal Suppositories (G & W Laboratories) p 545
    Allerest Headache Strength Tablets (Pharmacraft) p 618
    Anacin-3 Analgesic Tablets & Capsules (Whitehall) p 429, 671
    Aspirin-Free Arthritis Pain Formula by the Makers of Anacin Analgesic Tablets (Whitehall) p 429, 671
    Comtrex (Bristol-Myers) p 405, 524
    Congespirin Liquid Cold Medicine (Bristol-Myers) p 405, 525
    Coricidin Extra Strength Sinus Headache Tablets (Schering) p 424, 638
    Datril (Bristol-Myers) p 406, 525
    Datril 500 (Bristol-Myers) p 406, 525
    Daycare Multi-Symptoms Colds Medicine Liquid (Vicks Health Care) p 427, 656
    Dristan-AF Decongestant/Antihistamine/Analgesic Tablets (Whitehall) p 674
    Excedrin (Bristol-Myers) p 406, 526
    Excedrin P.M. (Bristol-Myers) p 406, 526
    Gemnisyn (Rorer) p 422, 631
    Headway Capsules and Tablets (Vicks Health Care) p 428, 657
    Liquiprin (Norcliff Thayer) p 416, 604
    Novahistine Sinus Tablets (Merrell Dow) p 593
    Nyquil Nighttime Colds Medicine (Vicks Health Care) p 428, 658
    Ornex Capsules (Menley & James) p 414, 586
    Percogesic Tablets (Endo) p 409, 543
    Pyrroxate Capsules (Upjohn) p 427, 654

Prepcort Hydrocortisone Cream 0.5%
(Whitehall) p 430, 677
Rectal Medicone Unguent (Medicone)
p 582
Resicort Cream (Mentholatum) p 588
Tronolane Cream (Abbott Consumer
Products) p 403, 503
Wellcortin Cream and Lotion
(Burroughs Wellcome) p 407, 529
Wellcortin Ointment (Burroughs
Wellcome) p 407, 529
Wyanoid Ointment (Wyeth) p 686

Suppositories
Acephen Acetaminophen Rectal
Suppositories (G & W Laboratories)
p 545
Anusol Suppositories (Parke-Davis)
p 418, 612
Aspirin Suppositories (G & W
Laboratories) p 546
Norwich Glycerin Suppositories
(Norwich-Eaton) p 607
Nupercainal Suppositories (Ciba)
p 407, 535
Pazo Hemorrhoid Ointment/
Suppositories (Bristol-Myers) p 527
Preparation H Hemorrhoidal
Suppositories (Whitehall) p 430, 677
Rectal Medicone Suppositories
(Medicone) p 581
Tronolane Suppositories (Abbott
Consumer Products) p 403, 503
Wyanoids Hemorrhoidal Suppositories
(Wyeth) p 430, 686

Other
Cleansing Pads by the Makers of
Preparation H Hemorrhoidal
Remedies (Whitehall) p 672
E. E. Dickinson's Witch Hazel
(Dickinson) p 408, 540
Lobana Perineal Cleanse (Ulmer) p 653
Mediconet (Medicone) p 581
Tucks Premoistened Pads (Parke-Davis)
p 419, 615

ANOREXICS
(see under APPETITE SUPPRESSANTS)

ANTACIDS
Antacids
Alka-Seltzer Effervescent Pain Reliever
& Antacid (Miles Laboratories)
p 415, 596
Alka-2 Chewable Antacid Tablets (Miles
Laboratories) p 415, 596
ALternaGEL Liquid (Stuart) p 425, 645
Amphojel Suspension & Suspension
without Flavor (Wyeth) p 430, 685
Amphojel Tablets (Wyeth) p 430, 685
Arm & Hammer Baking Soda (Church
& Dwight) p 534
Nephrox Suspension (Fleming) p 544
Phillip's Milk of Magnesia (Glenbrook)
p 410, 548
Riopan Antacid Chew Tablets (Ayerst)
p 513
Riopan Antacid Suspension (Ayerst)
p 404, 513
Riopan Antacid Swallow Tablets
(Ayerst) p 513
Tums (Norcliff Thayer) p 417, 605

Antacid Combinations
Alka-Seltzer Effervescent Antacid (Miles
Laboratories) p 415, 596
Aludrox Oral Suspension & Tablets
(Wyeth) p 430, 685
Bisodol Antacid Powder (Whitehall)
p 671
Bisodol Antacid Tablets (Whitehall)
p 672
Citrocarbonate Antacid (Upjohn) p 653
Delcid (Merrell Dow) p 590
Di-Gel (Plough) p 420, 621
Eno (Beecham Products) p 517
Gaviscon Antacid Tablets (Marion)
p 411, 560
Gaviscon Liquid Antacid (Marion)
p 411, 561
Gaviscon-2 Antacid Tablets (Marion)
p 411, 561
Gelusil Liquid & Tablets (Parke-Davis)
p 419, 613

Kolantyl (Merrell Dow) p 591
Kudrox Suspension (Double Strength)
(Kremers-Urban) p 552
Maalox Suspension (Rorer) p 423, 631
Maalox TC (Therapeutic Concentrate)
(Rorer) p 423, 632
Maalox Tablets (No.1 & No.2) (Rorer)
p 423, 631
Magnatril Suspension & Tablets
(Lannett) p 552
Marblen Suspensions & Tablets
(Fleming) p 544
Percy Medicine (Merrick) p 415, 595
Riopan Plus Chew Tablets (Ayerst)
p 514
Riopan Plus Suspension (Ayerst)
p 404, 514
Simeco Suspension (Wyeth) p 430,
686
WinGel (Consumer Products Div.,
Winthrop) p 684

Antacids with Antiflatulents
Di-Gel (Plough) p 420, 621
Gelusil-M (Parke-Davis) p 614
Gelusil-II Liquid & Tablets (Parke-Davis)
p 614
Maalox Plus Suspension (Rorer) p 423,
632
Maalox Plus Tablets (Rorer) p 423,
632
Mylanta Liquid (Stuart) p 426, 647
Mylanta Tablets (Stuart) p 426, 647
Mylanta-II Liquid (Stuart) p 426, 648
Mylanta-II Tablets (Stuart) p 426, 648
Riopan Plus Chew Tablets (Ayerst)
p 514
Riopan Plus Suspension (Ayerst)
p 404, 514
Simeco Suspension (Wyeth) p 430,
686

ANTIANEMIA
(see under HEMATINICS)

ANTIARTHRITICS
(see under ANALGESICS)

ANTIASTHMATICS
(see under BRONCHODILATORS)

ANTIBIOTICS, Topical
BPN Ointment (Norwich-Eaton) p 605
Baciguent Antibiotic Ointment (Upjohn)
p 653
Myciguent Antibiotic Ointment (Upjohn)
p 654
Mycitracin Antibiotic Ointment (Upjohn)
p 427, 654

ANTICONSTIPATION
(see under LAXATIVES)

ANTIDIARRHEALS
Charcocaps (Requa) p 421, 626
Kaopectate Anti-Diarrhea Medicine
(Upjohn) p 427, 654
Kaopectate Concentrate Anti-Diarrhea
Medicine (Upjohn) p 427, 654
Lactinex Tablets & Granules (Hynson,
Westcott & Dunning) p 410, 551
Pepto-Bismol Liquid & Tablets
(Norwich-Eaton) p 417, 608
Percy Medicine (Merrick) p 415, 595
Rheaban Tablets & Liquid (Leeming)
p 556

ANTIDOTES FOR ACUTE TOXIC
INGESTION
Charcocaps (Requa) p 421, 626

ANTIEMETICS
Emetrol (Rorer) p 422, 631
Pepto-Bismol Liquid & Tablets
(Norwich-Eaton) p 417, 608

ANTIFLATULENTS
(see also under ANTACIDS)
Allimin Filmcoated Tablets (Health
Care) p 410, 549
Charcocaps (Requa) p 421, 626
Gas-X Tablets (Creighton Products)
p 409, 538
Mylicon (Tablets & Drops) (Stuart)
p 426, 648

Mylicon-80 Tablets (Stuart) p 426,
648

ANTIFUNGALS
(see under DERMATOLOGICALS)

ANTIHISTAMINES
(see under ALLERGY RELIEF
PRODUCTS or under COLD
PREPARATIONS)

ANTILICE
(see under PEDICULICIDES)

ANTIMICROBIALS, Topical
Anbesol Gel Antiseptic Anesthetic
(Whitehall) p 429, 671
Anbesol Liquid Antiseptic Anesthetic
(Whitehall) p 429, 671
BPN Ointment (Norwich-Eaton) p 605
Bactine Antiseptic/Anesthetic First Aid
Spray (Miles Laboratories) p 415,
597
Betadine Solution (Purdue Frederick)
p 421, 624
Listerine Antiseptic (Warner-Lambert
Co.) p 428, 663
Medi-Quik (Lehn & Fink) p 558
Mercurochrome II (Becton Dickinson)
p 517
Norwich Bacitracin Ointment
(Norwich-Eaton) p 607
Ora 5 (McHenry) p 412, 565
S.T. 37 (Beecham Products) p 518

ANTIMOTION SICKNESS REMEDIES
Bonine (Pfipharmecs) p 419, 617
Dramamine Liquid (Searle Consumer
Products) p 425, 642
Dramamine Tablets (Searle Consumer
Products) p 425, 642
Marezine Tablets (Burroughs Wellcome)
p 527

ANTINAUSEANTS
Dramamine Liquid (Searle Consumer
Products) p 425, 642
Dramamine Tablets (Searle Consumer
Products) p 425, 642
Emetrol (Rorer) p 422, 631
Pepto-Bismol Liquid & Tablets
(Norwich-Eaton) p 417, 608

ANTIOBESITY PREPARATIONS
(see under APPETITE
SUPPRESSANTS)

ANTIPERSPIRANTS
(see under DERMATOLOGICALS)

ANTIPRURITICS
(see under DERMATOLOGICALS)

ANTIPYRETICS
(see under ANALGESICS)

ANTISEPTICS
(see under ANTIMICROBIALS,
Topical)

ANTITUSSIVES
(see under COUGH PREPARATIONS)

ANTIVERTIGO AGENTS
Bonine (Pfipharmecs) p 419, 617
Dramamine Liquid (Searle Consumer
Products) p 425, 642
Dramamine Tablets (Searle Consumer
Products) p 425, 642
Marezine Tablets (Burroughs Wellcome)
p 527
Nicotinex Elixir (Fleming) p 544

APPETITE SUPPRESSANTS
Anorexin Capsules (SDA
Pharmaceuticals) p 633
Anorexin One-Span Capsules (SDA
Pharmaceuticals) p 633
Appedrine, Maximum Strength
(Thompson Medical) p 426, 650
The Cambridge Diet Plan (Cambridge)
p 407, 529
Codexin Extra Strength Capsules (Arco)
p 511
Control Capsules (Thompson Medical)
p 426, 651

Dexatrim & Dexatrim Extra Strength
(Thompson Medical) p 426, 651

Dexatrim Extra Strength, Caffeine-Free
(Thompson Medical) p 426, 651

Dietac Diet Aid Capsules (Menley &
James) p 414, 584

Dietac Diet Aid Drops (Menley &
James) p 414, 584

Dietac Diet Aid Tablets (Menley &
James) p 414, 584

Dietac Once-A-Day Maximum Strength
Diet Aid Capsules (Menley & James)
p 414, 584

Dietac Twice-A-Day Maximum Strength
Diet Aid Capsules (Menley & James)
p 414, 584

Diet Gard 14 Day Diet Plan (Whitehall)
p 429, 672

E-Z Trim (Fox) p 545

Herbitol (PharmTech) p 419, 620

Pretts Tablets (Marion) p 412, 562

Prolamine Capsules, Super Strength
(Thompson Medical) p 426, 651

Super Odrinex (Fox) p 545

ARTHRITIS RELIEF
(see under ANALGESICS)

ASTHMA PREPARATIONS
(see under BRONCHODILATORS)

ASTRINGENTS
(see under DERMATOLOGICALS)

ATHLETE'S FOOT TREATMENT
**(see under DERMATOLOGICALS,
Antifungal)**

B

BACKACHE REMEDIES
(see under ANALGESICS)

BAD BREATH PREPARATIONS
**(see under ORAL HYGIENE AID &
MOUTHWASHES)**

BANDAGES
Other
Gelocast (Beiersdorf) p 520

BATH PREPARATIONS
Alpha Keri Bath Oil (Westwood) p 666
Balnetar (Westwood) p 666

BEE STING RELIEF
**(see under INSECT BITE & STING
PREPARATIONS)**

BIOFEEDBACK SYSTEMS
GSR 2 (Thought Technology) p 652
GSR/Temp 2 (Thought Technology)
p 652

BIRTH CONTROL PREPARATIONS
**(see under VAGINAL PREPARATIONS
& CONTRACEPTIVES-MALE)**

BRONCHITIS PREPARATIONS
**(see under COLD PREPARATIONS
& COUGH PREPARATIONS)**

BRONCHODILATORS
Bronkaid Mist (Consumer Products
Div., Winthrop) p 681

Bronkaid Mist Suspension (Consumer
Products Div., Winthrop) p 681

Bronkaid Tablets (Consumer Products
Div., Winthrop) p 682

Efed II Capsules (Alto) p 404, 509

Primatene Mist (Whitehall) p 430, 677

Primatene Mist Suspension (Whitehall)
p 677

Primatene Tablets - M Formula
(Whitehall) p 430, 678

Primatene Tablets - P Formula
(Whitehall) p 430, 678

BURN PREPARATIONS
**(see under DERMATOLOGICALS,
Antidermatitis)**

BURSITIS RELIEF
(see under ANALGESICS)

C

CANKER SORE PREPARATIONS
External
Cankaid (Becton Dickinson) p 516
Gly-Oxide Liquid (Marion) p 411, 561
Ora 5 (McHenry) p 412, 565

COLD PREPARATIONS
Antihistamines & Combinations
A.R.M. Allergy Relief Medicine Tablets
(Menley & James) p 413, 582

Alka-Seltzer Plus Cold Medicine (Miles
Laboratories) p 415, 596

Allerest Headache Strength Tablets
(Pharmacraft) p 618

Allerest Tablets & Capsules
(Pharmacraft) p 618

C3 Cold Cough Capsules (Menley &
James) p 414, 583

Chlor-Trimeton Decongestant Tablets &
Long Acting Decongestant Repetabs
Tablets (Schering) p 423, 636

Comtrex (Bristol-Myers) p 405, 524

Contac Capsules (Menley & James)
p 413, 583

Contac Severe Cold Formula (Menley &
James) p 414, 583

Coricidin 'D' Decongestant Tablets
(Schering) p 424, 636

Coricidin Demilets Tablets for Children
(Schering) p 424, 637

Coricidin Extra Strength Sinus
Headache Tablets (Schering) p 424,
638

Coricidin Medilets Tablets for Children
(Schering) p 424, 637

Coricidin Tablets (Schering) p 424,
636

Demazin Decongestant-Antihistamine
Repetabs Tablets & Syrup (Schering)
p 424, 638

Dimetane Decongestant Elixir (Robins)
p 422, 628

Dimetane Decongestant Tablets
(Robins) p 422, 628

Dimetane Elixir (Robins) p 422, 627

Dimetane Tablets (Robins) p 422, 627

Dristan Decongestant/Antihistamine/
Analgesic Capsules (Whitehall)
p 430, 673

Dristan Decongestant/Antihistamine/
Analgesic Tablets (Whitehall) p 430,
673

Dristan 12-Hour Nasal Decongestant
Capsules (Whitehall) p 673

Dristan Nasal Mist, Regular & Menthol
(Whitehall) p 429, 674

Dristan-AF
Decongestant/Antihistamine/
Analgesic Tablets (Whitehall) p 674

4-Way Long Acting Nasal Spray
(Bristol-Myers) p 406, 526

4-Way Nasal Spray (Bristol-Myers)
p 406, 526

Formula 44 Cough Mixture (Vicks
Health Care) p 427, 657

Novahistine Cough & Cold Formula
(Merrell Dow) p 591

Novahistine Cold Tablets (Merrell Dow)
p 593

Novahistine Elixir (Merrell Dow) p 593

Novahistine Sinus Tablets (Merrell Dow)
p 593

Nyquil Nighttime Colds Medicine (Vicks
Health Care) p 428, 658

Pyrroxate Capsules (Upjohn) p 427,
654

Ryna Liquid (Wallace) p 428, 661

Sinarest Tablets (Pharmacraft) p 620

Sine-Off Extra Strength Sinus Medicine
Non-Aspirin Tablets (Menley &
James) p 415, 586

Sine-Off Sinus Medicine Tablets-Aspirin
Formula (Menley & James) p 415,
587

Sinutab Extra Strength Capsules
(Warner-Lambert Inc.) p 429, 665

Sinutab Extra Strength Tablets
(Warner-Lambert Inc.) p 429, 665

Sinutab Tablets (Warner-Lambert Inc.)
p 429, 664

Sudafed Plus Tablets & Syrup
(Burroughs Wellcome) p 406, 528

Teldrin Spansule Capsules, 8 mg., 12
mg. (Menley & James) p 415, 587

Triaminic Syrup (Dorsey) p 408, 542

Triaminic-12 Sustained Release Tablets
(Dorsey) p 408, 542

Triaminicin Tablets (Dorsey) p 408,
542

Tussagesic Tablets & Suspension
(Dorsey) p 543

Vicks Formula 44 Cough Mixture (Vicks
Health Care) p 427, 657

Vicks Nyquil Nighttime Colds Medicine
(Vicks Health Care) p 428, 658

Viro-Med Tablets (Whitehall) p 679

Decongestants

Oral & Combinations
Afrinol Repetabs Tablets (Schering)
p 423, 635

Alka-Seltzer Plus Cold Medicine (Miles
Laboratories) p 415, 596

Bayer Children's Cold Tablets
(Glenbrook) p 547

CCP Tablets (Medique) p 582

Children's Hold (Beecham Products)
p 517

Chlor-Trimeton Decongestant Tablets &
Long Acting Decongestant Repetabs
Tablets (Schering) p 423, 636

Comtrex (Bristol-Myers) p 405, 524

Congespirin (Bristol-Myers) p 405, 525

Congespirin Liquid Cold Medicine
(Bristol-Myers) p 405, 525

Contac Capsules (Menley & James)
p 413, 583

Contac Jr. Childrens' Cold Medicine
(Menley & James) p 414, 583

Contac Severe Cold Formula (Menley &
James) p 414, 583

Coricidin Cough Syrup (Schering)
p 424, 636

Coricidin 'D' Decongestant Tablets
(Schering) p 424, 636

Coricidin Demilets Tablets for Children
(Schering) p 424, 637

Coricidin Extra Strength Sinus
Headache Tablets (Schering) p 424,
638

Coryban-D Capsules (Pfipharmecs)
p 419, 617

CoTylenol Children's Liquid Cold
Formula (McNeil Consumer Products)
p 413, 566

CoTylenol Cold Formula Tablets and
Capsules (McNeil Consumer
Products) p 413, 566

CoTylenol Liquid Cold Formula (McNeil
Consumer Products) p 413, 566

Dalca Decongestant/Analgesic Tablets
(Ascher) p 511

Daycare Multi-Symptom Colds Medicine
Capsules (Vicks Health Care) p 427,
656

Daycare Multi-Symptoms Colds
Medicine Liquid (Vicks Health Care)
p 427, 656

Demazin Decongestant-Antihistamine
Repetabs Tablets & Syrup (Schering)
p 424, 638

Dimacol Capsules (Robins) p 421, 627

Dimetane Decongestant Elixir (Robins)
p 422, 628

Dimetane Decongestant Tablets
(Robins) p 422, 628

Dristan Decongestant/Antihistamine/
Analgesic Capsules (Whitehall)
p 430, 673

Dristan Decongestant/Antihistamine/
Analgesic Tablets (Whitehall) p 430,
673

Dristan 12-Hour Nasal Decongestant
Capsules (Whitehall) p 673

Dristan-AF
Decongestant/Antihistamine/
Analgesic Tablets (Whitehall) p 674

COSMETICS

Brush-On Blush (Almay) p 508
Brush-On Eyeliner (Almay) p 508
Chip Resistant Top Coat (Almay) p 508
Clear Nail Enamel (Almay) p 508
Enamel Quick Dry (Almay) p 508
Eyebrow and Liner Pencil (Almay)
  p 508
Eye Color Pencils (Almay) p 508
Herpecin-L Cold Sore Lip Balm
  (Campbell) p 529
High Gloss Nail Guard (Almay) p 508
Lengthening Mascara (Almay) p 508
Lip Color Pencils (Almay) p 508
Lip Liner Pencils (Almay) p 508
Long Wearing Eye Color (Almay) p 508
Long Wearing Eye Color Duo (Almay)
  p 508
Maxi Extra-Long Thick Lash Mascara
  w/Sealer (Max Factor) p 412, 563
Maxi-Lash 24-Hour Polymer Mascara
  (Max Factor) p 412, 562
Maxi Stay-Fresh Crease Resistant Eye
  Shadow (Max Factor) p 412, 562
Maxi-Thick Double-Lash Mascara (Max
  Factor) p 412, 562
Maxi Unshine Oil Blotting Make-Up
  (Max Factor) p 412, 563
Maxi Unshine Oil Free Liquid Make-Up
  (Max Factor) p 412, 563
Maxi Unshine 100% Oil Free Blotting
  Powder (Max Factor) p 412, 563
Maxi Unshine 100% Oil Free Blushing
  Gel (Max Factor) p 412, 563
Maxi Unshine 100% Oil Free Blushing
  Powder (Max Factor) p 412, 563
Moisture Rich Lipstick (Cream &
  Frosted) (Almay) p 508
Moisture Whip Lip Conditioner
  (Maybelline) p 565
Moisture Whip Lipstick (Maybelline)
  p 565
Moisture Whip Liquid Make-up &
  Moisture Whip Cream Make-up
  (Maybelline) p 565
Moisture Whip Protective Facial
  Moisturizer (Maybelline) p 565
Nail Enamel Remover (Almay) p 508
Protective Base Coat (Almay) p 508
Protective Formula Nail Enamel (Almay)
  p 508
Ridge Filling Pre-Coat (Almay) p 508
Thickening Mascara (Almay) p 508
Waterproof Mascara (Almay) p 508

COUGH PREPARATIONS

Antitussives & Combinations

Ambenyl-D Decongestant Cough
  Formula (Marion) p 411, 560
Bayer Cough Syrup for Children
  (Glenbrook) p 547
Benylin Cough Syrup (Parke-Davis)
  p 418, 613
Benylin DM (Parke-Davis) p 418, 613
C3 Cold Cough Capsules (Menley &
  James) p 414, 583
Children's Hold (Beecham Products)
  p 517
Contac Jr. Childrens' Cold Medicine
  (Menley & James) p 414, 583
Contac Severe Cold Formula (Menley &
  James) p 414, 583
Coricidin Children's Cough Syrup
  (Schering) p 424, 637
Coricidin Cough Syrup (Schering)
  p 424, 636
Coryban-D Cough Syrup (Pfipharmecs)
  p 419, 617
Cosanyl Cough Syrup (Health Care)
  p 410, 549
Cosanyl-DM Cough Syrup (Health Care)
  p 410, 549
CoTylenol Cold Formula Tablets and
  Capsules (McNeil Consumer
  Products) p 413, 566
CoTylenol Liquid Cold Formula (McNeil
  Consumer Products) p 413, 566
Daycare Multi-Symptom Colds Medicine
  Capsules (Vicks Health Care) p 427,
  656
Daycare Multi-Symptoms Colds
  Medicine Liquid (Vicks Health Care)
  p 427, 656

Dimacol Capsules (Robins) p 421, 627
Dorcol Pediatric Cough Syrup (Dorsey)
  p 408, 541
Formula 44 Cough Control Discs (Vicks
  Health Care) p 657
Formula 44 Cough Mixture (Vicks
  Health Care) p 427, 657
Formula 44D Decongestant Cough
  Mixture (Vicks Health Care) p 427,
  657
Halls Mentho-Lyptus Cough Tablets
  (Warner-Lambert Co.) p 428, 663
Halls Mentho-Lyptus Decongestant
  Cough Formula (Warner-Lambert Co.)
  p 663
Hold (Beecham Products) p 518
Naldecon-CX Suspension (Bristol)
  p 523
Naldecon-DX Pediatric Syrup (Bristol)
  p 523
Novahistine Cough & Cold Formula
  (Merrell Dow) p 591
Novahistine Cough Formula (Merrell
  Dow) p 591
Novahistine DMX (Merrell Dow) p 592
Nyquil Nighttime Colds Medicine (Vicks
  Health Care) p 428, 658
Ornacol Capsules (Menley & James)
  p 414, 586
Robitussin-CF (Robins) p 422, 629
Robitussin-DM (Robins) p 422, 629
Ryna-C Liquid (Wallace) p 428, 661
St. Joseph Cough Syrup for Children
  (Plough) p 420, 622
Sucrets Cough Control Formula
  (Beecham Products) p 519
Sudafed Cough Syrup (Burroughs
  Wellcome) p 406, 527
Triaminic-DM Cough Formula (Dorsey)
  p 408, 541
Triaminicol Decongestant Cough Syrup
  (Dorsey) p 408, 543
Trind-DM (Mead Johnson Nutritional)
  p 580
Tussagesic Tablets & Suspension
  (Dorsey) p 543
Vaposteam (Vicks Health Care) p 658
Vicks Cough Syrup (Vicks Health Care)
  p 659
Vicks Formula 44 Cough Control Discs
  (Vicks Health Care) p 657
Vicks Formula 44 Cough Mixture (Vicks
  Health Care) p 427, 657
Vicks Formula 44D Decongestant
  Cough Mixture (Vicks Health Care)
  p 427, 657
Vicks Nyquil Nighttime Colds Medicine
  (Vicks Health Care) p 428, 658
Vicks Vaporub (Vicks Health Care)
  p 428, 660
Vicks Vaposteam (Vicks Health Care)
  p 658
Viro-Med Liquid (Whitehall) p 679
Viro-Med Tablets (Whitehall) p 679

Expectorants & Combinations

Breonesin Capsules (Breon) p 405,
  522
CCP Tablets (Medique) p 582
Cheracol D Cough Syrup (Upjohn)
  p 653
Coricidin Children's Cough Syrup
  (Schering) p 424, 637
Coricidin Cough Syrup (Schering)
  p 424, 636
Dimacol Capsules (Robins) p 421, 627
Dorcol Pediatric Cough Syrup (Dorsey)
  p 408, 541
Formula 44 Cough Mixture (Vicks
  Health Care) p 427, 657
Formula 44D Decongestant Cough
  Mixture (Vicks Health Care) p 427,
  657
Glytuss Tablets (Mayrand) p 565
Naldecon-CX Suspension (Bristol)
  p 523
Naldecon-DX Pediatric Syrup (Bristol)
  p 523
Naldecon-EX Pediatric Drops (Bristol)
  p 523
Novahistine Cough Formula (Merrell
  Dow) p 591
Novahistine DMX (Merrell Dow) p 592
Robitussin (Robins) p 422, 629

Robitussin-CF (Robins) p 422, 629
Robitussin-DM (Robins) p 422, 629
Robitussin-PE (Robins) p 422, 629
Ryna-CX Liquid (Wallace) p 428, 661
Sudafed Cough Syrup (Burroughs
  Wellcome) p 406, 527
Triaminic Expectorant (Dorsey) p 408,
  542
Tussagesic Tablets & Suspension
  (Dorsey) p 543
Vaposteam (Vicks Health Care) p 658
Vicks Cough Syrup (Vicks Health Care)
  p 659
Vicks Formula 44 Cough Mixture (Vicks
  Health Care) p 427, 657
Vicks Formula 44D Decongestant
  Cough Mixture (Vicks Health Care)
  p 427, 657
Vicks Vaporub (Vicks Health Care)
  p 428, 660
Vicks Vaposteam (Vicks Health Care)
  p 658
Viro-Med Liquid (Whitehall) p 679
Viro-Med Tablets (Whitehall) p 679

Lozenges

Chloraseptic Cough Control Lozenges
  (Norwich-Eaton) p 417, 606
Formula 44 Cough Control Discs (Vicks
  Health Care) p 657
Spec-T Sore Throat/Cough Suppressant
  Lozenges (Squibb) p 425, 644
Vicks Cough Silencers Cough Drops
  (Vicks Health Care) p 659
Vicks Throat Lozenges (Vicks Health
  Care) p 659

D

DANDRUFF & SEBORRHEA PREPARATIONS
(see under DERMATOLOGICALS, ANTIDANDRUFF)

DECONGESTANTS
(see under COLD PREPARATIONS)

DENTAL PREPARATIONS

Anbesol Gel Antiseptic Anesthetic
  (Whitehall) p 429, 671
Anbesol Liquid Antiseptic Anesthetic
  (Whitehall) p 429, 671
Cankaid (Becton Dickinson) p 516
Colgate MFP Fluoride Gel
  (Colgate-Palmolive) p 407, 535
Colgate MFP Fluoride Toothpaste
  (Colgate-Palmolive) p 407, 536
Fluorigard Anti-Cavity Dental Rinse
  (Colgate-Palmolive) p 407, 536
Gly-Oxide Liquid (Marion) p 411, 561
Ora 5 (McHenry) p 412, 565
Sensodyne Toothpaste (Block) p 521
Xero-Lube-Saliva Substitute (Scherer)
  p 634

DENTURE PREPARATIONS

Anbesol Gel Antiseptic Anesthetic
  (Whitehall) p 429, 671
Anbesol Liquid Antiseptic Anesthetic
  (Whitehall) p 429, 671
Cushion Grip (Plough) p 420, 621
Ora 5 (McHenry) p 412, 565

DEODORANTS

Cheq Antiperspirant/Deodorant (Almay)
  p 508
Cheq Extra-Dry
  Antiperspirant/Deodorant Spray
  (Aerosol) (Almay) p 508
Cheq Roll-On Antiperspirant/Deodorant
  (Almay) p 508
Cheq Soft Powder Extra Dry
  Antiperspirant Spray (Aerosol)
  (Almay) p 508
Chloresium Ointment & Solution
  (Rystan) p 633
Derifil Tablets & Powder (Rystan)
  p 633
NP-27 Powder (Norwich-Eaton) p 608
Norforms Feminine Deodorant &
  Suppositories (Norwich-Eaton) p 417,
  607

DERMATOLOGICALS

Abradant
Oxy-Scrub (Norcliff Thayer) p 417, 604
Pernox Lotion (Westwood) p 668
Pernox Scrub (Westwood) p 668

Analgesic
Calamatum Lotion, Ointment, Spray (Blair) p 520
Vicks Vaporub (Vicks Health Care) p 428, 660

Anesthetics, Topical
Bactine Antiseptic/Anesthetic First Aid Spray (Miles Laboratories) p 415, 597
Dermoplast (Ayerst) p 404, 513
Rhulicaine (Lederle) p 411, 554

Antiacne Preparations
Acnederm Lotion (Lannett) p 552
Acno Astringent (Baker/Cummins) p 514
Acno Lotion (Baker/Cummins) p 514
Acnomel Cream (Menley & James) p 413, 582
Bensulfoid Lotion (Poythress) p 623
Clearasil 5% Benzoyl Peroxide Lotion (Vicks Toiletry Products) p 427, 656
Clearasil Pore Deep Cleanser (Vicks Toiletry Products) p 427, 656
Clearasil Super Strength Acne Treatment Cream, Tinted (Vicks Toiletry Products) p 427, 655
Dry and Clear, Acne Medication, Lotion & Double Strength Cream (Whitehall) p 675
Dry and Clear Medicated Acne Cleanser (Whitehall) p 675
Fomac Foam (Dermik) p 538
Fostex 5% Benzoyl Peroxide Gel (Westwood) p 667
Fostex Medicated Cleansing Bar (Westwood) p 667
Fostex Medicated Cleansing Cream (Westwood) p 667
Fostex Medicated Cover-Up (Westwood) p 667
Fostril (Westwood) p 667
Hydrostat Lotion (Derma) p 538
Loroxide Acne Lotion (Dermik) p 539
Oxy-5 Lotion (Norcliff Thayer) p 417, 604
Oxy-10 Lotion (Norcliff Thayer) p 417, 604
Oxy-Scrub (Norcliff Thayer) p 417, 604
Oxy Wash (Norcliff Thayer) p 417, 605
Pernox Lotion (Westwood) p 668
Pernox Scrub (Westwood) p 668
Stri-Dex B.P. (Lehn & Fink) p 558
Stri-Dex Medicated Pads (Lehn & Fink) p 558
Topex 10% Benzoyl Peroxide Lotion Buffered Acne Medication (Vicks Toiletry Products) p 427, 656
Transact (Westwood) p 670
Vanoxide Acne Lotion (Dermik) p 539
Vlemasque Acne Mask (Dermik) p 539
Xerac (Persōn & Covey) p 617
Zacne Tablets (Nature's Bounty) p 603

Antibacterial
B.F.I. (Beecham Products) p 517
BPN Ointment (Norwich-Eaton) p 605
Bactine Antiseptic/Anesthetic First Aid Spray (Miles Laboratories) p 415, 597
Betadine Ointment (Purdue Frederick) p 421, 624
Betadine Skin Cleanser (Purdue Frederick) p 421, 624
Betadine Solution (Purdue Frederick) p 421, 624
Campho-Phenique Liquid (Consumer Products Div., Winthrop) p 682
Hibiclens Antimicrobial Skin Cleanser (Stuart) p 425, 646
Hibistat Germicidal Hand Rinse (Stuart) p 647
Hibitane Tincture (Tinted & Non-Tinted) (Stuart) p 647
Hydrostat Lotion (Derma) p 538
Isodine Antiseptic (Blair) p 520

Listerine Antiseptic (Warner-Lambert Co.) p 428, 663
Loroxide Acne Lotion (Dermik) p 539
Medi-Quik (Lehn & Fink) p 558
NP-27 Powder (Norwich-Eaton) p 608
Neosporin Ointment (Burroughs Wellcome) p 406, 527
Norwich Bacitracin Ointment (Norwich-Eaton) p 607
Oxy Wash (Norcliff Thayer) p 417, 605
Polysporin Ointment (Burroughs Wellcome) p 527
PRID Salve (Walker Pharmacal) p 660
Rhulicaine (Lederle) p 411, 554
Vanoxide Acne Lotion (Dermik) p 539

Antibacterial, Antifungal & Combinations
Caldesene Medicated Ointment (Pharmacraft) p 619
Caldesene Medicated Powder (Pharmacraft) p 619
Vioform Cream & Ointment (Ciba) p 535

Antiburn
Alo-Ointment (Aloe Cream) p 404, 509
Bactine Antiseptic/Anesthetic First Aid Spray (Miles Laboratories) p 415, 597
Balmex Ointment (Macsil) p 560
Betadine Ointment (Purdue Frederick) p 421, 624
BiCozene Creme (Creighton Products) p 409, 537
Desitin Ointment (Leeming) p 556
Hydrostat Lotion (Derma) p 538
Medi-Quik (Lehn & Fink) p 558
Neosporin Ointment (Burroughs Wellcome) p 406, 527
Polysporin Ointment (Burroughs Wellcome) p 527
Resinol Cream (Mentholatum) p 588
Resinol Ointment (Mentholatum) p 588
Rhulicaine (Lederle) p 411, 554
Unguentine Plus First Aid & Burn Cream (Norwich-Eaton) p 608

Antidandruff
DHS Tar Shampoo (Persōn & Covey) p 419, 616
DHS Zinc Dandruff Shampoo (Persōn & Covey) p 419, 616
Denorex Medicated Shampoo, Regular & Mountain Fresh Herbal (Whitehall) p 429, 672
Denorex Shampoo & Conditioner (Whitehall) p 429, 672
Doak Tar Shampoo (Doak) p 408, 541
Head & Shoulders (Procter & Gamble) p 623
Listerine Antiseptic (Warner-Lambert Co.) p 428, 663
Sebb Dandruff Treatment Lotion (Max Factor) p 412, 563
Tegrin Medicated Shampoo (Block) p 521
Zetar Shampoo (Dermik) p 539

Antidermatitis
Alo-Ointment (Aloe Cream) p 404, 509
Alo-Relief (Aloe Cream) p 404, 509
Bactine Hydrocortisone Skin Care Cream (Miles Laboratories) p 415, 597
Balmex Baby Powder (Macsil) p 560
Balmex Emollient Lotion (Macsil) p 560
Balmex Ointment (Macsil) p 560
BiCozene Creme (Creighton Products) p 409, 537
Borofax Ointment (Burroughs Wellcome) p 527
Caladryl Lotion & Cream (Parke-Davis) p 419, 613
Calamatum Lotion, Ointment, Spray (Blair) p 520
Cortaid Cream (Upjohn) p 427, 653
Cortaid Lotion (Upjohn) p 427, 653
Cortaid Ointment (Upjohn) p 427, 653
Cortef Feminine Itch Cream (Upjohn) p 427, 653
Cortef Rectal Itch Ointment (Upjohn) p 427, 654
Delacort (Mericon) p 589
Dermolate Anti-Itch Cream & Spray (Schering) p 424, 639

Dermolate Scalp-Itch Lotion (Schering) p 424, 639
Doak Tar Lotion (Doak) p 408, 541
E. E. Dickinson's Witch Hazel (Dickinson) p 408, 540
E. E. Dickinson's Witch Hazel Towelettes (Dickinson) p 408, 540
Estar Tar Gel (Westwood) p 666
Hytone Cream & Ointment ½% (Dermik) p 538
Kerodex Cream 51 (for dry or oily work) (Ayerst) p 404, 513
Kerodex Cream 71 (for wet work) (Ayerst) p 404, 513
Lanacort Antipruritic Hydrocortisone Acetate 0.5% Creme (Combe) p 537
Lobana Derm-Ade Cream (Ulmer) p 653
Pragmatar Ointment (Menley & James) p 414, 586
Prepcort Hydrocortisone Cream 0.5% (Whitehall) p 430, 677
Resicort Cream (Mentholatum) p 588
Resinol Cream (Mentholatum) p 588
Rhulicort Cream & Lotion (Lederle) p 411, 555
Solarcaine (Plough) p 420, 622
Tarpaste (Doak) p 541
Wellcortin Cream and Lotion (Burroughs Wellcome) p 407, 529
Wellcortin Ointment (Burroughs Wellcome) p 407, 529
Zincofax Skin Cream (Burroughs Wellcome) p 529
Ziradryl Lotion (Parke-Davis) p 419, 616

Antifungal & Combinations
Aftate (Plough) p 419, 620
B.F.I. (Beecham Products) p 517
Betadine Ointment (Purdue Frederick) p 421, 624
Betadine Skin Cleanser (Purdue Frederick) p 421, 624
Betadine Solution (Purdue Frederick) p 421, 624
Blis-To-Sol Liquid (Chattem) p 533
Blis-To-Sol Powder (Chattem) p 533
Cruex Antifungal Cream (Pharmacraft) p 619
Cruex Antifungal Powder (Pharmacraft) p 619
Desenex Foam (Pharmacraft) p 619
Desenex Ointment & Liquid (Pharmacraft) p 619
Desenex Powders (Pharmacraft) p 619
Desenex Soap (Pharmacraft) p 619
Hibiclens Antimicrobial Skin Cleanser (Stuart) p 425, 646
Hibistat Germicidal Hand Rinse (Stuart) p 647
Hibitane Tincture (Tinted & Non-Tinted) (Stuart) p 647
NP-27 Aerosol Powder (Norwich-Eaton) p 608
NP-27 Cream (Norwich-Eaton) p 607
NP-27 Liquid (Norwich-Eaton) p 608
NP-27 Powder (Norwich-Eaton) p 608
Tinactin Aerosol Powder 1% (Schering) p 425, 642
Tinactin 1% Cream, Solution & Powder (Schering) p 425, 642

Antiperspirants
Cheq Antiperspirant/Deodorant (Almay) p 508
Cheq Extra-Dry Antiperspirant/Deodorant Spray (Aerosol) (Almay) p 508
Cheq Roll-On Antiperspirant/Deodorant (Almay) p 508
Cheq Soft Powder Extra Dry Antiperspirant Spray (Aerosol) (Almay) p 508

Antipruritics, Topical
Alpha Keri Bath Oil (Westwood) p 666
Balneol (Rowell) p 633
Balnetar (Westwood) p 666
Benadryl Antihistamine Cream (Parke-Davis) p 418, 612
BiCozene Creme (Creighton Products) p 409, 537
Caladryl Lotion & Cream (Parke-Davis) p 419, 613

Oil Control Facial Cleanser (Almay) p 508
Oxy Wash (Norcliff Thayer) p 417, 605
Perineal/Ostomy Skin Cleanser (Consolidated) p 537
Pernox Scrub (Westwood) p 668
Purpose Brand Soap (Ortho Dermatological) p 418, 611
Satin Body Wash and Shampoo (Consolidated) p 537
Shepard's Soap (Dermik) p 539
Skin Principle Gentle Cleansing Bar (Max Factor) p 412, 564
Skin Principle Purifying Cleansing Lotion (Max Factor) p 412, 564
Tersaseptic Hygienic Skin Cleanser (Doak) p 408, 541

Sulfur & Salicylic Acid
Acno Lotion (Baker/Cummins) p 514
Fomac Foam (Dermik) p 538
Fostex Medicated Cleansing Bar (Westwood) p 667
Fostex Medicated Cleansing Cream (Westwood) p 667
Pernox Lotion (Westwood) p 668
Pernox Scrub (Westwood) p 668
Pragmatar Ointment (Menley & James) p 414, 586
Sebulex and Sebulex Cream (Westwood) p 669
Sebulex with Protein (Westwood) p 670
Sebutone & Sebutone Cream (Westwood) p 670

Sunburn Preparations
Alo-Relief (Aloe Cream) p 404, 509
Bactine Antiseptic/Anesthetic First Aid Spray (Miles Laboratories) p 415, 597
Balmex Ointment (Macsil) p 560
BiCozene Creme (Creighton Products) p 409, 537
Borofax Ointment (Burroughs Wellcome) p 527
Dermoplast (Ayerst) p 404, 513
Hydrostat Lotion (Derma) p 538
Lobana Derm-Ade Cream (Ulmer) p 653
Medi-Quik (Lehn & Fink) p 558
Resinol Ointment (Mentholatum) p 588
Rhulicaine (Lederle) p 411, 554
Solarcaine (Plough) p 420, 622
Unguentine Plus First Aid & Burn Cream (Norwich-Eaton) p 608

Sun Screens
Alo-Lip-Shield (Aloe Cream) p 403, 509
Alo-Sun Fashion Tan SPF 15 Sun Block Lotion (Aloe Cream) p 404, 509
Alo-Sun SPF 15 Sun Block Stick (Aloe Cream) p 509
Chap Stick Lip Balm (Robins) p 421, 627
Chap Stick Sunblock 15 Lip Balm (Robins) p 421, 627
Eclipse Sunscreen Lotion, Total (Alcohol Base) (Herbert) p 410, 550
Eclipse Sunscreen Lotion, Total (Moisturizing Base) (Herbert) p 410, 550
Formula 405 Solar Cream (Doak) p 540
Herpecin-L Cold Sore Lip Balm (Campbell) p 529
Mentholatum Lipbalm with Sunscreen (Mentholatum) p 588
Moisture Whip Lip Conditioner (Maybelline) p 565
Moisture Whip Lipstick (Maybelline) p 565
Moisture Whip Liquid Make-up & Moisture Whip Cream Make-up (Maybelline) p 565
Moisture Whip Protective Facial Moisturizer (Maybelline) p 565
PreSun 4 Lotion (Westwood) p 669
PreSun 8 Lotion, Creamy Lotion & Gel (Westwood) p 669
PreSun 15 Creamy Sunscreen Lotion (Westwood) p 669
PreSun 15 Lotion (Westwood) p 669
PreSun 15 Sunscreen Lip Protector (Westwood) p 669

Resinol Cream (Mentholatum) p 588
Shade Plus Sunscreen Lotion (SPF-8) (Plough) p 420, 622
Shade Sunscreen Lotion (SPF-6) (Plough) p 420, 622
Solbar (Persōn & Covey) p 617
Solbar Plus 15 (Persōn & Covey) p 617
Sundown Sunscreen, Extra Protection (Johnson & Johnson Baby Products Company) p 410, 551
Sundown Sunscreen, Maximal Protection (Johnson & Johnson Baby Products Company) p 410, 551
Sundown Sunscreen, Moderate Protection (Johnson & Johnson Baby Products Company) p 410, 551
Sundown Sunscreen, Ultra Protection (Johnson & Johnson Baby Products Company) p 410, 551
Super Shade (SPF-15) (Plough) p 420, 623

Wart Removers
Compound W Solution (Whitehall) p 672
Vergo Cream (Daywell) p 538
Wart-Off (Pfipharmecs) p 419, 618

Wet Dressings
Domeboro Powder Packets & Tablets (Miles Pharmaceuticals) p 599
E. E. Dickinson's Witch Hazel (Dickinson) p 408, 540
Tucks Premoistened Pads (Parke-Davis) p 419, 615

Other
Bactine Hydrocortisone Skin Care Cream (Miles Laboratories) p 415, 597
Balanced Makeup for Normal/Combination Skin (Almay) p 508
Borofax Ointment (Burroughs Wellcome) p 527
Brush-On Blush (Almay) p 508
Clean and Gentle Oil-Free Conditioner (Almay) p 508
Cortaid Cream (Upjohn) p 427, 653
Cortaid Lotion (Upjohn) p 427, 653
Cortaid Ointment (Upjohn) p 427, 653
Cortef Feminine Itch Cream (Upjohn) p 427, 653
Cortef Rectal Itch Ointment (Upjohn) p 427, 654
Cover-up Stick - light, medium, dark (Almay) p 508
Cuticle Treatment Oil (Almay) p 508
Deep Mist Gentle Gel Mask (Almay) p 508
Derma Medicone Ointment (Medicone) p 581
Diaparene Baby Wash Cloths (Glenbrook) p 409, 548
E. E. Dickinson's Witch Hazel Towelettes (Dickinson) p 408, 540
Extra Cover Cream Makeup (Almay) p 508
Extra Hold Protein Conditioning Hair Spray (Aerosol) (Almay) p 508
Ice Mint (Westwood) p 667
Medicone Dressing Cream (Medicone) p 581
Moisturizing Eye Makeup Remover Pads (Almay) p 508
Moisturizing Make-Up for Dry Skin (Almay) p 508
Natural Blush Cream Cheek Color (Almay) p 508
Oil-Free Make-Up (Almay) p 508
Oil-Free Moisture Lotion (Almay) p 508
PRID Salve (Walker Pharmacal) p 660
Protein Conditioning Hair Spray (Almay) p 508
Regular Hold Conditioning Hair Spray (Almay) p 508
Resicort Cream (Mentholatum) p 588
Resinol Cream (Mentholatum) p 588
Sebucare (Westwood) p 669
Shepard's Cream Lotion (Dermik) p 539
Shepard's Dry Skin Cream (Dermik) p 539
Shepard's Hand Cream (Dermik) p 539

Shepard's Soap (Dermik) p 539
Tried & True Hair Thickener (Max Factor) p 412, 564
Under Eye Cover Creme, Ivory, Natural (Almay) p 508

DIAGNOSTICS
Acu-Test In-Home Pregnancy Test (J.B. Williams) p 679
Microstix-Nitrite Kit (Ames Division, Miles) p 404, 509
Predictor In-Home Early Pregnancy Test (Whitehall) p 676

DIAPER RASH RELIEF
(see under DERMATOLOGICALS, Antidermatitis)

DIARRHEA AIDS
(see under ANTIDIARRHEALS)

DIET AIDS
(see under APPETITE SUPPRESSANTS)

DIETARY SUPPLEMENTS
Acidophilus Capsules (Nature's Bounty) p 600
Alfalfa Tablets (Nature's Bounty) p 600
Allbee C-800 Plus Iron Tablets (Robins) p 421, 626
Allbee C-800 Tablets (Robins) p 421, 626
Allbee with C Capsules (Robins) p 421, 626
Aloe Vera Juice (Forever Living) p 409, 545
Bee Pollen Tablets (Nature's Bounty) p 600
Brewer's Yeast Powder (Debittered) (Nature's Bounty) p 600
Brewer's Yeast Tablets (Nature's Bounty) p 600
The Cambridge Diet Plan (Cambridge) p 407, 529
Carnation Instant Breakfast (Carnation) p 530
Casec (Mead Johnson Nutritional) p 568
Chew-Iron Tablets (Nature's Bounty) p 601
Choline Tablets (Nature's Bounty) p 601
Criticare HN (Mead Johnson Nutritional) p 569
Enisyl 334 mg and 500 mg Tablets (Persōn & Covey) p 617
FemIron Tablets (J.B. Williams) p 680
FemIron Multi-Vitamins and Iron (J.B. Williams) p 680
Fibermed (Purdue Frederick) p 421, 625
Garlic Oil Capsules (Nature's Bounty) p 601
Garlic & Parsley Capsules (Nature's Bounty) p 601
Geritol Liquid - High Potency Iron & Vitamin Tonic (J.B. Williams) p 680
Geritol Mega Vitamins (J.B. Williams) p 680
Geritol Tablets - High Potency Iron & Vitamin Tablets (J.B. Williams) p 680
Ginseng, Manchurian Capsules & Tablets (Nature's Bounty) p 601
Glutamic Acid Tablets (Nature's Bounty) p 601
l-Glutamine Tablets (Nature's Bounty) p 602
Herbitol (PharmTech) p 419, 620
Incremin w/Iron Syrup (Lederle) p 554
Inositol Tablets (Nature's Bounty) p 601
Isocal Complete Liquid Diet (Mead Johnson Nutritional) p 571
Isocal HCN (Mead Johnson Nutritional) p 572
KLB6 Capsules (Nature's Bounty) p 602
Kelp Tablets (Nature's Bounty) p 602
Lecithin Capsules (Nature's Bounty) p 602
Lecithin Chewable Tablets (Nature's Bounty) p 602

Lecithin Granules (Nature's Bounty)
p 602
I-Lysine Tablets (Nature's Bounty)
p 602
Mega-B (Arco) p 511
Optilets-500 (Abbott) p 503
Orazinc (Mericon) p 589
PABA Tablets (Nature's Bounty) p 602
Pantothenic Acid Tablets (Nature's
Bounty) p 602
Protein Tablets (Nature's Bounty)
p 602
RNA Tablets (Nature's Bounty) p 602
RNA/DNA Tablets (Nature's Bounty)
p 602
Rutin Tablets (Nature's Bounty) p 602
Super Wate-On Emulsion (Fleetwood)
p 409, 544
Sustacal HC (Mead Johnson
Nutritional) p 578
Tryptophan Tablets (Nature's Bounty)
p 602
Ultra KLB6 Tablets (Nature's Bounty)
p 603
Ultra Vita-Time Tablets (Nature's
Bounty) p 603
Yeast Plus Tablets (Nature's Bounty)
p 603
Z-Bec Tablets (Robins) p 422, 629
Zinc Tabs (Mericon) p 589

DIGESTIVE AIDS
Charcocaps (Requa) p 421, 626
Cholagest (Anabolic) p 510
Festal (Hoechst-Roussel) p 410, 550
Pepto-Bismol Liquid & Tablets
(Norwich-Eaton) p 417, 608

DISHPAN HANDS AIDS
(see under DERMATOLOGICALS,
Antidermatitis)

DIURETICS
Aqua-Ban (Thompson Medical) p 426,
650
DeWitt's Pills for Backache & Joint
Pains (DeWitt) p 408, 539
Odrinil (Fox) p 545
Sunril Premenstrual Capsules
(Schering) p 424, 641
Water Pill Tablets (Nature's Bounty)
p 603
Water Pill w/Iron Tablets (Nature's
Bounty) p 603

DRY SKIN PREPARATIONS
(see under DERMATOLOGICALS,
Emollients)

E

EAR ACHE AIDS
(see under EAR PREPARATIONS)

EAR PREPARATIONS
Ear Wax Control Agents
Debrox Drops (Marion) p 411, 560
Ear Drops by Murine
(See Murine Ear Wax Removal
System/Murine Ear Drops) (Abbott
Consumer Products) p 403, 502
Kerid Ear Drops (Blair) p 520
Murine Ear Wax Removal
System/Murine Ear Drops (Abbott
Consumer Products) p 403, 502
Other
Star-Otic (Stellar) p 645

ECZEMA PREPARATIONS
(see under DERMATOLOGICALS,
Antidermatitis)

ELECTROLYTE REPLACEMENT, ORAL
Lytren (Mead Johnson Nutritional)
p 573

ENZYMES & DIGESTANTS
Cholagest (Anabolic) p 510
LactAid (SugarLo) p 426, 649
Papaya Enzyme Tablets (Nature's
Bounty) p 602

EXPECTORANTS
(see under COUGH PREPARATIONS)

EYE PREPARATIONS
(see under OPHTHALMICS)

F

FEVER BLISTER AIDS
(see under COLD SORE
PREPARATIONS)

FIBER SUPPLEMENT
Fibermed (Purdue Frederick) p 421,
625

FOODS
Allergy Diet
MBF (Meat Base Formula) Liquid
(Gerber) p 546
ProSobee (Mead Johnson Nutritional)
p 576
Complete Therapeutic
Carnation Instant Breakfast (Carnation)
p 530
Criticare HN (Mead Johnson
Nutritional) p 569
Isocal Complete Liquid Diet (Mead
Johnson Nutritional) p 571
Isocal HCN (Mead Johnson Nutritional)
p 572
Slender Diet Food For Weight Control
(Instant) (Carnation) p 530
Slender Diet Meal Bars For Weight
Control (Carnation) p 530
Slender Diet Meal For Weight Control
(Canned) (Carnation) p 530
Sustacal (Mead Johnson Nutritional)
p 577
Sustacal HC (Mead Johnson
Nutritional) p 578
Sustagen (Mead Johnson Nutritional)
p 579
Dietetic
Herbitol (PharmTech) p 419, 620
Slender Diet Food For Weight Control
(Instant) (Carnation) p 530
Slender Diet Meal Bars For Weight
Control (Carnation) p 530
Slender Diet Meal For Weight Control
(Canned) (Carnation) p 530
High Nitrogen
Criticare HN (Mead Johnson
Nutritional) p 569
Isocal HCN (Mead Johnson Nutritional)
p 572
Infant
(see under INFANT FORMULAS)
Lactose Free
Criticare HN (Mead Johnson
Nutritional) p 569
Isocal HCN (Mead Johnson Nutritional)
p 572
Portagen (Mead Johnson Nutritional)
p 575
Sustacal HC (Mead Johnson
Nutritional) p 578
Low Fat
Criticare HN (Mead Johnson
Nutritional) p 569
Slender Diet Meal For Weight Control
(Canned) (Carnation) p 530
Low Residue
Criticare HN (Mead Johnson
Nutritional) p 569
Isocal HCN (Mead Johnson Nutritional)
p 572
Sustacal HC (Mead Johnson
Nutritional) p 578
Low Sodium
Criticare HN (Mead Johnson
Nutritional) p 569
Isocal HCN (Mead Johnson Nutritional)
p 572
Lonalac (Mead Johnson Nutritional)
p 573
Medium Chain Triglycerides
Isocal HCN (Mead Johnson Nutritional)
p 572
MCT Oil (Mead Johnson Nutritional)
p 574

Portagen (Mead Johnson Nutritional)
p 575
Nonfat
Carnation Instant Nonfat Dry Milk
(Carnation) p 530
Slender Diet Food For Weight Control
(Instant) (Carnation) p 530
Other
The Cambridge Diet Plan (Cambridge)
p 407, 529

FOOT CARE PRODUCTS
(see under DERMATOLOGICALS)

FORMULAS
(see under INFANT FORMULAS)

G

GASTRITIS AIDS
(see under ANTACIDS)

GERMICIDES
(see under ANTIMICROBIALS)

H

HALITOSIS PREPARATIONS
(see under ORAL HYGIENE AID &
MOUTHWASHES)

HAY FEVER AIDS
(see under ALLERGY RELIEF
PRODUCTS)

HEADACHE RELIEF
(see under ANALGESICS)

HEAD LICE RELIEF
(see under PEDICULICIDES)

HEARTBURN AIDS
(see under ANTACIDS)

HEMATINICS
Femiron Tablets (J.B. Williams) p 680
Feosol Elixir (Menley & James) p 414,
585
Feosol Plus (Menley & James) p 414,
585
Feosol Spansule Capsules (Menley &
James) p 414, 585
Feosol Tablets (Menley & James)
p 414, 585
Ferancee Chewable Tablets (Stuart)
p 646
Ferancee-HP Tablets (Stuart) p 425,
646
Fergon Capsules (Breon) p 523
Fergon Tablets & Elixir (Breon) p 522
Fer-In-Sol Iron Drops, Syrup & Capsules
(Mead Johnson Nutritional) p 571
Ferro-Sequels (Lederle) p 411, 553
Ferrous Sulfate Tablets (Nature's
Bounty) p 601
Fumasorb Tablets (Marion) p 560
Geritol Liquid - High Potency Iron &
Vitamin Tonic (J.B. Williams) p 680
Geritol Mega Vitamins (J.B. Williams)
p 680
Geritol Tablets - High Potency Iron &
Vitamin Tablets (J.B. Williams) p 680
Incremin w/Iron Syrup (Lederle) p 554
Iron Tablets (Nature's Bounty) p 601
Mol-Iron Tablets, Liquid & Chronosule
Capsules (Schering) p 424, 641
Mol-Iron Tablets w/Vitamin C
(Schering) p 424, 641
Nu-Iron 150 Caps (Mayrand) p 565
Nu-Iron Elixir (Mayrand) p 565
Peritinic Tablets (Lederle) p 554
Simron (Merrell Dow) p 594
Simron Plus (Merrell Dow) p 595
Stuartinic Tablets (Stuart) p 426, 649
Tri-88 (Anabolic) p 510
Troph-Iron Liquid & Tablets (Menley &
James) p 415, 587

HEMORRHOIDAL PREPARATIONS
(see under ANORECTAL PRODUCTS)

HERPES PREPARATIONS
(see under COLD SORE PREPARATIONS)

HOUSEWIVES' DERMATITIS AIDS
(see under DERMATOLOGICALS, Antidermatitis)

I

INFANT FORMULAS

Concentrate
Enfamil Concentrated Liquid & Powder (Mead Johnson Nutritional) p 569
Enfamil w/Iron Concentrated Liquid & Powder (Mead Johnson Nutritional) p 570
I-Soyalac (Loma Linda) p 558
Nursoy Soy Protein Infant Formula (Wyeth) p 685
ProSobee (Mead Johnson Nutritional) p 576
SMA Iron Fortified Infant Formula (Wyeth) p 685
SMA lo-iron (Wyeth) p 685
Soyalac: Liquid Concentrate, Ready-to-Serve and Powder (Loma Linda) p 559

Corn Free
I-Soyalac (Loma Linda) p 558

High Protein
Casec (Mead Johnson Nutritional) p 568

Hypo-Allergenic
I-Soyalac (Loma Linda) p 558
MBF (Meat Base Formula) Liquid (Gerber) p 546
Nursoy Soy Protein Infant Formula (Wyeth) p 685
Nutramigen (Mead Johnson Nutritional) p 575
Pregestimil (Mead Johnson Nutritional) p 576
ProSobee (Mead Johnson Nutritional) p 576
Soyalac: Liquid Concentrate, Ready-to-Serve and Powder (Loma Linda) p 559

Iron Supplement
Enfamil w/Iron Concentrated Liquid & Powder (Mead Johnson Nutritional) p 570
Enfamil w/Iron Ready-To-Use (Mead Johnson Nutritional) p 570
Nursoy Soy Protein Infant Formula (Wyeth) p 685
SMA Iron Fortified Infant Formula (Wyeth) p 685

Lactose Free
I-Soyalac (Loma Linda) p 558
Nursoy Soy Protein Infant Formula (Wyeth) p 685
Portagen (Mead Johnson Nutritional) p 575
ProSobee (Mead Johnson Nutritional) p 576
Soyalac: Liquid Concentrate, Ready-to-Serve and Powder (Loma Linda) p 559

Low Phenylalanine
Lofenalac (Mead Johnson Nutritional) p 573

Medium Chain Triglycerides
Portagen (Mead Johnson Nutritional) p 575
Pregestimil (Mead Johnson Nutritional) p 576

Milk Free
I-Soyalac (Loma Linda) p 558
ProSobee (Mead Johnson Nutritional) p 576
Soyalac: Liquid Concentrate, Ready-to-Serve and Powder (Loma Linda) p 559

Protein Hydrolysate
Pregestimil (Mead Johnson Nutritional) p 576

Ready-to-feed
Enfamil Nursette (Mead Johnson Nutritional) p 570
Enfamil Ready-To-Use (Mead Johnson Nutritional) p 570
Enfamil w/Iron Ready-To-Use (Mead Johnson Nutritional) p 570
I-Soyalac (Loma Linda) p 558
Nursoy Soy Protein Infant Formula (Wyeth) p 685
SMA Iron Fortified Infant Formula (Wyeth) p 685
SMA lo-iron (Wyeth) p 685
Soyalac: Liquid Concentrate, Ready-to-Serve and Powder (Loma Linda) p 559

Sucrose Free
ProSobee (Mead Johnson Nutritional) p 576

INGROWN TOENAIL PREPARATIONS
Outgro Solution (Whitehall) p 676

INSECT BITE & STING PREPARATIONS
Alo-Ointment (Aloe Cream) p 404, 509
Alo-Relief (Aloe Cream) p 404, 509
Anbesol Gel Antiseptic Anesthetic (Whitehall) p 429, 671
Anbesol Liquid Antiseptic Anesthetic (Whitehall) p 429, 671
B.F.I. (Beecham Products) p 517
Bactine Antiseptic/Anesthetic First Aid Spray (Miles Laboratories) p 415, 597
Bactine Hydrocortisone Skin Care Cream (Miles Laboratories) p 415, 597
BiCozene Creme (Creighton Products) p 409, 537
Borofax Ointment (Burroughs Wellcome) p 527
Lanacort Antipruritic Hydrocortisone Acetate 0.5% Creme (Combe) p 537
Medi-Quik (Lehn & Fink) p 558
Nupercainal Cream & Ointment (Ciba) p 407, 534
Resinol Cream (Mentholatum) p 588
Resinol Ointment (Mentholatum) p 588
Topic Benzyl Alcohol Gel (Syntex) p 650
Unguentine Plus First Aid & Burn Cream (Norwich-Eaton) p 608

IRON DEFICIENCY PREPARATIONS
(see under HEMATINICS)

L

LAXATIVES

Bulk
Effersyllium Instant Mix (Stuart) p 425, 646
Hydrocil Instant (Rowell) p 633
Metamucil, Instant Mix (Searle Consumer Products) p 425, 643
Metamucil, Instant Mix, Orange Flavor (Searle Consumer Products) p 425, 644
Metamucil Powder (Searle Consumer Products) p 425, 643
Metamucil Powder, Orange Flavor (Searle Consumer Products) p 425, 643
Modane Bulk (Adria) p 504
Serutan Concentrated Powder (J.B. Williams) p 680
Serutan Concentrated Powder - Fruit Flavored (J.B. Williams) p 680
Serutan Toasted Granules (J.B. Williams) p 681
Syllact (Wallace) p 428, 662

Combinations
Correctol Laxative Tablets (Plough) p 420, 621
Dialose Plus Capsules (Stuart) p 425, 645
Doxidan (Hoechst-Roussel) p 410, 550
Haley's M-O (Consumer Products Div., Winthrop) p 682
Milkinol (Kremers-Urban) p 552
Modane Plus (Adria) p 505

Nature's Remedy (Norcliff Thayer) p 417, 604
Perdiem Granules (Rorer) p 423, 632
Peri-Colace (Mead Johnson Pharmaceutical) p 413, 580
Unilax Laxatives Tablets (Ascher) p 512

Fecal Softeners
Colace (Mead Johnson Pharmaceutical) p 413, 580
Correctol Laxative Tablets (Plough) p 420, 621
Dialose Capsules (Stuart) p 425, 645
Dialose Plus Capsules (Stuart) p 425, 645
DioMedicone Tablets (Medicone) p 581
Geriplex-FS Kapseals (Parke-Davis) p 614
Geriplex-FS Liquid (Parke-Davis) p 615
Kasof Capsules (Stuart) p 425, 647
Milkinol (Kremers-Urban) p 552
Modane Soft (Adria) p 504
Regutol (Plough) p 420, 621
Senokot-S Tablets (Purdue Frederick) p 421, 625
Surfak (Hoechst-Roussel) p 410, 550

Mineral Oil
Agoral, Plain (Parke-Davis) p 612
Haley's M-O (Consumer Products Div., Winthrop) p 682

Stimulant
Agoral Raspberry & Marshmallow Flavors (Parke-Davis) p 612
Black-Draught Granulated (Chattem) p 532
Black-Draught Syrup (Chattem) p 533
Black-Draught Tablets (Chattem) p 533
Carter's Little Pills (Carter Products) p 407, 532
Correctol Laxative Liquid (Plough) p 420, 621
Correctol Laxative Tablets (Plough) p 420, 621
Dialose Plus Capsules (Stuart) p 425, 645
Dulcolax Tablets & Suppositories (Boehringer Ingelheim) p 405, 521
Evac-U-Gen (Walker, Corp) p 660
Ex-Lax Chocolated Laxative (Ex-Lax Pharm.) p 409, 543
Ex-Lax Pills, Unflavored (Ex-Lax Pharm.) p 409, 544
Herbal Laxative Tablets (Nature's Bounty) p 601
Maltsupex Liquid & Powder (Wallace) p 428, 660
Modane Tablets & Liquid (Adria) p 505
Nature's Remedy (Norcliff Thayer) p 417, 604
Neoloid (Lederle) p 554
Norwich Glycerin Suppositories (Norwich-Eaton) p 607
Nytilax Tablets (Leeming) p 556
Phillip's Milk of Magnesia (Glenbrook) p 410, 548
Purge Concentrate (Fleming) p 545
Senokot Tablets/Granules (Purdue Frederick) p 421, 625
Senokot-S Tablets (Purdue Frederick) p 421, 625
Yellolax (Luyties) p 559

LICE TREATMENTS
(see under PEDICULICIDES)

LIP BALMS
Alo-Lip-Shield (Aloe Cream) p 403, 509
Alo-Sun SPF 15 Sun Block Stick (Aloe Cream) p 509
Chap Stick Lip Balm (Robins) p 421, 627
Chap Stick Sunblock 15 Lip Balm (Robins) p 421, 627
Herpecin-L Cold Sore Lip Balm (Campbell) p 529
Mentholatum Lipbalm with Sunscreen (Mentholatum) p 588
Moisture Whip Lip Conditioner (Maybelline) p 565
Moisture Whip Lipstick (Maybelline) p 565

Kerodex Cream 51 (for dry or oily work) (Ayerst) p 404, 513
Kerodex Cream 71 (for wet work) (Ayerst) p 404, 513
Resinol Cream (Mentholatum) p 588
Skin Screen (Cetylite) p 532

SKIN REMEDIES
(see under DERMATOLOGICALS)

SKIN WOUND PREPARATIONS

Cleansers
Bactine Antiseptic/Anesthetic First Aid Spray (Miles Laboratories) p 415, 597
Betadine Solution (Purdue Frederick) p 421, 624
Mercurochrome II (Becton Dickinson) p 517
Oil-O-Sol Liquid (Health Care) p 410, 549
S.T. 37 (Beecham Products) p 518

Healing Agents
Alo-Ointment (Aloe Cream) p 404, 509
Alo-Relief (Aloe Cream) p 404, 509
Chloresium Ointment & Solution (Rystan) p 633
Medicone Dressing Cream (Medicone) p 581
Neosporin Ointment (Burroughs Wellcome) p 406, 527
Polysporin Ointment (Burroughs Wellcome) p 527
PRID Salve (Walker Pharmacal) p 660
Zincofax Skin Cream (Burroughs Wellcome) p 529

Protectants
Johnson & Johnson First Aid Cream (Johnson & Johnson) p 410, 552
Medicone Dressing Cream (Medicone) p 581
Medi-Quik (Lehn & Fink) p 558
Rhulicaine (Lederle) p 411, 554
S.T. 37 (Beecham Products) p 518
Zinc Oxide Ointment (Norwich-Eaton) p 607

SLEEP AIDS
Miles Nervine Nighttime Sleep-Aid (Miles Laboratories) p 416, 598
Quiet World Analgesic/Sleeping Aid (Whitehall) p 678
Sleep-Eze Tablets (Whitehall) p 678
Sominex Sleep Aid (J.B. Williams) p 681
Unisom Nighttime Sleep-Aid (Leeming) p 557

SORE THROAT PREPARATIONS
(see under COLD PREPARATIONS, Lozenges)

STIFF NECK RELIEF
(see under ANALGESICS)

STIMULANTS
Efed II Capsules (Alto) p 404, 509
No Doz (Bristol-Myers) p 406, 526
Vivarin Stimulant Tablets (J.B. Williams) p 681

SUGAR SUBSTITUTES
Necta Sweet Non-Caloric Sweetener (Norwich-Eaton) p 607

SUN SCREENS
(see under DERMATOLOGICALS)

SUPPLEMENTS
(see under DIETARY SUPPLEMENTS)

T

TEETHING LOTIONS
Anbesol Gel Antiseptic Anesthetic (Whitehall) p 429, 671
Anbesol Liquid Antiseptic Anesthetic (Whitehall) p 429, 671

TENNIS ELBOW RELIEF
(see under ANALGESICS)

THROAT LOZENGES
Aspergum (Plough) p 419, 620

Cēpacol Anesthetic Troches (Merrell Dow) p 590
Cēpacol Throat Lozenges (Merrell Dow) p 589
Cēpastat Sore Throat Lozenges (Merrell Dow) p 590
Children's Cepastat Sore Throat Lozenges (Merrell Dow) p 590
Children's Hold (Beecham Products) p 517
Chloraseptic Cough Control Lozenges (Norwich-Eaton) p 417, 606
Chloraseptic Lozenges (Norwich-Eaton) p 417, 606
Chloraseptic Lozenges, Children's (Norwich-Eaton) p 417, 605
Formula 44 Cough Control Discs (Vicks Health Care) p 657
Hold (Beecham Products) p 518
Spec-T Sore Throat Anesthetic Lozenges (Squibb) p 425, 644
Spec-T Sore Throat/Cough Suppressant Lozenges (Squibb) p 425, 644
Spec-T Sore Throat/Decongestant Lozenges (Squibb) p 425, 644
Sucrets (Regular, Mentholated & Children's Cherry) (Beecham Products) p 518
Sucrets—Cold Decongestant Formula (Beecham Products) p 519
Sucrets Cough Control Formula (Beecham Products) p 519
Throat Discs Throat Lozenges (Marion) p 412, 562
Vicks Formula 44 Cough Control Discs (Vicks Health Care) p 657
Vicks Throat Lozenges (Vicks Health Care) p 659

TOOTH DESENSITIZERS
Red Cross Toothache Kit (Mentholatum) p 588
Sensodyne Toothpaste (Block) p 521

U

UNIT DOSE SYSTEMS
Peri-Colace (Mead Johnson Pharmaceutical) p 413, 580

V

VAGINAL PREPARATIONS

Contraceptives

Creams
Koromex'' Contraceptive Cream (Youngs) p 687

Foams
Emko Because Contraceptor Vaginal Contraceptive Foam (Schering) p 424, 639
Emko Pre-Fil Vaginal Contraceptive Foam (Schering) p 424, 640
Emko Vaginal Contraceptive Foam (Schering) p 424, 640
Koromex Contraceptive Foam (Youngs) p 687

Inserts, Suppositories
Encare Contraceptive Inserts (Norwich-Eaton) p 417, 606
Semicid Vaginal Contraceptive Suppositories (Whitehall) p 678

Jellies, Ointments
Koromex'' Contraceptive Jelly (Youngs) p 687
Koromex''-A Contraceptive Jelly (Youngs) p 687

Spermicides
Conceptrol Birth Control Cream (Ortho Consumer Products) p 417, 609
Conceptrol Disposable Gel (Ortho Consumer Products) p 417, 609
Delfen Contraceptive Foam (Ortho Consumer Products) p 418, 610
Gynol II Contraceptive Jelly (Ortho Consumer Products) p 418, 610
Intercept Contraceptive Inserts (Ortho Consumer Products) p 418, 610
Ortho-Creme Contraceptive Cream (Ortho Consumer Products) p 418, 611

Ortho-Gynol Contraceptive Jelly (Ortho Consumer Products) p 418, 611

Douches, Cleansing
Betadine Douche, Betadine Douche Kit & Betadine Medicated Douche (Purdue Frederick) p 420, 624
Massengill Disposable Douche (Beecham Products) p 518
Massengill Disposable Medicated Douche (Beecham Products) p 518
Massengill Liquid Concentrate (Beecham Products) p 518
Massengill Powder (Beecham Products) p 518
Nylmerate'' Solution Concentrate (Youngs) p 687

Other
Betadine Solution (Purdue Frederick) p 421, 624
Cortef Feminine Itch Cream (Upjohn) p 427, 653
Gynecort Antipruritic 0.5% Hydrocortisone Acetate Creme (Combe) p 408, 536
Norforms Feminine Deodorant & Suppositories (Norwich-Eaton) p 417, 607
Ortho Disposable Vaginal Applicators (Ortho Consumer Products) p 418, 611
Ortho Personal Lubricant (Ortho Consumer Products) p 418, 611
Transi-Lube (Youngs) p 687
Vagisil Feminine Itching Medication (Combe) p 408, 537

VITAMINS

Vitamins
Aqua-A (Anabolic) p 510
B12-Plus (Anabolic) p 510
KLB6 Capsules (Nature's Bounty) p 602
Tri-B3 (Anabolic) p 510
Tri-C-500 (Anabolic) p 511
Vitamin C Crystals (Nature's Bounty) p 600

Multivitamins
A.C.N. (Persōn & Covey) p 616
Acerola C (100 mg) (Nature's Bounty) p 600
Acerola C (300 mg) (Nature's Bounty) p 600
Allbee C-800 Tablets (Robins) p 421, 626
Allbee with C Capsules (Robins) p 421, 626
B-50 Tablets (Nature's Bounty) p 600
B-100 Tablets (Nature's Bounty) p 600
B-100 Time Release Tablets (Nature's Bounty) p 600
B-125 Tablets (Nature's Bounty) p 600
B Complex & B-12 Tablets (Nature's Bounty) p 600
B Complex & C (Time Release) Capsules (Nature's Bounty) p 600
B & C Liquid (Nature's Bounty) p 600
Brewer's Yeast Powder (Debittered) (Nature's Bounty) p 600
Brewer's Yeast Tablets (Nature's Bounty) p 600
Bugs Bunny Multivitamin Supplement (Miles Laboratories) p 415, 597
Bugs Bunny With Extra C Multivitamin Supplement (Miles Laboratories) p 415, 598
C-Complex Tablets (Nature's Bounty) p 600
Children's Chewable Vitamins (Nature's Bounty) p 601
Cod Liver Oil Concentrate Tablets w/Vitamin C (Schering) p 424, 636
Flintstones Multivitamin Supplement (Miles Laboratories) p 416, 597
Flintstones With Extra C Multivitamin Supplement (Miles Laboratories) p 416, 598
Geriplex-FS Kapseals (Parke-Davis) p 614
Geriplex-FS Liquid (Parke-Davis) p 615
Geritol Tablets - High Potency Iron & Vitamin Tablets (J.B. Williams) p 680

W

WART REMOVERS
(see under DERMATOLOGICALS, Keratolytics)

WEIGHT CONTROL PREPARATIONS
(see under APPETITE SUPPRESSANTS)

WET DRESSINGS
(see under DERMATOLOGICALS)

Active Ingredients Index

In this section the products described in the Product Information (White) Section are listed under their chemical (generic) name according to their principal ingredient(s). Products have been included under specific headings by the Publisher with the cooperation of individual manufacturers.

A

Acerola
C-Complex Tablets (Nature's Bounty) p 600

Acetaminophen
Acephen Acetaminophen Rectal Suppositories (G & W Laboratories) p 545
Allerest Headache Strength Tablets (Pharmacraft) p 618
Anacin-3 Analgesic Tablets & Capsules (Whitehall) p 429, 671
Aspirin-Free Arthritis Pain Formula by the Makers of Anacin Analgesic Tablets (Whitehall) p 429, 671
CCP Tablets (Medique) p 582
Comtrex (Bristol-Myers) p 405, 524
Congespirin Liquid Cold Medicine (Bristol-Myers) p 405, 524
Contac Jr. Childrens' Cold Medicine (Menley & James) p 414, 583
Contac Severe Cold Formula (Menley & James) p 414, 583
Coricidin Extra Strength Sinus Headache Tablets (Schering) p 424, 638
Coryban-D Cough Syrup (Pfipharmecs) p 419, 617
CoTylenol Children's Liquid Cold Formula (McNeil Consumer Products) p 413, 566
CoTylenol Cold Formula Tablets and Capsules (McNeil Consumer Products) p 413, 566
CoTylenol Liquid Cold Formula (McNeil Consumer Products) p 413, 566
Datril (Bristol-Myers) p 406, 525
Datril 500 (Bristol-Myers) p 406, 525
Daycare Multi-Symptom Colds Medicine Capsules (Vicks Health Care) p 427, 656
Daycare Multi-Symptoms Colds Medicine Liquid (Vicks Health Care) p 427, 656

Dristan-AF Decongestant/Antihistamine/ Analgesic Tablets (Whitehall) p 674
Excedrin (Bristol-Myers) p 406, 526
Excedrin P.M. (Bristol-Myers) p 406, 526
Gemnisyn (Rorer) p 422, 631
Goody's Headache Powders (Goody's) p 410, 548
Headway Capsules and Tablets (Vicks Health Care) p 428, 657
Liquiprin (Norcliff Thayer) p 416, 604
Novahistine Sinus Tablets (Merrell Dow) p 593
Nyquil Nighttime Colds Medicine (Vicks Health Care) p 428, 658
Ornex Capsules (Menley & James) p 414, 586
Pamprin Capsules (Chattem) p 407, 533
Pamprin Tablets (Chattem) p 407, 533
Percogesic Tablets (Endo) p 409, 543
Pyrroxate Capsules (Upjohn) p 427, 654
Quiet World Analgesic/Sleeping Aid (Whitehall) p 678
Sinarest Tablets (Pharmacraft) p 620
Sine-Aid Sinus Headache Tablets (McNeil Consumer Products) p 413, 567
Sine-Off Extra Strength No Drowsiness Formula (Menley & James) p 415, 587
Sine-Off Extra Strength Sinus Medicine Non-Aspirin Capsules (Menley & James) p 415, 586
Sine-Off Extra Strength Sinus Medicine Non-Aspirin Tablets (Menley & James) p 415, 586
Sinutab Extra Strength Capsules (Warner-Lambert Inc.) p 429, 665
Sinutab Extra Strength Tablets (Warner-Lambert Inc.) p 429, 665
Sinutab Tablets (Warner-Lambert Inc.) p 429, 664
Sinutab II Tablets (Warner-Lambert Inc.) p 429, 665

Sunril Premenstrual Capsules (Schering) p 424, 641
Tempra (Mead Johnson Nutritional) p 579
Trendar Premenstrual Tablets (Whitehall) p 679
Tylenol acetaminophen Children's Chewable Tablets, Elixir, Drops (McNeil Consumer Products) p 413, 567
Tylenol, Extra-Strength, acetaminophen Adult Liquid Pain Reliever (McNeil Consumer Products) p 413, 568
Tylenol, Extra-Strength, acetaminophen Capsules & Tablets (McNeil Consumer Products) p 413, 568
Tylenol, Regular Strength, acetaminophen Capsules & Tablets (McNeil Consumer Products) p 413, 567
Vanquish (Glenbrook) p 548
Vicks Nyquil Nighttime Colds Medicine (Vicks Health Care) p 428, 658
Viro-Med Liquid (Whitehall) p 679

Acetic Acid
Star-Otic (Stellar) p 645

Acetone Sodium Bisulfite
Nupercainal Suppositories (Ciba) p 407, 535

Acetylsalicylic Acid
(see under Aspirin)

Alcohol
Anbesol Gel Antiseptic Anesthetic (Whitehall) p 429, 671
Anbesol Liquid Antiseptic Anesthetic (Whitehall) p 429, 671
Coryban-D Cough Syrup (Pfipharmecs) p 419, 617
Denorex Medicated Shampoo, Regular & Mountain Fresh Herbal (Whitehall) p 429, 672
Denorex Shampoo & Conditioner (Whitehall) p 429, 672
Desenex Foot & Sneaker Spray (Pharmacraft) p 619

Lanolin

A and D Ointment (Schering) p 423, 634
Alpha Keri Bath Oil (Westwood) p 666
Balmex Emollient Lotion (Macsil) p 560
Chap Stick Lip Balm (Robins) p 421, 627
Chap Stick Sunblock 15 Lip Balm (Robins) p 421, 627
Derma Medicone Ointment (Medicone) p 581
Diaparene Baby Wash Cloths (Glenbrook) p 409, 548
Lobana Bath Oil (Ulmer) p 652
Lobana Body Lotion (Ulmer) p 652
Medicone Dressing Cream (Medicone) p 581
Mediconet (Medicone) p 581
pHisoDerm (Consumer Products Div., Winthrop) p 684
Rectal Medicone Unguent (Medicone) p 582
Shepard's Dry Skin Cream (Dermik) p 539
Shepard's Soap (Dermik) p 539

Lanolin Alcohol

pHisoDerm (Consumer Products Div., Winthrop) p 684
Skin Screen (Cetylite) p 532

Lard

PRID Salve (Walker Pharmacal) p 660

Laureth-4

Fostril (Westwood) p 667
Transact (Westwood) p 670

Lead Oleate

PRID Salve (Walker Pharmacal) p 660

Lecithin

KLB6 Capsules (Nature's Bounty) p 602
Lecithin Capsules (Nature's Bounty) p 602
Lecithin Chewable Tablets (Nature's Bounty) p 602
Lecithin with Vitamin D Capsules (Nature's Bounty) p 602
Ultra KLB6 Tablets (Nature's Bounty) p 603

Lidocaine

Medi-Quik (Lehn & Fink) p 558

Lidocaine Base

Xylocaine 2.5% Ointment (Astra) p 404, 513

Lidocaine Hydrochloride

Mercurochrome II (Becton Dickinson) p 517
Unguentine Plus First Aid & Burn Cream (Norwich-Eaton) p 608

Lipase

Festal (Hoechst-Roussel) p 410, 550

Live Yeast Cell Derivative

Preparation H Hemorrhoidal Ointment (Whitehall) p 430, 677
Preparation H Hemorrhoidal Suppositories (Whitehall) p 430, 677

Liver, Desiccated

Liver W/B-12 Tablets (Nature's Bounty) p 602

Liver Preparations

Tri-88 (Anabolic) p 510

l-Lysine

l-Lysine Tablets (Nature's Bounty) p 602

Lysine Hydrochloride

Enisyl 334 mg and 500 mg Tablets (Persōn & Covey) p 617

M

Magaldrate

Riopan Antacid Chew Tablets (Ayerst) p 513
Riopan Antacid Suspension (Ayerst) p 404, 513
Riopan Antacid Swallow Tablets (Ayerst) p 513
Riopan Plus Chew Tablets (Ayerst) p 514
Riopan Plus Suspension (Ayerst) p 404, 514

Magnesium

Beelith Tablets (Beach) p 516
Chelated Multi-Mineral Tablets (Nature's Bounty) p 601
Dolomite Tablets (Nature's Bounty) p 601
One-A-Day Multivitamin Supplement Plus Minerals (Miles Laboratories) p 416, 598

Magnesium Amino Acid Chelate

Chelated Magnesium Tablets (Nature's Bounty) p 601

Magnesium Carbonate

Bisodol Antacid Powder (Whitehall) p 671
Gaviscon Liquid Antacid (Marion) p 411, 561
Marblen Suspensions & Tablets (Fleming) p 544

Magnesium Carbonate Gel

Di-Gel (Plough) p 420, 621

Magnesium Gluconate

Magnesium Tablets (Nature's Bounty) p 602

Magnesium Hydroxide

Aludrox Oral Suspension & Tablets (Wyeth) p 430, 685
Ascriptin (Rorer) p 422, 630
Ascriptin A/D (Rorer) p 422, 630
Bisodol Antacid Tablets (Whitehall) p 672
Delcid (Merrell Dow) p 590
Di-Gel (Plough) p 420, 621
Gelusil-M (Parke-Davis) p 614
Gelusil-II Liquid & Tablets (Parke-Davis) p 614
Kolantyl (Merrell Dow) p 591
Kudrox Suspension (Double Strength) (Kremers-Urban) p 552
Maalox Plus Suspension (Rorer) p 423, 632
Maalox Plus Tablets (Rorer) p 423, 632
Maalox Suspension (Rorer) p 423, 631
Maalox TC (Therapeutic Concentrate) (Rorer) p 423, 632
Maalox Tablets (No.1 & No.2) (Rorer) p 423, 631
Magnatril Suspension & Tablets (Lannett) p 552
Mylanta Liquid (Stuart) p 426, 647
Mylanta Tablets (Stuart) p 426, 647
Mylanta-II Liquid (Stuart) p 426, 648
Mylanta-II Tablets (Stuart) p 426, 648
Phillip's Milk of Magnesia (Glenbrook) p 410, 548
Simeco Suspension (Wyeth) p 430, 686
WinGel (Consumer Products Div., Winthrop) p 684

Magnesium Oxide

B6-Plus (Anabolic) p 510
Beelith Tablets (Beach) p 516
Cal-M (Anabolic) p 510

Magnesium Salicylate

Dalca Decongestant/Analgesic Tablets (Ascher) p 511
Mobigesic Analgesic Tablets (Ascher) p 512

Magnesium Trisilicate

Gaviscon Antacid Tablets (Marion) p 411, 560
Gaviscon-2 Antacid Tablets (Marion) p 411, 561
Gelusil Liquid & Tablets (Parke-Davis) p 419, 613
Magnatril Suspension & Tablets (Lannett) p 552

Malt Soup Extract

Maltsupex Liquid & Powder (Wallace) p 428, 660

Manganese

Chelated Multi-Mineral Tablets (Nature's Bounty) p 601

Manganese Amino Acid Chelate

Chelated Manganese Tablets (Nature's Bounty) p 601

Manganese Gluconate

Manganese Tablets (Nature's Bounty) p 602

Meclizine Hydrochloride

Bonine (Pfipharmecs) p 419, 617

Medium Chain Triglycerides

MCT Oil (Mead Johnson Nutritional) p 574
Portagen (Mead Johnson Nutritional) p 575
Pregestimil (Mead Johnson Nutritional) p 576

Menthol

Absorbine Jr. (W. F. Young) p 430, 686
Afrin Menthol Nasal Spray (Schering) p 423, 634
Ben-Gay External Analgesic Products (Leeming) p 556
Black-Draught Syrup (Chattem) p 533
Cēpastat Sore Throat Lozenges (Merrell Dow) p 590
Cēpastat Sore Throat Spray/Gargle/Mouthwash (Merrell Dow) p 590
Children's Cepastat Sore Throat Lozenges (Merrell Dow) p 590
Deep-Down Pain Relief Rub (J.B. Williams) p 679
Denorex Medicated Shampoo, Regular & Mountain Fresh Herbal (Whitehall) p 429, 672
Denorex Shampoo & Conditioner (Whitehall) p 429, 672
Derma Medicone Ointment (Medicone) p 581
Dermassage Medicated Skin Lotion (Colgate-Palmolive) p 407, 536
Dermoplast (Ayerst) p 404, 513
Formula 44 Cough Control Discs (Vicks Health Care) p 657
Halls Mentho-Lyptus Cough Tablets (Warner-Lambert Co.) p 428, 663
Halls Mentho-Lyptus Decongestant Cough Formula (Warner-Lambert Co.) p 663
Heet Spray Analgesic (Whitehall) p 675
Icy Hot Balm (Searle Consumer Products) p 425, 643
Icy Hot Rub (Searle Consumer Products) p 425, 643
Listerine Antiseptic (Warner-Lambert Co.) p 428, 663
Medicone Dressing Cream (Medicone) p 581
Mentholatum Deep Heating Lotion (Mentholatum) p 588
Mentholatum Deep Heating Rub (Mentholatum) p 588
Mentholatum Ointment (Mentholatum) p 588
Mercurochrome II (Becton Dickinson) p 517
Panalgesic (Poythress) p 420, 623
Protexin Oral Rinse (Cetylite) p 532
Rectal Medicone Suppositories (Medicone) p 581
Rectal Medicone Unguent (Medicone) p 582
Rhulicaine (Lederle) p 411, 554
Rhulicream (Lederle) p 554

Rhuligel (Lederle) p 411, 554
Rhulispray (Lederle) p 554
Sinex Decongestant Nasal Spray (Vicks Health Care) p 428, 658
Soft 'N Soothe Anti-Itch Creme (Ascher) p 512
Soltice Quick-Rub (Chattem) p 533
Vaposteam (Vicks Health Care) p 658
Vatronol Nose Drops (Vicks Health Care) p 659
Vicks Cough Silencers Cough Drops (Vicks Health Care) p 659
Vicks Formula 44 Cough Control Discs (Vicks Health Care) p 657
Vicks Inhaler (Vicks Health Care) p 659
Vicks Sinex Decongestant Nasal Spray (Vicks Health Care) p 428, 658
Vicks Throat Lozenges (Vicks Health Care) p 659
Vicks Vaporub (Vicks Health Care) p 428, 660
Vicks Vaposteam (Vicks Health Care) p 658
Vicks Vatronol Nose Drops (Vicks Health Care) p 659

Methionine

Geritol Liquid - High Potency Iron & Vitamin Tonic (J.B. Williams) p 680

Methyl Nicotinate

Deep-Down Pain Relief Rub (J.B. Williams) p 679
Heet Spray Analgesic (Whitehall) p 675

Methyl Salicylate

Ben-Gay External Analgesic Products (Leeming) p 556
Bensulfoid Lotion (Poythress) p 623
Black-Draught Syrup (Chattem) p 533
Deep-Down Pain Relief Rub (J.B. Williams) p 679
Heet Analgesic Liniment (Whitehall) p 675
Heet Spray Analgesic (Whitehall) p 675
Icy Hot Balm (Searle Consumer Products) p 425, 643
Icy Hot Rub (Searle Consumer Products) p 425, 643
Listerine Antiseptic (Warner-Lambert Co.) p 428, 663
Mentholatum Deep Heating Lotion (Mentholatum) p 588
Mentholatum Deep Heating Rub (Mentholatum) p 588
Panalgesic (Poythress) p 420, 623
Sinex Decongestant Nasal Spray (Vicks Health Care) p 428, 658
Soltice Quick-Rub (Chattem) p 533
Vatronol Nose Drops (Vicks Health Care) p 659
Vicks Inhaler (Vicks Health Care) p 659
Vicks Sinex Decongestant Nasal Spray (Vicks Health Care) p 428, 658
Vicks Vatronol Nose Drops (Vicks Health Care) p 659

Methylbenzethonium Chloride

Diaparene Baby Powder (Glenbrook) p 409, 548
Lobana Body Powder (Ulmer) p 652

Methylcellulose

Murocel Ophthalmic Solution (Muro) p 599

Methylparaben

Transi-Lube (Youngs) p 687

Milk Of Magnesia

Haley's M-0 (Consumer Products Div., Winthrop) p 682

Mineral Oil

Agoral, Plain (Parke-Davis) p 612
Agoral Raspberry & Marshmallow Flavors (Parke-Davis) p 612
Alpha Keri Bath Oil (Westwood) p 666
Balneol (Rowell) p 633
Haley's M-0 (Consumer Products Div., Winthrop) p 682
Keri Lotion (Westwood) p 668
Lobana Bath Oil (Ulmer) p 652

Lobana Body Lotion (Ulmer) p 652
Milkinol (Kremers-Urban) p 552
Nephrox Suspension (Fleming) p 544
Shepard's Dry Skin Cream (Dermik) p 539
Vaseline Dermatology Formula Cream (Chesebrough) p 407, 534
Vaseline Dermatology Formula Lotion (Chesebrough) p 407, 534

Multivitamins

KLB6 Complete Tablets (Nature's Bounty) p 602
KLB6 Diet Mix (Nature's Bounty) p 602
Stress "1000" Tablets (Nature's Bounty) p 602
Stress Formula "605" Tablets (Nature's Bounty) p 602

Multivitamins with Minerals

Carnation Instant Breakfast (Carnation) p 530
Children's Chewable Vitamins with Iron (Nature's Bounty) p 601
Herbitol (PharmTech) p 419, 620
Mega V & M Tablets (Nature's Bounty) p 602
Multi-Mineral Tablets (Nature's Bounty) p 602
Optilets-500 (Abbott) p 503
Optilets-M-500 (Abbott) p 503
Slender Diet Food For Weight Control (Instant) (Carnation) p 530
Slender Diet Meal Bars For Weight Control (Carnation) p 530
Slender Diet Meal For Weight Control (Canned) (Carnation) p 530
Stress Formula "605" w/Iron Tablets (Nature's Bounty) p 602
Stress Formula "605" w/Zinc Tablets (Nature's Bounty) p 602
Surbex-750 with Iron (Abbott) p 503
Surbex-750 with Zinc (Abbott) p 504
Ultra Vita-Time Tablets (Nature's Bounty) p 603
Vita-Time Tablets (Nature's Bounty) p 603

N

Naphazoline Hydrochloride

Clear Eyes Eye Drops (Abbott Consumer Products) p 403, 502
4-Way Nasal Spray (Bristol-Myers) p 406, 526
Privine Nasal Spray & Solution 0.05% (Ciba) p 407, 535
20/20 Eye Drops (S.S.S. Company) p 634

Neomycin Sulfate

BPN Ointment (Norwich-Eaton) p 605
Myciguent Antibiotic Ointment (Upjohn) p 654
Mycitracin Antibiotic Ointment (Upjohn) p 427, 654
Neosporin Ointment (Burroughs Wellcome) p 406, 527

Niacin

Allbee C-800 Plus Iron Tablets (Robins) p 421, 626
Allbee C-800 Tablets (Robins) p 421, 626
Allbee with C Capsules (Robins) p 421, 626
B Complex & B-12 Tablets (Nature's Bounty) p 600
Brewer's Yeast Powder (Debittered) (Nature's Bounty) p 600
Brewer's Yeast Tablets (Nature's Bounty) p 600
Bugs Bunny Multivitamin Supplement (Miles Laboratories) p 415, 597
Bugs Bunny Plus Iron Multivitamin Supplement (Miles Laboratories) p 415, 597
Bugs Bunny With Extra C Multivitamin Supplement (Miles Laboratories) p 415, 598
Flintstones Multivitamin Supplement (Miles Laboratories) p 416, 597

Flintstones Plus Iron Multivitamin Supplement (Miles Laboratories) p 416, 597
Flintstones With Extra C Multivitamin Supplement (Miles Laboratories) p 416, 598
Niacin Tablets (Nature's Bounty) p 602
One-A-Day Core C 500 Multivitamin Supplement (Miles Laboratories) p 416, 598
One-A-Day Multivitamin Supplement (Miles Laboratories) p 416, 598
One-A-Day Multivitamin Supplement Plus Iron (Miles Laboratories) p 416, 598
One-A-Day Multivitamin Supplement Plus Minerals (Miles Laboratories) p 416, 598
One-A-Day Stressguard Vitamins (Miles Laboratories) p 416, 598
Tri-B3 (Anabolic) p 510
Z-Bec Tablets (Robins) p 422, 629

Niacinamide

A.C.N. (Persōn & Covey) p 616
B-100 Tablets (Nature's Bounty) p 600
B Complex & C (Time Release) Capsules (Nature's Bounty) p 600
B & C Liquid (Nature's Bounty) p 600
Geritol Liquid - High Potency Iron & Vitamin Tonic (J.B. Williams) p 680
Mega-B (Arco) p 511
Megadose (Arco) p 511
Niacinamide Tablets (Nature's Bounty) p 602
Tri-B-Plex (Anabolic) p 510

Nicotinic Acid
(see also under Niacin)

Nicotinex Elixir (Fleming) p 544

Nonfat Dry Milk

Carnation Instant Breakfast (Carnation) p 530
Carnation Instant Nonfat Dry Milk (Carnation) p 530
Slender Diet Food For Weight Control (Instant) (Carnation) p 530

Nonoxynol-9

Conceptrol Birth Control Cream (Ortho Consumer Products) p 417, 609
Conceptrol Disposable Gel (Ortho Consumer Products) p 417, 609
Delfen Contraceptive Foam (Ortho Consumer Products) p 418, 610
Emko Because Contraceptor Vaginal Contraceptive Foam (Schering) p 424, 639
Emko Pre-Fil Vaginal Contraceptive Foam (Schering) p 424, 640
Emko Vaginal Contraceptive Foam (Schering) p 424, 640
Encare Contraceptive Inserts (Norwich-Eaton) p 417, 606
Gynol II Contraceptive Jelly (Ortho Consumer Products) p 418, 610
Intercept Contraceptive Inserts (Ortho Consumer Products) p 418, 610
Koromex Contraceptive Foam (Youngs) p 687
Koromex^{II} Contraceptive Cream (Youngs) p 687
Ortho-Creme Contraceptive Cream (Ortho Consumer Products) p 418, 611
Semicid Vaginal Contraceptive Suppositories (Whitehall) p 678

Nutmeg Oil

Vicks Vaporub (Vicks Health Care) p 428, 660

O

Octoxynol

Koromex^{II} Contraceptive Cream (Youngs) p 687
Koromex^{II} Contraceptive Jelly (Youngs) p 687

Q

Quaternium 12
Lobana Perineal Cleanse (Ulmer) p 653

R

RNA
Brewer's Yeast Powder (Debittered) (Nature's Bounty) p 600
Brewer's Yeast Tablets (Nature's Bounty) p 600
RNA Tablets (Nature's Bounty) p 602
RNA/DNA Tablets (Nature's Bounty) p 602

Resorcinol
Acnomel Cream (Menley & James) p 413, 582
BiCozene Creme (Creighton Products) p 409, 537
Lanacane Medicated Creme (Combe) p 536
Resinol Cream (Mentholatum) p 588
Resinol Ointment (Mentholatum) p 588
Vagisil Feminine Itching Medication (Combe) p 408, 537

Riboflavin
Allbee C-800 Plus Iron Tablets (Robins) p 421, 626
Allbee C-800 Tablets (Robins) p 421, 626
Allbee with C Capsules (Robins) p 421, 626
B-2 Tablets (Nature's Bounty) p 600
B Complex & B-12 Tablets (Nature's Bounty) p 600
B Complex & C (Time Release) Capsules (Nature's Bounty) p 600
B & C Liquid (Nature's Bounty) p 600
Brewer's Yeast Powder (Debittered) (Nature's Bounty) p 600
Brewer's Yeast Tablets (Nature's Bounty) p 600
Bugs Bunny Multivitamin Supplement (Miles Laboratories) p 415, 597
Bugs Bunny Plus Iron Multivitamin Supplement (Miles Laboratories) p 415, 597
Bugs Bunny With Extra C Multivitamin Supplement (Miles Laboratories) p 415, 598
Flintstones Multivitamin Supplement (Miles Laboratories) p 416, 597
Flintstones Plus Iron Multivitamin Supplement (Miles Laboratories) p 416, 597
Flintstones With Extra C Multivitamin Supplement (Miles Laboratories) p 416, 598
Geritol Liquid - High Potency Iron & Vitamin Tonic (J.B. Williams) p 680
One-A-Day Core C 500 Multivitamin Supplement (Miles Laboratories) p 416, 598
One-A-Day Multivitamin Supplement (Miles Laboratories) p 416, 598
One-A-Day Multivitamin Supplement Plus Iron (Miles Laboratories) p 416, 598
One-A-Day Multivitamin Supplement Plus Minerals (Miles Laboratories) p 416, 598
Z-Bec Tablets (Robins) p 422, 629

Rose Hips
B Complex & C (Time Release) Capsules (Nature's Bounty) p 600
C-250 with Rose Hips Tablets (Nature's Bounty) p 600
C-300 with Rose Hips (Chewable) Tablets (Nature's Bounty) p 600
C-Complex Tablets (Nature's Bounty) p 600
C-Time 500 Tablets (Nature's Bounty) p 601
C-Time-1500 Tablets (Nature's Bounty) p 601
Zacne Tablets (Nature's Bounty) p 603

Rosin
PRID Salve (Walker Pharmacal) p 660

Rutin
C-Complex Tablets (Nature's Bounty) p 600
Rutin Tablets (Nature's Bounty) p 602

S

Saccharin
Necta Sweet Non-Caloric Sweetener (Norwich-Eaton) p 607

Salicylamide
DeWitt's Pills for Backache & Joint Pains (DeWitt) p 408, 539
Os-Cal-Gesic Tablets (Marion) p 562

Salicylic Acid
Acno Lotion (Baker/Cummins) p 514
Blis-To-Sol Liquid (Chattem) p 533
Blis-To-Sol Powder (Chattem) p 533
Clearasil Pore Deep Cleanser (Vicks Toiletry Products) p 427, 656
Compound W Solution (Whitehall) p 672
Derma+Soft Creme (Creighton Products) p 409, 538
Dry and Clear Medicated Acne Cleanser (Whitehall) p 675
Fomac Foam (Dermik) p 538
Fostex Medicated Cleansing Bar (Westwood) p 667
Fostex Medicated Cleansing Cream (Westwood) p 667
Freezone Solution (Whitehall) p 675
Mediplast (Beiersdorf) p 405, 520
Mosco Corn & Callus Remover (Moss) p 416, 599
NP-27 Powder (Norwich-Eaton) p 608
Oxipor VHC Lotion for Psoriasis (Whitehall) p 676
P&S Plus (Baker/Cummins) p 514
P&S Shampoo (Baker/Cummins) p 514
Panscol (Baker/Cummins) p 515
Pernox Lotion (Westwood) p 668
Pernox Scrub (Westwood) p 668
Pragmatar Ointment (Menley & James) p 414, 586
Sebucare (Westwood) p 669
Sebucare and Sebulex Cream (Westwood) p 669
Sebulex with Protein (Westwood) p 670
Sebutone & Sebutone Cream (Westwood) p 670
Stri-Dex Medicated Pads (Lehn & Fink) p 558
Wart-Off (Pfipharmecs) p 419, 618
Xseb Shampoo (Baker/Cummins) p 515
Xseb-T Shampoo (Baker/Cummins) p 515

Salicylsalicylic Acid
Momentum Muscular Backache Formula (Whitehall) p 676

Saline
Ocean Mist (Fleming) p 544

Salt Substitutes
NoSalt Salt Alternative (Norcliff Thayer) p 417, 604

Selenium
Selenium Tablets (Nature's Bounty) p 602

Selenium Sulfide
Selsun Blue Lotion (Abbott Consumer Products) p 403, 502

Senna
Black-Draught Granulated (Chattem) p 532
Black-Draught Syrup (Chattem) p 533
Black-Draught Tablets (Chattem) p 533
Herbal Laxative Tablets (Nature's Bounty) p 601
Perdiem Granules (Rorer) p 423, 632

Senna Concentrates
Senokot Tablets/Granules (Purdue Frederick) p 421, 625

Sennosides (A & B)
Nytilax Tablets (Leeming) p 556

Sesame Oil
Shepard's Cream Lotion (Dermik) p 539

Shark Liver Oil
Preparation H Hemorrhoidal Ointment (Whitehall) p 430, 677
Preparation H Hemorrhoidal Suppositories (Whitehall) p 430, 677

Silicone Preparations
Lobana Derm-Ade Cream (Ulmer) p 653
Skin Screen (Cetylite) p 532

Simethicone
Di-Gel (Plough) p 420, 621
Gas-X Tablets (Creighton Products) p 409, 538
Gelusil-M (Parke-Davis) p 614
Gelusil-II Liquid & Tablets (Parke-Davis) p 614
Maalox Plus Suspension (Rorer) p 423, 632
Maalox Plus Tablets (Rorer) p 423, 632
Mylanta Liquid (Stuart) p 426, 647
Mylanta Tablets (Stuart) p 426, 647
Mylanta-II Liquid (Stuart) p 426, 648
Mylanta-II Tablets (Stuart) p 426, 648
Mylicon (Tablets & Drops) (Stuart) p 426, 648
Mylicon-80 Tablets (Stuart) p 426, 648
Riopan Plus Chew Tablets (Ayerst) p 514
Riopan Plus Suspension (Ayerst) p 404, 514
Simeco Suspension (Wyeth) p 430, 686

Sodium Bicarbonate
Alka-Seltzer Effervescent Antacid (Miles Laboratories) p 415, 596
Alka-Seltzer Effervescent Pain Reliever & Antacid (Miles Laboratories) p 415, 596
Arm & Hammer Baking Soda (Church & Dwight) p 534
Bisodol Antacid Powder (Whitehall) p 671
Citrocarbonate Antacid (Upjohn) p 653
Lobana Body Powder (Ulmer) p 652
Massengill Liquid Concentrate (Beecham Products) p 518

Sodium Biphosphate
Preflex (Alcon/bp) p 403, 507

Sodium Borate
BoilnSoak (Alcon/bp) p 403, 507
Flex-Care (Alcon/bp) p 403, 507

Sodium Carboxymethylcellulose (see under Carboxymethylcellulose Sodium)

Sodium Chloride
Ayr Saline Nasal Drops (Ascher) p 511
Ayr Saline Nasal Mist (Ascher) p 511
HuMist Saline Nasal Mist (Scherer) p 634
Ocean Mist (Fleming) p 544
Thermotabs (Beecham Products) p 519

Sodium Citrate
Chlor-Trimeton Expectorant (Schering) p 635
Citrocarbonate Antacid (Upjohn) p 653
Eno (Beecham Products) p 517
Formula 44 Cough Mixture (Vicks Health Care) p 427, 657
Vicks Cough Syrup (Vicks Health Care) p 659
Vicks Formula 44 Cough Mixture (Vicks Health Care) p 427, 657
Viro-Med Liquid (Whitehall) p 679

U

Undecylenic Acid

Blis-To-Sol Liquid (Chattem) p 533
Cruex Antifungal Cream (Pharmacraft) p 619
Cruex Antifungal Powder (Pharmacraft) p 619
Desenex Foam (Pharmacraft) p 619
Desenex Ointment & Liquid (Pharmacraft) p 619
Desenex Powders (Pharmacraft) p 619
Desenex Soap (Pharmacraft) p 619
NP-27 Liquid (Norwich-Eaton) p 608

Urea

Carmol 10 Lotion (Syntex) p 650
Carmol 20 Cream (Syntex) p 650
Kerid Ear Drops (Blair) p 520

Urea Preparations

Debrox Drops (Marion) p 411, 560
Gly-Oxide Liquid (Marion) p 411, 561
Ultra Mide Moisturizer Lotion (Baker/Cummins) p 515

Uva Ursi Extract

DeWitt's Pills for Backache & Joint Pains (DeWitt) p 408, 539
Odrinil (Fox) p 545
Water Pill Tablets (Nature's Bounty) p 603
Water Pill w/Iron Tablets (Nature's Bounty) p 603

V

Vinegar

Massengill Disposable Douche (Beecham Products) p 518

Vitamin A

Aqua-A (Anabolic) p 510
Bugs Bunny Multivitamin Supplement (Miles Laboratories) p 415, 597
Bugs Bunny Plus Iron Multivitamin Supplement (Miles Laboratories) p 415, 597
Bugs Bunny With Extra C Multivitamin Supplement (Miles Laboratories) p 415, 598
Flintstones Multivitamin Supplement (Miles Laboratories) p 416, 597
Flintstones Plus Iron Multivitamin Supplement (Miles Laboratories) p 416, 597
Flintstones With Extra C Multivitamin Supplement (Miles Laboratories) p 416, 598
Halibut Liver Oil Capsules (Nature's Bounty) p 601
Lobana Derm-Ade Cream (Ulmer) p 653
Megadose (Arco) p 511
One-A-Day Core C 500 Multivitamin Supplement (Miles Laboratories) p 416, 598
One-A-Day Multivitamin Supplement (Miles Laboratories) p 416, 598
One-A-Day Multivitamin Supplement Plus Iron (Miles Laboratories) p 416, 598
One-A-Day Multivitamin Supplement Plus Minerals (Miles Laboratories) p 416, 598
One-A-Day Stressguard Vitamins (Miles Laboratories) p 416, 598
Oyster Calcium Tablets (Nature's Bounty) p 602
Tri-Vi-Sol (Mead Johnson Nutritional) p 580
Tri-Vi-Sol Vitamin Drops w/Iron (Mead Johnson Nutritional) p 580
Ultra "A" Capsules & Tablets (Nature's Bounty) p 603
Ultra "A & D" Tablets (Nature's Bounty) p 603
Vi-Penta Infant Drops (Roche) p 422, 630
Vi-Penta Multivitamin Drops (Roche) p 422, 630
Vitamin A Capsules & Tablets (Nature's Bounty) p 603

Vitamin A & D Tablets (Nature's Bounty) p 603
Zacne Tablets (Nature's Bounty) p 603

Vitamin A Palmitate

A.C.N. (Persōn & Covey) p 616

Vitamins A & D

Balmex Ointment (Macsil) p 560
Carnation Instant Nonfat Dry Milk (Carnation) p 530
Cod Liver Oil Concentrate Tablets, Capsules (Schering) p 424, 636
Cod Liver Oil Concentrate Tablets w/Vitamin C (Schering) p 424, 636
Lobana Peri-Gard (Ulmer) p 653
Megadose (Arco) p 511
Scott's Emulsion (Beecham Products) p 518
The Stuart Formula Tablets (Stuart) p 426, 649
Stuart Prenatal Tablets (Stuart) p 649

Vitamin B₁

Allbee C-800 Plus Iron Tablets (Robins) p 421, 626
Allbee C-800 Tablets (Robins) p 421, 626
Allbee with C Capsules (Robins) p 421, 626
B-1 Tablets (Nature's Bounty) p 600
B-100 Tablets (Nature's Bounty) p 600
B Complex & B-12 Tablets (Nature's Bounty) p 600
B Complex & C (Time Release) Capsules (Nature's Bounty) p 600
B & C Liquid (Nature's Bounty) p 600
Bugs Bunny Multivitamin Supplement (Miles Laboratories) p 415, 597
Bugs Bunny Plus Iron Multivitamin Supplement (Miles Laboratories) p 415, 597
Bugs Bunny With Extra C Multivitamin Supplement (Miles Laboratories) p 415, 598
Chew-Iron Tablets (Nature's Bounty) p 601
Flintstones Multivitamin Supplement (Miles Laboratories) p 416, 597
Flintstones Plus Iron Multivitamin Supplement (Miles Laboratories) p 416, 597
Flintstones With Extra C Multivitamin Supplement (Miles Laboratories) p 416, 598
Mega-B (Arco) p 511
Megadose (Arco) p 511
One-A-Day Core C 500 Multivitamin Supplement (Miles Laboratories) p 416, 598
One-A-Day Multivitamin Supplement (Miles Laboratories) p 416, 598
One-A-Day Multivitamin Supplement Plus Iron (Miles Laboratories) p 416, 598
One-A-Day Multivitamin Supplement Plus Minerals (Miles Laboratories) p 416, 598
One-A-Day Stressguard Vitamins (Miles Laboratories) p 416, 598
Orexin Softab Tablets (Stuart) p 648
The Stuart Formula Tablets (Stuart) p 426, 649
Stuart Prenatal Tablets (Stuart) p 649
Super Wate-On Emulsion (Fleetwood) p 409, 544
Tri-88 (Anabolic) p 510
Tri-B-Plex (Anabolic) p 510
Troph-Iron Liquid & Tablets (Menley & James) p 415, 587
Trophite Liquid & Tablets (Menley & James) p 415, 587
Z-Bec Tablets (Robins) p 422, 629

Vitamin B₂

Allbee C-800 Plus Iron Tablets (Robins) p 421, 626
Allbee C-800 Tablets (Robins) p 421, 626
Allbee with C Capsules (Robins) p 421, 626
B-2 Tablets (Nature's Bounty) p 600
B-100 Tablets (Nature's Bounty) p 600

B Complex & B-12 Tablets (Nature's Bounty) p 600
B Complex & C (Time Release) Capsules (Nature's Bounty) p 600
B & C Liquid (Nature's Bounty) p 600
Bugs Bunny Multivitamin Supplement (Miles Laboratories) p 415, 597
Bugs Bunny Plus Iron Multivitamin Supplement (Miles Laboratories) p 415, 597
Bugs Bunny With Extra C Multivitamin Supplement (Miles Laboratories) p 415, 598
Flintstones Multivitamin Supplement (Miles Laboratories) p 416, 597
Flintstones Plus Iron Multivitamin Supplement (Miles Laboratories) p 416, 597
Flintstones With Extra C Multivitamin Supplement (Miles Laboratories) p 416, 598
Mega-B (Arco) p 511
Megadose (Arco) p 511
One-A-Day Core C 500 Multivitamin Supplement (Miles Laboratories) p 416, 598
One-A-Day Multivitamin Supplement (Miles Laboratories) p 416, 598
One-A-Day Multivitamin Supplement Plus Iron (Miles Laboratories) p 416, 598
One-A-Day Multivitamin Supplement Plus Minerals (Miles Laboratories) p 416, 598
One-A-Day Stressguard Vitamins (Miles Laboratories) p 416, 598
The Stuart Formula Tablets (Stuart) p 426, 649
Stuart Prenatal Tablets (Stuart) p 649
Super Wate-On Emulsion (Fleetwood) p 409, 544
Tri-B-Plex (Anabolic) p 510
Z-Bec Tablets (Robins) p 422, 629

Vitamin B₃
(see under Niacin)

Vitamin B₆

Allbee C-800 Plus Iron Tablets (Robins) p 421, 626
Allbee C-800 Tablets (Robins) p 421, 626
Allbee with C Capsules (Robins) p 421, 626
B6-Plus (Anabolic) p 510
B-6 Tablets (Nature's Bounty) p 600
B-100 Tablets (Nature's Bounty) p 600
B Complex & C (Time Release) Capsules (Nature's Bounty) p 600
B & C Liquid (Nature's Bounty) p 600
Beelith Tablets (Beach) p 516
Bugs Bunny Multivitamin Supplement (Miles Laboratories) p 415, 597
Bugs Bunny Plus Iron Multivitamin Supplement (Miles Laboratories) p 415, 597
Bugs Bunny With Extra C Multivitamin Supplement (Miles Laboratories) p 415, 598
Flintstones Multivitamin Supplement (Miles Laboratories) p 416, 597
Flintstones Plus Iron Multivitamin Supplement (Miles Laboratories) p 416, 597
Flintstones With Extra C Multivitamin Supplement (Miles Laboratories) p 416, 598
KLB6 Capsules (Nature's Bounty) p 602
Mega-B (Arco) p 511
Megadose (Arco) p 511
One-A-Day Core C 500 Multivitamin Supplement (Miles Laboratories) p 416, 598
One-A-Day Multivitamin Supplement (Miles Laboratories) p 416, 598
One-A-Day Multivitamin Supplement Plus Iron (Miles Laboratories) p 416, 598
One-A-Day Multivitamin Supplement Plus Minerals (Miles Laboratories) p 416, 598

Product Identification Section

This section is designed to help you identify products and their packaging.

Participating manufacturers have included selected products in full color. Where capsules and tablets are included they are shown in actual size. Packages generally are reduced in size.

For more information on products included, refer to the description in the PRODUCT INFORMATION SECTION or check directly with the manufacturer.

While every effort has been made to reproduce products faithfully, this section should be considered only as a quick-reference identification aid.

INDEX BY MANUFACTURER

ABBOTT

Consumer Products Division

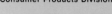

0.5 Fl. Oz.

CLEAR EYES®
For Immediate Redness
Removal

Also available in 1.5 Fl. Oz.

Consumer Products Division

0.5 Fl. Oz.

MURINE® REGULAR FORMULA
For Irritated Eyes

Also available in 1.5 Fl. Oz.

Consumer Products Division

0.5 Fl. Oz.

MURINE® PLUS
For **Faster** Redness Removal

Also available in 1.5 Fl. Oz.

Consumer Products Division

MURINE® EAR WAX REMOVAL SYSTEM
0.5 Fl.Oz.

MURINE® EAR DROPS
0.5 Fl. Oz.

Consumer Products Division

4 Fl. Oz.

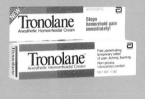

For Oily Hair

For Dry Hair

For Normal Hair

SELSUN BLUE®
Dandruff Shampoo

Also available in 7 and 11 Fl. Oz.

Consumer Products Division

1 Oz. Tube With Applicator

TRONOLANE™
Anesthetic Hemorrhoidal Cream

Also available in a 2 oz. tube.

Consumer Products Division

10 Suppositories

TRONOLANE™
Anesthetic Hemorrhoidal
Suppositories

Also available in size 20's.

ALCON/bp

15 ml
(½ fl. oz.)

ADAPETTES®
Hard & Soft Lens Rewetting/
Lubricating Solution

Alcon/bp

355 ml
(12 fl. oz.)

Also available: 237 ml (8 fl. oz.)

BOILnSOAK®
Soft Lens Rinsing, Storage & Heat
Disinfection Solution

Alcon/bp

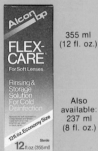

355 ml
(12 fl. oz.)

Also available: 237 ml (8 fl. oz.)

FLEX-CARE®
Soft Lens Rinsing, Storage & Cold
Disinfection Solution

Alcon/bp

45 ml
(1.5 fl. oz.)

PREFLEX®
Soft Lens Cleaning Solution

Alcon/bp

120 ml
(4 fl. oz.)

SOACLENS®
Hard Lens Soaking &
Wetting Solution

ALLERGAN

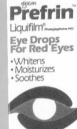

½ fl oz

Also available: 1 fl oz

LIQUIFILM® TEARS
Artificial Tears

Allergan

0.7 fl oz

PREFRIN™ LIQUIFILM®
Ocular Decongestant
(phenylephrine HCl 0.12%)

Allergan

½ fl oz

TEARS PLUS™
Artificial Tears

ALOE CREME

Protects lips while it helps heal chapping
and drying from summer and winter
weather.

ALO-LIP-SHIELD®
Lip Balm and Protectant

Also Available: An SPF 15 Ultra
Protection Stick by Alo-Sun®

Aloe Creme Laboratories

2 oz. jar

Also available in
4 oz. and 16 oz. jars

1 oz. tube

ALO-OINTMENT®
(70% aloe vera 'gel')

Aloe Creme Laboratories

2 oz. and 4 oz. sizes available

ALO-RELIEF®
Healing Lotion
(50% aloe vera 'gel')

Aloe Creme Laboratories

4 fl. oz.
Also available in 8 oz. size

ALO-SUN®
FASHION TAN® SPF 15
Sun Block Lotion

ALTO

or

Theionized® EFED II™
Decongestant/Stimulant

AMES DIVISION

Miles Laboratories Inc.

MICROSTIX®-NITRITE

Reagent Strip Kit

An Indicator of Urinary
Tract Infection

ASTRA

Available in 35g Tube

XYLOCAINE® 2.5% OINTMENT
(lidocaine)

AYERST

BEMINAL
STRESS PLUS™
with iron

BEMINAL
STRESS PLUS™
with zinc

Stress potency replacement
vitamins

Bottles of 60

Ayerst

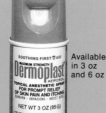

Available
in 3 oz
and 6 oz

DERMOPLAST®
Topical Anesthetic First Aid Spray
(20% benzocaine and 0.5% menthol)

Ayerst

KERODEX® 71
for Wet Work

KERODEX® 51
for Dry Work

Barrier Skin Cream
Available in 4 oz tubes
and 1 lb jars

Ayerst

Available in
12 fl oz
Suspension;
and Chew
and Swallow
Tablets
(60s and 100s)

RIOPAN®
(magaldrate)
Antacid

Ayerst

Available in
12 fl oz
Suspension;
and Chew
Tablets (60s)

RIOPAN PLUS®
(magaldrate and simethicone)
Antacid/Anti-Gas

Ayerst

For more detailed in-
formation on products
illustrated in this sec-
tion, consult the Prod-
uct Information Sec-
tion or manufacturers
may be contacted di-
rectly.

BAUSCH & LOMB

For Use With Soft Contact Lenses Only

STERILE DAILY CLEANER

Bausch & Lomb

For Use With Soft Contact Lenses Only

STERILE DISINFECTING SOLUTION

Bausch & Lomb

For Use With Soft & Hard Contact Lenses

STERILE LENS LUBRICANT

Bausch & Lomb

For Use With Soft Contact Lenses Only

**STERILE PRESERVED
SALINE SOLUTION**

Bausch & Lomb

STERILE SALINE SOLUTION

For Use With
Soft Contact Lenses Only

BEIERSDORF

16 oz.

4 oz.

EUCERIN®
Unscented Moisturizing Formula
for Dry Skin Care

Beiersdorf

8 fl. oz.

EUCERIN™ LOTION
Unscented Moisturizing Formula
for Dry Skin Care

Beiersdorf

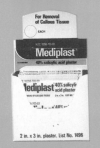

Available in individual packets

MEDIPLAST®
40% Salicylic Acid Plaster

For Removal of Callous Tissue

Boehringer Ingelheim Ltd.

Available in boxes of 2's, 4's,
8's and 50's.

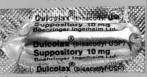

10 mg.

Dulcolax® Suppositories
(bisacodyl USP)

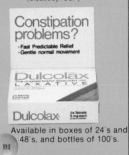

Available in boxes of 24's and
48's, and bottles of 100's.

12   5 mg.

Dulcolax® Tablets
(bisacodyl USP)

BREON

200 mg

Bottles of 24
and 100

BREONESIN®
(guaifenesin capsules, USP)

BRISTOL-MYERS

Bottles of 40's
& 100's

**ARTHRITIS STRENGTH
BUFFERIN®**
(aspirin)

Bristol-Myers

Bottles of 12's,
36's, 60's, 100's,
165's, 225's,
375's,
& 1000's

BUFFERIN®
(aspirin)

Bristol-Myers

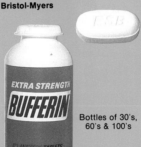

Bottles of 30's,
60's & 100's

**EXTRA STRENGTH
BUFFERIN® TABLETS**
(aspirin)

Bristol-Myers

Bottles of
50's & 75's

**EXTRA STRENGTH
BUFFERIN® CAPSULES**
(aspirin)

Bristol-Myers

Bottles of 6
& 10 oz.

COMTREX® LIQUID

Bristol-Myers

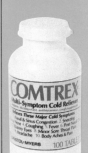

Bottles of 24's,
60's & 100's

COMTREX® TABLETS

Bristol-Myers

Bottles of 16's
& 36's

COMTREX® CAPSULES

Bristol-Myers

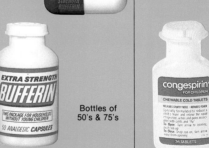

Bottles of
36's

CONGESPIRIN® COLD TABLETS

Bristol-Myers

3 oz.
Bottles

**CONGESPIRIN® LIQUID COLD
MEDICINE**

Bristol-Myers

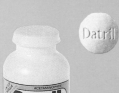

Bottles of 24's, 100's & 250's

DATRIL®
(acetaminophen)

Bristol-Myers

Bottles of 10's, 30's, 50's & 80's

EXCEDRIN P.M.®

Bristol-Myers

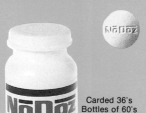

Carded 36's
Bottles of 60's

NO-DOZ® TABLETS
(caffeine)

Burroughs Wellcome

100

48

24

SUDAFED® TABLETS
Decongestant

Bristol-Myers

Bottles of 24's, 50's & 72's

EXTRA STRENGTH DATRIL™ TABLETS
(acetaminophen)

Bristol-Myers

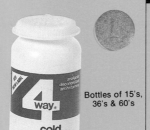

Bottles of 15's, 36's & 60's

4-WAY® COLD TABLETS

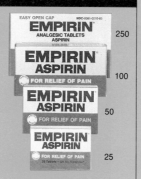

250

100

50

25

EMPIRIN® ASPIRIN TABLETS

Burroughs Wellcome

8 fl. oz.   4 fl. oz.

SUDAFED® COUGH SYRUP

Bristol-Myers

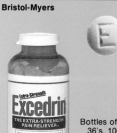

Bottles of 12's, 36's, 100's, 165's, 225's & 375's

EXCEDRIN® TABLETS
Aspirin/Acetaminophen/Caffeine

Bristol-Myers

Atomizers of ½ & 1 oz.

4-WAY® NASAL SPRAY

Burroughs Wellcome

1 oz.

½ oz.

NEOSPORIN® OINTMENT
Antibacterial

Burroughs Wellcome

4 fl. oz.   24

SUDAFED® PLUS SYRUP & TABLETS

Bristol-Myers

Bottles of 24's, 40's & 60's

EXCEDRIN® CAPSULES
Aspirin/Acetaminophen/Caffeine

Bristol-Myers

½ oz. Atomizers

4-WAY® LONG ACTING NASAL SPRAY
(xylometazoline hydrochloride)

Burroughs Wellcome

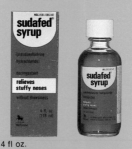

4 fl. oz.

SUDAFED® SYRUP
Decongestant

Also available in pints

Burroughs Wellcome

40

10

Also available in 100s
SUDAFED® S.A. CAPSULES

Burroughs Wellcome

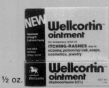

½ oz.

½ oz.

**WELLCORTIN™
CREAM AND OINTMENT**

Carter Products

2 sizes: 85 pills
and 30 pills

CARTER'S LITTLE PILLS
(5 mg. bisacodyl)

CIBA

Available in 2 oz and 1 oz tubes

NUPERCAINAL®
Anesthetic Ointment

Ciba

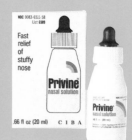

.66 fl oz (20 ml)

.66 fl oz

PRIVINE®
Nasal Solution

Burroughs Wellcome

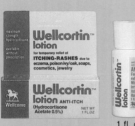

1 fl. oz.

WELLCORTIN™ LOTION

CHATTEM LABORATORIES

24's Packettes

48's Bottle

PAMPRIN®
Menstrual Relief Tablets

Ciba

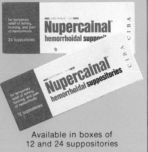

Available in boxes of
12 and 24 suppositories

NUPERCAINAL®
Hemorrhoidal Suppositories

COLGATE-PALMOLIVE

DERMASSAGE®
Medicated
Skin Lotion

CAMBRIDGE PLAN

Weight-loss powder as
part of a total plan and
nutrition supplement.

21-meal
container

Contains 100% RDA + trace elements
and electrolytes

CAMBRIDGE PLAN

CHESEBROUGH-POND'S

Cream
5.25 Oz.
Also available: 3 Oz.

For Severe
Cases of Dry   Lotion
Skin   16 Fl. Oz.

Also available: 5½ & 11 Oz.

**VASELINE®
DERMATOLOGY FORMULA**

Ciba

1½ oz

NUPERCAINAL®
Pain-Relief Cream

Colgate-Palmolive

FLUORIGARD™
Anti-Cavity Dental Rinse
With Fluoride

CARTER PRODUCTS

Division of Carter-Wallace Inc.

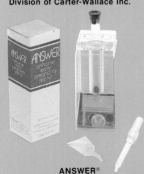

ANSWER®
At-home early pregnancy test kit

Chesebrough-Pond's

15 Oz.

Also available: 1¾ Oz., 3¼ Oz.,
7½ Oz. and
Scented Vaseline Nursery Jelly

**VASELINE®
Pure Petroleum Jelly**

Ciba

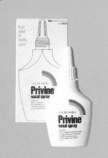

½ fl oz

PRIVINE®
Nasal Spray

Colgate-Palmolive

**COLGATE® MFP® FLUORIDE
TOOTHPASTE**

COLGATE® MFP® FLUORIDE GEL

Both available in 5 sizes

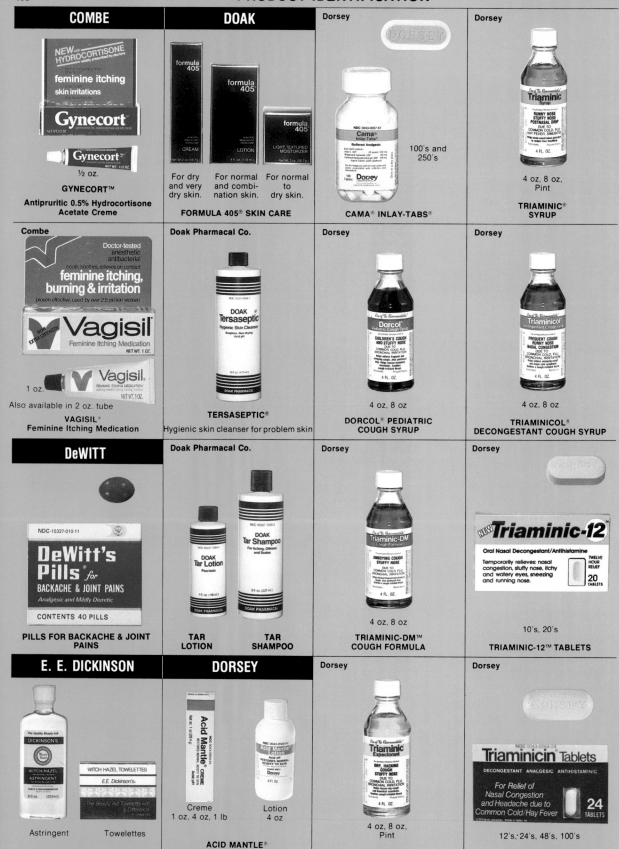

COMBE

GYNECORT™

½ oz.

Antipruritic 0.5% Hydrocortisone Acetate Creme

DOAK

FORMULA 405® SKIN CARE

For dry and very dry skin. — CREAM

For normal and combination skin. — LOTION

For normal to dry skin. — LIGHT-TEXTURED MOISTURIZER

Dorsey

CAMA® INLAY-TABS®

100's and 250's

Dorsey

TRIAMINIC® SYRUP

4 oz, 8 oz, Pint

Combe

VAGISIL®
Feminine Itching Medication

1 oz.

Also available in 2 oz. tube

Doak Pharmacal Co.

TERSASEPTIC®

Hygienic skin cleanser for problem skin

Dorsey

DORCOL® PEDIATRIC COUGH SYRUP

4 oz, 8 oz

Dorsey

TRIAMINICOL® DECONGESTANT COUGH SYRUP

4 oz, 8 oz

DeWITT

PILLS FOR BACKACHE & JOINT PAINS

DeWitt's Pills for BACKACHE & JOINT PAINS
Analgesic and Mildly Diuretic
CONTENTS 40 PILLS

Doak Pharmacal Co.

TAR LOTION

TAR SHAMPOO

Dorsey

TRIAMINIC-DM™ COUGH FORMULA

4 oz, 8 oz

Dorsey

TRIAMINIC-12™ TABLETS

NEW Triaminic-12

Oral Nasal Decongestant/Antihistamine

Temporarily relieves: nasal congestion, stuffy nose, itchy and watery eyes, sneezing and running nose.

TWELVE HOUR RELIEF 20 TABLETS

10's, 20's

E. E. DICKINSON

DICKINSON'S WITCH HAZEL

Astringent

Towelettes

DORSEY

ACID MANTLE® CREME AND LOTION
(aluminum acetate)

Creme
1 oz, 4 oz, 1 lb

Lotion
4 oz

Dorsey

TRIAMINIC® EXPECTORANT

4 oz, 8 oz, Pint

Dorsey

TRIAMINICIN® TABLETS

Triaminicin Tablets
DECONGESTANT ANALGESIC ANTIHISTAMINIC
For Relief of Nasal Congestion and Headache due to Common Cold/Hay Fever
24 TABLETS

12's, 24's, 48's, 100's

ENDO

Available in blister-strip boxes of 24 tablets and bottles of 100.

PERCOGESIC®
analgesic

Each tablet contains acetaminophen (APAP) 325 mg. and phenyltoloxamine citrate 30 mg.

Ex-Lax Pharmaceutical

DOCTOR-PRESCRIBED INGREDIENT HELPS RELIEVE SYMPTOMS OF INTESTINAL GAS

NEW GAS-X
SIMETHICONE—ANTIFLATULENT

FOR RELIEVING SYMPTOMS OF INTESTINAL GAS

30 Tablets, 80 mg. each

GAS-X®
(simethicone)

GEIGY

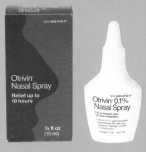

Otrivin® Nasal Spray
Relief up to 10 hours

½ fl oz (15 ml)

Otrivin® 0.1% Nasal Spray

OTRIVIN® 0.1%
Nasal Spray

Glenbrook

NEW PLASTIC BOTTLE
ORANGE FLAVORED
BAYER® CHILDREN'S
CHEWABLE ASPIRIN
WITH CHILD-GUARD CAP

36 TABLETS-81 MG (1¼ GR. EACH)

Available in bottle of 36 tablets

BAYER® CHILDREN'S CHEWABLE ASPIRIN

EX-LAX PHARMACEUTICAL

Medical Formula for Itching Skin
BiCOZENE CREME
NET WT. 1 OZ. (28 g.)

Medical Formula for Itching Skin
BiCOZENE CREME

1 oz. (28 g.)

BICOZENE® CREME

FLEETWOOD

Regular **Wate-On** Tablets

Super **Wate-On**

REGULAR WATE-ON® Tablets 96's

SUPER WATE-ON® Emulsion 16 oz.

High Calorie Nutritional and Vitamin Supplements for the Gaining of Weight.

Geigy

Otrivin® Nasal Drops
Relief up to 10 hours

.66 fl oz (20 ml)

Otrivin® 0.1% Nasal Solution

OTRIVIN® 0.1%
Nasal Drops

Otrivin® Pediatric Nasal Drops
Relief up to 10 hours

.66 fl oz (20 ml)

OTRIVIN® 0.05%
Pediatric Nasal Drops

Glenbrook

BAYER

NDC 12843-197-02
BAYER® TIMED-RELEASE ASPIRIN
TAKE EVERY 8 HOURS
72 TABLETS-EACH 650 MG. 10 GRS. ASPIRIN

For temporary relief of minor pain of **Arthritis**

THIS PACKAGE FOR HOUSEHOLDS WITHOUT YOUNG CHILDREN

Available in bottles of 30, 72, and 125 tablets

BAYER® TIMED-RELEASE ASPIRIN

Ex-Lax Pharmaceutical

Medical Formula for Hard Callused Skin
DERMA+SOFT CREME
ACTIVE INGREDIENT: Salicylic Acid 2.5%
NET WT. 1 oz. (28 Grams)

Medical Formula for Hard Callused Skin
DERMA+SOFT CREME

1 oz. (28 g.)

DERMA + SOFT® CREME

FOREVER LIVING PRODS.

Forever Living Products
ALOE VERA GELLY

4 Fl. Oz. (118 ml)

ALOE VERA GELLY

Geigy

PBZ

PBZ

Cream

PBZ®
(tripelennamine hydrochloride)

Glenbrook

100% Talc Free
Diaparene Corn Starch Baby Powder
Naturally Absorbent
NET WT 9 OZ.

Available in 4 oz., 9 oz. and 12½ oz. containers

DIAPARENE® BABY POWDER

Ex-Lax Pharmaceutical

Gentle, dependable overnight relief

FOR RELIEF OF CONSTIPATION
EX-LAX PILLS
30 PILLS-UNFLAVORED

FOR RELIEF OF CONSTIPATION
EX-LAX
THE CHOCOLATED LAXATIVE
18 TABLETS

Pill

Chocolated Tablet

EX-LAX®

Forever Living Products

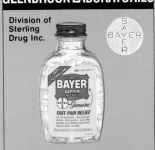

Forever Living Products
ALOE VERA JUICE
32 FL.OZ. (946 ML)

32 Fl. Oz. (946 ml)

ALOE VERA JUICE

GLENBROOK LABORATORIES

Division of Sterling Drug Inc.

BAYER

BAYER ASPIRIN
Genuine
FAST PAIN RELIEF

Available in packs of 12 tablets and bottles of 24's, 50's, 100's, 200's and 300's

BAYER® ASPIRIN

Glenbrook

150 cloth
Diaparene Baby Wash Cloths
PRE-MOISTENED POP-UP TOWELETTES WITH LANOLIN

Available in 70 cloth and 150 cloth canisters

DIAPARENE® BABY WASH CLOTHS

Glenbrook

Available in packages of 12, 30 and 60 Caplets®

MIDOL®

HEALTH CARE INDUSTRIES

Div. of ACCRA PAC, Inc.

Available in 30, 80, 160, 330 sizes

4¾ grains (308 mg.) per tablet

Dried garlic powder (Allium sativum, dehydrated)

ALLIMIN® FILMCOATED TABLET

HERBERT

Cooling Alcohol Lotion

Moisturizing Lotion

ECLIPSE® SUNCARE PRODUCTS

Hynson, Westcott & Dunning

Product must be refrigerated

Granules: 1 gram packet

Tablets: bottles of 50

LACTINEX®
Tablets & Granules
(Lactobacillus acidophilus and Lactobacillus bulgaricus)

Glenbrook

Available in regular and mint flavor 4 oz., 12 oz. and 26 oz.

PHILLIPS'® MILK OF MAGNESIA

Health Care Industries

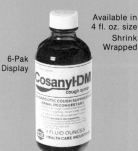

Available in 4 fl. oz. 1 pint and 1 gallon sizes

COSANYL® COUGH SYRUP
Each teaspoonful (5 ml.): Codeine phosphate,* 10 mg. d-pseudoephedrine HCl, 30 mg. Peach flavor: Alcohol, 6%
*(Warning: May be habit forming)

HOECHST-ROUSSEL

10 capsule pack and bottles of 30 and 100

Laxative and Stool Softener

DOXIDAN®
(docusate calcium USP and danthron USP)

JOHNSON & JOHNSON

8 Fl. Oz.
Also available:
4 Fl. Oz. & 12 Fl. Oz. sizes

1.5 Fl. Oz.
For hospital nursery use

JOHNSON'S BABY BATH

GOODY'S

6 Powders

HEADACHE POWDERS

Health Care Industries

6-Pak Display

Available in 4 fl. oz. size
Shrink Wrapped

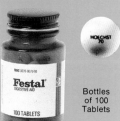

COSANYL-DM® COUGH SYRUP
Teaspoonful (5 ml.): d-methorphan, 15 mg. d-pseudoephedrine HCl, 30 mg. Peach flavor. Alcohol 6%

Hoechst-Roussel

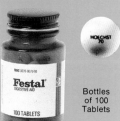

Bottles of 100 Tablets

Digestive Aid

FESTAL®
(digestive enzymes with bile constituents)

Johnson & Johnson

1.5 Oz.   .8 Oz.

FIRST AID CREAM

For more detailed information on products illustrated in this section, consult the Product Information Section or manufacturers may be contacted directly.

Health Care Industries

Available in 1 oz., 2 oz., 4 oz., pints and gallons

2 oz. STREEM-TOP™
OIL-O-SOL® LIQUID

Corn oil 52%, castor oil 40.8%, camphor oil 6.8%, hexylresorcinol 0.1%

Hoechst-Roussel

50 mg
Bottles of 30 and 100

240 mg
Bottles of 30 and 100

Stool Softener

Surfak®
(docusate calcium USP)

Johnson & Johnson

SPF 4   SPF 6   SPF 8   SPF 15

4 Fl. Oz.

SUNDOWN®
Sunscreen and Sunblock Protection

LEDERLE

**LEDERMARK™
Product Identification
Code**

Many Lederle tablets and capsules bear an identification code, and these codes are listed with each product pictured. A current listing appears in the Product Information Section of the 1982 Physicians' Desk Reference.

Lederle

NEW
The itch relieving power of Hydrocortisone in soothing Aquatain® cream.

Rhulicort anti-itch cream®

Rhulicort® anti-itch cream

20 gm Tube

**RHULICORT™ CREAM
Hydrocortisone 0.5%**

Lederle

S2

New advanced formula Stresstabs available 5/1/82

Bottles of 30 & 60

**STRESSTABS® 600 with IRON
High Potency Stress Formula
Vitamins**

Marion

GAVISCON 1175

GAVISCON® antacid
for fast relief of HEARTBURN acid indigestion

100-tablet bottle

GAVISCON antacid
for fast relief of HEARTBURN acid indigestion

30-tablet box (foil-wrapped 2's)

**GAVISCON®
Antacid Tablets**

Lederle

C1

Centrum®

BONUS OFFER
30 FREE WITH 100

Combopack
**CENTRUM®
High Potency Multivitamin/
Multimineral Formula**

Lederle

NEW
The itch relieving power of Hydrocortisone in soothing Aquatain® lotion.

Rhulicort

Effective, temporary relief from the itch and inflammation of:
Poison Ivy
Poison Oak
Poison Sumac
Insect Bites
Scalp Itch
Eczema
Allergic Rashes

60 ml Bottle

**RHULICORT™ LOTION
Hydrocortisone 0.5%**

Lederle

S3

New advanced formula Stresstabs available 5/1/82

Bottles of 30 & 60

**STRESSTABS® 600 with ZINC
High Potency Stress Formula
Vitamins**

Marion

GAVISCON liquid antacid
for relief of HEARTBURN acid indigestion

12 fl. oz.

**GAVISCON®
Liquid Antacid**

Lederle

Ferro-Sequels iron

Bottles of 30, 100 and 1000

**FERRO-SEQUELS®
Sustained Release Iron Capsules**

Lederle

RHULIGEL Analgesic-Anesthetic GEL
NET WT. 2 OZ. (56.7 Grams)

RHULIGEL Analgesic-Anesthetic Gel

2 oz Tube

**RHULIGEL®
Analgesic-Anesthetic Gel**

MARION

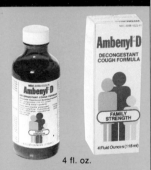

Ambenyl-D

Ambenyl-D DECONGESTANT COUGH FORMULA

FAMILY STRENGTH

4 fl. oz.

**AMBENYL®-D
Decongestant Cough Formula**

Marion

GAVISCON 2 1172

double-strength
GAVISCON-2 antacid tablets
for fast relief of HEARTBURN acid indigestion
48 CHEWABLE TABLETS in Convenient Foil Packets

Box of 48 foil-wrapped tablets

**GAVISCON®-2
Antacid Tablets**

Lederle

RHULICAINE

COOL RELIEF FROM SUNBURN PAIN

NET WT. 4 OZ.

4 oz Can

**RHULICAINE™
Anesthetic-Antiseptic
Medicated Spray**

Lederle

S1

New advanced formula Stresstabs available 5/1/82

Bottles of 30, 60 & 500

Stresstabs 600 HIGH POTENCY STRESS FORMULA VITAMINS

**STRESSTABS® 600
High Potency Stress Formula
Vitamins**

Marion

Debrox Drops
FOR EARWAX CONTROL
ECONOMY SIZE
MOST WIDELY RECOMMENDED BY DOCTORS FOR EARWAX REMOVAL

Debrox Drops
FOR EARWAX CONTROL
MOST WIDELY RECOMMENDED BY DOCTORS FOR EARWAX REMOVAL

1 fl. oz. (30 ml)   1/2 FL. OZ. (15 ml)

1 fl. oz.   ½ fl. oz.

**DEBROX®
Drops**

Marion

Gly-Oxide CLEANSING ANTISEPTIC for the MOUTH
LIQUID CARBAMIDE PEROXIDE
RECOMMENDED BY DOCTORS FOR CANKER SORES
AN AID TO REGULAR BRUSHING

Gly-Oxide CLEANSING ANTISEPTIC for the MOUTH
LIQUID CARBAMIDE PEROXIDE

2 fl. oz.   1/2 FL. OZ. (15 ml)

2 fl. oz.   ½ fl. oz.

GLY-OXIDE® Liquid

Marion

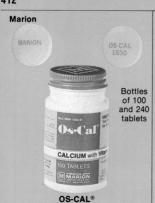

Bottles of 100 and 240 tablets

OS-CAL®
Tablets
(calcium with Vitamin D)

Max Factor & Co.

MAXI®
UNSHINE™
OIL-BLOTTING
MAKE-UP

MAXI®
UNSHINE™
100% OIL-FREE
BLUSHING GEL

Max Factor & Co.

Maxi-Thick™ Double Lash Mascara; Maxi-Lash™ 24 Hour Polymer Mascara; Maxi® Extra-long Thick Lash Mascara with Sealer.

MAXI® MASCARA
Dermatologist and Ophthalmologist tested

Max Factor & Co.

SEBB™
Shampoo and Lotion

Shampoo removes loose or flaking dandruff.
Lotion treats itchy scalp associated with dandruff.

Marion

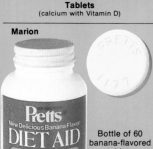

Bottle of 60 banana-flavored tablets

PRETTS®
Tablets
(diet control adjunct)

Max Factor & Co.

Dermatologist tested. Pure and gentle. Soaks up oily shine for hours. Available in six transparent shades.

MAXI® UNSHINE™
100% OIL-FREE BLOTTING POWDER

Max Factor & Co.

Purifying Cleansing Lotion

Gentle Cleansing Bar

Max Factor & Co.

TRIED & TRUE®
HAIR THICKENER

Marion

Box of 60 lozenges

THROAT DISCS®
Throat Lozenges

Max Factor & Co.

Dermatologist tested. Pure and gentle. Available in eight radiant shades.

Won't streak or change color.

MAXI® UNSHINE™
100% OIL-FREE BLUSHING POWDER

SKIN PRINCIPLE™
Basic Clarifying Lotion

McHENRY LABORATORIES

ORA5™
ORA5
ORA5

Oral Antibacterial Agent

Aids discomfort and inflammation of the mouth tissues associated with:

• Mouth Sores
• Denture Sores
• Ulcers
• Minor Irritations of the Mouth and Gums.

NDC #50185-0002-3B   Net Wt. ½ oz (3.7 ML.)

Oral Antibacterial Agent

ORA 5™

MAX FACTOR & CO.

Dermatologist tested. Pure, water base formula. Fragrance free. Available in 10 natural looking shades.
*Contains none of the natural oils associated with oily skin problems.
MAXI® UNSHINE™
OIL-FREE* MAKE-UP

Max Factor & Co.

Hypo-Allergenic; dermatologist and ophthalmologist tested; fragrance free. Formulated with oil blotters for long lasting color on oily skin.

MAXI® STAY-FRESH™
CREASE RESISTANT
EYE SHADOW

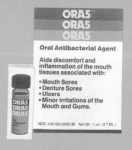

Daily Light Moisture Lotion

Daily Rich Moisture Lotion

Serious Moisture Supplement
SKIN PRINCIPLE™ PRODUCTS
Hypo-Allergenic   Fragrance Free

For more detailed information on products illustrated in this section, consult the Product Information Section or manufacturers may be contacted directly.

McNEIL CONSUMER

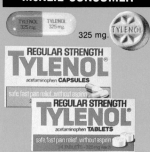

325 mg.

REGULAR STRENGTH TYLENOL® acetaminophen CAPSULES

safe, fast pain relief...without aspirin

REGULAR STRENGTH TYLENOL® acetaminophen TABLETS

safe, fast pain relief...without aspirin

Capsules: bottles of 24, 50 and 100.
Tablets: tins and vials of 12, and bottles
of 24, 50, 100 and 200.

REGULAR STRENGTH TYLENOL®
acetaminophen   Capsules & Tablets

McNeil Consumer

CHILDREN'S TYLENOL ELIXIR acetaminophen

Relieves children's fever and pain without aspirin complications

Available in 2 & 4 fl. oz. bottles with
child-resistant safety cap and convenient
dosage cup.

CHILDREN'S TYLENOL®
acetaminophen
Elixir

McNeil Consumer

Children's COTYLENOL LIQUID COLD FORMULA

relieves cold symptoms without aspirin complications

Available in 4 fl. oz. bottle
with child-resistant safety cap
and convenient dosage cup.

CHILDREN'S COTYLENOL®
Liquid Cold Formula

MENLEY & JAMES

ACNOMEL acne cream   NET WT. 1 OZ. (28 GRAMS)

ACNOMEL® ACNE CREAM
(resorcinol, sulfate, alcohol)

McNeil Consumer

500 mg.

EXTRA-STRENGTH TYLENOL® acetaminophen CAPSULES

extra pain relief contains no aspirin
50 Capsules—500 mg. each

EXTRA-STRENGTH TYLENOL® acetaminophen TABLETS

Capsules available in bottles of
24, 50, 100 and 165.

Tablets available in vials of 10 and
bottles of 30, 60 and 100.

EXTRA-STRENGTH TYLENOL®
acetaminophen
Capsules & Tablets

McNeil Consumer

INFANTS' TYLENOL DROPS

Relieves infants fever and pain without aspirin complications

Available in ½ fl. oz. bottle with
child-resistant safety cap and
calibrated dropper.

INFANTS' TYLENOL®
acetaminophen
Drops

McNeil Consumer

SINE AID

No Drowsiness Formula

SINE-AID®
For sinus headache pain and pressure
50 TABLETS

Available in bottles of
24, 50 & 100.

SINE-AID®
Sinus Headache Tablets

Menley & James

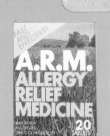

FAST AND EFFECTIVE!

A.R.M. ALLERGY RELIEF MEDICINE

HAY FEVER
ALLERGIES
SINUS CONGESTION

20 TABLETS

Packages of 20 and 40 tablets

**A.R.M.® ALLERGY RELIEF
MEDICINE**
(chlorpheniramine maleate,
phenylpropanolamine HCl)

McNeil Consumer

All sizes have
child-resistant
safety cap and
convenient
dosage cup.

EXTRA-STRENGTH TYLENOL® ADULT LIQUID PAIN RELIEVER

FAST, SAFE PAIN RELIEF WITHOUT ASPIRIN COMPLICATIONS

8 fl. oz. bottle

EXTRA-STRENGTH TYLENOL®
acetaminophen
Adult Liquid Pain Reliever

McNeil Consumer

COTYLENOL COLD FORMULA LONGER ACTING

relieves cold symptoms without aspirin complications

COTYLENOL COLD FORMULA LONGER ACTING

relieves cold symptoms without aspirin complications
50 Tablets

Capsules available in blister pack of
20 and bottle of 40.
Tablets available in blister pack
of 24 and bottles of 50 and 100.

COTYLENOL® COLD FORMULA
Capsules & Tablets

MEAD JOHNSON PHARM.

NDC 0087-0713-02

CAPSULES

COLACE DOCUSATE SODIUM (Dioctyl Sodium Sulfosuccinate) STOOL SOFTENER

50 mg
100 mg

Store at controlled room temperature (15°–30°C/59°–86°F.)

60 CAPSULES

Mead Johnson

Bottles of 30, 60, 250 and 1000
Stool Softener

COLACE®
(docusate sodium)

Menley & James

BENZEDREX INHALER

BENZEDREX® INHALER
(propylhexedrine, SK&F)

McNeil Consumer

80 mg.

Available in bottles
of 30.

CHILDREN'S TYLENOL® CHEWABLE TABLETS IMPROVED DOSAGE acetaminophen

Relieves children's fever and pain without aspirin complications
Fruit Flavored

CHILDREN'S TYLENOL®
acetaminophen
Chewable Tablets

Child-resistant safety cap.

McNeil Consumer

COTYLENOL COLD FORMULA LOWER ACTING

relieves cold symptoms without aspirin complications
5 FL. OZ.

Available in 5 fl. oz.
& 10 fl. oz. bottles.

All sizes have child-resistant safety
cap and convenient dosage cup.

**COTYLENOL® LIQUID COLD
FORMULA**

Mead Johnson Pharmaceutical Division

NDC 0087-0715-02

CAPSULES

PERI-COLACE CASANTHRANOL AND DOCUSATE SODIUM (Dioctyl Sodium Sulfosuccinate)

LAXATIVE PLUS STOOL SOFTENER

A GENTLE, PREDICTABLE LAXATIVE

60 CAPSULES

Mead Johnson

Bottles of 30, 60, 250 and 1000
Laxative and Stool Softener

PERI-COLACE®
(casanthranol and docusate sodium)

Menley & James

Packages of 10, 20, 30 and 40
capsules

10 CAPSULES

12 HOUR RELIEF

1 CAPSULE EVERY 12 HOURS

CONTAC
CONTINUOUS ACTION NASAL DECONGESTANT / ANTIHISTAMINE CAPSULES   10 CAPSULES

CONTAC®
CONTINUOUS ACTION
DECONGESTANT CAPSULES

Menley & James

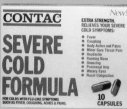

Packages of 10 and 20 capsules

**CONTAC®
SEVERE COLD FORMULA**

Menley & James

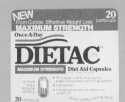

Packages of 20 and
40 capsules

**Once-A-Day
DIETAC™ MAXIMUM STRENGTH**
Diet Aid Capsules

Menley & James

In 36, 100 and 250
tablet bottles

ECOTRIN® TABLETS
Duentric® coated 5 gr. aspirin

Menley & James

FEOSOL PLUS®
Iron Plus Vitamins

Menley & James

Includes dose-
by-weight cup

**CONTAC JR.®
COLD MEDICINE FOR CHILDREN**

Menley & James

Packages of 24 and
48 capsules

**Twice-A-Day
DIETAC™ MAXIMUM STRENGTH**
Diet Aid Capsules

Menley & James

12 oz. bottle
FEOSOL® ELIXIR
(ferrous sulfate USP)

Menley & James

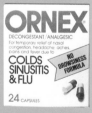

In 30 capsule packages

**ORNACOL® COUGH & COLD
CAPSULE & LIQUID**

Menley & James

C3® COLD-COUGH CAPSULES

Menley & James

**PRE-MEAL
DIETAC™** ½ Fl. Oz.
Diet Aid Drops

Menley & James

In 30 and 100 capsule bottles

FEOSOL® SPANSULE® CAPSULES
(ferrous sulfate USP)

Menley & James

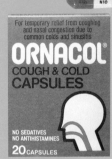

In 24, 48 and 100
capsule packages

ORNEX® CAPSULES
Decongestant/Analgesic

Menley & James

Packages of 14
and 28 capsules

**12 Hour
DIETAC™**
Diet Aid Capsules

Menley & James

42 Tablets

**Pre-Meal
DIETAC™**
Diet Aid Tablets

Menley & James

In 100 and 1,000 tablet bottles

FEOSOL® TABLETS
(ferrous sulfate USP)

Menley & James

Dermatologic Ointment

1 oz. tube
PRAGMATAR® OINTMENT

Menley & James

Packages of 24,
48, and 100 tablets

**SINE-OFF® TABLETS
ASPIRIN FORMULA**

Menley & James

In 12 and 24
packages; in
bottles of 50

8 mg.

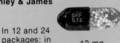

12-HOUR
ALLERGY RELIEF

Teldrin®

chlorpheniramine maleate TIMED-RELEASE CAPSULES

Relieves
runny nose,
sneezing and itchy,
watery eyes

12 CAPSULES   **8 mg.**

**TELDRIN®
TIMED-RELEASE CAPSULES**
(chlorpheniramine maleate)

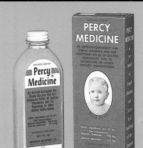

PERCY MEDICINE®
(bismuth subnitrate NF & calcium
hydroxide USP)

Miles Laboratories, Inc.

ALKA-2® CHEWABLE ANTACID
(Calcium Carbonate 500 mg)

Menley & James

EXTRA STRENGTH

Prompt relief from
sinus headache, pain,
pressure & congestion   20 TABLETS

**SINE-OFF® AF
EXTRA STRENGTH NON-ASPIRIN
TABLETS**

Menley & James

In 12 and 24
packages; in
bottles of 50   12 mg.

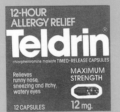

12-HOUR
ALLERGY RELIEF

Teldrin®

chlorpheniramine maleate TIMED-RELEASE CAPSULES

Relieves
runny nose,
sneezing and itchy,
watery eyes   MAXIMUM
STRENGTH

12 CAPSULES   **12 mg.**

**TELDRIN®
TIMED-RELEASE CAPSULES**
(chlorpheniramine maleate)

ORIGINAL

Alka-Seltzer®
BRAND

THE SOUND OF FAST RELIEF®

with SPECIALLY BUFFERED ASPIRIN
For ACID INDIGESTION or HEARTBURN
with HEADACHE, or MINOR PAINS.
Also UPSET STOMACH with HEADACHE
from OVERINDULGENCE.

36 TABLETS IN 18 FOIL PACKS

**ALKA-SELTZER® BRAND
EFFERVESCENT
PAIN RELIEVER & ANTACID**

Miles Laboratories, Inc.

**BACTINE® BRAND
ANTISEPTIC · ANESTHETIC
FIRST AID SPRAY**
Aerosol and Liquid

Menley & James

20 capsules

EXTRA STRENGTH
WITH NON-ASPIRIN PAIN RELIEVER

Prompt relief from
sinus headache, pain,
pressure & congestion   20 CAPSULES

**SINE-OFF®
EXTRA STRENGTH SINUS MEDICINE
NON-ASPRIN CAPSULES**

Menley & James

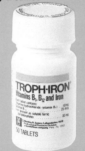

TROPH-IRON®
Vitamins B₁, B₁₂ and Iron

50 TABLETS

4 oz. liquid and
50 tablet bottle
**TROPH-IRON®
LIQUID AND TABLETS**
Vitamins B1, B12 and Iron

Miles Laboratories, Inc.

EFFERVESCENT ANTACID

Alka-Seltzer®
BRAND

Special Antacid Formula

For ACID INDIGESTION
HEARTBURN · SOUR STOMACH

36 TABLETS IN 18 FOIL PACKS

**ALKA-SELTZER® BRAND
EFFERVESCENT ANTACID**

Miles Laboratories, Inc.

Hydrocortisone (0.5%)
Skin Care Cream
Antipruritic (Anti-Itch)

Bactine
Hydrocortisone

For the temporary relief of
minor skin irritations,
itching, and rashes
due to eczema, dermatitis, insect bites,
poison ivy, oak, sumac

NET WT ½ OZ

**BACTINE® BRAND
HYDROCORTISONE (0.5%)
SKIN CARE CREAM**

Menley & James

NO DROWSINESS FORMULA   NEW!

EXTRA STRENGTH
WITH NON-ASPIRIN PAIN RELIEVER

Prompt relief from
sinus headache, pain,
pressure & congestion   20 CAPSULES

**SINE-OFF®
EXTRA STRENGTH NO DROWSINESS
CAPSULES**

Menley & James

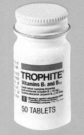

TROPHITE®
Vitamins B₁ and B₁₂

50 TABLETS

4 oz. liquid and
50 tablet bottle
**TROPHITE® LIQUID AND
TABLETS**
Vitamins B1, B12

Miles Laboratories, Inc.

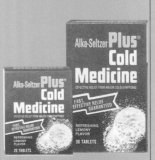

Alka-Seltzer Plus®
Cold Medicine

Alka-Seltzer Plus®
Cold Medicine

REFRESHING
LEMONY
FLAVOR

**ALKA-SELTZER PLUS®
COLD MEDICINE**

Miles Laboratories, Inc.

Bugs Bunny Extra C

Bugs Bunny Extra C

Bugs Bunny

Bugs Bunny
PLUS IRON

**BUGS BUNNY® BRAND
CHILDREN'S CHEWABLE VITAMINS
WITH EXTRA C, REGULAR,
AND PLUS IRON**

Miles Laboratories, Inc.

**FLINTSTONES® BRAND
CHILDREN'S CHEWABLE VITAMINS
WITH EXTRA C, REGULAR,
AND PLUS IRON**

Miles Laboratories, Inc.

**ONE A DAY® BRAND VITAMINS
PLUS IRON**

For the Extra Iron
Teens and Women Need

MOSS CHEMICAL CO., INC.

0.8 Oz.
(24 grams)

0.4 Oz.
(13 grams)

MOSCO®

Corn and Callus Remover

Nicholas Laboratories

2 oz. Tube

Oily Skin Formula

AMBI® SKIN CREAM

Miles Laboratories, Inc.

**MILES® NERVINE
NIGHTTIME SLEEP-AID**

Miles Laboratories, Inc.

**ONE A DAY® BRAND VITAMINS
PLUS MINERALS**

NATRA-BIO COMPANY

**NATRA-BIO™
28 Homeopathic Medicines**
1 oz. Dropper Bottles
sublingual administration

Nicholas Laboratories

4 oz. Jar

**AMBI® SKIN CREAM
WITH MOISTURIZERS**

Miles Laboratories, Inc.

ONE A DAY® BRAND VITAMINS

Miles Laboratories, Inc.

**ONE A DAY® STRESSGARD™
BRAND VITAMINS**

NICHOLAS LABORATORIES

2 oz. Tube

Dry Skin Formula

AMBI® SKIN CREAM

NORCLIFF THAYER

**A-200
PYRINATE®**
Liquid
A PEDICULICIDE

**KILLS
HEAD, CRAB and
BODY LICE
and their Eggs
ON CONTACT**

EXTERNAL USE ONLY
2 FLUID OUNCES

2 fl. oz.

A-200 PYRINATE® LIQUID

Also available:
A-200 Pyrinate Liquid, 4 fl. oz.
A-200 Pyrinate Gel, 1 oz.

Miles Laboratories, Inc.

**ONE A DAY® CORE C 500™
BRAND VITAMINS**

High Potency
500 mg Vitamin C
Plus 9 Essential Vitamins

For more detailed in-
formation on products
illustrated in this sec-
tion, consult the Prod-
uct Information Sec-
tion or manufacturers
may be contacted di-
rectly.

Nicholas Laboratories

2 oz. Tube

Normal Skin Formula

AMBI® SKIN CREAM

Norcliff Thayer

1.16 fl. oz.

35 ml.

LIQUIPRIN®

Norcliff Thayer

30 tablets

NATURE'S REMEDY®

Also available:
Box 12s and 60s

Norcliff Thayer

Bottle 75s,
Peppermint

TUMS®

Also available: Tums Single Roll and Three Roll Wrap, Peppermint and Assorted Flavors; Tums Bottle 75s, Assorted Flavors; Tums Bottle 150s, Peppermint and Assorted Flavors.

Norwich-Eaton

Original

Herbal

Original and Herbal Norforms available in cartons of 6, 12 and 24 deodorant suppositories.

**NORFORMS®
FEMININE DEODORANTS**

OPTIMOX, INC.

Multivitamin &
Multimineral
Supplement

OPTIVITE for Women

Norcliff Thayer

11 oz.

NOSALT™
Salt Alternative

NORWICH-EATON

Cherry   Menthol

Cherry   Menthol

Available: 6 oz. with sprayer, 12 oz. refill, 1.5 oz. nitrogen pressurized pocket spray.

CHLORASEPTIC® LIQUID

Norwich-Eaton

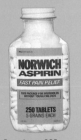

5 grains—325 mg.

NORWICH® ASPIRIN

Available in bottles of 100, 250 and 500 tablets.

ORTHO—CONS. PRODS.

Starter (2.46 oz. tube w/applicator package)
Refill (2.46 oz. tube only package)

CONCEPTROL® Birth Control Cream
(nonoxynol 9, 5%)

Norcliff Thayer

1 fl. oz.
OXY-10® LOTION

1 fl. oz.
OXY-5® LOTION

Norwich-Eaton

Cherry

Menthol

Grape

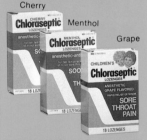

Available: all flavors in cartons of 18; Menthol & Cherry available in cartons of 45 lozenges.

CHLORASEPTIC® LOZENGES

Norwich-Eaton

Liquid available in 4 oz., 8 oz., 12 oz. and 16 oz. bottles

Tablets available in cartons of 24, 42 and 60.

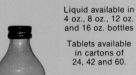

PEPTO-BISMOL® LIQUID AND TABLETS

Ortho—Cons. Prods.

CONCEPTROL DISPOSABLE

NEW! UNSCENTED GEL

6's (6 disposable prefilled applicators)
10's (10 disposable prefilled applicators)

CONCEPTROL® Disposable Contraceptive Gel
(nonoxynol 9, 4%)

Norcliff Thayer

2.65 oz.

OXY-SCRUB®
Abradant Cleanser

4 fl. oz.
OXY WASH™

Norwich-Eaton

Available: Cartons of 12 lozenges.

**CHLORASEPTIC®
COUGH CONTROL LOZENGES**

For more detailed information on products illustrated in this section, consult the Product Information Section or manufacturers may be contacted directly.

Ortho—Cons. Prods.

Lubricated and Non-Lubricated packages of 12's and 24's.

CONCEPTROL SHIELDS®
Latex Prophylactics

Ortho—Cons. Prods.

Packages of 12's
Lubricated

CONCEPTROL SUPREME®
Lubricated Thin Prophylactics

Ortho—Cons. Prods.

2 oz. tube

MASSÉ® Breast Cream

Ortho—Cons. Prods.

2 oz. and 4 oz. tubes

ORTHO® PERSONAL LUBRICANT

Available in boxes of 12, 24 and 48

1 Oz. Tube

ANUSOL®
Suppositories and Ointment

Ortho—Cons. Prods.

Starter (0.70 oz. vial w/applicator
package)
Refill (0.70 oz. and 1.75 oz. vial
only packages)

DELFEN® Contraceptive Foam
(nonoxynol 9, 12.5%)

Ortho—Cons. Prods.

ORTHO-CREME is intended for use
with a diaphragm

Starter (2.46 oz. tube w/applicator
package). Refill (2.46 oz. and 4.05
oz. tube only packages).

**ORTHO-CREME®
Contraceptive Cream**
(nonoxynol 9, 2.00%)

ORTHO—DERM. DIV.

**PURPOSE BRAND
DRY SKIN CREAM**

Parke-Davis

Available in 1 Oz. and 2 Oz. Tubes

**BENADRYL®
Antihistamine Cream**

Ortho—Cons. Prods.

Gynol II is intended for
use with a diaphragm.

Starter (2.85 oz. tube with
applicator package)
Refill (4.44 oz. tube only
package)

**GYNOL II®
Contraceptive Jelly**
(nonoxynol 9, 2%)

Ortho—Cons. Prods.

Packages of 18 applicators each

**ORTHO®
Disposable Vaginal Applicators**

Ortho—Derm. Div.

**PURPOSE BRAND
SHAMPOO**

Parke-Davis

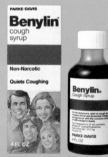

4 Fl. Oz.

**BENYLIN®
Cough Syrup**

Ortho—Cons. Prods.

Starter (12 inserts w/applicator
package)
Refill (12 inserts)

INTERCEPT®
Contraceptive Inserts

(nonoxynol 9, 5.56%)

Ortho—Cons. Prods.

ORTHO-GYNOL is intended for use
with a diaphragm

Starter (2.85 oz. tube w/applicator
package). Refill (2.85 oz. and 4.44
oz. tube only packages).

**ORTHO-GYNOL® Contraceptive
Jelly**
(diisobutylphenoxypolyethoxyethanol,
1.00%)

Ortho—Derm. Div.

**PURPOSE BRAND
SOAP**

Parke-Davis

4 Fl. Oz.

**BENYLIN DM®
Cough Syrup**

Parke-Davis

Available in 2½ and 6 Fl. Oz.

CALADRYL® LOTION

Parke-Davis

6 Fl. Oz.

ZIRADRYL® LOTION

Pfipharmecs

LI·BAN SPRAY
LICE CONTROL SPRAY

Net Wt. 5 oz (147.8 ml)

LI·BAN™ SPRAY

**HERBITOL®
with Tri-Herbal Complex™**

12 oz. and 32 oz. economy sizes

Drug-Free Diet Aid

Parke-Davis

100 tablets

50 tablets

Also available:
165 tablets

GELUSIL®
Antacid-Antiflatulent   12 Fl. Oz.

PERSŌN & COVEY

DHS™
Dermato-
logical
Hair and
Scalp
Shampoo

DHS™
Tar
Shampoo
Dermato-
logical
Hair and
Scalp
Shampoo

DHS™
Zinc
Dandruff
Shampoo

Pfipharmecs

4 fl. oz.

2 fl. oz.

RID™ PEDICULICIDE

PLOUGH, INC.

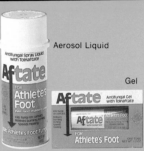

Aerosol Liquid

Gel

4.0 oz.   0.5 oz.

AFTATE® FOR ATHLETE'S FOOT
(tolnaftate)

Parke-Davis

Available in bottles of 130 and
250 tablets

MYADEC®

**High potency vitamin supplement
with minerals**

PFIPHARMECS

25 mg.

8 Chewable Tablets
per pack

BONINE® TABLETS
(meclizine HCl)

Pfipharmecs

Removes Warts
Safely and Effectively
**WART
TREATMENT KIT**
• Instructional Brochure
• Special Cleaning Brush
• Pinpoint Plastic Applicator

WART-OFF™

Plough, Inc.

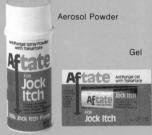

Aerosol Powder

Gel

3.5 oz.   0.5 oz.

AFTATE® FOR JOCK ITCH
(tolnaftate)

Parke-Davis

100 pads

40 pads

TUCKS®
Pre-Moistened Pads

Pfipharmecs

4 fl. oz.

Available in 12
& 24 capsules

**CORYBAN-D® COLD CAPSULES
& COUGH SYRUP**

For more detailed in-
formation on products
illustrated in this sec-
tion, consult the Prod-
uct Information Sec-
tion or manufacturers
may be contacted di-
rectly.

Plough, Inc.

Cherry
16 Tablet Size

Orange
16 Tablet Size

Also available in Orange and
Cherry flavors, 40 tablet sizes.

ASPERGUM®
(3½ grs. aspirin per tablet)

Plough, Inc.

Available in
15, 30, 60
and 90 tablet sizes.

Available in 8
and 16 fl. oz.
liquid sizes.

CORRECTOL® LAXATIVE
(100 mg. docusate sodium and 65 mg.
phenolphthalein per tablet)

Mild Laxative with Stool Softener

Plough, Inc.

Available in 30, 60 and 90
tablet sizes.

**REGUTOL®
STOOL SOFTENER**
(100 mg. docusate sodium per tablet)

Plough, Inc.

4 fl. oz.
SHADE®
Sunscreen
Lotion

4 fl. oz.
SHADE PLUS™
Water Resistant
Sunscreen Lotion

Shade® Sunscreen Lotion also
available in 2 and 8 fl. oz. sizes.

For Relief of Arthritis
Pain
and
Muscle Stiffness

4 oz. Bottle

Also available in 16 oz. and
64 oz. sizes.

**PANALGESIC®
MAXIMUM STRENGTH**
60% Total Salicylate Level

Plough, Inc.

CUSHION GRIP
ONE APPLICATION HOLDS DENTURES
UP TO 4 FULL DAYS

EASY TO APPLY
CUSHION GRIP
MODERN THERMOPLASTIC DENTURE ADHESIVE

Available in ¼ oz., ½ oz. and
1 oz. sizes.

CUSHION GRIP®
Denture Adhesive

Plough, Inc.

36 tablets per bottle

**ST. JOSEPH® ASPIRIN FOR
CHILDREN**
(1¼ grs. aspirin per tablet)

Plough, Inc.

4 fl. oz.

SUPER SHADE® 15
Sunblocking Lotion

Also available in 8 fl. oz.

8 oz.

Also available: Betadine Douche
½ oz. travel packettes.

BETADINE® DOUCHE

Plough, Inc.

Liquid

Tablets

Mint and Lemon/Orange flavors,
6 fl. oz. and 12 fl. oz. liquid plus 30,
60 and 90 tablet sizes.

DI-GEL®
(simethicone, aluminum hydroxide,
magnesium hydroxide)

Plough, Inc.

30 tablets per bottle

**ST. JOSEPH® COLD TABLETS
FOR CHILDREN**
(1¼ grs. aspirin and 3.125 mg.
phenylpropanolamine HCl per tablet)

Plough, Inc.

3 fl. oz.

3 oz.

Also available in 6 fl. oz. lotion,
5 oz. spray, 3.5 fl. oz. pump and
1 and 2 oz. First Aid Cream

**SOLARCAINE® FIRST AID
PRODUCTS**
(benzocaine and triclosan)

Purdue Frederick

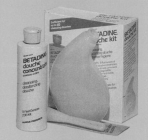

8 oz. bottle of concentrate; squeezable
syringe bottle and anatomically-correct
cannula

BETADINE® DOUCHE KIT

Plough, Inc.

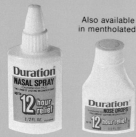

Also available
in mentholated.

Available in
½ fl. oz. and
1 fl. oz. sizes.

⅔ fl. oz.

**DURATION®
NASAL SPRAY AND NOSE DROPS**
(oxymetazoline HCl)

Plough, Inc.

Available in 2 fl. oz. and 4 fl. oz.
sizes.

**ST. JOSEPH® COUGH SYRUP
FOR CHILDREN**
(dextromethorphan hydrobromide)

For more detailed in-
formation on products
illustrated in this sec-
tion, consult the Prod-
uct Information Sec-
tion or manufacturers
may be contacted di-
rectly.

Purdue Frederick

Twin Pack

Single Unit

Completely disposable

BETADINE® MEDICATED DOUCHE

Purdue Frederick

1 oz. tube; 1 lb. & 5 lb. jars

BETADINE® OINTMENT

Purdue Frederick

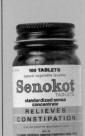

20 tablet pack; bottles of 50 and 100 tablets; unit strip pack of 100 tablets

SENOKOT® TABLETS

Purdue Frederick

Available in boxes of 14.

FIBERMED™

High-Fiber Supplements

A. H. Robins

Available in bottles of 30, 100 and 1000

ALLBEE® WITH C CAPSULES

Purdue Frederick

4 oz.

1 oz. and 4 oz. plastic bottles; Also available: Betadine® Skin Cleanser Foam

BETADINE® SKIN CLEANSER

Purdue Frederick

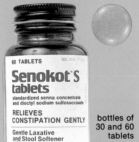

bottles of 30 and 60 tablets

SENOKOT® S TABLETS

REQUA

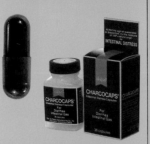

CHARCOCAPS®
Intestinal Distress Capsules
for
Diarrhea, Intestinal Gas

A. H. Robins

Ultra sunscreen protection (SPF-15)

Aids prevention and healing of dry, chapped, sun- and windburned lips.

CHAP STICK®
SUNBLOCK 15 Lip Balm

Purdue Frederick

8 oz.

BETADINE® SOLUTION

Purdue Frederick

Boxes of 12 and 50

**BETADINE®
ANTISEPTIC GAUZE PAD**

A. H. ROBINS

Consumer Products Division

Available in bottles of 60

ALLBEE® C-800 TABLETS

A. H. Robins

CHAP STICK®
Lip Balm

Purdue Frederick

2 oz., 6 oz., and 12 oz. canisters; Also available: Senokot® Suppositories and Senokot® Syrup

SENOKOT® GRANULES

Purdue Frederick

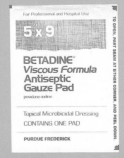

Available in 3″ x 9″ and 5″ x 9″ sizes.

**BETADINE® VISCOUS FORMULA
ANTISEPTIC GAUZE PAD**

A. H. Robins

Available in bottles of 60

ALLBEE® C-800 PLUS IRON TABLETS

A. H. Robins

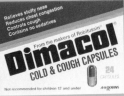

Available in consumer cartons of 12 and 24 and bottles of 100 and 500

DIMACOL® CAPSULES

A. H. Robins

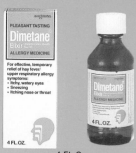

4 Fl. Oz.

DIMETANE® ELIXIR

(Brompheniramine Maleate Elixir, USP)

A. H. Robins

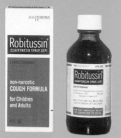

Available in bottles of 4 Fl. Oz.,
8 Fl. Oz., 16 Fl. Oz. and 128 Fl. Oz.

ROBITUSSIN® SYRUP

(Guaifenesin Syrup, USP)

A. H. Robins

Available in bottles of 60 and 500

Z-BEC® TABLETS

RORER

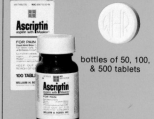

bottles of 50, 100,
& 500 tablets

ASCRIPTIN®

Aspirin, Alumina and Magnesia Tablets,
Rorer (Aspirin: [5 grains] 325 mg.
Maalox®: magnesium hydroxide, 75 mg
and dried aluminum hydroxide gel, 150
mg)

A. H. Robins

Available in consumer cartons of
24 and bottles of 100 and 500

DIMETANE® TABLETS

(Brompheniramine Maleate Tablets, USP)

A. H. Robins

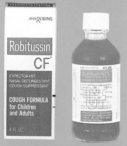

Available in bottles of 4 Fl. Oz.,
8 Fl. Oz. and 16 Fl. Oz.

ROBITUSSIN-CF® SYRUP

ROCHE

0.6 cc

0.3 cc

VI-PENTA® INFANT DROPS

William H. Rorer

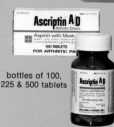

bottles of 100,
225 & 500 tablets

ASCRIPTIN® A/D

Aspirin, Alumina and Magnesia Tablets,
Rorer (Aspirin: [5 grains] 325 mg.
Maalox®: magnesium hydroxide, 150 mg
and dried aluminum hydroxide gel, 150
mg)

A. H. Robins

4 Fl. Oz.

**DIMETANE®
DECONGESTANT ELIXIR**

A. H. Robins

Available in bottles of 4 Fl. Oz.,
8 Fl. Oz., 16 Fl. Oz. and 128 Fl. Oz.

ROBITUSSIN-DM® SYRUP

Roche

0.6 cc

0.3 cc

VI-PENTA® MULTIVITAMIN DROPS

William H. Rorer

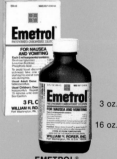

3 oz.

16 oz.

EMETROL®

(levulose [fructose], dextrose [glucose]
and phosphoric acid)

A. H. Robins

Available in consumer cartons of
24 and 48

**DIMETANE® DECONGESTANT
TABLETS**

A. H. Robins

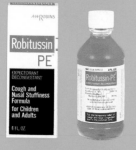

Available in bottles of 4 Fl. Oz.,
8 Fl. Oz. and 16 Fl. Oz.

ROBITUSSIN-PE® SYRUP

For more detailed in-
formation on products
illustrated in this sec-
tion, consult the Prod-
uct Information Sec-
tion or manufacturers
may be contacted di-
rectly.

William H. Rorer

bottles of
100

GEMNISYN™

(acetaminophen 325 mg [5 grains] and aspirin
325 mg [5 grains])

William H. Rorer

bottles of 5 oz.,
12 oz. & 26 oz.

MAALOX® SUSPENSION
Magnesia and Alumina Oral Suspension,
Rorer

William H. Rorer

Suspension
12 oz.

**MAALOX® TC
(Therapeutic Concentrate)**

(300 mg of magnesium hydroxide and
600 mg of aluminum hydroxide per 5 ml)

Schering

15 ml

**AFRIN® MENTHOL
NASAL SPRAY 0.05%**
(oxymetazoline hydrochloride, USP)

Schering

TW

**CHLOR-TRIMETON®
ALLERGY TABLETS**
(chlorpheniramine maleate, USP)

William H. Rorer

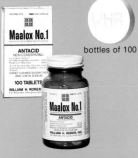

bottles of 100

MAALOX® NO. 1 TABLETS
Magnesia and Alumina Tablets, Rorer

(200 mg of magnesium hydroxide and
200 mg of aluminum hydroxide)

William H. Rorer

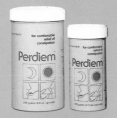

250 grams   100 grams

Granules

PERDIEM™
82 percent psyllium (Plantago Hydrocolloid)
18 percent senna (Cassia Pod Concentrate)

Schering

Nose Drops
0.05%

Pediatric
Nose Drops
0.025%

AFRIN® NOSE DROPS
(oxymetazoline hydrochloride, USP)

Schering

901

**CHLOR-TRIMETON®
DECONGESTANT TABLETS**
(4 mg chlorpheniramine maleate, USP
and 60 mg pseudoephedrine sulfate)

William H. Rorer

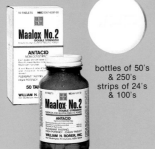

bottles of 50's
& 250's
strips of 24's
& 100's

MAALOX® NO. 2 TABLETS
Magnesia and Alumina Tablets, Rorer

(400 mg of magnesium hydroxide and
400 mg of aluminum hydroxide)

SCHERING

WMJ

4 oz tube

A and D Reg. ™ **OINTMENT**

Schering

AFRINOL® REPETABS® TABLETS

(pseudoephedrine sulfate 120 mg)

Schering

**LONG ACTING
CHLOR-TRIMETON®
DECONGESTANT REPETABS®**
(chlorpheniramine maleate and
pseudoephedrine sulfate)

William H. Rorer

Tablets
12's & 50's

Suspension
12 oz.

MAALOX® PLUS
Alumina, Magnesia and Simethicone
Oral Suspension and Tablets, Rorer

Schering

30 ml

AFRIN® NASAL SPRAY 0.05%
(oxymetazoline hydrochloride, USP)

Schering

4 oz
(118 ml)

**CHLOR-TRIMETON®
ALLERGY SYRUP**
(chlorpheniramine maleate, USP)

Schering

374

**CHLOR-TRIMETON®
LONG-ACTING ALLERGY
REPETABS® TABLETS**
(chlorpheniramine maleate, USP)

Schering/White Product Line

COD LIVER OIL CONCENTRATE CAPSULES

COD LIVER OIL CONCENTRATE TABLETS

COD LIVER OIL CONCENTRATE TABLETS W/VITAMIN C

Schering

CORICIDIN® DEMILETS® TABLETS

Schering

ADD or 133

4 oz (118 ml)

DEMAZIN® DECONGESTANT- ANTIHISTAMINE REPETABS® TABLETS AND SYRUP

Schering/Emko Product Line

40 g

EMKO® CONTRACEPTIVE FOAM
(nonoxynol-9)

Schering

4 oz (118 ml)

CORICIDIN® COUGH SYRUP   **CORICIDIN® CHILDREN'S COUGH SYRUP**

Schering

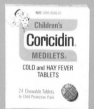

CORICIDIN® MEDILETS® TABLETS

Schering

30 g (1.0 oz.)   45 ml (1.5 fl. oz.)

DERMOLATE™ ANTI-ITCH CREAM AND SPRAY
(hydrocortisone 0.5%)

Schering/Emko Product Line

30 g

EMKO® PRE-FIL® CONTRACEPTIVE FOAM
(nonoxynol-9)

Schering

20 ml

CORICIDIN® DECONGESTANT NASAL MIST

Schering

CORICIDIN® SINUS HEADACHE TABLETS

Schering

30 g (1.0 oz.)   30 ml (1 fl. oz.)

DERMOLATE™ ANAL-ITCH OINTMENT AND SCALP-ITCH LOTION
(hydrocortisone 0.5%)

Schering/White Product Line

Chronosule® Capsules   Tablets

with Vitamin C Tablets

MOL-IRON®

Schering

871 or 524

CORICIDIN 'D'® DECONGESTANT TABLETS

Schering

PKD or SN or 171

CORICIDIN® TABLETS

Schering/Emko Product Line

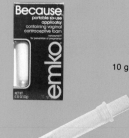

10 g

BECAUSE® CONTRACEPTOR®
(nonoxynol-9)

Schering

SUNRIL® PREMENSTRUAL CAPSULES

PRODUCT IDENTIFICATION

Schering

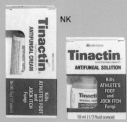

NK

15 g   10 ml

**TINACTIN®
CREAM AND SOLUTION**
(tolnaftate 1%)

Schering

100 g   **TINACTIN®**   45 g
**POWDER AEROSOL AND
POWDER**

SEARLE

DRAMAMINE®
(dimenhydrinate)
Tablets, packets
of 12 (as shown),
and bottles of 36
and 100.

DRAMAMINE® LIQUID
(dimenhydrinate syrup USP)
Liquid, 3 fl oz

Searle Consumer Products

Balm, 3½-oz and
7-oz jars

Rub, greaseless,
1¼-oz and 3-oz tubes

ICY HOT®
Analgesic Balm and Rub
for Muscle Aches and Arthritis

Searle Consumer Products

Orange Flavor   Regular

Powder, 7 oz, 14 oz, and 21 oz

**METAMUCIL®
A Natural-Fiber Laxative**

Searle Consumer Products

Orange Flavor   Regular

Single-dose packets,
cartons of 16 and 30

**INSTANT MIX METAMUCIL®
A Natural-Fiber Laxative**

SQUIBB

**SPEC-T® SORE THROAT ANESTHETIC
LOZENGES**

**SPEC-T® SORE THROAT/
DECONGESTANT LOZENGES**

**SPEC-T® SORE THROAT/COUGH
SUPPRESSANT LOZENGES**

E. R. Squibb & Sons

THERAGRAN-M® TABLETS
High Potency Vitamin Supplement
with Minerals

E. R. Squibb & Sons

THERAGRAN-Z® TABLETS
High Potency Vitamin-Mineral
Supplement with Zinc

STUART

5 oz.   12 oz.

ALternaGEL®
High-Potency Aluminum Hydroxide
Antacid

Stuart

Available in
bottles of
9 and 16 oz.

Convenience
Packet

EFFERSYLLIUM® INSTANT MIX
Bulk Laxative containing
Natural Dietary Fiber

Available in boxes of 12 and 24
Convenience Packets

Stuart

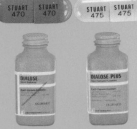

Bottles of 36, 100 and 500 capsules

DIALOSE™   **DIALOSE™ PLUS**
(docusate potassium,   (docusate potassium,
100 mg.)   100 mg. and casan-
    thranol, 30 mg.)

Stool Softeners

Stuart

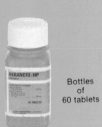

Bottles
of
60 tablets

FERANCEE®-HP
Hematinic

Stuart

4 oz.   8 oz.

HIBICLENS®
(chlorhexidine gluconate)

Antimicrobial Skin Cleanser

Stuart

Bottle of 60s
Available in bottles of 30 and 60 capsules

KASOF®
(docusate potassium, 240 mg.)

High Strength Stool Softener

Stuart

12 oz.

MYLANTA® LIQUID
Antacid/Anti-Gas

(magnesium and aluminum hydroxides
with simethicone)

Stuart

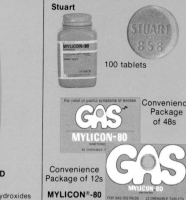

100 tablets

Convenience
Package
of 48s

Convenience
Package of 12s

MYLICON®-80
Antiflatulent

THOMPSON MEDICAL

Available in 30 & 60 tablet sizes.

**APPEDRINE®
APPETITE CONTROL TABLETS**

Thompson Medical Company, Inc.

Available in 1 oz. tubes.

CORTIZONE 5

Stuart

Available in boxes of 40 (not shown) and
100, bottles of 180, and flip-top Convenience Packs of 48

MYLANTA® TABLETS
Antacid/Anti-Gas

Stuart

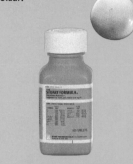

Bottles of 100 tablets

STUART FORMULA® TABLETS
Multivitamin/Multimineral Supplement

Thompson Medical Company, Inc.

Packages of 60 tablets.

AQUA-BAN®

Thompson Medical Company, Inc.

Available in
28 & 56
capsule sizes.

**DEXATRIM®
APPETITE CONTROL CAPSULES**

Stuart

12 oz.

Boxes of
60 tablets

MYLANTA®-II LIQUID and TABLETS
High Potency Antacid/Antiflatulent

Stuart

Bottles of 60 tablets

STUARTINIC®
Hematinic

Thompson Medical Company, Inc.

Available in 1.25 oz.,
3 oz., 5 oz. cream
& 6 oz. lotion.

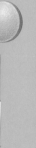

An effective aspirin-like analgesic for
temporary relief of occasional minor pains of

ARTHRITIS
Rheumatism, Back and Muscular Aches

ASPERCREME
CREME RUB

ASPERCREME™

Available in
10, 20 & 40
capsule sizes.

EXTRA-STRENGTH DEXATRIM®

Available in
10, 20 & 40
capsule sizes.

**CAFFEINE-FREE
EXTRA-STRENGTH DEXATRIM®**

Stuart

Bottles of 100 and
500 tablets

1 fl. oz.

MYLICON®
Antiflatulent

SugarLo

for milk lovers
who can't digest
the lactose
in milk

30 QUART SUPPLY

Reduces 70% of
the lactose in milk.
Just add 5 drops
to a quart

LactAid
lactase enzyme

4 qt. size, 12 qt. size, 30 qt. size

LactAid®
(lactase enzyme)

Thompson Medical Company, Inc.

NEW!
NO CAFFEINE · NO STIMULANTS
LOSE WEIGHT FAST
without going hungry

CONTROL
CLINICALLY PROVEN APPETITE SUPPRESSANT

NO CAFFEINE · NO STIMULANTS

STRONGEST 12-HOUR
APPETITE CONTROL FORMULA
available without prescription

Available in 14, 28 & 56 capsule sizes.

**CONTROL®
APPETITE CONTROL CAPSULES**

Thompson Medical Company, Inc.

**TAKE
WEIGHT
OFF**
AND KEEP IT OFF

SUPER STRENGTH
prolamine

Available in 20 & 50 capsule sizes.

**PROLAMINE™
APPETITE CONTROL CAPSULES**

UPJOHN

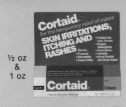

CORTAID® Cream

½ oz & 1 oz

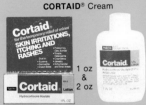

CORTAID® Lotion

1 oz & 2 oz

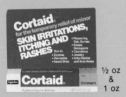

½ oz & 1 oz

CORTAID® Ointment

hydrocortisone acetate
(equivalent to hydrocortisone 0.5%)

Upjohn

½ oz tubes

CORTEF® Rectal   **CORTEF® Feminine**
Itch Ointment   **Itch Cream**

hydrocortisone acetate
(equivalent to hydrocortisone 0.5%)

Upjohn

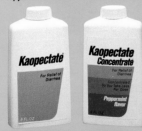

3, 8, 12 oz & 1 gallon   2, 8, 12 oz

KAOPECTATE®   **KAOPECTATE CONCENTRATE®**

Anti-Diarrhea Medicine

Upjohn

½ oz & 1 oz tubes

MYCITRACIN® Antibiotic Ointment

(bacitracin-polymyxin-neomycin
topical ointment)

Upjohn

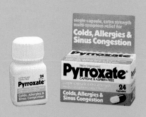

bottles of 24 & 500

PYRROXATE® Capsules

Upjohn

Available in:

Bottles of 30, 90, 180, 500   Bottles of 30, 90, 500

UNICAP M®   **UNICAP T®**
Tablets   Tablets
     High Potency

Vitamin-mineral supplement

For more detailed information on products illustrated in this section, consult the Product Information Section or manufacturers may be contacted directly.

VICKS TOILETRY DIV.

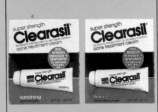

.65 and 1.0 oz. sizes available

**CLEARASIL®
Acne Treatment Cream**
(10% benzoyl peroxide)

Vicks Toiletry Div.

1 oz.

**CLEARASIL®
5% Benzoyl Peroxide Lotion
Acne Treatment**

Vicks Toiletry Div.

4 and 8 oz. sizes

**CLEARASIL®
Pore Deep Cleanser
For Oily Skin**
(0.5% salicylic acid)

Vicks Toiletry Div.

1 oz.

**TOPEX®
Acne Clearing Medication**
(10% benzoyl peroxide)

VICKS HEALTH CARE DIV.

Capsules
Imprinted
DAYCARE

Blister Packs of
20s, 36s and 60s

**DAYCARE®
Multi-Symptom Colds Medicine**

(acetaminophen, phenylpropanolamine hydrochloride, dextromethorphan hydrobromide)

Vicks Health Care Div.

Bottles of 6 oz. and 10 oz.

**DAYCARE®
Multi-Symptom Colds Medicine**

(acetaminophen, phenylpropanolamine hydrochloride, dextromethorphan hydrobromide)

Vicks Health Care Div.

Available in 3 oz., 6 oz., 8 oz.

**FORMULA 44®
Cough Mixture**
(dextromethorphan hydrobromide,
doxylamine succinate, sodium citrate)

Vicks Health Care Div.

Available in 3 oz., 6 oz., 8 oz.

**FORMULA 44D®
Decongestant Cough Mixture**
(dextromethorphan hydrobromide,
phenylpropanolamine hydrochloride,
guaifenesin)

Vicks Health Care Div.

Capsule Sizes: 16, 36, 49
Tablet Sizes: 20, 40, 60

VICKS® HEADWAY®

(acetaminophen, phenylpropanolamine
and chlorpheniramine)

Vicks Health Care Div.

Available in ½ oz.
and 1 oz. atomizers

**SINEX™ LONG-ACTING
Decongestant Nasal Spray**
(oxymetazoline hydrochloride)

Wallace

1 pint
(473 ml)

4 fl oz
(118 ml)

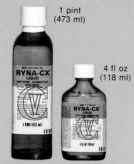

RYNA-C® LIQUID
(antitussive-antihistamine-decongestant)

WARNER-LAMBERT CO.

one test kit

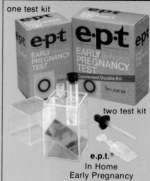

two test kit

e.p.t.®
In Home
Early Pregnancy
Test

Vicks Health Care Div.

6 oz. and 10 oz.

**NYQUIL® NIGHTTIME COLDS
MEDICINE**
(acetaminophen, doxylamine succinate,
ephedrine sulfate, dextromethorphan
hydrobromide)

WALLACE

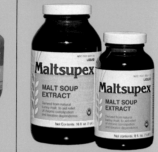

16 fl oz (1 pt)   8 fl oz (½ pt)
MALTSUPEX® LIQUID
(malt soup extract)

Wallace   Ⓒ

1 pint
(473 ml)

4 fl oz
(118 ml)

RYNA-C® LIQUID
(antitussive-decongestant-expectorant)

(labeled RYNA-CX® LIQUID)

Warner-Lambert Co.

**HALLS®
Mentho-Lyptus®
Cough Tablets**

Vicks Health Care Div.

1.5 oz., 3.0 oz.,
6 oz.

**VICKS® VapoRub®
Decongestant Vaporizing Ointment**

Special Vicks Medication
(camphor, menthol, spirits of turpentine,
eucalyptus oil, cedar leaf oil, nutmeg oil,
thymol)

Wallace

16 oz (1 lb)   8 oz (½ lb)
MALTSUPEX® POWDER
(malt soup extract)

Wallace

SYLLACT™
(powdered psyllium seed husks)

Warner-Lambert Co.

24 OZ. SIZE

**LISTERINE®
Antiseptic**

Vicks Health Care Div.

Available in ½ oz. and
1 oz. atomizers

**SINEX™
Decongestant Nasal Spray**
Special Vicks Blend of Aromatics
(menthol, eucalyptol, camphor, methyl
salicylate)

Wallace

1 pint
(473 ml)

4 fl. oz.
(118 ml)

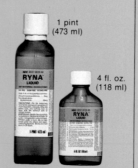

RYNA™ LIQUID
(antihistamine-decongestant)

For more detailed in-
formation on products
illustrated in this sec-
tion, consult the Prod-
uct Information Sec-
tion or manufacturers
may be contacted di-
rectly.

Warner-Lambert Co.

LISTERMINT®
Mouthwash and Gargle

Warner-Lambert Co.

LUBRIDERM®
Lotion

LUBATH®
Bath Oil

For Dry Skin Care

WHITEHALL

Available in Tins of 12 and Bottles of
30, 50, 100, 200 and 300 Tablets

ANACIN®
Analgesic Tablets

Whitehall

Available in Bottles of 30, 60 and
100 Tablets

ANACIN-3®
Analgesic Tablets
100% ASPIRIN-FREE

Whitehall

ASPIRIN-FREE
NEW **Arthritis Pain Formula**
Maximum Strength
BY THE MAKERS OF ANACIN ANALGESIC TABLETS
75 ACETAMINOPHEN TABLETS

Available in Bottles
of 30 and 75 Tablets

**ASPIRIN-FREE
ARTHRITIS PAIN FORMULA**
by the makers of ANACIN®

Analgesic Tablets

Warner-Lambert Co.

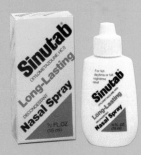

**SINUTAB®
LONG-LASTING DECONGESTANT
NASAL SPRAY**

Whitehall

Available in Bottles of 20,
40, 75 and 125 Capsules

ANACIN®
Analgesic Capsules

Whitehall

**MAXIMUM STRENGTH
ANACIN-3®**
100% ASPIRIN-FREE
CAPSULES
with Acetaminophen
72 ANALGESIC CAPSULES

Available in Bottles of 20, 40
and 72 Capsules

ANACIN-3®
Analgesic Capsules
100% ASPIRIN-FREE

Whitehall

Lotion:
4 oz. and
8 oz. Bottles

Lotion:
4 oz. and
8 oz. Bottles
Gel:
2 oz. and
4 oz. Tubes

Lotion:
4 oz. and
8 oz. Bottles

DENOREX®
Medicated Shampoo

WARNER-LAMBERT INC.

**SINUTAB®

Sinutab II
No Drowsiness Formula
(WITHOUT ANTIHISTAMINES)
Sinus Headache
and Congestion
Medication
30 TABLETS

**SINUTAB-II®

Whitehall

Available in Tins of 12 and Bottles of
20, 40, 75 and 150 Tablets

MAXIMUM STRENGTH ANACIN®
Analgesic Tablets

Whitehall

Anbesol

Liquid
Available in Bottles of
.31 oz. and .74 oz.

Anbesol GEL
Cold Sores/Fever Blisters
Toothache/Denture Irritation
Sore Gums/Teething Pain

Gel
Available in
.25 oz. Tube

ANBESOL®
Antiseptic—Anesthetic

Whitehall

Lose weight sensibly in
14 DAYS

**Diet Gard
14 DAY
DIET PLAN**
42 Capsules

Available in 42 Tablet and
42 Capsule Plans

DIET GARD™ 14 DAY PLAN
Appetite Suppressant

Warner-Lambert Inc.

Capsules

Tablets

****EXTRA-STRENGTH
SINUTAB®**

**Product of Warner-Lambert Inc.,
Santurce, P.R. 00911

Whitehall

**MAXIMUM STRENGTH
ANACIN®**
36 ANALGESIC
CAPSULES

Available in Bottles of 36 and
72 Capsules

MAXIMUM STRENGTH ANACIN®
Analgesic Capsules

Whitehall

**Arthritis
Pain
Formula**
with Double Buffering
BY THE MAKERS OF ANACIN
40 TABLETS

Available in Bottles of 40, 100 and
175 Tablets

ARTHRITIS PAIN FORMULA
by the makers of ANACIN®

Analgesic Tablets

Whitehall

DRISTAN NASAL MIST
DECONGESTANT
ANTIHISTAMINIC
½ FL. OZ (15ml)
Relieves Nasal Congestion / Hay Fever / Head Colds Distress

DRISTAN MENTHOL NASAL MIST
DECONGESTANT
ANTIHISTAMINIC
½ FL. OZ (15ml)
Relieves Nasal Congestion / Hay Fever / Head Colds Distress

Both Available in Bottles of
15 ml. and 30 ml.

DRISTAN®
Nasal Mist

Whitehall

Available in Bottles of 15 ml. and 30 ml.

Available in 15 ml. Bottle

DRISTAN®
Long Lasting Nasal Mist

Whitehall

Available in Boxes
of 12, 24 and 48 Suppositories

PREPARATION H®
Hemorrhoidal Suppositories

WYETH

100 tablets

**ALUDROX®
TABLETS and
SUSPENSION**

Antacid

12 Fl. Oz.

Wyeth

WYANOIDS®
Hemorrhoidal Suppositories

Whitehall

Available in Bottles of 24, 50 and
100 Tablets

DRISTAN® TABLETS
Decongestant/Antihistamine/Analgesic

Whitehall

Available in ½ oz. and 1 oz. Tubes

PREPCORT™
by the makers of Preparation H®

Hydrocortisone Cream 0.5%

Wyeth

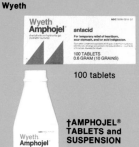

100 tablets

**†AMPHOJEL®
TABLETS and
SUSPENSION**

Antacid

12 Fl. Oz.

W. F. YOUNG, INC.

ABSORBINE JR.®
External Analgesic and
Athlete's Foot Preparation

Whitehall

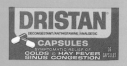

Available in Bottles of 16 and
36 Capsules

DRISTAN® CAPSULES
Decongestant/Antihistamine/Analgesic

Whitehall

Available in 15 cc.
Inhaler Unit and
15 cc. and 22.5 cc.
Refills.

PRIMATENE® MIST

Asthma Remedy

Wyeth

12 Fl. Oz.

SIMECO®
Antacid/Anti-Gas

The Indices are divided
into four sections:

Section 1

Manufacturers' Index

lists address and telephone
numbers of participating
manufacturers;

Section 2

Product Name Index

products are indexed
alphabetically;

Section 3

**Product Category
Index**—products are
indexed by category;

Section 4

**Active Ingredients
Index**—products are
indexed by active
ingredients.

Whitehall

Available in 1 oz. and 2 oz. Tubes

PREPARATION H®
Hemorrhoidal Ointment

Whitehall

P Formula

M Formula

Both Available in Bottles of 24 and
60 Tablets

PRIMATENE® TABLETS

Asthma Remedy

Wyeth

Lotion 6 Fl. Oz. with separate
eyecup bottle cap

½ Fl. Oz.

**COLLYRIUM
Eye Lotion
and Eyedrops**

Product Information

This section is made possible through the courtesy of the manufacturers whose products appear on the following pages. The information concerning each product has been prepared, edited and approved by the manufacturer.

Products described in PHYSICIANS' DESK REFERENCE For NONPRESCRIPTION DRUGS comply with labeling regulations. PDR copy may include all the essential information necessary for informed usage such as active ingredients, indications, actions, warnings, drug interactions, precautions, symptoms and treatment of oral overdosage, dosage and administration, professional labeling, and how supplied. In some cases additional information has been supplied to complement the foregoing. The Publisher has emphasized to manufacturers the necessity of describing products comprehensively so that all information essential for intelligent and informed use is available. In organizing and presenting the material in PHYSICIANS' DESK REFERENCE For NONPRESCRIPTION DRUGS, the Publisher is providing all the information made available to PDR by manufacturers.

In presenting the following material to the medical profession, the Publisher is not necessarily advocating the use of any product herein listed.

Abbott Laboratories
Consumer Products Division
NORTH CHICAGO, IL 60064

CLEAR EYES®
Eye Drops

Description: Clear Eyes® is a sterile isotonic buffered solution containing naphazoline hydrochloride 0.012%, boric acid, sodium borate and water. Edetate disodium 0.1% and benzalkonium chloride 0.01% are added as preservatives.
Indications: Clear Eyes is a decongestant ophthalmic solution specially designed to moisturize as it removes redness from eyes irritated due to plant allergies (pollen), overindulgence, fatigue, swimming, colds, wearing contact lenses, and use of eyes in reading, driving, TV and close work. Clear Eyes contains laboratory tested, and scientifically blended ingredients including an effective vasoconstrictor which narrows swollen blood vessels and rapidly whitens reddened eyes in a moisturizing formulation which produces a refreshing, soothing effect. Clear Eyes is a sterile, isotonic solution compatible with the natural fluids of the eye.
Warning: Clear Eyes should only be used for minor eye irritations.
Clear Eyes should not be used by individuals with glaucoma and serious eye diseases. In some instances redness or inflammation may be due to serious eye conditions such as acute iritis, acute glaucoma, or corneal trauma. When redness, pain, or blurring persist, discontinue use. A physician should be consulted at once. Remove contact lenses before using.
Dosage and Administration: One or two drops in eye(s) two or three times daily or as directed by physician. Do not touch bottle tip to any surface, since this may contaminate the solution. Keep container tightly closed. Keep this and all other medicines out of reach of children.
How Supplied: In 0.5 fl. oz. and 1.5 fl. oz. plastic dropper bottle.
[*Shown in Product Identification Section*]

EAR DROPS BY MURINE
See Murine Ear Wax Removal System/Murine Ear Drops

MURINE EAR WAX REMOVAL SYSTEM/MURINE EAR DROPS

Description: Carbamide peroxide 6.5% in anhydrous glycerin and a 1.0 fl. oz. soft rubber ear syringe. The MURINE EAR WAX REMOVAL SYSTEM is the only self-treatment method on the market for complete ear wax removal. Application of carbamide peroxide drops followed by warm water irrigation is the only effective, medically recommended way to remove hardened ear wax.
Actions: The carbamide peroxide formula in MURINE EAR DROPS is an aid in the removal of hardened cerumen from the ear canal. Anhydrous glycerin penetrates and softens wax while the release of oxygen from carbamide peroxide provides a mechanical action resulting in

the loosening of the softened wax accumulation. It is usually necessary to remove the loosened wax by gentle irrigation with warm water using the soft rubber ear syringe provided.
Indications: The MURINE EAR WAX REMOVAL SYSTEM is indicated as an aid in the removal of hardened or tightly packed cerumen from the ear canal or as an aid in the prevention of ceruminosis.
Caution: If redness, tenderness, pain, dizziness or ear drainage are present or develop, the medication should not be used or continued until a physician is seen. Do not use if ear drum is known to be perforated.
Dosage and Administration: For wax removal, place five drops into affected ear twice daily for three or four days. Tip of bottle should not enter ear canal. Remove softened wax after each application by gently flushing ear with warm (body temperature) water using the soft rubber ear syringe provided. Tip of syringe should be at the edge of the ear canal.
The ear canal can be kept free from accumulated hardened cerumen by regular usage of the MURINE EAR WAX REMOVAL SYSTEM.
How Supplied: The MURINE EAR WAX REMOVAL SYSTEM contains 0.5 fl. oz. drops and a 1.0 fl. oz. soft rubber ear syringe.
Also available in 0.5 fl. oz. drops only, MURINE EAR DROPS
[*Shown in Product Identification Section*]

MURINE® REGULAR FORMULA
Eye Drops

Description: Murine® Regular Formula is a sterile isotonic buffered solution containing glycerin, potassium chloride, sodium chloride, sodium phosphate (monobasic and dibasic), and water. Edetate disodium 0.05% and benzalkonium chloride 0.01% are added as preservatives.
Indications: Murine is non-staining, clear solution formulated to closely match the natural fluid of the eye for gentle, soothing relief from minor eye irritation. Use whenever desired to cleanse or refresh the eyes and to relieve minor irritation due to smog, sun glare, wind, dust, wearing contact lenses and overuse of the eyes in reading, driving, TV and close work.
Warning: Murine Regular Formula should only be used for minor eye irritations. If irritation persists or increases, discontinue use and consult your physician.
Dosage and Administration: Two or three drops into each eye several times a day or as directed by a physician. Do not touch bottle tip to any surface since this may contaminate solution. Remove contact lenses before using. Keep container tightly closed. Keep this and all medications out of reach of children.
How Supplied: In 0.5 fl. oz. and 1.5 fl. oz. plastic dropper bottle.
[*Shown in Product Identification Section*]

MURINE® PLUS
Eye Drops

Description: Murine® Plus is a sterile isotonic buffered solution containing tetrahydrozoline hydrochloride 0.05%, boric acid, sodium borate and water. Edetate disodium, 0.1% and benzalkonium chloride 0.01% are added as preservatives.
Indications: Murine Plus is a decongestant ophthalmic solution designed to refresh and soothe as it removes redness from eyes irritated due to swimming, plant allergies (pollen), overindulgence, colds, smog, sunglare, wind, dust, wearing contact lenses, and overuse of the eyes in reading, driving, TV and close work. Murine Plus contains laboratory tested, and scientifically blended ingredients including an effective vasoconstrictor which narrows swollen blood vessels and rapidly whitens reddened eyes in a formulation which produces a refreshing, soothing effect. Murine Plus is a sterile, isotonic solution compatible with the natural fluids of the eye.
Warning: Murine Plus should only be used for minor eye irritations.
Murine Plus should not be used by individuals with glaucoma and serious eye diseases. In some instances redness or inflammation may be due to serious eye conditions such as acute iritis, acute glaucoma, or corneal trauma. When redness, pain, or blurring persist, discontinue use. A physician should be consulted at once. Remove contact lenses before using.
Dosage and Administration: One or two drops in eye(s) two or three times daily or as directed by physician. Do not touch bottle tip to any surface, since this may contaminate the solution. Keep container tightly closed. Keep this and all other medicines out of reach of children.
How Supplied: In 0.5 fl. oz. and 1.5 fl. oz. plastic dropper bottle.
[*Shown in Product Identification Section*]

SELSUN BLUE®
(selenium sulfide)
Lotion

Selsun Blue is a non-prescription anti-dandruff shampoo containing a 1% concentration of selenium sulfide in a freshly scented, pH balanced formula to leave hair clean and manageable. Available in formulations for dry, oily or normal hair types.
Clinical testing has shown it to be safe and more effective than other leading shampoos in helping control dandruff symptoms with regular use.
Directions: Shake lotion well before using. Use just enough to lather, rinse thoroughly, and repeat. Use once or twice weekly for effective dandruff control.
Caution: For external use only. Keep this and all shampoos out of children's reach. Avoid getting shampoo in eyes—if this happens, rinse thoroughly with water. When used before or after bleaching, tinting or permanent waving, rinse hair for at least five minutes in cool running water. If irritation occurs, discontinue use. Protect from heat.

How Supplied: 4, 7 and 11 fl. oz. plastic bottles.
[*Shown in Product Identification Section*]

TRONOLANE™
(pramoxine hydrochloride)
Cream, Suppositories

Description: Tronolane contains pramoxine hydrochloride a surface anesthetic agent, chemically unrelated to the benzoate esters of the "caine" type, which is chemically designated as a 4-n-butoxyphenyl gammamorpholinopropyl-ether hydrochloride.

Indications: Tronolane is indicated for use as a topical anesthetic to relieve pain, burning, itching and discomfort that accompanies hemorrhoids. It also has a soothing, lubricant action on mucous membranes.

Tronolane contains an excellent rapidly acting topical anesthetic with surface analgesia that lasts up to 5 hours. It fills a conspicuous gap among anesthetics by combining: prompt and potent relief from surface pain or itching, with almost complete freedom from toxicity and sensitization. Since the drug is chemically unrelated to other anesthetics, cross-sensitization is unlikely. Patients who are already sensitized to the "caine" drugs or other anesthetics can generally use Tronolane with excellent results. Tronolane provides a desirable combination of properties—low toxicity, low sensitization, and structural individuality, together with prompt and adequate anesthetic effect.

Tronolane cream and suppositories provide adjunctive therapy for the symptomatic relief of pain and discomfort in external and internal hemorrhoids. The special emollient/emulsion base of the cream provides soothing lubrication making bowel movements easier and more comfortable. Tronolane cream is a bland, non-toxic, well balanced formula in a non-drying base which is non-greasy, not messy, and nonstaining to undergarments.

Warnings: If bleeding is present, consult physician. Certain persons can develop allergic reactions to ingredients in this product. During treatment, if condition worsens or persists 7 days, consult physician. For children under 12 years, use only as directed by physician.

Dosage and Administration: CREAM: Apply up to five times daily, especially morning, night and after bowel movements or as directed by physician.
External—Apply liberally to affected area. Intrarectal—Remove protective cover from clean applicator, lubricate with small amount of Tronolane, gently insert applicator into rectum and squeeze tube. Thoroughly cleanse applicator with soap after use.

Dosage and Administration: SUPPOSITORIES: Use up to five times daily, especially morning, night, and after bowel movements, or as directed by physician. Detach one suppository from pack. Tear notch at pointed end and remove wrapper before insertion. Insert suppository into the rectum, pointed end first.

How Supplied: Tronolane is available in 1-oz., 2-oz. cream tubes and 10, and 20 count suppository boxes.
[*Shown in Product Identification Section*]

If desired, additional information on any Abbott Product will be provided upon request to Abbott Laboratories.

Abbott Laboratories— Abbott Pharmaceuticals, Inc.
Pharmaceutical Products Division
NORTH CHICAGO, IL 60064

OPTILETS®-500
High potency multivitamin for use in treatment of multivitamin deficiency.*

OPTILETS-M-500®
High potency multivitamin for use in treatment of multivitamin deficiency.*
Mineral supplementation added.**

Description: A therapeutic formula of ten important vitamins, with and without minerals, in a small tablet with the Abbott Filmtab® coating. Each Optilets-500 tablet provides:

Vitamin C (as sodium ascorbate)	500 mg
Niacinamide	100 mg
Calcium Pantothenate	20 mg
Vitamin B$_1$ (thiamine mononitrate)	15 mg
Vitamin B$_2$ (riboflavin)	10 mg
Vitamin B$_6$ (pyridoxine hydrochloride)	5 mg
Vitamin A (as palmitate 1.5 mg, as acetate 1.5 mg— total 3 mg)	10,000 IU
Vitamin B$_{12}$ (cyanocobalamin)	12 mcg
Vitamin D (ergocalciferol)	(10 mcg) 400 IU
Vitamin E (as dl-alpha tocopheryl acetate)	30 IU

Each Optilets-M-500 Filmtab contains all the vitamins in the same quantities provided in Optilets-500, plus the following minerals:

Magnesium (as oxide)	80 mg**
Iron (as dried ferrous sulfate)	20 mg
Copper (as sulfate)	2 mg
Zinc (as sulfate)	1.5 mg**
Manganese (as sulfate)	1 mg
Iodine (as calcium iodate)	0.15 mg

* These products contain no folic acid and only dietary supplement levels of vitamins D and E.
** Below USRDA levels.

Dosage and Administration: Usual adult dosage is one Filmtab tablet daily, or as directed by physician.

How Supplied: Optilets-500 tablets are supplied in bottles of 30 (**NDC** 0074-4287-30) and 100 (**NDC** 0074-4287-13). Optilets-M-500 tablets are supplied in bottles of 30 (**NDC** 0074-4286-30) and 100 (**NDC** 0074-4286-13).
Abbott Laboratories
North Chicago, IL 60064
Ref. 02-5861-4/R9, 02-5551-4/R8

SURBEX-T®
High-Potency Vitamin B-Complex*
with 500 mg of Vitamin C

Description: Each Filmtab® tablet provides:

Vitamin C (as sodium ascorbate)	500 mg
Niacinamide	100 mg
Calcium Pantothenate	20 mg
Vitamin B$_1$ (thiamine mononitrate)	15 mg
Vitamin B$_2$ (riboflavin)	10 mg
Vitamin B$_6$ (pyridoxine hydrochloride)	5 mg
Vitamin B$_{12}$ (cyanocobalamin)	10 mcg

Indications: For use in treatment of Vitamin B-Complex* with Vitamin C deficiency.
* Contains no folic acid; not for treatment of folate deficiency.

Dosage and Administration: Usual adult dosage is one Filmtab tablet daily, or as directed by physician.

How Supplied: Orange-colored tablets in bottles of 50 (NDC 0074-4878-50), 100 (NDC 0074-4878-13), and 500 (NDC 0074-4878-53). Also supplied in Abbo-Pac® unit dose packages of 100 tablets in strips of 10 tablets per strip (NDC 0074-4878-11). ®Filmtab—Film-sealed Tablets, Abbott.
Abbott Pharmaceuticals, Inc.
North Chicago, IL 60064

SURBEX®-750 with IRON
High-potency B-complex with Iron, vitamin E and 750 mg vitamin C

Description: Each Filmtab® tablet provides:
VITAMINS

Vitamin C (as sodium ascorbate)	750 mg
Niacinamide	100 mg
Vitamin B$_6$ (pyridoxine hydrochloride)	25 mg
Calcium Pantothenate	20 mg
Vitamin B$_1$ (thiamine mononitrate)	15 mg
Vitamin B$_2$ (riboflavin)	15 mg
Vitamin B$_{12}$ (cyanocobalamin)	12 mcg
Folic Acid	400 mcg
Vitamin E (as dl-alpha tocopheryl acetate)	30 IU

MINERAL

Elemental Iron (as dried ferrous sulfate)	27 mg
equivalent to 135 mg ferrous sulfate	

Indications: For the treatment of vitamin C and B-complex deficiencies and to supplement the daily intake of iron and vitamin E.

Dosage and Administration: Usual adult dosage is one tablet daily or as directed by physician.

How Supplied: Bottles of 50 tablets (NDC 0074-8029-50)
Abbott Pharmaceuticals, Inc.
North Chicago, IL 60064
Ref. 03-0723-2/R2

Continued on next page

If desired, additional information on any Abbott Product will be provided upon request to Abbott Laboratories.

Abbott Pharm.—Cont.

SURBEX®–750 with ZINC
Zinc, vitamin B-complex and vitamins C and E for persons 12 years of age or older

Description: Daily dose (one Filmtab® tablet) provides:

VITAMINS		%U.S. R.D.A.*
Vitamin E	30 IU	100%
Vitamin C	750 mg	1250%
Folic Acid	0.4 mg	100%
Thiamine (B₁)	15 mg	1000%
Riboflavin (B₂)	15 mg	882%
Niacin	100 mg	500%
Vitamin B₆	20 mg	1000%
Vitamin B₁₂	12 mcg	200%
Pantothenic Acid	20 mg	200%
MINERAL		
Zinc**	22.5 mg	150%

* % U.S. Recommended Daily Allowance for Adults.
** Equivalent to 100 mg of zinc sulfate.
Ingredients: Sodium ascorbate, niacinamide, zinc sulfate, dl-alpha tocopheryl acetate, povidone, cellulose, pyridoxine hydrochloride, calcium pantothenate, thiamine mononitrate, riboflavin, cyanocobalamin, magnesium stearate, colloidal silicon dioxide, folic acid, in a film-coated tablet with vanillin flavoring and artificial coloring added.
Usual Adult Dose: One tablet daily.
How Supplied: Bottles of 50 tablets (NDC 0074-8152-50).
Abbott Pharmaceuticals, Inc.
North Chicago, IL 60064
Ref. 03-0724-2/R3

If desired, additional information on any Abbott Product will be provided upon request to Abbott Laboratories.

Adria Laboratories Inc.
5000 POST ROAD
DUBLIN, OH 43017

(includes products formerly marketed by Warren-Teed Laboratories)

MODANE® BULK
(psyllium and dextrose)

Description: MODANE BULK is a powdered mixture of equal parts of psyllium, a bulking agent, and dextrose, as a dispersing agent. Psyllium is a highly efficient dietary fiber derived from the husk of the seed of *Plantago ovata*. Each rounded teaspoonful contains approximately 3.5 g psyllium, 3.5 g dextrose, 2 mg sodium and 37 mg potassium, and provides 14 calories.
Clinical Pharmacology: Psyllium absorbs water and expands. When taken with adequate amounts of water, it increases the water content and bulk volume of the stool. The initial response usually occurs in 12 to 24 hours but, in patients who have used laxatives chronically, up to three days may elapse before the initial response.

Indications and Usage: MODANE BULK is indicated in the treatment of constipation resulting from a diet low in residue. It is used also as adjunctive therapy in patients with diverticular disease, spastic or irritable colon, hemorrhoids, in pregnancy, and in convalescent and senile patients.
Contraindications: Intestinal obstruction, fecal impaction.
Precautions *General*—Impaction or obstruction may occur if the bulk-forming agent is temporarily arrested in its passage through parts of the alimentary canal. In this case, water is absorbed and the bolus may become inspissated. Use of this product in patients with narrowing of the intestinal lumen may be hazardous. Inspissation should not occur in a normal gastrointestinal tract if the product is taken with one or more glasses of water.
Drug Interactions—Psyllium may combine with certain other drugs. Products containing psyllium should not be taken with salicylates, digitalis and other cardiac glycosides, or nitrofurantoin.
Adverse Reactions: Adverse reactions are uncommon, and most often have resulted from inadequate intake of water or from underlying organic disease. Esophageal, gastric, small intestinal and rectal obstruction have resulted from the accumulation of the mucilaginous components of psyllium.
Dosage and Administration: Adults and children over 12 years of age—ONE ROUNDED TEASPOONFUL ONE TO THREE TIMES DAILY STIRRED INTO AN 8 OUNCE GLASS OF WATER, JUICE OR OTHER SUITABLE LIQUID AND PREFERABLY FOLLOWED BY A SECOND GLASSFUL OF LIQUID. Children 6 to 12 years of age—one-half the adult dose in 8 ounces of liquid.
How Supplied: Each rounded teaspoonful of MODANE BULK powder contains approximately 3.5 g psyllium. NDC 0013-5025-72   14 oz. container. Store at room temperature.

MODANE® SOFT
(docusate sodium)
Capsules

Description: Each MODANE SOFT capsule contains docusate sodium 120 mg, and color additives including FD&C Yellow No. 5 (tartrazine) in a soft gelatin capsule. Docusate sodium is classified as a stool softener. Chemically, docusate sodium is sulfobutanedioc acid 1,4-bis(2-ethylhexyl) ester sodium salt. The chemical structure is:

$$\underset{\text{docusate sodium}}{\begin{array}{l} C_2H_5 \\ | \\ COOCH_2CH(CH_2)_3CH_3 \\ | \\ CH_2 \\ | \\ CH{-}SO_3Na \\ | \\ COOCH_2CH(CH_2)_3CH_3 \\ | \\ C_2H_5 \end{array}}$$

The empirical formula is $C_{20}H_{37}O_7SNa$

and the molecular weight is 444.56. At 25°C the solubility of docusate sodium in water is 15 g/l.
Clinical Pharmacology: Hydration of the stool has been attributed to the drug's surfactant effect on the intestinal contents which was assumed to facilitate penetration of the fecal mass by water and lipids. Although this emollient effect may exist, there is evidence that mucosal permeability is increased and water absorption is inhibited in the jejunum. Similar concentrations inhibit colonic absorption and/or increase intraluminal water and electrolytes. In these respects, it is similar to bile salts and in this manner, may also be considered as a stimulant laxative.
Docusate sodium is absorbed to some extent in the duodenum and proximal jejunum. It appears in the bile.
Indications and Usage: MODANE SOFT is indicated for the management of functional constipation associated with dry hard stools. It is especially useful when it is desirable to lessen the strain of defecation (e.g. in persons with painful rectal lesions, hernia or cardiovascular disease). The effect on the stools may not be apparent until 1–3 days after the first dose.
Contraindications: Mineral oil administration or when abdominal pain, nausea, vomiting, or other signs and/or symptoms of appendicitis are present.
Precautions: *General*—This product contains FD&C Yellow No. 5 (tartrazine) which may cause allergic-type reactions (including bronchial asthma) in certain susceptible individuals. Although the overall incidence of FD&C Yellow No. 5 (tartrazine) sensitivity in the general population is low, it is frequently seen in patients who also have aspirin hypersensitivity.
Drug Interactions—MODANE SOFT may increase the intestinal absorption of mineral oil and may increase the intestinal absorption and/or hepatic uptake of other drugs administered concurrently.
Carcinogenesis, Mutagenesis, Impairment of Fertility—There have been no long term studies of docusate to evaluate carcinogenic potential. There have been no studies to evaluate mutagenic potential or to determine whether docusate has the potential to impair fertility.
Teratogenic Effects—Pregnancy Category C. Animal reproduction studies have not been conducted with docusate. It is also not known whether MODANE SOFT can cause fetal harm when administered to a pregnant woman or can affect reproductive capacity. MODANE SOFT should be given to a pregnant woman only if clearly needed.
Nursing Mothers—It is not known whether this drug is excreted in human milk. Caution should be exercised when MODANE SOFT is administered to a nursing woman.
Pediatric Use—Because of its dosage size, MODANE SOFT is not recommended for use by children less than 6 years of age.

Adverse Reactions: Adverse reactions are uncommon. Diarrhea, cramping pains and rash have been reported.

Overdosage: Docusates have a low potential for toxicity. Single doses as large as 50 mg/kg have not produced adverse effects in children. Anorexia, vomiting and diarrhea may result from overdosage.

Dosage and Administration: Adults and children over 12 years of age—1 to 3 capsules daily. Children 6–12 years of age—one capsule daily.

How Supplied: Each MODANE SOFT green, soft gelatin capsule contains docusate sodium 120 mg coded 13 503.
NDC 0013-5031-13 Package of 30 Capsules
Store at controlled room temperature (59°–86°F, 15°–30°C).

MODANE®
(danthron)
Tablets and Liquid

Description: MODANE® Tablets (yellow)—Each tablet contains danthron 75 mg and color additives including FD&C Yellow No. 5 (tartrazine).
MODANE® MILD Tablets—Each tablet contains danthron 37.5 mg and color additives including FD&C Yellow No. 5 (tartrazine).
MODANE® Liquid—Each 5 ml (teaspoonful) contains danthron 37.5 mg and alcohol 5%. Danthron is classified as a stimulant laxative and is chemically 1,8-dihydroxyanthraquinone. Its chemical structure is:

danthron

The empirical formula is $C_{14}H_8O_4$ and the molecular weight is 240.21. It is practically insoluble in water.

Clinical Pharmacology: Stimulant cathartics act on the intestinal mucosa and have effects both on the net absorption of electrolytes and water and on motility. This group includes danthron, the docusates, castor oil, and bile acids. Despite similarity of their mechanism of action, there are differences among these drugs which are due, for the most part, to dosage and the major site of action, i.e. small intestine or colon.

Anthraquinone cathartics vary in their effects depending upon their anthraquinone content and the ease of liberation of the active constituents from their inactive precursor glycosides. Danthron, although a free anthraquinone, is similar to the pro-drug glycosides in its pharmacological properties. A soft or semifluid stool is passed 6 to 8 hours after administration of an anthraquinone glycoside cathartic such as danthron.

Danthron is absorbed from the small intestine to a limited extent, circulated through the portal system and into the general circulation and excreted in the bile, urine, saliva, colonic mucosa and milk.

Indications and Usage: MODANE is indicated for the management of constipation. It may be useful in the management of constipation in geriatric, cardiac, surgical and postpartum patients. MODANE may be useful in the management of constipation which may occur with or during the concomitant use of antihypertensive agents, ganglionic blocking agents, antihistamines, tranquilizers, sympathomimetics and anticholinergics. A soft or semifluid stool is passed 6 to 8 hours after administration. Adequate bulk should be provided in the diet and, if the diet does not provide sufficient bulk, by hydrophilic bulking agents. Poor bowel habits should be corrected.

Contraindications: Should not be used when abdominal pain, nausea, vomiting or other signs and/or symptoms of appendicitis are present.

Precautions: *General*—This product contains FD&C Yellow No. 5 (tartrazine) which may cause allergic-type reactions (including bronchial asthma) in certain susceptible individuals. Although the overall incidence of FD&C Yellow No. 5 (tartrazine) sensitivity in the general population is low, it is frequently seen in patients who also have aspirin hypersensitivity. MODANE may cause harmless pink discoloration of urine (the urine may be pink-red, red-violet or red-brown if alkaline). As with all laxatives, frequent or prolonged use may result in dependence.

Drug Interactions—The absorption of danthron from the gastrointestinal tract and/or its uptake by hepatic cells may be increased by the co-administration of docusate.

Carcinogenesis, Mutagenesis, Impairment of Fertility—There have been no long term studies of MODANE to evaluate carcinogenic potential. There have been no studies to evaluate mutagenic potential or whether MODANE has the potential to impair fertility.

Teratogenic Effects—Pregnancy Category C. Animal reproduction studies have not been conducted with danthron. It is also not known whether danthron can cause fetal harm when administered to a pregnant woman or can affect reproductive capacity. MODANE should be given to a pregnant woman only if clearly needed.

Nursing Mothers—Danthron is excreted in human milk and has been reported to increase bowel activity in infants nursed by women taking it. Caution should be exercised when MODANE is administered to a nursing woman.

Pediatric Use—In general stimulant cathartics should seldom be used in children.

Adverse Reactions: Adverse reactions are uncommon. These are in order of frequency: excessive bowel activity (griping, diarrhea, nausea, vomiting), peri-anal irritation, weakness, dizziness, palpitations and sweating. Temporary brownish mucosal staining has occurred with prolonged use. There has also been reported a suspected allergic reaction with facial swelling, redness and discomfort.

Overdosage: The lowest reported lethal dose in mice and rats is 500 mg/kg. Overdosage may be expected to result in excessive bowel activity. Treatment is symptomatic when the duration of effects is prolonged.

Dosage and Administration: MODANE Tablet (yellow)—Adults—1 tablet with evening meal.
MODANE MILD Tablets (half-strength, pink)—Adults—1 or 2 tablets with the evening meal. For adults who have previously responded with excessive bowel activity to a mild laxative or who are diet-restricted or who are bedfast and for children 6–12 years of age—1 tablet with the evening meal.
MODANE Liquid—Adults—1 to 2 teaspoonfuls with the evening meal. For adults who have previously responded with excessive bowel activity to a mild laxative or who are diet-restricted or who are bedfast and children who are 6–12 years of age—1 teaspoonful with the evening meal.

How Supplied:
Each MODANE Tablet contains danthron 75 mg in a yellow, round, sugar coated tablet, coded 13 501.
NDC 0013-5011-17 Bottle of 100 Tablets
NDC 0013-5011-23 Bottle of 1000 Tablets
NDC 0013-5011-18 STAT-PAK® (unit dose) 100 Tablets
NDC 0013-5011-07 Package of 10 Tablets
NDC 0013-5011-13 Package of 30 Tablets
Store at room temperature.
Each MODANE MILD Tablet contains danthron 37.5 mg in a pink, round, sugar coated tablet, coded 13 502.
NDC 0013-5021-17 Bottle of 100 Tablets
NDC 0013-5021-23 Bottle of 1000 Tablets
Store at room temperature.
Each 5 ml (teaspoonful) of MODANE Liquid contains danthron 37.5 mg in a red liquid.
NDC 0013-5033-51 Pint Bottles
Protect from cold.

MODANE® PLUS
(danthron and docusate sodium)
Tablets

Description: Each MODANE PLUS tablet contains danthron 50 mg and docusate sodium 100 mg and color additives including FD&C Yellow No. 5 (tartrazine). Danthron is classified as a stimulant cathartic and docusate sodium is a stool softener. Chemically docusate sodium is sulfobutanedioc acid 1,4-bis (2-ethylhexyl) ester sodium salt and danthron is 1,8-dihydroxyanthraquinone. The empirical formula of docusate sodium is $C_{20}H_{37}O_7SNa$ and its molecular weight is 444.56. The empirical formula of danthron is $C_{14}H_8O_4$ and its molecular weight is 240.21.

Continued on next page

Adria—Cont.

danthron   docusate sodium

Danthron is practically insoluble in water. At 25°C the solubility of docusate sodium in water is 15 g/l.

Clinical Pharmacology: Contact cathartics act on the intestinal mucosa and have effects both on the net absorption of electrolytes and water and on motility. This group includes danthron, the docusates, castor oil, and bile acids. Despite similarity of their mechanism of action, there are differences among these drugs which are due, for the most part, to dosage and the major site of action, i.e. small intestine or colon.

Anthraquinone cathartics vary in their effects depending upon their anthraquinone content and the ease of liberation of the active constituents from their precursor glycosides. Danthron, although a free anthraquinone, is similar to the prodrug glycosides in its pharmacological properties. A soft or semifluid stool is passed 6 to 8 hours after administration of an anthraquinone glycoside cathartic or danthron.

Hydration of the stool has been attributed to docusate sodium's surfactant effect on the intestinal contents which was assumed to facilitate penetration of the fecal mass by water and lipids. Although this emollient effect may exist, there is evidence that mucosal permeability is increased and water absorption is inhibited in the jejunum. Similar concentrations inhibit colonic absorption and/or increase intraluminal water and electrolytes. In these respects docusate sodium is similar to bile salts and in this manner may also be considered as a stimulant laxative.

Danthron is absorbed from the small intestine to a limited extent, circulated through the portal system and into the general circulation and excreted in the bile, urine, saliva, colonic mucosa and milk.

Docusate sodium is absorbed to some extent in the duodenum and proximal jejunum. It appears in the bile.

Indications and Usage: MODANE PLUS is indicated for the management of constipation where a combination of a stimulant plus a stool softener is needed. It may be useful in geriatric or inactive patients, following surgery, and in patients refractory to other laxatives (see MODANE, MODANE SOFT and MODANE BULK). Adequate bulk should be provided in the diet and, if the diet does not provide sufficient bulk, by hydrophilic bulking agents (MODANE BULK). Poor bowel habits should be corrected.

Contraindications: Mineral oil administration, or when abdominal pain, nausea, vomiting or other signs and/or symptoms of appendicitis are present.

Precautions: *General*—This product contains FD&C Yellow No. 5 (tartrazine) which may cause allergic-type reactions (including bronchial asthma) in certain susceptible individuals. Although the overall incidence of FD&C Yellow No. 5 (tartrazine) sensitivity in the general population is low, it is frequently seen in patients who also have aspirin hypersensitivity. It may cause harmless discoloration of urine (the urine may be pink-red, red-violet or red-brown if alkaline).

As with all laxatives, frequent or prolonged use may result in dependence.

Drug Interactions—Docusate sodium may increase the intestinal absorption and/or hepatic uptake of other drugs administered concurrently.

Carcinogenesis, Mutagenesis, Impairment of Fertility—There have been no long term studies of MODANE PLUS to evaluate carcinogenic potential. There have been no studies to evaluate mutagenic potential or to determine whether MODANE PLUS has the potential to impair fertility.

Teratogenic Effects—Pregnancy Category C. Animal reproduction studies have not been conducted with danthron and docusate sodium. It is also not known whether MODANE PLUS can cause fetal harm when administered to a pregnant woman or can affect reproductive capacity. MODANE PLUS should be given to a pregnant woman only if clearly needed.

Nursing Mothers—Danthron is excreted in human milk and has been reported to increase bowel activity in infants nursed by women taking it. Caution should be exercised when MODANE PLUS is administered to a nursing woman.

Pediatric Use—Because of its dosage size, MODANE PLUS is not recommended for use by children less than 12 years.

Adverse Reactions: Adverse reactions are uncommon. These are in order of frequency: Excessive bowel activity (griping, diarrhea, nausea, vomiting), peri-anal irritation, weakness, dizziness, palpitations and sweating. Temporary brownish mucosal staining has occurred with prolonged use. There have also been reports of rash and a report of facial swelling, redness and discomfort.

Overdosage: Docusates and danthron have low potential for toxicity. The oral LD_{50} values of danthron, docusate sodium and danthron—docusate sodium combination in mice were greater than 7 g/kg, 2.64 g/kg and 3.44 g/kg, respectively. The lowest reported lethal dose of danthron in mice and rats is 500 mg/kg. Single doses of docusate sodium, as large as 50 mg/kg, has not produced adverse effects in children. Overdosage may be expected to result in anorexia, vomiting and diarrhea. Treatment is symptomatic when the duration of effects is prolonged.

Dosage and Administration: Adults and children over 12 years of age—1 tablet daily with evening meal.

How Supplied: Each MODANE PLUS tablet contains a combination of danthron 50 mg and docusate sodium 100 mg in a brown, round, sugar coated tablet coded 13 504.

NDC 0013-5041-13   30 Tablet Package
NDC 0013-5041-17   Bottle of 100 Tablets
Store at room temperature
AHFS 56:12

MYOFLEX® CREME
(Triethanolamine Salicylate)

Description: Triethanolamine salicylate 10% in a non-greasy base. Nonirritating, nonburning, odorless, stainless, readily absorbed.

Actions: Topical Analgesic. Penetration assured with maximal salicylate appearing in urine 5 hours after application.

Indications: An effective analgesic rub for sore muscles, joint attachments, stiffness and strains; a helpful topical adjunct in arthritis and rheumatism. Excellent as a hand cream for patients with minor rheumatic stiffness and soreness of the hands. Excellent for sore feet.

Contraindications: Do not use in patient's manifesting idiosyncrasy to salicylates.

Warnings: For external use only. Avoid getting into eyes or on mucous membranes. To be used only according to directions. Keep out of the reach of children.

Precautions: Apply to affected parts only. Do not apply to irritated skin or if excessive irritation develops, consult physician. A 2 oz. tube contains the salicylate equivalent of about 56 grains of aspirin.

Adverse Reactions: None reported, but if applied to large skin areas may cause typical salicylate side effects such as tinnitus, nausea, or vomiting.

Dosage and Administration: Adults — Rub into area of soreness two or three times daily. Wrists, elbows, knees and ankles may be wrapped loosely with 2″ or 3″ elastic bandage after liberal application.

How Supplied:
NDC 0013-5404-61 Tubes, 2 oz.
NDC 0013-5404-74 Jars, 1 lb.

Alcon/bp
Alcon Laboratories, Inc.
6201 SOUTH FREEWAY
FORT WORTH, TX 76101

HARD CONTACT LENS PRODUCTS

CLENS®
A Concentrated Cleansing Solution for Hard Contact Lenses

Description: CLENS is a concentrated solution specially formulated for the effective cleansing of hard contact lenses. Routine use of CLENS helps prevent mucus, oil and other troublesome deposits from accumulating on the lens surfaces.

Warning: Should not be used as a soaking or wetting solution.

Contains: Active Ingredients: benzalkonium chloride 0.02%, edetate disodium 0.1%.

Supplied: 2 fl. oz plastic containers.

SOACLENS®
Dual-Purpose Soaking and Wetting Solution for Hard Contact Lenses

Description: SOACLENS is a carefully balanced, tear-like solution, buffered to closely approximate the pH and tonicity of the eye. Thimerosal 0.004% and edetate disodium 0.1% are added as preservatives.

The routine use of SOACLENS, for overnight storage of the lenses, facilitates maximum hydration and wettability. The convenient one-step soaking and wetting procedure helps assure prolonged comfort and wearing time.

Directions: Fill kit with sufficient SOACLENS to cover lens. Insert lens onto eye directly from SOACLENS bath or lens may be rinsed with water or a few drops of SOACLENS before reinsertion.

Supplied: 4 fl. oz. (120ml) plastic containers. A complimentary disposable storage case is supplied with each carton of SOACLENS.

[*Shown in Product Identification Section*]

SOFT CONTACT LENS PRODUCTS
(or lenses made from other new polymers)

ADAPETTES®
Sterile lubricating and rewetting solution for use with conventional hard contact lenses, soft (hydrophilic) contact lenses, and contact lenses made from other new polymers.[7]

Description: A sterile, buffered, isotonic, aqueous solution containing Adsorbobase®* (povidone with other water soluble polymers) with thimerosal 0.004% and edetate disodium 0.1% added as preservatives. ADAPETTES is designed for use, while the contact lens is on the eye, as a rewetting and/or lubricating solution. ADAPETTES may also help remove particulate material.

Administration: Place one drop of ADAPETTES on each lens 3 or 4 times a day or as needed. If minor irritation, discomfort or blurring occur while wearing the lenses, place a drop of ADAPETTES on the eye and blink 2 or 3 times.

Warning: If discomfort persists after using ADAPETTES, the patient should remove lenses and see an eye care practitioner.

Supplied: ½ fl. oz. (15 ml) plastic dropper vials.
*Patented
[*Shown in Product Identification Section*]

BOILnSOAK®
Sterile, preserved, saline solution for rinsing, storage and heat disinfection of soft (hydrophilic) contact lenses.[1]

Description: A sterile, buffered, isotonic, aqueous solution containing boric acid, sodium borate and sodium chloride 0.7%, preserved with thimerosal 0.001% and edetate disodium 0.1%.

Administration: After lenses have been cleaned with PREFLEX®, BOILnSOAK is used to rinse lenses free of loosened debris and traces of the cleaner. Disinfec-

tion of lenses is accomplished by immersing lenses in BOILnSOAK, in the carrying case, and heating them in a thermal unit designed for this procedure. If no thermal unit is available, lenses may be disinfected by immersing them in BOILnSOAK, in the carrying case, and dropping the sealed case into a pan of already boiling water. Remove the pan from heat after ten minutes and allow the water to cool before handling lenses.

Warnings: Fresh BOILnSOAK must be used daily for disinfection and storage. NEVER REUSE BOILnSOAK. Do not touch tip of bottle to any surface since this may contaminate solution. If irritation occurs and persists or increases, discontinue use and consult your eye care practitioner.

Supplied: 8 fl. oz. (237 ml) and 12 fl. oz. (355 ml) plastic containers.

[*Shown in Product Identification Section*]

FLEX–CARE®
Sterile solution for rinsing, storage and cold (chemical) disinfection of soft (hydrophilic) contact lenses or lenses made from other new polymers.[6]

Description: A sterile, buffered, isotonic, aqueous solution containing sodium chloride, sodium borate and boric acid, having a tonicity of approximately 289 mOsm. Thimerosal 0.001%, edetate disodium 0.1% and chlorhexidine 0.005% are added as preservatives. FLEX-CARE is used as the rinsing, storage and disinfection solution in conjunction with the PREFLEX® and FLEX-CARE cold (chemical) disinfection system.

Administration: After cleaning with PREFLEX, each lens should be thoroughly rinsed with FLEX-CARE (for approximately 10 seconds) to remove loosened debris and traces of the cleaner, prior to storage and disinfection of lenses in FLEX-CARE. Lenses should be completely submerged, in their storage case, and stored in FLEX-CARE for a minimum of 4 hours to assure disinfection. Prior to reinsertion of lenses, they should be rinsed with fresh FLEX-CARE.

Warnings: Fresh FLEX-CARE must be used daily for storage. NEVER REUSE FLEX-CARE. NEVER HEAT LENSES IN FLEX-CARE.
WHEN THE ENZYMATIC CONTACT LENS CLEANER (PAPAIN) IS USED IN CONJUNCTION WITH THIS PRODUCT, CARE MUST BE TAKEN TO EFFECTIVELY CLEAN AND THOROUGHLY RINSE THE LENS AFTER ENZYME TREATMENT AND BEFORE LENS DISINFECTION. Do not touch the dropper tip of bottle to any surface since this may contaminate the solution

Supplied: 12 fl. oz (355 ml) plastic containers.

[*Shown in Product Identification Section*]

PREFLEX®
Sterile cleaning solution for use with soft (hydrophilic) contact lenses or lenses made from other new polymers.[3]

Description: A sterile, buffered, isotonic, aqueous solution consisting of sodium phosphates, sodium chloride, tyloxapol, hydroxyethylcellulose and polyvinyl alcohol, with thimerosal 0.004% and edetate disodium 0.2% added as preservatives. Daily cleaning with PREFLEX helps prevent oil, mucus and other troublesome deposits from accumulating on the lens surfaces.

Administration: Before handling lenses, hands should be cleaned with non-cosmetic soap, rinsed thoroughly, and dried with a lint-free towel. Apply 3 drops of PREFLEX to each lens surface and thoroughly clean by rubbing between thumb and forefinger for at least 20 seconds. Lenses should be rinsed, disinfected and stored in accordance with the lens care procedures recommended by the eye care practitioner.

Warning: PREFLEX is not intended for use directly in the eye.

Supplied: 1.5 fl. oz. (45 ml) plastic containers.

[*Shown in Product Identification Section*]

1-7:

ACCUGEL™ (droxifilcon)
Strieter Laboratories

AMSOF® (deltafilcon A)
Lombart Lenses, Ltd.
Div. of American Sterilizer Co.

AOSOFT® (tetrafilcon A)
American Optical Corp.
Soft Contact Lens Division

AQUAFLEX® (tetrafilcon A)
UCO Optics, Inc.

AQUA-SOFT® (deltafilcon A)
Aquarius Soft Lens, Inc.

CUSTOM-FLEX™ (deltafilcon A)
Custom Contact Lens Lab., Inc.

DURASOFT® (phemfilcon A)
Wesley-Jessen, Inc.

DURASOFT® TT (phemfilcon A)
Wesley-Jessen, Inc.

FLEXLENS™ (hefilcon A) PHP
PHP (U.S. Pat. 3,721,657)
Trademark of Automated Optics, Inc.
Manufactured by Flexlens™, Inc.

GELFLEX® (dimefilcon A)
Dow Corning Ophthalmics, Inc.

HYDROCURVE® (hefilcon A) PHP
PHP (U.S. Pat. 3,721,657)
Trademark of Automated Optics, Inc.
Manufactured by Soft Lenses, Inc.

HYDROCURVE® II (bufilcon A)
Soft Lenses, Inc.

HYDRO-MARC® (etafilcon A)
Frontier Contact Lenses, Inc.

HYDRON® (polymacon)
National Patent Development Corp.

Continued on next page

Alcon/bp—Cont.

MIRACON™ (hefilcon B)
Bausch & Lomb Soflens Division
Bausch & Lomb, Inc.

NATURVUE® (hefilcon A) PHP
PHP (U.S. Pat. 3,721,657)
Trademark of Automated Optics, Inc.
Manufactured by Milton Roy Co.

NU-SOFT® (deltafilcon A)
Vent-Air Optics, Inc.

PERMALENS® (perfilcon A)
Cooper Laboratories

SOF-FORM® (deltafilcon A)
Sof-Form, Inc.
Div. of Salvatori Ophthalmics, Inc.

SOFLENS® (polymacon)
Bausch & Lomb Soflens Division
Bausch & Lomb, Inc.

SOFT-FLOW™ (deltafilcon A)
Medicornea, Inc.

SOFTICS™ (deltafilcon A)
Advanced Soft Optics, Inc.

SOFTSITE® (hefilcon A) PHP
PHP (U.S. Pat. 3,721,657)
Trademark of Automated Optics, Inc.
Manufactured by
Paris Contact Lens Laboratory

TRÈSOFT® (ocufilcon A)
Alcon Optic Division
Alcon Laboratories, Inc.

TRI POL 43® (deltafilcon A)
Comfortflex Hydrophilics, Inc.
Div. of Capitol Contact Lenses, Inc.

3-7:

CABCURVE™ (porofocon B)
Soft Lenses, Inc.

RX-56® (porofocon A)
Rynco Scientific Corp.

SOFTCON® (vifilcon A, cosmetic)
American Optical Corp.
Soft Contact Lens Division

1-3:

SOFTCON® (vifilcon A, therapeutic)
American Optical Corp.
Soft Contact Lens Division

3, 6, 7:

POLYCON® (silafocon A)
Syntex Ophthalmics, Inc.

3-6:

MESO® (cabufocon A)
Danker Laboratories, Inc.

IDENTIFICATION PROBLEM?

Consult the

Product Identification Section

where you'll find

products pictured

in full color.

Allergan Pharmaceuticals, Inc.
**2525 DUPONT DRIVE
IRVINE, CA 92713**

LIQUIFILM® TEARS
Artificial Tears

Active Ingredient: Polyvinyl alcohol 1.4% with chlorobutanol 0.5% as a preservative and sodium chloride.
Indications: Dry eye conditions and hard contact lens wear discomfort.
Actions: Soothes and lubricates dry eyes and promotes comfort and longer wearing of hard contact lenses.
Warnings: If irritation persists or increases, discontinue use. Keep container tightly closed. Do not touch dropper tip to any surface to prevent contamination. Not for use with soft contact lenses. Keep out of reach of children.
Precaution: (See Warnings).
Dosage and Administration: 1 drop in the eye as needed, or as directed by physician.
Professional Labeling: Same as outlined under Indications.
How Supplied: 15 ml and 30 ml plastic bottles.
[*Shown in Product Identification Section*]

PREFRIN™ LIQUIFILM®
decongestant ophthalmic solution

Active Ingredient: Phenylephrine HCl 0.12% polyvinyl alcohol 1.4%, and benzalkonium chloride 1:25,000.
Indications: Minor eye irritations.
Actions: Lubricates and whitens the eye; relieves and soothes minor eye irritations.
Warnings: Do not use in presence of narrow-angle glaucoma. If irritation persists or increases, discontinue use. Keep container tightly closed; do not touch dropper tip to any surface to avoid contamination. Not for use with soft contact lenses. Pupillary dilation may occur in some individuals.
Precaution: (See Warnings).
Dosage and Administration: 1 or 2 drops in each eye; repeat in 3 to 4 hours as needed.
Professional Labeling: Same as outlined under Indications.
How Supplied: 20 ml plastic bottle.
[*Shown in Product Identification Section*]

TEARS PLUS™
Artificial Tears

Active Ingredient: Polyvinyl alcohol 1.4% and povidone, with chlorobutanol 0.5% as a preservative and sodium chloride.
Indications: Dry eye conditions.
Actions: Soothes and lubricates dry eyes.
Warnings: If irritation persists or increases, discontinue use. Keep container tightly closed. Do not touch dropper tip to any surface to prevent contamination. Not for use with soft contact lenses. Keep out of reach of children.
Precaution: (See Warnings).
Dosage and Administration: 1 drop in the eye as needed or directed.

Professional Labeling: Same as outlined under Indications.
How Supplied: 15 ml plastic bottles.
[*Shown in Product Identification Section*]

Almay Hypoallergenic Cosmetics and Toiletries
Almay, Inc.
**850 THIRD AVENUE
NEW YORK, NY 10022**

Almay Hypoallergenic Cosmetics and Toiletries
Almay, Inc.
**PROFESSIONAL SERVICE DEPT.
APEX, NC 27502**

ALMAY HYPOALLERGENIC COSMETICS, SKIN CARE PRODUCTS AND TOILETRIES manufacture a complete line of high fashion cosmetics and skin care (treatment-aid) products including antiperspirant/deodorants; astringents; bath products; cleansers; conditioners; covering agents; moisturizers and emollients; hair and nail care products.

Cosmetics as well as skin care products are prepared for three skin types: normal/combination skin; dry skin and oily skin. ALL ALMAY PRODUCTS ARE FRAGRANCE-FREE AND FREE OF MASKING ODORS. All products are formulated in accordance with Almay's Cosmetic Control System to assure hypoallergenicity. The Rabbit Ear Assay for Comedogenicity has been added to the roster of safety testing. All of the Almay foundation lotions, moisture lotions and blushers have been shown to be non-comedogenic.

Almay manufactures two lines of skin care (treatment-aid) products, a Deep Mist collection for the care of normal/combination and dry skin and a special collection for the care of oily skin. Makeup, blushers and face powder are formulated for all skin types. For normal/combination skin Almay recommends Cold Cream Soap, Deep Mist Cleansing Lotion for soap-sensitive individuals; Deep Mist Purifying toner; Deep Mist Ultralight Moisture Lotion to alleviate dryness and Fresh Finish Balanced Makeup. Combination skin refers to T-Zone oiliness limited to the forehead, nose and chin with normal or somewhat dry cheeks and temples.

For dry to very dry skin Almay recommends Deep Mist Cleansing Cream which protects the skin by the desposition of a fine oily film; Deep Mist Purifying Freshener for toning; Deep Mist Moisture Cream to alleviate excessive dryness and Fresh Glow Moisturizing Makeup. For oily skin Almay recommends cleansing with Gentle Cleansing Soap for Oily Skin; Oil Control Purifying Pure Lotion and Fresh Look Oil-Free Makeup, a water-based makeup.

Extra Cover Cream Makeup may be used for all skin types when heavier coverage is required because of blemishes or other minor skin defects.

Super Shine Shampoo or Castile Shampoo, Clean and Gentle Oil-Free Conditioner and Protein Conditioning Hair Spray may be used as often as needed for all types of hair to enhance, luster, sheen and combability. These products are particularly helpful in the care of hair that has been chemically, mechanically or environmentally damaged, e.g. excessive sun exposure.

Almay's Hypo-allergenic cosmetics are high fashioned and are obtainable in a wide variety of shades.

Literature: Almay's Product Formulary and Cosmetic Guide lists products, ingredient disclosures and the action and uses of all products. A detailed description of the Almay Cosmetic Control System is likewise available as well as literature dealing with cosmetics.

[*Shown in Product Identification Section*]

Aloe Creme Laboratories
a division of ALO-SCHERER
   HEALTHCARE, INC.
P. O. BOX 5847
FORT LAUDERDALE, FL 33310

ALO-LIP-SHIELD®
ALO-SUN® SPF 15 SUN BLOCK STICK

Ingredients: Mineral Oil, Petrolatum, Beeswax, Lanolin Aloe Vera Gel, Cetyl Alcohol. ALO-LIP-SHIELD® contains Homosalate.

ALO-SUN® SPF 15 Sun Block Stick active ingredients: Octyl Dimethyl PABA, Benzophenone-3.

Indications: Aids prevention and healing of chapping and dryness from too much sun, wind, cold. ALO-SUN® SPF 15 Sun Block Stick provides ultra sunscreen protection.

Actions: Forms a protective barrier to protect lips and sensitive areas year round from drying effects of sun, wind and cold. The aloe vera gel and special emollients soften and moisturize and help heal the skin and forms an occlusive film thus inducing hydration, restoring suppleness to lips and preventing drying. ALO-LIP-SHIELD® also protects skin from the external environment and its sunscreen offers protection from exposure to the sun.

Also available ALO-SUN® SPF 15 Sun Block Stick, which provides the highest degree of sun burn protection available for application to sun-sensitive areas (lips, ears, nose, etc.).

Dosage and Administration: Apply evenly and liberally to lips and sensitive areas before exposure to sun, wind, cold. For dry chapped lips, apply as needed.

How Supplied:
ALO-LIP-SHIELD®—.15 oz. tube.
ALO-SUN® SPF 15 Sun Block Stick—.15 oz. tube.

ALO-OINTMENT®

Active Ingredient: Allantoin. Also contains 70% pure Aloe Vera gel protected in an exclusively compounded base— mineral oil, stearic acid, petrolatum, triethanolamine, beeswax, synthetic spermaceti, propylparaben, methylparaben. Contains no anesthetic drugs.

Indications: Topical application for temporary relief of and to aid healing and moisturize minor burns (sunburn, thermal and chemical), cuts, chafing, abrasions and skin irritations. Greaseless, non-staining and non-toxic.

Warnings: For external use only, not to be swallowed. Avoid contact with eyes. If irritation, rash or occasional skin sensitivity occur, wash off immediately and discontinue further use.

Dosage and Administration: Clean affected area thoroughly. Apply ALO-OINTMENT® generously over affected area. Repeat as often as necessary to keep the area moist and covered. If affected area requires a dressing, apply a sterile, non-adherent bandage. If relief is not obtained within 24 hours, consult a physician.

How Supplied: 1 oz. tube; 2 oz., 4 oz. and 16 oz. jars.

ALO-RELIEF®
Healing Lotion

Active Ingredient: Allantoin. Also contains 50% pure Aloe Vera gel protected in an exclusively compounded base—water, mineral oil, lanolin, stearic acid, triethanolamine, cetyl alcohol, carbomer 940, methylparaban, propylparaben.

Indications: Topical application for temporary relief and to aid healing of sunburn, minor burns, chafing, insect bites, abrasions, diaper rash and minor skin irritations. Greaseless, non-staining and contains no anesthetic drugs.

Warnings: For external use only, not to be swallowed. Avoid contact with eyes. In rare cases irritation or rash may appear. If this occurs, discontinue use.

Dosage and Administration: Apply evenly and generously over the affected area. Repeat as necessary.

How Supplied: 4 oz. and 2 oz. tubes.

ALO-SUN® FASHION TAN® SPF 15 SUN BLOCK LOTION

Active Ingredients: Octyl Dimethyl PABA, Benzophenone-3.

Indications: Sun Screen to help prevent sunburn. FASHION TAN® SPF 15 SUN BLOCK LOTION provides 15 times your natural sunburn protection. Provides the highest degree of sunburn protection available for all over application or for sun-sensitive areas (nose, ears, shoulders, etc.). Liberal and regular use may help prevent premature aging and wrinkling of skin and skin cancer due to long-term over exposure to the sun.

Actions: Sun screen.

Warnings: Avoid contact with eyes, not to be used internally. Discontinue use if signs of irritation or rash appear.

Dosage and Administration: Apply evenly and liberally to exposed skin. To insure maximum protection, reapply after swimming or exercise.

How Supplied: 4 fl. oz. and 8 fl. oz. Squeeze Bottle.

Alto Pharmaceuticals, Inc.
P.O. BOX 271369
TAMPA, FL 33688

EFED II™

Active Ingredients: Each Efed II capsule contains Theionized ephedrine sulfate 25 mg., phenylpropanolamine HCl 50 mg., and caffeine 125 mg.

Indications: Efed II fast acting ingredients give immediate relief from fatigue, drowsiness and stuffiness. It can also be used as a stimulant to aid in mental alertness; also as a decongestant and bronchodilator in the management of bronchial asthma.

Caution: If under medical care do not take without consulting a physician or pharmacist. Individuals with high blood pressure, heart disease, diabetes or thyroid disease should use only as directed by a physician. Should not be taken as a substitute for normal sleep. May interfere with sleep if taken within four hours of bedtime.

Warning: Do not exceed recommended dosage. Reduce dosage if nervousness or restlessness or sleeplessness occurs. Because of the ephedrine component, this medicine should be used with caution by elderly males or those with prostatic hypertrophy.

Adult Dosage: One capsule every four hours, not to exceed 4 capsules in a 24 hour period. Not recommended for children under 12 years of age.

How Supplied: Box of 24 capsules, available in Opaque Black or Opaque Yellow.

Ames Division
Miles Laboratories, Inc.
POST OFFICE BOX 70
ELKHART, IN 46515

MICROSTIX®–Nitrite Kit
In-home dip and read test for nitrite in urine, an indicator of urinary tract infection
For in vitro diagnostic use

Active Ingredient: Reagents: P-arsanilic acid and N [1-naphthyl] ethylenediamine dihydrochloride, plus a buffer in solid state reagent strip format.

Indications: MICROSTIX®-Nitrite is an in-home test kit that has reagent strip tests that will detect nitrite in urine, an indicator of urinary tract infection.

Actions: The three MICROSTIX®-Nitrite test strips are to be used to test first morning urine specimens on three consecutive mornings. To achieve best results, the urine should be retained in the bladder for at least four hours, and should be tested immediately upon urinating. Ninety percent of urinary tract infections are caused by bacteria that convert nitrate in the urine to nitrite. If nitrite is present in urine, the test strip will turn a pink color. When this positive result occurs, the person should contact her/his doctor for treatment.

Anabolic Laboratories, Inc.
17802 GILLETTE AVENUE
IRVINE, CA 92714

AQUA-A
Chewable, emulsified "water solublized" vitamin A tablets

Description: AQUA-A is a pleasant tasting emulsified vitamin A formula (from non-fish oil sources), providing excellent absorption. It is in a soft tablet form which may be chewed, dissolved in the mouth or swallowed providing 25,000 I.U. of vitamin A (palmitate) per tablet.
Indication: For use as a vitamin A supplement.
Warning: Keep out of the reach of children.
Dosage and Administration: One tablet daily to be chewed or allowed to dissolve in the mouth for faster and better absorption.
How Supplied: Bottle of 90 tablets.

B6-PLUS
Vitamin B6 supplement with Magnesium

Description: B6-PLUS combines vitamin B6 and magnesium which function together as coenzyme and cofactor in many reactions throughout the body, along with other supportive factors. Each tablet provides:

		% U.S. RDA*
Vitamin B6 (pyridoxine HCl)	50 mg	2500
Vitamin B1 (thiamine HCl)	10 mg	667
Vitamin B2 (riboflavin)	2.4 mg	141
Niacin	20 mg	100
Potassium (as potassium citrate)	50 mg	**
Magnesium (as magnesium oxide)	50 mg	12.5

In a base containing concentrate of adrenal substance.
Percentage of U.S. Recommended Daily Allowance for adults and children four or more years of age.
**RDA has not been established.
Indication: Vitamin B6 supplement.
Dosage and Administration: Usual adult dosage one or two tablets daily or as directed by physician.
How Supplied: Bottle of 100 tablets.

B12-PLUS
Vitamin B12 supplement

Description: Each tablet provides 250 mcg of vitamin B12 on an ion exchange resin designed to release the vitamin in the intestine insuring maximum absorption. Provides 4167% of the U.S. Recommended Daily Allowance for adults and children four or more years of age.
Indication: Vitamin B12 supplement.
Dosage and Administration: Usual adult dosage one or two tablets daily or as directed by physician.
How Supplied: Bottle of 120 or 60 tablets.

CAL-M
Calcium-Magnesium supplement

Description: Three tablets provide:

		% U.S. RDA*
Calcium (from calcium lactate)	250 mg	25
Magnesium (from magnesium oxide)	200 mg	50
Vitamin B1 (thiamine)	45 mg	3000
Vitamin B6 (pyridoxine HCl)	45 mg	2250
Niacin	90 mg	450
Vitamin D (ergocalciferol)	400 I.U.	100

*Percentage of U.S. Recommended Daily Allowance for adults and children four or more years of age.
Indication: CAL-M is a source of calcium and magnesium when it is desired to increase dietary intake of these minerals. CAL-M also contains other supportive factors including vitamin D which aids in the absorption of calcium.
Dosage and Administration: Usual adult dosage three tablets daily or as directed by physician.
How Supplied: Bottle of 90 tablets.

CHOLAGEST
Digestive aid

Description: CHOLAGEST is a complete formula containing digestive enzymes to aid in absorption of protein, fats and carbohydrates, and bile extract to aid in emulsifying fats. In addition, CHOLAGEST contains dehydrocholic acid which thins out thickened bile allowing for much smoother flow. Each tablet provides:

Pancreatic concentrate*	100 mg
Ox bile extract	65 mg
Dehydrocholic acid	20 mg

* Standardized to supply 10,000 Wilson Units of amylase, 9,000 Wilson Units of protease and 240 Wilson Units of lipase.
Indication: For use as a comprehensive formulation of natural enzymes to assist in the digestion of protein fats and carbohydrates.
Warning: Keep out of the reach of children.
Dosage and Administration: One or two tablets before each meal.
How Supplied: Bottle of 90 tablets.

TRI-88
Sustained release iron capsules

Description: TRI-88 is a sustained release formula containing iron, vitamins B12 and B1, and whole liver. Because the iron is slowly released over several hours and is present as the fumarate, intestinal disturbances and other uncomfortable side effects often associated with the administration of iron are minimized. Each capsule provides:

Iron (ferrous fumarate)	110 mg
Vitamin B1 (thiamine hydrochloride)	5 mg
Vitamin B12 (cyanocobalamin)	30 mcg
Whole liver	100 mg

Indication: For use as an iron supplement.
Warnings: Keep out of the reach of children. Not for pernicious anemia.
Dosage and Administration: One capsule daily after breakfast.
How Supplied: Bottle of 60 capsules. Available with child-resistant cap.

TRI-ADRENOPAN
Sustained release pantothenic acid capsules

Description: TRI-ADRENOPAN is a sustained release, high-potency pantothenic acid formula with vitamins C and B6, and other supportive factors. Two capsules provide:

Pantothenic acid (calcium pantothenate)	250 mg
Vitamin C (ascorbic acid)	100 mg
Vitamin B6 (pyridoxine hydrochloride)	25 mg

In a base containing whole adrenal substance, whole pituitary and liver.
Indication: For use as a pantothenic acid supplement.
Dosage and Administration: One or two capsules after breakfast and dinner.
How Supplied: Bottle of 60 capsules.

TRI-B3
Sustained release niacin capsules

Description: TRI-B3 is a sustained release niacin product supplied in specially coated pellets designed to release over several hours. This feature reduces or eliminates the flushing and skin irritation often present when administering straight niacin. Each capsule provides 300 mg of niacin.
Indications: For use as vitamin B3 (niacin) supplement.
Warning: Keep out of the reach of children.
Administration and Dosage: One capsule daily after breakfast.
How Supplied: Bottle of 90 capsules.

TRI-B-PLEX
Sustained release B-complex capsules

Description: TRI-B-PLEX is a complete, balanced, high-potency B-complex formula in sustained release form designed to release over an eight hour period ensuring maximum and efficient utilization and effectiveness. Two capsules provide:

Vitamin B1 (thiamine hydrochloride)	100 mg
Vitamin B2 (riboflavin)	40 mg
Niacinamide	200 mg
Vitamin B6 (pyridoxine hydrochloride)	50 mg
Folic acid	400 mcg
Vitamin B12 (cyanocobalamin)	25 mcg
Biotin	300 mcg
Pantothenic acid (calcium pantothenate)	100 mg

Indication: For use as a complete B-complex supplement.

Dosage and Administration: One capsule after breakfast and one after dinner.

How Supplied: Bottle of 60 capsules.

TRI–C–500
Sustained release vitamin C capsules

Description: TRI-C-500 is a high-potency, sustained release vitamin C product designed to maintain high blood and tissue levels of vitamin C throughout the day. TRI-C-500 provides 500 mg of vitamin C (ascorbic acid) per capsule.

Indication: For use as a vitamin C supplement.

Dosage and Administration: One capsule after breakfast and dinner.

How Supplied: Bottles of 120 and 60 capsules.

Arco Pharmaceuticals, Inc.
105 ORVILLE DRIVE
BOHEMIA, NY 11716

CODEXIN™ Extra Strength Capsules
Time Release Appetite suppressant and diuretic

Active Ingredients: Each continuous action capsule contains:
Phenylpropanolamine HCl ....75 mg.
Caffeine...200 mg.

Indication: For continuous all day appetite control.

Caution: For adult use only. Do not give this product to children under 12 years of age. Do not exceed recommended dose. If nervousness, dizziness, sleeplessness, rapid pulse, palpitations, or other symptoms occur discontinue medication and consult your physician. If you have, or are being treated for high blood pressure, heart diabetes, thyroid or other disease, or while pregnant, or nursing under the age of 18 do not take this drug except under the advice of a physician or pharmacist.

Precaution: If you are taking any prescription drugs or another medication containing Phenylpropanolamine do not take this drug except under the advice and supervision of a physician.

Dosage and Administration: One capsule in the morning between 10 and 11 o'clock with a full glass of water.

How Supplied: Continuous action capsules. Package of 21 and 42 with 1200 calorie diet plan.

MEGA–B®
(super potency vitamin B complex, sugar & starch free)

Composition: Each Mega-B Tablet contains the following Mega Vitamins:
B_1 (Thiamine Mononitrate) 100 mg.
B_2 (Riboflavin) 100 mg.
B_6 (Pyridoxine Hydrochloride) 100 mg.
B_{12} (Cyanocobalamin) 100 mcg.
Choline Bitartrate 100 mg.
Inositol 100 mg.
Niacinamide 100 mg.
Folic Acid 100 mcg.
Pantothenic Acid 100 mg.
d-Biotin 100 mcg.

Para-Aminobenzoic Acid (PABA) 100 mg.
In a base of yeast to provide the identified and unidentified B-Complex Factors.

Advantages: Each Mega-B capsule-shaped tablet provides the highest vitamin B complex available in a single dose. Mega-B was designed for those patients who require truly Mega vitamin potencies with the convenience of minimum dosage.

Indications: Mega-B is indicated in conditions characterized by depletions or increased demand of the water-soluble B-complex vitamins. It may be useful in the nutritional management of patients during prolonged convalescence associated with major surgery. It is also indicated for stress conditions, as an adjunct to antibiotics and diuretic therapy, pre and post operative cases, liver conditions, gastro-intestinal disorders interferring with intake or absorbtion of water-soluble vitamins, prolonged or wasting diseases, diabetes, burns, fractures, severe infections, and some psychological disorders.

Warning: NOT INTENDED FOR TREATMENT OF PERNICIOUS ANEMIA, OR OTHER PRIMARY OR SECONDARY ANEMIAS.

Dosage: Usual dosage is one Mega-B tablet daily, or varied, depending on clinical needs.

Supplied: Yellow capsule shaped tablets in bottles of 30, 100 and 500.

MEGADOSE™
(multiple mega-vitamin formula with minerals, sugar and starch free)

Composition:

Vitamin A	25,000 USP Units
Vitamin D	1,000 USP Units
Vitamin C w/Rose Hips	250 mg.
Vitamin E	100 IU
Folic Acid	400 mcg.
Vitamin B_1	80 mg.
Vitamin B_2	80 mg.
Niacinamide	80 mg.
Vitamin B_6	80 mg.
Vitamin B_{12}	80 mcg.
Bioten	80 mcg.
Pantothenic Acid	80 mg.
Choline Bitartrate	80 mg.
Inositol	80 mg.
Para-Aminobenzoic Acid	80 mg.
Rutin	30 mg.
Citrus Bioflavonoids	30 mg.
Betaine Hydrochloride	30 mg.
Glutamic Acid	30 mg.
Hesperidin Complex	5 mg.
Iodine (from Kelp)	0.15 mg.
Calcium Gluconate*	50 mg.
Zinc Gluconate*	25 mg.
Potassium Gluconate*	10 mg.
Ferrous Gluconate*	10 mg.
Magnesium Gluconate*	7 mg.
Manganese Gluconate*	6 mg.
Copper Gluconate*	0.5 mg.

*Natural mineral chelates in a base containing natural ingredients.

Dosage: One tablet daily.
Supplied: Capsule shaped tablets in bottles of 30, 100 and 250.

B. F. Ascher & Company, Inc.
15501 WEST 109th STREET
LENEXA, KS 66219
Mailing address:
P.O. BOX 827
KANSAS CITY, MO 64141

AYR® Saline Nasal Mist and Drops

AYR Mist or Drops restores vital moisture to provide prompt relief for dry, crusted and inflamed nasal membranes due to colds, low humidity, overuse of nasal decongestant drops and sprays, allergies, minor nose bleeds and other minor nasal irritations. AYR provides a soothing way to thin thick secretions and aid their removal from the nose and sinuses. AYR is not a decongestant and, therefore, can be used as often as needed without the side effects associated with overuse of decongestant nose drops and sprays.

SAFE & GENTLE ENOUGH FOR CHILDREN AND INFANTS
AYR Drops are particularly convenient for easy application with infants and children. AYR is formulated to prevent stinging, burning and irritation of delicate nasal tissue, even that of babies.

Directions For Use: SPRAY—Squeeze twice in each nostril as often as needed. DROPS—Two to four drops in each nostril every two hours as needed, or as directed by your physician.

AYR contains sodium chloride 0.65% buffered to a neutral pH and benzalkonium chloride and EDTA as antibacterial and antifungal preservatives.

How Supplied:
AYR Mist NDC 0225-0380-80 50 ml spray bottle
AYR Drops NDC 0225-0382-72 20 ml dropper bottle
Manufactured for B. F. Ascher & Company, Inc.

DALCA® Decongestant/Analgesic Tablets

Active Ingredients: Each DALCA tablet contains phenylpropanolamine hydrochloride 12.5 mg and magnesium salicylate 325 mg.

Indications: For the temporary relief of nasal congestion and headache, aches, pains and fever due to the common cold, sinusitis, hay fever, or other respiratory allergies.

Actions: DALCA helps clear nasal passages and temporarily restores freer breathing through the nose. DALCA helps decongest sinus passages and promotes sinus drainage. DALCA contains no sedatives or antihistamines and, therefore, does not produce drowsiness in most people. This makes DALCA especially suited for working people and others who must remain alert.

Continued on next page

Ascher—Cont.

Warnings: Do not give to children under 6 years of age except under the advice and supervision of a physician. If symptoms do not improve within 7 days or are accompanied by high fever, consult a physician before continuing use. Do not exceed recommended dosage because at higher doses nervousness, dizziness, or sleeplessness may occur. Do not take this product if you have stomach distress, ulcers, or bleeding problems, high blood pressure, heart disease, diabetes, thyroid disease, or if you are allergic to salicylates, except under the advice and supervision of a physician. Do not take this product during the last 3 months of pregnancy except under the advice and supervision of a physician.

Drug Interaction: Do not take this product if you are taking a prescription drug for anticoagulation (thinning the blood), diabetes, gout, arthritis, or an antihypertensive or antidepressant drug containing a monoamine oxidase inhibitor except under the advice and supervision of a physician.

Precaution: Keep Out Of Reach Of Children. In case of overdose, contact your physician or Poison Control Center immediately. Store in a dry place at room temperature.

Dosage and Administration: Adults: Two tablets every four hours. Do not exceed 12 tablets in 24 hours. Children (6 to 12 years): One tablet every four hours. Do not exceed 6 tablets in 24 hours.

How Supplied:
NDC 0225-0385-08   24 Tablets
NDC 0225-0385-04   48 Tablets
NDC 0225-0385-15   100 Tablets
Manufactured for B. F. Ascher & Company, Inc.

MOBIGESIC® Analgesic Tablets

Active Ingredients: 300 mg magnesium salicylate and 30 mg phenyltoloxamine citrate

Indications: MOBIGESIC is indicated for headaches, menstrual cramps, low back pain, muscular aches, toothaches, joint pain, discomfort of colds, flu, and sinusitis.

Actions: MOBIGESIC is a unique analgesic formulation which provides relief from pain and inflammation, relaxes muscles and reduces fever.

Warning: Keep this and all drugs out of the reach of children. In case of accidental overdose, call your doctor or poison control center immediately. Store at room temperature.

Usual Dosage: Adults—1 or 2 tablets every four hours, up to 10 tablets daily. Children (6 to 12 years)—1 tablet every 4 hours, up to 5 tablets daily. Do not use more than 10 days unless directed by physician.

Caution: When used for the temporary symptomatic relief of colds, if relief does not occur within 7 days (3 days for fever), discontinue use and consult physician. This preparation may cause drowsiness. Do not drive or operate machinery while taking this medication. Do not adminis-

ter to children under 6 years of age or exceed recommended dosage unless directed by physician.

How Supplied:
NDC 0225-0355-12   Package of 18 tablets
NDC 0225-0355-10   Bottle of 50 tablets
NDC 0225-0355-15   Bottle of 100 tablets
Manufactured for B.F. Ascher & Company, Inc.

MOBISYL® Analgesic Creme

Active Ingredient: Triethanolamine salicylate 10%

Description: MOBISYL is a greaseless, odorless, penetrating, analgesic creme.

Indications: For adults and children, 12 years of age and older, MOBISYL is indicated for the temporary relief of minor aches and pains of muscles and joints, such as simple backache, lumbago, arthritis, neuralgia, strains, bruises and sprains.

Actions: MOBISYL penetrates fast into sore, tender joints and muscles where pain originates. It works to reduce inflammation. Helps soothe stiff joints and muscles and gets you going again. There is no burning sensation when you apply MOBISYL, only soothing relief, and MOBISYL doesn't irritate normal skin. MOBISYL won't stain clothing and has no tell-tale medicine smell.

Warnings: For external use only. Avoid contact with the eyes. Discontinue use if condition worsens or if symptoms persist for more than 7 days, and consult a physician. Do not use on children under 12 years of age except under the advice and supervision of a physician. In case of accidental ingestion, seek professional assistance or contact a Poison Control Center immediately. Close cap tightly. Keep this and all drugs out of the reach of children. Store at room temperature.

Dosage and Administration: Place a liberal amount of MOBISYL Creme in your palm and massage into the area of pain and soreness three or four times a day, especially before retiring. MOBISYL may be worn under makeup or bandages.

How Supplied:
NDC 0225-0360-33   1.25 oz tubes
NDC 0225-0360-11   3.5 oz tubes
NDC 0225-0360-35   8 oz jars
Manufactured for B.F. Ascher & Co., Inc.

SOFT 'N SOOTHE® Creme

Active Ingredients: Benzocaine and menthol. Soft 'N Soothe also contains natural oat protein, lanolin oil, light weight mineral oil, and lanolin alcohol, to help give you soft, luxurious-feeling skin.

Indications: Soft 'N Soothe is medicated for the relief of itching and pain associated with dryness of skin, poison ivy, and non-poisonous insect bites. Soft 'N Soothe may also be used to relieve itching and pain in external anal and external vaginal areas.

Actions: Soft 'N Soothe is a greaseless, moisturizing creme for the relief of itching and pain. The vanishing, moisturiz-

ing creme penetrates the skin to aid in natural healing.

Warning: For external use only. Avoid contact with the eyes. Keep this and all medication out of reach of children. In case of accidental ingestion, seek professional assistance or contact a Poison Control Center immediately. Close cap tightly. Store at room temperature.

Precaution: If condition worsens, or if symptoms persist for more than 7 days, discontinue use of the product and consult a physician.

For use on children under 12, consult your physician.

Dosage and Administration: Apply Soft 'N Soothe liberally to affected areas. Repeat as needed 3 to 4 times daily and before retiring.

How Supplied:
NDC 0225-0370-09   50 gram tubes
Manufactured for B.F. Ascher & Company, Inc.

UNILAX™ Laxative Tablets

Active Ingredients: Each UNILAX tablet contains danthron 75 mg and docusate sodium 150 mg.

Indications: UNILAX is a dual-acting laxative and stool softener for the relief of constipation.

Actions: UNILAX promotes bowel movement by acting directly on the intestine and has an added ingredient which penetrates and softens the stool for gentle, effective relief of constipation.

Warnings: Do not use when abdominal pain, nausea or vomiting is present. Frequent or prolonged use of this preparation may result in dependence on laxatives. May cause a harmless discoloration of the urine. If you have noticed a sudden change in bowel habits that has persisted over a period of 2 weeks, consult a physician before using a laxative.

Dosage and Administration: Adults: One tablet daily (preferably at bedtime) or as directed by a physician. Do not use in children under 12 years old except under the advice and supervision of a physician.

How Supplied:
NDC 0225-0390-75   10 Tablets
NDC 0225-0390-85   20 Tablets
Manufactured for B. F. Ascher & Company, Inc.

IDENTIFICATION PROBLEM?

Consult the

Product Identification Section

where you'll find

products pictured

in full color.

Astra Pharmaceutical Products, Inc.
7 NEPONSET ST.
WORCESTER, MA 01606

XYLOCAINE® (lidocaine) 2.5% OINTMENT

Composition: Diethylaminoacet-2, 6-xylidide 2.5% in a water miscible ointment vehicle consisting of polyethylene glycols and propylene glycol.

Action and Uses: A topical anesthetic ointment for fast, temporary relief of pain and itching due to minor burns, sunburn, minor cuts, abrasions, insect bites and minor skin irritations. The ointment can be easily removed with water. It is ineffective when applied to intact skin.

Administration and Dosage: Apply topically in liberal amounts for adequate control of symptoms. When the anesthetic effect wears off additional ointment may be applied as needed.

Important Warning: *In persistent, severe or extensive skin disorders, advise patient to use only as directed. In case of accidental ingestion advise patient to seek professional assistance or to contact a poison control center immediately. Keep out of the reach of children.*

Caution: *Do not use in the eyes. Not for prolonged use. If the condition for which this preparation is used persists or if a rash or irritation develops, advise patient to discontinue use and consult a physician.*

How Supplied: Available in tube of 35 grams (approximately 1.25 ounces).

Ayerst Laboratories
Division of American Home
Products Corporation
685 THIRD AVE.
NEW YORK, NY 10017

BEMINAL STRESS PLUS™
Stress potency replacement vitamins

BEMINAL STRESS PLUS™
with Iron

Each tablet contains:	% U.S. RDA*
Vitamin B1 as	1717%
thiamine mononitrate, U.S.P. 25.0 mg	
Vitamin B2 as	735%
riboflavin, U.S.P. 12.5 mg	
Vitamin B3 as	504%
niacinamide 100.0 mg	
Vitamin B5 as	184%
calcium pantothenate, U.S.P. 20.0 mg	
Vitamin B6 as	411%
pyridoxine hydrochloride, U.S.P. 10.0 mg	
Vitamin B12 as	417%
cyanocobalamin 25.0 mcg	
Vitamin Bc as	100%
folic acid, U.S.P. 400.0 mcg	
Vitamin C as	1166%
sodium ascorbate, U.S.P. 787 mg	
Vitamin E as	150%
dl-α-tocopheryl acetate 45.0 I.U.	
Iron as	150%
ferrous fumarate, U.S.P. 82.2 mg	

*percentage of U.S. recommended daily allowance

BEMINAL STRESS PLUS™
with Zinc

Each tablet contains:	% U.S. RDA*
Vitamin B1 as	1717%
thiamine mononitrate, U.S.P. 25.0 mg	
Vitamin B2 as	735%
riboflavin, U.S.P. 12.5 mg	
Vitamin B3 as	504%
niacinamide 100.0 mg	
Vitamin B5 as	184%
calcium pantothenate, U.S.P. 20.0 mg	
Vitamin B6 as	411%
pyridoxine hydrochloride, U.S.P. 10.0 mg	
Vitamin B12 as	417%
cyanocobalamin 25.0 mcg	
Vitamin C as	1166%
sodium ascorbate, U.S.P. 787 mg	
Vitamin E as	150%
dl-α-tocopheryl acetate 45.0 I.U.	
Zinc as	300%
zinc sulfate 111.1 mg	

*percentage of U.S. recommended daily allowance

Indication: Dietary supplement.

Action and Uses: The BEMINAL STRESS PLUS formulas can help replenish the vitamins and minerals depleted by the stress of sickness, infections, and surgery. BEMINAL STRESS PLUS formulas may also be used where the demand on the body's store of vitamins and minerals may be increased by dieting, lack of sleep, the use of alcohol or cigarettes, jogging and other strenuous physical exercise.

Recommended Intake: *Adults,* one tablet daily.

How Supplied: BEMINAL STRESS PLUS with Iron—bottles of 60 tablets. BEMINAL STRESS PLUS with Zinc— bottles of 60 tablets.
[*Shown in Product Identification Section*]

DERMOPLAST®
Topical Anesthetic First Aid Spray

Contains (exclusive of propellants) 20% benzocaine and 0.5% menthol in a water-dispersible base of TWEEN® 85 and polyethylene glycol 400 monolaurate with methylparaben as a preservative.

A topical anesthetic and antipruritic spray providing soothing, temporary relief of skin pain, itching, and discomfort due to sunburn, minor wounds, insect bites, abrasions, burns and minor skin irritations. May be applied without touching sensitive affected areas. Widely used in hospitals for pain and itch of episiotomy, pruritus vulvae, postpartum hemorrhoids.

Warnings: FOR EXTERNAL USE ONLY. Avoid spraying in eyes. Contents under pressure. Do not puncture or incinerate. Do not expose to heat or temperatures above 120° F. Do not use near open flame. Use only as directed. Intentional misuse by deliberately concentrating and inhaling the contents can be harmful or fatal.

Do not take orally. Not for prolonged use. If the condition for which this preparation is used persists or if a rash or irritation develops, discontinue use and consult physician.

Directions for Use: Hold can in a convenient position 6–12 inches away from affected area. Point spray nozzle and

press button. To apply to face, spray in palm of hand. May be administered three or four times daily, or as directed by physician.

How Supplied: DERMOPLAST Aerosol Spray, in Net Wt 3 oz (85 g)—NDC 0046-1008-03; and in Net Wt 6 oz (170 g)—NDC 0046-1008-06.
[*Shown in Product Identification Section*]

KERODEX®
Skin Barrier Cream

Action and Uses: A specially formulated barrier hand cream to help protect against potentially irritating chemicals, compounds, and solutions in common use. When applied and used as directed, KERODEX provides a barrier film that helps to block contact with skin irritants. KERODEX No. 71 (water-repellent) is for use in handling or working with *wet* materials; No. 51 is for *dry* or *oily* work. KERODEX is greaseless and stainless.

Application: 1. Wash hands clean and dry *thoroughly*. 2. Squeeze out ½ inch of cream into palm of one hand. Rub hands together with a washing motion until cream is *lightly* and *evenly* distributed, leaving no excess. Make sure cream reaches under nails, around cuticles, between fingers, across wrists and backs of hands (forearms, if necessary). 3. A second application is recommended. **NOTE:** After applying KERODEX 71, "set" by holding hands under cold running water. Pat dry. After applying KERODEX 51, avoid contact with water. If hands become wet during work, reapply.

How Supplied: KERODEX (water-repellent cream for wet work), in 4 oz (113 g) tubes (NDC 0046-0071-04) and 1 lb jars (NDC 0046-0071-01). KERODEX (water-miscible cream for dry or oily work), in 4 oz (113 g) tubes (NDC 0046-0051-04) and 1 lb jars (NDC 0046-0051-01).
[*Shown in Product Identification Section*]

RIOPAN®
magaldrate
Antacid

RIOPAN is a chemical entity (not a physical mixture), providing the advantages of a true buffer-antacid (not simply a neutralizing agent): (1) rapid action; (2) uniform buffering action; (3) high acid-consuming capacity; (4) no alkalinization or acid rebound.

Low Sodium Content: Not more than 0.3 mg of sodium—per teaspoonful (5 ml) suspension—per chew tablet—per swallow tablet.

Acid-neutralizing Capacity— 13.5 mEq/5 ml or tablet.

Indications: For the relief of upset stomach associated with heartburn, sour stomach, and/or acid indigestion. For symptomatic relief of hyperacidity associated with the diagnosis of peptic ulcer, gastritis, peptic esophagitis, gastric hyperacidity, and hiatal hernia.

Directions: RIOPAN (magaldrate) Antacid *Suspension*—Recommended dosage, one or two teaspoonfuls, between meals and at bedtime, or as directed by the physician. RIOPAN Antacid *Chew Tablets*

Continued on next page

Ayerst—Cont.

—Recommended dosage, one or two tablets, between meals at bedtime, or as directed by the physician. Chew before swallowing. RIOPAN Antacid *Swallow Tablets*—Recommended dosage, one or two tablets, between meals at bedtime, or as directed by the physician. Take with enough water to swallow promptly.

Drug Interaction Precaution: Do not use in patients taking a prescription antibiotic drug containing any form of tetracycline.

Warnings: Patients should not take more than 20 teaspoonfuls (or 20 tablets) in a 24-hour period or use this maximum dosage for more than two weeks, except under the advice and supervision of a physician. If you have kidney disease, do not use this product except under the advice and supervision of a physician.

How Supplied: RIOPAN Antacid *Suspension*—Each teaspoonful (5 ml) contains 480 mg magaldrate, in 12 fl oz (355 ml) bottles (NDC 0046-0933-12). Individual Cups, 1 fl oz (30 ml) ea., tray of 10—10 trays per packer (NDC 0046-0933-99). RIOPAN Antacid *Chew Tablets*—Each tablet contains 480 mg magaldrate. Packages of 60 (NDC 0046-0928-60) and 100 (NDC 0046-0928-81) in individual film strips (10 x 6 and 10 x 10, respectively). RIOPAN Antacid *Swallow Tablets* —Each tablet contains 480 mg magaldrate. Packages of 60 (NDC 0046-0927-60) and 100 (NDC 0046-0927-81) in individual film strips (6 x 10 and 10 x 10, respectively).

[*Shown in Product Identification Section*]

RIOPAN PLUS®
magaldrate and SIMETHICONE
Antacid/Anti-Gas

Each teaspoonful (5 ml) of Suspension contains:

Magaldrate	480 mg
Simethicone	20 mg

Each Chew Tablet contains:

Magaldrate	480 mg
Simethicone	20 mg

Low Sodium Content: Not more than 0.3 mg per teaspoonful (5 ml) or Chew Tablet.

Acid-neutralizing Capacity— 13.5 mEq/5 ml or Chew Tablet.

Indications: For the relief of upset stomach associated with heartburn, sour stomach, and/or acid indigestion, accompanied by the symptoms of gas. For symptomatic relief of hyperacidity associated with the diagnosis of peptic ulcer, gastritis, peptic esophagitis, gastric hyperacidity, and hiatal hernia. For postoperative gas pain or for use in endoscopic examinations.

Directions: RIOPAN PLUS (magaldrate and SIMETHICONE) *Suspension* —Recommended dosage, one or two teaspoonfuls between meals and at bedtime, or as directed by the physician.

RIOPAN PLUS *Chew Tablets*—Recommended dosage, one or two tablets, between meals and at bedtime, or as directed by the physician. Chew before swallowing.

Drug Interaction Precaution: Do not use in patients taking a prescription antibiotic drug containing any form of tetracycline.

Warnings: Patients should not take more than 20 teaspoonfuls (or 20 tablets) in a 24-hour period or use this maximum dosage for more than two weeks, except under the advice and supervision of a physician. If you have kidney disease, do not use this product except under the advice and supervision of a physician.

How Supplied: RIOPAN PLUS *Suspension*—in 12 fl oz (355 ml) plastic bottles (NDC 0046-0937-12). Individual Cups, 1 fl oz (30 ml) ea.—10—10 trays per packer (NDC 0046-0937-99). RIOPAN PLUS *Chew Tablets*—in bottles of 60 (NDC 0046-0930-60).

[*Shown in Product Identification Section*]

Baker/Cummins
Div. of Key Pharmaceuticals, Inc.
50 N.W. 176TH STREET
MIAMI, FLORIDA 33169

ACNO ASTRINGENT

Composition: Isopropyl alcohol, water, laureth-23, fragrance, tetrasodium EDTA.

Actions and Uses: ACNO ASTRINGENT is formulated to aid in removing excess oil and grime associated with acne conditions. It contains a lipophylic surfactant which enhances its lipid solvent properties.

Directions: Saturate a cotton pad and wipe areas to be cleaned two or three times daily.

Caution: For external use only. Avoid contact with eyes or mucous membranes. Keep out of the reach of children.

Warning: Flammable

How Supplied: ACNO ASTRINGENT is available in 8-fluid ounce bottles.

ACNO LOTION

Composition: Active ingredients—3% sulfur and 2% salicylic acid.

Actions and Usage: ACNO LOTION is an effective aid for acne and related skin conditions. The vehicle used in ACNO LOTION is pleasant and cosmetically elegant.

Directions: Shake well before using. Cleanse affected areas and apply twice daily unless otherwise directed by physician.

Caution: For external use only. Discontinue use if excessive irritation of the skin develops. Avoid contact with eyes or mucous membranes. Keep out of the reach of children.

How Supplied: ACNO LOTION is available in 2-fluid ounce bottles.

P&S® LIQUID

Composition: P&S Liquid is a specially prepared mixture of liquid paraffin oil, sodium chloride and phenol, less than 1%.

Action and Uses: P&S Liquid provides safe and effective management of scaling conditions of the scalp resulting from psoriasis or seborrhea. It has a relatively high capacity to remove scale from lesions without the disagreeable greasiness, odor, staining and irritation so common to preparations used in psoriasis.

Directions: Shake well before using. Apply P&S Liquid liberally to scalp lesions. Gently massage to loosen scales and crusts, without breaking skin. Use this treatment at night before retiring, and shampoo each morning after treatment. Repeat daily as needed. If other topical agents are used during the day, nightly use of P&S Liquid will aid in removing the heavy scale of psoriasis.

Caution: Do not apply to large portions of body surfaces. If irritation should occur during treatment—discontinue use. Keep preparation out of eyes.

How Supplied: P&S Liquid available in 4 and 8 fl oz bottles.

P&S® PLUS

Description: A moisturizing gel formulated to remove scales while it moisturizes and soothes affected areas of skin and scalp. P&S PLUS penetrates quickly to promote relief from itching and flaking. It is a moisturizing tar gel with an aqueous base. (Due to coal tar solution the formulation contains 6.4% alcohol). Staining is minimal.

Composition: P&S PLUS contains 8% Coal Tar Solution (1.6% crude coal tar) and 2% salicylic acid as active ingredients.

Actions and Uses: Helps remove scales of skin and scalp and helps relieve the discomfort of psoriasis and other scaling conditions.

Directions: Apply to affected areas of skin and scalp once or twice daily or as directed by physician.

Caution: For external use only. Avoid contact with eyes. Flush with water if product gets into eyes. Do not use on highly inflamed or broken skin. If undue irritation develops, wash off with soap and water and consult physician if necessary. After application, avoid excessive exposure to direct sunlight, unless directed by physician. Keep this and all drugs out of children's reach.

How Supplied: P&S PLUS is available in 3.5 ounce jars.

P&S® SHAMPOO
Antiseborrheic Shampoo

Composition: P&S Shampoo contains 2% Salicylic Acid and 0.5% Lactic Acid as active ingredients.

Action and Uses: P&S Shampoo, used regularly, helps control scaling problems of the scalp associated with psoriasis and severe seborrhea. While this unique formulation was designed to complement the action of P&S Liquid treatment, it also effectively controls scaling problems between such treatments while leaving hair clean, fresh and manageable.

Directions: Wet hair thoroughly, apply P&S Shampoo, lather and rinse. Reapply, lather and rinse again. Repeat if necessary, or as directed by physician.

Caution: For external use only. Discontinue use if excessive irritation of the skin develops. Avoid contact with eyes or mucous membranes. Keep out of the reach of children.

How Supplied: P&S Shampoo available in 4 fluid ounce bottles.

PANSCOL®
Lotion and Ointment

Composition: PANSCOL Lotion and Ointment are specially compounded emollients containing 3% salicylic acid, 2% lactic acid and less than 1% phenol.

Action and Uses: PANSCOL Lotion and Ointment provide emollient action for dry, scaly skin and relief of associated itching. PANSCOL Ointment may be preferred for more severe scaling conditions.

Directions: Apply to dry, scaly areas twice daily unless otherwise directed by physician.

Caution: For external use only. Discontinue use if excessive irritation of the skin develops. Avoid contact with eyes or mucous membranes. Keep out of the reach of children.

How Supplied: PANSCOL Lotion available in 4 fl. oz. bottles. PANSCOL Ointment available in 3 oz. jars.

ULTRA MIDE MOISTURIZER

Composition: Water, urea 25%, mineral oil, lanolin, oil, glycerin, propylene glycol, petrolatum, glyceryl stearate, PEG-50 stearate, cetyl alcohol, propylene glycol stearate SE, lactic acid, sorbitan laurate, fragrance, potassium sorbate, tetrasodium EDTA.

Actions and Uses: ULTRA MIDE is formulated with selected emollients and moisturizers to render dry, rough skin soft and pliable.

Directions: Apply one to four times daily unless otherwise directed by physician.

Caution: For external use only. Store in cool place.

How Supplied: ULTRA MIDE MOISTURIZER is available in 6-fluid ounce bottles.

XSEB® SHAMPOO

Composition: Contains 4% salicylic acid and a blend of surface active agents to potentiate the keratolytic effect of the salicylic acid.

Action & Uses: Xseb Shampoo helps provide temporary control of scaling associated with dandruff and seborrheic dermatitis.

Directions: Wet hair thoroughly, apply Xseb Shampoo, massaging into scalp for 2–3 minutes. Rinse and reapply. Shampoo once or twice weekly or as directed by physician.

As Oily Skin Cleanser: Massage into moistened skin. Leave on for 2–3 minutes before rinsing off.

Caution: For external use only. Discontinue use if excessive irritation of the skin develops. Avoid contact with eyes or mucous membranes. Keep out of the reach of children.

How Supplied: Xseb Shampoo is available in 4-fluid ounce bottles.

XSEB®–T SHAMPOO

Composition: Contains 10% coal tar solution and 4% salicylic acid in a blend of surface active agents.

Action & Uses: Helps control scaling and itching associated with seborrhea, psoriasis and chronic eczematous conditions of the scalp.

Directions: Wet hair thoroughly. Apply Xseb-T Shampoo, massaging into scalp for 2–3 minutes. Rinse and reapply. Use twice weekly or as directed by physician.

Caution: For external use only. Discontinue use if excessive irritation of the skin develops. Avoid contact with eyes or mucous membranes. Keep out of the reach of children.

How Supplied: Xseb-T Shampoo is available in 4-fluid ounce bottles.

Bausch & Lomb, Inc.
Personal Products Division
1400 N. GOODMAN ST.
ROCHESTER, NY 14692

BAUSCH & LOMB®
STERILE DAILY CLEANER

Sterile cleaning solution for use with heat (thermal) or cold (chemical) disinfection of soft (hydrophilic) contact lenses or lenses made from other new polymers.

Description: A sterile, buffered, isotonic aqueous solution consisting of sodium phosphates, sodium chloride, tyloxapol, hydroxyethylcellulose, and polyvinyl alcohol, with thimerosal 0.004% and edetate disodium 0.2% added as preservatives.

Action: When lenses are thoroughly cleaned with BAUSCH & LOMB® Sterile Daily Cleaner and rinsed, mucus and other deposits which may accumulate on the lens surfaces are removed.

Administration: Wash and rinse hands thoroughly before handling lenses. Apply 3 drops BAUSCH & LOMB® Daily Cleaner to each lens surface and thoroughly clean lenses by rubbing between fingers for 20 seconds. Thoroughly rinse lenses free of debris with BAUSCH & LOMB® Sterile Saline Solution or Sterile Preserved Saline Solution if you use heat (thermal) disinfection, or with BAUSCH & LOMB® Disinfecting Solution if you use cold (chemical) disinfection. Disinfect and store lenses in accordance with the lens care procedures recommended by eye care practitioner.

Warnings: BAUSCH & LOMB® Sterile Daily Cleaner is not intended for use directly in the eye. Store at room temperature. Lens care procedures as recommended by practitioner must be followed daily. Failure to follow these procedures may result in development of serious eye infections.

Contraindications: This solution is contraindicated in patients with a history of allergic hypersensitivity to mercury compounds (thimerosal).

How Supplied: 1.5 FL. OZ. (45ml) plastic bottles.
[*Shown in Product Identification Section*]

BAUSCH & LOMB®
STERILE DISINFECTING SOLUTION

Sterile Solution for Rinsing, Storing and cold (chemical) Disinfection of soft (hydrophilic) contact lenses or lenses made from other new polymers.

Description: A suitably buffered aqueous solution containing sodium chloride, sodium borate and boric acid and having a tonicity of approximately 289 mOsm. Preserved with thimerosal 0.001, edetate disodium 0.1% and chlorhexidine 0.005%.

Administration: After cleaning with BAUSCH & LOMB® Sterile Daily Cleaner, thoroughly rinse both lens surfaces with BAUSCH & LOMB® Sterile Disinfecting Solution for approximately 10 seconds to remove debris. Place lens in lens storage case and fill each well of the case with enough BAUSCH & LOMB® Sterile Disinfecting Solution to cover the lens. Always check to see that the lens is completely submerged. To ensure disinfection, the lens must be stored in BAUSCH & LOMB® Sterile Disinfecting Solution for a minimum of 4 hours before reinsertion. Prior to reinsertion of lenses, rinse thoroughly with fresh BAUSCH & LOMB® Sterile Disinfecting Solution.

Warnings: Fresh BAUSCH & LOMB® Sterile Disinfecting Solution must be used daily for storage. NEVER REUSE BAUSCH & LOMB® Sterile Disinfecting Solution. Lens care procedures, as recommended by practitioner, must be followed daily. Failure to follow these procedures may result in development of serious eye infections. NEVER HEAT LENSES IN BAUSCH & LOMB® Sterile Disinfecting Solution. Do not touch the dropper tip of the BAUSCH & LOMB® Sterile Disinfecting Solution to any surface, since this may contaminate the solution. When Enzymatic Contact Lens Cleaner (Papain) is used in conjunction with Disinfecting Solution, care must be taken to effectively clean and thoroughly rinse the lens after enzyme treatment and before lens disinfection. Store at room temperature. Keep from freezing.

Contraindications: This solution is contraindicated in patients with history of allergic hypersensitivity to mercury compound (thimerosal).

How Supplied: 8 FL. OZ. (237ml) and 12 FL. OZ. (335ml) plastic bottles.
[*Shown in Product Identification Section*]

BAUSCH & LOMB®
STERILE LENS LUBRICANT

A sterile lubricating and rewetting solution for use with conventional

Continued on next page

Bausch & Lomb—Cont.

hard and soft (hydrophilic) contact lens, and contact lenses made from other new polymers.

Description: A sterile buffered isotonic aqueous solution consisting of povidone with Polyoxyethylene. Thimerosal 0.004% and edetate disodium 0.1% added as preservatives.

Actions: Rewets the lens and may help remove particulate material.

Administration: Place one drop of BAUSCH & LOMB® Sterile Lens Lubricant on each lens 3 or 4 times a day or as needed. If minor irritation, discomfort, or blurring occur while wearing lenses, place a drop of BAUSCH & LOMB® Sterile Lens Lubricant on the eye and blink 2 or 3 times.

Warnings: If discomfort persists after using BAUSCH & LOMB® Sterile Lens Lubricant, remove lenses and see eye care practitioner. Do not touch the dropper tip of the BAUSCH & LOMB® Sterile Lens Lubricant bottle to any surface, since this may contaminate the solution. Protect from light, store at room temperature.

Contraindications: This solution is contraindicated in patients with a history of allergic hypersensitivity to mercury compounds (thimerosal).

How Supplied: 0.5 FL. OZ. (15ml) plastic bottles.

[*Shown in Product Identification Section*]

BAUSCH & LOMB® STERILE PRESERVED SALINE SOLUTION

For use in heat disinfection, rinsing and storage of soft (hydrophilic) contact lenses.

Description: A sterile buffered isotonic aqueous solution containing boric acid, sodium borate and sodium chloride 0.7%. Preserved with thimerosal 0.001% and edetate disodium 0.1%.

Administration: After cleaning lenses with BAUSCH & LOMB® Sterile Daily Cleaner, BAUSCH & LOMB® Sterile Preserved Saline is used to rinse lenses free of loosened debris and traces of the cleaner. Disinfection of lenses is accomplished by immersing lenses in BAUSCH & LOMB® Sterile Preserved Saline Solution in the carrying case and heating them in a BAUSCH & LOMB® Disinfecting Unit. If no heating unit is available, lenses may be disinfected by immersing them in BAUSCH & LOMB® Sterile Preserved Saline Solution in the carrying case and dropping the sealed case into a pan of already boiling water. Remove the pan from heat after ten minutes and allow the water to cool before removing your lenses.

Warnings: Fresh BAUSCH & LOMB® Sterile Preserved Saline Solution must be used daily for disinfection and storage. NEVER REUSE BAUSCH & LOMB® Sterile Preserved Saline Solution. Lens care procedures, as recommended by practitioner, must be followed daily.

Failure to follow these procedures may result in development of serious eye infections. Do not touch the dropper tip of the BAUSCH & LOMB Sterile Preserved Saline Solution bottle to any surface, since this may contaminate the solution. Store at room temperature.

Contraindications: This solution is contraindicated in patients with a history of allergic hypersensitivity to mercury compounds (thimerosal).

How Supplied: 4 FL. OZ. (118ml), 8 FL. OZ. (237 ml), and 12 FL. OZ. (355ml) plastic bottles.

[*Shown in Product Identification Section*]

BAUSCH & LOMB® STERILE SALINE SOLUTION (Preservative-free)

For heat disinfection, rinsing, and storage of soft (hydrophilic) contact lenses.

Description: A sterile isotonic aqueous solution of 0.9% sodium chloride. It contains no antimicrobial agents.

Administration: Rinsing lenses with entire contents of BAUSCH AND LOMB® Saline Solution packet after cleaning will remove loosened debris. Disinfection of lenses is accomplished by immersing the lenses in BAUSCH & LOMB® Saline Solution in the BAUSCH & LOMB® Lens Carrying Case and heating in a BAUSCH & LOMB® Disinfecting Unit. If a Disinfecting Unit is not available, lenses may be disinfected by immersing them in BAUSCH & LOMB® Saline Solution in the lens carrying case and dropping the sealed case into a pan of already boiling water. Remove the pan from heat after ten minutes and allow the water to cool before removing lenses.

Warnings: Fresh BAUSCH & LOMB® Saline Solution must be used daily for disinfection and storage. NEVER REUSE BAUSCH & LOMB® Saline Solution, as eye infection might result. Do not touch pouring area of the BAUSCH & LOMB® Saline Solution package to any surface since this may contaminate the solution. Store at room temperature. Lens care procedures as recommended by practitioner must be followed daily. Failure to follow these procedures may result in development of serious eye infections. If irritation occurs and persists or increases, discontinue use and consult eye care practitioner.

How Supplied: ⅓ FL. OZ. (10ml) single-dose foil packets in cartons of 14 and 35.

[*Shown in Product Identification Section*]

Products are cross-indexed by generic and chemical names in the

YELLOW SECTION

Beach Pharmaceuticals
Division of BEACH PRODUCTS, INC.
5220 SOUTH MANHATTAN AVE.
TAMPA, FL 33611

BEELITH Tablets
Magnesium Oxide with Vitamin B₆

Each tablet contains: Magnesium oxide 600 mg and pyridoxine hydrochloride (Vitamin B_6) 25 mg equivalent to B_6 20 mg.

Dosage: The usual adult dose is one or two tablets daily.

Actions and Uses: BEELITH is a dietary supplement for patients deficient in magnesium and/or pyridoxine. Each tablet yields approximately 362 mg of elemental magnesium & supplies 1000% of the Adult U.S. Recommended Daily Allowance (RDA) for vitamin B_6 & 90% of the RDA for magnesium.

Precaution: Excessive dosage might cause laxation.

Caution: Use only under the supervision of a physician. Use with caution in renal insufficiency.

Drug Interaction Precautions: Do not take this product if you are presently taking a prescription antibiotic drug containing any form of tetracycline.

Warning: Keep this and all drugs out of the reach of children. In case of accidental overdose, seek professional assistance or contact a Poison Control Center immediately.

Storage: Keep tightly closed. Store at controlled room temperature 15°C–30°C (59°F–86°F).

How Supplied: Bottles of 100 and 500 tablets.

Becton Dickinson Consumer Products
365 W. PASSAIC STREET
ROCHELLE PARK, NJ 07662

CANKAID®
(carbamide peroxide 10%)
Antiseptic Treatment for the Mouth

Active Ingredient: Carbamide peroxide 10% in specially prepared anhydrous glycerol. Artificial flavor added.

Indications and Actions: CANKAID gives quick, temporary relief from minor mouth irritations such as canker sores, sore or injured gums, and inflammation caused by dentures, mouth appliances (orthodontics), or dental procedures. CANKAID cleanses oral wounds and inflammation gently but thoroughly with its antiseptic, microfoaming action. CANKAID coats and clings to tissue, prolonging its soothing, protective effects.

Precaution: If severe or persistent symptoms occur in the mouth or throat, consult physician or dentist promptly. Do not administer to children under three years of age unless directed by physician or dentist. Keep out of reach of children.

Dosage and Administration: Do not dilute. Use four times daily, or as directed by physician or dentist. Apply directly onto affected area with painless, no touch tip. To treat widespread inflammation or hard to reach areas, apply 10 drops onto tongue; mix with saliva; swish thoroughly; expectorate.

How Supplied: CANKAID comes in liquid form, in ¾ fl. oz. plastic bottles.

MERCUROCHROME II™
Antiseptic/Double Anesthetic First Aid Spray and Liquid

Active Ingredients: Lidocaine HCl, Menthol, Benzalkonium Chloride, Isopropyl Alcohol 5%

Actions and Indications: MERCUROCHROME II contains a safe and effective germ killing ingredient plus two pain relieving anesthetics. It is indicated for minor burns, cuts, scrapes, insect bites, and sunburn. It does not sting or irritate injured skin. MERCUROCHROME II is colorless; it will not stain clothes or skin.

Precaution: For external use only. In case of deep or puncture wounds, or serious burns, consult physician. If irritation or swelling develops or persists, or if infection occurs, discontinue use and consult physician. KEEP OUT OF REACH OF CHILDREN. Do not use near the eyes. In case of accidental ingestion seek professional assistance. Do not use in large quantities, particularly over raw surfaces or blistered areas. Benzalkonium chloride is inactivated by contact with soap.

Dosage and Administration: SPRAY—Hold bottle 3 to 6 inches from skin surface; spray until affected area is completely wetted.

LIQUID—Apply directly onto affected area with attached applicator rod.

How Supplied: 2 fl. oz. pump spray bottle, 1 fl. oz. applicator bottle.

Beecham Products
DIVISION OF BEECHAM INC.
POST OFFICE BOX 1467
PITTSBURGH, PA 15230

B.F.I.®
Antiseptic First-Aid Powder

Active Ingredient: Bismuth-Formic-Iodide 16.0%. Other ingredients—Boric Acid, Bismuth Subgallate, Zinc Phenolsulfonate, Potassium Alum, Thymol, Amol (mono-n-amyl hydroquinone ether), Menthol, Eucalyptol, and inert diluents.

Indications: For cuts, abrasions, minor burns, skin irritations, athlete's foot and dermatitis due to poison ivy and poison oak.

Actions: B.F.I. First-Aid Powder promotes healing of cuts, scratches, abrasions and minor burns. Relieves itching, chafing and irritations from prickly heat, sunburn, mosquito bites, athlete's foot and poison ivy and oak.

Warnings: Keep out of reach of children. If redness, irritation, swelling or pain persists or increases or if infection occurs, discontinue use and consult physician. For deep or puncture wounds or serious burns, consult physician.

Symptoms and Treatment of Oral Overdosage: In the event of ingestion of large quantities, consult a physician, local poison control center, or the Rocky Mt. Poison Control Center at (303)-629-1123, 24 hours a day.

Dosage and Administration: Freely sprinkle B.F.I. on the injured area to completely cover the area. Avoid use on extensive denuded (raw) areas particularly on infants and children.

How Supplied: ¼ oz., 1¼ oz. and 8 oz. shaker top container.

CHILDREN'S HOLD®
4 Hour Cough Suppressant and Decongestant Lozenge

Active Ingredient: 3.75 mg. dextromethorphan HBr and 6.25 mg. phenylpropanolamine HCl per lozenge.

Indications: Suppresses coughs for up to 4 hours and helps provide relief of nasal congestion up to 4 hours.

Actions: Dextromethorphan is the most widely-used, non-narcotic/non-habit forming antitussive. Taken in a 5-10 mg. dose, it has been recognized as being effective for children (3-12 years) in relieving the discomfort of coughs up to 4 hours by reducing coughing intensity and frequency. Phenylpropanolamine is also non-narcotic and non-habit forming, and works as a decongestant.

Warnings: Persons with diabetes, high blood pressure, heart or thyroid disease should use only as directed by a physician. If symptoms persist or are accompanied by high fever, consult physician promptly. Do not administer to children under 3. Do not exceed recommended dosage. Keep this and all other medications out of the reach of children.

Drug Interaction: Avoid the use of medications containing phenylpropanolamine when under treatment with monoamine oxidase inhibitors unless under the advice and supervision of a physician.

Symptoms and Treatment of Oral Overdosage: The principal symptoms of overdose are restlessness, dizziness, anxiety. Should these symptoms appear or a large overdose be suspected, seek professional advice by contacting your physician, the local poison control center, or The Rocky Mt. Poison Control Center at (303)-629-1123, 24 hrs. a day.

Dosage and Administration: Children over 6 years: Take 2 suppressants one after the other, every 4 hours. Children 3-6 years: One suppressant every 4 hours. Let dissolve fully.

How Supplied: 10 individually wrapped lozenges come packaged in a plastic tube container.

CUPREX®
Pediculicide

Active Ingredient: Tetrahydronaphthalene—30.97%; Copper Oleate—.03%

Indications: For the elimination of head lice, crab lice, body lice and their nits.

Actions: Cuprex provides an effective treatment for the elimination of lice and nits in the forms indicated above.

Warnings: Keep out of reach of children. Flammable—keep away from heat and open flame. Harmful if swallowed. Keep away from eyes. Store out of direct sunlight. Do not use more than twice in 48 hour period. Where skin is raw, broken or infected, consult a physician.

Precaution: Excessive or prolonged contact with the skin may produce erythema, edema, itching, and burning. In the event of excessive contact with skin or eyes, flush with copious amounts of clear water.

Symptoms and Treatment of Oral Overdosage: If ingestion is suspected, consult your physician, your local poison control center, or the Rocky Mt. Poison Control Center at (303)-629-1123, 24 hours a day.

Dosage and Administration: For Head Lice and Nits: Apply gently but thoroughly to scalp and hair using small quantities at a time. After 15 minutes, wash hair and scalp thoroughly with soap and warm water. While still damp, comb hair with a fine comb. For Crab Lice and Nits: Apply thoroughly on effected hairy areas. After 15 minutes, wash thoroughly with soap and warm water; while still damp, comb hair with fine comb. It is not necessary to shave the hair in uncomplicated cases. Body Lice and Nits: Treat skin and hair as for crab lice. General Instructions: If repeat application is required, apply a bland ointment or oil between treatments to avoid drying of skin. All infested clothing should be deloused to prevent reinfestation.

How Supplied: 3 and 16 fl. oz. bottles.

ENO®
Sparkling Antacid

Active Ingredient: When mixed with water, one level teaspoon of Eno produces 1620 mg. of sodium tartrate and 1172 mg. of sodium citrate. Contains 819 mg. of sodium per teaspoonful.

Indications: For relief from the symptoms of sour stomach, acid indigestion, and heartburn.

Actions: Eno is a good tasting, fast acting and effective antacid. It is free of aspirin or sugar and is 100% antacid.

Warnings: If under 60 years of age, don't take more than 6 teaspoonfuls in a 24 hour period. If over 60, don't take over 3 teaspoonfuls. Don't use maximum dosage for over 2 weeks, or use the product if on a sodium restricted diet, except under the advice of a physician. May have a laxative effect. Keep out of reach of children.

Symptoms and Treatment of Oral Overdosage: In case of a large overdose, consult your physician, your local poison control center, or the Rocky Mt. Poison Control Center at (303)-629-1123, 24 hours a day.

Dosage and Administration: Adults —1 level teaspoonful in 6 ozs. of water. May be repeated every 4 hours. Children 4-6—¼ level teaspoonful; children 7-15—½ level teaspoonful.

How Supplied: 3½ and 7 oz. bottles.

Continued on next page

Beecham—Cont.

HOLD®
4 Hour Cough Suppressant Lozenge

Active Ingredient: 7.5 mg. dextromethorphan HBr per lozenge.

Indications: Suppresses coughs for up to 4 hours.

Actions: Dextromethorphan is the most widely used, non-narcotic/non-habit forming antitussive. A 10-20 mg. dose has been recognized as being effective in relieving the discomfort of coughs up to 4 hours by reducing cough intensity and frequency.

Warnings: If cough persists or is accompanied by high fever, consult a physician promptly. Do not administer to children under 6. Keep this and all other medications out of the reach of children. DO NOT EXCEED RECOMMENDED DOSE.

Drug Interaction: No known drug interaction.

Symptoms and Treatment of Oral Overdosage: The principal symptom of over dosage with dextromethorphan HBr is slowing of respiration. Should a large overdose be suspected seek professional assistance by contacting your physician, the local poison control center, or The Rocky Mt. Poison Control Center at (303)-629-1123, 24 hrs. a day.

Dosage and Administration: Adults (12 years and older): Take 2 suppressants one after the other, every 4 hours as needed. Children (6-12 years): One suppressant every 4 hours as needed. Let dissolve fully.

How Supplied: 10 individually wrapped suppressants come packaged in a plastic tube container.

MASSENGILL®
Disposable Douches
MASSENGILL®
Liquid Concentrate
MASSENGILL® Powder

Ingredients:
DISPOSABLES: Vinegar and Water—Water and Vinegar.
Country Flowers—Water, SD Alcohol 40, Lactic Acid, Sodium Lactate, Octoxynol-9, Cetylpyridinium Chloride, Sorbic Acid Disodium EDTA, Fragrance, D&C Red #19.
Mountain Herbs—Water, Octoxynol-9, SD Alcohol 40, Lactic Acid, Sodium Lactate, Cetylpyridinium Chloride, Sorbic Acid, Fragrance, Disodium EDTA, D&C Yellow #10, FD&C Blue #1.
LIQUID CONCENTRATE: Water, SD Alcohol 40, Lactic Acid, Sodium Bicarbonate, Octoxynol-9, Fragrance, D&C Yellow #10, FD&C Yellow #6. (Alcohol 19.6%)
POWDER: Salt, Ammonium Alum., Fragrance, D&C Yellow #10, FD&C Yellow #6.

Indications: Recommended for routine cleansing at the end of menstruation, after use of contraceptive creams or jellies (check the contraceptive package instructions first) or to rinse out the residue of prescribed vaginal medication (as directed by physician).

Actions: The buffered acid solutions of Massengill Douches are valuable adjuncts to specific vaginal therapy following the prescribed use of vaginal medication or contraceptives and in feminine hygiene.

Directions:
DISPOSABLES: Hold bottle upright and twist nozzle in either direction until nozzle stops (about one-half turn). The unit is now ready to use. Product is completely disposable.
LIQUID CONCENTRATE: Fill cap ¾ full, to measuring line, and pour contents into douche bag containing 1 quart of warm water. Mix thoroughly.
POWDER: Dissolve two rounded teaspoonfuls in a douche bag containing 1 quart of warm water. Mix thoroughly.

Warning: Vaginal cleansing douches should not be used more than twice weekly except on the advice of a physician. If irritation occurs, discontinue use.

How Supplied: Disposable—6 oz. disposable plastic bottle.
Liquid Concentrate—4 oz., 8 oz., plastic bottles. Packettes—12's.
Powder—4 oz., 8 oz., 16 oz., 22 oz. Packettes—10's, 12's.

MASSENGILL® Disposable Medicated Douche

Active Ingredient: Cepticin™ (0.23% povidone-iodine).

Indications: For symptomatic relief of minor irritation and itching associated with vaginitis due to monilia, Trichomonas vaginalis and Gardnerella vaginalis.

Action: Povidone-iodine is widely recognized as an effective broad spectrum microbicide against both gram negative and gram positive bacteria, fungi, yeasts and protozoa. While remaining active in the presence of blood, serum or bodily secretions, it possesses none of the irritating properties of iodine.

Warnings: If symptoms persist after seven days of use, or if redness, swelling or pain develop during treatment, consult a physician. Women with iodine-sensitivity should not use this product. You may douche during menstruation if you douche gently. Do not douche during pregnancy unless directed by a physician. Douching does not prevent pregnancy. Keep out of the reach of children.

Dosage and Administration: Dosage is provided as a single unit concentrate to be added to 6 oz. of sanitized water supplied in a disposable bottle. A specially designed nozzle is provided. After use the unit is discarded. Use once daily for up to 7 days.

How Supplied: 6 oz. bottle of sanitized water with 0.17 oz. vial of povidone-iodine and nozzle.

SCOTT'S EMULSION®
Vitamin A and D Food Supplement

Active Ingredient: Cod Liver Oil which provides 5,000 International Units of Vitamin A per 4 teaspoons of Scott's Emulsion (100% of RDA) and 400 International Units of Vitamin D per 4 teaspoons (100% of RDA).

Indications: Provides daily requirements of Vitamin A and D.

Actions: Scott's Emulsion supplies natural Vitamins A and D from cod liver oil. The product is in a highly emulsified form for more rapid absorption by the body. Flavoring agents are included to help mask the flavor of cod liver oil.

Dosage and Administration: 4 teaspoons per day provides 100% of the adult RDA for Vitamins A and D.

How Supplied: 6¼ and 12½ fl. oz. bottles.

S.T.37®
Antiseptic Solution

Active Ingredient: .1% hexylresorcinol in a glycerin-aqueous solution

Indications: For use on cuts, abrasions, burns, scalds, sunburn and the hygienic care of the mouth.

Actions: S.T.37 is a non-stinging, non-staining antiseptic solution that provides soothing protection and helps relieve pain of burns, cuts, abrasions and mouth irritations.

Warnings: If redness, irritation, swelling or pain persists or increases or if infection occurs, discontinue use and consult physician. In case of deep or puncture wounds or serious burns, consult physician. Keep out of reach of children.

Symptoms and Treatment of Oral Overdosage: In case of a large overdose of S.T. 37, seek professional assistance. Contact a physician, the local poison control center, or call the Rocky Mt. Poison Control Center at (303)-629-1123, 24 hours a day.

Dosage and Administration: For cuts, burns, scalds and abrasions apply undiluted, bandage lightly keeping bandage wet with S.T.37 antiseptic solution. For hygienic care of the mouth, dilute with 1 or 2 parts of warm water.

How Supplied: 5 and 12 fl. oz. bottles.

SUCRETS® (Regular, Mentholated, and Children's Cherry-Flavored)
Sore Throat Lozenges

Active Ingredient: Hexylresorcinol, 2.4 mg. per lozenge

Indications: Temporary relief of minor sore throat pain and mouth irritations.

Actions: Hexylresorcinol's soothing demulcent/anesthetic action quickly relieves minor throat irritations.

Warnings: Do not administer to children under 3 years of age unless directed by a physician. Keep all medications out of the reach of children. Persistent sore throat or sore throat accompanied by high fever, headache, nausea or vomiting usually indicates a severe infection and may be serious. Consult a physician promptly in such case, or if sore throat persists more than 2 days.

Drug Interaction: No known drug interaction

Symptoms and Treatment of Oral Overdosage: Should a large overdose of Sucrets (Regular, Mentholated or Children's Cherry-Flavored) be suspected, with symptoms of profuse sweating, nausea, vomiting and diarrhea, seek professional assistance. Call your physician, local poison control center or the Rocky Mountain Poison Control Center at (303)-629-1123, 24 hrs. a day.

Dosage and Administration: Use as needed. For best results dissolve slowly—do not chew.

Professional Labeling: Same as those outlined under Indications.

How Supplied: Sucrets-Regular: Available in tins of 24 and jars of 55 individually wrapped lozenges. Sucrets-Mentholated and Sucrets-Children's Cherry Flavored are available in tins of 24 lozenges.

SUCRETS®–Cold Decongestant
Formula
Decongestant Lozenges

Active Ingredient: Phenylpropanolamine hydrochloride, 25 mg./per lozenge

Indications: For fast temporary relief of nasal congestion.

Warnings: Do not exceed recommended dosage because at higher dosages nervousness, dizziness or sleeplessness may occur. If symptoms do not improve within 7 days or are accompanied by high fever, consult a physician before continuing use. Do not take this product if you have high blood pressure, heart disease, diabetes or thyroid disease except under the advice of a physician.

Drug Interaction: Avoid the use of medications containing phenylpropanolamine when under treatment with monamine oxidase inhibitors unless under the advice and supervision of a physician.

Symptoms and Treatment of Oral Overdosage: The principal symptoms of an overdose are restlessness, dizziness, anxiety. Should these symptoms appear or a large overdose be suspected, seek professional assistance. Call your physician, the local poison control center or the Rocky Mt. Poison Control Center at (303)-629-1123, 24 hours a day.

Dosage and Administration: Adults (12 years and over): Slowly dissolve one lozenge in the mouth. One additional lozenge every 3 hours, but do not exceed 6 lozenges in 24 hours. Do not exceed recommended dosage. Children (under 12 years): Only as directed by a physician.

Professional Labeling: Same as those outlined under Indications.

How Supplied: Available in tins of 24 lozenges.

SUCRETS® COUGH CONTROL
FORMULA
Cough Control Lozenges

Active Ingredient: Dextromethorphan hydrobromide, 7.5 mg./lozenge.

Indications: For temporary suppression of cough and relief of minor throat irritation.

Actions: Dextromethorphan is the most widely used non-narcotic/non-habit forming antitussive. A 10-20 mg. dose in adults (7.5 mg in children over 6) has been recognized as being effective in relieving the frequency and intensity of cough for up to 4 hours.

Warnings: If cough persists or is accompanied by high fever, consult a physician

promptly. Do not use more than two days or administer to children under 6 unless directed by a physician. Keep out of the reach of children.

Drug Interaction: No known drug interaction.

Symptoms and Treatment of Oral Overdosage: Slowing of respiration is the principal symptom of dextromethorphan HBr overdose. Should a large overdose be suspected, seek professional assistance. Call your physician, the local poison control center or the Rocky Mt. Poison Control Center at (303)-629-1123, 24 hours a day.

Dosage and Administration: Adults (12 years and over): Take 2 lozenges every 4 hours as needed. Let dissolve fully in mouth. Children (6–12 years): One lozenge every 4 hours as needed. Let dissolve fully in mouth. Do not exceed recommended dosage.

Professional Labeling: Same as those outlined under Indications.

How Supplied: Available in tins of 24 lozenges.

THERMOTABS®
Buffered Salt Tablets

Active Ingredient: Per tablet—sodium chloride—450 mg.; potassium chloride—30 mg.; calcium carbonate—18 mg.; dextrose—200 mg.

Indications: To minimize fatigue and prevent muscle cramps and heat prostration due to excessive perspiration.

Actions: Thermotabs are designed for tennis players, joggers, golfers and other athletes who experience excessive perspiration. Also for use in steel mills, industrial plants, kitchens, stores, or other locations where high temperatures cause heat fatigue, cramps or heat prostration.

Warnings: Keep out of reach of children.

Precaution: Individuals on a salt-restricted diet should use THERMOTABS only under the advice and supervision of a physician.

Symptoms and Treatment of Oral Overdosage: Signs of salt overdose include diarrhea and muscular twitching. If an overdose is suspected, contact a physician, the local poison control center, or call the Rocky Mt. Poison Control Center at (303)-629-1123, 24 hours a day.

Dosage and Administration: One tablet with a full glass of water, 5 to 10 times a day depending on temperature and conditions.

How Supplied: 100 and 1,000 tablet bottles; 500 tablet wall dispenser.

Products are cross-indexed by

generic and chemical names

in the

YELLOW SECTION

Beiersdorf, Inc.
DUKE PLACE
SOUTH NORWALK, CT 06854

AQUAPHOR®
Ointment Base
NDC Number–10356-020-01

Composition: Petrolatum, mineral oil, mineral wax, wool wax alcohol.

Actions and Uses: Aquaphor is a stable, neutral, odorless, anhydrous ointment base. Miscible with water or aqueous solutions several times its own weight, Aquaphor forms smooth, creamy water-in-oil emulsions. Also, recommended for use as a topical preparation for extremely dry skin.

Administration and Dosages: Aquaphor will absorb many times its own weight of water or aqueous solution. Use Aquaphor in compounding virtually any ointment using aqueous solutions alone or in combination with other oil-based substances, and all common topical medications.

Precautions: For external use only.

How Supplied:
1 lb. plastic jars—List Number 0020
5 lb. plastic jars—List Number 0021
45 lb. drum—List Number 0022

EUCERIN® Creme
Unscented Moisturizing Formula
NDC Number–10356-090-01

Composition: Water, petrolatum, mineral oil, mineral wax, wool wax alcohol, 2-bromo-2 nitropropane-1, 3-diol.

Actions and Uses: A gentle, unscented water-in-oil emulsion. Eucerin helps alleviate excessive dry skin and may be helpful in conditions such as chapped or chafed skin, sunburn, windburn, and itching associated with dryness.

Administration and Dosages: Apply freely to affected areas of the skin as often as necessary or as directed by physician.

Precautions: For external use only.

How Supplied:
16 oz. jar—List Number 0090
4 oz. jar—List Number 3797

EUCERIN™ Lotion
Unscented Moisturizing Formula

Composition: Water, Mineral Oil, Isopropyl Myristate, PEG-40 Sorbitan Peroleate, Lanolin Acid Glycerin Ester, Sorbitol, Propylene Glycol, Beeswax, Magnesium Sulfate, Aluminum Stearate, Lanolin Alcohol, BHT, Methylchloroisothiazolinone·Methylisothiazolinone.

Actions and Uses: Eucerin Lotion is a gentle, light moisturizing formula that works itself deep into the pores of the skin, to help replace lost moisture and augment the return of natural oils. Used daily, Eucerin Lotion keeps skin feeling soft, moist, and fresh all over.

Administration and Dosage: Apply Eucerin Lotion all over body—hands,

Continued on next page

Beiersdorf—Cont.

arms, legs, and feet—to help moisturize, smooth and soothe rough, dry skin.

Precautions: For external use only.

How Supplied: 8 fluid oz. plastic bottles.

List Number 3793

GELOCAST®
GELOCAST® Unna Boot
NDC Number–10356-103-02

Composition: Water, glycerin, sorbitol, gelatin, magnesium aluminum silicate, zinc oxide, calamine, methylparaben, imidazolidinyl urea, propylparaben, and dimethicone.

Actions and Uses: For the compression treatment of venous insufficiency conditions such as stasis ulcers, stasis dermatitis, chronic lymphangitis, and varicose veins with ulceration. Also, indications for use in Orthopedics and in the treatment of post-fracture conditions and as an aid in helping prevent edema.

Administration and Dosage: Thoroughly wash the extremity with soap and water, towel dry, then sponge with alcohol. Remove Gelocast bandage from sealed, inner pouch.

Wrap the extremity by winding the bandage around knee or elbow. Maintain even pressure on the bandage, and avoid folds by molding to body contours. Allow Gelocast to dry, then cover with a layer of plain gauze to prevent adhering to other material (stocking or bed linen). Gelocast may be left in place from one to two weeks. To remove bandage, simply cut lengthwise with a pair of scissors.

Precautions: If skin sensitivity or irritation develops, discontinue use and consult a physician.

How Supplied:

$4'' \times 10$ yards Unna Boot—List Number 0100

$3'' \times 10$ yards Unna Boot—List Number 0103

MEDIPLAST®
40% Salicylic acid plaster
NDC Number–10356-703-03

Active Ingredient: 40% Salicylic Acid.

Indications: For removal of callous tissue.

Actions: Mediplast is a 40% salicylic acid plaster that is used for the softening of callous tissue and the removal of warts. Convenient to use, Mediplast is self-adhesive and can be cut to fit the affected area. Mediplast stays in place while it works to soften the calloused area.

Warnings

Caution: Not to be applied to healthy tissue. Do not use each application for more than 24 hours. If re-application to calloused part is necessary, allow time in between applications.

Upon evidence of irritation, remove plaster immediately and do not re-apply. Consult your physician. Do not use on inflamed sites or if diabetic or if circula-

tory impairments exist. Keep out of reach of children. For external use only.

Dosage and Administration: Cut out piece of plaster to dimension of calloused tissue. Remove backing paper and apply plaster. Use the envelope to store remaining plaster for next use. Store at room temperature 15-30 C (59-86F).

Professional Labeling: Same as those outlined under Indications.

How Supplied: 25 individually wrapped plasters per box.

List Number 1496

[*Shown in Product Identification Section*]

Blair Laboratories, Inc.
Affiliate, The Purdue Frederick Company
50 WASHINGTON STREET
NORWALK, CT 06856

CALAMATUM® LOTION
(Calamine, zinc oxide, phenol, camphor and benzocaine 3%)
Antipruritic/Anesthetic/Analgesic

Description: CALAMATUM Lotion is a soothing, greaseless lotion containing astringent, anesthetic, analgesic and antipruritic ingredients.

Composition: CALAMATUM Lotion contains calamine, zinc oxide, phenol, camphor and benzocaine 3% in a nongreasy base.

Indications: CALAMATUM Lotion helps relieve itching and minor pain of poison ivy, oak and sumac; of insect and chigger bites; of rashes, prickly heat and minor skin irritations.

Action: CALAMATUM Lotion provides prompt medicated relief of itching and helps prevent scratching that might spread infection or cause scarring. It soothes and dries skin irritations. CALAMATUM Lotion dries to form its own "bandage" that stays on until washed off.

Caution: Do not bandage. Do not use in the eye. When symptoms are severe, recurrent, or persistent, or if sensitivity arises, consult a physician. Keep out of reach of children. Keep from freezing.

Administration: Shake well. Spread in a thin film over the affected area three or four times a day until relieved. Wash off once daily with warm water.

How Supplied: $3\frac{3}{4}$ fluid ounces (111 ml) in plastic bottles.

Also Available: CALAMATUM® Ointment ($1\frac{1}{2}$ oz.) providing the same ingredients as CALAMATUM Lotion in a soothing greaseless ointment. CALAMATUM® Spray (3 oz.—85 g) is a cooling, soothing spray containing benzocaine 1.05%, calamine, zinc oxide, menthol, camphor, and isopropanol 19.9% by weight.

ISODINE® ANTISEPTIC
(povidone–iodine 10%)
Antiseptic/Germicide

Description: ISODINE Antiseptic is a topical antiseptic microbicide which essentially retains the broad-range, nonselective microbicidal activity of iodine, yet is virtually free of the undesirable fea-

tures associated with tincture of iodine. Unlike tincture of iodine, topically applied ISODINE Antiseptic can be bandaged or taped.

Composition: ISODINE Antiseptic is an aqueous solution of povidone-iodine. ISODINE Antiseptic is a film-forming, water-soluble iodine complex, virtually nonstinging and nonirritating to skin, wounds and mucous membranes.

Actions: ISODINE Antiseptic kills bacteria (including antibiotic-resistant strains), fungi, viruses, protozoa and yeasts. It maintains germicidal activity in the presence of blood, pus and serum. The golden-brown film formed by topically applied ISODINE Antiseptic can be easily washed off skin and natural fabrics.

Indications: ISODINE Antiseptic helps prevent infection in minor cuts, scratches, abrasions and minor burns. This potent, yet gentle, antiseptic kills germs promptly.

Caution: In case of deep or puncture wounds or serious burns, or if redness, irritation, swelling or pain persists or increases, or if infection occurs, consult physician. Keep out of reach of children.

Administration: Apply full strength to injured area. Cover with gauze or adhesive bandage if desired.

Supplied: 1 oz. plastic bottles.

KERID® EAR DROPS
(Urea and glycerin in propylene glycol)
Earwax Removal Aid

Description: KERID Ear Drops are an improved preparation to help loosen and remove excess earwax easily and effectively.

Composition: Active ingredients are urea and glycerine in propylene glycol. Preservatives are methyl paraben and propyl paraben.

Action and Uses: KERID Ear Drops help soften and loosen earwax so that it may simply wash out when gently flushed with water. Helps prevent "swimmer's ear." When used routinely (once or twice a month), KERID Ear Drops help prevent earwax buildup.

Caution: Do not use in presence of inflammation, pain or fever. If irritation develops, consult a physician.

Administration: Fill ear canal with KERID Ear Drops. Insert cotton plug in ear and allow drops to remain for 30 to 60 minutes. Gently wash ear canal with warm water. In stubborn cases where a second application is necessary, repeat procedure, allow to remain overnight, gently wash out in morning. As with all medication, keep out of reach of children.

How Supplied: 8 cc. bottle with cellophane-wrapped blunt-end dropper.

Products are

indexed alphabetically

in the

PINK SECTION

Block Drug Company, Inc.
257 CORNELISON AVENUE
JERSEY CITY, NJ 07302

SENSODYNE® TOOTHPASTE
Desensitizing dentifrice

Description: Each tube contains strontium chloride hexahydrate (10%) in a pleasantly flavored cleansing/polishing dentifrice.

Actions/Indications: Tooth hypersensitivity is a dentally recognized condition in which individuals experience pain from exposure to hot, cold, sweet or sour stimuli, from chewing fibrous foods, or from tactile stimuli (e.g. toothbrushing.) Hypersensitivity usually occurs when the protective enamel covering on teeth wears away (which happens most often at the gum line) and exposes the dentin underneath.

Running through the dentin are microscopic small "tubules" which, according to many authorities, carry the pain impulses to the nerve of the tooth.

Sensodyne provides a unique ingredient—strontium chloride which is believed to be deposited in the tubules where it blocks the pain. The longer Sensodyne is used, the more of a barrier it helps build against pain.

The effect of Sensodyne may not be manifested immediately and may require a few weeks or longer of use for relief to be obtained. A number of clinical studies in the U.S. and other countries have provided substantial evidence of Sensodyne's performance attributes. Complete relief of hypersensitivity has been reported in approximately 65% of users and measurable relief or reduction in hypersensitivity in approximately 90%. Sensodyne has been commercially available for over 17 years and has received wide dental endorsement.

Contraindications: Subjects with severe dental erosion should brush properly and lightly with any dentifrice to avoid further removal of tooth structure. Subjects with identified idiosyncracies to dentifrice flavorants may also react to those in Sensodyne.

Dosage: Use twice a day as in regular dental care.

NOTE: Individuals should be instructed to use SENSODYNE frequently and in place of their regular dentifrice since relief from pain tends to be cumulative. If relief does not occur after 3 months, a dentist should be consulted.

How Supplied: SENSODYNE Toothpaste is supplied as a paste in tubes of 4 oz. and 2.1 oz.

(U.S. Patent No. 3,122,483)

TEGRIN® MEDICATED SHAMPOO

Highly effective shampoo for moderate-to-severe dandruff and the relief of flaking, itching, and scaling associated with eczema, seborrhea, and psoriasis. Two commercial product versions are available: a cream shampoo and a lotion shampoo, each in two scents.

Description: Each tube of cream shampoo or bottle of lotion shampoo contains 5% special alcohol extract of coal tar in a pleasantly scented, high-foaming, cleansing shampoo base with emollients, conditioners and other formula components.

Actions/Indications: Coal Tar is obtained in the destructive distillation of bituminous coal and is a highly effective agent for the local therapy of a number of dermatological disorders. The action of tar is believed to be keratoplastic, antiseptic, antipruritic and astringent. The special extract of coal tar used in the Tegrin products is prepared in such a way as to reduce the pitch and other irritant components found in crude coal tar without reduction in therapeutic potency.

Coal tar extract has been used clinically for many years as a remedy for dandruff and for scaling associated with scalp disorders such as eczema, seborrhea, and psoriasis. Its mechanism of action has not been fully established, but it is believed to retard the rate of turnover of epidermal cells with regular use. A number of clinical studies have demonstrated the performance attributes of Tegrin Shampoo against dandruff and seborrheic dermatitis. In addition to relieving the above symptoms, Tegrin shampoo used regularly, maintains scalp and hair cleanliness and leaves the hair lustrous and manageable.

Contraindications: For External Use Only—Should irritation develop, discontinue use. Avoid contact with eyes. Keep out of reach of children.

Dosage: Use regularly as a shampoo. Wet hair thoroughly. Rub Tegrin liberally into hair and scalp. Rinse thoroughly. Briskly massage a second application of the shampoo into a rich lather. Rinse thoroughly.

How Supplied:
Tegrin Cream Shampoo is supplied in 2 oz., 3.2 oz., and 5 oz. collapsible tubes. Tegrin Lotion Shampoo is supplied in 3.75 and 6.6 oz. plastic bottles.

TEGRIN® for Psoriasis Lotion and Cream

Description: Each tube of cream or bottle of lotion contains special crude coal tar extract (5%) and allantoin (1.7%) in a greaseless, stainless vehicle.

Actions/Indications: Crude coal tar is obtained in the destructive distillation of bituminous coal and is a highly effective agent for the local therapy of a number of dermatological disorders. The action of tar is believed to be keratoplastic, antiseptic, antipruritic and astringent. The special coal tar extract used in the Tegrin products is prepared in such a way as to reduce the pitch and other irritant components found in crude coal tar. Allantoin (5-Ureidohydantoin) is a debriding and dispersing agent for psoriatic scales and is believed to accelerate proliferation of normal skin cells. The combination of coal tar extract and allantoin used in Tegrin has been demonstrated in a number of controlled clinical studies to have a high level of efficacy in controlling the itching and scaling of psoriasis.

Contraindications: Discontinue medication should irritation or allergic reactions occur. Avoid contact with eyes and mucous membranes. Keep out of reach of children.

Dosage and Administration: Apply 2 to 4 times daily as needed, massaging thoroughly into affected areas. A hot bath before application will help to soften heavy scales. Once condition is under control, maintenance therapy should be individually adjusted. Occlusive dressings are not required.

How Supplied: Tegrin Lotion 6 fl. oz., Tegrin Cream 2 oz. and 4.4 oz. tubes.

Boehringer Ingelheim Ltd.
90 EAST RIDGE
POST OFFICE BOX 368
RIDGEFIELD, CT 06877

DULCOLAX®
brand of bisacodyl USP
Tablets of 5 mg.................BI-CODE 12
Suppositories of 10 mg..BI-CODE 52
Laxative

Description: Dulcolax is a contact laxative acting directly on the colonic mucosa to produce normal peristalsis throughout the large intestine. Its unique mode of action permits either oral or rectal administration, according to the requirements of the patient. Because of its gentleness and reliability of action without side effects, Dulcolax may be used whenever constipation is a problem. In preparation for surgery, proctoscopy, or radiologic examination, Dulcolax provides satisfactory cleansing of the bowel, obviating the need for an enema.

Dulcolax is a colorless, tasteless compound that is practically insoluble in water and alkaline solution. It is designated chemically bis(p-acetoxyphenyl)-2-pyridylmethane.

Actions: Dulcolax differs markedly from other laxatives in its mode of action: it is virtually nontoxic, and its laxative effect occurs on contact with the colonic mucosa, where it stimulates sensory nerve endings to produce parasympathetic reflexes resulting in increased peristaltic contractions of the colon. Administered orally, Dulcolax is absorbed to a variable degree from the small bowel but such absorption is not related to the mode of action of the compound. Dulcolax administered rectally in the form of suppositories is negligibly absorbed. The contact action of the drug is restricted to the colon, and motility of the small intestine is not appreciably influenced. Local axon reflexes, as well as segmental reflexes, are initiated in the region of contact and contribute to the widespread peristaltic activity producing evacuation. For this reason, Dulcolax may often be employed satisfactorily in patients with ganglionic blockage or spinal cord damage (paraplegia, poliomyelitis, etc.).

Indications: *Acute Constipation:* Taken at bedtime, Dulcolax tablets are almost invariably effective the following morning. When taken before breakfast, they usually produce an effect within six hours. For a prompter response and to

Continued on next page

Boehringer Ingelhelm—Cont.

replace enemas, the suppositories, which are usually effective in 15 minutes to one hour, can be used.

Chronic Constipation and Bowel Retraining: Dulcolax is extremely effective in the management of chronic constipation, particularly in older patients. By gradually lengthening the interval between doses as colonic tone improves, the drug has been found to be effective in redeveloping proper bowel hygiene. There is no tendency to "rebound".

Preparation for Radiography: Dulcolax tablets are excellent in eliminating fecal and gas shadows from x-rays taken of the abdominal area. For barium enemas, no food should be given following the administration of the tablets, to prevent reaccumulation of material in the cecum, and a suppository should be given one to two hours prior to examination.

Preoperative Preparation: Dulcolax tablets have been shown to be an ideal laxative in emptying the G.I. tract prior to abdominal surgery or to other surgery under general anesthesia. They may be supplemented by suppositories to replace the usual enema preparation. Dulcolax will not replace the colonic irrigations usually given patients before intracolonic surgery, but is useful in the preliminary emptying of the colon prior to these procedures.

Postoperative Care: Suppositories can be used to replace enemas, or tablets given as an oral laxative, to restore normal bowel hygiene after surgery.

Antepartum Care: Either tablets or suppositories can be used for constipation in pregnancy without danger of stimulating the uterus.

Preparation for Delivery: Suppositories can be used to replace enemas in the first stage of labor provided that they are given at least two hours before the onset of the second stage.

Postpartum Care: The same indications apply as in postoperative care, with no contraindication in nursing mothers.

Preparation for Sigmoidoscopy or Proctoscopy: For unscheduled office examinations, adequate preparation is usually obtained with a single suppository. For sigmoidoscopy scheduled in advance, however, administration of tablets the night before in addition will result in adequate preparation almost invariably.

Colostomies: Tablets the night before or a suppository inserted into the colostomy opening in the morning will frequently make irrigations unnecessary, and in other cases will expedite the procedure.

Contraindication: There is no contraindication to the use of Dulcolax, other than an acute surgical abdomen.

Precaution: Dulcolax tablets contain FD&C Yellow No. 5 (tartrazine) which may cause allergic-type reactions (including bronchial asthma) in certain susceptible individuals. Although the overall incidence of FD&C Yellow No. 5 (tartrazine) sensitivity in the general population is low, it is frequently seen in patients who also have aspirin hypersensitivity.

Adverse Reactions: As with any laxative, abdominal cramps are occasionally noted, particularly in severely constipated individuals.

Dosage:

Tablets

Tablets must be swallowed whole, not chewed or crushed, and should not be taken within one hour of antacids or milk.

Adults: Two or three (usually two) tablets suffice when an ordinary laxative effect is desired. This usually results in one or two soft, formed stools. Tablets when taken before breakfast usually produce an effect within 6 hours, when taken at bedtime usually in 8–12 hours.

Up to six tablets may be safely given in preparation for special procedures when greater assurance of complete evacuation of the colon is desired. In producing such thorough emptying, these higher doses may result in several loose, unformed stools.

Children: One or two tablets, depending on age and severity of constipation, administered as above. Tablets should not be given to a child too young to swallow them whole.

Suppositories

Adults: One suppository at the time a bowel movement is required. Usually effective in 15 minutes to one hour.

Children: Half a suppository is generally effective for infants and children under two years of age. Above this age, a whole suppository is usually advisable.

Combined

In preparation for surgery, radiography and sigmoidoscopy, a combination of tablets the night before and a suppository in the morning is recommended (see Indications).

How Supplied: Dulcolax, brand of bisacodyl: Yellow, enteric-coated tablets of 5 mg in boxes of 24, 48 and bottles of 100, 1000 and unit strip packages of 100; suppositories of 10 mg in boxes of 2, 4, 8, 50 and 500.

Note: Dulcolax suppositories and tablets should be stored at temperatures not above 86°F (30°C).

Also Available: Dulcolax® Bowel Prep Kit. Each kit contains:

  1 Dulcolax suppository of 10 mg bisacodyl;

  4 Dulcolax tablets of 5 mg bisacodyl; Complete patient instructions.

Clinical Applications: Dulcolax can be used in virtually any patient in whom a laxative or enema is indicated. It has no effect on the blood picture, erythrocyte sedimentation rate, urinary findings, or hepatic or renal function. It may be safely given to infants and the aged, pregnant or nursing women, debilitated patients, and may be prescribed in the presence of such conditions as cardiovascular, renal, or hepatic diseases.

026-G   (11/81)

[Shown in Product Identification Section]

Breon Laboratories Inc.
90 PARK AVENUE
NEW YORK, NY 10016

BREONESIN®
brand of guaifenesin capsules, USP

Description: Each red, oval-shaped BREONESIN capsule contains 200 mg of guaifenesin in an easy to swallow, soft gelatin capsule.

Indications: BREONESIN is indicated for the temporary relief of coughs. BREONESIN is an expectorant which helps to loosen phlegm (sputum) and bronchial secretions, and acts to thin mucus. Coughs due to minor throat and bronchial irritation that occur with the common cold are temporarily relieved.

Warnings: Persistent cough may indicate a serious condition. Consult your physician if cough persists for more than 1 week, recurs, or is accompanied by high fever, rash or persistent headache. Do not take this product for persistent coughs due to smoking, asthma or emphysema, or coughs accompanied by excessive secretions, except under the advice and supervision of your physician.

Dosage: Adults and Children 12 years of age and over: 1 or 2 capsules every 4 hours, not to exceed 12 capsules in a 24-hour period. Children under 12 years: as directed by your physician.

Store at controlled room temperature, between 15°C and 30°C (59°F and 86°F).

Supplied by:

BREON LABORATORIES INC.
New York, N.Y. 10016
Mfg. by R.P. Scherer Corp.
Monroe, N.C. 28110

[Shown in Product Identification Section]

FERGON®
brand of ferrous gluconate
FERGON ELIXIR

Composition: FERGON (brand of pure ferrous gluconate) is stabilized to maintain a minimum of ferric ions. It contains not less than 11.5 per cent iron. Each FERGON tablet contains 320 mg. FERGON Elixir 6% contains 300 mg per teaspoon.

Action and Uses: FERGON preparations produce rapid hemoglobin regeneration in patients with iron deficiency anemias. FERGON is better utilized and better tolerated than other forms of iron because of its low ionization constant and solubility in the entire pH range of the gastrointestinal tract. It does not precipitate proteins or have the astringency of more ionizable forms of iron, does not interfere with proteolytic or diastatic activities of the digestive system, and will not produce nausea, abdominal cramps, constipation or diarrhea in the great majority of patients.

FERGON preparations are indicated in anemias amenable to iron therapy: (1) hypochromic anemia of infancy and childhood; (2) idiopathic hypochromic anemia; (3) hypochromic anemia of pregnancy; and (4) anemia associated with chronic blood loss.

Administration and Dosage: Adults—one or two FERGON tablets or one or two teaspoons of FERGON Elixir three times daily. Children 6–12 years—one FERGON tablet or one teaspoon of FERGON Elixir one to three times daily, as directed by the physician. Infants—30 drops of FERGON Elixir, gradually increasing to 1 teaspoon daily.

How Supplied: FERGON, tablets of 320 mg (5 grains), bottles of 100, 500 and 1,000. FERGON Elixir 6% (5 grains per teaspoon), bottles of 1 pint.

FERGON registered trademark of Sterling Drug Inc.

FERGON® CAPSULES

Composition: Each FERGON Capsule contains 435 mg of ferrous gluconate, yielding 50 mg of elemental iron.

Action and Uses: FERGON preparations produce rapid hemoglobin regeneration in patients with iron deficiency anemias. FERGON is better utilized and better tolerated than other forms of iron because of its low ionization constant and solubility in the entire pH range of the gastrointestinal tract. It does not precipitate proteins or have the astringency of more ionizable forms of iron, does not interfere with proteolytic or diastatic activities of the digestive system, and will not produce nausea, abdominal cramps, constipation or diarrhea in the great majority of patients. The pellets of ferrous gluconate contained in FERGON Capsules are coated to permit maximum availability of iron in the upper small bowel, the site of maximum absorption. FERGON preparations are indicated in anemias amenable to iron therapy: (1) hypochromic anemia of infancy and childhood; (2) idiopathic hypochromic anemia; (3) hypochromic anemia of pregnancy; and (4) anemia associated with chronic blood loss.

Administration and Dosage: 1 FERGON Capsule daily for mild to moderate iron deficiency anemia. For more severe anemia the dosage may be increased.

How Supplied: FERGON Capsules, bottles of 30.

Bristol Laboratories
(Division of Bristol-Myers Co.)
SYRACUSE, NY 13201

NALDECON-CX® SUSPENSION ©

Description: Each teaspoonful (5 ml) of Naldecon-CX Suspension contains:
Phenylpropanolamine
  hydrochloride .... 18 mg
Guaifenesin .... 200 mg
Codeine Phosphate .... 10 mg
  (Warning: May be Habit Forming)

Indications: Provide prompt relief from cough and nasal congestion due to the common cold, bronchitis, nasopharyngitis, and influenza. Codeine temporarily quiets non-productive coughing by its antitussive action while guaifenesin's expectorant action helps loosen phlegm and bronchial secretions. Phenylpropanolamine reduces swelling of nasal passages and shrinks swollen membranes. This combination production is antihistamine and alcohol free.

Contraindications: Hypersensitivity to guaifenesin, codeine or sympathomimetic amines.

Warnings: Nervousness, dizziness or sleeplessness may occur if recommended dosage is exceeded. Do not give this product to a child with high blood pressure, heart disease, diabetes or thyroid disease except under the advice and supervision of a physician. Do not give this product to a child presently taking a prescription drug containing a monamine oxidase inhibitor except under the advice and supervision of a physician. Do not administer this product for persistent or chronic cough associated with asthma or emphysema or when cough is accompanied by excessive secretions, except under the care and advice of a physician. A persistent cough may be a sign of a serious condition. If cough persists for more than 1 week, tends to recur, or is accompanied by high fever, rash or persistent headaches, consult a physician.

Dosage and Administration: Children 2 to 6 years—½ teaspoon 4 times daily. 6 to 12 years—1 teaspoon 4 times daily. Over 12 years—2 teaspoons 4 times daily.

How Supplied: Naldecon-CX Suspension—4 oz. and pint bottles.

NALDECON-DX®
Pediatric Syrup

Description: Each teaspoonful (5 ml.) of Naldecon-DX Syrup contains:
dextromethorphan
  hydrobromide ....7.5 mg
phenylpropanolamine
  hydrochloride ....9 mg
guaifenesin ....100 mg
alcohol 5%

Indications: Provide prompt relief from cough and nasal congestion due to the common cold, bronchitis, nasopharyngitis and recurrent bronchial coughing. Dextromethorphan temporarily quiets non-productive coughing by its antitussive action while guaifenesin's expectorant action helps loosen phlegm and bronchial secretions. Phenylpropanolamine reduces swelling of nasal passages; shrinks swollen membranes. This combination product is antihistamine-free.

Contraindications: Hypersensitivity to guaifenesin, dextromethorphan or sympathomimetic amines.

Warnings: Nervousness, dizziness or sleeplessness may occur if recommended dosage is exceeded. Do not give this product to a child with high blood pressure, heart disease, diabetes or thyroid disease except under the advice and supervision of a physician. Do not give this product to a child presently taking a prescription drug containing a monamine oxidase inhibitor except under the advice and supervision of a physician. Do not administer this product for persistent or chronic cough such as occurs with asthma or emphysema or when cough is accompanied by excessive secretions except under the care and advice of a physician. A persistent cough may be a sign of a serious condition. If cough persists for more than 1 week, tends to recur, or is accompanied

by high fever, rash or persistent headaches, consult a physician.

Dosage and Administration: Children 2 to 6 years—1 teaspoonful 4 times daily. Over 6 years—2 teaspoons 4 times daily.

How Supplied: Naldecon-DX Syrup in 4 oz. and pint bottles.

(1) 8/80

NALDECON–EX®
Pediatric Drops

Description: Each 1 ml. drop of Naldecon-EX contains:
phenylpropanolamine
  hydrochloride ....9 mg
guaifenesin ....30 mg
alcohol 0.6%

Indications: Combined decongestant/ expectorant designed specifically to promptly reduce the swelling of nasal membranes and to help loosen phlegm and bronchial secretions through productive coughing. This dual action is of particular value in infants with common cold, acute bronchitis, bronchiolitis, tracheobronchitis, nasopharyngitis and croup. This combination product is antihistamine-free.

Contraindications: Hypersensitivity to guaifenesin or sympathomimetic amines.

Warnings: Nervousness, dizziness or sleeplessness may occur if recommended dosage is exceeded. Do not give this product to a child with high blood pressure, heart disease, diabetes or thyroid disease except under the advice and supervision of a physician. Do not give this product to a child presently taking a prescription drug containing a monamine oxidase inhibitor except under the advice and supervision of a physician. Do not administer this product for persistent or chronic cough such as occurs with asthma or emphysema or when cough is accompanied by excessive secretions except under the care and advice of a physician. A persistent cough may be a sign of a serious condition. If cough persists for more than 1 week, tends to recur, or is accompanied by high fever, rash or persistent headaches, consult a physician.

Dosage and Administration: Dose should be adjusted to age or weight and be given 4 times a day (see calibrations on dropper). Administer by mouth only.

1–3 Months: (8–12 lbs.)	¼ ml
4–6 Months: (13–17 lbs.)	½ ml
7–9 Months: (18–20 lbs.)	¾ ml
10 Months or over (21 lbs. or more)	1 ml

Bottle label dosage reads as follows: children under 2 years of age: use only as directed by a physician.

How Supplied: Naldecon-EX Pediatric Drops in 20 ml. bottles with calibrated dropper.

(1) 8/80

Bristol-Myers Products
(Div. of Bristol-Myers Co.)
345 PARK AVENUE
NEW YORK, NY 10154

ARTHRITIS STRENGTH BUFFERIN®
Analgesic

Composition: Aspirin 7½ gr. (486 mg.) in a formulation buffered with Di-Alminate,® Bristol-Myers' brand of Aluminum Glycinate 1.125 gr. (72.9 mg.) and Magnesium Carbonate 2.25 gr. (145.8 mg.).

Action and Uses: ARTHRITIS STRENGTH BUFFERIN is specially formulated to give temporary relief from the minor aches and pains, stiffness, swelling and inflammation of arthritis and rheumatism. ARTHRITIS STRENGTH BUFFERIN also reduces pain and fever of colds and "flu" and provides fast, effective pain relief for: simple headache, lower back muscular aches from fatigue, sinusitis, neuralgia, neuritis, tooth extraction, muscle strain, athletic soreness, painful distress associated with normal menstrual periods. The leading aspirin substitute acetaminophen cannot provide relief from inflammation.
ARTHRITIS STRENGTH BUFFERIN PROVIDES INGREDIENTS FOR STOMACH PROTECTION JUST LIKE REGULAR BUFFERIN WHICH HELP PREVENT THE STOMACH UPSET PLAIN ASPIRIN OFTEN CAUSES.

Contraindications: Hypersensitivity to salicylates.

Caution: If pain persists for more than 10 days or redness is present or in Arthritic or Rheumatic conditions affecting children under 12, consult physician immediately. Do not take without consulting physician if under medical care. WARNING: Keep this and all medicines out of children's reach. In case of accidental overdose, contact a physician immediately.

Administration and Dosage: Two tablets with water. Repeat after four hours if necessary. Do not exceed 8 tablets in any 24 hour period. If dizziness, impaired hearing or ringing in ear occurs, discontinue use. Not recommended for children.

Overdose: (Symptoms and Treatment) Typical of aspirin.

How Supplied: Tablets in bottles of 40 and 100. Samples available upon request.

Product Identification: White elongated tablet.

Literature Available: Upon request.
[Shown in Product Identification Section]

BUFFERIN® Analgesic

Composition: Aspirin 5 gr. (324 mg.) in a formulation buffered with Di-Alminate®, Bristol-Myers's brand of Aluminum Glycinate ¾ gr. (48.6 mg.), and Magnesium Carbonate 1½ gr. (97.2 mg.).

Action and Uses: Bufferin® is for relief of simple headache; and for temporary relief of: minor arthritic pain, painful discomforts and fever of colds and "flu", menstrual cramps, muscular aches from fatigue and toothache. Bufferin® helps prevent the stomach upset often caused by plain aspirin.

Contraindications: Hypersensitivity to salicylates.

Caution: If pain persists for more than 10 days or redness is present or, in Arthritic or Rheumatic conditions affecting children under 12, consult physician immediately. Do not take without consulting physician if under medical care. Consult a dentist for toothache promptly.

Warning: Keep this and all medicines out of children's reach. In case of accidental overdose, consult a physician immediately.

Dosage: 2 tablets every four hours as needed. Do not exceed 12 tablets in 24 hours, unless directed by a physician. For children 6-12, one-half dose. Under 6, consult physician.

Overdose: (Symptoms and treatment) Typical of aspirin.

How Supplied: Tablets in bottles of 12, 36, 60, 100, 165, 225, and 375. For hospital and clinical use: bottle—1,000; boxed 200x2 tablet foil packets. Samples available on request.

Product Identification Mark: White tablet with letter "B" on one surface.

Literature Available: Upon request.
[Shown in Product Identification Section]

EXTRA–STRENGTH BUFFERIN®

Composition: Each tablet and capsule contains aspirin 500 mg. in a formulation buffered with Di-Alminate®, Bristol-Myers' brand of Aluminum Glycinate 75 mg. and Magnesium Carbonate 150 mg.

Action and Uses: Extra-Strength BUFFERIN provides fast extra-strength pain relief, and is gentler on the stomach than plain aspirin. Each 2 tablet/capsule dose contains 1000 mg. of aspirin, the maximum quantity recommended without a prescription. Extra-Strength BUFFERIN is formulated to help prevent the stomach upset that plain aspirin can cause. Provides relief of headaches, menstrual cramps, toothache, muscular aches, painful discomforts and fever of colds or flu, and temporary relief from the minor aches, pain and inflammation of arthritis and rheumatism.

Contraindications: Hypersensitivity to salicylates.

Caution: If pain persists for more than 10 days, or redness is present, or in arthritic or rheumatic conditions affecting children under 12, consult a physician immediately. Do not take without consulting a physician if under medical care. Consult a dentist for toothache promptly.

Warning: KEEP THIS AND ALL MEDICINES OUT OF CHILDREN'S REACH. IN CASE OF ACCIDENTAL OVERDOSE, CONSULT A PHYSICIAN IMMEDIATELY.

Administration and Dosage: Tablets—2 tablets every 4 hours as needed. Do not exceed 8 tablets in 24 hours, or give to children 12 or under, unless directed by a physician. Capsules—2 capsules every 4 hours as needed. Do not exceed 8 capsules in 24 hours, or give to children 12 or under, unless directed by a physician.

How Supplied: Bottles of 30, 60 and 100 tablets. Capsules in bottles of 24's, 50's and 75's. All sizes packaged in child resistant closures except 60's (for tablets); 50's (for capsules) which are sizes not recommended for households with young children.

Product Identification Mark: White, elongated tablets with "ESB" imprinted on one side. White and blue capsules with "EXTRA-STRENGTH BUFFERIN" (all caps) imprinted on 3 sides.
[Shown in Product Identification Section]

COMTREX®
Multi-Symptom Cold Reliever

Composition: Each tablet, fluid ounce (30 ml.), and capsule contains:
[See table below].

Actions and Uses: COMTREX® contains safe and effective fast acting ingredients including a non-aspirin analgesic, a decongestant, an antihistamine and a cough reliever. COMTREX relieves these major cold symptoms: nasal and sinus congestion, runny nose, sneezing post nasal drip, watery eyes, coughing, fever, minor sore throat pain (systemically), headache, body aches and pain.

Contraindications: Hypersensitivity to acetaminophen or antihistamines.

Caution: Do not take without consulting a physician if under medical care. Do not drive a car or operate machinery while taking this cold remedy as it may cause drowsiness.

Warning: Keep this and all medicine out of children's reach. In case of accidental overdose, consult a physician immediately. Persistent cough may indicate the presence of a serious condition. Persons with a high fever or persistent cough, or with high blood pressure, diabetes, heart or thyroid disease should not use this preparation unless directed by a physician. Do not use for more than 10 days unless directed by a physician.

Administration and Dosage:
Tablets—Adults: 2 tablets every 4 hours as needed not to exceed 12 tablets in 24 hours. Children 6-12 years: ½ the adult dose. Under 6, consult a physician.
Liquid—Adults: 1 fluid ounce (30 ml.) every 4 hours as needed, not to exceed 6

	COMTREX Tablets	COMTREX Liquid	COMTREX Capsules
Acetaminophen	325 mg.	650 mg.	325 mg.
Phenylpropanolamine HCl:	12 ½ mg.	25 mg.	12 ½ mg.
Chlorpheniramine Maleate:	1 mg.	2 mg.	1 mg.
Dextromethorphan HBr	10 mg.	20 mg.	10 mg.
Alcohol:	—	20% by Volume	—

fluid ounces (180 ml.) in 24 hours. Children 6-12 years: ½ the adult dose. Under 6, consult a physician.

Capsules—Adults: 2 capsules every 4 hours as needed not to exceed 12 capsules in 24 hours. Children 6–12 years: ½ the adult dose. Under 6, consult a physician.

Overdose: The signs and symptoms observed would be those produced by the acetaminophen, which may cause hepatotoxicity in some patients. Since clinical and laboratory evidence may be delayed up to 1 week, close clinical monitoring and serial hepatic enzyme determinations are recommended.

How Supplied: Tablets in bottles of 24's, 50's. Capsules in bottles of 16's and 36's. Liquid in 6 oz. and 10 oz. plastic bottles. Samples available on request.

Product Identification Mark: Yellow tablet with letter "C" on one surface. Orange and Yellor capsules with "Bristol-Myers" and "Comtrex" on one side.

Literature Available: Upon request.
[*Shown in Product Identification Section*]

CONGESPIRIN®
Chewable Cold Tablets for Children

Composition: Each tablet contains aspirin 81 mg. (1¼ grains) phenylephrine hydrochloride (1¼ mg.).

Action and Uses: For the temporary relief of nasal congestion, fever, aches and pains of the common cold or "flu". Plus an effective nasal decongestant to help relieve stuffiness, runny nose and sneezing from colds.

Dosage and Administration:
Under Age 2 consult your physician
2–3 YRS. ....2 TABLETS
4–5 YRS. ....3 TABLETS
6–8 YRS. ....4 TABLETS
9–10 YRS. ....5 TABLETS
11 YRS ....6 TABLETS
12+ YRS. ....8 TABLETS
Repeat dose in four hours if necessary. Do not give more than four doses per day unless prescribed by your physician.

Contraindications: Hypersensitivity to acetaminophen.

Caution: If child is under medical care, do not administer without consulting physician. Do not exceed recommended dosage. Consult your physician if symptoms persist or if high fever, high blood pressure, heart disease, diabetes or thyroid disease is present. Do not administer for more than 10 days unless directed by your physician.

Warning: KEEP THIS AND ALL MEDICINES OUT OF CHILDREN'S REACH. IN CASE OF ACCIDENTAL OVERDOSAGE, CONTACT A PHYSICIAN IMMEDIATELY.

How Supplied: Tablets in bottles of 36.

Product Identification Mark: Two layer (orange/white) circular tablet with letter "C" imprinted on the orange side.

CONGESPRIN®
Liquid Cold Medicine

Composition: Each 5 ml. teaspoon contains Acetaminophen 130 mg., Phenylpropanolamine Hydrochloride 6 ¼ mg., Alcohol 10% by volume.

Action and Uses: Reduces fever and relieves aches and pains associated with colds and "flu". Contains an effective decongestant for the temporary relief of nasal congestion due to the common cold, hay fever or other respiratory allergies. Reduces swelling of nasal passages, shrinks swollen membranes, restores freer breathing.

Dosage and Administration:
Children 3–5, 1 teaspoon every 3–4 hours.
Children 6–12, 2 teaspoons every 3–4 hours.
Children under 3 years use only as directed by your physician.
Do not give more than 4 doses a day unless directed by your physician.

Contraindications: Hypersensitivity to acetaminophen.

Caution: If child is under medical care, do not administer without consulting physician. Do not exceed recommended dosage. Consult your physician if symptoms persist or if high fever, high blood pressure, heart disease, diabetes or thyroid disease is present. Do not administer for more than 10 days unless directed by your physician.

Warning: KEEP THIS AND ALL MEDICINES OUT OF CHILDREN'S REACH. IN CASE OF ACCIDENTAL OVERDOSAGE, CONTACT A PHYSICIAN IMMEDIATELY.

How Supplied: In 3 oz. plastic, unbreakable bottles.
[*Shown in Product Identification Section*]

DATRIL® Analgesic

Composition: Each tablet contains acetaminophen 325 mg.

Actions and Uses: The **DATRIL** formula contains a safe, effective, non-aspirin analgesic that relieves pain fast, without causing the gastric bleeding that aspirin tablets can cause. DATRIL is also less likely to cause the nausea and stomach upset that plain aspirin tablets can cause. DATRIL provides relief from the pain of: ● Headache ● Colds or "flu" ● Bursitis ● Menstrual discomfort ● Sinusitis ● Muscular aches due to fatigue or overexertion ● Muscular backache ● Neuralgia. **DATRIL** also helps reduce fever of colds or "flu" and provides temporary relief from toothache and minor arthritic or rheumatic aches and pain. For most persons with peptic ulcer **DATRIL** may be used safely and comfortably when taken as directed for recommended conditions.

Contraindications: There have been rare reports of skin rash or glossitis attributed to acetaminophen. Discontinue use if a sensitivity reaction occurs. However, acetaminophen is usually well tolerated by aspirin-sensitive patients.

Caution: If pain persists for more than 10 days or redness is present or in arthritic or rheumatic conditions affecting children under 12, consult physician immediately. Do not take without consulting a physician if under medical care. Consult a dentist for toothache promptly.

Warning: Do not give to children under 6 or use for more than 10 days unless directed by a physician. Keep this and all

medicines out of reach of children. In case of accidental overdose contact a physician promptly.

Dosage: 2 tablets every four hours, 1 to 4 times daily as needed, or as directed by a physician. For children 6–12 years of age use half the adult dose.

Overdose: A massive overdose of acetaminophen may cause hepatotoxicity in some patients. Since clinical and laboratory evidence may be delayed up to 1 week, close clinical monitoring and serial hepatic enzyme determinations are recommended.

How Supplied: Tablets in bottles of 24 and 100. Samples available on request.

Product Identification Mark: White tablet with name "Datril" on one surface.

Literature Available: Upon request.
[*Shown in Product Identification Section*]

DATRIL 500™

Composition: Each tablet contains acetaminophen 500 mg.

Actions and Uses: DATRIL 500 has been specially developed to provide fast, extra-strength pain relief. It contains a non-aspirin ingredient (acetaminophen) which is less likely to irritate the stomach than plain aspirin. DATRIL 500 is fast-acting. DATRIL 500 Extra-Strength tablets are for the temporary relief of minor aches, pains, headaches and fever. For most persons with peptic ulcer DATRIL 500 may be used when taken as directed for recommended conditions.

Contraindications: There have been rare reports of skin rash or glossitis attributed to acetaminophen. Discontinue use if a sensitivity reaction occurs. However, acetaminophen is usually well tolerated by aspirin-sensitive patients.

Caution: Severe or recurrent pain or high or continued fever may be indicative of serious illness. Under these conditions consult a physician.

Warning: Do not give to children 12 and under or use for more than 10 days unless directed by a physician. Keep this and all medicines out of reach of children. In case of accidental overdose contact a physician immediately.

Dosage: Adults: Two tablets. May be repeated in 4 hours if needed. Do not exceed 8 tablets in any 24 hour period.

Overdose: A massive overdose of acetaminophen may cause hepatotoxicity in some patients. Since clinical and laboratory evidence may be delayed up to 1 week, close clinical monitoring and serial hepatic enzyme determinations are recommended.

How Supplied: Tablets in bottles of 24's, 50's and 72's. Samples available on request.

Product Identification Mark: White tablet with DATRIL 500 on one surface.

Literature Available: Upon request.
[*Shown in Product Identification Section*]

Continued on next page

Bristol-Myers—Cont.

EXCEDRIN® Analgesic

Composition: Each tablet and capsule contains Acetaminophen 250 mg.; Aspirin 250 mg.; and Caffeine 65 mg.

Action and Uses: The Extra-Strength Excedrin formula provides fast, effective relief from pain of: headache, sinusitis, colds or 'flu', muscular aches and menstrual discomfort. Also recommended for temporary relief of toothaches and minor arthritic pains.

Contraindications: Hypersensitivity to salicylates or acetaminophen.

Caution: If sinus or arthritis pain persists (say for a week), or if skin redness is present, or in arthritic conditions affecting children under 12, consult physician immediately. Consult dentist for toothache promptly. Do not take without consulting physician if under medical care.

Warning: Do not exceed 8 tablets/capsules in 24 hours or use for more than 10 days unless directed by physician, or give to children under 12. **Keep this and all medicines out of children's reach. In case of accidental overdose, contact a physician immediately.**

Administration and Dosage: Tablets —Individuals 12 and over, take 2 tablets every 4 hours as needed. Capsules—Individuals 12 and over, take 2 capsules every 4 hours as needed.

How Supplied: Bottles of 12, 36, 60, 100, 165, 225, and 375 tablets. Capsules in bottles of 24's, 40's and 60's. A metal tin of 12 tablets. All sizes packaged in child resistant closures except 100's (for tablets); 60's (for capsules) which is a size not recommended for households with young children.

Product Identification Mark: White, circular tablet with letter "E" imprinted on both sides. Red capsules with "EXCEDRIN" printed on 2 sides.

Literature Available: Upon request.

EXCEDRIN P.M.® Nighttime Analgesic

Composition: Each tablet contains Acetaminophen 500 mg. and Pyrilamine Maleate 25 mg.

Action and Uses: Excedrin P.M. has a special formula that provides prompt relief of nighttime pain and aids sleep for people with headache, bursitis, colds or "flu", sinusitis, muscle aches and menstrual discomfort. Also recommended for temporary relief of toothaches and minor arthritic pain.

Contraindications: There have been rare reports of skin rash or glossitis attributed to acetaminophen. Discontinue use if a sensitivity reaction occurs. However, acetaminophen is usually well tolerated by aspirin-sensitive patients.

Caution: If sinus or arthritis pain persists (say for a week) or if skin redness is present, or in arthritic conditions affecting children under 12 consult physician immediately. Do not drive a car or operate machinery after use. Consult dentist for toothache promptly. Do not take without consulting physician if under medical care.

Warning: Do not exceed 2 tablets in 24 hours, or give to children under 12 or use for more than 10 days unless directed by physician. KEEP THIS AND ALL MEDICINES OUT OF CHILDREN'S REACH. IN CASE OF ACCIDENTAL OVERDOSE, CONTACT A PHYSICIAN IMMEDIATELY. If sleeplessness persists for more than two weeks, consult your physician. Imsomnia may be a symptom of serious underlying medical ailments. Take this product with caution if alcohol is being consumed. DO NOT TAKE THIS PRODUCT IF YOU HAVE ASTHMA, GLAUCOMA OR ENLARGEMENT OF THE PROSTATE GLAND EXCEPT UNDER THE ADVICE AND SUPERVISION OF A PHYSICIAN.

Administration and Dosage: Adults take two tablets at bedtime to help relieve pain and aid sleep.

How Supplied: Bottles of 10, 30, 50, and 80 tablets. All sizes packaged in child resistant closures except 50's, which is a size not recommended for households with young children.

Product Identification Mark: Blue/green circular tablet with letters "PM" imprinted on one side.

[*Shown in Product Identification Section*]

4-WAY® Cold Tablets

Composition: Each tablet contains aspirin 324 mg., phenylpropanolamine HCl 12½ mg., and chlorpheniramine maleate 2 mg.

Action and Uses: For temporary relief of minor aches and pains, fever, nasal congestion and runny nose as may occur in the common cold.

Dosage and Administration:
Adults—2 tablets every 4 hours, if needed. Do not exceed 6 tablets in 24 hours. Children 6–12 years—1 tablet every 4 hours. Do not exceed 4 tablets in 24 hours. Under age 6, consult a physician.

Warning: Do not take without consulting a physician if under medical care.

Contraindications: Hypersensitivity to aspirin or antihistamines.

Caution: This preparation may cause drowsiness. Do not drive or operate machinery while taking this medication. Individuals with high blood pressure, heart disease, diabetes, or thyroid disease should use only as directed by physician. Do not exceed recommended dosage.

KEEP THIS AND ALL MEDICINES OUT OF CHILDREN'S REACH. IN CASE OF ACCIDENTAL OVERDOSE, CONTACT PHYSICIAN IMMEDIATELY.

How Supplied: Carded 15's and bottles of 36's and 60's.

Product Identification Mark: Pink and White tablet with number "4" on one surface.

[*Shown in Product Identification Section*]

4-WAY® Nasal Spray

Composition: Phenylephrine hydrochloride 0.5%, naphazoline hydrochloride 0.05%, pyrilamine maleate 0.2%, in a buffered isotonic aqueous solution with thimerosal, 0.005%, added as a preservative. Also available in a mentholated formula.

Action and Uses: For relief of nasal congestion, runny nose, sneezing, and itching nose, which may be symptoms of common cold, sinusitis, nasal allergies, or hay fever.

Dosage and Administration: With head in a normal upright position, put atomizer tip into nostril. Squeeze atomizer with firm, quick pressure while inhaling. Adults-spray twice into each nostril. Children 6-12-spray once. Under 6-consult physician. Repeat in three hours, if needed.

Warning: Overdosage in young children may cause marked sedation. Do not exceed recommended dosage. Follow directions carefully. If symptoms persist, consult physician. The use of this dispenser by more than one person may spread infection. Keep out of children's reach.

How Supplied: Atomizers of ½ fluid ounce and 1 fluid ounce.

[*Shown in Product Identification Section*]

4-WAY® Long Acting Nasal Spray

Composition: Xylometazoline Hydrochloride 0.1% in a buffered isotonic aqueous solution. Thimerosal, 0.005%, added as a preservative. Also available in a mentholated formula.

Action and Uses: Provides temporary relief of nasal congestion due to the common cold, sinusitis, hayfever or other upper respiratory allergies.

Dosage and Administration: With head in a normal upright position, put atomizer tip into nostril. Squeeze atomizer with firm, quick pressure while inhaling. Adults: Spray 2 or 3 times in each nostril every 8 to 10 hours. For children under 12, consult physician.

Warning: For adult use only. Do not give this product to children under 12 years except under the advice and supervision of a physician. Do not exceed recommended dosage because symptoms may occur such as burning, stinging, sneezing, or an increase of nasal discharge. Do not use this product for more than 3 days. If symptoms persist, consult a physician. The use of this dispenser by more than one person may spread infection.

KEEP OUT OF CHILDREN'S REACH

How Supplied: Atomizers of ½ fluid ounce.

[*Shown in Product Identification Section*]

NO DOZ® TABLETS

Composition: Each tablet contains 100 mg. Caffeine. No Doz is non-habit forming.

Action and Uses: Helps restore mental alertness.

Dosage and Administration:
For Adults: 2 tablets initially, thereafter, 1 tablet every three hours should be sufficient.

Caution: Do not take without consulting physician if under medical care. No stimulant should be substituted for normal sleep in activities requiring physical alertness.

KEEP THIS AND ALL MEDICINES OUT OF THE REACH OF CHILDREN.
How Supplied: Carded 15's and 36's and bottles of 60's.
Product Identification Mark: A white tablet with No Doz on one side.
[*Shown in Product Identification Section*]

PAZO® HEMORRHOID OINTMENT/SUPPOSITORIES

Composition: Triolyte®, Bristol-Myers brand of the combination of benzocaine (0.8%) and ephedrine sulphate (0.24%); zinc oxide (4.0%); camphor (2.18%), in an emollient base.
Action and Uses: Pazo helps shrink swelling of inflamed hemorrhoid tissue. Provides prompt, temporary relief of burning itch and pain in many cases.
Administration:
Ointment—Apply stainless Pazo well up in rectum night and morning, and after each bowel movement. Repeat as often during the day as may be necessary to maintain comfort. Continue for one week after symptoms subside. When applicator is used, lubricate applicator first with Pazo. Insert slowly, then simply press tube.
Suppositories—Remove foil and insert one Pazo suppository night and morning, and after each bowel movement. Repeat as often during the day as may be necessary to maintain comfort. Continue for one week after symptoms subside.
Warning: If the underlying condition persists or recurs frequently, despite treatment, or if any bleeding or hard irreducible swelling is present, consult your physician.
Keep out of children's reach. Keep in a cool place.
How Supplied:
Ointment—1-ounce and 2-ounce tubes with plastic applicator.
Suppositories—Boxes of 12 and 24 wrapped in silver foil.
Literature Available: Yes.

Burroughs Wellcome Co.
**3030 CORNWALLIS ROAD
RESEARCH TRIANGLE PARK,
NC 27709**

BOROFAX® Ointment

Description: Contains 5% boric acid in an emollient base with high lanolin content.
Indications: Relief of discomfort of chapped skin, chafed skin, diaper rash, dry skin, abrasions, sunburn, windburn, insect bites, other skin irritations.
Actions: Provides a water-resistant protective film which soothes affected area, promotes rapid healing. Keeps infant's tender skin soft, smooth, free from irritation, especially in diaper area.
Directions: *Not to be applied to the eye.* Apply to inflamed areas three or four times daily.
How Supplied: Tubes, $\frac{3}{4}$ oz., $1\frac{3}{4}$ oz.

EMPIRIN® ASPIRIN

Description: Each tablet contains 325 mg (5 grs) aspirin.
Indications: Adults: headache, minor muscular aches and pains, menstrual pain, toothache, pain of neuralgia; pain, discomfort, and fever of colds and flu; pain and discomfort associated with minor sore throat; sleeplessness caused by minor pain and discomfort; minor pain of arthritis, rheumatism, bursitis, lumbago, sciatica.
Children: headache, minor muscular aches and pains, toothache, discomfort and fever of colds and flu.
Actions: Acts to reduce pain as well as inflammation and fever.
Warning: Do not take this product if you are allergic to aspirin, have asthma, a gastric ulcer or its symptoms, or are taking a medication that affects the clotting of blood, except under the advice of a physician.
Dosage and Administration: For adults: 1 or 2 tablets with a full glass of water; repeat every 4 hours as needed, up to 12 tablets a day.
For children:

under 3 years—consult your physician	
3 to under 4 years	$\frac{1}{2}$ tablet
4 to under 6 years	$\frac{3}{4}$ tablet
6 to under 9 years	1 tablet
9 to under 11 years	$1\frac{1}{4}$ tablets
11 to under 12 years	$1\frac{1}{2}$ tablets
12 and over	same as adult

Take with a full glass of water. Indicated dosage may be repeated every 4 hours up to 5 times a day. High or continued fever, severe or persistent sore throat especially when accompanied by high fever, headache, nausea or vomiting, may be serious. Consult your physician.
How Supplied: Bottles of 25, 50, 100, 250. Note: Bottles of 250 available without child-resistant cap for people who have no children in the house and for the elderly or handicapped.
[*Shown in Product Identification Section*]

MAREZINE® Tablets

Description: Scored tablets, cyclizine hydrochloride 50 mg.
Indication: Motion sickness — land, sea, air.
Actions: Helps treat nausea and vomiting associated with motion sickness.
Warnings: Drowsiness may occur; use caution in operating motor vehicles or other machinery. Do not take this product in the presence of glaucoma or enlargement of the prostate except under the advice and supervision of a physician. Do not give to children under 6 years of age except under the advice and supervision of a physician.
KEEP THIS AND ALL MEDICINES OUT OF CHILDREN'S REACH. Store at 15°–30°C (59°–86°F) in a dry place.
Dosage and Administration: Adults and children 12 years and older: one tablet $\frac{1}{2}$ hour before departure, to be repeated every 4 to 6 hours if required. Not to exceed four tablets per day. Children 6–12, $\frac{1}{2}$ tablet up to three times daily.
How Supplied: Boxes, 12 scored tablets. Bottles of 100, 1000.

NEOSPORIN® Ointment

Description: Contains three antibacterial components: polymyxin B, bacitracin, neomycin. Each gram contains Aerosporin® (polymyxin B sulfate) 5,000 units, bacitracin zinc 400 units, neomycin sulfate 5 mg (equivalent to 3.5 mg neomycin base), special white petrolatum qs.
Indications: For first aid: to help prevent bacterial infection of minor cuts, burns, abrasions; as an aid to healing.
Actions: Gentle occlusive base helps soften dry lesions. Low melting point of base enables ointment to spread quickly and evenly without caking. Won't sting, burn or irritate skin.
Warning: In case of deep or puncture wounds or serious burns consult physician. If redness, irritation, swelling or pain persists or increases or if infection occurs, discontinue use and consult physician. Do not use in the eyes.
Directions: May be applied to affected area as needed, 2 to 5 times daily.
How Supplied: Tubes, $\frac{1}{2}$ oz (with applicator tip), 1 oz.
[*Shown in Product Identification Section*]

POLYSPORIN® Ointment

Description: Contains two antibacterial components: polymyxin B and bacitracin. Each gram contains Aerosporin® (polymyxin B sulfate) 10,000 units, bacitracin zinc 500 units, special white petrolatum qs.
Indications: Helps prevent bacterial infection in minor cuts, burns, abrasions.
Actions: Provides antibacterial protection; especially useful in patients sensitive to neomycin. Bland base won't sting or burn tender lesions. Works even under occlusive dressings or bandages.
Warning: In case of deep or puncture wounds or serious burns, consult physician. If redness, irritation, swelling or pain persists or increases or if infection occurs, discontinue use and consult physician. Do not use in the eyes.
Directions: May be applied to affected area as needed.
How Supplied: Tubes, $\frac{1}{2}$ oz with applicator tip, 1 oz.

SUDAFED® Cough Syrup
Cough Formula For Children and Adults

Description: Each 5 ml (1 teaspoonful) contains pseudoephedrine hydrochloride 30 mg, dextromethorphan hydrobromide 10 mg, guaifenesin 100 mg, alcohol 2.4%.
Indications: Temporary relief of coughing and nasal congestion due to colds or flu. Relief without drowsiness.
Actions: Suppresses unproductive coughing; loosens thick mucosal secretions; decongests stuffy noses; doesn't cause drowsiness.
Warnings: Do not give to children under 2 years except as directed by a physician. Do not exceed recommended dosage because at higher doses nervousness, dizziness or sleeplessness may occur. If cough persists for more than 7 days,

Continued on next page

Burroughs Wellcome—Cont.

tends to recur or is accompanied by high fever, rash or persistent headache, consult a physician before continuing use. Do not take this product for persistent or chronic cough such as occurs with smoking, asthma or emphysema, or where cough is accompanied by excessive secretions, or if you have high blood pressure, heart disease, diabetes, difficulty in urination due to enlargement of the prostate gland, asthma, glaucoma or thyroid disease except under the advice and supervision of a physician. Consult your physician if pregnant or nursing, or taking other medication.

Drug Interaction Precaution: Do not take this product if you are presently taking a prescription antihypertensive or antidepressant drug containing a monoamine oxidase inhibitor except under the advice and supervision of a physician.

Store at 15°–30°C (59°–86°F) and protect from light.

KEEP THIS AND ALL MEDICINES OUT OF CHILDREN'S REACH. In case of accidental overdose, seek professional assistance or contact a Poison Control Center immediately.

Dosage and Administration: Adults and children over 12 years: 2 teaspoonfuls every 4 hours. Children 6–12 years: 1 teaspoonful every 4 hours. Children 2–5 years: ½ teaspoonful every 4 hours. For children under 2 years, consult physician. Do not exceed 4 doses in 24 hours.

How Supplied: Bottles, 8 oz family size; bottles, 4 fl. oz.

[*Shown in Product Identification Section*]

SUDAFED® Tablets
30 mg, Sugar Coated
SUDAFED® Syrup
30 mg/5cc tsp, Raspberry Flavored

Description: Each tablet contains 30 mg pseudoephedrine hydrochloride. Each 5 cc teaspoonful contains 30 mg pseudoephedrine hydrochloride.

Indications: Relieves nasal/sinus congestion associated with allergies, sinusitis, and the common cold. *Decongests without drowsiness.*

Actions: Clears stuffy nose and head within 15–30 minutes; decongestant effect lasts for at least 4 hours.

Caution: Do not exceed recommended dosage unless directed by a physician. If symptoms persist for 5 days or are accompanied by high fever, consult your physician before continuing use. Reduce dosage if nervousness, dizziness, sleeplessness, nausea or headache occur. Individuals with high blood pressure, heart disease, diabetes, urinary retention, glaucoma or thyroid disease should use only as directed by a physician. Consult your physician if pregnant or nursing, or taking other medication.

Dosage and Administration: Adults and children over 12 years, 2 tablets every 4 hours. Children 6–12 years, 1 tablet every 4 hours. Children 2–5 years, SUDAFED® Syrup, ½ teaspoonful every 4 hours. Do not exceed 4 doses in 24

hours. For children under 2 years of age, give only as directed by a physician.

How Supplied: SUDAFED® Tablets, 30 mg, boxes of 24, 48. Bottles of 100. SUDAFED® Syrup, 30 mg/5cc teaspoonful, bottles of 4 fl. oz., 1 pint. [*Shown in Product Identification Section*]

SUDAFED® Tablets
60 mg, Sugar Coated, Adult Strength

Description: Each tablet contains 60 mg pseudoephedrine hydrochloride.

Indications: Temporary relief of nasal/sinus congestion associated with the common cold, sinusitis, hay fever and allergies. Decongests without drowsiness.

Actions: Opens up congested noses and sinuses, reaching places inaccessible to drops and sprays; makes breathing easier. No antihistamine so should not cause drowsiness; no analgesic so fever isn't masked.

Caution: Do not exceed recommended dosage unless directed by a physician. If symptoms persist for 5 days or are accompanied by high fever, consult your physician before continuing use. Reduce dosage if nervousness, dizziness, sleeplessness, nausea or headache occur. Individuals with high blood pressure, heart disease, diabetes, urinary retention, glaucoma or thyroid disease should use only as directed by a physician. Consult your physician if pregnant or nursing, or taking other medication.

Dosage and Administration: Adults and children over 12 years of age, 1 tablet every 4 hours. For children 6–12 years, use Sudafed® 30 mg Tablets, 1 tablet every 4 hours. For children 2–5 years, use Sudafed® Syrup, ½ teaspoonful every 4 hours. Do not exceed 4 doses in 24 hours. For children under 2 years of age, give only as directed by a physician.

How Supplied: Bottles of 100, 1000. [*Shown in Product Identification Section*]

SUDAFED® Plus Tablets
SUDAFED® Plus Syrup

Description: Each scored tablet contains pseudoephedrine hydrochloride 60 mg and chlorpheniramine maleate 4 mg. Each 5 ml syrup contains pseudoephedrine hydrochloride 30 mg and chlorpheniramine maleate 2 mg.

Indications: Decongestant *plus* antihistamine effect. Relieves nasal/sinus congestion associated with the common cold *PLUS* sneezing and other hay fever symptoms, for example: watery, itchy eyes; runny nose.

Actions: Clears areas unreached by nose drops, sprays, inhalants. Provides longer relief than some nose drops and sprays.

Warnings: May cause excitability especially in children. Do not give to children under 6 years except as directed by a physician. May cause drowsiness. Do not exceed recommended dosage because at higher doses nervousness, dizziness or sleeplessness may occur. If symptoms do not improve within 7 days, or are accompanied by a high fever, consult a physician before continuing use. Do not take

this product if you have high blood pressure, heart disease, (diabetes), thyroid disease, asthma, glaucoma or difficulty in urination due to enlargement of the prostate gland except under the advice and supervision of a physician. Consult your physician if pregnant or nursing, or taking other medication.

Drug Interaction Precaution: Do not take this product if you are presently taking a prescription antihypertensive or antidepressant drug containing a monoamine oxidase inhibitor except under the advice and supervision of a physician.

Caution: Avoid driving a motor vehicle or operating heavy machinery. Avoid alcoholic beverages while taking this product.

KEEP THIS AND ALL MEDICINES OUT OF CHILDREN'S REACH. In case of accidental overdose, seek professional assistance or contact a Poison Control Center immediately.

Dosage and Administration: Tablets: Adults and Children over 12 years of age, 1 tablet every 4 hours. Children 6–12 years, ½ tablet every 4 hours. For children under age 6, consult a physician.

Syrup: Adults and children over 12 years of age, 2 teaspoonfuls every 4 hours. Children 6–12 years, 1 teaspoonful every 4 hours. For children under 6 years of age, consult a physician. Do not exceed 4 doses in 24 hours.

How Supplied: Tablets, boxes of 24. Syrup, bottles, 4 fl. oz. [*Shown in Product Identification Section*]

SUDAFED® S.A. Capsules
Sustained Action

Description: Each capsule contains: 120 mg pseudoephedrine hydrochloride.

Indications: Temporary relief of nasal congestion; helps decongest sinus openings, without drowsiness.

Actions: Clears stuffy nose and head—up to 12 hours relief. Contains no antihistamine so won't cause drowsiness—no analgesic so fever isn't masked.

Warnings: Do not exceed recommended dosage because at higher doses nervousness, dizziness, or sleeplessness may occur. If symptoms do not improve within 7 days or are accompanied by high fever, consult a physician before continuing use. Do not take this preparation if you have high blood pressure, heart disease, diabetes, or thyroid disease except under the advice and supervision of a physician.

Drug Interaction Precaution: Do not take this product if you are presently taking a prescription antihypertensive or antidepressant drug containing a monoamine oxidase inhibitor except under the advice and supervision of a physician.

Dosage and Administration: One capsule every 12 hours. Do not give to children under 12 years old.

How Supplied: Capsules of 120 mg (clear red top and clear body. Box of 10 capsules and bottles of 40 and 100 capsules.

[*Shown in Product Identification Section*]

WELLCOME® LANOLINE

Description: A highly purified lanolin obtained from the fat of lamb's wool.

Indications: For all ages. Replaces natural oils in skin and hair. Useful in foot care of diabetics when impaired circulation causes skin of feet to be dry, cracked, fissured.

Actions: Soothes chapped, irritated skin dried out by soaps, detergents, weather; alleviates scaliness and dryness of scalp.

Directions: May be applied to the face, hands, scalp, feet or other areas of the body's skin as often as needed. For best results, apply after washing while the skin is still damp. Massage gently into skin, removing excess Lanoline with a tissue.

How Supplied: Tubes, 1¾ oz (49.6 g).

WELLCORTIN™ Cream
WELLCORTIN™ Lotion
WELLCORTIN™ Ointment

Description: WELLCORTIN™ CREAM contains 0.5% hydrocortisone acetate. WELLCORTIN™ LOTION contains 0.5% hydrocortisone acetate. WELLCORTIN™ OINTMENT contains 0.5% hydrocortisone.

Indications: Temporary relief of itching and rashes associated with exzema, poison ivy/oak, cosmetics, soaps, jewelry. For itchy anal areas.

Actions: Action of steroid breaks itch-scratch-itch cycle.

Warnings: For external use only. Avoid contact with eyes. If condition worsens or if symptoms persist for more than 7 days, discontinue use of this product and consult a physician. Do not use on children under two years of age except under the advice and supervision of a physician.

Directions: Adults and children 2 years and older: apply to affected area not more than 3 to 4 times daily. For children under 2 years of age, there is no recommended dosage except under the advice and supervision of a physician.

How Supplied: WELLCORTIN™ CREAM, tubes, ½ oz. WELLCORTIN™ LOTION, bottles, 1 fl. oz. WELLCORTIN™ OINTMENT, tubes, ½ oz.

[*Shown in Product Identification Section*]

ZINCOFAX® Skin Cream

Description: A pleasantly scented skin cream containing zinc oxide 15% finely dispersed in a base containing lanolin.

Indications: Soothes and promotes healing in diaper rash, small cuts and fissures, minor skin irritations, abrasions, chafed skin.

Actions: Spreads smoothly and easily over affected area, hastening healing. Coats the skin without caking.

Directions: May be applied as needed; easily removed with soap and water.

How Supplied: Tubes, 1¾ oz.

Cambridge Plan International
WORLD HEADQUARTERS
GARDEN ROAD
MONTEREY, CA 93940

THE CAMBRIDGE DIET™

Ingredients: Nonfat milk solids, fructose, calcium sodium caseinate, soy flour, sodium citrate, monocalcium phosphate, potassium chloride, artificial flavors, magnesium oxide, calcium carrageenan, ascorbic acid, dl-alpha tocopheryl acetate, ferrous fumarate, niacinamide, zinc oxide, manganese sulfate, calcium pantothenate, vitamin A palmitate, artificial coloring, cupric sulfate, pyridoxine hydrochloride, thiamine hydrochloride, riboflavin, vitamin D_2, folic acid, sodium molybdate, biotin, potassium iodide, sodium selenite, chromic chloride, vitamin K_1, cyanocobalamin.

Indications: To make each meal of the Cambridge Diet, mix 1 level scoop of the diet food with 8 or 9 ounces of chilled water, three times daily.

Important Notice: Consult your doctor before starting this diet. In particular, individuals who have heart and cardiovascular conditions, stroke, kidney disease, diabetes, gout, hypoglycemia, chronic infections, the very elderly, growing children, adolescents, or anyone under medical care for any other condition should diet only under direct medical supervision. Your doctor can advise you whether you have any of the above conditions or for any reason should not be on this or any other diet. We will be happy to work along with you and your doctor to see that you achieve the exact results desired. Pregnant women and nursing mothers should not be on any weight-loss program.

The Cambridge Diet formula is designed for use as a sole source of nutrition for periods not to exceed four consecutive weeks at any one time.

The Cambridge Diet contains 100% of the United States RDA of vitamins and minerals, plus trace elements and electrolytes—the essential nutrients you need for health and vitality—but with only 330 calories. Cambridge is available in a bouquet of delicious flavors, including chocolate, strawberry, vanilla, and eggnog, beef, tomato and chicken soup, and a chocolate dessert. The diet also includes 33 grams of protein (75% of the US RDA), 44 grams of carbohydrates, and 3 grams of fat.

The diet was developed after 8½ years of research and testing by Alan Howard, Ph.D. and Ian McLean Baird, M.D. of the University of Cambridge, England. The fat loss on this diet is comparable to that achieved by starvation without the harmful side effects. From the precise ratio of carbohydrate to protein to fat, nitrogen balance is achieved. All the trace elements and electrolytes specified

as essential by the National Academy of Sciences are contained in The Cambridge Diet.

The average weight loss of 16 to 20 pounds in four weeks has been achieved by people who could not lose weight with any other low-calorie program.

Studies showed that in clinical tests no harmful side effects were experienced; however, after three weeks, serum cholesterol was decreased by 21 percent, triglycerides were reduced by 45 percent, and serum lipids in hyperlipaemic patients were normalized.

How Supplied: By independent distributors. For more information, contact Cambridge Plan International, World Headquarters, Garden Road, Monterey, California, 93940.

[*Shown in Product Identification Section*]

Campbell Laboratories, Inc.
300 EAST 51st STREET
P.O. BOX 812, F.D.R. STATION
NEW YORK, NY 10022

HERPECIN-L® Cold Sore Lip Balm

Composition: A soothing, emollient, cosmetically pleasant lip balm incorporating pyridoxine HCl; allantoin; the sunscreen, octyl p-(dimethylamino)-benzoate (Padimate O); and titanium dioxide in a balanced, acidic lipid system. (All ingredients appear on the package. Does not contain any "caines", antibiotics, phenol or camphor.)

Actions and Uses: HERPECIN-L® relieves dryness and chapping by providing a lipid barrier to help restore normal moisture balance to labial tissues. The sunscreen is effective in 2900-3200 AU range while titanium dioxide blocks, scatters and reflects the sun's rays. Pyridoxine is reputed to act as a co-enzyme in the metabolism of amino acids.

Administration: (1) *Recurrent "cold sores, sun and fever blisters"*: Simply put, users report the sooner and more often applied, the better the results. Frequent sufferers report that with *prophylactic* use (B.I.D./P.R.N.), their attacks are fewer and less severe. Most recurrent herpes labialis patients are aware of the *prodromal* symptoms: tingling, itching, burning. At this stage, or if the lesion has already developed, HERPECIN-L should be applied liberally as often as convenient—at least *every hour* (qq. hor.). The prodrome will often persist and remind the patient to continue to reapply HERPECIN-L. (2) *Outdoor sun/winter protection:* Apply during and after exposure (and after swimming) and again at bedtime (h.s.). (3) *Dry, chapped lips:* Apply as needed.

Note: HERPECIN-L is for peri-oral use only; not for "canker sores" (aphthous stomatitis). Primary attacks, usually in children and young adults, are normally intra-oral and accompanied by foul breath, pain and fever. Lasting up to six weeks, they are most resistant to treatment. Adjunctive therapy for pain, fever

Continued on next page

Campbell—Cont.

and secondary infection may be indicated. "Mouth breathing" is often causative of excessive chapping. Malocclusion (narrowed bite) may be suspected in angular chelosis.

Adverse Reactions: A few, rare instances of topical sensitivity to pyridoxine HCl (Vitamin B_6) have been reported. Discontinue use if allergic reaction develops.

Contraindications: HERPECIN-L does not contain any steroids; oral or topical corticosteroids are normally contraindicated in *herpes* infections.

How Supplied: 2.5 gm. swivel tubes. O.T.C.

Samples Available: Yes.

Carnation Company
**5045 WILSHIRE BLVD.
LOS ANGELES, CA 90036**

CARNATION® INSTANT BREAKFAST

Active Ingredients: Protein sources (nonfat dry milk, whey, caseinate); multivitamins and minerals.

Indications: When one envelope of Carnation instant breakfast is mixed with 8 fl. oz. (237 ml) vitamin D milk as directed, it is to be used as a meal replacement or as a supplement to the regular diet by children ages 4 years and over and adults. As such, it is indicated for low fiber/roughage diets, for burn patients, for those who temporarily cannot chew solid food, and for certain high-protein diets when a supplement is needed. When prepared with 8 fl. oz. nonfat milk, the product is also indicated for low-fat, low-cholesterol, and low-calorie diets.

Actions: When mixed with vitamin D whole milk as directed, one serving provides 280 kilocalories, 35% U.S. RDA for protein, and at least 25% U.S. RDA for all vitamins and minerals for which a U.S. RDA has been established, except for biotin. When mixed with 8 fl. oz. nonfat milk, one serving provides 220 kilocalories.

Drug Interaction: No known drug interaction.

Symptoms and Treatment of Oral Overdosage: No known symptoms of overdosage. Overconsumption might lead to excessive kilocalorie intake. Based on medical judgment, not on actual clinical experience, persons with lactose intolerance might develop temporary G.I. gas or diarrhea, depending on degree of overdosage.

Dosage and Administration: One envelope is to be mixed with 8 fl. oz. vitamin D milk. May be taken orally or by stomach tube.

Professional Labeling: Same as those described under Indications and Actions.

How Supplied: Available in either 6- or 10-envelope cartons, each envelope containing 1.21 to 1.26 oz (34.3 to 35.7 g), depending on flavor variety: Vanilla,

Chocolate, Strawberry, Eggnog, Chocolate Malt, and Coffee.

CARNATION® INSTANT NONFAT DRY MILK

Active Ingredients: Nonfat dry milk, 2203 I.U. % vitamin A palmitate, 440 I.U. % vitamin D_2.

Indications: For use by individuals wishing to reduce fat and caloric intakes by replacing nonfat milk for regular full-fat milk in the diet.

Actions: When mixed according to package directions, one 8-fl.-oz. (237-ml) serving provides 80 kilocalories and 0.16 g fat.

Warnings: Not recommended for use as a base for formula preparation for infants less than 6 months old.

Drug Interaction: No known drug interaction.

Dosage and Administration: After reconstituting Carnation instant nonfat dry milk with the appropriate amount of water (100 g by weight mixed with 950 ml water, or 350 ml by volume mixed with 950 ml water equals 1 litre), to be consumed orally, as an alternative to fresh whole milk in the diet.

How Supplied: Available either in 3.2 oz. (90.7 g) envelopes which reconstitute to one quart (in either 5- or 10-envelope cartons), or in boxes containing bulk powder in amounts which reconstitute to the following volumes of fluid milk: 3 qt, 8 qt, 14 qt, 20 qt, and 50 qt.

SLENDER® DIET FOOD FOR WEIGHT CONTROL (INSTANT)

Active Ingredients: Nonfat dry milk, multivitamins and minerals; 0.0009% BHA added to strawberry flavor as a preservative.

Indications: One envelope of Slender instant is to be mixed with 6 fl. oz. (178 ml) vitamin D milk. It is to be used as a meal replacement to maintain or slowly lose weight, or as a complete dietary replacement for more rapid weight loss when at least four servings are consumed daily as the total diet. Slender instant is intended for children ages 4 years and older and adults.

Actions: When consumed as directed, one serving of Slender instant supplies 225 kilocalories, 25% of the U.S. RDA for protein, and 25% of U.S. RDA of all vitamins and minerals for which a U.S. RDA has been established. Safety, and efficacy for weight loss, for patients consuming four servings per day have been clinically demonstrated for a period of three weeks.

Drug Interaction: No known drug interaction.

Symptoms and Treatment of Oral Overdosage: No known symptoms exist. Overconsumption might lead to excessive kilocalorie intake. Based on medical judgment, not on actual clinical experience, persons with lactose intolerance might develop temporary G.I. gas or diarrhea, depending on degree of overdosage.

Dosage and Administration: Taken orally, one or more daily servings (up to

four per day), each mixed with 6 fl. oz. vitamin D milk.

Professional Labeling: Same information as outlined under Indications and Actions.

How Supplied: Available in 1.05 to 1.07 oz. envelopes (depending on flavor variety), which come in cartons containing 4 envelopes. Available flavors are Dutch Chocolate, Chocolate, Vanilla, Strawberry Yogurt, Lemon Yogurt, and Raspberry Yogurt.

SLENDER® DIET MEAL FOR WEIGHT CONTROL (CANNED)

Active Ingredients: Skim milk, multivitamins, and minerals.

Indications: For use as a meal replacement to maintain or slowly lose weight, or as a complete dietary replacement for more rapid weight loss when at least four servings are consumed daily. Slender liquid is intended for children ages 4 years and older and adults.

Actions: One serving of Slender liquid (one 10-fl.-oz. can) supplies 225 kilocalories, 25% of the U.S. RDA for protein, and 25% of U.S. RDA of all vitamins and minerals for which a U.S. RDA has been established. Safety, and efficacy for weight loss, for patients consuming four servings per day have been clinically demonstrated for a period of three weeks.

Drug Interactions: No known drug interaction.

Symptoms and Treatment of Oral Overdosage: No known symptoms exist. Overconsumption might lead to excessive kilocalorie intake. Based on medical judgment, not on actual clinical experience, persons with lactose intolerance might develop temporary G.I. gas or diarrhea, depending on degree of overdosage.

Dosage and Administration: Taken orally, one or more daily servings up to four servings per day.

Professional Labeling: Same information as outlined under Indications and Actions.

How Supplied: Available in 10-fl.-oz. (296-ml; 313-g) cans in the following varieties: Chocolate, Chocolate Fudge, Milk Chocolate, Chocolate Malt, Vanilla, Strawberry, Banana, Peach.

SLENDER® DIET MEAL BARS FOR WEIGHT CONTROL

Active Ingredients: Protein sources, including peanuts, whey, calcium caseinate, egg white, and soy; multivitamins and minerals.

Indications: For use as a meal replacement to maintain or slowly lose weight, or as a complete dietary replacement for more rapid weight loss when at least four servings are consumed daily. Slender bars are intended for children ages 4 years and older and adults.

Actions: One serving of two Slender diet meal bars supplies 275 kilocalories, 25% of the U.S. RDA for protein, and 25% of U.S. RDA of all vitamins and minerals for which a U.S. RDA has been established. Safety, and efficacy for weight loss, for patients consuming four servings per day have been clinically demonstrated for a period of three weeks.

Drug Interaction: No known drug interaction.

Symptoms and Treatment of Oral Overdosage: No known symptoms exist. Overconsumption might lead to excessive kilocalorie intake.

Dosage and Administration: Taken orally, one or more daily servings (of two bars), up to four servings per day.

Professional Labeling: Same information as outlined under Indications and Actions.

How Supplied: Available in two-bar pouches, four pouches per carton. Each bar weighs 0.98 to 1.00 oz. (27.6 to 28.6 g), depending on flavor variety. Available flavors are Chocolate, Chocolate Peanut Butter, Vanilla, Chocolate Chip, Chocolate Fudge, Chocolate Caramel Nut, Strawberry Yogurt, Lemon Yogurt, Raspberry Yogurt.

Carter Products
Division of Carter-Wallace, Inc.
767 FIFTH AVENUE
NEW YORK, NY 10153

ANSWER®
At–Home Early Pregnancy
Test Kit (Results in 2 Hours)

Active Ingredients: Each kit contains: HCG antiserum (rabbit) and HCG on sheep red blood cells, dried (test tube with chemical material) and a Buffer solution (plastic vial with test liquid).

Indications: A diagnostic aid for early determination of pregnancy, based on the presence of Human Chorionic Gonadotropin (HCG) in the urine. The sensitivity of ANSWER is such that pregnancy can often be determined as early as the 9th day after an expected menstrual period.

Actions: ANSWER is a rapid, specific test. Based on its sensitivity, most urine specimens contain an adequate concentration of HCG to be detected nine days after the day the period was expected. In studies conducted with untrained people, 96% of the time the test was performed correctly. This number is based on reports which include a population of normal pregnant and non-pregnant females comparing results to results obtained by trained laboratory personnel.

Directions for Use:

A. **Urine Collection—Before you start the test.**

Collect a small amount of your first morning urine in a clean, well-rinsed glass container. The container must be washed and rinsed absolutely clean since any trace of detergent could give a false reading.

The test should be performed immediately. However, if you cannot do this, keep the urine sample covered in the refrigerator until you are ready to do the test. Sediment may form, but do not shake the container of urine. Only the clear urine at the top of the container should be used. Be sure to test your urine

the same day it is collected. Be sure to bring urine to room temperature before testing.

Note: If urine is cloudy, pink, or red in color or has a strong odor, do not perform the test, as certain substances can cause false test results.

B. **Performance of the test.**

1. Remove test tube from stand and tap it gently to make sure the chemical material is at the bottom of the test tube. Remove stopper from the test tube and replace tube in stand. Keep the stopper because you will use it later.

2. Fill dropper with urine by squeezing the rubber bulb.

3. Empty 2 drops of urine from dropper into test tube.

4. Remove plastic vial and hold with tip pointing up making sure no liquid is in the neck of the vial. Snap off tip of vial and squeeze all contents of the vial into the test tube.

5. Replace stopper in test tube. Remove test tube from stand and turn over several times until chemical material is completely mixed with liquid.

6. Replace test tube in the stand. Place the stand (with the mirror facing you) on a solid surface away from vibration, such as on a heavy chest or bookcase where it will not be hit or bumped or otherwise disturbed, and where the mirror can be easily seen. Allow to remain UNDISTURBED at room temperature for 2 hours.

Keep stand away from heat, vibration, and direct sunlight. Do not place stand on the refrigerator or on the same table or kitchen counter as a mixer or blender since these can cause vibrations when they are running. Do not place it on the stove, next to a heater, or in the window because heat or direct sunlight can disturb the test. Make sure stand is not moved during this 2-hour period.

Note: If stand is moved or jarred during the initial 2-hour waiting period, take tube from stand, shake several times and return it to stand for another 2 hours undisturbed. This re-shaking procedure can be done only once and only within the first 2 hours.

C. **How to read the test (results).**

The test is to be read no sooner than 2 hours and no later than 4 hours after the tube is placed in the stand above the mirror.

Do not pick up or touch stand or tube. Read results by looking at the bottom of the tube in the mirror at base of stand. If the image you see in the mirror shows no ring as in illustration 1, pregnancy hormone is not detected.

If the image you see in the mirror shows a well-formed ring or doughnut-like ring, as in illustrations 2 and 3, pregnancy hormone is detected.

Continued on next page

Carter—Cont.

PREGNANCY HORMONE NOT DETECTED

No Ring

PREGNANCY HORMONE DETECTED

Ring

Ring

Important: This test is not intended to replace your doctor's diagnosis: If your test result shows pregnancy hormone detected, this should be confirmed by your doctor. If your result shows pregnancy hormone not detected, you may want to retest in one week. If you miss a second period, see your doctor.

Warnings: DO NOT REUSE, USE ONLY ONCE AND DISCARD.

Sometimes, around the time of "change of life" or in the case of certain diseases, ANSWER will show the presence of a hormone resembling the pregnancy hormone in your urine, even though you may not be pregnant. If your test result shows pregnancy hormone is detected, you should see your doctor. If you have missed a period or for any reason you think that you may be pregnant no matter what the result of the test, you should see your doctor. Don't guess; if you are not sure of your test result, consult your doctor.

ANSWER is not meant to replace an examination by your doctor. If you have been taking medication, the test may not work. In this case, you should have a test performed by your doctor or a professional laboratory. No test is perfect. Laboratory test results and a doctor's examination go hand in hand. Although the ANSWER method of detecting pregnancy is reliable, it is not 100% accurate. False results (pregnancy hormone detected when there is no pregnancy or pregnancy hormone not detected when the woman is pregnant) can occur in about 5% of women tested.

Precaution:
- Store the whole kit in a cool, dry place, not more than 30°C (86°F). Do not put in the freezer.
- ANSWER is not for internal use (it is for in vitro diagnostic use). Keep it out of the reach of children.

- Use only as directed. Do not use earlier than 9 days after the day you expected your period.
- Do not use after the expiration date stamped on the box.
- If the liquid in the plastic vial is cloudy, do not use the kit. Return to place of purchase for a new kit.

How Supplied: Available in kits of one test each. Each kit includes a test tube containing Human Chorionic Gonadotropin antiserum (rabbit) and Human Chorionic Gonadotropin on sheep red blood cells, dried; a plastic vial containing a buffer solution; a dropper for transferring urine; and a stand for conducting the test. The stand includes a mirror for convenient reading without disturbing the test.

[*Shown in Product Identification Section*]

CARTER'S LITTLE PILLS®
A Stimulant Laxative

Active Ingredient: 5 mg bisacodyl, U.S.P. in each enteric coated pill.

Indications: For effective short-term relief of simple constipation (infrequent or difficult bowel movement).

Actions: Bisacodyl is a stimulant laxative that promotes bowel movement by one or more direct actions on the intestine.

Directions for Use: Adult dosage is 1 to 3 pills (usually 2) at bedtime. Children over 3 years of age, 1 pill at bedtime.

Warnings: Do not chew. Do not give to children under 3 years of age or to persons who cannot swallow without chewing. Do not use this product when abdominal pain, nausea, or vomiting are present. Do not take this product within one hour before or after taking an antacid and/or milk. This product may cause abdominal discomfort, faintness, rectal burning or mild cramps. Store in a cool place at temperatures not above 86°F (30°C).

Prolonged or continued use of this product can lead to laxative dependence and loss of normal bowel function. Serious side effects from prolonged use or overdose can occur.

If you have noticed a sudden change in bowel habits that persists over a period of two weeks, consult a physician before using a laxative. This product should be used only occasionally, but in any event, no longer than daily for one week, except on the advice of a physician.

Drug Interaction Precaution: No known drug interaction.

Treatment of Overdosage: In case of accidental overdose seek professional assistance or contact a Poison Control Center immediately.

Professional Labeling: For effective short-term relief of simple constipation. For use in preparation of the patient for surgery or for preparation of the colon for x-ray and endoscopic examination.

How Supplied: Available in packages of 30 pills and 85 pills.

[*Shown in Product Identification Section*]

Cetylite Industries, Inc.
9051 RIVER ROAD
P.O. BOX CN6
PENNSAUKEN, NJ 08110

PROTEXIN ORAL RINSE
Deodorant Mouthwash

Ingredients: SD Alcohol 38B, Polysorbate 80 USP, Water, Flavor, Zinc Chloride, Artificial Color.

Indications: Oral debris, ropy saliva, offensive oral odors, unpleasant aftertaste.

Actions: Clears the mouth of debris and ropy saliva and leaves a pleasant, freshening, long-lasting taste.

Warnings: To be used only as directed.

Precaution: None needed.

Dosage and Administration: As per label.

Professional Labeling: None needed.

How Supplied: 3 two ounce bottles of concentrate per package. Each bottle makes up to two (2) gallons of mouthwash. Available in 2 flavors—Peppermint Menthol or Cinnamon Clove.

SKIN SCREEN
Skin Protectant

Ingredients: Isopropanol, Propylene Glycol, Silicone, Lanolin Derivative, Oil of Mink.

Indications: For use on technicians' hands as well as the lip areas and facial hair of patients to reduce the sticking of cements or other dental and laboratory adhesive materials.

Actions: The specially formulated ingredients provide long lasting protection against the repeated use of soaps and detergents.

Warnings: For external use only.

Drug Interaction: None known.

Precaution: None needed.

Symptoms and Treatment of Oral Overdosage: Not applicable.

Dosage and Administration: Externally, freely as needed.

Professional Labeling: None.

How Supplied: Three 4 ounce bottles per package.

Chattem Laboratories
Division of Chattem, Inc.
1715 WEST 38TH STREET
CHATTANOOGA, TN 37409

GRANULATED BLACK-DRAUGHT®
Senna Laxative

Active Ingredients: Senna especially compounded with other vegetable products as blending agents.

Indications: Indicated for relief of simple constipation. All laxatives are intended for occasional use only.

Warnings: Keep this and all drugs out of the reach of children. In case of accidental overdose seek professional assistance or contact a poison control center immediately.

Precautions: Not to be used when abdominal pain, nausea, vomiting or other symptoms of appendicitis are present.

During pregnancy laxatives should be taken only on the advice of a physician.

Dosage and Administration: Place ¼ to ½ level teaspoonful on tongue. Wash down at once with water. This is an average dose. Experience will determine exact dose. To take Black-Draught as a tea: steep 1 level teaspoonful in ½ cup very hot water 3 to 5 minutes. Strain through clean cloth. Add sugar if desired. Average dose: ¼ to ½ cup Black-Draught tea. ½ teaspoon contains 1.65 grams senna equivalent.

How Supplied: Net wt. ¾ oz. granulated-package.

Syrup of
BLACK-DRAUGHT®
Laxative

Active Ingredient: Casanthranol (90 mg. per tbs.). Compounded with Senna, Rhubarb, Anise, Methyl Salicylate, Cinnamon, Clove, Nutmeg, Peppermint, Spearmint and Menthol as flavorings. Alcohol 5%.

Indications: Indicated for relief of simple constipation. All laxatives are intended for occasional use only.

Warnings: Keep this and all drugs out of the reach of children. In case of accidental overdose seek professional assistance or contact a poison control center immediately.

Precautions: Not to be used when abdominal pain, nausea, vomiting or other symptoms of appendicitis are present. During pregnancy laxatives should be taken only on the advice of physician.

Dosage and Administration: Adults —1 teaspoonful to one tablespoonful. Children—(2–12 years) ½ adult dose. Take before meals or at bedtime.

How Supplied: Net 2 fluid ounces and net 5 fluid ounces.

BLACK-DRAUGHT®
Lax-Senna Tablets

Active Ingredients: Senna especially compounded with other vegetable products as blending agents.

Indications: Indicated for relief of simple constipation. All laxatives are intended for occasional use only.

Warnings: Keep this and all drugs out of the reach of children. In case of accidental overdose seek professional assistance or contact a poison control center immediately.

Precautions: Not to be used when abdominal pain, nausea, vomiting or other symptoms of appendicitis are present. During pregnancy laxatives should be taken only on the advice of a physician.

Dosage and Administration: Adults —average dose 2 tablets preferably at bedtime. Dose may be increased to 3 tablets or decreased to 1 tablet to suit individual requirements. Each tablet contains 600 mg. senna equivalent.

How Supplied: 30 tablets per package.

BLIS-TO-SOL®
Liquid

Active Ingredients: Salicylic Acid and Undecylenic Acid.

Indications: For relief of Athlete's Foot, Ringworm and other skin fungus infections.

Warnings: Keep this and all drugs out of the reach of children. In case of accidental ingestion, seek professional assistance or contact a poison control center immediately.

Precautions: If swelling develops or symptoms persist or increase, discontinue use and consult a physician.

Dosage and Administration: Apply generous amounts of Blis-To-Sol liquid to infected area morning and night until infected outer layer of skin begins to shed. Then apply once or twice a week until skin appears healthy.

How Supplied: Net 1 and 2 fluid ounce packages.

BLIS-TO-SOL®
Powder

Active Ingredients: Benzoic Acid and Salicylic Acid.

Indications: An anti-infective to relieve and help prevent infection of Athlete's Foot, Ringworm, Jockey Itch and minor fungus skin irritations.

Warnings: Keep out of the reach of children.

Dosage and Administration: Cleanse affected parts and dry thoroughly. Dust on powder and rub into the skin to help prevent infection or reinfection of athlete's foot. Dust powder between toes and over the feet and inside of shoes everyday. Blis-To-Sol powder quickly soothes itching, prolongs fungicidal action, aids in healing; also helps check foot odor.

How Supplied: Net wt. 2 oz. package.

MAXIMUM CRAMP RELIEF
FORMULA
PAMPRIN®
MENSTRUAL RELIEF CAPSULES

Active Ingredients: Each capsule contains Acetaminophen 500 mg., Pamabrom 25 mg., and Pyrilamine Maleate 15 mg.

Indications: Formulated to relieve the pain of cramps. Maximum Cramp Relief Formula contains over 50% more aspirin-free pain reliever plus two special ingredients that have been clinically tested in relieving cramps, headache, low backache, water weight gain and bloating, premenstrual tension, nervousness and irritability.

Warning: KEEP THIS AND ALL DRUGS OUT OF THE REACH OF CHILDREN. In case of accidental overdose, seek professional assistance or contact a poison control center immediately.

Precautions: If drowsiness occurs, do not drive or operate machinery. Do not use for more than 10 consecutive days without consulting your physician. Do not exceed recommended dosage.

Dosage and Administration: Two capsules and repeat every three or four hours as needed not to exceed 8 capsules in a 24 hour period.

How Supplied: 4 capsules in 4 foil packettes—16's and bottle of 32's.

PAMPRIN®
MENSTRUAL RELIEF TABLETS

Active Ingredients: Each tablet contains Acetaminophen 325 mg., Pamabrom 25 mg., and Pyrilamine Maleate 12.5 mg.

Indications: To be taken at the first sign of premenstrual discomfort for safe effective relief of cramps, low backache, headache, water weight gain and bloating, premenstrual tension, nervousness and irritability.

Warning: Keep this and all drugs out of the reach of children. In case of accidental overdose, seek professional assistance or contact a poison control center immediately.

Precautions: If drowsiness occurs, do not drive or operate machinery. Do not use for more than 10 consecutive days without consulting your physician. Do not exceed recommended dosage.

Dosage and Administration: Two tablets and repeat every three or four hours as needed not to exceed 8 tablets in a 24 hour period.

How Supplied: 8 tablets in 3 foil packettes—24's and bottle of 48's.

SOLTICE®
Analgesic Quick-Rub

Active Ingredients: Menthol, Methyl Salicylate, Camphor and Eucalyptus Oil.

Indications: For minor muscular soreness and to relieve discomfort of colds.

Warning: Keep this and all drugs out of the reach of children. In case of accidental ingestion, seek professional assistance or contact a poison control center immediately.

Precautions: Do not apply to sensitive membranes (such as nose or mouth) or to broken or irritated skin. Do not apply near eyes or on children less than five years old unless on the advice of a physician. FOR EXTERNAL USE ONLY.

Dosage and Administration: To relieve discomforts of a cold, rub Soltice generously on chest and neck to provide comforting warmth to the chest area. To help relieve nasal congestion, apply small amount of Soltice just below the nose. For added relief, melt a teaspoonful of Soltice in boiling water and breathe in the medicated vapors. For muscular soreness bathe with hot water, dry thoroughly, then massage Soltice generously onto the affected areas to increase local blood circulation.

How Supplied: Net wt. 1.33 oz. package and net wt. 3.75 oz. package.

Products are cross-indexed

by product classifications

in the

BLUE SECTION

Chesebrough-Pond's Inc.
33 BENEDICT PLACE
GREENWICH, CT 06830

VASELINE® Dermatology Formula™ Cream

Composition:
Active ingredients: Petrolatum USP, Mineral Oil USP, Dimethicone.
Other ingredients: Water, Glycerin, Myreth-3 Myristate, Cetearyl Alcohol, Triethanolamine, Carbomer-934, Ceteareth-20, DMDM Hydantoin, Methylparaben, Fragrance, Propylparaben.
Actions and Uses: Developed with dermatologists, this exclusive, concentrated formula is clinically proven to help heal chapping, scaling, raw cracked skin, redness, soreness and itching caused by severely dry skin. Formulated to penetrate as deep as the dryness, it helps heal even rough areas such as knees, elbows and heels. When used as directed, this cream can restore severely dry skin to its healthy, normal condition.
Administration and Dosage: Apply liberally to affected areas as often as needed. It is recommended that harsh soap and hot water be avoided as these may adversely affect dry skin conditions.
How Supplied: Dermatology Formula™ Cream is available in 3 and 5.25 oz. jars.
[*Shown in Product Identification Section*]

VASELINE® Dermatology Formula™ Lotion

Composition:
Active ingredients: Petrolatum USP, Mineral Oil USP, Dimethicone.
Other ingredients: Water, Glycerin, Stearic Acid, Glycol Stearate and Other Ingredients, Acetylated Lanolin Alcohol, Glyceryl Stearate, Triethanolamine, PEG-40 Stearate, Magnesium Aluminum Silicate, Cetyl Alcohol, Methylparaben, Fragrance, Propylparaben, Carbomer-934, Disodium EDTA, DMDM Hydantoin.
Actions and Uses: Developed with dermatologists, this exclusive formula is clinically proven to help heal chapping, scaling, raw cracked skin, redness, soreness and itching caused by severely dry skin. Vaseline® Dermatology Formula™ is formulated to incorporate the superior skin protection, moisturizing and softening properties of petrolatum. The product has superior aesthetics and is non-greasy to maximize patient compliance with the treatment regimen. Clinical studies conducted during winter months on patients with severely dry skin showed dramatic relief of all dry skin signs and symptoms after only 4 days.
Administration and Dosage: Apply liberally to affected areas as often as needed. It is recommended that harsh soaps and hot water be avoided as these may adversely affect dry skin conditions.
How Supplied: Dermatology Formula™ Lotion is available in 5.5, 11 and 16 oz. plastic bottles.
[*Shown in Product Identification Section*]

VASELINE® Pure Petroleum Jelly Skin Protectant

Composition: White Petrolatum U.S.P.
Indications: A soothing protectant for minor skin irritations such as burns, scrapes, abrasions, chafing, detergent hands, dry or chapped skin and sunburn. Provides temporary relief of external hemorrhoids and scaling due to psoriasis. Helps prevent diaper rash, soothes chapped skin and temporarily soothes minor sunburn due to its emollient and lubricant properties.
Directions: Cleanse affected areas with soap and water prior to application, then apply generously to provide a continuous protective film.
Drug Interaction: No known drug interactions. Product is innocuous, physiologically inert with no known sensitization potential.
How Supplied: 1 oz. and 3¾ oz. plastic tubes.
1¾ oz., 3¾ oz., 7½ oz. and 15 oz. plastic jars.
[*Shown in Product Identification Section*]

Church & Dwight Co., Inc.
20 KINGSBRIDGE ROAD
PISCATAWAY, NJ 08854

ARM & HAMMER® BAKING SODA
Antacid

Active Ingredient: Sodium Bicarbonate, U.S.P.
Indications: For relief of heartburn, sour stomach and/or acid indigestion.
Actions: Arm & Hammer Baking Soda provides rapid, effective neutralization of stomach acids. Each ½ teaspoon dose will neutralize 20.9 mEq of acid.
Warnings: Except under the advice and supervision of a physician (1) do not take more than eight ½ teaspoons per person up to 60 years old or four ½ teaspoons per person 60 years or older in a 24-hour period, (2) do not use this product if you are on a sodium restricted diet, or (3) do not use the maximum dose for more than 2 weeks.
Dosage and Administration: ½ teaspoon in a glass of water every 2 hours up to maximum dosage, or as directed by a physician.
How Supplied: Available in 8 oz., 16 oz. and 32 oz. boxes.

IDENTIFICATION PROBLEM?

Consult the

Product Identification Section

where you'll find

products pictured

in full color.

CIBA Pharmaceutical Company
Division of CIBA-GEIGY Corporation
SUMMIT, NJ 07901

NUPERCAINAL®
Anesthetic Ointment
Pain-Relief Cream

> **Caution:**
> **Nupercainal** products are not for prolonged or extensive use and should never be applied in or near the eyes.
> **Consult labels before using.**
> **Keep this and all medications out of reach of children.**
> NUPERCAINAL SHOULD NOT BE SWALLOWED. SWALLOWING OR USE OF A LARGE QUANTITY IS HAZARDOUS, PARTICULARLY TO CHILDREN. CONSULT A PHYSICIAN OR POISON CONTROL CENTER IMMEDIATELY.

Indications: Nupercainal Ointment and Cream are fast-acting, long-lasting pain relievers that you can use for a number of painful skin conditions. **Nupercainal Anesthetic Ointment** is for hemorrhoids and for general use. **Nupercainal Pain-Relief Cream** is for general use only. The **Cream** is half as strong as the **Ointment**.
How to use Nupercainal Anesthetic Ointment (for general use). This soothing Ointment helps lubricate dry, inflamed skin and gives fast, temporary relief of pain and itching. It is recommended for sunburn, nonpoisonous insect bites, minor burns, cuts and scratches. **DO NOT USE THIS PRODUCT IN OR NEAR YOUR EYES.**
Apply to affected areas gently. If necessary, cover with a light dressing for protection. Do not use more than 1 ounce of Ointment in a 24-hour period for an adult, do not use more than one-quarter of an ounce in a 24-hour period for a child. If irritation develops, discontinue use and consult your doctor.
How to use Nupercainal Anesthetic Ointment for fast, temporary relief of pain and itching due to hemorrhoids (also known as piles).
Remove cap from tube and set it aside. Attach the white plastic applicator to the tube. Squeeze the tube until you see the Ointment begin to come through the little holes in the applicator. Using your finger, lubricate the applicator with the Ointment. Now insert the entire applicator gently into the rectum. Give the tube a good squeeze to get enough Ointment into the rectum for comfort and lubrication. Remove applicator from rectum and wipe it clean. Apply additional Ointment to anal tissues to help relieve pain, burning, and itching. For best results use Ointment morning and night and after each bowel movement. After each use detach applicator, and wash it off with soap and water. Put cap back on tube before storing. In case of rectal bleeding, discontinue use and consult your doctor.

Pain-Relief Cream for general use. This Cream is particularly effective for fast, temporary relief of pain and itching associated with sunburn, cuts, scratches, minor burns and non-poisonous insect bites. **DO NOT USE THIS PRODUCT IN OR NEAR YOUR EYES.** Apply liberally to affected area and rub in gently. This Cream is water-washable, so be sure to reapply after bathing, swimming or sweating. If irritation develops, discontinue use and consult your doctor.

Nupercainal Anesthetic Ointment contains 1% (one percent) dibucaine USP in a lubricant base. Available in tubes of 1 and 2 ounces.

Nupercainal Pain-Relief Cream contains 0.5% (one-half of one percent) dibucaine USP in a water-soluble base. Available in 1 ½ ounce tubes.

Dibucaine USP is officially classified as a "topical anesthetic" and is one of the strongest and longest lasting of all pain relievers. It is not a narcotic.

C81-17 (5/81)

[Shown in Product Identification Section]

NUPERCAINAL™
Suppositories

Caution:
Nupercainal Suppositories are not for prolonged or extensive use. Contact with the eyes should be avoided.
Consult labels before using.
Keep this and all medications out of reach of children.
NUPERCAINAL SUPPOSITORIES SHOULD NOT BE SWALLOWED. SWALLOWING CAN BE HAZARDOUS, PARTICULARLY TO CHILDREN. IN THE EVENT OF ACCIDENTAL SWALLOWING CONSULT A PHYSICIAN OR POISON CONTROL CENTER IMMEDIATELY.

Indications: Nupercainal Suppositories are for the temporary relief from itching, burning, and discomfort due to hemorrhoids or other anorectal disorders.

How to use Nupercainal Suppositories for hemorrhoids (also known as piles) or other anorectal disorders.
Tear off suppository along the perforated line. Remove foil wrapper. Insert the suppository, rounded end first, well into the anus until you can feel it moving into your rectum. For best results, use one suppository after each bowel movement and as needed, but not to exceed 6 in a 24-hour period. Each suppository is sealed in its own foil packet to reduce danger of leakage when carried in pocket or purse. **To prevent melting, do not store above 86°F (30°C).**

Nupercainal Suppositories contain 2.4 gram cocoa butter, .25 gram zinc oxide, .1 gram bismuth subgallate, and acetone sodium bisulfite as preservative.

No longer contains dibucaine.

Mfd. by: G & W Laboratories, Inc.
South Plainfield
New Jersey 07080

Dist. by:
CIBA Pharmaceutical Company
Division of CIBA-GEIGY Corporation
Summit, New Jersey 07901

C81-14 (5/81)

[Shown in Product Identification Section]

PRIVINE®
0.05% Nasal Solution
0.05% Nasal Spray

Caution: Do not use Privine if you have glaucoma. Privine is an effective nasal decongestant **when you use it in the recommended dosage.** If you use too much, too long, or too often, Privine may be harmful to your nasal mucous membranes and cause burning, stinging, sneezing or an increased runny nose. Do not use Privine by mouth.

Keep this and all medications out of the reach of children. Do not use Privine with children under 6 years of age, except with the advice and supervision of a doctor.
OVERDOSAGE IN YOUNG CHILDREN MAY CAUSE MARKED SEDATION AND IF SEVERE, EMERGENCY TREATMENT MAY BE NECESSARY. IF NASAL STUFFINESS PERSISTS AFTER 3 DAYS OF TREATMENT, DISCONTINUE USE AND CONSULT A DOCTOR.

Privine is a nasal decongestant that comes in two forms: Nasal Solution (in a bottle with a dropper) and Nasal Spray (in a plastic squeeze bottle). Both are for prompt, and prolonged relief of nasal congestion due to common colds, sinusitis, hay fever, etc.

How to use Nasal Solution. Squeeze rubber bulb to fill dropper with proper amount of medication. For best results, tilt head as far back as possible and put two drops of solution into your right nostril. Then lean head forward, inhaling and turning your head to the left. Refill dropper by squeezing bulb. Now tilt head as far back as possible and put two drops of solution into your left nostril. Then lean head forward, inhaling, and turning your head to the right.

Use only 2 drops in each nostril. Do not repeat this dosage more than every 3 hours.

The Privine dropper bottle is designed to make administration of the proper dosage easy and to prevent accidental overdosage. Privine will not cause sleeplessness, so you may use it before going to bed.

Important: After use, be sure to rinse the dropper with very hot water. This helps prevent contamination of the bottle with bacteria from nasal secretions. Use of the dispenser by more than one person may spread infection.

Note: Privine Nasal Solution may be used on contact with glass, plastic, stainless steel and specially treated metals used in atomizers. Do not let the solution come in contact with reactive metals, especially aluminum. If solution becomes discolored, it should be discarded.

How to use Nasal Spray. For best results do **not** shake the plastic squeeze bottle.
Remove cap. With head held upright, spray twice into each nostril. Squeeze the

bottle sharply and firmly while sniffing through the nose.

For best results use every 4 to 6 hours. Do not use more often than every 3 hours. Avoid overdosage. Follow directions for use carefully.

Privine Nasal Solution contains 0.05% naphazoline hydrochloride USP with benzalkonium chloride as a preservative. Available in bottles of .66 fl. oz. (20 ml) with dropper, and bottles of 16 fl. oz. (473 ml). Privine Nasal Spray contains 0.05% naphazoline hydrochloride USP with benzalkonium chloride as a preservative. Available in plastic squeeze bottles of ½ fl. oz. (15 ml).

C80-5 (1/80)

[Shown in Product Identification Section]

VIOFORM®
(iodochlorhydroxyquin USP)

Listed in USP, a Medicare designated compendium.

Indications and Directions For Use: A soothing antifungal and antibacterial preparation for the treatment of inflamed conditions of the skin, such as eczema, athlete's foot and other fungal infections.

Apply to the affected area 2 or 3 times a day or use as directed by physician.

Caution: May prove irritating to sensitized skin in rare cases. If this should occur, discontinue treatment and consult physician. May stain.

KEEP OUT OF REACH OF CHILDREN.

How Supplied:
Ointment, 3% iodochlorhydroxyquin in a petrolatum base; tubes of 1 ounce.
Cream, 3% iodochlorhydroxyquin in a water-washable base; tubes of 1 ounce.

(7/80)

Colgate-Palmolive Company
A Delaware Corporation
300 PARK AVENUE
NEW YORK, NY 10022

COLGATE MFP® FLUORIDE GEL

Active Ingredient: Sodium Monofluorophosphate (MFP®) 0.76% in a spearmint flavored gel toothpaste base.

Other Ingredients: Sorbitol, Glycerin, Hydrated Silica, Water, PEG-12, Sodium Lauryl Sulfate, Flavor, Sodium Benzoate, Cellulose Gum, Sodium Saccharin, Titanium Dioxide, FD&C Blue No. 1.

Indications: The gel toothpaste with the anti-cavity ingredient MFP® fluoride providing maximum fluoride protection by a toothpaste and a fresh clean taste for the whole family.

Actions: Clinical tests have shown COLGATE'S MFP® fluoride to be an effective aid in the reduction of the incidence of cavities. It is approved as a decay-preventive dentifrice by the American Dental Association.

Contraindications: Sensitivity to any ingredient in this product.

Continued on next page

Colgate-Palmolive—Cont.

Directions: Brush regularly as part of a dental health program.
How Supplied: 1.4 oz., 2.6 oz., 4.6 oz., 6.4 oz., 8.2 oz. tubes.
[*Shown in Product Identification Section*]

COLGATE MFP® FLUORIDE TOOTHPASTE

Active Ingredient: Sodium Monofluorophosphate (MFP®) 0.76% in a doublemint flavored toothpaste base.
Other Ingredients: Dicalcium Phosphate Dihydrate, Water, Glycerin, Sodium Lauryl Sulfate, Cellulose Gum, Flavor, Sodium Benzoate, Tetrasodium Pyrophosphate, Sodium Saccharin.
Indications: The toothpaste with the anti-cavity ingredient MFP® fluoride providing maximum fluoride protection by a toothpaste.
Actions: Clinical tests have shown COLGATE'S MFP® fluoride to be an effective aid in the reduction of the incidence of cavities. It is approved as a decay-preventive dentifrice by the American Dental Association.
Contraindications: Sensitivity to any ingredient in this product.
Directions: Brush regularly as part of a dental health program.
How Supplied: 0.75 oz., 1.50 oz., 3.0 oz., 5.0 oz., 7.0 oz., 9.0 oz. tubes.
[*Shown in Product Identification Section*]

DERMASSAGE MEDICATED SKIN LOTION

Active Ingredient: 0.11% Menthol
Other Ingredients: Water, mineral oil, TEA-stearate, propylene glycol, stearic acid, diammonium phosphate, methylparaben, lanolin, triclosan, fragrance, urea, propylparaben.
Indications: Dermassage Medicated Skin Lotion is a rich, creamy formula that replaces lost moisture and helps soothe and smooth away rough, dry, chapped skin.
Actions: Dermassage Medicated Skin Lotion contains moisturizers and emollients that work deep into pores to soften the skin and prevent dryness from becoming soreness. The active ingredient (menthol) works as an anti-pruritic and a mild analgesic.
Contraindications: Sensitivity to any ingredient in this product.
Warnings: For External Use Only. Not for use on mucous membranes.
Dosage and Administration: Used daily Dermassage helps keep skin feeling soft and moist. Apply as desired to relieve the itching and irritation of dry, sore skin.
How Supplied:
6 oz.
10 oz.
15 oz.
Dermassage Medicated Skin Lotion is supplied in white opaque plastic bottles.
[*Shown in Product Identification Section*]

FLUORIGARD ANTI-CAVITY DENTAL RINSE

Fluorigard is accepted by the American Dental Association.

Active Ingredient: Sodium Fluoride (0.05%) in a neutral solution.
Other Ingredients: Water, Glycerin, SD Alcohol 38-B (6%), Poloxamer 338, Poloxamer 407, Sodium Benzoate, Sodium Saccharin, Benzoic Acid, Flavor, FD & C Blue No. 1, FD & C Yellow No. 5.
Indications: Good tasting Fluorigard Anti-Cavity Dental Rinse is fluoride in liquid form. It helps get cavity-fighting fluoride to back teeth, as well as front teeth; even floods those dangerous spaces between teeth where brushing might miss. 70% of all cavities happen in back teeth and between teeth.
Actions: Fluorigard Anti-Cavity Dental Rinse is a 0.05% Sodium Fluoride solution which has been proven effective in reducing cavities.
Contraindications: Sensitivity to any ingredient in this product.
Warnings: Do not swallow. For rinsing only. Not to be used by children under 6 years of age unless recommended by a dentist. Keep out of reach of young children. If an amount considerably larger than recommended for rinsing is swallowed, give as much milk as possible and contact a physician immediately.
Directions: Use once daily after thoroughly brushing teeth. For persons 6 years of age and over, fill measuring cap to 10 ml. level (2 teaspoons), rinse around and between teeth for one minute, then spit out. For maximum benefit, use every day and do not eat or drink for at least 30 minutes afterward. Rinsing may be most convenient at bedtime. This product may be used in addition to a fluoride toothpaste.
How Supplied:
6 oz.
10 oz.
16 oz.
1 Gallon Professional Size for use in dentists offices only.
[*Shown in Product Identification Section*]

Combe Incorporated
1101 WESTCHESTER AVENUE
WHITE PLAINS, NY 10604

GYNECORT™ Antipruritic
0.5% Hydrocortisone Acetate Creme

Active Ingredient: 0.5% Hydrocortisone Acetate
Indications: GYNECORT antipruritic creme medication was specifically formulated for temporary relief of external genital and rectal itching. It also relieves minor skin irritations, itching and rashes due to dermatitis on other parts of the body. GYNECORT is a highly emollient white vanishing cream which is soothing to delicate external vaginal tissue. It is hypoallergenic (contains no potentially irritating perfume), greaseless and non-staining.
Action: Hydrocortisone Acetate is an anti-inflammatory corticosteroid[1,2],

whose mechanism of action has been widely investigated. Current thinking points to the following modes of action: (1) controlling the rate of protein synthesis; (2) reducing the amounts of prostaglandin substrate available for the enzyme.[3] Corticosteroids are also known to reduce immune hypersensitivity by reducing the inflammatory response.[1]
Warning: For external use only. Avoid contact with the eyes. If condition worsens or if symptoms persist for more than 7 days, discontinue use and consult a physician. Do not use on children under 2 years of age except under the advice and supervision of a physician. Keep out of reach of children.
Dosage and Administration: Apply to affected area three or four times daily. For children under 2 years of age there is no recommended dosage except under the advice and supervision of a physician.
How Supplied: Available in ½ oz. tubes.
References:
1. Goodman and Gilman, The Pharmacological Basis of Therapeutics, Page 1487, 5th Ed., MacMillan, 1975.
2. Su-Chen L. Hong, Lawrence Levine, J. Bio. Chem., Vol. 251, No. 18, pp. 5814-5816, 1976.
3. Ryszard J. Gryglewski, et al., Prostoglandins, Vol. 10, No. 2, pp. 343–35, August 1975.
[*Shown in Product Identification Section*]

LANACANE® Medicated Creme

Active Ingredients: 6.0% Benzocaine; 2.0% Resorcinol.
Indications: LANACANE Creme Medication is specially formulated to give prompt, temporary relief from dry skin itching, vaginal and rectal itching, rashes, insect bites, sunburn, chafing, poison ivy, poison oak, chapping, sore detergent hands, minor burns and other irritated skin conditions. LANACANE checks bacteria to help speed natural healing.
Actions: Benzocaine is a local anesthetic of low toxicity considered to be one of the safest and most widely used of the over-the-counter topical anesthetics. Temporary anesthesia is elicited by penetrating the cutaneous barriers and blocking sensory receptors for the perception of pain and itching. Resorcinol activity is both antimicrobial and mildly keratolytic.
Warnings: Read enclosed circular carefully before using. Not for prolonged use. Do not get into the eyes. Some skin and membrane irritations may be caused by internal systemic disorders. If condition persists for more than seven days or worsens, discontinue use and consult your physician. Keep out of reach of children.
Drug Interaction Precaution: Benzocaine has been known to occasionally cause allergic dermatitis. Cross-reactions have been reported with paraphenylenediamine, a hair dye, sulfonamide and sun screens containing paraaminobenzoic acid esters.

Dosage and Administration: Apply LANACANE Creme Medication liberally to the affected area. Repeat as needed three or four times daily.

How Supplied: Available in 1.0 and 2.0 oz. tubes.

LANACORT™ Antipruritic
Hydrocortisone Acetate 0.5% Creme

Active Ingredient: 0.5% Hydrocortisone Acetate.

Indication: Lanacort™ Creme is specially formulated to provide relief from minor skin irritation, rashes, itching due to eczema (symptoms are redness, itching, and flaking), dermatitis (an irritated condition of the skin including inflammation and redness)... also due to soaps, detergents, cosmetics, jewelry, poison ivy, oak, sumac; insect bites; and for genital and rectal itching.

Action: Hydrocortisone Acetate is an anti-inflammatory corticosteroid[1,2], whose mechanism of action has been widely investigated. Current thinking points to the following modes of action: (1) controlling the rate of protein synthesis; (2) reducing the amounts of prostaglandin substrate available for the enzyme.[3] Corticosteroids are also known to reduce immune hypersensitivity by reducing the inflammatory response.[1]

Warning: For external use only. Avoid contact with the eyes. If conditions worsen or if symptoms persist for more than 7 days, discontinue use and consult a physician. Do not use on children under 2 years of age except under the advice and supervision of a physician. Keep out of reach of children.

Dosage and Administration: Apply to affected area 3 or 4 times daily. For children under 2 years of age there is no recommended dosage except under the advice and supervision of a physician.

How Supplied: Available in 0.5 and 1.0 oz. tubes.

References:
1. Goodman and Gilman, The Pharmacological Basis of Therapeutics, Page 1487, 5th Ed., MacMillan, 1975.
2. Su-Chen L. Hong, Lawrence Levine, J. Bio. Chem., Vol. 251, No. 18, pp. 5814–5816, 1976.
3. Ryszard J. Gryglewski, et al., Prostoglandins, Vol. 10, No. 2, pp. 343–35 August 1975.

VAGISIL® Feminine Itching Medication

Active Ingredients: 5.0% Benzocaine; 2.0% Resorcinol.

Indications: VAGISIL Medication has been formulated to give prompt, effective relief from the discomfort of minor itching, burning, and other irritations in the external vaginal area. VAGISIL forms a cooling, protective film over irritated tissues. Helps check bacteria to speed natural healing. Lightly scented, stainless, greaseless.

Actions: Benzocaine is a local anesthetic of low toxicity considered to be one of the safest and most widely used of the over-the-counter topical anesthetics. Temporary anesthesia is elicited by penetrating the cutaneous barriers and blocking sensory receptors for the perception of pain and itching. Resorcinol activity is both antimicrobial and mildly keratolytic.

Warnings: Read enclosed circular carefully before using. Not for prolonged use. Do not get into eyes. Some skin and membrane irritations may be caused by internal systemic disorders. If condition persists for more than seven days or worsens, discontinue use and consult physician. Keep out of reach of children.

Drug Interaction Precaution: Benzocaine has been known to occasionally cause allergic dermatitis. Cross-reactions have been reported with para-phenylenediamine, a hair dye, sulfonamide and sun screens containing para-aminobenzoic acid esters.

Dosage and Administration: Apply VAGISIL Creme Medication liberally to the affected area. Repeat as needed three or four times daily.

How Supplied: Available in 1.0 and 2.0 oz. tubes.

[Shown in Product Identification Section]

Consolidated Chemical, Inc.
Healthcare Products Division
3224 S. KINGSHIGHWAY
ST. LOUIS, MO 63139

FORMULA MAGIC®

Composition: Talc, USP, Mineral Oil, Magnesium Carbonate, Fragrance, DMDM Hydantoin.

Action: USP Talc based body powder and nursing lubricant. Aids in preventing excoriation and friction chafing. Aids in controlling odor.

Precautions: Non-irritating to skin. Non-toxic orally (LD_{50} 15g/kg body weight). Slightly irritating to eyes. In case of eye contact flush with water.

Dosage and Administration: Apply liberally to body and rub gently into skin.

How Supplied: 4 oz., 12 oz.

PERINEAL/OSTOMY SKIN CLEANSER

Composition: Water, Cocamidopropylamine Oxide, Witch Hazel, Coco Betaine, DMDM Hydantoin, Fragrance, FD&C Red #33, FD&C Blue #1.

Action: A gentle, effective spray cleanser for cleaning, refreshing, and deodorizing the perineal area, stoma sites, and ostomy appliances.

Precautions: Non-irritating to skin. Non-toxic orally (LD_{50} 15g/kg). May cause slight eye discomfort. In case of eye contact flush with water.

Dosage and Administration: Spray directly on the entire perineal area, or the peristomal skin and in the ostomy appliance for quick odor control and cleaning. See label for full instructions.

How Supplied: 8 oz., 1 gallon.

SATIN™

Composition: Water, Ammonium Laureth Sulfate, Cocamide DEA, PEG 8, Glycol Stearate, Sodium Cocyl Sarcosinate, Lanolin Oil, Chloroxylenol, Citric Acid, Sodium EDTA, Fragrance, D&C Yellow #10.

Action: Skin cleanser and shampoo for daily hygiene and odor control.

Precautions: Non-irritating to skin. Non-toxic orally (LD_{50} 15g/kg). Moderate eye irritant. In case of eye contact flush with water.

Dosage and Administration: Apply directly to wet skin or hair or to a pre-dampened washcloth. Wash in normal manner. Rinse thoroughly.

How Supplied: 4 oz., 8 oz., 16 oz., 1 gallon.

SKIN MAGIC™

Composition: Water, Stearic Acid, Mineral Oil, Isostearyl Alcohol, Propylene Glycol, Stearamide DEA, Triethanolamine, Cetyl Alcohol, Myristyl Propionate, Methylparaben, Fragrance, Propylparaben, Carbomer 934P, Sodium Borate, Lanolin Oil, DMDM Hydantoin.

Action: Emollient body rub and skin lotion. Soothes and moisturizes dry irritated skin.

Precautions: Non-irritating to skin. Non-toxic orally (LD_{50} 15g/kg). Slight eye irritant. In case of eye contact flush with water.

Dosage and Administration: Apply liberally topically and massage into skin.

How Supplied: 4 oz., 8 oz., 1 gallon.

Creighton Products Corporation
a Sandoz Company
(see also Ex-Lax Pharmaceutical Co., Inc.)
605 THIRD AVENUE
NEW YORK, NY 10158

BiCOZENE® Creme External Analgesic

Active Ingredients: Benzocaine 6%, resorcinol 1.67% in a specially prepared cream base.

Indications: For the temporary relief of pain and itching due to minor burns, sunburn, minor cuts, abrasions, insect bites, and minor skin irritations. For all kinds of external itching skin conditions; vaginal, rectal, poison ivy, heat rash, chafing, eczema, and common itching of the skin.

Actions: Benzocaine is a topical anesthetic and resorcinol is a topical antipruritic, at the concentrations used in BiCozene Creme. Both exert their actions by depressing cutaneous sensory receptors.

Warnings: Caution: Use only as directed. Keep away from the eyes. Not for prolonged use. If the condition for which this preparation is used persists, or if a rash or irritation develops, discontinue use and consult a physician. For external use only. **Warning**—Keep out of the reach of children.

Drug Interaction Precautions: No known drug interaction.

Continued on next page

Creighton—Cont.

Dosage and Administration: Apply to affected area morning, night, and as needed.
How Supplied: BiCozene Creme is available in 1-ounce tubes.
[*Shown in Product Identification Section*]

DERMA+SOFT® Creme

Active Ingredient: Salicylic acid 2.5% in a specially prepared cream base.
Actions: The unique stainless, greaseless creme formula of Derma-Soft softens and removes corns and calluses.
Warnings: Do not apply Derma-Soft to moles, birthmarks, or warts. **Caution:** Derma-Soft should not be used by diabetics or persons with poor circulation. For external use only. Store in a cool, dry place. KEEP ALL MEDICINES OUT OF THE REACH OF CHILDREN.
Drug Interaction Precautions: No known drug interactions.
Dosage and Administration: Thoroughly wash area to be treated. Dry with a rough, clean towel, rubbing off any loose dead skin. Apply Derma-Soft directly on corns and calluses. Avoid applying to healthy skin. Use treatment daily for two weeks. In stubborn cases, continue use for another two weeks. If condition persists, see your physician.
How Supplied: Derma-Soft Creme is available in 1-oz. tubes.
[*Shown in Product Identification Section*]

GAS-X®
High–Capacity Antiflatulent

Active Ingredient: Each tablet contains 80 mg. simethicone.
Indications: For relief of the pain and pressure symptoms of excess gas in the digestive tract, which is often accompanied by complaints of bloating, distention, fullness, pressure, pain, cramps or excess anal flatus.
Actions: GAS-X acts in the stomach and intestines to disperse and reduce the formation of mucus-trapped gas bubbles. The GAS-X defoaming action reduces the surface tension of gas bubbles so that they are more easily eliminated.
Warning: Keep this and all medicines out of the reach of children.
Drug Interaction Precautions: No known drug interaction.
Dosage and Administration: Adults: Chew thoroughly and swallow one or two tablets as needed after meals and at bedtime. Do not exceed six tablets in 24 hours, except under the advice and supervision of a physician.
Professional Labeling: GAS-X may be useful in the alleviation of postoperative gas pain, and for use in endoscopic examination.
How Supplied: GAS-X is available in white, chewable, scored tablets in boxes of 30 tablets and convenience packages of 12 tablets.
[*Shown in Product Identification Section*]

Daywell Laboratories Corporation
78 UNQUOWA PLACE
FAIRFIELD, CT 06430

VERGO® Cream

Composition: Vergo contains Pancin®, a special formulation of calcium pantothenate, ascorbic acid and starch.
Action and Uses: Vergo is a conservative, painless and safe treatment of warts. Vergo is very gentle, even for diabetics. It is not liquid. It is not caustic. It can be used on all parts of the body, even on the face. Vergo will not burn, blister, scar or injure surrounding tissue. Vergo is easily applied by finger. The ingredients are essential to the soundness of tissues and skin and will relieve the pain of warts and promote healing. Vergo is not irritating and there are no contraindications to its use. The average treatment time is from 2 to 8 weeks depending on the size of the wart and the response of the patient. It is important that the directions be carefully followed and that treatment be continued without interruption as long as necessary. Mosaic-type warts are more resistant and usually require longer treatment for relief.
Administration and Dosage: Cleanse area with soap and water; rinse thoroughly. Apply Vergo liberally to wart. Do not massage or rub in. Cover with plain Band-Aid® or gauze and adhesive tape. Change dressing and apply Vergo twice a day, morning and evening.
Side Effects: None known.
How Supplied: In one-half ounce tubes.
Product Identification Mark: Vergo®.
Literature Available: Yes.

Derma Labs, Inc.
802 EASY STREET
P. O. BOX 40266
GARLAND, TEXAS 75042

HYDROSTAT LOTION

Active Ingredients: Water, Stabilized* Aloe Vera Gel, glyceryl stearate & stearyl stearate, propylene glycol, SD alcohol 40, dimethypolysiloxane, palmitamidopropyl dimethylamine, methylparaben, propylparaben, phosphoric acid, tocopherol, and hydrolyzed animal protein.
Descripion: Hydrostat is a soothing NON-OILY, NON-STEROID anti-inflammatory and germicidal moisturizer with analgesic and healing benefits of Stabilized* Aloe Vera leaf gel.
Actions: The penetrating action of Hydrostat lotion promptly restores normal moisture to dry sensitive areas while destroying bacterial, viral and fungal organisms to help maintain healthy skin. It may be indicated in acne or other conditions aggravated by excessive oils. Hydrostat also may be used as a pre-make-up lotion in the morning and after cleansing at bedtime.
Directions for Use: Apply liberally and continuously with light massage for about 5 minutes, 4 times per day or as directed by a physician.
How Supplied: Bottle, 4 fl. oz (120 ml.).
*Aloe Vera of America, Inc. U.S. Pat. 3,892,853

Dermik Laboratories, Inc.
1777 WALTON ROAD, DUBLIN HALL
BLUE BELL, PA 19422

FOMAC® FOAM
(medicated foam cleanser)

Description: Salicylic acid 2% in a soap-free, mild detergent system. Patent No. 4147782.
Indications: Acne and oily skin.
Directions: DO NOT SHAKE. Invert container and squeeze a puff of Fomac Foam into palm of hand and massage, gently but thoroughly, into affected area until foam disappears. For best results, do not wet skin. Leave on skin 3 - 5 minutes, then rinse well with lukewarm water and pat dry. Use once or twice daily, or as recommended by physician. Discontinue use of all soaps or other skin cleansers.
Precautions: If redness or irritation occurs or increases, reduce frequency of applications. If irritation persists, discontinue use and consult your physician.
Keep away from eyes.
For external use only.
Keep out of the reach of children.
Keep tightly closed.
Store at room temperature.
How Supplied: 3 fl. oz. non-aerosol bottle.

HYTONE® CREAM ½%
HYTONE® OINTMENT ½%
(hydrocortisone ½%)

Active Ingredient: Hydrocortisone 0.5%.
Indications: For the temporary relief of minor skin irritations, itching, and rashes due to eczema, dermatitis, insect bites, poison ivy, poison oak, poison sumac, soaps, detergents, cosmetics, and jewelry, and for itchy genital and anal areas.
Actions: Provides temporary relief of itching and minor skin irritations.
Warnings: For External Use Only. Avoid contact with eyes. If condition worsens, or if symptoms persist for more than 7 days, discontinue use of this product and consult a physician. Do not use on children under 2 years of age except under the advice and supervision of a physician. KEEP OUT OF THE REACH OF CHILDREN.
Dosage and Administration: For adults and children 2 years of age and older: Apply to affected area not more than 3 or 4 times daily, or as directed by physician.
How Supplied: Tube, 1 ounce.

SHEPARD'S CREAM LOTION
Skin Lubricant—Moisturizer

Composition: Water, sesame oil, SD alcohol 40-B, stearic acid, propylene glycol, ethoxydiglycol, glycerin, triethanolamine, glyceryl stearate, letyl alcohol, may contain fragrance ("scented" only), simethicone, methylparaben, propylparaben, vegetable oil, monoglyceride citrate, BHT and citric acid.

Indications: For generalized dryness and itching, sunburn, "winter-itch"; dry skin; heat rash.

Actions and Uses: Shepard's Cream Lotion is a rich lotion containing soothing Oil of Sesame.

Dosage and Administration: Apply as often as needed. Use particularly after bathing and exposure to sun, water, soaps and detergents.

How Supplied: Scented and Unscented 8 oz. bottle and 16 oz. pump bottle.

SHEPARD'S DRY SKIN CREAM
Concentrated Moisturizer

Composition: Lanolin, mineral oil, petrolatum and ceresin.

Indications: For day or night lubrication of severe and persistent dry skin.

Actions: Rich in lanolin, contains no water, helps retain moisture that makes skin feel soft, smooth, supple; for problem dry skin particularly on hands, elbows, feet and legs.

Dosage and Administration: A small amount is rubbed into dry skin areas as needed.

How Supplied: Unscented, 3 1/4 oz. jars.

SHEPARD'S HAND CREAM
Concentrated
Moisturizer—Non-greasy Emollient

Composition: Water, glyceryl stearate, ethoxydiglycol, propylene glycol, glycerin, stearic acid, isopropyl myristate, cetyl alcohol, urea, lecithin, may contain fragrance ("scented" only) methylparaben and propylparaben.

Indications: For problem dry skin of the hands, face, elbows, feet, legs. Helps resist effects of soaps, detergents and chemicals.

Actions: Soothing, rich lubricant containing isopropyl myristate in a non-greasy or sticky base containing no lanolin or mineral oil. Shepard's Hand Cream helps retain moisture that makes skin feel soft, smooth, supple.

Dosage and Administration: A small amount is rubbed into dry skin areas as needed.

How Supplied: Scented and Unscented, 4 oz. jars.

SHEPARD'S MOISTURIZING SOAP
Cleanser for Dry Skin

Composition: Soap (Sodium Tallowate & Cocoate Types), Water, Glycerin, Fragrance, Coconut Acid, Sodium Chloride, Lanolin, Titanium Dioxide, o-Tolyl Biguanide

Indications: As a daily cleanser of dry skin of the face, hands, or in the bath or shower. Shepard's Soap helps to give the skin an overall smoothness.

Actions: A lightly scented, non-detergent moisturizing soap containing lanolin that cleanses the skin while helping to minimize the excessive drying inherent in most detergent-type soaps.

Dosage and Administration: Use regularly to cleanse face and hands as well as in the bath or shower.

How Supplied: 4 oz. bars.

VANOXIDE® ACNE LOTION
(Dries on Clear)
LOROXIDE® ACNE LOTION
(Flesh Tinted)

Description: Vanoxide® Lotion contains (as dispensed) benzoyl peroxide 5%, incorporated in lotion that dries on clear. Loroxide® Lotion contains (as dispensed) benzoyl peroxide 5.5%, incorporated in a flesh-tinted lotion.

Actions: Provides keratolytic, peeling and drying action.

Indications: An aid in the treatment of acne and oily skin.

Contraindications: These products are contraindicated for use by patients having known hypersensitivity to benzoyl peroxide or any other component of these preparations.

Precautions: For external use only. Keep away from eyes. Do not add any other medicaments or substances to these lotions unless specifically directed by physician to do so. Patients should be observed carefully for possible local irritation or sensitivity during long-term topical therapy. If any irritation or sensitivity is observed, discontinue use and consult physician. Apply with caution on neck and/or other sensitive areas. There may be a slight, transitory stinging or burning sensation on initial application which invariably disappears on continued use. Ultraviolet and cold quartz light should be employed in lesser amounts as these lotions are keratolytic and drying. Harsh, abrasive cleansers should not be used simultaneously with these lotions. Colored or dyed garments may be bleached by the oxidizing action of benzoyl peroxide. Occurrence of excessive redness or peeling indicates that the amount and frequency of application should be reduced. Keep out of the reach of children.

Adverse Reactions: The sensitizing potential of benzoyl peroxide is low; but it can, on occasion, produce allergic reaction.

Directions: Shake well before using. Apply a thin film to affected areas with light massaging to blend in each application 1 or 2 times daily or in accordance with the physician's directions.

How Supplied: Vanoxide® Lotion-Bottles, 25 grams (0.88 oz.) and 50 grams (1.76 oz.) net weights as dispensed. Loroxide® Lotion-Bottles, 25 grams (0.88 oz.) net weight as dispensed. A "Dermik Color Blender™" is provided with Loroxide® Lotion which enables the patient to alter the basic shade of the lotion to match the skin color.

VLEMASQUE®
Acne Mask Treatment

Active Ingredient: Contains sulfurated lime solution 6%, S.D. alcohol 7% in a drying clay mask.

Indications: For the treatment of acne.

Warnings: Keep away from eyes. In case of contact, flush eyes thoroughly. For external use only. If any irritation appears, stop treatment immediately and consult physician.

Dosage and Administration: Daily, apply generous layer over entire face and neck, or as directed by physician. Avoid eyes, nostrils and lips. Leave on for 20-25 minutes. Remove with lukewarm water, using a gentle circular motion. Pat dry.

How Supplied: 4 oz. Jars.

ZETAR® SHAMPOO

Active Ingredients: WHOLE Coal Tar (as Zetar®) 1.0%, and parachlorometaxylenol 0.5% in a golden foam shampoo which produces soft, fluffy abundant lather.

Actions and Indications: Antiseptic, antibacterial, antiseborrheic. Loosens and softens scales and crusts. Indicated in psoriasis, seborrhea, dandruff, cradle-cap and other oily, itchy conditions of the body and scalp.

Contraindications: Acute inflammation, open or infected lesions.

Precautions: If undue skin irritation develops or increases, discontinue use and consult physician. In rare instances, temporary discoloration of blond, bleached, or tinted hair may occur. Avoid contact with eyes.

Dosage and Administration: Massage into moistened scalp. Rinse. Repeat; leave on 5 minutes. Rinse thoroughly.

How Supplied: 6 oz. plastic bottles.

DeWitt International Corporation
5 N. WATSON ROAD
TAYLORS, SC 29687

DEWITT'S PILLS FOR BACKACHE AND JOINT PAINS

Active Ingredients: Salicylamide, Potassium Nitrate, Uva Ursi, Buchu and Caffeine.

Indications: For backache and joint pains, muscular aches, headaches and mild urinary irritations caused by non-organic disturbances of a minor nature.

Actions: Analgesic ingredients help in relief of minor pains. Mild diuretic action helps eliminate retained fluids, flushes out bladder wastes and irritations that often cause physical distress including too frequent or difficult passage of urine.

Warnings: Keep this and all medicines out of the reach of children. In case of accidental overdose, seek professional assistance or contact a Poison Control Center immediately.

Drug Interaction: No known drug interactions.

Continued on next page

DeWitt—Cont.

Precaution: A few pills will turn the urine blue or green because of the presence of Methylene Blue as a coloring agent.

Symptoms and Treatment of Oral Overdosage:

Symptoms: Vomiting; epigastric pain; profuse perspiration; headache; dizziness; tinnitus; visual disturbances; delirium; restlessness, excitement, convulsions; pulse rapid, feeble; BP low; pallor; skin eruptions; dyspnea. Urine shows salicylate reaction: ferric chloride produces port-wine color (not affected by prior boiling).

Treatment: Lavage or emetics; saline cathartic. I.V. fluids containing sodium bicarbonate or lactate 40 to 60 mEq/L and potassium 30 to 40 mEq/L at a rate of 3 to 5 L/sq.M of BSA to correct acid-base disturbances (acidosis common in young children) and to promote excretion. Treatment otherwise supportive. Dialysis in extreme cases (for peritoneal dialysis, 5% normal serum albumin [human] should be used).

Dosage and Administration: For adult use only. Take 3 pills before meals and 3 pills at bedtime, up to a maximum of 12 pills per day. Swallow with a glass of water. Drink plenty of water between meals.

Professional Labeling: Same as those outlined under indications.

How Supplied: Individual blistering of pills packaged in cartons of 20, 40 and 80 pills.

[*Shown in Product Identification Section*]

The E. E. Dickinson Co.
40-46 N. MAIN STREET
ESSEX, CT 06426

E. E. DICKINSON'S WITCH HAZEL

Active Ingredient: Witch hazel distillate.

Description: Contains Witch hazel distillate and SD Alcohol 40; Alcohol 14% by volume.

Actions and Uses: E. E. Dickinson's Witch Hazel should be used whenever the use of an astringent is indicated. Witch hazel provides temporary relief of mild irritations to the skin. E. E. Dickinson's Witch Hazel may also be used with 50% glycerine and 10% purified water in a preparation for the treatment of external hemorrhoids.

Warning: For external use only. Avoid excessive heat.

How Supplied: 4, 8, 16, 32 fluid ounce and one gallon bottles. Also available in 30 and 55 gallon drums.

[*Shown in Product Identification Section*]

E. E. DICKINSON'S WITCH HAZEL TOWELETTES

Active Ingredient: Witch hazel distillate.

Description: Contains a 5½″ × 8″ towelette premoistened with witch hazel distillate, packaged individually, in foil wrappers.

Actions and Uses: E. E. Dickinson's Witch Hazel Towelette should be used whenever the use of an astringent is indicated. Witch hazel provides temporary relief of mild irritations to the skin.

Warning: Avoid excessive heat.

How Supplied: Boxes of 24 individually wrapped towelettes. Plastic bags of 12 individually wrapped towelettes.

[*Shown in Product Identification Section*]

Doak Pharmacal Co., Inc.
700 SHAMES DRIVE
WESTBURY, NY 11590

FORMULA 405 SKIN CARE

Deep-Action Skincare. Scientific. Substantive. Effective. Dry Skin Treatment Products.

Formula 405 Preparations penetrate deep into the stratum corneum where they help the cells retain the natural moisture as they move up through your visible skin. Healthy moisture balance is maintained.

FORMULA 405 SKIN CARE PRODUCTS:

ENRICHED CREAM

Description: Contains a special patented agent, a true moisturizer—Pregnenolone Succinate. For dry and very dry skin.

Action: With its special agent, actually penetrates the stratum corneum where it is absorbed and retained, working to "plump out" aging lines caused by moisture deficiency.

Dosage and Administration: Just a little smoothed over face and throat every night. Dry and very dry skin will find it effective worn sparingly under makeup.

How Supplied: 2 oz. tube.

LIGHT TEXTURED MOISTURIZER

Description: Light, non-greasy cream with patented agent, Pregnenolone Succinate.

Action: Instantly absorbed, it works invisibly to revive dry, dull skin. . . . Return it to softness, smoothness, clarity. For normal to dry skin.

Dosage and Administration: For day with or without makeup. . . A light night treatment, too. (Some women find that a combination of light textured moisturizer during the day and cream at night is ideal.)

How Supplied: 2 oz. and 4 oz. jars.

MOISTURIZING LOTION

Description: Contains same patented agent mentioned above. The lotion is a light, flowing version of Formula 405 Cream. For normal and combination skin.

Action: Its deep-action moisturizing benefits are effective for the entire body and under makeup too.

Dosage and Administration: May be applied sparingly to all parts of body requiring moisturization.

How Supplied: 4 fl. oz. bottle.

EYE CREAM

Description: An eye cream containing an exclusive blend of beneficial, proven ingredients, including Pregnenolone Succinate. Fragrance-free.

Action: Rapidly absorbed. Especially formulated to protect and care for the delicate skin tissue around the eyes.

Dosage and Administration: Apply sparingly around eyes.

How Supplied: ½ oz. jar.

SKIN CLEANSER AND PATENTED BUFFING MITT

Description: A skin cleansing treatment which does what dermatologists believe a cleanser should do. A soapless cleanser that is a mild epidermal abrasive.

Action: Gets skin microscopically clean through mild epidermal abrasion—Formula 405 Soapless Cleanser foams up with water to lift away makeup and clogging dirt while the gentle friction of the mitt sloughs away flaking surface skin cells that dull skin.

How Supplied: 8 fl. oz. Cleansing Lotion with Face Mitt in one package.

THERAPEUTIC BATH OIL

Description: Contains moisturizers and lubricants to help control dry and itchy skin. Non-greasy.

Action: Quickly dispersed in warm water, this formula actually cleans your skin as it moisturizes, softens and smooths away dryness, tautness, itching.

Administration: A fifteen-minute treatment bath a few times a week—just with Formula 405 Bath Oil, no soap. (Will not leave ring around tub.)

How Supplied: 8 fl. oz. bottle.

MOISTURIZING SOAP

Description: Cleans gently, yet thoroughly, and moisturizes at the same time. Fragrance-free.

Action: Quickly helps restore smoothness and softness to sensitive areas of body that are dry, irritated and sore, gentle enough to be effective even on tender skin.

How Supplied: Bar 3.8 oz.

SOLAR CREAM

Description: A total sun block containing Paba and Titanium Dioxide. Protection factor of 15. Need not be reapplied for 4–6 hours. Tinted flesh color.

Action: A total sunscreen that lasts 4 to 6 hours even while swimming. Developed for complete protection from sun's rays—not just against burning of sensitive skin, but against the aging effects the sun can have on all skins.

Administration: A fine-textured, flesh-tinted cream that may be smoothed on skin during exposure to sun's rays. Can be worn under or instead of regular makeup. May be used alternately with an ordinary suntan lotion.

How Supplied: 1 oz. tube.

DOAK OIL

Description: Contains 2% Tar Distillate "Doak".

Actions: Antipruritic, skin-softening and moisturizing therapeutic Bath Oil.

How Supplied: 8 fl. oz. bottle.

DOAK OIL FORTE

Description: Nonstaining antipruritic, skin-softening and moisturizing therapeutic Bath Oil containing 10% Tar Distillate "Doak".

Actions: Useful in treatment of Psoriasis.

How Supplied: 4 fl. oz. bottle.

DOAK TAR SHAMPOO

Description: Anti-seborrheic Tar Shampoo. Tar distillate "Doak" 3% incorporated in Tersaseptic.

Action: Soapless Tar Shampoo that foams up to help treat dandruff, Seborrhea and Psoriasis of the scalp.

Dosage and Administration: Use as directed.

How Supplied: 8 fl. oz.

DOAK TAR SHAMPOO

Description: Anti-seborrheic Tar Shampoo. Tar distillate "Doak" 3% incorporated in Tersaseptic.

Action: Soapless Tar Shampoo that foams up to help treat dandruff, Seborrhea and Psoriasis of the scalp.

Dosage and Administration: Use as directed.

How Supplied: 8 fl. oz.

LAVATAR TAR BATH

Description: Nonstaining antipruritic, skin-softening and moisturizing Bath Oil containing 25% Tar Distillate "Doak".

Action: Added to bath water, aids in the treatment of generalized pruritus, psoriasis and atopic dermatitis.

How Supplied: 4 and 16 fl. oz. bottles.

TARPASTE

Description: Tar Distillate "Doak" 5% incorporated in Lassar's Paste.

Action: Ideal for chronic eczematoid dermatitis, infantile eczema and psoriasis.

How Supplied: 1 oz. tube, 4 oz. jar.

TERSASEPTIC HYGIENIC SKIN CLEANSER

Description: Sudsing, soapless skin and scalp cleanser; employing anionic and nonionic surfactants. Mild and nondrying acid pH.

Dosage and Administration: Use as directed.

How Supplied: 16 fl. oz. bottles.

Dorsey Laboratories
Division of Sandoz, Inc.
P.O. BOX 83288
LINCOLN, NE 68501

ACID MANTLE® CREME AND ACID MANTLE® LOTION

Description: A greaseless, water-miscible preparation containing buffered aluminum acetate.

Indications: Provides relief from mild skin irritation due to exposure to soaps, detergents, chemicals, alkalis. Aids in the treatment of diaper rash, acne, eczema and dry, rough, scaly skin from varied causes.

Application: Apply several times daily, especially after wet work.

Caution: Limited compatibility and stability with Vitamin A, neomycin and water-soluble antibiotics. For external use only. Not for ophthalmic use.

How Supplied: Creme: 1 oz tubes; 4 oz and 1 lb jars. Lotion: 4 oz.

[*Shown in Product Identification Section*]

CAMA® INLAY-TABS®

Description: Each CAMA INLAY-TAB contains: aspirin USP 600 mg (10 grains); magnesium hydroxide, USP 150 mg; aluminum hydroxide dried gel USP 150 mg.

Indications: An analgesic in arthritis and rheumatism.

Contraindications: Hypersensitivity to salicylates.

Warnings: The antipyretic effect of salicylates may mask the diagnostic importance of persistent fever.

Precautions: The occasional occurrence of mild salicylism may require adjustment of dosage.

Adverse Reactions: Overdosage of salicylates will cause tinnitus, nausea, vomiting and gastrointestinal upsets and bleeding.

Dosage and Administration: Adults —one tablet every four hours. Physicians may increase the dosage as required to provide satisfactory relief of symptoms. Usually, a dose of one to two tablets four times daily is adequate.

How Supplied: Cama Inlay-Tabs (white with salmon inlay) in bottles of 100 and 250.

[*Shown in Product Identification Section*]

DORCOL® PEDIATRIC COUGH SYRUP

Description: Each teaspoonful (5 ml) of DORCOL Pediatric Cough Syrup contains: phenylpropanolamine hydrochloride 6.25 mg, guaifenesin 50 mg, dextromethorphan hydrobromide 5 mg, alcohol 5%.

Indications: Provides prompt relief of cough and nasal congestion due to the common cold. The expectorant component helps loosen bronchial secretions. The decongestant, expectorant and antitussive are provided in an antihistamine-free formula.

Contraindications: DORCOL Pediatric Cough Syrup is contraindicated in the presence of hypersensitivity to any of the ingredients. The use of pressor amines

such as phenylpropanolamine hydrochloride is contraindicated in those patients taking monamine oxidase inhibitors for antihypertensive or antidepressant indications.

Precautions: Exercise prescribing caution in patients with persistent or chronic cough such as occurs with chronic bronchitis, bronchial asthma, or emphysema. Use with caution in patients with hypertension, hyperthyroidism cardiovascular disease or diabetes mellitus.

Adverse Reactions: Occasional blurred vision, cardiac palpitations, flushing, gastrointestinal upsets, nervousness, dizziness, or sleeplessness may occur.

Dosage and Administration: Children 6–12 years—2 teaspoonfuls every 4 hours. Children 2–6 years—1 teaspoonful every 4 hours. The suggested dosage in pediatric patients 3 months to 2 years of age is 3 drops per kilogram of body weight administered every four hours. For nighttime cough relief, give the last dose at bedtime.

How Supplied: DORCOL Pediatric Cough Syrup (grape-colored) in 4 fl oz and 8 fl oz bottles.

[*Shown in Product Identification Section*]

TRIAMINIC–DM® COUGH FORMULA

Description: Each teaspoonful (5 ml) of TRIAMINIC-DM Cough Formula contains: phenylpropanolamine hydrochloride 12.5 mg and dextromethorphan hydrobromide 10 mg in a nonalcoholic vehicle.

Indications: Provides prompt, temporary relief of cough and nasal congestion due to the common cold. The decongestant and antitussive are provided in an antihistamine free formula.

Contraindications: TRIAMINIC-DM Cough Formula is contraindicated in the presence of hypersensitivity to any of the ingredients. The use of pressor amines such as phenylpropanolamine hydrochloride is contraindicated in those patients taking monamine oxidase inhibitors for antihypertensive or antidepressant indications.

Precautions: Exercise prescribing caution in patients with persistent or chronic cough such as occurs with chronic bronchitis, bronchial asthma, or emphysema. Use with caution in patients with hypertension, hyperthyroidism cardiovascular disease or diabetes mellitus.

Adverse Reactions: Occasional blurred vision, cardiac palpitations, flushing, gastrointestinal upsets, nervousness, dizziness, or sleeplessness may occur.

Dosage and Administration: Adults —2 teaspoonfuls every 4 hours. Children 6–12—1 teaspoonful every 4 hours. Children 2–6 years—½ teaspoonful every 4 hours. The suggested dosage in pediatric patients 3 months to 2 years of age is 1½ drops per kilogram of body weight administered every 4 hours.

Continued on next page

Dorsey—Cont.

How Supplied: TRIAMINIC-DM Cough Formula (dark red) in 4 fl oz and 8 fl oz bottles.
[*Shown in Product Identification Section*]

TRIAMINIC® EXPECTORANT

Description: Each teaspoonful (5 ml) of TRIAMINIC Expectorant contains: phenylpropanolamine hydrochloride 12.5 mg, guaifenesin 100 mg, alcohol 5%.

Indications: Provides prompt relief of cough and nasal congestion due to the common cold. The expectorant component helps loosen bronchial secretions. The decongestant and expectorant are provided in an antihistamine-free formula.

Contraindications: TRIAMINIC Expectorant is contraindicated in the presence of hypersensitivity to any of the ingredients. The use of pressor amines such as phenylpropanolamine hydrochloride is contraindicated in those patients taking monamine oxidase inhibitors for antihypertensive or antidepressant indications.

Precautions: Exercise prescribing caution in patients with persistent or chronic cough such as occurs with chronic bronchitis, bronchial asthma, or emphysema. Use with caution in patients with hypertension, hyperthyroidism cardiovascular disease or diabetes mellitus.

Adverse Reactions: Occasional blurred vision, cardiac palpitations, flushing, gastrointestinal upsets, nervousness, dizziness, or sleeplessness may occur.

Dosage and Administration: Adults —2 teaspoonfuls every 4 hours. Children 6–12 years—1 teaspoonful every 4 hours. Children 2–6—½ teaspoonful every 4 hours. The suggested dosage in pediatric patients 3 months to 2 years of age is 4 to 5 drops per kilogram of body weight administered every four hours.

How Supplied: TRIAMINIC Expectorant (yellow) in 4 fl oz, 8 fl oz and pint bottles.
[*Shown in Product Identification Section*]

TRIAMINIC® SYRUP

Description: Each teaspoonful (5 ml) of TRIAMINIC Syrup contains: phenylpropanolamine hydrochloride 12.5 mg and chlorpheniramine maleate 2 mg in a nonalcoholic vehicle.

Indications: For the temporary relief of nasal congestion, sneezing, and itchy watery eyes that may occur in hay fever or other upper respiratory allergies, the common cold and sinusitis.

Contraindications: TRIAMINIC Syrup is contraindicated in the presence of hypersensitivity to any of the ingredients. The use of pressor amines such as phenylpropanolamine hydrochloride is contraindicated in those patients taking monamine oxidase inhibitors for antihypertensive or antidepressant indications.

Precautions: Caution should be observed in operating a motor vehicle or performing potentially hazardous tasks requiring mental alertness. Alcoholic beverages and other CNS depressants may potentiate the sedative effects of antihistamines. Caution should be observed in the presence of hypertension, hyperthyroidism, cardiovascular disease or diabetes mellitus. Because of anticholinergic action of antihistamines they should be administered with caution to patients with bronchial asthma, narrow angle glaucoma, stenosing peptic ulcer, pyloroduodenal obstruction, prostatic hypertrophy or other bladder neck obstruction.

Adverse Reactions: Drowsiness, blurred vision, palpitations, flushing, gastrointestinal upsets, nervousness, dizziness, or sleeplessness may occur. May cause excitability especially in children.

Dosage and Administration: Adults —two teaspoonfuls every 4 hours. Children 6–12 years—1 teaspoonful every 4 hours, children 2–6—½ teaspoonful every 4 hours. The suggested dosage in pediatric patients 3 months to 2 years of age is 4 to 5 drops per kilogram of body weight administered every four hours.

How Supplied: TRIAMINIC Syrup (orange), in 4 fl oz, 8 fl oz and pint bottles.
[*Shown in Product Identification Section*]

TRIAMINIC-12™ Sustained Release Tablets

Each tablet contains: phenylpropanolamine hydrochloride 75 mg and chlorpheniramine maleate 12 mg.
TRIAMINIC-12 Tablets contain the nasal decongestant, phenylpropanolamine, and the antihistamine, chlorpheniramine, in a formulation providing 12 hours of symptomatic relief.
NOTE: This product's formula differs from the original TRIAMINIC formula in that the two antihistamines have been replaced by a 12-hour dosage of a single antihistamine.

Indications: For the temporary relief of nasal congestion due to the common cold, hay fever or other upper respiratory allergies and associated with sinusitis. Helps decongest sinus openings, sinus passages; promotes nasal and/or sinus drainage; temporarily restores freer breathing through the nose.
For temporary relief of running nose, sneezing, itching of the nose or throat and itchy and watery eyes as may occur in allergic rhinitis (such as hay fever).

Dosage: Adults and children over 12 years of age—1 tablet every 12 hours. Unless directed by physician, do not exceed 2 tablets in 24 hours.

Warnings: Do not give this product to children under 12 years except under the advice and supervision of a physician. Do not take this preparation if you have high blood pressure, heart disease, diabetes, thyroid disease, asthma, glaucoma or difficulty in urination due to enlargement of the prostate gland except under the advice and supervision of a physician. Do not exceed the recommended dosage because at higher doses nervousness, dizziness, or sleeplessness may occur. This preparation may cause drowsiness; this preparation may cause excitability, especially in children. If symptoms do not improve within seven days or are accompanied by high fever, consult a physician before continuing use.

Caution: Avoid driving a motor vehicle or operating heavy machinery. Avoid alcoholic beverages while taking this product.
Keep this and all drugs out of the reach of children. In case of accidental overdose, seek professional assistance or contact a Poison Control Center immediately.

Drug Interaction Precaution: Do not take this product if you are presently taking a prescription antihypertensive or antidepressant drug containing a monamine oxidase inhibitor except under the advice and supervision of a physician.

How Supplied: Triaminic-12 Tablets (orange) in blister packs of 10 and 20.
[*Shown in Product Identification Section*]

TRIAMINICIN® CHEWABLES

Description: Each TRIAMINICIN Chewable contains: phenylpropanolamine hydrochloride 6.25 mg, chlorpheniramine maleate 0.5 mg.

Indications: For relief of children's nasal congestion due to the common cold or nasal allergies.

Precautions: Patients should be advised not to drive a car or operate dangerous machinery if drowsiness occurs. Use with caution in the presence of hypertension, hyperthyroidism, cardiovascular disease or diabetes.

Adverse Reactions: Occasional drowsiness, blurred vision, cardiac palpitations, flushing, dizziness, nervousness or gastrointestinal upsets.

Dosage: Children 2 to 6—1 chewable tablet 4 times a day; children 6 to 12—2 chewable tablets 4 times a day.

How Supplied: TRIAMINICIN Chewables (hexagonal, yellow) in blister packs of 24.

TRIAMINICIN® TABLETS

Description: Each TRIAMINICIN TABLET contains: phenylpropanolamine hydrochloride 25 mg, chlorpheniramine maleate 2 mg, aspirin 450 mg, caffeine 30 mg.

Indications: For prompt, temporary relief of nasal congestion, simple headache, and minor aches and pains due to the common cold, hay fever and similar conditions.

Contraindications: Sensitivity to salicylates.

Precautions: Patients should be advised not to drive a car or operate dangerous machinery if drowsiness occurs. Use with caution in the presence of hypertension, hyperthyroidism, cardiovascular disease or diabetes.

Adverse Reactions: Occasional drowsiness, blurred vision, cardiac palpitations, flushing, dizziness, nervousness or gastrointestinal upsets.

Dosage: Adults—One tablet four times a day.

How Supplied: Triaminicin Tablets (yellow) in blister packs of 12, 24, 48 and bottles of 100.
[*Shown in Product Identification Section*]

TRIAMINICOL® DECONGESTANT COUGH SYRUP

Description: Each teaspoonful (5 ml) of TRIAMINICOL Decongestant Cough Syrup contains: phenylpropanolamine hydrochloride 12.5 mg, pheniramine maleate 6.25 mg, pyrilamine maleate 6.25 mg, dextromethorphan hydrobromide 15 mg, ammonium chloride 90 mg, in a palatable nonalcoholic vehicle.
Indications: For relief of coughs, especially when accompanied by stuffed and runny noses, due to the common cold. It combines the effective, nonnarcotic, antitussive action of dextromethorphan hydrobromide with a proven nasal decongestant.
Contraindications: TRIAMINICOL Decongestant Cough Syrup is contraindicated in the presence of hypersensitivity to any of the ingredients. The use of pressor amines such as phenylpropanolamine hydrochloride is contraindicated in those patients taking monamine oxidase inhibitors for antihypertensive or antidepressant indications.
Precautions: Exercise prescribing caution in patients with persistent or chronic cough such as occurs with chronic bronchitis, bronchial asthma, or emphysema. Patients should be advised not to drive a car or operate dangerous machinery if drowsiness occurs. Use with caution in the presence of hypertension, hyperthyroidism, cardiovascular disease or diabetes.
Adverse Reactions: Occasional drowsiness, blurred vision, cardiac palpitations, flushing, dizziness, nervousness or gastrointestinal upsets.
Dosage and Administration: Adults —2 teaspoonfuls every 4 hours; children 6 to 12—1 teaspoonful every 4 hours; children 2 to 6—½ teaspoonful every 4 to 6 hours. For nighttime cough relief, give the last dose at bedtime.
How Supplied: TRIAMINICOL Decongestant Cough Syrup (dark red) in 4 fl oz and 8 fl oz.
[*Shown in Product Identification Section*]

TUSSAGESIC® TABLETS and TUSSAGESIC® SUSPENSION

Description: Each Tussagesic Timed Release Tablet contains: phenylpropanolamine hydrochloride 25 mg, pheniramine maleate 12.5 mg, pyrilamine maleate 12.5 mg, dextromethorphan hydrobromide 30 mg, terpin hydrate 180 mg, acetaminophen 325 mg.
Each teaspoonful (5 ml) of Tussagesic Suspension contains: phenylpropanolamine hydrochloride 12.5 mg, pheniramine maleate 6.25 mg, pyrilamine maleate 6.25 mg, dextromethorphan hydrobromide 15 mg, terpin hydrate 90 mg, acetaminophen 120 mg.
Indications: For prompt relief of symptoms associated with the common cold such as cough, nasal congestion, simple headache and minor muscular aches

and pains. Tussagesic contains the effective, nonnarcotic antitussive, dextromethorphan hydrobromide; a proven decongestant; an expectorant; and the well-tolerated analgesic, acetaminophen.
Precautions: Patients should be advised not to drive a car or operate dangerous machinery if drowsiness occurs. Use with caution in the presence of hypertension, hyperthyroidism, cardiovascular disease or diabetes.
Adverse Reactions: Occasional drowsiness, blurred vision, cardiac palpitations, flushing, dizziness, nervousness or gastrointestinal upsets.
Dosage and Administration: Tablets: Adults—1 tablet, swallowed whole, in morning, midafternoon and before retiring. Suspension: Children 1 to 6—½ teaspoonful every 4 hours; children 6 to 12—1 teaspoonful every 4 hours; adults—2 teaspoonfuls every 4 hours.
How Supplied: Tussagesic Tablets (orange) in bottles of 100. Tussagesic Suspension (orange) in pint bottles.

URSINUS® INLAY–TABS®

Description: Each URSINUS INLAY-TAB contains: Calurin® (calcium carbaspirin) equivalent to 300 mg aspirin; phenylpropanolamine hydrochloride 25 mg; pheniramine maleate 12.5 mg; pyrilamine maleate 12.5 mg.
Indications: For prompt, temporary relief of nasal congestion, simple headache and minor aches and pains associated with sinusitis and the common cold. Ursinus contains Calurin, the freely-soluble aspirin complex, to provide prompt analgesic action. Orally effective phenylpropanolamine hydrochloride with two antihistamines decongests and promotes drainage of nasal passages.
Contraindications: Sensitivity to salicylates.
Precautions: Patients should be advised not to drive a car or operate dangerous machinery if drowsiness occurs. Use with caution in the presence of hypertension, hyperthyroidism, cardiovascular disease, or diabetes.
Adverse Reactions: Drowsiness, blurred vision, cardiac palpitations, flushing, dizziness, nervousness or gastrointestinal upsets may occur occasionally.
Dosage and Administration: Adults —One tablet four times daily.
How Supplied: Ursinus Inlay-Tabs (white with yellow inlay) in bottles of 24 and 100.

Products are cross-indexed by

generic and chemical names

in the

YELLOW SECTION

Endo Laboratories, Inc.
Subsidiary of the DuPont Company
ONE RODNEY SQUARE
WILMINGTON, DE 19898

PERCOGESIC®
Analgesic Tablets

Description: Each tablet contains:
Acetaminophen (APAP)..............325 mg
Phenyltoloxamine citrate............. 30 mg
Uses: For relief of mild to moderate pain and discomfort due to simple headache; for temporary relief of such pain associated with muscle and joint soreness, neuralgia, sinusitis, minor menstrual cramps, the common cold or grippe, toothache, and minor aches and pains of rheumatism and arthritis.
Precautions: If arthritic or rheumatic pain persists for more than 10 days; in the presence of redness or swelling; or in arthritic or rheumatic conditions affecting children under 12 years of age, consult a physician immediately. When used for the temporary symptomatic relief of colds, if relief does not occur within three days, discontinue use and consult physician. This preparation may cause drowsiness. Do not drive or operate machinery while taking this medication. Do not administer to children under six years of age or exceed recommended dosage unless directed by physician.
Administration and Dosage: Adults—1 or 2 tablets every 4 hours; maximum daily dose 8 tablets. Children: 6-12 years—one-half adult dose; maximum daily dose 4 tablets. Do not use for more than 10 days unless directed by physician.
Warning: Keep this and all drugs out of reach of children. In case of accidental overdose, seek professional assistance or contact a poison control center immediately.
How Supplied: PERCOGESIC® tablets are available in blister-strip boxes of 24 tablets and bottles of 100.
PERCOGESIC® is an Endo registered U.S. trademark.
LK
[*Shown in Product Identification Section*]

Ex-Lax Pharmaceutical Co., Inc.
a Sandoz Company
(see also Creighton Products Corporation)
605 THIRD AVENUE
NEW YORK, NY 10158

EX-LAX® Chocolated Laxative

Active Ingredient: Yellow phenolphthalein, 90 mg per tablet.
Indications: For short-term relief of constipation.
Actions: Yellow phenolphthalein was previously categorized as a "stimulant" laxative. Recent research appears to indicate that phenolphthalein acts primarily by its effect on intestinal absorption

Continued on next page

Ex-Lax—Cont.

of water and electrolytes, thus causing propulsive activity. The main mode of action appears to be as a noncompetitive inhibitor of the enzymes, sodium and potassium adenosine triphosphatase, resulting in failure of salt and water absorption.

Warnings: Caution: Do not take any laxative when abdominal pain, nausea, or vomiting are present. Frequent or prolonged use of this or any other laxative may result in dependence on laxatives. If skin rash appears, do not use this or any other preparation containing phenolphthalein.

Ex-Lax is a medicine, not a candy. **Warning:** Keep this and all other medicines out of the reach of children.

Drug Interaction Precautions: No known drug interaction.

Dosage and Administration: Adults: 1 to 2 tablets, preferably at bed time. Children over 6 years: ½ to 1 tablet. Adult dosage may be slightly increased or decreased to suit individual requirements. If slightly increased adult dose is necessary, take it the following day.

How Supplied: Available in boxes of 6, 18, 48, and 72 chewable chocolate-flavored tablets.

[Shown in Product Identification Section]

EX–LAX® Pills, Unflavored Laxative

Active Ingredient: Yellow phenolphthalein, 90 mg per tablet.

Indications: For short-term relief of constipation.

Actions: Yellow phenolphthalein was previously categorized as a "stimulant" laxative. Recent research appears to indicate that phenolphthalein acts primarily by its effect on intestinal absorption of water and electrolytes, thus causing propulsive activity. The main mode of action appears to be as a noncompetitive inhibitor of the enzymes, sodium and potassium adenosine triphosphatase, resulting in failure of salt and water absorption.

Warnings: Caution: Do not take any laxative when abdominal pain, nausea, or vomiting are present. Frequent or prolonged use of this or any other laxative may result in dependence on laxatives. If skin rash appears, do not use this or any other preparation containing phenolphthalein.

Ex-Lax is a medicine, not a candy. **Warning:** Keep this and all other medicines out of the reach of children.

Drug Interaction Precautions: No known drug interaction.

Dosage and Administration: Adults: 1 to 2 tablets with a glass of water, preferably at bed time. Children over 6 years: 1 tablet. Adult dosage may be increased or decreased to suit individual requirements. If increased adult dose is necessary, take it the following day.

How Supplied: Available in boxes of 8, 30, and 60 unflavored pills.

[Shown in Product Identification Section]

Fleetwood Company
1500 BROOK DRIVE
DOWNERS GROVE, IL 60515

SUPER WATE–ON® EMULSION

Description: A high caloric, energy giving nutritional supplement ideal for use in weight gaining or weight maintaining programs, and in supplying the extra energy sources many persons need.

Nutritional Information: Daily dose of 3 ounces provides 541 calories taken alone or 991 calories taken with whole milk. (1 ounce of Super Wate-On mixed with 8 ounces of whole milk taken 3 times daily).

Super Wate-On is 62% fats, 10.6% carbohydrates. It also contains the following amounts of vitamins and minerals:

	*(R.D.A.)
400 IU Vitamin D	100%
2.25 mg Thiamine (Vitamin B$_1$)	150%
2.55 mg Riboflavin (Vitamin B$_2$)	150%
30 mg Niacin	150%
3.0 mg Vitamin B$_6$	150%
9.0 mcg Vitamin B$_{12}$	150%
15.0 mg Pantothenic Acid	150%
27.0 mg Iron	150%

Ingredients: Soybean Oil, Water, Sugar, Polyoxyethlene 20 Sorbitan Monostearate, Propylene Glycol, Sorbitan Monostearate, Ferric Ammonium Citrate, Artificial Flavor, Exanthan Gum, Sorbic Acid, Methyl Paraben, Propyl Paraben, Panthenol, Niacinamide, L-Lysine Monohydrochloride, Riboflavin 5 Phosphate, Buthlated Hydroxyanisole, Thiamine Hydrochloride, Pyndoxine Hydrochloride, Calciferol, Cyanocobalamin.

Dosage: Adults and Children 4 or more years of age. Take 1 ounce (2 tablespoonfuls) mixed in an 8 ounce glass of whole milk three times daily AFTER or between meals. Mix thoroughly using spoon, mixer or blender. May be taken direct from spoon.

Availability: Most pharmacies stock WATE-ON or can quickly obtain supply from local wholesalers.

Samples: Available at no cost to physicians that make request to above address.

How Supplied: 16 ounce bottle with weight-gaining plan booklet. Choice of 5 flavors.

OTHER WATE-ON® FORMS
AVAILABLE
REGULAR WATE-ON TABLETS 96's
REGULAR WATE-ON EMULSION 16 oz.
SUPER WATE-ON TABLETS 96's
SUPER WATE-ON P-410 SHAKE MIX 16 oz.
FLEETWOOD's RED LABEL IRON & VITAMIN TONIC 16 oz.
(SUPER WATE-ON products contain about 44% more calories than comparable Regular WATE-ON products).

[Shown in Product Identification Section]

Products are cross-indexed by

generic and chemical names in the

YELLOW SECTION

Fleming & Company
1600 FENPARK DR.
FENTON, MO 63026

MARBLEN Suspensions and Tablet

Composition: A modified 'Sippy Powder' antacid containing magnesium and calcium carbonates;

Action and Uses: The peach/apricot (pink) or unflavored (green) antacid suspensions are sugar-free and neutralize 18 mEq acid per teaspoonful with a low sodium content of 18mg per fl. oz. Each pink tablet consumes 18.0 mEq acid.

Administration and Dosage: One teaspoonful rather than a tablespoonful or one tablet to reduce patient cost by ⅔.

How Supplied: Plastic pints and bottles of 100 and 1000.

NEPHROX SUSPENSION
(aluminum hydroxide)
Antacid Suspension

Composition: A watermelon flavored aluminum hydroxide (320mg as gel)/mineral oil (10% by volume) antacid per teaspoonful.

Action and Uses: A sugar-free/saccharin-free pink suspension containing no magnesium and low sodium (19mg/oz). Extremely palatable and especially indicated in renal patients. Each teaspoon consumes 9 mEq acid.

Administration and Dosage: Two teaspoonfuls or as directed by a physician.

Caution: To be taken only at bedtime. Do not use at any other time or administer to infants, expectant women, and nursing mothers except upon the advice of a physician as this product contains mineral oil.

How Supplied: Plastic pints and gallons.

NICOTINEX Elixir
nicotinic acid

Composition: Contains niacin 50 mg./tsp. in a sherry wine base (amber color).

Action and Uses: Produces flushing when tablets fail. To increase micro-circulation of inner-ear in Meniere's, tinnitus and labyrinthine syndromes. For 'cold hands & feet', and as a vehicle for additives.

Administration and Dosage: One or two teaspoonsful on fasting stomach.

Side Effects: Patients should be warned of dermal flush. Ulcer and gout patients may be affected by 14% alcoholic content.

Contraindications: Severe hypotension and hemorrhage.

How Supplied: Plastic pints and gallons.

OCEAN MIST
(buffered saline)

Composition: Special isotonic saline, buffered with sodium bicarbonate to proper pH so as not to irritate the nose.

Action and Uses: Rhinitis medicamentosa, rhinitis sicca and atrophic rhinitis. For patients 'hooked on nose drops' and glaucoma patients on diuretics having dry nasal capillaries. OCEAN may be used as a mist or drop.

Administration and Dosage: One or two squeezes in each nostril.

Supplied: Plastic 45cc spray bottles and pints.

PURGE
(flavored castor oil)

Composition: Contains 95% castor oil (USP) in a sweetened lemon flavored base that completely masks the odor and taste of the oil.

Indications: Preparation of the bowel for x-ray, surgery and proctological procedures, IVPs, and constipation.

Dosage: Infants—1–2 teaspoonfuls. Children—adjust between infant and adult dose. Adult—2–4 tablespoonfuls.

Precaution: Not indicated when nausea, vomiting, abdominal pain or symptoms of appendicitis occur. Pregnancy, use only on advice of physician.

Supplied: Plastic 1 oz. & 2 oz. bottles.

Forever Living Products, Inc.
P.O. BOX 29041
PHOENIX, AZ 85038

ALOE VERA GELLY

Aloe Vera Gelly is a smooth translucent gelly formulated with 100% stabilized aloe vera gel. Standardized for topical application with a pure aloe vera base, Aloe Vera Gelly has a smoothing moisturizing effect on the skin.

Indications: Aloe Vera Gelly can be used for dry or chafed skin, itching, non-poisonous insect bites, diaper rash, and other problems related to the skin and tissues.

Directions for Use: Thoroughly cleanse area. Apply Aloe Vera Gelly liberally. Repeat applications as required.

How Supplied: 4 oz. (118 ml.) container.

ALOE VERA JUICE

Aloe Vera Juice can be consumed like any other fruit, vegetable or plant juice. It appears to have supplemental value in a variety of medical conditions. Digestive processes have been noted to improve. Many have reported to feel more energetic.

How Supplied: Available in 32 fl. oz. (946 ml.) jugs.

Products are

indexed alphabetically

in the

PINK SECTION

Fox Pharmacal, Inc.
1750 W. McNAB ROAD
FT. LAUDERDALE, FL 33310

E–Z TRIM™
Timed-release Diet Aid Capsules

Active Ingredient: Phenylpropanolamine HCl ....75 mg.

Indications: Phenylpropanolamine is a sympathomimetic amine with demonstrated appetite-suppressant effects. For use in programs of weight reduction adjunctively to reduced caloric intake.

Warnings: Do not exceed recommended dosage. Do not take this product for periods exceeding three months. Do not give this product to children under 12 years. Do not take this product if you are taking another medication containing phenylpropanolamine HCl. If you have or are being treated for high blood pressure, heart disease, diabetes, thyroid disease or depression or are pregnant or nursing, do not take this product except under the supervision of a physician. If you become nervous, sleepless or dizzy, stop the medication.

Dosage and Administration: Take one capsule at mid-morning.

How Supplied: Consumer packages of 22 capsules.

ODRINIL™ Natural Diuretic

Active Ingredients: Powdered Extract of Buchu; Powdered Extract of Uva Ursi; Powdered Extract of Corn Silk; Powdered Extract of Juniper; Caffeine.

Indications: To aid in the relief of simple water retention or "bloating" such as experienced in the premenstrual period and not associated with disease conditions.

Actions: Herbal extracts contained in this product have been recommended for centuries to aid in the excretion of excess sodium and thereby overcome excessive water retention that results from salt retention. Caffeine is widely recognized as having similar diuretic properties.

Warnings: This product is not indicated for water retention that results from kidney, heart or other systemic disease. It should not be used when such diseases or conditions are present except on the advice of a physician.

Drug Interaction Precautions: None.

Dosage and Administration: One tablet with a glass of water after each meal and before retiring when premenstrual bloating is experienced. The product has no value as a preventative, but is only effective when water retention is present.

How Supplied: Packages of 60 tablets.

SUPER ODRINEX™ Reducing Aid

Active Ingredients:
Phenylpropanolamine HCl ....25 mg.
Caffeine ....100 mg.

Indications: For use in short term (8–12 weeks) programs of weight reduction adjunctively to reduced caloric intake.

Actions: Phenylpropanolamine is a sympathomimetic amine with demon-

strated appetite-suppressant effects. Clinical trials have shown that individuals on restricted caloric intake lose several times as much weight when taking SUPER ODRINEX adjunctively to the dietary restrictions as patients on the same dietary restrictions but receiving placebo tablets.

Warnings: Individuals being treated for high blood pressure, heart disease, diabetes, thyroid disease or depression or are pregnant or nursing, should not take this product except under the supervision of a physician. Do not exceed recommended dosage. Discontinue use when desired weight is attained. For adult use only. Do not administer this product to children under the age of 12 except on the advice of a physician.

Drug Interaction Precautions: Do not use concurrently with Cough, Cold or Allergy preparations which contain a decongestant.

Precautions: Some sensitive persons may experience nervousness or insomnia, especially if they are prone to excessive intake of coffee, tea, cocoa or soft drinks containing caffeine.

Overdosage: Ingestion of marked overdoses is not usually life-threatening, but marked drowsiness or jitteryness may occur. The persistence of these symptoms is short-lived.

Dosage and Administration: One tablet with a glass of water three times daily, ½ hour before meals. For use by Adults only.

How Supplied: In packages of 50 or 110 tablets, each containing Phenylpropanolamine HCl 25 mg. and Caffeine 100 mg.

G & W Laboratories, Inc.
111 COOLIDGE STREET
SOUTH PLAINFIELD, NJ 07080

ACEPHEN
Acetaminophen Rectal Suppositories

Active Ingredient: Acetaminophen

Indications: For the temporary relief of fever, minor aches, pains, and headaches.

Warning: Adults—do not use consistently for more than 10 days, except on the advice of a physician. Children—do not use more than 5 days, except on the advice of a physician. **Keep this and all drugs out of the reach of children. In case of accidental ingestion, seek professional assistance or contact a poison control center immediately.**

Dosage and Administration: 650 mg.:
Adults: One suppository every 4–6 hours. No more than a total of 4 suppositories in any 24 hour period. Children (6–12 years): One half suppository every 4–6 hours. No more than a total of 4 suppositories in any 24 hour period.
120 mg.:
Children (3–6 years): One suppository every 4–6 hours. No more than 6 supposi-

Continued on next page

G & W Laboratories—Cont.

tories in any 24 hour period. Children (under 3): Consult a physician.
STORE BELOW 80°F. OR REFRIGERATE.
How Supplied: Available in 650 mg. and 120 mg. Packaged in boxes of 12's.

ASPIRIN SUPPOSITORIES

Description: Each suppository contains aspirin 125 mg., 300 mg., or 600 mg., in a specially blended hydrogenated vegetable oil base.
Indications and Use: For the relief of headaches and simple muscular aches and pains. Note: Store in a cool place 8°–15°C. (46°–59°F).
Caution: For children under 4 years of age, consult a physician.
Warning: Keep this and all drugs out of the reach of children. In case of accidental ingestion, seek professional assistance or contact a poison control center immediately.
Dosage and Administration: Remove foil wrapper and insert one suppository well up into rectum 3 or 4 times daily as required.
How Supplied:
125 mg.—Pediatric Suppositories
300 mg. and 600 mg.—Adult Suppositories
Boxes of 12's.

(See Manufacturers' Index for additional products available.)

GEIGY Pharmaceuticals
Division of CIBA-GEIGY Corporation
ARDSLEY, NY 10502

OTRIVIN®
xylometazoline hydrochloride USP
Adult Nasal Spray and Drops 0.1%
Pediatric Nasal Drops 0.05%

Description: Otrivin, xylometazoline HCl, a sympathomimetic amine, is a white, odorless, crystalline powder which is soluble in water and freely soluble in alcohol. Chemically, it is 2-(4- tert-butyl-2, 6-dimethylbenzyl)-2-imidazoline monohydrochloride.
This preparation is available in 0.1% solution for adults and 0.05% solution for children under 12.
Nasal Spray contains 0.1% and *Nasal Drops* contain 0.1% or 0.05% xylometazoline hydrochloride USP, potassium phosphate monobasic, potassium chloride, sodium phosphate dibasic, sodium chloride, and benzalkonium chloride 1:5,000 as preservative in water.
Actions: Its sympathomimetic (adrenergic) action constricts the smaller arterioles of the nasal passages, effecting a decongesting action. This vasoconstriction results from alpha-adrenergic receptor stimulation of vascular smooth muscle.
Indications: For decongestion of the nasal mucosa.
Contraindications: Narrow-angle glaucoma. Concurrent MAO inhibitor ther-

apy. Tricyclic antidepressant therapy. Hypersensitivity to any component of this preparation.
Sensitivity to even small doses of adrenergic substances as manifested by sleeplessness, dizziness, lightheadedness, weakness, tremulousness, or cardiac arrhythmias.
Warnings: Systemic effects from the use of topical decongestants may occur due to rapid absorption through the nasal mucous membrane and from gastrointestinal absorption if given in excess so that the solution is swallowed. Such reactions are most likely to occur in infants and the elderly.
Because of the possibility of generalized vasoconstriction and tachycardia, nose drops (as all sympathomimetic amines) should be used very cautiously in patients with hypertension, heart disease, including angina, hyperthyroidism and advanced arteriosclerotic conditions.
Overdosage may produce profound CNS depression in children, possibly requiring intensive supportive treatment.
Usage in Pregnancy: Clinical data are inadequate to establish conditions for safe use of nose drops in pregnancy.
Directions:
Nasal Spray 0.1%—Spray 2 or 3 times into each nostril every 8–10 hours. With head upright, squeeze sharply and firmly while inhaling (sniffing) through the nose.
Nasal Drops 0.1%—For adults and children 12 years and older. Put 2 or 3 drops into each nostril every 8 to 10 hours. Tilt head as far back as possible. Immediately bend head forward toward knees, hold a few seconds, then return to upright position.
Pediatric Nasal Drops 0.05%—For children 2 to 12 years of age. Put 2 or 3 drops into each nostril every 8 to 10 hours. Tilt head as far back as possible. Immediately bend head forward toward knees, hold a few seconds, then return to upright position.
How Supplied: *Otrivin Nasal Spray/Nasal Drops* are available in unbreakable plastic spray packages of ½ fl oz (15 ml) and in plastic dropper bottles of .66 fl oz (20 ml).
Otrivin Pediatric Nasal Drops Available in plastic dropper bottles of .66 fl oz (20 ml).

(8/80)
[*Shown in Product Identification Section*].

PBZ®
tripelennamine hydrochloride
Antihistamine Cream

Description: PBZ Cream is a topical antihistaminic preparation containing 2% tripelennamine hydrochloride.
Indications: For the temporary relief of itching due to minor skin disorders, ivy and oak poisoning, hives, sunburn, insect bites (nonpoisonous), and stings.
Directions: Apply gently to the affected area 3 or 4 times daily or according to physician's directions.
Caution: If the condition persists or irritation develops, discontinue use and consult physician. Do not use in eyes.

KEEP OUT OF REACH OF CHILDREN.
How Supplied: *Cream,* 2% tripelennamine hydrochloride in a water-washable base; tubes of 1 ounce.

(1/80)
[*Shown in Product Identification Section*]

The full prescribing information for each GEIGY drug is contained herein and is that in effect as of December 1, 1981.

Gerber Products Company
FREMONT, MI 49412

MBF* (Meat Base Formula) Liquid Hypoallergenic Infant feeding Formula, Gerber

Composition: Hypoallergenic liquid formula made from water, beef hearts, sugar, sesame oil, modified tapioca starch, tricalcium phosphate, calcium citrate, potassium chloride, iodized salt, magnesium chloride, sodium ascorbate, ferrous sulfate, tocopheryl acetate, thiamin hydrochloride, vitamin A palmitate, calcium pantothenate, pyridoxine hydrochloride, vitamin D, cupric sulfate, phytonadione (vitamin K_1), folic acid, potassium iodide and biotin.
Nutrient Content: 1:1 dilution contains 20 cal/fl.oz., 12.2% solids, 2.6% protein, 3.2% fat and 6.0% carbohydrate with a Ca/P ratio of 1.5. Vitamin and mineral content per 15 fl. oz. can is:

Vitamin A	1600.0 I.U.
Vitamin D	360.0 I.U.
Vitamin K	24.0 mcg
Vitamin E	6.6 I.U.
Vitamin C	54.0 mg
Vitamin B_1 (Thiamin)	0.54 mg
Vitamin B_2 (Riboflavin)	0.90 mg
Vitamin B_6 (Pyridoxine)	0.78 mg
Vitamin B_{12}	7.8 mcg
Niacin	3.6 mg
Folic Acid	24.0 mcg
Pantothenic Acid	1.8 mg
Biotin	9.0 mcg
Choline	90.0 mg
Inositol	150.0 mg
Calcium	900.0 mg
Phosphorus	600.0 mg
Magnesium	36.0 mg
Iron	12.0 mg
Iodine	30.0 mcg
Zinc	3.0 mg
Copper	0.36 mg
Manganese	30.0 mcg
Sodium	246.0 mg
Potassium	486.0 mg
Chloride	438.0 mg

Action and Uses: A nutritionally adequate formula for infants and children intolerant to cow's and goat's milk whose symptoms may be diarrhea, colic, eczema, upper respiratory, etc. Useful in the management of milk induced steatorrhea, and prophylactic feedings.
Administration and Dosage: Provides 20 cal/fl.oz. when diluted 1:1; similar to other milk-based and soy-based infant formulas. Concentrated liquid added to previously boiled (not hot) water is to be

divided among prescribed number of bottles, easily fed thru cross-cut nipples. MBF's content of essential nutrients conforms to the infant formula standard established by the U.S. Food and Drug Administration in 1971 and the 1980 American Academy of Pediatrics infant formula recommendations.

Side Effects: None.
Precautions: None.
Contraindications: None.
How Supplied: Concentrated Liquid, 15 fl. oz. cans.
Literature Available: Yes.
*Trademark

Glenbrook Laboratories
Division of Sterling Drug Inc.
90 PARK AVENUE
NEW YORK, NY 10016

BAYER® ASPIRIN AND BAYER® CHILDREN'S CHEWABLE ASPIRIN
Aspirin (Acetylsalicylic Acid)

Composition: Bayer Aspirin—Aspirin 5 grains. (325 mg.)
Bayer Children's Chewable Aspirin—Aspirin 1¼ grains (81 mg.) per orange flavored chewable tablet.

Action and Uses: Analgesic, antipyretic, anti-inflammatory. For relief of headache; painful discomfort and fever of colds and flu; sore throats; muscular aches and pains; temporary relief of minor pains of arthritis, rheumatism, bursitis, lumbago, sciatica; toothache, teething pains, and pain following dental procedures; neuralgia and neuritic pain; functional menstrual pain; sleeplessness when caused by minor painful discomforts; painful discomfort and fever accompanying immunizations.

Administration and Dosage: The following dosages are those provided in the packaging, as appropriate for self-medication. Larger or more frequent dosage may be necessary as appropriate to the condition or needs of the patient.
Bayer Aspirin—5 grain (325 mg.) tablets
Adult Dose: One or two tablets with water. May be repeated every four hours as necessary up to 12 tablets a day.
Children's Dose: To be administered only under adult supervision.
Under 2 years ....per physician
2 to under 4 years ....½ tablet
4 to under 6 years ....¾ tablet
6 to under 9 years ....1 tablet
9 to under 11 years ....1¼ tablets
11 to under 12 years ....1½ tablets
Over 12 years ....same as adult
Indicated dosage may be repeated every 4 hours, up to but not more than five times a day. Larger dosage may be prescribed per physician.
Bayer Children's Chewable Aspirin—1¼ grain (81 mg.) tablets
DOSAGE
To be administered only under adult supervision. For children under 2, consult physician.

Age (years)	Weight (lbs)	Dosage
2 up to 4	27 to 35	2 tablets
4 up to 6	36 to 45	3 tablets
6 up to 9	46 to 65	4 tablets
9 up to 11	66 to 76	5 tablets
11 up to 12	77 to 83	6 tablets
12 and over	84 and over	8 tablets

Indicated dosage may be repeated every 4 hours, up to but not more than five times a day. Larger dosage may be prescribed per physician.

Contraindications: Hypersensitivity to salicylates. To be used with caution in presence of peptic ulcer, asthma, or with anticoagulant therapy.

How Supplied:
Bayer Aspirin 5 grains (325 mg.)—
NDC-12843-101-10, packs of 12 tablets
NDC-12843-101-11, bottles of 24 tablets
NDC-12843-101-17, bottles of 50 tablets
NDC-12843-101-12, bottles of 100 tablets
NDC-12843-101-20, bottles of 200 tablets
NDC-12843-101-13, bottles of 300 tablets
Child-resistant safety closures on 12s, 24s, 50s, 200s, 300s. Bottle of 100s available without safety closure for households without small children.
Bayer Children's Chewable Aspirin 1¼ grains (81 mg.)—
NDC-12843-131-05, bottle of 36 tablets with child-resistant safety closure.
Samples available on request.
[Shown in Product Identification Section]

BAYER® CHILDREN'S COLD TABLETS

Composition: Each tablet contains phenylpropanolamine HCl 3.125 mg., aspirin 1¼ gr. (81 mg.); the tablets are orange flavored and chewable.

Action and Uses: Bayer Children's Cold Tablets combine two effective ingredients: a gentle decongestant to relieve nasal congestion and ease breathing, and genuine Bayer Aspirin to reduce fever and relieve minor aches and pains of colds and flu.

Administration and Dosage: The following dosage is provided in the packaging:
Under 3 years - consult physician
3 years - 1 tablet
4 to 5 years - 2 tablets
6 to 12 years - 4 tablets
Indicated dosage may be repeated every four hours up to but not more than four times a day. Larger or more frequent dosage may be necessary as appropriate to the condition or needs of the patient.

Contraindications: Side effects at higher doses may include nervousness, dizziness, sleeplessness. To be used with caution in presence of high blood pressure, heart disease, diabetes, asthma, or thyroid disease.

How Supplied: NDC-12843-181-01, bottles of 30 tablets with child-resistant safety closure.
Samples available on request.

BAYER® COUGH SYRUP FOR CHILDREN

Composition: Each 5 ml. (1 tsp.) contains phenylpropanolamine HCl 9 mg. and dextromethorphan hydrobromide 7.5 mg., alcohol 5% Cherry flavored.

Action and Uses: Bayer Cough Syrup for Children combines two effective ingredients in a syrup with a very appealing cherry flavor: a gentle nasal decongestant and a cough suppressant.

Administration and Dosage: The following dosage is provided on the packaging:
Under 2 years ....per physician
2–5 years: 1 teaspoon every 4 hours, not to exceed 4 teaspoons every 24 hours.
6–12 years: 2 teaspoons every 4 hours, not to exceed 8 teaspoons every 24 hours.

Contraindications and Precautions: To be used with caution in presence of high blood pressure, heart disease, diabetes, asthma, or thyroid disease.
How Supplied: NDC-12843-401-02, 3.0 oz. bottles. Samples available on request.

BAYER® TIMED-RELEASE ASPIRIN
(aspirin)

Description: Each oblong white scored tablet contains 10 grains (650 mg.) of aspirin in microencapsulation form.

Indications: Bayer Timed-Release Aspirin is indicated for the temporary relief of low grade pain amenable to relief with salicylates, such as in rheumatoid arthritis, osteoarthritis, spondylitis, bursitis and other forms of rheumatism, as well as in many common musculoskeletal disorders. It possesses the same advantages for other types of prolonged aches and pains, such as minor injuries, dental pain and dysmenorrhea. Its long-lasting effectiveness should also make it valuable as an analgesic in simple headache, colds, grippe, flu and other similar conditions in which aspirin is indicated for symptomatic relief, either by itself or as an adjunct to specific therapy.

Dosage: Two Bayer Timed-Release Aspirin tablets q. 8 h. provide effective long-lasting pain relief. This two-tablet (20 grain or 1300 mg.) dose of timed-release aspirin promptly produces salicylate blood levels greater than those achieved by a 10-grain (650 mg.) dose of regular aspirin, and in the second 4 hour period produces a salicylate blood level curve which approximates that of two successive 10-grain (650 mg.) doses of regular aspirin at 4 hour intervals. The 10-grain (650 mg.) scored Bayer Timed-Release Aspirin tablets permit administration of aspirin in multiples of 5 grains (325 mg.), allowing individualization of dosage to meet the specific needs of the patient. For the convenience of patients on a regular aspirin dosage schedule, two 10-grain (650 mg.) Bayer Timed-Release Aspirin tablets may be administered with water every 8 hours. Whenever possible, two tablets (20 grains or 1300 mg.) should be given before retiring to provide effective analgesic and anti-inflammatory action—for relief of pain throughout the night and lessening of stiffness upon arising. Do not exceed 6 tablets in 24 hours. Bayer Timed-Release Aspirin has been made in a special capsule-shaped tablet to permit easy swallowing. However, for patients who do have difficulty, Bayer

Continued on next page

Glenbrook—Cont.

Timed-Release Aspirin tablets may be gently crumbled in the mouth and swallowed with water without loss of timed-release effect. There is no bitter "aspirin" taste. For children under 12, per physician.

Side Effects: Side effects encountered with regular aspirin may be encountered with Bayer Timed-Release Aspirin. Tinnitus and dizziness are the ones most frequently encountered.

Contraindications and Precautions: Bayer Timed-Release Aspirin is contraindicated in patients with marked aspirin hypersensitivity, and should be given with extreme caution to any patient with a history of adverse reaction to salicylates. It may cautiously be tried in patients intolerant to aspirin because of gastric irritation, but the usual precautions for any form of aspirin should be observed in patients with gastric ulcers, bleeding tendencies, asthma, or hypoprothrombinemia.

Supplied:
Tablets in Bottle of 30's
NDC-12843-191-72
Tablets in Bottle of 72's
NDC-12843-191-74
Tablets in Bottle of 125's
NDC-12843-191-76
All sizes packaged in child-resistant safety closure except 72's which is a size recommended for households without young children.
Samples available upon request.
[*Shown in Product Identification Section*]

DIAPARENE® BABY POWDER

Description: Powder comprised of corn starch, magnesium carbonate, fragrance, and methylbenzethonium chloride.

Action and Uses: Diaparene Baby Powder has a corn starch base for high absorbency to help keep baby skin dry and for soothing diaper rash, prickly heat, and chafing.

Administration and Dosage: Apply liberally to baby's skin after bath and with each diaper change.

How Supplied: Canister sizes of 4 oz., 9 oz., 12½ oz.
[*Shown in Product Identification Section*]

DIAPARENE™ BABY WASH CLOTHS

Description: Wash cloths are impregnated with a cleansing solution containing water, SD alcohol-40, propylene glycol, lanolin, sodium nonoxynol-9-phosphate, sorbic acid, citric acid, disodium phosphate, oleth-20, and fragrance.

Action and Uses: Diaparene Baby Wash Cloths contain lanolin and a mild cleansing solution to clean and condition baby's skin.

Administration and Dosage: Wipe baby's skin with solution-impregnated wash cloths as required.

How supplied: Canisters in sizes of 70 and 150 wash cloths.
[*Shown in Product Identification Section*]

MIDOL®

Composition: Each Caplet® contains Aspirin 454 mg (7 grains); Cinnamedrine Hydrochloride 14.9 mg; Caffeine 32.4 mg.

Action and Uses: Analgesic, antispasmodic. For fast relief of functional menstrual pain, cramps, irritability; headache, aches from swelling, and the irritability associated with premenstrual tension; headache, and low backache associated with menstruation.

Usage Adult Dosage: Two Caplets with water. Repeat two Caplets every four hours as needed, up to eight Caplets per day.

How Supplied: White, capsule-shaped Caplets.
NDC-12843-151-34, strip packs of 12 Caplets
NDC 12843-151-02, sample size of 6 caplets
NDC-12843-151-36, bottles of 30 Caplets
NDC-12843-151-38, bottles of 60 Caplets
Child-resistant safety closures on bottles of 30 to 60 Caplets.

Samples Supplied: Available upon request.
[*Shown in Product Identification Section*]

PHILLIPS' MILK OF MAGNESIA

Composition: A suspension of magnesium hydroxide, meeting all USP specifications.

Action and Uses: Phillips' Milk of Magnesia is a mild saline laxative and is indicated for the relief of constipation especially in patients with hemorrhoids, obstetric patients, cardiacs, and in geriatric patients where straining at stool is contraindicated. Phillips' also acts as an antacid, and is effective for the relief of symptoms associated with gastric hyperacidity.

Administration and Dosage: As a laxative, adults 2 to 4 tbsp. followed by a glass of water. Children-infants 1 tsp.; over one year ¼ to ½ adult dose, depending on age. As a antacid, 1 to 3 tsps. with a little water, up to four times a day. Children-1 to 12 years: ¼ to ½ adult dose up to four times a day.

Contraindications: Abdominal pain, nausea, vomiting or other symptoms of appendicitis.

How Supplied: Phillips' Milk of Magnesia is available in regular and mint in bottles of:

Regular

4 fl. oz.	NDC-12843-353-01
12 fl. oz.	NDC-12843-353-02
26 fl. oz.	NDC-12843-353-03

Mint

4 fl oz.	NDC-12843-363-04
12 fl. oz.	NDC-12843-363-05
26 fl. oz.	NDC-12843-363-06

Also available in tablet form.
[*Shown in Product Identification Section*]

VANQUISH®

Composition: Each Caplet contains aspirin 227 mg., acetaminophen 194 mg., caffeine 33 mg., dried aluminum hydroxide gel 25 mg.; magnesium hydroxide 50 mg.

Action and Uses: A buffered analgesic, antipyretic for relief of headache; muscular aches and pains; neuralgia and neuritic pain; pain following dental procedures; for painful discomforts and fever of colds and flu; functional menstrual pain, headache and pain due to cramps; temporary relief from minor pains of arthritis, rheumatism, bursitis, lumbago, sciatica.

Usual Adult Dosage: Two caplets with water. May be repeated every four hours if necessary up to 12 tablets per day. Larger or more frequent doses may be prescribed by physician if necessary.

Contraindications: Hypersensitivity to salicylates.
(To be used with caution during anticoagulant therapy or in asthmatic patients.)

How Supplied: White, capsule-shaped Caplets in bottles of:
  15 Caplets NDC 12843-17142
  30 Caplets NDC 12843-17144
  60 Caplets NDC 12843-17146
100 Caplets NDC 12843-17148

Goody's Manufacturing Corporation
436 SALT STREET
WINSTON-SALEM, NC 27108

GOODY'S HEADACHE POWDERS

Active Ingredient: 520 mg. Aspirin, 260 mg. Acetaminophen 32.5 mg. Caffeine

Indications: For relief of pain due to simple headache, muscular aches and pains, headaches accompanying head colds.

Actions: Combination of active ingredients have analgesic, antipyretic and anti-inflammatory activity.

Warnings: Do not take more than recommended dosage or take regularly for more than 10 days without consulting your physician. Keep out of reach of children. In case of accidental overdose, contact a physician immediately.

Symptoms and Treatment of Oral Overdosage: Symptoms consist of dizziness, ringing in the ears, nausea, diarrhea, incoherent speech, and coma. Treatment varies but drinking two glasses of milk will dilute and slow absorption. Activated charcoal may be given orally in a 5 ml/kg dose. Emptying the stomach is advised.

Dosage and Administration: Adults: one powder with water or other liquid. May be repeated in 3 or 4 hours. Do not take more than 4 powders in any 24 hour period. For children under 12, only as directed by a physician.

How Supplied: Available in 2 dose envelope, 6 dose small box, 24 and 50 dose carton.
[*Shown in Product Identification Section*]

Products are cross-indexed by
generic and chemical names in the
YELLOW SECTION

Health Care Industries
Division of Accra Pac, Inc.
2825 MIDDLEBURY STREET
ELKHART, IN 46515

ALLIMIN® Filmcoated Tablets
Antiflatulent Tablets

Active Ingredient: Dried garlic powder (Allium sativum, dehydrated), 4¾ grains (308 mg.) per tablet. Filmcoated (sugarless) for ease of swallowing.

Indications: For expelling gas from stomach and intestines. Is indicated when entrapped gas is associated with tension of gastrointestinal muscles and/ or sphincters.

Actions: Allimin® relaxes the smooth muscle of the tense gastrointestinal tract and sphincters, thus allowing entrapped gas to escape.

Warnings: Keep this and all medications out of reach of children. There is no known case of hypersensitivity, but in such an event, discontinue use and consult a physician. If symptoms persist consult physician.

Drug Interaction: No known drug interaction.

Symptoms and Treatment of Oral Overdosage: These symptoms are based on medical judgment and not on clinical studies: Nausea and vomiting may occur with overdosage. Discontinue use, drink at least 6 to 8 fl. oz. of milk or water for dilution effect and consult physician.

Dosage and Administration: Two (2) tablets after meals when needed. Swallow whole with liquids: water, milk, fruit or vegetable juices.

Professional Labeling: Same as outlined above.

How Supplied: Cartons of 30 pouched tablets and plastic bottles of 80, 160, and 330 tablets. (NDC #036038-)
[Shown in Product Identification Section]

COSANYL® Cough Syrup   ©
Cough suppressant/nasal
decongestant

Active Ingredients: Each teaspoonful (5 ml.): Codeine phosphate, 10 mg. (Warning: May be habit forming); d-pseudoephedrine HCl, 30 mg. Peach flavor. Alcohol, 6%.

Indications: For the temporary relief of cough, and for temporary relief of nasal congestion due to the common cold or inhaled irritants causing upper respiratory allergies.

Actions: Codeine is a well-known, centrally acting anti-tussive. d-pseudoephedrine reduces congestion of the nasopharyngeal mucosa.

Warnings: May cause or aggravate constipation. Consult a physician or act under his advice for children on other drugs or under 2 years of age, for chronic cough, if one has high blood pressure, heart, thyroid, diabetic, pulmonary diseases, shortness of breath. Do not exceed recommended dosage. If after 7 days, cough persists, or with fever, rash, headache, consult a physician. Keep all drugs out of childrens' reach.

Drug Interaction Precaution: Consult a physician or act under his advice and supervision for concomitant use with a prescription antihypertensive or anti-depressant drug containing a monoamine oxidase inhibitor. Avoid use with alcoholic beverages.

Symptoms and Treatment of Oral Overdosage: These symptoms are based on medical judgment and not on clinical studies: Depending on degree of oral overdosage, codeine symptoms may include: depressed respiration in severe cases, and in other cases, somnolence, sedation. Use with alcoholic beverages could cause a comatose state. Although d-pseudoephedrine in recommended doses won't normally cause symptoms of sympathomimetic overstimulation, signs of marked overdose may include hypertension, headache, tachycardia, flushing, etc. Codeine and d-pseudoephedrine effects in overdose, may tend to counteract one another to some degree. But for extreme overdose, prompt gastric evacuation and supportive care is indicated and in this event or in case of accidental ingestion, seek professional assistance or contact a Poison Control Center immediately.

Dosage and Administration: Adults: 2 teaspoonful every 6 hours. Maximum 8 teaspoonful in 24 hours. Children (6 to under 12 years): ½ of adult dose above. Children (2 to under 6 years): ¼ of adult dose. Screw safety cap on tightly.

Professional Labeling: Same as outlined above.

How Supplied: 4 fl. oz. with safety cap. Pharmacy dispensing units are pints and gallons. (NDC #11010-001-)
[Shown in Product Identification Section]

COSANYL-DM® Cough Syrup
Non-narcotic cough
suppressant/nasal decongestant

Active Ingredients: Teaspoonful (5 ml.): d-methorphan, 15 mg; d-pseudoephedrine HCl, 30 mg. Peach flavor. Alcohol 6%.

Indications: For the temporary relief of cough, and for temporary relief of nasal congestion due to the common cold or upper respiratory allergies.

Actions: d-methorphan is a well-known, centrally acting anti-tussive with a 6 to 8 hour duration of action for nighttime relief. d-pseudoephedrine reduces congestion of the naso-pharyngeal mucosa.

Warnings: Consult a physician or act under his advice for children on other drugs or under 2 years of age, for chronic cough, if one has high blood pressure, heart, thyroid, diabetic, pulmonary diseases, shortness of breath. Do not exceed recommended dosage. If after 7 days, cough persists, or with fever, rash, headache, consult a physician. Keep all drugs out of childrens' reach.

Drug Interaction Precaution: Consult a physician or act under his advice and supervision for concomitant use with a prescription antihypertensive or anti-depressant drug containing a monoamine oxidase inhibitor. Avoid use with alcoholic beverages.

Symptoms and Treatment of Oral Overdosage: Symptoms are based on medical judgment and not clinical studies: d-pseudoephedrine in recommended doses normally won't cause sympathomimetic side effects but particularly sensitive persons, especially with overdosage, may experience nervousness, restlessness, sleeplessness or other signs of overstimulation of the sympathetic nervous system. In such an event, discontinue use and seek professional assistance to establish a reduced dosage. In case of marked overdosage or accidental ingestion, seek professional assistance or contact a Poison Control Center immediately.

Dosage and Administration: Adults: 2 teaspoonful every 6 to 8 hours. Maximum 8 teaspoonful in 24 hours. Children (6 to under 12 years): ½ of adult dose above. Children (2 to under 6 years): ¼ of adult dose. For night time cough relief, give the last dose at bedtime.

Professional Labeling: Same as outlined above.

How Supplied: 4 fl. oz. shrink-wrapped, in 6-Pak Display unit. (NDC #11010-002-04)
[Shown in Product Identification Section]

OIL-O-SOL® Liquid
Skin wound cleanser/dressing

Active Ingredients: Corn oil 52%, Castor oil 40.8%, Camphor oil 6.8%, Hexylresorcinol 0.1% (all % are wt. to wt.)

Indications: For minor cuts, scratches, and surface abrasions. For minor burns, non-venomous insect bites. Can be used to treat minor sunburn.

Actions: Corn oil is a natural vegetable oil which provides emollient effects. Castor oil is a quick drying natural oil for a protectant effect. Camphor oil provides mild local analgesic and rubefacient action and topical cooling effect to ease pain. Hexylresorcinol is added for its topical anti-bacterial effects, which helps to prevent infection.

Warnings: For EXTERNAL USE ONLY. Keep out of the eyes and mucous membranes. If burns or wounds are deep or extensive, consult a physician. If redness, irritation, swelling or pain persist, or if infection occurs, discontinue use, see physician.

Drug Interaction Precaution: No known drug interactions.

Symptoms and Treatment of Oral Overdosage: Since Oil-O-Sol® is for EXTERNAL USE ONLY, oral ingestion would be accidental or other mis-use. These symptoms are based on medical judgment and not on clinical studies: Corn oil, Castor oil, and Hexylresorcinol are all edible and have a high order of safety in these concentrations. Accidental ingestion may cause indigestion, nausea, vomiting, or catharsis. In extreme oral misuse, camphor could have CNS toxic effects of an overstimulation type. In such an extreme case, dilute by drinking large amounts of water and immediately seek professional assistance or contact a Poison Control Center. When used

Continued on next page

Health Care—Cont.

EXTERNALLY as recommended, Oil-O-Sol® overdose has never occurred.

Usage and Administration: Clean area thoroughly with mild soap and water. Then clean with Oil-O-Sol.® Saturate a sterile gauze pad with Oil-O-Sol® and apply to injured part. For ready-to-use speed and convenience, use Oil-O-Sol® STREEM-TOP™ with pump applicator.

Professional Labeling: Same as outlined above.

How Supplied: 1, 2, 4 fl. oz. liquid, 2 oz. STREEM-TOP™ pump. Economy sizes, pint and gallon. (NDC #0543-0001-)
[*Shown in Product Identification Section*]

Herbert Laboratories
Dermatology Division of Allergan Pharmaceuticals, Inc.
2525 DUPONT DRIVE
IRVINE, CA 92713

TOTAL ECLIPSE®
Sunscreen Lotion (Moisturizing Base & Alcohol Base)—(SPF 15)

Active Ingredient:
Total Eclipse (SPF 15) (Moisturizing Base): Padimate O (octyl dimethyl PABA) and oxybenzone (benzophenone-3)
Total Eclipse (SPF 15) (Alcohol Base): Oxybenzone (benzophenone-3), padimate O (octyl dimethyl PABA) and glyceryl PABA with alcohol (81%)
Indications: Prevention of harmful effects of sun
Actions: Selectively screens the harmful rays of the sun to help prevent sunburn, premature aging and skin cancer. Total Eclipse (Moisturizing and Alcohol base) screens the burning and tanning rays for the most sun-sensitive skin either dry or oily respectively.
Warnings: For external use only. Do not use if sensitive to benzocaine, sulfonamides, aniline dyes, PABA or related compounds. Avoid contact with eyes or eyelids. If contact occurs, rinse thoroughly with water. If irritation develops, discontinue use. If it persists, consult a physician. Keep out of reach of children. May stain some fabrics. Total Eclipse (alcohol base)—Avoid flame.
Drug Interaction: No known drug interaction.
Symptoms and Treatment of Oral Overdosage: Total Eclipse (Moisturizing Base): Push fluids.
Total Eclipse (Alcohol Base): Induce emesis by aspiration or gastric lavage. Then push fluids.
Dosage and Administration: Apply liberally & evenly to all exposed skin; Total Eclipse (Moisturizing Base)—(every 6-8 hours). Apply in thin, even film to all exposed skin; Total Eclipse (alcohol base)—(every 6-8 hours).
Professional Labeling: Same as outlined under Indications.

How Supplied: Both Total Eclipses: 4 oz plastic bottles.
[*Shown in Product Identification Section*]

Hoechst-Roussel Pharmaceuticals Inc.
SOMERVILLE, NJ 08876

DOXIDAN®
Laxative with Stool Softener

Active Ingredients: Doxidan is a combination of 60 mg docusate calcium USP, 50 mg danthron USP and up to 1.5% alcohol (w/w).
Actions: Doxidan has a highly effective stool softener and a mild peristaltic stimulant that acts mainly in the lower bowel. Due to the effectiveness of the stool softening component, Doxidan produces soft, formed, easily evacuated stools, with the least possible disturbance of normal body physiology.
Indications: Doxidan is a safe, gentle laxative for the management of constipation. It has proved clinically effective in the management of constipation in geriatric or inactive patients, obstetric patients, and following surgery, particularly anorectal procedures. It may be used as a safe and effective evacuant prior to x-ray examination of the colon in preparing patients for barium enema.
Warnings: Do not use when abdominal pain, nausea, or vomiting is present. Frequent or prolonged use of this preparation may result in dependence on laxatives. A harmless pink or orange discoloration may appear in alkaline urine. In some patients occasional cramping may occur.
Dosage and Administration: Adults and children over 12—one or two capsules daily. Children 6 to 12—one capsule daily. Best given at bedtime, Doxidan will usually provide a gentle evacuation in 8 to 12 hours. Dosage should be maintained for 2 to 3 days or until bowel movements return to normal. For use in children under 6, consult a physician.
How Supplied: Packs of 10; bottles of 30, 100 (NSN 6505-00-074-3169) and 1,000 (NSN 6505-00-890-1247) maroon, soft-gelatin capsules; and in Unit Dose 100s (10×10 strips) (NSN 6505-00-118-1700, 6505-00-163-7700A).
[*Shown in Product Identification Section*]

FESTAL®
Digestive Aid

Active Ingredients: Each enteric-coated tablet contains the following: lipase 6,000 NF units; amylase 30,000 NF units; protease 20,000 NF units; hemicellulase 50 mg; and bile constituents 25 mg.
Actions: Festal provides a high degree of protected digestive activity in a formula of standardized enzyme and bile constituents. Enteric coating of the tablet prevents release of ingredients in the stomach, so that high enzymatic activity is delivered to the site in the intestinal tract where digestion normally takes place.

Indications: Festal is indicated in any condition where normal digestion is impaired by insufficiency of natural digestive enzymes, or when additional digestive enzymes may be beneficial. These conditions often manifest complaints of discomfort due to excess intestinal gas, such as bloating, cramps and flatulence. The following are conditions or situations where Festal may be helpful: pancreatic insufficiency, enteritis, postgastrectomy syndrome, chronic pancreatitis, pancreatic necrosis, chronic hepatitis, gallbladder disease, surgical patients following cholecystectomy, subtotal gastrectomy, pancreatectomy and other surgery of the upper gastrointestinal tract, removal of gas prior to x-ray examination; and in the healthy individual who may experience temporary digestive deficiency due to over-indulgence in excessively fatty meals.
Dosage and Administration: Usual adult dose is one or two tablets with each meal, or as directed by a physician.
How Supplied: Bottles of 100 and 500 white, enteric-coated tablets for oral use.
[*Shown in Product Identification Section*]

SURFAK®
Stool Softener

Active Ingredient: Each 240 mg capsule contains 240 mg docusate calcium USP and up to 3% alcohol (w/w). Each 50 mg capsule contains 50 mg docusate calcium USP and up to 1.3% alcohol (w/w).
Actions: Surfak provides homogenization and formation of soft, easily evacuated stools without disturbance of body physiology, discomfort of bowel distention, oily leakage or interference with vitamin absorption. Surfak is non-habit forming.
Indications: Surfak is indicated for the prevention and treatment of constipation in conditions in which hard stools may cause discomfort, or in those conditions where laxative therapy is undesirable or contraindicated. Surfak is useful in patients who require only stool softening without propulsive action to accomplish defecation. Surfak does not cause peristaltic stimulation, and because of its safety it may be effectively used in patients with heart conditions, anorectal conditions, obstetrical patients, following surgical procedures, ulcerative colitis, diverticulitis and bedridden patients.
Warnings: Surfak has no known side effects or disadvantages, except for the unusual occurrence of mild, transitory cramping pains.
Dosage and Administration: Adults—one red 240 mg capsule daily for several days or until bowel movements are normal. Children and adults with minimal needs—one to three orange 50 mg capsules daily. For use in children under 6, consult a physician.
How Supplied: 240 mg red, soft gelatin capsules—bottles of 30 (NSN 6505-00-117-8607), 100 (NSN 6505-00-926-8844), 500 (NSN 6505-00-148-9815) and unit dose 100s (10 x 10 strips) (NSN 6505-00-118-1449); 50 mg orange, soft gelatin capsules—bottles of 30 and 100.
[*Shown in Product Identification Section*]

Holland-Rantos Company, Inc.
P.O. BOX 385
865 CENTENNIAL AVE.
PISCATAWAY, NJ 08854

See YOUNGS DRUG PRODUCTS CORPORATION

Hynson, Westcott & Dunning
Division of Becton Dickinson and Co.
CHARLES & CHASE STS.
BALTIMORE, MD 21201

LACTINEX® TABLETS AND GRANULES
Composition: A viable mixed culture of *Lactobacillus acidophilus* and *L. bulgaricus* with the naturally occurring metabolic products that are produced by these organisms.
Action and Uses: Lactinex has, been found to be useful in the treatment of uncomplicated diarrhea (including that due to antibiotic therapy) and acute fever blisters (cold sores).
Indications and Dosage: (for adults and children):
Gastrointestinal Disturbances—4 tablets or 1 packet of granules added to or taken with cereal, food, milk, fruit juice or water; three or four times a day.
Fever Blisters (Cold Sores)—4 tablets or 1 packet of granules chewed and swallowed three or four times a day. Each dose may be followed by a small amount of milk, fruit juice or water.
Lactinex Must Be Refrigerated
Individuals sensitive to milk products should not use Lactinex.
How Supplied: Tablets—bottles of fifty (NDC 0011-8368-50). Granules, boxes of twelve, 1 gram packets (unit dose dispensing), (NDC 0011-8367-12).
Literature Available: On request.
[*Shown in Product Identification Section*]

Johnson & Johnson
Baby Products Company
GRANDVIEW ROAD
SKILLMAN, NJ 08558

JOHNSON'S Baby Bath
Infant Bathing Product
Description: JOHNSON'S Baby Bath is an effective, extremely mild, clear liquid surfactant (cleansing) system especially formulated for bathing infants and children. When mixed with water it produces a cleansing lather which is superior in mildness to the skin and eyes.
Indications: JOHNSON'S Baby Bath is indicated for routine bathing of infants, children, and adults when an extremely mild, and effective cleansing action is desired.
Composition: The ingredients in JOHNSON'S Baby Bath and their intended function are as follows: Water (vehicle), Sodium Trideceth Sulfate (Anionic Surfactant), Cocamidopropyl Sultaine (Amphoteric Surfactant), PEG-150 Distearate (Nonionic Thickener & Emollient), PPG-15 Stearyl Ether (Emollient), Benzyl Alcohol (Microbiological Preservative), Sodium Phosphate (Buffer Component), Quaternium-15 (Microbiological Preservative), Fragrance, Disodium Phosphate (Buffer Component), Tetrasodium EDTA (Chelating Agent).
Clinical Studies:
Skin Irritation Potential
Occlusive patch testing of adult volunteers compared the cumulative irritation potential of 50% solutions of JOHNSON'S Baby Bath and another liquid baby bath. This exaggerated exposure technique indicated a significantly lower irritation potential for JOHNSON'S Baby Bath (44% of maximum irritation potential vs 83% for the other liquid baby bath). Pure bar soap, even at 1% concentration, is too irritating to be used in such a test.

MAXIMUM CUMULATIVE IRRITATION

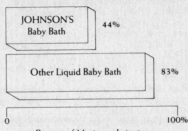

Percent of Maximum Irritation

Arm Immersion Studies
Arm immersion studies assessed the relative irritation potential of soaps and a mild detergent bar versus JOHNSON'S Baby Bath. In one study JOHNSON'S Baby Bath was found to be milder than the leading pure bar soap, the leading deodorant bar, the leading toilet soap bar, and a leading mild detergent complexion bar.

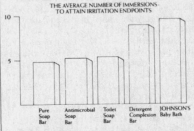

THE AVERAGE NUMBER OF IMMERSIONS TO ATTAIN IRRITATION ENDPOINTS

Human Ocular Sting and Irritation Potential
It is particularly important that a skin cleanser used for infants be gentle and non-irritating to human eyes.
After results obtained from preclinical tests showed no significant eye damage, the adult human ocular sting and irritation potential of both a normal use and a three times normal use (~24%) concentration of JOHNSON'S Baby Bath were assessed. A test solution was instilled into the lower cul-de-sac of one eye of volunteer subjects and sterile water into the other. All such clinical studies have shown that JOHNSON'S Baby Bath is as gentle to human eyes as water, even at three times normal use concentration.
Directions for Use: Pour onto wet washcloth or hand, work up lather, apply to body, rinse.
How Supplied: JOHNSON'S Baby Bath is available in three convenient sizes: 4 fluid ounce, 8 fluid ounce, and 12 fluid ounce. The 8 and 12 fluid ounce sizes have dispenser top caps which are easily opened with one hand. A 1.5 fluid ounce size is also available for professional use only, suitable for individual patient bassinets.

SUNDOWN® SUNSCREENS
Moderate Protection (SPF 4)
Extra Protection (SPF 6)
Maximal Protection (SPF 8)
Ultra Protection (SPF 15)

Active Ingredients:
Moderate Protection: Padimate O (Octyl dimethyl PABA)
Extra Protection: Padimate O (Octyl dimethyl PABA) and Oxybenzone
Maximal and Ultra Protection: Padimate O (Octyl dimethyl PABA), Oxybenzone and Octyl salicylate
Indications: Sunscreens to help prevent harmful effects from the sun. SUNDOWN Moderate, Extra, Maximal and Ultra Protection provide 4, 6, 8, and 15 times your natural sunburn protection, respectively. Moderate and Extra Protection permit tanning, Maximal Protection permits minimal tanning and Ultra Protection permits no tanning. Liberal and regular use may help reduce the chance of premature aging and wrinkling of the skin, and skin cancer, due to overexposure to the sun. Moderate, Extra and Maximal Protection are waterproof requiring reapplication after 80 minutes in the water or excessive perspiration. Ultra Protection is water resistant and should be reapplied after 40 minutes in the water or after excessive perspiration.
Actions: Absorption of Ultraviolet light
Warnings: For external use only. Avoid contact with eyes. Discontinue use if signs of irritation or rash appear. Use on children under 6 months of age only with the advice of physician. Keep out of reach of children.
Symptoms and Treatment of Oral Overdose: If ingested, remove material from stomach by gastric lavage or emesis induction. Give demulcent or milk. Observe and treat symptomatically. If appropriate monitor serum electrolytes. Flush eyes with a gentle stream of tepid water or isotonic saline.
Dosage and Administration: Shake well. Apply generously and evenly to all exposed areas. Reapply after prolonged swimming or excessive perspiration.
How Supplied: 4 fluid ounce bottles.

Products are cross-indexed by generic and chemical names in the **YELLOW SECTION**

Johnson & Johnson Products, Inc.
501 GEORGE STREET
NEW BRUNSWICK, NJ 08903

JOHNSON & JOHNSON FIRST AID CREAM
Skin Wound Protectant

Active Ingredient: Contains: Cetyl alcohol, Glyceryl stearate, Isopropyl palmitate, Stearyl alcohol, Synthetic beeswax as the skin wound protectants.
Indications: For minor cuts, scrapes and burns.
Actions: Helps protect minor skin wounds against contamination.
Warnings: Not for use on large, deep, or puncture wounds, serious burns or animal bites. If redness, irritation, swelling, or pain persists or increases, or if infection occurs, discontinue use and consult physician. Should not be used for more than ten days. If condition worsens or persists, see your physician. Not for use in eyes or on chronic skin conditions.
Drug Interaction Precaution: No known drug interaction.
Symptoms and Treatment of Oral Overdosage: There is no known history of any oral ingestion/toxicity case. However, animal studies reveal significant safety with oral ingestion; the lethal dose in both rats and mice exceeds 40 ml/kg of body weight. Therefore, only symptomatic treatment and observation would be required in the case of ingestion.
[Shown in Product Identification Section]

Kremers-Urban Company
BOX 2038
MILWAUKEE, WI 53201

KUDROX® SUSPENSION (DOUBLE STRENGTH) ANTACID

Composition: A pleasantly flavored SUSPENSION containing a concentrated combination of aluminum hydroxide gel and magnesium hydroxide in d-sorbitol.
One teaspoonful of KUDROX Liquid contains not more than 0.65 mEq (15 mg.) of sodium.
Action and Uses: A palatable antacid to alleviate acid indigestion, heartburn and/or sour stomach, or whenever antacid therapy is the treatment indicated for symptomatic relief of hyperacidity associated with the diagnosis of peptic ulcer, gastritis, peptic esophagitis, gastric hyperacidity, and hiatal hernia. The ratio of aluminum hydroxide to magnesium hydroxide is such that undesirable bowel effects are minimal. Each 5cc dose of SUSPENSION will neutralize approximately 25 mEq of HCl. High concentration of the active ingredients produces prompt, long lasting neutralization without the acid rebound associated with calcium carbonate containing antacids.
Dosage: KUDROX SUSPENSION, half that ordinarily employed with other liquid antacids. Usual dose only 1 teaspoonful 30 minutes after meals and at bedtime. May be taken undiluted or mixed with water or milk. In peptic ulcer, 2 to 4 teaspoonfuls after meals and at bedtime.
Warning: Antacids containing magnesium hydroxide or magnesium salts should be administered cautiously in patients with renal insufficiency.
Drug Interaction Precaution: This product should not be taken if the patient is currently taking a prescription drug containing any form of tetracycline.
Supplied: KUDROX SUSPENSION, 12 oz. plastic bottles (NDC 0091-4475-42).

MILKINOL®

Composition: MILKINOL is a unique formulation containing liquid petrolatum for lubrication with a special mixture of emulsifiers to aid in penetration and softening of fecal mass and to disperse oil in any beverage.
Action and Uses: Pleasant, dependable MILKINOL provides safe, gentle lubrication for the constipation problem. No oily taste, no purgative griping, not habit forming, sugar free.
Dosage: Adults 1 to 2 tablespoonfuls. Children over 6: 1 to 2 teaspoonfuls. Infants, young children, expectant mothers, aged or bedridden patients, use only as directed by physician. Pour MILKINOL in a glass, add ¼ glass fruit juice, soft drink, milk, or even water. Stir and drink.
Precautions: Prolonged usage, without intermission is not advised. Should be given at bedtime ONLY.
Supplied: 8 oz. glass bottles (NDC 0091-7580-08).

The Lannett Company, Inc.
9000 STATE ROAD
PHILADELPHIA, PA 19136

ACNEDERM™ LOTION

Composition: Grease-free, water-washable, non-staining suspension containing dispersible sulfur 5%, zinc sulfate 1% and zinc oxide 10% in a flesh-tinted powder foundation base. Isopropyl alcohol, 21% by volume.
Action and Uses: Medication of acne lesions. Combats oiliness of skin and excessive keratinization of sebaceous glands; promotes drying and peeling in acne, seborrheic dermatitis, rosacea, tinea corporis and tinea versicolor.
Administration and Dosage: Apply several times daily and at bedtime to affected areas, either with finger tips or sponge. Allow to dry and remove excess with powder puff or cleansing tissue.
Precautions: Discontinue treatment if excessive dryness or skin irritation occurs.
How Supplied: Bottles of 2 fl. oz.
Literature Available: Yes.

MAGNATRIL™ SUSPENSION AND TABLETS

Composition: Each tablet contains: Aluminum Hydroxide Gel (dried) 4 grs., Magnesium Trisilicate 7 grs., Magnesium Hydroxide 2 grs. Each teaspoonful of suspension contains: Colloidal suspension of Magnesium and Aluminum Hydroxides with 4 grs. Magnesium Trisilicate.
Action and Uses: Indicated to alleviate the symptoms of heartburn, sour stomach, and/or acid indigestion.
Drug Interaction Precautions: Do not take this product if you are presently taking a prescription of antibiotic drug containing any form of tetracycline.
Warning: Do not take more than 16 teaspoonsful in a 24 hour period, or use the maximum dosage of this product for more than 2 weeks, except under the advice and supervision of a physician. Do not use this product except under the advice and supervision of a physician if you have kidney disease.
Administration and Dosage: Tablets — Adults: 2 tablets well chewed, 1 or 2 hours following meals, or whenever symptoms are pronounced. Suspension —Adults, 1 to 4 teaspoonsful in water or milk four times a day, twenty minutes after meals and at bedtime, or as directed by a physician.
How Supplied: Tablets—Boxes of 50 and 100 cellophane-stripped tablets. Suspension—Bottles of 12 fl. oz.
Literature Available: Yes.

Lederle Laboratories
A Division of American Cyanamid Co.
WAYNE, NJ 07470

LEDERMARK™
Product Identification Code
Many Lederle tablets and capsules bear an identification code. A current listing appears in the Product Information Section of the 1982 PDR for Prescription Drugs.

CENTRUM®
High Potency
Multivitamin-Multimineral Formula
Composition: Each tablet contains:

	For Adults Percentage of U.S. Recommended Daily Allowance (U.S. RDA)
Vitamin A (as Acetate)	5000 I.U. (100%)
Vitamin E (as dl-Alpha Tocopheryl Acetate)	30 I.U. (100%)
Vitamin C (as Ascorbic Acid)	90 mg (150%)
Folic Acid (as Folacin)	400 mcg (100%)
Vitamin B₁ (as Thiamine Mononitrate)	2.25 mg (150%)
Vitamin B₂ (as Riboflavin)	2.6 mg (153%)
Niacinamide	20 mg (100%)
Vitamin B₆ (as Pyridoxine Hydrochloride)	3 mg (150%)
Vitamin B₁₂ (as Cyanocobalamin)	9 mcg (150%)
Vitamin D	400 I.U. (100%)
Biotin	45 mcg (15%)
Pantothenic Acid (as Calcium Pantothenate)	10 mg (100%)

Calcium (as Dibasic
Calcium Phosphate).....162 mg (16%)
Phosphorus (as Dibasic
Calcium Phosphate).....125 mg (13%)
Iodine (as
Potassium Iodide).......150 mcg (100%)
Iron (as
Ferrous Fumarate).........27 mg (150%)
Magnesium (as
Magnesium Oxide).......100 mg (25%)
Copper (as
Cupric Oxide)....................3 mg (150%)
Manganese (as
Manganese Sulfate).......7.5 mg*
Potassium (as
Potassium Sulfate)........7.5 mg*
Zinc (as Zinc Sulfate).....22.5 mg (150%)
*Recognized as essential in human nutrition, but no U.S. RDA established.
Recommended Intake: Adults, 1 tablet daily.
How Supplied:
Capsule-shaped tablets, light peach, engraved LL— bottles of 100 tablets
[*Shown in Product Identification Section*]

FERRO-SEQUELS®
(sustained release iron)
Capsules

Composition: Each capsule contains 150 mg. of ferrous fumarate equivalent to approximately 50 mg. of elemental iron, so prepared that it is released over a 5 to 6 hour period, and 100 mg. of docusate sodium (DSS) to counteract constipating effect of iron.
Indications: For the treatment of iron deficiency anemias.
Dosage: 1 capsule, once or twice daily or as prescribed by the physician.
Precautions: In case of accidental overdose, seek professional assistance or contact a Poison Control Center immediately. Keep out of the reach of children.
How Supplied: Capsules (hard shell, light green) printed "Lederle" and "Ferro-Sequels"—bottles of 30, 100, and 1,000; unit-dose 10 × 10's.
Military and USPHS Depots:
NSN 6505-00-149-0103, 30's
NSN 6505-00-074-2981, 1000's
NSN 6505-00-131-8870, individually sealed 100's

FILIBON®
(prenatal tablets)

Each tablet contains:

	For Pregnant or Lactating Women Percentage of U.S. Recommended Daily Allowance (U.S. RDA)
Vitamin A (as Acetate)	5000 I.U. (63%)
Vitamin D₂	400 I.U. (100%)
Vitamin E (as *dl*-Alpha Tocopheryl Acetate)	30 I.U. (100%)
Vitamin C (Ascorbic Acid)	60 mg (100%)
Folic Acid (Folacin)	0.4 mg (50%)
Vitamin B₁ (as Thiamine Mononitrate)	1.5 mg (88%)
Vitamin B₂ (as Riboflavin)	1.7 mg (85%)
Niacinamide	20 mg (100%)
Vitamin B₆ (as Pyridoxine Hydrochloride)	2 mg (80%)

Vitamin B₁₂ (as
Cyanocobalamin)........... 6 mcg (75%)
Calcium (as Calcium
Carbonate)..................... 125 mg (10%)
Iodine (as Potassium
Iodide)..........................150 mcg (100%)
Iron(asFerrousFumarate) 18 mg (100%)
Magnesium (as
Magnesium Oxide)....... 100 mg (22%)
A phosphorus-free vitamin and mineral dietary supplement for use in prenatal care and lactation.
Recommended Intake: 1 daily, or as prescribed by the physician.
How Supplied: Capsule-shaped tablets (film-coated, pink) engraved LL—bottles of 100.

GEVRABON®
(vitamin-mineral supplement)

Composition: Each fluid ounce (30 ml.) contains:

	For Adults Percentage of U.S. Recommended Daily Allowance (U.S. RDA)
Vitamin B₁ (as Thiamine Hydrochloride)	.5 mg (333%)
Vitamin B₂ (as Riboflavin-5-Phosphate Sodium)	2.5 mg (147%)
Niacinamide	50 mg (250%)
Vitamin B₆ (Pyridoxine Hydrochloride)	1 mg (50%)
Vitamin B₁₂ (as Cyanocobalamin)	1 mcg (17%)
Pantothenic Acid (as D-Pantothenyl Alcohol)	10 mg (100%)
Iodine (as Potassium Iodide)	100 mcg (67%)
Iron (as Ferrous Gluconate)	15 mg (83%)
Magnesium (as Magnesium Chloride)	2 mg (0.5%)
Zinc (as Zinc Chloride)	2 mg (13%)
Inositol	100 mg.
Choline (as Tricholine Citrate)	100 mg.
Manganese (as Manganese Chloride)	2 mg.

Alcohol 18%
*Recognized as essential in human nutrition but no U.S. RDA established.
Indications: For use as a nutritional supplement.
Administration and Dosage: Adult: One ounce (30 ml.) daily or as prescribed by the physician as a nutritional supplement.
How Supplied: Liquid (sherry flavor)—decanters of 16 fl. oz. and bottles of 1 gallon.
VA Depots:
NSN 6505-01-091-7541A

GEVRAL®
Multivitamin and Multimineral Supplement for Adults and Children 4 or More Years of Age
TABLETS

Composition: Each tablet contains:

	For Adults Percentage of U.S. Recommended Daily Allowance (U.S. RDA)
Vitamin A (as Acetate)	5000 I.U. (100%)

Vitamin E (as *dl*-Alpha
Tocopheryl Acetate)... 30 I.U. (100%)
Vitamin C (as Ascorbic
Acid)................................ 60 mg (100%)
Folic Acid (as Folacin) .. 0.4 mg (100%)
Vitamin B₁ (as Thiamine Mononitrate)..... 1.5 mg (100%)
Vitamin B₂ (as
Riboflavin).................... 1.7 mg (100%)
Niacinamide................. 20 mg (100%)
Vitamin B₆ (as Pyridoxine Hydrochloride)............ 2 mg (100%)
Vitamin B₁₂ (as
Cyanocobalamin)......... 6 mcg (100%)
Calcium (as Dibasic
Calcium Phosphate)... 162 mg (16%)
Phosphorus (as Dibasic
Calcium Phosphate)... 125 mg (13%)
Iodine (as Potassium
Iodide)..........................150 mcg (100%)
Iron (as Ferrous
Fumarate)..................... 18 mg (100%)
Magnesium (as
Magnesium Oxide)..... 100 mg (25%)
Indications: Supplementation of the diet.
Administration and Dosage: One tablet daily or as prescribed by the physician.
How Supplied: Tablets (film-coated, brown) engraved LL—bottle of 100.

GEVRAL® T
High Potency
Multivitamin and Multimineral Supplement for Adults and Children 4 or More Years of Age
TABLETS

Each tablet contains:

	Percentage of U.S. Recommended Daily Allowance (U.S. RDA)
Vitamin A (as Acetate)	5000 I.U. (100%)
Vitamin E (as *dl*-Alpha Tocopheryl Acetate)	45 I.U. (150%)
Vitamin C (as Ascorbic Acid)	90 mg (150%)
Folic Acid (as Folacin)	0.4 mg (100%)
Vitamin B₁ (as Thiamine Mononitrate)	2.25 mg (150%)
Vitamin B₂ (as Riboflavin)	2.6 mg (153%)
Niacinamide	30 mg (150%)
Vitamin B₆ (as Pyridoxine Hydrochloride)	3 mg (150%)
Vitamin B₁₂ (as Cyanocobalamin)	9 mcg (150%)
Vitamin D₂	400 I.U. (100%)
Calcium (as Dibasic Calcium Phosphate)	162 mg (16%)

Continued on next page

Lederle—Cont.

Phosphorus (as Dibasic
   Calcium Phosphate)... 125 mg (13%)
Iodine (as Potassium
   Iodide)............................225 mcg (150%)
Iron (as Ferrous
   Fumarate)..................... 27 mg (150%)
Magnesium (as
   Magnesium Oxide)..... 100 mg (25%)
Copper (as Cupric oxide) 1.5 mg (150%)
Zinc (as Zinc Oxide)....... 22.5 mg (150%)
Indications: For the treatment of vitamin and mineral deficiencies.
Dosage: 1 tablet daily or as prescribed by physician.
How Supplied: Tablets (film coated, maroon). Printed LL—bottle of 100.

INCREMIN®
WITH IRON • SYRUP
(vitamins plus iron)
Dietary Supplement

Composition: Each teaspoonful (5 ml.) contains:
Elemental Iron (as Ferric
   Pyrophosphate)............................30 mg.
L-Lysine HCl ....300 mg.
Thiamine HCl (B$_1$)..........................10 mg.
Pyridoxine HCl (B$_6$)..........................5 mg.
Vitamin B$_{12}$
   (Cyanocobalamin) ....25 mcgm.
Sorbitol ....3.50 Gm.
Alcohol...0.75%
Each teaspoonful (5 ml.) supplies the following Minimum Daily Requirements:

	Child under 6	Child over 6	Adults
Vitamin B$_1$	20 MDR	13⅓ MDR	10 MDR
Iron	4 MDR	3 MDR	3 MDR

Indications: For the prevention and treatment of iron deficiency anemia in children and adults. Keep this and all medications out of the reach of children.
Administration and Dosage:
Children
One teaspoonful (5 ml.) daily for the prevention of iron deficiency anemia. Three teaspoonfuls (15 ml.) daily in divided doses for treatment.
Adults
One teaspoonful (5 ml.) for prevention. Four teaspoonfuls (20 ml.) daily in divided doses for treatment.
How Supplied: Syrup (cherry flavor)—bottles of 4 and 16 fl. oz.

LEDERPLEX®
Dietary Supplement of B-Complex Vitamins for Adults and Children 4 or More Years of Age
Capsules—Liquid—Tablets

Each Capsule or Tablet Contains:
For Adults-
Percentage of U.S.
Recommended Daily
Allowance (U.S. RDA)
Vitamin B$_1$ (as Thiamine
   Mononitrate) .... 2.25 mg (150%)
Vitamin B$_2$ (as
   Riboflavin) .... 2.6 mg (153%)

Niacinamide..................... 30 mg (150%)
Vitamin B$_6$ (as Pyridoxine
   Hydrochloride)............. 3 mg (150%)
Vitamin B$_{12}$ (as
   Cyanocobalamin)........ 9 mcg (150%)
Pantothenic Acid (as Calcium
   Pantothenate).............. 15 mg (150%)
Indications: For the prevention of Vitamin B complex deficiencies.
Dosage: *Children*—1 capsule or tablet daily.
Adults—1 capsule or tablet daily.

Each 10 ml (2 teaspoonfuls) contains:
Vitamin B$_1$ (as Thiamine
   Hydrochloride)............ 2.25 mg (150%)
Vitamin B$_2$ (Riboflavin) 2.6 mg (153%)
Niacinamide..................... 30 mg (150%)
Vitamin B$_6$ (as Pyridoxine
   Hydrochloride)............. 3 mg (150%)
Vitamin B$_{12}$ (as Cobalamin
   Concentrate NF) 9 mcg (150%)
Pantothenic Acid (as
   Panthenol) .... 15 mg (150%)
Preservative:
   Sodium Benzoate .... 0.1% w/w
Indications: For the prevention of Vitamin B complex deficiencies:
Recommended intake:
Adults—10 ml. or 2 teaspoonfuls daily.
How Supplied: Capsules (hard shell, brown)—bottles of 100. Liquid (orange flavor)—bottles of 12 fl. oz. Tablets (coated brown)—bottles of 100.

NEOLOID®
(emulsified castor oil)

Composition: NEOLOID Emulsified Castor Oil U.S.P. 36.4% (w/w) with preservative, emulsifying and flavoring agents in water. NEOLOID is an emulsion with an exceptionally bland, pleasant taste.
Indications: For the treatment of isolated bouts of constipation.
Administration and Dosage:
Infants—½ to 1½ teaspoonfuls.
Children—Adjust between infant and adult dose.
Adult— Average dose, 2 to 4 tablespoonfuls, or as prescribed by the physician.
Precautions: Not to be used when abdominal pain, nausea, vomiting, or other symptoms of appendicitis are present. Frequent or continued use of this preparation may result in dependence on laxatives. Do not use during pregnancy except on competent advice. Keep this and all drugs out of the reach of children. In case of accidental overdosage seek professional assistance or contact a Poison Control Center immediately.
How Supplied: Bottles of 4 fl. oz. (peppermint flavor).

PERITINIC®
(hematinic with vitamins and fecal softener)
Tablets

Each tablet contains:
Elemental Iron
   (as Ferrous Fumarate).............100 mg.
Docusate Sodium U.S.P. (DSS)
   (to counteract the constipating effect of iron)......100 mg.

Vitamin B$_1$
   (as Thiamine Mononitrate)......7.5 mg.
   (7 ½ MDR)
Vitamin B$_2$ (Riboflavin)................7.5 mg.
   (6¼ MDR)
Vitamin B$_6$
   (Pyridoxine Hydrochloride)......7.5 mg.
Vitamin B$_{12}$
   (Cyanocobalamin) ....50 mcg.
Vitamin C (Ascorbic Acid)..........200 mg.
   (6⅔ MDR)
Niacinamide (3 MDR)....................30 mg.
Folic Acid ....0.05 mg.
Pantothenic Acid
   (as D-Pantothenyl Alcohol).......15 mg.
MDR—Adult Minimum Daily Requirement
Precaution: In case of accidental overdose, seek professional assistance or contact a Poison Control Center immediately. Keep out of the reach of children.
Action and Uses: In the prevention of nutritional anemias, certain vitamin deficiencies, and iron-deficiency anemias.
Administration and Dosage:
Adults: 1 or 2 tablets daily.
How Supplied: Tablets (maroon, capsule-shaped, film coated)—bottles of 60.

RHULICAINE™

Active Ingredient: Benzocaine, Triclosan, and Menthol. SD 40 Alcohol 32% w/w, Isopropyl Alcohol 9% w/w.
Indications:
SOOTHES • ANTISEPTIC • AIDS HEALING
Prompt cooling relief of sunburn pain. Antiseptic protection for minor skin irritations: cuts, burns, scrapes and scratches.
FOR EXTERNAL USE ONLY.
Precaution: Not for deep or puncture wounds or serious burns. Not for prolonged use. If condition for which this preparation is used persists, or if infection, rash or irritation develops, discontinue use and consult a physician.
Dosage and Administration: Use several times daily, or as necessary for relief of pain and antiseptic protection.
How Supplied: 4 oz can.
[*Shown in Product Identification Section*]

RHULICREAM®
RHULIGEL®
RHULISPRAY®
(analgesic-anesthetic)

Composition: RHULICREAM: A soothing, bland ointment containing as active ingredients:
Zirconium oxide .... 1 %
Benzocaine .... 1 %
Menthol .... 0.7 %
Camphor.. 0.3 %
Inactive Ingredients:
Isopropyl alcohol............................ 8.8 %
Methylparaben............................... 0.08 %
Propylparaben................................ 0.02 %
RHULIGEL: Active ingredients are:
Phenylcarbinol .... 2 % w/w
Menthol USP....................... 0.3 % w/w
Camphor USP....................... 0.3 % w/w
Alcohol .... 31 % w/w
RHULISPRAY: A cool, soothing, conve-

nient spray that is nonstaining because it dries instantly.

Active ingredients are: (percent w/w)
Phenylcarbinol 0.674%
Menthol 0.025%
Camphor 0.253%
Calamine 4.710%
Benzocaine 1.153%
Isopropyl Alcohol 28.767%
Inactive Ingredients and
Propellant 64.418%

All:
Indications: For the temporary relief of itching, pain, and discomfort of ivy and oak poisoning, nonpoisonous insect bites, mild sunburn and other minor skin irritations.
Administration and Dosage: Apply to affected area 2 or 3 times daily and at bedtime.
Precautions: Avoid application around the eyes and genitalia, or on infected wounds. A physician should be consulted if the condition persists.
How Supplied: RHULICREAM: Tubes of 1 oz. and 2 oz. RHULIGEL: Tubes of 2 oz. RHULI-SPRAY: (Hydrocarbon Aerosol) 2 and 4 oz. cans.
[*Shown in Product Identification Section*]

RHULICORT™
(Hydrocortisone 0.5% in soothing AQUATAIN™)
Cream and Lotion

Active Ingredient: Hydrocortisone Acetate equivalent to 0.5% Hydrocortisone
Preservative: Benzyl Alcohol 2.0%
Indications: For the temporary relief of minor skin irritations, itching, and rashes due to poison ivy, poison oak, poison sumac, insect bites, eczema, dermatitis, soaps, detergents, cosmetics, and jewelry, and for itchy genital and anal areas.
Directions for Use: *For adults and children 2 years of age and older*—apply to affected area not more than 3 to 4 times daily. For children under 2 years of age there is no recommended dosage except under the advice and supervision of a physician.
Warnings: For external use only. Avoid contact with eyes. If condition worsens, or if symptoms persist for more than 7 days, discontinue use of this product and consult a physician. Do not use on children under 2 years of age except under the advice and supervision of a physician. Keep this and all drugs out of the reach of children. In case of accidental ingestion, seek professional assistance or contact a Poison Control Center immediately.
How Supplied:
Cream - 20 gm tubes
Lotion - 60 ml bottles.
[*Shown in Product Identification Section*]

STRESSCAPS®
(Stress formula B+C vitamins)

Each capsule contains:
For Adults-Percentage
of U.S.
Recommended Daily
Allowance (U.S. RDA)

Vitamin B₁ (as Thiamine
Mononitrate) .... 10 mg (667%)
Vitamin B₂ (as Riboflavin)10 mg (588%)
Vitamin B₆ (as Pyridoxine
Hydrochloride)............ 2 mg (100%)
Vitamin B₁₂
(as Cyanocobalamin).. 6 mcg (100%)
Vitamin C (as Ascorbic
Acid)............................ 300 mg (500%)
Niacinamide.................. 100 mg (500%)
Pantothenic Acid (as Calcium
Pantothenate).............. 20 mg (200%)
Indications: For the treatment of vitamin deficiencies.
Dosage and Administration: Adults, 1 capsule daily or as directed by the physician.
How Supplied: *Capsules* (hard shell, opaque brown)—bottles of 30, 100, and 500.

STRESSTABS® 600
High Potency
Stress Formula Vitamins

Each tablet contains:
For Adults-
Percentage of U.S.
Recommended Daily
Allowance (U.S. RDA)

Vitamin E (as *dl*-Alpha
Tocopheryl Acetate)... 30 I.U. (100%)
Vitamin C (L-Ascorbic
Acid)............................600 mg (1000%)
B₁ (as Thiamine
Mononitrate) .... 15 mg (1000%)
Vitamin B₂ (as
Riboflavin) .... 15 mg (882%)
Niacinamide ....100 mg (500%)
Vitamin B₆ (as Pyridoxine
Hydrochloride)............ 5 mg (250%)
Vitamin B₁₂
(as Cyanocobalamin) 12 mcg (200%)
Pantothenic Acid (as Calcium
Pantothenate USP).... 20 mg (200%)
Recommended Intake: Adults, 1 tablet daily or as directed by physician.
Supplied: Capsule-shaped tablets (film-coated orange)-bottles of 30, 60 and 500; unit-dose 10 x 10's.
VA Depot:
NSN 6505-00-375-4618A
[*Shown in Product Identification Section*]

STRESSTABS® 600 with IRON
High Potency
Stress Formula Vitamins

Each tablet contains:
For Adults-
Percentage of U.S.
Recommended Daily
Allowance (U.S. RDA)

Vitamin E (as *dl*-Alpha
Tocopheryl Acetate) ..30 I.U. (100%)
Vitamin C (L-Ascorbic
Acid) ....600 mg (1000%)
Folic Acid (as
Folacin) .... 400 mcg (100%)
Vitamin B₁ (as Thiamine
Mononitrate) .... 15 mg (1000%)
Vitamin B₂ (as
Riboflavin) .... 15 mg (882%)
Niacinamide ....100 mg (500%)
Vitamin B₆ (as Pyridoxine
Hydrochloride) .... 25 mg (1250%)
Vitamin B₁₂
(as Cyanocobalamin) 12 mcg (200%)
Pantothenic Acid (as Calcium
Pantothenate USP) ... 20 mg (200%)
Iron (as Ferrous
Fumarate) .... 27 mg (150%)
Recommended Intake: Adults, 1 tablet daily or as directed by physician.
Supplied: Capsule-shaped tablets (film-coated, orange-red, scored)—bottles of 30 and 60.
[*Shown in Product Identification Section*]

STRESSTABS® 600 with ZINC
High Potency
Stress Formula Vitamins

Each tablet contains:
For Adults-
Percentage of U.S.
Recommended Daily
Allowance (U.S. RDA)

Vitamin E (as *dl*-Alpha
Tocopheryl Acetate) 45 I.U. (150%)
Vitamin C
(L-Ascorbic Acid).....600 mg. (1000%)
Folic Acid (as
Folacin).....................400 mcg. (100%)
Vitamin B₁ (as Thiamine Mononitrate)....20 mg. (1333%)
Vitamin B₂
(as Riboflavin)............10 mg. (588%)
Niacinamide.................100 mg. (500%)
Vitamin B₆ (as Pyridoxine Hydrochloride)....10 mg. (500%)
Vitamin B₁₂ (as Cyano-
Cobalamin) ....25 mcg. (417%)
Pantothenic Acid (as Calcium
Pantothenate USP) 25 mg. (250%)
Copper (as Cupric
Oxide)............................3 mg. (150%)
Zinc (as Zinc Sulfate)23.9 mg. (159%)
Recommended Intake: Adults, 1 tablet daily or as directed by the physician.
Supplied: Capsule-shaped Tablet (film coated, peach color)—bottles of 30 and 60.
[*Shown in Product Identification Section*]

ZINCON®
Dandruff Shampoo

Contains pyrithione zinc 1%, a clinically proven anti-dandruff compound to help control dandruff flaking. Used regularly, ZINCON leaves hair clean and easy to manage. It is recommended by dermatologists, does not cause dry or oily hair, has a pleasant fragrance and may be used on gray or dyed hair.
How Supplied: 4 fl. oz. and 8 fl. oz. unbreakable plastic bottles.

The information on each product appearing here is based on labelling effective in November, 1981 and is either the entire official brochure or an accurate condensation therefrom. Official brochures are enclosed in product packages. Information concerning all Lederle products may be obtained from the Professional Services Department, Lederle Laboratories, Pearl River, New York 10965.

Leeming Division
Pfizer, Inc.
**100 JEFFERSON ROAD
PARSIPPANY, NJ 07054**

BEN–GAY® External Analgesic Products

Description: Ben-Gay is a combination of methyl salicylate and menthol in a suitable base for topical application. In addition to the Original Ointment (methyl salicylate, 18.3%; menthol, 16%), Ben-Gay is offered as a Greaseless/Stainless Ointment (methyl salicylate, 15%; menthol, 10%), an Extra Strength Balm (methyl salicylate, 30%; menthol, 8%), a Lotion and a Clear Gel (both of which contain methyl salicylate, 15%; menthol, 7%).

Action and Uses: Methyl salicylate and menthol are external analgesics which stimulate sensory receptors, including receptors of warmth and cold. This produces a counter-irritant response which alleviates the more severe pain in the joints and muscles where applied to provide transient, temporary symptomatic relief.

Several double blind clinical studies of Ben-Gay products have shown the effectiveness of the menthol-methyl salicylate combination in counteracting minor pain of skeletal muscle stress and arthritis.

Three studies involving a total of 102 normal subjects in which muscle soreness was experimentally induced showed statistically significant beneficial results from use of the active product vs. placebo for lowered Muscle Action Potential (spasms), greater rise in threshold of muscular pain and greater reduction in perceived muscular pain.

Six clinical studies of a total of 207 subjects suffering from minor pain and skeletal muscular spasms due to osteoarthritis and rheumatoid arthritis showed the active product to give statistically significant beneficial results vs. placebo for lowered Muscle Action Potential (spasm), greater relief of perceived pain, increased range of motion of the affected joints and increased digital dexterity.

Directions: Rub generously into painful area, then massage gently until Ben-Gay disappears. Repeat as necessary.

Warning: Use only as directed. Keep away from children to avoid accidental poisoning. Do not swallow. If swallowed, induce vomiting, call a physician. Keep away from eyes, mucous membrane, broken or irritated skin. If skin irritation develops, pain lasts 10 days or more, redness is present, or with arthritis-like conditions in children under 12, call a physician.

DESITIN® OINTMENT

Description: Desitin Ointment is a combination of Zinc Oxide (40%), Cod Liver Oil (high in Vitamins A & D), and Talc in a petrolatum-lanolin base suitable for topical application.

Actions and Uses: Desitin Ointment is designed to provide relief of diaper rash, superficial wounds and burns, and other minor skin irritations. It helps prevent incidence of diaper rash, protects against urine and other irritants, soothes chafed skin and promotes healing.

Relief and protection is afforded by the combination of Zinc Oxide, Cod Liver Oil, Lanolin and Petrolatum. They provide a physical barrier by forming a protective coating over skin or mucous membrane which serves to reduce further effects of irritants on the affected area and relieves burning, pain or itch produced by them. In addition to its protective properties, Zinc Oxide acts as an astringent that helps heal local irritation and inflammation by lessening the flow of mucus and other secretions.

Several studies have shown the effectiveness of Desitin Ointment in the relief and prevention of diaper rash.

Two clinical studies involving 90 infants demonstrated the effectiveness of Desitin Ointment in curing diaper rash. The diaper rash area was treated with Desitin Ointment at each diaper change for a period of 24 hours, while the untreated site served as controls. A significant reduction was noted in the severity and area of diaper dermatitis on the treated area.

Ninety-seven (97) babies participated in a 12-week study to show that Desitin Ointment helps prevent diaper rash. Approximately half of the infants (49) were treated with Desitin Ointment on a regular daily basis. The other half (48) received the ointment as necessary to treat any diaper rash which occurred. The incidence as well as the severity of diaper rash was significantly less among the babies using the ointment on a regular daily basis.

In a comparative study of the efficacy of Desitin Ointment vs. a baby powder, forty-five babies were observed for a total of eight weeks. Results support the conclusion that Desitin Ointment is a better prophylactic against diaper rash than the baby powder.

Several other studies show that Desitin Ointment helps relieve other skin disorders, such as contact dermatitis.

Directions: To prevent diaper rash, apply Desitin Ointment to the diaper area—especially at bedtime when exposure to wet diapers may be prolonged. If diaper rash is present, or at the first sign of redness, minor skin irritation or chafing, simply apply Desitin Ointment three or four times daily as needed. In superficial noninfected surface wounds and minor burns, apply a thin layer of Desitin Ointment, using a gauze dressing, if necessary. For external use only.

How Supplied: Desitin Ointment is available in 1.25 ounce (35g), 2.25 ounce (63g), 4.25 (120g) 8 ounce (226g) tubes, and 1-lb. (452g) jars.

NYTILAX® TABLETS (sennosides A and B)

Description: Each blue Nytilax Tablet contains 12 mg. of crystalline Sennosides A and B calcium salts, the most highly purified form available for these glycosides, derived from the *Cassia Acutifolia* plant and standardized by chemical rather than biological assay.

Actions and Uses: Indicated for relief of chronic or occasional functional constipation. Recent additional support has been given to the current theory that upon ingestion, the sugar glycosides Sennosides A and B are transported without chemical change through the alimentary canal to the colon, where they are hydrolyzed to their aglycone derivatives by the colonic flora, leading to localized nerve plexus stimulation and peristalsis-induced defecation. The effect is gentle and predictable, with well-formed stools being produced, usually within 8–10 hours. Contrary to a previously published opinion, the clinical evidence now available strongly indicates that the senna glycosides are not excreted into the milk of lactating mothers and, therefore, have no effect on the bowel function of nursing infants. The high chemical purity of the Sennoside A and B calcium salts facilitates individualized dosage regulation and further minimizes the possibility of rare adverse reactions such as loose stools or abdominal discomfort. Sennosides A and B, as contained in Nytilax Tablets, have been found in numerous clinical studies to be highly effective for varieties of functional constipation: chronic, geriatric, antepartum and postpartum, drug-induced, pediatric and surgical-related, and in lower bowel x-ray preparative procedures.

Dosage and Administration:

Adults—1 or 2 tablets at bedtime. If you do not readily respond to laxatives, take 3 tablets at bedtime.

Children—Consult a physician.

Warnings: Do not take any laxative when abdominal pain, nausea or vomiting are present. Frequent or prolonged use of laxatives may result in dependence.

Keep out of the reach of children.

How Supplied: Boxes of 12 or 24 tablets.

RHEABAN® TABLETS and LIQUID (attapulgite)

Description: Rheaban is an anti-diarrheal medication containing activated attapulgite and is offered in liquid and tablet forms.

The liquid is mint-flavored with each fluid ounce containing 4.2 grams of activated attapulgite.

Each white Rheaban tablet contains 600 mg. of collodial activated attapulgite.

Rheaban contains no narcotics, opiates or other habit-forming drugs.

Actions and Uses: Rheaban is indicated for relief of diarrhea and the cramps and pains associated with it. Attapulgite, which has been activated by thermal treatment, is a highly sorptive substance which absorbs nutrients and digestive enzymes as well as noxious gases, irritants, toxins and some bacteria and viruses that are common causes of diarrhea.

In clinical studies to show the effectiveness in relieving diarrhea and its symptoms, 100 subjects suffering from acute gastroenteritis with diarrhea participated in a double-blind comparison of Rheaban to a placebo. Patients treated with the attapulgite product showed significantly improved relief of diarrhea and its symptoms vs. the placebo.

Dosage and Administration:

LIQUID

Adults—2 tablespoons after initial bowel movement, 1 tablespoon after subsequent bowel movements.

Children 6 to 12 years—1 tablespoon after initial bowel movement, ½ tablespoon after each subsequent bowel movement.

Children 3 to 6 years—½ tablespoon after initial bowel movement, ½ tablespoon after each subsequent bowel movement.

Infant and Children under 3 years— Only as directed by physician.

TABLETS

Adults—2 tablets after initial bowel movement, 2 tablets after each subsequent bowel movement.

Children 6 to 12 years—1 tablet after initial bowel movement, 1 tablet after each subsequent bowel movement.

Children 3 to 6 years—Use Rheaban Liquid.

Warnings: Do not use for more than two days, or in the presence of high fever. Tablets should not be used for children under 6 years of age, and liquid should not be used for children under 3 years of age, unless directed by physician. If diarrhea persists consult a physician.

How Supplied:
  Liquid—5.5 ounce bottles
  Tablets—Boxes of 12 tablets

UNISOM® NIGHTTIME SLEEP-AID (doxylamine succinate)

Description: Pale blue oval scored tablets containing 25 mg. of doxylamine succinate, 2-(α-(2-dimethylaminoethoxy)α-methylbenzyl) pyridine succinate.

Action and Uses: Doxylamine succinate is an antihistamine of the ethanolamine class, which characteristically shows a high incidence of sedation. In a comparative clinical study of over 20 antihistamines on more than 3000 subjects, doxylamine succinate 25 mg. was one of the three most sedating antihistamines, producing a significantly reduced latency to end of wakefulness and comparing favorably with established hypnotic drugs such as secobarbital and pentobarbital in sedation activity. It was chosen as the antihistamine, based on dosage, causing the earliest onset of sleep. In another clinical study, doxylamine succinate 25 mg. scored better than secobarbital 100 mg. as a nighttime hypnotic. Two additional, identical clinical studies involving a total of 121 subjects demonstrated that doxylamine succinate 25 mg. reduced the sleep latency period by a third, compared to placebo. Duration of sleep was 26.6% longer with doxylamine succinate, and the quality of sleep was rated higher with the drug than with placebo. An EEG study of 6 subjects confirmed the results of these studies.

Administration and Dosage: One tablet 30 minutes before retiring. Not for children under 12 years of age.

Side Effects: Occasional anticholinergic effects may be seen.

Precautions: Unisom® should be taken only at bedtime.

Contraindications: Asthma, glaucoma, enlargement of the prostate gland. This product should not be taken by pregnant women, or those who are nursing a baby.

Warnings: Should be taken with caution if alcohol is being consumed. Product should not be taken if patient is concurrently on any other drug, without prior consultation with physician. Should not be taken for longer than two weeks unless approved by physician.

How Supplied: Boxes of 8, 16 or 32 tablets.

VISINE® Eye Drops (tetrahydrozoline HCl)

Description: Visine is a sterile, isotonic, buffered ophthalmic solution containing tetrahydrozoline hydrochloride 0.05%, boric acid, sodium borate, sodium chloride and water. It is preserved with benzalkonium chloride 0.01% and disodium edetate 0.1%.

Indications: Visine is a decongestant ophthalmic solution designed to provide symptomatic relief of conjunctival edema and hyperemia secondary to ocular allergies, minor irritations, and so called non-specific or catarrhal conjunctivitis. Beneficial effects include amelioration of burning, irritation, pruritus, soreness, and excessive lacrimation. Relief is afforded by tetrahydrozoline hydrochloride, a sympathomimetic agent, which brings about decongestion by vasoconstriction. Reddened eyes are rapidly whitened by this effective vasoconstrictor, which limits the local vascular response by constricting the small blood vessels. The onset of vasoconstriction becomes apparent within minutes and the effect is prolonged. While some vasoconstrictors may produce a dilation of the pupil or cause rebound hyperemia, there is no evidence that the use of Visine, with tetrahydrozoline hydrochloride, results in either condition.

The effectiveness of Visine in relieving conjunctival hyperemia and associated symptoms has been demonstrated by numerous clinicals, including several double blind studies, involving more than 2,000 subjects suffering from acute or chornic hyperemia induced by a variety of conditions. Visine was found to be efficacious in providing relief from conjunctival hyperemia and associated symptoms in over 90% of subjects.

Dosage and Administration: Place one or two drops in each eye two or three times a day or as directed by a physician. To avoid contamination of this product, do not touch tip of container to any other surface. Replace cap after using.

Warning: Visine should be used only for minor eye irritations. If relief is not obtained within 72 hours, or if irritation or redness persists or increases, discontinue use and consult your physician. In some instances irritation or redness is due to serious eye conditions such as infection, foreign body in the eye, or chemical corneal trauma requiring the atten-

tion of a physician. If you experience severe eye pain, headache, rapid change of vision, sudden appearance of floating spots, acute redness of the eyes, pain on exposure to light, or double vision, consult a physician at once. If you have glaucoma, do not use this product except under the advice and supervision of a physician. Not for use while soft or hard contact lenses are in eye.

How Supplied: In 0.5 fl. oz., 0.75 fl. oz. and 1.0 fl. oz. plastic dispenser bottle and 0.5 fl. oz. plastic bottle with dropper.

VISINE® A.C. Eye Drops (tetrahydrozoline hydrochloride and zinc sulfate)

Description: Visine A.C. is a sterile, isotonic, buffered ophthalmic solution containing tetrahydrozoline hydrochloride 0.05%, zinc sulfate 0.25%, boric acid, sodium citrate, sodium chloride, and water. It is preserved with benzalkonium chloride 0.01% and disodium edetate 0.1%.

Indications: Visine A.C. is an ophthalmic solution combining the effects of the decongestant tetrahydrozoline hydrochloride with the astringent effects of zinc sulfate. It is designed to provide symptomatic relief of conjunctival edema and hyperemia secondary to ocular allergies, minor irritation due to colds and other causes, as well as the so called non-specific or catarrhal conjunctivitis. Beneficial effects include amelioration of burning, irritation, pruritus, soreness, excessive lacrimation and removal of mucus from the eye. Relief is afforded by both ingredients, tetrahydrozoline hydrochloride and zinc sulfate. Tetrahydrozoline hydrochloride is a sympathomimetic agent, which brings about decongestion by vasoconstriction. Reddened eyes are rapidly whitened by this effective vasoconstrictor, which limits the local vascular response by constricting the small blood vessels. The onset of vasoconstriction becomes apparent within minutes and the effect is prolonged. While some vasoconstrictors produce a dilation of the pupil or cause rebound hyperemia, there is no evidence that the use of Visine, with tetrahydrozoline hydrochloride, results in either condition. Zinc sulfate is an ocular astringent which, by precipitating protein, helps to clear mucus from the outer surface of the eye.

The effectiveness of Visine A.C. in relieving conjunctival hyperemia and associated symptoms induced by cold and allergy has been clinically demonstrated. In one double blind study involving cold and allergy sufferers experiencing acute episodes of minor eye irritation, Visine A.C. produced statistically significant beneficial results versus a placebo of normal saline solution in relieving irritation of bulbar conjunctiva, irritation of palpebral conjunctiva, and mucous build-up. Treatment with Visine A.C. also significantly improved burning and itching symptoms.

Dosage and Administration: Place one or two drops in each eye two or three

Continued on next page

Leeming—Cont.

times a day or as directed by a physician. To avoid contamination of this product, do not touch tip of container to any other surface. Replace cap after using.

Warning: Visine A.C. should be used only for minor eye irritations. If relief is not obtained within 72 hours, or if irritation or redness persists or increases, discontinue use and consult your physician. In some instances irritation or redness is due to serious eye conditions such as infection, foreign body in the eye, or other mechanical or chemical corneal trauma requiring the attention of a physician. If you experience severe eye pain, headache, rapid change in vision, sudden appearance of floating spots, acute redness of the eyes, pain on exposure to light, or double-vision consult a physician at once. If you have glaucoma, do not use this product except under the advice and supervision of a physician. Not for use while soft or hard contact lenses are in eye.

How Supplied: In 0.5 fl. oz. and 1.0 fl. oz. plastic dispenser bottle.

Lehn & Fink Products Company
Division of Sterling Drug Inc.
225 SUMMIT AVENUE
MONTVALE, NJ 07645

MEDI–QUIK®
Antiseptic-Anesthetic First Aid Spray

Description:
Aerosol Spray: Lidocaine 2%, Benzalkonium Chloride 0.135%, Camphor 0.2%
Pump Spray: Lidocaine HCl 2.3%, Benzalkonium Chloride 0.135%
Indications: First aid spray for sunburn, minor cuts, scrapes, poison ivy, burns, insect bites.
Action: Antiseptic-Anesthetic First-Aid Spray.
Caution: "Not for deep or puncture wounds or serious burns. Not for prolonged use. If the condition for which Medi-Quik is used persists, or irritation, redness, swelling or pain persists or increases, or a rash or infection develops, discontinue use and consult physician."
Dosage and Administration: "Hold can 4 to 6 inches from surface. Press button on top of can. Spray only until area is wetted. This will dry quickly to a water-washable, non-staining film. May be repeated as necessary."
How Supplied: Spray can of 3 oz. and Pump Spray of 4 oz.

STRI–DEX®
Medicated Pads for acne vulgaris

Description: Clear, stainless solution containing salicylic acid 0.5%, alcohol 28% by volume in a vehicle consisting of water, sulfonated alkyl benzenes, citric acid, sodium carbonate, fragrance and simethicone.
Indications: Aid in the topical treatment of acne vulgaris.

Action: Comedolytic on microcomedones. Helps prevent development of comedones and inflammatory lesions. Softens blackheads, helps resolve comedones and inflammatory lesions and helps prevent infection. Removes dirt, bacteria and oil.
Precautions: "Keep away from eyes. If skin irritation develops, discontinue use and consult physician."
Symptoms and Treatment of Oral Overdosage: None with ingestion of small amounts. Larger amounts can cause gastrointestinal irritation with nausea and vomiting. Treatment: dilute with milk or water. Empty stomach only if very large quantities ingested.
Dosage and Administration: "1. Wash and dry face. 2. Wipe the Stri-Dex Medicated Pad over your face in the morning and at night. 3. Girls-apply your makeup over the Stri-Dex medication. Boys-apply in place of your regular shaving lotion."
Professional Labeling: Patient should be informed that a certain amount of dryness or peeling is to be expected.
How Supplied: Containers containing 42 pads or 75 pads.

STRI–DEX® B.P.
10% Benzoyl Peroxide Cream for acne vulgaris

Description: 10% Benzoyl Peroxide in a greaseless, colorless, odorless vanishing cream.
Indications: For topical treatment of acne vulgaris.
Action: Effective antibacterial against P. acnes. Also provides peeling and drying action. Helps clear comedones, papules and pustules and prevent formation of new lesions. Reduces skin oiliness.
Caution: "Avoid contact with eyes, lips and mouth. If excessive dryness or undue irritation of the skin develops, discontinue use and consult physician. May bleach dyed fabrics."
Directions: "Wash acne areas thoroughly and apply cream once a day initially, then two or three times a day, or as directed by a physician."
Symptoms and Treatment of Oral Overdosage: Irritating and toxic if swallowed. Dilute with demulcents such as milk or eggwhite.
How Supplied: Tubes of 1 oz.

IDENTIFICATION PROBLEM?

Consult the

Product Identification Section

where you'll find

products pictured

in full color.

Loma Linda Foods
RIVERSIDE, CA 92515

I–SOYALAC®   K PAREVE

Description: A corn free, milk free nutritionally balanced formula for infants. Liquid products are packed in solderless cans, eliminating lead from this source. i-Soyalac contains a negligible amount of soy carbohydrates and has a high polyunsaturated fatty acid ratio together with a liberal supply of Vitamin E. (For the significance of this, see Potter and Nestel, "The effects of dietary fatty acids and cholesterol on the milk lipids of lactating women, and the plasma cholesterol of breast-fed infants." Am., J. Clin. Nutr. 29, 54, 1976; Hodgson et al. "Comparison of serum cholesterol in children fed high, moderate, or low cholesterol milk diets during neonatal period." Metabolism 25, 739, 1976; Widdowson et al. "Body fat of British and Dutch infants." Brit. Med. J., March 22, 653, 1975). When prepared as directed, one quart of i-Soyalac daily, contains essential nutrients in balanced combination and sufficient quantities to provide adequate nutrition for infants.

Action and Uses: When breast milk is not available or the supply is inadequate, i-Soyalac provides a highly satisfactory alternative or supplement. It is especially valuable for all—infants, children, and adults—who may be sensitive to animal milk and/or corn products. It may also be prescribed for low cholesterol diets; for pre-operative and post-operative diets; for fortifying any milk free diet; for geriatric cases, etc.

Preparation: Standard dilution is—
Ready to Serve —as canned
Concentrate —one part mixed with an equal part water
Powder (can) —four scoops to one cup water
Powder (pouch) —contents of one pouch to 8 fl. oz. of water

Typical Analysis: Standard Dilution

i-SOYALAC		
	NUTRIENTS PER 100	
	KILO-CALORIES	PER LITER
Protein (g)	3.1	21
Fat (g)	5.5	37
Carbohydrate (g)	9.8	66
Calories		680
Calories Per Fluid Ounce 20		
Essential Fatty Acids (linoleate) (g)	2.8	19
Vitamins:		
A (IU)	310	2100
D (IU)	62	420
K (mcg)	7.8	53
E (IU)	2.3	16
C (ascorbic acid) (mg)	9.4	63
B_1 (thiamine) (mg)	0.078	0.53

B$_2$ (riboflavin) (mg)	0.093	0.63
B$_6$ (pyridoxine) (mg)	0.062	0.42
B$_{12}$ (mcg)	0.31	2.1
Niacin (mg)	1.2	8.5
Folic acid (mcg)	15	106
Pantothenic acid (mg)	0.47	3.2
Biotin (mcg)	7.8	53
Choline (mg)	15	106
Inositol (mg)	15	106

Minerals:

Calcium (mg)	93	630
Phosphorus (mg)	62	420
Magnesium (mg)	9.4	63
Iron (mg)	1.9	13
Iodine (mcg)	7.0	48
Zinc (mg)	0.78	5.3
Copper (mg)	0.078	0.53
Manganese (mcg)	78	530
Sodium (mg)	50	340
Potassium (mg)	120	790
Chloride (mg)	78	530

Supply:
i-Soyalac Ready to Serve liquid:
   32 fl. oz. cans, 6 cans per case
i-Soyalac Double Strength Concentrate:
   13 fl. oz. cans, 12 cans per case
i-Soyalac Powder—Cans:
   1 lb. cans, 12 cans per case
i-Soyalac Powder—Pouches:
   34 g. pouches, 18 pouches per case

SOYALAC® K PAREVE

Description: A milk free nutritionally balanced formula for infants. Liquid products are packed in solderless cans, eliminating lead from this source. Soyalac has a high polyunsaturated to saturated fatty acid ratio together with a liberal supply of Vitamin E. (For the significance of this, see Potter and Nestel, "The effects of dietary fatty acids and cholesterol on the milk lipids of lactating women, and the plasma cholesterol of breast-fed infants." Am., J. Clin. Nutr. 29, 54, 1976; Hodgson et al. "Comparison of serum cholesterol in children fed high, moderate, or low cholesterol milk diets during neonatal period." Metabolism 25, 739, 1976; Widdowson et al. "Body fat of British and Dutch infants." Brit. Med. J., March 22, 653, 1975). When prepared as directed, one quart of Soyalac daily contains essential nutrients in balanced combination and sufficient quantities to provide adequate nutrition for infants.
Action and Uses: Soyalac provides a highly satisfactory alternative or supplement for infants when breast milk is not available or the supply is inadequate. It is especially valuable for all infants, children, and adults - who may be sensitive to dairymilk, or who prefer a vegetarian diet. It may also be prescribed successfully for use in hypocholestrogenic diets; for pre-operative and post-operative diets; for fortifying any milk free diet; for geriatric cases, etc.

Preparation: Standard dilution is—
Ready to Serve—as canned
Concentrate—one part mixed with an equal part of water
Powder (can)—four scoops to one cup of water
Powder (pouch)—contents of one pouch to 8 fl. oz. of water

Typical Analysis: Standard Dilution

SOYALAC

NUTRIENTS	PER 100 KILO-CALORIES	PER LITER
Protein (g)	3.1	21
Fat (g)	5.5	37
Carbohydrate (g)	9.8	66
Calories		680
Calories Per Fluid Ounce		20
Essential Fatty Acids (linoleate) (g)	2.8	19

Vitamins:

A (IU)	310	2100
D (IU)	62	420
K (mcg)	7.8	53
E (IU)	2.3	16
C (ascorbic acid) (mg)	9.4	63
B$_1$ (thiamine) (mg)	0.078	0.53
B$_2$ (riboflavin) (mg)	0.093	0.63
B$_6$ (Pyridoxine) (mg)	0.062	0.42
B$_{12}$ (mcg)	0.31	2.1
Niacin (mg)	1.2	8.5
Folic acid (mcg)	15	106
Pantothenic acid (mg)	0.47	3.2
Biotin (mcg)	7.8	53
Choline (mg)	15	106
Inositol (mg)	15	106

Minerals:

Calcium (mg)	93	630
Phosphorus (mg)	62	420
Magnesium (mg)	11	74
Iron (mg)	1.9	13
Iodine (mcg)	7	48
Zinc (mg)	0.78	5.3
Copper (mg)	0.078	0.53
Manganese (mcg)	156	1060
Sodium (mg)	51	350
Potassium (mg)	110	740
Chloride (mg)	58	390

Supply:
Soyalac Ready to Serve liquid:
   32 fl. oz. cans, 6 cans per case
Soyalac Double Strength Concentrate:
   13 fl. oz. cans, 12 cans per case
Soyalac Powder—Cans:
   1 lb. cans, 12 cans per case
Soyalac Powder—Pouches:
   34 g. pouches, 18 pouches per case

Luyties Pharmacal Company
4200 LACLEDE AVENUE
ST. LOUIS, MO 63108

YELLOLAX

Description: YELLOLAX is a combination of time proven Yellow-phenolphthalein, and the Homeopathic ingredients, Bryonia and Hydrastis. Clinically YELLOLAX is an oral laxative. Each tablet contains two grains of yellow phenolphthalein and the Bryonia and Hydrastis approximately one fortieth grain each.
Action: Yellow-phenolphthalein is an effective and safe laxative, which is not contraindicated in pregnancy. Homeopathic Bryonia is used to treat constipation and the pain associated with constipation. Homeopathic Bryonia tends to increase mucous membrane moisture. Homeopathic Hydrastis is also included in the treatment of constipation because, the Homeopathic Hydrastis provides some relief of constipation and the associated pain and headaches by relaxing mucous membranes and encouraging their secretion. YELLOLAX has been safely used in pregnancy, children, and as conjunctive treatment with hemorrhoidal complications.
Indications: YELLOLAX is indicated in the management of simple constipation. YELLOLAX is also indicated in those conditions which require a gentle laxative.
Contraindications: YELLOLAX and all laxatives are contraindicated in appendicitis. All laxatives containing phenolphthalein are contraindicated in patients who have hypersensitivity to phenolphthalein.
Warnings: Do not use laxatives in cases of severe colic, nausea and other symptoms of appendicitis. Do not use laxatives habitually nor continually. If condition persists consult physician. Keep this and all medication out of the reach of children. DO NOT exceed the recommended dosage.
Caution: Frequent or prolonged use may result in laxative dependence. If skin rash appears, discontinue use.
Side Effects: The phenolphthalein may impart a red color to the urine, (phenolphthalein is also used as a pH indicator), this is normal.
Dosage: For adults one or two tablets chewed before retiring. For children over six a quarter tablet to half tablet before retiring. Tablets should be well chewed. For younger children consult physician.
Supplied: Compressed tablets packed in glass bottles of 36 (NDC 0618-0832-55) and 100 (NDC 0618-0832-12), and in repackers of 1000 tablets.

Products are cross-indexed by generic and chemical names in the
YELLOW SECTION

Macsil, Inc.
1326 FRANKFORD AVENUE
PHILADELPHIA, PA 19125

BALMEX® BABY POWDER

Composition: Contains BALSAN® (specially purified balsam Peru), zinc oxide, talc, starch, calcium carbonate.
Action and Uses: Absorbent, emollient, soothing—for diaper irritation, intertrigo, and other common dermatological conditions. In acute, simple miliaria, itching ceases in minutes and lesions dry promptly. For routine use after bathing and each diaper change.
How Supplied: 4 oz. shaker top cans.

BALMEX® EMOLLIENT LOTION

Gentle and effective scientifically compounded infant's skin conditioner.
Composition: Contains a special lanolin oil (non-sensitizing, dewaxed, moisturizing fraction of lanolin), BALSAN® (specially purified balsam Peru) and silicone.
Action and Uses: The special Lanolin Oil aids nature lubricate baby's skin to keep it smooth and supple. Balmex Emollient Lotion is also highly effective as a physiologic conditioner on adult's skin.
How Supplied: Available in 6 oz. dispenser-top plastic bottles.

BALMEX® OINTMENT

Composition: Contains BALSAN® (specially purified balsam Peru), vitamins A and D, zinc oxide, and bismuth subnitrate in an ointment base containing silicone.
Action and Uses: Emollient, protective, anti-inflammatory, promotes healing—for diaper rash, minor burns, sunburn, and other simple skin conditions; also decubitus ulcers, skin irritations associated with ileostomy and colostomy drainage. Nonstaining, readily washes out of diapers and clothing.
How Supplied: 1, 2, 4 oz. tubes; 1 lb. plastic jars (½ oz. tubes for Hospitals only).

Marion Laboratories, Inc.
Pharmaceutical Division
MARION INDUSTRIAL PARK
10236 BUNKER RIDGE ROAD
KANSAS CITY, MO 64137

AMBENYL®-D Decongestant Cough Formula
Antitussive, Expectorant, Nasal Decongestant

Two teaspoonfuls (10 ml) contain the following active ingredients:
Guaifenesin (glyceryl
  guaiacolate) .... 200 mg
Pseudoephedrine
  hydrochloride .... 60 mg
Dextromethorphan
  hydrobromide .... 30 mg
Also contains 9.5% Alcohol.
Indications: Ambenyl®-D is for temporary relief of nasal congestion due to the common cold or associated with sinusitis, helps loosen phlegm, calms cough impulses without narcotics and temporarily helps you cough less.
Directions for Use: Adult Dose (12 years and over)—Two teaspoonfuls every six hours. Child Dose (6–12 years)—One teaspoonful every six hours. (2–6 years) —One-half teaspoonful every six hours. No more than four doses per day.
Warnings: Do not give this product to children under two years except under the advice and supervision of a physician. Do not take this product for persistent or chronic cough such as occurs with smoking, asthma, or emphysema, or where cough is accompanied by excessive secretions except under the advice and supervision of a physician.
Do not exceed recommended dosage because at higher doses nervousness, dizziness, or sleeplessness may occur.
Caution: A persistent cough may be a sign of a serious condition. If cough persists for more than one week, tends to recur, or is accompanied by high fever, rash, or persistent headache, consult a physician.
If symptoms do not improve within seven days or are accompanied by high fever, consult a physician before continuing use. Do not take this product if you have high blood pressure, heart disease, diabetes, or thyroid disease, except under the advice and supervision of a physician.
Drug Interaction Precaution: Do not take this product if you are presently taking a prescription antihypertensive or antidepressant drug containing a monoamine oxidase inhibitor except under the advice and supervision of a physician.
Store at a controlled room temperature (59°–86°F).
Keep this and all drugs out of reach of children.
In case of accidental overdose, seek professional assistance or contact a poison control center immediately.
How Supplied: Ambenyl-D Decongestant Cough Formula is supplied in a 4-fluid-ounce bottle.
[*Shown in Product Identification Section*]

DEBROX® Drops

Description: Carbamide peroxide 6.5% in specially prepared anhydrous glycerol.
Actions: Debrox® penetrates, softens and facilitates removal of earwax, without causing the wax to swell. Upon direct contact with earwax, carbamide peroxide releases oxygen to form a dense foam which helps to break up wax accumulations. These actions result in a chemomechanical cleansing, debriding effect. Any remaining wax may be removed by flushing with warm water, using a soft rubber bulb ear syringe. Avoid excessive pressure.
Indications: Debrox provides a safe, nonirritating method of removing earwax. Aids in the prevention of ceruminosis. Used regularly, Debrox Drops helps keep the ear canal free from blockage due to accumulated earwax.
Caution: Consult physician if redness, irritation, swelling or pain persists or increases.
Dosage and Administration: Use directly from bottle. Tilt head sideways and squeeze bottle gently so that 5-10 drops flow into ear. Tip of bottle should not enter ear canal. Keep drops in ear for several minutes while head remains tilted or by inserting cotton. Repeat twice daily for at least 3-4 days or as directed by physician. Any remaining wax may be removed by flushing with warm water, using a soft rubber bulb ear syringe.
AVOID CONTACT WITH EYES. Keep this and all drugs out of the reach of children. In case of accidental ingestion, seek professional assistance or contact a poison control center immediately. Protect from heat and direct sunlight.
How Supplied: Debrox Drops in ½- or 1-fl.-oz. plastic squeeze bottles with applicator spouts.
[*Shown in Product Identification Section*]

FUMASORB® Tablets
(iron therapy)

Each tablet contains:
Elemental Iron (as 200 mg of
  ferrous fumarate) .... 66 mg
Indications: For prophylaxis treatment of iron deficiencies or anemias due to partial or complete iron deficiency.
Dosage: Prophylaxis—one (1) tablet daily for adults and children over 5 years. Treatment—one (1) tablet three (3) times a day or as directed by a physician. For infants—as directed by a physician. To minimize gastric disturbances, take after meals or with food.
How Supplied: Available in bottles of 100 tablets.
Keep out of reach of children.
Store at room temperature.

GAVISCON® Antacid Tablets

Composition: Each chewable tablet contains the following active ingredients:
Aluminum hydroxide dried gel... 80 mg
Magnesium trisilicate .... 20 mg
and the following inactive ingredients: sucrose, alginic acid, sodium bicarbonate, starch, calcium stearate and flavoring.
Actions: Unique formulation produces soothing foam which floats on stomach contents. Foam containing antacid precedes stomach contents into the esophagus when reflux occurs to help protect the sensitive mucosa from further irritation. GAVISCON acts locally without neutralizing entire stomach contents to help maintain integrity of the digestive process. Endoscopic studies indicate that GAVISCON® Antacid Tablets are equally as effective in the erect or supine patient.
Indications: For temporary relief of heartburn, sour stomach, and/or acid indigestion.
Directions: Chew two to four tablets four times a day or as directed by a physician. Tablets should be taken after meals and at bedtime or as needed. For best results follow by a half glass of water or

other liquid. DO NOT SWALLOW WHOLE.

Warnings: Except under the advice and supervision of a physician: do not take more than 16 tablets in a 24-hour period or 16 tablets daily for more than 2 weeks; do not use this product if you are on a sodium restricted diet. Each GAVISCON Tablet contains approximately 0.8 mEq sodium.

Drug Interaction Precautions: Do not take this product if you are presently taking a prescription antibiotic drug containing any form of tetracycline.

Store at a controlled room temperature. Keep this and all drugs out of the reach of children. In case of accidental overdose, seek professional assistance or contact a poison control center immediately.

How Supplied: Available in bottle of 100 tablets and in foil-wrapped 2's in box of 30 tablets.

[*Shown in Product Identification Section*]

GAVISCON® Liquid Antacid

Each tablespoonful (15 ml) contains the following active ingredients:

Aluminum hydroxide .... 95 mg
Magnesium carbonate .... 412 mg

And the following inactive ingredients: water, sorbitol solution, glycerin, sodium alginate, xanthan gum, edetate disodium, methylparaben, propylparaben, flavorings and colors.

Indications: For the relief of heartburn, sour stomach, and/or acid indigestion, and upset stomach associated with heartburn, sour stomach, and/or acid indigestion.

Directions: Shake well before using. Take one to two tablespoonfuls four times a day or as directed by a physician. GAVISCON Liquid should be taken after meals and at bedtime, followed by a half glass of water.

Warnings: Except under the advice and supervision of a physician: do not take more than eight tablespoonfuls in a 24-hour period or eight tablespoonfuls daily for more than two weeks. May have laxative effect. Do not use this product if you have a kidney disease; do not use this product if you are on a sodium restricted diet. Each tablespoonful of GAVISCON Liquid contains approximately 1.7 mEq sodium.

Drug Interaction Precautions: Do not take this product if you are presently taking a prescription antibiotic drug containing any form of tetracycline.

Keep tightly closed. Avoid freezing. Store at a controlled room temperature.

Keep this and all drugs out of the reach of children.

In case of accidental overdose, seek professional assistance or contact a poison control center immediately.

How Supplied: 12 fluid ounces (355 ml).

[*Shown in Product Identification Section*]

GAVISCON®-2 Antacid Tablets

Each chewable tablet contains the following active ingredients:

Aluminum hydroxide dried gel 160 mg
Magnesium trisilicate .... 40 mg

and the following inactive ingredients: sucrose, alginic acid, sodium bicarbonate, starch, calcium stearate and flavoring.

Indications: For temporary relief of heartburn, sour stomach, and/or acid indigestion.

Directions: Chew one to two tablets four times a day or as directed by a physician. Tablets should be taken after meals and at bedtime or as needed. For best results follow by a half glass of water or other liquid. DO NOT SWALLOW WHOLE.

Warnings: Except under the advice and supervision of a physician: do not take more than 8 tablets in a 24-hour period or 8 tablets daily for more than 2 weeks; do not use this product if you are on a sodium-restricted diet. Each GAVISCON-2 Tablet contains approximately 1.6 mEq sodium.

Drug Interaction Precautions: Do not take this product if you are presently taking a prescription antibiotic drug containing any form of tetracycline.

Store at a controlled room temperature in a dry place.

Keep this and all drugs out of the reach of children. In case of accidental overdose, seek professional assistance or contact a poison control center immediately.

How Supplied: Box of 48 foil-wrapped tablets.

[*Shown in Product Identification Section*]

GLY-OXIDE® Liquid

Description: Carbamide peroxide 10% in specially prepared anhydrous glycerol. Artificial flavor added. Not NF.

Actions: GLY-OXIDE® is a safe, stabilized oxygenating agent. Specifically formulated for topical oral administration, it provides unique chemomechanical cleansing and debriding action, which allows normal healing to occur.

Indications: Local treatment and hygienic prevention (as an aid to professional care) of minor oral inflammation such as canker sores, denture irritation and post-dental procedure irritation. GLY-OXIDE Liquid provides effective aid to oral hygiene when normal cleansing measures are inadequate or impossible (e.g., total-care geriatric patients). As an adjunct to oral hygiene (orthodontics, dental appliances) after regular brushing.

Precautions: Severe or persistent oral inflammation or denture irritation may be serious. If these or unexpected effects occur, consult physician or dentist promptly.

Dosage and Administration: DO NOT DILUTE—use directly from the bottle. Apply 4 times daily after meals and at bedtime, or as directed by a dentist or physician. Place several drops on affected area; expectorate after 2-3 minutes, or place 10 drops onto tongue, mix with saliva, swish for several minutes, expectorate. Do not rinse. Foams on contact with saliva.

Avoid contact with eyes. Protect from heat and direct sunlight. Keep this and all drugs out of the reach of children. In case of accidental ingestion, seek professional assistance or contact a poison control center immediately.

How Supplied: GLY-OXIDE Liquid in ½-fl.-oz. and 2-fl.-oz. non-spill plastic squeeze bottles with applicator spouts.

[*Shown in Product Identification Section*]

METASEP® Shampoo
(medicated shampoo concentrate)

Avoids drying hair. Will not discolor gray, blond or bleached hair.

Active Ingredient: Parachlorometaxylenol 2%.

Other Ingredients: Isopropyl alcohol NF 9%, sodium lauryl sulfate, water, lauramide DEA, laneth-10 acetate, citric acid USP, fragrance.

Indications: Use as an aid in relief of dandruff and associated conditions.

Directions: Wet hair thoroughly. Apply METASEP® Medicated Shampoo and massage to foamy lather. Allow lather to remain five minutes. Rinse hair thoroughly and repeat.

Caution: Avoid contact with eyes.

How Supplied: 4-fluid-ounce bottle. Store at room temperature.

Keep out of reach of children.

OS-CAL® Tablets
(calcium with vitamin D)

Each tablet contains: 625 mg of calcium carbonate from oyster shell which provides:

Elemental calcium............. 250 mg
Ergocalciferol (Vitamin D₂)..... 125 USP Units

Indications: Os-Cal Tablets provide a source of calcium when it is desired to increase the dietary intake of this mineral. Os-Cal also contains Vitamin D₂ to aid in the absorption of calcium.

Directions: Take one tablet three times a day at mealtime. Three tablets daily provide:

	Quantity	%U.S.RDA* for Adults
Calcium	750 mg	75%
Vitamin D₂	375 units	94%

*Percent U.S. Recommended Daily Allowance

Store at room temperature.

Keep this and all drugs out of reach of children. In case of accidental overdose, seek professional assistance or contact a poison control center immediately.

How Supplied: Bottles of 100, 240, 500, and 1000 tablets.

[*Shown in Product Identification Section*]

OS-CAL® 500 Tablets
(calcium supplement)

Each tablet contains: 1,250 mg of calcium carbonate from oyster shell which provides:

Elemental calcium .... 500 mg

Indications: Os-Cal 500 Tablets provide a source of calcium where it is desired or recommended by a physician to increase the dietary intake of this mineral.

Directions: Take one tablet two or three times a day at mealtime or as directed.

Continued on next page

Marion—Cont.

Two tablets daily provide:

	Quantity	%U.S.RDA†
Calcium	1,000 mg	100%*
		77%**

Three tablets daily provide:

	Quantity	%U.S.RDA†
Calcium	1,500 mg	150%*
		115%**

†Percent U.S. Recommended Daily Allowance.
*For adults and children 12 or more years of age.
**For pregnant and lactating women.
Keep this and all drugs out of reach of children. In case of accidental overdose, seek professional assistance or contact a poison control center immediately.
How Supplied: Bottles of 60 tablets.

OS–CAL FORTE®Tablets
(multivitamin and mineral supplement)

Each tablet contains:
Vitamin A (palmitate) 1668 USP Units
Ergocalciferol
  (Vitamin D₂)................. 125 USP Units
Thiamine mononitrate
  (Vitamin B₁)................................ 1.7 mg
Riboflavin (Vitamin B₂)................ 1.7 mg
Pyridoxine hydrochloride
  (Vitamin B₆).................................. 2.0 mg
Cyanocobalamin (Vitamin B₁₂) 1.6 mcg
Ascorbic acid (Vitamin C)............ 50 mg
dl-alpha-tocopherol acetate
  (Vitamin E).................................. 0.8 IU
Niacinamide .... 15 mg
Calcium (from oyster shell*)...... 250 mg
Iron (as ferrous fumarate)............. 5 mg
Copper (as sulfate)........................ 0.3 mg
Iodine (as potassium iodide)...... 0.05 mg
Magnesium (as oxide)................... 1.6 mg
Manganese (as sulfate)................. 0.3 mg
Zinc (as sulfate)............................ 0.5 mg
*Trace minerals from oyster shell: copper, iron, magnesium, manganese, silica and zinc.
Indication: Multivitamin and mineral supplement.
Dosage: One tablet three times daily or as directed by physician.
How Supplied: Bottles of 100 tablets.
Keep this and all drugs out of reach of children. In case of accidental overdose, seek professional assistance or contact a poison control center immediately.
Store at room temperature.

OS–CAL–GESIC® Tablets
(antiarthritic)

Each tablet contains:
Salicylamide .... 400 mg
Calcium (from oyster shell) .... 100 mg
Ergocalciferol
  (Vitamin D₂)....................50 USP Units
Indication: For temporary relief of symptoms associated with arthritis.
Dosage: Initially: 2 tablets hourly for 3 or 4 doses. Maintenance: 1 or 2 tablets 4 times daily.
How Supplied: OS-CAL-GESIC® is available in bottles of 100 tablets.
Keep this and all drugs out of reach of children. In case of accidental overdose,

seek professional assistance or contact a poison control center immediately.
Store at room temperature.

OS–CAL® Plus Tablets
(multivitamin and multimineral supplement)

Each tablet contains:
Calcium (from oyster shell*)...... 250 mg
Ergocalciferol
  (Vitamin D₂)................ 125 USP Units
*Trace minerals from oyster shell: copper, iron, magnesium, manganese, silica and zinc.
Plus:
Vitamin A (palmitate) 1666 USP Units
Vitamin C (ascorbic acid)............. 33 mg
Vitamin B₂ (riboflavin).............. 0.66 mg
Vitamin B₁ (thiamine
  mononitrate)............................... 0.5 mg
Vitamin B₆ (pyridoxine HCl)...... 0.5 mg
Vitamin B₁₂ (cyanocobalamin) 0.03 mcg
Niacinamide................................. 3.33 mg
Iron (as ferrous fumarate) .... 16.6 mg
Zinc (as the sulfate).................... 0.75 mg
Manganese (as the sulfate)....... 0.75 mg
Copper (as the sulfate)............. 0.036 mg
Iodine (as potassium iodide) ... 0.036 mg
Indications: As a multivitamin and multimineral supplement.
Dosage: One (1) tablet three times a day before meals or as directed by a physician. For children under four years of age, consult a physician.
How Supplied: Bottles of 100 tablets.
Store at room temperature.
Keep this and all drugs out of reach of children. In case of accidental overdose, seek professional assistance or contact a poison control center immediately.

PRETTS® Tablets
(diet control adjunct)

Each Pretts® Tablet contains:
Alginic acid.................................. 200 mg
Sodium carboxymethyl-
  cellulose .... 100 mg
Sodium bicarbonate .... 70 mg
Contains FD&C Yellow No. 5 (tartrazine) as a color additive.
Indications: For use as an adjunct to diet control. Pretts Tablets provide bulk to help satisfy the feeling of hunger caused by emptiness, making it easier for you to adhere to your specific diet regimen.
Those on a sodium-restricted diet should consult their physician.
Actions: Pretts Tablets, when chewed, introduce a bulky foam into the gastrointestinal tract to create a feeling of fullness and to help alleviate hunger pangs; this serves as an aid in helping the patient eat less.
Dosage and Administration: Take two to four tablets with a full glass of water three or four times a day, or as needed. Chew each tablet individually, followed by small sips of water. Do not swallow tablets whole!
Store at room temperature.
Protect from moisture.
Keep out of reach of children.
How Supplied: Bottles of 60 tablets. Tablets imprinted with MARION/1177.
[*Shown in Product Identification Section*]

THROAT DISCS® Throat Lozenges
Description: Each lozenge contains capsicum, peppermint, anise, cubeb, glycyrrhiza extract (licorice), and linseed.
Indications: Effective for soothing, temporary relief of minor throat irritations from hoarseness and coughs due to colds.
Precautions: For severe or persistent cough or sore throat, or sore throat accompanied by high fever, headache, nausea, and vomiting, consult physician promptly. Not recommended for children under 3 years of age.
Dosage: Allow lozenge to dissolve slowly in mouth. One or two should give the desired relief. Do not use more than four lozenges per hour.
How Supplied: Box of 60 lozenges.
[*Shown in Product Identification Section*]

Max Factor & Co.
1655 N. McCADDEN PLACE
HOLLYWOOD, CA 90028

MAXI® STAY-FRESH™
Crease Resistant Eye Shadow

Description: A crease resistant powder eye shadow formulated especially for persons with oily skin.
Actions: Provides velvety, long lasting eye color that will not streak or smudge. Resists creasing even on oily skin. Formulated with oil blotters to control oily shine and build-up on eye lids. Product is hypo-allergenic, fragrance free, dermatologist tested and ophthalmologist tested to insure minimal potential for sensitization. Available in (8) shades:

Pure Lilac	Winewood
Fresh Grape	Wild Heather
Acorn	Periwinkle
Peach Bisque	Country Sage

How Supplied: Self-service/blister card package contains net wt. .08 oz. compact with sponge tip applicator.
[*Shown in Product Identification Section*]

MAXI-THICK™
Double-Lash Mascara

Description: A quick-drying mascara formulated to increase the thickness of eyelashes by more than 100%.
Actions: Thickening formula applies and dries rapidly to double the thickness of the lashes in less than 60 seconds. Resists smudging and flaking to insure fresh-looking lashes for hours.
Ophthalmologist and dermatologist tested for safety and gentleness.
Available in black, brownish-black, brown.
Removes easily with soap and water or use ophthalmologist-tested MAXI® Quick & Clean Eye Make-Up Remover Gel or any mineral oil based make-up remover.
How Supplied: Self-service/blister card package holds tube containing .42 fl. oz. net wt. mascara with brush wand.
[*Shown in Product Identification Section*]

MAXI-LASH™
24-Hour Mascara

Description: A waterproof, polymer formula mascara with 24-hour durability.

Actions: Exclusive polymer formula builds thick, long lashes that last for hours. Waterproof formula is so tear-proof and smudgeproof it can even be slept in without affecting the results. Special spiral shaped brush colors, curls and separate lashes.

Dermatologist and ophthalmologist tested to insure minimal potential for sensitization.

Available in black, brownish-black and brown.

Removes easily with ophthalmologist-tested MAXI® Quick & Clean Eye Make-Up Remover Gel or any mineral oil based make-up remover.

How Supplied: Self-service/blister card package holds tube containing .42 fl. oz. mascara with brush wand.

[*Shown in Product Identification Section*]

MAXI® Extra-Long
Thick Lash Mascara with Sealer

Description: A fast-drying, water-resistant mascara formulated to keep lashes looking long and thick for hours.

Actions: Fiber-free formula lengthens and thickens lashes. Contains a water-resistant sealer to help prevent mascara from smearing, smudging and flaking. Gentle conditioning formulation has been dermatologist and ophthalmologist tested to insure minimal potential for sensitization. Includes a lavish brush designed to separate lashes as it colors.

Available in black, brownish-black, brown and navy.

Removes easily with ophthalmologist-tested MAXI® Quick & Clean Eye Make-Up Remover Gel.

How Supplied: Self-service/blister card package holds tube containing .42 fl. oz. mascara with brush wand.

[*Shown in Product Identification Section*]

MAXI® UNSHINE™
Oil Blotting Make-Up

Description: A water-based, oil blotting make-up in a creamy liquid formula created for persons with oily skin that may be sensitive and blemish prone.

Actions: Oil-blotting formula provides extra coverage to hide flaws with a clean, natural looking finish. Actually blots oil to control shine hour after hour. Will not clog pores.

Hypo-allergenic, fragrance free and dermatologist tested to insure minimal potential for sensitization. Should be used with other UNSHINE™ products for best results. Available in 5 matte shades: Fresh Buff, Soft Ivory, Natural Beige, Pure Biege, Soft Amber.

How Supplied: Self-service/blister card package contains 1 fl. oz. make-up in a convenient plastic squeeze tube.

[*Shown in Product Identification Section*]

MAXI® UNSHINE™
Oil Free* Liquid Make-Up

Description: A waterbased, fragrance free, hypo-allergenic liquid make-up for persons with oily skin or skin which is oily in patches.

Actions/Benefits: Provides light, even coverage. Facial shine, caused by accumulation of surface skin lipids, is minimized. Product has been dermatologically tested to insure minimal potential for sensitization. Should be used with the other MAXI®UNSHINE™ products for best effect.

*Contains none of the natural oils associated with oily skin problems.

Shade Range: Available in ten (10) shades: Buff, Bisque, Soft Beige, Warm Honey, Beige Blush, Deep Beige, Natural Tan, Golden Tan, Tawny Bronze and Mahogany.

How Supplied: Available in 1 fluid ounce glass bottle. Bottle also available in self-service/blister carded package.

[*Shown in Product Identification Section*]

MAXI® UNSHINE™
100% Oil Free Blotting Powder

Description: A pure and gentle oil absorbing make-up powder base for persons with oily skin or skin which is oily in patches. Hypo-allergenic.

Actions/Benefits: Oil absorbing action keeps skin looking and feeling fresh by absorbing surface skin lipids. Helps prevent make-up from streaking; maintains matte appearance. Product has been dermatologically tested to insure minimal potential for sensitization. Should be used with the other MAXI® UNSHINE™ products for best effect.

Shade Range: Available in a selection of six transparent shades: Transparent Natural, Transparent Buff, Transparent Beige, Transparent Tan, Transparent Tawny, and Transparent Bronze.

How Supplied: Self service/blister carded package contains .33 ounce compact with washable sponge puff applicator.

[*Shown in Product Identification Section*]

MAXI® UNSHINE™
100% Oil Free Blushing Gel

Description: A waterbased blushing gel formulated for persons with oily or combination skin that may be sensitive and blemish prone.

Actions: 100% oil-free formula provides sheer, natural looking cheek color. Gentle water base blends quickly and is long lasting. Color will not streak or blotch. Hypo-allergenic, fragrance free and dermatologist tested to insure minimal potential for sensitization. Should be used with other MAXI® UNSHINE™ products for best results.

Available in 4 shades: Clear Pink, Clear Plum, Clear Peach, Clear Peachbronze.

How Supplied: Self-service/blister card package contains ½ fl. oz. gel in a convenient plastic squeeze tube.

[*Shown in Product Identification Section*]

MAXI® UNSHINE™
100% Oil Free Blushing Powder

Description: A pure and gentle blusher for persons with oily skin or skin which is oily in patches. Hypo-allergenic.

Actions/Benefits: Provides light, even coloration to cheeks. Oil absorbing action keeps skin looking fresh, minimizes oily shine caused by accumulation of surface skin lipids.

Product has been dermatologically tested to insure minimal potential for sensitization. Should be used with other MAXI® UNSHINE™ products for best effect.

Shade Range: Available in a selection of eight shades: Blushing Pink, Warm Cinnamon, Blushing Peach, Fresh Raspberry, Natural Pink, Blushing Coral, Tawny Burgundy, and Rich Plum.

How Supplied: Self service/blister carded package contains .15 ounce compact with washable sponge puff applicator.

[*Shown in Product Identification Section*]

SEBB® Dandruff Treatment Lotion

Active Ingredients: Benzethonium Chloride, and N-trichloromethylmercapto-4-cyclohexene -1, 2 - dicarboximide (captan) in a 19% alcoholic lotion.

Description: For temporary relief of dandruff and itchy scalp associated with dandruff.

Actions/Benefits: Clinical studies show the active ingredients in SEBB Lotion significantly reduce the degree of flaking in cases of dandruff.

Dosage and Administration: Shake well (settled ingredients are important). For best results start treatment with a clean scalp. So before first SEBB Lotion application, shampoo hair thoroughly, then towel dry. Use SEBB Lotion daily until condition is under control, then only as often as necessary. Shampooing is not necessary each time SEBB Lotion is applied. Just shampoo as often as normal.

Application for Men: Apply SEBB Lotion liberally, moistening entire scalp area well. After applying SEBB Lotion, regular hair grooming aids may be used.

Application for Women: Moisten entire scalp area well with SEBB Lotion by parting hair sectionally and using saturated cotton pad or eye dropper. Allow SEBB Lotion to dry on scalp. SEBB Lotion is odorless and will not discolor hair. No special rinsing or massaging is necessary. SEBB Lotion does not interfere with the use of regular hair beautifying aids.

How Supplied: Available in 8 fluid ounce glass bottle.

[*Shown in Product Identification Section*]

SEBB® Dandruff Shampoo

Description: SEBB shampoo has been designed especially for oily scalps and to help remove dandruff flakes. Leaves hair shiny and manageable.

Composition: Contains water, TEA-lauryl sulfate, coconut acid, triethanolamine, disodium monooleamidosulfosuccinate, cocamide DEA, sodium lauryl sulfate, PEG-8 disterarate, hydroxypropyl methylcellulose, tetrasodium EDTA, fragrance, sodium o-phenyl phenate, chloroxylenol, FD&C yellow No. 5, FD&C yellow No. 6.

Dosage and Administration: Apply a small amount to wet hair. Lather and rinse. Apply again. Massage scalp gently,

Continued on next page

Max Factor—Cont.

yet thoroughly. Leave on hair for 2–3 minutes, then rinse.

How Supplied: Available in an 8 fluid ounce plastic bottle.

[*Shown in Product Identification Section*]

SKIN PRINCIPLE™

SKIN PRINCIPLE Skin Support System is a serious line of hypo-allergenic skin care formulated to help skin breathe. It consists of cleansing, clarifying and moisturizing products especially formulated for Oily/Partly Oily, Normal, Dry/-Partly Dry skin types.

All products are hypo-allergenic, fragrance free, dermatologist tested and clinically tested.

SKIN PRINCIPLE™
Gentle Cleansing Bar

Composition: Sodium Tallowate, Water, Sodium Cocoate, Glycerin, Sodium Stearate, Octyl Hydroxystearate, Urea, Butylene Glycol, Dimethicone, Rosemary Oil, Menthol, Polyamino Sugar Condensate, Glycine, Potassium and Ammonium PCA, Leucine, Glucose Glutamate, Serine, Proline, Collagen Amino Acids, Tyrosine, Tryptophan, Aspartic Acid, Valine, Alanine, Isoleucine, Sodium Lactate, Methylparaben, Propylparaben, BHT, Trisodium HEDTA, Titanium Dioxide, Iron Oxides, D&C Red No. 33.

Actions: Lathers away make-up, dirt, excess oil and skin-dulling dead cells to help skin breathe as it cleanses. Recommended for: Oily/Partly Oily and Normal Skin.

Administration: Twice daily, morning and night.

How Supplied: 6 oz. net wt. solid bar (in plastic covered soap dish).

SKIN PRINCIPLE™
Purifying Cleansing Lotion

Composition: Water, Mineral Oil, Isopropyl Palmitate, Butylene Glycol, Glyceryl Stearate, PEG-100 Stearate, Isocetyl Stearate, Sorbitan Stearate, Urea, Matricaria Oil, Allantoin, Benzophenone-9, Carbomer-941, Triethanolamine, Polyamino Sugar Condensate, Glycine, Potassium and Ammonium PCA, Leucine, Glucose Glutamate, Serine, Proline, Collagen Amino Acids, Tyrosine, Tryptophan, Aspartic Acid, Valine, Alanine, Isoleucine, Sodium Lactate, Methylparaben, Propylparaben, Quaternium-15, BHA, D&C Green No. 5, FD&C Red No. 4, FD&C Yellow No. 5.

Actions: Cleanses and helps skin breathe by gently removing make-up, dirt, grime and skin-dulling dead cells. Recommended for: Dry/Partly Dry and Normal Skin.

Administration: Twice daily, morning and night.

How Supplied: 8.3 fl. oz. lotion (plastic bottle).

SKIN PRINCIPLE™
Basic Clarifying Lotion

Composition: Water, SD Alcohol 40, Horse Chestnut Extract, Butylene Glycol, Alcloxa, Matricaria Oil, Polysorbate 20, Benzophenone-4, Polyamino Sugar Condensate, Glycine, Potassium and Ammonium PCA, Leucine, Glucose Glutamate, Serine, Proline, Collagen Amino Acids, Tyrosine, Tryptophan, Aspartic Acid, Valine, Alanine, Isoleucine, Sodium Lactate, Lactic Acid, Methylparaben, Propylparaben, Imidazolidinyl Urea, D&C Red. No. 19, FD&C Yellow No. 5.

Actions: Removes final traces of cleanser. Works with body chemistry to tone, refine and normalize pH balance. Prepares skin for moisturizing benefits. Recommended for: Oily/Partly Oily, Normal, Dry/Partly Dry Skin.

Caution: For dry skin, dampen cotton ball with water before use.

Administration: Twice daily, morning and night after cleansing. Oily skin types may reapply throughout day as needed.

How Supplied: 8.3 fl. oz. liquid (plastic bottle).

SKIN PRINCIPLE™
Daily Light Moisture Lotion

Composition: Water, Butylene Glycol, Octyl Palmitate, Glyceryl Stearate, Myristyl Myristate, Sorbitan Stearate, PEG-100 Stearate, Squalane, Urea, Sesame Oil, Matricaria Oil, Collagen, Hydrogenated Cottonseed, Glyceride, Caprylic Capric Triglyceride, Ribonucleic Acid, Benzophenone-9, Cetearyl, Alcohol, Cetareth-20, Polysorbate 60, Dimethicone, Carbomer-941, Triethanolamine, Polyamino Sugar Condensate, Glycine, Potassium and Ammonium PCA, Leucine, Glucose Glutamate, Serine, Proline, Collagen Amino Acids, Tyrosine, Tryptophan, Aspartic Acid, Valine, Alanine, Isoleucine, Sodium Lactate, Methylparaben, Propylparaben, Quaternium-15, Imidazolidinyl Urea, BHA, D&C Green No. 5, FD&C Red No. 4, FD&C Yellow No. 5.

Actions: Non-occlusive formula provides moisture where needed. Helps combat drying effects of the environment. Softens and smoothes skin. Suitable for under make-up. Recommended for: Partly Oily and Normal Skin.

Caution: Avoid oily T-zone.

Administration: Twice daily, morning and night.

How Supplied: 4.2 fl. oz. lotion (bottle).

SKIN PRINCIPLE™
Daily Rich Moisture Lotion

Composition: Water, Butylene Glycol, Octyl Palmitate, Glyceryl Stearate, PEG-100 Stearate, Myristyl Myristate, Sorbitan Stearate, Squalane Urea, Hybrid Safflower Oil, Sesame Oil, Sunflower Seed Oil, Matricaria Oil, Collagen, Caprylic Capric Triglyceride, Ribonucleic Acid, Benzophenone-9, Cetaryl Alcohol, Ceteareth-20, Polysorbate 60, Dimethicone, Carbomer-941, Triethanolamine, Polyamino Sugar Condensate, Glycine,

Potassium and Ammonium PCA, Leucine, Glucose Glutamate, Serine, Proline, Collagen Amino Acids, Tyrosine, Tryptophan, Aspartic Acid, Valine, Alanine, Isoleucine, Sodium Lactate, Methylparaben, Propylparaben, Quaternium-15, Imidazolidinyl Urea, BHA, D&C Green No. 5, FD&C Red No. 4, FD&C Yellow No. 5.

Actions: Non-occlusive moisture lotion works with body chemistry to renew and rebalance moisture reserves. Enhances elasticity to instantly soften and smoothe skin. Suitable for under make-up. Recommended for: Dry/Partly Dry Skin.

Administration: Twice daily, morning and night.

How Supplied: 4.2 fl. oz. lotion (bottle).

SKIN PRINCIPLE™
Serious Moisture Supplement

Composition: Water, Isostearyl Neopentanoate, Isocetyl Stearate, Hybrid Safflower Oil, Sesame Oil, Sunflower Seed Oil, Butylene Glycol, Sorbitan Stearate, Glyceryl Stearate, PEG-100 Stearate, Squalane, Caprylic Capric Triglyceride, Matricaria Oil, Urea, Collagen, Ceteareth-20, Cetearyl Alcohol, Cetyl Alcohol, Elastin, Ribonucleic Acid, Ascorbic Acid, Tocopherol, Sodium Citrate, Benzophenone-9, Dimethicone, Polyamino Sugar Condensate, Glycine, Potassium and Ammonium PCA, Leucine, Glucose Glutamate, Serine, Proline, Collagen Amino Acids, Tyrosine, Tryptophan, Aspartic Acid, Valine, Alanine, Isoleucine, Xanthan Gum, Sodium Lactate, Ethylparaben, Methylparaben, Propylparaben, Quaternium-15, Imidazolidinyl Urea, BHA, Trisodium EDTA, D&C Green No. 5, D&C Red No. 19, FD&C Yellow No. 5.

Actions: Non-occlusive moisture concentrate. Minimizes dry skin lines to help skin appear younger and fresher looking. Suitable for use under make-up by extra dry skin types. Recommended for: Dry/Partly Dry Skin or a mature complexion.

Administration: Once nightly. Extra-dry skin types may also use in the morning under make-up if desired.

How Supplied: 2 oz. cream (glass jar).

TRIED & TRUE® Hair Thickener

Ingredients: Water, PVP/VA Copolymer, Cetearyl Octanoate, PPG-40 Butyl Ether, Lanolin, Styrene/Acrylate Copolymer, Cetyl Lactate, Sodium Carbomer-941, PEG-8 Disterate, Laureth-23, Htdrolyzed Animal Protein, Propylene Glycol, Allantoin Acetyl Methionine, Sodium Carbomer-934, Fragrance, Methylparaben, Propylparaben, Quaternium-15.

Description: A protein formula body builder designed for fine, limp hair.

Actions: Increases the dimensions of the hair by coating the hair shaft. Adds body, fullness and bounce to hair that's limp and lifeless. Helps make hair look thicker.

Dosage and Administration: Shampoo and towel dry hair before use. Massage a small amount into hair. (Approximately the size of a quarter for shoulder length hair. Vary amount to length of hair.) Comb through <u>thoroughly</u>. Blow dry, comb or set hair as usual.

How Supplied: Tried & True is available in both lotion and cream concentrate form (ideal for men's short hair grooming needs). Lotion is packaged in unbreakable plastic bottles in 4 fl. oz. and 7.75 fl. oz. sizes. Cream concentrated form available in 3 oz. net wt. plastic tube.

Maybelline
3030 JACKSON AVENUE
MEMPHIS, TN 38151

MOISTURE WHIP®
LIP CONDITIONER
Lip Balm with Sunscreen

Active Ingredient: Padimate O
Indications: A hypoallergenic lip balm which moisturizes lips. It will help protect lips from the sun (Sun Protection Factor of 2) and also chapping and drying effects of the wind and cold. Keeps lips feeling soft and moist. It has no taste or color.
Actions: Sunscreen and moisturization.
Dosage and Administration: Use daily and reapply as needed for maximum protection. Can be used under lip color.
How Supplied: .15 oz. tube.

MOISTURE WHIP® LIPSTICK
Lipstick with Sunscreen

Active Ingredient: Padimate O
Indications: A hypoallergenic, moisturizing lipstick in fashionable shades. It will help protect lips from the sun (Sun Protection Factor of 2) and help prevent dryness and chapping. Keeps lips soft and moist.
Actions: Sunscreen and moisturization.
Dosage and Administration: Use daily and reapply as needed for maximum protection.
How Supplied: .12 oz. tube. Comes in 30 shades.

MOISTURE WHIP®
LIQUID MAKE-UP AND
MOISTURE WHIP®
CREAM MAKE-UP
Foundation Make-up with Sunscreen

Active Ingredient: Padimate O
Indications: A hypoallergenic foundation make-up which is moisturizing. Used daily it will help protect skin from the premature aging effects of too much sun (Sun Protection Factor of 2). Feels light and sheer.
Actions: Sunscreen and moisturization.
Dosage and Administration: Use daily.
How Supplied: 1 fl. oz. liquid (bottle) and 1 oz. cream (jar). Both come in eight shades.

MOISTURE WHIP® PROTECTIVE
FACIAL MOISTURIZER
Facial Moisturizer with Sunscreen

Active Ingredient: Padimate O
Indications: A facial moisturizer that does more than just moisturize. Used daily, it will help protect skin from the premature aging effects of too much sun (Sun Protection Factor of 2) and thus help prevent wrinkles from coming along too soon. The product absorbs quickly and is fragrance free. Suitable for use under makeup.
Actions: Sunscreen and moisturization.
Dosage and Administration: Use daily first thing in the morning, the last thing at night.
How Supplied: 4 fl. oz. lotion (bottle) and 2 oz. cream (jar).

Mayrand, Inc.
P.O. BOX 8869
FOUR DUNDAS CIRCLE
GREENSBORO, NC 27419-0869

ENTAB-650
Analgesic

Composition: Each light green enteric coated tablet contains:
Aspirin (10 gr) .... 650 mg.
Action and Use: For the relief of pain and inflammation associated with arthritis and rheumatism. It may also be used for relief of minor aches and pains in other conditions. However, onset of action is slower than other types of aspirin due to the enteric coating which allows the aspirin to pass through the stomach protecting against stomach upset. Therefore, ENTAB-650 is best suited for long term maintenance therapy, i.e. arthritis.
Warning: Do not use if under medical care without your physician's approval. If pain persists for more than 10 days, or redness is present, or in conditions affecting children under 12 years of age, consult a physician immediately. Discontinue use if dizziness, ringing in ears, or impaired hearing occurs.
Keep this and all medicine out of children's reach. In case of accidental overdose, contact a physician or poison control center immediately. Keep bottle well closed and store at controlled room temperature (59°-86°F.)
Usual Dosage: 1 tablet every 4 hours, as necessary. Do not exceed 6 tablets in 24 hours unless directed by a physician.
How Supplied: Light green enteric coated tablets imprinted with letters M/R in bottles of 100, NDC 0259-0347-01.

GLYTUSS TABS
Expectorant Tablets

Composition: Each tablet contains:
Guaifenesin .... 200 mg.
Actions and Use: Guaifenesin is an expectorant that enhances the output of respiratory tract fluid by reducing the viscosity of the fluid. This results in a less dry, more productive cough.
Indications: Glytuss is useful in the treatment of dry, unproductive coughing

associated with the common cold, influenza and bronchitis.
Warning: Persons with high fever, or persistent cough that recurs should consult a physician since one or more of these symptoms may indicate a serious condition. Glytuss should not be taken for persistent coughs associated with smoking, asthma or emphysema, or coughs associated with excessive secretions, except under supervision of a physician.
How Supplied: Bottles of 100 tablets, NDC 0259-0288-01. Tablets are imprinted Mayrand.

NU–IRON 150 Caps
NU–IRON Elixir
(polysaccharide-iron complex)
Iron Supplement

Composition: NU-IRON is a highly water soluble complex of iron and a low molecular weight polysaccharide. Each NU-IRON 150 Capsule contains 150 mg. elemental iron. Each 5 ml. (teaspoonful) of NU-IRON Elixir contains 100 mg. elemental iron, alcohol 10% (Sugar free).
Action and Uses: NU-IRON is a non-ionic, easily assimilated, relatively non-toxic form of iron. Full therapeutic doses may be achieved with virtually no gastrointestinal side effects. There is no metallic aftertaste and no staining of teeth.
Indications: For treatment of uncomplicated iron deficiency anemia.
Contraindications: Hemochromatosis, hemosiderosis or a known hypersensitivity to any of the ingredients.
Usual Dosage: ADULTS; One or two NU-IRON 150 Caps daily, or one to two teaspoonfuls NU-IRON Elixir daily. CHILDREN; 6 to 12 years old; one teaspoonful NU-IRON Elixir daily; 2 to 6 years old: ½ teaspoonful daily; under 2 years: ¼ teaspoonful daily.
How Supplied: NU-IRON 150 Caps in bottles of 100. NU-IRON Elixir in 8 fl. oz. bottles.

McHenry Laboratories, Inc.
118 WELLS-LEE BUILDING
EDNA, TX 77957

ORA 5™

Active Ingredients: Copper Sulfate, Iodine, Potassium Iodide and Alcohol, 1.5%
Indications: Ora 5 is indicated for denture sores, mouth sores, sores and cuts due to eating utensils, corn chips, sore gum tissue after dental work.
Actions: Ora 5 promotes healing, reduces trauma, soreness and inflammation to gingival tissue.
Warnings: Pregnant or lactating women, hyperthyroid conditions or those who are hypersensitive should not use.
Precautions: Ora 5 should not be swallowed. It may stain fabric or fingernails. Color may vary if container is not closed. Contact physician if swallowed.
This product should not be substituted for professional care when there are

Continued on next page

McHenry—Cont.

lumps in the mouth, soreness over a large area, toothache or bleeding. Ora 5 may produce a temporary burning sensation. Keep out of the reach of children.

Directions: For small/local areas: Use Ora 5 soaked with a cotton swab for approximately 1 to 2 minutes. For inaccessible areas: Use a cotton pellet soaked in Ora 5 for same time.

How Supplied: Shipped 10 packages to a carton.

McNeil Consumer Products Company
McNEILAB, INC.
FORT WASHINGTON, PA 19034

COTYLENOL® Cold Formula Tablets and Capsules

Description: Each CoTYLENOL Tablet or Capsule contains acetaminophen 325 mg., chlorpheniramine maleate 2 mg., pseudoephedrine hydrochloride 30 mg. and dextromethorphan hydrobromide 15 mg.

Actions and Indications: CoTYLENOL Cold Formula Tablets and Capsules combine the non-salicylate analgesic-antipyretic acetaminophen with the decongestant pseudoephedrine hydrochloride, the cough suppressant dextromethorphan hydrobromide and the antihistamine chlorpheniramine maleate to help relieve nasal congestion and coughing, as well as fever, aches, pains and general discomfort associated with colds and other upper respiratory infections.

While the acetaminophen component is equal to aspirin in analgesic and antipyretic effectiveness, it is unlikely to produce many of the side effects associated with aspirin and aspirin-containing products.

Usual Dosage: Adults: Two tablets or capsules every six hours, not to exceed 8 tablets or capsules per day. Children (6–12 years): One tablet or capsule every six hours, not to exceed 4 tablets or capsules per day.

Note: Since CoTYLENOL Cold Formula Tablets and Capsules are available without prescription, the following appears on the package label: "WARNING: Do not exceed the recommended dosage or administer to children under 6. Reduce dosage if nervousness, restlessness, or sleeplessness occurs. Persistent cough may indicate a serious condition. Persons with a high fever, rash, or persistent cough or headache or asthma, emphysema or with glaucoma, high blood pressure, heart disease, diabetes, thyroid disease, enlargement of the prostate gland, or who are presently taking a prescription drug for the treatment of high blood pressure or emotional disorders, do not take, except under the advice and supervision of a physician. This preparation may cause drowsiness. Do not drive or operate machinery while taking this medication. If symptoms do not improve within five days, consult a physician be-

fore continuing use. Keep this and all medication out of the reach of children. In case of accidental overdosage, contact a physician immediately."

Overdosage: Acetaminophen in massive overdosage may cause hepatic toxicity in some patients. In all cases of suspected overdose, immediately call your regional poison center or the Rocky Mountain Poison Center's toll-free number (800-525-6115) for assistance in diagnosis and for directions in the use of N-acetylcysteine as an antidote. Adverse effects are rare when acetaminophen is used as recommended. However, as with all drugs, overdosage may cause serious toxicity.

How Supplied: Tablets (colored yellow, imprinted "CoTYLENOL")—blister packs of 24's and bottles of 50 and 100. Capsules (colored dark green and light yellow, imprinted "CoTYLENOL")—blister packs of 20 and bottles of 40.

[*Shown in Product Identification Section*]

CoTYLENOL® Liquid Cold Formula

Description: Each 30 ml (1 fl. oz.) contains acetaminophen 650 mg, chlorpheniramine maleate 4 mg, pseudoephedrine hydrochloride 60 mg, and dextromethorphan hydrobromide 30 mg (alcohol 7.5%).

Actions and Indications: CoTYLENOL Liquid Cold Formula combines the nonsalicylate analgesic-antipyretic acetaminophen with the decongestant pseudoephedrine hydrochloride, the cough suppressant dextromethorphan hydrobromide and the antihistamine chlorpheniramine maleate to help relieve nasal congestion and coughing, as well as the fever, aches, pains and general discomfort associated with colds and other upper respiratory infections. While the acetaminophen component is equal to aspirin in analgesic and antipyretic effectiveness, it is unlikely to produce many of the side effects associated with aspirin and aspirin-containing products.

Usual Dosage: Measuring cup is provided and marked for accurate dosing. Adults: 1 fluid ounce (2 tbsps.) every 6 hours as needed, not to exceed 4 doses in 24 hours. Children (6-12 yrs.): ½ the adult dose (1 tbsp.) every 6 hours as indicated on the measuring cup provided, not to exceed 4 doses in 24 hours.

Note: Since CoTylenol Liquid Cold Formula is available without a prescription, the following appears on the package label: "WARNING: Do not exceed the recommended dosage or administer to children under 6. Reduce dosage if nervousness, restlessness or sleeplessness occurs. Persistent cough may indicate a serious condition. Persons with a high fever, rash or persistent cough or headache or asthma, emphysema or with glaucoma, high blood pressure, heart disease, diabetes, thyroid disease, enlargement of the prostate gland, or who are presently taking a prescription drug for the treatment of high blood pressure or emotional disorders, do not take, except under the advice and supervision of a physician. This preparation may cause

drowsiness. Do not drive or operate machinery while taking this medication. If symptoms do not improve within five days, consult a physician before continuing use. Keep this and all medication out of the reach of children. In case of accidental overdosage, contact a physician immediately."

Overdosage: Acetaminophen in massive overdosage may cause hepatic toxicity in some patients. In all cases of suspected overdose, immediately call your regional poison center or the Rocky Mountain Poison Center's toll-free number (800-525-6115) for assistance in diagnosis and for directions in the use of N-acetylcysteine as an antidote. Adverse effects are rare when acetaminophen is used as recommended. However, as with all drugs, overdosage may cause serious toxicity.

How Supplied: Cherry/mint flavored mentholated (colored amber) bottles of 5 and 10 oz. with child-resistant safety cap and special dosage cup graded in ounces and tablespoons.

[*Shown in Product Identification Section*]

Children's CoTYLENOL®
Liquid Cold Formula

Description: Children's CoTYLENOL Liquid Cold Formula is stable, cherry-flavored, red in color and contains 8.5% alcohol. Each teaspoon (5 ml.) contains acetaminophen 160 mg., chlorpheniramine maleate 1 mg., and phenylpropanolamine hydrochloride 6.25 mg.

Actions and Indications: Children's CoTYLENOL Liquid Cold Formula combines the nonsalicylate analgesic-antipyretic acetaminophen with the decongestant phenylpropanolamine hydrochloride and the antihistamine chlorpheniramine maleate to help relieve nasal congestion, dry runny noses and prevent sneezing as well as to relieve the fever, aches, pains and general discomfort due to colds and "flu".

While the acetaminophen component is equal to aspirin in analgesic and antipyretic effectiveness, it is unlikely to produce the following side effects often associated with aspirin or aspirin-containing products: allergic reactions, even in aspirin-sensitive children or those with a history of allergy in general; "therapeutic toxicity" in feverish children, since electrolyte imbalance and acid-base changes are not likely to occur; gastric irritation even in children with an already upset stomach.

Dosage: Measuring cup is provided and marked for accurate dosing. 2–3 years—1 teaspoonful; 4–5 years—1½ teaspoonfuls; 6–8 years—2 teaspoonfuls; 9–10 years—2½ teaspoonfuls; 11 years—3 teaspoonfuls, every 4 hours, as needed, not to exceed 4 doses in 24 hours.

Note: Since Children's CoTYLENOL Cold Formula is available without prescription, the following information appears on the package label: "WARNING: Do not exceed the recommended dosage. Reduce dosage if nervousness, restlessness or sleeplessness occurs. Do not use if glaucoma, high blood pressure, heart disease, diabetes, or thyroid disease is present. This preparation may cause drowsiness. This medication may cause excitability in children. If presently taking a prescription drug for the treatment of high blood pressure or emotional disorders, or if you have asthma, do not use except under advice and supervision of a physician. Do not drive or operate machinery while taking this medication. If symptoms do not improve within seven days, or are accompanied by high fever or persistent cough, consult a physician before continuing use. KEEP THIS AND ALL MEDICATION OUT OF THE REACH OF CHILDREN. IN CASE OF ACCIDENTAL OVERDOSE, CONTACT A PHYSICIAN IMMEDIATELY.

Overdosage: Acetaminophen in massive overdosage may cause hepatic toxicity in some patients. In all cases of suspected overdose, immediately call your regional poison center or the Rocky Mountain Poison Center's toll-free number (800-525-6115) for assistance in diagnosis and for directions in the use of N-acetylcysteine as an antidote. Adverse effects are rare when acetaminophen is used as recommended. However, as with all drugs, overdosage may cause serious toxicity.

How Supplied: Bottle of 4 fl. oz. with child-resistant safety cap.

[Shown in Product Identification Section]

SINE-AID®
Sinus Headache Tablets

Description: Each SINE-AID Tablet contains acetaminophen 325 mg. and phenylpropanolamine hydrochloride 25 mg.

Actions: Acetaminophen is a clinically proven analgesic-antipyretic. Acetaminophen produces analgesia by elevation of the pain threshold and antipyresis through action on the hypothalamic heat-regulating center. Phenylpropanolamine hydrochloride is a sympathomimetic amine and provides vasoconstriction to the nasopharyngeal mucosa. Although similar in action to ephedrine, phenylpropanolamine HCl is less likely to cause CNS stimulation.

Indications: SINE-AID provides effective symptomatic relief from sinus headache pain and pressure caused by sinusitis. Since it contains no antihistamine, SINE-AID will not produce the drowsiness that may interfere with work, driving an automobile or operating dangerous machinery. SINE-AID is particularly well-suited in patients with aspirin allergy, hemostatic disturbances (including anticoagulant therapy), and bleeding diatheses (e.g. ulcer, gastritis, hiatus hernia).

Precautions and Adverse Reactions: Acetaminophen has rarely been found to produce any side effects. It is usually well-tolerated by aspirin-sensitive patients. If a rare sensitivity reaction occurs, the drug should be stopped. In patients with high blood pressure, diabetes, or thyroid disease, phenylpropanolamine hydrochloride should be used with caution and only as directed by a physician. Do not use in patients receiving MAO inhibitors.

Usual Dosage: Adult dosage: Two tablets every four hours, no more than 6 tablets in any 24-hour period.

Note: Since SINE-AID tablets are available without a prescription, the following appears on the package labels: "CAUTION: Individuals with high blood pressure, heart disease, diabetes, thyroid disease, and children under 12 should use only as directed by a physician. Do not exceed recommended dosage unless directed by a physician. WARNING: If symptoms of sinusitis or colds persist after 3 days, consult a physician. Keep this and all medications out of the reach of children. In case of accidental overdose, contact a physician immediately."

Overdosage: Acetaminophen in massive overdosage may cause hepatic toxicity in some patients. In all cases of suspected overdose, immediately call your regional poison center or the Rocky Mountain Poison Center's toll-free number (800-525-6115) for assistance in diagnosis and for directions in the use of N-acetylcysteine as an antidote. Adverse effects are rare when acetaminophen is used as recommended. However, as with all drugs, overdosage may cause serious toxicity.

How Supplied: Tablets (colored white, imprinted "SINE-AID")—bottles of 24, 50 and 100.

[Shown in Product Identification Section]

Children's TYLENOL®
acetaminophen
Chewable Tablets, Elixir, Drops

Description: Each Children's TYLENOL Chewable Tablet contains 80 mg. acetaminophen in a fruit flavored tablet. Children's TYLENOL acetaminophen Elixir is stable, cherry flavored, red in color and contains 7% alcohol. Infants' TYLENOL Drops are stable, fruit flavored, orange in color and contain 7% alcohol. Children's TYLENOL Elixir: Each 5 ml. contains 160 mg. acetaminophen.
Infant's TYLENOL Drops: Each 0.8 ml. (one calibrated dropperful) contains 80 mg. acetaminophen.

Actions: TYLENOL acetaminophen is an antipyretic and analgesic clinically proven in pediatric use. TYLENOL acetaminophen produces antipyresis through action on the hypothalamic heat-regulating center and analgesia by elevation of the pain threshold.

Indications: Children's TYLENOL Chewable Tablets, Elixir and Drops are designed for treatment of infants and children with conditions requiring reduction of fever or relief of pain—such as mild upper respiratory infections (tonsillitis, common cold, "grippe"), headache, myalgia, post-immunization reactions, post-tonsillectomy discomfort and gastroenteritis. In conjunction with antibiotics or sulfonamides, TYLENOL acetaminophen is useful as an analgesic and antipyretic in many bacterial or viral infections, such as bronchitis, pharyngitis, tracheobronchitis, sinusitis, pneumonia, otitis media, and cervical adenitis.

Precautions and Adverse Reactions: If a rare sensitivity reaction occurs, the drug should be stopped. TYLENOL acetam-

inophen has rarely been found to produce any side effects. It is usually well tolerated by aspirin-sensitive patients.

Usual Dosage: Doses may be repeated 4 or 5 times daily, but not to exceed 5 doses in 24 hours. Children's TYLENOL Chewable Tablets: 1–2 years: one and one half tablets. 2–3 years: two tablets. 4–5 years: three tablets. 6–8 years: four tablets. 9–10 years: five tablets. 11–12 years: six tablets.
Children's TYLENOL Elixir: (special cup for measuring dosage is provided) 4–11 months: one-half teaspoon. 2–23 months: three-quarters teaspoon, 2–3 years: one teaspoon. 4–5 years: one and one-half teaspoons. 6–8 years: 2 teaspoons. 9–10 years: two and one-half teaspoons. 11–12 years: three teaspoons.
Infants' TYLENOL Drops: 0–3 months: 0.4 ml. 4–11 months: 0.8 ml. 12–23 months: 1.2 ml. 2–3 years: 1.6 ml. 4–5 years: 2.4 ml.

Note: Since Children's TYLENOL acetaminophen Chewable Tablets, Elixir and Drops are available without prescription as an analgesic, the following appears on the package labels: "WARNING: Consult your physician if fever persists for more than three days or if pain continues for more than five days. Keep this and all medication out of the reach of children. In cases of accidental overdosage, contact a physician immediately."

Overdosage: Acetaminophen in massive overdosage may cause hepatic toxicity in some patients. In all cases of suspected overdose, immediately call your regional poison center or the Rocky Mountain Poison Center's toll-free number (800-525-6115) for assistance in diagnosis and for directions in the use of N-acetylcysteine as an antidote. Adverse effects are rare when acetaminophen is used as recommended. However, as with all drugs, overdosage may cause serious toxicity.

How Supplied: Chewable Tablets (colored pink, scored, imprinted "TYLENOL")—Bottles of 30. Elixir (colored red)—bottles of 2 and 4 fl. oz. Drops (colored orange)—bottles of ½ oz. (15 ml.) with calibrated plastic dropper.
All packages listed above have child-resistant safety caps.

[Shown in Product Identification Section]

Regular Strength
TYLENOL® acetaminophen
Tablets and Capsules

Description: Each Regular Strength TYLENOL Tablet or Capsule contains acetaminophen 325 mg.

Actions: TYLENOL acetaminophen is a clinically proven analgesic and antipyretic. TYLENOL acetaminophen produces analgesia by elevation of the pain threshold and antipyresis through action on the hypothalamic heat-regulating center.

Indications: TYLENOL acetaminophen provides effective analgesia in a wide variety of arthritic and rheumatic conditions involving musculoskeletal pain, as well as in other painful disorders such as headache, dysmenorrhea, myalgias and

Continued on next page

McNeil Consumer—Cont.

neuralgias. In addition, TYLENOL acetaminophen is indicated as an analgesic and antipyretic in diseases accompanied by discomfort and fever, such as the common cold and other viral infections. TYLENOL acetaminophen is particularly well-suited as an analgesic-antipyretic in the presence of aspirin allergy, hemostatic disturbances (including anticoagulant therapy), and bleeding diatheses (e.g. hemophilia) and upper gastrointestinal disorders (e.g., ulcer, gastritis, hiatus hernia).

Precautions and Adverse Reactions: If a rare sensitivity reaction occurs, the drug should be stopped. TYLENOL acetaminophen has rarely been found to produce any side effects. It is usually well-tolerated by aspirin-sensitive patients.

Usual Dosage: *Adults:* One to two tablets or capsules every 4–6 hours. Not to exceed 12 tablets or capsules per day. *Children* (6 to 12): One-half to one tablet 3 or 4 times daily. (TYLENOL acetaminophen Chewable Tablets, Elixir and Drops are available for greater convenience in younger patients.)

Note: Since TYLENOL acetaminophen tablets and capsules are available without prescription as an analgesic, the following appears on the package labels: "Consult a physician for use by children under 6 or for use longer than 10 days. WARNING: Keep this and all medication out of the reach of children. In case of accidental overdosage, contact a physician immediately." In connection with its use for temporary relief of minor aches and pains of arthritis and rheumatism: "Caution: If pain persists for more than 10 days, or redness is present, or in arthritic or rheumatic conditions affecting children under 12 years, consult a physician immediately."

Overdosage: Acetaminophen in massive overdosage may cause hepatic toxicity in some patients. In all cases of suspected overdose, immediately call your regional poison center or the Rocky Mountain Poison Center's toll-free number (800-525-6115) for assistance in diagnosis and for directions in the use of N-acetylcysteine as an antidote. Adverse effects are rare when acetaminophen is used as recommended. However, as with all drugs, overdosage may cause serious toxicity.

How Supplied: Tablets (colored white, scored, imprinted "TYLENOL")—tins and vials of 12 and bottles of 24, 50, 100 and 200. Capsules (colored gray and white, imprinted "TYLENOL 325 mg")—bottles of 24, 50 and 100.

Also available: For additional pain relief, Extra-Strength TYLENOL® Capsules and Tablets, 500 mg. and Extra-Strength TYLENOL® Adult Liquid Pain Reliever (colored green; 1 fl. oz. = 1000 mg.).

[*Shown in Product Identification Section*]

Extra-Strength TYLENOL® acetaminophen Tablets and Capsules

Description: Each Extra-Strength TYLENOL Tablet or Capsule contains acetaminophen 500 mg.

Actions: TYLENOL acetaminophen is a clinically proven analgesic and antipyretic. Acetaminophen produces analgesia by elevation of the pain threshold and antipyresis through action on the hypothalamic heat-regulating center.

Indications: For relief of pain and fever. Extra-Strength TYLENOL Tablets and Capsules provide increased analgesic strength for minor conditions when the usual doses of mild analgesics are insufficient.

Precautions and Adverse Reactions: If a rare sensitivity reaction occurs, the drug should be stopped. TYLENOL acetaminophen has rarely been found to produce any side effects. It is usually well-tolerated by aspirin-sensitive patients.

Usual Dosage: Adults: Two tablets or capsules 3 or 4 times daily. No more than a total of eight tablets or capsules in any 24-hour period.

Note: Since Extra-Strength TYLENOL Tablets and Capsules are available without a prescription, the following appears on the package labels: "Severe or recurrent pain or high or continued fever may be indicative of serious illness. Under these conditions, consult a physician. WARNING: Keep this and all medication out of the reach of children. In case of accidental overdosage, contact a physician immediately."

Overdosage: Acetaminophen in massive overdosage may cause hepatic toxicity in some patients. In all cases of suspected overdose, immediately call your regional poison center or the Rocky Mountain Poison Center's toll-free number (800-525-6115) for assistance in diagnosis and for directions in the use of N-acetylcysteine as an antidote. Adverse effects are rare when acetaminophen is used as recommended. However, as with all drugs, overdosage may cause serious toxicity.

How Supplied: Tablets (colored white, imprinted "TYLENOL" and "500")—vials of 10 and bottles of 30, 60 and 100; Capsules (colored red and white, imprinted "TYLENOL 500 mg.")—bottles of 24, 50 and 100.

Also Available: For adults who prefer liquids or can't swallow solid medication, Extra-Strength TYLENOL® Adult Liquid Pain Reliever (1 fl. oz. = 1000 mg.).

[*Shown in Product Identification Section*]

Extra-Strength TYLENOL® acetaminophen Adult Liquid Pain Reliever

Description: Each 15 ml. (½ fl. oz. or one tablespoonful) contains 500 mg. acetaminophen (alcohol 8½%).

Actions: TYLENOL acetaminophen is a clinically proven analgesic and antipyretic. Acetaminophen produces analgesia by elevation of the pain threshold and antipyresis through action on the hypothalamic heat-regulating center.

Indications: TYLENOL acetaminophen provides fast, effective relief of pain and/or fever for adults who prefer liquids or can't swallow solid medication, e.g., the aged, patients with easily triggered gag reflexes, extremely sore throats, or those on liquid diets.

Precautions and Adverse Reactions: If a rare sensitivity reaction occurs, the drug should be stopped. TYLENOL acetaminophen has rarely been found to produce any side effects. It is usually well-tolerated by aspirin-sensitive patients.

Usual Dosage: Extra-Strength TYLENOL Adult Liquid is an adult preparation. Not for use in children under 12. Measuring cup is marked for accurate dosage.

Extra-Strength Dose—1 fl. oz. (30 ml or 2 tablespoonful, 1000 mg) which is equivalent to two 500 mg Extra-Strength TYLENOL Tablets or Capsules. Take every 4 to 6 hours, no more than 4 doses in any 24 hour period.

Note: Since Extra-Strength TYLENOL Adult Liquid Pain Reliever is available without a prescription, the following appears on the package labels: "Severe or recurrent pain or high or continued fever may be indicative of serious illness. Under these conditions, consult a physician. WARNING: Keep this and all medication out of the reach of children. In case of accidental overdosage, contact a physician immediately."

Overdosage: Acetaminophen in massive overdosage may cause hepatic toxicity in some patients. In all cases of suspected overdose, immediately call your regional poison center or the Rocky Mountain Poison Center's toll-free number (800-525-6115) for assistance in diagnosis and for directions in the use of N-acetylcysteine as an antidote. Adverse effects are rare when acetaminophen is used as recommended. However, as with all drugs, overdosage may cause serious toxicity.

How Supplied: Mint-flavored liquid (colored green), 8 fl. oz. bottle, with child resistent safety cap and special dosage cup.

[*Shown in Product Identification Section*]

Mead Johnson Nutritional Division
Mead Johnson & Company
2404 W. PENNSYLVANIA ST.
EVANSVILLE, IN 47721

CASEC® powder
Calcium caseinate

Composition: Consists of dried, soluble calcium caseinate (88% protein) derived from skim milk curd and lime water (calcium carbonate) by a special process. Contains only 42.6 mg sodium per 6 packed level tbsp (1 ounce).

Action and Uses: Supplementing infant formulas or breast feeding when extra protein is desired. Supplementing diets of children and adults, including sodium restricted diets and diets low in fat or cholesterol.

Precautions: Additional water should be given as needed to meet the infant's daily water requirement.

Preparation: Use 2 packed level tbsp powder to 6 fl oz water. Feed from dropper, spoon or nursing bottle. For protein supplementation—give as needed. Each ounce of mixture provides about 1.3 g protein.

How Supplied: Casec® powder
NDC 0087-0390-02   Cans of 3⅓ oz (94.5 g)

CE-VI-SOL®
Vitamin C supplement drops
For Infants

Composition: Each 0.6 ml supplies 35 mg ascorbic acid.

Action and Uses: Dietary supplement of vitamin C for infants.

Administration and Dosage: 0.6 ml (35 mg) or as indicated. Dropper calibrated for doses of 0.6 and 0.3 ml (35 and 17.5 mg ascorbic acid).

How Supplied: Ce-Vi-Sol® drops (with calibrated dropper)
NDC 0087-0400-01 Bottles of 1⅔ fl oz (50 ml)

CRITICARE™ HN
Ready-To-Use High Nitrogen
Elemental Diet

Composition: Water, maltodextrin, enzymatically hydrolyzed casein, modified corn starch, safflower oil, potassium citrate, calcium gluconate, calcium glycerophosphate, magnesium chloride, choline bitartrate, L-methionine, carrageenan, L-tyrosine, diacetyl tartaric acid esters of mono- and diglycerides, magnesium oxide, L-tryptophan, vitamins (vitamin A palmitate, cholecalciferol, dl-alpha-tocopheryl acetate, sodium ascorbate, folic acid, thiamine hydrochloride, riboflavin, niacinamide, pyridoxine hydrochloride, cyanocobalamin, biotin, calcium pantothenate and phytonadione) and minerals (potassium iodide, ferrous gluconate, copper gluconate, zinc gluconate and manganese gluconate).

Criticare HN provides approximately 70% free amino acids and 30% small peptides found to be more efficiently utilized than free amino acids alone. Criticare HN provides 72 g protein/2000 Calories and the following nutrients:

Proximate analysis (g/100 ml)

Protein equivalent (N x 6.25)	3.8
Fat	0.3
Carbohydrate	22.2
Ash	0.7
Water	83.1

[See table above].

Actions and Uses: Criticare HN is the first complete, high nitrogen, elemental nutrition in a commercially sterile, ready-to-use liquid form for patients with impaired digestion and absorption. It is intended for use with inflammatory bowel disease, chronic pancreatitis, G.I. fistulas, short gut syndrome, radiation/chemotherapeutic enteropathy, cystic fibrosis, non-specific malabsorption/maldigestion states, and transitions from TPN to enteral nutrition. Criticare HN

	Per 8 fl oz	% U.S. RDA Adults & Children 4 or More Years of Age	Per 2000 Cal (64 fl oz)	% U.S. RDA Adults & Children 4 or More Years of Age
Calories	250	*	2000	*
Protein equivalent, g	9	20	72	160
Fat, g	0.8	*	6	*
Carbohydrate, g	52.5	*	420	*
Vitamin A, IU	625	12.5	5000	100
Vitamin D, IU	50	12.5	400	100
Vitamin E, IU	9.4	31	75	250
Vitamin C (Ascorbic acid), mg	37.5	63	300	500
Folic acid (Folacin), mg	0.05	12.5	0.4	100
Thiamine (Vitamin B$_1$), mg	0.48	31	3.8	250
Riboflavin (Vitamin B$_2$), mg	0.54	31	4.3	250
Niacin, mg	6.25	31	50	250
Vitamin B$_6$, mg	0.63	31	5	250
Vitamin B$_{12}$, mcg	1.9	31	15	250
Biotin, mg	37.5	12.5	300	100
Pantothenic acid, mg	3.1	31	25	250
Vitamin K, mcg	31	*	250	*
Choline, mg	62.5	*	500	*
Calcium, mg	125	12.5	1000	100
Phosphorus, mg	125	12.5	1000	100
Iodine, mcg	19	12.5	150	100
Iron, mg	2.25	12.5	18	100
Magnesium, mg	50	12.5	400	100
Copper, mg	0.25	12.5	2	100
Zinc, mg	2.5	17	20	133
Manganese, mg	0.63	*	5	*
Chloride, mg	250	*	2000	*
Potassium, mg	313	*	2500	*
Sodium, mg	150	*	1200	*

*U.S. Recommended Daily Allowance (U.S. RDA) not established.

provides easily digested nutrients providing these important characteristics:

Commercially sterilized liquid free from pathogens and any micro-organism capable of reproducing under normal, non-refrigerated conditions of storage and distribution.

Easy to digest and absorb proteins consisting of amino acids and small peptides.

Appropriate vitamin and mineral levels for the nutritionally stressed patient.

CRITICARE HN contains at least 100% of the U.S. RDA's for all vitamins and minerals in 2000 Calories with extra amounts of vitamin C and B-complex vitamins to meet the increased requirements for these vitamins in the critically ill patient.

High quality fat from safflower oil meets essential fatty acid requirements, yet is low enough for efficient digestion and absorption.

Lactose-free formulation and a moderate osmolality (650 mOsm/kg H$_2$O) to assure rapid patient adaptation and good patient tolerance.

Preparation: It is recommended that Criticare HN be tube fed and that tube feeding be initiated as follows:

Day 1—1:1 dilution of Criticare HN with water at 50 ml/hour (or full strength at 25 ml/hr).

Day 2—full strength at 50 ml/hour.

Day 3—full strength up to 100–125 ml/hour.

Administration via infusion pump or continuous gravity drip is recommended.

Unused Criticare HN should be covered, kept refrigerated and used within 48 hours of opening.

If used with an oral feeding, it is advisable to counsel patients that the flavor of Criticare HN differs significantly from other liquid diets because of the special characteristics of the protein.

Tube Feeding Precaution: Additional water should be given as needed to meet the patient's requirements. Particular attention should be given to water supply for comatose and unconscious patients and others who cannot express the usual sensation of thirst.

Additional water is important also when renal concentrating ability is impaired, when there is extensive breakdown of tissue protein, or when water requirements are high, as in fever, burns or under dry atmospheric conditions.

Criticare HN provides 831 ml of water per 1000 ml of formula.

How Supplied: Criticare™ HN liquid
NDC 0087-0563-41 Bottles of 8 fl oz

ENFAMIL® concentrated liquid •
powder
Infant formula

Composition: Infant formula nearly identical to mother's milk. Caloric distribution: 9% from protein, 50% from fat, 41% from carbohydrate.

Each quart of ENFAMIL formula (normal dilution, 20 kcal/fl oz) supplies 640

Continued on next page

Mead Johnson Nutritional—Cont.

kilocalories, 14.2 g protein, 35 g fat, 66.2 g carbohydrate and the following vitamins and minerals.

Vitamin A, IU	1600
Vitamin D, IU	400
Vitamin E, IU	12
Vitamin C (Ascorbic acid), mg	52
Folic acid (Folacin), mg	0.1
Thiamine (Vitamin B₁), mg	0.5
Riboflavin (Vitamin B₂), mg	0.6
Niacin, mg	8
Vitamin B₆, mg	0.4
Vitamin B₁₂, mcg	2
Pantothenic acid, mg	3
Choline, mg	45
Calcium, mg	500
Phosphorus, mg	420*
Iodine, mcg	65
Iron, mg	1.4

(Supply 5 mg iron per quart from other sources)

Magnesium, mg	45
Copper, mg	0.6
Zinc, mg	4
Manganese, mg	1
Chloride, mg	450
Potassium, mg	640
Sodium, mg	220

*Enfamil powder contains 400 mg phosphorus

NOTE: FER-IN-SOL® iron supplement drops are a convenient source of added iron.

Action and Uses: For feeding of full term and premature infants and a supplementary formula for breast-fed babies. "When breast-feeding is unsuccessful, inappropriate or stopped early, infant formulas provide the best alternative for meeting nutritional needs during the first year."[1]

Preparation: For 20 kcal/fl oz: With concentrated liquid—1 part to 1 part water. With powder—1 level scoop to each 2 fl oz water; or 1 level cup to water sufficient to make a quart of formula.

Precautions: Prepared formula not fed immediately and opened cans of liquid should be stored in the refrigerator and used within 48 hours.

How Supplied: Powder, 16-oz (1-lb) cans with measuring scoop. Concentrated liquid, 40 kcal/fl oz 13-fl oz cans.

Also available, Enfamil concentrated liquid or powder with iron; 12 mg iron per quart of 20 kcal/fl oz Concentrated liquid, 13-fl oz cans. Powder, 16-oz (1-lb) cans with scoop.

[1]AAP Committee On Nutrition: Commentary on Breast-Feeding and Infant Formulas, Including Proposed Standards for Formulas. Pediatrics 57:279, 1976.

ENFAMIL® with Iron concentrated liquid ●powder Infant formula

Composition: Infant formula nearly identical to mother's milk, with added iron (12 mg/qt). Caloric distribution: 9% from protein, 50% from fat, 41% from carbohydrate. Except for the higher iron content, the normal dilution (20 kcal/fl oz) has the same vitamin and mineral content as Enfamil (see Enfamil).

Action and Uses: For feeding of full term and premature infants to supply a daily intake of iron with the formula. Feeding of infants with special needs for exogenous iron, such as: premature infants, offspring of anemic mothers, infants of multiple births, infants with low birth weights and those who grow rapidly, infants who have minor losses of blood at birth or in surgery. As a supplementary formula for breast-fed infants. "When breast-feeding is unsuccessful, inappropriate or stopped early, infant formulas provide the best alternative for meeting nutritional needs during the first year."[1] For older infants the formula provides an easily digestible "beverage milk" plus a supplement of iron. One quart (32 fl oz) of formula supplies 12 mg of iron.

Preparation: For 20 kcal/fl oz: With concentrated liquid—1 part to 1 part water. With powder—1 level scoop to each 2 fl oz water; or 1 level cup to water sufficient to make a quart of formula.

Precautions: If therapeutic or larger supplementary amounts of iron are indicated, the iron content of the formula should be taken into account (12 mg iron per qt) in calculating the total iron dosage. Prepared Enfamil with Iron formula not fed immediately and opened cans of Enfamil with Iron liquid should be stored in the refrigerator and used within 48 hours.

How Supplied: Liquid—13-fl oz cans. Powder—16-oz (1-lb) cans.

[1]AAP Committee on Nutrition: Commentary on Breast-Feeding and Infant Formulas, Including Proposed Standards for Formulas. Pediatrics 57:279, 1976.

ENFAMIL NURSETTE® Infant formula

Composition: Glass formula bottle filled with ready-to-feed Enfamil® (infant formula) 20 kcal/fl oz) (See Enfamil concentrated liquid and powder for nutrient values.)

Action and Uses: A very convenient form of Enfamil for routine formula feeding at home or away. Especially useful for first weeks at home, infants of working mothers, infant travel, emergency feedings, or as a supplementary formula for breast-fed babies. "When breast-feeding is unsuccessful, inappropriate or stopped early, infant formulas provide the best alternative for meeting nutritional needs during the first year."[1]

Preparation: Remove cap, attach any standard sterilized nipple unit and feed baby. The Nursette bottle needs no refrigeration until opened and can be fed at room temperature. Interchangeable with Enfamil Ready-To-Use liquid in cans and formulas in normal dilution (20 kcal/fl oz) prepared from Enfamil concentrated liquid or powder.

Note: Contents remaining in bottle after feeding should be discarded. Nipples and collar rings should be washed, rinsed and sterilized before reuse.

How Supplied: Available in convenient 4 fl oz, 6 fl oz, and 8 fl oz Nursette® bottles, packed four bottles to a sealed carton, six 4-packs per case.

Enfamil Nursette with Iron also available in 6-fl oz bottles.

[1]AAP Committee On Nutrition: Commentary on Breast-Feeding and Infant Formulas, Including Proposed Standards for Formulas. Pediatrics 57:279, 1976.

ENFAMIL® ready-to-use Infant formula

Composition: Filled cans of ready-to-feed Enfamil infant formula 20 kcal/fl oz (see Enfamil concentrated liquid and powder for nutrient values.)

Action and Uses: A very convenient form of Enfamil for routine formula feeding at home. Especially useful for feeding of infants during first weeks at home, infants of working mothers, infant travel, emergency feedings, as a supplementary formula for breast-fed babies. "When breast-feeding is unsuccessful, inappropriate or stopped early, infant formulas provide the best alternative for meeting nutritional needs during the first year."[1]

Preparation: Pour liquid into sterilized nursing bottle without diluting. No refrigeration is necessary for the unopened cans. The formula need not be heated before feeding baby. Interchangeable with formulas in normal dilution (20 kcal/fl oz) prepared from Enfamil concentrated liquid or powder and Enfamil Nursette® in filled formula bottles.

Precautions: Opened cans of Enfamil Ready-To-Use formula should be stored in refrigerator and used within 48 hours.

How Supplied: 8-fl oz cans, in an easy to carry handy six-can pack, 4 packs per case, and 32-fl oz (1-qt.) cans, six cans per case.

[1]AAP Committee on Nutrition: Commentary on Breast-Feeding and Infant Formulas, Including Proposed Standards for Formulas. Pediatrics 57:279, 1976.

ENFAMIL® with Iron ready-to-use Infant formula

Composition: Filled cans of ready-to-feed Enfamil with Iron infant formula 20 kcal/fl oz (see Enfamil with Iron concentrated liquid & powder for nutrient values.)

Action and Uses: A very convenient form of Enfamil with Iron for routine formula feeding at home or away, especially useful for routine feeding of infants during first weeks at home, infants of working mothers, infant travel, emergency feedings, as a supplementary formula for breast-fed babies. "When breast-feeding is unsuccessful, inappropriate or stopped early, infant formulas provide the best alternative for meeting nutritional needs during the first year."[1]

Preparation: Pour desired amount of liquid into sterilized nursing bottle without diluting. No refrigeration is necessary for unopened cans. The formula need not be heated before feeding baby. Interchangeable with formulas in nor-

	Per 250 Cal (8 fl oz)	Adults & Children 4 or more yrs. % U.S. RDA	Per 375 Cal (12 fl oz)	Adults & Children 4 or more yrs. % U.S. RDA	Per 2000 Cal (64 fl oz)	Adults & Children 4 or more yrs. % U.S. RDA
Calories	250	*	375	*	2000	*
Protein, g	8.1	12	12.1	19	65	100
Fat, g	10.5	*	15.7	*	84	*
Carbohydrate, g	31.2	*	46.9	*	250	*
Vitamin A, IU	625	12	937	19	5000	100
Vitamin D, IU	50	12	75	19	400	100
Vitamin E, IU	9.4	32	14	47	75	250
Vitamin C (Ascorbic acid), mg	37.5	62	56	94	300	500
Folic acid (Folacin), mcg	50	12	75	19	400	100
Thiamine (Vitamin B$_1$), mg	0.48	32	0.72	47	3.8	250
Riboflavin (Vitamin B$_2$), mg	0.54	32	0.81	47	4.3	250
Niacin, mg	6.2	32	9.4	47	50	250
Vitamin B$_6$, mg	0.62	32	0.93	47	5	250
Vitamin B$_{12}$, mcg	1.9	32	2.8	47	15	250
Biotin, mcg	40	12	60	19	300	100
Pantothenic acid, mg	3.1	32	4.7	47	25	250
Vitamin K$_1$, mcg	31	*	47	*	250	*
Choline, mg	62.5	*	93.7	*	500	*
Calcium, mg	150	15	225	22	1200	120
Phosphorus, mg	125	12	188	19	1000	100
Iodine, mcg	19	12	28	19	150	100
Iron, mg	2.25	12	3.4	19	18	100
Magnesium, mg	50	12	75	19	400	100
Copper, mg	0.25	12	0.37	19	2	100
Zinc, mg	2.5	17	3.7	25	20	133
Manganese, mg	0.6	*	0.9	*	5	*
Chloride, mg	250	*	375	*	2000	*
Potassium, mg	312	*	468	*	2500	*
Sodium, mg	125	*	187	*	1000	*

*U.S. Recommended Daily Allowance (U.S. RDA) has not been established.

mal dilution (20 kcal/fl oz) prepared from Enfamil with Iron concentrated liquid or powder. One quart (32 fl oz) of Enfamil with Iron Ready-To-Use infant formula supplies 12 mg of iron.

Precautions: If therapeutic or larger supplementary amounts of iron are indicated, the iron content of the formula should be taken into account (12 mg per qt) in calculating the total iron dosage. Opened cans of Enfamil with Iron Ready-To-Use formula should be stored in the refrigerator and used within 48 hours.

How Supplied: 8-fl oz cans, in an easy to carry handy six-can pack, 4 packs per case, and 32-fl oz (1-qt) cans, six cans per case.

[1]AAP Committee On Nutrition: Commentary on Breast-Feeding and Infant Formulas, Including Proposed Standards for Formulas. Pediatrics 57:279, 1976.

FEMININS® tablets
Multivitamin-mineral supplement for women taking oral contraceptives

Composition: Each tablet supplies:

	% U.S. RDA* Adults	
Vitamin A, IU	5000	100
Vitamin D, IU	400	100
Vitamin E, IU	10	33
Vitamin C (Ascorbic acid), mg	200	333
Folic acid (Folacin), mg	0.1	25
Thiamine (Vitamin B$_1$), mg	1.5	100
Riboflavin (Vitamin B$_2$), mg	3	176
Niacin, mg	15	75
Vitamin B$_6$, mg	25	1250
Vitamin B$_{12}$, mcg	10	167
Pantothenic acid, mg	10	100
Iron, mg	18	100
Zinc, mg	10	67

*U.S. Recommended Daily Allowance

Ingredients: Vitamin A acetate, ergocalciferol, dl-alpha-tocopheryl acetate, sodium ascorbate, folic acid, thiamine mononitrate, riboflavin, niacinamide, pyridoxine hydrochloride, cyanocobalamin, calcium pantothenate, ferrous fumarate, zinc oxide, and artificial coloring.

Action and Uses: Daily diet supplementation during use of oral contraceptives. Feminins tablets provide vitamin and mineral supplementation for the special needs of women taking oral contraceptives.

Administration and Dosage: One tablet a day, or as indicated.

How Supplied: Feminins® tablets NDC 0087-0470-01   Bottles of 100

FER-IN-SOL®
Iron supplement
- drops
- syrup
- capsules

Ferrous sulfate, Mead Johnson

Composition:

	Supplies	
	Ferrous Sulfate	As Elemental Iron
Fer-In-Sol	mg	mg
Drops (per 0.6 ml dose)	75	15
Syrup (per 5 ml teaspoonful)	90	18
Capsule (1 capsule) (dried)	190	60

Action and Uses: Source of supplemental iron.

Administration and Dosage:

drops

0.6 ml daily supplies 15 mg of elemental iron, 100% of the U.S. RDA for infants and 150% of the U.S. RDA for children under 4 years of age.

Give in water or in fruit or vegetable juice.

Fer-In-Sol should be given immediately after meals. When an infant or child is taking iron, stools may appear darker in color. This is to be expected and should be no cause for concern. When drops containing iron are given to young babies, some darkening of the membrane covering the baby's teeth may occur. This is not serious or permanent. The enamel of the teeth is not affected. Should this darkening or staining occur, it may be removed by rubbing the baby's teeth with a little baking soda on a small cloth once a week.

syrup

1 teaspoon (5 ml) daily supplies 18 mg of elemental iron, 100% of the U.S. RDA for adults and children 4 or more years of age.

capsules

One capsule daily supplies 60 mg of elemental iron, 333% of the U.S. RDA for pregnant or lactating women.

How Supplied: Fer-In-Sol® drops (with calibrated 'Safti-Dropper')
NDC 0087-0740-02 Bottles of 1-⅔ fl oz (50 ml)
6505-00-664-0856 (1-⅔ fl oz, 50 ml) Defense
Fer-In-Sol® syrup
NDC 0087-0741-01 Bottles of 16 fl oz
Fer-In-Sol® capsules
NDC 0087-0742-01 Bottles of 100

ISOCAL®
Complete liquid diet

Composition: Water, maltodextrin, soy oil, calcium caseinate, sodium caseinate, medium chain triglycerides (fractionated coconut oil), soy protein isolate, potassium citrate, lecithin, calcium citrate, magnesium chloride, calcium chloride, dibasic calcium phosphate, dibasic magnesium phosphate, sodium citrate, carra-

Continued on next page

Mead Johnson Nutritional—Cont.

geenan, potassium chloride, vitamins (vitamin A palmitate, ergocalciferol, dl-alpha-tocopheryl acetate, sodium ascorbate, folic acid, thiamine hydrochloride, riboflavin, niacinamide, pyridoxine hydrochloride, cyanocobalamin, biotin, calcium pantothenate, phytonadione, and choline chloride) and minerals (potassium iodide, ferrous sulfate, cupric sulfate, zinc sulfate and manganese sulfate). [See table on **preceding** page].

Actions and Uses: Isocal is a complete liquid diet specifically formulated to provide well-balanced nutrition when used as the sole source of nourishment. The formulation of Isocal is especially designed to meet the special nutritional requirements of tube-fed patients and provide these unique characteristics:

An isotonic osmolality to avoid the problems associated with formulas of high osmotic concentrations: e.g., diarrhea, cramps, vomiting, nausea.

No lactose—to preclude the diarrhea and other side effects associated with lactose intolerance.

MCT oil (Medium Chain Triglycerides) as a component of the fat source is easily digestible and well absorbed.

100% of the U.S. RDA's for protein and all known essential vitamins and minerals in 2000 Calories. Also, additional amounts of vitamin C and the B-complex vitamins are of particular value to many tube-fed patients.

Preparation and Administration: Isocal is ready to feed and requires no additional water; shake well before opening. Unopened Isocal should be stored at room temperature. After opening, Isocal should be covered and refrigerated if not used immediately.

Nasogastric tube feedings with Isocal, Complete Liquid Diet, may be given using a standard tube feeding set, or the Isocal Tube Feeding Set. Feedings may be given by continuous drip or at intervals. The rate should be adjusted for the best comfort and needs of the individual patient. When initiating feedings it is recommended that the volume given be no more than 8 fluid ounces. This amount should be administered over a period of about 30 minutes.

Isocal has a bland, unsweetened taste because it is specifically formulated for tube feedings. However, patients on long-term oral diet may prefer the taste of Isocal to the sweet taste of some oral liquid nutritional supplements.

Precautions: Additional water should be given as needed to meet the patient's requirements. Particular attention should be given to water supply for comatose and unconscious patients and others who cannot express the usual sensations of thirst. Additional water is important also when renal-concentrating ability is impaired, when there is extensive breakdown of tissue protein, or when water

requirements are high, as in fever. Tube feeding preparations should be at room temperature during administration.

How Supplied: Isocal® Complete Liquid Diet
NDC 0087-0355-01 Cans of 8 fl oz
NDC 0087-0355-02 Cans of 12 fl oz
NDC 0087-0355-44 Cans of 32 fl oz (1 quart)
NDC 0087-0356-01 Bottles of 8 fl oz
VA 8940-00-624899(8-fl-oz cans)

Also Available:
NDC 0087-0357-01 Isocal Tube Feeding Set

ISOCAL® HCN
High calorie and nitrogen nutritionally complete Liquid Tube-Feeding Formula

Composition: Water, corn syrup, soybean oil, calcium caseinate, sodium caseinate, medium chain triglycerides (fractionated coconut oil), lecithin, potassium citrate, magnesium chloride, dibasic magnesium phosphate, calcium chloride, calcium citrate, potassium chloride, carrageenan, vitamins (vitamin A palmitate, cholecalciferol, dl-alpha-tocopheryl acetate, sodium ascorbate, folic acid, thiamine hydrochloride, riboflavin, niacinamide, pyridoxine hydrochloride, cyanocobalamin, biotin, calcium pantothenate, phytonadione and choline bitartrate) and minerals (potassium iodide, ferrous sulfate, cupric sulfate, zinc sulfate and manganese sulfate).

Proximate analysis (g/100 ml)

Protein	7.5
Fat	9.1
Carbohydrate	22.5
Minerals (ash)	0.8
Water	70.9

Isocal HCN provides 112.5 grams of protein per 1500 ml from 100% caseinates, the PER standard; a 30% MCT oil: 70% soy oil fat blend for excellent absorption; and 100% of all essential vitamins and minerals in 1500 ml (see table). [See table below].

Actions and Uses: Isocal HCN is a complete, concentrated liquid tube feeding diet specifically formulated to provide patients with generous calorie (2.0 Cal/ml; 3000 Cal/1500 ml) and protein levels (112.5 g protein/1500 ml) in limited volume. The higher levels of vitamins C, E, B-complex, copper and zinc provided are often recommended for various types of stress. The level of Vitamin K, 250 mcg/1500 ml, does not interfere with anticoagulant therapy. Isocal HCN is of particular value to patients who are hypermetabolic (from burns, major trauma, thyrotoxicoses, etc.), fluid-restricted (from neurosurgery, congestive heart failure, etc.) or are volume-restricted (cardiac or cancer cachexia, chronic obstructive lung disease) and require tube feeding. Other unique characteristics include:

A moderate osmolality to assure rapid patient adaptation. No lactose—to avoid problems associated with lactose intolerance.

	Per 8 fl oz	% U.S. RDA Adults & Children 4 or More Years of Age	Per 3000 Cal (1500 ml)	% U.S. RDA Adults & Children 4 or More Years of Age
Calories	473	*	3000	*
Protein, g	17.7	39	112.5	250
Fat, g	21.5	*	136.5	*
Carbohydrate, g	53.2	*	337.5	*
Vitamin A, IU	790	16	5000	100
Vitamin D, IU	63	16	400	100
Vitamin E, IU	11.8	39	75	250
Vitamin C (Ascorbic acid), mg	47.3	79	300	500
Folic acid (Folacin), mg	0.06	16	0.4	100
Thiamine (Vitamin B_1), mg	0.6	39	3.8	250
Riboflavin (Vitamin B_2), mg	0.68	39	4.3	250
Niacin, mg	7.9	39	50	250
Vitamin B_6, mg	0.79	39	5	250
Vitamin B_{12}, mcg	2.4	39	15	250
Biotin, mg	0.05	16	0.3	100
Pantothenic acid, mg	3.9	39	25	250
Vitamin K, mcg	39	*	250	*
Choline, mg	79	*	500	*
Calcium, mg	158	16	1000	100
Phosphorus, mg	158	16	1000	100
Iodine, mcg	24	16	150	100
Iron, mg	2.8	16	18	100
Magnesium, mg	63	16	400	100
Copper, mg	0.47	24	3	150
Zinc, mg	4.7	32	30	200
Manganese, mg	0.8	*	5	*
Chloride, mg	284	*	1800	*
Potassium, mg	331	*	2100	*
Sodium, mg	189	*	1200	*

*U.S. Recommended Daily Allowance (U.S. RDA) has not been established.

MCT oil (Medium Chain Triglycerides) as a component of the fat source is easily digested and well absorbed. Isocal HCN may be used as a nutritional supplement in situations: where taste perceptions have been altered by therapy and illness; where variety is indicated during long-term full liquid diet use; during the transition from tube feedings to conventional supplements and normal diets. Flavorings may be added to Isocal HCN to suit individual preferences.

Preparation: It is recommended that Isocal HCN be tube fed and that tube feeding be initiated as follows:

Day 1—1:1 dilution of Isocal HCN to water at 50 ml/hour (or full strength at 25 ml/hr).

Day 2—full strength at 50 ml/hour.

Day 3—full strength up to 100–125 ml/hour.

Administration via infusion pump is recommended.

Precaution: Additional water may be given as needed to meet the patient's requirements. Particular attention should be given to water supply for comatose and unconscious patients, those who cannot express the usual sensation of thirst and patients with impaired renal concentrating capacity, extensive breakdown of tissue protein, or when water requirements are high, e.g. fever, burns, and dry atmospheric conditions. Isocal HCN provides 709 ml of water per 1000 ml of formula.

How Supplied: Isocal® HCN liquid
NDC 0087-0462-42 cans of 8 fl oz

LOFENALAC® powder
Low phenylalanine food

Composition: 49.2% corn syrup solids, 18.7% specially processed casein hydrolysate (an enzymic digest of casein containing amino acids and small peptides, processed to remove most of the phenylalanine), 18% corn oil, 9.57% modified tapioca starch, 1.45% calcium citrate, 0.8% L-tyrosine, 0.76% dibasic calcium phosphate, 0.58% dibasic potassium phosphate, 0.2% L-tryptophan, 0.18% L-histidine hydrochloride monohydrate, 0.12% potassium citrate, 0.1% magnesium oxide, 0.1% L-methionine, 0.04% calcium hydroxide, vitamins (vitamin A palmitate, cholecalciferol, dl-alpha-tocopheryl acetate, sodium ascorbate, folic acid, thiamine hydrochloride, riboflavin, niacinamide, pyridoxine hydrochloride, cyanocobalamin, biotin, calcium pantothenate, phytonadione, choline chloride and inositol), and minerals (ferrous sulfate, cupric sulfate, zinc sulfate, manganese sulfate, and sodium iodide). *Proximate analysis* (powder): protein equivalent (N × 6.25) 15%, fat 18%, carbohydrate 59.6%, minerals (ash) 3.6%, moisture 3%. Phenylalanine content of Lofenalac powder is approximately 0.08% (not more than 0.1% nor less than 0.06%). Each 100 g of powder supplies about 460 kilocalories and 80 mg phenylalanine. One packed level scoop contains 9.5 g. Each quart of formula in normal dilution supplies these vitamins and minerals.

Protein, equivalent (N × 6.25) g	Per Qt. 21+
Vitamin A, IU	1600
Vitamin D, IU	400
Vitamin E, IU	10
Vitamin C (Ascorbic acid), mg	52
Folic acid (Folacin), mcg	100
Thiamine (Vitamin B₁), mg	0.5
Riboflavin (Vitamin B₂), mg	0.6
Niacin, mg	8
Vitamin B₆, mg	0.4
Vitamin B₁₂, mcg	2
Biotin, mcg	50
Pantothenic acid, mg	3
Vitamin K₁, mcg	100
Choline, mg	85
Inositol, mg	30
Calcium, mg	600
Phosphorus, mg	450
Iodine, mcg	45
Iron, mg	12
Magnesium, mg	70
Copper, mg	0.6
Zinc, mg	4
Manganese, mg	1
Chloride, mg	450
Potassium, mg	650
Sodium, mg	300

+The protein is incomplete since it contains an inadequate amount of the essential amino acid, phenylalanine, for normal growth. With added phenylalanine, the PER is greater than that of casein.

Action and Uses: For use as basic food in low phenylalanine dietary management of infants and children with phenylketonuria. Provides essential nutrients without the high phenylalanine content (approx. 5%) present in natural food proteins.

Preparation: 20 kcal/fl oz Formula for Infants: To make a quart of formula, add one packed level cup (139 g) of Lofenalac powder to 29 fl oz water. For smaller amounts of formula, add 1 packed level measuring scoop (9.5 g) of powder to each 2 fluid ounces of water.

To prepare as a beverage for older children (about 30 kcal/fl oz), add one cup of powder to 2½ cups of warm water; mix with beater until smooth, then store in refrigerator. Prescribe a specific amount of this mixture daily, and carefully add specific amounts of other foods to the diet.

When fed at the level of 50 kilocalories per pound of body weight (110 kcal/kg), this product provides about 9 mg phenylalanine per pound (20 mg/kg). This is within a phenylalanine range (20 to 30 mg/kg) recommended as needed by phenylketonuric patients for growth. Other foods should be given as required to provide needed calories and bring phenylalanine intake to adequate, but not excessive, level. The diet and the phenylalanine intake must be adapted to individual needs.

Store bottled formula in refrigerator and use within 24 hours.

Contraindications: Lofenalac (low phenylalanine food) should not be used for normal infants and children, but should be used only as part of the diet of patients with phenylketonuria. Continued usage must be carefully

and frequently supervised by the physician and the diet periodically adjusted on the basis of frequent tests of urine and blood.

How Supplied: Lofenalac®powder
NDC 0087-0340-01 Cans of 40 oz (2½ lb)

Consult Lofenalac® product brochure for details.

LONALAC® powder
Low sodium, high protein beverage mix

Composition: Lactose, casein, coconut oil, monobasic calcium phosphate, potassium carbonate, calcium citrate, potassium citrate, calcium hydroxide, calcium chloride, potassium chloride, magnesium oxide, calcium carbonate, vitamin A palmitate, thiamine hydrochloride, riboflavin, niacinamide, artificial color and flavor.

Each 100 g of Lonalac powder supplies 27 g protein, 28 g fat and 38 g carbohydrate. Each quart (20 Cal/fl oz) contains the following vitamins and minerals:

Vitamin A, IU	960
Thiamine (Vitamin B₁), mg	0.4
Riboflavin (Vitamin B₂), mg	1.7
Niacin, mg	0.8
Calcium, mg	1100
Phosphorus, mg	1000
Iron, mg	1
Magnesium, mg	90
Potassium, mg	1200
Sodium mg	25

It contains only 25 mg sodium per quart of normal dilution, in contrast to 480 mg per quart of milk.

Action and Uses: A substitute for milk when dietary sodium restriction is prescribed, as in congestive heart failure, hypertension, nephrosis, acute nephritis, toxemia of pregnancy, hepatic cirrhosis with ascites, and therapy with certain drugs.

Preparation: For 20 Cal/fl oz: add 1 cup (125 g) Lonalac powder to 3½ cups of water. Concentrated preparation: ½ cup Lonalac powder to 1 cup water. Store bottled formula in refrigerator and use within 24 hours.

Precautions: Care should be taken to avoid additional sodium intake from other dietary or non-dietary sources. Subjects receiving low sodium diets must be observed for signs of sodium deprivation such as weakness, exhaustion and abdominal cramps. In long term management (using Lonalac), additional sources of sodium must be given since Lonalac is almost void of the essential nutrient sodium.

How Supplied: Lonalac® powder
NDC 0087-0391-01 Cans of 16 oz (1 lb)
VA 8940-00-191-6565 (1 lb can)

LYTREN®
Oral electrolyte solution

Lytren provides important electrolytes plus carbohydrate in a balanced formulation. It is designed for oral administration when food intake is discontinued.

Composition:
Ingredients: Water, corn syrup solids, dextrose, sodium citrate, potassium chloride, citric acid, sodium biphosphate, po-

Continued on next page

Mead Johnson Nutritional—Cont.

tassium citrate, calcium chloride, and magnesium sulfate.

Concentrations of Electrolytes (9 kcal/fl oz):

Electrolyte	mEq/L	Approximate mEq/4 fl oz (118 ml)	mOsm/L
Sodium	30	3.5	30
Potassium	25	3	25
Calcium	4	0.5	2
Magnesium	4	0.5	2
Chloride	25	3	25
Citrate	36	4	12
Sulfate	4	0.5	2
Phosphate	5	0.6	5
Total*	133	15.6	103

*NOTE: Lytren oral electrolyte solution is nearly isotonic (compared to extracellular fluid) and has an osmolality of approximately 290 mOsm per kilogram of water.

Indications: When intake of the usual foods and liquids is discontinued, oral feedings of Lytren solution may be used:
- To supply water and electrolytes for maintenance.
- To replace mild to moderate fluid losses.

Such oral electrolyte feedings have particular application in mild and moderate diarrheas, to forestall dehydration,[1-6] and in postoperative states.

Intake and Administration: Feed by nursing bottle, glass or straw.

Administration of Lytren solution should be begun as soon as intake of usual foods and liquids is discontinued, and before serious fluid losses or deficits develop.

Intake of Lytren solution should approximate the patient's calculated daily water requirements, for maintenance and for replacement of losses. The prescribed quantity may be divided and used throughout the day as desired or appropriate. (Note: No more than this amount of Lytren should be given. Additional liquid to satisfy thirst should be water or other non-electrolyte-containing fluids.)

●For infants and young children. The water requirement should be calculated on the basis of body surface area. Estimated daily water requirements such as the following may be used as a general guide:

    For maintenance in illness—1500 ml (50 fl oz) per square meter.[7]

    For maintenance plus replacement of moderate losses (as in diarrhea or vomiting)—2400 ml (80 fl oz) per square meter.[7]

Daily amount of Lytren solution based on these estimated requirements is shown in the Intake Guide table. Intake should be adjusted according to the size of the individual patient and the clinical conditions.

●For older children and adults. When fluid losses are mild to moderate, amounts such as the following may be given daily: Children 5 to 10 years—1 to 2 quarts. Older children and adults—2 to 3 quarts.

Intake should be adjusted on the basis of clinical indications, amount of fluid loss, patient's usual water intake and other relevant factors.

[See table below].

●Lytren In conjunction with other fluids. When severe fluid losses or accumulated deficits require parenteral fluid therapy, Lytren solution by mouth <u>may be</u> given simultaneously to supply <u>part</u> of the estimated fluid requirement. After emergency needs have been met, Lytren solution alone may be used.

Contraindications:

Lytren should not be used:

●In the presence of severe, continuing diarrhea or other critical fluid losses requiring parenteral fluid therapy.

●In intractable vomiting, adynamic ileus, intestinal obstruction or perforated bowel.

●When renal function is depressed (anuria, oliguria) or homeostatic mechanisms are impaired.

Precautions: Lytren oral electrolyte solution should only be used in the recommended volume intakes in order to avoid excessive electrolyte ingestion. Do not mix with, or give with, other electrolyte-containing liquids, such as milk or fruit juices.

Urgent needs in severe fluid imbalances must be met parenterally. When Lytren solution by mouth is used in addition to parenteral fluids, do not exceed total water and electrolyte requirements.

Intake of Lytren should be reduced promptly and steadily upon reintroduction of other electrolyte-containing foods into the diet. Should be administered on physician's orders only.

How Supplied:

Lytren—8 fl oz, Ready to Use.

Lytren is also available in the hospital in an 8-fl oz Nursette® Disposable Bottle and Beniflex® Disposable Nurser System.

References:
1. Darrow DC: Pediatrics *9*:519–533 (May) 1952. 2. Harrison HE: Pediat Clin North America, May 1954. pp 335–348. 3. Vaughan VC, III, in Nelson WE: Textbook of Pediatrics, ed 7, Philadelphia, WB Saunders Company, 1959, pp 187–189. 4. Brooke CE, Anast CS: JAMA *179*:148–153 (March) 1962. 5. Darrow DC, Welsh JS: J Pediat *56*:204–210 (Feb) 1960. 6. Cooke RE: JAMA *167*:1243–1246 (July 5) 1958. 7. Worthen HG, Raile RB: Minnesota Med *37*:558–564 (Aug) 1954. 8. McLester JS, Darby WJ: Nutrition and Diet in Health and Disease, ed 6, Philadelphia, WB Saunders Company, 1952, pp 32–34.

MCT® Oil
Medium chain triglycerides oil

Composition: MCT Oil contains triglycerides of medium chain fatty acids which are more easily digested and absorbed than conventional food fat.

MCT Oil is bland tasting and light yellow in color. It provides 8.3 Cal/g. One tablespoon (15 ml) weighs 14 g and contains 115 Cal. It is a lipid fraction of coconut oil and consists primarily of the triglycerides of C_8 and C_{10} saturated fatty acids. Approximate percentages are:

Fatty Acid	%
Shorter than C_8	6
C_8 (Octanoic)	67
C_{10} (Decanoic)	23
Longer than C_{10}	< 4

Actions and Uses: MCT Oil is a special dietary supplement for use in the nutritional management of children and adults who cannot efficiently digest and absorb conventional long chain food fats. One tablespoonful 3 to 4 times per day or as recommended by the physician. MCT Oil should be mixed with fruit juices, used on salads and vegetables, incorporated into sauces for use on fish, chicken, or lean meat, or used in cooking or baking. Recipes or professional literature available upon request.

Precaution: In persons with advanced cirrhosis of the liver, large amounts of medium chain triglycerides in the diet may result in elevated blood and spinal fluid levels of medium chain fatty acids (MCFA), due to impaired hepatic clearance of these fatty acids, which are rapidly absorbed via the portal vein. These elevated levels have been reported to be associated with reversible coma and precoma in certain subjects with advanced cirrhosis, particularly with portacaval shunts. Therefore, diets containing high levels of medium chain triglyceride fat should be used with caution in persons with hepatic cirrhosis and complications

LYTREN INTAKE GUIDE
for infants and young children

(Adjust to meet individual needs)

*Averages of Benedict-Talbot estimated surface areas for boys and girls.[8]	Body Weight Kg	Body Weight Lb	Average Surface Area Sq Meter*	Maintenance Approx. Fl Oz†	Maintenance plus Replacement of Moderate Losses Approx. Fl Oz‡
†Based on water requirement	3	6–7	0.2	10	16
of 1500 ml (50 fl oz) per sq	5	11	0.29	15	23
meter.[7]	7	15	0.38	19	30
‡Based on water requirement	10	22	0.49	25	40
of 2400 ml (80 fl oz) per sq	12	26	0.55	28	44
meter.[7]	15	33	0.64	32	51
	18	40	0.76	38	61

LYTREN SOLUTION DAILY INTAKE

thereof, such as portacaval shunts or tendency to encephalopathy.

Use of MCT Oil-containing products in abetalipoproteinemia is not indicated.

How Supplied: MCT Oil

NDC 0087-0365-03 Bottles of 1 quart

NUTRAMIGEN® powder
Protein hydrolysate formula

Composition: Ingredients: 43.3% sugar (sucrose), 19.2% casein enzymically hydrolyzed and charcoal-treated to reduce allergenicity, 18% corn oil, 16.5% modified tapioca starch, 1.12% dibasic calcium phosphate, 0.91% potassium citrate, 0.34% calcium citrate, 0.3% calcium hydroxide, 0.1% magnesium oxide, 0.057% potassium chloride, vitamins (vitamin A palmitate, ergocalciferol, dl-alpha-tocopheryl acetate, sodium ascorbate, folic acid, thiamine hydrochloride, riboflavin, niacinamide, pyridoxine hydrochloride, cyanocobalamin, biotin, calcium pantothenate, phytonadione, choline chloride and inositol), and minerals (ferrous sulfate, manganese sulfate, cupric sulfate, zinc sulfate, and sodium iodide).

One quart of Nutramigen formula (4.9 oz Nutramigen Powder) supplies 640 kilocalories and the following vitamins and minerals:

Vitamin A, IU	1600
Vitamin D, IU	400
Vitamin E, IU	10
Vitamin C, mg	52
Folic acid, mcg	100
Thiamine, mg	0.5
Riboflavin, mg	0.6
Niacin, mg	8
Vitamin B$_6$, mg	0.4
Vitamin B$_{12}$, mcg	2
Biotin, mg	0.05
Pantothenic acid, mg	3
Vitamin K$_1$, mcg	100
Choline, mg	85
Inositol, mg	30
Calcium, mg	600
Phosphorus, mg	450
Iodine, mcg	45
Iron, mg	12
Magnesium, mg	70
Copper, mg	0.6
Zinc, mg	4
Manganese, mg	1
Chloride, mg	450
Potassium, mg	650
Sodium, mg	300

Action and Uses: Feeding of infants and children allergic or intolerant to ordinary food proteins (intact proteins). Provides a formula with predigested protein for infants with diarrhea or other gastrointestinal disturbances. Provides lactose-free feedings in galactosemia.

Precautions: Initial feedings of Nutramigen should be diluted to 10 kcal/fl oz and gradually increased to 20 kcal/fl oz over a period of 3 to 5 days. Individuals with lengthy episodes of diarrhea and/or receiving antibiotics may require supplemental vitamin K.

Preparation: For 10 kcal/fl oz: 1 packed level scoop to 4 fl oz water, or ½ cup, packed level, to water sufficient to make a quart of formula. For 20 kcal/fl oz: 1 packed level scoop powder (9.5 g) to 2 fl oz

water, or 1 level cup (139 g) to water sufficient to make a quart of formula. Store bottled formula in refrigerator and use within 24 hours.

How Supplied: Nutramigen® powder

NDC 0087-0338-01 Cans of 16 oz (1 lb), with scoop.

POLY-VI-SOL®
Multivitamin supplement
drops • chewable tablets

Composition: Usual daily doses supply:

	Drops 1.0 ml	Chewable Tablet 1 tablet
Vitamin A, IU	1500	2500
Vitamin D, IU	400	400
Vitamin E, IU	5	15
Vitamin C, mg	35	60
Folic acid, mg	—	0.3
Thiamine, mg	0.5	1.05
Riboflavin, mg	0.6	1.2
Niacin, mg	8	13.5
Vitamin B$_6$, mg	0.4	1.05
Vitamin B$_{12}$, mcg	2	4.5

Action and Uses: Daily vitamin supplementation for infants and children. Chewable tablets useful also for adults.

Administration and Dosage: Usual doses as above, or as indicated.

How Supplied: Poly-Vi-Sol® multivitamin supplement drops: (with 'Safti-Dropper' marked to deliver 1.0 ml)

NDC 0087-0402-02 Bottles of 1 fl oz (30 ml)

NDC 0087-0402-03 Bottles of 1⅔ fl oz (50 ml)

6505-00-104-8433 (50 ml) (Defense)

Poly-Vi-Sol® multivitamin supplement chewable tablets

NDC 0087-0412-02 Bottles of 24
NDC 0087-0412-03 Bottles of 100
NDC 0087-0412-05 Bottles of 1000

Poly-Vi-Sol® multivitamin supplement chewable tablets in Circus Shapes:

NDC 0087-0414-01 Bottles of 24
NDC 0087-0414-02 Bottles of 100

POLY-VI-SOL® with Iron
Multivitamin and Iron supplement
chewable tablets

Composition: Each tablet supplies same vitamins as Poly-Vi-Sol tablets (see above) plus 12 mg iron (from 40 mg ferrous fumarate).

Action and Uses: Daily vitamin and iron supplement for adults and children.

Administration and Dosage: 1 tablet daily.

How Supplied: Poly-Vi-Sol® multivitamin and iron supplement chewable tablets.

NDC 0087-0455-02 Bottles of 100
NDC 0087-0455-04 Bottles of 1000

Poly-Vi-Sol® multivitamin and iron supplement chewable tablets in Circus Shapes.

NDC 0087-0456-02 Bottles of 100

POLY-VI-SOL® with Iron
Multivitamin and Iron supplement
drops

Composition: Each 1.0 ml supplies:

Vitamin A, IU	1500
Vitamin D, IU	400
Vitamin E, IU	5
Vitamin C, mg	35
Thiamine, mg	0.5
Riboflavin, mg	0.6
Niacin, mg	8
Vitamin B$_6$, mg	0.4
Iron, mg	10

Action and Uses: Daily vitamin and iron supplement for infants.

Administration and Dosage: Drop into mouth with 'Safti-Dropper.' Dose: 1.0 ml daily, or as indicated.

How Supplied: Poly-Vi-Sol® multivitamin and iron supplement drops (with dropper marked to deliver 1 ml)

NDC 0087-0405-01 Bottles of 1⅔ fl oz (50 ml)

PORTAGEN®
Nutritionally complete dietary with
Medium Chain Triglycerides
U.S. Patent No. 3,450,819

Composition: Corn syrup solids, medium chain triglycerides (fractionated coconut oil), sodium caseinate, sugar (sucrose), corn oil, calcium citrate, potassium chloride, dibasic magnesium phosphate, dicalcium phosphate, potassium citrate, lecithin, vitamins (vitamin A palmitate, ergocalciferol, dl-alpha-tocopheryl acetate, sodium ascorbate, folic acid, thiamine hydrochloride, riboflavin, niacinamide, pyridoxine hydrochloride, cyanocobalamin, biotin, calcium pantothenate, phytonadione, and choline chloride), and minerals (ferrous sulfate, cupric sulfate, zinc sulfate, manganese sulfate, and sodium iodide).

One packed level cup (136 g) of Portagen powder supplies 640 Calories (20 Cal/fl oz) and 1½ packed level measuring cups (207 g) of Portagen powder supplies 960 Calories (30 Cal/fl oz) plus the following nutrients:

	One Quart 20 Cal/ fl oz	One Quart 30 Cal/ fl oz
Protein, g	22.4	33.6
Fat, g	30.5	45.8
Carbohydrate, g	73.6	110.4
Vitamin A, IU	5000	7500
Vitamin D, IU	500	750
Vitamin E, IU	20	30
Vitamin C (Ascorbic acid), mg	52	78
Folic acid (Folacin), mcg	100	150
Thiamine (Vitamin B$_1$), mg	1	1.5
Riboflavin (Vitamin B$_2$), mg	1.2	1.8
Niacin, mg	13	20
Vitamin B$_6$, mg	1.3	2
Vitamin B$_{12}$, mcg	4	6
Biotin, mcg	50	75
Pantothenic acid, mg	6.7	10
Vitamin K$_1$, mcg	100	150
Choline, mg	85	125
Calcium, mg	600	900
Phosphorus, mg	450	675
Iodine, mcg	45	70
Iron, mg	12	18
Magnesium, mg	130	200

Continued on next page

Mead Johnson Nutritional—Cont.

Copper, mg	1	1.5
Zinc, mg	6	9
Manganese, mg	2	3
Chloride, mg	550	825
Potassium, mg	800	1200
Sodium, mg	300	450

Action and Uses: A nutritionally complete dietary is prepared by adding Portagen powder to water.

This dietary may be used, according to physician recommendation, as the major or sole constituent of the diet. Or, it may be used as a beverage to be consumed with each meal, or it may be incorporated in various recipes. Recipes or professional literature available upon request.

The fat blend of Portagen contains 87% Medium Chain Triglycerides, which are glycerol esters of Octanoic (C_8) and Decanoic (C_{10}) acids; along with corn oil which provides linoleic acid, an essential fatty acid.

When compared to conventional food fat, Medium Chain Triglycerides or medium chain fatty acids are: (1) more rapidly hydrolyzed, (2) not dependent on bile salts for emulsification, (3) carried by the portal circulation, and (4) not dependent on chylomicron formation or lymphatic transport.

Portagen may be used where conventional food fats are not well digested or absorbed. Impaired fat absorption may be a nutritional problem in the following conditions: *Intraluminal defect in hydrolysis of fat,* decreased pancreatic lipase (pancreatic insufficiency and cystic fibrosis of the pancreas) or decreased bile salts (chronic liver disease, biliary atresia, and biliary obstruction); *Mucosal defect in absorption of fat,* decreased permeability (sprue and idiopathic steatorrhea) or decreased surface (intestinal resection and blind loop syndrome) or defective lipoprotein lipase system (hyperchylomicronemia); and *Lymphatic defect in transport of fat* with intestinal lymphatic obstruction (lymphangiectasia, chylothorax, chyluria, chylous ascites and exudative enteropathy).

Preparation: *To Prepare as a Beverage (30 kilocalories per fluid ounce):* Add 1½ packed level cups of Portagen powder (203 g) to 3 cups of water. Mix with electric mixer, egg beater or fork until smooth. Then stir in enough water to make 1 quart of beverage.

To Prepare as an Infant Formula (in normal dilution of 20 kilocalories per fluid ounce): Add 1 packed level cup (136 g) of Portagen powder to 3 cups of water. Mix with electric mixer, egg beater or fork until smooth. Then stir in enough water to make 1 quart of formula.

Store bottled formula in refrigerator and use within 24 hours.

Precautions: Recent studies indicate that contrary to earlier recommendations, Portagen should not be used in cases of abetalipoproteinemia (faulty chylomicron formation). The usual intake of water should be maintained when Portagen beverage is used as the sole ar-

ticle or major part of the diet. In persons with advanced cirrhosis of the liver, large amounts of medium chain triglycerides in the diet may result in elevated blood and spinal fluid levels of medium chain fatty acids (MCFA), due to impaired hepatic clearance of these fatty acids, which are rapidly absorbed via the portal vein. These elevated levels have been reported to be associated with reversible coma and pre-coma in certain subjects with advanced cirrhosis, particularly with portacaval shunts. Therefore, diets containing high levels of medium chain triglyceride fat should be used with caution in persons with hepatic cirrhosis and complications thereof, such as portacaval shunts or tendency to encephalopathy.

How Supplied: Portagen® Powder
NDC 0087-0387-01 Cans of 16 oz (1 lb)

PREGESTIMIL®
Protein hydrolysate formula with medium chain triglycerides and added amino acids

Composition: 52.4% corn syrup solids, 15.5% casein enzymically hydrolyzed and charcoal-treated to reduce allergenicity, 10.5% corn oil, 10.3% modified tapioca starch, 7.7% medium chain triglycerides (fractionated coconut oil), 1.1% calcium citrate, 0.88% potassium citrate, 0.79% dibasic calcium phosphate, 0.18% lecithin, 0.15% L-cystine, 0.15% L-tyrosine, 0.08% magnesium oxide, 0.07% potassium chloride, 0.06% L-tryptophan, vitamins (vitamin A palmitate, ergocalciferol, dl-alpha-tocopheryl acetate, sodium ascorbate, folic acid, thiamine hydrochloride, riboflavin, niacinamide, pyridoxine hydrochloride, cyanocobalamin, biotin, calcium pantothenate, phytonadione, choline chloride, and inositol) and minerals (ferrous sulfate, cupric sulfate, zinc sulfate, manganese sulfate and sodium iodide).

One quart of Pregestimil formula (20 kcal/fl oz) supplies 18 g protein equivalent, 25.7 g fat, 86.4 g carbohydrate and the following vitamins and minerals.

		% U. S. RDA Children Under 4 Years of Age
Vitamin A, IU	2000	80
Vitamin D, IU	400	100
Vitamin E, IU	15	150
Vitamin C, mg	52	130
Folic acid, mcg	100	50
Thiamine, mg	0.5	71
Riboflavin, mg	0.6	75
Niacin, mg	8	89
Vitamin B₆, mg	0.4	57
Vitamin B₁₂, mcg	2	67
Biotin, mg	0.05	33
Pantothenic acid, mg	3	60
Vitamin K₁, mcg	100	*
Choline, mg	85	*
Inositol, mg	30	*
Calcium, mg	600	75
Phosphorus, mg	400	50
Iodine, mcg	45	64
Iron, mg	12	120
Magnesium, mg	70	35
Copper, mg	0.6	60
Zinc, mg	4	50
Manganese, mg	0.2	*
Chloride, mg	550	*

Potassium, mg	700	*
Sodium, mg	300	*

*U.S. Recommended Daily Allowance (U.S. RDA) has not been established.

Action and Uses: Provides very easily digestible and assimilable fat, carbohydrate, and protein for feeding of infants and children with severe problems of diarrhea, dietary intolerance, disaccharidase deficiency, or malabsorption. For the nutritional management of infants following intestinal resection where temporary deficiency of intestinal enzymes may be found, or in infants with cystic fibrosis. In infants with severe malabsorption problems of non-specific etiologies, such as chronic diarrhea, nutritional maintenance with Pregestimil permits trial of specific disaccharides, milk protein or regular dietary fats to determine if the dietary intolerance is due to a component of conventional feedings.

Precautions: Initial feedings of Pregestimil should be diluted to 10 kcal/fl oz or less and gradually increased to 20 kcal/fl oz over a period of 3 to 5 days. Individuals with lengthy episodes of diarrhea and/or receiving antibiotics may require supplemental vitamin K. This product is not recommended for routine use in highly stressed low birthweight infants. Some of these infants may be at increased risk of developing gastrointestinal complications.

Preparation: For 10 kcal/fl oz: add one packed level scoop (enclosed) (9.7 g) of Pregestimil powder to each 4 fl oz (120 ml) of water. Always add powder to water. To make a quart of 10 kcal/fl oz formula, add 1/2 packed level cup (71 g) of powder to 29 fl oz (858 ml) of water. For 20 kcal/fl oz: add one packed level scoop (9.7 g) of Pregestimil powder to each 2 fl oz (60 ml) of water. To make a quart of 20 kcal/fl oz formula, add one packed level cup (141 g) of powder to 29 fl oz (858 ml) of water.

Caution: Store remaining liquid formula in refrigerator in a covered container and use within 24 hours after mixing.

How Supplied: Pregestimil® powder
NDC 0087-0367-01 Cans of 16 oz (1 lb) with measuring scoop

PROSOBEE® concentrated liquid
● ready-to-use
Milk-free formula with soy protein isolate

ProSobee Concentrated Liquid
Ingredients: 74.9% Water, 13.4% corn syrup solids, 5.3% soy oil, 4.1% soy protein isolate, 1.3% coconut oil, 0.3% tribasic calcium phosphate, 0.2% lecithin, 0.16% tribasic potassium citrate, 0.1% salt, 0.09% magnesium chloride, 0.031% L-methionine, 0.022% calcium carbonate, 0.007% carrageenan, vitamins (vitamin A palmitate, ergocalciferol, dl-alpha-tocopheryl acetate, sodium ascorbate, folic acid, thiamine hydrochloride, riboflavin, niacinamide, pyridoxine hydrochloride, cyanocobalamin, biotin, calcium pantothenate, phytonadione, choline chloride and inositol) and minerals (potassium iodide, ferrous sulfate, cupric

sulfate, zinc sulfate and manganese sulfate).

ProSobee Ready-To-Use:

Ingredients: 87.1% Water, 6.9% corn syrup solids, 2.7% soy oil, 2.1% soy protein isolate, 0.7% coconut oil, 0.15% tribasic calcium phosphate, 0.1% lecithin, 0.08% tribasic potassium citrate, 0.05% salt, 0.04% magnesium chloride, 0.016% L-methionine, 0.01% carrageenan, 0.004% calcium carbonate, vitamins (vitamin A palmitate, ergocalciferol, dl-alpha-tocopheryl acetate, sodium ascorbate, folic acid, thiamine hydrochloride, riboflavin, niacinamide, pyridoxine hydrochloride, cyanocobalamin, biotin, calcium pantothenate, phytonadione, choline chloride and inositol) and minerals (potassium iodide, ferrous sulfate, cupric sulfate, zinc sulfate and manganese sulfate).

One quart of ProSobee formula, normal dilution (20 kcal/fl oz) supplies 640 kilocalories and the following vitamins and minerals:

Vitamin A, IU	2000
Vitamin D, IU	400
Vitamin E, IU	10
Vitamin C (Ascorbic acid), mg	52
Folic acid (Folacin), mcg	100
Thiamine (Vitamin B_1), mg	0.5
Riboflavin (Vitamin B_2), mg	0.6
Niacin, mg	8
Vitamin B_6, mg	0.4
Vitamin B_{12}, mcg	2
Biotin, mcg	50
Pantothenic acid, mg	3
Vitamin K_1, mcg	100
Choline, mg	50
Inositol, mg	30
Calcium, mg	600
Phosphorus, mg	475
Iodine, mcg	65
Iron, mg	12
Magnesium, mg	70
Copper, mg	0.6
Zinc, mg	5
Manganese, mg	0.2
Chloride, mg	520
Potassium, mg	780
Sodium, mg	275

Action and Uses: Formula for infants sensitive to milk, infants potentially allergic to milk on the basis of a family history of allergy and infants with galactosemia. As a milk substitute for children and adults with poor tolerance to milk. As a dietary trial food when milk sensitivity or lactose or sucrose intolerance is suspected.

Preparation: *Concentrated liquid:* For 20 kcal/fl oz, 1 part ProSobee concentrated liquid to 1 part water. ProSobee may be used to replace milk as a beverage or in cooking. A pleasant-tasting beverage is made with two parts ProSobee concentrated liquid to one part water.

How Supplied: ProSobee®
List 308-01 Cans of 13 fl oz Concentrated Liquid (40 kcal/fl oz)
List 309-01 Cans of 32 fl oz (1 qt) Ready-To-Use (20 kcal/fl oz)
List 309-42 Cans of 8 fl oz Ready-To-Use (20 kcal/fl oz)

SUSTACAL®
- **liquid (ready to use)**
- **powder (mix with milk)**
- **pudding (ready-to-eat)**
Nutritionally complete food

Composition: Vanilla Liquid—
Ingredients: Water, sugar (sucrose), corn syrup, calcium caseinate, partially hydrogenated soy oil, soy protein isolate, sodium caseinate, potassium citrate, artificial flavor, dibasic magnesium phosphate, salt (sodium chloride), potassium chloride, calcium carbonate, dibasic calcium phosphate, sodium citrate, lecithin, carrageenan, vitamins (vitamin A palmitate, ergocalciferol, dl-alpha-tocopheryl acetate, sodium ascorbate, folic acid, thiamine hydrochloride, riboflavin, niacinamide, pyridoxine hydrochloride, cyanocobalamin, biotin, calcium pantothenate, phytonadione and choline bitartrate) and minerals (sodium iodide, ferric pyrophosphate, ferrous sulfate, zinc sulfate and manganese sulfate).
(In addition to the above, Chocolate liquid contains Dutch process cocoa [alkalized], and artificial color.) Eggnog flavored liquid contains artificial color.
Proximate analysis (g/100 ml)

Protein	6.1
Fat	2.3
Carbohydrate	14
Ash	1.1
Water	84.2

Each 12-fl-oz can of Sustacal supplies 21.7 g protein, 8.3 g fat, 49.6 g carbohydrate, 360 Calories (1 Calorie per ml) and the following vitamins and minerals:

		% U.S. RDA Adults and Children 4 or More Years of Age
Vitamin A, IU	1670	33
Vitamin D, IU	133	33
Vitamin E, IU	10	33
Vitamin C (Ascorbic acid), mg	20	33
Folic acid (Folacin), mg	0.133	33
Thiamine (Vitamin B_1), mg	0.5	33
Riboflavin (Vitamin B_2), mg	0.6	35
Niacin, mg	7	35
Vitamin B_6, mg	0.7	35
Vitamin B_{12}, mcg	2	33
Biotin, mcg	100	33
Pantothenic acid, mg	3.5	35
Vitamin K_1, mcg	83.3	*
Choline, mg	83.3	*
Calcium, mg	360	36
Phosphorus, mg	330	33
Iodine, mcg	50	33
Iron, mg	6	33
Magnesium, mg	135	33
Copper, mg	0.7	35
Zinc, mg	5	33
Manganese, mg	1	*
Chloride, mg	560	*
Potassium, mg	740	*
Sodium, mg	333	*

*U.S. RDA (Recommended Daily Allowance) not established.

Vanilla Powder—Nonfat dry milk, sugar, corn syrup solids, artificial flavor, dibasic magnesium phosphate, vitamins (vitamin A palmitate, ergocalciferol, dl-alpha-tocopheryl acetate, sodium ascorbate, folic acid, thiamine hydrochloride, niacinamide, pyridoxine hydrochloride, cyanocobalamin, biotin and calcium pantothenate) and minerals (ferrous sulfate, cupric carbonate, zinc sulfate, and manganese sulfate). (In addition to the above, Chocolate Powder contains Dutch process cocoa [alkalized], and lecithin.)
With the exception of lactose, one pouch of Sustacal powder mixed with 8-fl oz whole milk provides essentially the same nutritional value as a 12 fl oz can of Sustacal.

Vanilla Pudding—Water, nonfat milk, sugar, partially hydrogenated soy oil, modified food starch, artificial flavor, dibasic magnesium phosphate, sodium stearoyl lactylate, dibasic sodium phosphate, carrageenan, artificial color (includes FD&C Yellow No. 5), and vitamins and minerals (vitamin A palmitate, sodium ascorbate, thiamine hydrochloride, riboflavin, niacinamide, ferric pyrophosphate, cholecalciferol, dl-alpha-tocopheryl acetate, pyridoxine hydrochloride, folic acid, cyanocobalamin, zinc sulfate, cupric sulfate, biotin and calcium pantothenate).

In addition to the above, Chocolate contains Dutch process cocoa (alkalized) but no FD&C Yellow No. 5. Butterscotch does not contain FD&C Yellow No. 5.

Proximate Analysis (% w/w):

Protein	4.8
Fat	6.7
Carbohydrate	22.6
Ash	1.2
Water	64.6

Each 5-oz tin of Sustacal Pudding supplies the following nutrients:

		% RDA
Calories	240	*
Protein, g	6	15
Fat, g	10	*
Cholesterol, mg (less than 5 mg per 100 g)**	<5	
Carbohydrate, g	32	*
Caloric Distribution, %		
Protein	11	
Fat	36	
Carbohydrate	53	
Vitamin A, I U	750	15
Vitamin D, I U	60	15
Vitamin E, I U	4.5	15
Vitamin C (Ascorbic Acid), mg	9	15
Folic acid (Folacin), mcg	60	15
Thiamine (Vitamin B_1), mg	0.23	15
Riboflavin (Vitamin B_2), mg	0.26	15
Niacin, mg	3	15
Vitamin B_6, mg	0.3	15
Vitamin B_{12}, mcg	0.9	15
Biotin, mcg	50	15
Pantothenic acid, mg	1.5	15
Calcium, mg	220	20
Phosphorus, mg	220	20

Continued on next page

Mead Johnson Nutritional—Cont.

Iodine, mcg	22.5	15
Iron, mg	2.7	15
Magnesium, mg	60	15
Copper, mg	0.3	15
Zinc, mg	2.25	15
Manganese, mg	0.67	*
Chloride, mg	200.0	*
Potassium, mg	320.0	*
Sodium, mg		
(85 mg per 100 g)	120	*

*No established U. S. RDA

**This information on cholesterol content is provided for individuals who, on the advice of a physician, are modifying their dietary intake of cholesterol.

Action and Uses: Sustacal liquid and powder are ideally formulated to provide for the nutritional needs of the broad range of patients requiring an oral supplement or high protein diet (21.7 g protein in one 12 fl oz serving). Sustacal is of particular value to patients in these situations: **lactose intolerance** (Sustacal liquid is lactose-free); **anorexia and food prejudice** (excellent taste in a choice of vanilla, chocolate, and eggnog flavors); **malnutrition/vitamin and mineral deficiencies** (each 12 fl oz can provides between 33–36% of U.S. RDA's for every vitamin and mineral for which U.S. RDA's are established); **ill, injured, surgical and convalescent patients and those with impediments to eating and swallowing.**

Sustacal Pudding is a convenient and well-accepted means of providing supplemental nutrition. Routine usage of Sustacal Pudding is appropriate for the majority of patients requiring nutritional supplementation and is especially appropriate to help avoid taste fatigue and form monotony associated with liquid supplements. Sustacal Pudding's nutritional balance is compatible with most normal complete diets.

Preparation: Liquid: ready to serve in 30 Cal/fl oz dilution (one Cal per milliliter). Powder: mix contents of one packet instantly with 8-fl oz whole milk to prepare a 40-calorie-per-fluid-ounce dilution. To prepare powder in 30 Calorie per-fluid-ounce dilution, add 90 ml (3 fl oz) of water to this mixture. Makes approximately 12 fluid ounces. Both forms may be used orally or by tube. Vanilla flavor is recommended for tube feeding if chocolate allergy is suspected.

In initiating tube feeding, particularly for malnourished patients, it may be advisable to start with 1/3 to 1/2 the desired daily caloric ration and with a half-strength concentration; then increase gradually over next few days.

Precautions: When Sustacal is used as the sole food, give additional water as needed for adequate daily intake. This is particularly important for unconscious or semiconscious patients. Do not begin postoperative tube feedings until peristalsis is reestablished. Electrolyte content of Sustacal should be considered for cardiac patients and others who tend to have edema.

Store bottled formula in refrigerator and use same day or next.

How Supplied: Sustacal® Vanilla liquid and powder.
  NDC 0087-0351-42 Cans of 8 fl oz
  NDC 0087-0351-01 Cans of 12 fl oz
  NDC 0087-0351-44 Cans of 32 fl oz (1 quart)
  NDC 0087-0353-01 Packets of 1.9 oz, 4 packets per carton
  NDC 0087-0353-43 Cans of 3.8 lb
  VA8940-00-627857 (8 fl oz, van.)
  VA8940-00-876-9044 (12 fl oz, van.)
Sustacal® Chocolate liquid and powder.
  NDC 0087-0350-01 Cans of 12 fl oz
  NDC 0087-0352-01 Packets of 1.9 oz, 4 packets per carton
  VA8940-00-035-6129 (12 fl oz, choc.)
Sustacal® Eggnog liquid.
  NDC 0087-0457-42 Cans of 8 fl oz, 12 cans per case
  NDC 0087-0457-44 Cans of 32 fl oz, 6 cans per case
Sustacal® Pudding
  NDC 0087-0409-41 Vanilla, 5 oz tins, 4 tins per carton, 12 cartons per case
  NDC 0087-0410-41 Chocolate, 5 oz tins, 4 tins per carton, 12 cartons per case
  NDC 0087-0415-41 Butterscotch, 5 oz tins, 4 tins per carton, 12 cartons per case
  VA8940-01-074-3125 (Vanilla, 5 oz tins)
  VA8940-01-074-3124 (Chocolate, 5 oz tins)
  VA8940-01-074-3123 (Butterscotch, 5 oz tins)

SUSTACAL® HC
High Calorie Nutritionally Complete Food

Composition: (Eggnog Flavored Liquid) Water, corn syrup solids, partially hydrogenated soybean oil, sugar, calcium caseinate, sodium caseinate, potassium chloride, dibasic magnesium phosphate, artificial flavor, calcium carbonate, sodium citrate, lecithin, carrageenan, potassium citrate, artificial color, vitamins (vitamin A palmitate, cholecalciferol, dl-alpha-tocopheryl acetate, sodium ascorbate, folic acid, thiamine hydrochloride, riboflavin, niacinamide, pyridoxine hydrochloride, cyanocobalamin, biotin, calcium pantothenate, phytonadione and choline bitartrate) and minerals (sodium iodide, ferric pyrophosphate, ferrous sulfate, cupric sulfate, zinc sulfate and manganese sulfate). Sustacal HC is available in vanilla and eggnog flavors.

Proximate analysis (g/100 ml)

Protein	6.1
Fat	5.8
Carbohydrate	19
Ash	0.8
Water	77.5

Each 8-fl oz can of Sustacal HC supplies 14.4 g protein, 13.6 g fat, 45.0 g carbohydrate, 360 Calories (1.5 Cal/ml) and the following vitamins and minerals.

	% U.S. RDA Adults & Children 4 or More Years of Age	
Vitamin A, IU	1000	20
Vitamin D, IU	80	20
Vitamin E, IU	6	20
Vitamin C (Ascorbic Acid), mg	18	30
Folic Acid (Folacin), mcg	120	30
Thiamine (Vitamin B_1), mg	0.45	30
Riboflavin (Vitamin B_2), mg	0.51	30
Niacin, mg	6	30
Vitamin B_6, mg	0.6	30
Vitamin B_{12}, mcg	1.8	30
Biotin, mcg	90	30
Pantothenic Acid, mg	3	30
Vitamin K_1, mcg	50	*
Choline, mg	50	*
Calcium, mg	200	20
Phosphorus, mg	200	20
Iodine, mcg	30	20
Iron, mg	3.6	20
Magnesium, mg	80	20
Copper, mg	0.4	20
Zinc, mg	3	20
Manganese, mg	0.6	*
Chloride, mg	300	*
Potassium, mg	350	*
Sodium, mg	200	*

*U.S. RDA (Recommended Daily Allowance) not established.

Actions and Uses: Sustacal HC liquid is formulated to meet the supplemental or total nutritional needs of patients requiring generous calorie and protein intake (1.5 Cal/ml; 14.4 g protein/8 fl oz) while limiting total fluid volume. Sustacal HC is of particular value to patients in these situations: hypermetabolic states (burn, major trauma, thyrotoxicosis, etc.); fluid restrictions (neurosurgery, congestive heart failure, etc.); volume restrictions (cardiac or cancer cachexia, chronic obstructive lung disease); and lactose intolerance (Sustacal HC is lactose free). Sustacal HC contains high quality protein (from 100% caseinate) providing 32% of the U.S. RDA for protein per 8 fl oz. The moderate level of sodium (200 mg/8 fl oz) provides added flexibility in sodium-restricted diets.

Preparation: Sustacal HC is ready to drink. Shake well before opening. Unopened Sustacal HC should be stored at room temperature. Refrigerate unused Sustacal HC and use within 48 hours. Acceptance by some patients is enhanced if Sustacal HC liquid is chilled before serving. Very ill patients should be directed to sip the liquid slowly.

Preparation for Tube Feeding: If Sustacal HC is used for this purpose, initial feedings should be diluted to half strength (0.75 Cal/ml) on the first day and three-fourths strength (1.12 Cal/ml) on the second day. This will allow the body to adjust to the osmolality of Sustacal HC Liquid. As tolerance is established, Sustacal HC Liquid can be fed full strength—1.5 Cal/ml.

Tube Feeding Precaution: Additional water should be given as needed to meet the patient's requirements. Particular attention should be given to water supply for comatose and unconscious patients and others who cannot express the usual sensation of thirst. Additional water is important also when renal concentrating ability is impaired, when there is extensive breakdown of tissue protein, or when water requirements are high, as in fever, burns or under dry atmospheric conditions. Sustacal HC provides 775 ml of water per 1000 ml of formula.

How Supplied: Sustacal® HC vanilla flavored liquid.

NDC 0087-0460-42 cans of 8 fl oz

Sustacal HC eggnog flavored liquid

NDC 0087-0461-42 cans of 8 fl oz

SUSTAGEN® powder
Nutritional supplement

Composition: Nonfat milk, corn syrup solids, powdered whole milk, calcium caseinate, dextrose, artificial vanilla flavor, vitamins (vitamin A palmitate, ergocalciferol, dl-alpha-tocopheryl acetate, ascorbic acid, folic acid, thiamine hydrochloride, riboflavin, niacinamide, pyridoxine hydrochloride, cyanocobalamin, biotin, calcium pantothenate, phytonadione, and choline bitartrate), and minerals (ferrous sulfate, dibasic magnesium phosphate, cupric carbonate, zinc sulfate, and manganese sulfate).

Chocolate-flavored Sustagen also contains sugar and cocoa. High in protein, low in fat; generous in vitamins, calcium and iron. Easily mixed with water to make a pleasant-tasting beverage or a feeding via nasogastric tube.

One pound of Sustagen powder supplies 107 g protein, 300 g carbohydrate, 15.9 g fat and the following vitamins and minerals:

Vitamin A, IU	5000
Vitamin D, IU	400
Vitamin E, IU	45
Vitamin C (Ascorbic acid), mg	300
Folic acid (Folacin), mcg	400
Thiamine (Vitamin B₁), mg	3.8
Riboflavin (Vitamin B₂), mg	4.3
Niacin, mg	50
Vitamin B₆, mg	5
Vitamin B₁₂, mcg	15
Biotin, mcg	300
Pantothenic acid, mg	25
Vitamin K₁, mcg	250
Choline, mg	500
Calcium, mg	3200
Phosphorus, mg	2400
Iodine, mcg	150
Iron, mg	18
Magnesium, mg	400
Copper, mg	2
Zinc, mg	20
Manganese, mg	5
Chloride, mg	2700
Potassium, mg	3200
Sodium, mg	1200

*Chocolate powder supplies 3500 mg of potassium

Actions and Uses: Orally or by tube, provides a complete diet or extra nutritional support for ill, injured, surgical, and convalescent patients and those with impediments to eating or swallowing. Useful in peptic ulcer for buffering effect plus nutrition.

Preparation: Oral dilution: Mix equal parts (by volume) of Sustagen powder and water. This yields about 50 Cal/fl oz. One pound (3 packed level cups) Sustagen powder and 3 cups water make about a quart. ⅔ packed level cup Sustagen powder and ⅔ cup water make a single serving.

Refrigerate reconstituted Sustagen and use within 24 hours.

Tube-feeding dilution: Use 400 g Sustagen powder to 800 ml water for 1 liter. This mixture yields about 45 Cal/fl oz. More dilute mixtures may be utilized if desired. **In initiating tube feeding,** particularly for malnourished patients, it may be advisable to start with ⅓ to ½ the desired daily caloric ration and with a halfstrength concentration; then increased gradually over next few days. Vanilla flavor is recommended for tube feeding if chocolate allergy is suspected.

Precautions: When Sustagen is used as the sole food, give additional water as needed for adequate daily intake. This is particularly important for unconscious or semiconscious patients. Do not begin post-operative tube feedings until peristalsis is reestablished. Electrolyte content of Sustagen should be considered for cardiac patients and others who tend to have edema.

How Supplied: Sustagen® vanilla

NDC 0087-0393-01 Cans of 16 oz (1 lb)

NDC 0087-0393-03 Cans of 5 lb

VA 8940-00-584-2702 (Cans of 5 lb)

Sustagen chocolate

NDC 0087-0394-01 Cans of 16 oz (1 lb)

TEMPRA®
Acetaminophen

DROPS AND SYRUP–for infants and younger children.

Composition: Tempra is acetaminophen, a safe and effective analgesic-antipyretic. It is not a salicylate. It contains no phenacetin or caffeine. It has no effect on prothrombin time. Tempra offers prompt, non-irritating therapy. Because it provides significant freedom from side effects, it is particularly valuable for patients who do not tolerate aspirin well.

Action and Uses: Tempra drops and syrup are useful for reducing fever and for the temporary relief of minor aches, pains and discomfort associated with the common cold or "flu," inoculations or vaccination. Tempra syrup is valuable in reducing pain following tonsillectomy and adenoidectomy.

Administration and Dosage: 3 or 4 times daily or as needed. DROPS (1 gr per 0.6 ml) and SYRUP (2 gr per 5 ml tsp.)—

Age	Drops	Syrup
Under 1	0.6 ml	½ tsp
1 to 3	0.6-1.2 ml	½-1 tsp
3 to 6	1.2 ml	1 tsp
6 to 12	2.4 ml	2 tsp

Drops given with calibrated 'Safti-Dropper' or mixed with water or fruit juices. Syrup given by teaspoon.

Precaution: Acetaminophen has been reported to potentiate the effect of orally administered anticoagulants.

Contraindications: The only known contraindication is possible rare sensitivity to acetaminophen or to one of the ingredients of the drops or syrup. Acetaminophen may be contraindicated in the patient with known glucose-6-phosphate dehydrogenase deficiency.

Side Effects: Infrequent, nonspecific side effects have been reported with the therapeutic use of acetaminophen.

Overdosage: The occurrence of acetaminophen overdose toxicity is uncommon in children. The pediatric age group appears less vulnerable than adults to developing hepatotoxicity, even with large overdoses.

In the event of a child ingesting a large overdose of acetaminophen, **immediately** contact a Poison Control Center or Mead Johnson Medical Affairs Department for information on the antidotes used to treat acetaminophen overdosage. Following the ingestion of a large quantity of acetaminophen, patients may be asymptomatic for several days. Likewise, clinical laboratory evidence of hepatotoxicity may be delayed for up to a week. Parents' estimates of the quantity of a drug ingested are often also unreliable. Therefore, any report of the ingestion of an overdose should be corroborated by assaying for the acetaminophen plasma concentration. Since plasma levels at specific time points following an overdose correlate closely with the potential occurrence and probable severity of hepatotoxicity, it is important to accurately determine the elapsed time from ingestion of an overdose to the time of plasma acetaminophen determination.

Close clinical monitoring and serial hepatic enzyme studies are recommended for patients who delay presentation until several days following a reported acetaminophen overdose.

Note: A prescription is not required for Tempra drops or syrup as an analgesic. To prevent its misuse by the layman, the following information appears on the package label: Do not use for more than 10 days or administer to children under 3 years of age unless so directed by your physician.

How Supplied: Tempra® (acetaminophen) drops: (With calibrated 'Safti-Dropper.')

NDC 0087-0730-01 Bottles of 15 ml

Tempra® (acetaminophen) syrup:

NDC 0087-0733-04 Bottles of 4 fl oz

NDC 0087-0733-03 Bottles of 16 fl oz

No ℞ required.

Literature Available: Yes.

TRIND® liquid
antihistamine • nasal decongestant

Composition:

	per 5 ml teaspoonful
Phenylpropanolamine hydrochloride	12.5 mg
Chlorpheniramine Maleate	2.0 mg

Contains 5% alcohol

Action and Uses: Trind contains two active ingredients to effectively relieve cold symptoms for children and adults. Pleasant tasting, orange-flavored liquid clears nasal passages, dries runny nose, relieves itchy, watery eyes and helps stop sneezing.

Continued on next page

Mead Johnson Nutritional—Cont.

Dosage: One dose 3 or 4 times a day, as needed. Use enclosed dosage cup to measure correct dosage.

Age	Approximate Weight Range*	Dosage
Under 2	Under 25 lb	As directed by physician
2–5	25–52 lb	½ tsp
6–12	53–99 lb	1 tsp
Adult	100 lb and over	2 tsp

*If child is significantly under or overweight, consult a physician for appropriate dosage.

Warning: If symptoms do not improve within 3-5 days, or are accompanied by fever, consult a physician before continuing use. Do not take this product except under the advice and supervision of a physician if you have asthma, glaucoma, high blood pressure, heart disease, diabetes, thyroid disease, or difficulty in urination due to enlargement of the prostate. May cause excitability in children. Do not take recommended dosage because at higher doses nervousness, dizziness, or sleeplessness may occur. Caution: May cause marked drowsiness. Avoid alcoholic beverages, driving a motor vehicle or operating machinery.

How Supplied: Trind® liquid (available without prescription)

NDC 0087-0750-44 Bottles of 5 fl oz

TRIND-DM® liquid
cough suppressant • antihistamine • nasal decongestant

Composition:

	per 5 ml teaspoonful
Phenylpropanolamine hydrochloride	12.5 mg
Dextromethorphan hydrobromide	7.5 mg
Chlorpheniramine Maleate	2.0 mg

Contains 5% alcohol

Action and Uses: Trind-DM contains three active ingredients to effectively relieve cough and cold symptoms for children and adults.

Pleasant tasting, fruit-flavored liquid suppresses cough, clears nasal passages, dries runny nose, relieves itchy, watery eyes and helps stop sneezing.

Dosage: One dose 3 or 4 times a day, as needed. Use enclosed dosage cup to measure correct dosage.

Age	Approximate Weight Range*	Dosage
Under 2	Under 25 lb	As directed by physician
2–5	25–52 lb	½ tsp
6–12	53–99 lb	1 tsp
Adult	100 lb and over	2 tsp

*If child is significantly under or overweight, consult a physician for appropriate dosage.

Warning: If symptoms do not improve within 3–5 days, or are accompanied by fever, consult a physician before continuing use. Do not take this product except under the advice and supervision of a physician if you have asthma, glaucoma, high blood pressure, heart disease, diabe-

tes, thyroid disease, or difficulty in urination due to enlargement of the prostate. May cause excitability in children. Do not exceed recommended dosage because at higher doses nervousness, dizziness, or sleeplessness may occur. Caution: A persistent cough may be a sign of a serious condition. If cough persists, tends to recur, is accompanied by fever, rash, persistent headache, or if symptoms do not improve within 3–5 days, consult a physician before continuing use. May cause marked drowsiness. Avoid alcoholic beverages, driving a motor vehicle or operating machinery.

How Supplied: Trind-DM® Liquid: (Available without prescription.)

NDC 0087-0753-44 Bottles of 5 fl oz

TRI-VI-SOL®
Vitamins A, D and C Supplement
infants' drops • chewable tablets

	Drops 1.0 ml	1 Tablet
Vitamin A, IU	1500	2500
Vitamin D, IU	400	400
Vitamin C, mg	35	60

Action and Uses: Tri-Vi-Sol drops and tablets provide vitamins A, D and C.

How Supplied: Tri-Vi-Sol® drops: (with 'Safti-Dropper' marked to deliver 1 ml)

NDC 0087-0403-02 Bottles of 1 fl oz (30 ml)

NDC 0087-0403-03 Bottles of 1⅔ fl oz (50 ml)

Tri-Vi-Sol® tablets:

NDC 0087-0413-02 Bottles of 100 tablets

TRI-VI-SOL® with Iron
Vitamins A, D, C and Iron
Infants' Drops

Composition: Each 1.0 ml supplies same vitamins as in Tri-Vi-Sol® vitamin drops (see above) plus 10 mg iron.

Action and Uses: Tri-Vi-Sol with Iron vitamins A, D, C and Iron for infants.

Administration and Dosage: Drop into mouth with 'Safti-Dropper'. Dose: 1.0 ml daily, or as indicated.

How Supplied: Tri-Vi-Sol® vitamin drops with Iron (with dropper marked to deliver 1 ml)

NDC 0087-0453-03 Bottles of 1⅔ fl oz (50 ml)

Mead Johnson
Pharmaceutical Division
Mead Johnson & Company
2404 W. PENNSYLVANIA ST.
EVANSVILLE, INDIANA 47721

COLACE®
Docusate sodium, Mead Johnson
capsules • syrup • liquid (drops)

Description: Colace (Docusate sodium) is a stool softener.

Actions and Uses: Colace, a surface-active agent, helps to keep stools soft for easy, natural passage. Not a laxative, thus not habit forming. Useful in constipation due to hard stools, in painful anorectal conditions, in cardiac and other conditions in which maximum ease of

passage is desirable to avoid difficult or painful defecation, and when peristaltic stimulants are contraindicated. *Note:* When peristaltic stimulation is needed due to inadequate bowel motility, see Peri-Colace® (laxative and stool softener).

Contraindications: There are no known contraindications to Colace.

Side Effects: The incidence of side effects—none of a serious nature—is exceedingly small. Bitter taste, throat irritation, and nausea (primarily associated with the use of the syrup and liquid) are the main side effects reported. Rash has occurred.

Administration and Dosage: *Orally*—Suggested daily Dosage: *Adults and older children:* 50 to 200 mg. *Children 6 to 12:* 40 to 120 mg. *Children 3 to 6:* 20 to 60 mg. *Infants and children under 3:* 10 to 40 mg. The higher doses are recommended for initial therapy. Dosage should be adjusted to individual response. The effect on stools is usually apparent one to three days after the first dose. Give Colace liquid in half a glass of milk or fruit juice or in infant formula, to mask bitter taste. *In enemas*—Add 50 to 100 mg. Colace (5 to 10 ml. Colace liquid) to a retention or flushing enema.

How Supplied: Colace® capsules, 50 mg.

NDC 0087-0713-01 Bottles of 30
NDC 0087-0713-02 Bottles of 60
NDC 0087-0713-03 Bottles of 250
NDC 0087-0713-05 Bottles of 1000
NDC 0087-0713-07 Cartons of 100 single unit packs

Colace® capsules, 100 mg.

NDC 0087-0714-43 Cartons of 10 single unit packs
NDC 0087-0714-01 Bottles of 30
NDC 0087-0714-02 Bottles of 60
NDC 0087-0714-03 Bottles of 250
NDC 0087-0714-05 Bottles of 1000
NDC 0087-0714-07 Cartons of 100 single unit packs

Note: Colace capsules should be stored at controlled room temperature (15°–30°C. or 59°–86°F.)

Colace® liquid, 1% solution; 10 mg./ml. (with calibrated dropper)

NDC 0087-0717-04 Bottles of 16 fl. oz.
NDC 0087-0717-02 Bottles of 30 ml.
6505-00-045-7786 (Bottle of 30 ml) Defense

Colace® syrup, 20 mg./5-ml. teaspoon; contains not more than 1% alcohol

NDC 0087-0720-01 Bottles of 8 fl. oz.
NDC 0087-0720-02 Bottles of 16 fl. oz.

PERI-COLACE® capsules • syrup
Casanthranol and docusate sodium

Description: Peri-Colace is a combination of the mild stimulant laxative Peristim (casanthranol, Mead Johnson) and the stool-softener Colace (docusate sodium, Mead Johnson). Each capsule contains 30 mg of Peristim and 100 mg of Colace; the syrup contains 30 mg of Peristim and 60 mg of Colace per 15-ml tablespoon (10 mg of Peristim and 20 mg of Colace per 5-ml teaspoon) and 10% alcohol.

Action and Uses: Peri-Colace provides gentle peristaltic stimulation and helps to keep stools soft for easier passage. Bowel movement is induced gently—usually overnight or in 8 to 12 hours. Nausea, griping, abnormally loose stools, and constipation rebound are minimized. Useful in management of chronic or temporary constipation.

Note: To prevent hard stools when laxative stimulation is not needed or undesirable, see Colace (stool softener).

Side Effects: The incidence of side effects—none of a serious nature—is exceedingly small. Nausea, abdominal cramping or discomfort, diarrhea, and rash are the main side effects reported.

Administration and Dosage:

Adults—1 or 2 capsules, or 1 or 2 tablespoons syrup at bedtime, or as indicated. In severe cases, dosage may be increased to 2 capsules or 2 tablespoons twice daily, or 3 capsules at bedtime. *Children*—1 to 3 teaspoons of syrup at bedtime, or as indicated.

Warnings: Do not use when abdominal pain, nausea, or vomiting are present. Frequent or prolonged use of this preparation may result in dependence on laxatives.

Overdosage: In addition to symptomatic treatment, gastric lavage, if timely, is recommended in cases of large overdosage.

How Supplied: Peri-Colace® Capsules
NDC 0087-0715-43 Cartons of 10 single unit pack
NDC 0087-0715-01 Bottles of 30
NDC 0087-0715-02 Bottles of 60
NDC 0087-0715-03 Bottles of 250
NDC 0087-0715-05 Bottles of 1000
NDC 0087-0715-07 Cartons of 100 single unit packs

Note: Peri-Colace capsules should be stored at controlled room temperatures (15°–30°C or 59°–86°F).
Peri-Colace® Syrup
NDC 0087-0721-01 Bottles of 8 fl. oz.
NDC 0087-0721-02 Bottles of 16 fl. oz.

Medicone Company
225 VARICK ST.
NEW YORK, NY 10014

DERMA MEDICONE® Ointment

Composition: Each gram contains:
Benzocaine.................................. 20.0 mg.
8-Hydroxyquinoline sulfate...... 10.5 mg.
Menthol.. 4.8 mg.
Ichthammol................................. 10.0 mg.
Zinc oxide..................................137.3 mg.
Petrolatum, Lanolin, perfume............q.s.

Action and Uses: For prompt, temporary relief of intolerable itching, burning and pain associated with minor skin irritations. A bland, non-toxic, well balanced formula in a non-drying base which will not disintegrate or liquefy at body temperature and is not washed away by urine, perspiration or exudate. Exerts a soothing, cooling influence on irritated skin surfaces by affording mild anesthesia to control the scratch reflex, promotes healing of the affected area and checks the spread of infection. Useful for symptomatic relief in a wide variety of pruritic skin irritations resulting from insect bites, prickly heat, eczema, chafed and raw skin surfaces, sunburn, fungus infections, plant poisoning, pruritus ani and pruritus vulvae—mouth sores, cracked lips, under dentures.

Administration and Dosage: Apply liberally directly to site of irritation and gently rub into affected area for better penetration and absorption. Cover area with gauze if necessary.

Precautions: Do not use in the eyes. If the condition for which this preparation is used persists, or if rash or irritation develops, discontinue use and consult physician.

How Supplied: 1 ounce tubes and one pound jars.

DioMEDICONE® Tablets

Composition: Each tablet contains: 50 mg. dioctyl sodium sulfosuccinate (a surface tension reducing wetting agent) and excipient q.s. to prevent hard stool formation.

Action and Uses: A gentle-acting, non-habit forming stool-softener for effective management of simple constipation due to hard, dry fecal matter. A medically accepted, clinically proven mode of treatment in preventing hard stool formation. Reduces surface tension of intestinal fluids, permitting better infiltration of waste matter, producing a soft pliable fecal mass, making evacuation easy and comfortable. Reduces straining. Does not irritate the intestinal tract or produce peristalsis. Useful in hemorrhoidal and anorectal conditions, during and after pregnancy and whenever smooth, easy bowel evacuation is essential such as in cardiac conditions and before and following surgery. May be safely used as directed, by anyone over 6 years of age.

Administration and Dosage: Children 6 to 12 years: 1 or 2 tablets (50 to 100 mg.) daily with water. Adults and older children: 1 to 4 tablets (50 to 200 mg.) daily with water. Initial dosages may be reduced as normal bowel function is restored. Note: The effect of DioMEDICONE in producing soft, pliable stools usually takes 2 to 3 days.

How Supplied: 50 mg. tablets in vials of 50 tablets.

MEDICONE® DRESSING Cream

Composition: Each gram contains:
Benzocaine...................................... 5.0 mg.
8-Hydroxyquinoline sulfate...... 0.5 mg.
Cod liver oil ....125.0 mg.
Zinc oxide....................................125.0 mg.
Menthol.. 1.8 mg.
Petrolatum, Lanolin, talcum, paraffin & perfume............................q.s.

Action and Uses: Meets the first requisite in the treatment of minor burns, wounds and other denuded skin lesions by exerting mild, cooling anesthetic action for the prompt temporary relief of pain, burning and itching. A stable, non-toxic anesthetic dressing which does not liquefy or wash off at body temperature, nor is it decomposed by exudate, urine or perspiration. Promotes granulation and aids epithelization of affected tissue. The anesthetic, antipruritic, antibacterial properties make Medicone Dressing ideal for the treatment of 1st and 2nd degree burns, minor wounds, abrasions, diaper rashes and a wide variety of pruritic skin irritations.

Administration and Dosage: The smooth, specially formulated consistency allows comfortable application directly to the painful, irritated affected area. It may be spread on gauze before application or covered with gauze as desired.

Precautions: Do not use in the eyes. If the condition for which this preparation is used persists or if a rash or irritation develops, discontinue use and consult physician.

How Supplied: Tubes of 1 ounce and 1 lb. jars.

MEDICONET®
(medicated rectal wipes)

Composition: Each cloth wipe medicated with Benzalkonium chloride, 0.02%; Ethoxylated lanolin, 0.5%; Methylparaben, 0.15%; Hamamelis water, 50%; Glycerin, 10%; Purified water, USP and Perfume, q.s.

Action and Uses: Soft disposable cloth wipes which fulfill the important requisite in treating anal discomfort by providing the facility for gently and thoroughly cleansing the affected area. For the temporary relief of intolerable pain, itching and burning in minor external hemorrhoidal, anal and outer vaginal discomfort. Lanolized, delicately scented, durable and delightfully soft. Antiseptic, antipruritic, astringent. Useful as a substitute for harsh, dry toilet tissue. May also be used as a compress in the pre- and post-operative management of anorectal discomfort. The hygienic Mediconet pad is generally useful in relieving pain, burning and itching in diaper rash, sunburn, heat rash, minor burns and insect bites.

How Supplied: Boxes of 20 individually packaged, pre-moistened cleansing cloths.

RECTAL MEDICONE®
SUPPOSITORIES

Composition: Each suppository contains:
Benzocaine .... 2 gr.
8-Hydroxyquinoline sulfate............¼ gr.
Zinc oxide.. 3 gr.
Menthol..¹⁄₇ gr.
Balsam Peru .... 1 gr.
Cocoa butter—vegetable & petroleum oil base; Certified color added ....q.s.

Action and Uses: A soothing, non-toxic, comprehensive formula carefully designed to meet the therapeutic requirements in adequately treating simple hemorrhoids and minor anorectal disorders. Performs the primary function of promptly alleviating pain, burning and itching temporarily by exerting satisfactory local anesthesia. The muscle spasm, present in many cases of painful anal and rectal conditions, is controlled and together with the emollients provided, helps the patient to evacuate the bowel

Continued on next page

Medicone—Cont.

comfortably and normally. The active ingredients reduce congestion and afford antisepsis, accelerating the normal healing process. Used pre- and post-surgically in hemorrhoidectomy, in prenatal and postpartum care and whenever surgery is contraindicated for the comfort and well-being of the patient during treatment of an underlying cause.

Administration and Dosage: One suppository in the morning and one at night and after each stool, or as directed. Use of the suppositories should be continued for 10 to 15 days after cessation of discomfort to help protect against recurrence of symptoms. See Rectal Medicone Unguent for concurrent internal-external use.

Precautions: If a rash or irritation develops, or bleeding from the rectum occurs, discontinue use and consult physician.

How Supplied: Boxes of 12 and 24 individually foil-wrapped green suppositories.

RECTAL MEDICONE® UNGUENT

Composition: Each gram contains:
Benzocaine................................. 20   mg.
8-Hydroxyquinoline sulfate...... 5   mg.
Menthol.. 4   mg.
Zinc oxide.................................100   mg.
Balsam Peru .... 12.5   mg.
Petrolatum 625   mg.
Lanolin.......................................210   mg.
Certified color added

Action and Uses: A soothing, effective formulation which affords prompt, temporary relief of pain, burning and itching by exerting surface anesthetic action on the affected area in minor internal-external hemorrhoids and anorectal disorders. The active ingredients promote healing and protect against irritation, aiding inflamed tissue to retrogress to normal. The emollient petrolatum-lanolin base provides lubrication making bowel movements easier and more comfortable. Accelerates the normal healing process. Non-toxic. Rectal Medicone Unguent and Rectal Medicone Suppositories are excellent for concurrent management of internal-external irritations.

Administration and Dosage: For internal use—attach pliable applicator and lubricate tip with a small amount of Unguent to ease insertion. Apply liberally into affected area morning and night and after each stool or as directed. When used externally, cover area with gauze. When used with Rectal Medicone Suppositories, insert a small amount of Unguent into the rectum before inserting suppository.

Precautions: If a rash or irritation develops or rectal bleeding occurs, discontinue use and consult physician.

How Supplied: 1½ ounce tubes with pliable rectal applicator.

Medique Products
8050 N. LAWNDALE
SKOKIE, IL 60076

CCP Cough and Cold Tablets

Active Ingredients: Each tablet contains: Phenylpropanolamine HCl 25 mg., Acetaminophen 325 mg., Caffeine 64.8 mg., Guaifenesin 100 mg.

Will not cause drowsiness.

Indications: For temporary relief of symptoms of the Common Cold; nasal congestion, minor aches and pains, post nasal drip associated with the common cold and sinusitus.

Warning: Do not take this for persistent or chronic cough or where cough is accompanied by excessive secretions, consult a physician. Discontinue use if rapid pulse, dizziness or palpitations occur.

Caution: If cough persists for more than 1 week, tends to recur or is accompanied by high fever, or persistent headache, consult a physician. Do not exceed recommended dosage. Do not take if you have high blood pressure, heart disease, diabetes, or thyroid disease, consult a physician. Do not take this product if you are presently taking as antihypertensive or antidepressant drug, consult a physician.

Dosage: Adult: One tablet four times a day.

How Supplied:
1000 Bottle—NDC-47682-106-04
500 Industrial Pak—NDC-47682-106-13
100 Industrial Pak—NDC-47682-106-33

Menley & James Laboratories
a SmithKline company
ONE FRANKLIN PLAZA
P. O. BOX 8082
PHILADELPHIA, PA 19101

A.R.M.® Allergy Relief Medicine
Fast and effective relief

Product Information: Allergies are caused by sensitivity to things like grass and tree pollen, dust, pollution—even pet dander. For allergy sufferers, A.R.M. represents a new era in non-prescription allergy care.

Product Benefits: A.R.M. combines two important medicines in one safe, fast-acting tablet:

- The highest level of antihistamine available without prescription-for better relief of sneezing, runny nose and itchy, weepy eyes.
- A clinically-proven sinus decongestant to help ease breathing and drain sinus congestion for hours.

Dosage: One tablet every 4 hours, not to exceed 4 tablets daily. Children (6-12 years): one-half the adult dose (break tablet in half). Children under 6 years use only as directed by physician.

Warning: Do not exceed recommended dosage. If symptoms do not improve within 7 days, or are accompanied by high fever, consult a physician before continuing use. Stop use if dizziness, sleeplessness or nervousness occurs. If you have or are being treated for depression, high blood pressure, glaucoma, diabetes, asthma, difficulty in urination due to enlarged prostate, heart disease or thyroid disease, use only as directed by physician. During pregnancy, use only as directed by a physician since safe use in pregnancy has not been clearly established. Do not take this product if you are taking another medication containing phenylpropanolamine.

Avoid alcoholic beverages while taking this product. Do not drive or operate heavy machinery as this preparation may cause drowsiness.

May cause excitability, especially in children. Keep this and all medicines out of reach of children. In case of accidental overdose, consult physician or poison control center immediately.

Formula: Each A.R.M. tablet contains chlorpheniramine maleate, 4.0 mg., phenylpropanolamine HCl, 37.5 mg.

How Supplied: Consumer packages of 20 and 40 tablets.

[*Shown in Product Identification Section*]

ACNOMEL® CREAM
acne therapy

Description: *Cream*—sulfur, 8%; resorcinol, 2%; alcohol, 11% (w/w); in a stable, grease-free, flesh-tinted vehicle. Standard strength for home application, morning or night.

Action and Uses: Acnomel provides effective acne therapy. Easily applied, flesh-tinted, it conceals as it heals. Because Acnomel is virtually invisible when applied, it is well accepted by even the most self-conscious person.

Directions: Wash and dry affected areas thoroughly. Apply a thin coating with fingertips or a moist sponge two or three times daily. Do not rub in.

Warning: If undue skin irritation develops or increases, discontinue use and consult physician. Do not apply to acutely inflamed area. Keep out of eyes and off eyelids. Keep this and all medicines out of reach of children. In case of accidental ingestion, contact a physician or poison control center immediately.

How Supplied: *Cream*—in specially lined 1 oz. tubes.

Remarks: Do not dilute or compound. When prescribing write for original container.

[*Shown in Product Identification Section*]

BENZEDREX® INHALER
nasal decongestant

Composition: Each Benzedrex Inhaler is packed with propylhexedrine, 250 mg.; menthol, 12.5 mg.; and aromatics.

Action and Uses: It relieves—*in a matter of seconds*—the congestion of head colds and hay fever. Also useful for the relief of ear block and pressure pain in air travelers.

Benzedrex rarely causes undesirable stimulation or interferes with sleep.

Directions: Insert in nostril. Close other nostril. Inhale twice. Treat other nostril the same way. Avoid excessive use.

Inhaler loses potency after 2 or 3 months' use but some aroma may linger.

Warning: Keep this and all medicines out of reach of children. In the case of accidental overdose or ingestion of contents, seek professional assistance or contact a poison control center immediately.

How Supplied: In single plastic tubes.

[*Shown in Product Identification Section*]

C3®
Cold Cough Capsules

Product Information: All-day or all-night temporary relief from nasal congestion and coughing due to the common cold. C3 acts through your system to check coughing; relieves nasal congestion, sneezing, running nose and watery eyes. Just one capsule taken in the morning and one at bedtime maintain a prolonged, around-the-clock therapeutic action in your system of a highly effective medical formula.

Dosage: 1 capsule every 12 hours.

Caution: Children under 12 years of age and individuals with high blood pressure, heart disease, diabetes, or thyroid disease should use only as directed by physician. Not recommended for children under 6 years of age. If high fever is present or cough persists, see a physician as these symptoms may indicate a serious condition. Do not exceed recommended dosage. Do not take this product for persistent or chronic cough such as occurs with smoking, asthma, or emphysema, or where cough is accompanied by excessive secretions except on the advice of a physician.

Warning: Do not take this product if you are taking another medication containing phenylpropanolamine. Keep this and all medicines out of the reach of children. In case of accidental overdose, get professional aid or call a poison control center immediately. Do not drive or operate machinery as this preparation may cause drowsiness.

Formula: Each capsule contains chlorpheniramine maleate 4 mg., phenylpropanolamine hydrochloride 50 mg., dextromethorphan hydrobromide 30 mg.

How Supplied: Consumer package of 10 capsules.

[*Shown in Product Identification Section*]

CONTAC®
Continuous Action Decongestant Capsules

Product Information: Contac provides an increased amount of decongestant and antihistamine to give prolonged, round-the-clock relief from nasal congestion due to the common cold, hay fever and sinusitis. With just one capsule in the morning and one at bedtime, you feel better all day, sleep better all night, to awake refreshed, breathing freely without congestion.

Product Benefits: Each Contac continuous action capsule contains over 600 "tiny time pills". Some go to work right away for fast relief. The rest are scientifically timed to dissolve slowly, to give up to 12 hours of prolonged relief. Contac provides increased amounts of:

- A DECONGESTANT to help clear nasal and sinus passages and to reduce swollen nasal and sinus tissues.
- AN ANTIHISTAMINE to help relieve itchy, watery eyes; sneezing, running nose and postnasal drip.

Dosage: One capsule every 12 hours.

Warnings: Children under 12 should use only as directed by physician. Do not exceed recommended dosage. If symptoms do not improve within 7 days, or are accompanied by high fever, consult a physician before continuing use. Stop use if dizziness, sleeplessness or nervousness occurs.

Individuals with high blood pressure, glaucoma, diabetes, asthma, difficulty in urination due to enlarged prostate, heart disease or thyroid disease should use only as directed by physician. Do not take this product if you are taking another medication containing phenylpropanolamine.

Avoid alcoholic beverages while taking this product. Do not drive or operate heavy machinery as this preparation may cause drowsiness.

May cause excitability, especially in children. Keep this and all medicines out of reach of children. In case of accidental overdose, consult physician or poison control center immediately. Store at controlled room temperature (59°–86°F.).

Drug Interaction Precaution: Do not take if you are presently taking a prescription antihypertensive or antidepressant drug containing a monoamine oxidase inhibitor except under the advice and supervision of a physician.

Formula: Each capsule contains phenylpropanolamine hydrochloride 75.0 mg.; chlorpheniramine maleate 8.0 mg.

How Supplied: Consumer packages of 10, 20 and 40 capsules. Also, Industrial Dispensary Package of 200 capsules (2's in strip dispenser) for industrial dispensaries only.

[*Shown in Product Identification Section*]

CONTAC®
Severe Cold Formula

Product Information: Two capsules every 6 hours help relieve discomforts of the severe cold (colds with flu-like symptoms such as fever, coughing, aches and pains).

Product Benefits: Contac Severe Cold Formula contains a non-aspirin analgesic, a cough suppressant, a decongestant and an antihistamine. These safe and effective ingredients provide temporary relief from these major cold symptoms: fever, coughing, body aches and pain, minor sore throat pain, headache, running nose, postnasal drip, sneezing, watery eyes and nasal congestion, sinus pressure, sinus congestion.

Dosage: Two capsules every 6 hours, not to exceed 8 capsules daily. Children under 12 should use only as directed by physician.

Warnings: Do not exceed recommended dosage. If symptoms do not improve within 7 days, or worsen, or are accompanied by high fever, or difficulty in breathing, consult a physician before continuing use. Persistent cough may

indicate the presence of a serious condition. Stop use if dizziness, sleeplessness, or nervousness occurs. Individuals with high blood pressure, glaucoma, diabetes, asthma, difficulty in urination due to enlarged prostate, heart disease or thyroid disease should use only as directed by physician. Avoid alcoholic beverages while taking this product. Do not drive or operate heavy machinery as this preparation may cause drowsiness. May cause excitability especially in children. Keep this and all medicines out of reach of children. In case of accidental overdose, consult physician or poison control center immediately. Store at controlled room temperature (59°–86°F.).

Formula: Each capsule contains Pseudoephedrine Hydrochloride 30 mg.; Acetaminophen 500 mg. (500 mg. is a nonstandard dose of acetaminophen, as compared to the standard of 325 mg.); Dextromethorphan Hydrobromide 15 mg.; Chlorpheniramine Maleate 1 mg.

How Supplied: Consumer packages of 10 and 20 capsules.

CONTAC JR.®
The Complete Cold Medicine For Children

Product Information: For congestion, coughing, body aches and fever due to colds. Relieves symptoms with these reliable medicines:

A gentle decongestant. For temporary relief of nasal congestion. Helps your child breathe more freely. A safe, sensible, non-narcotic cough quieter. Calms worrisome coughs due to colds.

A trusted, non-aspirin pain reliever and fever reducer. Provides temporary relief of muscular aches and pains, headaches, discomforts of fever due to colds and "flu."

Product Benefits: The good medicines in Contac Jr. were specially chosen to help relieve your child's congestion, coughing, body aches and fever due to colds-without harsh drugs. Medical authorities know that for children, dose by weight-not age-means the dose you give is right for consistent controlled relief. Use the enclosed Contac Jr. Accu-Measure® Cup to select the right dose for your child's body weight.

Dosage: One dose every four hours, not to exceed 6 times daily. Use the enclosed Contac Jr. Accu-Measure Cup to measure the right dose for your child. You control the proper dose according to your child's body weight so the strength is always right. For dose by teaspoon see bottle label.

Caution: Do not exceed recommended dosage for your child's body weight. For children under 31 lbs. or under 3 years of age, consult a physician.

Warning: If symptoms persist for 7 days or are accompanied by high fever, severe or recurrent pain, or if child has diabetes or heart disease, consult your physician. Keep this and all medicines out of children's reach. In case of accidental overdose, contact a physician immediately. Do not take this product if you are taking

Continued on next page

Menley & James—Cont.

another medication containing phenyl-propanolamine.

Formula: Each 5 cc (average teaspoon) contains: phenylpropanolamine HCl 9.375 mg.; acetaminophen 162.5 mg.; dextromethorphan hydrobromide 5.0 mg.; alcohol 10% by volume.

How Supplied: A clear red liquid in 4 oz. size bottle.

[*Shown in Product Identification Section*]

DIETAC™
Once-A-Day Diet Aid Capsules

Product Benefits:
- Timed-release-just one capsule controls your appetite for 12 hours.
- Helps you lose weight.
- Contains a mild stimulant to help relieve fatigue often caused by dieting.

Dosage: Take one capsule each morning.

Warning: Do not exceed recommended dosage. Do not take this product for periods exceeding three months. Do not give this product to children under 12 years. Do not take this product if you are taking another medication containing phenylpropanolamine. If you have or are being treated for high blood pressure, heart disease, diabetes, thyroid disease or depression, take this product only under the supervision of a physician. If you become nervous, sleepless or dizzy, stop the medication. The recommended dose of this product contains about as much caffeine as a cup of coffee so take with caution while taking caffeine-containing beverages such as coffee, tea or cola drinks.

Keep this and all medicines out of reach of children. In case of accidental overdose, contact a physician or poison control center immediately.

Formula: Each capsule contains phenylpropanolamine HCl 50 mg. (appetite suppressant); caffeine 200 mg. (mild stimulant).

How Supplied: Consumer packages of 14 and 28 capsules

Also Available:
Once-A-Day Dietac Maximum Strength Capsules 20's & 40's.
Twice-A-Day Dietac Maximum Strength Capsules 24's & 48's.
Pre-Meal Dietac Diet Aid Tablets 42's.
Pre-Meal Dietac Diet Aid Drops ½ oz.

[*Shown in Product Identification Section*]

DIETAC™
Diet Aid Drops

Product Benefits:
- Provides a clinically proven safe and effective appetite suppressant.
- Effectively curbs your appetite at meals.
- Helps you lose weight.
- Caffeine-free-can be used in coffee, tea or cola—in the evening, too.

Dosage: Add five drops to your hot or cold beverage 30 minutes before each meal.

DO NOT EXCEED 5 DROPS PER DOSE. DO NOT EXCEED 3 DOSES PER DAY.

Warning: Do not exceed recommended dosage. Do not take this product for periods exceeding three months.

Do not give this product to children under 12 years. Do not take this product if you are taking another medication containing phenylpropanolamine. If you have or are being treated for high blood pressure, heart disease, diabetes, thyroid disease or depression, take this product only under the supervision of a physician. If you become nervous, sleepless, or dizzy, stop the medication.

Keep this and all medicines out of reach of children. In case of accidental overdose, contact a physician or poison control center immediately.

Formula: Each 0.2 ml. (approximately 5 drops) contains phenylpropanolamine HCl 25 mg. (appetite suppressant).

How Supplied: In consumer packages with ½ oz. bottle.

Also Available:
Once-A-Day Dietac Maximum Strength Diet Aid Capsules 20's & 40's.
Twice-A-Day Dietac Maximum Strength Diet Aid Capsules 24's & 48's.
Once-A-Day Dietac Diet Aid Capsules 14's & 28's.
Pre-Meal Dietac Diet Aid Tablets 42's.

[*Shown in Product Identification Section*]

DIETAC™
Pre–Meal Diet Aid Tablets

Product Benefits:
- Provides a clinically proven safe and effective appetite suppressant.
- Curbs your appetite at meals.
- Helps you lose weight.
- Caffeine-free-can be used in the evening.

Dosage: Take one tablet 30 minutes before each meal. Do not exceed 3 tablets per day.

Warning: Do not exceed recommended dosage. Do not take this product for periods exceeding three months. Do not give this product to children under 12 years. Do not take this product if you are taking another medication containing phenylpropanolamine. If you have or are being treated for high blood pressure, heart disease, diabetes, thyroid disease or depression, take this product only under the supervision of a physician. If you become nervous, sleepless or dizzy, stop the medication.

Keep this and all medicines out of reach of children. In case of accidental overdose, contact a physician or poison control center immediately.

Formula: Each tablet contains phenylpropanolamine HCl 25 mg. (appetite suppressant).

How Supplied: In consumer packages of 42 tablets.

Also Available:
Once-A-Day Dietac Maximum Strength Diet Aid Capsules 20's & 40's.
Twice-A-Day Dietac Maximum Strength Diet Aid Capsules 24's & 48's.
Once-A-Day Dietac Diet Aid Capsules 14's & 28's.
Pre-Meal Dietac Diet Aid Drops ½ oz.

[*Shown in Product Identification Section*]

DIETAC®
Maximum Strength
Once-A-Day Diet Aid
Capsules

Product Benefits:
- No stronger, longer-lasting appetite suppressant available without a prescription
- Timed-release—Just one capsule controls your appetite for 12 hours
- Helps you lose weight
- Caffeine-free
- Provides clinically-proven safe and effective appetite suppressant.

Dosage: Take one capsule each morning.

Warning: Do not exceed recommended dosage. Do not take this product for periods exceeding three months. Do not give this product to children under 12 years. Do not take this product if you are taking another medication containing phenylpropanolamine. If you have or are being treated for high blood pressure, heart disease, diabetes, thyroid disease or depression, take this product only under the supervision of a physician. If you become nervous, sleepless or dizzy, stop the medication.

Keep this and all medicines out of reach of children. In case of accidental overdose, contact a physician or poison control center immediately.

Formula: Each capsule contains phenylpropanolamine HCl 75 mg. (appetite suppressant).

How Supplied: In consumer packages of 20's & 40's.

Also Available:
Once-A-Day Dietac Diet Aid Capsules 14's & 28's.
Twice-A-Day Dietac Maximum Strength Diet Aid Capsules 24's & 48's.
Pre-Meal Dietac Diet Aid Tablets 42's.
Pre-Meal Dietac Diet Aid Drops ½ oz.

[*Shown in Product Identification Section*]

DIETAC®
Maximum Strength
Twice-A-Day Diet Aid
Capsules

Product Benefits:
- No stronger appetite suppressant available without a prescription.
- Caffeine-free.
- Provides clinically-proven safe and effective appetite suppressant.

Dosage: Take two capsules daily, one at 10 A.M. another at 4 P.M.

Warning: Do not exceed recommended dosage. Do not take this product for periods exceeding three months. Do not give this product to children under 12 years. Do not take this product if you are taking another medication containing phenylpropanolamine. If you have or are being treated for high blood pressure, heart disease, diabetes, thyroid disease or depression, take this product only under the supervision of a physician. If you become nervous, sleepless or dizzy, stop the medication.

Keep this and all medicines out of reach of children. In case of accidental overdose, contact a physician or poison control center immediately.

Formula: Each capsule contains phenylpropanolamine HCl 37.5 mg. (appetite suppressant).

How Supplied: In consumer packages of 24's and 48's.

Also Available:
Once-A-Day Dietac Maximum Strength Diet Aid Capsules 20's & 40's.
Once-A-Day Dietac Diet Aid Capsuls 14's & 28's.
Pre-Meal Dietac Diet Aid Tablets 42's.
Pre-Meal Dietac Diet Aid Drops ½ oz.

[*Shown in Product Identification Section*]

ECOTRIN®
Enteric-coated Aspirin

When aspirin is needed and gastric discomfort makes therapy with uncoated aspirin tablets impractical—particularly for temporary relief of minor aches and pains of arthritis and rheumatism.

Each Ecotrin tablet contains aspirin, specially processed with Duentric® coating to protect against the possibility of stomach discomfort and upset often associated with aspirin therapy. Technical advances allow these Ecotrin tablets to be smaller and easier to swallow than before, yet have precisely the same strength.

Formula: Each tablet contains 325 mg. (5 gr.) aspirin.

Usual Dosage: 1 or 2 tablets every 4 hours, as necessary. Do not exceed 12 tablets in 24 hours unless directed by a physician.

High aspirin dosage is recommended in arthritis and rheumatic conditions (40–80 gr. daily) and in acute rheumatic fever (up to 120 gr. daily), in divided doses. In arthritic and rheumatic conditions, concomitant use of Ecotrin often permits a reduction in steroid dosage.

Warning: If under medical care, do not use without physician's approval. If pain persists more than 10 days or redness is present, or in arthritic or rheumatic conditions affecting children under 12, consult a physician immediately. Discontinue use if dizziness, ringing in ears or impaired hearing occurs.

Keep this and all medicines out of reach of children. In case of accidental overdose, contact a physician or poison control center immediately.

EASY-OPENING CAP available on 250 tablet bottle—intended for households without children.

How Supplied: 5 grain tablets, in bottles of 36, 100, 250 and 1000.

[*Shown in Product Identification Section*]

FEOSOL® ELIXIR
Hematinic

Description: Feosol Elixir, an unusually palatable iron elixir, provides the body with ferrous sulfate—iron in its most efficient form. The standard elixir for simple iron deficiency and iron-deficiency anemia when the need for such therapy has been determined by a physician. Each 5 ml. (1 teaspoonful) contains ferrous sulfate USP, 220 mg. (44 mg. of elemental iron); alcohol, 5%.

Usual Dosage: *Adults*—1 to 2 teaspoonfuls three times daily. *Children*—½ to 1 teaspoonful three times daily preferably between meals. *Infants*—as directed by physician. Mix with water or fruit juice to avoid temporary staining of teeth; do not mix with milk or wine-based vehicles.

Warning: The treatment of any anemic condition should be under the advice and supervision of a physician. Since oral iron products interfere with absorption of oral tetracycline antibiotics, these products should not be taken within two hours of each other. Occasional gastrointestinal discomfort (such as nausea) may be minimized by taking with meals and by beginning with one teaspoonful the first day, two the second, etc. until the recommended dosage is reached. Iron-containing medication may occasionally cause constipation or diarrhea, and liquids may cause temporary staining of the teeth (this is less likely when diluted). Keep this and all medicines out of reach of children. In case of accidental overdose, contact a physician or poison control center immediately.

How Supplied: A clear orange liquid in 12 fl. oz. bottles.

Also Available: Feosol® Tablets, Feosol® Spansule® capsules.

[*Shown in Product Identification Section*]

FEOSOL® SPANSULE® CAPSULES
Hematinic

Description: Feosol *Spansule* capsules provide the body with ferrous sulfate—iron in its most efficient form—for simple iron deficiency and iron-deficiency anemia, when the need for such therapy has been determined by a physician.

The special *Spansule* capsule formulation—ferrous sulfate in pellets—reduces stomach upset, a common problem with iron.

Formula: Each capsule contains 167 mg. of dried ferrous sulfate USP (50 mg. of elemental iron), equivalent to 250 mg. of ferrous sulfate USP.

Usual Dosage: *Adults and Children*—One to two Feosol *Spansule* capsules daily, depending on severity of iron deficiency. Children too young to swallow the capsule can be given the contents in a spoonful of soft, cool food (applesauce, custard, etc.). *Children under 6*—Use Feosol® Elixir.

Warnings: The treatment of any anemic condition should be under the advice and supervision of a physician. Since oral iron products interfere with absorption of oral tetracycline antibiotics, these products should not be taken within two hours of each other. Keep this and all medicines out of reach of children. In case of accidental overdose, contact a physician or poison control center immediately. Iron-containing medicine may occasionally cause constipation or diarrhea.

How Supplied: Bottles of 30, 100 and 500 capsules; in Single Unit Packages of 100 capsules (intended for institutional use only).

Also available in Tablets and Elixir.

[*Shown in Product Identification Section*]

FEOSOL® TABLETS
Hematinic

Description: Feosol Tablets provide the body with ferrous sulfate, iron in its most efficient form, for iron deficiency and iron-deficiency anemia when the need for such therapy has been determined by a physician. The distinctive triangular-shaped tablet has a special coating to prevent oxidation and improve palatability.

Formula: Each tablet contains 200 mg. of dried ferrous sulfate USP (65 mg. of elemental iron), equivalent to 325 mg. (5 grains) of ferrous sulfate USP.

Usual Dosage: *Adults*—one tablet 3 to 4 times daily, after meals and upon retiring. *Children 6 to 12 years*—one tablet three times a day after meals. *Children under 6 years and infants*—use Feosol® Elixir.

Warning: The treatment of any anemic condition should be under the advice and supervision of a physician. Since oral iron products interfere with absorption of oral tetracycline antibiotics, these products should not be taken within two hours of each other.

Occasional gastrointestinal discomfort (such as nausea) may be minimized by taking with meals and by beginning with one tablet the first day, two the second, etc. until the recommended dosage is reached. Iron-containing medication may occasionally cause constipation or diarrhea.

Keep this and all medicines out of reach of children. In case of accidental overdose, contact a physician or poison control center immediately.

How Supplied: Bottles of 100 and 1000 tablets; in Single Unit Packages of 100 tablets (intended for institutional use only).

Also available in Spansule® capsules and Elixir.

[*Shown in Product Identification Section*]

FEOSOL PLUS®
Iron plus vitamins

Description: For use in iron deficiency and iron-deficiency anemia where additional vitamins are indicated.

Modified Formula (No prescription required)

Formula: Each Feosol Plus capsule contains:

Dried ferrous sulfate ....200 mg.
  (equivalent to 325 mg. ferrous sulfate USP; 65 mg. of elemental iron)
Folic acid ....0.2 mg.
Ascorbic acid
  (Vitamin C) ....50 mg.
Thiamine HCl
  (Vitamin B$_1$) ....2 mg.
Riboflavin
  (Vitamin B$_2$) ....2 mg.
Pyridoxine HCl
  (Vitamin B$_6$) ....2 mg.
Vitamin B$_{12}$
  (activity equivalent) ....5 mcg.
  (derived from streptomyces fermentation)
Nicotinic acid (niacin) ....20 mg.

Continued on next page

Menley & James—Cont.

Usual Dosage: *Adults and Children (over 3 yrs.)* One capsule twice daily or as directed by physician.

Warning: The treatment of any anemic condition should be under the advice and supervision of a physician.

Since oral iron products tend to interfere with absorption of oral tetracycline antibiotics, these products should not be taken within two hours of each other. Keep this and all medicines out of reach of children. In case of accidental overdose, contact a physician or poison control center immediately. Iron-containing medication may occasionally cause constipation or diarrhea.

How Supplied: Bottles of 100 capsules.

[*Shown in Product Identification Section*]

ORNACOL®
Relieves coughing and nasal congestion.

Description: Ornacol is specifically formulated for temporary relief from coughing and nasal congestion due to the common cold and sinusitis.

Ornacol contains no sedatives or antihistamines and, therefore, does not produce drowsiness in most people. This makes it especially suited for working people and others who must remain alert.

Composition: Each red and gray Ornacol Cough & Cold Capsule contains: 30 mg. dextromethorphan hydrobromide; 25 mg. phenylpropanolamine hydrochloride.

Dosage: Ornacol Capsules: *Adults and children over 12*—one capsule four times a day.

Children—consult your physician.

Warning: Persistent cough may indicate the presence of a serious condition. Persons with a high fever or persistent cough should not use this preparation unless directed by a physician. Do not take this product if you are taking another medication containing phenylpropanolamine.

Individuals with high blood pressure, heart disease, diabetes or thyroid disease should use only as directed by a physician. If relief does not occur within three days, discontinue use and consult a physician.

Keep this and all medicines out of reach of children. In case of accidental overdose, contact a physician or a poison control center immediately.

Supplied: Ornacol Cough & Cold Capsules in packages of 20.

[*Shown in Product Identification Section*]

ORNEX®
decongestant/analgesic

Composition: Each blue and white Ornex capsule contains: 18 mg. phenylpropanolamine hydrochloride; 325 mg. acetaminophen.

Action: For temporary relief of nasal congestion, headache, aches, pains and

fever due to colds, sinusitis and flu. No antihistamine drowsiness.

Dosage: Adults—Two capsules every 4 hours. Do not exceed 8 capsules in 24 hours. Children (6 to 12 years)—One capsule every 4 hours. Do not exceed 4 capsules in 24 hours.

Warning: Do not give to children under 6 years or use for more than 10 days, unless directed by physician. Individuals with high blood pressure, heart disease, diabetes or thyroid disease should use only as directed by physician. Do not take this product if you are taking another medication containing phenylpropanolamine.

This package is child-safe; however, keep this and all medicines out of reach of children. In case of accidental overdose, contact a physician or poison control center immediately.

Supplied: In consumer packages of 24 and 48 capsules, in bottles of 100 capsules. Also, Dispensary Packages of 800 capsules for industrial dispensaries and student health clinics only.

[*Shown in Product Identification Section*]

PRAGMATAR® OINTMENT

Description: Cetyl alcohol-coal tar distillate, 4%; precipitated sulfur, 3%; salicylic acid, 3%—in an oil-in-water emulsion base.

Action and Uses: Pragmatar is highly effective in a wide range of common skin disorders both in adults and in children: seborrheic affections, especially of the scalp, including dandruff and "cradle cap"; subacute and chronic dermatitis; eczematous eruptions; fungous infections, including "athlete's foot", etc. *Note:* For use in infants and when otherwise desired, Pragmatar may be diluted by mixing a few drops of water with a small quantity of the ointment in the palm of the hand.

Precautions: Keep out of eyes and off eyelids. Use with care near the groin or on acutely inflamed areas. Do not use on blistered surfaces. If rash or irritation develops, discontinue use.

Administration and Dosage: *On the scalp:* Part hair and massage into small areas before retiring. Apply sparingly but thoroughly to entire scalp. Remove with a light shampoo the following morning. Use no more often than once daily. *On other areas:* Use small quantities, confining application to affected surfaces. Apply no more often than once daily.

Warning: Keep this and all medicines out of reach of children. In case of accidental ingestion, contact a physician or poison control center immediately.

How Supplied: 1 oz. tubes.

[*Shown in Product Identification Section*]

SINE-OFF® Extra Strength
Sinus Medicine
Non-Aspirin Capsules
Relieves headache and congestion

Product Information: Sine-Off Extra Strength Sinus Medicine Non-Aspirin Capsule provides extra strength relief from headache, pain, pressure and congestion due to sinusitis, allergic sinusitis

or the common cold. This formula contains **acetaminophen,** a pain reliever that is unlikely to cause gastric irritation or allergic reactions often associated with aspirin-containing products.

Product Benefits: Eases headache pain and pressure • promotes sinus drainage • shrinks swollen membranes to relieve congestion • relieves postnasal drip.

Dosage: Adults and children over 12 years of age: 2 capsules every 6 hours, not to exceed 8 capsules in any 24-hour period. Children under 12 should use only as directed by physician.

Warnings: Do not exceed recommended dosage. If symptoms do not improve within 7 days, consult a physician before continuing use. Individuals being treated for depression, high blood pressure, asthma, heart disease, diabetes, thyroid disease, glaucoma or enlarged prostate should use only as directed by a physician.

Avoid alcoholic beverages while taking this product. Do not drive or operate heavy machinery as this preparation may cause drowsiness.

Stop use if dizziness, sleeplessness or nervousness occurs. Safe use in pregnancy has not been established. Therefore, product should be used during pregnancy only as directed by a physician. Do not take this medication if you are taking another product containing phenylpropanolamine.

May cause excitability, especially in children. This package is child-safe; however, keep this and all medicines out of reach of children. In case of accidental overdose, contact a physician immediately.

Formula: Each capsule contains: Chlorpheniramine maleate, 2.0 mg.; phenylpropanolamine HCl, 18.75 mg.; acetaminophen, 500 mg. **(500 mg. is a non-standard dosage of acetaminophen, as compared to the standard of 325 mg.).**

How Supplied: Consumer packages of 20 capsules.

Also Available: Sine-Off® Extra Strength Sinus Medicine Non-Aspirin Tablets 20's. Sine-Off® Sinus Medicine Tablets with Aspirin in 24's, 48's, 100's.

[*Shown in Product Identification Section*]

SINE-OFF® Extra Strength
Sinus Medicine
Non-Aspirin Tablets
Relieves sinus headache and congestion

Product Information: Sine-Off provides extra strength relief from headache, pain, pressure and congestion due to sinusitis, allergic sinusitis, or the common cold. This formula contains acetaminophen, a pain reliever that is unlikely to cause gastric irritation or allergic reactions often associated with aspirin-containing products.

Product Benefits: Eases headache pain and pressure; promotes sinus drainage; shrinks swollen membranes to relieve congestion; relieves drip.

Dosage: Adults and children over 12 years of age, 2 tablets per dose. Allow at least 6 hours between doses. Do not exceed 8 tablets in any 24 hour period.

Warning: Individuals with high blood pressure, heart disease, diabetes, thyroid disease, high fever, or glaucoma should use only as directed by physician. Do not drive or operate heavy machinery as this preparation may cause drowsiness. Consult your physician if symptoms persist or before exceeding the recommended dosage. Do not take this medication if you are taking another product containing phenylpropanolamine. Keep this and all medicines out of reach of children. In case of accidental overdose, contact a physician immediately.

Formula: Each tablet contains chlorpheniramine, 2.0 mg.; phenylpropanolamine HCl, 18.75 mg.; acetaminophen 500 mg. (500 mg. is a non-standard extra strength dosage of acetaminophen, as compared to the standard of 325 mg.).

How Supplied: Consumer packages of 20 tablets.

Also Available: Sine-Off® Tablets with Aspirin in 24's, 48's, 100's. Sine-Off® Extra Strength Non-Aspirin Tablets 20's.

[*Shown in Product Identification Section*]

SINE–OFF® Extra Strength No Drowsiness Formula

Product Information: New No Drowsiness Formula Sine-Off Extra Strength Capsules provide extra strength relief from headache and sinus pain. Relieves pressure and congestion due to sinusitis, allergic sinusitis or the common cold. This formula contains acetaminophen, a pain reliever that is unlikely to cause gastric irritation or allergic reactions often associated with aspirin-containing products.

Product Benefits: Eases headache, pain and pressure. Promotes sinus drainage • shrinks swollen membranes to relieve congestion • does not cause drowsiness.

Dosage: Adults and children over 12 years of age: 2 capsules every 6 hours, not to exceed 8 capsules in any 24-hour period. Children under 12 should use only as directed by physician.

Warnings: Do not exceed recommended dosage. If symptoms do not improve within 7 days, consult a physician before continuing use. Individuals being treated for depression, high blood pressure, heart disease, diabetes, thyroid disease should use only as directed by a physician. Do not take this product if you are taking another medication containing phenylpropanolamine.

Stop use if dizziness, sleeplessness or nervousness occurs. This package is child-safe; however, keep this and all medicines out of reach of children. In case of accidental overdose, contact a physician immediately. Store at controlled room temperature (59°–86°F.).

Formula: Each capsule contains: 18.75 mg. phenylpropanolamine hydrochloride, 500 mg. acetaminophen (500 mg. is a non-standard dosage of acetaminophen, as compared to the standard of 325 mg.).

How Supplied: Consumer packages of 20 capsules.

Also Available:
Sine-Off® Tablets with Aspirin
Sine-Off® Extra Strength Tablets
Sine-Off® Extra Strength Capsules

SINE–OFF® Sinus Medicine Tablets–Aspirin Formula
Relieves sinus headache and congestion

Product Information: Sine-Off relieves headache, pain, pressure and congestion due to sinusitis, allergic sinusitis, or the common cold.

Product Benefits: Eases headache, pain and pressure; promotes sinus drainage; shrinks swollen membranes to relieve congestion; relieves postnasal drip.

Dosage: Adults: 2 tablets every 4 hours, not to exceed 8 tablets daily. Children (6–12) one-half the adult dosage. Children under 6 years use only as directed by physician.

Warning: Individuals with high blood pressure, heart disease, diabetes, thyroid disease, high fever, or glaucoma should use only as directed by physician. Do not drive or operate heavy machinery as this preparation may cause drowsiness. Consult your physician if symptoms persist or before exceeding the recommended dosage. Do not take this medication if you are taking another product containing phenylpropanolamine. This package is child-safe; however, keep this and all medicines out of reach of children. In case of accidental overdose, contact a physician immediately.

Formula: Chlorpheniramine maleate 2.0 mg.; phenylpropanolamine HCl 18.75 mg. aspirin 325.0 mg.

How Supplied: Consumer packages of 24, 48 and 100 tablets

Also Available: Sine-off® Extra Strength Non-Aspirin Capsules 20's, and Extra Strength Non-Aspirin Tablets 20's.

[*Shown in Product Identification Section*]

TELDRIN®
Chlorpheniramine maleate Timed-Release Allergy Capsules, 8 mg. and Maximum Strength 12 mg.

Description: Each Teldrin Timed-Release capsule contains chlorpheniramine maleate, 8 mg. or Maximum Strength 12 mg., so formulated that a portion of the antihistamine dose is released initially, and the remaining medication is released gradually over a prolonged period.

Indications: Teldrin provides up to 12 hours of relief from hay fever/upper respiratory allergy symptoms: sneezing; runny nose; itchy, watery eyes.

Dosage: DOSAGE SHOULD BE INDIVIDUALIZED ACCORDING TO THE NEEDS AND THE RESPONSE OF THE USER.

Adults and children over 12 years of age: Just one capsule in the morning, and one in the evening. Do not give to children under 12 without the advice and consent of a physician. Not to exceed 24 mg. (2 capsules) in 24 hours.

Warning: Do not take this product if you have asthma, glaucoma, or difficulty in urination due to enlargement of the prostate gland, except under the advice and supervision of a physician.

Do not drive or operate heavy machinery as this preparation may cause drowsiness. Avoid alcoholic beverages while taking this product. May cause excitability, especially in children. Keep this and all medicines out of the reach of children. In case of accidental overdose, contact a physician or poison control center immediately.

How Supplied: 8 mg. and Maximum Strength 12 mg. Timed-Release capsules in packages of 12 and 24 capsules, in bottles of 50 and 500; in Single Unit Packages of 100 (intended for institutional use only).

[*Shown in Product Identification Section*]

TROPH–IRON®
Vitamins B₁, B₁₂ and Iron

Description: Each 5 ml. (1 teaspoonful) and each tablet contains thiamine hydrochloride (vitamin B_1), 10 mg.; cyanocobalamin (vitamin B_{12}), 25 mcg.; elemental iron, 30 mg., present as soluble ferric pyrophosphate.

Indications: For deficiencies of vitamins B_1, B_{12} and iron.

Dosage and Administration: Adults and children 4 years of age and over. One 5 ml. teaspoonful or one tablet daily—or as directed by physician.

The treatment of any anemic condition should be under the advice and supervision of a physician. Since oral iron products interfere with absorption of oral tetracycline antibiotics, these products should not be taken within two hours of each other.

Iron-containing medications may occasionally cause gastrointestinal discomfort, such as nausea, constipation or diarrhea.

Warning: Keep this and all medicines out of reach of children. In case of accidental overdose, contact a physician or poison control center immediately.

How Supplied: Liquid—a clear red liquid in 4 fl. oz. (118 ml) bottles; Tablets—bottles of 50. (While its effectiveness is in no way affected, Troph-Iron liquid may darken as it ages.)

[*Shown in Product Identification Section*]

TROPHITE®
Vitamins B₁ and B₁₂

Description: Each 5 ml (1 teaspoonful) and each tablet contains thiamine hydrochloride (vitamin B_1), 10 mg.; and cyanocobalamin (vitamin B_{12}), 25 mcg.

Indications: For deficiencies of vitamins B_1 and B_{12}.

Dosage and Administration: Adults and children 4 years of age and over: One 5 ml. teaspoonful or one tablet daily—or as directed by physician. Children under 4 years: ½ teaspoonful daily.

Trophite Liquid may be mixed with water, milk, or fruit or vegetable juices immediately before taking.

Warning: Keep this and all medicines out of reach of children. In case of acci-

Continued on next page

Menley & James—Cont.

dental overdose, contact a physician or poison control center immediately.
How Supplied: Liquid—4 fl. oz. (118 ml.) bottles. Tablets—bottles of 50.
[*Shown in Product Identification Section*]

The Mentholatum Company
1360 NIAGARA STREET
BUFFALO, NY 14213

MENTHOLATUM DEEP HEATING®
LOTION
Topical Analgesic

Active Ingredient: Methylsalicylate 20%, Menthol 6%.
Indications: For the temporary relief of minor arthritic and rheumatic pain. Also helps relieve muscle soreness and stiffness. Also for muscle tightness due to chest colds.
Actions: Acts as a counterirritant by stimulating cutaneous sensory receptors.
Warnings: For external use only. Keep this and all drugs out of the reach of children. In case of accidental ingestion, seek professional assistance or contact a Poison Control Center immediately. Use only as directed. If pain persists for more than 10 days, or redness is present, or in conditions affecting children under 12 years of age, consult a physician immediately. Discontinue use if excessive irritation of the skin develops. Avoid getting into the eyes or on mucous membranes.
Dosage and Administration: Massage on affected area until it is absorbed into the skin. Repeat as necessary.
Professional Labeling: Same as those under indications.
How Supplied: 2 oz. (safety cap) and 4 oz. bottles.

MENTHOLATUM DEEP HEATING®
RUB
Topical Analgesic

Active Ingredient: Methylsalicylate 12.7%, Menthol 5.8%.
Indications: For the temporary relief of minor arthritic and rheumatic pain. Also helps relieve muscle soreness and stiffness. Also for muscle tightness due to chest colds.
Actions: Acts as a counterirritant by stimulating cutaneous sensory receptors.
Warnings: For external use only. Keep this and all drugs out of the reach of children. In case of accidental ingestion, seek professional assistance or contact a Poison Control Center immediately. Use only as directed. If pain persists for more than 10 days, or redness is present, or in conditions affecting children under 12 years of age, consult a physician immediately. Discontinue use if excessive irritation of the skin develops. Avoid getting into the eyes or on mucous membranes.
Dosage and Administration: Massage on affected area until it is absorbed into the skin. Repeat as necessary.
Professional Labeling: Same as those under indications.

How Supplied: 1¼, 3⅓ and 5 oz. aluminum tubes.

MENTHOLATUM® LIPBALM with SUNSCREEN
Lipbalm with sunscreen

Active Ingredient: Octyldimethyl PABA 8% in a petrolatum base.
Indications: Aids in the prevention and healing of winter chapped lips. Also prevents sunburned lips. Over exposure to sun may lead to lip cancer. Liberal and regular use over the years may reduce the sun's harmful effects.
Actions: Octyldimethyl paba is an effective sunscreen agent. Petrolatum is an effective skin moisturizing agent.
Warnings: For external use only. Avoid contact with the eyes. Discontinue use if signs of irritation or rash appear.
Dosage and Administration: For dry, chapped lips apply as needed. To help prevent dry, chapped sun or windburned lips, apply to lips before, during or following exposure to sun, wind, water and cold weather.
How Supplied: ⅙ oz. Lipsticks in regular, or Cherry, Strawberry and Lemon Ice flavors.

MENTHOLATUM® OINTMENT
Topical Analgesic, Skin protectant

Active Ingredient: Menthol 1.35%, Camphor 9% in a petrolatum base.
Indications: For the symptomatic relief of nasal congestion, bronchial mucous congestion, coughs, muscular tightness and muscular aches and pains due to cold. Also for chapped irritated skin, sunburn, scalds and insect bites.
Actions: Menthol and camphor are cutaneous sensory receptor depressants and thus produce a local analgesia. Petrolatum is an effective skin moisturizing agent.
Warnings: For conditions that persist or are accompanied by fever, see your doctor. For external use only. Do not place in mouth or nostrils. Keep this and all medicines out of the reach of children. In case of accidental ingestion, seek professional assistance or contact a poison control center immediately.
Dosage and Administration: To help relieve discomforts of head colds, chest colds, congestion, coughs, sore throat and that all-over "achy" feeling-rub Mentholatum Ointment on chest, throat and back. For most effective results, cover these areas with a warm cloth. Repeat as often as necessary. To help ease stuffy nose, place a dab of Mentholatum Ointment below each nostril. For skin soreness due to colds, sneezing or runny nose, spread a thin layer over irritated areas, lips and outside of nostrils. Also recommended for: chapped skin, sunburn, scalds, insect bites.
How Supplied: 1 and 3 oz. plastic jars and 1 oz. & ⅖ oz. tubes.

RED CROSS TOOTHACHE KIT
Toothache Drops

Active Ingredient: Eugenol 85%.
Indications: For the temporary relief of discomfort of a tooth with throbbing,

persistent pain until a dentist can be seen.
Actions: Eugenol is an effective dental analgesic acting on tooth nerve endings to eliminate pain.
Warnings: Avoid touching tissue other than the tooth cavity. Keep this and all drugs out of reach of children.
Dosage and Administration: Rinse with water to remove food particles. Use tweezers to moisten pellet and place in cavity.
How Supplied: As a kit containing ⅛ fl. oz. (3.7 ml) bottle of drops, a pair of tweezers and a box of cotton pellets.

RESICORT® CREAM
Hydrocortisone Cream

Active Ingredient: Hydrocortisone acetate 0.5% in a cream base.
Indications: For the temporary relief of minor skin irritations, itching and rashes due to eczema, dermatitis, insect bites, poison ivy, poison oak, poison sumac, soaps, detergents, cosmetics, jewelry, and itchy genital and anal areas.
Actions: Hydrocortisone acetate is a topical anti-inflamatory and an antipruritic.
Warnings: For external use only. Avoid contact with eyes. If condition worsens or if symptoms persist more than 7 days discontinue use and consult a physician. Do not use on children under 2 years except under the advice of a physician. Keep this and all drugs out of the reach of children.
Dosage and Administration: For adults and children 2 years and older, apply to affected area 3 to 4 times daily.
How Supplied: ½ oz. tubes.

RESINOL® CREAM
Antipruritic, Topical

Active Ingredient: Zinc oxide 4.5%, Calamine 3.5%, Resorcinol 2% in a greaseless emulsion type base.
Indications: Soothes and relieves the itching discomfort of minor skin irritations due to windburn, chafing, chapping, minor burns and sunburn, piles or hemorrhoids, Athlete's Foot, Poison Ivy or Poison Oak, non-poisonous insect bites, dry rough skin, prickly heat, and diaper rash.
Actions: The zinc oxide and calamine act as astringents and drying agents in the treatment of poison ivy and oak. The resorcinol acts as an antipruritic.
Warnings: Should not be applied to blistered or raw areas of the skin. Keep this and all medications out of reach of children.
Dosage and Administration: Rub gently into the affected area. Repeat as necessary (3 to 4 times a day).
How Supplied: Available in 1¼ oz. tubes.

RESINOL® OINTMENT
Antipruritic, Topical

Active Ingredient: Zinc Oxide 12%, Calamine 6%, Resorcinol 2% in a petrolatum base.
Indications: Soothes and relieves the itching discomfort of minor skin irrita-

tions due to windburn, chafing, chapping, minor burns and sunburn, piles or hemorrhoids, Athlete's Foot, Poison Ivy or Poison Oak, non-poisonous insect bites, dry rough skin, prickly heat, and diaper rash.

Actions: The zinc oxide and calamine act as astringents and drying agents in the treatment of poison ivy or oak. The resorcinol acts as antipruritic.

Warnings: Should not be applied to blistered or raw areas of the skin. Keep this and all medications out of reach of children.

Dosage and Administration: Rub gently into the affected area. Repeat as necessary (3 to 4 times a day).

How Supplied: Available in 1¼ & 3½ oz. plastic jars.

STOP 'n GROW®
Nail Biting Deterrent

Active Ingredient: Sucrose octaacetate 6%, Denatonium Benzoate 0.15% in a nail lacquer base.

Indications: To aid as a deterrent to nail biting.

Actions: The two bitter compounds act as a deterrent to nailbiting by making insertion of finger nails into the mouth very unpleasant.

Warnings: For external use only. Keep this and all drugs out of the reach of children. In case of accidental ingestion, seek professional assistance or contact a Poison Control Center immediately. Keep away from heat and flame.

Dosage and Administration: Apply over entire nail and cuticle daily. Let dry. Repeat application after washing hands and at bedtime. Continue using at least three months after habit is broken.

How Supplied: 0.22 fl. oz. (6.5 ml) bottle with brush applicator.

Mericon Industries, Inc.
P.O. BOX 5759
PEORIA, IL 61601

DELACORT
(hydrocortisone USP ½%)

Active Ingredient: Hydrocortisone USP ½%.

Indications: For the temporary relief of minor skin irritations, itching and rashes due to eczema, dermatitis, insect bites, poison ivy, poison oak, poison sumac; soaps; detergents, cosmetics, and jewelry, and for itchy genital and anal areas.

Warnings: For external use only. Avoid contact with the eyes. If condition worsens, or if symptoms persist for more than 7 days discontinue use (of this product) and consult a physician. Do not use on children 2 years of age except under the advice and supervision of a physician.

Precaution: KEEP OUT OF REACH OF CHILDREN.

Dosage and Administration: For adults and children 2 years of age and older: Apply to affected area 3 or 4 times daily.

How Supplied: 2 oz. and 4 oz. squeeze bottle.

ORAZINC®
(zinc sulfate)

Active Ingredient: Zinc Sulfate U.S.P. 220 mg. and 110 mg. Capsules.

Indications: A Dietary Supplement containing Zinc.

Warnings: Should be taken with milk or meals to alleviate possible gastric distress.

Symptoms and Treatment of Oral Overdosage: Nausea, mild diarrhea or rash—to control, reduce dosage or discontinue.

Dosage and Administration: One capsule daily or as recommended by Physician.

How Supplied: Bottles of 100 and 1000 Capsules each.

ZINC TABS
(zinc sulfate U.S.P.)

Active Ingredient: Zinc (As Zinc Sulfate U.S.P.) 15 mg. and 25 mg. Tablets.

Indications: A Dietary Supplement containing Zinc.

Warnings: Should be taken with milk or meals to alleviate possible gastric distress.

Symptoms and Treatment of Oral Overdosage: Nausea, mild diarrhea or rash—to control, reduce dosage or discontinue.

Dosage and Administration: One capsule daily or as recommended by Physician.

How Supplied: Bottles of 100 and 1000 Capsules each.

Merrell Dow Pharmaceuticals Inc.
Subsidiary of The Dow Chemical Company
P. O. BOX 68511
9550 ZIONSVILLE ROAD
INDIANAPOLIS, IN 46268

CĒPACOL® Mouthwash/Gargle

Description:
Ceepryn® (cetylpyridinium chloride).. 1:2000
Alcohol 14%
Phosphate buffers and aromatics
Cēpacol is a soothing, pleasant tasting mouthwash/gargle. It has a low surface tension, approximately ½ that of water. This property is the basis of the spreading action in the oral cavity as well as its foaming action. Cēpacol leaves the mouth feeling fresh and clean and helps provide soothing, temporary relief of dryness and minor irritations.

Uses: Recommended as a mouthwash and gargle for daily oral care; as an aromatic mouth freshener to provide a clean feeling in the mouth; as a soothing, foaming rinse to freshen the mouth.

Used routinely before dental procedures, helps give patient confidence of not offending with mouth odor. Often employed as a foaming and refreshing rinse before, during, and after instrumentation and dental prophylaxis. Convenient as a mouth-freshening agent after taking dental impressions. Helpful in reducing

the unpleasant taste and odor in the mouth following gingivectomy.

Used in hospitals as a mouthwash and gargle for daily oral care. Also used to refresh and soothe the mouth following emesis; inhalation therapy, and intubations, and for swabbing the mouths of patients incapable of personal care.

Warning: Keep out of reach of children.

Instructions For Use: Rinse vigorously after brushing or any time to freshen the mouth. Particularly useful after meals or before social engagements. Aromatic Cēpacol leaves the mouth feeling refreshingly clean.

Use full strength every two or three hours as a soothing, foaming gargle, or as directed by a physician or dentist. May also be mixed with warm water.

How Supplied:
6 oz., 12 oz., 18 oz., 24 oz., and a unit package of 4/2-quart bottles
4 oz. Hospital Bedside Bottles (not for retail sale)
4 oz. Dental Chairside Bottles (not for retail sale)
14 oz. Direct Stream Dispenser (not for retail sale)
Professional Unit of 4/2-quart bottles with dispensing pump (not for retail sale)

CĒPACOL® Throat Lozenges

Description:
Ceepryn® (cetylpyridinium chloride)..1:1500
Benzyl alcohol 0.3%
Aromatics
Yellow mint-flavored hard candy base
Cetylpyridinium chloride (Ceepryn) is a cationic quaternary ammonium compound. This is a surface-active agent, which in aqueous solution, has a surface tension lower than that of water. Cetylpyridinium chloride in the concentration used in Cēpacol is non-irritating to tissues.

Indications: Cēpacol Lozenges stimulate salivation to help provide soothing temporary relief of dryness and minor irritation of mouth and throat and resulting cough.

Warning: Severe sore throat or sore throat accompanied by high fever or headache or nausea and vomiting, or any sore throat persisting more than two days may be serious. Consult a physician promptly. Persons with a high fever or persistent cough should not use this preparation unless directed by physician. Do not administer to children under 3 years of age unless directed by physician. Keep this and all medication out of children's reach.

Instructions For Use: May be used as needed. Allow to dissolve slowly in the mouth.

How Supplied:
Trade Package: 27 lozenges in 3 pocket packs of 9 each.
Professional Package: 400 lozenges in 100 foil strips of 4 each.

Continued on next page

Merrell Dow—Cont.

CEPACOL® Anesthetic Troches

Description:
Ceepryn® (cetylpyridinium chloride).................. 1:1500
Benzocaine
Aromatics
Green citrus-flavored hard candy base
Cetylpyridinium chloride (Ceepryn) is a cationic quaternary ammonium compound, which is a surface-active agent. Aqueous solutions of cetylpyridinium chloride have a surface tension lower than that of water.
Cetylpyridinium chloride in the concentration used in Cēpacol is non-irritating to tissues.

Actions:
Anesthetic effect for pain relief
Stimulates salivation—Relieves dryness
Indications: *Sore Throat:* For fast, temporary relief of pain and discomfort due to minor sore throat. For temporary relief of pain and discomfort associated with tonsillitis and pharyngitis. *Mouth Irritations:* For fast, temporary relief of pain and discomfort due to minor mouth irritations. For temporary relief of discomfort associated with stomatitis. For adjunctive, temporary relief of pain and discomfort following periodontal procedures and minor surgery of the mouth.
Warning: Severe sore throat or sore throat accompanied by high fever or headache or nausea and vomiting, or any sore throat persisting more than two days may be serious. Consult a physician promptly. Do not administer to children under 3 years of age unless directed by physician. Keep this and all medication out of children's reach.
Instructions For Use: May be used as needed. Allow to dissolve slowly in the mouth.
How Supplied:
Trade Package: 18 troches in 2 pocket packs of 9 each.
Professional Package: 200 troches in 100 foil strips of 2 each.

CEPASTAT®
sore throat spray/gargle and lozenges
Description:
Sore Throat Spray/Gargle
A liquid available as a spray or gargle containing phenol (1.4%) and glycerin in a pleasant, soothing, aqueous solution.
Lozenges
Cooling sugar-free lozenges containing phenol (1.45%) and menthol (0.12%) in a sorbitol base flavored with eucalyptus oil.
Indications:
Sore Throat Spray/Gargle and Lozenges
1. Sore throat:
   For prompt temporary relief of minor pain or discomfort associated with pharyngitis or tonsillitis or following tonsillectomy.
2. Sore mouth or gums:
   For prompt temporary relief of minor pain or discomfort associated with pericoronitis or periodontitis or with dental procedures such as extrac-

tions, gingivectomies, and other minor oral surgery.
Action:
Sore Throat Spray/Gargle
Phenol is a recognized topical anesthetic. Glycerin provides a soothing effect.
Lozenge
Phenol is a recognized topical anesthetic. Menthol provides a cooling sensation to aid in symptomatic relief and adds to the lozenge effect in stimulating salivary flow.
Warning*:
Sore Throat Spray/Gargle and Lozenges
Do not exceed recommended dosage. If soreness is severe, persists for more than 2 days, or is accompanied by high fever, headache, nausea or vomiting, consult your physician or dentist promptly. Do not give to children under 6 years unless directed by physician or dentist. Do not use for more than 10 days at a time.
KEEP OUT OF REACH OF CHILDREN.
Note To Diabetics*: Each lozenge contains approximately 2 grams of carbohydrate as sorbitol.
Instructions For Use:
Sore Throat Spray/Gargle
For minor sore throat pain:
   As gargle, use full strength. Limit gargling to 15 seconds and expel. As spray, spray 5 times (children 6 to 12 years, spray 3 times) and expel. Repeat either gargle or spray every 2 hours, if necessary.
For discomforts of mouth or gums:
   As gargle, use full strength. Swish around sore or painful areas for 15 seconds and expel. Repeat every 2 hours, if necessary.
Lozenges
Adults
   Dissolve 1 lozenge in mouth every 2 hours. Do not exceed 9 lozenges per day.
Children (6 to 12 years of age)
   Dissolve 1 lozenge in mouth every 3 hours. Do not exceed 4 lozenges per day.
How Supplied:
Sore Throat Spray
   3-ounce bottles with sprayer
Gargle
   14-ounce bottles without sprayer
All bottles are shatterproof plastic.
Lozenges
   300 lozenges in 100 strips of 3 each
   Boxes of 18 lozenges as 2 pocket packs of 9 lozenges each

*This section appears on the label for the consumer.

Children's
CEPASTAT®
sore throat lozenges

Description: Cherry-flavored, sugar-free lozenges containing phenol 0.73% and menthol 0.12% in a sorbitol base. Specially formulated for children 6 years of age and older.
Indications:
1. Sore throat:
   For prompt temporary relief of minor pain or discomfort associated with pharyngitis or tonsillitis or following tonsillectomy.

2. Sore mouth or gums:
   For prompt temporary relief of minor pain or discomfort associated with pericoronitis or periodontitis or with dental procedures such as extractions, gingivectomies, and other minor oral surgery.
Action: Phenol is a recognized topical anesthetic. Menthol provides a cooling sensation to aid in symptomatic relief and adds to the lozenge effect in stimulating salivary flow.
Warnings*: Do not exceed recommended dosage. If soreness is severe, persists for more than 2 days, or is accompanied by high fever, headache, nausea, or vomiting, consult your physician or dentist promptly. Do not give to children under 6 years unless directed by physician or dentist. Do not use for more than 10 days at a time.
KEEP OUT OF REACH OF CHILDREN.
Note To Diabetics*: Each lozenge contains approximately 2 grams of carbohydrate as sorbitol.
Directions*: DO NOT CHEW. 6 to 12 years: 1 lozenge every 3 hours, followed by another after the first one dissolves, if needed during the 3-hour period; do not use more than 2 in 3 hours or more than 10 daily. Over 12 years: 1 lozenge every 2 hours, followed by another after the first dissolves, if needed during the 2-hour period; do not use more than 2 in 2 hours or more than 18 daily. Under 6 years: consult your physician or dentist.
How Supplied: Boxes of 18 lozenges as 2 pocket packs of 9 lozenges each

*This section appears on the label for the consumer.

DELCID®

Description: Each teaspoonful (5 ml.) contains a balanced combination of 600 mg. aluminum hydroxide [$Al(OH)_3$] and 665 mg. magnesium hydroxide [$Mg(OH)_2$]. The sodium content is not more than 15 mg. per teaspoonful.
Actions: The balanced ratio of antacids provides reduction of gastric acidity and gives symptomatic comfort to the patient. The acid neutralizing capacity is 42 mEq. for each 5 ml.
Indications: Delcid is used to relieve the symptoms of hyperacidity associated with peptic ulcer, gastritis, peptic esophagitis, gastric hyperacidity, and hiatal hernia, and to relieve the following symptoms: heartburn, sour stomach, or acid indigestion.
Warnings*: Do not take more than 6 teaspoonfuls in a 24-hour period or use the maximum dosage of this product for more than 2 weeks, except under the advice and supervision of a physician. May have laxative effect. Do not use this product except under the advice and supervision of a physician if you have kidney disease. Keep this and all drugs out of the reach of children. In case of accidental overdose, seek professional assistance or contact a poison control center immediately.
Drug Interaction Precautions*: Do not take this product if you are presently

taking a prescription antibiotic drug containing any form of tetracycline.

Adverse Reactions: Miscellaneous reports include diarrhea, nausea, and vomiting.

Dosage and Administration: 1 teaspoonful, ½ to 1 hour after meals and at bedtime or as directed.

Directions: Take as needed to alleviate symptoms: 1 teaspoonful every 4 hours, or as directed by a physician.

How Supplied: 8 fl. oz. plastic bottles

---

*This section appears on the label for the consumer.

KOLANTYL®

Description: Each teaspoonful (5 ml.) of Kolantyl Gel contains:

Aluminum hydroxide
  [Al (OH)₃] ....150 mg.

Magnesium hydroxide
  [Mg(OH)₂] ....150 mg.

Each Kolantyl Wafer contains:

Aluminum hydroxide ....180 mg.
  (supplied as dried aluminum
  hydroxide gel)

Magnesium hydroxide ....170 mg.

Actions: The balanced ratio of antacids provides reduction of gastric acidity and gives symptomatic comfort to the patient. The acid neutralizing capacity is 10.5 mEq. for each 5 ml. of gel and 10.8 mEq. for each wafer.

Indications: Kolantyl is used to relieve the symptoms of hyperacidity associated with peptic ulcer, gastritis, peptic esophagitis, gastric hyperacidity, and hiatal hernia, and to relieve the following symptoms: heartburn, sour stomach, or acid indigestion.

Warnings*: Do not take more than 12 teaspoonfuls of gel or 12 wafers in a 24-hour period or use the maximum dosage of this product for more than 2 weeks, except under the advice and supervision of a physician. May have laxative effect. Do not use this product except under the advice and supervision of a physician if you have kidney disease. Keep this and all drugs out of the reach of children. In case of accidental overdose, seek professional assistance or contact a poison control center immediately.

Drug Interaction Precautions*: Do not take this product if you are presently taking a prescription antibiotic drug containing any form of tetracycline.

Adverse Reactions: Miscellaneous reports include nausea and vomiting, abdominal discomfort, stomatitis, rash, dizziness, and diarrhea.

Dosage and Administration:
Kolantyl Gel: 1 to 4 teaspoonfuls ½ to 1 hour after meals and at bedtime or as directed. May be taken undiluted or mixed with milk or water, particularly if the patient is on a regular milk regimen. Kolantyl Wafers: 1 to 4 wafers ½ to 1 hour after meals and at bedtime or as directed. Wafers may be chewed or allowed to dissolve in the mouth.

Directions:
Kolantyl Gel—Take as needed to alleviate symptoms: 1 to 4 teaspoonfuls every 4 hours, or as directed by a physician.

Kolantyl Wafers—Take as needed to alleviate symptoms: 1 to 4 wafers every 4 hours, or as directed by a physician. Wafers may be chewed or allowed to dissolve in the mouth.

How Supplied:
Kolantyl Gel: 6 oz. and 12 oz. bottles
Kolantyl Wafers: boxes of 32 wafers, boxes of 96 wafers, and boxes of 400 wafers in sealed strips of 4 wafers each

---

*This section appears on the label for the consumer.

NOVAHISTINE® COUGH FORMULA
Antitussive–Expectorant
Liquid

Description: Each 5 ml teaspoonful contains: dextromethorphan hydrobromide, 10 mg. and guaifenesin (glyceryl guaiacolate), 100 mg. The formulation also contains alcohol, 7.5%.

Actions: Dextromethorphan suppresses the cough reflex by a direct effect on the cough center in the medulla of the brain. Although it is chemically related to morphine, it produces no analgesia or addiction. Its antitussive activity is about equal to that of codeine.

Guaifenesin (glyceryl guaiacolate) acts as an expectorant by increasing respiratory tract fluid which reduces the viscosity of tenacious secretions, thus making expectoration easier.

Indications: For the control of exhausting cough spasms and to convert a dry, nonproductive cough to a productive one. Generally, such coughs include those associated with colds, influenza and pertussis. It may also be used to provide symptomatic cough relief in some chronic respiratory disorders, such as tuberculosis or bronchitis, especially when these are associated with dry, nonproductive coughing.

Contraindications: NOVAHISTINE COUGH FORMULA is contraindicated in persistent or chronic cough such as occurs with smoking, asthma, or emphysema, or when cough is accompanied by excessive secretions, except on advice of a physician.

This drug is contraindicated in patients with hypersensitivity or idiosyncrasy to the formula ingredients.

Warnings: Patients taking MAO inhibitors should not be given drug preparations containing dextromethorphan. If cough persists for more than 1 week, tends to recur, or is accompanied by high fever, rash or persistent headache, consult a physician.

Precautions: Dextromethorphan is incompatible with penicillins, tetracyclines, salicylates, phenobarbital and high concentrations of iodides.

  Note: Guaifenesin interferes with the colorimetric determination of 5-hydroxyindoleacetic acid (5-HIAA) and vanillylmandelic acid (VMA).

Adverse Reactions: These occur infrequently with usual doses. When they occur, adverse reactions may include nausea and dizziness, gastrointestinal upset or vomiting.

Dosage and Administration: Adults and children 12 years or older, 2 teaspoonfuls every 4 hours. Children 6 to under 12 years, 1 teaspoonful every 4 hours. Children 2 to under 6 years, ½ teaspoonful every 4 hours. Not more than 4 doses in 24 hours. For children under 2 years of age give only as directed by a physician.

How Supplied: In 4 fluid ounce bottles and 8 fluid ounce bottles.

NOVAHISTINE® COUGH & COLD FORMULA
Antitussive-Decongestant-
Antihistamine
Liquid

Description: Each 5 ml. teaspoonful of NOVAHISTINE COUGH & COLD FORMULA contains dextromethorphan hydrobromide, 10 mg., pseudoephedrine hydrochloride, 30 mg., and chlorpheniramine maleate, 2 mg. The formulation also contains alcohol, 5%.

Actions: Dextromethorphan suppresses the cough reflex by a direct effect on the cough center in the medulla of the brain. Although it is chemically related to morphine, it produces no analgesia or addiction. Its antitussive activity is about equal to that of codeine.

Pseudoephedrine is an orally effective nasal decongestant. Pseudoephedrine is a sympathomimetic amine with peripheral effects similar to epinephrine and central effects similar to, but less intense than, amphetamines. It has the potential for excitatory side-effects. At the recommended oral dosage, pseudoephedrine has little or no pressor effect in normotensive adults. Patients have not been reported to experience the rebound congestion sometimes experienced with frequent, repeated use of topical decongestants.

Chlorpheniramine is an antihistaminic drug which possesses anticholinergic and sedative effects. It is considered one of the most effective and least toxic of the histamine antagonists. Chlorpheniramine antagonizes many of the pharmacologic actions of histamine. It prevents released histamine from dilating capillaries and causing edema of the respiratory mucosa.

Indications: For the relief of exhausting, nonproductive cough and nasal congestion associated, for example, with the common cold, acute upper respiratory infections, sinusitis, and hay fever or upper respiratory allergies.

Contraindications: NOVAHISTINE COUGH & COLD FORMULA is contraindicated in persistent or chronic cough such as occurs with smoking, asthma, or emphysema, or when cough is accompanied by excessive secretions, except on advice of a physician. It is also contraindicated in patients with narrow-angle glaucoma, urinary retention, peptic ulcer, or during an asthmatic attack, patients with severe hypertension, severe coronary artery disease, and patients on MAO inhibitor therapy.

Continued on next page

Merrell Dow—Cont.

Nursing Mothers: Pseudoephedrine is contraindicated in nursing mothers because of the higher than usual risk for infants from sympathomimetic amines.

Hypersensitivity: This drug is contraindicated in patients with hypersensitivity or idiosyncrasy to antitussives, sympathomimetic amines or antihistamines. Patient idiosyncrasy to adrenergic agents may be manifested by insomnia, dizziness, weakness, tremor or arrhythmias.

Warnings: Use judiciously and sparingly in patients with hypertension, diabetes mellitus, ischemic heart disease, increased intraocular pressure, hyperthyroidism, or prostatic hypertrophy. Sympathomimetics may produce central nervous system stimulation and convulsions or cardiovascular collapse with accompanying hypotension.

Do not exceed recommended dosage.

Use in Pregnancy: The safety of pseudoephedrine for use during pregnancy has not been established.

Use in Elderly: The elderly (60 years and older) are more likely to have adverse reactions to sympathomimetics. Overdosage of sympathomimetics in this age group may cause hallucinations, convulsions, CNS depression, and death. Antihistamines may cause excitability, especially in children. If cough persists for more than 1 week, tends to recur, or is accompanied by high fever, rash or persistent headache, consult a physician.

Precautions: Drugs containing pseudoephedrine should be used with caution in patients with diabetes, hypertension, cardiovascular disease and hyperreactivity to ephedrine. The antihistaminic agent may cause drowsiness and ambulatory patients who operate machinery or motor vehicles should be cautioned accordingly.

Adverse Reactions: These occur infrequently with usual doses. When they occur, adverse reactions may include nausea and dizziness, gastrointestinal upset or vomiting.

Because of the pseudoephedrine in NOVAHISTINE COUGH & COLD FORMULA, hyperreactive individuals may display ephedrine-like reactions such as tachycardia, palpitations, headache, dizziness or nausea. Sympathomimetic drugs have been associated with certain untoward reactions including fear, anxiety, tenseness, restlessness, tremor, weakness, pallor, respiratory difficulty, dysuria, insomnia, hallucinations, convulsions, CNS depression, arrhythmias and cardiovascular collapse with hypotension.

Patients may experience mild sedation. Possible side effects from the antihistamine may include dry mouth, dizziness, weakness, anorexia, nausea, vomiting, headache, nervousness, polyuria, heartburn, diplopia, dysuria and, very rarely, dermatitis.

Drug Interactions: MAO inhibitors and beta adrenergic blockers increase the effects of pseudoephedrine (sympa-

thomimetics). Sympathomimetics may reduce the antihypertensive effects of methyldopa, mecamylamine, reserpine and veratrum alkaloids.

Antihistamines have been shown to enhance one or more of the effects of tricyclic antidepressants, barbiturates, alcohol and other central nervous system depressants.

Dosage and Administration: Adults and children 12 years or older, 2 teaspoonfuls every 4 to 6 hours. Children 6 to under 12 years, 1 teaspoonful every 4 to 6 hours. Children 2 to under 6 years, ½ teaspoonful every 4 to 6 hours. Not more than 4 doses in 24 hours. For children under 2 years of age, at the discretion of the physician.

Note: NOVAHISTINE COUGH & COLD FORMULA does not require a prescription. The package label has dosage instructions as follows: Adults and children 12 years or older, 2 teaspoonfuls every 4 to 6 hours. Children 6 to under 12 years, 1 teaspoonful every 4 to 6 hours. Not more than 4 doses in 24 hours. For children under 6 years of age give only as directed by a physician.

How Supplied: In 4 fluid ounce bottles and 8 fluid ounce bottles.

NOVAHISTINE® DMX
Antitussive-Decongestant
Liquid

Description: Each 5 ml. teaspoonful of NOVAHISTINE DMX contains: dextromethorphan hydrobromide, 10 mg., pseudoephedrine hydrochloride, 30 mg., and guaifenesin (glyceryl guaiacolate), 100 mg. Dextromethorphan, a synthetic non-narcotic antitussive, is the dextrorotatory isomer of 3-methoxy-N- methylmorphinan. Pseudoephedrine hydrochloride is the salt of a pharmacologically active stereoisomer of ephedrine (1-phenyl-2-methylamino propanol). The formulation also contains alcohol, 10%.

Actions: Dextromethorphan suppresses the cough reflex by a direct effect on the cough center in the medulla of the brain. Although it is chemically related to morphine, it produces no analgesia or addiction. Its antitussive activity is about equal to that of codeine.

Pseudoephedrine hydrochloride is an orally effective nasal decongestant. Pseudoephedrine is a sympathomimetic amine with peripheral effects similar to epinephrine and central effects similar to, but less intense than, amphetamines. Therefore, it has the potential for excitatory side effects. Pseudoephedrine at the recommended oral dosage has little or no pressor effect in normotensive adults. Patients taking pseudoephedrine orally have not been reported to experience the rebound congestion sometimes experienced with frequent, repeated use of topical decongestants. Pseudoephedrine is not known to produce drowsiness.

Guaifenesin (glyceryl guaiacolate) acts as an expectorant by increasing respiratory tract fluid which reduces the viscosity of tenacious secretions, thus making expectoration easier.

Indications: NOVAHISTINE DMX is indicated when exhausting, nonproduc-

tive cough accompanies respiratory tract congestion. It is useful in the symptomatic relief of upper respiratory congestion associated with the common cold, influenza, bronchitis, and sinusitis.

Contraindications: Sympathomimetic amines are contraindicated in patients with severe hypertension, severe coronary artery disease, and in patients on MAO inhibitor therapy. Patient idiosyncrasy to adrenergic agents may be manifested by insomnia, dizziness, weakness, tremor or arrhythmias.

Nursing mothers: Pseudoephedrine is contraindicated in nursing mothers because of the higher than usual risk for infants from sympathomimetic amines.

Hypersensitivity: This drug is contraindicated in patients with hypersensitivity or idiosyncrasy to sympathomimetic amines, dextromethorphan, or to other formula ingredients.

Warnings: Sympathomimetic amines should be used judiciously and sparingly in patients with hypertension, diabetes mellitus, ischemic heart disease, increased intraocular pressure, hyperthyroidism and prostatic hypertrophy. Sympathomimetics may produce central nervous system stimulation with convulsions or cardiovascular collapse with accompanying hypotension. See, however, Contraindications.

Use in pregnancy: The safety of pseudoephedrine for use during pregnancy has not been established.

Use in elderly: The elderly (60 years and older) are more likely to have adverse reactions to sympathomimetics. Overdosage of sympathomimetics in this age group may cause hallucinations, convulsions, CNS depression, and death.

Precautions: Pseudoephedrine should be used with caution in patients with diabetes, hypertension, cardiovascular disease and hyperreactivity to ephedrine. See, however, Contraindications.

Adverse Reactions: Adverse reactions occur infrequently with usual oral doses of NOVAHISTINE DMX. When they occur, adverse reactions may include gastrointestinal upset and nausea. Because of the pseudoephedrine in NOVAHISTINE DMX, hyperreactive individuals may display ephedrine-like reactions such as tachycardia, palpitations, headache, dizziness or nausea. Sympathomimetic drugs have been associated with certain untoward reactions including fear, anxiety, tenseness, restlessness, tremor, weakness, pallor, respiratory difficulty, dysuria, insomnia, hallucinations, convulsions, CNS depression, arrhythmias, and cardiovascular collapse with hypotension.

Note: Guaifenesin interferes with the colorimetric determination of 5-hydroxyindoleacetic acid (5-HIAA) and vanillylmandelic acid (VMA).

Drug Interactions: MAO inhibitors and beta adrenergic blockers increase the effects of pseudoephedrine (sympathomimetics). Sympathomimetics may reduce the antihypertensive effects of methyldopa, mecamylamine, reserpine, and veratrum alkaloids.

Dosage: Adults and older children, two teaspoonfuls, 3 to 4 times a day. Children 6 to 12 years of age, one teaspoonful, 3 to 4 times a day. Children 2 to 5 years of age, one-half teaspoonful, 3 to 4 times a day. May be given to children under 2 at the discretion of the physician.

Note: NOVAHISTINE DMX does not require a prescription. The package label has dosage instructions as follows:

Adults, and children over 12 years of age, two teaspoonfuls, every 4 to 6 hours. Children 6 to 12 years of age, one teaspoonful, every 4 to 6 hours. Children 2 to 5 years of age, one-half teaspoonful, every 4 to 6 hours. Not more than four doses every 24 hours. For children under 2 years of age, give only as directed by a physician.

How Supplied: As a red syrup in 4 fluid ounce bottles and 8 fluid ounce bottles.

NOVAHISTINE® ELIXIR
NOVAHISTINE® COLD TABLETS
Decongestant—Antihistaminic

Description: Each 5 ml. teaspoonful of elixir or each tablet contains: phenylpropanolamine hydrochloride, 18.75 mg., chlorpheniramine maleate, 2 mg. The elixir also contains alcohol, 5%.

Actions: NOVAHISTINE, Elixir or Cold Tablets, has decongestant and antihistaminic actions. Phenylpropanolamine hydrochloride, an orally effective nasal decongestant, is a sympathomimetic amine similar in action to ephedrine but with less central nervous system stimulation. Phenylpropanolamine, at the recommended oral dosage, has no significant effect on blood pressure and pulse rate in normotensive adults. Patients taking phenylpropanolamine orally have not been reported to experience the rebound congestion sometimes experienced with frequent, repeated use of topical decongestants.

Chlorpheniramine maleate, an antihistaminic effective for the symptomatic relief of allergic rhinitis, possesses mild anticholinergic and sedative effects. Chlorpheniramine antagonizes many of the pharmacologic actions of histamine. It prevents released histamine from dilating capillaries and causing edema of the respiratory mucosa.

Indications: NOVAHISTINE Elixir or Cold Tablets are indicated for the temporary relief of nasal congestion and eustachian tube congestion associated with the common cold, sinusitis, and hay fever (allergic rhinitis). They also provide temporary relief of runny nose, sneezing, itching of nose or throat and itchy and watery eyes as may occur in hay fever (allergic rhinitis). May be given concomitantly, when indicated, with analgesics and antibiotics.

Contraindications: Sympathomimetic amines are contraindicated in patients with severe hypertension, severe coronary artery disease, in patients on MAO inhibitor therapy, and in nursing mothers.

Antihistamines are contraindicated in patients with narrow-angle glaucoma, urinary retention, peptic ulcer, during an asthmatic attack, and in patients receiving MAO inhibitors.

NOVAHISTINE Elixir or Cold Tablets are contraindicated in patients with hyersensitivity or idiosyncrasy to sympathomimetic amines or antihistamines.

Warnings: If sympathomimetic amines are used in patients with hypertension, diabetes mellitus, ischemic heart disease, increased intraocular pressure, hyperthyroidism, or prostatic hypertrophy, judicious caution should be exercised. The elderly (60 years and older) are more likely to have adverse reactions to sympathomimetics. Safety for use during pregnancy has not been established. Antihistamines may cause excitability, especially in children.

At dosages higher than the recommended dose, nervousness, dizziness, or sleeplessness may occur.

Precautions: Caution should be exercised if used in patients with high blood pressure, heart disease, diabetes or thyroid disease. The antihistamine may cause drowsiness, and ambulatory patients who operate machinery or motor vehicles should be cautioned accordingly.

Adverse Reactions: Drugs containing sympathomimetic amines have been associated with certain untoward reactions including fear, anxiety, tenseness, restlessness, tremor, weakness, pallor, respiratory difficulty, dysuria, insomnia, hallucinations, convulsions, CNS depression, arrhythmias, and cardiovascular collapse with hypotension. Phenylpropanolamine is considered safe and relatively free of unpleasant side-effects, when taken at recommended dosage. However, there have been isolated reports of individuals experiencing an acute hypertensive episode after taking therapeutic doses of phenylpropanolamine-containing preparations.

Patients sensitive to antihistamine drugs may experience mild sedation. Other side-effects from antihistamines may include dry mouth, dizziness, weakness, anorexia, nausea, vomiting, headache, nervousness, polyuria, heartburn, diplopia, dysuria, and, very rarely, dermatitis.

Drug Interactions: MAO inhibitors and beta adrenergic blockers increase the effects of sympathomimetics. Sympathomimetics may reduce the antihypertensive effects of methyldopa, mecamylamine, reserpine and veratrum alkaloids. Antihistamines have been shown to enhance one or more of the effects of tricyclic antidepressants, barbiturates, alcohol, and other central nervous system depressants.

Dosage: Adults, 2 teaspoonfuls or tablets every 4 hours; children 6 to 12 years, 1 teaspoonful or tablet every 4 hours; children 2 to 5 years, ½ teaspoonful every 4 hours. *Do not exceed 4 doses in a 24-hour period.* For children under 2 years, at the discretion of the physician.

Note: NOVAHISTINE Elixir or Cold Tablets do not require a prescription.

The package label has dosage instructions as follows:

Adults, 2 teaspoonfuls or tablets every 4 hours; children 6 to 12 years, 1 teaspoonful or tablet every 4 hours. Not more than 4 doses in 24 hours. For children under 6 years, consult a physician.

How Supplied: NOVAHISTINE Elixir, as a green liquid in 4 fluid ounce bottles and 8 fluid ounce bottles.

NOVAHISTINE Cold Tablets in unit dose packages of 24 tablets and 48 tablets.

NOVAHISTINE®
SINUS TABLETS
Analgesic-Decongestant-Antihistamine

Description: Each NOVAHISTINE SINUS TABLET contains acetaminophen, 325 mg., pseudoephedrine hydrochloride, 30 mg., and chlorpheniramine maleate, 2 mg.

Actions: Combines the actions of a nasal decongestant, pseudoephedrine; an antihistamine, chlorpheniramine; and an analgesic, acetaminophen.

Acetaminophen is a synthetic non-narcotic derivative of paraminophenol with an analgesic effect similar to that of aspirin. Unlike aspirin, acetaminophen has no anti-inflammatory or uricosuric activity. It produces less gastric irritation than salicylates, does not appear to depress prothrombin levels at recommended doses and usually can be taken by persons sensitive to aspirin.

Pseudoephedrine hydrochloride, an orally effective nasal decongestant, is a sympathomimetic amine with peripheral and central effects. It has the potential for excitatory side-effects. Pseudoephedrine at the recommended oral dosage has little or no pressor effect in normotensive adults. Patients taking pseudoephedrine orally have not been reported to experience the rebound congestion sometimes experienced with frequent, repeated use of topical decongestants.

Chlorpheniramine maleate is one of the most effective and least toxic of the histamine antagonists. The antihistaminic action of chlorpheniramine prevents released histamine from dilating capillaries and causing edema of the respiratory mucosa. It also possesses anticholinergic and sedative effects.

Indications: NOVAHISTINE SINUS TABLETS provide temporary relief of nasal and upper respiratory tract congestion, sneezing, runny nose, watery eyes, myalgia, and headache associated with colds and other viral infections, sinusitis, influenza, and seasonal and perennial nasal allergies.

May be given concomitantly, when indicated, with antibiotics.

Contraindications: Patients with severe hypertension, severe coronary artery disease, on MAO inhibitor therapy, narrow angle glaucoma, urinary retention, peptic ulcer, during an asthmatic attack, seriously impaired liver and kid-

Continued on next page

Merrell Dow—Cont.

ney function, gastrointestinal bleeding, severe or recurrent pain, in nursing mothers and hypersensitivity to its ingredients.

Repeated administration of acetaminophen-containing products is contraindicated in patients with anemia or cardiac, pulmonary, renal and hepatic disease.

Warnings: Drugs containing sympathomimetics should be used judiciously and sparingly in patients with hypertension, diabetes mellitus, ischemic heart disease, increased intraocular pressure, hyperthyroidism, or prostatic hypertrophy. Sympathomimetics may produce central nervous system stimulation and convulsions or cardiovascular collapse with accompanying hypotension. Antihistamines may impair mental and physical abilities required for the performance of potentially hazardous tasks, such as driving a vehicle or operating machinery, and mental alertness in children. Acetaminophen should be used judiciously in patients with pre-existing anemias, peptic ulcer and diminished hepatic or renal function.

Safety in pregnancy has not been established. The elderly (60 years and older) are more likely to have adverse reactions to sympathomimetics and antihistamines.

Precautions: Patients with hypertension, cardiovascular, liver and kidney disease, anemia, hyperreactivity to ephedrine, or a history of bronchial asthma, (see Contraindications) should not exceed recommended dose.

Adverse Reactions: Sympathomimetics have been associated with certain untoward reactions including fear, anxiety, tenseness, restlessness, tremor, weakness, pallor, respiratory difficulty, dysuria, insomnia, hallucinations, convulsions, CNS depression, arrhythmias, and cardiovascular collapse with hypotension.

Possible side-effects of antihistamines are drowsiness, restlessness, dizziness, weakness, dry mouth, anorexia, nausea, headache and nervousness, blurring of vision, heartburn, dysuria and very rarely, dermatitis.

Side-effects of acetaminophen associated with higher than recommended doses include anorexia, nausea, vomiting, excitement (CNS stimulation) and abdominal pain. Chronic ingestion has in rare occasions caused methemoglobinemia, agranulocytosis, thrombocytopenia, hemolytic anemia and renal necrosis.

Drug Interactions: MAO inhibitors and beta adrenergic blockers increase the effect of sympathomimetics and the anticholinergic (drying) effects of antihistamines. Sympathomimetics may reduce the antihypertensive effects of methyldopa, mecamylamine, reserpine and veratrum alkaloids. Concomitant use of antihistamines with alcohol, tricyclic antidepressants, barbiturates and other central nervous system depressants may have an additive effect.

Dosage and Administration: Adults, 2 tablets every 4 hours; children 6 to 12 years, 1 tablet every 4 hours. Not more than 4 doses in 24 hours. For children under 6 years, at the discretion of a physician.

Overdosage: Acetaminophen in massive overdosage has caused liver damage and fatal hepatic necrosis.

How Supplied: Boxes of 24 tablets and 48 tablets. Tablets are white with the Dow diamond on one side and number 71 on the other.

RESOLVE® COLD SORE & FEVER BLISTER RELIEF
1% dyclonine hydrochloride U.S.P. Topical Anesthetic Gel
FOR EXTERNAL USE

Description: Each gram of RESOLVE contains dyclonine hydrochloride (4'-butoxy-3-piperidinopropiophenone hydrochloride) 10 mg.

Actions: RESOLVE produces surface anesthesia when applied topically to inflamed or abraded skin or to mucous membranes. Effective anesthesia varies with the individual and the area, but usually begins within 2 to 10 minutes after application and may persist for an hour or longer. Relief of local symptoms may continue after tactile sensibility has returned.

Indications: RESOLVE is useful for the relief of local discomfort due to cold sores (fever blisters). For best results the gel should be applied within the first few hours after the appearance of local symptoms of tingling, itching, burning or pain.

Contraindications: RESOLVE is contraindicated in patients known to be hypersensitive (allergic) to the anesthetic or other ingredients of the formulation. Do not use in the eyes.

Warnings: RESOLVE is for external use only. Skin irritation may occur but it is usually slight.

As with other topical anesthetics, RESOLVE should not be used repeatedly or to cover extensive areas because of the possibility of systemic absorption. Discontinue use if bacterial infection develops.

Precautions: RESOLVE should be used with caution in areas from which rapid or significant systemic absorption could occur, such as broken or abraded skin or oral mucosa. The drug should also be used cautiously in patients sensitive to various allergens including drugs or those with a strong family history of allergy.

Development of secondary or delayed cutaneous hypersensitivity on repeated usage is possible. Since this reaction may resemble an exacerbation or progression of the cold sore, it could lead to an increased number of applications when, in fact, further applications should be stopped. Thus, if local irritation or sensitivity occurs, the use of RESOLVE should be discontinued.

Usage in Pregnancy. Safe use during pregnancy has not been established.

Adverse Reactions: Systemic reactions could result from high plasma levels of dyclonine due to extensive applica-

tion or rapid absorption. Cardiovascular and central nervous system reactions have occurred after instillation of 20 to 30 ml. of 1% dyclonine HCl solution into the trachea, esophagus, or bladder preliminary to endoscopy. Because of slow percutaneous absorption, such reactions are unlikely to occur following application of recommended dosages of RESOLVE. However, hypersensitivity or other idiosyncratic systemic reactions cannot be ruled out at any dosage.

Local irritant reactions (primary) have been observed in some laboratory animals. In guinea pigs and in about 15% of human volunteers, repeated applications of 0.5 ml. of a 2% dyclonine HCl solution with occluded dressing produced secondary or delayed skin hypersensitivity. Such hypersensitivity could also be produced by RESOLVE. Continued use on a cold sore which appears worse or spreading is therefore not recommended.

Dosage and Administration:
RESOLVE should be applied sparingly on cold sores and as soon as possible after the first symptoms of tingling, itching, burning, or pain. The area of discomfort and a narrow margin of the surrounding normal skin should be covered by one to two drops of RESOLVE. Running or dripping and spreading of the gel to the other lip should be avoided. Applications may be timed to follow such activities as eating, brushing of teeth, and washing of face to avoid removal of medication.

RESOLVE may be applied approximately every four hours. If the cold sore appears to progress or spread, the use of RESOLVE should be discontinued (see also Precautions and Adverse Reactions).

How Supplied: In 0.10 oz. (3 gm.) plastic tubes.

SIMRON™

Description:
Each maroon, soft-gelatin Simron capsule contains:

    Elemental iron ....10 mg.
    (supplied as ferrous gluconate)
    Sacagen™ (polysorbate 20).....400 mg.

Actions: Ferrous gluconate provides a source of elemental iron that will prevent and correct iron deficiency and iron-deficiency anemia. Sacagen (polysorbate 20) is polyoxyethylene 20 sorbitan monolaurate. It is an amber-colored liquid intended to enhance iron absorption and, as a surfactant, aids in the prevention of constipation.

Indications: For the prevention and treatment of iron deficiency and iron-deficiency anemia.

Simron is unusually well tolerated in patients who cannot tolerate other oral iron preparations and in patients with gastrointestinal disease, including peptic ulcer and ulcerative colitis.

Simron is indicated in the treatment of iron-deficiency anemia of patients with a potential for upper gastrointestinal bleeding because it rarely produces black stools, which could mask evidence of bleeding. Simron is indicated in the treatment of iron-deficiency anemia of patients with ulcerative colitis because only small amounts of unabsorbed irritant iron salts are present in the stool. Simron is indicated in the prevention and treatment of iron deficiency and iron-deficiency anemia of pregnancy.

Contraindications: Simron is contraindicated in the treatment of patients with disease associated with increased iron storage (hemochromatosis).

Warnings: Simron should be stored out of the reach of children because of the possibility of iron intoxication from accidental overdosage. Individuals with normal iron balance should not chronically take iron.

Precautions: When anemia is diagnosed, the type of anemia should be established. When iron-deficiency anemia is diagnosed, the cause of the iron deficiency should be established.

Ferrous iron compounds taken by mouth can impair the absorption of tetracycline and tetracycline derivatives. Antacids given concomitantly with iron compounds will decrease the absorption of iron.

Adverse Reactions: The incidence of adverse gastrointestinal reactions is reduced with Simron. Gastric irritation, nausea, constipation, and diarrhea are rarely observed.

Dosage and Administration: For the prevention and treatment of iron deficiency and iron-deficiency anemia the recommended dose is 1 Simron capsule three times a day *between meals*. This supplies 30 mg. elemental iron. It should be noted that in patients with continued blood loss it may be necessary to exceed the recommended dose of Simron to obtain optimum therapeutic effect.

Overdosage: As little as 1 gram of elemental iron ingested orally may be toxic. Onset of symptoms usually occurs approximately 30 minutes after ingestion. Initially, gastrointestinal symptoms predominate (vomiting, diarrhea, melena). Shock, dyspnea, lethargy, and coma may follow. Metabolic acidosis may then occur.

Standard measures used to treat acute iron intoxication may include the following: 1) induced vomiting, 2) gastric lavage with 1% sodium bicarbonate, 3) general supportive measures for the treatment of shock and acidosis. Deferoxamine mesylate (Desferal®) should be given intramuscularly for patients not in shock, and intravenously for patients in shock. The manufacturer's recommendations should be consulted for details of administration. Some authors recommend 8000 mg. deferoxamine in 50 ml. of water via nasogastric tube.

How Supplied: Bottles of 100 soft-gelatin capsules

SIMRON PLUS®

Description: Each maroon, soft-gelatin capsule contains:

Elemental iron ....10 mg.
   (supplied as ferrous gluconate)
Sacagen™ (polysorbate 20) ....400 mg.
Ascorbic acid....................................50 mg.
   (supplied as sodium ascorbate)

Pyridoxine hydrochloride.............1.0 mg.
Folic acid ....0.1 mg.
Vitamin B$_{12}$...................................3.33 mcg.
   (supplied as cyanocobalamin)

Actions: Ferrous gluconate provides a source of elemental iron that will prevent and correct iron deficiency and iron-deficiency anemia. Sacagen (polysorbate 20) is polyoxyethylene 20 sorbitan monolaurate. It is an amber-colored liquid intended to enhance iron absorption and, as a surfactant, aids in the prevention of constipation.

In addition, factors necessary for normal hematopoiesis are supplied: ascorbic acid (as sodium ascorbate), pyridoxine hydrochloride, folic acid, and vitamin B$_{12}$ (as cyanocobalamin).

Indications: For the prevention and treatment of iron deficiency and iron-deficiency anemia or anemia due to decreased erythrocyte formation except pernicious anemia or anemias due to bone marrow deficiencies. Simron Plus is indicated in the prevention and treatment of iron deficiency and iron-deficiency anemia of pregnancy.

Contraindications: Simron Plus is contraindicated in the treatment of patients with disease associated with increased iron storage (hemochromatosis).

Warnings: Simron Plus should be stored out of the reach of children because of the possibility of iron intoxication from accidental overdosage. Individuals with normal iron balance should not chronically take iron. Folic acid alone is improper therapy in the treatment of pernicious anemia and other megaloblastic anemias where vitamin B$_{12}$ is deficient.

Precautions: When anemia is diagnosed, the type of anemia should be established. When iron-deficiency anemia is diagnosed, the cause of the iron deficiency should be established.

Ferrous iron compounds taken by mouth can impair the absorption of tetracycline and tetracycline derivatives. Antacids given concomitantly with iron compounds will decrease the absorption of iron. This preparation is not a reliable substitute for parenterally administered cyanocobalamin (vitamin B$_{12}$) in the management of pernicious anemia.

Parenteral cyanocobalamin should be used in patients receiving folic acid unless pernicious anemia has been ruled out, since folic acid may correct blood disorders of pernicious anemia while nervous system changes progress. Periodic examinations and laboratory studies of pernicious anemia patients are essential.

Adverse Reactions: The incidence of adverse gastrointestinal reactions is reduced with Simron Plus. Gastric irritations, nausea, constipation, and diarrhea are rarely observed. Allergic sensitization has been reported following both oral and parenteral administration of folic acid.

Dosage and Administration: The recommended dose of Simron Plus is 1 capsule three times a day between meals.

Overdosage: As little as 1 gram of elemental iron ingested orally may be toxic. Onset of symptoms usually occurs ap-

proximately 30 minutes after ingestion. Initially, gastrointestinal symptoms predominate (vomiting, diarrhea, melena). Shock, dyspnea, lethargy, and coma may follow. Metabolic acidosis may then occur.

Standard measures used to treat acute iron intoxication may include the following: 1) induced vomiting, 2) gastric lavage with 1% sodium bicarbonate, 3) general supportive measures for the treatment of shock and acidosis. Deferoxamine mesylate (Desferal®) should be given intramuscularly for patients not in shock, and intravenously for patients in shock. The manufacturer's recommendation should be consulted for details of administration. Some authors recommend 8000 mg. deferoxamine in 50 ml. of water via nasogastric tube.

How Supplied: Bottles of 100 soft-gelatin capsules

Merrick Medicine Company

P. O. BOX 1489 (76703)
501-503 S. 8TH STREET (76706)
WACO, TX

PERCY® MEDICINE
For relief of simple diarrhea and excess acid conditions of the stomach.

Active Ingredients: The active ingredients in an aqueous solution of 10 ml adult dose are as follows:

Bismuth Subnitrate NF .... 959.0 mg.
Calcium Hydroxide USP .... 21.9 mg.

The solution contains 5% alcohol, used as a preservative.

Indications: An antacid-astringent for simple diarrhea and for temporary relief of gastric discomfort due to overeating or other dietary indiscretions.

Drug Interaction Precautions: No known drug interaction.

Dosage and Directions For Use: Shake well before using. Administer orally 3 or 4 times daily as required. Vary dosage according to age. For use in infants and children under 6 years of age, consult your physician:

AGE BY YEARS	DOSAGE
6 to 12	1 to 1½ teaspoonfuls
12 to 18	1 to 2 teaspoonfuls
Over 18 and adults	2 teaspoonfuls

Normally, the clear liquid portion of this product (before shaking) is a light lemon color with a sweet palatable flavor. After a long period of time, the color may darken and flavor change. If the product is found to have lost its sweet agreeable flavor and light color, use is not recommended. PERCY MEDICINE may cause stool to darken temporarily.

Warning: Do not use for more than 2 days or in the presence of high fever or in infants or children under 6 years of age unless directed by a physician.

Professional Labeling: Same as those outlined under indications.

Continued on next page

Merrick—Cont.

How Supplied: Available only in 3 fl. oz. glass bottle encased in an outer carton (NDC 0322-2222-03), (UPC 0322-2222-03). [*Shown in Product Identification Section*]

Miles Laboratories, Inc.
P. O. BOX 340
ELKHART, IN 46515

ALKA–SELTZER® Effervescent Pain Reliever & Antacid

Active Ingredient: Each tablet contains: aspirin 324 mg., heat treated sodium bicarbonate 1904 mg., citric acid 1000 mg. ALKA-SELTZER® in water contains principally the antacid sodium citrate and the analgesic sodium acetylsalicylate. Buffered pH is between 6 and 7.

Indications: ALKA-SELTZER® Effervescent Pain Reliever & Antacid is an analgesic and an antacid and is indicated for relief of sour stomach, acid indigestion or heartburn with headache or body aches and pains. Also for fast relief of upset stomach with headache from overindulgence in food and drink—especially recommended for taking before bed and again on arising. Effective for pain relief alone: headache or body and muscular aches and pains.

Actions: When the ALKA-SELTZER® Effervescent Pain Reliever & Antacid tablet is dissolved in water, the acetylsalicylate ion differs from acetylsalicylic acid chemically, physically and pharmacologically. Being fat insoluble, it is not absorbed by the gastric mucosal cells. Studies and observations in animals and man including radiochrome determinations of fecal blood loss, measurement of ion fluxes and direct visualization with gastrocamera, have shown that, as contrasted with acetylsalicylic acid, the acetylsalicylate ion delivered in the solution does not alter gastric mucosal permeability to permit back-diffusion of hydrogen ion, and gastric damage and acute gastric mucosal lesions are therefore not seen after administration of the product. ALKA-SELTZER® Effervescent Pain Reliever & Antacid has the capacity to neutralize gastric hydrochloric acid quickly and effectively. In-vitro, 154 ml. of 0.1 N hydrochloric acid are required to decrease the pH of one tablet of ALKA-SELTZER® Effervescent Pain Reliever & Antacid in solution to 4.0. Measured against the in vitro standard established by the Food and Drug Administration one tablet neutralizes 17.2 mEq of acid. In vivo, the antacid activity of two ALKA-SELTZER® Effervescent Pain Reliever & Antacid tablets is comparable to that of 10 ml. of milk of magnesia. ALKA-SELTZER® Effervescent Pain Reliever & Antacid is able to resist pH changes caused by the continuing secretion of acid in the normal individual and to maintain an elevated pH until emptying occurs.

ALKA-SELTZER® Effervescent Pain Reliever & Antacid provides highly water soluable acetylsalicylate ions which are fat insoluble. Acetylsalicylate ions are not absorbed from the stomach. They empty from the stomach and thereby become available for absorption from the duodenum. Thus, fast drug absorption and high plasma acetylsalicylate levels are achieved. Plasma levels of salicylate following the administration of ALKA-SELTZER® Effervescent Pain Reliever & Antacid solution (acetylsalicylate ion equivalent to 648 mg. acetylsaliylic acid) can reach 29 mg./liter in 10 minutes and rise to peak levels as high as 55 mg./liter within 30 minutes.

Warnings: Except under the advice and supervision of a physician, do not take more than, Adults: 8 tablets in a 24 hour period. (60 years of age or older: 4 tablets in a 24 hour period), Children (6–12), 4 tablets in a 24 hour period, (3–5), 2 tablets in a 24 hour period, or use the maximum dosage for more than 10 days (5 days for children). Do not use if you are allergic to aspirin or have asthma, if you have a coagulation (bleeding) disease, or if you are on a sodium restricted diet. Each tablet contains 551 mg. of sodium. Keep this and all drugs out of the reach of children.

Dosage and Administration: ALKA-SELTZER® Effervescent Pain Reliever and Antacid is taken in solution, approximately three ounces of water per tablet is sufficient. Adults: 2 tablets every 4 hours. Children: (6–12) 1 tablet, (3–5) ½ tablet, every 4–6 hours; children under 3, as directed by a physician. CAUTION: If symptoms persist or recur frequently, or if you are under treatment for ulcer, consult your physician.

How Supplied: Tablets: in bottles of 8 and 25; individually foil sealed; box of 12; dispenser boxes of 36 tablets in 18 foil twin packs; 100 tablets in 50 foil twin packs; carton of 72 tablets in 36 foil twin packs. Product Identification Mark: "Alka-Seltzer" embossed on each tablet. [*Shown in Product Identification Section*]

ALKA–SELTZER® Effervescent Antacid

Active Ingredient: Each tablet contains heat treated sodium bicarbonate 958 mg., citric acid 832 mg., potassium bicarbonate 312 mg. ALKA-SELTZER® Effervescent Antacid in water contains principally the antacids sodium citrate and potassium citrate.

Indications: ALKA-SELTZER® Effervescent Antacid is indicated for relief of acid indigestion, sour stomach or heartburn.

Actions: The ALKA-SELTZER® Effervescent Antacid solution provides quick and effective neutralization of gastric acid. Measured by the in vitro standard established by the Food and Drug Administration one tablet will neutralize 10.6 mEq of acid.

Warnings: Except under the advice and supervision of a physician, do not take more than: Adults: 8 tablets in a 24 hour period (60 years or older: 7 tablets in a 24 hour period), Children 4 tablets in a 24 hour period; or use the maximum dosage of this product for more than 2 weeks. Do not use this product if you are on a sodium restricted diet. Each tablet contains 296 mg. of sodium. Keep this and all drugs out of the reach of children.

Dosage and Administration: ALKA-SELTZER® Effervescent Antacid is taken in solution; approximately 3 oz. of water per tablet is sufficient. Adults: one or two tablets every 4 hours as needed. Children: ½ the adult dosage.

How Supplied: individually foil sealed, box of 12; dispenser boxes of 20 tablets in 10 foil twin packs; 36 tablets in 18 foil twin packs. [*Shown in Product Identification Section*]

ALKA–2® Chewable Antacid Tablets

Active Ingredient: Each ALKA-2 chewable antacid tablet contains calcium carbonate 500 mg.

Indications: ALKA-2 is an antacid for occasional use to obtain relief from transient symptoms of acid indigestion, heartburn, and sour stomach.

Actions: ALKA-2 provides quick and effective neutralization of gastric acidity. Measured by the in vitro standard established by the Food and Drug Administration, each tablet will neutralize 10/mEq of acid.

Warnings: Do not take more than 16 tablets in a 24-hour period or use the maximum dosage of this product for more than 2 weeks, except under the advice and supervision of a physician. May cause constipation. Keep this and all drugs out of the reach of children.

Dosage and Administration: Chew 1 or 2 tablets every two hours or as directed by a physician. Not to exceed 16 tablets in a 24 hour period.

How Supplied: Tablets: rolls of 10, triple roll, 10 tablets per roll; bottle of 85 **Product Identification Mark:** "Alka 2" embossed on each tablet. [*Shown in Product Identification Section*]

ALKA-SELTZER PLUS® Cold Medicine

Active Ingredient:
Each dry ALKA-SELTZER PLUS® Cold Tablet contains the following active ingredients: Phenylpropanolamine bitartrate 24.08 mg., chlorpheniramine maleate 2.0 mg., aspirin 324.0 mg. The product is dissolved in water prior to ingestion and the aspirin is converted into its soluble ionic form, sodium acetylsalicylate.

Indications: For relief of the symptoms of head colds, common flu, sinus congestion and hay fever.

Actions: Each tablet contains: A decongestant which helps restore free breathing, shrink swollen nasal tissue and relieve sinus congestion due to head colds or hay fever. An antihistamine which helps relieve the runny nose, sneezing, sniffles, itchy watering eyes that accompany colds or hay fever. Specially buffered aspirin which relieves headache, scratchy sore throat, general body aches and the feverish feeling of a cold and common flu.

Warnings: Do not use if you are allergic to aspirin or have asthma, or if you have a coagulation (bleeding) disease. If symptoms do not improve in 7 days or are accompanied by high fever or if fever persists for more than 3 days consult a physician before continuing use. Do not take this product if you have glaucoma or difficulty in urination due to enlargement of the prostate gland except under the advice and supervision of a physician. Avoid alcoholic beverages while taking this product.

Caution: Individuals with high blood pressure, diabetes, heart or thyroid disease or on a sodium restricted diet should use only as directed by a physician. Each tablet contains 515 mg. of sodium. Product may cause drowsiness: use caution if operating heavy machinery or driving a vehicle. Keep this and all drugs out of the reach of children.

Dosage and Administration:
ALKA-SELTZER PLUS® is taken in solution; approximately 3 ounces of water per tablet is sufficient. Adults: two tablets every 4 hours up to 8 tablets in 24 hours. Children (6–12): Half of adult dosage. Children under 6 years: Consult your physician.

How Supplied: Tablets: carton of 20 tablets in 10 foil twin packs; carton of 36 tablets in 18 foil twin packs.

Product Identification Mark:
"Alka-Seltzer Plus" embossed on each tablet.
[*Shown in Product Identification Section*]

BACTINE® Antiseptic·Anesthetic First Aid Spray

Active Ingredients: Benzalkonium Chloride 0.13% w/w, Lidocaine, HCl. 2.5% w/w

Indications: Antiseptic/anesthetic for helping prevent infecton, cleanse wounds, and for the temporary relief of pain and itching due to insect bites, minor burns, sunburn, minor cuts and minor skin irritations.

Warnings: (Aerosol Spray and Liquid Spray)
For external use only. Do not use in large quantities, particularly over raw surfaces or blistered areas. Avoid spraying in eyes, mouth, ears or on sensitive areas of the body. This product is not for use on wild or domestic animal bites. If you have an animal bite or puncture wound, consult your physician immediately. If condition worsens or if symptoms persist for more than 7 days, discontinue use of this product and consult a physician. Do not bandage tightly. Keep this and all drugs out of reach of children. In case of accidental ingestion, seek professional assistance or contact a Poison Control Center immediately.
(Aerosol Only): Contents under pressure. Do not puncture or incinerate. Do not store at temperature above 120° F. Use only as directed. Intentional misuse by deliberately concentrating and inhaling the contents can be harmful or fatal.

Dosage and Administration: For adults and children 2 years of age or older. For superficial skin wounds, cuts, scratches, scrapes. Cleanse affected area thoroughly.
Directions: (Liquid) First Aid Spray To spray, hold bottle upright 2 to 3 inches from injured area and squeeze repeatedly. To pour, hold bottle down. To aid in removing foreign particles, dab injured area with clean gauze saturated with product. For sunburn, minor burns, insect bites, and minor skin irritations, apply to affected area of skin for temporary relief. To spray, hold bottle upright 2 to 3 inches from affected area and squeeze repeatedly. To pour, hold bottle down. Product can be applied to affected area with clean gauze saturated with product. (Aerosol First Aid Spray)
Shake well. For adults and children 2 years of age and older. For superficial skin wounds, cuts, scratches, scrapes, cleanse affected area thoroughly. Hold can upright 2 to 3 inches from injured area and spray until wet. To aid in removing foreign particles, dab injured area with clean gauze saturated with product. For sunburn, minor burns, insect bites, and minor skin irritations, hold can upright 2 to 3 inches from injured area and spray until wet. Product can be applied to affected area with clean gauze saturated with product.
How Supplied: 2 oz., 4 oz. liquid spray, 16 oz. liquid, 3 oz. aerosol.
[*Shown in Product Identification Section*]

BACTINE® Brand Hydrocortisone Skin Care Cream Antipruritic

Active Ingredient: Hydrocortisone 0.5%
Indications: For the temporary relief of minor skin irritations, itching, and rashes due to eczema, dermatitis, insect bites, poison ivy, poison oak, poison sumac, soaps, detergents, cosmetics, and jewelry.
Warnings: For external use only. Avoid contact with the eyes. If condition worsens or if symptoms persist for more than seven days, discontinue use and consult a physician.
Do not use on children under 2 years of age except under the advice and supervision of a physician.

Keep this and all drugs out of the reach of children. In case of accidental ingestion, seek professional assistance or contact a Poison Control Center immediately.
Directions: For adults and children 2 years of age and older. Gently massage into affected skin area not more than 3 or 4 times daily.
How Supplied: ½ oz. plastic tube.
[*Shown in Product Identification Section*]

BUGS BUNNY® Children's Chewable Vitamins (Multivitamin Supplement)
BUGS BUNNY® Children's Chewable Vitamins Plus Iron (Multivitamin Supplement with Iron)
FLINTSTONES® Children's Chewable Vitamins Plus Iron (Multivitamin Supplement with Iron)
FLINTSTONES® Children's Chewable Vitamins (Multivitamin Supplement)

Vitamin Ingredients: Each multivitamin supplement with iron contains the ingredients listed in the chart below. [See table above].
BUGS BUNNY® Children's Chewable Vitamins and FLINTSTONES® Children's Chewable Vitamins provide the same quantities of vitamins, but do not provide iron.
Indication: Dietary supplementation
Dosage and Administration: One chewable tablet daily. For adults and children two years and older; tablet must be chewed.
Precaution:
IRON SUPPLEMENTS ONLY.
Contains iron, which can be harmful in large doses. Close tightly and keep out of reach of children. In case of overdose contact a Poison Control Center immediately.
How Supplied: All four products are supplied in bottles of 60 and 100.
[*Shown in Product Identification Section*]

One Tablet Provides		% of U.S. RDA	
Vitamins	Quantity	For Children 2 to 4 Years of Age	For Adults and Children over 4 Years of Age
Vitamin A	2500 I.U.	100	50
Vitamin D	400 I.U.	100	100
Vitamin E	15 I.U.	150	50
Vitamin C	60 mg.	150	100
Folic Acid	0.3 mg.	150	75
Thiamine	1.05 mg.	150	70
Riboflavin	1.20 mg.	150	70
Niacin	13.50 mg.	150	67
Vitamin B_6	1.05 mg.	150	52
Vitamin B_{12}	4.5 mcg.	150	75
Mineral:			
Iron (Elemental)	15 mg.	150	83

Continued on next page

Miles Labs.—Cont.

FLINTSTONES® With Extra C
Multivitamin Supplement

BUGS BUNNY® With Extra C
Multivitamin Supplement

Vitamin Ingredients: Each multivitamin supplement contains the ingredients listed in the chart below.

Indication: Dietary supplementation
Dosage and Administration: One chewable tablet daily for adults and children two years and older; tablet must be chewed.
How Supplied: Bottles of 60's
[*Shown in Product Identification Section*]

MILES® Nervine Nighttime Sleep–Aid

Active Ingredient: Each capsule-shaped tablet contains pyrilamine maleate 25 mg.
Indications: Nighttime sleep-aid. Helps you fall asleep and relieves occasional sleeplessness.
Actions: Antihistamines act on the central nervous system and produce drowsiness.
Warnings: Use only as directed. Do not give to children under 12 years of age. Do not take this product when: pregnant or nursing a baby; alcohol is being consumed. NOT FOR PROLONGED USE. If sleeplessness persists continuously for more than 2 weeks, consult your physician. Insomnia may be a symptom of serious underlying medical illness. Keep this and all drugs out of the reach of children. In case of accidental overdose, seek professional assistance or contact a Poison Control Center immediately. DO NOT TAKE THIS PRODUCT IF YOU HAVE ASTHMA, GLAUCOMA OR ENLARGEMENT OF THE PROSTATE GLAND EXCEPT UNDER THE ADVICE AND SUPERVISION OF A PHYSICIAN.
Dosage and Administration: Two tablets at bedtime or as directed by a physician. Maximum during 24 hours—4 tablets.
How Supplied: Bottles of 12's, 30's, and 50's capsule-shaped tablets.
[*Shown in Product Identification Section*]

ONE–A–DAY® Vitamins
(Multivitamin Supplement)

ONE–A–DAY® Vitamins Plus Iron
(Multivitamin Supplement with Iron)

Ingredients:
One tablet daily of ONE-A-DAY® Vitamins Plus Iron provides:

Vitamins	Quantity	% of U.S. RDA
Vitamin A	5,000 I. U.	100
Vitamin E	15 I. U.	50
Vitamin C	60 mg.	100
Folic Acid	0.4 mg.	100
Thiamine	1.5 mg.	100
Riboflavin	1.7 mg.	100
Niacin	20 mg.	100
Vitamin B$_6$	2 mg.	100
Vitamin B$_{12}$	6 mcg.	100
Vitamin D	400 I. U.	100

Mineral	Quantity	% of U.S. RDA
Iron (Elemental)	18 mg.	100

ONE-A-DAY® Vitamins provides the same quantities of vitamins as ONE-A-DAY® Vitamins Plus Iron but does not contain iron.
Indication: Dietary supplementation.
Dosage and Administration: One tablet daily for adults and teens.
Precaution: For ONE-A-DAY Vitamins Plus Iron Only. Contains iron, which can be harmful in large doses. Close tightly and keep out of reach of children. In case of overdose, contact a physician or Poison Control Center immediately.
How Supplied: ONE-A-DAY® Vitamins, bottles of 25, 60, 100, 250, and 365. ONE-A-DAY® Vitamins Plus Iron, bottles of 60, 100, 240, and 365.
[*Shown in Product Identification Section*]

ONE–A–DAY® Vitamins Plus Minerals
(Multivitamin/Multimineral Supplement for adults and teens)

Ingredients:
One tablet daily of ONE-A-DAY® Vitamins Plus Minerals provides:

Vitamins	Quantity	% of U.S. RDA
Vitamin A	5,000 I.U.	100
Vitamin E	30 I.U.	100
Vitamin C	60 mg.	100
Folic Acid	0.4 mg.	100
Thiamine	1.5 mg.	100
Riboflavin	1.7 mg.	100
Niacin	20 mg.	100
Vitamin B$_6$	2 mg.	100
Vitamin B$_{12}$	6 mcg.	100
Vitamin D	400 I.U.	100
Pantothenic Acid	10 mg.	100
Biotin	30 mcg.	10

Minerals	Quantity	% of U.S. RDA
Iron (Elemental)	18 mg.	100
Calcium	129.6 mg.	13
Phosphorus	100 mg.	10
Iodine	150 mcg.	100
Magnesium	100 mg.	25
Copper	2 mg.	100
Zinc	15 mg.	100
Chromium	10 mcg.	*
Selenium	10 mcg.	*
Molybdenum	10 mcg.	*
Manganese	2.5 mg.	*
Potassium	5 mg.	*

*No U.S. RDA established
Indication: Dietary supplementation.
Dosage and Administration: One tablet daily for adults and teens.
Precaution: Contains iron, which can be harmful in large doses. Close tightly and keep out of reach of children. In case of overdose, contact a physician or Poison Control Center immediately.
How Supplied: Bottles of 30, 60, and 100.
[*Shown in Product Identification Section*]

ONE–A–DAY® CORE C 500™ Vitamins
(Multivitamin Supplement for adults and children 12 or more years of age.)

ONE–A–DAY® Plus Extra C
High Potency 500 mg Vitamin C Plus 9 Essential Vitamins

Vitamin ingredients: One tablet daily of ONE-A-DAY® Core C 500™ provides:

Vitamins	Quantity	% of U.S. RDA
Vitamin A	5,000 I.U.	100
Vitamin E	15 I.U.	50
Vitamin C	500 mg.	833
Folic Acid	0.4 mg.	100
Thiamine	1.5 mg.	100
Riboflavin	1.7 mg.	100
Niacin	20 mg.	100
Vitamin B$_6$	2 mg.	100
Vitamin B$_{12}$	6 mcg.	100
Vitamin D	400 I.U.	100

Indication: Dietary supplementation.
Dosage and Administration: One tablet daily.
How Supplied: Bottles of 60's.
[*Shown in Product Identification Section*]

ONE–A–DAY® STRESSGARD™ Vitamins
(B Complex Plus C Stress Formula) High Potency Multivitamin/Multimineral Supplement For Adults

Ingredients:

Vitamins	Quantity	% of U.S. RDA
Vitamin A	5000 I.U.	100
Vitamin C	600 mg.	1000
Thiamine (B$_1$)	15 mg.	1000
Riboflavin (B$_2$)	10 mg.	588
Niacin	100 mg.	500
Vitamin D	400 I.U.	100
Vitamin E	30 I.U.	100

One Tablet Provides		% of U.S. RDA	
		For Children 2 To 4 Years of Age	For Adults and Children Over 4 Years of Age
Vitamins	Quantity		
Vitamin A	2500 I.U.	100	50
Vitamin D	400 I.U.	100	100
Vitamin E	15 I.U.	150	50
Vitamin C	250 mg.	625	417
Folic Acid	0.3 mg.	150	75
Thiamine	1.05 mg.	150	70
Riboflavin	1.20 mg.	150	70
Niacin	13.50 mg.	150	67
Vitamin B$_6$	1.05 mg.	150	52
Vitamin B$_{12}$	4.5 mcg.	150	75

Vitamin B$_6$	5 mg.	250
Folic Acid	400 mcg.	100
Vitamin B$_{12}$	12 mcg.	200
Pantothenic Acid	20 mg.	200

Minerals	Quantity	% of U.S. RDA
Iron (Elemental)	18 mg.	100
Zinc	15 mg.	100
Copper	2 mg.	100

Indication: Dietary supplementation.

Dosage and Administration: Adults —one tablet daily with food.

Precaution: Contains iron, which can be harmful in large doses. Close tightly and keep out of reach of children. In case of overdose, contact a physician or Poison Control Center immediately.

How Supplied: Bottles of 60.

[*Shown in Product Identification Section*]

Miles Pharmaceuticals
Division of Miles Laboratories, Inc.
400 MORGAN LANE
WEST HAVEN, CT 06516

DOMEBORO® Powder Packets, Effervescent Tablets (acid pH) Astringent Wet Dressing

One packet or tablet dissolved in a pint of water makes a modified Burow's Solution approximately equivalent to a 1:40 dilution, two packets or tablets a 1:20 dilution, and four packets or tablets a 1:10 dilution.

Buffered to an acid pH.

Contains: Aluminum sulfate and calcium acetate.

Indications: A soothing wet dressing for relief of inflammatory conditions of the skin such as insect bites, poison ivy, swellings and bruises or athlete's foot.

Directions: Dissolve one or two packets or tablets in a pint (large glass) of water and stir. When the powder disperses, shake resulting mixture. Do not strain or filter. Bandage the site of application loosely. Pour mixture on bandage every 15 to 30 minutes to keep dressing moist. Continue for 4 to 8 hours unless otherwise directed by physician. Do not use plastic or other impervious material to prevent evaporation without consulting your physician.

Caution: Keep away from eyes. For external use only. Store below 86°F. (30°C.), avoid freezing. Material in diluted form may be stored for 7 days at room temperature.

How Supplied:
Powder Packets: Boxes of 12 and 100. Each packet contains 2.2 gm. Individually foil-wrapped *Tablets:* Boxes of 12, 100 and 1000.

Products are cross-indexed

by product classifications

in the

BLUE SECTION

Moss Chemical Company, Inc.
183 ST. PAUL STREET
ROCHESTER, NY 14604

MOSCO CORN AND CALLUS REMOVER

Active Ingredient: Salicylic Acid.

Indications: MOSCO salve removes hard corns and calluses.

Actions: MOSCO salve soothingly penetrates the hardest, most annoying corns and calluses, while loosening and lifting them away in just a few days. MOSCO eliminates the use of pads, liquids or dangerous blades. MOSCO is the most simple and easiest preparation to apply to the corn and callus. MOSCO's stable ingredients provide for long lasting shelf life if securely capped. MOSCO is the proven salve remedy since 1910. Money back guarantee.

Warnings: Apply only as directed. Not to be used by diabetics or persons with impaired circulation. Keep out of the reach of children. If accidently ingested, immediately contact physician or poison control center.

Precautions: Apply MOSCO on corn or callus ONLY. Avoid contact with surrounding skin.

Dosage and Administration: Wash foot clean. Rub small amount into hard corn or callus only, not on skin, for 4 nights, then soak foot in warm water. Repeat treatment if necessary.

Professional Labeling: Same as outlined under indications.

How Supplied: MOSCO is available in 0.4 oz. (13g) and 0.8 oz. (24g) safe plastic jar.

[*Shown in Product Identification Section*]

Muro Pharmaceutical, Inc.
890 EAST STREET
TEWKSBURY, MA 01876

DUOLUBE™

Contains: White petrolatum and liquid petrolatum.

Supplied: 3.5 g tubes.

MURO TEARS™
Artificial Tears

Ingredients: Hydroxypropyl methylcellulose, dextran 40, sodium and potassium chloride (total chlorides 0.85%). Also contains benzalkonium chloride 0.01% as a preservative, disodium EDTA and purified water. Buffered with sodium borate and boric acid.

How Supplied: 15 ml plastic dropper bottles.

MUROCEL
(methylcellulose) 1%

How Supplied: 15 and 30 ml plastic dropper bottles.

SALINEX NASAL MIST
Buffered Isotonic Saline Mist

Ingredients: Sodium Chloride 0.4%, propylene glycol, hydroxypropyl methylcellulose, benzalkonium chloride 0.01% as preservative.

Indications: Rhinitis Medicamentosa and Rhinitis Sicca. For relief of nasal congestion associated with overuse of nasal sprays, drops and inhalers.

To alleviate crusting due to nose bleeds to compensate for nasal stuffiness and dryness to lack of humidity.

Directions: Squeeze twice in each nostril as needed.

How Supplied: 50 ml plastic spray bottle.

Natra-Bio Company
1427 1/2 SANTA MONICA MALL
SANTA MONICA, CA 90401

NATRA-BIO

Description: Twenty-Eight 100% Natural, herbally based, homeopathic medicines, 1-oz. dropper bottle each unit approx. 50 doses for sublingual administration 3–5 times daily, more frequently in acute cases. 20% alcohol solution.

Actions: Promotes relief by stimulating the body's defense mechanisms to accelerate the relief of symptoms naturally.

Contraindications: None.

Warnings: Can occasionally cause temporary worsening of symptoms. Homeopathically this is a positive sign that body's defenses are working, however if excessive discomfort occurs reduce frequency.

501 Indigestion
502 Cough
503 Nervousness
504 Injuries
505 Fever
506 Neuralgia Pains
507 Sinus
508 Arthritis
509 Sore Throat
510 Menstrual
511 Nausea
512 Chest Cold
513 Head Cold
514 Earache
515 Headache and Pain
516 Prostate
517 Menopause
518 Bedwetting
519 Hayfever
520 Hemorrhoids
521 Laxative
522 Bladder Irritation
523 Insomnia
524 Diarrhea
525 Herpes
526 Acne
527 Flu
528 Exhaustion

[*Shown in Product Identification Section*]

Nature's Bounty, Inc.
105 ORVILLE DRIVE
BOHEMIA, NY 11716

ACEROLA "C" (100 mg.)

Each chewable tablet contains:
Vitamin C with
  Rose Hips and Acerola ....100 mg.
Citrus Bioflavonoids
  Complex .... 5 mg.
Supplied: Tablets, bottles of 100, 500.

ACEROLA "C" (300 mg.)

Each chewable tablet contains:
Vitamin C with
  Rose Hips and Acerola .... 300 mg.
Citrus Bioflavonoids
  Complex .... 5 mg.
Supplied: Tablets, bottles of 100, 500.

ACIDOPHILUS

Aid in maintaining healthy balance of
intestinal flora.
Each capsule contains live lactobacillus
acidophilus
Supplied: Capsules, bottles of 100.

ALFALFA (500 mg.)

Supplied: Tablets, bottles of 100, 500,
1000.

B–1 (100 mg.)
  Tablets, bottles of 100
B–1 (250 mg.)
  Tablets, bottles of 100
B–1 (500 mg.)
  Tablets, bottles of 100

B–2 (100 mg.)
  Tablets, bottles of 100

B–6 (50 mg.)
  Tablets, bottles of 100, 250
B–6 (100 mg.)
  Tablets, bottles of 100, 250, 500
B–6 (500 mg.)
  Tablets, bottles of 100, 500

Each tablet contains:

			MDR*
Vitamin B-1	100 mg.	....	10,000 %
Vitamin B-2	100 mg.	....	8,200 %
Vitamin B-6	100 mg.	....	**
Vitamin B-12	100 mcg.	....	**
Niacinamide	100 mg.	....	1,000 %
Folic Acid	100 mcg.	....	**
Pantothenic Acid	100 mg.	....	**
d-Biotin	100 mcg.	....	***
Para Aminobenzoic Acid (PABA)	100 mg.	....	***
Chlorine Bitartrate	100 mg.	....	***
Inositol	100 mg.	....	***

*MDR, Minimum Daily Requirement
**Need in human nutrition established but no MDR established
***Need in human nutrition has not been established.

B–12 (25 mcg.)
  Tablets, bottles of 100, 500
B–12 (50 mcg.)
  Tablets, bottles of 100, 500
B–12 (100 mcg.)
  Tablets, bottles of 100, 250
B–12 (250 mcg.)
  Tablets, bottles of 100, 250
B–12 (500 mcg.)
  Tablets, bottles of 100, 250
B–12 (1000 mcg.)
  Tablets, bottles of 100, 250
B–12 (1500 mcg.) Long Acting
  Tablets, bottles of 100, 500

B–50®
(Vitamin B Complex)
  Tablets, bottles of 50, 100, 250, 500

B–100®
Ultra B—Complex Vitamin
Sugar and Starch Free
[See table below].
Recommended Intake: Adults, 1 tab-
let daily or as directed by physician.
Supplied: Capsule-shaped tablets (pro-
tein-coated)—bottles of 50, 100 and 250.

B–100® (TIME RELEASE)
(Vitamin B Complex)
  Tablets, bottles of 50, 100

B–125®
(Vitamin B Complex)
  Tablets, bottles of 50, 100

B & C LIQUID

Each teaspoon (5cc.) contains:
Vitamin C ....300 mg.
Vitamin B-1
  (thiamine hydrochloride) ...... 15 mg.
Vitamin B-2
  (riboflavin) .... 10 mg.
Vitamin B-6
  (pyridoxine hydrochloride) ... 5 mg.
Vitamin B-12
  (cobalamin concentrate) .... 5 mcg.
Niacinamide ....100 mg.
d-Panthenol .... 20 mg.
Supplied: 4 oz. bottle.

B–COMPLEX AND B–12

Each tablet contains:
Protease (from natural
  Carica Papaya) .... 10 mg.

Vitamins:
B–12 (from Cobalamin) .... 25 mcg.
B–1 (Thiamine) .... 7 mg.
B–2 (Riboflavin) .... 14 mg.
Niacin .... 4.5 mg.
Supplied: Tablets, bottles of 90.

B–COMPLEX & C
(TIME RELEASE)

Each time release capsule contains vita-
mins:
C (with rose hips) ....200 mg.
B-1 (Thiamine) .... 10 mg.
B-2 (Riboflavin) .... 10 mg.
B-6 (Pyridoxine HCl) .... 5 mg.
B-12 (Cobalamin) .... 10 mcg.
Niacinamide .... 50 mg.
Calcium Pantothenate .... 10 mg.
Supplied: Capsules, bottles of 100.

BEE POLLEN (500 mg.)
  Tablets, bottles of 100, 250
BEE POLLEN "1000" ™
  Tablets, bottles of 100

BIOTIN (300 mcg.)
  Tablets, bottles of 100

BONE MEAL W/VIT. D
  Tablets, bottles of 100, 250, 500, 1000

BREWER'S YEAST POWDER
(DEBITTERED)

A specially cultivated brewer's yeast containing B complex vitamins in natural
high potency.
Supplied: 16 oz. can.

BREWER'S YEAST
  Tablets, bottles of 250, 500, 1000

C–250 W/ROSE HIPS
  Tablets, bottles of 100, 500
C–300 W/ROSE HIPS (CHEWABLE)
  Tablets, bottles of 100, 250
C–500 W/ROSE HIPS
  Tablets, bottles of 100, 250, 500
C–1000 W/ROSE HIPS
  Tablets, bottles of 100, 250, 500

C–COMPLEX

Each tablet contains:
Vitamin C with rose hips ......500 mg.
Bioflavonoids ....100 mg.
Rutin (Buckwheat) .... 50 mg.
Hesperidin Complex .... 25 mg.
Acerola .... 1.0 mg.
Supplied: Tablets, bottles of 100, 250.

VITAMIN C CRYSTALS

One teaspoonful provides:
Vitamin C ....5000 mg.
Supplied: 6 oz. bottle.

C–LIQUID

One teaspoon supplies:
Vitamin C with Rose Hips ...... 300 mg.
Supplied: 4 oz. bottles.

C-TIME 500™
with Rose Hips
Sustained Release Tablets
Sugar and Starch Free

Each tablet contains: (U.S.R.D.A.)
Vitamin C
  with Rose Hips .... 500 mg. (833%)
Recommended Intake: Adults, 1 tablet daily or as directed by physician.
Supplied: Capsule-shaped tablets (protein-coated to provide gradual release of Vitamin C over a prolonged period of time). Bottles of 100, 500.

C-TIME 750™ (TIME RELEASE)
  Tablets, bottles of 100, 250

C-TIME 1500™
with Rose Hips
Sustained Release Tablets
Sugar and Starch Free

Each tablet contains: (U.S.R.D.A.)
Vitamin C
  with Rose Hips ..... 1500 mg. (2500%)
Recommended Intake: Adults, 1 tablet daily or as directed by physician.
Supplied: Capsule-shaped tablets (protein-coated to provide gradual release of Vitamin C over a prolonged period of time). Bottles of 30, 100 and 250.

CALCIUM ASCORBATE (500 mg.)
  Tablets, bottles of 100

CALCIUM LACTATE (10 gr.)
  Tablets, bottles of 100, 250, 500, 1000

CHELATED CALCIUM

Each tablet contains:
Calcium Amino Acid
  Chelate .... 750 mg.
  (equivalent to 150 mg. elemental Calcium)
Supplied: Tablets, bottles of 100, 500.

CHELATED CHROMIUM

Each tablet contains:
Chromium Amino Acid
  Chelate .... 50 mg.
  (equivalent to 1000 mcg. of elemental Chromium)
Supplied: Tablets, bottles of 100, 500.

CHELATED COPPER

Each tablet contains:
Copper Amino Acid Chelate ...... 20 mg.
  (equivalent to 2 mg. of elemental Copper)
Supplied: Tablets, bottles of 100.

CHELATED MAGNESIUM

Each tablet contains:
Magnesium Amino Acid
  Chelate .... 500 mg.
  (equivalent to 100 mg. of elemental Magnesium)
Supplied: Tablets, bottles of 100.

CHELATED MANGANESE

Each tablet contains:
Manganese Amino Acid
  Chelate .... 50 mg.
  (equivalent to 5 mg. of elemental Manganese)
Supplied: Tablets, bottles of 100.

CHELATED MULTI-MINERALS

A multiple mineral amino acid chelate of 10 minerals.
Supplied: Tablets, bottles of 100, 250.

CHELATED POTASSIUM

Each tablet contains:
Potassium Amino Acid
  Complex .... 495 mg.
  (equivalent to 99 mg. of elemental Potassium)
Supplied: Tablets, bottles of 100, 250.

CHELATED ZINC

Each tablet contains:
Zinc Amino Acid Chelate .... 150 mg.
  (equivalent to 15 mg. of elemental Zinc)
Supplied: Tablets, bottles of 100, 250.

CHEW-IRON

Each chewable tablet contains:
Ferrous Fumarate .... 150 mg.
  (elemental iron 50 mg)
B-12 (Cobalamin) .... 33 mcg.
B-1 (Thiamine) .... 10 mg.
Protease (from natural
  Papaya) .... 10 mg.
Supplied: Tablets, bottles of 100, 250.

CHILDREN'S CHEWABLE VITAMINS

A popular chewable vitamin formula containing 10 essential vitamins.
Supplied: Tablets, bottles of 100, 250, 500.

CHILDREN'S CHEWABLE VITAMINS WITH IRON

A popular chewable vitamin formula containing 10 essential vitamins with iron (15 mg.).
Supplied: Tablets, bottles of 100, 250, 500.

CHOLINE (650 mg.)
  Tablets, Bottles of 100, 500

CHROMIUM, GTF (50 mcg.)
  Tablets, bottles of 100, 500
CHROMIUM, GTF (200 mcg.)
  Tablets, bottles of 50, 100, 500

CITRUS BIOFLAVONOIDS (1000 mg.)
Supplied: Tablets, bottles of 100.

DOLOMITE
  Tablets, bottles of 100, 250, 500, 1000

E-200 (d-ALPHA TOCOPHEROL ACETATE)
  Capsules, Bottles of 100, 250, 500, 1000
E-400 (d-ALPHA TOCOPHEROL ACETATE)
  Capsules, bottles of 100, 250, 500, 1000

E-200 (NATURAL COMPLEX)
  Capsules, bottles of 100, 250, 500, 1000
E-400 (NATURAL COMPLEX)
  Capsules, bottles of 100, 250
E-600 (NATURAL COMPLEX)
  Capsules, bottles of 50, 100, 250
E-1000 (NATURAL COMPLEX)
  Capsules, bottles of 50, 100, 250

EMULSIFIED E-200
  Capsules, bottles of 100

FERROUS SULFATE (5 gr.)
  Tablets, bottles of 250, 500

FOLIC ACID (400 mcg.)
  Tablets, bottles of 250
FOLIC ACID (800 mcg.)
  Tablets, bottles of 250

GARLIC OIL (15 gr.)
  Capsules, bottles of 100, 500
GARLIC OIL (77 gr.)
  Capsules, bottles of 100, 500

GARLIC & PARSLEY (7½ minim)

Each capsule contains:
Concentrated garlic oil ....10 mg.
Concentrated parsley .... 1 mg.
Supplied: Capsules, bottles of 100, 250, 500.

GINSENG, MANCHURIAN™ (250 mg.)
  Capsules, bottles of 50, 100, 250, 500
GINSENG, MANCHURIAN™ (500 mg.)
  Tablets, bottles of 50, 100, 250

GLUTAMIC ACID (500 mg.)
  Tablets, bottles of 100, 500

HALIBUT LIVER OIL

Each capsule contains:
Vitamin A (from halibut
  liver oil) .... 5000 USP Units
Vitamin D (from halibut
  liver oil) .... 85 USP Units
Supplied: Capsules, bottles of 100.

HERBAL LAXATIVE

A gentle vegetable and herb laxative.
Supplied: Tablets, bottles of 100.

INOSITOL (650 mg.)
  Tablets, bottles of 100, 500

IRON
(Ferrous Gluconate, 5 gr.)
  Tablets, bottles of 100, 250, 500

Continued on next page

Nature's Bounty—Cont.

KELP
Tablets, bottles of 250, 500, 1000

KLB6®
Natural Diet Aid
Six capsules contain:
Vitamin B-6
(Pyridoxine HCl) .... 21 mg.
Cider Vinegar ....240 mg.
Soya Lecithin ....600 mg.
Kelp ....150 mg.
Supplied: Capsules, bottles of 100, 250, 500.

KLB6 COMPLETE®
The famous KLB6® formula with wheat bran (500 mg) and 100% of RDA of 10 essential vitamins.
Supplied: Capsules, bottles of 100, 250, 500.

KLB6 DIET MIX®
Vanilla and Carob
Balanced low-calorie meal replacement fortified with kelp, lecithin and Vitamin B6.
Supplied: 14 oz. can.

L-GLUTAMINE (500 mg.)
Tablets, bottles of 50, 100, 500

L-LYSINE (500 mg.)
Tablets, bottles of 100, 500

LECITHIN (1200 mg.)
Capsules, bottles of 100, 250

LECITHIN, CHEWABLE (1200 mg)
Supplied: Tablets, bottles of 100, 250.

LECITHIN W/VIT. D
Each capsule contains:
Soya Lecithin ....259.2 mg.
Soy Bean Oil ....170.2 mg.
Vitamin D ....150 USP units
Supplied: Capsules, bottles of 100.

LECITHIN GRANULES
Each tablespoon contains 7.5 gms of lecithin.
Supplied: 14 oz. can.

LIVER W/B-12
Tablets, bottles of 100, 250

MAGNESIUM
(Magnesium Gluconate, 30 mg.)
Supplied: Tablets, bottles of 100.

MANGANESE
(Manganese Gluconate, 50 mg.)
Supplied: Tablets, bottles of 100.

MEGA B® W/C
High B-Complex formula with Vitamin C (500 mg).
Supplied: Tablets, bottles of 60, 180.

MEGA V & M™
Mega potency multiple vitamin and mineral formula.
Supplied: Tablets, bottles of 30, 60, 100, 250.

MULTI-MINERALS
A multiple mineral formula containing nine essential minerals.
Supplied: Tablets, bottles of 100, 250.

NATURE'S BOUNTY HAIR BOOSTER™
Vitamin-Mineral Complex for the hair.
Supplied: Tablets, bottles of 100.

NATURE'S BOUNTY SLIM®
100% Natural High Protein Powder plus Vitamins.
Supplied: 16 oz. can.

NIACIN (100 mg.)
Tablets, bottles of 100, 500
NIACIN (250 mg.)
Tablets, bottles of 100

NIACINAMIDE (500 mg.)
Tablets, bottles of 100, 250

OYSTER CALCIUM
Each tablet contains:
Calcium ....375 mg.
Vitamin A ....800 I.U.
Vitamin D-2 ....200 I.U.
Supplied: Tablets, bottles of 100, 500.

PABA
(Para-Aminobenzoic Acid, 100 mg.)
Tablets, bottles of 250, 500, 1000
PABA
(Para-Aminobenzoic Acid, 500 mg.)
Tablets, bottles of 100

PANTOTHENIC ACID (100 mg.)
Tablets, bottles of 100, 250
PANTOTHENIC ACID (200 mg.)
Tablets, bottles of 100, 250

PAPAYA ENZYME (1 gr.)
Aid to starch and protein digestion.
Supplied: Tablets, bottles of 100, 250.

POTASSIUM
(Potassium Gluconate, 83.5 mg.)
Tablets, bottles of 100, 250

POTASSIUM & B-6
Each tablet contains:
Potassium ....30 mg.
Vitamin B-6
(pyridoxine HCl) ....50 mg.
Supplied: Tablets, bottles of 90, 250.

PROTEIN (250 mg.)
A food supplement from soya, dried malt extract and dry milk powder.
Supplied: Tablets, bottles of 100, 250, 500.

PROTEIN FOR BODY BUILDING™
100% Natural High Protein Powder
Supplied: 16 oz. cans

RNA
(100 mg from brewer's yeast)
Supplied: Tablets, bottles of 100.

RNA/DNA
(100 mg of each from brewer's yeast)
Supplied: Tablets, bottles of 100.

RUTIN (50 mg.)
Tablets, bottles of 250, 500

SELENIUM (50 mcg.)
Tablets, bottles of 100, 250
SELENIUM (200 mcg.)
Tablets, bottles of 50, 100, 500

SPIRULINA (500 mg.)
Tablets, bottles of 90

STRESS FORMULA "605" ™
Hi-potency stress formula vitamins.
Supplied: Tablets, bottles of 60, 250.

STRESS FORMULA "605" ™ W/IRON
Hi-potency stress formula vitamins with iron (27 mg).
Supplied: Tablets, bottles of 60, 250.

STRESS FORMULA "605" ™ W/ZINC
Hi-potency stress formula with zinc (23.9 mg.).
Supplied: Tablets, bottles of 60, 250.

STRESS "1000"™
Sugar, Starch and Preservative Free

Each tablet provides:		%USRDA*
Vitamin C (with Rose Hips)	1000 mg.	1667
Vitamin E (d-alpha Tocopheryl Acetate)	30 I.U.	100
Thiamine (Vitamin B-1) (as Thiamine Mononitrate)	15 mg.	1000
Riboflavin (Vitamin B-2)	15 mg.	882
Niacinamide	100 mg.	500
Vitamin B-6 (as Pyridoxine Hydrochloride)	5 mg.	205
Vitamin B-12 (Cyanocobalamin)	12 mcg.	200
Pantothenic Acid (Calcium Pantothenate USP)	20 mg.	183

*Percentage of the U.S. government recommended daily allowance for adults and children four or more years of age.
Supplied: Tablets, bottles of 30, 60, 90, 250.

SUPEROXIDE DISMUTASE (SOD)
2000 Units
Supplied: Tablets, bottles of 50, 100, 500.

TRYPTOPHAN (200 mg.)
Tablets, bottles of 30, 100
TRYPTOPHAN (667 mg.)
Tablets, bottles of 30, 100

ULTRA "A"
(Vitamin A, 25,000 USP Units)
Capsules, bottles of 100, 250
ULTRA "A"
(Vitamin A, 25,000 USP Units)
Tablets, bottles of 100, 1000

ULTRA "A & D"
(25,000 UNITS OF VIT. A & 1,000 UNITS OF VIT. D)
Tablets, bottles of 100, 1000

ULTRA "D"
(1000 USP units Vit. D)
Supplied: Tablets, bottles of 100, 500.

ULTRA KLB6™
Three tablets contain:
Lecithin ....1200 mg.
Vitamin B-6 .... 350 mg.
Kelp .... 100 mg.
Cider Vinegar .... 240 mg.
Supplied: Tablets, bottles of 100, 250, 500.

ULTRA VITA-TIME™
Ultra potency vitamins, minerals, amino acids and lipotropic formula.
Supplied: Tablets, bottles of 50, 100, 250, 500.

VITAMIN A (10,000 USP UNITS)
Capsules, bottles of 100, 250, 500
VITAMIN A (10,000 USP UNITS)
Tablets, bottles of 100, 250, 500, 1000

VITAMIN A & D
(10,000 UNITS VIT. A & 400 UNITS VIT. D)
Tablets, bottles of 100, 500

VITAMIN D (400 USP UNITS)
Tablets, bottles of 100

VITAMIN K (100 mcg.)
Tablets, bottles of 100, 500

VITA-TIME™
High potency vitamins, minerals and amino acids.
Supplied: Tablets, bottles of 100, 250, 500, 1000.

WATER PILL (NATURAL DIURETIC)
Each tablet contains:
Buchu Leaves Powder ....50 mg.
Uva Ursi Leaves Powder ....50 mg.
Parsley Leaves Powder ....50 mg.
Juniper Berries Powder ....10 mg.
Potassium ....20 mg.
Supplied: Tablets, bottles of 50, 100, 250.

WATER PILL WITH IRON (NATURAL DIURETIC)
Each tablet contains:
Same as above plus:
Iron (ferrous gluconate) ....6 mg.
Supplied: Tablets, bottles of 50, 100, 250.

WATER PILL W/POTASSIUM
Capsules, bottles of 50, 100, 250

WHEAT GERM OIL (6 minim)
Capsules, bottles of 100
WHEAT GERM OIL (14 minim)
Capsules, bottles of 100
WHEAT GERM OIL (20 minim)
Capsules, bottles of 100, 250

YEAST PLUS VITAMIN
B12, B-Complex with minerals and amino acids.
Supplied: Tablets, bottles of 100, 250.

ZACNE®
Each tablet contains:
Zinc Gluconate .... 25 mg.
Vitamin C
with Rose Hips .... 75 mg.
B-6 (Pyridoxine HCl) .... 10 mg.
Vitamin A
(fish liver oils) .... 500 I.U.
Vitamin E .... 25 I.U.
Directions: As a dietary supplement, two tablets three times daily before meals.
Supplied: Tablets, bottles of 100, 500.
[Shown in Product Identification Section]

ZINC (10 mg.)
(Zinc Gluconate)
Tablets, bottles of 100, 250, 500, 1000
ZINC (25 mg.)
Tablets, bottles of 100, 500
ZINC (50 mg.)
Tablets, bottles of 100, 500
ZINC (100 mg.)
Tablets, bottles of 100, 500

Nicholas Laboratories, Inc.
99 MORRIS AVENUE
P.O. BOX 110
SPRINGFIELD, NJ 07081

AMBI® SKIN CREAM
Dry, Normal, Oily and with Moisturizers
Active Ingredients: Dry Skin Formula and Skin Cream with Moisturizers contain Hydroquinone 2%, Octyl Dimethyl PABA 2%. Oily Skin Formula and Normal Skin Formula contain Hydroquinone 2%, Glyceryl PABA 2.8%.
Indications: Lightens dark pigment and skin discolorations.
Precaution: For external use only. Avoid contact with eyes and mouth. Discontinue use if no improvement is seen after 2 months. Not recommended for use by children under 12 years of age. To prevent a return of uneven coloration, avoid overexposure to sunlight.
Directions: Apply twice daily, rub in gently until cream vanishes.
Professional Labeling: Skin toning cream, skin bleaching agent.
How Supplied: Ambi Skin Cream; Dry, Normal and Oily available in 2 oz. aluminum tubes. Ambi Skin Cream with Moisturizers available in 4 oz. plastic jar.

Norcliff Thayer Inc.
ONE SCARSDALE ROAD
TUCKAHOE, NY 10707

A-200 Pyrinate® Liquid, Gel

A-200 Pyrinate® Liquid
Description: Active Ingredients: pyrethrins 0.165%, piperonyl butoxide technical 2.00% (equivalent to 1.60% (butylcarbityl) (6-propylpiperonyl) ether and 0.40% related compounds), deodorized kerosene 5.00%. Inert ingredients 92.835%.
A-200 Pyrinate® Gel
Description: Active Ingredients: pyrethrins 0.333%, piperonyl butoxide technical 4.00% (equivalent to 3.2% (butylcarbityl) (6-propylpiperonyl) ether and 0.8% related compounds), deodorized kerosene 5.333%. Inert ingredients 90.334%.
Actions: A-200 Pyrinate is an effective pediculicide for control of head lice (Pediculus humanus capitis), pubic lice (Phthirus pubis) and body lice (Pediculus humanus corporis), and their nits.
Indications: A-200 Pyrinate Liquid and Gel are indicated for the treatment of human pediculosis—head lice, body lice and pubic lice, and their eggs. A-200 Pyrinate Gel is specially formulated for pubic lice and head lice in children, where control of application is desirable.
Contraindications: A-200 Pyrinate is contraindicated in individuals hypersensitive to any of its ingredients or allergic to ragweed.
Precautions: A-200 Pyrinate is for external use only. It is harmful if swallowed or inhaled. It may be irritating to the eyes and mucous membranes. In case of accidental contact with eyes, they should be immediately flushed with water. If skin irritation or signs of infection are present, a physician should be consulted.
Administration and Dosage: Apply sufficient A-200 Pyrinate to completely "wet" the hair and scalp or skin of any infested area. Allow application to remain no longer than 10 minutes. Wash and rinse with plenty of warm water. Remove dead lice and eggs from hair with fine comb. To restore body and luster to hair following scalp applications, follow with a good shampoo. If necessary, this treatment may be repeated, but should not exceed two applications within 24 hours.
In order to prevent reinfestation with lice, all clothing and bedding must be sterilized or treated concurrent with the application of this preparation.
How Supplied: A-200 Pyrinate Liquid in 2 and 4 fl. oz. bottles. A-200 Pyrinate Gel in 1 oz. tubes.
Literature Available: Patient literature available upon request.
[Shown in Product Identification Section]

Continued on next page

Norcliff Thayer—Cont.

ESOTÉRICA® MEDICATED FADE CREAM
Regular
Facial
Fortified Scented with Sunscreen
Fortified Unscented with Sunscreen

Composition: Regular and Facial:
Active Ingredient: Hydroquinone 2%. Other Ingredients: Water, glyceryl stearate, isopropyl palmitate, propylene glycol, ceresin, mineral oil, stearyl alcohol, propylene glycol stearate, PEG-6-32 stearate, poloxamer 188, steareth-20, laureth-23, dimethicone, sodium lauryl sulfate, citric acid, sodium bisulfite, methylparaben, propylparaben, trisodium EDTA, BHA.
Fortified Scented and Unscented with Sunscreen:
Active Ingredients: Hydroquinone 2%, padimate O 3.3%, oxybenzone 2.5%. Other Ingredients: Water, glyceryl stearate, isopropyl palmitate, ceresin, propylene glycol, stearyl alcohol, PEG-6-32 stearate, poloxamer 188, mineral oil, steareth-20, laureth-23, steareth-10, allantoin ascorbate, dimethicone, sodium lauryl sulfate, methylparaben, propylparaben, sodium bisulfite, BHA, trisodium EDTA.
Fragrance in all except Fortified Unscented with Sunscreen.
Indications: Regular and Fortified Scented and Unscented with Sunscreen: Indicated for helping fade darkened skin areas including age spots, liver spots, freckles and melasma on the face, hands, legs and body and when used as directed helps prevent their recurrence. Facial: Specially designed to help fade darkened skin areas including age spots, liver spots, freckles and melasma on the face and when used as directed helps prevent their recurrence. It has emollients to help moisturize while it lightens, so it makes an excellent night cream as well.
Actions: Esotérica Medicated helps bleach and lighten hyperpigmented skin.
Contraindications: Should not be used by persons with known sensitivity to hydroquinone.
Warnings: Do not use if skin is irritated. Some individuals may be sensitive to the active ingredient(s) in this cream. Discontinue use if irritation appears. Avoid contact with eyes. Excessive exposure to the sun should be avoided. For external use only.
Fortified Scented and Unscented with Sunscreen: Not for use in the prevention of sunburn.
Directions: Apply Esotérica to areas you wish to lighten and rub in well. Use cream in the morning and at bedtime for at least six weeks for maximum results. Esotérica is greaseless and may be used under makeup.
How Supplied: 3 oz. glass jars.

LIQUIPRIN®
(acetaminophen)

Description: Liquiprin is a nonsalicylate analgesic and antipyretic particularly suitable for children. Each 1.25 ml (top mark on dropper) contains 60 mg (1 gr.) of acetaminophen. Liquiprin is raspberry flavored, reddish pink solution, and does not contain alcohol.
Actions: Liquiprin safely and effectively reduces fever and pain at any age without the hazards of salicylate therapy (e.g., gastric mucosal irritation).
Indications: Liquiprin is indicated as treatment of infants and children with conditions requiring reduction of fever and/or relief of pain such as mild upper respiratory infections (tonsillitis, common cold, flu), teething, headache, myalgia, postimmunization reactions, post-tonsillectomy discomfort and gastroenteritis. As adjunctive therapy with antibiotics or sulfonamides, Liquiprin may be useful as an analgesic and antipyretic in bacterial or viral infections, such as bronchitis, pharyngitis, tracheobronchitis, sinusitis, pneumonia, otitis media and cervical adenitis.
Precautions and Adverse Reactions: If a sensitivity reaction occurs, the drug should be discontinued. Liquiprin Drops has rarely been found to produce side effects. It is usually well tolerated by patients who are sensitive to products containing aspirin.
Usual Dosage: Liquiprin should be administered at 4-hour intervals 3 to 4 times daily in the following dosages:
Under 3 years: Up to 120 mg (two dropperfuls filled to 60 mg top mark)
3 years: 120 mg (two dropperfuls filled to 60 mg top mark)
4 to 5 years: 180 mg (three dropperfuls filled to 60 mg top mark)
How Supplied: Liquiprin is available in a 1.16 fl. oz. (35 ml) plastic bottle with a calibrated dropper and child-resistant cap.
[*Shown in Product Identification Section*]

NATURE'S REMEDY®
Laxative

Active Ingredients: Cascara sagrada 150 mg, aloe 100 mg.
Indications: For gentle, overnight relief of constipation.
Actions: Nature's Remedy has two natural active ingredients that give gentle, overnight relief of constipation. These ingredients, cascara sagrada and aloe, gently stimulate the body's natural function.
Warnings: Do not take any laxative when nausea, vomiting, abdominal pain, or other symptoms of appendicitis are present. Frequent or prolonged use of laxatives may result in dependence on them.
Dosage and Administration: Adults, swallow two tablets daily along with a full glass of water; children (8–15 yrs.), one tablet daily; or as directed by a physician.
How Supplied: Beige, film-coated tablets with foil-backed blister packaging in boxes of 12s, 30s and 60s.
[*Shown in Product Identification Section*]

NOSALT™
Salt Alternative

Composition: Food seasoning to be used as an alternative or substitute for salt (NaCl) at the table and in cooking to help regulate dietary sodium intake. Contains potassium chloride, potassium bitartrate, potassium glutamate, adipic acid, fumaric acid, polyethylene glycol 400, disodium inosinate. Looks, sprinkles and tastes like salt, contains less than 10 mg of sodium per 100 g which is considered to be dietetically sodium free. Contains approximately 35 mEq (1,368 mg) of potassium per ½ level teaspoon.
Uses: Sprinkled on food or in cooking, in the same proportion as regular salt, gives food salt flavor while helping to reduce sodium intake. Appropriate for persons on low sodium diets, as for example, those whose sodium intake has been restricted for medical reasons.
Caution to Physicians: The potassium intake of persons receiving potassium-sparing diuretics or potassium supplementation should be evaluated. Potassium chloride should not be used in patients with hyperkalemia, oliguria, and severe kidney disease.
Consumer Warning: For normal, healthy people. Persons having diabetes, heart or kidney disease, or persons receiving medical treatment should consult a physician before using a salt alternative or substitute.
How Supplied: 11 oz. container with shaker top.
[*Shown in Product Identification Section*]

OXY-5® LOTION
OXY-10® LOTION
Benzoyl Peroxide Lotion 5% and 10%

Description: 5% or 10% benzoyl peroxide in a colorless, odorless, greaseless lotion base.
Indications: A topical aid in the treatment of acne vulgaris.
Action: Provides antibacterial activity against Propionibacterium acnes plus the drying and desquamation necessary in the topical treatment of acne.
Dosage and Administration: Shake well before using. Wash affected area with soap and water. Dry well. Dab lotion on existing pimples and smooth into oily acne-prone areas. Apply one to three times daily or as required.
Contraindications: Should not be used by patients with known sensitivity to benzoyl peroxide.
Caution: Avoid contact with eyes, lips and mucous membranes. For external use only. Discontinue use if excessive irritation or dryness develops. May bleach hair and colored fabrics.
How Supplied: 1 fl. oz. plastic bottles.
[*Shown in Product Identification Section*]

OXY-SCRUB®
Abradant Cleanser

Description: Oxy-Scrub is a skin cleanser containing dissolving abradant granules and is useful for opening plugged pores and for removing excess oil. Oxy-Scrub can't over-abrade as can cleansers with non-dissolving abradant particles.

Composition: Contains dissolving abradant granules (sodium tetraborate decahydrate) in a base containing a unique combination of surface active soapless cleaning agents.

Directions: Use in place of your usual soap or cleanser. Wet face with warm water. Squeeze Oxy-Scrub onto fingertips and gently massage into face. Continue massaging and adding water until abradant granules are completely dissolved. (About one minute.) Rinse thoroughly with warm water and dry. Use once or twice daily, or as required.

Caution: Avoid contact with eyes. If particles get into eyes, flush thoroughly with water and avoid rubbing eyes. Discontinue use if skin irritation or excessive dryness develops. Not to be used on infants or children under 3 years of age. Do not use on inflamed skin. Keep out of reach of children.

How Supplied: 2.65 oz. plastic tubes. [*Shown in Product Identification Section*]

OXY WASH™ Antibacterial Skin Wash

Active Ingredient: Benzoyl peroxide 10%

Indications: Kills acne bacteria. Thoroughly cleanses acne-prone skin. Removes excess oils.

Actions: Antibacterial skin wash. Helps remove the cause of acne pimples to aid in keeping skin clean, clear and healthy looking.

For a complete anti-acne program, follow Oxy Wash with Oxy-5® acne-pimple medication. Or for stubborn and adult acne, use Oxy-10® extra strength acne-pimple medication.

Contraindications: Should not be used by patients with known sensitivity to benzoyl peroxide.

Warnings: Avoid contact with eyes, lips and mucous membranes. If excessive dryness or undue irritation of the skin develops, discontinue use and consult physician. Colored or dyed garments may be bleached by the oxidizing action of benzoyl peroxide. To prevent bleaching, avoid contact with hair. For external use only. Keep out of reach of children.

Dosage and Administration: Shake well. Wet area to be washed. Apply Oxy Wash massaging gently for 1 to 2 minutes. Rinse thoroughly. Use 2 to 3 times daily or as directed by physician.

How supplied: 4 fl. oz. plastic bottles. [*Shown in Product Identification Section*]

TUMS® Antacid Tablets

Active Ingredient: Calcium carbonate, Precipitated U.S.P. 500 mg

Indications: For fast relief of acid indigestion, heartburn and sour stomach.

Actions: A novel antacid composition providing liquid effectiveness in a low cost, pleasant-tasting tablet. TUMS tablets are free of the chalky aftertaste usually associated with calcium carbonate therapy and remain pleasant-tasting even during long-term therapy. TUMS lowers the upper limit of the pH range

without affecting the innate antacid efficiency of calcium carbonate. One tablet, when tested *in vitro* according to the *Federal Register* procedure (*Fed. Reg.* 39:19862, June 4, 1974), neutralizes 10 mEq of 0.1 N HCl. This high neutralization capacity combined with a rapid rate of reaction makes TUMS an ideal antacid for management of conditions associated with hyperacidity. The mild, water-insoluble active ingredient of TUMS is non-systemic. It effectively neutralizes free acid yet does not cause systemic alkalosis in the presence of normal renal function. A double-blind placebo controlled clinical study demonstrated that calcium carbonate taken at a dosage of 16 TUMS tablets daily for a two-week period was non-constipating/non-laxative.

Tums is a low sodium antacid. Each tablet contains less than 3 mg of sodium.

Contraindications: Renal disease, hypercalcemia, concurrent administration with large amounts of milk.

Warnings: TUMS should not be used by patients who are severely debilitated or suffering from kidney failure. For Self-Medication: Do not take more than 16 tablets in a 24-hour period or use the maximum dosage of this product for more than 2 weeks, except under the advice and supervision of a physician.

Dosage and Administration: Chew 1 or 2 TUMS tablets as symptoms occur. Repeat hourly if symptoms return, or as directed by a physician. No water is required. Simulated Drip Method: The pleasant-tasting TUMS tablet may be kept between the gum and cheek and allowed to dissolve gradually by continuous sucking to prolong the effective relief time.

Professional Labeling: Indicated in the management of peptic ulcer, gastritis, gastric hyperacidity, hiatal hernia and peptic esophagitis.

How Supplied: Peppermint and Assorted Flavors of Cherry, Lemon, Orange and Wintergreen are available in 12-tablet rolls, 3-roll wraps, and bottles of 75 and 150 tablets. [*Shown in Product Identification Section*]

Norwich-Eaton Pharmaceuticals
Division of MortonNorwich Consumer Products Group 17 EATON AVENUE NORWICH, NY 13815

BPN® TRIPLE ANTIBIOTIC OINTMENT

Active Ingredient: A triple antibiotic ointment in an inert petrolatum base. Each gram contains: Bacitracin 500 units, Polymixin B 5,000 units, (as Sulfate), Neomycin base (as Sulfate) 3.5 mg.

Indications: A topical antibiotic ointment to help prevent infection in minor cuts and abrasions; an aid to healing.

Warnings: In case of deep or puncture wounds or serious burns consult physician. If redness, irritation, swelling or pain persists, or increases or if infection

occurs, discontinue use and consult physician. Do not use in the eyes.

Dosage and Administration: Spread liberally over affected area once or twice daily; cover with a dry, sterile dressing. For external use only.

How Supplied: Tubes of ½ ounce.

CHILDREN'S CHLORASEPTIC® LOZENGES

Active Ingredient: Each Children's Chloraseptic Lozenge contains 5 mg. benzocaine in a grape flavored base of sugar and corn syrup solids.

Actions: Children's Chloraseptic Lozenges provide prompt, temporary relief of minor sore throat pain which may accompany conditions such as tonsillitis, pharyngitis and in post-tonsillectomy soreness, and discomfort of minor mouth and gum irritations.

Dosage and Administration: Allow one lozenge to dissolve slowly in the mouth. Repeat hourly if needed. Do not take more than 12 lozenges per day. Not for children under 3 unless directed by a physician.

How Supplied: Carton of 18 lozenges. [*Shown in Product Identification Section*]

MENTHOL CHLORASEPTIC® LIQUID
CHERRY CHLORASEPTIC® LIQUID
MENTHOL CHLORASEPTIC® AEROSOL SPRAY
CHERRY CHLORASEPTIC® AEROSOL SPRAY

Active Ingredient: An alkaline solution containing phenol and sodium phenolate (total phenol 1.4%). In addition, Menthol and Cherry Chloraseptic 1.5 oz Spray contain compressed nitrogen as a propellant.

Indications: Pleasant-tasting Chloraseptic is an antiseptic, anesthetic, deodorizing mouthwash and gargle. It is an alkaline solution designed specifically to maintain oral hygiene and to relieve local soreness and irritation without "caines." Chloraseptic may be used as a topical anesthetic while antibacterials are used systemically in the treatment of infection. Chloraseptic acts promptly, often providing effective surface anesthesia in minutes. It is a valuable adjunct for temporary relief of pain and discomfort and will reduce oral bacterial flora temporarily to improve oral hygiene. Chloraseptic is indicated for prompt temporary relief of discomfort due to the following conditions: *Medical* —oropharyngitis and throat infections; acute tonsillitis; posttonsillectomy soreness; peritonsillar abscess; oropharyngeal manifestations of postnasal drip; throat and mouth dryness (smoker's cough); and before intubation (anti-gag) and after (for soreness); *Dental*—after oral surgery or extractions; aphthous ulcers and infectious stomatitis; Vincent's infection; gingivitis; preinjection topical anesthesia; insertion of immedi-

Continued on next page

Norwich-Eaton—Cont.

ate denture; pericoronitis; and x-rays and impressions (anti-gag).

Dosage and Administration: Chloraseptic Mouthwash and Gargle—*Irritated throat:* Advise patient to spray 5 times (children 6-12 years of age, 3 times) and swallow. May be used as a gargle. Repeat every 2 hours if necessary. *After oral surgery:* Advise patient to allow full-strength solution to run over affected areas for 15 seconds without swishing, then expel remainder. Repeat every 2 hours if necessary. Not for children under 6 years of age unless directed by a physician or dentist. *Adjunctive gingival therapy:* Rinse vigorously with full-strength solution for 15 seconds, working between teeth, then expel remainder. Repeat every 2 hours if necessary. *Daily deodorizing mouthwash and gargle:* Dilute with equal parts of water and rinse thoroughly, or spray full strength, then expel remainder.

Chloraseptic Spray: *Irritated throat:* Advise patient to spray throat about 2 seconds (children 6 to 12 years about 1 second) and swallow. Repeat every 2 hours if necessary. After oral surgery: Advise patient to spray affected area for 1 to 2 seconds, allow solution to remain for 15 seconds, without swishing, then expel remainder. Repeat every 2 hours if necessary. *Adjunctive gingival therapy:* Spray affected area for about 2 seconds, swish for 15 seconds working between teeth, then expel remainder. Repeat every 2 hours if necessary. *Daily deodorizing spray:* Spray, rinse thoroughly, and expel remainder. Not for children under 6 years of age unless directed by a physician or dentist.

Packaging: Menthol Chloraseptic—6 oz. bottle with sprayer, 8 and 12 oz. bottles without sprayer, and 1.5 oz. spray can. Cherry Chloraseptic—6 oz. bottle with sprayer, 12 oz. bottle without sprayer, and 1.5 oz. spray can. No prescription necessary.

[Shown in Product Identification Section]

MENTHOL CHLORASEPTIC® LOZENGES
CHERRY CHLORASEPTIC® LOZENGES

Description: Each Chloraseptic Lozenge contains phenol, sodium phenolate (total phenol 32.5 mg).

Action and Uses: Chloraseptic Lozenges provide prompt temporary relief of discomfort due to mouth and gum irritations and of minor sore throat due to colds. They are anesthetic and antiseptic—and also may be used as a topical adjunct to systemic antibacterial therapy for severe cases. For prompt temporary relief of pain and discomfort associated with the following conditions: *Medical* —oropharyngitis and throat infections; acute tonsillitis; posttonsillectomy soreness; peritonsillar abscess; oropharyngeal manifestations of postnasal drip; and throat and mouth dryness (smoker's cough); *Dental*—after oral surgery; aphthous ulcers and infectious stomatitis;

Vincent's infection; gingivitis; and pericoronitis.

Administration and Dosage: Adults: Dissolve 1 lozenge in the mouth every 2 hours; do not exceed 8 lozenges per day. Children 6-12 years: Dissolve 1 lozenge in the mouth every 3 hours; <u>do not exceed 4 lozenges per day</u>. Not for children under 6 unless directed by a physician or dentist.

Packaging: Menthol and Cherry Chloraseptic Lozenges—packages of 18, and 45 lozenges.

No prescription necessary.

[Shown in Product Identification Section]

CHLORASEPTIC® COUGH CONTROL LOZENGES

Description: Each CHLORASEPTIC Cough Control Lozenge contains phenol and sodium phenolate (total phenol 32.5 mg.), and a 10 mg. therapeutic dose of dextromethorphan hydrobromide.

Action and Uses: CHLORASEPTIC Cough Control Lozenges provide fast relief of minor sore throat pain and control coughs due to colds. Each lozenge contains two active ingredients. One is the same agent contained in CHLORASEPTIC, a widely used medication for relief of minor sore throat pain. This ingredient acts as a local anesthetic stopping sore throat pain by temporarily blocking the nerve impulse transmission to the ninth cranial nerve. The second agent, dextromethorphan hydrobromide, a non-narcotic antitussive, acts by selective suppression of the central cough mechanism. Dual-active CHLORASEPTIC Cough Control Lozenges provide temporary symptomatic relief of coughs and minor sore throat pain.

Administration and Dosage: Adults: Dissolve one lozenge slowly in mouth every two hours; do not exceed eight lozenges per day. Children 6 to 12 years: Dissolve one lozenge slowly in mouth every four hours; do not exceed four lozenges per day. Do not administer to children under 6 years of age unless directed by a physician.

Caution: Persistent cough may indicate the presence of a serious condition. Persons with a high fever or persistent cough should not use this preparation unless directed by physician. Consult physician promptly if sore throat is severe or lasts more than two days, or if accompanied by high fever, headache, nausea or vomiting.

Warning: Do not take this product for persistent cough such as occurs with smoking, asthma, emphysema, or where cough is accompanied by excessive secretions except with the advice and supervision of a physician.

Packaging: Pocket-size box of 12 lozenges.

[Shown in Product Identification Section]

CHLORASEPTIC® GEL

Description: Chloraseptic Gel contains phenol, sodium phenolate (total phenol 1.4%) in a special adherent base.

Indications: For prompt, temporary relief of discomfort from minor mouth and gum irritations.

Warnings: If irritation or pain persists, discontinue use and consult physician or dentist. Do not administer to children under 6 years of age unless directed by a physician.

Administration: Apply directly to the affected areas. Repeat as necessary.

How Supplied: Chloraseptic Gel is available in $\frac{1}{4}$-oz. tubes.

ENCARE®
Vaginal Contraceptive Inserts

Description: ENCARE is an effervescent vaginal contraceptive insert containing a premeasured dose of the spermicide nonoxynol 9 (2.27%).

Action: When used as directed, ENCARE dissolves and gently effervesces into a spermicidal barrier that immobilizes and kills sperm on contact.

Indications: Prevention of pregnancy. ENCARE is useful in managing a broad-spectrum of contraceptive indications. **Primary contraception:** when oral contraceptives or the IUD are contraindicated; for patients concerned about the risk of hormonal or mechanical side-effects; when sexual activity is infrequent or intermittent. **Transitional contraception:** during the initial cycle of oral contraception, or in the three months following IUD insertion, when O.C. users desire pregnancy and unprotected intercourse should not occur immediately; prior to surgical procedures if hormones are contraindicated. **Adjunctive contraception:** for O.C. users to keep on hand for use when consecutive pills are missed; with the IUD, for extra midcycle protection; with condoms for additional contraceptive effectiveness.

Effectiveness: ENCARE is not as effective as the pill or IUD in actual use, but is approximately as effective as vaginal foam contraceptives. Use-effectiveness will depend on how correctly and consistently patients follow package instructions.

Precautions: When pregnancy is medically contraindicated, the contraceptive program should be determined by a physician. If allergic reactions to cream, foam, jelly, or suppository-type contraceptives have been experienced, a physician should be consulted before use.

Adverse Reactions: In some instances, irritation of the vagina or penis accompanies use of the product. If this occurs, use should be discontinued. As ENCARE effervesces, there may be some sensation of warmth; however, this should not be cause for concern. Some users report that this sensation diminishes through repeated use.

Dosage and Administration: ENCARE must be inserted according to instructions and at least **ten minutes** before intercourse. Best protection will occur when inserted deep in the vagina, close to the cervix.

Contraceptive protection lasts during the period from ten minutes to one hour following insertion. A new ENCARE must be inserted each time intercourse is repeated. The patient should wait at least six hours after intercourse before douching, if a douche is desired.

How Supplied: Boxes of 12 inserts. EN-CARE should be stored at a temperature below 86°F (30°C). Should the product inadvertently be exposed to higher temperatures, hold under cold water for two minutes before removing protective wrap.

Eaton-Merz Laboratories, Inc.
Distributed by Eaton-Merz Laboratories, Inc.
Manufactured by Norwich-Eaton Pharmaceuticals
Norwich, New York 13815
Division of Morton-Norwich Products, Inc.
[*Shown in Product Identification Section*]

NECTA SWEET® NON-CALORIC SWEETENER

Active Ingredient:
12.3 mg. sodium saccharin per ¼ grain tablet
24.6 mg. sodium saccharin per ½ grain tablet
49.2 mg. sodium saccharin per 1 grain tablet

Indications: A non-nutritive, artificial sweetener for persons who must restrict their intake of sugar.

Actions: Instant dissolving tablets containing no proteins, fat, available carbohydrates or calories.

Warning: Use of this product may be hazardous to your health. This product contains saccharin which has been determined to cause cancer in laboratory animals.

How Supplied: Available in ¼ grain, ½ grain and 1 grain tablets packaged 500 and 1000 per bottle.

NORFORMS® FEMININE DEODORANT SUPPOSITORIES

Norforms Unscented Ingredients: PEG-20, PEG-6, PEG-20 Palmitate, Methylbenzethonium Chloride, Methylparaben, Lactic Acid.

Norforms Herbal Ingredients: PEG-20, PEG-6, PEG-20 Palmitate, Fragrance, Methylbenzethonium Chloride, Methylparaben, Lactic Acid.

Usage: Internal Feminine Deodorant

Actions: Norforms' deodorant action effectively controls feminine odor in most women for over 8 full hours. They begin working internally the minute they are inserted, spreading a film over the walls of the vagina.

Warnings: If one wishes to become pregnant, Norforms or any internal personal hygiene product should not be used for 6 hours prior to or following intercourse. **Norforms are not recommended for contraception,** but any product introduced into the vaginal area during that time may sometimes interfere with conception.

Most obstetricians advise against the use of products such as douches, sprays or vaginal deodorants during pregnancy. The subject of vaginal hygiene during this time should be discussed with a physician before using Norforms.

Several symptoms may signal **unrelated** medical problems during Norforms use: 1. A discharge which is unusual in color, consistency or amount. 2. A burning or itching sensation in the vaginal area. 3. An abnormal or stronger than usual odor. A physician should be consulted immediately if any of these symptoms occur—especially if they are accompanied by unusual swelling or tenderness, fever, or by pains or cramps in the lower abdomen.

Dosage and Administration: One deodorant suppository a day or as needed. Each deodorant suppository can be easily inserted into the vagina with a finger, or the inserter which is available in the package. Can be used during menstruation in conjunction with a tampon or pad.

Professional Labeling: Same as those outlined under Usage.

How Supplied: Available in both unscented and herbal fragranced forms. Package sizes include 6, 12 and 24 deodorant suppositories.
[*Shown in Product Identification Section*]

NORWICH® ASPIRIN

Active Ingredient: Aspirin 5 Grain (325 mg)

Indications: For pain relief of simple headache and the fever of colds and flu.

Actions: Analgesic, antipyretic

Warnings: Keep all medicines out of reach of children. In case of accidental overdose, contact a physician immediately. Do not take if asthmatic, or during last 3 months of pregnancy except under advice and supervision of physician.

Caution: Do not take if you have ulcers, ulcer symptoms or bleeding problems. If taking medicines for anticoagulation (thinning the blood), diabetes, gout or arthritis, consult physician. Discontinue use if ringing in the ears occurs.

Dosage and Administration: Adults: 1 or 2 tablets every 3-4 hours up to 6 times a day. Children: under 3 years, consult physician; 3-6 years, ½-1 tablet; over 6 years, 1 tablet. May be taken every 3-4 hours up to 3 times a day.

Professional Labeling: Same as outlined under Indications.

How Supplied: In bottles of 100, 250 and 500 tablets.
[*Shown in Product Identification Section*]

NORWICH® BACITRACIN ANTIBIOTIC OINTMENT

Active Ingredient: Bacitracin Ointment U.S.P. (500 units Bacitracin per gram in an ointment base)

Indications: An antibiotic ointment to help prevent infection in minor cuts, burns, abrasions.

Warnings: In case of deep or puncture wounds or serious burns, consult physician. If redness, irritation, swelling or pain persists or increases or if infection occurs, discontinue use and consult physician. Do not use in the eyes.

Dosage and Administration: Apply once or twice a day to injured area and cover with a sterile gauze bandage.

How Supplied: Tubes of ½ oz. and 1 oz.

NORWICH® GLYCERIN SUPPOSITORIES

Active Ingredient: Glycerin

Indications: A convenient aid for prompt yet gentle relief of simple constipation.

Action: Laxative

Warning: Do not use when abdominal pain, nausea, or vomiting are present. Frequent or prolonged use of this preparation may result in dependence on laxatives.

Dosage and Administration: Insert one suppository into the rectum. Keep in place five minutes or longer. Repeat as needed. For infants and small children: hold larger end of infants size suppository, insert tapered end well up into the rectum; keep in place five minutes or longer. The suppository need not melt completely to produce laxative action.

Professional Labeling: Same as those outlined under Indications.

How Supplied: Adult formula available in shatterproof jars containing 12, 24 and 50 suppositories. Infant formula available in shatterproof jars containing 12, and 24 suppositories.

NORWICH-EATON ZINC OXIDE OINTMENT

Active Ingredient: 20% Zinc Oxide in a white ointment base with mineral oil.

Indications: For temporary relief of: minor skin irritations, diaper rash, discomfort due to hemorrhoids. A protective coating for inflamed tissue.

Directions: For minor skin irritations and diaper rash: apply liberally as often as necessary. For hemorrhoids: wash area with mild soap and warm water, rinse. Apply freely or as directed by physician. Do not exceed six applications per 24 hours or between bowel movements. Not for internal use.

Warnings: For external use only. Do not put this product into the rectum by using fingers or any mechanical device or applicator. Do not apply over puncture wounds, infections or lacerations. Avoid contact with the eyes. Follow recommended dosage except as directed by physician. If symptoms persist for more than 7 days, or if rectal bleeding occurs, consult physician. Keep all medicines out of reach of children.

How Supplied: Tubes of 1 oz. and 2¼ oz.

NP–27® CREAM

Active Ingredient: 8-Hydroxyquinoline Benzoate 2.5%

Indications: For Athlete's Foot and Ringworm

Actions: Antifungal/anti-itch. Deep acting antifungal NP-27 quickly relieves itching and discomfort of Athlete's Foot and Ringworm. Combats and controls infection-causing fungi; helps restore normal skin even in severe or persistent cases.

Warnings: In case of fungal infections of nails, or if symptoms persist, consult a physician. Diabetics should not use this

Continued on next page

Norwich-Eaton—Cont.

or any topical foot medication without first consulting a physician.

Dosage and Administration: After vigorously washing affected area, rub NP-27 Cream gently into skin until cream disappears, then apply a generous second coating of cream over area. Repeat treatment morning and night. After symptoms have disappeared, continue treatment once a day for another week.

How Supplied: 1½ oz. tubes.

NP-27® LIQUID

Active Ingredient: Undecylenic Acid 10% w/w.

Indications: For Athlete's Foot & Ringworm

Action: Antifungal

Warnings: Temporary smarting may occur. Avoid getting into eyes. In case of ringworm of nails or scalp, or if symptoms persist, see physician. Persons with impaired circulation, including diabetics, should not use this or any topical foot medication, without first consulting a physician. Keep all medicines out of reach of children. In case of accidental ingestion, seek professional assistance or contact a Poison Control Center.

Dosage and Administration: Cleanse affected and adjacent areas night and morning with soap and water. Spray NP-27 Liquid liberally on the affected area. Continue for a week after symptoms disappear to help prevent recurrence.

How Supplied: Available in 2 oz. and 4 oz. bottles.

NP-27® POWDER

Active Ingredient: Salicylic Acid 1.5%

Indications: For Athlete's Foot

Actions: Antifungal/anti-itch. Guards against fungus growth; protects broken skin from infection; helps prevent odor.

Warnings: Diabetics should not use this or any topical foot medication without consulting a physician.

Dosage and Administration: Sprinkle a generous quantity of NP-27 Powder on feet, especially between toes, daily.

How Supplied: Available in 1¾ oz. bottles.

NP-27® SPRAY POWDER

Active Ingredient: Zinc Undecylenate 20%

Indications: For effective relief of Athlete's Foot discomfort.

Actions: antifungal/anti-itch

Warnings: For external use only. Use only as directed. Diabetics should not use this or any topical foot medication without first consulting a physician. Avoid spraying in eyes. Contents under pressure. Do not puncture or incinerate. Do not store at temperature above 120°F. Keep out of reach of children. Use only as directed. Intentional misuse by deliberately concentrating and inhaling the contents can be harmful or fatal.

Dosage and Administration: Shake well before using. Hold NP-27 spray

about 5 inches from affected area. Spray area completely, especially between toes.

How Supplied: 4 oz. and 8 oz. cans.

PEPTO–BISMOL® Liquid and Tablets
For upset stomach, indigestion and nausea.
Controls common diarrhea.

Active Ingredient: Bismuth subsalicylate, 300 mg. per tablet or 262 mg. per 15 ml. (tablespoon). Contains no sugar.

Indications: For indigestion—soothes irritated stomach with a protective coating action. For nausea brings fast, sure relief from distress of that queasy, nauseated feeling. For diarrhea, controls common diarrhea within 24 hours, without constipating, relieving gas pains and abdominal cramps.

Keep all medicines out of reach of children.

Caution: This product contains salicylates. If taken with aspirin and ringing of the ears occur, discontinue use. If taking medicines for anticoagulation (thinning the blood), diabetes, or gout, consult physician before taking this product. If diarrhea is accompanied by high fever or continues more than 2 days, consult a physician.

Note: The beneficial medication may cause a temporary darkening of the stool and tongue.

Dosage Directions: LIQUID

Adults—2 tablespoonfuls.

Children—according to age:

10 to 14 years—4 teaspoonfuls

 6 to 10 years—2 teaspoonfuls

 3 to 6 years—1 teaspoonful

Repeat above dosage every ½ to 1 hour, if needed until 8 doses are taken.

TABLETS

Adults—2 Tablets

Children—(6 to 10 years)   1 Tablet

Children—(3 to 6 years)   ½ Tablet

Chew or dissolve in mouth. Repeat every ½ to one hour as needed to maximum of 8 doses.

[*Shown in Product Identification Section*]

UNGUENTINE® PLUS FIRST AID & BURN CREAM

Active Ingredients: An antiseptic, anesthetic moisturizing cream containing lidocaine hydrochloride 2%, parachlorometaxylenol 2%, phenol 0.5% in a moisturizing cream base.

Indications: An anesthetic/antiseptic moisturizing cream to help stop pain, prevent infection and promote healing in sunburn, minor burns, windburn, chapping, cuts and minor itch due to insect bites.

Warnings: Consult physician in cases of deep or puncture wounds, serious burns, infection or persistent pain or if irritation or swelling develops.

Dosage and Administration: Apply to affected parts and protect with gauze if necessary.

How Supplied: Tubes of ½ oz., 1 oz. and 2 oz.

Optimox, Inc.
801 DEEP VALLEY DRIVE
SUITE 1
PALOS VERDES PENINSULA, CA
90274

OPTIVITE™ for Women
(Multiple Megavitamin Formula with Amino Acid Chelated Minerals and Digestive Aids)

Composition:

Six (6) Tablets Provide:

Vitamins

 Liposoluble

Vitamin A (Palmitate) (Water Dispersed)	12,500 I.U.
Vitamin E (d'Alpha Tocopherol)	100 I.U.
Vitamin D3 (Cholecalciferol)	100 I.U.

Hydrosoluble (Sustained Release)

Folic Acid	200 mcg
Vitamin B1 (Thiamin HCl)	25 mg
Vitamin B2 (Riboflavin)	25 mg
Niacinamide	25 mg
Vitamin B6 (Pyridoxine HCl)	300 mg
Vitamin B12 (Cobal. Conc.)	62.5 mcg
Biotin	62.5 mcg
Pantothenic Acid (d'Cal. Pan)	25 mg
Choline Bitartrate	312.5 mg
Inositol	25 mg
Para Amino Benzoic Acid	25 mg
Vitamin C (Ascorbic Acid)	1,500 mg
Bioflavonoid	250 mg
Rutin	25 mg

Minerals

Calcium (Amino Acid Chelate)	125 mg
Magnesium (Amino Acid Chelate)	250 mg
Iodine (Hydrolyzed Protein Complex)	75 mcg
Iron (Amino Acid Chelate)	16 mg
Copper (Amino Acid Chelate)	0.5 mg
Zinc (Amino Acid Chelate)	25 mg
Manganese (Amino Acid Chelate)	10 mg
Potassium (Hydrolyzed Protein Complex)	47.5 mg
Selenium (Hydrolyzed Protein Complex)	100 mcg
Chromium (Hydrolyzed Protein Complex)	100 mcg

Digestive Aids

Amylase Activity	15,000 NF Units
Protease Activity	15,000 NF Units
Lipase Activity	1,200 NF Units
Betaine Acid HCl	100 mg

Indications: OPTIVITE for Women has been formulated for the adult premenopausal woman to help her cope with the tensions and stresses of everyday living. This is a multi-vitamin-mineral combination with emphasis on vitamin C, vitamin B-6 and the minerals magnesium and zinc. These nutrients are most susceptible to loss and poor utilization in women on hormonal contraceptive pills and with premenstrual distress.

Because of the relatively high amount of vitamin B-6 present, OPTIVITE for Women is particularly useful in alleviating the premenstrual complaints of nervous tension, irritability, breast tenderness and congestion, weight gain and bloating due to water/salt retention and incrased extracellular fluid, craving for sweets, increased appetite, loss of energy, inability to cope and perform. OPTIVITE for Women is also effective in correcting the nutritional imbalance caused by the use of hormonal contraceptive pills. The high amount of magnesium present together with B-6 and zinc help regulate the menstrual cycle and decrease the intensity of low abdominal cramps occurring with menstruation.

Vitamin A, at the dose present in OPTIVITE for Women together with zinc and vitamin B-6, help minimize the premenstrual flares of oily skin and acne occurring in some women.

OPTIVITE for Women does not replace but works together with a good nutritional program, adequate exercise, preferably outdoor, and proper rest.

Dosage and Administration: Since vitamins and minerals come naturally with food and our digestive system is accustomed to handle them together with food, OPTIVITE for Women works best when taken with a full meal. The effect lasts 8–12 hours and it is best taken with breakfast for day workers. It is recommended to build up the dose slowly by starting with 2 pills a day and increasing by 2 pills every week. Adjust the dose according to need. Most women need 2–6 tablets a day except one week before periods when the need increases. Do not exceed 12 tablets a day.

How Supplied: Yellow and modified capsule shaped tablets (riboflavin coated) in bottles of 126 and 252 tablets.

References:

1. Abraham, G.E.: Premenstrual tension, In Current Problems in OB Gyn. August 1980, page 1. Yearbook Medical Publishers, Chicago Levanthal, M. (Ed.).
2. Abraham, G.E.: Primary dysmenorrhea, Clin. Obstet, Gynecol. 21:139, 1978.
3. Abraham, G.E. and Hargrove, J.T.: Effect of vitamin B-6 on premenstrual symtomatology in women with premenstrual tension syndromes: A double blind crossover study. Infertility 3:155, 1980.
4. Abraham, G.E. and Lubran, M.M.: Serum and red cell magnesium levels in patients with premenstrual tension. Am. J. Clin. Nutr. 34:2364–2366, 1981.
5. Anderson, K.E., Bodansky, O. and Kappas, A. Effects of Oral Contraceptives on Vitamin Metabolism. Advances in Clin. Chem. 18:247–287, 1976.
6. Kumar, D., Zourlas, P.A., and Barnes, A.C. In Vitro and In Vivo Effects of Magnesium Sulfate on Human Uterine Contractility. Am. J. Obstet. Gynecol. 86:1036, 1963.
7. Larsson-Cohn, U. Oral Contraceptives and Vitamins: A Review. Am. J. Obstet, Gynecol. 121:84–90, 1975.
8. Hargrove, J.T. and Abraham, G.E.: Effect of vitamin B-6 on infertility in women with the premenstrual tension syndrome. Infertility 2:315, 1980.
9. Michaelson G., Juhlin L., Vahlquist A.: Effects of oral zinc and vitamin A in acne. Arch. Dermatol. 113–31, 1977.

Ortho Pharmaceutical Corporation
Consumer Products Division
RARITAN, NJ 08869

CONCEPTROL®
Birth Control Cream

Description: A contraceptive cream containing the active spermicide Nonoxynol-9, in an oil-in-water emulsion at pH 4.5.

Indication: Contraception.

Action and Uses: A spermicidal cream for intravaginal contraception.

Warning: Occasional burning and/or irritation of the vagina or penis have been reported. In such cases, the medication should be discontinued and a physician consulted. Not effective if taken orally. Keep out of reach of children. When pregnancy is contraindicated, the contraceptive program should be discussed with a physician.

Dosage and Administration: CONCEPTROL should be inserted prior to each intercourse. One applicatorful of CONCEPTROL inserted just before intercourse is adequate for only one time. An additional applicatorful is required each time intercourse is repeated. If intercourse has not occurred within one hour after application of CONCEPTROL, repeat the application before intercourse. If a douche is desired for cleansing purposes, wait at least six hours following intercourse. Refer to directions and diagrams for detailed instructions. CONCEPTROL is an easy to use, pleasant and reliable method of birth control. While no method of contraception can provide an absolute guarantee against becoming pregnant, for maximum protection, CONCEPTROL Cream must be used according to directions.

How Supplied: CONCEPTROL Cream available in packages containing a 2.46 oz. Starter tube with applicator and 2.46 oz. Refill tube only.
[*Shown in Product Identification Section*]

CONCEPTROL® Disposable Contraceptive Gel

Description: An unscented, unflavored, colorless, greaseless and non-staining gel in convenient, easy-to-use disposable plastic applicators. Each applicator is filled with a single, pre-measured dose containing the active spermicide nonoxynol-9 at pH 4.5.

Actions and Uses: A spermicidal gel for use whenever control of conception is desirable.

Warning: Occasional burning and/or irritation of the vagina or penis have been reported. If this occurs, discontinue use and consult a physician.

Dosage and Administration: CONCEPTROL Disposable should be inserted prior to each intercourse. One applicatorful of CONCEPTROL inserted just before intercourse is adequate for one time only. An additional applicatorful is required each time intercourse is repeated. If intercourse has not occurred within one hour after the application of CONCEPTROL, repeat the application of CONCEPTROL.

Douching is not recommended after using CONCEPTROL Gel. However, if desired for cleansing purposes, wait at least six hours following last intercourse to allow for full spermicidal activity of CONCEPTROL Gel.

While no method of contraception can provide an absolute guarantee against becoming pregnant, for maximum protection, CONCEPTROL Gel must be used according to directions.

How Supplied: CONCEPTROL Gel in packages of 6 and 10 disposable applicators, premeasured, prefilled, prewrapped.
[*Shown in Product Identification Section*]

CONCEPTROL SHIELDS®
Latex Prophylactics

Advantages: Advanced Design—Each prophylactic is specially contoured for greater comfort and sensitivity. Sensitive—All CONCEPTROL SHIELDS are made from a premium quality, thin latex. Lubrication — CONCEPTROL SHIELDS are available with a special "dry" lubricant that is less messy; they are also available non-lubricated. Reservoir—CONCEPTROL SHIELDS have a reservoir tip to aid in the prevention of spillage.

How Supplied: CONCEPTROL SHIELDS are available lubricated and non-lubricated, in packages of 12's and 24's.
[*Shown in Product Identification Section*]

CONCEPTROL SUPREME®
Thin Prophylactics

Advantages: Advanced Design—Each prophylactic is designed to be extra light for a more natural feeling. Sensitive—ALL CONCEPTROL SUPREME prophylactics are made from a premium quality, very thin latex. Lubrication—ALL CONCEPTROL SUPREME prophylactics are lubricated with a special "dry" lubricant that's less messy. Reservoir—Each CONCEPTROL SUPREME prophylactic has a reservoir tip to aid in the prevention of spillage.

How Supplied: CONCEPTROL SUPREME prophylactics are available lubricated in packages of 12.
[*Shown in Product Identification Section*]

Continued on next page

Ortho Pharm.—Cont.

DAISY 2®
Home Pregnancy Test

Active Ingredients: Human Chorionic Gonadotropin (HCG) on red blood cells, HCG antiserum, and diluent solution.

Indications: An in-vitro pregnancy test for use in the home that can detect the presence of HCG in the urine as early as six (6) days past last missed period.

Actions: DAISY 2® provides a double-check test method that accurately detects the presence or absence of HCG in urine in just one hour. It is the same pregnancy test method used in many hospitals.

Dosage and Administration: Perform the test according to instructions. If, after one hour, a dark brown ring appears in the test tube, the patient is probably pregnant. If no ring is visible, no pregnancy hormone has been detected and the patient is probably not pregnant. All home pregnancy test kits recommend a second test if the first test indicates that the patient is not pregnant, and her period does not begin within a week. This second test is needed because the patient may have miscalculated her period, or her body may not have accumulated enough hormone for a true reading. Also, the accuracy of test results can be affected by various factors, so many women like the reassurance that comes from double-checking their results. DAISY 2® makes this double-checking easy and convenient by providing two complete and identical tests in each kit. In addition, a toll-free telephone number is included in each package insert. This service is staffed by registered nurses who can answer any questions the patient may have about her results, or how she performed the test.

How Supplied: Each DAISY 2® Kit contains everything needed to perform two tests: Two test tubes with reagents, two vials of diluent solution, two droppers, one lid, a stand with mirror for reading test results, and complete directions.

DELFEN®
Contraceptive Foam

Description: A contraceptive foam in an aerosol dosage formulation containing 12.5% Nonoxynol-9 and buffered to normal vaginal pH 4.5.

Indication: Contraception.

Action and Uses: A spermicidal foam for intravaginal contraception.

Warning: Burning and/or irritation of the vagina or penis have been reported. In such cases, the medication should be discontinued and a physician consulted. Not effective if taken orally. Do not burn or puncture container. Keep out of reach of children.

When pregnancy is contraindicated, the contraceptive program should be discussed with a physician.

Dosage and Administration: Insert DELFEN Contraceptive Foam just prior to each intercourse. You may have inter-

course any time up to one hour after you have inserted the foam. If you repeat intercourse, insert another applicatorful of DELFEN Foam. After shaking the vial, place the measured-dose (5cc) applicator over the top of the vial, then press applicator down very gently. Fill to the top of the barrel threads. Remove applicator to stop flow of foam. Insert the filled applicator well into the vagina and depress the plunger. Remove the applicator with the plunger in depressed position. If a douche is desired for cleansing purposes, wait at least six hours after intercourse. Refer to directions and diagrams for detailed instructions. DELFEN Foam is a reliable method of birth control. While no method of birth control can provide an absolute guarantee against becoming pregnant, for maximum protection, DELFEN Foam must be used according to directions.

How Supplied: DELFEN Contraceptive Foam 0.70 oz. Starter vial with applicator. Also available in 0.70 oz. and 1.75 oz. Refill vial only.

[*Shown in Product Identification Section*]

GYNOL II®
Contraceptive Jelly

Description: A colorless, unscented, unflavored, greaseless and non-staining contraceptive jelly containing the active spermicide nonoxynol-9 and having a pH of 4.5

Actions and Uses: A spermicidal jelly to be used in conjunction with a diaphragm whenever control of conception is desirable. Esthetically pleasing.

Dosage and Administration: Used in conjuction with a vaginal diaphragm. Prior to insertion, put an applicatorful (about a teaspoonful) of GYNOL II Contraceptive Jelly into the cup of the dome of the diaphragm and spread a small amount around the edge with your fingertip. This will aid in insertion and provide protection.

Some doctors recommend that the diaphragm be inserted every night to affort maximum protection.

It is also important to remember that if intercourse occurs more than six hours after insertion, or if repeated intercourse takes place, an additional application of GYNOL II is necessary. DO NOT REMOVE THE DIAPHRAGM—simply add more GYNOL II with the applicator provided in the applicator package, being careful not to dislodge the diaphragm.

Remember, another application of GYNOL II is required each time intercourse is repeated, regardless of how little time has transpired since the diaphragm has been in place. In addition, it is essential that the diaphragm remain in place for at least 6 hours after intercourse. Removal of the diaphragm before this time may increase the risk of becoming pregnant. There is no urgency in removing the diaphragm—it may remain in position for up to 24 hours. If a douche is desired for cleansing purposes, wait at least six hours after intercourse. While no method of contraception can provide an absolute guarantee against becoming pregnant, for maximum protection,

GYNOL II must be used according to directions.

How Supplied: 81 gm starter tube with measured dose applicator and large size 126 gm refill package.

[*Shown in Product Identification Section*]

INTERCEPT®
Contraceptive Inserts

Description: A single dose vaginal contraceptive insert containing the active ingredient nonoxynol-9, 5.56% at pH 4.5.

Indication: Contraception

Action: A spermicidal insert for intravaginal contraception.

Warning: Should sensitivity to the ingredients or irritation of the vagina or penis develop, discontinue use and consult a physician. Not effective if taken orally. Keep out of reach of children. When pregnancy is contraindicated, the contraceptive program should be discussed with a physician.

Dosage and Administration: INTERCEPT should be inserted into the vagina at least ten minutes prior to male penetration to insure proper dispersion. INTERCEPT provides protection from ten minutes to one hour after product insertion. Insert a new INTERCEPT Contraceptive Insert each time intercourse is repeated. If a douche is desired for cleansing purposes, wait at least six hours following intercourse.

INTERCEPT is an effective method of contraception. No product, however, can provide an absolute guarantee against becoming pregnant.

How Supplied: INTERCEPT Contraceptive Inserts are available in a starter package containing 12 inserts with applicator and in a 12 insert refill package.

[*Shown in Product Identification Section*]

MASSÉ®
Breast Cream

Composition: MASSE Breast Cream.

Action and Uses: MASSE Breast Cream is especially designed for care of the nipples of pregnant and nursing women.

Administration and Dosage:

BEFORE BIRTH

During the last two or three months of pregnancy, it is often desirable to prepare the nipple and the nipple area of the breast for eventual nursing. In these cases, MASSE is used once or twice daily in the following manner: Carefully cleanse the breast with a soft, clean cloth and plain water and dry. Squeeze a ribbon of MASSE, approximately an inch long, and lightly massage into the nipple and immediate surrounding area. Do so until the cream has completely disappeared. The massage motion should be gentle and outward.

AFTER BABY IS BORN

During the nursing period MASSE is used as follows: BEFORE AND AFTER EACH NURSING cleanse the breasts with a clean cloth and water. After drying squeeze a ribbon of MASSE, approximately an inch long, and gently massage into the nipple and the immediate surrounding area.

Contraindications: MASSE should not be used in cases of acute mastitis or breast abscess.

Caution: In cases of excessive tenderness or irritation of any kind, consult your physician.

How Supplied: MASSE Breast Cream is available in a 2 oz. tube.

[*Shown in Product Identification Section*]

ORTHO–CREME®
Contraceptive Cream

Description: ORTHO-CREME Contraceptive Cream is a pure white and pleasantly scented cream of cosmetic consistency. ORTHO-CREME is a greaseless, non-staining and non-irritating spermicidal cream which contains the active ingredient Nonoxynol-9.

Action and Uses: A spermicidal vaginal cream for use with a vaginal diaphragm when control of conception is desirable. Esthetically pleasing.

Dosage and Administration: Used in conjunction with a vaginal diaphragm. Prior to insertion, put an applicatorful (about a teaspoonful) of ORTHO-CREME Contraceptive Cream into the cup of the dome of the diaphragm and spread a small amount around the edge with the fingertip. This will aid in insertion and provide protection.

Some doctors recommend that the diaphragm be inserted every night to afford maximum protection.

It is also important to remember that if intercourse occurs more than six hours after insertion, or if repeated intercourse takes place, an additional application of ORTHO-CREME is necessary. DO NOT REMOVE THE DIAPHRAGM—simply add more ORTHO-CREME with the applicator provided in the applicator package, being careful not to dislodge the diaphragm.

Remember, another application of ORTHO-CREME is required each time intercourse is repeated, regardless of how little time has transpired since the diaphragm has been in place.

In addition, it is essential that the diaphragm remain in place for at least six hours after intercourse. Removal of the diaphragm before this time may increase the risk of becoming pregnant. There is no urgency in removing the diaphragm —it may remain in position for up to 24 hours. If a douche is desired for cleansing purposes, wait at least 6 hours after intercourse. Refer to directions and diagrams for detailed instructions. While no method of contraception can provide an absolute guarantee against becoming pregnant, for maximum protection, ORTHO-CREME must be used according to directions.

How Supplied: 2.46 oz. Starter tube with measured-dose applicator. Regular size 2.46 oz. Refill tube only. Large size 4.05 oz. Refill tube only.

[*Shown in Product Identification Section*]

ORTHO® Disposable
Vaginal Applicators

Action and Uses: ORTHO Disposable applicators are made of paperboard and are designed to provide a simple, clean, accurate method for inserting tubed vaginal jellies and creams into the vagina. The applicator may be readily filled directly from the tube used and then discarded.

How Supplied: Packages of 18 applicators each.

[*Shown in Product Identification Section*]

ORTHO–GYNOL®
Contraceptive Jelly

Description: ORTHO-GYNOL Contraceptive Jelly is a water dispersible spermicidal jelly having a pH of 4.5 which contains the active ingredient p-diisobutylphenoxypolyethoxyethanol.

Action and Uses: A spermicidal vaginal jelly for use with a vaginal diaphragm whenever the control of conception is desirable. Esthetically acceptable.

Dosage and Administration: Used in conjunction with a vaginal diaphragm. Prior to insertion, put an applicatorful (about a teaspoonful) of ORTHO-GYNOL Contraceptive Jelly into the cup of the dome of the diaphragm and spread a small amount around the edge with the fingertip. This will aid in insertion and provide protection.

Some doctors recommend that the diaphragm be inserted every night to afford maximum protection.

It is also important to remember that if intercourse occurs more than six hours after insertion, or if repeated intercourse takes place, an additional application of ORTHO-GYNOL is necessary. DO NOT REMOVE THE DIAPHRAGM—simply add more ORTHO-GYNOL with the applicator provided in the applicator package, being careful not to dislodge the diaphragm.

Remember, another application of ORTHO-GYNOL is required each time intercourse is repeated, regardless of how little time has transpired since the diaphragm has been in place.

In addition, it is essential that the diaphragm remain in place for at least six hours after intercourse. Removal of the diaphragm before this time may increase the risk of becoming pregnant. There is no urgency in removing the diaphragm —it may remain in position for up to 24 hours. If a douche is desired for cleansing purposes, wait at least 6 hours after intercourse. Refer to directions and diagrams for complete instructions. While no method of contraception can provide an absolute guarantee against becoming pregnant, for maximum protection ORTHO-GYNOL must be used according to directions.

How Supplied: 2.85 oz. Starter tube with measured-dose applicator. Regular size 2.85 oz. Refill tube only. Large size 4.44 oz. Refill tube only.

[*Shown in Product Identification Section*]

ORTHO® PERSONAL LUBRICANT

Description: ORTHO PERSONAL LUBRICANT is especially formulated as a sexual lubricant that is designed to be gentle and non-irritating for both women and men. It is a non-staining, water soluble jelly that is safe for delicate tissue.

Dosage and Administration: Apply a one (1″) to two (2″) inch ribbon of product, or desired amount, to external vaginal area and/or penis. Repeat applications may be used by one or both partners. If desired, this product may be used inside the vagina.

For easy insertion of rectal thermometers, tampons, douche nozzles and enema nozzles, use desired amount.

How Supplied: ORTHO PERSONAL LUBRICANT is available in 2 oz. and 4 oz. tubes.

[*Shown in Product Identification Section*]

Ortho Pharmaceutical Corporation
DERMATOLOGICAL DIVISION
RARITAN, NJ 08869

PURPOSE Brand Dry Skin Cream

Composition: Contains purified water, petrolatum, propylene glycol, glyceryl stearate, sodium lactate, almond oil, steareth-20, cetyl alcohol, cetyl esters wax, mineral oil, steareth-2, xanthan gum, sorbic acid, lactic acid and fragrance.

Action and Uses: PURPOSE Dry Skin Cream is formulated especially to meet the need for an effective dry skin cream that dermatologists can recommend. PURPOSE Dry Skin Cream moisturizes dry, chapped and irritated skin and provides effective, lasting relief from drying and scaling. PURPOSE Dry Skin Cream smoothes easily into skin for all-over body care.

Administration and Dosage: Instruct patients to use PURPOSE Dry Skin Cream as any other dry skin cream.

How Supplied: 3 oz. tube.

[*Shown in Product Identification Section*]

PURPOSE Brand Shampoo

Composition: Contains water, amphoteric 19, PEG-44 sorbitan laurate, PEG-150 distearate, sorbitan laurate, boric acid, fragrance, and benzyl alcohol.

Action and Uses: PURPOSE Shampoo is formulated especially to meet the need for a mild shampoo that Dermatologists can recommend. PURPOSE Shampoo helps control oily scalp and hair and helps remove the scales of dandruff leaving hair clean and manageable. Safe for color-treated hair. PURPOSE Shampoo works into a rich, pleasant lather. It may be used daily.

Administration and Dosage: Instruct patients to use PURPOSE Shampoo as any other shampoo.

How Supplied: 7 fluid oz. plastic bottle.

[*Shown in Product Identification Section*]

PURPOSE Brand Soap

Composition: Contains sodium and potassium salts of fatty acids, glycerin, water and mild fragrance.

Continued on next page

Ortho Derm.—Cont.

Action and Uses: Extraordinary mild PURPOSE Soap was created to wash tender, sensitive skin. Formulated especially to meet the need for a mild soap that Dermatologists can recommend. This translucent washing bar is non-medicated and completely free of harsh detergents or other ingredients that might dry or irritate skin.

Administration and Dosage: Wash face with PURPOSE Soap two or three times a day or as directed by your physician. Rinse with warm water. For complete skin care, use it also for bath and shower.

How Supplied: 3.6 oz. bar in plastic soap dish.

[*Shown in Product Identification Section*]

Parke-Davis
Division of Warner-Lambert Company
201 TABOR ROAD
MORRIS PLAINS, NJ 07950 USA

AGORAL® Plain
AGORAL® Raspberry
AGORAL® Marshmallow

Description: Each tablespoonful (15 ml) of Agoral Plain (white) contains 4.2 grams mineral oil in a thoroughly homogenized emulsion with agar, tragacanth, acacia, egg albumin, glycerin and water.

Each tablespoonful (15 ml) of Agoral Raspberry (pink) or of Agoral Marshmallow (white) contains 4.2 grams mineral oil and 0.2 grams phenolphthalein in a thoroughly homogenized emulsion with agar, tragacanth, acacia, egg albumin, glycerin and water.

Actions: Agoral, containing mineral oil, facilitates defecation by lubricating the fecal mass and softening the stool. More effective than nonemulsified oil in penetrating the feces, Agoral thereby greatly reduces the possibility of oil leakage at the anal sphincter. Phenolphthalein gently stimulates motor activity of the lower intestinal tract. Agoral's combined lubricating-softening and peristaltic actions can help to restore a normal pattern of evacuation.

Indications: Relief of constipation. Agoral may be especially required when straining at stool is a hazard, as in hernia, cardiac, or hypertensive patients; during convalescence from surgery; before and after surgery for hemorrhoids or other painful anorectal disorders; for patients confined to bed.

The management of chronic constipation should also include attention to fluid intake, diet and bowel habits.

Contraindication: Sensitivity to phenolphthalein.

Dosage and Management:
(Taken at bedtime, laxation may be expected the next morning.)

	Adults	**Children over 6 years**
Agoral Plain (without phenolphthalein)	1 to 2 tblsp.	2 to 4 tsp.
Agoral Raspberry	½ to 1 tblsp.	1 to 2 tsp.
Agoral Marshmallow	½ to 1 tblsp.	1 to 2 tsp.

Take at bedtime only, unless other time is advised by physician.

Agoral may be taken alone or in milk, water, fruit juice, or any miscible food. Expectant or nursing mothers, bedridden or aged patients, young children or infants should use only on advice of physician.

Supplied: Agoral Plain (without phenolphthalein), plastic bottles of 16 fl oz (N 0071-2071-23). Agoral (raspberry flavor), plastic bottles of 16 fl oz (N 0071-2072-23). Agoral (marshmallow flavor), plastic bottles of 8 fl oz (N 0071-2070-20) and 16 fl oz (N 0071-2070-23).

ANUSOL®
Suppositories/Ointment

Description:

	Anusol Suppositories each contains	Anusol Ointment each gram
Bismuth subgallate	2.25%	—
Bismuth Resorcin Compound	1.75%	—
Benzyl Benzoate	1.2 %	12 mg
Peruvian Balsam	1.8 %	18 mg
Zinc Oxide	11.0 %	110 mg
Analgine™ (pramoxine hydrochloride)	—	10 mg

Also contain the following inactive ingredients: dibasic calcium phosphate and certified coloring in a hydrogenated vegetable oil base.

Also contains the following inactive ingredients: dibasic calcium phosphate and kaolin in a liquid petrolatum-cocoa butter-polyethylene wax base containing glyceryl monooleate and glyceryl stearate.

Actions: Anusol Suppositories and Anusol Ointment help to relieve pain, itching and discomfort arising from irritated anorectal tissues. They have a soothing, lubricant action on mucous membranes. Analgine (pramoxine hydrochloride) in Anusol Ointment is a rapidly acting local anesthetic for the skin and mucous membranes of the anus and rectum. Analgine is also chemically distinct from procaine, cocaine, and dibucaine and can often be used in the patient previously sensitized to other surface anesthetics. Surface analgesia lasts for several hours.

Indications: Anusol Suppositories and Anusol Ointment are adjunctive therapy for the symptomatic relief of pain and discomfort in: external and internal hemorrhoids, proctitis, papillitis, cryptitis, anal fissures, incomplete fistulas, and relief of local pain and discomfort following anorectal surgery.

Anusol Ointment is also indicated for pruritus ani.

Contraindications: Anusol Suppositories and Anusol Ointment are contraindicated in those patients with a history of hypersensitivity to any of the components of the preparations.

Precautions: Symptomatic relief should not delay definitive diagnoses or treatment.

If irritation develops, these preparations should be discontinued. These preparations are not for ophthalmic use.

Adverse Reactions: Upon application of Anusol Ointment, which contains Analgine (pramoxine HCl), a patient may occasionally experience burning, especially if the anoderm is not intact. Sensitivity reactions have been rare; discontinue medication if suspected.

Dosage and Administration: Anusol Suppositories—Adults: Remove foil wrapper and insert suppository into the anus. Insert one suppository in the morning and one at bedtime, and one immediately following each evacuation.

Anusol Ointment—Adults: After gentle bathing and drying of the anal area, remove tube cap and apply freely to the exterior surface and gently rub in. Ointment should be applied every 3 or 4 hours, or, when necessary, every 2 hours. NOTE: If staining from either of the above products occurs, the stain may be removed from fabric by hand or machine washing with household detergent.

How Supplied: Anusol Suppositories—boxes of 12 (N 0071-1088-07), 24 (N 0071-1088-13) and 48 (N 0071-1088-18); in silver foil strips.

Anusol Ointment—1-oz tubes (N 0071-3075-13) with plastic applicator.

Store between 59°F and 86°F (15° and 30°C).

[*Shown in Product Identification Section*]

BENADRYL® Antihistamine Cream

Description: Greaseless disappearing cream contains 2% Benadryl (diphenhydramine hydrochloride) in a water-miscible ointment base.

Indications: For relief of itching due to insect bites and other minor skin irritations (rashes, inflammation). FOR EXTERNAL USE ONLY.

Warning: Should not be applied to blistered, raw or oozing areas of the skin. If burning sensation results, discontinue use. In case of accidental ingestion, seek professional assistance or contact a Poison Control Center immediately.

Caution: Do not use in eyes. If condition persists or a rash or irritation develops, discontinue use and consult a physician.

Directions: Apply locally for itching three or four times daily or as directed by the physician.

How Supplied:
1-oz tubes (N 0071-3058-13)
2-oz tubes (N 0071-3058-15)

[*Shown in Product Identification Section*]

BENYLIN®
Cough Syrup

Description: Each teaspoonful (5 ml) contains Benadryl® (diphenhydramine hydrochloride), 12.5 mg. Alcohol, 5%.

Indications: For the temporary relief of cough due to minor throat and bronchial irritation as may occur with the common cold or with inhaled irritants.

Warnings: May cause marked drowsiness. Keep this and all drugs out of the reach of children. In case of accidental overdosage, seek professional assistance or contact a poison control center immediately. Do not give to children under 6 years of age except under the advice and supervision of a physician. May cause excitability, especially in children. Do not take this product for persistent or chronic cough such as occurs with smoking, asthma, emphysema, or when cough is accompanied by excessive secretions, or if you have epilepsy, glaucoma, or difficulty in urination due to enlargement of the prostate gland except under the advice and supervision of a physician.

Caution: Avoid driving a motor vehicle or operating heavy machinery, or drinking alcoholic beverages. A persistent cough may be a sign of a serious condition. If cough persists for more than one week, tends to recur, or is accompanied by high fever, rash, or persistent headache, consult a physician.

Directions: Adults—two teaspoonfuls every four hours, not to exceed twelve teaspoonfuls in twenty-four hours; Children (6 to under 12 years), one teaspoonful every four hours not to exceed six teaspoonfuls in twenty-four hours; or as directed by a physician. Children (2 to under 6 years) one-half teaspoonful every four hours not to exceed three teaspoonfuls in twenty-four hours. Use in children under 2 years of age is only at the discretion of the physician.

How Supplied: N 0071-2195-Benylin Cough Syrup is supplied in 4-oz, 1-pt, 1-gal bottles, and unit-dose bottles of 5 ml and 10 ml.

Store below 86°F (30°C). Protect from freezing.

[*Shown in Product Identification Section*]

BENYLIN DM®
dextromethorphan cough syrup

Description: Each teaspoonful (5 ml) contains 10 mg dextromethorphan hydrobromide and 5% alcohol; also contains, sugar; water; glucose liquid; glycerin; ammonium chloride; sodium citrate; raspberry imitation flavor; citric acid; caramel; menthol; and D&C Red 33. Nonnarcotic; Contains No Antihistamine

Indications: Antitussive—For the temporary relief of coughs due to minor throat and bronchial irritation as may occur with the common cold or with inhaled irritants

Warnings: Keep this and all drugs out of the reach of children. In case of accidental overdosage, seek professional assistance or contact a poison control center immediately. Do not give this product to children under 2 years of age, except

under the advice and supervision of a physician. Do not take this product for persistent or chronic cough such as occurs with smoking, asthma, or emphysema, or where cough is accompanied by excessive secretions, except under the advice and supervision of a physician.

Caution: A persistent cough may be a sign of a serious condition. If cough persists for more than 1 week, tends to recur, or is accompanied by high fever, rash, or persistent headache, consult a physician.

Dosage: For the temporary relief of cough—

Adults—1 to 2 teaspoonfuls every 4 hours, or 3 teaspoonfuls every 6 to 8 hours, not to exceed 12 teaspoonfuls in 24 hours

Children 6 to under 12 years—½ to 1 teaspoonful every 4 hours, or 1½ teaspoonfuls every 6 to 8 hours, not to exceed 6 teaspoonfuls in 24 hours

Children 2 to under 6 years—¼ to ½ teaspoonful every 4 hours, or ¾ teaspoonful every 6 to 8 hours, not to exceed 3 teaspoonfuls in 24 hours

Children under 2 years—there is no recommended dosage, except under the advice and supervision of a physician

How Supplied: N 0071-2401-17: 4-oz bottles in cartons of 12.

[*Shown in Product Identification Section*]

CALADRYL® Lotion
CALADRYL Cream

Description: Caladryl Lotion—A drying, antihistaminic, calamine-Benadryl® lotion containing calamine, 1% Benadryl (diphenhydramine hydrochloride), camphor, and 2% alcohol

Caladryl Cream—a drying, antihistaminic, calamine-Benadryl cream containing 1% Benadryl (diphenhydramine hydrochloride) and camphor.

Indications: For relief of itching due to mild poison ivy or oak, insect bites, or other minor skin irritations, and soothing relief of mild sunburn

Warnings: Should not be applied to blistered, raw, or oozing areas of the skin. Discontinue use if burning sensation or rash develops or condition persists. Remove by washing with soap and water. Use on extensive areas of the skin or for longer than seven days only as directed by a physician.

Caution: Keep away from eyes or other mucous membranes.

FOR EXTERNAL USE ONLY

Keep this and all drugs out of the reach of children. In case of accidental ingestion, seek professional assistance or contact a Poison Control Center immediately.

Directions: Caladryl Cream—Apply topically three or four times daily. Cleanse skin with soap and water and dry area before each application. Caladryl Lotion—SHAKE WELL. Apply topically three or four times daily. Cleanse skin with soap and water and dry area before each application.

How Supplied: N 0071-3226-14: Caladryl Cream; 1½-oz tubes

N0071-3181: Caladryl Lotion—2½-oz (75 ml) squeeze bottles and 6-oz bottles. [*Shown in Product Identification Section*]

GELUSIL®
Antacid–Antiflatulent
Liquid/Tablets

Each teaspoonful (5 ml) or tablet contains:
200 mg aluminum hydroxide
200 mg magnesium hydroxide
25 mg simethicone

Advantages:
- High acid-neutralizing capacity
- Low sodium content
- Simethicone for antiflatulent activity
- Good taste for better patient compliance
- Fast dissolution of chewed tablets for prompt relief

Indications: Gelusil, a carefully balanced combination of two widely used antacids and the antiflatulent simethicone, is effective for the relief of symptoms associated with heartburn, sour stomach, and acid indigestion with gas. Gelusil provides symptomatic relief of hyperacidity associated with the diagnosis of peptic ulcer, gastritis, peptic esophagitis, gastric hyperacidity and hiatal hernia, and it alleviates or relieves the symptoms of gas and postoperative gas pain.

Actions and Uses: The proven neutralizing powers of aluminum hydroxide and of magnesium hydroxide combine to give Gelusil dependable antacid action without the acid rebound sometimes associated with calcium carbonate.

The pleasant peppermint-flavored taste of Gelusil Liquid and Tablets encourages patient acceptance of, and compliance with, recommended antacid-antiflatulence regimens.

Gelusil Tablets are easy to chew and are specifically formulated to dissolve readily, providing prompt onset of action and reliable relief of symptoms.

Gelusil is appropriate whenever there is a need for well-accepted, effective antacid-antiflatulent therapy.

Dosage and Administration: Two or more teaspoonfuls or tablets one hour after meals and at bedtime, or as directed by a physician.

Tablets should be chewed.

The following information is provided to facilitate treatment:

Gelusil	LIQUID	TABLETS
Acid-neutralizing capacity	24 mEq/ 10 ml	22 mEq/ 2 tabs
Sodium	0.7 mg/ 5 ml	0.8 mg/ tab
Lactose	0	0

This product information was prepared in December, 1981. On these and other Parke-Davis Products, detailed information may be obtained by addressing PARKE-DAVIS, Division of Warner-Lambert Company, Morris Plains, NJ 07950 USA.

Continued on next page

Parke-Davis—Cont.

Warnings: Do not take more than 12 tablets or teaspoonfuls in a 24-hour period, or use this maximum dosage for more than two weeks, or use this product if you have kidney disease, except under the advice and supervision of a physician.

Keep this and all drugs out of the reach of children.

Drug Interaction Precaution: Do not take this product if you are presently taking a prescription antibiotic drug containing any form of tetracycline.

All aluminum-containing antacids, including Gelusil, may prevent proper absorption of tetracycline.

How Supplied:

N 0071-2036—Liquid—In plastic bottles of 6 fl oz and 12 fl oz.

N 0071-0034—Tablets—White, embossed Gelusil P-D 034—individual strips of 10 in boxes of 50, 100 and 1000; 165 tablets loose-packed in plastic bottles. [*Shown in Product Identification Section*]

GELUSIL–M®
Antacid–Antiflatulent
Liquid/Tablets

Each teaspoonful (5 ml) or tablet contains:
300 mg aluminum hydroxide
200 mg magnesium hydroxide
25 mg simethicone

Advantages:
- High acid-neutralizing capacity
- Low sodium content
- Simethicone for antiflatulent activity
- Good taste for better patient compliance
- Fast dissolution of chewed tablets for prompt relief

Indications: Gelusil-M, a carefully balanced combination of two widely used antacids and the antiflatulent simethicone, is effective for the relief of symptoms associated with heartburn, sour stomach, and acid indigestion with gas. Gelusil-M provides symptomatic relief of hyperacidity associated with the diagnosis of peptic ulcer, gastritis, peptic esophagitis, gastric hyperacidity and hiatal hernia, and it alleviates or relieves the symptoms of gas and postoperative gas pain.

Actions and Uses: The proven neutralizing power of aluminum hydroxide and magnesium hydroxide combine to give Gelusil-M dependable antacid action without the acid rebound sometimes associated with calcium carbonate. The pleasant spearmint-flavored taste of Gelusil-M Liquid and Tablets encourages patient acceptance of, and compliance with, recommended antacid-antiflatulence regimens.

Gelusil-M Tablets are easy to chew and are specifically formulated to dissolve readily, providing prompt onset of action and reliable relief of symptoms.

Gelusil-M is appropriate whenever there is a need for well-accepted, effective antacid-antiflatulent therapy.

Dosage and Administration: Two or more teaspoonfuls or tablets one hour after meals and at bedtime, or as directed by a physician.

Tablets should be chewed.

The following information is provided to facilitate treatment:

Gelusil-M	LIQUID	TABLETS
Acid-neutralizing capacity	30 mEq/ 10 ml	25 mEq/ 2 tabs
Sodium	1.2 mg/ 5 ml	1.3 mg/ tab
Lactose	0	0

Warnings: Do not take more than 10 teaspoonfuls or tablets in a 24-hour period, or use this maximum dosage for more than two weeks, or use this product if you have kidney disease, except under the advice and supervision of a physician.

Keep this and all drugs out of the reach of children.

Drug Interaction Precaution: Do not take this product if you are presently taking a prescription antibiotic drug containing any form of tetracycline.

All aluminum-containing antacids, including Gelusil-M, may prevent proper absorption of tetracycline.

How Supplied:

N 0071-2043—Liquid—In plastic bottles of 12 fl oz.

N 0071-0045—Tablets—White, embossed P-D 045— individual strips of 10 in boxes of 100.

GELUSIL–II®
Antacid-Antiflatulent
Liquid/Tablets
High Potency

Each teaspoonful (5 ml) or tablet contains:
400 mg aluminum hydroxide
400 mg magnesium hydroxide
30 mg simethicone

Advantages:
- High acid-neutralizing capacity
- Low sodium content
- Simethicone for antiflatulent activity
- Good taste for better patient compliance
- Fast dissolution of chewed tablets for prompt relief
- Double strength antacid

Indications: Gelusil-II, a carefully balanced, high-potency combination of two widely used antacids and the antiflatulent simethicone, is effective for the relief of symptoms associated with heartburn, sour stomach, and acid indigestion with gas. Gelusil-II provides symptomatic relief of hyperacidity associated with the diagnosis of peptic ulcer, gastritis, peptic esophagitis, gastric hyperacidity and hiatal hernia, and it alleviates or relieves the symptoms of gas and postoperative gas pain.

Actions and Uses: The proven neutralizing powers of aluminum hydroxide and magnesium hydroxide combine to give Gelusil-II dependable antacid action without the acid rebound sometimes associated with calcium carbonate. The higher potency of Gelusil-II is achieved by greater concentration of antacid ingredients per dosage unit.

The pleasant taste of Gelusil-II Liquid (citrus-flavored) and Tablets (orange-flavored) encourages patient acceptance of, and compliance with, recommended antacid-antiflatulence regimens.

Gelusil-II Tablets are easy to chew and are specifically formulated to dissolve readily, providing prompt onset of action and reliable relief of symptoms.

Gelusil-II is appropriate whenever there is a need for well-accepted, effective antacid-antiflatulent therapy.

Dosage and Administration: Two or more teaspoonfuls or tablets one hour after meals and at bedtime, or as directed by a physician. Tablets should be chewed.

The following information is provided to facilitate treatment:

Gelusil-II	LIQUID	TABLETS
Acid-neutralizing capacity	48 mEq/ 10 ml	42 mEq/ 2 tabs
Sodium	1.3 mg/ 5 ml	2.1 mg/ tab
Lactose	0	0

Warnings: Do not take more than 8 tablets or teaspoonfuls in a 24-hour period, or use this maximum dosage for more than two weeks, or use this product if you have kidney disease, except under the advice and supervision of a physician.

Keep this and all drugs out of the reach of children.

Drug Interaction Precaution: Do not take this product if you are presently taking a prescription antibiotic containing any form of tetracycline.

All aluminum-containing antacids, including Gelusil-II, may prevent proper absorption of tetracycline.

How Supplied:

N 0071-0042—Liquid—In plastic bottles of 12 fl oz.

N 0071-0043—Tablets—Double-layered white/orange, embossed W/C 043 or P-D 043—individual strips of 10 in boxes of 80.

GERIPLEX-FS® KAPSEALS®

Composition: Each Kapseal represents:
Vitamin A ....(1.5 mg) 5,000 IU*
  (acetate)
Vitamin C.. 50 mg
  (ascorbic acid)†
Vitamin B₁ .... 5 mg
  (thiamine mononitrate)
Vitamin B₂ .... 5 mg
  (riboflavin)
Vitamin B₁₂, crystalline
  (cyanocobalamin) .... 2 mcg
Choline dihydrogen
  citrate .... 20 mg
Nicotinamide .... 15 mg
  (niacinamide)
Vitamin E (*dl*-alpha tocopheryl acetate) .... (5 mg) 5 IU*

Ferrous sulfate‡ .... 30 mg
Copper sulfate .... 4 mg
Manganese sulfate
(monohydrate) .... 4 mg
Zinc sulfate .... 2 mg
Calcium phosphate, dibasic
(anhydrous) .... 200 mg
Taka-Diastase® (aspergillus
oryzae enzymes) .... 2½ gr.
Docusate sodium .... 100 mg

---

* International Units
†Supplied as sodium ascorbate
‡Supplied as dried ferrous sulfate equivalent to the labeled amount of ferrous sulfate
Action and Uses: A preparation containing vitamins, minerals, and a fecal softener for middle-aged and older individuals. The fecal softening agent, docusate sodium, acts to soften stools and make bowel movements easier.
Administration and Dosage: USUAL DOSAGE —One capsule daily, with or immediately after a meal.
How Supplied: N 0071-0544-24—Bottles of 100. Parcode® No. 544.

GERIPLEX-FS®
LIQUID
Geriatric Vitamin Formula with Iron and a Fecal Softener

Composition: Each 30 ml represents vitamin B_1 (thiamine hydrochloride), 1.2 mg; vitamin B_2 (as riboflavin-5'-phosphate sodium), 1.7 mg; vitamin B_6 (pyridoxine hydrochloride), 1 mg; vitamin B_{12} (cyanocobalamin) crystalline, 5 mcg; niacinamide, 15 mg; iron (as ferric ammonium citrate, green), 15 mg; Pluronic® F-68,* 200 mg; alcohol, 18%.
Administration and Dosage: USUAL ADULT DOSAGE—Two tablespoonfuls (30 ml) daily or as recommended by the physician.
How Supplied: N 0071-2454-23—16-oz bottles.

---

*Pluronic is a registered trademark of BASF Wyandotte Corporation for polymers of ethylene oxide and propylene oxide.

MYADEC®

Each tablet represents:		% of US Recommended Daily Allowances (US RDA)
Vitamins		
Vitamin A	10,000 IU*	200%
Vitamin D	400 IU	100%
Vitamin E	30 IU	100%
Vitamin C	250 mg	417%
Folic Acid	0.4 mg	100%
Thiamine	10 mg	667%
Riboflavin	10 mg	588%
Niacin†	100 mg	500%
Vitamin B_6	5 mg	250%
Vitamin B_{12}	6 mcg	100%
Pantothenic Acid	20 mg	200%
Minerals		
Iodine	150 mcg	100%
Iron	20 mg	111%
Magnesium	100 mg	25%
Copper	2 mg	100%
Zinc	20 mg	133%
Manganese	1.25 mg	‡

Ingredients: Sodium ascorbate, magnesium oxide, microcrystalline cellulose, niacinamide, ferrous fumarate, ascorbic acid, zinc sulfate monohydrate, gelatin, vitamin E acetate, polyvinylpyrrolidone, calcium pantothenate, hydroxypropyl methylcellulose, silicon dioxide, riboflavin, thiamine mononitrate, magnesium stearate, pyridoxine hydrochloride, propylene glycol, cupric sulfate anhydrous, sugar, manganese sulfate monohydrate, vitamin A acetate, ethylcellulose, citric acid anhydrous, polysorbate 80, folic acid, wax, potassium iodide, vitamin D_2, titanium dioxide, vanillin, FD&C Yellow No. 6, FD&C Blue No. 2, FD&C Red No. 3, and vitamin B_{12}.

---

* International Units
† Supplied as niacinamide
‡ No US Recommended Daily Allowance (US RDA) has been established for this nutrient.
Actions and Uses: High potency vitamin supplement with minerals for adults.
Dosage: One tablet daily
How Supplied: N 0071-0335. In bottles of 130 and 250.
[*Shown in Product Identification Section*]

NATABEC® KAPSEALS®

Each capsule represents:

Vitamins	
Vitamin A	4,000 IU*
Vitamin D	400 IU
Vitamin C (ascorbic acid)	50 mg
Thiamine (vitamin B_1)	3 mg
Riboflavin (vitamin B_2)	2.0 mg
Nicotinamide†	20 mg
Vitamin B_6	3 mg
Vitamin B_{12}	5 mcg
Minerals	
Precipitated Calcium carbonate	600 mg
Dried Ferrous Sulfate	150 mg

---

*IU = International Units
†Supplied as niacinamide
Action and Uses: A multivitamin and mineral supplement for use during pregnancy and lactation.
Dosage: One capsule daily, or as directed by physician.
How Supplied: N 0071-0390-24. In bottles of 100. Parcode® 390.
The color combination of the banded capsule is a Warner-Lambert trademark.

THERA-COMBEX H-P®
High-Potency Vitamin B Complex with 500 mg Vitamin C

Composition: Each Kapseal contains:
Ascorbic acid
(vitamin C) .... 500 mg
Thiamine (vitamin B_1)
mononitrate .... 25 mg
Riboflavin
(vitamin B_2) .... 15 mg
Pyridoxine hydrochloride
(vitamin B_6) .... 10 mg
Vitamin B_{12}
(cyanocobalamin) .... 5 mcg
Nicotinamide
(niacinamide) .... 100 mg
dl-Panthenol .... 20 mg
Uses: For the prevention or treatment of vitamin B complex and vitamin C deficiencies.
Dosage: One or two capsules daily
How Supplied: N 0071-0550-24—Bottles of 100. Parcode® No. 550

TUCKS®
Pre-moistened Hemorrhoidal/Vaginal Pads

Indications: Temporarily relieve external discomfort of simple hemorrhoids.
—Soothe, cool, and comfort itching, burning, and irritation of sensitive rectal and outer vaginal areas.
—As a compress, to help relieve discomfort from rectal/vaginal surgical stitches.
—Effective hygienic wipe to cleanse rectal area of irritation-causing residue.
—Solution buffered to help prevent further irritation.
Directions: For external use only. Use as a wipe following bowel movement, during menstruation, or after napkin or tampon change. Or, as a compress, apply to affected area 10 to 15 minutes as needed. Change compresses every 5 minutes.
Warnings: In case of rectal bleeding, consult physician promptly. In case of continued irritation, discontinue use and consult a physician. Keep this and all medication out of the reach of children. In case of accidental ingestion seek professional assistance or contact a Poison Control Center immediately.
Contains: Soft pads pre-moistened with a solution containing 50% Witch Hazel, 10% Glycerin USP, Purified Water USP deionized q.s., Methylparaben USP 0.1% and Benzalkonium Chloride USP 0.003% as preservatives. Buffered to acid pH.
Store between 59 and 86 F.
How Supplied: Jars of 40 and 100. Also available as Tucks Take-Alongs®, individual, foil-wrapped, nonwoven wipes, 12 per box
Tucks—N 0071-1703
Tucks Take-Alongs—N 0071-1704-01
[*Shown in Product Identification Section*]

TUCKS® OINTMENT, CREAM

Composition: Tucks Ointment and Cream contain a specially formulated aqueous phase of 50% witch hazel

Continued on next page

This product information was prepared in December, 1981. On these and other Parke-Davis Products, detailed information may be obtained by addressing PARKE-DAVIS, Division of Warner-Lambert Company, Morris Plains, NJ 07950 USA.

Parke-Davis—Cont.

(hamamelis water). Both have an acid pH, pleasant odor, and are nonstaining.
Action and Uses: Both non-staining Tucks Ointment and Tucks Cream exert a temporary soothing, cooling, mildly astringent effect on such superficial irritations as simple hemorrhoids, vaginal and rectal area itch, post episiotomy discomfort and anorectal surgical wounds. Neither the Ointment or Cream contain steroids or skin sensitizing "caine" type topical anesthetics.
Warning: Symptomatic relief should not delay definitive diagnosis and treatment. If itching or irritation continue, discontinue use and consult your physician. In case of rectal bleeding, consult physician promptly.
Dosage and Administration: Apply locally three or four times daily. Applicator provided for rectal instillation.
How Supplied: Tucks Ointment and Tucks Cream (water-washable) in 40-g tubes with rectal applicators
Tucks Ointment—N 0071-3021-14
Tucks Cream—N 0071-3022-14
                       7000G070

ZIRADRYL® Lotion

Description: A zinc oxide-Benadryl lotion of 2% Benadryl® (diphenhydramine hydrochloride) and 2% zinc oxide; contains 2% alcohol.
Indications: For relief of itching in ivy or oak poisoning.
Warning: Should not be applied to extensive, or raw, oozing areas, or for a prolonged time, except as directed by a physician. Hypersensitivity to any of the components may occur.
Caution: Do not use in the eyes. If the condition for which this preparation is used persists or if a rash or irritation develops, discontinue use and consult physician.
FOR EXTERNAL USE ONLY
Directions: *SHAKE WELL*
For relief of itching, cleanse affected area and apply generously three or four times daily. Temporary stinging sensation may follow application. Discontinue use if stinging persists. Easily removed with water.
How Supplied: N 0071-3224-19: 6-oz bottles
[*Shown in Product Identification Section*]

IDENTIFICATION PROBLEM?

Consult the

Product Identification Section

where you'll find

products pictured

in full color.

Persōn & Covey, Inc.
616 ALLEN AVENUE
GLENDALE, CA 91201

A.C.N.®
Water-miscible Vitamin A,C, and Niacinamide Tablets

Description:
Each tablet contains: <u>% of U.S. RDA*</u>
Vitamin A ....25,000 I.U.   500
Ascorbic Acid ....250 mg   417
Niacinamide ....25 mg   125
*Percentage of U.S. Recommended Daily Allowance.
Indication: For use as a dietary supplement.
Dosage: One tablet daily as a dietary supplement. For adults and children 4 or more years of age.
Warnings: Keep all medication out of the reach of children. Keep in tight, light-resistant container.
How Supplied: In bottles of 100 tablets.
NDC 0096-0014-11

DHS™ Conditioning Rinse

DHS Conditioning Rinse is specially formulated for dermatological hair care.
DHS Conditioning Rinse helps control static electricity, eliminate tangles, mend split ends and improve elasticity. DHS Conditioning Rinse helps make hair easier to comb and manage while adding lustre and body.
Directions: Shampoo and rinse well. (We suggest DHS™ Shampoo.) Then apply a generous amount of DHS Conditioning Rinse and work evenly through the hair to the ends for 60 seconds. Rinse with warm water for 30 seconds.
Caution: For external use only. Keep out of the reach of children. Avoid contact with the eyes.
Contains: Purified Water, Glyceryl Stearate, Quaternium-31, Panthenol, Cetearyl Alcohol, Dimethicone Copolyol, Fragrance, FD&C Yellow #6.
How Supplied: 8 fluid ounce plastic bottles with easy to use dispenser.
NDC #0096-0726-08

DHS™ Shampoo
Dermatological Hair and Scalp Shampoo

DHS™ contains a unique blend of special cleansing agents that provide a luxurious lather which cleans the hair and scalp.
DHS™ conditioners reduce the need for after rinses and leave the hair lustrously clean.
DHS™ is especially formulated for pH balance. DHS may be used daily.
Directions: (1) Wet hair thoroughly; apply DHS, lather and rinse. Reapply DHS, lather and rinse again. Repeat as necessary or as directed by your physician.
Caution: For external use only. Keep out of the reach of children. Avoid contact with the eyes.
Contents: purified water, TEA-lauryl sulfate, sodium-chloride, PEG-8 distea-

rate, cocamide DEA, cocamide MEA, fragrance and FD&C yellow #6.
How Supplied: 8 fluid and 16 fluid ounce plastic bottles with easy to use dispenser.
NDC 0096-0727-08
NDC 0096-0727-16
[*Shown in Product Identification Section*]

DHS™ Tar Shampoo
Dermatological Hair and Scalp Shampoo

DHS™ Tar Shampoo aids in the control of the scaling of seborrhea (dandruff) and psoriasis of the scalp.
Directions: (1) Wet hair thoroughly; apply a liberal quantity of DHS™ Tar Shampoo and massage into a lather. (2) Rinse thoroughly and repeat application. (3) Allow lather to remain on scalp for about 5 minutes. (4) Use DHS Tar Shampoo once or twice weekly or as directed by your physician.
Caution: Avoid contact with the eyes. In case of contact, wash out with water. If irritation occurs, discontinue use and consult physician.
Warning: Keep out of the reach of children. For external use only.
DHS™ Tar Shampoo contains: Tar, equivalent to 0.5% Coal Tar U.S.P., TEA-lauryl sulfate, purified water, sodium chloride, PEG-8 disterate, cocamide DEA, cocamide MEA.
How Supplied: 4 and 8 fluid ounce plastic bottles with easy to use dispenser.
NDC 0096-0728-04
NDC 0096-0728-08
[*Shown in Product Identification Section*]

DHS™ Zinc Dandruff Shampoo
2% Zinc Pyrithione

DHS™ Zinc Shampoo aids in the control of dandruff/seborrheic dermatitis of the scalp.
Directions: Shake well before using. (1) Wet hair thoroughly; apply a liberal quantity of DHS™ Zinc and massage into a lather. (2) Rinse thoroughly and repeat application. (3) Allow lather to remain on scalp for about 5 minutes. (4) Use DHS Zinc at least twice weekly for the first two weeks then regularly thereafter, or as directed by physician.
Caution: Avoid contact with eyes. In case of contact, wash out with water. If irritation occurs, discontinue use and consult physician.
Warning: Keep out of the reach of children. For external use only.
DHS™ Zinc contains: 2% zinc pyrithione, purified water, TEA-lauryl sulfate, PEG-8 distearate, sodium chloride, cocamide DEA, cocamide MEA, magnesium aluminum silicate, hydroxypropyl methylcellulose, fragrance, and FD&C yellow #6.
How Supplied: 6 fluid ounce plastic bottles.
NDC 0096-0729-06
[*Shown in Product Identification Section*]

ENISYL™ Tablets
Lysine Hydrochloride

Composition: Each tablet contains Lysine 334 mg and 500 mg respectively (from the hydrochloride).

Indication: For use as a dietary supplement.

Dosage: Adults: one to three tablets daily as a dietary supplement.

Actions: Improves utilization of vegetable proteins such as rice, wheat, corn, etc.

Warnings: Keep out of the reach of children. Keep in tight, light-resistant container.

How Supplied: In bottles of 100 and 250 tablets. 334 and 500 mg.
NDC 0096-0777-11   NDC 0096-0777-52
NDC 0096-0778-11   NDC 0096-0778-52

SOLBAR®
Dioxybenzone and Oxybenzone Cream, U.S.P.

Composition:
Dioxybenzone, U.S.P. 3%
Oxybenzone, U.S.P. 3%

Action and Uses: When properly applied, Solbar® protects the skin from sunburning and aids in the prevention of visible changes in the skin such as wrinkling, drying and freckling due to overexposure to sun.

Directions: Smooth Solbar® gently and evenly on exposed skin areas. Do not rub. Allow to dry. Solbar will leave a transparent film containing the sum protectant, which is colorless, odorless, tasteless, non-staining, and cosmetically acceptable for men or women. Apply Solbar before exposure to sun. Reapply after swimming, bathing or prolonged exposure.

Caution: If irritation or sensitization occurs, discontinue use and consult a physician. Avoid contact with eyes. Protect from freezing.
Keep out of the reach of children.

How Supplied: Packaged in 2½ oz. polyethylene plastic tubes. NDC 0096-0680-75

SOLBAR® Plus 15

Solbar® Plus 15: Specially formulated to provide ultra protection from the sun's burning and tanning rays. Provides a high degree of sunburn protection for sun sensitive skin and fair skinned persons, blondes, brunettes and redheads. Fragrant-free formula ... contains no drying alcohol.

Directions: Smooth evenly on all exposed skin. To ensure maximum protection reapply after swimming or exercise.

Caution: For external use only. If irritation or sensitization occurs discontinue use and consult a physician. Avoid contact with the eyes. Keep this and all drugs out of the reach of children. Solbar® Plus 15 contains: Oxybenzone USP 5%, Ethyl Dihydroxypropyl PABA 5%, Purified Water, Isopropyl Palmitate, PPG-20 Lanolin Ether, PPG-2 Lanolin Ether, Glyceryl Stearate, PEG-100 Stearate, Carbomer 934, PEG-15 Cocamine, Sodium Hydroxide, Methylparaben, Propylparaben.

How Supplied: 4 ounce plastic tube.
NDC 0096-0681-04

XERAC®
(alcohol gel)

Composition:
Isopropyl Alcohol 44%
Microcrystalline Sulfur 4%

Effects: A medicated antiseptic gel to promote drying and peeling of the skin. An aid in the management of acne. Invisible when applied to the skin.

Directions: Apply a thin film to affected areas one to three times daily, or as directed by physician.

Precautions: Avoid overuse. If undue skin irritation develops or becomes excessive, discontinue use and consult physician. Avoid contact with eyes. Keep this and all medication out of the reach of children. For external use only.

How Supplied: 45 g (1-½ oz.) plastic tube.
NDC 0096-0787-45

Pfipharmecs Division
PFIZER INC.
235 EAST 42ND STREET
NEW YORK, NY 10017

BONINE®
(meclizine hydrochloride)
Chewable Tablets

Actions: BONINE is an antihistamine which shows marked protective activity against nebulized histamine and lethal doses of intravenously injected histamine in guinea pigs. It has a marked effect in blocking the vasodepressor response to histamine, but only a slight blocking action against acetylcholine. Its activity is relatively weak in inhibiting the spasmogenic action of histamine on isolated guinea pig ileum.

Indications: BONINE is effective in the management of nausea, vomiting and dizziness associated with motion sickness.

Contraindications: Meclizine HCl is contraindicated in individuals who have shown a previous hypersensitivity to it.

Warnings: Since drowsiness may, on occasion, occur with the use of this drug, patients should be warned of this possibility and cautioned against driving a car or operating dangerous machinery. Patients should avoid alcoholic beverages while taking this drug. Due to its potential anticholinergic action, this drug should be used with caution in patients with asthma, glaucoma, or enlargement of the prostate gland.

Usage in Children:
Clinical studies establishing safety and effectiveness in children have not been done; therefore, usage is not recommended in children under 12 years of age.

Usage in Pregnancy:
Meclizine HCl, or any other medication, should be used during pregnancy only if clearly necessary.

Adverse Reactions: Drowsiness, dry mouth, and on rare occasions, blurred vision have been reported.

Dosage and Administration: For motion sickness 1 or 2 tablets of BONINE should be taken one hour prior to embarkation. Therefore, the dose may be repeated every 24 hours for the duration of the journey.

How Supplied: BONINE (meclizine HCl) is available in convenient packets of 8 chewable tablets of 25 mg. meclizine HCl.
[*Shown in Product Identification Section*]

CORYBAN®–D CAPSULES
Decongestant Cold Capsules

Composition: Each capsule contains:
Caffeine U.S.P. ....30 mg.
Chlorpheniramine maleate
   U.S.P......................................2 mg.
Phenylpropanolamine HCl ....25 mg.

How Supplied: In bottles of 24 or packs of 12, light and dark blue capsules.
[*Shown in Product Identification Section*]

CORYBAN®–D COUGH SYRUP
With Decongestant

Composition: Each 5 ml (1 teaspoonful) contains:
Dextromethorphan HBr U.S.P....7.5 mg.
Guaifenesin ....50 mg.
Phenylephrine HCl..........................5 mg.
Acetaminophen ....120 mg.
Alcohol*...7.5%
* Small loss unavoidable

How Supplied: Coryban-D Cough Syrup is available in 4-ounce dripless spout bottles. Sorbitol, which is contained in this product, is a nutritive, carbohydrate sweetening agent which is metabolized more slowly than sugar.

Do not refrigerate.
[*Shown in Product Identification Section*]

LI-BAN™ Spray
Lice Control Spray

THIS PRODUCT IS NOT FOR USE ON HUMANS OR ANIMALS

Active Ingredient:
(5-Benzyl-3-Furyl) methyl 2, 2-dimethyl-3-(2-methylpropenyl) cyclopropanecarboxylate
                                           0.500%
Related Compounds   0.068%
Aromatic petroleum
   hydrocarbons   0.664%
Inert Ingredients   98.768%
                                         100.000%

Actions: A highly active synthetic pyrethroid for the control of lice and louse eggs on garments, bedding, furniture and other inanimate objects.

Warnings: Avoid contamination of feed and foodstuffs. Cover or remove fishbowls. **Harmful if swallowed.** If lice infestations should occur on humans, consult either your physician or pharmacist for a product for use on humans.
Physical and Chemical Hazards: Contents under pressure. Do not use or store near heat or open flame. Do not puncture or incinerate container. Exposure to temperatures above 130° F may cause bursting.

Continued on next page

Pfipharmecs—Cont.

Direction For Use: It is a violation of Federal law to use this product in a manner inconsistent with its labeling.

Shake well before each use. Remove protective cap. Aim spray opening away from person. Push button to spray. **Caution: Avoid spraying in eyes. Avoid breathing spray mist. Avoid contact with skin. In case of contact wash immediately with soap and water. Vacate room and ventilate before reoccupying.**

To kill lice and louse eggs: Spray in an inconspicuous area to test for possible staining or discoloration. Inspect again after drying, then proceed to spray entire area to be treated.

Hold container upright with nozzle away from you. Depress valve and spray from a distance of 8 to 10 inches.

Spray each square foot for 3 seconds. Spray only those garments, parts of bedding, including mattresses and furniture that cannot be either laundered or dry cleaned.

Allow all sprayed articles to dry thoroughly before use. Repeat treatment as necessary.

Buyer assumes all risks of use, storage or handling of this material not in strict accordance with direction given herewith.

DISPOSAL OF CONTAINER
Wrap container and dispose of in trash. Do not incinerate.

How Supplied: 5 ounce aerosol can.
[*Shown in Product Identification Section*]

RID™
Liquid Pediculicide

Description: Rid is a liquid pediculicide whose active ingredients are: pyrethrins 0.3%, piperonyl butoxide, technical 3.00%, equivalent to 2.4% (butylcarbityl) (6-propylpiperonyl) ether and to 0.6% related compounds, petroleum distillate 1.20% and benzyl alcohol 2.4%. Inert ingredients 93.1%.

Actions: RID kills head lice (Pediculus humanus capitis), body lice (Pediculus humanus humanus), and pubic or crab lice (Phthirus pubis).

The pyrethrins act as a contact poison and affect the parasite's nervous system, resulting in paralysis and death. The efficacy of the pyrethrins is enhanced by the synergist, piperonyl butoxide.

Indications: RID is indicated for the treatment of infestations of head lice, body lice and pubic (crab) lice.

Warning: RID should not be used by ragweed sensitized persons.

Precautions: This product is for external use only. It is harmful if swallowed. It should not be inhaled. It should be kept out of the eyes and contact with mucous membranes should be avoided. If accidental contact with eyes occurs, flush immediately with water. In case of infection or skin irritation, discontinue use and consult a physician. Consult a physician if infestation of eyebrows or eyelashes occurs. Avoid contamination of

feed or foodstuffs. Do not reuse container. Destroy when empty.
Do not transport or store below 32°F (0°C).

Dosage and Administration: (1) Apply RID undiluted to hair and scalp or to any other infested area until entirely wet. Do not use on eyelashes or eyebrows. (2) Allow RID to remain on area for 10 minutes but no longer. (3) Wash thoroughly with warm water and soap or shampoo. (4) Dead lice and eggs may require removal with fine-toothed comb provided. A second application is seldom needed. If necessary, treatment may be repeated but do not exceed two consecutive applications within 24 hours.

Many experts have recommended that a second treatment 7–10 days after the first to kill any newly hatched nymphs. Since lice infestations are spread by contact, each family member should be examined carefully. If infested, he or she should be treated promptly to avoid spread or reinfestation of previously treated individuals. Contaminated clothing and other articles, such as hats, etc. should be dry cleaned, boiled or otherwise treated until decontaminated to prevent reinfestation or spread.

How Supplied: In 2 and 4 fl. oz. bottles. Fine-toothed comb to aid in removal of dead lice and nits and patient instruction booklet are included in each package of RID.
[*Shown in Product Identification Section*]

WART-OFF™

Active Ingredient: Salicylic Acid, U.S.P., 17%, in Flexible Collodion, U.S.P. Wart-Off™ Solution contains approx. 20.5% Alcohol and 54.2% Ether—small losses are unavoidable.

Indications: Removal of Warts

Warnings: Keep this and all medications out of reach of children to avoid accidental poisoning.

Flammable—Do not use near fire or flame. For external use only. In case of accidental ingestion, contact a physician or a Poison Control Center immediately. Do not use near eyes or on mucous membranes. Diabetics or other people with impaired circulation should not use Wart-Off™. Do not use on moles, birthmarks or unusual warts with hair growing from them. If wart persists, see your physician. If pain should develop, consult your physician.

Dosage and Administration: Wart-Off™ to warts For Use: Read warning and enclosed instructional brochure. **Apply Wart-Off™ to warts only. Do not apply to surrounding skin. Make sure that surrounding skin is protected from accidental application.** Before applying, soak affected area in hot water for several min- utes. If any tissue has been loosened, remove by rubbing surface of wart gently with special brush enclosed in Wart-Off™ package. Dry thoroughly. Warts are contagious, so don't share your towel. Apply once or twice daily. Using plastic applicator attached to cap, apply one drop at a time until entire wart is covered. Lightly cover with small adhesive bandage. Re-

place cap tightly. This treatment may be used daily for three to four weeks if necessary.

How Supplied: 0.5 fluid ounce bottle with pinpoint plastic applicator, special cleaning brush and instructional brochure.
[*Shown in Product Identification Section*]

Pharmacraft Division
PENNWALT CORPORATION
755 JEFFERSON ROAD
ROCHESTER, NY 14623

ALLEREST® TABLETS, CHILDREN'S CHEWABLE TABLETS, HEADACHE STRENGTH TABLETS, TIMED RELEASE CAPSULES

Active Ingredients:
acetaminophen
 Headache Strength, 325 mg.
chlorpheniramine maleate
 Tablets, 2 mg.
 Children's Chewables, 1 mg.
 Headache Strength, 2 mg.
 Timed Release, 4 mg.
phenylpropanolamine HCl
 Tablets, 18.7 mg.
 Children's Chewables, 9.4 mg.
 Headache Strength, 18.7 mg.
 Timed Release, 50 mg.

Indications: Allerest is indicated for symptomatic relief of hay fever, pollen allergies, upper respiratory allergies (perennial allergic rhinitis), allergic colds, sinusitis and nasal passage congestion. Those symptoms include headache pain, sneezing, runny nose, itching or watery eyes and itching nose and throat.

Actions: Allerest contains the antihistamine chlorpheniramine maleate which acts to suppress the symptoms of allergic rhinitis. In addition, it contains the decongestant phenylpropanolamine which acts to reduce swelling of the upper respiratory tract mucosa. Headache Strength also contains acetaminophen to relieve headache pain.

Contraindications: Known hypersensitivity to the ingredients in this drug.

Warnings: Allerest should be used with caution in patients with cardiac disorders, hypertension, hyperthyroidism or diabetes. Since drowsiness may occur, patients should be instructed not to operate a car or machinery.

Adverse Reactions: Drowsiness; excitability, especially in children; nervousness; and dizziness.

Dosage and Administration: TABLETS AND HEADACHE STRENGTH —Adult, 2 tablets every 4 hours. Not to exceed 8 tablets in 24 hours. Children (6–12)—half the adult dose. Dosage for children under 6 should be individualized under the supervision of a physician. CHILDREN'S CHEWABLE TABLETS—Children (6–12) 2 tablets every 4 hours. Not to exceed 8 tablets in 24 hours. Children under 6 consult a physician. Adults double the children's dose. TIMED RELEASE CAPSULES—Adults, 1 capsule in the morning and one capsule in the evening. If symptoms are especially severe, one capsule every 8 hours may be taken. Not to exceed 3 capsules in 24 hours. Do not give to children under 12 years without physician's approval.

Overdosage: Acetaminophen in massive overdosage may cause hepatotoxicity.

Drug Interaction Precautions: Not to be taken by patients currently taking a prescription antihypertensive or antidepressant drug containing a monoamine oxidase inhibitor except under the advice and supervision of a physician. Antihistamines and oral nasal decongestants have additive effects with alcohol and other CNS depressants.

How Supplied: TABLETS packaged on blister cards in 24 and 48 count cartons, and in 75 count glass bottles. CHILDREN'S CHEWABLE TABLETS packaged on blister cards in 24 count cartons. HEADACHE STRENGTH TABLETS packaged on blister cards in 24 count cartons. CAPSULES supplied in bottles of 10 count.

CaldeCORT® CREAM, SPRAY AND RECTAL-ITCH OINTMENT

Active Ingredient: hydrocortisone acetate (equivalent to hydrocortisone 0.5%)

Indications: Provides temporary relief from itching, minor skin irritations and rashes due to eczema, dermatitis, insect bites, poison ivy, poison oak, poison sumac, soaps, detergents, cosmetics and jewelry, and for itchy genital and anal areas.

Actions: Anti-dermatitis cream, spray and ointment for the temporary relief from itching and minor skin irritations.

Warnings: For external use only. Avoid contact with the eyes. If condition worsens, or if symptoms persist for more than 7 days, discontinue use of this product and consult a physician. Do not use on children under 2 years of age except under the advice and supervision of a physician.

Dosage and Administration: For adults and children 2 years of age and older: Apply to affected area not more than 3 or 4 times daily. For children under 2 years of age: There is no recommended dosage except under the advice and supervision of a physician.

How Supplied: Anti-Itch Cream, ½ and 1 oz. tubes; Anti-Itch Spray, 1½ oz. can; and greaseless Rectal-Itch Ointment, ¼ and ½ oz. tubes.

CALDESENE® MEDICATED POWDER AND OINTMENT

Active Ingredients:
calcium
undecylenate
  Powder, 10%
zinc oxide
  Cream

Indications: Caldesene Medicated Powder is indicated to help heal, relieve and prevent diaper rash, prickly heat and chafing. Medicated Ointment helps prevent diaper rash and soothe minor skin irritations.

Actions: Antifungal and antibacterial Medicated Powder inhibits the growth of bacteria and fungi which cause diaper rash. Also, forms a protective coating to repel moisture, soothe and comfort minor skin irritations, helps heal and prevent chafing and prickly heat. Medicated Ointment forms a protective skin coating to repel moisture and promote healing of diaper rash, while its natural ingredients protect irritated skin against wetness. Soothes minor skin irritations, superficial wounds and burns.

Warnings: Keep this and all drugs out of the reach of children. In case of accidental ingestion, seek professional assistance or contact a Poison Control Center immediately.

Dosage and Administration: Cleanse and dry affected area. Smooth on Caldesene 3–4 times daily, or after each diaper change, or as directed by a physician.

How Supplied: Medicated Powder, 2.0 oz. and 5.0 oz. shaker containers. Medicated Ointment; 1.25 oz. collapsible tubes.

CRUEX® ANTIFUNGAL POWDER AND CREAM

Active Ingredients:
calcium
undecylenate
  Squeeze Powder, 10%
zinc undecylenate
  Spray Powder & Cream, 20%
undecylenic acid
  Spray Powder 2%, Cream 3%

Indications: Recommended for the relief and prevention of Jock Itch (Tinea cruris) and relief of excessive perspiration, itching, chafing, rash and irritation in the groin area. Cruex relieves odor too.

Actions: Antifungal Powder and Cream are effective in the treatment of superficial fungous infections of the skin.

Warnings: For external use only. Keep away from eyes and other mucous membranes. Use only as directed. If symptoms do not improve in 4 weeks, discontinue use and consult your physician. Do not use if skin is pustular or severely broken—consult your physician. Keep this and all drugs out of the reach of children. In case of accidental ingestion, seek professional assistance or contact a Poison Control Center immediately. For aerosol container only; contents under pressure. Do not puncture or incinerate. Flammable mixture, do not use near a fire or flame. Do not store at temperature above 120° F. Use only as directed. Intentional misuse by deliberately concentrating and inhaling the contents can be harmful or fatal.

Dosage and Administration: Cleanse and dry the affected area. Apply Cruex Medicated Powder to affected area once or twice a day or as directed by a physician. Apply Cruex Medicated Cream liberally as often as needed or as directed by a physician. For the best results rub cream into the skin.

How Supplied: Antifungal Powder, 1.8 oz., 3.5 oz. and 5.5 oz. aerosol containers; 1.5 oz. plastic squeeze bottle. Antifungal Cream, .5 oz. tube.

DESENEX® ANTIFUNGAL POWDER, PENETRATING FOAM, OINTMENT, FOOT & SNEAKER SPRAY, LIQUID AND SOAP

Active Ingredients:
undecylenic acid
  Powder, 2%
  Ointment, 5%
  Penetrating Foam, 10%
  Liquid, 10%
  Soap, 2%
zinc undecylenate
  Powder, 20%
  Ointment, 20%
isopropyl alcohol
  Penetrating Foam, 35.2%
  Liquid, 47%
aluminum chlorhydrex PG
  Foot & Sneaker Spray
alcohol
  Foot & Sneaker Spray, 89.3%,v/v

Indications: Desenex is indicated for the topical treatment of Athlete's Foot (T. rubrum, T. mentagrophytes, T. floccosum) and ringworm of the body exclusive of the nails and scalp.

Action: Medicated Powders, Ointment and Penetrating Foam are effective antifungal treatment of superficial fungous infections of the skin. Penetrating Foam quickly dissolves into a highly concentrated liquid. Foot & Sneaker Spray is a formulated liquid that dries to a fine powder to protect feet from odor causing perspiration wetness. Powder also helps keep feet dry and comfortable. Medicated Liquid is effective antifungal and antibacterial treatment of superficial infections of the skin.

Warnings: For external use only. If symptoms do not improve in 4 weeks, discontinue use and consult your physician. Desenex is not recommended for nail or scalp infections. Keep this and all drugs out of the reach of children. In case of accidental ingestion, seek professional assistance or contact a Poison Control Center immediately. For Liquid and Foam; Do not use near eyes. For Spray-On Powder, Foot & Sneaker Spray and Penetrating Foam only; Contents under pressure. Do not puncture or incinerate. Flammable mixture, do not use near fire or flame. Do not store at temperature above 120° F. Use only as directed. Intentional misuse by deliberately concentrating and inhaling the contents can be harmful or fatal.

Dosage and Administration: Cleanse affected and adjacent areas morning and evening with soap (such as Desenex Soap) and water. Powder—dust powder gently on the skin. To assure continued prophylaxis against fungous infections, dust powder freely between the toes and over the feet. Ointment—apply liberally every night before retiring. If condition persists, a physician or foot specialist should be contacted. Soap—work up into rich lather using hot or warm water. Rinse and dry thoroughly. Use at least twice daily or as recommended by a physician or foot specialist. Frequent use is recommended to obtain maximum effectiveness. Liquid and Spray—hold the bottle or can at a convenient angle and press

Continued on next page

Pharmacraft—Cont.

down on the valve, aiming spray at affected areas from a distance of 4 to 6 inches. Spray liberally in between and around toes for Athlete's Foot. Foot & Sneaker Spray—shake can well, hold 6 inches from area and spray onto the soles of your feet, and between toes daily. To curtail foot, shoe and sneaker odor, spray liberally over entire inside area of shoes and sneakers. After spraying, allow sneakers to dry one minute before wearing. Penetrating Foam—Shake well. INVERT CONTAINER and direct Penetrating Foam between toes and other infected foot areas. Apply twice daily or as needed.

How Supplied: Spray-On Powder; 2.7 oz. and 5.5 oz. aerosol containers. Powder, 1.5 oz. and 3.0 oz. shaker containers. Ointment; 0.9 oz. and 1.8 oz. tubes. Liquid; 1.5 oz. pump spray bottle. Foot & Sneaker Spray; 2.7 oz. aerosol container. Penetrating Foam; 1.5 oz. aerosol container. Soap; 3.25 oz. bar.

SINAREST® TABLETS

Active Ingredients:
acetaminophen:
  Tablets, 325 mg.
  Extra Strength, 500 mg.
chlorpheniramine maleate
  Tablets 2 mg.
  Extra Strength, 2 mg.
phenylpropanolamine HCl
  Tablets, 18.7 mg.
  Extra Strength, 18.7 mg.
Indications: Sinarest is indicated for symptomatic relief from the headache pain, pressure and congestion associated with sinusitis, allergic rhinitis or the common cold.
Actions: Sinarest contains an antihistamine (chlorpheniramine maleate) and a decongestant (phenypropanolamine) for the relief of sinus and nasal passage congestion as well as an analgesic (acetaminophen) to relieve pain and discomfort.
Contraindications: Known hypersensitivity to any of the ingredients in this compound.
Warnings: Sinarest should be used with caution in patients with high blood pressure, heart disease, diabetes or thyroid disease. Since drowsiness may occur, patients should be instructed not to operate a car or machinery. This product should not be taken for more than 10 consecutive days.
Adverse Reactions: Drowsiness; excitability, especially in children; nervousness; and dizziness.
Dosage and Administration: SINAREST TABLETS—Adult—take 2 tablets every 4 hours. Not to exceed 8 tablets in 24 hours. Children (6–12 years)—One half of adult dosage. Dosage for children under 6 should be individualized under the supervision of a physician. EXTRA STRENGTH TABLETS—Adults and Children over 12—take 2 tablets every 6 hours. Not to exceed 8 tablets in 24 hours. Not recommended for children 12 and under.

Overdosage: Acetaminophen in massive overdosage may cause hepatotoxicity.
Drug Interaction Precaution: Not to be taken by patients currently taking a prescription antihypertensive or antidepressant drug containing a monoamine oxidase inhibitor except under the advice and supervision of a physician. Antihistamines and oral nasal decongestants have additive effects with alcohol and other CNS depressants.
How Supplied: Blister packages of 20 and 40 tablets and 80 tablet bottle. Extra Strength tablets: package of 24 tablets.

PharmTech Research Inc.
1750 MONTGOMERY STREET
SAN FRANCISCO, CA 94111

HERBITOL®

Active Ingredients: The Herbitol Diet System consists of a specially formulated whole protein powder with rice fiber and provides 100% of the U.S. Recommended Daily Allowance of vitamins and minerals. Contains Tri-Herbal Complex™ (A specialized formula consisting of dandelion, gotu-kola, echinacea and spices), Soy protein isolate, amylum, fructose, calcium sodium caseinate, natural flavors, vegetable fiber, ascorbic acid, whey, nonfat milk solids, magnesium oxide, vitamin E acetate, DL-methionine, Pyridoxine hydrochloride, ferrous mumarate, lecithin, soybean oil, brewers yeast, corn bran flour, riboflavin, niacinamide, zinc oxide, calcium pantothenate, vitamin A palmitate, copper sulfate, choline bitartrate, inositol, thiamine hydrochloride, vitamin D2, folic acid, biotin, potassium iodide, selenium kelp and cyanocobalamin.
Indications: The Herbitol Diet System is indicated for those seeking a nutritionally balanced diet plan providing 800 or more calories per day including one regular meal.
Actions: A safe, effective aid to healthful weight reduction and diet control. Should vitamin needs be increased by stress, Herbitol® has an extra measure of protection against possible B Complex and C & E vitamin deficiency.
Warnings: Use only as directed in the accompanying diet plan. Do not use as the sole or primary source of calories for weight reduction.
Drug Interaction: None
Precautions: None
Symptoms and Treatment of Oral Overdosage: None
Dosage and Administration: Add one level 1 oz. scoop (provided) of Herbitol® to exactly 8 oz. of low-fat white or low-fat chocolate milk. Blend or shake 5–10 seconds. Pour into a small bowl—chill until set into a pudding. Dosage: twice a day and a balanced evening meal.
Professional Labeling: Same as those listed under indications.
How Supplied: Available in display box, 12 oz. Introductory and 32 oz. Economy sizes with literature and instruc-

tions. See photo in Product Identification section.
[*Shown in Product Identification Section*]

Plough, Inc.
3030 JACKSON AVENUE
MEMPHIS, TN 38151

AFTATE®
Antifungal
Sprinkle Powder/Aerosol Spray Powder
Aerosol Spray Liquid/Gel

Active Ingredients: Tolnaftate 1% (Also contains: Aerosol Spray Liquid—36% alcohol; Aerosol Spray Powder—14% alcohol.)
Indications: AFTATE affords excellent topical treatment and prophylaxis of tinea pedis, tinea cruris, tinea corporis, and tinea manuum due to infection with *Trichophyton rubrum, Trichophyton mentagrophytes and Epidermophyton floccosum.*
Actions: AFTATE is a highly active synthetic fungicidal agent that is effective in the treatment of superficial fungus infections of the skin. It is inactive systemically, virtually nonsensitizing, and does not ordinarily sting or irritate intact or broken skin, even in the presence of acute inflammatory reactions.
Warnings: For external use only. Keep out of eyes. Not recommended for nail and scalp infections. If symptoms do not improve in ten (10) days or if irritation occurs, discontinue use unless directed otherwise by a physician.
Dosage and Administration: Liberal use, twice daily.
How Supplied:
AFTATE for Athlete's Foot
  Sprinkle Powder—2.25 oz. bottle.
  Aerosol Spray Powder—3.5 oz. can
  Gel—.5 oz. tube.
  Aerosol Spray Liquid—4 oz. can.
AFTATE for Jock Itch
  Aerosol Spray Powder—3.5 oz. can.
  Sprinkle Powder—1.5 oz. bottle.
  Gel—.5 oz. tube.
[*Shown in Product Identification Section*]

ASPERGUM®
Analgesic
Gum Tablet

Active Ingredients: Each gum tablet contains aspirin 3½ gr.
Indications: For temporary relief of minor sore throat pain, simple headache, aches and pains of colds and flu, and muscular aches and pains.
Actions: ASPERGUM is a convenient way to administer aspirin to children and adults who cannot or will not gargle properly or who cannot readily swallow tablets.
Warnings: Do not use more than 2 days or administer to children under 3 years of age unless directed by a physician.
Do not exceed maximum dosage (in adults) of 16 tablets in 24 hours; (in children 6–12 years) of 8 tablets in 24 hours, unless directed by physician; (in children 3–6 years) of 3 tablets in 24 hours.

Precaution: ASPERGUM is not intended for treatment of severe or persistent sore throat pain, high fever, headache, nausea or vomiting.

Dosage and Administration: Adults—chew 2 tablets; repeat as required up to a maximum of 16 in any 24 hour period, or as directed by physician. Children—6 to 12 years—chew 1 to 2 tablets as required up to 8 daily, or as directed by physician. Children—3 to 6 years—chew 1 tablet as required up to 3 daily. Children under 3 years of age, consult physician.

How Supplied:
ASPERGUM tablets in chewing gum form. Individual blister packaging.
Orange flavored: boxes of 16 and 40 tablets.
Cherry flavored: boxes of 16 and 40 tablets.
[*Shown in Product Identification Section*]

CORRECTOL®
Laxative
Tablets/Liquid
Active Ingredients: Tablets—Yellow phenolphthalein, 65 mg. and docusate sodium, 100 mg. per tablet. Liquid—Yellow phenolphthalein, 65 mg per tablespoonful.
Indications: For temporary relief of constipation.
Actions: Yellow phenolphthalein—stimulant laxative; docusate sodium—fecal softener.
Warnings: Not to be taken in case of nausea, vomiting, abdominal pain, or signs of appendicitis. Take only as needed—as frequent or continued use of laxatives may result in dependence on them. If skin rash appears, do not use this or any other preparation containing phenolphthalein.
Dosage and Administration
Dosage: Adults—1 or 2 tablets or tablespoonfuls daily as needed, at bedtime or on arising.
Children over 6 years—1 tablet or tablespoonful daily as needed.
How Supplied: Tablets—Individual foil-backed blister packaging in boxes of 15, 30, 60 and 90 tablets. Liquid—8 and 16 fl. oz. bottles.
[*Shown in Product Identification Section*]

CUSHION GRIP®
Thermoplastic Denture Adhesive
Indications: A soft pliable thermoplastic adhesive which creates a secure seal to help reduce looseness, shifting, clicking of dentures.
Actions: Securely holds dentures comfortably for up to 4 days. Won't wash off in water. Even after repeated cleaning. CUSHION GRIP remains in place, remains soft and pliable... recreates a secure seal each time dentures are reinserted. CUSHION GRIP is safe for plastic and porcelain plates.
Caution: Intended for use only on non-defective dentures. Ill-fitting, broken or irritating dentures may impair health of patient. Periodic dental examination is recommended at least every six months.
Directions for Use: Refer patient to detailed instructions supplied with each

Age (Years)	Weight (lbs.)	Dosage
Under 2	Below 27	As directed by physician.
2 through 3	27 to 35	2 tablets
4 through 5	36 to 45	3 tablets
6 through 8	46 to 65	4 tablets
9 through 10	66 to 76	5 tablets
11 years	77 to 83	6 tablets
12 and over	84 and over	8 tablets

package.
How Supplied: In tubes of ¼, ½ and 1 oz.
[*Shown in Product Identification Section*]

DI-GEL®
Antacid · Anti-Gas
Tablets/Liquid
Active Ingredients: DI-GEL Tablets: Each tablet contains: Simethicone 25 mg., aluminum hydroxide-magnesium carbonate codried gel 282 mg., magnesium hydroxide 85 mg.
Sodium Content: 10.6 mg. per tablet.
DI-GEL Liquid: Each teaspoonful contains: Simethicone 25 mg., aluminum hydroxide (equivalent to aluminum hydroxide dried gel, U.S.P.) 282 mg., magnesium hydroxide 87 mg.
Sodium Content: 8.5 mg. per teaspoonful.
Indications: For fast, temporary relief of acid indigestion, heartburn, sour stomach and accompanying painful gas symptoms.
Actions: The antacid system in DI-GEL relieves and soothes acid indigestion, heartburn and sour stomach. At the same time, the simethicone "defoamers" eliminate gas.
When air becomes entrapped in the stomach, heartburn and acid indigestion can result, along with sensations of fullness, pressure and bloating.
Warnings: Do not take more than 20 teaspoonfuls or tablets in a 24 hour period, or use the maximum dosage of this product for more than 2 weeks, except under the advice and supervision of a physician. If you have kidney disease or if you are on a sodium restricted diet, do not use this product except under the advice and supervision of a physician. May cause constipation or have a laxative effect.
Drug Interaction: This product should not be taken if patient is presently taking a prescription antibiotic drug containing any form of tetracycline.
Dosage and Administration: Two teaspoonfuls or tablets every 2 hours, or after or between meals and at bedtime, not to exceed 20 teaspoonfuls or tablets per day, or as directed by a physician.
How Supplied:
DI-GEL Liquid in Mint and Lemon/Orange Flavors - 6 and 12 fl. oz. bottles.
DI-GEL Tablets in Mint and Lemon/Orange Flavors - In boxes of 30, 60 and 90 in handy portable blister packaging.
[*Shown in Product Identification Section*]

DURATION® Long Lasting Topical Nasal Spray/Nose Drops/ Mentholated Nasal Spray Nasal Decongestant

Active Ingredients: Oxymetazoline HCl 0.05%

Preservative: Phenylmercuric Acetate 0.002% (Mentholated Nasal Spray also contains the following aromatics: menthol, camphor, eucalyptol.)
Indications: Temporary relief, for up to 12 hours, of nasal congestion due to colds, hay fever and sinusitis.
Actions: The sympathomimetic action of DURATION constricts the smaller arterioles of the nasal passages, producing a prolonged, gentle and predictable decongesting effect up to 12 hours.
Warnings: Do not exceed recommended dosage because symptoms may occur such as burning, stinging, sneezing, or increase of nasal discharge. Do not use this product for more than 3 days. If symptoms persist, consult a physician. The use of dispenser by more than one person may spread infection.
Dosage and Administration:
DURATION Nasal Spray—With head upright, spray 2 or 3 times in each nostril twice daily—morning and evening. To spray, squeeze bottle quickly and firmly. Not recommended for children under 6.
DURATION Nose Drops—Tilt head back, apply 2 or 3 drops into each nostril twice daily—morning and evening. Not recommended for children under 6.
Used at bedtime, DURATION helps restore freer nasal breathing throughout the night.
How Supplied:
DURATION Nasal Spray—½ & 1 fl. oz. Plastic Squeeze Bottle
DURATION Mentholated Nasal Spray—½ fl. oz. Plastic Squeeze Bottle
DURATION Nose Drops—⅔ fl. oz. Bottle.
[*Shown in Product Identification Section*]

REGUTOL®
Stool Softener
Tablets
Active Ingredients: Each tablet contains 100 mg. docusate sodium.
Indications: For relief of constipation.
Actions: REGUTOL contains docusate sodium which aids natural regularity and promotes easier elimination by moistening and softening dry, hard, constipating waste. REGUTOL does not cause cramps or spasms.
Dosage and Administration: Adults and children over six years old—1 tablet twice a day until regularity is restored.
How Supplied: REGUTOL tablets in boxes of 30, 60 and 90 individual blister packaging.
[*Shown in Product Identification Section*]

ST. JOSEPH® Aspirin for Children
Pediatric Analgesic/Antipyretic
Chewable Tablets
Active Ingredient: Aspirin 81 mg. (1¼ grain) per tablet.

Continued on next page

Plough—Cont.

Indications: For temporary reduction of fever, relief of minor aches and pains of cold and flu.

Actions: Analgesic/Antipyretic

Precaution: Do not administer this product for more than 5 days. If symptoms persist or new ones occur, consult physician. If fever persists for more than three days, or recurs, consult physician. Severe or persistent sore throat, high fever, headaches, nausea or vomiting may be serious. Discontinue use and consult physician if not relieved in 24 hours.

Dosage and Administration:
Dosage by Age and Weight
To be administered only under adult supervision.
[See table on **preceding** page].
May be repeated in 4 hours but not more than 5 times a day unless prescribed by physician.
ST. JOSEPH Aspirin for Children may be given one of five ways. Always follow with ½ glass of water, milk, or fruit juice.
1. CHEWED, followed by liquid.
2. SWALLOWED whole, followed by liquid.
3. DISSOLVED on tongue, followed by liquid.
4. CRUSHED or dissolved in a teaspoon of liquid.
5. POWDERED for infant use, when so directed by physician.

How Supplied: Chewable orange flavored tablets in plastic bottles of 36 tablets. Child-resistant packaging.
[*Shown in Product Identification Section*]

ST. JOSEPH® Cold Tablets for Children
Pediatric Analgesic/Antipyretic/Nasal Decongestant

Active Ingredients: Aspirin, 81 mg. (1¼ grain) and phenylpropanolamine hydrochloride 3.125 mg. per tablet.

Indications: Temporary reduction of fever, relief of minor aches and pains, nasal congestion, runny nose, difficult nasal breathing accompanying colds and flu.

Actions: Aspirin provides analgesia and antipyresis. Phenylpropanolamine hydrochloride restricts the smaller arterioles of nasal passages resulting in a nasal decongestant effect. Helps decongest sinus openings and sinus passages, thus promoting sinus drainage.

Precaution: Do not administer this product for more than 5 days. If symptoms persist or new ones occur, consult physician. If fever persists for more than

Age (Years)	Weight (lbs.)	Dosage
Under 2	Below 27	As directed by physician.
2 through 3	27 to 35	2 tablets
4 through 5	36 to 45	3 tablets
6 through 8	46 to 65	4 tablets
9 through 10	66 to 76	5 tablets
11 years	77 to 83	6 tablets
12 years and older	84 and over	8 tablets

three days, or recurs, consult physician. Severe or persistent sore throat with high fever, headaches, nausea or vomiting may be serious. Discontinue use and consult physician if not relieved in 24 hours.

Dosage and Administration:
Dosage by Age and Weight
To be administered only under adult supervision.
[See table above].
May be repeated in 4 hours if necessary, but not more than 4 times a day unless prescribed by physician.

How Supplied: Chewable orange flavored tablets in plastic bottles of 36 tablets. Child-resistant packaging.
[*Shown in Product Identification Section*]

ST. JOSEPH® Cough Syrup for Children
Pediatric
Antitussive Syrup

Active Ingredient: Dextromethorphan hydrobromide 7.5 mg. per 5 cc.

Indications: For relief of coughing of colds and flu for up to 8 hours.

Actions: Antitussive

Warning: Should not be administered to children for persistent or chronic cough such as occurs with asthma or emphysema or where cough is accompanied by excessive secretions except under physician's advice.

Dosage and Administration:
Dosage:
[See table below].

How Supplied: Cherry tasting syrup in plastic bottle of 2 and 4 fl. ozs.
[*Shown in Product Identification Section*]

SHADE®
Sun Protection Factor 6
Sunscreen Lotion

Active Ingredient: Homosalate 8% and oxybenzone 3%.

Indications: Sunscreen to help prevent sunburn. SHADE Sunscreen Lotion 6 provides 6 times your natural sunburn protection. For allover application or for spot use on unprotected areas. Liberal and regular use may help reduce chances

of premature aging and wrinkling of the skin, and skin cancer, due to long-term overexposure to sun.

Actions: Sunscreen.

Warnings: Avoid contact with eyes or mouth. Discontinue use if signs of irritation or rash appear.

Dosage and Administration: Apply evenly and liberally to exposed skin. Reapply after swimming or exercise.

How Supplied: In plastic bottles of 4- and 8-fl. ozs.
[*Shown in Product Identification Section*]

SHADE PLUS™
Sun Protection Factor 8
Water Resistant Sunscreen Lotion

Active Ingredients: 7% Padimate 0 and 3% oxybenzone.

Indications: For maximal protection in and out of the water. SHADE PLUS provides 8 times your natural sunburn protection. Provides maximal sunburn protection for people with sun-sensitive skin. Excellent for use on children. Liberal and regular use may help reduce chances of premature aging and wrinkling of skin, and skin cancer, due to long-term overexposure to sun.

Actions: Sunscreen.

Dosage and Administration: Apply evenly and liberally to exposed skin. To insure maximum protection, reapply after swimming or exercise.

How Supplied: 4 fl. oz. plastic bottles.
[*Shown in Product Identification Section*]

SOLARCAINE®
Antiseptic · Topical Anesthetic
Lotion/Cream/Aerosol Spray Liquid

Active Ingredients:
SOLARCAINE Aerosol Spray—to deliver benzocaine 9.4% (w/w), triclosan 0.18% (w/w). Also contains isopropyl alcohol 24% (w/w) in total contents.
SOLARCAINE Lotion—Benzocaine and triclosan.
SOLARCAINE Cream—Benzocaine and triclosan.

Indications: Medicated first aid to provide fast temporary relief of sunburn pain, minor burns, cuts, scrapes, chapping and skin injuries, poison ivy, detergent hands, insect bites (non-venomous).

Actions: Benzocaine provides local anesthetic action to relieve itching and pain. Triclosan provides antimicrobial activity.

Caution: Not for use in eyes. Not for deep or puncture wounds or serious burns, nor for prolonged use. If condition persists, or infection, rash or irritation develops, discontinue use.

Age	Weight	Dosage
Under 2 years	below 27 lbs.	As directed by Physician.
2 to under 6 yrs.	27 to 45 lbs.	1 teaspoonful every 6 to 8 hours. (Not to exceed 4 teaspoonfuls daily.)
6 to under 12 yrs.	46 to 83 lbs.	2 teaspoonfuls every 6 to 8 hours. (Not to exceed 8 teaspoonfuls daily.)
12 years and older	84 and greater	4 teaspoonfuls every 6 to 8 hours. (Not to exceed 16 teaspoonfuls daily.)

Warnings: For Aerosol Spray—Flammable—Do not spray while smoking or near fire. Do not spray into eyes or mouth. Avoid inhalation. Contents under pressure. For external use only.

Dosage and Administration: Lotion and Cream—Apply freely as needed. Spray—Hold 3 to 5 inches from injured area. Spray until wet. To apply to face, spray on palm of hand. Use often for antiseptic protection.

How Supplied:
SOLARCAINE Aerosol Spray—3- and 5-oz. cans.
SOLARCAINE Lotion—3- and 6-fl oz. bottles.
SOLARCAINE Cream—1- and 2-oz. tubes.
[*Shown in Product Identification Section*]

SUPER SHADE®
Sun Protection Factor 15
Sunblocking Sunscreen Lotion

Active Ingredients: 7% Padimate 0 and 3% oxybenzone.

Indications: Sunscreen to help prevent sunburn. SUPER SHADE Sunblocking Lotion 15 provides 15 times your natural sunburn protection. Provides the highest degree of sunburn protection for allover application or spot use on face, shoulders, etc. Liberal and regular use may help reduce chances of premature aging and wrinkling of skin, and skin cancer, due to long-term overexposure to sun. Contains no drying alcohol, no parabens. Virtually non-staining, does not sting skin.

Actions: Sunscreen.

Warnings: Avoid contact with eyes or mouth. Discontinue use if signs of irritation or rash appear.

Dosage and Administration: Apply evenly and liberally to exposed skin. Resists removal by perspiration and water, but to insure maximum protection, reapply after swimming or exercise.

How Supplied: 4 fl. oz. and 8 fl. oz. Squeeze Bottle.
[*Shown in Product Identification Section*]

Wm. P. Poythress & Co. Incorporated
16 N. 22nd ST.
POST OFFICE BOX 26946
RICHMOND, VA 23261

BENSULFOID® LOTION

Composition: A greaseless, cosmetic lotion containing Bensulfoid, 6% (a fusion of finely divided sulfur, 33% by weight, onto colloidal bentonite); methyl salicylate 5%; thymol, 0.5%; zinc oxide, 6%; alcohol, 12% by volume. Preservative: 0.1%.

Action and Uses: For the topical treatment of acne. Bensulfoid Lotion massages into the skin, penetrating the epidermal layer and exerting keratolytic, germicidal and fungicidal actions on the acne lesions. The effectiveness of the lotion is greatly enhanced by this penetration into the pores and therefore it need

not be applied but once a day. When used as directed there is no evidence of medication on the skin. Bensulfoid Lotion may be used as a cosmetic base.

Method of Application: Wash gently each morning and evening with soap and warm water, and after drying skin apply the lotion. With a finger tip gently massage Bensulfoid Lotion into the skin a little at a time until completely absorbed, using the smallest amount that will cover the acne area. Conspicuous blemishes may be retouched for the sake of appearance. Bensulfoid Lotion can be used regularly or intermittently as needed.

Precautions: If chapping occurs, discontinue for a few days. If undue skin irritation develops or increases, discontinue use and consult physician. Avoid getting into the eyes. Contact with blond, white or red hair may cause temporary discoloration. Persons with sensitive skins may experience a transient warming or smarting sensation.

How Supplied: In 2-ounce bottles.
Literature Available: Yes.

PANALGESIC

Composition: Methyl salicylate, 50%; aspirin, 8%; menthol and camphor, 4%; emollient oils, 20%; alcohol, 18% by weight.

Action and Uses: Panalgesic, an external application for relief of superficial aches and pains, supplies salicylates in the proper environment for maximum skin absorption, producing counterirritation, analgesia, local anesthesia, and asepsis. Panalgesic lessens the discomfort of muscular fatigue, and of trauma, and increases the blood level of salicylate by dermal absorption.

Method of Application: Apply externally to affected area with a gentle massage 3 or 4 times daily.

Warning: Do not use otherwise than as directed. Keep out of reach of children to avoid accidental poisoning. Discontinue use if excessive irritation of the skin develops. Avoid getting into eyes or on mucous membrane.

How Supplied: 4-ounce; 1-pint; one-half gallon bottles.

Procter & Gamble
P. O. BOX 171
CINCINNATI, OH 45201

HEAD & SHOULDERS® Shampoo
Antidandruff Shampoo

Active Ingredient: 2.0% pyrithione zinc suspended in an anionic detergent system. Cosmetic ingredients are also included.

Indications: For effective control of dandruff and seborrheic dermatitis of the scalp.

Actions: Pyrithione zinc is substantive to the scalp and remains after rinsing, allowing for therapeutic action until subsequent shampooing.

Precautions: Not to be taken internally. Keep out of children's reach. Avoid getting shampoo in eyes—if this happens, rinse eyes with water.

Dosage and Administration: Frequency of usage is dependent on severity of scalp condition. Results from clinical testing recommend a minimum of four shampooings before full antiseborrheic effectiveness should be expected. Head & Shoulders is gentle enough to use for every shampoo.

How Supplied: Lotion form available in 4.0 fl. oz., 7.0 fl. oz., 11.0 fl. oz., and 15.0 fl. oz. unbreakable plastic bottles. Cream form available in 2.5 oz., 4.0 oz., and 7.0 oz. tubes.

Composition: LOTION—Regular Formula: Pyrithione zinc in a shampoo base of water, TEA-lauryl sulfate, cocamide MEA, triethanolamine, magnesium aluminum silicate, hydroxypropyl methylcellulose, fragrance, FD&C Green No. 3, and D&C Green No. 5. LOTION—Conditioning Formula: Pyrithione zinc in a shampoo base of water, TEA-lauryl sulfate, triethanolamine, coconut acid, cocamide MEA, magnesium aluminum silicate, hydroxypropyl methylcellulose, fragrance, FD&C Green No. 3., and D&C Green No. 5. CREAM—Regular Formula ONLY: Pyrithione zinc in a shampoo base of water, sodium cocoglyceryl ether sulfonate, sodium chloride, sodium lauroyl sarcosinate, cocamide DEA, cocoyl sarcosine, fragrance, FD&C Green No. 3, and D&C Green No. 5.

SCOPE®
Oral Rinse

Description: Scope is an oral rinse, green in color, with a pleasant tasting, fresh wintergreen flavor. It has a low surface tension, approximately ½ that of water. Scope refreshes the mouth and leaves it feeling clean.

Composition: Cetylpyridinium chloride (.045%), domiphen bromide (.005%) and SD alcohol 38F (18.5%) in a mouthwash base of water, glycerin, polysorbate 80, flavor, sodium saccharin, FD&C Blue No. 1 and FD&C Yellow No. 5.

Consumer Use: For mouth refreshment and as an aid to daily oral care. Scope also helps provide soothing, temporary relief of dryness and minor irritations of the mouth and throat.

Dental Office Use: Scope is used before, during and after instrumentation and dental prophylaxis in the interest of enhancing patient comfort, as well as to provide dentists with a more pleasant working environment. Scope's low surface tension also makes it ideal for preparing oral surfaces for impressions. A pre-impression rinse with Scope helps remove debris and ropy saliva from the oral cavity. It is also used for mouth freshening after taking impressions. Scope is guaranteed not to clog dental spray units (it contains no sugar).

Consumer Usage Instructions: Rinse or gargle for 20 seconds with one ounce of Scope first thing in the morning, after

Continued on next page

Procter & Gamble—Cont.

meals or when needed for mouth refreshment.

Consumer Precautions: Keep out of reach of children. Do not administer to any child under six years of age. Any sore throat may be serious; consult your doctor promptly.

Dental Office Precautions: Keep out of reach of children. Not to be used undiluted. Because of high alcohol content, avoid contact with eyes and ingestion of the undiluted concentrate.

How Supplied: Scope is supplied to consumers in 6, 12, 18, 24 and 40 fl. oz. bottles and is available to the dental profession in a one gallon concentrate (each gallon makes 3.5 gallons of regular Scope). A pump attachment for the gallon container, 18 oz. operatory decanters and a spray attachment for the decanter are available for office use.

The Purdue Frederick Company
50 WASHINGTON STREET NORWALK, CT 06856

BETADINE® SOLUTION
(povidone-iodine 10%)
Topical antiseptic, germicide

Action and Uses: For preoperative prepping of operative site, including the vagina, and as a general topical microbicide for: disinfection of wounds; emergency treatment of lacerations and abrasions; second– and third–degree burns; as a prophylactic anti-infective agent in hospital and office procedures, including postoperative application to incisions to help prevent infection; trichomonal, monilial, and nonspecific infectious vaginitis; oral moniliasis (thrush); bacterial and mycotic skin infections; decubitus and stasis ulcers; preoperatively, in the mouth and throat, as a swab. BETADINE Solution is microbicidal, and not merely bacteriostatic. It *kills* gram-positive and gram-negative bacteria (including antibiotic-resistant strains), fungi, viruses, protozoa and yeasts.

Administration: Apply full strength as often as needed as a paint, spray, or wet soak. May be bandaged. In preoperative prepping, avoid "pooling" beneath the patient.

How Supplied: ½ oz., 8 oz., 16 oz. (1 pt.), 32 oz. (1 qt.) and 1 gal. plastic bottles and 1 oz. packettes.

Also Available: BETADINE SOLUTION SWAB AIDS for degerming small areas of skin or mucous membranes prior to injections, aspirations, catheterization and surgery; boxes of 100 packettes. Also: disposable BETADINE SOLUTION SWABSTICKS, in packettes of 1's and 3's.

[*Shown in Product Identification Section*]

BETADINE® DOUCHE
(povidone-iodine)

A pleasantly scented solution, clinically effective in nonspecific infectious vaginitis and against vaginal moniliasis and *Trichomonas vaginalis* vaginitis. Also effective as a cleansing douche.

Advantages: Low surface tension, with uniform wetting action to assist penetration into vaginal crypts and crevices. Active in the presence of blood, pus, or vaginal secretions. Virtually nonirritating to vaginal mucosa. Will not stain skin or natural fabrics.

Directions for Use: As a Therapeutic Douche: Two (2) tablespoonfuls to a quart of lukewarm water once daily. As a Routine Cleansing Douche: One (1) tablespoonful to a quart of lukewarm water once or twice per week.

How Supplied: 1 oz., 8 oz., 1 gallon plastic bottles. Disposable ½ oz. (1 tablespoonful) packettes.

Also Available: BETADINE Douche Kit is supplied as individual units, each containing:

(1) 8 oz. plastic bottle of BETADINE Douche concentrate;
(2) 14 oz., squeezable, plastic syringe bottle;
(3) anatomically-correct cannula;
(4) instruction booklet.

The 8 oz. bottle of BETADINE Douche concentrate is sufficient for up to 40 cleansing douches.

Directions for Use:

As a Therapeutic Douche: Add one (1) tablespoonful of BETADINE Douche concentrate to the 14 oz. syringe bottle which is then filled to the top with lukewarm water. Douche, then repeat the procedure. For daily use.

As a Routine Cleansing Douche: Add BETADINE Douche concentrate to FIRST FILL-LINE on syringe bottle. Add lukewarm water up to WATER FILL-LINE. For use once or twice a week.

Also Available: BETADINE® Medicated Douche is a hygienic, **disposable,** convenient method to provide symptomatic relief of minor vaginal soreness, irritation, itching.

BETADINE Medicated Douche is supplied as individual units, each containing:

(1) 0.18 fl. oz. (5.2 ml) BETADINE Douche Concentrate;
(2) 6 fl. oz. (177 ml) of sanitized water in a squeezable, plastic syringe bottle with nozzle (when mixed, a 0.25% solution of povidone-iodine is formed);
(3) instruction booklet.

The syringe bottle and nozzle are completely disposable to avoid contamination from previously used douche accessories. Also supplied in a "Twin Pack."

[*Shown in Product Identification Section*]

BETADINE® SKIN CLEANSER
(povidone-iodine)

BETADINE Skin Cleanser is a sudsing antiseptic liquid cleanser. It essentially retains the nonselective microbicidal action of iodine, yet virtually without the undesirable features associated with iodine. BETADINE Skin Cleanser kills gram-positive and gram-negative bacteria (including antibiotic-resistant strains), fungi, viruses, protozoa and yeasts. It forms a rich golden lather; virtually nonirritating; nonstaining to skin and natural fabrics.

Indications: BETADINE Skin Cleanser aids in degerming the skin of patients with common pathogens, including Staphylococcus aureus. To help prevent the recurrence of acute inflammatory skin infections caused by iodine-susceptible pyogenic bacteria. In pyodermas, as a topical adjunct to systemic antimicrobial therapy. To help prevent spread of infection in acne pimples.

Directions for Use: Wet the skin and apply a sufficient amount of Skin Cleanser to work up a rich golden lather. Allow lather to remain about 3 minutes. Then rinse. Repeat 2-3 times a day or as needed.

Caution: In rare instances of local sensitivity, discontinue use by the individual.

How Supplied: 1 fl. oz. and 4 fl. oz. plastic bottles.

Note: Blue stains on starched linen will wash off with soap and water.

[*Shown in Product Identification Section*]

BETADINE® OINTMENT
(povidone-iodine)

Action: BETADINE Ointment, in a water-soluble base, is a topical agent active against organisms commonly encountered in skin and wound infections. BETADINE Ointment kills gram-positive and gram-negative bacteria (including antibiotic-resistant strains), fungi, viruses, protozoa and yeasts.

The broad-spectrum activity of BETADINE Ointment provides microbicidal action against most commonly occurring skin bacteria. Its range of antibacterial activity encompasses many bacteria—including antibiotic-resistant forms.

The active ingredient in BETADINE Ointment substantially retains the broad-spectrum germicidal activity of iodine without the undesirable features or disadvantages of iodine. BETADINE Ointment is virtually nonirritating, does not block air from reaching the site of application, and washes easily off skin and natural fabrics. The site to which BETADINE Ointment is applied can be bandaged.

Indications: Therapeutically, BETADINE Ointment may be used as an adjunct to systemic therapy where indicated; for primary or secondary topical infections caused by iodine-susceptible organisms such as infected burns, infected surgical incisions, infected decubitus or stasis ulcers, pyodermas, secondarily infected dermatoses, and infected traumatic lesions.

Prophylactically: BETADINE Ointment may be used to prevent microbial contamination in burns, incisions and other topical lesions; for degerming skin in hyperalimentation, catheter care, the umbilical area or circumcision. The use of BETADINE Ointment for abrasions, minor cuts, and wounds, may prevent the development of infections and permit wound healing.

Administration: Apply directly to affected area as needed. May be bandaged.

How Supplied: $^1/_{32}$ oz. and $^1/_8$ oz. packettes; 1 oz. tubes; 16 oz. (1 lb.) and 5 lb. jars.

FIBERMED™
High–Fiber Supplements

Description: FIBERMED High-Fiber Supplements provide a uniform, measured quantity of natural dietary fiber with precision in a palatable, ready-to-eat form. Each FIBERMED Supplement contains 5.0 grams of dietary fiber—supplied by corn, wheat and oats.

FIBERMED overcomes problems associated with other fiber-containing products—problems such as variable fiber content, inconvenience and monotonous taste. FIBERMED Supplements are exceptional among high-fiber products because of their convenience and good taste, qualities which encourage good compliance. Ready-to-eat FIBERMED Supplements can be eaten anytime, anyplace. They can be eaten with milk, coffee, tea, juice, soup or fruit; or dunked in a beverage. As with any healthful diet, drinking adequate fluids is important. FIBERMED Supplements (only 60 calories per supplement) are satisfying and help reduce the desire for snacks and desserts that are highly caloric.

Ingredients: Corn Bran, Brown Sugar, Wheat Flour, Corn Starch, Wheat Bran, Oat Flakes, Corn Germ Meal, Vegetable Shortening (Partially Hydrogenated Soybean Oil), Sodium Bicarbonate, Vanilla Flavor, Peanut Butter Flavor, Ammonium Bicarbonate, Baking Acid, Sodium Propionate, Salt and Citric Acid.

Nutrition Information Per Serving:

Serving Size	1 supplement
Servings per package	14
Calories	60
Protein	1 g
Carbohydrate	14 g*
Fat	2 g

Percentage of U.S. Recommended Daily Allowances (% U.S. RDA):

Riboflavin (Vitamin B$_2$)	2
Niacin	2
Iron	4

Contains less than 2% of the U.S. RDA of Protein, Vitamin A, Vitamin C, Thiamine and Calcium.

*Includes 4.6 g of simple carbohydrates (brown sugar) and 9.4 g of complex carbohydrates.

Usage: Dietary fiber, as contained in FIBERMED, increases the softness and size of stools and regulates the time required for food wastes to travel through the gastrointestinal tract.

Because of its influence on gastrointestinal function, dietary fiber may be beneficial in disorders related to the consistency of stools and to gastrointestinal transit time. Diverticular disease, hiatus hernia, hemorrhoids and irritable bowel syndrome are among such disorders involving digestive functions that a diet high in fiber can benefit. (This data is presented solely as background information on the effect of fiber on gastrointestinal function.)

FIBERMED Supplements are indicated when it is desirable to regulate gastrointestinal transit time and to increase stool weight. Because of their taste and convenience, FIBERMED Supplements are the product of choice to significantly increase intake of dietary fiber in uniform amounts.

Two FIBERMED Supplements a day provide a high level of dietary fiber—10 grams—more dietary fiber than a serving of high-fiber cereal.

Supplied: FIBERMED Supplements are supplied in boxes of 14. For most individuals, 14 is a week's supply.

[*Shown in Product Identification Section*]

SENOKOT® TABLETS/GRANULES
(standardized senna concentrate)

Action and Uses: Indicated for relief of functional constipation (chronic or occasional). SENOKOT Tablets/Granules contain a natural vegetable derivative, purified and standardized for uniform action. The current theory of the mechanism of action is that glycosides are transported to the colon, where they are changed to aglycones that stimulate Auerbach's plexus to induce peristalsis. This virtually colon-specific action is gentle, effective and predictable, usually inducing comfortable evacuation of well-formed stool within 8-10 hours. Found effective even in many previously intractable cases of functional constipation, SENOKOT preparations may aid in rehabilitation of the constipated patient by facilitating regular elimination. At proper dosage levels, SENOKOT preparations are virtually free of adverse reactions (such as loose stools or abdominal discomfort) and enjoy high patient acceptance. Numerous and extensive clinical studies show their high degree of effectiveness in varieties of functional constipation: chronic, geriatric, antepartum and postpartum, drug-induced, and pediatric, as well as in functional constipation concurrent with heart disease or anorectal surgery.

Contraindications: Acute surgical abdomen.

Administration and Dosage: Preferably at bedtime. GRANULES (deliciously cocoa-flavored): Adults: 1 level tsp. (maximum—2 level tsp. b.i.d.). For older, debilitated, and OB/GYN patients, the physician may consider prescribing ½ the initial adult dose. Children above 60 lb.: ½ level tsp. (maximum—1 level tsp. b.i.d.). TABLETS: Adults: 2 tablets (maximum—4 tablets b.i.d.). For older, debilitated, and OB/-GYN patients, the physician may consider prescribing ½ the initial dose. Children above 60 lb.: 1 tablet (maximum—2 tablets b.i.d.). To meet individual requirements, if comfortable bowel movement is not achieved by the second day, decrease or increase dosage daily by ½ level tsp. or 1 tablet (up to maximum) until optimal dose for evacuation is established.

How Supplied: Granules: 2, 6, and 12 oz. plastic canisters. Tablets: Box of 20, bottles of 50 and 100.
SENOKOT Tablets Unit Strip Packs in boxes of 100 tablets; each tablet individually sealed in see-through pockets.

[*Shown in Product Identification Section*]

SENOKOT®-S
(docusate sodium and standardized senna concentrate)
Stool Softener/Natural Laxative Combination

Action and Uses: SENOKOT-S Tablets are designed to relieve both aspects of functional constipation—dry, hard stools and bowel inertia. They provide a classic stool softener combined with a natural neuroperistaltic stimulant: docusate sodium softens the stool for smoother and easier evacuation, while standardized senna concentrate gently stimulates Auerbach's plexus in the colonic wall. This coordinated dual action of the two ingredients results in colon-specific, predictable laxative effect, usually in 8–10 hours. Administering the tablets at bedtime allows the patient an uninterrupted night's sleep, with a comfortable evacuation in the morning. Flexibility of dosage permits fine adjustment to individual requirements. At proper dosage levels, SENOKOT-S Tablets are virtually free from side effects. SENOKOT-S Tablets are highly suitable for relief of postsurgical and postpartum constipation, and effectively counteract drug-induced constipation. They facilitate regular elimination in impaction-prone and elderly patients, and are indicated in the presence of cardiovascular disease where straining must be avoided, as well as in the presence of hemorrhoids and anorectal disease.

Contraindications: Acute surgical abdomen.

Administration and Dosage: (preferably at bedtime) Recommended Initial Dosage: ADULTS—2 tablets (maximum dosage—4 tablets b.i.d.); CHILDREN (above 60 lbs.)—1 tablet (maximum dosage—2 tablets b.i.d.). For older or debilitated patients, the physician may consider prescribing half the initial adult dose. To meet individual requirements, if comfortable bowel movement is not achieved by the second day, dosage may be decreased or increased by 1 tablet, up to maximum, until the most effective dose is established.

Supplied: Bottles of 30 and 60 Tablets.
[*Shown in Product Identification Section*]

Reed & Carnrick
**1 NEW ENGLAND AVENUE
PISCATAWAY, NJ 08854**

R&C SPRAY™ Lice Control Insecticide

Description: Active ingredients: 3-Phenoxybenzyl d-cis and trans 2,2-dimethyl-3-(2-methylpropenyl)

cyclopropanecarboxylate	0.382%
Other Isomers	0.018%
Petroleum Distillates	4.255%
Inert Ingredients:	95.345%

	100.000%

Actions: R&C SPRAY is specially formulated to kill lice and their nits on inanimate objects.

Continued on next page

Reed & Carnrick—Cont.

Indications: R&C SPRAY is recommended for use only on bedding, mattresses, furniture and other objects infested or possibly infested with lice which cannot be laundered or dry cleaned.

Warnings: Contents under pressure. Do not use or store near heat or open flame. Do not puncture or incinerate container. Exposure to temperatures above 130°F may cause bursting. It is a violation of Federal law to use this product in a manner inconsistent with its labeling. NOT FOR USE ON HUMANS OR ANIMALS.

Caution: Avoid spraying in eyes. Avoid breathing spray mist. Avoid contact with the skin. In case of contact, wash immediately with soap and water. Harmful if swallowed. Vacate room after treatment and ventilate before reoccupying. Avoid contamination of feed and foodstuffs. Remove pets, birds and cover fish aquariums before spraying.

Directions: SHAKE WELL BEFORE AND OCCASIONALLY DURING USE. Spray on an inconspicuous area to test for possible staining or discoloration. Inspect after drying, then proceed to spray entire area to be treated.

Hold container upright with nozzle away from you. Depress valve and spray from a distance of 8 to 10 inches.

Spray each square foot for about three seconds. For mattresses, furniture, or similar objects (that cannot be laundered or dry cleaned): Spray thoroughly. Do not use article until spray is dry. Repeat treatment as necessary. Do not use in commercial food processing, preparation, storage or serving areas.

How Supplied: In 5 oz. aerosol container.

EPA REG NO   36232-2
EPA EST NO   (C) 11598-CT-1
                 (D) 11525-RI-1

Requa Manufacturing Company, Inc.
1 SENECA PLACE
GREENWICH, CT 06830

CHARCOCAPS®
Activated Charcoal Capsules

Active Ingredient: Activated vegetable charcoal U.S.P., 260 mg per capsule

Indications: Relief of intestinal gas, diarrhea, gastrointestinal distress associated with indigestion. Also for the prevention of non-specific pruritus associated with kidney dialysis treatment.

Actions: Adsorbent, detoxicant, soothing agent. Reduces the volume of intestinal gas and allays related discomfort.

Warnings: As with all anti-diarrheals—not for children under 3 unless directed by physician. If diarrhea persists more than two days or is accompanied by high fever, consult physician.

Drug Interaction: Activated Charcoal USP can adsorb medication while they are in digestive tract.

Precaution: Take two hours before or one hour after medication including oral contraceptives.

Symptoms and Treatment of Oral Overdosage: Overdosage has not been encountered. Medical evidence indicates that high dosage or prolonged use does not cause side effect or harm the nutritional state of the patient.

Dosage and Administration: Two capsules after meals or at first sign of discomfort. Repeat as needed up to eight doses (16 capsules) per day.

Professional Labeling: None.

How Supplied: Bottles of 36 capsules [*Shown in Product Identification Section*]

A. H. Robins Company, Inc.
CONSUMER PRODUCTS DIVISION
3800 CUTSHAW AVENUE
RICHMOND, VIRGINIA 23230

ALLBEE® C–800 TABLETS
ALLBEE® C–800 plus IRON TABLETS

Allbee C-800

One tablet daily provides:	Percentage of U.S. Recommended Daily Allowances (U.S. RDA)	
Vitamin E	150	45 I.U.
Vitamin C	1333	800 mg
Thiamine (Vitamin B$_1$)	1000	15 mg
Riboflavin (Vitamin B$_2$)	1000	17 mg
Niacin	500	100 mg
Vitamin B$_6$	1250	25 mg
Vitamin B$_{12}$	200	12 mcg
Pantothenic Acid	250	25 mg

Ingredients: Ascorbic Acid, Niacinamide, Starch, Vitamin E Acetate, Hydrolyzed Protein, Calcium Pantothenate, Artificial Color, Pyridoxine Hydrochloride, Hydroxypropyl Methylcellulose, Riboflavin, Stearic Acid, Povidone, Thiamine Mononitrate, Silicon Dioxide, Ethylcellulose, Propylene Glycol, Lactose, Magnesium Stearate, Polysorbate 20, Vanillin, Gelatin, Sorbic Acid, Sodium Benzoate, Cyanocobalamin.

Allbee C-800 plus Iron

One tablet daily provides:	Percentage of U.S. Recommended Daily Allowances (U.S. RDA)	
Vitamin Composition		
Vitamin E	150	45.0 I.U.
Vitamin C	1333	800.0 mg
Folic Acid	100	0.4 mg
Thiamine (Vitamin B$_1$)	1000	15.0 mg
Riboflavin (Vitamin B$_2$)	1000	17.0 mg
Niacin	500	100.0 mg
Vitamin B$_6$	1250	25.0 mg
Vitamin B$_{12}$	200	12.0 mcg
Pantothenic Acid	250	25.0 mg
Mineral Composition		
Iron	150	27.0 mg

Ingredients: Ascorbic Acid, Niacinamide, Ferrous Fumarate, Starch, Vitamin E Acetate, Hydrolyzed Protein, Calcium Pantothenate, Artificial Color, Pyridoxine Hydrochloride, Hydroxypropyl Methylcellulose, Povidone, Riboflavin, Stearic Acid, Thiamine Mononitrate, Silicon Dioxide, Ethylcellulose, Propylene Glycol, Lactose, Magnesium Stearate, Polysorbate 20, Vanillin, Gelatin, Folic Acid, Sorbic Acid, Sodium Benzoate, Cyanocobalamin.

Actions and Uses: The components of Allbee C-800 have important roles in general nutrition, healing of wounds, and prevention of hemorrhage. Allbee C-800 is recommended for nutritional supplementation of these components in conditions such as febrile diseases, chronic or acute infections, burns, fractures, surgery, physiologic stress, alcoholism, prolonged exposure to high temperature, geriatrics, gastritis, peptic ulcer, and colitis; and in weight-reduction and other special diets.

In dentistry, Allbee C-800 is recommended for nutritional supplementation of its components in conditions such as herpetic stomatitis, aphthous stomatitis, cheilosis, herpangina and gingivitis.

In addition, Allbee C-800 Plus Iron is recommended as a nutritional source of iron. The iron is present as ferrous fumarate, a well-tolerated salt. The ascorbic acid in the formulation enhances the absorption of iron.

Precautions: Do not take Allbee C-800 Plus Iron within two hours of oral tetracycline antibiotics, since oral iron products interfere with absorption of tetracycline. Not intended for treatment of iron-deficiency anemia.

Adverse Reactions: Iron-containing medications may occasionally cause gastrointestinal discomfort, nausea, constipation or diarrhea.

Dosage: The recommended OTC dosage for adults and children twelve or more years of age is one tablet daily. Under the direction and supervision of a physician, the dose and frequency of administration may be increased in accordance with the patient's requirements.

How Supplied: Allbee C-800—orange, film-coated, elliptically-shaped tablets in bottles of 60 (NDC 0031-0677-62). Allbee C-800 Plus Iron—red, film-coated, elliptically-shaped tablets in bottles of 60 (NDC 0031-0678-62).

[*Shown in Product Identification Section*]

ALLBEE® WITH C CAPSULES

One capsule daily provides:	Percentage of U.S. Recommended Daily Allowance (U.S. RDA)	
Vitamin C	500	300.0 mg
Thiamine (Vitamin B$_1$)	1000	15.0 mg
Riboflavin (Vitamin B$_2$)	600	10.2 mg
Niacin	250	50.0 mg
Vitamin B$_6$	250	5.0 mg
Pantothenic Acid	100	10.0 mg

Ingredients: Ascorbic Acid; Gelatin; Niacinamide; Lactose; Corn Starch; Thiamine Mononitrate; Calcium Pantothenate; Riboflavin; Magnesium Stearate; Pyridoxine Hydrochloride; Light Mineral Oil; FD&C Yellow No. 5; Vanillin; Artificial Color.

Action and Uses: Allbee with C is a high potency formulation of B and C vitamins. Its components have important roles in general nutrition, healing of wounds, and prevention of hemorrhage. It is recommended for deficiencies of B-vitamins and ascorbic acid in conditions such as febrile diseases, chronic or acute infections, burns, fractures, surgery, toxic conditions, physiologic stress, alcoholism, prolonged exposure to high temperature, geriatrics, gastritis, peptic ulcer, and colitis; and in conditions involving special diets and weight-reduction diets.

In dentistry, Allbee with C is recommended for deficiencies of B-vitamins and ascorbic acid in conditions such as herpetic stomatitis, aphthous stomatitis, cheilosis, herpangina, gingivitis.

Precaution: This product contains FD&C Yellow No. 5 (tartrazine) which may cause allergic-type reactions (including bronchial asthma) in certain susceptible individuals. Although the overall incidence of FD&C Yellow No. 5 (tartrazine) sensitivity in the general population is low, it is frequently seen in patients who have aspirin hypersensitivity.

Dosage: The recommended OTC dosage for adults and children twelve or more years of age, other than pregnant or lactating women, is one capsule daily. Under the direction and supervision of a physician, the dose and frequency of administration may be increased in accordance with the patient's requirements.

How Supplied: Yellow and green capsules, monogrammed AHR and 0674, in bottles of 30 (NDC 0031-0674-56), 100 (NDC 0031-0674-63), 1,000 capsules (NDC 0031-0674-74) and in Dis-Co® Unit Dose Packs of 100 (NDC 0031-0674-64).

[*Shown in Product Identification Section*]

CHAP STICK® Lip Balm

Active Ingredients: 44% Petrolatums, 1.5% Padimate O (2-ethyl-hexyl p-dimethylaminobenzoate, 1% Lanolin, 1% Isopropyl Myristate, .5% Cetyl Alcohol.

Indications: Aids prevention and healing of dry, chapped, sun and windburned lips.

Actions: A specially designed lipid complex hydrophobic base containing Padimate O which forms a barrier to prevent moisture loss and protect lips from the drying effects of cold weather, wind and sun which cause chapping. The special emollients soften the skin by forming an occlusive film thus inducing hydration, restoring suppleness to the lips, and preventing drying from evaporation of water that diffuses to the surface from the underlying layers of tissue. Chap Stick also protects the skin from the external environment and its sunscreen offers protection from exposure to the sun.

Warning: Discontinue use if signs of irritation appear.

Symptoms and Treatment of Oral Ingestion: The oral LD_{50} in rats is greater than 5 gm/kg. There have been no reported overdoses in humans. There are no known symptoms of overdosage.

Dosage and Treatment: For dry, chapped lips apply as needed. To help prevent dry, chapped sun or windburned lips, apply to lips as needed before, during and following exposure to sun, wind, water and cold weather.

Professional Labeling: None.

How Supplied: Available in 4.25 gm tubes in Regular, Mint, Cherry, Orange, Grape, Lemon-Lime, and Strawberry flavors.

[*Shown in Product Identification Section*]

CHAP STICK® SUNBLOCK 15
Lip Balm

Active Ingredients: 44% Petrolatums, 7% Padimate O, 3% Oxybenzone, 0.5% Lanolin, 0.5% Isopropyl Myristate, 0.5% Cetyl Alcohol.

Indications: Ultra Sunscreen Protection (SPF-15). Aids prevention and healing of dry, chapped, sun and windburned lips. Overexposure to sun may lead to premature aging of skin and lip cancer. Liberal and regular use may help reduce the sun's harmful effects.

Actions: Ultra sunscreen protection for the lips, plus the attributes of Chap Stick® Lip Balm. The emollients in the specially-designed lipid complex hydrophobic base soften the lips by forming an occlusive film while the two sunscreens have specific ultraviolet absorption ranges which overlap to offer ultra sunscreen protection (SPF-15).

Warning: Discontinue use if signs of irritation appear.

Symptoms and Treatment of Oral Ingestion: Toxicity studies indicate this product to be extremely safe. The oral LD_{50} in rats is greater than 5 gm./kg. There are no known symptoms of overdosage.

Dosage and Treatment: For ultra sunscreen protection, apply evenly and liberally to lips before exposure to sun. Reapply as needed. For dry, chapped lips, apply as needed. To help prevent dry, chapped, sun, and windburned lips, apply to lips as needed before, during, and following exposure to sun, wind, water, and cold weather.

How Supplied: 4.25 gm. tube.

[*Shown in Product Identification Section*]

DIMACOL® CAPSULES

Composition: Each capsule contains:
Guaifenesin, USP ....100 mg
Pseudoephedrine
  Hydrochloride, USP ....30 mg
Dextromethorphan
  Hydrobromide, USP ....15 mg

Actions: Dimacol helps reduce nasal congestion and suppresses cough associated with the common cold and other upper respiratory disorders.

Guaifenesin enhances the output of lower respiratory tract fluid. The enhanced flow of less viscid secretions promotes ciliary action, and facilitates the removal of inspissated mucus. As a result, dry unproductive coughs become more productive and less frequent. *Pseudoephedrine hydrochloride* is an orally effective nasal decongestant. Through its vasoconstrictor action, pseudoephedrine gently but promptly reduces edema and congestion of nasal passages. *Dextromethorphan hydrobromide* is a synthetic, non-narcotic cough suppressant. The antitussive effectiveness of dextromethorphan has been demonstrated in both animal and clinical studies, and the incidence of toxic effects has been remarkably low.

Indications: Dimacol is indicated for the management of cough accompanied by nasal mucosal congestion and edema, and nasal hypersecretion, associated with the common cold, upper respiratory infection and sinusitis.

Contraindications: Hypersensitivity to any of the ingredients. Dimacol should not be administered to patients receiving MAO inhibitors.

Precautions: Administer with caution in the presence of hypertension, heart disease, peripheral vascular disease, diabetes or hyperthyroidism. As with all products containing sympathomimetic amines, use with caution in patients with prostatic hypertrophy or glaucoma.

Note: Guaifenesin has been shown to produce a color interference with certain clinical laboratory determinations of 5-hydroxyindoleacetic acid (5-HIAA) and vanilmandelic acid (VMA).

Adverse Reactions: The following adverse reactions may possibly occur: nausea, vomiting, dry mouth, nervousness, insomnia.

Dosage and Administration: Adults and children over 12 years of age, one capsule three times a day.

How Supplied: Orange and green capsules in bottles of 100 (NDC 0031-1650-63), and 500 (NDC 0031-1650-70) and consumer packages of 12 (NDC 0031-1650-46) and 24 (NDC 0031-1650-54) (individually packaged).

[*Shown in Product Identification Section*]

DIMETANE®
brand of Brompheniramine Maleate, USP
Tablets—4 mg
Elixir—2 mg/5 ml
  Alcohol, 3%

Actions: Brompheniramine maleate is an antihistamine, with anticholinergic (drying) and sedative side effects. Antihistamines appear to compete with histamine for cell receptor sites on effector cells.

Indications: For effective, temporary relief of hay fever/upper respiratory allergy symptoms: itchy, watery eyes; sneezing; itching nose or throat.

Contraindications: *Use in Newborn or Premature Infants.* This drug should

Continued on next page

Prescribing information on A. H. Robins products listed here is based on official labeling in effect December 1, 1981, with Indications, Contraindications, Warnings, Precautions, Adverse Reactions, and Dosage stated in full.

Robins—Cont.

not be used in newborn or premature infants.

Use in Nursing Mothers. Because of the higher risk of antihistamines for infants generally and for newborns and prematures in particular, antihistamine therapy is contraindicated in nursing mothers.

Use in Lower Respiratory Disease. Antihistamines **should NOT** be used to treat lower respiratory tract symptoms including asthma.

This drug is also contraindicated in the following conditions: hypersensitivity to brompheniramine maleate and other antihistamines of similar chemical structure; monoamine oxidase inhibitor therapy (see Drug Interaction section).

Warnings: Antihistamines should be used with considerable caution in patients with: narrow angle glaucoma; stenosing peptic ulcer; pyloroduodenal obstruction; symptomatic prostatic hypertrophy; bladder neck obstruction.

Use in Children. In infants and children, especially, antihistamines in **overdosage** may cause hallucinations, convulsions, or death.

As in adults, antihistamines may diminish mental alertness in children. In the young child, particularly, they may produce excitation.

Use in Pregnancy. Experience with this drug in pregnant women is inadequate to determine whether there exists a potential for harm to the developing fetus.

Use with CNS Depressants. Dimetane has additive effects with alcohol and other CNS depressants (hypnotics, sedatives, tranquilizers, etc.)

Use in Activities Requiring Mental Alertness. Patients should be warned about engaging in activities requiring mental alertness, such as driving a car or operating appliances, machinery, etc.

Use in the Elderly (approximately 60 years or older). Antihistamines are more likely to cause dizziness, sedation, and hypotension in elderly patients.

Precautions: As with other antihistamines, Dimetane has an atropine-like action and, therefore, should be used with caution in patients with: history of bronchial asthma; increased intraocular pressure; hyperthyroidism; cardiovascular disease; hypertension.

Drug Interactions: MAO inhibitors prolong and intensify the anticholinergic (drying) effects of antihistamines.

Adverse Reactions: The most frequent adverse reactions are italicized:

General: Urticaria, drug rash, anaphylactic shock, photosensitivity, excessive perspiration, chills, dryness of mouth, nose, and throat.

Cardiovascular System: Hypotension, headache, palpitations, tachycardia, extrasystoles.

Hematologic System: Hemolytic anemia, thrombocytopenia, agranulocytosis.

Nervous System: Sedation, sleepiness, dizziness, disturbed coordination, fatigue, confusion, restlessness, excitation, nervousness, tremor, irritability, insomnia, euphoria, paresthesias, blurred vision, diplopia, vertigo, tinnitus, acute labyrinthitis, hysteria, neuritis, convulsions.

G.I. System: Epigastric distress, anorexia, nausea, vomiting, diarrhea, constipation.

G.U. System: Urinary frequency, difficult urination, urinary retention, early menses.

Respiratory System: Thickening of bronchial secretions, tightness of chest and wheezing, nasal stuffiness.

Overdosage: Antihistamine overdosage reactions may vary from central nervous system depression to stimulation. Stimulation is particularly likely in children. Atropine-like signs and symptoms—dry mouth; fixed, dilated pupils; flushing; and gastrointestinal symptoms may also occur.

If vomiting has not occurred spontaneously, the patient should be induced to vomit. This is best done by having him drink a glass of water or milk after which he should be made to gag. Precautions against aspiration must be taken, especially in infants and children.

If vomiting is unsuccessful, gastric lavage is indicated within 3 hours after ingestion and even later if large amounts of milk or cream were given beforehand. Isotonic and ½ isotonic saline is the lavage solution of choice.

Saline cathartics, such as milk of magnesia, by osmosis draw water into the bowel and therefore, are valuable for their action in rapid dilution of bowel content.

Stimulants should not be used.

Vasopressors may be used to treat hypotension.

Dosage and Administration: The recommended OTC dosage is:

Adults and children 12 years of age and over: 1 tablet or 2 teaspoonfuls every four to six hours, not to exceed 6 tablets or 12 teaspoonfuls in 24 hours.

Children 6 to under 12 years: ½ tablet or 1 teaspoonful every four to six hours, not to exceed 3 tablets or 6 teaspoonfuls in 24 hours.

Children under 6 years: use as directed by a physician.

Under physician supervision, children 2 to under 6 years: ½ teaspoonful every four to six hours, not to exceed 3 teaspoonfuls in 24 hours.

How Supplied: 4 mg tablets are available as peach-colored, compressed, scored tablets in cartons of 24 individually packaged blister units (NDC 0031-1857-54), and in bottles of 100 (NDC 0031-1857-63) and 500 (NDC 0031-1857-70). 2 mg per 5 ml peach-colored liquid is available in bottles of 4 fl. oz. (NDC 0031-1807-12), 1 pint (NDC 0031-1807-25) and 1 gallon (NDC 0031-1807-29).

[*Shown in Product Identification Section*]

DIMETANE® DECONGESTANT ELIXIR
DIMETANE® DECONGESTANT TABLETS

Elixir:
Each 5 ml (1 teaspoonful) contains:
Phenylephrine
   Hydrochloride, USP ....5 mg
Brompheniramine
   Maleate, USP ....2 mg
Alcohol 2.3 percent

Tablet:
Each tablet contains:
Phenylephrine
   Hydrochloride, USP ....10 mg
Brompheniramine
   Maleate, USP ....4 mg

Indications: For temporary relief of nasal congestion due to the common cold, sinusitis, hay fever or other upper respiratory allergies; runny nose, sneezing, itching of the nose or throat and itchy and watery eyes as may occur in allergic rhinitis (such as hay fever). Temporarily restores freer breathing through the nose.

Contraindications: Hypersensitivity to any of the ingredients; marked hypertension.

Warnings: May cause excitability, especially in children. Use with caution in children under 2 years. Prescribe cautiously for patients with asthma, glaucoma, difficulty in urination due to enlargement of the prostate gland, high blood pressure, heart disease, diabetes or thyroid disease and for patients who are receiving MAO inhibitors or antihypertensive medication. May cause drowsiness. Doses in excess of the recommended dosage may cause nervousness, dizziness or sleeplessness.

Cautions: Patients should be warned about driving a motor vehicle, operating heavy machinery, or consuming alcoholic beverages while taking this product.

Recommended Dosage: *Elixir:* Adults and children 12 years of age and over: 2 teaspoonfuls every 4 hours, not to exceed 12 teaspoonfuls in a 24-hour period; children 6 to under 12 years: 1 teaspoonful every 4 hours, not to exceed 6 teaspoonfuls in a 24-hour period; children 2 to under 6 years: ½ teaspoonful every 4 hours, not to exceed 3 teaspoonfuls in a 24-hour period.

Tablets: Adults and children 12 years of age and over: 1 tablet every 4 hours, not to exceed 6 tablets in a 24-hour period; children 6 to under 12 years: ½ tablet every 4 hours, not to exceed 3 tablets in a 24-hour period.

How Supplied: *Tablets*—light blue, capsule shaped tablets in cartons of 24 (NDC 0031-2117-54) and 48 (NDC 0031-2117-59) individually packaged blister units.

Elixir—red colored, grape flavored liquid in 4 fl. oz. bottle (NDC 0031-2127-12).

[*Shown in Product Identification Section*]

ROBITUSSIN®
ROBITUSSIN–CF®
ROBITUSSIN–DM®
ROBITUSSIN–PE®

Composition: *Robitussin* contains Guaifenesin, USP 100 mg in 5 ml (1 teaspoonful) of palatable aromatic syrup; alcohol 3.5%. *Robitussin-CF* contains in each 5 ml (1 teaspoonful): Guaifenesin, USP 100 mg, Phenylpropanolamine Hydrochloride, USP 12.5 mg, Dextromethorphan Hydrobromide, USP 10 mg; alcohol 4.75%. *Robitussin-DM* contains in each 5 ml (1 teaspoonful): Guaifenesin, USP 100 mg and Dextromethorphan Hydrobromide, USP 15 mg; alcohol 1.4%. *Robitussin-PE* contains in each 5 ml (1 teaspoonful): Guaifenesin, USP 100 mg and Pseudoephedrine Hydrochloride, USP 30 mg; alcohol 1.4%.

Action and Uses: All four preparations employ the expectorant action of guaifenesin which enhances the output of respiratory tract fluid (RTF). The enhanced flow of less viscid secretions promotes ciliary action, and facilitates the removal of inspissated mucus. As a result, unproductive coughs become more productive and less frequent. *Robitussin* is therefore, useful in combatting coughs associated with the common cold, bronchitis, laryngitis, tracheitis, pharyngitis, pertussis, influenza and measles, and for coughs provoked by chronic paranasal sinusitis. In *Robitussin-CF* the guaifenesin is supplemented with phenylpropanolamine which provides mild vasoconstrictor action resulting in a nasal decongestant effect and dextromethorphan, a synthetic, non-narcotic, centrally-acting cough suppressant. In *Robitussin-DM*, the guaifenesin is supplemented by dextromethorphan. In *Robitussin-PE*, the expectorant action of guaifenesin is supplemented by a sympathomimetic amine, pseudoephedrine, which helps reduce mucosal congestion and edema in the nasal passages.

Contraindications: Hypersensitivity to any of the components. *Robitussin-DM* is also contraindicated in patients who are receiving MAO inhibitors. *Robitussin-CF* and *Robitussin-PE* are also contraindicated in marked hypertension, hyperthyroidism or in patients who are receiving MAO inhibitors or antihypertensive medication.

Precautions: *Robitussin-CF* and *Robitussin-PE* should be administered with caution to patients with hypertension, cardiac disorders, diabetes or peripheral vascular disease. As with all products containing sympathomimetic amines, these products should be used with caution in patients with prostatic hypertrophy or glaucoma.

Note: Guaifenesin has been shown to produce a color interference with certain clinical laboratory determinations of 5-hydroxyindoleacetic acid (5-HIAA) and vanillylmandelic acid (VMA).

Adverse Reactions: No serious side effects have been reported from guaifenesin or dextromethorphan. Possible adverse reactions of *Robitussin-CF* and *Robitussin-PE* include nausea, vomiting, dry mouth, nervousness, insomnia, restlessness or headache.

Dosage: The following dosages are recommended for *Robitussin* and *Robitussin-CF:* Adults and children 12 years of age and over: 2 teaspoonfuls every four hours, not to exceed 12 teaspoonfuls in a 24-hour period; children 6 to under 12 years: 1 teaspoonful every four hours, not to exceed 6 teaspoonfuls in a 24-hour period; children 2 to under 6 years: ½ teaspoonful every four hours, not to exceed 3 teaspoonfuls in a 24-hour period; children under 2 years: use only as directed by physician. *Robitussin-DM:* Adults and children 12 years of age and over: 2 teaspoonfuls every six to eight hours, not to exceed 8 teaspoonfuls in a 24-hour period; children 6 to under 12 years: 1 teaspoonful every six to eight hours, not to exceed 4 teaspoonfuls in a 24-hour period; children 2 to under 6 years: ½ teaspoonful every six to eight hours, not to exceed 2 teaspoonfuls in a 24-hour period; children under 2 years: use only as directed by physician. *Robitussin-PE:* Adults and children 12 years of age and over: 2 teaspoonfuls every four hours, not to exceed 8 teaspoonfuls in a 24-hour period; children 6 to under 12 years: 1 teaspoonful every four hours, not to exceed 4 teaspoonfuls in a 24-hour period; children 2 to under 6 years: ½ teaspoonful every four hours, not to exceed 2 teaspoonfuls in a 24-hour period; children under 2 years: use as directed by physician.

How Supplied: *Robitussin* (wine-colored) in bottles of 4 fl. oz. (NDC 0031-8624-12), 8 fl. oz. (NDC 0031-8624-18), pint (NDC 0031-8624-25) and gallon (NDC 0031-8624-29). *Robitussin-DM* (cherry-colored) in bottles of 4 fl. oz. (NDC 0031-8684-12), 8 fl. oz. (NDC 0031-8684-18), pint (NDC 0031-8684-25), and gallon (NDC 0031-8684-29). *Robitussin-CF* (red-colored) in bottles of 4 fl. oz. (NDC 0031-8677-12), 8 fl. oz. (NDC 0031-8677-18), and pint (NDC 0031-8677-25). *Robitussin-PE* (orange-red) in bottles of 4 fl. oz. (NDC 0031-8695-12), 8 fl. oz. (NDC 0031-8695-18) and pint (NDC 0031-8695-25). *Robitussin* also available in 1 fl. oz. bottles (4 x 25's-NDC 0031-8624-02) and Dis-Co® Unit Dose Packs of 10 x 10's in 5 ml (NDC 0031-8624-23), 10 ml (NDC 0031-8624-26) and 15 ml (NDC 0031-8624-28). *Robitussin-DM* also available in Dis-Co® Unit Dose Packs of 10 x 10's in 5 ml (NDC 0031-8684-23) and 10 ml (NDC 0031-8684-26).

[*Shown in Product Identification Section*]

Z–BEC® Tablets

One tablet daily provides:

Vitamin Composition	Percentage of U.S. Recommended Daily Allowance (U.S. RDA)	
Vitamin E	150	45.0 I.U.
Vitamin C	1000	600.0 mg
Thiamine (Vitamin B$_1$)	1000	15.0 mg
Riboflavin (Vitamin B$_2$)	600	10.2 mg
Niacin	500	100.0 mg
Vitamin B$_6$	500	10.0 mg
Vitamin B$_{12}$	100	6.0 mcg
Pantothenic Acid	250	25.0 mg

Mineral Composition		
Zinc	150	22.5 mg*

*22.5 mg zinc (equivalent to zinc content in 100 mg Zinc Sulfate, USP)

Ingredients: Niacinamide Ascorbate; Ascorbic Acid; Microcrystalline Cellulose; Zinc Sulfate; Vitamin E Acetate; Hydrolyzed Protein; Calcium Pantothenate; Modified Starch; Hydroxypropyl Methylcellulose; Thiamine Mononitrate; Stearic Acid; Pyridoxine Hydrochloride; Riboflavin; Silicon Dioxide; Polysorbate 20; Magnesium Stearate; Lactose; Povidone; Propylene Glycol; Artificial Color; Vanillin; Hydroxypropyl Cellulose; Gelatin; Sorbic Acid; Sodium Benzoate; Cyanocobalamin.

Actions and Uses: Z-BEC is a high potency formulation. Its components have important roles in general nutrition, healing of wounds, and prevention of hemorrhage. It is recommended for deficiencies of these components in conditions such as febrile diseases, chronic or acute infections, burns, fractures, surgery, leg ulcers, toxic conditions, physiologic stress, alcoholism, prolonged exposure to high temperature, geriatrics, gastritis, peptic ulcer, and colitis; and in conditions involving special diets and weight-reduction diets.

In dentistry, Z-BEC is recommended for deficiencies of its components in conditions such as herpetic stomatitis, aphthous stomatitis, cheilosis herpangina and gingivitis.

Precaution: Not intended for the treatment of pernicious anemia.

Dosage: The recommended OTC dosage for adults and children twelve or more years of age, other than pregnant or lactating women, is one tablet daily with food or after meals. Under the direction and supervision of a physician, the dose and frequency of administration may be increased in accordance with the patient's requirements.

How Supplied: Green film-coated, capsule shaped tablets in bottles of 60 (NDC 0031-0689-62) and 500 (NDC 0031-0689-70).

[*Shown in Product Identification Section*]

Prescribing information on A. H. Robins products listed here is based on official labeling in effect December 1, 1981, with Indications, Contraindications, Warnings, Precautions, Adverse Reactions, and Dosage stated in full.

Products are

indexed alphabetically

in the

PINK SECTION

Roche Laboratories
Division of Hoffmann-La Roche Inc.
**340 KINGSLAND STREET
NUTLEY, NJ 07110**

VI-PENTA® INFANT DROPS
VI-PENTA® MULTIVITAMIN DROPS

The following text is complete prescribing information based on official labeling in effect December 1, 1981.

Composition: Vi-Penta Infant Drops and Vi-Penta Multivitamin Drops are designed to fill the vitamin needs of specific age groups. (See Composition Table below.)

Action and Uses: Vi-Penta Drops are water miscible and can be mixed with food or infant formula, or placed directly on the tongue.

Vi-Penta Infant Drops—a selective formula for prevention of vitamin deficiencies in infants and young children. *Vi-Penta Multivitamin Drops*—a comprehensive formula for daily nutritional support in adults as well as children of all ages. It is an especially convenient dosage form when a small volume liquid vitamin supplement is desired, such as to supplement the diets of those patients with conditions which permanently or temporarily impair their ability to swallow, chew or consume normal amounts and/or kinds of food.

Dosage: The average daily dose is 0.6 cc; therapeutic doses should be given according to the needs of the patient.

How Supplied: Vi-Penta Infant Drops and Vi-Penta Multivitamin Drops—fruit flavored, 50-cc bottles packaged with calibrated dropper.
[*Shown in Product Identification Section*]

William H. Rorer, Inc.
**500 VIRGINIA DRIVE
FORT WASHINGTON, PA 19034**

ASCRIPTIN®
Aspirin, Alumina and Magnesia Tablets, Rorer
Aspirin with

Formula: Each tablet contains:
Aspirin .... (5 grains) 325 mg
Maalox®:
　Magnesium Hydroxide .... 75 mg
　Dried Aluminum
　Hydroxide Gel .... 75 mg

Description: Ascriptin® is an excellent analgesic, antipyretic and anti-inflammatory agent for general use, particularly where there is concern over aspirin-induced gastric distress. When large doses are used, as in arthritis and rheumatic disorders, gastric discomfort is rare.

Indications: As an analgesic for the relief of pain in such conditions as headache, neuralgia, minor injuries and dysmenorrhea. As an analgesic and antipyretic in colds and influenza. As an analgesic and anti-inflammatory agent in arthritis and other rheumatic diseases. As an inhibitor of platelet aggregation, see TIA's indications.

Usual adult dose: Two or three tablets four times daily. For children under 12, at the discretion of the physician. As an inhibitor of platelet aggregation, see TIA's dosage information.

For Recurrent TIA's in Men

Indications: For reducing the risk of recurrent transient ischemic attacks (TIA's) or stroke in men who have had transient ischemia of the brain due to fibrin platelet emboli. There is inadequate evidence that aspirin or buffered aspirin is effective in reducing TIA's in women at the recommended dosage. There is no evidence that aspirin or buffered aspirin is of benefit in the treatment of completed strokes in men or women.

Precautions: (1) Patients presenting with signs and symptoms of TIA's should have a complete medical and neurologic evaluation. Consideration should be given to other disorders which resemble TIA's.
(2) Attention should be given to risk factors: it is important to evaluate and treat, if appropriate, other diseases associated with TIA's and stroke such as hypertension and diabetes.
(3) Concurrent administration of absorbable antacids at therapeutic doses may increase the clearance of salicylates in some individuals. The concurrent administration of nonabsorbable antacids may alter the rate of absorption of aspirin, thereby resulting in a decreased acetylsalicylic acid/salicylate ratio in plasma. The clinical significance on TIA's of these decreases in available aspirin is unknown.

Dosage: 1300 mg a day, in divided doses of 650 mg twice a day or 325 mg four times a day.

Warning: Keep this and all drugs out of the reach of children. In case of accidental overdose, seek professional assistance or contact a poison control center immediately.

Supplied: Bottles of 50 tablets (NDC 0067-0135-50), 100 tablets (NDC 0067-0135-68) and 225 tablets (NDC 0067-0135-77) with child-resistant caps. Bottles of 500 tablets (NDC 0067-0135-74) without child-resistant closures (for arthritic patients). Military Stock #NSN 6505-00-135-2783. V.A. Stock #6505-00-890-1979A (bottles of 500).
[*Shown in Product Identification Section*]

ASCRIPTIN® A/D
Arthritic Doses
Ascriptin® A/D Arthritic Doses with added Maalox® for increased buffering in Arthritic Doses.
Aspirin, Alumina and Magnesia Tablets, Rorer

Formula: Each capsule shaped tablet contains:
Aspirin .... (5 grains) 325 mg
Maalox®:
　Magnesium Hydroxide .... 150 mg
　Dried Aluminum
　Hydroxide Gel .... 150 mg

Description: Ascriptin® A/D is a highly buffered, analgesic, anti-inflammatory and antipyretic agent for use in the treatment of rheumatoid arthritis, osteoarthritis and other arthritic conditions. It is formulated with added Maalox® to provide increased neutralization of gastric acid thus improving the likelihood of GI tolerance when large antiarthritic doses of aspirin are used.

Vi-Penta Composition Table

Each 0.6 cc of Vi-Penta Infant Drops provides:	% minimum daily requirements (MDR)	
	Infants (under 1 year)	Young Children (1–6 years)
Vitamin A (as the palmitate) 5000 U.S.P. Units	333%	166%
Vitamin D₂ .... 400 U.S.P. Units	100%	100%
Vitamin C .... 50 mg	500%	250%
Vitamin E (as *dl*-α-tocopheryl acetate) 2 Int. Units	*	*

Each 0.6 cc of Vi-Penta Multivitamin Drops provides:	% minimum daily requirements (MDR)		
	Infants (under 1 year)	Children (1-6 years)	(6-12 years)
Vitamin A (as the palmitate) 5000 U.S.P. Units	333%	166%	166%
Vitamin D₂ .... 400 U.S.P. Units	100%	100%	100%
Vitamin C .... 50 mg	500%	250%	250%
Vitamin B₁ (as hydrochloride) .... 1 mg	400%	200%	133%
Vitamin B₂ (as riboflavin-5'-phosphate sodium) .... 1 mg	166%	111%	111%
Vitamin B₆ .... 1 mg	*	*	*
Vitamin E (as *dl*-α-tocopheryl acetate) 2 Int. Units	*	*	*
d-Biotin .... 30 mcg	†	†	†
Niacinamide .... 10 mg	*	200%	133%
D-Panthenol (equiv. to 11.6 mg Calcium pantothenate) .... 10 mg	†	†	†

*MDR for these vitamins has not been determined.
†The need for these vitamins in human nutrition has not been established.

Indications: As an analgesic, anti-inflammatory and antipyretic agent in rheumatoid arthritis, osteoarthritis and other arthritic conditions.

Usual Adult Dose: Two or three tablets, four times daily, or as directed by the physician for arthritis therapy. For children under twelve, at the discretion of the physician.

Drug Interaction Precautions: Do not use if patient is taking a tetracycline antibiotic.

Warning: Keep this and all drugs out of the reach of children. In case of accidental overdose, seek professional assistance or contact a poison control center immediately.

Supplied: Available in bottles of 100 tablets (NDC 0067-0137-68) and 225 tablets (NDC 0067-0137-77) with child-resistant caps, and in special bottles of 500 tablets (without child-resistant closures) for arthritic patients (NDC 0067-0137-74).

[*Shown in Product Identification Section*]

EMETROL®
For nausea and vomiting

Decription: Emetrol is an oral solution containing balanced amounts of levulose (fructose) and dextrose (glucose) and orthophosphoric acid with controlled hydrogen ion concentration. Pleasantly mint flavored.

Action: Emetrol quickly relieves nausea and vomiting by local action on the wall of the hyperactive G.I. tract. It reduces smooth-muscle contraction in direct proportion to the amount used. Unlike systemic antiemetics, Emetrol works almost immediately to control both nausea and active vomiting—and it is free from toxicity or side effects.

Indications: For nausea and vomiting.

Advantages:

1. *Fast action*—works almost immediately by local action on contact with the hyperactive G.I. tract.

2. *Effectiveness*—reported completely effective in epidemic vomiting—reduces smooth-muscle contractions in direct proportion to the amount used—stops both nausea and active vomiting.

3. *Safety*—no toxicity or side effects—won't mask symptoms of organic pathology.

4. *Convenience*—can be recommended over the phone for any member of the family, even the children—no Rx required.

5. *Patient acceptance*—a low cost that patients appreciate—a pleasant mint flavor that both children and adults like.

Usual dose: *Epidemic and other functional vomiting (intestinal "flu", G.I. grippe, etc.); or nausea and vomiting due to psychogenic factors:* Infants and children, one or two teaspoonfuls at 15 minute intervals until vomiting ceases; adults, one or two tablespoonfuls in same manner. If first dose is rejected, *resume dosage schedule in five minutes. Regurgitation in infants:* One or two teaspoonfuls ten or fifteen minutes before each feeding; in refractory cases, two or three teaspoonfuls one-half hour before feedings. "*Morning sickness*": One or two tablespoonfuls on arising, repeated every three hours or whenever nausea threatens.

Emetrol may also be used in motion sickness and in nausea and vomiting due to drug therapy or inhalation anesthesia; in teaspoonful dosage for young children, tablespoonful dosage for older children and adults.

Important: *DO NOT DILUTE or permit oral fluids immediately before or for at least 15 minutes after dose.*

Warning: Keep this and all drugs out of the reach of children. In case of accidental overdose, seek professional assistance or contact a poison control center immediately.

Supplied: Bottles of 3 fluid ounces (89 ml) (NDC 0067-0240-58) and 1 pint (473 ml) (NDC 0067-0240-74).

[*Shown in Product Identification Section*]

GEMNISYN™
(acetaminophen and aspirin)
Double Strength Analgesic For Pain

Description: Each Gemnisyn™ tablet contains aspirin 325 mg (5 gr) and acetaminophen 325 mg (5 gr) for increased assurance of analgesia in adults compared to a standard analgesic dosage unit.

Indications: For relief of pain requiring increased analgesic strength when the usual doses of mild analgesics are inadequate.

Contraindications: Sensitivity to aspirin or acetaminophen.

Adult Dosage: 1 or 2 Gemnisyn tablets every 4 to 6 hours while pain persists, not to exceed 6 tablets in any 24-hour period.

Warning: Use with caution in the presence of peptic ulcer, asthma, liver damage or with anticoagulant therapy. Not recommended for children under 12. Patient Precaution: If pain persists for more than 10 days, consult your physician.

Keep this and all drugs out of the reach of children. In case of accidental overdose, seek professional assistance or contact a poison control center immediately.

Overdosage: A massive overdosage of acetaminophen may cause hepatotoxicity. Since clinical and laboratory evidence may be delayed for up to one week, close clinical monitoring and serial hepatic enzyme determinations are recommended.

Supplied: Plastic bottle of 100 tablets. NDC 0067-0171-68

[*Shown in Product Identification Section*]

MAALOX®
Antacid
Magnesia and Alumina Oral Suspension and Tablets, Rorer
A Balanced Formulation of Magnesium and Aluminum Hydroxides

Description: Maalox Suspension is a balanced combination of magnesium and aluminum hydroxides... first in order of preference for all routine purposes of antacid medication. The high neutralizing power of magnesium hydroxide and the established acid binding capacity of aluminum hydroxide support the reputation of Maalox for reliable antacid action.

MAALOX® SUSPENSION: 225 mg Aluminum Hydroxide Equivalent to Dried Gel, USP, and 200 mg Magnesium Hydroxide per 5 ml.

MAALOX® No. 1 TABLETS: 200 mg Magnesium Hydroxide, 200 mg Dried Aluminum Hydroxide Gel.

MAALOX® No. 2 TABLETS: 400 mg Magnesium Hydroxide, 400 mg Dried Aluminum Hydroxide Gel.

Acid Neutralizing Capacity
Maalox® Suspension—27 mEq/2 teaspoonfuls
Maalox No. 1 Tablets—17 mEq/2 tablets
Maalox No. 2 Tablets—18 mEq/tablet
Sodium Content
Maalox® Suspension—1.35 mg/tsp. (5 ml) or .06 mEq (5 ml)
Maalox No. 1 Tablets—0.84 mg/tablet or 0.036 mEq/tablet
Maalox No. 2 Tablets—1.84 mg/tablet or .08 mEq/tablet

Indications: As an antacid for symptomatic relief of hyperacidity associated with the diagnosis of peptic ulcer, gastritis, peptic esophagitis, gastric hyperacidity, heartburn or hiatal hernia.

Advantages: Many patients prefer Maalox whether they are taking it for occasional heartburn or routinely on an ulcer therapy regimen. Once started on Maalox, patients tend to stay on Maalox because it tastes good, it's effective and it will not cause constipation... three important reasons for Maalox when prolonged therapy is necessary.

Directions for use:

MAALOX® SUSPENSION: Two to four teaspoonfuls, four times a day, taken twenty minutes to one hour after meals and at bedtime, or as directed by a physician.

MAALOX NO. 1 TABLETS: Two to four tablets, well chewed, twenty minutes to one hour after meals and at bedtime, or as directed by a physician.

MAALOX NO. 2 TABLETS: One or two tablets, well chewed, twenty minutes to one hour after meals and at bedtime, or as directed by a physician. May be followed with milk or water.

Patient Warnings:
Do not take more than 16 teaspoonfuls of Maalox Suspension, 16 Maalox No. 1 Tablets or 8 Maalox No. 2 Tablets in a 24-hour period or use the maximum dosage for more than 2 weeks or use if you have kidney disease, except under the supervision of a physician.

Drug Interaction Precaution: Do not use with patients taking a prescription antibiotic drug containing any form of tetracycline.

Keep this and all drugs out of the reach of children.

Supplied:
MAALOX SUSPENSION is available in bottles of 12 fluid ounces (355 ml) (NDC 0067-0330-73), plastic bottles of 5 fluid ounces (148 ml) (NDC 0067-0330-62) and 26 fluid ounces (769 ml) (NDC 0067-0330-44).

Continued on next page

Rorer—Cont.

Military Stock #NSN 6505-00-680-0133;
V.A. Stock #6505-00-074-0993A [bottles
of 6 fluid ounces (177 ml)].
MAALOX NO. 1 TABLETS (400 mg)
available in bottles of 100 tablets (NDC
0067-0335-68).
MAALOX NO. 2 TABLETS (800 mg)
available in bottles of 50 (NDC 0067-
0337-50) and 250 tablets (NDC 0067-0337-
70). Also available in boxes of 24 (NDC
0067-0337-24) and 100 (NDC 0067-0337-
67) tablets in easy-to-carry strips.
V.A. Stock #6505-00-993-3507A [boxes
of 100 tablets (in cellophane strips)].
[*Shown in Product Identification Section*]

MAALOX® PLUS
Antacid-Antiflatulent
Alumina, Magnesia and Simethicone
Oral Suspension and Tablets, Rorer

☐ Lemon swiss creme flavor... the
taste preferred by physician and patient.
☐ Physician-proven Maalox® formula
for antacid effectiveness.
☐ Simethicone, at a recognized clinical
dose, for antiflatulent action.

Description: Maalox® Plus, a balanced combination of magnesium and
aluminum hydroxides plus simethicone,
is a non-constipating, lemon-flavored,
antacid-antiflatulent.
Composition: To provide symptomatic
relief of hyperacidity plus alleviation of
gas symptoms, each teaspoonful/tablet
contains:

Active Ingredients	Maalox Plus Per Tsp. (5 ml)	Per Tablet
Magnesium Hydroxide	200 mg	200 mg
Aluminum Hydroxide	225 mg	200 mg
Simethicone	25 mg	25 mg

To aid in establishing proper dosage
schedules, the additional information is
provided:

Minimum Recommended Dosage:		
	Per 2 Tsp. (10 ml)	Per 2 Tablets
Acid neutralizing capacity	27 mEq	17 mEq
Sodium content	2.6 mg	2.0 mg
Sugar content	None	1.1 g
Lactose content	None	None

Indications: As an antacid for symptomatic relief of hyperacidity associated
with the diagnosis of peptic ulcer, gastritis, peptic esophagitis, gastric hyperacidity, heartburn or hiatal hernia. As an

antiflatulent to alleviate the symptoms
of gas, including postoperative gas pain.
Advantages: Among antacids, Maalox
Plus is uniquely palatable—an important feature which encourages patients
to follow your dosage directions. Maalox
Plus has the time proven, nonconstipating, low sodium Maalox formula—useful
for those patients suffering from the
problems associated with hyperacidity.
Additionally, Maalox Plus contains simethicone to alleviate discomfort associated
with entrapped gas.
Directions for Use:
MAALOX® PLUS SUSPENSION: Two
to four teaspoonfuls, four times a day,
taken twenty minutes to one hour after
meals and at bedtime, or as directed by a
physician.
MAALOX® PLUS TABLETS: Two to
four tablets, well chewed, four times a
day, taken twenty minutes to one hour
after meals and at bedtime, or as directed
by a physician.
Patient Warnings: Do not take more
than 16 teaspoonfuls or 16 tablets in a 24-
hour period or use the maximum dosage
for more than two weeks or use if you
have kidney disease except under the
advice and supervision of a physician.
Drug Interaction Precaution: Do not
use with patients taking a prescription
antibiotic containing any form of tetracycline. As with all aluminum-containing antacids, Maalox Plus may prevent
the proper absorption of the tetracycline.
Keep this and all drugs out of the reach
of children. In case of accidental overdose, seek professional assistance or contact a poison control center immediately.
Supplied:
MAALOX PLUS SUSPENSION is available in a plastic 12 fluid ounce (355 ml)
bottle (NDC 0067-0332-71).
MAALOX PLUS TABLETS are available in bottles of 50 tablets (NDC 0067-
0339-50) and boxes of 100 tablets (NDC
0067-0339-67) in handy portable strips
and convenience packs of 12 tablets
(NDC 0067-0339-29).
[*Shown in Product Identification Section*]

MAALOX® TC
(Therapeutic Concentrate)

Descriptions and Actions: Maalox®
TC is a potent, concentrated, balanced
formulation of 300 mg magnesium hydroxide and 600 mg aluminum hydroxide
per teaspoonful (5 ml). This formulation
produces a therapeutic concentrated antacid that exceeds standard antacids in
acid neutralizing capacity and acid consuming capacity.
Maalox® TC is formulated to reduce the
need to alter therapy due to treatment
induced changes in bowel habits. Palatability is enhanced by a pleasant-tasting
peppermint flavor.

Acid Neutralizing Capacity	28.3 mEq/5 ml
Acid Consuming Capacity	49.2/ml*

Sodium Content:

mg Na/ml	.16
mg Na/mEq ANC	.03

*(ml N/10 HCl/gm)
Indications: Maalox® TC antacid is
indicated for the symptomatic relief of
hyperacidity associated with the diagnosis of peptic ulcer and other gastrointestinal conditions where a high degree of
acid neutralization is desired.
Directions for Use: One or two teaspoonfuls as needed between meals and
at bedtime or as directed by a physician.
Higher dosage regimens may be employed under the direct supervision of a
physician in the treatment of active peptic ulcer disease.
Patient Warnings
Warning: Do not take more than 8 teaspoonfuls in a 24-hour period, or use the
maximum dosage of this product for
more than two weeks or use if you have
kidney disease except under the advice
and supervision of a physician.
Keep this and all drugs out of the reach
of children. In case of accidental overdose, seek professional assistance or contact a poison control center immediately.
Drug Interaction Precaution: Do not
take this product if you are presently
taking a prescription antibiotic drug containing any form of tetracycline.
Supplied: Maalox® TC is available in
bottles of 12 fluid ounces (355 ml) (NDC
0067-0334-73).
[*Shown in Product Identification Section*]

PERDIEM™

Actions: Perdiem™ with its gentle
action does not produce disagreeable side
effects. The vegetable mucilages of Perdiem soften the stool and provide pain-
free evacuation of the bowel. Perdiem is
effective as an aid to elimination for the
hemorrhoid or fissure patient prior to
and following surgery.
Composition: Contains Natural Vegetable Derivatives. Active ingredients are
82 percent psyllium (Plantago Hydrocolloid) and 18 percent senna (Cassia Pod
Concentrate).
Indication: For relief of constipation.
Patient Warning: Should not be used
in the presence of undiagnosed abdominal pain. Frequent or prolonged use
without the direction of a physician is
not recommended. Such use may lead to
laxative dependence. Should not be used
in patients with a history of esophageal
disorders.
Directions For Use—ADULTS: In the
evening and/or before breakfast, 1–2
rounded teaspoonfuls of Perdiem granules should be placed in the mouth and
swallowed with at least 8 fl. oz of cool
beverage. Additional liquid would be
helpful. Perdiem granules should not be
chewed.
After Perdiem takes effect (usually after
24 hours, but possibly not before 36–48
hours): reduce the morning and evening
doses to one rounded teaspoonful. Subsequent doses should be adjusted after adequate laxation is obtained.

In Obstinate Cases: Perdiem may be taken more frequently, up to two rounded teaspoonfuls every six hours.

For Patients Habituated to Strong Purgatives: Two rounded teaspoonfuls of Perdiem in the morning and evening may be required along with half the usual dose of the purgative being used. The purgative should be discontinued as soon as possible and the dosage of Perdiem granules reduced when and if bowel tone shows lessened laxative dependence.

For Colostomy Patients: To ensure formed stools, give one to two rounded teaspoonfuls of Perdiem in the evening.

During Pregnancy: Give one to two rounded teaspoonfuls each evening.

For Clinical Regulation: For patients confined to bed, for those of inactive habits, and in the presence of cardiovascular disease where straining must be avoided, one rounded teaspoonful of Perdiem taken once or twice daily will provide regular bowel habits.

For children: From age 7–11 years, give one rounded teaspoonful one to two times daily. From age 12 and older, give adult dosage.

Note: It is extremely important that Perdiem be taken with at least 8 oz of cool liquid. Psyllium containing preparations, because of their bulk-forming action, should be used with caution in patients with hiatal hernia.

Keep this and all drugs out of the reach of children. In case of accidental overdose, seek professional assistance or contact a poison control center immediately.

How Supplied: Granules; 100 gram (3.5 oz) (NDC 46213-0690-68) and 250 gram (8.8 oz) (NDC 46213-0690-70) canisters.

Dist. by William H. Rorer, Inc.

[*Shown in Product Identification Section*]

Rowell Laboratories, Inc.
210 WEST MAIN STREET
BAUDETTE, MN 56623

BALNEOL®
Perianal cleansing lotion

Composition: Contains water, mineral oil, propylene glycol, glyceryl stearate/PEG-100 stearate, PEG-40 stearate, laureth-4, PEG-4 dilaurate, lanolin oil, sodium acetate, carbomer-934, triethanolamine, sorbic acid, dioctyl sodium sulfosuccinate, fragrance, acetic acid.

Action and Uses: BALNEOL is a soothing, emollient cleanser for hygienic cleansing of irritated perianal and external vaginal areas. It helps relieve itching and other discomforts, helps stop irritation due to toilet tissue. BALNEOL gently yet thoroughly cleanses and provides a soothing, protecting film.

Administration and Dosage: For cleansing without discomfort after each bowel movement, a small amount of BALNEOL is spread on tissue or cotton and used to wipe the perianal area. Also used between bowel movements and at bedtime for additional comfort. For cleansing and soothing the external vagi-

nal area: to be used on clean tissue or cotton as often as necessary.

Caution: In all cases of rectal bleeding, consult physician promptly. If irritation persists or increases, discontinue use and consult physician.

How Supplied: 4 oz. plastic bottle.

HYDROCIL® INSTANT

Description: A concentrated hydrophilic mucilloid containing 95% psyllium. Hydrocil Instant mixes instantly, is sugar-free, low in potassium and contains less than 10 mg. of sodium per dose.

Indications: Hydrocil Instant is a natural bulk forming fiber useful in the treatment of constipation and other conditions as directed by a physician.

Directions: The usual adult dose is one packet or scoopful poured into an 8 oz. glass. Add water, fruit juices or other liquid and stir. It mixes instantly. Drink immediately. Take in the morning and night or as directed by a physician. Follow each dose with another glass of liquid.

How Supplied: In unit-dose packets of 3.7 grams that are available in boxes of 30's or 500's. Also in 250 gram jars with a measuring scoop. Each packet or scoopful, 3.7 grams, contains one usual adult dose of psyllium hydrophilic mucilloid, 3.5 grams.

Rystan Company, Inc.
470 MAMARONECK AVE.
WHITE PLAINS, NY 10605

CHLORESIUM® Ointment and Solution
Healing and Deodorizing Agent

Composition: Ointment: 0.5% water-soluble chlorophyll derivatives (Rystan brand, 100% concentration) in a hydrophilic base. Solution: 0.2% chlorophyll derivatives in isotonic saline solution.

Action and Uses: To promote normal healing, relieve pain and inflammation and reduce malodors in wounds, burns, surface ulcers, cuts, abrasions and skin irritations.

Administration and Dosage: Ointment: Apply generously and cover with gauze, linen or other appropriate dressing. Dressings preferably changed no more often than every 48 to 72 hours. Solution: Apply full strength as continuous wet dressing, or instill directly into sinus tracts, fistulae, deep ulcers or cavities. As a mouthwash, use half strength.

Side Effects: CHLORESIUM Ointment and Solution are soothing and nontoxic. Sensitivity reactions are extremely rare, and only a few instances of slight itching or irritation have been reported.

How Supplied: Ointment: 1 oz. and 4 oz. tubes, 1 lb. jars. Solution: 2 oz., 8 oz. and 32 oz. bottles.

DERIFIL® Tablets and Powder
Fecal and Urinary Deodorizer

Composition: 100 mg. water-soluble chlorophyll derivatives (Rystan brand,

100% concentration) per tablet or per teaspoonful of prepared solution.

Action and Uses: Oral tablet or solution for control of fecal and urinary odors in colostomy, ileostomy or incontinence; also to deodorize certain necrotic, ulcerative lesions such as decubitus ulcers; also urinary and fecal fistulas and certain breath and body odors not related to faulty hygiene.

Administration and Dosage: In incontinence, one tablet by mouth (or one teaspoonful of solution prepared by dissolving 1 oz. of powder in 1 pint of water) daily at mealtime or any other convenient time. For other conditions, the effective dosage varies with the severity of the odor problem (ordinarily within the range of one to three tablets daily) and is best determined by trial and error. NOTE: Deodorizing effect is cumulative, may require up to seven days to reach maximum. If preferred, tablets may be placed directly in the ostomy appliance.

Side Effects: No toxic effects have been reported from use of DERIFIL, even at high dosage levels for extended periods. A temporary, mild laxative effect may be noted, and the stool is commonly stained dark green. Isolated instances of stomach discomfort or cramps have been reported on high dosages of DERIFIL.

How Supplied: Bottles of 30, 100 and 1000 tablets; 1 oz. and 10 oz. bottles of powder.

SDA Pharmaceuticals, Inc.
919 THIRD AVENUE
NEW YORK, NY 10022

ANOREXIN™
Capsules
Anorectic for simple exogenous obesity contains:
phenylpropanolamine HCl 25 mg
caffeine 100 mg

One-Span™
Sustained Release Capsules contains:
phenylpropanolamine HCl 50 mg
caffeine 200 mg

Description: Each capsule contains phenylpropanolamine HCl, an anorexiant, and caffeine, a mild stimulant.

Indication: ANOREXIN is indicated as adjunctive therapy in a regimen of weight reduction based on caloric restriction in the management and control of simple exogenous obesity.

Caution: Do not exceed recommended dosage. Discontinue use if rapid pulse, dizziness or palpitations occur. Do not use if high blood pressure, heart, kidney, diabetes, thyroid or other disease is present, or if pregnant or lactating, nor to be used by anyone under the age of 18, except on physician's advice. Keep this and all drugs out of the reach of children. In case of accidental overdose seek professional assistance or contact a Poison Control Center immediately.

Precaution: Avoid use if taking prescription, anti-hypertensive or anti-de-

Continued on next page

SDA Pharmaceuticals—Cont.

pressive drugs containing monoamine oxidase inhibitors or other medication containing sympathomimetic amines. Avoid continuous use longer than 3 months.

Adverse Reactions: Side effects are rare when taken as directed. Nausea or nasal dryness may occasionally occur.

Dosage and Administration:

ANOREXIN™ Capsules: One capsule 30–60 minutes before each meal three times a day with one or two full glasses of water.

ANOREXIN™ One-Span™ Sustained Release Capsules: One capsule with a full glass of water once a day mid-morning (10:00 A.M.)

How Supplied:

ANOREXIN™ Capsules: Bottles of 50, packaged with 1200 calorie ANOREXIN Diet Plan.

ANOREXIN™ One-Span™ Sustained Release Capsules: Bottles of 21, packaged with 1200 calorie ANOREXIN Diet Plan.

A U.S. Government advisory panel of medical and scientific experts has determined the combination of active ingredients in this product as safe and effective when taken as directed for appetite control to aid in weight reduction by caloric restriction.

Reference: Griboff, Solomon, I., M.D., F.A.C.P. et al., A Double-Blind Clinical Evaluation of a Phenylpropanolamine-Caffeine Combination and a Placebo in the Treatment of Exogenous Obesity, Current Therapeutic Research 17, 6:535, 1975 (June).

Silverman, H. I., D.Sc., Kreger, B., M.D., Lewis, G., M.D., et al., Lack of Side Effects From Orally Administered Phenylpropanolamine and Phenylpropanolamine with Caffeine: A Controlled Three-Phase Study, Current Therapeutic Research 28, 2:18, 1980 (Aug.).

S.S.S. Company
71 UNIVERSITY AVENUE, S.W.
POST OFFICE BOX 4447
ATLANTA, GA 30302

20/20 Eye Drops
(naphazoline hydrochloride 0.012%)

Active Ingredients: Naphazoline Hydrochloride 0.012%, buffered with Sodium Carbonate, preserved with Thimerosal, 0.0050%.

Indications: For the temporary relief of minor eye irritation due to smoke, wind blown pollen, dust, smog and hayfever.

Actions: Naphazoline, an occular decongestant, constricts the small arterioles on the surface of the eye and thus helps remove the redness. Eyes are soothed and cleared in a few minutes.

Warnings: If irritation persists or increases, discontinue use and consult a physician. Do not touch the dispenser tip

or allow it to be exposed longer than necessary. Keep the container tightly closed.

Drug Interaction Precaution: No known drug interaction.

Dosage and Administration: Use two drops in each eye for the relief of minor eye irritation. May be repeated.

How Supplied: Available in a 0.5 fl. oz. plastic bottle.

Scherer Laboratories, Inc.
14335 GILLIS ROAD
DALLAS, TEXAS 75234

HuMIST
Humidifying Saline Nasal Mist

Composition: Sodium chloride 0.65% with 0.35% chlorabutanol (as a preservative) in a soothing, buffered, isotonic solution that is physiologically compatable with nasal membranes.

Actions and Uses: HuMIST, saline nasal mist, provides immediate safe relief from the discomfort of dry nasal mucosa, with no danger from continuous use. HuMIST is an ideal moisturizer for adjunctive use with systemic nasal decongestants, and whenever nasal dryness is caused by lack of humidity, dusty or air conditioned atmospheres, drug therapy, or overuse of decongestant sprays and inhalers. HuMIST also alleviates "crusting" following nosebleeds, surgery, and/or cauterization.

Dosage and Administration: Spray twice into each nostril. May also be used as drops. Use as often as needed.

How Supplied: 45 cc plastic squeeze bottle.

XERO–LUBE
Saliva Substitute–Oral Lubricant

XERO-LUBE has been accepted by the Council on Dental Therapeutics of the American Dental Association.

Composition: XERO-LUBE closely resembles normal human saliva in electrolyte content, viscosity, and pH. XERO-LUBE is pleasantly flavored and the fluoride concentration is 2 parts per million.

Actions and Uses: XERO-LUBE provides immediate effective safe relief of dry mouth (Xerostomia) symptoms. The moistening and lubricating actions are sustained because of the saliva-like viscosity.

Warnings: Keep this and all medicines out of children's reach.

Dosage and Administration: Aim and depress plunger to spray directly into mouth. May be used as often as needed to moisten the oral cavity. XERO-LUBE may be swallowed or expectorated.

How Supplied: XERO-LUBE is available in a 6 fluid ounce plastic bottle with a pump-spray top.

Schering Corporation
GALLOPING HILL ROAD
KENILWORTH, NJ 07033

A and D Ointment
REG. T.M.

Description: An ointment containing the emollients, anhydrous lanolin and petrolatum.

Indications: *Diaper rash*—**A and D Ointment** provides prompt, soothing relief for diaper rash and helps heal baby's tender skin; forms a moisture-proof shield that helps protect against urine and detergent irritants; comforts baby's skin and helps prevent chafing.

Chafed Skin—**A and D Ointment** helps skin retain its vital natural moisture; quickly soothes chafed skin in adults and children and helps prevent abnormal dryness.

Abrasions and Minor Burns—**A and D Ointment** soothes and helps relieve the smarting and pain of abrasions and minor burns, encourages healing and prevents dressings from sticking to the injured area.

Warning: Keep this and all drugs out of the reach of children.

Overdosage: In case of accidental ingestion, seek professional assistance or contact a poison control center immediately.

Dosage and Administration: *Diaper Rash*—Simply apply a thin coating of **A and D Ointment** at each diaper change. A modest amount is all that is needed to provide protective and healing action.

Chafed Skin—Gently smooth a small quantity of **A and D Ointment** over the area to be treated.

Abrasions, Minor Burns—Wash with lukewarm water and mild soap. When dry, apply **A and D Ointment** liberally. When a sterile dressing is used, change the dressing daily and apply fresh **A and D Ointment**. If no improvement occurs after 48 to 72 hours or if condition worsens, consult your physician.

How Supplied: A and D Ointment is available in 1½-ounce (42.5 g) and 4-ounce (113 g) tubes and 1-pound (454 g) jars.

Store away from heat.

Copyright© 1973, 1977, Schering Corporation. All rights reserved.

[*Shown in Product Identification Section*]

AFRIN®
Nasal Spray 0.05%
Menthol Nasal Spray 0.05%
Nose Drops 0.05%
Pediatric Nose Drops 0.025%

Description: AFRIN products contain oxymetazoline hydrochloride, the longest acting topical nasal decongestant available. Each ml of AFRIN Nasal Spray and Nose Drops contains oxymetazoline hydrochloride, USP 0.5 mg (0.05%); aminoacetic acid 3.8 mg; sorbitol solution, USP 57.1 mg; phenylmercuric acetate 0.02 mg; benzalkonium chloride 0.2 mg; sodium hydroxide to adjust the pH to a weak acid solution (5.5-6.5); and purified water, q.s. 1 ml.

Each ml of AFRIN Pediatric Nose Drops contains oxymetazoline hydrochloride, USP 0.25 mg (0.025%); aminoacetic acid 3.8 mg; sorbitol solution, USP 57.1 mg; phenylmercuric acetate 0.02 mg; benzalkonium chloride 0.2 mg; hydrochloric acid to adjust the pH to a weak acid solution (4.0-5.0); and purified water, q.s. 1 ml.

AFRIN Menthol Nasal Spray contains cooling aromatic vapors of menthol, eucalyptol and camphor in addition to the ingredients of AFRIN Nasal Spray.

Indications: For temporary relief of nasal congestion "associated with" or "accompanying" colds, hay fever and sinusitis.

Actions: The sympathomimetic action of AFRIN products constrict the smaller arterioles of the nasal passages, producing a prolonged, gentle and predictable decongesting effect. In just a few minutes a single dose, as directed, provides prompt, temporary relief of nasal congestion that lasts up to 12 hours. AFRIN products last up to 3 or 4 times longer than most ordinary nasal sprays.

AFRIN products used at bedtime help restore freer nasal breathing through the night.

Warnings: Do not exceed recommended dosage because symptoms may occur, such as burning, stinging, sneezing or increase of nasal discharge. Do not use these products for more than 3 days. If symptoms persist, consult a physician. The use of the dispensers by more than one person may spread infection. Keep these and all medicines out of the reach of children.

Overdosage: In case of accidental ingestion, seek professional assistance or contact a Poison Control Center immediately.

Dosage and Administration: Because AFRIN has a long duration of action, twice-a-day administration—in the morning and at bedtime—is usually adequate.

AFRIN Nasal Spray and Menthol Nasal Spray, 0.05%—For adults and children 6 years of age and over: With head upright, spray 2 or 3 times into each nostril twice daily—morning and evening. To spray, squeeze bottle quickly and firmly and sniff briskly. Not recommended for children under six.

AFRIN Nose Drops—For adults and children 6 years of age and over: Tilt head back, apply 2 or 3 drops into each nostril twice daily—morning and evening. Immediately bend head forward toward knees. Hold a few seconds, then return to upright position. Not recommended for children under six.

AFRIN Pediatric Nose Drops—Children 2 through 5 years of age: Tilt head back, apply 2 or 3 drops into each nostril twice daily—morning and evening. Promptly move head forward toward knees. Hold a few seconds, then return child to upright position. For children under 2 years, use only as directed by a physician.

How Supplied: AFRIN Nasal Spray 0.05% (1:2000), 15 ml and 30 ml plastic squeeze bottles.

AFRIN Menthol Nasal Spray 0.05% (1:2000), 15 ml plastic squeeze bottle.
AFRIN Nose Drops, 0.05% (1:2000), 20 ml dropper bottle.
AFRIN Pediatric Nose Drops, 0.025% (1:4000), 20 ml dropper bottle.
[*Shown in Product Identification Section*]

AFRINOL®
Repetabs® Tablets
Long-Acting Nasal Decongestant

Active Ingredients: Each Repetabs Tablet contains: 120 mg pseudoephedrine sulfate. Half the dose (60 mg) is released after the tablet is swallowed and the other half is released hours later; continuous relief is provided for up to 12 hours . . . without drowsiness.

Indications: For temporary relief of nasal congestion due to the common cold, hay fever or other upper respiratory allergies, and nasal congestion associated with sinusitis.

Actions: Promotes nasal and/or sinus drainage, helps decongest sinus openings, sinus passages.

Warnings: Do not exceed recommended dosage because at higher doses nervousness, dizziness or sleeplessness may occur. Do not take this preparation if you have high blood pressure, heart disease, diabetes, or thyroid disease, except under the advice and supervision of a physician. If symptoms do not improve within 7 days or are accompanied by high fever, consult a physician before continuing use. Keep this and all drugs out of the reach of children.

Drug Interactions: Do not take this product if you are presently taking a prescription antihypertensive or antidepressant drug containing a monoamine oxidase inhibitor, except under the advice and supervision of a physician.

Overdosage: In case of accidental overdose, seek professional assistance or contact a poison control center immediately.

Dosage and Administration: Adults and children 12 years and over—One tablet every 12 hours. AFRINOL is not recommended for children under 12 years of age.

How Supplied: AFRINOL Repetabs Tablets—Boxes of 12 and bottles of 100. Store between 2° and 30°C (36° and 86° F) Protect from excessive moisture.
[*Shown in Product Identification Section*]

CHLOR-TRIMETON®
Allergy Syrup
Allergy Tablets
Long Acting Allergy REPETABS® Tablets

Active Ingredients: Each Allergy Tablet contains: 4 mg CHLOR-TRIMETON (brand of chlorpheniramine maleate, USP); Each REPETABS® Tablet contains: 8 mg CHLOR-TRIMETON (brand of chlorpheniramine maleate). Half the dose (4 mg) is released after the tablet is swallowed, and the other half is released hours later; continuous relief is provided for up to 12 hours.

Each teaspoonful (5 ml) of Allergy Syrup contains: 2 mg CHLOR-TRIMETON (brand of chlorpheniramine maleate) in a pleasant-tasting syrup containing approximately 7% alcohol.

Indications: For temporary relief of hay fever/upper respiratory allergy symptoms: sneezing; running nose; watery, itchy eyes.

Actions: The active ingredient in CHLOR-TRIMETON is an antihistamine with anticholinergic (drying) and sedative side effects. Antihistamines appear to compete with histamine for cell receptor sites on effector cells.

Warnings: May cause drowsiness. May cause excitability especially in children. Do not take these products if you have asthma, glaucoma or difficulty in urination due to enlargement of the prostate gland, or give the REPETABS Tablets to children under 12 years, or the Allergy Syrup and Tablets to children under 6 years, except under the advice and supervision of a physician. Keep these and all drugs out of the reach of children.

Precautions: Avoid driving a motor vehicle or operating heavy machinery. Avoid alcoholic beverages while taking these products.

Overdosage: In case of accidental overdose, seek professional assistance or contact a Poison Control Center immediately.

Dosage and Administration: Allergy Syrup—Adults and Children 12 years and over: Two teaspoonfuls (4 mg) every 4 to 6 hours, not to exceed 12 teaspoonfuls in 24 hours; Children 6 through 11 years: one teaspoonful (2 mg) every 4 to 6 hours, not to exceed 6 teaspoonfuls in 24 hours; For children under 6 years, consult a physician.

Allergy Tablets—Adults and Children 12 years and over: One tablet (4 mg) every 4 to 6 hours, not to exceed 6 tablets in 24 hours. Children 6 through 11 years: One half the adult dose (break tablet in half) every 4 to 6 hours, not to exceed 3 whole tablets in 24 hours. For children under 6 years, consult a physician.

Allergy REPETABS Tablets—Adults and Children 12 years and over: One tablet (8 mg) in the morning and one tablet in the evening, not to exceed 3 tablets in 24 hours. For children under 12 years, consult a physician.

Professional Labeling: Dosage—Allergy Syrup: Children 2 through 5 years: ½ teaspoonful (1 mg) every 4 to 6 hours; Allergy Tablets: Children 2 through 5 years: one-quarter tablet (1 mg) every 4 to 6 hours.

Allergy REPETABS Tablets—Children 6 to 12 years: One tablet (8 mg) at bedtime or during the day, as indicated.

How Supplied: CHLOR-TRIMETON Allergy Tablets, 4 mg, yellow compressed, scored tablets impressed with the Schering trademark and product identification letters, TW or numbers, 080; box of 24, bottles of 100 and 1000, canisters of 5000.

Continued on next page

Information on Schering products appearing on these pages is effective as of January 1, 1982.

Schering—Cont.

CHLOR-TRIMETON Allergy Syrup: 2 mg per 5 ml, blue-green-colored liquid; 4-fluid ounce (118 ml) and 128-fluid ounce (3.2 liters) bottles. Protect from light; however, if color fades potency will not be affected.

CHLOR-TRIMETON Allergy REPE-TABS Tablets, 8 mg, sugar-coated, yellow tablets branded in red with the Schering trademark and product identification letters, CC or numbers, 374; boxes of 24, 48, bottles of 100 and 1000, canister of 5000.

Store the tablets and syrup between 2° and 30°C (36° and 86°F).

[*Shown in Product Identification Section*]

Note: also available—CHLOR-TRIME-TON Expectorant (brand of antihistamine-decongestant expectorant-antitussive); each 5 ml (1 teaspoonful) contains 2 mg chlorpheniramine maleate, USP; 10 mg phenylephrine hydrochloride, USP; 100 mg ammonium chloride, NF; 50 mg sodium citrate; 50 mg guaifenesin, NF, and alcohol 1 per cent or less, in a cherry-flavored demulcent syrup.

CHLOR–TRIMETON® Decongestant Tablets
Long Acting CHLOR–TRIMETON® Decongestant REPETABS® Tablets

Active Ingredients: Each tablet contains: 4 mg. CHLOR-TRIMETON (brand of chlorpheniramine maleate, USP) and 60 mg. pseudoephedrine sulfate.

Each REPETABS Tablet contains: 8 mg CHLOR-TRIMETON (brand of chlorpheniramine maleate) and 120 mg pseudoephedrine sulfate. Half the dose of each ingredient is released after the tablet is swallowed and the other half is released hours later providing continuous long-lasting relief up to 12 hours.

Indications: For temporary relief of nasal congestion due to hay fever and associated with sinusitis.

Actions: The antihistamine, chlorpheniramine maleate, provides temporary relief of running nose, sneezing, itching of the nose or throat, and itchy and watery eyes as may occur in allergic rhinitis (such as hayfever). The decongestant, pseudoephedrine sulfate reduces swelling of nasal passages; shrinks swollen membranes; and temporarily restores freer breathing through the nose.

Warnings: If symptoms do not improve within seven days or are accompanied by high fever, consult your physician before continuing use. May cause drowsiness. May cause excitability especially in children. Do not exceed recommended dosage because at higher doses nervousness, dizziness or sleeplessness may occur. Do not give the Decongestant Tablets to children under 6 years or the REPETABS Tablets to children under 12 years except under the advice and supervision of a physician. Do not take these products if you have asthma, glaucoma, difficulty in urination due to enlargement of the prostate gland, high blood pressure, heart disease, diabetes or thy-

roid disease, except under the advice and supervision of a physician.

Drug Interaction: Do not take this product if you are presently taking a prescription antihypertensive or antidepressant medication containing a monoamine oxidase inhibitor, except under the advice and supervision of a physician.

Precautions: Avoid driving a motor vehicle or operating heavy machinery. Avoid alcoholic beverages while taking this product. Keep these and all drugs out of the reach of children.

Overdosage: In case of accidental overdose, seek professional assistance or contact a Poison Control Center immediately.

Dosage and Administration: Tablets—ADULTS AND CHILDREN 12 YEARS AND OVER: One tablet every 4 hours, not to exceed 4 tablets in 24 hours. CHILDREN 6 THROUGH 11 YEARS—One half the adult dose (break tablet in half) every 4 hours not to exceed 2 whole tablets in 24 hours. For children under 6 years, consult a physician. REPETABS Tablets—ADULTS AND CHILDREN 12 YEARS AND OVER: one tablet every 12 hours.

Professional Labeling: Tablets—Children 2-5 years—one quarter the adult dose every 4 hours, not to exceed 1 tablet in 24 hours.

How Supplied: CHLOR-TRIMETON Decongestant Tablets—boxes of 24 and 48. Long Acting CHLOR-TRIMETON Decongestant REPETABS Tablets boxes of 12.

[*Shown in Product Identification Section*]

COD LIVER OIL CONCENTRATE
Tablets
Capsules
Tablets with Vitamin C

Active Ingredients: Tablets—A pleasantly flavored concentrate of cod liver oil with Vitamins A & D added. Each tasty, chewable tablet provides 4000 IU of vitamin A and 200 IU of vitamin D.

Capsules—A concentrate of cod liver oil with Vitamin A, with Vitamin D added. Each capsule provides: 10,000 IU of vitamin A and 400 IU of vitamin D.

Tablets with Vitamin C—A pleasantly-flavored concentrate of cod liver oil with Vitamins A, D and C added. Each tablet provides, 4000 IU of Vitamin A, 200 IU of Vitamin D and 50 mg of Vitamin C.

Tablets may be chewed or swallowed. Cod Liver Oil Concentrate Tablets and Tablets with Vitamin C contain FD&C Yellow No. 5 (tartrazine) as a color additive.

Indications: Cod Liver Oil Concentrate Tablets and Capsules are recommended for prevention and treatment of diseases due to deficiencies in Vitamins A and D. The tablets with Vitamin C are recommended for prevention and treatment of diseases due to deficiencies of Vitamins A, D and C.

Warnings: Keep this and all drugs out of the reach of children.

Overdosage: In case of accidental overdose, seek professional assistance or

contact a Poison Control Center immediately.

Dosage and Administration: Tablets: Two tablets daily, or as prescribed by a physician, taken preferably before meals.

Capsules: One capsule daily, or as prescribed by a physician, taken preferably before meals.

Tablets with Vitamin C: Two tablets daily, taken preferably before meals.

How Supplied: Cod Liver Oil Concentrate Tablets: bottles of 100 and 240. Cod Liver Oil Concentrate Capsules: bottles of 40 and 100. Cod Liver Oil Concentrate Tablets with Vitamin C: bottles of 100 tablets.

[*Shown in Product Identification Section*]

CORICIDIN® Tablets
CORICIDIN 'D'® Decongestant Tablets
CORICIDIN® Cough Syrup
CORICIDIN® Decongestant Nasal Mist

Active Ingredients: CORICIDIN Tablets—2 mg CHLOR-TRIMETON® (brand of chlorpheniramine maleate, USP); 325 mg (5gr) aspirin, USP.

CORICIDIN 'D' Decongestant Tablets—2 mg chlorpheniramine maleate, USP; 12.5 mg phenylpropanolamine hydrochloride, NF; 325 mg (5 gr) aspirin, USP.

CORICIDIN Cough Syrup—Each teaspoonful (5 ml) of fruit-flavored syrup contains 10 mg dextromethorphan hydrobromide; 12.5 mg phenylpropanolamine hydrochloride; 100 mg guaifenesin and less than 0.5% alcohol.

CORICIDIN Decongestant Nasal Mist—0.5% phenylephrine hydrochloride, USP.

Indications: CORICIDIN Tablets—For effective, temporary relief of cold and flu symptoms.

CORICIDIN 'D' Decongestant Tablets—For congested cold, flu and sinus symptoms.

CORICIDIN Cough Syrup—For temporary relief of coughs and stuffy noses.

CORICIDIN Decongestant Nasal Mist—For temporary relief of nasal congestion due to the common cold, hay fever or sinusitis.

Actions: CORICIDIN Tablets relieve annoying cold symptoms such as minor aches and pains, fever, sneezing, running nose and watery/itchy eyes.

CORICIDIN 'D' Tablets relieve the same annoying cold symptoms as well as stuffy nose, nasal membrane swelling and sinus headache.

CORICIDIN Cough Syrup helps loosen the phlegm in a non-productive cough, temporarily soothes irritated throat membranes, suppresses annoying coughs and helps relieve stuffy noses.

CORICIDIN Decongestant Nasal Mist is "symptom specific" and designed to shrink swollen nasal membranes promptly and help restore freer breathing through the nose.

Warnings: CORICIDIN Tablets—Drink a full glass of water with each dose. Adults should not take this product for more than 10 days; children 6 through 11 not more than 5 days. If fever persists or recurs, neither adults nor children should use for more than 3 days. If symptoms persist or new ones occur, consult your physician. May cause drowsiness. May cause excitability, especially in children. This product contains aspirin. Do not take this product if you are allergic to aspirin or if you have asthma, glaucoma, difficulty in urination due to enlargement of the prostate gland, stomach distress, ulcers or bleeding problems, or give this product to children under 6 years, except under the advice and supervision of a physician. Stop taking this product if ringing in the ears or other symptoms occur. Use during pregnancy ONLY under your doctor's direction. Keep this and all drugs out of the reach of children.

CORICIDIN 'D' Decongestant Tablets—Drink a full glass of water with each dose. Adults should not take this product for more than 7 days; children 6 through 11 not more than 5 days. If fever persists or recurs, neither adults nor children should use for more than 3 days. If symptoms persist or new ones occur, consult your physician. May cause drowsiness. May cause excitability especially in children. Do not exceed recommended dosage because at higher doses nervousness, dizziness or sleeplessness may occur. This product contains aspirin. Do not take this product if you are allergic to aspirin or if you have asthma, glaucoma, difficulty in urination due to enlargement of the prostate gland, stomach distress, ulcers or bleeding problems, high blood pressure, heart disease, diabetes or thyroid disease, or give this product to children under 6 years, except under the advice and supervision of a physician. Stop taking this product if ringing in the ears or other symptoms occur. Use during pregnancy ONLY under your doctor's direction. Keep this and all drugs out of the reach of children.

CORICIDIN Cough Syrup—Do not exceed recommended dosage because at higher doses nervousness, dizziness or sleeplessness are more likely to occur. This product should not, except under the direction of a physician, be used for persistent or chronic cough such as occurs with smoking, asthma or emphysema or where cough is accompanied by excessive secretions. CORICIDIN Cough Syrup should not be used in children under 2 years of age or by persons with high blood pressure, heart disease, diabetes or thyroid disease, except under the advice and supervision of a physician. Keep this and all drugs out of the reach of children.

CORICIDIN Decongestant Nasal Mist —Do not exceed recommended dosage because symptoms may occur such as burning, stinging, sneezing, or increase of nasal discharge. Do not use this product for more than 3 days. If symptoms persist, consult a physician. The use of this dispenser by more than one person may spread infection. For adult use only. Do not give this product to children under 12 years of age except under the advice and supervision of a physician. Keep this and all medicines out of the reach of children.

Drug Interactions: CORICIDIN Tablets—Do not take this product if you are presently taking a prescription drug for anticoagulation (thinning of the blood), diabetes, gout or arthritis, except under the advice and supervision of a physician.

CORICIDIN 'D' Decongestant Tablets—Do not take this product if you are presently taking a prescription antihypertensive or antidepressant drug containing a monoamine oxidase inhibitor or a prescription drug for anticoagulation (thinning of the blood), diabetes, gout or arthritis, except under the advice and supervision of a physician.

CORICIDIN Cough Syrup—Do not take this product if you are presently taking a prescription antihypertensive or antidepressant drug containing a monoamine oxidase inhibitor, except under the advice and supervision of a physician.

Precautions: CORICIDIN Tablets and CORICIDIN 'D' Decongestant Tablets —Avoid alcoholic beverages while taking these products. Also avoid driving a motor vehicle or operating heavy machinery.

CORICIDIN Cough Syrup—A persistent cough may be a sign of a serious condition. If cough or other symptoms persist for more than one week, tend to recur or are accompanied by high fever, rash or persistent headache, consult a physician before continuing use.

Overdosage: In case of accidental overdose of the tablets or syrup or accidental ingestion of the nasal mist, seek professional assistance or contact a Poison Control Center immediately.

Dosage and Administration: CORICIDIN Tablets—Adults and children 12 years and over—2 tablets every 4 hours not to exceed 12 tablets in 24 hours. Children 6 through 11 years: 1 tablet every 4 hours not to exceed 5 tablets in 24 hours.

CORICIDIN 'D' Decongestant Tablets —Adults and children 12 years and over: 2 tablets every 4 hours not to exceed 12 tablets in 24 hours. Children 6 through 11 years: 1 tablet every 4 hours not to exceed 5 tablets in 24 hours.

CORICIDIN Cough Syrup—NEW DOSAGE: Read carefully. Adults and chldren 12 years and over: 2 teaspoonfuls every 4 hours. Children 6–11 years: 1 teaspoonful every 4 hours. Children 2–5 years: ½ teaspoonful every 4 hours. Do not exceed 6 doses per day.

CORICIDIN Decongestant Nasal Mist— For adults and children 12 years of age and over: With head upright spray two or three times in each nostril, not more frequently than every four hours.

How Supplied: CORICIDIN Tablets— bottles of 12, 24, 60, 100 and 1000. Dispensing Package, box of 100 packets, 4 tablets in each packet.

CORICIDIN 'D' Decongestant Tablets— bottles of 12, 24, 50, and 100. Dispensing Package, box of 100 packets, 4 tablets in each packet.

CORICIDIN Cough Syrup—bottles of 4 oz. (118 ml).

Store the tablets and syrup between 2° and 30°C (36° and 86°F). Protect the tablets from moisture.

CORICIDIN Decongestant Nasal Mist— Plastic squeeze bottles of ⅔ fl. oz. (20 ml).

[*Shown in Product Identification Section*]

CORICIDIN® MEDILETS® Tablets for Children
CORICIDIN® DEMILETS® Tablets for Children
CORICIDIN® Children's Cough Syrup

Active Ingredients: CORICIDIN MEDILETS Tablets—1.0 mg CHLOR-TRIMETON® (brand of chlorpheniramine maleate, USP); 80 mg (1¼ gr) aspirin.
CORICIDIN DEMILETS Tablets—1.0 mg chlorpheniramine maleate, USP; 80 mg (1¼ gr) aspirin; 6.25 mg phenylpropanolamine hydrochloride.
CORICIDIN Children's Cough Syrup —Each teaspoonful (5 ml) contains: 5 mg dextromethorphan hydrobromide; 6.25 mg phenylpropanolamine hydrochloride; 100 mg guaifenesin and less than 0.5% alcohol.

Indications: CORICIDIN MEDILETS Tablets—For temporary relief of cold and flu symptoms in children. CORICIDIN DEMILETS Tablets—For temporary relief of children's congested cold, flu and sinus symptoms.
CORICIDIN Children's Cough Syrup— For temporary relief of children's cough symptoms and stuffy nose.

Actions: CORICIDIN MEDILETS Tablets provide relief of minor aches, pains, fever, running nose, sneezing and watery/itchy eyes that may accompany colds and flu.
CORICIDIN DEMILETS Tablets provide relief of annoying cold and flu symptoms: running nose, stuffy nose, sneezing, watery/itchy eyes, minor aches, pains and fever.
CORICIDIN Children's Cough Syrup provides temporary relief of cough symptoms, decongests stuffy noses, helps loosen the phlegm in a non-productive cough and temporarily soothes irritated throat membranes.

Warnings: CORICIDIN MEDILETS Tablets—Give water with each dose. Do not give this product for more than 5 days, but if fever is present, persists or recurs limit use to 3 days; if symptoms persist or new ones occur, consult your physician. This product may cause drowsiness; therefore, driving a motor vehicle or operating heavy machinery must be avoided while taking it. Alcoholic beverages must also be avoided while taking this product. It may cause excitability, especially in children. This product contains aspirin. Do not give this product to persons who are allergic to aspirin or to those who have asthma, glaucoma, difficulty in urination due to enlargement of the prostate gland, stomach distress, ulcers or bleeding problems, or to children less than 6 years old, except under the

Continued on next page

Information on Schering products appearing on these pages is effective as of January 1, 1982.

Schering—Cont.

advice and supervision of a physician. If ringing in the ears or other symptoms occur, stop giving this product. Use during pregnancy ONLY under a doctor's direction. Keep this and all drugs out of the reach of children.

CORICIDIN DEMILETS Tablets—Give water with each dose. Do not give this product for more than 5 days, but if fever is present, persists or recurs, limit dosage to 3 days; if symptoms persist or new ones occur, consult a physician. This product may cause drowsiness, therefore, driving a motor vehicle or operating heavy machinery must be avoided while taking it. Alcoholic beverages must also be avoided while taking this product. It may cause excitability, especially in children. Do not exceed recommended dosage because at higher doses nervousness, dizziness, elevation of blood pressure or sleeplessness are more likely to occur. This product contains aspirin. Do not administer this product to persons who are allergic to aspirin or to those who have asthma, glaucoma, difficulty in urination due to enlargement of the prostate gland, stomach distress, ulcers or bleeding problems, high blood pressure, heart disease, diabetes or thyroid disease, or give this product to children less than 6 years old, except under the advice and supervision of a physician. Use during pregnancy ONLY under a doctor's direction. If ringing in the ears or other symptoms occur, stop giving this product. Keep this and all drugs out of the reach of children.

CORICIDIN Children's Cough Syrup—Do not exceed recommended dosage because at higher doses nervousness, dizziness or sleeplessness are more likely to occur. This product should not, except under the direction of a physician, be used for persistent or chronic cough such as occurs with smoking, asthma or emphysema or where cough is accompanied by excessive secretions. CORICIDIN Children's Cough Syrup should not be used in children under 2 years of age or in persons with high blood pressure, heart disease, diabetes or thyroid disease, except under the advice and supervision of a physician. A persistent cough may be a sign of a serious condition. If cough or other symptoms persist for more than one week, tend to recur or are accompanied by high fever, rash or persistent headache, consult a physician before continuing use. Keep this and all drugs out of the reach of children.

Drug Interactions: CORICIDIN MEDILETS Tablets—Do not give this product to persons who are presently taking a prescription drug for anticoagulation (thinning of the blood), diabetes, gout or arthritis, except under the advice and supervision of a physician.

CORICIDIN DEMILETS Tablets—Do not give this product to persons who are presently taking a prescription antihypertensive or antidepressant medication containing a monoamine oxidase inhibitor or a prescription drug for anticoagu-

lation (thinning of the blood), diabetes, gout or arthritis, except under the advice and supervision of a physician. CORICIDIN Children's Cough Syrup—Do not give this product to persons who are presently taking a prescription antihypertensive or antidepressant drug containing a monoamine oxidase inhibitor, except under the advice and supervision of a physician.

Overdosage: In case of accidental overdose, seek professional assistance or contact a Poison Control Center immediately.

Dosage and Administration: CORICIDIN MEDILETS Tablets—Under 6 years: As directed by physician. Children 6 through 11 years: Two MEDILETS Tablets every 4 hours not to exceed 12 tablets in a 24-hour period, or as directed by physician.

CORICIDIN DEMILETS Tablets—Under 6 years: As directed by physician. 6 through 11 years: Two DEMILETS Tablets every 4 hours not to exceed 12 tablets in a 24-hour period, or as directed by physician.

CORICIDIN Children's Cough Syrup—Children 2 through 5 years: 1 teaspoonful every 4 hours not to exceed 6 teaspoonfuls in a 24-hour period. Children 6 through 11 years: 2 teaspoonfuls every 4 hours not to exceed 12 teaspoonfuls in a 24-hour period.

How Supplied: CORICIDIN MEDILETS Tablets—boxes of 24 and 36, individually wrapped in a child's protective pack.

CORICIDIN DEMILETS Tablets—boxes of 24 and 36, individually wrapped in a child's protective pack.

Store the tablets between 2° and 30°C (36° and 86°F). Protect from excessive moisture.

CORICIDIN Children's Cough Syrup—bottles of 4 fl. oz. (118 ml).

[*Shown in Product Identification Section*]

CORICIDIN® Extra Strength Sinus Headache Tablets

Active Ingredients: Each tablet contains: acetaminophen 500 mg (500 mg is a non-standard extra strength tablet of acetaminophen, as compared to the standard of 325 mg); CHLOR-TRIMETON (brand of chlorpheniramine maleate) 2 mg; phenylpropanolamine hydrochloride 12.5 mg.

Indications: For temporary relief of sinus headache and congestion.

Actions: CORICIDIN Sinus Headache Tablets have been formulated with an antihistamine for temporary relief of the running nose that often accompanies upper respiratory allergies and sinusitis; a non-aspirin pain reliever for temporary relief of sinus headache pain and a decongestant for temporary relief of nasal membrane swelling, thus promoting freer breathing.

Warnings: Consult your physician: if symptoms persist, do not improve within 7 days, if new symptoms occur, or if fever persists for more than 3 days (72 hours) or recurs. May cause drowsiness. May cause excitability, especially in children. Do not exceed recommended dosage be-

cause severe liver damage may occur and at higher doses nervousness, dizziness or sleeplessness are more likely to occur. Except under the advice and supervision of a physician, this product should not be used in children less than 12 years old or by persons with high blood pressure, heart disease, diabetes or thyroid disease, asthma, glaucoma or difficulty in urination due to enlargement of the prostate gland. Keep this and all drugs out of the reach of children.

Drug Interactions: Do not take this product if you are presently taking a prescription antihypertensive or, antidepressant medication containing a monoamine oxidase inhibitor, except under the advice and supervision of a physician.

Precautions: Avoid alcoholic beverages while taking this product. Also, avoid driving a motor vehicle or operating heavy machinery.

Overdosage: In case of accidental overdose, seek professional assistance or contact a poison control center immediately.

Dosage and Administration: Adults and children 12 years and older: 2 tablets every 6 hours not to exceed 8 tablets in a 24-hour period, or as directed by a physician. Swallow one tablet at a time.

Store between 2° and 30°C (36° and 86°F). Protect from excessive moisture.

How Supplied: Box of 24.

[*Shown in Product Identification Section*]

DEMAZIN®
Decongestant-Antihistamine
REPETABS® Tablets
Syrup

Active Ingredients: Each REPETABS® Tablet contains: 20 mg. phenylephrine and 4 mg CHLOR-TRIMETON® (brand of chlorpheniramine maleate, USP). Half the dose is in the outside coating for rapid absorption and prompt effect. The other half is in the inner core coated for repeat action.

Each teaspoonful (5 ml.) of syrup contains 2.5 mg. phenylephrine hydrochloride, USP and 1 mg. CHLOR-TRIMETON® (brand of chlorpheniramine maleate, USP) in a pleasant-tasting syrup containing approximately 7.5% alcohol. DEMAZIN Syrup contains FD&C Yellow No. 5 (tartrazine) as a color additive.

Indications: For temporary relief of nasal congestion, watery eyes, running nose, and sneezing associated with hay fever, sinus congestion and the common cold.

Actions: Phenylephrine hydrochloride is a sympathomimetic agent which acts as an upper respiratory and pulmonary decongestant and mild bronchodilator. It exerts desirable sympathomimetic action with relatively little central nervous system excitation, so that wakefulness and nervousness are reduced to a minimum. Chlorpheniramine maleate antagonizes many of the characteristic effects of histamine. It is of value clinically in the prevention and relief of many allergic manifestations.

The oral administration of phenylephrine hydrochloride with chlorpheniramine maleate produces a complementary action on congestive conditions of the upper respiratory tract, thus often obviating the need for topical nasal therapy.

Warnings: If symptoms do not improve within 7 days or are accompanied by high fever consult a physician before continuing use. May cause drowsiness. May cause excitability especially in children. Do not exceed recommended dosage because at higher doses nervousness, dizziness or sleeplessness are more likely to occur. Except under the advice and supervision of a physician, these products should not be used in children under 6 years of age or by persons with high blood pressure, heart disease, diabetes, thyroid disease, asthma, glaucoma or difficulty in urination due to enlargement of the prostate gland.

Keep these and all drugs out of the reach of children.

Drug Interaction: Do not take this product if you are presently taking a prescription antihypertensive or antidepressant drug containing a monoamine oxidase inhibitor, except under the advice and supervision of a physician.

Precautions: Avoid alcoholic beverages while taking these products. Also avoid driving a motor vehicle or operating heavy machinery.

Overdosage: In case of accidental overdose, seek professional assistance or contact a Poison Control Center immediately.

Dosage and Administration: Tablets—Adults and children 12 years and over: One tablet morning and evening. Children under 12 years, consult a physician. Syrup—Adults: Two teaspoonfuls four times daily or as directed by a physician. Children 6 to 12 years: One teaspoonful four times daily or as directed by a physician. For children under 6 years, consult a physician. Not more than 4 doses every 24 hours.

Professional Labeling: Dosage: Syrup—Children 2 to 5 years: 1 teaspoonful, four times daily.

How Supplied: DEMAZIN REPETABS Tablets, blue, sugar-coated tablets branded in red with the Schering trademark and either product identification letters, ADD or numbers, 133; box of 24 tablets and bottles of 100 and 1000.

DEMAZIN Syrup, blue-colored liquid, bottles of 4 fluid ounces (118 ml) and 128 fluid ounces (1 gallon). Store the syrup between 2° and 25°C (36° and 77°F).

[*Shown in Product Identification Section*]

DERMOLATE™ Anti-Itch Cream
DERMOLATE™ Anti-Itch Spray
DERMOLATE™ Anal-Itch Ointment
DERMOLATE™ Scalp-Itch Lotion

Active Ingredients: DERMOLATE Anti-Itch Cream contains hydrocortisone 0.5% in a greaseless, vanishing cream.

DERMOLATE Anti-Itch Spray contains hydrocortisone 0.5% in a clear, cooling, fast-drying spray. Alcohol content 24%.

DERMOLATE Anal-Itch Ointment contains hydrocortisone 0.5% in a soothing, lubricating ointment.

DERMOLATE Scalp-Itch Lotion contains hydrocortisone 0.5% in a clear, non-greasy liquid that dries in minutes. Isopropyl alcohol content 47%.

Indications: DERMOLATE Anti-Itch Cream and Spray—For the temporary relief of minor skin irritations, itching and rashes due to eczema, dermatitis, insect bites, poison ivy, poison oak, poison sumac, soaps, detergents, cosmetics and jewelry.

DERMOLATE Anal-Itch Ointment—For the temporary relief of itchy anal areas. Also for minor skin irritations and itching due to eczema and dermatitis.

DERMOLATE Scalp-Itch Lotion—For temporary relief of itching and minor scalp irritation due to scalp dermatitis.

Actions: DERMOLATE Anti-Itch Cream and Spray provide temporary relief of itching and minor skin irritation.

DERMOLATE Anal-Itch Ointment provides temporary relief of anal itching, minor skin irritations and itching due to eczema and dermatitis.

DERMOLATE Scalp-Itch Lotion provides temporary relief of itching and minor scalp irritation due to scalp dermatitis.

Warnings: All DERMOLATE forms are for external use only. Avoid contact with the eyes. Discontinue use and consult a physician if condition worsens or if symptoms persist for more than seven days. Do not use on children under 2 years of age except under the advice and supervision of physician. Keep these and all drugs out of the reach of children.

Overdosage: In case of accidental ingestion, seek professional assistance or contact a Poison Control Center immediately.

Dosage and Administration: DERMOLATE Anti-Itch Cream—*For adults and children 2 years of age and older:* Gently massage into affected skin area not more than 3 or 4 times daily. *For children under 2 years of age,* there is no recommended dosage except under the advice and supervision of a physician.

DERMOLATE Anti-Itch Spray—*For adults and children 2 years of age and older:* Spray on affected skin area not more than 3 or 4 times daily. *For children under 2 years of age,* there is no recommended dosage except under the advice and supervision of a physician.

DERMOLATE Anal-Itch Ointment—*Adults and children 2 years of age and older:* Apply to affected area not more than 3 to 4 times daily. *For children under 2 years of age,* there is no recommended dosage except under the advice and supervision of a physician.

DERMOLATE Scalp-Itch Lotion—*For adults and children 2 years of age and older:* Part the hair and apply directly to the scalp by squeezing a small amount onto affected areas. Massage into the scalp and repeat this process until desired coverage is achieved. Maintain normal hair care but do not wash out DERMOLATE Lotion immediately after application. Apply to affected scalp areas not more than 3 to 4 times daily. *For children under 2 years of age,* there is no recommended dosage except under the advice and supervision of a physician.

How Supplied: DERMOLATE Anti-Itch Cream—30 g (1.0 oz.) tube, and 15 g (½ oz) tubes and institutional package, 50 × 2g (1/15 oz) tubes.

DERMOLATE Anti-Itch Spray—45 ml (1.5 fl. oz.) pump spray bottle.

DERMOLATE Anal-Itch Ointment—30 g (1.0 fl. oz.) tube.

DERMOLATE Scalp-Itch Lotion—30 ml (1 fl. oz.) plastic squeeze bottle.

Store all forms between 2° and 30°C (36° and 86°F).

Protect the spray from freezing.

[*Shown in Product Identification Section*]

EMKO® BECAUSE®
Vaginal Contraceptive Foam

Description: A non-hormonal, non-scented aerosol foam contraceptive in a portable applicator/foam unit containing six applications of an 8.0% concentration of the spermicide nonoxynol-9.

Indications: Vaginal contraceptive intended for the prevention of pregnancy. BECAUSE Foam provides effective protection alone or it may be used instead of spermicidal jelly or cream to give added protection with a diaphragm.

BECAUSE Foam also may be used to give added protection to other methods of contraception: with a condom; as a backup to the IUD or oral contraceptives during the first month of use; in the event more than one oral contraceptive pill is forgotten and extra protection is needed during that menstrual cycle.

Actions: Each applicatorful of BECAUSE Foam provides the correct amount of nonoxynol-9, the most widely used spermicide, to prevent pregnancy effectively. The foam covers the inside of the vagina and forms a layer of spermicidal material between the sperm and the cervix. The powerful spermicide prevents pregnancy by killing sperm after contact. BECAUSE Foam is effective immediately upon insertion. No waiting period is needed for effervescing or melting to take place since BECAUSE is introduced into the vagina as a foam.

Warnings: If vaginal or penile irritation occurs and continues, a physician should be consulted. Not effective orally. Where pregnancy is contraindicated, further individualization of the contraceptive program may be needed. Do not burn, incinerate or puncture container. Keep this and all drugs out of the reach of children and in case of accidental ingestion, call a Poison Control Center, emergency medical facility, or a doctor.

Dosage and Administration: Although no contraceptive can guarantee 100% effectiveness, for reliable protection against pregnancy follow directions. One applicatorful of BECAUSE Contraceptive Foam must be inserted before each act of sexual intercourse. BECAUSE Foam can be inserted immediately or up to one hour before inter-

Continued on next page

Information on Schering products appearing on these pages is effective as of January 1, 1982.

Schering—Cont.

course. If more than one hour has passed before intercourse or if intercourse is repeated, another applicatorful of BECAUSE Foam must be inserted.

Directions for Use: The BECAUSE CONTRACEPTOR has a foam container attached to an applicator barrel.

With the container pushed all the way into the barrel, shake well. Pull the container upward until it stops. Tilt container to side to release foam into barrel. Allow foam to fill barrel to about one inch from end and return container to straight position. Foam will expand to fill remainder of barrel.

Hold contraceptor at top of the barrel part and gently insert applicator barrel deep into the vagina (close to the cervix). For ease of insertion, lie on your back with knees bent. With applicator barrel in place, push container all the way into the barrel. This deposits the foam properly. Remove the Contraceptor with the container still pushed all the way in the applicator barrel to avoid withdrawing any of the foam. No waiting period is needed before intercourse. BECAUSE Contraceptive Foam is effective immediately after proper insertion.

As with other vaginal contraceptive foam, cream and jelly products, douching is *not* recommended after using BECAUSE Foam. However, if douching is desired for cleansing purposes, you *must* wait at least six hours following your last act of sexual intercourse to allow BECAUSE Foam's full spermicidal activity to take place. Refer to package insert directions and diagrams for further details and applicator cleansing instructions.

How to Use the BECAUSE CONTRACEPTOR with a Diaphragm.

Insert one applicatorful of BECAUSE Foam directly into the vagina according to above directions and then insert diaphragm. After insertion, BECAUSE Foam is effective immediately and remains effective up to one hour before intercourse. If more than one hour has passed or you are going to repeat intercourse, insert another applicatorful of BECAUSE Foam *without removing your diaphragm.*

Storage: Contents under pressure. Do not burn, incinerate, or puncture the applicator. Store at normal room temperature. Do not expose to extreme heat or open flame or store at temperatures above 120°F. If stored at temperatures below 60°F, warm to room temperature before using.

How Supplied: Disposable 10 gm CONTRACEPTOR containing six applications of BECAUSE Contraceptive Foam. This foam is also available in two other forms, PRE-FIL® Foam with the "fill-in-advance" applicator and EMKO® Foam with the regular applicator.

[*Shown in Product Identification Section*]

EMKO®
Vaginal Contraceptive Foam

Description: A non-hormonal, non-scented aerosol foam contraceptive containing an 8.0% concentration of the spermicide nonoxynol-9.

Indications: Vaginal contraceptive intended for the prevention of pregnancy. EMKO Foam provides effective protection alone or it may be used instead of spermicidal jelly or cream to give added protection with a diaphragm.

EMKO Foam also may be used to give added protection to other methods of contraception: with a condom; as a backup to the IUD or oral contraceptives during the first month of use; in the event more than one oral contraceptive pill is forgotten and extra protection is needed during that menstrual cycle.

Actions: Each applicatorful of EMKO Foam provides the correct amount of nonoxynol-9, the most widely used spermicide, to prevent pregnancy effectively. The foam covers the inside of the vagina and forms a layer of spermicidal material between the sperm and the cervix. The powerful spermicide prevents pregnancy by killing sperm after contact. EMKO Foam is effective immediately upon insertion. No waiting period is needed for effervescing or melting to take place since EMKO is introduced into the vagina as a foam.

Warnings: If vaginal or penile irritation occurs and continues, a physician should be consulted. Where pregnancy is contraindicated, further individualization of the contraceptive program may be needed. Do not burn, incinerate or puncture can. Keep this and all drugs out of the reach of children and in case of accidental ingestion, call a Poison Control Center, emergency medical facility, or a doctor.

Dosage and Administration: Although no contraceptive can guarantee 100% effectiveness, for reliable protection against pregnancy read and follow directions carefully. One applicatorful of EMKO Contraceptive Foam must be inserted before each act of sexual intercourse. EMKO Foam can be inserted immediately or up to one hour before intercourse. If more than one hour has passed before intercourse or if intercourse is repeated, another applicatorful of EMKO Foam must be inserted.

Directions for Use:

Check Foam Supply with Weigh Cap.

With the cap on the can, hold the can in midair by the white button. As long as the black is showing, a full dose of foam is available. When the black begins to disappear, purchase a new can of EMKO Foam. USE *only if black is showing* to assure a full application. SHAKE CAN WELL before filling applicator. *Remove cap and place the can in an upright position on a level surface.* Place the EMKO regular applicator in an upright position over valve on top of can. Press down on the applicator gently. Allow foam to fill to the ridge in applicator barrel. The plunger will rise up as the foam fills the applicator. Remove the filled applicator from the can to stop flow. Hold the filled applicator by the barrel and gently insert deep into the vagina (close to the cervix). For ease of insertion, lie on your back with knees bent. With the applicator in

place, push plunger into applicator until it stops. This deposits the foam properly. Remove the applicator with the plunger still pushed all the way in to avoid withdrawing any of the foam. No waiting period is needed before intercourse. EMKO Contraceptive Foam is effective immediately after proper insertion. As with other vaginal contraceptive foam, cream, and jelly products, douching is *not* recommended after using EMKO Foam. However, if douching is desired for cleansing purposes, you *must* wait at least six hours following your last act of sexual intercourse to allow EMKO Foam's full spermicidal activity to take place. Refer to package insert directions and diagrams for further details and applicator cleansing instructions.

How to Use EMKO with a Diaphragm.

Insert one applicatorful of EMKO Foam directly into the vagina according to above directions and then insert your diaphragm. After insertion, EMKO Foam is effective immediately and remains effective up to one hour before intercourse. If more than one hour has passed or you are going to repeat intercourse, insert another applicatorful of EMKO Foam *without removing your diaphragm.*

Storage: Contents under pressure. Do not burn, incinerate or puncture can. Store at normal room temperature. Do not expose to extreme heat or open flame or store at temperatures above 120°F. If stored at temperatures below 60°F, warm to room temperature before using.

How Supplied: EMKO Contraceptive Foam, 40 gm can with applicator and storage purse. Refill cans without applicator and purse available in 40 gm and 90 gm sizes. All sizes feature a unique weighing cap that indicates when a new foam supply is needed. EMKO Foam also comes in two other forms, PRE-FIL® with the "fill-in-advance" applicator and BECAUSE® CONTRACEPTOR®, the portable six-use, combination foam/applicator unit.

[*Shown in Product Identification Section*]

EMKO® PRE–FIL®
Vaginal Contraceptive Foam

Description: A non-hormonal, non-scented aerosol foam contraceptive, for use with the "fill-in-advance" applicator, containing 8.0% concentration of the spermicide nonoxynol-9.

Indications: Vaginal contraceptive intended for the prevention of pregnancy. PRE-FIL Foam provides effective protection alone or it may be used instead of spermicidal jelly or cream to give added protection with a diaphragm.

PRE-FIL Foam also may be used to give added protection to other methods of contraception: with a condom; as a backup to the IUD or oral contraceptives during the first month of use; in the event more than one oral contraceptive pill is forgotten and extra protection is needed during that menstrual cycle.

Actions: Each applicatorful of PRE-FIL Foam provides the correct amount of nonoxynol-9, the most widely used spermicide, to prevent pregnancy effectively.

The foam covers the inside of the vagina and forms a layer of spermicidal material between the sperm and the cervix. The powerful spermicide prevents pregnancy by killing sperm after contact. PRE-FIL Foam is effective immediately upon insertion. No waiting period is needed for effervescing or melting to take place since PRE-FIL is introduced into the vagina as a foam.

Warnings: If vaginal or penile irritation occurs and continues, a physician should be consulted. Where pregnancy is contraindicated, further individualization of the contraceptive program may be needed. Do not burn, incinerate or puncture can. Keep this and all drugs out of the reach of children and in case of accidental ingestion, call a Poison Control Center, emergency medical facility, or a doctor.

Dosage and Administration: Although no contraceptive can guarantee 100% effectiveness, for reliable protection against pregnancy read and follow directions carefully. One applicatorful of PRE-FIL Contraceptive Foam must be inserted before each act of sexual intercourse. PRE-FIL Foam can be inserted immediately or up to one hour before intercourse. If more than one hour has passed before intercourse or if intercourse is repeated, another applicatorful of PRE-FIL Foam must be inserted.

Directions for Use:
Check Foam Supply with Weigh Cap. With the cap on the can, hold the can in midair by the white button. As long as the black is showing, a full dose of foam is available. When the black begins to disappear, purchase a new can of PRE-FIL FOAM. USE *only if black is showing* to assure a full application. SHAKE CAN GENTLY before filling applicator.
Remove cap and place the can in an upright position on a level surface.
PRE-FIL Foam can only be used with the special "fill-in-advance" applicator. The PRE-FIL applicator has two parts: an inner tube and an outer barrel. Remove inner tube from outer barrel. Place *inner* tube in upright position over valve on top of can and press down until pink plunger stops rising. Continue to press for a few seconds before removing inner tube from can. To be sure inner tube is completely filled, press pink plunger. If it can be depressed, inner tube is not full—repeat filling procedure.
Place inner tube into outer barrel. *The foam can only be released when the inner tube is inside the outer barrel.* Gently insert applicator deep into the vagina (close to the cervix). For ease of insertion, lie on your back with knees bent. With the applicator in place, push pink plunger back into applicator until it stops. This deposits the foam properly. Remove the applicator with the plunger still pushed all the way in to avoid withdrawing any of the foam. No waiting period is needed before intercourse. PRE-FIL Contraceptive Foam is effective immediately after proper insertion.
PRE-FIL's "fill-in-advance" applicator can be filled and stored, ready for use either immediately or up to seven days.

As with other vaginal contraceptive foam, cream and jelly products, douching is *not* recommended after using PRE-FIL Foam. However, if douching is desired for cleansing purposes, you *must* wait at least six hours following your last act of sexual intercourse to allow PRE-FIL Foam's full spermicidal activity to take place. Refer to package insert directions and diagrams for further details and applicator cleansing instructions.
How to Use PRE-FIL with a Diaphragm Insert one applicatorful of PRE-FIL Foam directly into the vagina according to above directions and then insert diaphragm. After insertion, PRE-FIL Foam is effective immediately and remains effective up to one hour before intercourse. If more than one hour has passed or you are going to repeat intercourse, insert another applicatorful of PRE-FIL Foam *without removing your diaphragm.*
Storage: Contents under pressure. Do not burn, incinerate or puncture can or filled applicator. Store at normal room temperature. Do not expose to extreme heat or open flame or store at temperatures above 120°F. If stored at temperatures below 60°F, warm to room temperature before using. Prefilled applicator may be stored up to seven days.
How Supplied: EMKO PRE-FIL Contraceptive Foam, 30 gm can with applicator and purse. Refill can without applicator and purse in 60 gm size. Both sizes feature a unique weighing cap that indicates when a new supply of foam is needed. This foam also comes in two other forms, EMKO® Foam with the regular applicator and BECAUSE® CONTRACEPTOR®, the portable six-use, combination foam/applicator unit.
[*Shown in Product Identification Section*]

MOL–IRON®
Tablets
Liquid
CHRONOSULE® Capsules
Tablets with Vitamin C
CHRONOSULE® Capsules with Vitamin C

Active Ingredients: MOL-IRON products contain a specially processed preparation of ferrous sulfate. They are highly effective and unusually well tolerated even by children and pregnant women.
Tablets: Each tablet contains 195 mg. ferrous sulfate, USP (39 mg. elemental iron).
Liquid: Each 4 ml teaspoonful of loganberry-flavored liquid contains 195 mg. ferrous sulfate, USP (39 mg. elemental iron) and alcohol 4.75%.
CHRONOSULE Capsules: Each capsule contains 390 mg. ferrous sulfate, USP (78 mg. elemental iron) in sustained release form.
Tablets with Vitamin C: Each tablet contains 195 mg. ferrous sulfate (39 mg. elemental iron) and 75 mg. ascorbic acid.
MOL-IRON Tablets, Tablets with Vitamin C, and CHRONOSULE capsules contain FD&C Yellow No. 5 (tartrazine) as a color additive.
Indications: For the prevention and treatment of iron-deficiency anemias. The CHRONOSULE capsules supply ad-

equate amounts of iron in the form of specially coated beadlets, fabricated to disintegrate gradually over a 6 to 8 hour period, effecting a continued release of absorbable ferrous iron while traversing the stomach and small intestine.
Unpleasant side effects are minimized.
Warnings: Keep these and all drugs out of the reach of children. In case of accidental overdose, seek professional assistance or contact a Poison Control Center immediately.
Dosage and Administration: Tablets—(Taken preferably after meals): Adults and Children 12 years and older—1 or 2 tablets 3 times daily; Children 6 through 11 years—1 tablet 3 times daily; or as prescribed by a physician.
Liquid—(Taken preferably after meals): Adults and Children 12 years and older—1 or 2 teaspoonfuls 3 times daily; Children 6 through 11 years—1 teaspoonful 3 times daily; Children 2 through 5 years—1 teaspoonful 2 times daily; Children less than 2 years old—½ teaspoonful 3 times daily; or as prescribed by a physician. The liquid should be administered in a small quantity of water or fruit juice (not milk).
CHRONOSULE Capsules—(Taken preferably after meals): Adults and Children 12 years and older—1 CHRONOSULE capsule once or twice daily; Children 6 through 11 years—1 capsule daily; or as prescribed by a physician.
Tablets with Vitamin C—(Taken preferably between meals): Adults and Children 12 years and older—1 or 2 tablets 3 times daily; Children 6 through 11 years—1 tablet 3 times daily; or as prescribed by a physician.
How Supplied: MOL-IRON Tablets—maroon colored tablets, bottles of 100 and 1000; MOL-IRON Liquid—bottles of 16 fl. oz.; MOL-IRON CHRONOSULE Capsules—bottles of 30 and 250; MOL-IRON Tablets with Vitamin C—bottles of 100.
Store the tablet and capsule forms between 2° and 30°C (36° and 86°F) and the liquid between 15° and 30°C (59° and 86°F).
[*Shown in Product Identification Section*]

SUNRIL® Premenstrual Capsules

Active Ingredients: Each capsule contains: Acetaminophen 300 mg, an effective analgesic. Pamabrom 50 mg (2-amino- 2-methyl- 1-propanol- 8-bromo-theophyllinate), a mild, effective diuretic. Pyrilamine maleate 25 mg, a mild antihistamine.
Indications: For relief of premenstrual tension, edema and related pain.
Warning: Keep out of reach of children.
Precautions: Do not drive or operate machinery while taking this medication as this preparation may cause drowsiness. Limit dosage to no more than 10 consecutive days unless recommended by your physician. Should not be used by anyone with a known sensitivity to any one of the ingredients.

Information on Schering products appearing on these pages is effective as of January 1, 1982.

Continued on next page

Schering—Cont.

Overdosage: In case of accidental overdose, seek professional assistance or contact a Poison Control Center immediately.

Dosage and Administration: 1 capsule every 3 to 4 hours. Do not exceed 4 capsules within a 24 hour period. Start using at first sign of discomfort, usually 4 to 7 days before onset of menstruation.

How Supplied: SUNRIL® Premenstrual Capsules are pink and lavender capsules; available in bottles of 100.

[*Shown in Product Identification Section*]

TINACTIN® Antifungal
Cream 1%
Solution 1%
Powder 1%
Powder (1%) Aerosol

Description: TINACTIN Cream 1% is a white homogeneous, nonaqueous preparation containing the highly active synthetic fungicidal agent, tolnaftate. Each gram contains 10 mg. tolnaftate solubilized in polyethylene glycol-400 and propylene glycol with carboxypolymethylene, monoamylamine, titanium dioxide, and butylated hydroxytoluene.

TINACTIN Solution 1% contains in each ml. tolnaftate, 10 mg. and butylated hydroxytoluene, 1 mg. in a nonaqueous, homogeneous vehicle of polyethylene glycol-400. The solution solidifies at low temperatures but liquefies readily when warmed, retaining its potency.

Each gram of TINACTIN Powder 1% contains tolnaftate 10 mg. in a vehicle of corn starch and talc.

TINACTIN Powder Aerosol contains 91 mg. tolnaftate in a vehicle of butylated hydroxytoluene, talc, and polyethylene-polypropylene glycol monobutyl ether. It also contains 14% denatured alcohol and sufficient inert propellant of isobutane to make 100 grams. The spray deposits a white clinging powder containing a concentration of 1% tolnaftate.

Indications: TINACTIN Cream and Solution are highly active antifungal agents that are effective in killing superficial fungi of the skin which cause tinea pedis (athlete's foot), tinea cruris (jock itch) and tinea corporis (body ringworm). TINACTIN Powder and Powder Aerosol are effective in killing superficial fungi of the skin which cause tinea cruris (jock itch) and tinea pedis (athlete's foot). All forms begin to relieve burning, itching and soreness within 24 hours. Symptoms are usually cleared in 2 to 3 weeks. Where skin is thickened, treatment may take 4 to 6 weeks. The powder and powder aerosol forms aid the drying of naturally moist areas and begin to relieve burning and itching within 24 hours.

Actions: The active ingredient in TINACTIN is a highly active synthetic fungicidal agent that is effective in the treatment of superficial fungus infections of the skin. It is inactive systemically, virtually nonsensitizing, and does not ordinarily sting or irritate intact or broken skin, even in the presence of acute inflammatory reactions.

TINACTIN products are odorless, greaseless, and do not stain or discolor the skin, hair, or nails.

Warnings: Keep these and all drugs out of the reach of children.

TINACTIN Powder Aerosol: Avoid spraying in eyes. Contents under pressure. Do not puncture or incinerate. Flammable mixture, do not use or store near heat or open flame. Exposure to temperatures above 120°F. may cause bursting. Never throw container into fire or incinerator. Use only as directed. Intentional misuse by deliberately concentrating and inhaling the contents can be harmful or fatal.

Precautions: If burning or itching do not improve within 10 days, become worse, or if irritation occurs, discontinue use and consult your physician or podiatrist.

TINACTIN products are for external use only. Keep out of eyes.

TINACTIN Cream and Solution are not recommended for nail or scalp infections. TINACTIN Powder and Powder Aerosol are not recommended for use on scalp.

Overdosage: In case of accidental ingestion, seek professional assistance or contact a Poison Control Center immediately.

Dosage and Administration: TINACTIN Cream—Wash and dry infected area morning and evening. Then apply one-half inch ribbon of cream and rub gently on infected area. Spread evenly. To help prevent recurrence, continue treatment for two weeks after disappearance of all symptoms.

TINACTIN Solution—Wash and dry infected area morning and evening. Then apply two or three drops and massage gently to cover the infected area. To help prevent recurrence, continue treatment for two weeks after disappearance of all symptoms.

TINACTIN Powder—Sprinkle powder liberally on all areas of infection and in shoes or socks. To help prevent recurrence of athlete's foot or jock itch, bathe daily, dry carefully and apply TINACTIN Powder.

TINACTIN Powder Aerosol—Shake well before using. Spray from a distance of 6 to 10 inches. Spray powder liberally on all areas of infection and in shoes or socks. To help prevent recurrence of jock itch or athlete's foot, bathe daily, dry carefully and apply TINACTIN Powder Aerosol.

How Supplied: TINACTIN Antifungal Cream 1%, 15 g (½ oz.) collapsible tube with dispensing tip. TINACTIN Antifungal Solution 1%, 10 ml (⅓ oz.) plastic squeeze bottle. TINACTIN Antifungal Powder 1%, 45 g (1.5 oz.) plastic container. TINACTIN Antifungal Powder (1%) Aerosol, 100 g (3.5 oz.) spray can. Store the aerosol between 35° and 86°F (2° and 30°C).

[*Shown in Product Identification Section*]

Information on Schering products appearing on these pages is effective as of January 1, 1982.

Searle Consumer Products
Division of Searle
   Pharmaceuticals Inc.
BOX 5110
CHICAGO, IL 60680

DRAMAMINE® Liquid
(dimenhydrinate syrup USP)

DRAMAMINE® Tablets
(dimenhydrinate USP)

Active Ingredient: Dimenhydrinate is the chlorotheophylline salt of the antihistaminic agent diphenhydramine. Dimenhydrinate contains not less than 53% and not more than 56% of diphenhydramine, and not less than 44% and not more than 47% of 8-chlorotheophylline, calculated on the dried basis.

Indications: Dramamine is indicated for the prevention and treatment of the nausea, vomiting or vertigo of motion sickness. Such an illness may arise from the motion of ships, planes, trains, automobiles, buses, swings, or even amusement park rides. Regardless of the cause of motion sickness, Dramamine has been found to be effective in its prevention or treatment.

Actions: While the precise mode of action of dimenhydrinate is not known, it has a depressant action on hyperstimulated labyrinthine function.

Warning: Caution should be used when Dramamine is given in conjunction with certain antibiotics which may cause ototoxicity, since Dramamine is capable of masking ototoxic symptoms and an irreversible state may be reached.

Precautions: Drowsiness may be experienced by some patients, especially on high dosage, although this action frequently is not undesirable in some conditions for which the drug is used. However, because of possible drowsiness, patients taking Dramamine should be cautioned against operating automobiles or dangerous machinery. Patients should also avoid alcoholic beverages while taking medication. Dramamine should not be used in the presence of asthma, glaucoma, or enlargement of the prostate gland, except on advice of a physician.

Dosage and Administration
Dramamine Tablets: To prevent motion sickness, the first dose should be taken one-half to one hour before starting your activity. Additional medication depends on travel conditions. *Adults*—Nausea or vomiting may be expected to be controlled for approximately four hours with 50 mg of Dramamine, and prevented by a similar dose every four hours. Its administration may be attended by some degree of drowsiness in some patients, and 100 mg every four hours may be given in conditions in which drowsiness is not objectionable or is even desirable. The usual adult dosage is 1 to 2 tablets every four to six hours, not to exceed 8 tablets in 24 hours. *Chil-*

dren 6 to 12 years: ½ to 1 tablet every six to eight hours, not to exceed 3 tablets in 24 hours. Children 2 to 6 years: Up to ½ tablet every six to eight hours, not to exceed 1½ tablets in 24 hours. Children may also be given Dramamine cherry-flavored liquid in accordance with directions for use. Not for frequent or prolonged use except on advice of a physician. Do not exceed recommended dosage.

Dramamine Liquid: To prevent motion sickness, the first dose should be taken one-half to one hour before starting your activity. Additional medication depends on travel conditions. Dosage: Adults: 4 to 8 teaspoonfuls (4 ml per teaspoonful) every four to six hours, not to exceed 32 teaspoonfuls in 24 hours. Children 6 to 12 years: 2 to 4 teaspoonfuls every six to eight hours, not to exceed 12 teaspoonfuls in 24 hours. Children 2 to 6 years: 1 to 2 teaspoonfuls every six to eight hours, not to exceed 6 teaspoonfuls in 24 hours. Children under 2 years: Only on advice of a physician.

Not for frequent or prolonged use except on advice of a physician. Do not exceed recommended dosage. Use of a measuring device is recommended for all liquid medication.

How Supplied: Tablets—scored, white tablets of 50 mg, with SEARLE debossed on one side and 1701 on the other side, in packages of 12 and bottles of 36 (OTC). Also available in unit-dose packets of 100, and in bottles of 100, 500, 1,000, and 2,500. Liquid—12.5 mg per 4 ml, ethyl alcohol 5%, bottles of 3 oz (OTC). Also available in pint bottles.

[Shown in Product Identification Section]

ICY HOT® BALM
(topical analgesic balm)
ICY HOT® RUB
(topical analgesic cream)

Active Ingredients:
ICY HOT BALM—methyl salicylate 29%, menthol 8%.
ICY HOT RUB—methyl salicylate 12%, menthol 9%.

Description: Icy Hot Balm and Icy Hot Rub are topically applied analgesics containing two active ingredients, methyl salicylate and menthol. It is the particular concentration of these ingredients, in combination with inert ingredients, that results in the distinct combined heating/cooling sensation of Icy Hot.

Actions: Icy Hot is classified as a counterirritant which, when rubbed into the intact skin, provides relief of deep-seated pain through a counterirritant action rather than through a direct analgesic effect. In acting as a counterirritant, Icy Hot replaces the patient's perception of pain with another sensation that blocks deep pain temporarily by its action on or near the skin surface.

Warnings: Use only as directed. Keep away from children to avoid accidental poisoning. Keep away from eyes, mouth, genitalia, mucous membranes, and broken, irritated, or very sensitive skin. Do not swallow. If swallowed, induce vomiting and call a physician. If skin irritation develops, discontinue use. Consult a phy-

sician if pain lasts 10 days or more, if redness is present, or before using on children under 12 years of age.

Adverse Reactions: The most common adverse reactions that may occur with Icy Hot use are skin irritation and blistering. The most serious adverse reaction is severe toxicity that occurs if the product is ingested.

Directions for Use: Apply to painful area; massage until Icy Hot is completely absorbed. Repeat as necessary.

How Supplied:
ICY HOT BALM is available in jars in two sizes—3½ oz and 7 oz.
ICY HOT RUB is available in tubes in two sizes—1¼ oz and 3 oz.
[Shown in Product Identification Section]

METAMUCIL®
(psyllium hydrophilic mucilloid)

Description: Metamucil is a bulk laxative that provides a bland, nonirritating bulk and promotes normal elimination. It contains refined hydrophilic mucilloid, a highly efficient dietary fiber derived from the husk of the psyllium seed (Plantago ovata). An equal amount of dextrose, a carbohydrate, is added as a dispersing agent. Each dose contains about 1 mg of sodium, 31 mg of potassium, and 14 calories. Carbohydrate content is approximately 3.5 g; psyllium mucilloid content is 3.4 g.

Indications: Metamucil is indicated in the management of chronic constipation, in irritable bowel syndrome, as adjunctive therapy in constipation of duodenal ulcer and diverticular disease, in the bowel management of patients with hemorrhoids, and for constipation during pregnancy, convalescence, and senility.

Actions: Metamucil is uniform, instantly miscible, palatable, and nonirritative in the gastrointestinal tract.

Dosage and Administration: The usual adult dosage is one rounded teaspoonful (7 g) stirred into a standard 8-oz glass of cool water or other suitable liquid and taken orally one to three times a day, depending on the need and response. It may require continuing use for 2 or 3 days to provide optimal benefit. Best results are observed if each dose is followed by an additional glass of liquid.

Contraindications: Intestinal obstruction, fecal impaction.

How Supplied: Powder, containers of 7 oz, 14 oz, and 21 oz.
[Shown in Product Identification Section]

INSTANT MIX METAMUCIL®
(psyllium hydrophilic mucilloid)

Description: Instant Mix Metamucil is provided in premeasured, single-dose packets for oral use. It contains refined hydrophilic mucilloid, a highly efficient dietary fiber, derived from the husk of the psyllium seed (Plantago ovata), together with citric acid, sucrose (a carbohydrate), potassium bicarbonate, calcium carbonate, flavoring, and sodium bicarbonate. Each dose contains approximately 7 mg of sodium, 60 mg of calcium, 280 mg of potassium, and less than 4 cal-

ories. Carbohydrate content is about 0.9 g; psyllium mucilloid content is 3.6 g.

Indications: Instant Mix Metamucil is indicated for its smoothage effect in the management of chronic constipation, in irritable bowel syndrome, as adjunctive therapy in constipation of duodenal ulcer and diverticular disease, in the bowel management of patients with hemorrhoids, and for constipation during pregnancy, convalescence, and senility.

Actions: Instant Mix Metamucil, effervescent and requiring no stirring, is uniform, instantly miscible, palatable, and nonirritative in the gastrointestinal tract.

Contraindications: Intestinal obstruction, fecal impaction.

Dosage and Administration: The usual adult dosage is the contents of one packet, taken one to three times daily as follows: 1. Entire contents of a packet are poured into a standard 8-oz water glass. 2. The glass is slowly filled with cool water. 3. Entire contents are drunk immediately. (An additional glass of water may be taken for best results.)

How Supplied: Cartons of 16 and 30 single-dose packets.
[Shown in Product Identification Section]

Orange Flavor METAMUCIL®
Powder
(psyllium hydrophilic mucilloid)

Description: Metamucil is a bulk laxative that provides a bland, nonirritating bulk and promotes normal elimination. It contains refined hydrophilic mucilloid, a highly efficient dietary fiber, derived from the husk of the psyllium seed (Plantago ovata), with sucrose (a carbohydrate) as a dispersing agent, citric acid, flavoring and coloring. Each dose contains about 1 mg of sodium, 31 mg of potassium, and 28 calories. Carbohydrate content is approximately 7.1 g; psyllium mucilloid content is 3.4 g.

Indications: Metamucil is indicated in the management of chronic constipation, in irritable bowel syndrome, as adjunctive therapy in constipation of duodenal ulcer and diverticular disease, in the bowel management of patients with hemorrhoids, and for constipation during pregnancy, convalescence, and senility.

Actions: Metamucil is uniform, instantly miscible, palatable, and nonirritative in the gastrointestinal tract.

Contraindications: Intestinal obstruction, fecal impaction.

Dosage and Administration: The usual adult dosage is one rounded tablespoonful (11 g) stirred into a standard 8-oz glass of cool water and taken orally one to three times a day, depending on the need and response. It may require continuing use for 2 or 3 days to provide optimal benefit. Best results are observed if each dose is followed by an additional glass of liquid.

How Supplied: Powder, containers of 7 oz, 14 oz, and 21 oz.
[Shown in Product Identification Section]

Continued on next page

Searle Consumer—Cont.

Orange Flavor
INSTANT MIX METAMUCIL®
(psyllium hydrophilic mucilloid)

Description: Orange Flavor Instant Mix Metamucil is provided in premeasured, single-dose packets for oral use. It contains refined hydrophilic mucilloid, a highly efficient dietary fiber derived from the husk of the psyllium seed *(Plantago ovata)*, together with sucrose (a carbohydrate), citric acid, potassium bicarbonate, flavoring, coloring, and sodium bicarbonate. Each dose contains approximately 6 mg of sodium, 307 mg of potassium, and 4½ calories. Carbohydrate content is about 1.1 g; psyllium mucilloid content is 3.6 g.

Indications: Instant Mix Metamucil is indicated in the management of chronic constipation, in irritable bowel syndrome, as adjunctive therapy in constipation of duodenal ulcer and diverticular disease, in the bowel management of patients with hemorrhoids, and for constipation during pregnancy, convalescence, and senility.

Actions: Instant Mix Metamucil, effervescent and requiring no stirring, is uniform, instantly miscible, palatable, and nonirritative in the gastrointestinal tract.

Contraindications: Intestinal obstruction, fecal impaction.

Dosage and Administration: The usual adult dosage is the contents of one packet, taken one to three times daily as follows: 1. Entire contents of a packet are poured into a standard 8-oz water glass. 2. The glass is slowly filled with cool water. 3. Entire contents are drunk immediately. (An additional glass of water may be taken for best results.)

How Supplied: Cartons of 16 and 30 single-dose packets.

[*Shown in Product Identification Section*]

The preceding prescribing information for Searle Consumer Products was current as of February 1, 1982.

E. R. Squibb & Sons, Inc.
GENERAL OFFICES
P.O. BOX 4000
PRINCETON, NJ 08540

SPEC-T®
Sore Throat Anesthetic Lozenges

Active Ingredient: Benzocaine 10 mg.
Indications: For temporary relief of minor sore throat pain due to colds.
Actions: Benzocaine, one of the strongest pain relievers you can buy without a prescription, acts fast to provide soothing temporary relief of minor sore throat pain.
Warnings: Severe or persistent sore throat or sore throat accompanied by high fever, headache, nausea and vomiting may be serious; in such cases consult a physician promptly. Do not use more than 2 days or administer to children un-

der 6 without physician's instructions. Keep this and all drugs out of the reach of children.
Oral Overdosage: In case of accidental overdose, seek professional assistance or contact a poison control center immediately.
Dosage and Administration: Adults and children over 6 years—dissolve 1 lozenge slowly. For best results do not chew. Use as needed. Children under 6 years —only as directed by a physician.
How Supplied: Available in (red) packages of 10 individually wrapped lozenges.
[*Shown in Product Identification Section*]

SPEC-T®
Sore Throat/Cough Suppressant Lozenges

Active Ingredient: Benzocaine 10 mg; dextromethorphan hydrobromide 10 mg.
Indications: For temporary relief of minor sore throat pain and coughs due to colds.
Actions: Benzocaine, one of the strongest pain relievers you can buy without a prescription, plus dextromethorphan, a widely recommended non-narcotic cough suppressant, offer a combination which acts fast to 1) provide soothing temporary relief of minor sore throat pain, and 2) quiet rasping coughs due to colds which may be causing throat discomfort.
Warnings: Severe or persistent sore throat or sore throat accompanied by high fever, headache, nausea and vomiting may be serious; in such cases consult a physician promptly. Persistent cough may indicate presence of a serious condition. Persons with high fever or persistent cough should not use this preparation unless directed by a physician. Do not use more than 2 days or administer to children under 6 unless directed by a physician. Keep this and all drugs out of the reach of children.
Oral Overdosage: In case of accidental overdose, seek professional assistance or contact a poison control center immediately.
Dosage and Administration: Adults and children over 6 years—dissolve 1 lozenge slowly. For best results do not chew. Lozenge may be repeated every 3 hours but should not exceed 6 lozenges in 24 hours. Children under 6—only as directed by a physician.
How Supplied: Available in (yellow) packages of 10 individually wrapped lozenges.
[*Shown in Product Identification Section*]

SPEC-T®
Sore Throat/Decongestant Lozenges

Active Ingredient: Benzocaine 10 mg; phenylephrine hydrochloride 5 mg; phenylpropanolamine hydrochloride 10.5 mg.
Indications: For temporary relief of minor sore throat pain and nasal congestion due to colds.
Actions: Benzocaine, one of the strongest pain relievers you can buy without a prescription, plus phenylpropanolamine and phenylephrine, which provide effec-

tive decongestant action, offer a combination which acts fast to 1) provide soothing temporary relief of minor sore throat pain, and 2) reduce nasal congestion due to colds including postnasal drip which may contribute to throat discomfort.
Warnings: Severe or persistent sore throat or sore throat accompanied by high fever, headache, nausea and vomiting may be serious; in such cases consult a physician promptly. Individuals with high blood pressure, heart disease, diabetes, or thyroid disease should use only as directed by a physician. Do not use more than 2 days or administer to children under 12 unless directed by a physician. Keep this and all drugs out of the reach of children.
Oral Overdosage: In case of accidental overdose, seek professional assistance or contact a poison control center immediately.
Dosage and Administration: Adults and children over 12 years—dissolve 1 lozenge slowly. For best results do not chew. Lozenge may be repeated every 3 hours but should not exceed 6 lozenges in 24 hours. Children under 12—only as directed by a physician.
How Supplied: Available in (green) packages of 10 individually wrapped lozenges.
[*Shown in Product Identification Section*]

THERAGRAN® LIQUID
(High Potency Vitamin Supplement)

Each 5 ml. teaspoonful contains:

		Percent US RDA*
Vitamin A (3 mg)	10,000 IU	200
Vitamin D (10 mcg)	400 IU	100
Vitamin C	200 mg	333
Thiamine	10 mg	667
Riboflavin	10 mg	588
Niacin	100 mg	500
Vitamin B6	4.1 mg	205
Vitamin B12	5 mcg	83
Pantothenic Acid	21.4 mg	214

*US Recommended Daily Allowance
Usage: For 12 year olds and older—1 teaspoonful daily.
The following statement appears on the label: "Use of this product may be hazardous to your health. This product contains saccharin which has been determined to cause cancer in laboratory animals".
How Supplied: In bottles of 4 fl. oz.
Storage: Store at room temperature; avoid excessive heat.

THERAGRAN® TABLETS
(High Potency Vitamin Supplement)

Each tablet contains:

		Percent US RDA*
Vitamin A (3 mg)	10,000 IU	200
Vitamin D (10 mcg)	400 IU	100
Vitamin E (15 mg)	15 IU	50
Vitamin C	200 mg	333
Thiamine	10.3 mg	687
Riboflavin	10 mg	588
Niacin	100 mg	500
Vitamin B6	4.1 mg	205
Vitamin B12	5 mcg	83
Pantothenic Acid	18.4 mg	184

*US Recommended Daily Allowance

Usage: For 12 year olds and older—1 tablet daily.
How Supplied: Bottles of 1000; Handy Packs of 30, 60, 100, and 180; and Unimatic® cartons of 100.
Storage: Store at room temperature; avoid excessive heat.

THERAGRAN-M® TABLETS
(High Potency Vitamin Supplement with Minerals)

Each tablet contains:

		Percent US RDA*
Vitamins		
Vitamin A (3 mg)	10,000 IU	200
Vitamin D (10 mcg)	400 IU	100
Vitamin E (15 mg)	15 IU	50
Vitamin C	200 mg	333
Thiamine	10.3 mg	687
Riboflavin	10 mg	588
Niacin	100 mg	500
Vitamin B$_6$	4.1 mg	205
Vitamin B$_{12}$	5 mcg	83
Pantothenic Acid	18.4 mg	184
Minerals		
Iodine	150 mcg	100
Iron	12 mg	67
Magnesium	65 mg	16
Copper	2 mg	100
Zinc	1.5 mg	10
Manganese	1 mg	**

*US Recommended Daily Allowance
**US RDA not established
Usage: For 12 year olds and older—1 tablet daily.
How Supplied: Bottles of 1000; Handy Packs of 30, 60, 100, and 180; and Unimatic® cartons of 100.
Storage: Store at room temperature; avoid excessive heat.
[Shown in Product Identification Section]

THERAGRAN-Z® TABLETS
(High Potency Vitamin-Mineral Supplement with Zinc)

Each tablet contains:

		Percent US RDA*
Vitamins		
Vitamin A (3 mg)	10,000 IU	200
Vitamin D (10 mcg)	400 IU	100
Vitamin E (15 mg)	15 IU	50
Vitamin C	200 mg	333
Thiamine	10.3 mg	687
Riboflavin	10 mg	588
Niacin	100 mg	500
Vitamin B$_6$	4.1 mg	205
Vitamin B$_{12}$	5 mcg	83
Pantothenic Acid	18.4 mg	184
Minerals		
Iodine	150 mcg	100
Iron	12 mg	67
Copper	2 mg	100
Zinc	22.5 mg	150
Manganese	1 mg	**

*US Recommended Daily Allowance
**US RDA not established
Usage: For 12 year olds and older—1 tablet daily.
How Supplied: Bottles of 30 and 60.
Storage: Store at room temperature; avoid excessive heat.
[Shown in Product Identification Section]

Stellar Pharmacal Corp.
Div./Star Pharmaceuticals, Inc.
P.O. BOX 600354
N. MIAMI BEACH, FL 33160

STAR-OTIC®
Antibacterial, Antifungal, Nonaqueous Ear Solution
For Prevention of "Swimmer's Ear"

Active Ingredients: Acetic acid 1.0% nonaqueous, Burow's solution 10%, Boric acid 1.0%, in a propylene glycol vehicle, with an acid pH and a low surface tension.
Indications: For the prevention of otitis externa, commonly called "Swimmer's Ear".
Actions: Star-Otic is antibacterial, antifungal, hydrophilic, has an acid pH and a low surface tension. Acetic acid and boric acid inhibit the rapid multiplication of microorganisms and help maintain the lining mantle of the ear canal in its normal acid state. Burow's solution (aluminum acetate) is a mild astringent. Propylene glycol reduces moisture in the ear canal.
Warning: Do not use in ear if tympanic membrane (ear drum) is perforated or punctured.
Drug Interaction Precaution: No known drug interaction. Virtually non-sensitizing and safe to use as directed.
Symptoms and Treatment of Overdosage: Discontinue use if undue irritation or sensitivity occurs.
Dosage and Administration: Adults and Children: For the prevention of otitis externa (Swimmer's Ear) instill 2–3 drops of Star-Otic in each ear before and after swimming or bathing in susceptible persons, or as directed by physician.
Professional Labeling: Same as those outlined under Indications.
How Supplied: Available in 15 cc measured drop, safety tip, plastic bottle.

Stuart Pharmaceuticals
Div. of ICI Americas Inc.
WILMINGTON, DE 19897

ALternaGEL®
Liquid
High-Potency Aluminum Hydroxide Antacid

Composition: ALternaGEL is available as a white, pleasant-tasting, low sodium, high-potency aluminum hydroxide liquid antacid.
Each 5 ml. teaspoonful contains 600 mg. aluminum hydroxide (equivalent to dried gel, USP) providing 12 milliequivalents (mEq) of acid-neutralizing capacity (ANC), and less than 2 mg. (.087 mEq) of sodium per teaspoonful.
Indications: ALternaGEL is indicated for the symptomatic relief of hyperacidity associated with peptic ulcer, gastritis, peptic esophagitis, gastric hyperacidity, hiatal hernia, and heartburn.
ALternaGEL will be of special value to those patients for whom magnesium-containing antacids are undesirable, such as patients with renal insufficiency, patients requiring control of attendant G.I. complications resulting from steroid or other drug therapy, and patients experiencing the laxation which may result from magnesium or combination antacid regimens.
Directions for Use: One or two teaspoonfuls, as needed, between meals and at bedtime, or as directed by a physician. May be followed by a sip of water if desired.
Patient Warnings: As with all medications, ALternaGEL should be kept out of the reach of children.
ALternaGEL may cause constipation. Except under the advice and supervision of a physician, more than 18 teaspoonfuls should not be taken in a 24-hour period, or the maximum recommended dosage taken for more than two weeks.
Drug Interaction Precaution: ALternaGEL should not be taken concurrently with an antibiotic containing any form of tetracycline.
How Supplied: ALternaGEL is available in bottles of 12 fluid ounces and 5 fluid ounces.
NDC 0038-0860.
[Shown in Product Identification Section]

DIALOSE™ Capsules
Stool Softener

Composition: Each capsule contains docusate potassium, 100 mg.
Action and Uses: DIALOSE is indicated for treating constipation due to hardness, or lack of moisture in the intestinal contents. DIALOSE is an effective stool softener, whose gentle action will help to restore normal bowel function gradually, without griping or acute discomfort.
Dosage and Administration:
Adults: Initially, one capsule three times a day.
Children, 6 years and over: One capsule at bedtime, or as directed by physician.
Children, under 6 years: As directed by physician.
It is helpful to increase the daily intake of fluids by taking a glass of water with each dose. When adequate laxation is obtained, the dose may be adjusted to meet individual needs.
How Supplied: Bottles of 36, 100, and 500 pink capsules, identified "STUART 470". Also available in 100 capsule unit dose boxes (10 strips of 10 capsules each).
NDC 0038-0470.
[Shown in Product Identification Section]

DIALOSE™ PLUS Capsules
Stool Softener
plus Peristaltic Activator

Composition: Each capsule contains: docusate potassium, 100 mg. and casanthranol, 30 mg.
Action and Uses: DIALOSE PLUS Is indicated for the treatment of constipation generally associated with any of the following: hardness, or lack of moisture in the intestinal contents, or decreased intestinal motility.

Continued on next page

Stuart—Cont.

DIALOSE PLUS combines the advantages of the stool softener, docusate potassium, with the peristaltic activating effect of casanthranol.

Warning: As with any laxative, DIALOSE PLUS should not be used when abdominal pain, nausea, or vomiting are present. Frequent or prolonged use may result in dependence on laxatives.

Dosage and Administration:

Adults: Initially, one capsule two times a day.

Children: As directed by physician. When adequate laxation is obtained the dose may be adjusted to meet individual needs.

It is helpful to increase the daily intake of fluids by taking a glass of water with each dose.

How Supplied: Bottles of 36, 100, and 500 yellow capsules, identified "STUART 475". Also available in 100 capsule unit dose boxes (10 strips of 10 capsules each).

NDC 0038-0475.

[*Shown in Product Identification Section*]

EFFERSYLLIUM® Instant Mix
Bulk Laxative

Composition: Each rounded teaspoonful, or individual packet (7 g.) contains psyllium hydrocolloid, 3 g.

Actions and Uses: EFFERSYLLIUM produces a soft, lubricating bulk which promotes natural elimination.

EFFERSYLLIUM is not a one-dose, fast-acting purgative or cathartic. Administration for several days may be needed to establish regularity.

Effersyllium contains less than 7 mg. sodium per rounded teaspoonful.

Dosage and Administration:

Adults: One rounded teaspoonful, or one packet, in a glass of water one to three times a day, or as directed by physician. *Children, 6 years and over:* One level teaspoonful, or one-half packet (3.5 g.) in one-half glass of water at bedtime, or as directed by physician. *Children, under 6 years:* As directed by physician.

Note: To avoid caking, always use a dry spoon to remove EFFERSYLLIUM from its container. Dosage should be placed in a dry glass. Add water, stir and drink immediately. REPLACE CAP TIGHTLY. KEEP IN A DRY PLACE.

Warning: As with all medication, keep out of the reach of children.

How Supplied: Bottles of 9 oz. and 16 oz. of tan, granular powder. Convenient pouch package 7 g. per packet in boxes of 12 or 24.

NDC 0038-0440.

[*Shown in Product Identification Section*]

FERANCEE®
Chewable Tablets

Composition: Each tablet contains: iron (from 200 mg. ferrous fumarate), 67 mg. and Vitamin C (as ascorbic acid, 49 mg. and sodium ascorbate, 114 mg.), 150 mg. Contains FD&C Yellow #5 (tartrazine) as a color additive.

Action and Uses: A pleasant tasting hematinic for iron-deficiency anemias, FERANCEE is particularly useful when chronic blood loss, onset of menses, or pregnancy create additional demands for iron supplementation. Because ferrous fumarate is unusually well-tolerated, FERANCEE can be administered between meals when iron absorption is maximal. The peach-cherry flavored chewable tablets dissolve quickly in the mouth and may be either chewed or swallowed.

Dosage and Administration:

Adults: Two tablets daily, or as directed by physician.

Children over 6 years of age: One tablet daily, or as directed by physician.

Children under 6 years of age: As directed by physician.

How Supplied: Bottles of 100 brown and yellow, two-layer tablets identified "STUART 650" on brown layer. A childproof cap is standard on each bottle as a safeguard against accidental ingestion by children.

NDC 0038-0650.

FERANCEE®–HP Tablets

Composition: Each tablet contains: iron (from 330 mg. ferrous fumarate), 110 mg.; Vitamin C (as ascorbic acid, 350 mg. and sodium ascorbate, 281 mg.), 600 mg. Contains FD&C Yellow #5 (tartrazine) as a color additive.

Action and Uses: FERANCEE-HP is a high potency formulation of iron and Vitamin C and is intended for use as either:

(1) intensive therapy for the acute and/or severe iron deficiency anemia where a high intake of elemental iron is required, or

(2) a maintenance hematinic for those patients needing a daily iron supplement to maintain normal hemoglobin levels.

The use of well-tolerated ferrous fumarate provides high levels of elemental iron with a low incidence of gastric distress. The inclusion of 600 mg. of Vitamin C per tablet serves to maintain more of the iron in the absorbable ferrous state.

Precautions: Because FERANCEE-HP contains 110 mg. of elemental iron per tablet, it is recommended that its use be limited to adults, i.e. over age 12 years. As with all medication, FERANCEE-HP should be kept out of the reach of children.

Dosage and Administration:

For acute and/or severe iron deficiency anemia, two or three tablets per day taken one tablet per dose after meals. (Each tablet provides 110 mg. elemental iron).

For maintenance of normal hemoglobin levels in most patients with a history of recurring iron deficiency anemia, one tablet per day taken after a meal should be sufficient.

How Supplied: FERANCEE-HP is supplied in bottles of 60 red, film coated, oval shaped tablets.

NDC 0038-0863.

Note: A childproof safety cap is standard on each bottle of 60 tablets as a safeguard against accidental ingestion by children.

[*Shown in Product Identification Section*]

HIBICLENS® Antiseptic
Antiseptic Antimicrobial Skin
Cleanser
(chlorhexidine gluconate)

Description: HIBICLENS is an antiseptic antimicrobial skin cleanser possessing bactericidal activities. HIBICLENS contains 4% chlorhexidine gluconate, chemically unique hexamethylenebis biguanide, in a mild, sudsing base adjusted to pH 5.0–6.5 for optimal activity and stability as well as compatability with the normal pH of the skin.

Action: HIBICLENS is bactericidal on contact. It has antiseptic activity and a persistent antimicrobial effect against a wide range of microorganisms, including gram-positive bacteria, and gram-negative bacteria such as *Pseudomonas aeruginosa.* The effectiveness of HIBICLENS is not significantly reduced by the presence of organic matter, such as pus or blood.[1]

In a study[2] simulating surgical use, the immediate bactericidal effect of HIBICLENS after a single six-minute scrub resulted in a 99.9% reduction in resident bacterial flora, with a reduction of 99.98% after the eleventh scrub. Reductions on surgically gloved hands were maintained over the six-hour test period.

HIBICLENS displays persistent antimicrobial action. In one study[2], 93% of a radiolabeled formulation of HIBICLENS remained present on uncovered skin after five hours.

HIBICLENS prevents skin infection thereby reducing the risk of cross-infection.

Indications: HIBICLENS is indicated for use as a surgical scrub, as a healthcare personnel handwash, for preoperative showering and bathing, and as a skin wound cleanser and general skin cleanser.

Safety: The extensive use of chlorhexidine gluconate for over 20 years outside the United States has produced no evidence of absorption of the compound through intact skin. The potential for producing skin reactions is extremely low. HIBICLENS can be used many times a day without causing irritation, dryness, or discomfort. When used for cleaning superficial wounds, HIBICLENS will neither cause additional tissue injury nor delay healing.

Precautions: HIBICLENS is for topical use only. The sudsing formulation may be irritating to the eyes. If HIBICLENS should get into the eyes, rinse out promptly and thoroughly with water. Keep out of ears. Chlorhexidine gluconate, like various other antimicrobial agents, has been reported to cause deafness when instilled in the middle ear. In the presence of a perforated eardrum particular care should be taken to prevent exposure of inner ear tissues to HIBICLENS.

HIBICLENS should not be used by persons with sensitivity to any of its components. Adverse reactions, including dermatitis and photosensitivity, are rare, but if they do occur, discontinue use. Keep this and all other drugs out of the reach of children. AVOID EXCESSIVE HEAT (104°F).

Directions for Use:
skin wound and general skin cleansing
Thoroughly rinse area to be cleansed with water. Apply sufficient HIBICLENS and wash gently. Rinse again thoroughly.

health-care personnel use
SURGICAL HAND SCRUB
Wet hands and forearms with water. Scrub for 3 minutes with about 5 ml. of HIBICLENS and a wet brush, paying particular attention to the nails, cuticles, and interdigital spaces. A separate nail cleaner may be used. Rinse thoroughly. Wash for an additional 3 minutes with 5 ml. of HIBICLENS and rinse under running water. Dry thoroughly.
HAND WASH
Wet hands with water. Dispense about 5 ml. of HIBICLENS into cupped hands and wash in a vigorous manner for 15 seconds. Rinse and dry thoroughly.

How Supplied: In plastic disposable bottles: for general handwashing locations, 4 oz. and 8 oz. with dispenser caps, and 16 oz. filled globes; for surgical scrub areas, 32 oz. and 1 gal. The 32 oz. bottle is designed for a special foot-operated wall dispenser. A hand-operated wall dispenser is available for the 16 oz. globe. Hand pumps are available for 16 oz., 32 oz., and 1 gal. sizes. NDC 0038-0575.

References:
1. Lowbury EJL, and Lilly HA: The effect of blood on disinfection of surgeons' hands, Brit. J. Surg. 61:19–21 (Jan.) 1974.
2. Peterson AF, Rosenberg A, Alatary SD: Comparative evaluation of surgical scrub preparations, Surg. Gynecol. Obstet. 146:63–65 (Jan.) 1978.
[*Shown in Product Identification Section*]

HIBISTAT™
(chlorhexidine gluconate)
Germicidal Hand Rinse

Description: HIBISTAT is a germicidal hand rinse effective against a wide range of microorganisms. HIBISTAT is a clear, colorless liquid containing 0.5% w/w chlorhexidine gluconate in 70% isopropyl alcohol with emollients.

Actions and Uses: HIBISTAT is indicated for health-care personnel use as a germicidal hand rinse. HIBISTAT is for hand hygiene on physically clean hands. It is used in those situations where hands are physically clean, but in need of degerming, when routine handwashing is not convenient or desirable. HIBISTAT provides rapid germicidal action and has a persistent effect.

HIBISTAT should be used in-between patients and procedures where there are no sinks available or continued return to the sink area is inconvenient or time-consuming. HIBISTAT can be used as an al-

ternative to detergent-based products when hands are physically clean. Also, HIBISTAT is an effective germicidal hand rinse following a soap and water handwash.

Cautions: Keep out of eyes and ears. If HIBISTAT should get into eyes or ears, rinse out promptly and thoroughly with water. Chlorhexidine gluconate has been reported to cause deafness when instilled in the middle ear through perforated ear drums. Irritation or other adverse reactions, such as dermatitis or photosensitivity are rare; but if they do occur, discontinue use. Keep this and all other drugs out of the reach of children.

AVOID EXCESSIVE HEAT (104°F).

Directions for Use: Dispense about 5 ml. of HIBISTAT into cupped hands and rub vigorously until dry (about 15 seconds), paying particular attention to nails and interdigital spaces. HIBISTAT dries rapidly in use. No water or toweling are necessary.

How Supplied: In plastic disposable bottles of 4 oz. and 8 oz. with flip-top cap. NDC 0038-0585.

HIBITANE® Tincture (Tinted)
HIBITANE® Tincture (Non-Tinted)
(chlorhexidine gluconate)
Patient Preoperative Skin Preparation

Description: HIBITANE Tincture is a patient preoperative skin preparation possessing both a rapid and persistent antimicrobial effect against a wide range of microorganisms. It contains 0.5% chlorhexidine gluconate in 70% isopropyl alcohol.

Actions and Uses: HIBITANE Tincture offers wide-range bactericidal activity for the preparation of the skin at the surgical site and prior to skin puncture or vessel puncture. It provides rapid action on contact and maintains persistent antimicrobial effect, not being significantly affected by pus or blood. HIBITANE Tincture (Tinted) contains a skin colorant to provide visible demarcation of the skin. HIBITANE Tincture (Non-Tinted) is slightly colored, but will not tint the skin. Both products are nondetergent and ready to use without dilution.

Cautions: Keep out of eyes and ears. If HIBITANE Tincture should get into eyes or ears, rinse immediately and thoroughly with water. Chlorhexidine gluconate has been reported to cause deafness when instilled in the middle ear through perforated ear drums. Irritation or other adverse reactions such as dermatitis or photosensitivity are rare, but if they do occur, discontinue use. HIBITANE Tincture may be irritating if used on mucosal tissue. Keep this and all other drugs out of the reach of children. AVOID EXCESSIVE HEAT (104°F).

Directions for Use: Apply HIBITANE Tincture liberally to surgical site and swab for at least 2 minutes. Dry with a sterile towel. Repeat this procedure for an additional 2 minutes, and allow skin to air dry.

How Supplied: HIBITANE Tincture (Tinted) is supplied in plastic disposable bottles of 4 oz. NDC 0038-0580.
HIBITANE Tincture (Non-Tinted) is supplied in plastic disposable bottles of 4 oz. and 1 gal. pour package bottles. NDC 0038-0583.

KASOF® Capsules
High Strength Stool Softener

Composition: Each KASOF capsule contains docusate potassium, 240 mg.
Action and Uses: KASOF provides a highly efficient wetting action to restore moisture to the bowel, thus softening the stool to prevent straining. KASOF is especially valuable for the severely constipated, as well as patients with anorectal disorders, such as hemorrhoids and anal fissures. KASOF is ideal for patients with any condition that can be complicated by straining at stool, for example, cardiac patients. The action of KASOF does not interfere with normal peristalsis and generally does not cause griping or extreme sensation of urgency. KASOF is sodium-free, containing a unique potassium formulation, without the problems associated with sodium intake. The simple, one-a-day dosage helps assure patient compliance in maintaining normal bowel function.
Dosage and Administration: Adults: 1 KASOF capsule daily for several days, or until bowel movements are normal and gentle. It is helpful to increase the daily intake of fluids by drinking a glass of water with each dose.
How Supplied: KASOF is available in bottles of 30 and 60 brown, gelatin capsules, identified "Stuart 380".
NDC 0038-0380.
[*Shown in Product Identification Section*]

MYLANTA®
Liquid and Tablets
Antacid/Antiflatulent

Composition: Each chewable tablet or each 5 ml. (one teaspoonful) of liquid contains:
Aluminum hydroxide
  (Dried Gel, USP in tablet and equiv. to
  Dried Gel, USP in liquid)........200 mg.
Magnesium hydroxide ....200 mg.
Simethicone.....................................20 mg.
Sodium Content: 0.68 mg. (0.03 mEq) sodium per 5 ml. teaspoonful of liquid; 0.77 mg. (0.03 mEq) per tablet.
Acid Neutralizing Capacity: Each teaspoonful of MYLANTA liquid will neutralize 12.7 mEq of acid. Each MYLANTA tablet will neutralize 11.5 mEq.
Indications: MYLANTA, a well-balanced combination of two antacids and simethicone, provides consistently dependable relief of symptoms associated with gastric hyperacidity, and mucus-entrapped air or "gas". These indications include:
  Common heartburn (pyrosis)
  Hiatal hernia
  Peptic esophagitis

Continued on next page

Stuart—Cont.

Gastritis
Peptic ulcer

The soft, easy-to-chew tablets and exceptionally pleasant tasting liquid encourage patients' acceptance, thereby minimizing the skipping of prescribed doses. MYLANTA is appropriate whenever there is a need for effective relief of temporary gastric hyperacidity and mucus-entrapped gas.

Directions for Use: One or two teaspoonfuls of liquid or one or two tablets, well-chewed, every two to four hours between meals and at bedtime, or as directed by physician.

Patient Warnings: Keep this and all drugs out of the reach of children.

Except under the advice and supervision of a physician: Do not take more than 24 teaspoonfuls or 24 tablets in a 24 hour period or use the maximum dose for more than two weeks. Do not use this product if you have kidney disease.

Drug Interaction Precaution: Do not use with patients who are presently taking a prescription antibiotic containing any form of tetracycline.

How Supplied: MYLANTA is available as a white, pleasant tasting liquid suspension, and as a two-layer yellow and white chewable tablet, identified on yellow layer "STUART 620". Liquid supplied in bottles of 5 oz. and 12 oz. Tablets supplied in boxes of individually wrapped 40's and 100's, economy size bottles of 180, and consumer convenience packs of 48. Also available for hospital use in liquid unit dose cups of 1 oz., and bottles of 5 oz.

NDC 0038-0610 (liquid). NDC 0038-0620 (tablets).

[*Shown in Product Identification Section*]

MYLANTA®-II
Liquid and Tablets
High Potency Antacid/Antiflatulent

Composition: Each chewable tablet or each 5 ml. (one teaspoonful) of liquid contains:

Aluminum hydroxide
(Dried Gel, USP in tablet and equiv. to Dried Gel, USP in liquid) 400 mg.
Magnesium hydroxide 400 mg.
Simethicone 30 mg.

Sodium Content: 1.14 mg. (0.05 mEq) sodium per 5 ml. teaspoonful of liquid; 1.3 mg. (0.06 mEq) per tablet.

Acid Neutralizing Capacity: Each teaspoonful of MYLANTA-II liquid will neutralize 25.4 mEq of acid. Each MYLANTA-II tablet will neutralize 23.0 mEq.

Indications: MYLANTA-II is a high-potency antacid with an antiflatulent. The soft, easy-to-chew tablets and exceptionally pleasant tasting liquid encourage patient acceptance, thereby minimizing the skipping of prescribed doses. MYLANTA-II provides consistently dependable relief of the symptoms of peptic ulcer and other problems related to acid hypersecretion. The high potency of MYLANTA-II is achieved through its concentration of noncalcium antacid ingredients. Thus MYLANTA-II can produce both rapid and long-lasting neutralization without the acid rebound associated with calcium carbonate. The balanced formula of aluminum and magnesium hydroxides minimizes undesirable bowel effects. Simethicone is effective for the relief of concomitant distress caused by mucus-entrapped gas and swallowed air.

Directions for Use: One or two teaspoonfuls of liquid, or one or two tablets, well-chewed, between meals and at bedtime, or as directed by physician.

Because patients with peptic ulcer vary greatly in both acid output and gastric emptying time, the amount and schedule of dosages should be varied accordingly.

Patient Warnings: Keep this and all drugs out of the reach of children.

Except under the advice and supervision of a physician: Do not take more than 12 teaspoonfuls or 12 tablets in a 24 hour period or use the maximum dose for more than two weeks. Do not use this product if you have kidney disease.

Drug Interaction Precaution: Do not use with patients who are presently taking a prescription antibiotic containing any form of tetracycline.

How Supplied: MYLANTA-II is available as a white, pleasant tasting liquid suspension, and a two-layer green and white chewable tablet, identified on green layer "STUART 851". Liquid supplied in 12 oz. bottles. Tablets supplied in boxes of 60 individually wrapped chewable tablets. Also available for hospital use in liquid unit dose cups of 1 oz., and bottles of 5 oz.

NDC 0038-0852 (liquid). NDC 0038-0851 (tablets).

[*Shown in Product Identification Section*]

MYLICON® Tablets and Drops
Antiflatulent

Composition: Each tablet or 0.6 ml. of drops contains simethicone, 40 mg.

Action and Uses: For relief of the painful symptoms of excess gas in the digestive tract. MYLICON is a valuable adjunct in the treatment of many conditions in which the retention of gas may be a problem, such as: postoperative gaseous distention, air swallowing, functional dyspepsia, peptic ulcer, spastic or irritable colon, diverticulitis.

The defoaming action of MYLICON relieves flatulence by dispersing and preventing the formation of mucus-surrounded gas pockets in the gastrointestinal tract. MYLICON acts in the stomach and intestines to change the surface tension of gas bubbles enabling them to coalesce; thus the gas is freed and is eliminated more easily by belching or passing flatus.

Dosage and Administration:

Tablets—One or two tablets four times daily after meals and at bedtime. May also be taken as needed or as directed by a physician. TABLETS SHOULD BE CHEWED THOROUGHLY.

Drops—0.6 ml. four times daily after meals and at bedtime. May also be taken as needed or as directed by a physician. Shake well before using.

How Supplied: Bottles of 100 and 500 white, scored, chewable tablets, identified front "STUART", reverse "450," and dropper bottles of 30 ml. (1 fl. oz.) pink, pleasant tasting liquid. Also available in 100 tablet unit dose boxes (10 strips of 10 tablets each).

NDC 0038-0450 (tablets).
NDC 0038-0630 (drops).

[*Shown in Product Identification Section*]

MYLICON®-80 Tablets
High-Capacity Antiflatulent

Composition: Each tablet contains simethicone, 80 mg.

Action and Uses: For relief of the painful symptoms of excess gas in the digestive tract. MYLICON-80 is a high capacity antiflatulent for adjunctive treatment of many conditions in which the retention of gas may be a problem, such as the following: air swallowing, functional dyspepsia, postoperative gaseous distension, peptic ulcer, spastic or irritable colon, diverticulitis.

MYLICON-80 has a defoaming action that relieves flatulence by dispersing and preventing the formation of mucus-surrounded gas pockets in the gastrointestinal tract. MYLICON-80 acts in the stomach and intestines to change the surface tension of gas bubbles enabling them to coalesce; thus, the gas is freed and is eliminated more easily by belching or passing flatus.

Dosage and Administration: One tablet four times daily after meals and at bedtime. May also be taken as needed or as directed by a physician. TABLETS SHOULD BE CHEWED THOROUGHLY.

How Supplied: Economical bottles of 100 and convenience packages of individually wrapped 12 and 48 pink, scored, chewable tablets identified "STUART 858". Also available in 100 tablet unit dose boxes (10 strips of 10 tablets each).

NDC 0038-0858.

[*Shown in Product Identification Section*]

OREXIN® SOFTAB® Tablets

Composition: Each tablet contains: thiamine mononitrate, 10 mg.; Vitamin B_6 (as pyridoxine hydrochloride), 5 mg.; and Vitamin B_{12} (cyanocobalamin), 25 mcg.

Action and Uses: OREXIN is a high-potency vitamin supplement providing thiamine mononitrate and Vitamins B_6 and B_{12}.

OREXIN SOFTAB tablets are specially formulated to dissolve quickly in the mouth. They may be chewed or swallowed. Dissolve tablet in a teaspoonful of water or fruit juice if liquid is preferred.

Dosage and Administration: One tablet daily, or as directed by physician.

How Supplied: Bottles of 100 pale pink SOFTAB tablets, identified "STUART". NDC 0038-0280.

PROBEC®-T Tablets

Composition: Each tablet contains: Vitamin C (as ascorbic acid, 67 mg. and sodium ascorbate, 600 mg.), 600 mg.; thiamine mononitrate, 15 mg.; riboflavin, 10 mg.; Vitamin B_6 (as pyridoxine hydrochloride), 5 mg.; Vitamin B_{12} (cyanoco-balamin), 5 mcg.; niacinamide, 100 mg.; calcium pantothenate, 20 mg. Contains FD&C yellow #5 (tartrazine) as a color additive.

Actions and Uses: PROBEC-T is a high-potency B complex supplement with 600 mg. of Vitamin C in easy to swallow odorless tablets.

Dosage and Administration: One tablet a day with a meal, or as directed by physician.

How Supplied: Bottles of 60, salmon colored, capsule-shaped tablets. NDC 0038-0840.

THE STUART FORMULA® Tablets

Composition: Each tablet contains:

Vitamins: Vitamin A (as palmitate), 5000 I.U.; Vitamin D (ergocalciferol), 400 I.U.; Vitamin E (as dl-alpha tocopheryl acetate), 15 I.U.; Vitamin C (as ascorbic acid), 60 mg.; folic acid, 0.4 mg.; thiamine (as thiamine mononitrate), 1.5 mg.; riboflavin, 1.7 mg.; niacin (as niacinamide), 20 mg.; Vitamin B_6 (as pyridoxine hydrochloride), 2 mg.; Vitamin B_{12} (cyanocobalamin), 6 mcg.

Minerals: calcium 160 mg.; phosphorus, 125 mg.; iodine, 150 mcg.; iron (from 54 mg. ferrous fumarate) 18 mg.; magnesium, 100 mg.

Actions and Uses: The STUART FORMULA tablet provides a well-balanced multivitamin/multimineral formula intended for use as a daily dietary supplement for adults and children over age four.

Dosage and Administration: One tablet daily or as directed by a physician.

How Supplied: Bottles of 100, 250 and 500 white round tablets. Childproof safety caps are standard on the 100 and 250 tablet bottles as a safeguard against accidental ingestion by children. NDC 0038-0866.

[*Shown in Product Identification Section*]

STUART PRENATAL® Tablets

Composition: Each tablet contains:

Vitamins:	% U.S. RDA*	
A (as acetate)	100%	8,000 I.U.
D (ergocalciferol)	100%	400 I.U.
E (as dl-alpha tocopheryl acetate)	100%	30 I.U.
C (ascorbic acid)	100%	60 mg.
Folic Acid	100%	0.8 mg.
Thiamine (as thiamine mononitrate)	100%	1.7 mg.
Riboflavin	100%	2 mg.
Niacin (as niacinamide)	100%	20 mg.
B_6 (as pyridoxine hydrochloride)	160%	4 mg.
B_{12} (cyanocobalamin)	100%	8 mcg.
Minerals:		
Calcium (from 679 mg. calcium sulfate anhydrous)	15%	200 mg.
Iodine (from potassium iodide)	100%	150 mcg.
Iron (from 182 mg. ferrous fumarate)	333%	60 mg.
Magnesium (from magnesium oxide)	22%	100 mg.

* Recommended Daily Allowance

Action and Uses: STUART PRENATAL is a multivitamin/multimineral supplement for pregnant and lactating women. It provides vitamins equal to 100% or more of the U.S. RDA for pregnant and lactating women, plus essential minerals, including 60 mg. of elemental iron as well-tolerated ferrous fumarate, and 200 mg. of elemental calcium (non-alkalizing and phosphorus-free). Stuart Prenatal also contains .8 mg. folic acid.

Dosage and Administration: During and after pregnancy, one tablet daily after a meal, or as directed by a physician.

How Supplied: Bottles of 100 and 500 pink capsule-shaped tablets. A childproof safety cap is standard on 100 tablet bottles as a safeguard against accidental ingestion by children. NDC 0038-0270.

STUARTINIC® Tablets

Composition: Each tablet contains: iron (from 300 mg. ferrous fumarate), 100 mg.; Vitamin C (as ascorbic acid, 300 mg. and sodium ascorbate, 225 mg.), 500 mg.; Vitamin B_{12} (cyanocobalamin), 25 mcg.; thiamine mononitrate, 6 mg.; riboflavin, 6 mg.; Vitamin B_6 (as pyridoxine hydrochloride), 1 mg.; niacinamide, 20 mg.; calcium pantothenate, 10 mg. Contains FD&C yellow #5 (tartrazine) as a color additive.

Action and Uses: STUARTINIC is a complete hematinic for patients with history of iron deficiency anemia who also lack adequate amounts of B-complex vitamins due to poor diet.

The use of well-tolerated ferrous fumarate in STUARTINIC provides a high level of elemental iron with a low incidence of gastric distress. The inclusion of 500 mg. of Vitamin C per tablet serves to maintain more of the iron in the absorbable ferrous state. The B-complex vitamins improve nutrition where B-complex deficient diets contribute to the anemia.

Precautions: Because STUARTINIC contains 100 mg. of elemental iron per tablet, use should be confined to adults, i.e. over age 12 years. As with all medications, STUARTINIC should be kept out of the reach of children.

Dosage and Administration: One tablet daily taken after a meal to maintain normal hemoglobin levels in most patients with chronic iron deficiency anemia resulting from inadequate diet. Higher doses of STUARTINIC can be taken as directed by the physician.

How Supplied: STUARTINIC is supplied in bottles of 60 and 500 yellow, film coated, oval shaped tablets. NDC 0038-0862.

Note: A childproof safety cap is standard on each bottle of 60 tablets. The physician should prescribe or recommend the bottle of 60 tablets, where appropriate, to provide that additional safeguard against accidental ingestion by children.

[*Shown in Product Identification Section*]

SugarLo Company
POST OFFICE BOX 111
PLEASANTVILLE, NJ
08232-0111

LACTAID®
(lactase enzyme)

Description: Each 5 drop dosage contains not less than 1000 NLU (Neutral Lactase Units) of Beta-D-galactosidase derived from Kluyveromyces lactis yeast. The enzyme is in a liquid carrier of glycerol (50%), water (30%), and inert yeast dry matter (20%). 4–5 drops hydrolyzes approximately 70% of the lactose in 1 quart of milk at refrigerator temperature, @ 42°F–6°C in 24 hours, or will do the same in 2 hours @ 85°F–30°C. Additional time and/or enzyme required for 100% lactose conversion. 1 U.S. quart of milk will contain approximately 50 gm lactose prior to lactose hydrolysis and will contain 15 gm or less, after. Hydrolysis converts the lactose into its simple sugar components, glucose and galactose.

Actions: Converts the disaccharide lactose into its monosugar components, glucose and galactose.

Indications: Lactase insufficiency in the patient, suspected from g.i. disturbances after consumption of milk or milk content products: e.g., bloat, distension, flatulence, diarrhea; or identified by a lactose tolerance test.

Precautions: Diabetics should be aware that the milk sugar will now be metabolically available and must be taken into account (25 gm glucose and 25 gm galactose per quart). No reports received of any diabetics' reactions. Galactosemics may not have milk in any form, lactase enzyme modified or not. No drug interactions. Overdose impossible.

Usage: Added to milk. 4–5 drops per quart depending on level of lactose conversion desired.

Toxicity: None. LactAid is not a drug but a food which modifies another food to make it more digestible.

Other Uses: Veterinary indications: treatment of milk for animals with gastric surgery; sick young animals; sick or healthy older animals.

How Supplied: Retail sale units of 4, 12 or 30 dosages at 5 drops per dose. Bulk institutional size also available. Sample and full product information to doctors, dietitians and institutions, on request. Also from dairies in some locations in U.S. as ready to drink hydrolyzed LactAid milk, with the enzyme modification having been done at the dairy to a 70% conversion level. Persons who find this 70% level to be inadequate can further modify the milk at home by utilizing the LactAid liquid drops covered in this description. Any store unable to purchase from its wholesaler can order direct from SugarLo Company.

[*Shown in Product Identification Section*]

Syntex Laboratories, Inc
STANFORD INDUSTRIAL PARK
PALO ALTO, CA 94304

CARMOL® 10
10% urea lotion
for total body
dry skin care.

Active Ingredient: Urea 10% in a blend of purified water, stearic acid, isopropyl palmitate, propylene glycol dipelargonate, PEG-8 dioleate, propylene glycol, PEG-8 distearate, cetyl alcohol, sodium laureth sulfate, trolamine, carbomer 940, xanthan gum; scented with hypoallergenic fragrance.
Indications: For total body dry skin care.
Actions: Keratolytic and antipruritic. CARMOL 10 is non-occlusive, contains no mineral oil or petrolatum. CARMOL 10 is hypoallergenic; contains no lanolin, parabens or other preservatives.
Precautions: For external use only. Discontinue use if irritation occurs. Keep out of the reach of children. In case of accidental ingestion, seek professional assistance or contact a poison control center immediately.
Dosage and Administration: Rub in gently on hands, face or body. Repeat as necessary.
How Supplied: 6 fl. oz. bottle.

CARMOL® 20
20% Urea Cream
Extra strength for
rough, dry skin

Active Ingredients: Urea 20% in a non-lipid vanishing cream containing purified water, isopropyl myristate, isopropyl palmitate, stearic acid, propylene glycol, trolamine, sodium laureth sulfate, carbomer 940, hypoallergenic fragrance, xanthan gum.
Indications: Especially useful on rough, dry skin of hands, elbows, knees and feet.
Actions: Keratolytic. Contains no parabens, lanolin or mineral oil.
Precautions: For external use only. Keep away from eyes. Use with caution on face or broken or inflamed skin; transient stinging may occur. Discontinue use if irritation occurs. Keep out of the reach of children. In case of accidental ingestion, seek professional assistance or contact a poison control center immediately.
Dosage and Administration: Apply once or twice daily or as directed. Rub in well.
How Supplied: 3 oz. tubes, 1 lb. jars.

TOPIC®
Benzyl alcohol gel
Relieves itching

Active Ingredients: 5% benzyl alcohol in a cooling, mildly drying gel base that contains camphor, menthol, 30% isopropyl alcohol, purified water, hectorite, propylene glycol, sodium laureth sulfate, perfume and color. The unique gel base is greaseless, non-occlusive and water-washable.
Indications: For temporary relief of itching caused by contact dermatitis (such as poison oak and ivy), insect bites, miliaria (heat rash), allergic dermatitis and localized neurodermatitis.
Actions: Antipruritic. TOPIC combines the antipruritic action of benzyl alcohol with the cooling effect of its alcohol gel base.
Precautions: For external use only. Keep away from eyes. Not for use on acutely inflamed skin. May sting temporarily on broken skin. Discontinue use if irritation develops. Keep out of the reach of children. In case of accidental ingestion, seek professional assistance or contact a poison control center immediately.
Dosage and Administration: Shake tube before using. Apply a thin film of TOPIC. Repeat as needed.
How Supplied: 2 oz. tubes.

Thompson Medical Company, Inc.
919 THIRD AVENUE
NEW YORK, NY 10022

MAXIMUM STRENGTH APPEDRINE®
Anorectic for Weight Control

Each tablet contains:

phenylpropanolamine HCl	25 mg
caffeine	100 mg

Each three tablets contain:

Vitamin A	5000 IU
Vitamin D	400 IU
Vitamin E	30 IU
Vitamin C (Ascorbic Acid)	60 mg
Folic Acid	0.4 mg
Vitamin B_1 (Thiamine HCl)	1.5 mg
Vitamin B_2 (Riboflavin)	1.7 mg
Niacinamide	20 mg
Vitamin B_6 (Pyridoxine HCl)	2 mg
Vitamin B_{12} (Cyanocobalamin)	6 mcg
d-Calcium Pantothenate	10 mg

Description: Each tablet contains phenylpropanolamine HCl, an anorexiant and caffeine, a mild stimulant and one third of the recommended daily adult requirement of major vitamins.
Indications: Maximum Strength APPEDRINE is indicated as adjunctive therapy in the management of simple exogenous obesity in a regimen of weight reduction and control based on caloric restriction.
Caution: Do not exceed recommended dosage. Discontinue use if rapid pulse, dizziness or palpitations occur. Do not use, if high blood pressure, heart, diabetes, kidney, thyroid or other disease is present or if pregnant, nursing or by anyone under the age of 18 except on the advice of a physician. Keep this and all drugs out of the reach of children. In case of accidental overdose, seek professional assistance or contact a Poison Control Center immediately.
Precaution: Avoid use if taking prescription, anti-hypertensive and anti-depressive drugs containing monoamine oxidase inhibitors or other medication containing sympathomimetic amines. Avoid continuous use longer than 3 months.
Adverse Reactions: Side effects are rare when taken as directed. Nausea or nasal dryness may occasionally occur.
Dosage and Administration: Adults: One tablet 30–60 minutes before each meal three times a day with one or two full glasses of water.
How Supplied: Maximum Strength APPEDRINE® packages of 30 and 60 tablets packaged with 1200 Calorie Maximum Strength Appedrine Diet Plan.
Reference: Griboff, Solomon, I., M.D., F.A.C.P. et al., A Double-Blind Clinical Evaluation of a Phenylpropanolamine-Caffeine Combination and a Placebo in the Treatment of Exogenous Obesity, Current Therapeutic Research 17, 6:535, 1975 (June).
Silverman, H. I., D.Sc., Kreger, B., M.D., Lewis, G., M.D., et al., Lack of Side Effects From Orally Administered Phenylpropanolamine with Caffeine: A Controlled Three-Phase Study, Current Therapeutic Research 28, 2:18, 1980 (Aug.).
[*Shown in Product Identification Section*]

AQUA-BAN®

Active Ingredient: Ammonium Chloride 325 mg., Caffeine 100 mg. Enteric Coated
Indications: For control of temporary weight gain by promoting loss of abnormal water storage due to onset of menstrual period.
Warnings: Do not exceed recommended dosage. Discontinue use if rapid pulse, dizziness, sleeplessness or palpitations occur. Do not use if high blood pressure, heart, kidney or other disease is present except upon the advice of a physician; discontinue use if signs of acidosis appear.
Dosage and Administration: 2 tablets, three times a day, after meals starting 4 or 5 days before expected menstrual period. Discontinue at onset of period. Do not take for longer than 5 days in any one month.
How Supplied: Packages of 60 tablets (2 month supply).
References: Hoffman, Jerome J., M.D., A Double-Blind Crossover Clinical Trial of an Over the Counter Diuretic in the Treatment of Premenstrual Tension and Weight Gain, Current Therapeutic Research, 26, 5-575, 1979 (Nov.)
[*Shown in Product Identification Section*]

ASPERCREME™

Description: 10% Triethanolamine Salicylate in a pleasantly scented lotion and cream.
Actions: External analgesic with rapid penetration and absorption.
Indications: An effective salicylate analgesic for temporary relief from minor pains of arthritis, rheumatism and muscular aches. Moderately effective in relieving the sensation of burning and tingling, frequently occurring in the hands and feet of elderly patients.
Contraindications: Do not use in patients manifesting idiosyncrasy to salicylates.

Warning: Use only as directed. If pain persists for more than ten days or in arthritic or rheumatic conditions affecting children under twelve years of age, consult a physician immediately. Keep out of reach of children.

Precautions: For external use only. Occasionally where this product has been used extensively, moderate peeling of the skin may occur. This is a normal reaction to salicylates on the skin, and should not warrant discontinuance of the use of the product.

Dosage and Administration: Apply to painful areas with gentle massage until absorbed into skin, three or four times daily, especially before retiring. Relief lasts for hours.

How Supplied: Lotion; 6 oz plastic bottle. Cream; 3 oz, 5 oz and 1 ¼ oz. plastic tubes.

References: Golden, Emanuel L., M.D., A Double-Blind Comparison of Orally Ingested Aspirin and a Topically Applied Salicylate Cream in the Relief of Rheumatic Pain, Current Therapeutic Research, 24, 5:524, 1978 (Sept.).

CONTROL™ Capsules
Prolonged action anorectic for weight control containing
phenylpropanolamine HCl 75 mg

Description: Phenylpropanolamine HCl is a sympathomimetic, related to ephedrine but with less CNS stimulation. Useful as an anorexiant.

Indication: CONTROL is indicated as adjunctive therapy in a regimen of weight reduction based on caloric restriction in the management and control of simple exogenous obesity.

Caution: For Adults use only.
Do not exceed recommended dose. If nervousness, dizziness, sleeplessness, rapid pulse, palpitations or other symptoms occur discontinue medication and consult your physician. If you have or are being treated for high blood pressure, heart, diabetes, thyroid or other disease, or while pregnant, or nursing or under the age of 18 do not take this drug except under the advice of a physician. Keep this and all drugs out of the reach of children. In case of accidental overdose seek professional assistance or contact a Poison Control Center immediately.

Precaution: Avoid use if taking prescription, anti-hypertensive and anti-depressive drugs containing monoamine oxidase inhibitors or other medication containing sympathomimetic amines. Avoid continuous use for longer than 3 months.

Adverse Reactions: Side effects are rare when taken as directed. Nausea or nasal dryness may occasionally occur.

Dosage and Administration: One capsule with a full glass of water once a day at mid-morning (10:00 A.M.).

How Supplied: CONTROL™ Capsules—Packages of 14, 28 and 56 capsules, packaged with 1200 Calorie CONTROL Diet Plan.

References: Silverman, H. I., D.Sc., Kreger, B., M.D., Lewis, G., M.D., et al. Lack of Side Effects from Orally Administered Phenylpropanolamine and Phen-

ylpropanolamine With Caffeine: A Controlled Three Phase Study, Current Therapeutic Research 28, 2:18, 1980 (Aug).
[*Shown in Product Identification Section*]

DEXATRIM™ Capsules
Prolonged action anorectic for weight control contains

phenylpropanolamine HCl	50 mg
caffeine	200 mg

DEXATRIM™ Extra Strength Capsules

phenylpropanolamine	75 mg
caffeine	200 mg

Caffeine-Free Extra Strength DEXATRIM™

phenylpropanolamine	75 mg.

Description: Phenylpropanolamine hydrochloride is a sympathomimetic, related to ephedrine but with less CNS stimulation. Useful as an anorexiant. Caffeine is a mild stimulant.

Indication: DEXATRIM, Extra Strength DEXATRIM Capsules and Caffeine-Free Extra Strength Dexatrim are indicated as adjunctive therapy in a regimen of weight reduction based on caloric restriction in the management and control of simple exogenous obesity. Studies comparing DEXATRIM to prescription anorexiants have shown DEXATRIM to be equally effective in helping to suppress appetite and in resultant weight loss. DEXATRIM, however, unlike prescription products, has been shown to induce little to no untoward CNS effects. When DEXATRIM was compared to mazindol in a six-week, double-blind study employing 67 outpatients[1] similar weight losses were reported for all subjects. DEXATRIM patients reported no significant adverse effects, while 18% of the mazindol patients reported side effects which included nervousness, nausea and insomnia.
In a six week double-blind parallel study comparing phenylpropanolamine HCl to diethylpropion similar weight losses occurred in 62 clinically obese patients. Ninety-six percent of the patients receiving phenylpropanolamine HCl and 87% of the patients receiving diethylpropion lost weight.[2]

Caution: Do not exceed recommended dosage. Discontinue use if rapid pulse, dizziness or palpitations occur. Do not use if high blood pressure, heart, diabetes, kidney, thyroid or other disease is present or if pregnant, nursing or by anyone under the age of 18 except on the advice of a physician. Keep this and all drugs out of the reach of children. In case of accidental overdose seek professional assistance or contact a Poison Control Center immediately.

Precaution: Avoid use if taking prescription, anti-hypertensive and anti-depressive drugs containing monoamine oxidase inhibitors or other medication containing sympathomimetic amines. Avoid continuous use for longer than 3 months.

Adverse Reactions: Side effects are rare when taken as directed. Nausea or nasal dryness may occasionally occur.

Dosage and Administration:
DEXATRIM™ Capsules: One capsule with a full glass of water mid-morning (10:00 AM)

How Supplied:
DEXATRIM™ Capsules: Packages of 28 or 56 with 1200 calorie DEXATRIM Diet Plan
Extra Strength DEXATRIM™ Capsules and Caffeine Free Extra Strength Dexatrim Capsules: Packages of 20 and 40 with 1200 calorie DEXATRIM Diet Plan.

A U.S. Government advisory panel of medical and scientific experts has determined the combination of active ingredients in this product is safe and effective when taken as directed for appetite control to aid in weight reduction by caloric restriction.

---

1. Report on file, Professional Services, Thompson Medical Company, Inc. 919 Third Avenue, New York, New York 10022.
2. Report on file, Professional Services, Thompson Medical Company, Inc. 919 Third Avenue, New York, New York 10022.
References: Silverman, H. I., D.Sc., Kreger, B., M.D., Lewis, G., M.D., et al., Lack of Side Effects From Orally Administered Phenylpropanolamine and Phenylpropanolamine with Caffeine: A Controlled Three-Phase Study, Current Therapeutic Research 28, 2:18, 1980 (Aug.).
[*Shown in Product Identification Section*]

Super Strength PROLAMINE™ Capsules
Continuous Action Anorectic for Weight Control

Each capsule contains:

phenylpropanolamine HCl	37.5 mg
caffeine	140 mg

Description: Each capsule contains phenylpropanolamine hydrochloride an anorexiant and caffeine, a mild stimulant.

Indication: Super Strength PROLAMINE is indicated as adjunctive therapy in the regimen of weight reduction based on caloric restriction in the management and control of simple exogenous obesity.
In a six-week double-blind study of 70 obese patients comparing phenylpropanolamine HCl to a placebo, 35% of the subjects taking phenylpropanolamine HCl experienced a weight loss of 8 pounds or more. Only 9% of the subjects taking placebo lost that amount of weight. Results were statistically significant at the 0.05 probability level.[1]

Caution: Do not exceed recommended dosage. Discontinue use if rapid pulse, dizziness, or palpitations occur. Do not take if you have high blood pressure, heart disease, diabetes, kidney, thyroid, or other disease or if pregnant or lactating. Keep this and all drugs out of the

Continued on next page

Thompson—Cont.

reach of children. In case of accidental overdose seek professional assistance or contact a Poison Control Center immediately.

Precaution: Avoid use if taking prescription, anti-hypertensive and anti-depressive drugs containing monoamine oxidase inhibitors or other medication containing sympathomimetic amines. Avoid continuous use for longer than 3 months.

Adverse Reactions: Side effects are rare when taken as directed. Nausea or nasal dryness may occasionally occur.

Dosage and Administration: one capsule at 10 A.M. and 1 capsule at 4 P.M.

How Supplied: Super Strength PRO-LAMINE™ Capsules: Packages of 20 and 50 packaged with 1200 Calorie PRO-LAMINE Diet Plan.

A U.S. Government advisory panel of medical and scientific experts has determined the combination of active ingredients in this product as safe and effective when taken as directed for appetite control to aid in weight reduction by caloric restriction.

1. Report on file, Professional Services, Thompson Medical Company, Inc. 919 Third Avenue, New York, New York 10022

References: Silverman, H. I., D.Sc., Kreger, B., M.D., Lewis, G., M.D., et al. Lack of Side Effects from Orally Administered Phenylpropanolamine and Phenylpropanolamine With Caffeine: A Controlled Three-Phase Study, Current Therapeutic Research 28, 2:18, 1980 (Aug.).

[*Shown in Product Identification Section*]

Thought Technology Ltd.
**2180 BELGRAVE AVENUE
SUITE #47
MONTREAL, QUEBEC, CANADA
H4A2L8**

GSR 2™ and GSR/TEMP 2™
Biofeedback Relaxation Systems

Description: The GSR 2 kit contains a hand-held, battery-operated GSR unit, 30-minute learning system on tape cassette or record, instruction booklet, an earphone for private listening. The GSR/TEMP 2 in addition to the above, contains a temperature probe, thermometer, read-out meter, remote electrodes, and rugged carrying case.

Indications: For stress-related symptoms and conditions, either alone or as an adjunct to pharmacological treatment, these systems help patients learn stress control. By themselves,

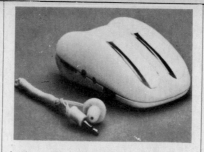

Actions: The GSR 2 and GSR/TEMP 2 monitor fluctuations in skin resistance caused by alterations in sympathetic nervous system activity and translate them into an audible tone which increases in pitch with rising stress, and decreases with relaxation. By learning to lower the tone, patients learn to lower stress levels. The monitor is activated automatically by resting fingers on built-in sensor plates. The GSR/TEMP 2 System monitors peripheral vascular constriction resulting in skin temperature fluctuations, in addition to skin resistance. Both systems are inexpensive and portable, so they can be used virtually anywhere, any time your patient wants to practice stress control.

Warnings: None

Also Available: 1) Sound control accessory: provides control of stereo volume. 2) Light control accessory: provides control of lamp brightness. 3) Acuprobe accessory: permits you to locate acupuncture points. 4) A complete line of clinical biofeedback equipment.

How Supplied: All U.S. orders are sent from Thought Technology's N.Y. warehouse, via U.P.S.

Ulmer Pharmacal Company
**(Div. of Physicians and Hospitals Supply Company)
2440 FERNBROOK LANE
MINNEAPOLIS, MN 55441**

LOBANA® BATH OIL

Contains: Mineral Oil, Lanolin Oil, PEG-4 Dilaurate, Fragrance and Coloring.

Description: A fragrant bath supplement that is readily dispersible in water.

Actions: Conditions as it soothes and softens dry, itching skin. Helps maintain natural skin moisture and increase moisture penetration.

Warnings: For External Use Only. In presence of an open wound or infection, consult a physician for proper treatment.

Directions:
BATH: Add one or two capfuls directly to water in tub or whirlpool. Allow bathing for at least ten minutes. Pat dry with towel.
SHOWER: Apply, then rub onto wet skin. Rinse. Pat dry with towel.

Supplied:

4 fl. oz.	Catalog No. 3030-06
16 fl. oz.	Catalog No. 3030-02
gallon	Catalog No. 3030-16

LOBANA® BODY LOTION

Contains: Deionized Water, Mineral Oil, Triethanolamine Stearate, Stearic Acid, Lanolin, Cetyl Alcohol, Potassium Stearate, Propylene Glycol, Methylparaben, Propylparaben and Fragrance.

Description: Greaseless, rapid absorption and the absence of residual sticky film assures easy application for hand and body massage.

Actions: Lanolin rich to help keep the skin soft. Contains no evaporating alcohol which drys the skin. Protected by a preservative system which guards against microbial contamination.

Warnings: For External Use Only. If sensitivity occurs, discontinue use.

Supplied:

4 fl. oz. bottle	Catalog No. 1540-06
8 fl. oz. bottle	Catalog No. 1540-12
gallon	Catalog No. 1540-16

LOBANA® BODY POWDER

Contains: Corn Starch, Sodium Bicarbonate and Methylbenzethonium Chloride

Description: Helps to protect the skin from symptoms of chafing, rubbing and friction while minimizing body odor.

Actions: Absorbs moisture, perspiration and noxious secretions as it lubricates those surfaces that are in continuous contact. Provides effective deodorant action.

Warning: For External Use Only.

Directions: For routine use after a bed linen or diaper change, bath or massage.

Supplied:
8 ounce shaker bottle
                    Catalog No. 1538-88

LOBANA® BODY SHAMPOO

Contains: Chloroxylenol (a broad-spectrum antimicrobial ingredient) in a mild, sudsing base with conditioners and emollients.

Description: A pH balanced body and hair cleanser.

Actions: Conditions while it cleans, while providing bacteriostatic and fungistatic activity. Gives a desirable "after feel". Extra rich in emollients to keep the skin soft.

Warning: For External Use Only.

Directions: Apply to a moistened washcloth, directly to the skin or to moistened hair. Bathe/shampoo and rinse in normal manner.

Supplied:

8 fl. oz	NDC 0127-2411-12
Gallon	NDC 0127-2411-16
5-gallon	NDC 0127-2411-07

LOBANA® CONDITIONING SHAMPOO

Contains: Deionized Water, TEA Lauryl Sulfate, Coco Betaine, Cocamide DEA, Quaternium 33, Ethyl Hexanediol, Sodium Chloride, Citric Acid, Fragrance, Quaternium 15 and Coloring.

Description: A pH balanced shampoo that conditions as it cleans the hair.

Actions: Adds fullness and body to the hair. Leaves conditioned hair feeling soft and manageable.

Supplied:

8 fl. oz. bottle	Catalog No. 2080-12
gallon	Catalog No. 2080-16

LOBANA® DERM-ADE CREAM

Contains: Vitamins A, D and E in a vanishing cream base with moisturizers, emollients and Silicone.

Description: Provides relief from diaper rash, minor burns, sunburn and other minor skin irritations—including those associated with ileostomy and colostomy drainage on the skin.

Actions: Soothes and softens irritated skin and promotes healing. Forms a protective film against urine and other irritants. Helps to retain natural skin moisture.

Warnings: For external use only. If infection or other signs develop, discontinue use and consult a physician.

Directions: Apply liberally as required. If necessary clean the affected area prior to application.

How Supplied:

2 oz. jar	NDC 0127-1722-77
8 oz. jar	NDC 0127-1722-88

LOBANA® LIQUID HAND SOAP

Contains: Chloroxylenol, a broad-spectrum antimicrobial ingredient.

Description: A pH balanced, pearlescent, pleasantly scented Health-care Personnel Handwash with conditioners and emollients.

Warning: For External Use Only.

Directions: Wet skin and spread soap on hands and forearms. Scrub well and rinse thoroughly after washing.

Supplied:

14 fl. oz. portable dispenser

	NDC 0127-3220-08
Wall Dispenser, 24 oz.	3220-W
Gallon	NDC 0127-3220-16

LOBANA® PERI-GARD

Contains: Vitamins A & D in an emollient ointment base with Chloroxylenol.

Actions: A water-resistant ointment recommended for the perineal area that protects the skin from irritation caused by urine, feces or drainage.

Warning: Should infection be present, consult a physician for proper treatment.

Directions: Apply directly to the perineal area.

Supplied:

2 oz. jar	NDC 0127-1365-77
8 oz. jar	NDC 0127-1365-88

LOBANA® PERINEAL CLEANSE

Contains: Quaternium 12 in a mild, sudsing base with conditioners and emollients.

Description: For routine use to remove feces, urine and vomit and destroy their odors.

Actions: Eliminates source of skin irritation as it destroys odors. The perineal area is left fresh, clean and soft.

Warnings: For external use only. If infections or other signs develop, discontinue use and consult a physician.

Directions: Spray on patient problem areas, and soiled linen. Wipe with cloth or underpad. Spray on a wet cloth and use to gently wash the affected skin area. Then wipe with a clean, wet cloth.

Supplied:

4 oz. sprayer	NDC 0127-1085-06
8 oz. sprayer	NDC 0127-1085-12
gallon	NDC 0127-1085-16
5-gallon	NDC 0127-1085-07
15 gallon	NDC 0127-1085-15

The Upjohn Company
KALAMAZOO, MI 49001

BACIGUENT® Antibiotic Ointment

Active Ingredient: Each gram contains 500 units of bacitracin.

Indications: Baciguent is a first aid ointment to help prevent infection and aid in the healing of minor cuts, burns and abrasions.

How Supplied: Available in ½ oz, 1 oz and 4 oz tubes.

CHERACOL D® Cough Syrup

Active Ingredients: Each teaspoonful (5 ml) contains dextromethorphan hydrobromide, 10 mg, and guaifenesin, 100 mg, in a pleasant-tasting vehicle. Contains 4.75% alcohol.

Indications: Cheracol D Cough Syrup helps quiet dry, hacking coughs, and helps loosen phlegm and mucus. Recommended for adults and children 2 years of age and older.

Dosage and Administration: Adults: 2 teaspoonfuls. Children 2 to 6 years: ½ teaspoonful. These doses may be repeated every four hours if necessary.

How Supplied: Available in 2 oz, 4 oz and 6 oz bottles.

CITROCARBONATE® Antacid

Active Ingredients: When dissolved, each 3.9 grams (1 teaspoonful) contains sodium bicarbonate, 0.78 gram and sodium citrate, 1.82 grams. Each teaspoonful contains 30.46 mEq (700.6 mg) of sodium.

Indications: For the temporary relief of heartburn, acid indigestion, and sour stomach.

Dosage and Administration: Adults: 1 to 2 teaspoonfuls (not to exceed 5 teaspoonfuls per day) in a glass of cold water after meals. Children 6 to 12 years: ¼ to ½ adult dose. For children under 6 years: Consult physician. Persons 60 years or older: ½ to 1 teaspoonful after meals.

How Supplied: Available in 4 oz and 8 oz bottles.

CORTAID® Cream
CORTAID® Ointment
CORTAID® Lotion
(hydrocortisone acetate)

Antipruritic

Description: Cortaid Cream contains hydrocortisone acetate (equivalent to 0.5% hydrocortisone) in a greaseless, odorless, vanishing cream that leaves no residue. Cortaid Ointment contains hydrocortisone acetate (equivalent to 0.5% hydrocortisone) in a soothing, lubricating ointment. Cortaid Lotion contains hydrocortisone acetate (equivalent to 0.5% hydrocortisone) in a greaseless, odorless, vanishing lotion.

Indications: All Cortaid forms are indicated for the temporary relief of minor skin irritations, itching and rashes due to eczema, dermatitis, insect bites, poison ivy, poison oak, poison sumac, soaps, detergents, cosmetics, and jewelry, and for itchy genital and anal areas.

Uses: The vanishing action of Cortaid Cream makes it cosmetically acceptable when the skin rash treated is on an exposed part of the body such as the hands or arms. Cortaid Ointment is best used where protection, lubrication and soothing of dry and scaly lesions is required; the ointment is also preferred for treating itchy genital and anal areas. Cortaid Lotion is thinner than the cream and is especially suitable for hairy body areas such as the scalp or arms.

Warnings: All Cortaid formulations are for external use only. Avoid contact with the eyes. If condition worsens or if symptoms persist for more than 7 days, discontinue use of this product and consult a physician. Do not use on children under 2 years of age except under the advice and supervision of a physician. Keep this and all drugs out of the reach of children. In case of accidental ingestion, seek professional assistance or contact a poison control center immediately.

Dosage and Administration: For adults and children 2 years of age and older. Apply the cream, ointment, or lotion by gently massaging Cortaid into the affected area not more than 3 to 4 times daily.

How Supplied: Cortaid (hydrocortisone acetate) is available in: Cream ½ oz and 1 oz tubes; Ointment ½ oz and 1 oz tubes; Lotion 1 oz and 2 oz bottles.
[Shown in Product Identification Section]

CORTEF® Feminine Itch Cream
(hydrocortisone acetate)
Antipruritic

Description: Cortef Feminine Itch Cream contains hydrocortisone acetate (equivalent to hydrocortisone 0.5%) in an odorless, vanishing cream base that quickly disappears into the skin to avoid staining of clothing.

Indications: For effective temporary relief of minor skin irritations and itching of the external vaginal area. It relieves the itch and takes the redness out of the skin to break the annoying itch/scratch cycle.

Warnings: For external use only. Avoid contact with the eyes. If condition worsens, or if symptoms persist for more than 7 days, discontinue use of this product and consult a physician. Do not use on children under 2 years of age except under the advice and supervision of a physician. Keep this and all drugs out of the reach of children. In case of accidental ingestion, seek professional assistance or contact a poison control center immediately.

Continued on next page

Upjohn—Cont.

Dosage and Administration: Apply to affected area not more than 3 to 4 times daily.

How Supplied: *Cortef* Feminine Itch Cream (hydrocortisone acetate) is available in ½ oz tubes.

[*Shown in Product Identification Section*]

CORTEF® Rectal Itch Ointment
(hydrocortisone acetate)
Antipruritic

Description: *Cortef* Rectal Itch Ointment contains hydrocortisone acetate (equivalent to hydrocortisone 0.5%) in a soothing, lubricating ointment. *Cortef* is odorless and spreads easily to provide continuous coating of the affected area.

Indications: For effective temporary relief of minor skin irritations and itching of the external rectal area. It relieves the itch and takes the redness out of the skin to break the annoying itch/scratch cycle.

Warnings: For external use only. Avoid contact with the eyes. If condition worsens, or if symptoms persist for more than 7 days, discontinue use of this product and consult a physician. Do not use on children under 2 years of age except under the advice and supervision of a physician. Keep this and all drugs out of the reach of children. In case of accidental ingestion, seek professional assistance or contact a poison control center immediately.

Dosage and Administration: Apply to affected area not more than 3 to 4 times daily.

How Supplied: *Cortef* Rectal Itch Ointment (hydrocortisone acetate) is available in ½ oz tubes.

[*Shown in Product Identification Section*]

KAOPECTATE®
Anti-Diarrhea Medicine

Active Ingredients: Each fluid ounce (2 tablespoonfuls) contains kaolin, 90 grains; pectin, 2 grains, in a pleasant-tasting liquid. Contains no alcohol.

Indications: For the relief of diarrhea. Relieves diarrhea within 24 hours without constipating.

Dosage and Administration: For best results, take full recommended dose at first sign of diarrhea and after each bowel movement or as needed. Adults: 4 to 8 tablespoonfuls. Children over 12 years: 4 tablespoonfuls. Children 6 to 12 years: 2 to 4 tablespoonfuls. Children 3 to 6 years: 1 to 2 tablespoonfuls. Infants and children under 3 years old: only as directed by a physician.

How Supplied: Available in 3 oz unit-dose, 8 oz, 12 oz, and gallon bottles; bilingual labeling in Spanish and English available for 8 oz and 12 oz bottles.

[*Shown in Product Identification Section*]

KAOPECTATE CONCENTRATE®
Anti-Diarrhea Medicine

Active Ingredients: Each fluid ounce (2 tablespoonfuls) contains kaolin, 135 grains; pectin, 3 grains, in a mint-flavored liquid. Contains no alcohol.

Indications: For the relief of diarrhea. Relieves diarrhea within 24 hours without constipating.

Dosage and Administration: For best results, take full recommended dose at first sign of diarrhea and after each bowel movement or as needed. Adults: 3 to 6 tablespoonfuls. Children over 12 years: 3 tablespoonfuls. Children 6 to 12 years: 2 tablespoonfuls. Children 3 to 6 years: 1 tablespoonful. Infants and children under 3 years: only as directed by a physician.

How Supplied: Available in 2 oz unit-dose, 8 oz and 12 oz bottles.

[*Shown in Product Identification Section*]

MYCIGUENT® Antibiotic Ointment

Active Ingredient: Each gram contains 5 mg of neomycin sulfate (equivalent to 3.5 mg neomycin).

Indications: *Myciguent* is a first aid ointment to help prevent infection and aid in the healing of minor cuts, burns and abrasions.

How Supplied: Available in ½ oz, 1 oz and 4 oz tubes.

MYCITRACIN® Antibiotic Ointment

Active Ingredients: Each gram contains 500 units of bacitracin, 5 mg of neomycin sulfate (equivalent to 3.5 mg neomycin) and 5000 units of polymyxin B sulfate.

Indications: *Mycitracin* is a first aid ointment to help prevent infection and aid in the healing of minor cuts, burns and abrasions.

How Supplied: Available in 1/32 oz unit-dose, ½ oz and 1 oz tubes.

[*Shown in Product Identification Section*]

PYRROXATE® Capsules
Nasal Decongestant/Antihistamine/Analgesic Capsules

Description: *Pyrroxate* provides single-capsules, multisymptom relief for colds, allergies, nasal/sinus congestion, runny nose, sneezing, watery eyes, and because it contains the non-aspirin analgesic **acetaminophen**, *Pyrroxate* gives temporary relief of occasional minor aches, pains, headache, and helps in the reduction of fever. *Pyrroxate* is caffeine and aspirin-free.

Ingredients: Each *Pyrroxate* capsule contains: Chlorpheniramine Maleate, 4 mg; Phenylpropanolamine HCl, 25 mg; Acetaminophen, 500 mg. The 500 mg (7.69 gr) strength of acetaminophen per capsule is non-standard, as compared to the established standard of 325 mg (5 gr) acetaminophen per capsule.

Indications: *Pyrroxate* Capsules are for the temporary relief of runny nose, sneezing, itching of the nose or throat; for the temporary relief of nasal congestion due to the common cold, allergies (hay fever), and sinus congestion; for the temporary relief of occasional aches, pains, and headache; and for the reduction of fever.

Actions: Chlorpheniramine Maleate is an antihistamine effective in controlling runny nose, sneezing, watery eyes, and itching of the nose and throat. Phenylpropanolamine HCl is an oral nasal decongestant effective in relieving nasal/sinus congestion due to the common cold or allergies (hay fever). Acetaminophen is a clinically effective analgesic and antipyretic without aspirin side effects.

Warnings: Do not take this product for more than 7 days. If symptoms persist, do not improve, or new ones occur, or if fever persists for more than 3 days, discontinue use and consult your physician. Do not take this product if you have asthma, glaucoma, difficulty in urination due to the enlargement of the prostate gland, high blood pressure, diabetes, thyroid disease, or if you are presently taking a prescription antihypertensive or antidepressant drug containing a monamine oxidase inhibitor, except under the advice and supervision of a physician. Do not exceed recommended dosage because severe liver damage may occur and at higher doses, nervousness, dizziness or sleeplessness may occur. Do not take this product for the treatment of arthritis except under the advice and supervision of a physician.

Cautions: Avoid alcoholic beverages, driving a motor vehicle, or operating heavy machinery while taking this product. This product may cause drowsiness or excitability, especially in children. Keep this and all drugs out of the reach of children. In case of accidental overdose, seek professional assistance or contact a poison control center immediately.

Dosage and Administration: Take 1 capsule every 4 hours or as directed by a physician. Do not take more than 6 capsules in a 24-hour period. Do not administer to children under 12 years of age.

How Supplied: Black/yellow capsules available in bottles of 24 and 500.

[*Shown in Product Identification Section*]

UNICAP® Capsules/Tablets
Multivitamin Supplement

Indications: Dietary multivitamin supplement of ten essential vitamins in capsule or tablet form for adults and children 4 or more years of age.

Ingredients:	Each capsule (or tablet) contains:	% U.S. RDA*
Vitamin A	5000 Int. Units	100
Vitamin D	400 Int. Units	100
Vitamin E	15 Int. Units	50
Vitamin C	60 mg	100
Folic Acid	400 mcg	100
Thiamine	1.5 mg	100
Riboflavin	1.7 mg	100
Niacin	20 mg	100
Vitamin B$_6$	2 mg	100
Vitamin B$_{12}$	6 mcg	100

*Percentage of U.S. Recommended Daily Allowance

How Supplied: Available in bottles of 90, 240 and 1000 capsules; bottles of 60 and 90 tablets.

UNICAP CHEWABLE® Tablets

Indications: Dietary multivitamin supplement with ten essential vitamins in an orange-flavored chewable tablet for **children** 4 or more years of age.

Ingredients:

	Each tablet contains:	% U.S. RDA*
Vitamin A	5000 Int. Units	100
Vitamin D	400 Int. Units	100
Vitamin E	15 Int. Units	50
Vitamin C	60 mg	100
Folic Acid	400 mcg	100
Thiamine	1.5 mg	100
Riboflavin	1.7 mg	100
Niacin	20 mg	100
Vitamin B6	2 mg	100
Vitamin B12	6 mcg	100

* Percentage of U.S. Recommended Daily Allowance

How Supplied: Available in bottle of 90 tablets.

UNICAP M® Tablets

Indications: Dietary supplement of 11 essential vitamins plus iron and five more minerals for persons 12 or more years of age.

Ingredients:

	Each tablet contains:	% U.S. RDA*
Vitamin A	5000 Int. Units	100
Vitamin D	400 Int. Units	100
Vitamin E	15 Int. Units	50
Vitamin C	60 mg	100
Folic Acid	400 mcg	100
Thiamine	1.5 mg	100
Riboflavin	1.7 mg	100
Niacin	20 mg	100
Vitamin B6	2 mg	100
Vitamin B12	6 mcg	100
Pantothenic Acid	10 mg	100
Iodine	150 mcg	100
Iron	18 mg	100
Copper	2 mg	100
Zinc	15 mg	100
Manganese	1 mg	+
Potassium	5 mg	+

* Percentage of U.S. Recommended Daily Allowance.
+ No U.S. RDA has been established for this nutrient.

How Supplied: Available in bottles of 30, 90, 180 and 500 tablets.
[*Shown in Product Identification Section*]

UNICAP PLUS IRON™ Tablets

Indications: Dietary multivitamin supplement with 11 essential vitamins and iron for persons 12 or more years of age.

Ingredients:

	Each tablet contains:	% U.S. RDA*
Vitamin A	5000 Int. Units	100
Vitamin D	400 Int. Units	100
Vitamin E	15 Int. Units	50
Vitamin C	60 mg	100
Folic Acid	400 mcg	100
Thiamine	1.5 mg	100
Riboflavin	1.7 mg	100
Niacin	20 mg	100
Vitamin B6	2 mg	100
Vitamin B12	6 mcg	100
Pantothenic Acid	10 mg	100
Iron	18 mg	100

* Percentage of U.S. Recommended Daily Allowance.

How Supplied: Available in bottles of 60 and 90 tablets.

UNICAP SENIOR® Tablets

Indications: Dietary supplement of ten essential vitamins plus six minerals for adults. Especially formulated for adults 51 years and older who need only 10 mg of iron.

Ingredients:

	Each tablet contains:	% U.S. RDA*
Vitamin A	5000 Int. Units	100
Vitamin E	15 Int. Units	50
Vitamin C	60 mg	100
Folic Acid	400 mcg	100
Thiamine	1.2 mg	80
Riboflavin	1.7 mg	100
Niacin	14 mg	70
Vitamin B6	2 mg	100
Vitamin B12	6 mcg	100
Pantothenic Acid	10 mg	100
Iodine	150 mcg	100
Iron	10 mg	56
Copper	2 mg	100
Zinc	15 mg	100
Manganese	1 mg	+
Potassium	5 mg	+

* Percentage of U.S. Recommended Daily Allowance
+ No U.S. RDA has been established for this nutrient.

How Supplied: Available in bottle of 90 tablets.

UNICAP T® Tablets
High Potency
Vitamin-Mineral Supplement

Indications: High potency dietary supplement of 11 essential vitamins and six minerals for persons 12 or more years of age.

Ingredients:

	Each tablet contains:	% U.S. RDA*
Vitamin A	5000 Int. Units	100
Vitamin D	400 Int. Units	100
Vitamin E	15 Int. Units	50
Vitamin C	300 mg	500
Folic Acid	400 mcg	100
Thiamine	10 mg	667
Riboflavin	10 mg	588
Niacin	100 mg	500
Vitamin B6	6 mg	300
Vitamin B12	18 mcg	300
Pantothenic Acid	10 mg	100
Iodine	150 mcg	100
Iron	18 mg	100
Copper	2 mg	100
Zinc	15 mg	100
Manganese	1 mg	+
Potassium	5 mg	+

* Percentage of U.S. Recommended Daily Allowance
+ No U.S. RDA has been established for this nutrient.

How Supplied: Available in bottles of 30, 90 and 500 tablets.
[*Shown in Product Identification Section*]

Products are cross-indexed by generic and chemical names in the
YELLOW SECTION

Vicks Toiletry Products Division
RICHARDSON-VICKS INC.
TEN WESTPORT ROAD
WILTON, CT 06897

CLEARASIL® Super Strength Acne Treatment Cream Vanishing and Tinted

Active Ingredients: Benzoyl Peroxide 10% in an odorless, greaseless cream base, containing water, propylene glycol, bentonite, glyceryl stearate SE, isopropyl myristate, cellulose gum, dimethicone, methylparaben, and propylparaben. The tinted formula also contains titanium dioxide and iron oxides.

Indications: For the topical treatment of acne vulgaris.

Actions: CLEARASIL Super Strength Acne Treatment Cream contains benzoyl peroxide, an antibacterial and keratolytic as well as bentonite as an oil absorbant. The product 1) helps heal and prevent acne pimples, 2) helps absorb excess skin oil often associated with acne blemishes, 3) helps your skin look fresh. The Vanishing formula works invisibly. The Tinted formula hides pimples while its works.

Warnings: Persons with a known sensitivity to benzoyl peroxide should not use this medication. Excessive dryness may occur especially when used by persons with unusually dry, sensitive, or maturing skin. If itching, redness, burning, swelling or undue dryness occurs, discontinue use. If symptoms persist, consult a physician promptly. For external use only. Keep from eyes, lips, mouth and sensitive areas of the neck. Colored or dyed fabrics may be bleached by the oxidizing action of this product. Keep this and all medicine out of the reach of children.

Symptoms and Treatment of Ingestion: These symptoms are based upon medical judgement, not on actual experience. Theoretically, ingestion of very large amounts may cause nausea, vomiting, abdominal discomfort and diarrhea. Treatment is symptomatic, with bedrest and observation.

Directions For Use: 1. Wash thoroughly. (Clearasil® Antibacterial Soap and Clearasil® Pore Deep Cleanser are excellent products to use in your cleansing regimen.) **2.** Try this sensitivity test. Apply cream sparingly with fingertips to one or two small affected areas during the first three days. If no discomfort or reaction occurs, apply up to two times daily, wherever pimples and oil are a problem. **3.** If bothersome dryness or peeling occurs, reduce dosage to one application per day or every other day.

How Supplied: Available in both Vanishing and Tinted formulas in 1 oz. and .65 oz. squeeze tubes.
[*Shown in Product Identification Section*]

Continued on next page

Vicks Toiletry—Cont.

CLEARASIL®
5% Benzoyl Peroxide Lotion
Acne Treatment

Active Ingredients: Benzoyl Peroxide 5% in a colorless, greaseless lotion which contains water, propylene glycol, glyceryl stearate SE, bentonite, cellulose gum, isopropyl myristate, sodium citrate, dimethicone, methylparaben, propylparaben.

Indications: For the topical treatment of acne vulgaris.

Actions: CLEARASIL 5% Benzoyl Peroxide Lotion contains benzoyl peroxide, an antibacterial and keratolytic. The product **1. Helps heal and prevent acne pimples.** Benzoyl peroxide dries up existing pimples and kills acne causing bacteria to help prevent new ones. In fact, benzoyl peroxide is the strongest acne pimple medicine you can buy without a prescription.
2. Helps absorb excess skin oil often associated with acne blemishes. Contains bentonite which is a unique oil absorbing ingredient that allows Clearasil Lotion to absorb **more** excess skin oil than 5% benzoyl peroxide alone.
3. Helps your skin look fresh. Extra oil absorption helps your skin look less oily, more natural.
4. Works invisibly. A colorless, odorless, and greaseless lotion.

Warnings: Persons with a known sensitivity to benzoyl peroxide should not use this medication. Excessive dryness may occur especially when used by persons with unusually dry, sensitive, or maturing skin. If itching, redness, burning, swelling or undue dryness occurs, discontinue use. If symptoms persist, consult a physician promptly. For external use only. Keep from eyes, lips, mouth and sensitive areas of the neck. Colored or dyed fabrics may be bleached by the oxidizing action of this product. Keep this and all medicine out of the reach of children.

Symptoms and Treatment of Ingestion: These symptoms are based upon medical judgement, not on actual experience. Theoretically, ingestion of very large amounts may cause nausea, vomiting, abdominal discomfort and diarrhea. Treatment is symptomatic, with bedrest and observation.

Directions For Use:
SHAKE WELL BEFORE USING.
1. Wash thoroughly. (Clearasil® Antibacterial Soap and Clearasil® Pore Deep Cleanser are excellent products to use in your cleansing regimen) **2.** Try this sensitivity test. Apply lotion sparingly with fingertips to one or two small affected areas during the first three days. If no discomfort or reaction occurs, apply up to two times daily, wherever pimples and oil are a problem **3.** If bothersome dryness or peeling occurs, reduce dosage to one application per day or every other day.

How Supplied: Available in a 1 fl. oz. squeeze bottle.

[*Shown in Product Identification Section*]

CLEARASIL®
Pore Deep Cleanser

Active Ingredient: Salicylic Acid (0.5%).

Indications: Topical Skin Cleanser.

Actions: Clearasil® Pore Deep Cleanser contains a comedolytic agent that penetrates deep into pores to clean out oil and dead skin cells that can clog pores and cause pimples.

Warnings: For external use only. May be irritating to the eyes. Keep away from extreme heat or flame.

Drug Interaction: None known.

Symptoms and Treatment of Ingestion: If large amounts ingested, nausea, vomiting, gastrointestinal irritation may develop. Bed rest and observation are indicated if ingested.

Directions for Use: Saturate cotton pad and apply 2-3 times per day. Do not rinse after use.

How Supplied: 4 and 8 oz. plastic bottles.

[*Shown in Product Identification Section*]

TOPEX®
10% Benzoyl Peroxide Lotion
Buffered Acne Medication

Active Ingredient: 10% Benzoyl Peroxide in a colorless, greaseless lotion which is fragrance-free and contains water, propylene glycol, stearic acid, PEG-20 stearate, glyceryl stearate, isopropyl palmitate, zinc laurate, benzoic acid.

Indications: For the topical treatment of acne vulgaris.

Actions: TOPEX 10% Benzoyl Peroxide Lotion contains benzoyl peroxide, an antibacterial and keratolytic. The product 1) dries and helps heal acne lesions (pimples), 2) reduces comedones (blackheads and whiteheads), 3) kills bacteria associated with acne lesions, and 4) helps prevent acne lesions from forming.

Warnings: Persons with a known sensitivity to benzoyl peroxide should not use this medication. Persons with unusually dry, sensitive, or maturing skin may experience excessive dryness. If itching, redness, burning, swelling or undue dryness occurs, discontinue use. If symptoms persist, consult a physician promptly. For external use only. Keep from eyes, lips, mouth and sensitive areas of the neck. Colored or dyed fabrics may be bleached by the oxidizing action of this product. Keep this and all medicine out of the reach of children.

Symptoms and Treatment of Ingestion: These symptoms are based upon medical judgement, not on actual experience. Theoretically, ingestion of very large amounts may cause nausea, vomiting, abdominal discomfort and diarrhea. Treatment is symptomatic, with bedrest and observation.

Directions For Use: Follow your normal cleansing routine. Shake bottle well. Some people are sensitive to the active ingredients of acne medications, so for the first three days apply lotion sparingly with fingertips to one or two small affected areas. If no discomfort or reaction occurs, apply one to three times daily to areas where pimples normally

appear to help prevent breakouts and to existing pimples to clear them fast. Gently rub in lotion until it disappears. Although Topex has been specially formulated to address the problem of the overdrying effects of benzoyl peroxide, some people may still experience bothersome dryness or flaking; if so, reduce number of daily applications.

How Supplied: Available in a 1 fl. oz. squeeze bottle.

[*Shown in Product Identification Section*]

Vicks Health Care Division
RICHARDSON-VICKS INC.
TEN WESTPORT ROAD
WILTON, CT 06897

DAYCARE LIQUID
DAYCARE CAPSULES
Multi-Symptom Colds Medicine

Active Ingredients: LIQUID — per fluid ounce (2 tbs.) or **CAPSULE** — per two capsules, contains Acetaminophen 650mg., Dextromethorphan HBr 20mg., Phenylpropanolamine HCl 25mg. DAYCARE LIQUID also contains Alcohol 10%.

Indications: For temporary relief of major colds symptoms as follows:
Nasal congestion, coughing, aches and pains, fever, and cough irritated throat of a cold or flu without drowsy side effects.

Actions: VICKS DAYCARE is a decongestant, antitussive, analgesic and antipyretic. It helps clear stuffy nose, congested sinus openings. Calms, quiets coughing. Eases headache pain and the ache-all-over feeling. Reduces fever due to colds and flu. It relieves these symptoms without drowsiness. DAYCARE LIQUID is also a demulcent, it sooths a cough irritated throat.

Warning: Do not administer to children under 6 years of age unless directed by a physician. Persistent cough may indicate the presence of a serious condition. Persons with a high fever or persistent cough or with high blood pressure, diabetes, heart or thyroid disease should not use this preparation unless directed by a physician. Do not use more than ten days unless directed by a physician.
Do not exceed recommended dosage unless directed by a physician. As with all medication, keep out of reach of children.

Symptoms and Treatment of Overdosage: These symptoms are based upon medical judgement, not on actual experience, since no significant incidence of overdose has been brought to our attention in clinical or consumer experience. Ingestion of very large amounts may cause dizziness, drowsiness, nausea, diarrhea, insomnia, nervousness, anxiety, tremors, tachycardia, extrasystoles, headache, sweating, confusion and delerium. Treatment is symptomatic, with bedrest and observation.

Dosage:
ADULTS one fluid ounce (2 tbs.) LIQUID, or 2 CAPSULES.
CHILDREN (6 to 12 years) One-half ounce (1 tbs.) LIQUID, or 1 CAPSULE

every 4 hours. Maximum 4 doses per day.

How Supplied: Available in: **LIQUID** with child resistant cap—6 and 10 fl. oz. bottles; **CAPSULES** in child resistant packages—8 (trial size), 20, 36 and 60. [*Shown in Product Identification Section*]

FORMULA 44® COUGH CONTROL DISCS

Active Ingredients per disc: Dextromethorphan (equivalent to Dextromethorphan Hydrobromide) 5 mg., Benzocaine 1.25 mg., Special Vicks Medication (menthol, anethole, peppermint oil) 0.35% in a dark brown sugar base.

Indications: Provides temporary relief from coughs and relieves throat irritation caused by colds, flu, bronchitis.

Actions: VICKS FORMULA 44 COUGH CONTROL DISCS are antitussive, local anesthetic and demulcent cough drops. They calm, quiet coughs and help coat and soothe irritated throats.

Warning: Do not exceed recommended dosage. Do not administer to children under 4 unless directed by physician. Persistent cough may indicate presence of a serious condition. Persons with high fever or persistent cough should not use this preparation unless directed by physician. As with all medication, keep out of reach of children.

Symptoms and Treatment of Overdosage: These symptoms are based upon medical judgement, not on actual experience, since no significant incidence of overdose has been brought to our attention in clinical or consumer experience. Though unlikely, ingestion of large amounts may cause dizziness, drowsiness, nausea, vomiting, diarrhea, central excitement and a possibility of cyanosis in young children. Treatment is symptomatic, with bedrest and observation.

Dosage:
ADULTS (12 years and over) 2 discs. Dissolve in mouth. Two additional discs every three hours as needed.
CHILDREN (4 to 12 years) 1 disc. Dissolve in mouth. One additional disc every three hours as needed.

How Supplied: Available as individual foil wrapped portable packets in boxes of 24.

FORMULA 44® COUGH MIXTURE

Active Ingredients per 2 tsp. (10 ml.): Dextromethorphan Hydrobromide 15 mg., Doxylamine Succinate 7.5 mg., Sodium Citrate 500 mg. in a pleasant tasting, dark brown syrup base. Also contains Alcohol 10%.

Indications: For the temporary relief of coughs due to colds, flu, bronchitis.

Actions: VICKS FORMULA 44 COUGH MIXTURE is an antitussive, antihistamine, demulcent and expectorant. Calms and quiets coughs. Reduces sneezing and sniffling. Coats, soothes irritated throat.

Warning: Do not exceed recommended dosage unless directed by a physician. Do not administer to children under 6 years

of age unless directed by a physician. Persistent cough may indicate the presence of a serious condition. Persons with a high fever or persistent cough should not use the product unless directed by a physician. FORMULA 44 may cause drowsiness. Do not drive or operate machinery while taking the product. If relief does not occur within three days, discontinue use and consult a physician. As with all medication, keep out of reach of children.

Symptoms and Treatment of Overdosage: These symptoms are based on medical judgement and not on clinical experience, since no significant incidence of overdose has been brought to our attention in clinical or consumer experience. Presenting symptom is drowsiness. Nausea, vomiting, dizziness, ataxia, mydriasis and headache may ensue with ingestion of excessive amounts. Treatment is symptomatic, with bedrest and observation.

Dosage:
Adults: 12 years and over—2 teaspoonfuls
Children: 6 to 12 years: 1 teaspoonful
Repeat every 4 hours as needed.
No more than 6 doses per day.

How Supplied: Available in 3 fl. oz., 6 fl. oz. and 8 fl. oz. bottles. [*Shown in Product Identification Section*]

FORMULA 44D® DECONGESTANT COUGH MIXTURE

Active Ingredients per 2 tsp. (10 ml): Dextromethorphan Hydrobromide 20 mg., Phenylpropanolamine Hydrochloride 25 mg., Guaifenesin 100 mg. in a red, cherry-flavored, cooling syrup. Also contains Alcohol 10%.

Indications: Relieves coughs, decongests nasal passages and loosens upper chest congestion due to colds, flu, bronchitis.

Actions: VICKS FORMULA 44D is an antitussive, nasal decongestant, expectorant and demulcent. It calms, quiets coughs; relieves nasal congestion; loosens phlegm, mucus; and coats, soothes an irritated throat.

Warning: Do not exceed recommended dosage unless directed by physician. Do not administer to children under 2 years of age unless directed by physician. Persistent cough may indicate the presence of a serious condition. Persons with a high fever or persistent cough or with high blood pressure, diabetes, heart or thyroid disease should not use this preparation unless directed by physician. As with all medication, keep out of reach of children.

Symptoms and Treatment of Overdosage: These symptoms are based upon medical judgement, not on actual experience, since no significant incidence of overdose has been brought to our attention in clinical or consumer experience. Ingestion of large amounts may cause drowsiness, dizziness, nausea, vomiting, diarrhea, central excitement, restlessness, anxiety, sweating, tremor, extrasystoles, confusion and delerium.

Treatment is symptomatic, with bedrest and observation.

Dosage:
ADULTS (12 years and over): 2 teaspoonfuls
CHILDREN (6–12 years): 1 teaspoonful
(2–6 years): ½ teaspoonful

No more than 6 doses per day. Repeat every 4 hours as needed.

How Supplied: Available in 3 fl. oz., 6 fl. oz. and 8 fl. oz. bottles. [*Shown in Product Identification Section*]

HEADWAY CAPSULES
HEADWAY TABLETS
For colds, sinus, allergy.

Active Ingredients per two capsules or tablets: Acetaminophen 650mg., Phenylpropanolamine HCl 37.5mg., Chlorpheniramine Maleate 4mg.

Indications: Relieves nasal congestion, runny nose, sneezing, itchy watery eyes, aches and pains caused by a cold, sinus or allergy problem.

Actions: HEADWAY is a nasal decongestant, antihistamine, analgesic and antipyretic. It provides hours of effective relief from symptoms of head colds, sinus and nasal allergies.

Warning: This preparation may cause excitability, especially in children. This medication may cause drowsiness. Avoid alcoholic beverages, driving a motor vehicle, and operating heavy machinery while taking this medication. Do not give to children under 6 years of age or exceed the recommended dosage unless directed by a physician. Persons having asthma, glaucoma, high blood pressure, heart disease, diabetes, thyroid disease, high fever, or difficulty in urination due to enlargement of the prostate gland should not use this product except under the advice and supervision of a physician. Do not use for more than 10 days unless directed by physician. In case of accidental overdose, seek professional assistance or contact a Poison Control Center immediately.

Symptoms and Treatment of Overdosage: These symptoms are based upon medical judgement, not on actual experience, since no significant incidence of overdose has been brought to our attention in clinical or consumer experience. Large overdoses may cause nausea, vomiting, drowsiness, dizziness, ataxia, mydriasis, insomnia, nervousness, tachycardia and headache. Treatment is symptomatic, with bedrest and observation.

Dosage:
ADULTS—2 capsules or tablets
CHILDREN (6–12 years) 1 capsule or tablet
Dose every 4 hours, not to exceed 4 doses per day.

How Supplied: Child-proof sealed packets. Available in 16, 36 and 48 sizes for Capsules and 20, 40 and 60 sizes for tablets. [*Shown in Product Identification Section*]

Continued on next page

Vicks Health Care—Cont.

NYQUIL®
Nighttime Colds Medicine
in oral liquid form.

Active Ingredients per fluid oz. (2 tbs.): Acetaminophen 600 mg., Doxylamine Succinate 7.5 mg., Ephedrine Sulfate 8.0 mg., and Dextromethorphan Hydrobromide 15.0 mg. Also contains Alcohol 25%, and FD&C Yellow No. 5 (tartrazine).

Indications: For the temporary relief of major cold and flu symptoms, as follows: nasal & sinus congestion, coughing, sneezing, minor sorethroat pain, aches and pains, runny nose, headache, fever.

Actions: Decongestant, antipyretic, antihistaminic, antitussive, analgesic. Helps decongest nasal passages and sinus openings, relieves sniffles and sneezing, eases aches and pains, reduces fever, soothes headache, minor sore throat pain, and quiets coughing due to a cold. By relieving these symptoms, also helps patient get to sleep to get the rest he needs.

Warning: This preparation may cause drowsiness. Do not drive or operate machinery while taking this medication. Do not give to children under ten, unless directed by physician. If relief does not occur within three days, discontinue use and consult physician. Reduce dosage if nervousness, restlessness or sleeplessness occurs. Do not use if high blood pressure, heart disease, diabetes or thyroid disease is present unless directed by physician.

Persistent cough may indicate a serious condition. Persons with a high fever or persistent cough should not use this preparation unless directed by a physician. Do not exceed recommended dosage. As with all medication, keep out of reach of children.

Symptoms and Treatment of Overdosage: These symptoms are based on medical judgement and not on actual clinical experience, since no significant incidence of overdose has been brought to our attention in clinical or consumer experience. Presenting symptom of overdosage is drowsiness. Large overdoses may cause emesis, ataxia, nausea, vomiting, restlessness, vertigo, dysuria, palpitations, tinnitus, diaphoresis, insomnia. Treatment is symptomatic, with bedrest and observation.

Dosage and Dosage Form: A green, anise-flavored oral liquid (syrup). A plastic measuring cup with 1 and 2 tablespoonful gradations is supplied.
ADULTS (12 and over): One fluid ounce (2 tablespoonfuls) at bedtime.
CHILDREN 10 to 12: One half ounce (1 tablespoonful) at bedtime.
If confined to bed or at home, a total of 4 doses may be taken per day, each 4 hours apart.

How Supplied: Available in 6 fl. oz. and 10 fl. oz. bottles.
[Shown in Product Identification Section]

SINEX™
Decongestant Nasal Spray

Active Ingredients: Phenylephrine Hydrochloride 0.5%, Cetylpyridinium Chloride 0.04%, Special Vicks Blend of Aromatics (menthol, eucalyptol, camphor, methyl salicylate). Also contains Thimerosol 0.001% as a preservative.

Indications: To provide temporary relief of nasal and sinus congestion of head colds and hay fever.

Actions: VICKS SINEX is a decongestant nasal spray. The product shrinks swollen membranes to restore freer breathing; gives fast relief of nasal stuffiness and congested sinus openings; allows congested sinuses to drain; and instantly cools irritated nasal passages.

Warning: Do not exceed recommended dosage. Follow directions for use carefully. For children under 6 years, consult your physician. If condition persists consult physician. As with all medication, keep out of reach of children.

Symptoms and Treatment of Ingestion: These symptoms are based upon medical judgement, not on actual experience, since no significant incidence of overdose or ingestion has been brought to our attention in clinical or consumer experience. Though unlikely, ingestion of very large amounts may cause restlessness, anxiety, ventricular arrhythmias, nausea and gastrointestinal upset. Treatment is symptomatic, with bedrest and observation.

Directions For Use: Keep head and dispenser upright. May be used every 3 hours as needed.
ADULTS: Spray quickly, firmly 2 times up each nostril, sniffing the spray upward.
CHILDREN 6 to 12 years: Spray 1 time up each nostril.
How Supplied: Available in ½ fl. oz. and 1 fl. oz. plastic spray bottles.
[Shown in Product Identification Section]

SINEX™ LONG-ACTING
Decongestant Nasal Spray

Active Ingredient: Oxymetazoline Hydrochloride 0.05% in an aqueous solution containing mentholated vapors. Also contains thimerosal 0.001% as a preservative.

Indications: For temporary relief of nasal congestion due to the common cold, hay fever or other upper respiratory allergies or nasal congestion associated with sinusitis.

Actions: Oxymetazoline constricts the arterioles of the nasal passages—resulting in a nasal decongestant effect which lasts up to twelve hours, restoring freer breathing through the nose. SINEX LONG-ACTING helps decongest sinus openings and sinus passages thus promoting sinus drainage.

Warning: Do not exceed recommended dosage because symptoms may occur such as burning, stinging, sneezing or increase of nasal discharge. Do not use the product for more than three days. If symptoms persist, consult a physician. The use of this dispenser by more than one person may spread infection. In case

of accidental ingestion, seek professional assistance or contact a Poison Control Center immediately. As with all medication, keep out of reach of children.

Symptoms and Treatment of Oral Ingestion: These symptoms are based upon medical judgement, not on actual experience, since no significant incidence of overdose or ingestion has been brought to our attention in clinical or consumer experience. Depending upon the amount of oral ingestion, somnolence, sedation, or deep coma may occur. With excessive ingestion, profound CNS depression may be accompanied by hypertension, bradycardia, and decreased cardiac output, which may be followed by rebound hypotension and cardiovascular collapse. Prompt gastric evacuation and intensive supportive care is indicated following marked overdosage.

Dosage and Aministration: With head upright, spray 2 or 3 times in each nostril twice daily (morning and evening) or as directed by a physician. Squeeze quickly, firmly, and sniff deeply. Not recommended for children under 6 years of age.

How Supplied: Available in ½ fl. oz. and 1 fl. oz. plastic spray bottles.
[Shown in Product Identification Section]

VAPOSTEAM®
Liquid Medication for
Hot Steam Vaporizers.

Active Ingredients: Polyoxyethylene Dodecanol 1.8%, Aromatics (eucalyptus oil, camphor, menthol) 12.4%, Tincture of Benzoin 5%, in a liquid vehicle. Also contains Alcohol 55%.

Indications: For the symptomatic relief of colds, coughs, chest congestion.

Actions: VAPOSTEAM increases the action of steam to help relieve colds symptoms in the following ways: relieves coughs of colds, even croupy coughs, eases stuffy nasal congestion, loosens phlegmy chest congestion, and moistens dry, irritated breathing passages.

Warning: VAPOSTEAM is for hot steam medication only. Do not ingest. Persistent coughing may indicate the presence of a serious condition. If symptoms persist, discontinue use and consult physician. Persons with high fever or persistent cough should not use this preparation except as directed by a physician. Keep away from open flame or extreme heat. Do not direct steam from vaporizer towards face. As with all medication, keep out of reach of children.

Symptoms and Treatment of Ingestion: Based on the medical literature and clinical judgement, ingestion of large amounts may cause nausea, vomiting, epigastric pain, discomfort and weakness, coma and death. Treatment should consist of cautious gastric lavage, barbiturates for convulsions, Metrazol for coma and supportive therapy as indicated.

Dosage and Administration: In a hot steam vaporizer: Use one tablespoonful of VAPOSTEAM with each quart of water added to the vaporizer. In an open bowl: Simply add VAPOSTEAM to any ordinary bowl of hot water—2 teaspoonfuls for each pint of water—and breathe in the medicated vapors.

How Supplied: Available in 4 fl. oz. and 6 fl. oz. bottles.

VATRONOL®
Nose Drops

Active Ingredients: Ephedrine Sulfate 0.5%, Special Vicks Aromatic Blend (menthol, eucalyptol, camphor, methyl salicylate) 0.06% in an aqueous base. Also contains Thimerosal 0.001% as a preservative.

Indications: Relieves nasal congestion caused by head colds and hay fever.

Actions: VICKS VATRONOL is a decongestant nose drop. It helps restore freer breathing by relieving nasal stuffiness and congested sinus openings. VATRONOL also cools irritated nasal passages.

Warning: Do not exceed recommended dosage. Overdosage may cause nervousness, restlessness, or sleeplessness. Do not use for more than 4 consecutive days or administer to children under 6, unless directed by a physician. As with all medication, keep out of reach of children.

Symptoms and Treatment of Ingestion: These symptoms are based upon medical judgement, not on actual experience, since no significant incidence of overdose or ingestion has been brought to our attention in clinical or consumer experience. Ingestion of very large quantities may cause restlessness, anxiety, sweating, tremor, rapid pulse, extrasystoles, confusion, delirium, nausea and gastrointestinal upset. Treatment is symptomatic, with bedrest and observation.

Dosage:
  ADULTS: Fill dropper to upper mark.
  CHILDREN (6–12 years): Fill dropper to lower mark.
Apply up one nostril, repeat in other nostril.
Repeat every 4 hours as needed.

How Supplied: Available in ½ fl. oz. and 1 fl. oz. dropper bottles.

VICKS® COUGH SILENCERS
Cough Drops

Active Ingredients per lozenge: Dextromethorphan (expressed as Dextromethorphan Hydrobromide) 2.5 mg., Benzocaine 1 mg., Special Vicks Medication (menthol, anethole, peppermint oil) 0.35% in a cooling green, sugar base.

Indications: Provides all-day relief from coughs of colds, excessive smoking, dry or irritated throats when used as directed.

Actions: VICKS COUGH SILENCERS are antitussive, local anesthetic and demulcent throat lozenges.

Warning: Do not administer to children under 4 years of age unless directed by a physician. Severe or persistent cough, sore throat, or sore throat accompanied by fever, headache, nausea and vomiting may be serious. Consult physician promptly. Persons with a high fever or persistent cough should not use this preparation unless directed by a physician. As with all medication, keep out of reach of children.

Symptoms and Treatment of Overdosage: These symptoms are based upon medical judgement, not on actual experience, since no significant incidence of overdose has been brought to our attention in clinical or consumer experience. Though unlikely, ingestion of large quantities may cause dizziness, drowsiness, nausea, vomiting, gastrointestinal upset, diarrhea, central excitement, and a possibility of cyanosis in young children. Treatment is symptomatic, with bedrest and observation.

Dosage: Age 12 and over, 2 drops, dissolve in mouth one at a time, then 1 or 2 each hour as needed. Ages 4 to 12, 1 drop, dissolve in mouth then 1 drop each hour as needed. Do not exceed recommended dosage.

How Supplied: Available in boxes of 15's.

VICKS® COUGH SYRUP
Expectorant, Antitussive Cough Syrup

Active Ingredients per tsp. (5 ml.): Dextromethorphan Hydrobromide 3.5 mg., Guaifenesin 25 mg., Sodium Citrate 200 mg. in a red, cherry-flavored, syrup base. Also contains Alcohol 5%.

Indications: Provides temporary relief of coughs due to colds, helps loosen phlegm and rid passageways of bothersome mucus, and soothes a cough-irritated throat.

Actions: VICKS COUGH SYRUP is an antitussive, expectorant and demulcent. It calms, quiets coughs of colds, flu and bronchitis; loosens phlegm, promotes drainage of bronchial tubes; and coats and soothes a cough irritated throat.

Warning: Do not exceed recommended dosage. Do not administer to children under 2 years of age unless directed by a physician. Persistent cough may indicate the presence of a serious condition. Persons with a high fever or persistent cough should not use this preparation unless directed by a physician. As with all medication, keep out of reach of children.

Symptoms and Treatment of Overdosage: These symptoms are based upon medical judgement, not on actual experience, since no significant incidence of overdose has been brought to our attention in clinical or consumer experience. Ingestion of large amounts may cause drowsiness, dizziness, nausea, vomiting, diarrhea, central excitement and alkalosis. Treatment is gastric lavage and symptomatic treatment with bedrest and observation.

Dosage:
  ADULTS (12 years and over): 3 teaspoonfuls
  CHILDREN (6–12 years): 2 teaspoonfuls
      (2–6 years): 1 teaspoonful
Repeat every 4 hours as needed.

How Supplied: Available in 3 fl. oz. and 6 fl. oz. bottles.

VICKS® INHALER
with decongestant action

Active Ingredients per inhaler: l-Desoxyephedrine 50 mg., Special Vicks Medication (menthol, camphor, methyl salicylate, bornyl acetate) 150 mg.

Indications: Provides temporary relief of nasal congestion of colds and hay fever. Decongests sinus openings.

Actions: VICKS INHALER is an intranasal inhaled decongestant. It shrinks swollen membranes and provides fast relief from a stuffy nose.

Warning: As with all medication, keep out of reach of children.

Symptoms and Treatment of Ingestion: These symptoms are based upon medical judgement, not on actual experience, since no significant incidence of overdose or ingestion has been brought to our attention in clinical or consumer experience. Though VICKS INHALER is unlikely to be ingested, consumption of large quantities of its active ingredients may cause dizziness, nervousness, headache, tachycardia, nausea and vomiting. Treatment is symptomatic, with bedrest and observation.

Directions For Use: Inhale medicated vapor through each nostril while blocking off other nostril. Use as often as needed.

VICKS INHALER is medically effective for 3 months after first use.

How Supplied: Available as a cylindrical plastic nasal inhaler (net wt. 0.007 oz.).

VICKS® THROAT LOZENGES

Active Ingredients per lozenge: Benzocaine 5 mg., Cetylpyridinium Chloride 1.66 mg., Special Vicks Medication (menthol, camphor, eucalyptus oil) in a red cooling sugar base.

Indications: For fast-acting temporary relief of minor sore throat pain, and minor coughs due to colds.

Actions: VICKS THROAT LOZENGES are local anesthetic and demulcent cough drops. They temporarily soothe minor sore throat irritations —ease pain —and relieve irritation and dryness of mouth and throat.

Warning: Do not exceed recommended dosage. Severe or persistent cough, sore throat, or sore throat accompanied by high fever, headache, nausea, and vomiting may be serious. Consult physician promptly. Do not use more than 2 days or administer to children under 3 years of age unless directed by physician. As with all medication, keep out of reach of children.

Symptoms and Treatment of Overdosage: These symptoms are based upon medical judgement, not on actual experience, since no significant incidence of overdose has been brought to our attention in clinical or consumer experience. Though unlikely, ingestion of large amounts may cause nausea, vomiting, gastrointestinal upset, central excitement, and a possibility of cyanosis in

Continued on next page

Vicks Health Care—Cont.

young children. Treatment is symptomatic, with bedrest and observation.

Dosage: ADULTS AND CHILDREN 3 years and over: allow one lozenge to dissolve slowly in mouth. Repeat hourly as needed.

How Supplied: Box of 12's.

VICKS® VAPORUB®
Decongestant Vaporizing Ointment

For use as a rub or in steam.

Active Ingredients: Special Vicks Medication (menthol, spirits of turpentine, eucalyptus oil, camphor, cedar leaf oil, nutmeg oil, thymol) 14% in a petrolatum base.

Indications: For the symptomatic relief of nasal congestion (up to 8 hours), bronchial mucous congestion, coughs, laryngitis and huskiness, muscular tightness and muscular aches and pains due to colds. Also for chapped hands.

Actions: The inhaled vapors of VICKS VAPORUB have a decongestant, and antitussive effect. Applied externally, the medication acts as a local analgesic. The ointment is soothing to chapped hands and skin.

Warning: For external application and use in steam only. Do not swallow or place in nostrils. If fever is present or cough or other symptoms persist, see your doctor. In case of illness in very young children, it is wise to consult your physician. To avoid possibility of fire, never expose VAPORUB to flame or place VAPORUB in any container in which you are heating water. Do not direct steam from vaporizer toward face. As with all medication, keep out of reach of children.

Symptoms and Treatment of Ingestion: These symptoms are based upon medical judgement, not on actual experience, since no significant incidence of overdose or ingestion has been brought to our attention in clinical or consumer experience. Ingestion of large quantities may cause nausea, vomiting, abdominal discomfort, diarrhea. Theoretically, very large quantities could cause weakness, vertigo, convulsions and drowsiness. If the extent of accidental ingestion is not known, treatment should consist of cautious gastric lavage. Otherwise, supportive and symptomatic treatment as necessary. If indicated, saline cathartics, demulcents and barbiturates for convulsions. Do not induce emesis.

Dosage:

AS A RUB: For relief of head and chest cold symptoms and coughs due to colds. Rub on throat, chest and back. Cover with a dry warm cloth if desired. Repeat as needed, especially at bedtime for continuous breathing relief.

For relief of muscle tightness, apply hot, moist towel to affected area. Remove towel, then massage well with VAPORUB. Cover with a dry, warm cloth if desired.

For chapped hands and skin, apply liberally as a dressing.

IN STEAM: Fill medicine cup of vaporizer with VICKS VAPORUB and follow directions of vaporizer manufacturer. VAPORUB may also be used in a steam bowl. Fill a bowl ¾ full with steaming water and add 2 teaspoonfuls of VAPORUB (after removing from heat). Then inhale steaming vapors. Add extra steaming water as steam decreases.

How Supplied: Available in 1.5 oz., 3.0 oz. and 6.0 oz. plastic jars.

[*Shown in Product Identification Section*]

Walker, Corp & Co., Inc.
P.O. BOX 1320
EASTHAMPTON PL. &
N. COLLINGWOOD AVE.
SYRACUSE, NY 13201

EVAC-U-GEN®

Description: Evac-U-Gen® is available as purple scored tablets, each containing 97.2 mg. of yellow phenolphthalein.

Action and Uses: For temporary relief of occasional constipation and to help restore a normal pattern of evacuation. A mild, non-griping, stimulant laxative in chewable, anise-flavored form, Evac-U-Gen provides softening of the feces through selective action on the intramural nerve plexus of intestinal smooth muscle, and increases the propulsive peristaltic activity of the colon.

Indications: Because of its gentle action and non-toxic nature, Evac-U-Gen is a particularly suitable laxative in pregnancy, in the presence of hemorrhoids, for children and the elderly. It is especially useful when straining at the stool is a hazard, as in hernia, cardiac or hypertensive patients.

Contraindications: Contraindicated in patients with a history of sensitivity to phenolphthalein. Evac-U-Gen should not be used when abdominal pain, nausea, vomiting, or other symptoms of appendicitis are present.

Side Effects: If skin rash appears, use of Evac-U-Gen or other preparations containing phenolphthalein should be discontinued. May cause coloration of feces or urine if they are sufficiently alkaline.

Warning: Frequent or prolonged use may result in dependence on laxatives.

Administration and Dosage: Adults: chew one or two tablets night or morning. **Children:** 3 to 10 years, chew ½ tablet daily. Intensity of action is proportional to dosage, but individually effective doses vary. Evac-U-Gen is usually active 6 to 8 hours after administration, but residual action may last 3 to 4 days.

How Supplied: Evac-U-Gen is available in bottles of 35, 100, 500, 1000, 2000 and 6000 tablets.

Products are cross-indexed by generic and chemical names in the

YELLOW SECTION

Walker Pharmacal Company
4200 LACLEDE AVENUE
ST. LOUIS, MO 63108

PRID SALVE
(Smile's PRID Salve)
Drawing Salve and Anti-infectant

Active Ingredients: Ichthammol (Ammonium Ichthosulfonate) Phenol (Carbolic Acid) Lead Oleate, Rosin, Bees Wax, Lard.

Description: PRID has a very stiff consistency and is almost black in color.

Indication: PRID is an anti-infective salve, which also serves as a skin protective ointment. As a drawing salve, PRID softens the skin around the foreign body, and assists the natural rejection. PRID also helps to prevent the spread of infection. PRID aids in relieving the discomfort of minor skin irritations, superficial cuts, scratches and wounds. PRID is also helpful in the treatment of boils and carbuncles. PRID has been used with some success in the treatment of acne and furunculosis as well as other skin disorders.

Warning: When applied to fingers or toes, do not use a bandage; use loose gauze so as to not interfere with circulation. Apply according to directions for use and in no case to large areas of the body without a physician's direction. Keep out of eyes.

Caution: If PRID salve is not effective in 10 days, see your physician.

Directions For Use: Wash affected parts thoroughly with hot water; dry and apply PRID at least twice daily on a clean bandage or gauze. After irritation subsides, repeat application once a day for several days. DO NOT irritate by squeezing or pressing skin area.

How Supplied: PRID is packaged in a telescoping orange metal can containing 20 grams of PRID salve.

Wallace Laboratories
HALF ACRE ROAD
CRANBURY, NJ 08512

MALTSUPEX®
(malt soup extract)
Powder, Liquid, Tablets

Composition: 'Maltsupex' is a nondiastatic extract from barley malt which is available in powder, liquid, and tablet form. 'Maltsupex' has a gentle laxative action and promotes soft, easily passed stools. Each **Tablet** contains 750 mg of 'Maltsupex' and approximately 0.15 to 0.25 mEq of potassium. Each tablespoonful (0.5 fl oz) of **Liquid** and each heaping tablespoonful of **Powder** contains approximately 16 grams of Malt Soup Extract and 3.1 to 5.5 mEq of potassium.

Indications: 'Maltsupex' is indicated for the dietary management and treatment of functional constipation in infants and children. It is also useful in treating constipation in adults, including those with laxative dependence.

Warnings: Do not use when abdominal pain, nausea or vomiting are present. If constipation persists, consult a physician. Keep this and all medications out of the reach of children.

'Maltsupex' Powder and Liquid only—Do not use these products except under the advice and supervision of a physician if you have kidney disease.

Precautions: In patients with diabetes, allow for carbohydrate content of approximately 14 grams per tablespoonful of **Liquid** (56 calories), 13 grams per tablespoonful of **Powder** (52 calories), and 0.6 grams per **Tablet** (3 calories).

Tablets only: This product contains FD&C Yellow No. 5 (tartrazine) which may cause allergic-type reactions (including bronchial asthma) in certain susceptible individuals. Although the overall incidence of FD&C Yellow No. 5 (tartrazine) sensitivity in the general population is low, it is frequently seen in patients who also have aspirin hypersensitivity.

Dosage and Administration: General—The recommended daily dosage of 'Maltsupex' may vary from 6 to 32 grams for infants (2 years or less) and 12 to 64 grams for children and adults, accompanied by adequate fluid intake with each dose. Use the smallest dose that is effective and lower dosage as improvement occurs. Use heaping measures of the **Powder.** 'Maltsupex' **Liquid** mixes more easily if stirred first in one or two ounces of warm water.

Powder and Liquid (Usual Dosage) — **Adults:** 2 tablespoonfuls (32 g) twice daily for 3 or 4 days, or until relief is noted, then 1 to 2 tablespoonfuls at bedtime for maintenance, as needed. Drink a full glass (8 oz) of liquid with each dose. **Children:** 1 or 2 tablespoonfuls in 8 ounces of liquid once or twice daily (with cereal, milk or preferred beverage). **Bottle-Fed Infants (over 1 month):** ½ to 2 tablespoonfuls in the day's total formula, or 1 to 2 teaspoonfuls in a single feeding to correct constipation. To prevent constipation (as when switching to whole milk) add 1 to 2 teaspoonfuls to the day's formula or 1 teaspoonful to every second feeding. **Breast-Fed Infants (over one month):** 1 to 2 teaspoonfuls in 2 to 4 ounces of water or fruit juice once or twice daily.

Tablets—Adults: Start with 4 tablets (3 g) four times daily (with meals and bedtime) and adjust dosage according to response. Drink a full glass (8 oz) of liquid with each dose.

How Supplied: 'Maltsupex' is supplied in 8 ounce (NDC 0037-9101-12) and 16 ounce (NDC 0037-9101-08) jars of 'Maltsupex' Powder; 8 fluid ounce (NDC 0037-9001-12) and 1 pint (NDC 0037-9001-08) bottles of 'Maltsupex' Liquid; and in bottles of 100 'Maltsupex' Tablets (NDC 0037-9201-01).

'Maltsupex' **Powder** and **Liquid** are Distributed by

WALLACE LABORATORIES
Division of
CARTER-WALLACE, INC.
Cranbury, New Jersey 08512
'Maltsupex' **Tablets** are Manufactured by

WALLACE LABORATORIES
Division of
CARTER-WALLACE, INC.
Cranbury, New Jersey 08512
Rev. 10/80

[*Shown in Product Identification Section*]

RYNA™
(Liquid)
RYNA-C®					C
(Liquid)
RYNA-CX®					C
(Liquid)

Description:
Each 5 ml (one teaspoonful) of **RYNA Liquid** contains:
Chlorpheniramine maleate...............2 mg
Pseudoephedrine hydrochloride....30 mg
in a clear, slightly yellow colored, lemon-vanilla flavored demulcent base containing no sugar, dyes, or alcohol.
Each 5 ml (one teaspoonful) of **RYNA-C Liquid** contains, in addition:
Codeine phosphate...........................10 mg
(WARNING: May be habit-forming)
in a colorless, cinnamon-flavored, demulcent base containing no sugar, dyes, or alcohol.
Each 5 ml (one teaspoonful) of **RYNA-CX Liquid** contains:
Codeine phosphate...........................10 mg
(WARNING: May be habit-forming)
Pseudoephedrine hydrochloride....30 mg
Guaifenesin.....................................100 mg
in a clear, colorless, cherry-vanilla-menthol flavored demulcent base containing no sugar, dyes, or alcohol.

Actions:
Chlorpheniramine maleate in RYNA and RYNA-C is an antihistamine that antagonizes the effects of histamine.
Codeine Phosphate in RYNA-C and RYNA-CX is a centrally-acting antitussive that relieves cough.
Pseudoephedrine hydrochloride in RYNA, RYNA-C and RYNA-CX is a sympathomimetic nasal decongestant that acts to shrink swollen mucosa of the respiratory tract.
Guaifenesin in RYNA-CX is an expectorant that increases mucus flow to help prevent dryness and relieve irritated respiratory tract membranes.

Indications:
RYNA is indicated for the temporary relief of the concurrent symptoms of nasal congestion, sneezing, itchy and watery eyes, and running nose as occurs with the common cold or allergic rhinitis.
RYNA-C is indicated for the above when cough is also a concurrent symptom.
RYNA-CX is indicated for the temporary relief of the concurrent symptoms of dry, nonproductive cough and nasal congestion.

Directions:
Adults: 2 teaspoonfuls every 6 hours.

Children 6–under 12 years: 1 teaspoonful every 6 hours.
Children 2–under 6 years: ½ teaspoonful every 6 hours (see WARNINGS).
Do not exceed 4 doses in 24 hours.

Warnings:
Do not give these products to children taking other medications. Do not give RYNA or RYNA-C to children under 6 years, nor RYNA-CX to children under 2 years except under the advice and supervision of a physician. Do not exceed recommended dosage unless directed by a physician because nervousness, dizziness, or sleeplessness may occur at higher doses. If symptoms do not improve within 3 days or are accompanied by high fever, discontinue use and consult a physician.

For RYNA-C and RYNA-CX only: Codeine may cause or aggravate constipation. A persistent cough may be a sign of a serious condition.

Do not take these products except under the advice and supervision of a physician if you have any of the following symptoms or conditions: cough that persists more than 3 days or tends to recur; chronic cough, such as occurs with smoking, asthma, or emphysema; cough accompanied by excessive secretions, high-fever, rash, or persistent headache; chronic pulmonary disease or shortness of breath; high blood pressure; thyroid disease or diabetes.

For RYNA and RYNA-C only: Do not take these products except under the advice and supervision of a physician if you have asthma, glaucoma, or difficulty in urination due to enlargement of the prostate. Both products contain an antihistamine which may cause excitability, especially in children, or drowsiness or which may impair mental alertness. Combined with alcohol, sedatives, or other depressants may have an additive effect. Do not drive motor vehicles, operate machinery, or drink alcoholic beverages while taking these products.

KEEP THIS AND ALL DRUGS OUT OF THE REACH OF CHILDREN. IN CASE OF ACCIDENTAL OVERDOSE, SEEK PROFESSIONAL ASSISTANCE OR CONTACT A POISON CONTROL CENTER IMMEDIATELY.

Drug Interaction Precaution: Do not take these products if you are presently taking a prescription antihypertensive or antidepressant drug containing a monoamine oxidase inhibitor, except under the advice and supervision of a physician.

How Supplied:
RYNA: bottles of 4 fl oz (NDC 0037-0638-66), one pint (NDC 0037-0638-68).
RYNA-C: bottles of 4 fl oz (NDC 0037-0522-66), one pint (NDC 0037-0522-68).

Continued on next page

Wallace—Cont.

RYNA-CX: bottles of 4 fl oz (NDC 0037-0801-66), one pint (NDC 0037-0801-68).

Rev. 10/80

[*Shown in Product Identification Section*]
WALLACE LABORATORIES
Division of
CARTER-WALLACE, INC.
Cranbury, New Jersey 08512

SYLLACT®
(Powdered Psyllium Seed Husks)

Description: Each rounded teaspoonful of fruit-flavored 'Syllact' contains approximately 3.3 g of powdered psyllium seed husks and an equal amount of dextrose as a dispersing agent, and provides about 14 calories. Potassium sorbate, methyl- and propylparaben are added as preservatives.

Actions: The active ingredient in 'Syllact' is hydrophilic mucilloid, nonabsorbable dietary fiber derived from the powdered husks of natural psyllium seed, which acts by increasing the water content and bulk volume of stools. It gives 'Syllact' a bland, non-irritating, laxative action and promotes physiologic evacuation of the bowel.

Indications: 'Syllact' is indicated for the treatment of constipation and, when recommended by a physician, in other disorders where the effect of additional bulk and fiber is desired.

Warnings: Do not swallow dry. Drink a full glass (8 oz) of water or other liquid with each dose. If constipation persists, consult a physician. Do not use if fecal impaction, intestinal obstruction, or abdominal pain, nausea or vomiting are present. Keep this and all medications out of the reach of children.

Dosage and Administration: The actual daily dosage depends on the need and response of the patient. Adults may take up to 9 teaspoonfuls daily, in divided doses, for several days to provide optimum benefit when constipation is chronic or severe. Lower the dosage as improvement occurs. Use a dry spoon to measure powder. Tighten lid to keep out moisture.

Usual Adult Dosage—One rounded teaspoonful of 'Syllact' in a full glass (8 oz) of cool water or other beverage taken orally one to three times daily. If desired, an additional glass of liquid may be taken after each dose.

Children's Dosage—6 years and older—Half the adult dosage with the same fluid intake requirement.

How Supplied: 'Syllact' Powder—in 10 oz jars (NDC 0037-9501-13).

Rev. 6/80

[*Shown in Product Identification Section*]
WALLACE LABORATORIES
Division of
CARTER-WALLACE, INC.
Cranbury, New Jersey 08512

Warner-Lambert Company
201 TABOR ROAD
MORRIS PLAINS, NJ 07950

Warner-Lambert Inc.
SANTURCE, P.R. 00911

e.p.t.®
In-Home Early Pregnancy Test
For *In-Vitro* Diagnostic Use

Reagents: HCG (Human Chorionic Gonadotropin) on Sheep Red Blood Cells, HCG Antiserum (Rabbit)

Indications: For use in detecting HCG hormone in the urine to detect pregnancy.

Actions: E.P.T. is a urine test. E.P.T. is a fast, highly accurate, easy, completely safe and completely private way for a woman to determine whether she is pregnant. E.P.T. is a simple urine test, designed to be done by a woman herself in her own home.

E.P.T. will answer the question "Am I pregnant?" in two hours. E.P.T. is for external use only—it is for *In Vitro* Diagnostic Use.

How E.P.T. works and when you'll want to use it.

When you become pregnant you begin to produce a hormone called HCG—Human Chorionic Gonadotropin. This hormone appears in your urine. When the HCG level is high enough, E.P.T. will detect the presence of the HCG in the urine. This HCG level occurs at about the *ninth day* after the day on which you expected your period. It is possible to get a positive result before the ninth day (indicating you may be pregnant) although in many cases the level of HCG will not be sufficient to give an accurate, clear reading before that time. We advise that you wait until at least your ninth "late day" so that you can test with greater confidence.

If you should obtain a negative result with E.P.T. and yet your period still does not begin, repeat the test one week later. (You may have miscalculated your dates.) If you get a second negative reading, and your period has still not begun, check with your doctor. If E.P.T. indicates that you are pregnant, of course you will want to see your doctor at once for advice on health measures for proper fetal development.

Directions:
Read all the following information carefully

IT IS IMPORTANT THAT YOU FOLLOW THESE INSTRUCTIONS WITH CARE TO ACHIEVE AN ACCURATE RESULT. When instructions are followed, no other in-home use test is more accurate than E.P.T.

Urine collection: For maximum accuracy test from the ninth day after you have missed an expected period. Wash kit lid with soap or detergent. Rinse it absolutely clean. Traces of soap or detergent could cause a false reading. You need two hours for the test, so if you haven't this much time in the morning, cover and store your urine specimen in

the refrigerator. Sediment may form but do not shake the specimen. Use the urine at the top of the container. Be sure to do the test the day the urine was collected. *Use only first morning urine.* Use first morning urine because if you are pregnant, this urine contains more HCG than urine collected at any other time of day. Accurate results may depend on your using *first morning urine.*

1. Remove the glass test tube from the support. Take off the rubber stopper and put the tube back into the support. Keep the stopper—you will need it later.
2. Fill the dropper with first morning urine.
3. Hold the dropper vertically above the test tube. Do not touch test tube with the dropper tip. Place three free-falling drops of the urine into the test tube (try to use just three drops but remember that a tiny bit more or less will not hurt the test.)
4. Twist off the top of the plastic vial and squeeze all the contents into the test tube.
5. Take the test tube from the support and press the rubber stopper back into place. SHAKE VIGOROUSLY FOR AT LEAST 10 SECONDS to mix contents adequately.
6. Replace the test tube in the support.
7. IMPORTANT: Put the support holding the test tube on a flat, solid surface free from vibrations. *Put it where it will not be disturbed or jiggled,* but where there is good light for reading the result. Do not put it on a windowsill or radiator where it will be subject to sunlight or heat. A bookshelf, the top of a heavy chest, desk or table are good choices. Be sure though, that you put the suppport where you will be able to read the results in the mirror without having to disturb it.
8. LET THE TEST TUBE AND STAND REMAIN UNDISTURBED FOR TWO HOURS BEFORE READING THE RESULTS. DO NOT RISK A FALSE READING BY MOVING OR OTHERWISE INTERFERING WITH THE TEST TUBE AND STAND. Although you may be able to read your result from about 1 to 2½ hours after you started the test, the most reliable time to read it is at 2 hours.
9. READING E.P.T. RESULTS
When two hours have passed, E.P.T. is ready to give you the results of your test. *Do not touch the support, but look into the mirror* under the test tube.

POSITIVE: A DONUT-SHAPED RING (MUST HAVE A HOLE IN THE CENTER).

This ring can vary in clarity, thickness and color. Any ring indicates that your urine does contain pregnancy hormone; and you can assume you are pregnant. You should now plan to consult your physician, who is best able to advise you.

NEGATIVE: NO RING, JUST A DEPOSIT—NO RING.

This means that no pregnancy hormone has been detected, and you probably are not pregnant. Your overdue period should begin soon. In the unlikely event that a week passes and you still have not menstruated, you should perform another test, using a new E.P.T. kit; because 1) you may have miscalculated your period; 2) there may not yet have been sufficient HCG in your urine at the time of the first test; or 3) the test might have been performed incorrectly. If a second test still gives a negative result, there is little chance that you are pregnant. However, there could be other important reasons why your period has not begun and you should see your physician. REMEMBER: Do not touch the test tube and support until you have read the result in the mirror. The pattern reflected in the mirror from the bottom of the test tube is the only reading that counts. Read the result two hours after you started the test.

Limits of the Test: If you allow the test to stand for much longer than two hours, a false or confusing ring may develop. The result you see at two hours is the result by which you should be guided. Each E.P.T. test tube of reagents, vial of special purified water and dropper are not reuseable. Although E.P.T. is highly accurate in detecting pregnancy, a low incidence of false results (positive when no pregnancy exists, or negative when pregnancy is present) can occur (see Table 1 and Table 2).

What the results mean

A positive result indicates that your urine contains HCG and you can assume you are pregnant. When tested by consumers, E.P.T. was 97% accurate when a positive result was obtained. You should now consult with your physician who is best able to guide you.

A negative result means that no HCG has been detected. When tested by consumers, E.P.T. was 84% accurate when a negative result was obtained. There is the possibility that your urine gave a false negative result because of miscalculating your menstrual cycle and as a result there may not have been enough HCG in the urine. If a week passes and you still have not started menstruating you should do the test again. If it is still negative in this later test there is little chance that you are pregnant, but because there could be other important reasons why you have not started menstruating you should see your doctor without delay.

Storage: Store below 86° Fahrenheit (30° Centigrade).
Do not freeze.

How Supplied: One E.P.T. kit including test tube of reagents, vial of special purified water, dropper, lid, mirror and support in carton with package insert. An E.P.T. 2-test kit including two test tubes of reagents, two vials of special purified water, two droppers, one lid, mirror and plastic support in carton with package insert.
E.P.T. is an *In Vitro* diagnostic test; not for internal use.
E.P.T. is made in Ireland and distributed by Warner-Lambert Company.
[*Shown in Product Identification Section*]

Table 1
Laboratory Evaluation of e.p.t.
(Single Test Results)

# of Urine Samples Tested	e.p.t. result	Clinical Diagnosis	e.p.t. Accuracy
200	197 Positive*	198 Pregnant	99.5%
	3 Negative**	2 Not Pregnant	

  *Positive indicates pregnancy
 **Negative indicates no pregnancy

Table 2
Consumer Use Tests
(Single Test Performed at Home by Individuals)

Actual Clinical State	Test Readings	
	Positive	Negative
Pregnant	451 (Accurate)	36 (Inaccurate)
Not Pregnant	15 (Inaccurate)	183 (Accurate)
Total Tests	466	219

Conclusion
1. First test is 97% accurate if positive reading is obtained.
2. First test is 84% accurate if negative reading is obtained: however, a repeat test one week later improves the accuracy to 96%.

HALLS® MENTHO–LYPTUS®
Cough Tablets

Active Ingredients: Each tablet contains eucalyptus oil and menthol.
Indications: For temporary relief of minor throat irritation and cough due to colds and to allergies. Makes nasal passages feel clearer.
Warning: Persistent cough may indicate presence of a serious condition. Persons with high fever or persistent cough should use this preparation only as directed by a physician.
Dosage: Allow to dissolve slowly in mouth. Repeat as often as necessary.
How Supplied: Halls Mentho-Lyptus Cough Tablets are available in single sticks of 9 tablets each, in 3-stick packs, and in bags of 30 tablets. They are available in four flavors: Regular, Cherry, Honey-Lemon and Ice Blue. There is also a Sugar Free Regular flavor available in single sticks of 5 tablets each.
[*Shown in Product Identification Section*]

HALLS® MENTHO-LYPTUS®
Decongestant Cough Formula

Active Ingredients: Per 2 teaspoonfuls:
Dextromethorphan
  Hydrobromide .... 15 mg
Phenylpropanolamine
  Hydrochloride .... 37.5 mg
Menthol .... 14 mg
Eucalyptus Oil .... 12.7 mg
Also contains Alcohol, 22%
Indications: To control coughs, soothe throat and help clear nasal passages.
Actions: Halls quickly soothes raw throat and relieves cough. Then once in your bloodstream, Halls rushes its non-narcotic cough medication to the brains cough control center. Safely relieves the persistent urge to cough up to 4 full hours.

Halls makes nasal passages feel clearer. Halls contains a concentration of vaporizing ingredients which send cooling, penetrating vapors deep into nasal passages. This "vapor action" makes stuffy nasal passages feel clearer in seconds. Halls relieves sinus congestion. The decongestant cough formula contains a medically proven ingredient which actually relieves congestion in the sensitive areas of your sinus. This provides hours of comforting relief from sinus congestion.
Warnings: Keep out of the reach of children.
Do not administer to children under 6 years of age unless directed by physician. Persistent cough may indicate the presence of a serious condition.
Persons with high fever, persistent cough, high blood pressure, heart disease, diabetes or thyroid disease should use only as directed by physician.
If relief does not occur within 3 days, discontinue use and consult physician.
Dosage: Age 12 years and over: 2 teaspoonfuls every 4 hours. Do not exceed 4 doses (8 teaspoonfuls) per day. Do not exceed recommended dosage. Children 6-12: ½ adult dosage.
Storage: Keep tightly closed. Store at room temperature.
How Supplied: Halls Mentho-lyptus Decongestant Cough Formula is available in 3 Fl. Oz. bottles.

LISTERINE® Antiseptic

Active Ingredients: Thymol, Eucalyptol, Methyl Salicylate and Menthol. Also contains: Water, Alcohol 26.9%, Benzoic Acid, Poloxamer 407 and Caramel.

Continued on next page

Warner-Lambert—Cont.

Indications: For general oral hygiene, bad breath, minor cuts, scratches, insect bites, infectious dandruff.

Actions: Listerine Antiseptic, a unique combination of aromatic oils in a hydroalcoholic vehicle, provides long lasting oral deodorant activity. Its antibacterial action against odor causing bacteria, its odor-masking properties, and its low surface tension which aids in the removal of oral debris, account for its efficacy as an oral mouthwash and gargle.

Warnings: Do not administer to children under three years of age. Keep this and all drugs out of the reach of children. Not for ingestion.

Directions: For bad breath and general oral hygiene—Rinse full strength for 30 seconds with 2/3 ounce (4 teaspoonfuls) morning and night.
For minor cuts, scratches and insect bites—apply directly to injury.
For infectious dandruff symptoms—massage on scalp.

Storage: Cold weather may cloud Listerine. Its antiseptic properties are not affected.

How Supplied: Listerine Antiseptic is supplied in 3, 6, 12, 18, 24 and 32 Fl. Oz. bottles.
[*Shown in Product Identification Section*]

LISTERMINT®
Mouthwash and Gargle

Ingredients: Water, SD Alcohol 38-B, Glycerin, Poloxamer 407, Sodium Lauryl Sulfate, Sodium Citrate, Sodium Saccharin, Flavoring, Zinc Chloride, Citric Acid, D&C Yellow No. 10, FD&C Green No. 3.

Indications: Listermint is a green, mint flavored, pleasant tasting mouthwash and gargle which is recommended for daily oral care and provides a refreshing mouth feeling and long lasting breath protection.

Directions: Rinse and gargle for 30 seconds with a half mouthful of Listermint first thing in the morning, after meals or when needed for mouth refreshment and clean breath.

How Supplied: Listermint is supplied to consumers in 6, 12, 18, 24 and 32 Fl. Oz. bottles.
[*Shown in Product Identification Section*]

LISTERMINT®
Cinnamon Mouthwash and Gargle

Ingredients: Water, SD Alcohol 38-B, Glycerin, Poloxamer 407, Sodium Lauryl Sulfate, Flavoring, Sodium Citrate, Sodium Saccharin, Zinc Chloride, Citric Acid, FD&C Red No. 40.

Indications: Listermint Cinnamon is a red, cinnamon flavored, zesty tasting mouthwash and gargle which is recommended for daily oral care and provides a refreshing mouth feeling and long lasting breath protection.

Directions: Rinse and gargle for 30 seconds with half a mouthful of Listermint Cinnamon first thing in the morning, after meals or when needed for mouth refreshment and clean breath.

How Supplied: Listermint Cinnamon is supplied to consumers in 6, 12, 18 and 24 Fl. Oz. bottles.
[*Shown in Product Identification Section*]

LUBATH® BATH OIL

Composition: Contains mineral oil, PPG-15 Stearyl Ether, Oleth-2, Nonoxynol-5, Fragrance, D&C Green No. 6.

Actions and Uses: Lubath is a lanolin-free, mineral oil based, bath oil designed for softening and soothing dry skin during the bath. The formula disperses into countless droplets of oil that coat the skin and help lubricate and soften. It is equally effective in hard or soft water and provides an excellent way to moisturize the skin.

Administration and Dosage: One to two capfuls (16 oz. size) or two to four capfuls (8 oz. and 4 oz. size) in bath, or apply with moistened cloth in shower and rinse. For use as a skin cleanser, rub into wet skin and rinse.

Precautions: Avoid getting in eyes, if this occurs, flush with clear water. When using any bath oil, take precautions against slipping. For external use only.

How Supplied: Available in 4, 8 and 16 fl. oz. plastic bottles.
[*Shown in Product Identification Section*]

LUBRIDERM® CREAM
Dry Skin Cream

Composition:
Scented: Contains Water, Mineral Oil, Petrolatum, Glycerin, Glyceryl Stearate, PEG-100 Stearate, Squalane, Lanolin, Lanolin Alcohol, Lanolin Oil, Cetyl Alcohol, Sorbitan Laurate, Fragrance, Methylparaben, Butylparaben, Propylparaben, Quaternium-15.
Unscented: Contains Water, Mineral Oil, Petrolatum, Glycerin, Glyceryl Stearate, PEG-100 Stearate, Squalane, Lanolin, Lanolin Alcohol, Lanolin Oil, Cetyl Alcohol, Sorbitan Laurate, Methylparaben, Butylparaben, Propylparaben, Quaternium-15.

Actions and Uses: Lubriderm Cream is an emollient cream indicated for relieving extremely dry, chapped skin. The formula contains emollients which help restore and maintain the skin's normal suppleness while smoothing, soothing and softening.

Administration and Dosage: Apply several times daily.

Precautions: For external use only.

How Supplied: Available in 4 oz. tubes. Scented also available in 1.5 oz. tubes.

LUBRIDERM® LOTION
Skin Lubricant Moisturizer

Composition:
Scented—Contains Water, Mineral Oil, Petrolatum, Sorbitol, Lanolin, Lanolin Alcohol, Stearic Acid, Triethanolamine, Cetyl Alcohol, Fragrance, Butylparaben, Methylparaben, Propylparaben, Sodium Chloride.
Unscented—Contains Water, Mineral Oil, Petrolatum, Sorbitol, Lanolin, Lanolin Alcohol, Stearic Acid, Triethanolamine, Cetyl Alcohol, Butylparaben, Methylparaben, Propylparaben, Sodium Chloride.

Actions and Uses: Lubriderm Lotion is an oil-in-water emulsion indicated for use in softening, soothing and moisturizing dry chapped skin. Lubriderm relieves the roughness, tightness and discomfort associated with dry or chapped skin and helps protect the skin from further drying.
Lubriderm's extra rich formula smoothes easily into skin without leaving a sticky film.

Administration and Dosage: Apply as often as needed to hands, face and body for skin protection.

Precautions: For external use only.

How Supplied:
Scented: Available in 4, 8 and 16 fl. oz. plastic bottles.
Unscented: Available in 8 and 16 fl. oz. plastic bottles.
[*Shown in Product Identification Section*]

SINUTAB® Tablets*
*Product of Warner-Lambert Inc.

Active Ingredients: Each tablet contains:
Acetaminophen ....325 mg.
Phenylpropanolamine HCl ....25 mg.
Phenyltoloxamine Citrate ....22 mg.

Indications: For temporary relief of sinus headache and congestion.

Actions: Sinutab® contains an analgesic (acetaminophen) to relieve pain, a decongestant (phenylpropanolamine hydrochloride) to reduce congestion of the nasopharyngeal mucosa, and an antihistamine (phenyltoloxamine citrate) to help control allergic symptoms.
Acetaminophen is both analgesic and antipyretic. Because acetaminophen is not a salicylate, Sinutab® can be used by patients who are allergic to aspirin.
Phenylpropanolamine hydrochloride, a sympathomimetic amine, provides vasoconstriction of the nasopharyngeal mucosa resulting in a nasal decongestant effect.
Phenyltoloxamine citrate is an antihistamine to provide relief of running nose, sneezing, itching of the nose or throat, and itchy and watery eyes as may occur in allergic rhinitis.

Warnings: Do not give to children under 6 years of age or use for more than 10 days unless directed by a physician. Keep this and all drugs out of the reach of children.

Caution: Do not exceed recommended dosage. Individuals with high blood pressure, heart disease, diabetes, thyroid disease, or those using monoamine oxidase inhibitors, should use only as directed by physician. This preparation may cause drowsiness. Do not drive or operate machinery while taking this medication.

Dosage: Adults: 2 tablets initially, followed by 1 tablet every 4 hours. Do not exceed 6 tablets in 24 hours. Otherwise, as directed by a physician. Children (6–12 years): one-half the adult dosage.

Storage: Store at room temperature.

How Supplied: Sinutab® tablets are pink, uncoated and scored so that tablets may be split in half. They are supplied in safety-capped bottles of 100 tablets and in child-resistant blister packs in boxes of 12 and 30 tablets.

SINUTAB-II® Tablets*
*Product of Warner-Lambert Inc.

Active Ingredients: Each tablet contains:
Acetaminophen ....325 mg.
Phenylpropanolamine HCl ....25 mg.
Indications: For temporary relief of sinus headache and congestion.
Actions: Sinutab-II® contains: an analgesic (acetaminophen) to relieve pain, and a decongestant (phenylpropanolamine hydrochloride) to reduce congestion of the nasopharyngeal mucosa. It contains no antihistamine which can cause drowsiness, and thus there is no interference with driving or the operation of machinery.
Acetaminophen is both analgesic and antipyretic. Because acetaminophen is not a salicylate, Sinutab-II® can be used by patients who are allergic to aspirin. Phenylpropanolamine hydrochloride, a sympathomimetic amine, provides vasoconstriction of the nasopharyngeal mucosa, resulting in a nasal decongestant effect.
Warnings: Do not give to children under 6 years of age or use for more than 10 days unless directed by a physician. Keep this and all drugs out of the reach of children.
Caution: Do not exceed recommended dosage. Individuals with high blood pressure, heart disease, diabetes, thyroid disease, or those using monoamine oxidase inhibitors, should use only as directed by a physician.
Dosage: Adults: 2 tablets initially, followed by 1 tablet every 4 hours. Do not exceed 6 tablets in 24 hours. Otherwise, as directed by a physician. Children (6–12 years): one-half the adult dosage.
Storage: Store at room temperature.
How Supplied: Sinutab-II® tablets are green, uncoated and scored so that tablets may be split in half. They are supplied in child-resistant blister packs in boxes of 12 and 30 tablets.

SINUTAB® Extra Strength Capsule Formula*
*Product of Warner-Lambert Inc.

Active Ingredients: Each capsule contains:
Acetaminophen ....500 mg.
Phenylpropanolamine HCl .....18.75 mg.
Chlorpheniramine Maleate ....2 mg.
Indications: For temporary relief of sinus headache and congestion, to promote nasal and sinus drainage, and to alleviate running nose as may occur in allergic rhinitis (such as hay fever).
Actions: Sinutab® Extra Strength Capsule Formula contains an analgesic (acetaminophen) to relieve pain, a decongestant (phenylpropanolamine hydrochloride) to reduce congestion of the nasopharyngeal mucosa, and an antihistamine (chlorpheniramine maleate) to help control allergic symptoms.
Acetaminophen is both analgesic and antipyretic. Because acetaminophen is not a salicylate, Sinutab® Extra

Strength Capsule Formula can be used by patients who are allergic to aspirin. Phenylpropanolamine hydrochloride, a sympathomimetic amine, provides vasoconstriction of the nasopharyngeal mucosa resulting in a nasal decongestant effect.
Chlorpheniramine maleate is an antihistamine incorporated to provide relief of running nose, sneezing, itching of the nose or throat, and itchy and watery eyes as may occur in allergic rhinitis.
Warnings: Do not give this product to children under 12 years of age except under the advice and supervision of a physician. May cause drowsiness. May cause excitability especially in children. Except under the advice and supervision of a physician, do not take this product if you have asthma, glaucoma, difficulty in urination due to enlargement of the prostate gland, high blood pressure, heart disease, diabetes, or thyroid disease. Do not exceed recommended dosage because at higher dosage nervousness, dizziness, sleeplessness, or severe liver damage may occur. If symptoms persist, do not improve within 7 days, or are accompanied by high fever, or if new symptoms occur, consult a physician before continuing use. Do not take this product for more than 10 days.
Keep this and all drugs out of the reach of children. In case of accidental overdose, seek professional assistance or contact a Poison Control Center immediately.
Drug Interaction Precaution: Do not take this product if you are presently taking a prescription antihypertensive or antidepressant drug containing a monoamine oxidase inhibitor except under the advice and supervision of a physician.
Caution: Avoid driving a motor vehicle or operating heavy machinery, and avoid alcoholic beverages while taking this product.
Dosage: Adults: 2 capsules every 6 hours, not to exceed 8 capsules in 24 hours. Otherwise, as directed by a physician.
Storage: Store at room temperature.
How Supplied: Sinutab® Extra Strength Capsule Formula capsules are red and yellow. They are supplied in child-resistant blister packs in boxes of 24 capsules.

SINUTAB® Extra Strength Tablets*
*Product of Warner-Lambert Inc.

Active Ingredients: Each tablet contains:
Acetaminophen ....500 mg.
Phenylpropanolamine HCl ....25 mg.
Phenyltoloxamine Citrate ....22 mg.
Indications: For temporary relief of sinus headache and congestion, to promote nasal and sinus drainage, and to alleviate running nose as may occur in allergic rhinitis (such as hay fever).
Actions: Sinutab® Extra Strength Tablets contain: an analgesic (acetaminophen) to relieve pain, a decongestant (phenylpropanolamine hydrochloride) to reduce congestion of the nasopharyngeal mucosa, and an antihistamine (phenyl-

toloxamine citrate) to help control allergic symptoms.
Acetaminophen is both analgesic and antipyretic. Because acetaminophen is not a salicylate, Sinutab® Extra Strength Tablets can be used by patients who are allergic to aspirin.
Phenylpropanolamine hydrochloride, a sympathomimetic amine, provides vasoconstriction of the nasopharyngeal mucosa, resulting in a nasal congestant effect.
Phenyltoloxamine citrate is an antihistamine to provide relief of running nose, sneezing, itching of the nose or throat, and itchy and watery eyes as may occur in allergic rhinitis.
Warnings: Do not give this product to children under 12 years of age except under the advice and supervision of a physician. May cause drowsiness. May cause excitability especially in children. Except under the advice and supervision of a physician do not take this product if you have asthma, glaucoma, difficulty in urination due to enlargement of the prostate gland, high blood pressure, heart disease, diabetes, or thyroid disease. Do not exceed recommended dosage because at higher doses nervousness, dizziness, sleeplessness or severe liver damage may occur. If symptoms persist, do not improve within 7 days, or are accompanied by high fever, or if new symptoms occur, consult a physician before continuing use. Do not take this product for more than 10 days.
Keep this and all drugs out of the reach of children. In case of accidental overdose, seek professional assistance or consult a Poison Control Center immediately.
Drug Interaction Precaution: Do not take this product if you are presently taking a prescription antihypertensive or antidepressant drug containing a monoamine oxidase inhibitor except under the advice and supervision of a physician.
Caution: Avoid driving a motor vehicle or operating heavy machinery and avoid alcoholic beverages while taking this product.
Dosage: Adults: 2 tablets every 6 hours, or 2 tablets 3 times a day, not to exceed 6 tablets in 24 hours. Otherwise as directed by a physician.
Storage: Store at room temperature.
How Supplied: Sinutab® Extra Strength Tablets are yellow and uncoated. They are supplied in child-resistant blister packs in boxes of 24 tablets.

SINUTAB® Long-Lasting Decongestant Nasal Spray

Active Ingredient: An isotonic aqueous buffered solution of xylometazoline hydrochloride 0.1%. Preserved with benzalkonium chloride.
Indications: For temporary relief of nasal congestion and to promote sinus drainage. Relief lasts for 8 to 10 hours.
Actions: Xylometazoline hydrochloride possesses sympathomimetic properties

Continued on next page

Warner-Lambert—Cont.

resulting in a decongestant effect on nasal mucosa.

Warnings: Follow directions for use carefully. For adult use only. Do not give this product to children under 12 years except under the advice and supervision of a physician. Do not exceed recommended dosage because symptoms may occur such as burning, stinging, sneezing, or increase of nasal discharge. Do not use this product for more than 3 days. If symptoms persist, consult a physician. The use of this dispenser by more than one person may spread infection.
KEEP THIS AND ALL DRUGS OUT OF THE REACH OF CHILDREN. In case of accidental ingestion, seek professional assistance or contact a Poison Control Center immediately.

Directions: Hold head in normal upright position. Hold bottle upright and place tip loosely in the nostril. Squeeze quickly and firmly. Sniff with each spray.

Dosage: Adults: 2 to 3 sprays in each nostril every 8 to 10 hours, not to exceed 3 times in 24 hours, or use as directed by physician.

Storage: Store at room temperature.

How Supplied: Sinutab® Long-Lasting Decongestant Nasal Spray is supplied in ½ Fl. Oz. (15 ml.) plastic squeeze-spray bottles.

Warren-Teed Laboratories

Warren-Teed products are now marketed by Adria Laboratories Inc.
Please see the Adria product monographs.

Westwood Pharmaceuticals Inc.
468 DEWITT ST.
BUFFALO, NY 14213

ALPHA KERI®
Therapeutic bath oil

Composition: Contains mineral oil, lanolin oil, Hydroloc™ brand of Westwood's PEG-4 dilaurate, fragrance, benzophenone-3, D&C green 6.

Action and Uses: ALPHA KERI is a water-dispersible, antipruritic oil for care of dry skin. ALPHA KERI effectively deposits a thin, uniform, emulsified film of oil over the skin. This film helps relieve itching, lubricates and softens the skin. ALPHA KERI BATH OIL is an all-over skin moisturizer. Only ALPHA KERI contains Hydroloc™— the unique emulsifier that provides a more uniform distribution of the therapeutic oils to moisturize dry skin. ALPHA KERI is valuable as an aid in the treatment of dry, pruritic skin and mild skin irritations such as chronic atopic dermatitis; pruritus senilis and hiemalis; contact dermatitis; "bath-itch"; xerosis or asteatosis; ichthyosis; soap dermatitis; psoriasis.

Administration and Dosage: ALPHA KERI *should always be used with water, either added to water or rubbed on to wet skin.* Because of its inherent cleansing properties it is not necessary to use soap when ALPHA KERI is being used.
For exact dosage, label directions should be followed.
BATH: Added as directed to bathtub of water. For optimum relief: 10 to 20 minute soak.
SHOWER: Small amount is poured into wet washcloth and rubbed on to wet skin. Rinse. Pat dry.
SPONGE BATH: Added as directed to a basin of warm water then rubbed over entire body with washcloth.
SITZ BATH: Added as directed to tub water. Soak should last for 10 to 20 minutes.
INFANT BATH: Added as directed to basin or bathinette of water.
SKIN CLEANSING OTHER THAN BATH OR SHOWER: A small amount is rubbed on to wet skin, which is then patted dry.

Precaution: The patient should be warned to guard against slipping in tub or shower.

How Supplied: 4 fl. oz. (NDC 0072-3600-04), 8 fl. oz. (NDC 0072-3600-08; NSN 6505-00-890-2027) 16 fl. oz. (NDC 0072-3600-16) plastic bottles. Also available for patients who prefer to shower—ALPHA KERI SPRAY—5 oz. (NDC 0072-3600-05) aerosol container, ALPHA KERI SOAP—4 oz. (NDC 0072-3500-04) bar.

ALPHA KERI® SOAP

Composition: Contains sodium tallowate, sodium cocoate, water, mineral oil, fragrance, PEG-75, glycerin, titanium dioxide, lanolin oil, sodium chloride, BHT, EDTA, D&C green 5, D&C yellow 10.

Action and Uses: ALPHA KERI SOAP, rich in emollient oils, thoroughly cleanses as it soothes and softens the skin.

Indications: Adjunctive use in dry skin care.

Administration and Dosage: To be used as any other soap.

How Supplied: 4 oz. (NDC 0072-3500-04) bar.

BALNETAR®
Water-dispersible Emollient Tar

Composition: Contains WESTWOOD® TAR (equivalent to 2.5% Coal Tar USP).

Action and Uses: For temporary relief of itching and scaling due to psoriasis, eczema, and other tar-responsive dermatoses. Tar ingredient is chemically and biologically standardized to insure uniform therapeutic activity. BALNETAR exerts keratoplastic, antieczematous, antipruritic, and emollient actions. It deposits microfine particles of tar over the skin in a lubricant-moisturizing film that helps soften and remove scales and crusts, making the skin smoother and more supple. BALNETAR is an impor-tant adjunct in a wide range of dermatoses, including: atopic dermatitis; chronic eczematoid dermatitis; seborrheic dermatitis.

Contraindications: Not indicated when acute inflammation is present.

Administration and Dosage: BALNETAR *should always be used with water. . . either added to water or rubbed onto wet skin.*
IN THE TUB—Add as directed to a bathtub of water (3–6 capfuls). Soap is not used. The patient soaks for 10 to 20 minutes and then pats dry.
FOR DIRECT APPLICATION—A small amount is rubbed onto the wet skin. Excess is wiped off with tissue to help prevent staining of clothes or linens.
FOR SCALP APPLICATION —A small amount is rubbed onto the wet scalp with fingertips.

Caution: If irritation persists, discontinue use. May temporarily discolor blond, bleached or tinted hair. In rare cases BALNETAR may cause allergic sensitization attributable to coal tar.

Precaution: After use of BALNETAR, patient should avoid exposure to direct sunlight unless sunlight is being used therapeutically in a supervised, modified Goeckerman regimen. Contact with the eyes should be avoided. Patient should be cautioned against slipping when BALNETAR is used in bathtub. Also advise patient that use in a plastic or fiberglass tub may cause staining of the tub.

How Supplied: 8 fl. oz. (NDC 0072-4200-08; NSN 6505-00-928-5890) plastic shatter-proof bottle.

ESTAR®
Therapeutic Tar Gel

Composition: WESTWOOD® TAR (biologically equivalent to 5% Coal Tar USP) in a hydroalcoholic gel (29% alcohol).

Actions and Uses: A therapeutic aid in the treatment of eczema, psoriasis, and other tar-responsive dermatoses such as atopic dermatitis, lichen simplex chronicus, and nummular eczema. ESTAR exerts keratoplastic, antieczematous, and antipruritic actions. It is equivalent in its photodynamic activity to 5% crude coal tar in either hydrophilic ointment or petrolatum. ESTAR provides the characteristic benefits of tar therapy in a form that is readily accepted by patients and nursing staff, due to its negligible tar odor and staining potential, and the superior cosmetic qualities of its gel base. ESTAR is suitable for use in a modified Goeckerman regimen, either in the hospital or on an outpatient basis; it also can be used in follow-up treatment to help maintain remissions. Substantivity to the skin can be demonstrated by examination with a Wood's light, which shows residual microfine particles of tar on the skin several days after application.

Contraindications: ESTAR should not be applied to acutely inflamed skin or used by individuals who are known to be sensitive to coal tar.

Administration and Dosage:
Psoriasis: ESTAR can be applied at bedtime in the following manner: the patient should massage ESTAR into af-

fected areas, allowing the gel to remain for five minutes, and then remove excess by patting with tissues. This procedure minimizes staining of skin and clothing, leaving behind an almost invisible layer of the active tar. If any staining of fabric should occur, it can be removed easily by standard laundry procedures.

The same technique of application may be used the following morning. If dryness occurs, an emollient may be applied one hour after ESTAR.

Because of ESTAR's superior substantivity and cosmetic qualities, patients who might otherwise be hospitalized for tar/UV therapy can now be treated as outpatients. The patient can easily apply ESTAR at bedtime and the following morning, then report for UV treatment that day. Laboratory tests and clinical experience to date suggest that it may be advisable to carefully regulate the length of UV exposure.

Chronic atopic dermatitis, lichen simplex chronicus, nummular eczema, and seborrheic dermatitis: One or two applications per day, as described above, are suggested. If dryness occurs, an emollient may be applied one hour after ESTAR and between applications as needed.

Caution: PROTECT TREATED AREAS FROM DIRECT SUNLIGHT FOR AT LEAST 24 HOURS AFTER APPLICATION, UNLESS OTHERWISE DIRECTED. ESTAR SHOULD NOT BE USED ON HIGHLY INFLAMED OR BROKEN SKIN. DO NOT APPLY TO GENITAL AREA. If used on the scalp, temporary discoloration of blond, bleached, or tinted hair may occur. If undue irritation develops or increases, the usage schedule should be changed or ESTAR discontinued. Contact with the eyes should be avoided. In case of contact, flush eyes with water.

Slight staining of clothing may occur. Standard laundry procedures will usually remove stains. For external use only.

How Supplied: 3 oz. (NDC 0072-7600-01; NSN 6505-01-056-2916) plastic tube.

FOSTEX® 5% BENZOYL PEROXIDE GEL
Antibacterial Acne Gel

Composition: Contains 5% benzoyl peroxide.

Action and Uses: FOSTEX 5% PEROXIDE GEL is a penetrating, disappearing gel which helps kill bacteria that can cause acne. Helps prevent new pimples before they appear. Drying action promotes gentle peeling to help clear acne involved skin.

Indications: A topical aid for the control of acne vulgaris.

Administration and Dosage: After washing, rub FOSTEX 5% BENZOYL PEROXIDE GEL into affected areas twice daily. In fair-skinned individuals or in excessively dry climates, start with only one application daily. The desired degree of dryness and peeling may be obtained by regulating frequency of use.

Caution: Avoid contact with eyes, lips and mucous membranes. In case of contact, flush with water. Persons with very sensitive skin or a known allergy to ben-

zoyl peroxide should not use this medication. If itching, redness, burning or swelling occurs, discontinue use. For external use only. May bleach dyed fabrics. Keep this and all drugs out of the reach of children. Store at controlled room temperature (59°-86°C).

How Supplied: 1.5 oz. (NDC 0072-3300-02) plastic tube.

FOSTEX® MEDICATED CLEANSING BAR
Acne Skin Cleanser

Composition: Contains 2% sulfur, 2% salicylic acid plus a combination of soapless cleansers and wetting agents.

Action and Uses: FOSTEX MEDICATED CLEANSING BAR is a surface-active, penetrating anti-seborrheic cleanser for therapeutic washing of the skin in the local treatment of acne and other skin conditions characterized by excessive oiliness. Degreases, dries and mildly desquamates.

Administration and Dosage: Use FOSTEX MEDICATED CLEANSING BAR instead of soap. Wash entire affected area 2 or 3 times daily, or as physician directs. Rinse well. The desired degree of dryness and peeling may be obtained by regulating frequency of use.

Caution: Avoid contact with eyes. In case of contact, flush with water. If undue skin irritation develops or increases, discontinue use and consult physician. For external use only.

How Supplied: 3¾ oz. (NDC 0072-3000-01; NSN 6505-00-116-1315) bar.

FOSTEX® MEDICATED CLEANSING CREAM
Acne Skin Cleanser and Dandruff Shampoo

Composition: Contains 2% sulfur, 2% salicylic acid, plus a combination of soapless cleansers and wetting agents.

Action and Uses: A penetrating antiseborrheic cleanser for the local treatment of acne, dandruff and other seborrheic skin conditions characterized by excessive oiliness. Degreases, dries and mildly desquamates.

Administration and Dosage: AS A WASH: Wet skin; wash entire affected area with FOSTEX MEDICATED CLEANSING CREAM instead of soap. Rinse thoroughly. Use 2 or 3 times daily, or as physician directs. The desired degree of dryness and peeling may be obtained by regulating frequency of use. AS A SHAMPOO: Use liberal amount on wet scalp and hair. Shampoo thoroughly, rinse, and repeat shampoo. Rinse thoroughly. No other shampoos are required. To help keep scalp free from excessive oiliness or scaling, use FOSTEX MEDICATED CLEANSING CREAM as often as necessary, or as physician directs.

Caution: Avoid contact with eyes. In case of contact, flush with water. If undue skin irritation develops or increases, discontinue use and consult physician. For external use only.

How Supplied: 4 oz. (NDC 0072-3200-01; NSN 6505-01-030-9067) plastic tube.

FOSTEX® MEDICATED COVER-UP
Medicated Acne Cover-Up

Composition: 2% sulfur in a flesh-tinted, greaseless base.

Action and Uses: FOSTEX MEDICATED COVER-UP is an acne cream which degreases, dries and mildly desquamates skin in the local treatment of acne and other skin conditions characterized by excessive oiliness.

Administration and Dosage: After thoroughly cleansing the skin, FOSTEX MEDICATED COVER-UP should be smoothed on with fingertips and cover the entire affected area; moisten fingertips to help blend easily into the skin. If necessary, smooth in extra amount on individual blemishes. May also be used for blemishes on the chest, shoulders and back. Apply FOSTEX MEDICATED COVER-UP day and night. Adjust frequency of use to keep blemish area comfortably dry but not so dry that skin becomes irritated.

Caution: Avoid contact with eyes, lips and mucous membranes. In case of contact, flush with water. If undue skin irritation develops or increases, discontinue use and consult physician. For external use only.

How Supplied: 1 oz. (NDC 0072-4100-01) plastic tube.

FOSTRIL®
Drying Lotion for Acne

Composition: Contains 2% sulfur in a greaseless base with laureth-4.

Action and Uses: Promotes drying and peeling of the skin in the treatment of acne. Daily use of FOSTRIL should result in a desirable degree of dryness and peeling in about 7 days. FOSTRIL removes excess oil and follicular obstruction, helping to remove comedones. It also helps prevent epithelial closure of pores and formation of new lesions.

Administration and Dosage: A thin film is applied to affected areas once or twice daily, or as directed.

Caution: If undue skin irritation develops or increases, adjust usage schedule or discontinue use. Anti-inflammatory measures may be used if necessary. For external use only. Contact with eyes should be avoided. In case of contact, flush eyes thoroughly with water.

How Supplied: 1 oz. (NDC 0072-3800-01; NSN 6505-00-116-1159) tube.

ICE MINT® FOOT CREME

Composition: Water, stearic acid, syn. cocoa butter, lanolin oil, camphor, menthol, beeswax, mineral oil, sodium borate, triethanolamine, camphor oil, dioctyl sodium sulfosuccinate, eucalyptus oil, peppermint oil, white thyme oil.

Indications: ICE MINT, with lanolin, cools and refreshes tired feet as it softens corns and callouses. It soothes, cools and softens dry and chapped skin.

Warnings: Keep out of reach of children. For external use only.

Continued on next page

Westwood—Cont.

Dosage and Administration: Rub ICE MINT on feet with fingertips. Wash hands after application.

How Supplied: 4 oz. (NDC 0072-1100-4) jar.

KERI® CREME
Concentrated Moisturizer— Nongreasy Emollient

Composition: Contains water, mineral oil, talc, sorbitol, ceresin, lanolin alcohol/mineral oil, magnesium stearate, glyceryl oleate/propylene glycol, isopropyl myristate, methylparaben, propylparaben, fragrance, quaternium-15.

Actions and Uses: KERI CREME is a concentrated moisturizer and nongreasy emollient for problem dry skin—hands, face, elbows, feet, legs. KERI CREME helps retain moisture that makes skin feel soft, smooth, supple. Helps resist the drying effects of soaps, detergents and chemicals.

Administration and Dosage: A small amount is rubbed into dry skin areas as needed.

How Supplied: 2.25 oz. (NDC 0072-5800-01) tube.

KERI® FACIAL CLEANSER

Composition: Water, glycerin, squalane, propylene glycol, glyceryl stearate/PEG-100 stearate, stearic acid, steareth-20, lanolin alcohol, magnesium aluminum silicate, cetyl alcohol, beeswax, PEG-20-sorbitan beeswax, methylparaben, propylparaben, quaternium-15, fragrance.

Indications: KERI FACIAL CLEANSER is a gentle, soapless moisturizing cleanser.

Precaution: Avoid contact with eyes.

Dosage and Administration: Use KERI FACIAL CLEANSER in place of soap. Apply a sufficient amount to facial area, massaging the area to be cleansed. Rinse thoroughly with water and pat dry. To remove make-up, apply generously and wipe off with a facial tissue.

How Supplied: 4 oz. (NDC 0072-8600-04) plastic bottle.

KERI® FACIAL SOAP

Composition: KERI® LOTION concentrate in a gentle, non-detergent soap containing: sodium tallowate, sodium cocoate, water, mineral oil, octyl hydroxystearate, fragrance, glycerin, titanium dioxide, PEG-75, lanolin oil, dioctyl sodium sulfosuccinate, PEG-4 dilaurate, propylparaben, PEG-40 stearate, glyceryl monostearate, PEG-100 stearate, sodium chloride, BHT, EDTA.

Action and Uses: KERI FACIAL SOAP helps keep skin soft while thoroughly cleansing.

Administration and Dosage: To be used as facial soap.

How Supplied: 3.25 oz. (NDC 0072-4900-03) bar.

KERI® LOTION and KERI LOTION, FRESHLY SCENTED
Skin Lubricant—Moisturizer

Composition: Contains mineral oil, water, propylene glycol, glyceryl stearate/PEG-100 stearate, PEG-40 stearate, PEG-4 dilaurate, laureth-4, lanolin oil, methylparaben, propylparaben, fragrance, carbomer-934, triethanolamine, dioctyl sodium sulfosuccinate, quaternium-15. FRESHLY SCENTED: FD&C blue 1, D&C yellow 10.

Action and Uses: KERI LOTION lubricates and helps hydrate the skin, making it soft and smooth. It relieves itching, helps maintain a normal moisture balance and supplements the protective action of skin lipids. Indicated for generalized dryness and itching; detergent hands; chapped or chafed skin; sunburn; "winter-itch"; aging, dry skin; diaper rash; heat rash.

Administration and Dosage: Apply as often as needed. Use particularly after bathing and exposure to sun, water, soaps and detergents.

How Supplied: 6½ oz. (NDC 0072-4600-56; NSN 6505-01-009-2897), 13 oz. (NDC 0072-4600-63) and 20 oz. (NDC 0072-4600-70) plastic bottles. Also available as KERI LOTION FRESHLY SCENTED —6½ oz. (NDC 0072-4500-56), 13 oz. (NDC 0072-4500-63), and 20 oz. (NDC 0072-4500-70) plastic bottles.

LOWILA® CAKE
Soap-free Skin Cleanser

Composition: Contains dextrin, sodium C14-16 olefin sulfonate, water, boric acid, urea, sorbitol, mineral oil, PEG-14 M, lactic acid, dioctyl sodium sulfosuccinate, cellulose gum, fragrance.

Action and Uses: LOWILA CAKE is indicated when soap should not be used, for cleansing skin that is sensitive or irritated, or in dermatitic and eczematous conditions. Used for general bathing, infant bathing, routine washing of hands and face and shampooing. The pH of LOWILA CAKE helps protect the skin's normal acid mantle and create an environment favorable to therapy and healing.

Administration and Dosage: LOWILA CAKE is used in place of soap. Lathers well in both hard and soft water.

How Supplied: 3¾ oz. (NDC 0072-2300-01) bar.

PERNOX®
Medicated Lathering Scrub Cleanser for Acne

Composition: Contains 2% sulfur, 1.5% salicylic acid, in a combination of soapless cleansers, wetting agents, and abradant polyethylene granules.

Actions and Uses: A lathering scrub cleanser for acne, oily skin. PERNOX provides microfine, uniform-size scrub particles with a rounded surface area to enable patients to achieve effective and gentle desquamation as they wash their skin. PERNOX helps loosen and remove comedones, dries, peels and degreases acne skin. It lathers abundantly and leaves the skin feeling smooth.

Contraindications: Not indicated when acute inflammation is present or in nodular or cystic acne.

Administration and Dosage: After wetting the skin, PERNOX is applied with the fingertips and massaged onto the skin for about one-half to one minute. The skin is then thoroughly rinsed. May be used instead of soap one to two times daily, or as directed.

Caution: If undue skin irritation develops or increases, adjust usage schedule or discontinue use. If necessary, anti-inflammatory measures may be used after discontinuance. For external use only. Contact with eyes should be avoided. In case of contact, flush eyes thoroughly with water.

How Supplied: 2 oz (NDC 0072-5200-02; NSN 6505-01-035-1719) and 4 oz. (NDC 0072-5200-04) tubes; lemon scented: 2 oz. (NDC 0072-5300-02) and 4 oz. (NDC 0072-5300-04) tubes.

PERNOX® LOTION
Lathering Abradant Scrub Cleanser for Acne

Composition: Contains 2% sulfur, 1.5% salicylic acid, in a combination of soapless cleansers, wetting agents, and abradant polyethylene granules.

Actions and Uses: PERNOX LOTION is a therapeutic abradant scrub cleanser in lotion form that is to be used routinely instead of soap. It gently desquamates or peels acne or oily skin. PERNOX LOTION also removes excessive oil from the skin surface and will produce mild drying of the affected skin areas when used regularly. It helps skin feel fresher and smoother with each wash.

Contraindications: Not indicated when acute inflammation is present or in nodular or cystic acne.

Administration and Dosage: To be shaken well before using. PERNOX may be used instead of soap one or two times daily or as directed. The skin should be wet first and PERNOX applied with the fingertips. The lather should be massaged onto skin for one-half to one minute. The patient then rinses thoroughly and pats dry.

Caution: If undue skin irritation develops or increases, adjust usage schedule or discontinue use. For external use only. Contact with eyes should be avoided. In case of contact, flush eyes with water.

How Supplied: 5 oz. (NDC 0072-7900-05) plastic bottle.

PERNOX® SHAMPOO
For Oily Hair

Composition: A blend of biodegradable cleansers and hair conditioners, containing: sodium laureth sulfate, water, lauramide DEA, quaternium 22, PEG-75 lanolin/hydrolyzed animal protein, sodium chloride, fragrance, lactic acid, sorbic acid, disodium EDTA, FD&C yellow 6, FD&C blue 1.

Actions and Uses: A gentle but thorough shampoo especially formulated to cleanse, control and condition oily hair. Especially suitable for adjunctive use with acne patients. PERNOX SHAM-

POO works into a rich, pleasant lather, leaves the hair lustrous and manageable. Its special conditioners help prevent tangles and fly away hair. Gentle enough to be used every day. It contains a refreshing natural scent.

Administration and Dosage: A liberal amount is massaged into wet hair and scalp. A good lather is worked up, massaging thoroughly. This is followed by a rinse and repeat application. A final rinse is used. No other shampoos or hair conditioners are necessary. May be used as needed.

Caution: For external use only. Contact with the eyes should be avoided. In case of contact, flush eyes with water.

How Supplied: 8 fl. oz. (NDC 0072-5500-08) shatterproof plastic bottle.

PRESUN® 4 SUNSCREEN LOTION
Moderate Sunscreen Protection

Composition: Contains 4% octyl dimethyl PABA, 10% SD alcohol 40.

Action and Uses: PRESUN 4 provides 4 times an individual's natural protection. Liberal and regular use may help reduce the chance of premature aging of the skin and skin cancer from overexposure to the sun. PRESUN 4 provides moderate protection, permits tanning, and reduces the chance of sunburn.

Administration and Dosage: Apply liberally and evenly 30 minutes before exposure. Reapply after swimming or excessive sweating. If used, cosmetics or emollients may be applied after PRESUN.

Caution: For external use only. Keep out of the reach of children. Discontinue use if irritation or rash appears. AVOID CONTACT WITH EYES.

How Supplied: 4 oz. (NDC 0072-5900-04) plastic bottle.

PRESUN® 8
LOTION, CREAMY LOTION, AND GEL
Maximal Sunscreen Protection

Composition: LOTION: Contains 5% (w/w) aminobenzoic acid (PABA), 55% (w/w) SD alcohol 40. CREAMY LOTION: Contains 5% aminobenzoic acid (PABA), 15% SD alcohol 40. GEL: Contains 5% (w/w) aminobenzoic acid (PABA), 55% (w/w) SD alcohol 40.

Action and Uses: PRESUN 8 provides 8 times an individual's natural protection. Liberal and regular use may reduce the chance of premature aging of the skin and skin cancer from overexposure to the sun. PRESUN 8 permits limited tanning and reduces the chance of sunburn. It gives maximal protection in the erythemogenic range, screening out the burning rays of the sun.

Contraindications: Do not use if sensitive to aminobenzoic acid, benzocaine, sulfonamides or aniline dyes.

Administration and Dosage: Apply liberally and evenly one hour before exposure. Let dry before dressing. Reapply after swimming or excessive sweating. If used, cosmetics or emollients may be applied after PRESUN.

Caution: For external use only. Keep out of the reach of children. Avoid contact with light-colored fabric, as staining may result. Avoid flame. Discontinue use if irritation or rash appears. AVOID CONTACT WITH EYES.

How Supplied: Lotion: 4 fl. oz. (NDC 0072-5400-04; NSN 6505-01-037-8636) and 7 fl. oz. (NDC 0072-5400-07) plastic bottles. Creamy Lotion: 4 oz. (NDC 0072-8502-04) plastic bottle. Gel: 3 oz. (NDC 0072-7700-03) plastic tube.

PRESUN® 15 SUNSCREEN LOTION
Ultra Sunscreen Protection

Composition: 5% Aminobenzoic acid (PABA), 5% octyl dimethyl PABA, 3% oxybenzone, 58% SD alcohol 40.

Actions and Uses: PRESUN 15 provides 15 times an individual's natural protection. Liberal and regular use may reduce the chance of premature aging of the skin and skin cancer from overexposure to the sun. PRESUN 15 permits no tanning and provides the highest degree of sunburn protection.

Contraindications: Do not use if sensitive to aminobenzoic acid, benzocaine, sulfonamides or aniline dyes.

Administration and Dosage: Shake well. Apply liberally and evenly one hour before exposure. Let dry before dressing. Reapply after swimming or excessive sweating. If used, cosmetics or emollients may be applied after PRESUN.

Caution: For external use only. Keep out of the reach of children. Avoid contact with light-colored fabric, as staining may result. Avoid flame. Discontinue use if irritation or rash appears. AVOID CONTACT WITH EYES.

How Supplied: 4 oz. (NDC 0072-8800-04) plastic bottle.

PRESUN® 15 CREAMY
SUNSCREEN LOTION
Water-resistant Creamy Sunscreen Protection

Composition: 8% Octyl dimethyl PABA, 3% oxybenzone, 8% SD alcohol 40.

Actions and Uses: PRESUN 15 CREAMY provides 15 times an individual's natural protection and resists wash-off by swimming or perspiration. Liberal and regular use may help reduce the chance of premature aging of the skin and skin cancer from overexposure to the sun. PRESUN 15 CREAMY provides the highest degree of sunburn protection.

Contraindications: Do not use if sensitive to aminobenzoic acid, benzocaine, sulfonamides or aniline dyes.

Administration and Dosage: Shake well. Before sun exposure, gently smooth liberal amount evenly onto **dry skin. Do not rub in.** PRESUN 15 CREAMY resists removal by perspiration and swimming, thereby reducing the need for frequent reapplication. To ensure maximum effectiveness, reapply to dry skin after excessive perspiration or prolonged swimming.

Caution: For external use only. Keep out of the reach of children. AVOID

CONTACT WITH EYES. Discontinue use if irritation or rash appears.

How Supplied: 4 oz. (NDC 0072-8900-04) plastic bottle.

PRESUN® 15 SUNSCREEN LIP PROTECTOR

Active Ingredient: 8% octyl dimethyl PABA, 3% oxybenzone.

Indications: For dry, chapped, cracked lips associated with sun and wind exposure.

Dosage and Administration: Apply PRESUN LIP PROTECTOR to lips as required.

How Supplied: .15 oz. (NDC 0072-8703-01) tube.

SEBUCARE®
Antiseborrheic Scalp Lotion

Composition: 1.8% salicylic acid, 61% alcohol, water, PPG-40 butyl ether, laureth-4, dihydroabietyl alcohol, fragrance.

Action and Uses: An aid in the treatment of dandruff, seborrhea capitis and other scaling conditions of the scalp. SEBUCARE helps control scaling, oiliness and itching. The unique base helps soften brittle hair and grooms the hair, thus eliminating the need for hair dressing which often impedes antiseborrheic treatment. SEBUCARE should be used every day in conjunction with therapeutic shampoos such as SEBULEX® or FOSTEX® CREAM.

Administration and Dosage: SEBUCARE is applied directly to scalp and massaged thoroughly with fingertips. Comb or brush as usual. Grooms as it medicates. Use once or twice daily or as directed.

Precaution: Volatile—Flame should be avoided. Contact with eyes should be avoided. In case of contact, flush eyes thoroughly with water. For external use only.

How Supplied: 4 fl. oz. (NDC 0072-4800-04) plastic bottle.

SEBULEX® and
SEBULEX CREAM
Antiseborrheic Treatment Shampoo

Composition: Contains 2% sulfur and 2% salicylic acid in SEBULYTIC® brand of surface-active cleansers and wetting agents.

Action and Uses: A penetrating therapeutic shampoo for the temporary relief of itchy scalp and the scaling of dandruff, SEBULEX helps relieve itching, remove dandruff, excess oil. It penetrates and softens the crusty, matted layers of scales adhering to the scalp, and leaves the hair soft and manageable.

Administration and Dosage: SEBULEX LIQUID should be shaken before being used. SEBULEX or SEBULEX CREAM is massaged onto wet scalp. Lather should be allowed to remain on scalp for about 5 minutes and then rinsed. Application is repeated, followed by a thorough rinse. Initially, SEBULEX or SEBULEX CREAM can be used daily,

Continued on next page

Westwood—Cont.

or every other day, or as directed, depending on the condition. Once symptoms are under control, one or two treatments a week usually will maintain control of itching, oiliness and scaling.

Caution: If undue skin irritation develops or increases, discontinue use. For external use only. Contact with eyes should be avoided. In case of contact, flush eyes thoroughly with water.

How Supplied: SEBULEX in 4 oz. (NDC 0072-2700-04) and 8 oz. (NDC 0072-2700-08) plastic bottles; SEBULEX CREAM in 4 oz. (NDC 0072-2800-04) tube.

SEBULEX® CONDITIONING SHAMPOO WITH PROTEIN
Antiseborrheic Treatment and Conditioning Shampoo

Composition: Contains 2% sulfur, 2% salicylic acid, water, sodium octoxynol-3 sulfonate, sodium lauryl sulfate, lauramide DEA, acetamide MEA, amphoteric-2, hydrolyzed animal protein, magnesium aluminum silicate, propylene glycol, methylcellulose, PEG-14 M, fragrance, disodium EDTA, dioctyl sodium sulfosuccinate, FD & C blue 1, D&C yellow 10.

Action and Uses: SEBULEX CONDITIONING SHAMPOO provides effective temporary control of the scaling and itching of dandruff and seborrheic dermatitis, while adding protein to the hair shaft to increase its manageability.

Administration and Dosage: SEBULEX CONDITIONING SHAMPOO should be shaken well before use. Shampoo five minutes. For optimum dandruff control and conditioning, leave shampoo on for the full five minutes. Rinse. Repeat. Use two or three times weekly to maintain control, although daily use may be continued. Consult physician for severe or unresponsive scalp conditions.

Caution: If undue skin irritation develops or increases, use should be discontinued. Contact with eyes should be avoided. In case of contact, eyes should be flushed thoroughly with water.

How Supplied: 4 oz. (NDC 0072-2600-04) and 8 oz. (NDC 0072-2600-08) plastic bottles.

SEBUTONE® and SEBUTONE CREAM
Antiseborrheic Tar Shampoo

Composition: WESTWOOD® TAR (equivalent to 0.5% Coal Tar USP), 2% sulfur and 2% salicylic acid in SEBULYTIC® brand of surface-active cleansers and wetting agents.

Action and Uses: A surface-active, penetrating therapeutic shampoo for the temporary relief of itchy scalp and the scaling of stubborn dandruff and psoriasis. Provides prompt and prolonged relief of itching, helps control oiliness and rid the scalp of scales and crust. Tar ingredient is chemically and biologically standardized to produce uniform therapeutic activity. Wood's light demonstrates residual microfine particles of tar on the

scalp several days after a course of SEBUTONE shampoo. In addition to its antipruritic and antiseborrheic actions, SEBUTONE also helps offset excessive scalp dryness with a special moisturizing emollient.

Administration and Dosage: SEBUTONE liquid should be shaken before being used. A liberal amount of SEBUTONE or SEBUTONE CREAM is massaged onto the wet scalp for 5 minutes and the scalp is then rinsed. Application is repeated, followed by a thorough rinse. Use as often as necessary to keep the scalp free from itching and scaling or as directed. No other shampoo or soap washings are required.

Caution: If undue skin irritation develops or increases, discontinue use. In rare instances, temporary discoloration of white, blond, bleached or tinted hair may occur. Contact with the eyes is to be avoided. In case of contact flush eyes with water.

How Supplied: SEBUTONE in 4 oz. (NDC 0072-5000-04) and 8 oz. (NDC 0072-5000-08) plastic bottles; SEBUTONE CREAM in 4 oz. (NDC 0072-5100-01) tube.

TRANSACT®
Transparent Medicated Acne Gel

Composition: Contains 2% sulfur and 37% alcohol in a greaseless gel base with laureth-4.

Action and Uses: TRANSACT is a transparent, nonstaining and greaseless gel, which leaves a fresh, clean fragrance on the skin. It dries, peels and degreases the skin of acne patients. Its effect is controlled by frequency of application and climatic conditions.

Administration and Dosage: After washing acne skin thoroughly, a thin film is applied to affected areas once daily or as directed. A brief tingling sensation may be expected upon application. Patient should anticipate beneficial drying and peeling in 5 to 7 days. Since TRANSACT is a highly active drying agent it should be used sparingly when initiating therapy, particularly for patients with sensitive skin. 1. Patients with tender skin may best be started on one application every other day. 2. Most other patients can be started on one daily application. 3. When patients develop tolerance, applications may be increased to two and then three times daily to maintain an adequate therapeutic effect. 4. TRANSACT is also for use on the shoulders and back. In dry or cold climates skin is more reactive to TRANSACT and frequency of use should be reduced. During warm, humid months, frequency of use may be increased.

Caution: If undue skin irritation develops, usage schedule should be adjusted or TRANSACT discontinued. For external use only. Avoid contact with the eyes. In case of contact, flush eyes with water.

How Supplied: 1 oz. (NDC 0072-5600-01) plastic tube.

Whitehall Laboratories
Division of American Home Products Corporation
685 THIRD AVENUE
NEW YORK, NY 10017

ANACIN®
Analgesic Tablets and Capsules

Active Ingredients: Each tablet or capsule contains: Aspirin 400 mg., Caffeine 32 mg.

Indications and Actions: Anacin relieves pain of headache, neuralgia, neuritis, sprains, muscular aches, discomforts and fever of colds, pain caused by tooth extraction and toothache, menstrual discomfort. Anacin also temporarily relieves the minor aches and pains of arthritis and rheumatism.

Warnings: Keep this and all medicines out of children's reach. In case of accidental overdose, contact a physician immediately.

Precautions: If pain persists for more than 10 days, or redness is present, or in arthritic or rheumatic conditions affecting children under 12 years of age, consult a physician immediately.

Dosage: Two tablets or capsules with water every 4 hours, as needed. Do not exceed 10 tablets or 10 capsules daily. For children 6–12, half the adult dosage.

Professional Labeling: Same as those outlined under Indications.

How Supplied: Tablets: In tins of 12's and bottles of 30's, 50's, 100's, 200's and 300's. Capsules: In bottles of 20's, 40's, 75's and 125's.

[*Shown in Product Identification Section*]

MAXIMUM STRENGTH ANACIN®
Analgesic Tablets and Capsules

Active Ingredients: Aspirin 500 mg. and Caffeine 32 mg. per tablet and capsule.

Indications and Actions: Maximum Strength Anacin provides fast, effective, temporary relief of headaches, minor aches, pains and fever . . . temporary relief of minor aches and pains of arthritis and rheumatism . . . discomforts and fever of colds or "flu" . . . pain caused by tooth extraction and discomfort associated with normal menstrual periods.

Precautions: If pain persists for more than 10 days, or redness is present, or in arthritic or rheumatic conditions affecting children under 12 years of age, consult a physician immediately.

Warning: Keep this and all medicines out of the reach of children.

Dosage: Adults: Initial dose 2 tablets or capsules with water, may be followed by 1 tablet or capsule after 3 hours or 2 tablets or capsules after 6 hours. Do not exceed 8 tablets or capsules in any 24 hour period. Not recommended for children under 12 years of age.

How Supplied: Tablets: Tins of 12's and bottles of 20's, 40's, 75's, and 150's. Capsules: bottles of 36's and 72's.

[*Shown in Product Identification Section*]

ANACIN–3®
Analgesic Tablets and Capsules

Active Ingredients: Each tablet and capsule contains acetaminophen 500 mg. and caffeine 32 mg.

Indications and Actions: Anacin-3 is a safe and effective 100% aspirin-free analgesic product that acts fast to provide relief from pain of headache, colds or "flu", sinusitis, muscle strain, backache and menstrual discomfort. Anacin-3 is recommended for temporary relief of minor arthritis pain, toothaches and to reduce fever.

Warnings: Do not give to children under 12 or use for more than 10 days unless directed by a physician. Keep this and all medicines out of reach of children. In case of accidental overdose, contact a physician immediately.

Caution: If pain persists for more than 10 days or redness is present or in arthritic or rheumatic conditions affecting children under 12, consult a physician immediately. Do not take without consulting a physician if under medical care. Promptly consult a dentist for toothache.

Dosage and Administration: Adults: Two tablets or capsules 3 or 4 times a day. Do not exceed 8 tablets or capsules in any 24-hour period.

Professional Labeling: Same as those outlined under Indications.

How Supplied: Tablets in bottles of 30's, 60's, and 100's. Capsules in bottles of 20's, 40's, and 72's.

[*Shown in Product Identification Section*]

ANBESOL® Gel
Antiseptic Anesthetic

Description: Anbesol Gel is a safe and effective antiseptic-anesthetic that can be used by all family members for the temporary relief of minor mouth pain, especially for cold sores and fever blisters.

Active Ingredients: Benzocaine (6.3%), Phenol (0.5%), Alcohol (70%).

Indications: For fast temporary pain relief of cold sores, fever blisters, toothache, teething, denture irritation and sore gums.

Actions: Helps dry and relieve the pain of cold sores, fever blisters. Temporarily deadens sensations of nerve endings to provide relief of pain and discomfort; reduces oral bacterial flora temporarily as an aid in oral hygiene.

Warnings: Not for use under dentures. Do not use near eyes. Keep this and all medicines out of the reach of children.

Precautions: Not for prolonged use. If the condition persists or irritation develops, discontinue use and consult your physician or dentist. For denture irritation, apply a thin layer and do not reinsert denture until irritation/pain is relieved. Rinse mouth before reinserting. If irritation/pain persists, contact your dentist.

Dosage and Administration: For topical application to the affected area on the lips or within the mouth.

Professional Labeling: Same as outlined under Indications.

How Supplied: Clear gel—.25 oz. tube.

[*Shown in Product Identification Section*]

ANBESOL® Liquid
Antiseptic Anesthetic

Description: Anbesol Liquid is a safe and effective antiseptic-anesthetic solution that can be used by all family members for temporary relief of minor mouth pain and for first aid needs.

Active Ingredients: Benzocaine (6.3%), Phenol (0.5%), Povidone-Iodine (Yields 0.04% available Iodine), Alcohol (70%).

Indications: For temporary relief of pain due to denture irritation, toothache, teething, cold sores/fever blisters as well as minor cuts, scrapes and burns.

Actions: Temporarily deadens sensations of nerve endings to provide relief of pain and discomfort; reduces oral bacterial flora temporarily as an aid in oral hygiene.

Warnings: Do not use near eyes. Keep this and all medicines out of the reach of children.

Precautions: Not for prolonged use. If pain, redness, rash, irritation or swelling persists, or if infection occurs, discontinue use and see your physician or dentist. In case of deep or puncture wounds or serious burns, consult your doctor.

Dosage and Administration: For topical application to the skin and mucous membranes. Apply freely, locally to affected area.

Professional Labeling: Same as outlined under Indications.

How Supplied: Amber liquid. Two sizes—.31 and .74 fluid ounce bottles.

[*Shown in Product Identification Section*]

ARTHRITIS PAIN FORMULA
By the Makers of Anacin® Analgesic Tablets

Active Ingredients: Each tablet contains 7½ grains microfined aspirin. Also contains two buffers, 20 mg. dried Aluminum Hydroxide Gel and 60 mg. Magnesium Hydroxide.

Indications: Fast, temporary relief from minor aches and pain of arthritis and rheumatism and low back pain. Also relieves the pain of headache, neuralgia, neuritis, sprains, muscular aches, discomforts and fever of colds, pain caused by tooth extraction and toothache, and menstrual discomfort.

Actions: Arthritis Pain Formula contains 50% more pain relief medicine than ordinary aspirin or regular buffered aspirin. Arthritis Pain Formula also provides extra stomach protection because, in addition to containing two buffers, the pain reliever is microfined. This means the pain relieving particles are so fine they dissolve rapidly and so are less apt to cause stomach upset.

Warnings: Keep this and all medications out of children's reach. In case of accidental overdose, contact a physician immediately. In arthritic or rheumatic conditions, if pain persists for more than 10 days, or redness is present, consult a physician immediately.

Dosage and Administration: Convenient daily schedule for adults: 2 tablets, 3 or 4 times a day with water. Do not exceed 8 tablets in any 24 hour period. For children under 12, consult your physician.

Professional Labeling: Same as stated under "Indications".

How Supplied: In plastic bottles of 40, 100 and 175 tablets.

[*Shown in Product Identification Section*]

ASPIRIN-FREE ARTHRITIS PAIN FORMULA
By the Makers of Anacin® Analgesic Tablets

Active Ingredients: Each tablet contains 500 mg. Acetaminophen.

Indications: Aspirin-Free Arthritis Pain Formula provides temporary relief from minor aches and pain of arthritis and rheumatism. Aspirin-Free Arthritis Pain Formula contains acetaminophen, and is unlikely to cause gastric irritation occasionally associated with aspirin or aspirin-containing products. Aspirin-Free Arthritis Pain Formula can be used by most persons with peptic ulcer when taken as directed for recommended conditions. Additionally, Aspirin-Free Arthritis Pain Formula is unlikely to cause allergic reaction to people sensitive to aspirin, and is particularly appropriate for these people. Aspirin-Free Arthritis Pain Formula also helps relieve pain of headache, low back pain, toothache, menstrual discomfort and fever.

Actions: Aspirin-Free Arthritis Pain Formula tablets contain acetaminophen, a clinically proven safe and effective analgesic.

Warnings: Keep this and all medications out of children's reach. In case of accidental overdose, contact a physician immediately.

Caution: In conditions affecting children under 12 years of age or if pain persists for more than 10 days or redness is present, consult a physician immediately.

Dosage and Administration: Adult Dosage: 2 tablets, 3 or 4 times a day. Do not exceed 8 tablets in any 24 hour period.

Professional Labeling: Same as those stated under "Indications."

How Supplied: In plastic bottles of 30 and 75 tablets.

[*Shown in Product Identification Section*]

BISODOL®
Antacid Powder

Active Ingredients: Per teaspoonful: Sodium Bicarbonate 644 mg., Magnesium Carbonate 475 mg.

Indications: Antacid to relieve the symptoms of acid indigestion, heartburn, and sour stomach.

Actions: Bisodol Powder is a combination of two well-established antacids, Magnesium Carbonate and Sodium Bicarbonate.

Warnings: Do not take more than four teaspoonfuls in a 24-hour period, or use the maximum dosage for more than two weeks, except under the advice and su-

Continued on next page

Whitehall—Cont.

pervision of a physician. Do not use this product except under advice and supervision of a physician if you have kidney disease. May cause constipation or have laxative effect. Do not use this product except under the advice and supervision of a physician if you are on a sodium restricted diet. Each teaspoonful contains 6.8 mEq. (157 mg.) of sodium.

Keep this and all medicines out of the reach of children. In case of accidental overdose, seek professional assistance or contact a poison control center immediately.

Dosage and Administration: <u>Adults</u>: Take one teaspoonful of Bisodol in a glass of water after meals and at bedtime, or as directed by a physician.

<u>Children under 12 years</u>: As directed by a physician.

Professional Labeling: Same as those outlined under Indications.

How Supplied: White powder in 3 oz. and 5 oz. cans.

BISODOL®
Antacid Tablets

Active Ingredients: Calcium Carbonate 194 mg., Magnesium Hydroxide 178 mg. per tablet.

Indications: Antacid to relieve the symptoms of acid indigestion, heartburn, and sour stomach.

Actions: Bisodol Tablets are a combination of two well-established antacids, Calcium Carbonate and Magnesium Hydroxide. Bisodol Tablets contain virtually no sodium (0.036 mg./tablet).

Warnings: Do not take more than 16 tablets in a 24-hour period, or use the maximum dosage for more than two weeks, except under the advice and supervision of a physician.

Do not use this product, except under the advice and supervision of a physician, if you have kidney disease. May cause constipation or have laxative effect.

Keep out of reach of children. In case of accidental overdose, seek professional assistance or contact a poison control center immediately.

Dosage and Administration: <u>Adults</u>: One to two tablets every two hours, or as directed by a physician. Chew thoroughly or, if preferred, swallow with a glass of water or milk.

<u>Children under 12 years</u>: As directed by a physician.

Professional Labeling: Same as those outlined under Indications.

How Supplied: White uncoated tablets in tins of 30 and bottles of 100.

CLEANSING PADS
By The Makers of Preparation H®
Hemorrhoidal Remedies

Active Ingredients: Witch hazel (50% w/v) and Glycerin (10% w/v).
Indications: Hemorrhoidal tissue irritation, anal cleansing wipe; everyday hygiene of the outer vaginal area, final cleansing step at diaper changing time.

Actions: Cleansing Pads are scientifically developed, soft cloth pads which are impregnated with a solution specially designed to gently soothe, freshen and clean the anal or genital area. Cleansing Pads are superior for a multitude of types of personal hygiene uses and are especially recommended for hemorrhoid sufferers.

Warnings: In case of rectal bleeding, consult physician promptly. In case of continued irritation, discontinue use and consult a physician.

Precaution: Keep this and all medicines out of the reach of children.

Dosage and Administration: As a personal wipe—use as a final cleansing step after regular toilet tissue or instead of tissue, in cases of special sensitivity. As a compress—hemorrhoid sufferers will get additional relief by using Cleansing Pads as a compress. Fold pad and hold in contact with inflamed anal tissue for 15 to 30 minutes. Repeat several times daily while inflammation lasts.

How Supplied: Jars of 40's and 100's.

COMPOUND W®
Solution

Active Ingredients: Each drop of Compound W Solution contains Salicylic Acid 14.2% w/w and Glacial Acetic Acid 9% w/w in a flexible collodion vehicle; Ether 57%.

Indications: Removes common warts quickly—painlessly.

Actions: Warts are common benign skin lesions caused by an infectious virus which stimulates mitosis in the basal cell layer resulting in the production of elevated epithelial growths. The keratolytic action of Salicylic and Acetic Acids in a flexible collodion vehicle causes the cornified epithelium to swell, soften, macerate and then desquamate.

Warnings: Flammable—do not use near fire or flame. For external use only. In case of accidental ingestion, seek professional assistance or contact a poison control center immediately. Do not use on face or on mucous membranes. If you are a diabetic, or have impaired circulation, do not use as it may cause serious complications. Do not use on moles, birthmarks, or on areas that do not have the typical appearance of the common wart. Keep this and all medicines out of the reach of children. Store at room temperature. Replace cap tightly.

Dosage and Administration: Use twice daily—morning and night. Soak the affected area in hot water for five minutes. If any tissue has been loosened, remove by rubbing with a washcloth or soft brush. Dry thoroughly. Using glass rod provided, completely cover the wart only with solution. To avoid irritating the skin surrounding the wart, confine the solution to the wart only. Allow the liquid to dry, then re-apply. The area covered with the medicine will appear white. Follow this procedure twice daily for the next 6 to 7 days. Most warts should clear within this time period. However, if the wart still remains, continue the treatment for up to another seven days.

Professional Labeling: Same as those outlined under Indications.
How Supplied: Compound W is available in .31 fluid oz. clear bottles with glass applicators.

DENOREX®
Medicated Shampoo
DENOREX®
Mountain Fresh Herbal Scent
Medicated Shampoo
DENOREX®
Shampoo and Conditioner

Active Ingredients:
Lotion: Coal Tar Solution 9.0%, Menthol 1.5%, Alcohol 7.5%. Also contains TEA-Lauryl Sulfate, Water, Lauramide DEA, Stearic Acid, Chloroxylenol.

Shampoo and Conditioner: Coal Tar Solution 9.0%, Menthol 1.5%, Alcohol 7.5%. Also contains TEA-Lauryl Sulfate, Water, Lauramide DEA, PEG-27 Lanolin, Quaterium 23, Fragrance, Chloroxylenol, Hydroxypropyl Methylcellulose, Citric Acid.

Gel: Coal Tar Solution 9.0%, Menthol 1.5%, Alcohol 7.5%. Also contains TEA-Lauryl Sulfate, Water, Hydroxypropyl Methylcellulose, Chloroxylenol.

Indications: Helps relieve scaling —itching—flaking of dandruff, seborrhea and psoriasis. Regular use promotes cleaner, healthier hair and scalp.

Actions: Denorex Shampoo is antiseborrheic and antipruritic. Loosens and softens scales and crusts. Coal tar helps correct abnormalities of keratinization by decreasing epidermal proliferation and dermal infiltration. Denorex also contains the antipruritic agent, menthol, which is "one of the most widely used antipruritics in dermatologic therapy of various diseases accompanied by itching". (The United States Dispensatory—26th Edition.)

Warnings: For external use only. Discontinue treatment if irritation develops. Avoid contact with eyes. Keep this and all medicines out of children's reach.

Directions: For best results, shampoo every other day during first 10 days of treatment, and two or three times a week thereafter. For severe scalp problems use daily. Wet hair thoroughly and briskly massage until a rich lather is obtained. Rinse and repeat. Scalp may tingle slightly during treatment.

Professional Labeling: Same as stated under Indications.

How Supplied:
Lotion: 4 oz. and 8 oz. Bottles in Regular Scent, Mountain Fresh Herbal Scent, and Shampoo and Conditioner.
Gel: 2 oz. Tube in Regular Scent
4 oz. Tube in Regular Scent
[*Shown in Product Identification Section*]

DIET GARD™
14 DAY DIET PLAN
Appetite Suppressant
Capsules and Tablets

Active Ingredient: Phenylpropanolamine HCl 25 mg., (appetite suppressant), per capsule or tablet.

Description: Diet Gard 14 Day Diet Plan is a unique and complete weight reduction regimen for fast, sensible weight loss in only 14 days. Plan provides:

- A safe and effective pre-meal appetite suppressant that is maximum strength in each daily dosage to effectively curb the appetite. No extra caffeine stimulant.
- Special 14 day menu plan of 1,000 to 1,250 calories per day developed by a leading nutritionist at a major university. This menu plan is nutritionally balanced to provide the daily requirement of protein and carbohydrates.
- Capsules or tablets and menus are packaged in a convenient pocket size carrying case.

Warning: Do not exceed recommended dosage. If nervousness, dizziness or sleeplessness occurs, stop the medication and consult your physician. If you have or are being treated for high blood pressure, heart disease, diabetes, thyroid disease, or depression, do not take the product except under the supervision of a physician. Do not give this product to children under the age of 12. KEEP THIS AND ALL MEDICINES OUT OF CHILDREN'S REACH. In case of accidental overdose, contact a physician immediately. Diet Gard can safely and effectively be used for periods longer than 14 days, but use of this product should not exceed three months. Do not take this product if you are taking any other medication containing phenylpropanolamine.

Dosage: Take one capsule or tablet 30 minutes before each meal with a full glass of water. Do not exceed 3 capsules or tablets per day. Eat three meals each day and follow the daily Diet Gard 14 Day menu as described. Those with extra pounds to lose should skip a few days, then start another 14 Day Plan.

Professional Labeling: Same as those outlined under Description.

How Supplied: The Diet Gard 14 Day Plan is available in cartons of 42 capsules or tablets.

Each Diet Gard 14 Day Plan carton contains two portable compliance folders: one folder for Week One and one folder for Week Two. Each folder provides a 7-day supply of capsules or tablets plus a complete lunch and dinner menu for each of the 7 days. The dieter selects breakfast from numerous choices. The entire regimen—capsules or tablets, menus, and instructions—was designed to assist the dieter in accurately following the plan. It also fits neatly into a briefcase or handbag so it can be carried with the dieter at all times.

[*Shown in Product Identification Section*]

DRISTAN®
12-Hour Nasal Decongestant Capsules

Active Ingredients: Each Dristan 12-Hour Nasal Decongestant Capsule contains: Chlorpheniramine Maleate 4 mg., Phenylephrine Hydrochloride 20 mg.

Indications: Dristan 12-Hour Nasal Decongestant Capsules provide 12 hour relief from nasal congestion, runny nose, watery, itchy eyes and sneezing due to the common cold and hay fever/allergies.

Actions: Dristan 12-Hour Capsules contain a decongestant to help restore free breathing by reducing swollen nasal membranes and by draining nasal passages, plus an antihistamine to help control sneezing, excessive nasal discharge and watery, itchy eyes due to the common cold and hay fever/allergies.

Chlorpheniramine Maleate is an antihistamine effective in the control of rhinorrhea, sneezing and lacrimation associated with elevated histimine levels in disorders of the respiratory tract.

Phenylephrine HCl is an oral nasal decongestant (Sympathomimetic Amine) effective as a vasoconstrictor to help reduce nasal/sinus congestion.

Warnings: Do not exceed recommended dosage or give to children under 12 years of age unless directed by a physician. Not to be used by individuals with high blood pressure, heart disease, diabetes, or thyroid disease without consulting a physician. Do not drive or operate machinery while taking this medication, as this preparation may cause drowsiness in some persons.

Precaution: Keep this and all medicines out of the reach of children.

Dosage and Administration: Usual dose of 1 capsule provides 12 hours of prolonged action, after which the dosage may be repeated. Do not exceed 1 capsule every 12 hours.

Professional Labeling: Same as those outlined under Indications.

How Supplied: Timed-release capsules in packages of 6's, 10's and 15's.

DRISTAN®
Decongestant/Antihistamine/ Analgesic Capsules

Active Ingredients: Each Dristan Capsule contains: Phenylpropanolamine HCl 12.5 mg., Chlorpheniramine Maleate 2 mg., Aspirin 325 mg., and Caffeine 16.2 mg. to counteract possible drowsiness from the antihistamine.

Indications: Dristan Decongestant/ Antihistamine/Analgesic Capsules are indicated for temporary relief of concurrent symptoms of colds, sinusitis, hay fever, or other upper respiratory allergies: nasal congestion, sneezing, runny nose, fever, headache and minor aches and pains.

Actions: Each ingredient in Dristan Capsules is selected for temporary relief of symptoms of colds, sinusitis, hay fever, or other upper respiratory allergies. Each capsule contains aspirin as an analgesic and antipyretic, an oral nasal decongestant to reduce swollen mucosa of the upper respiratory tract, and an antihistamine as a rhinitis suppressant.

Aspirin is both analgesic and antipyretic. Therapeutic doses of aspirin will effectively reduce an elevated body temperature. Also, aspirin is effective in reducing the discomfort of pain associated with headache.

Phenylpropanolamine HCl is an oral nasal decongestant (Sympathomimetic Amine), effective as a vasoconstrictor to help reduce nasal/sinus congestion.

Chlorpheniramine Maleate is an antihistamine effective in the control of rhinorrhea, sneezing, and lacrimation associated with elevated histamine levels and disorders of the respiratory tract.

Warnings: May cause drowsiness. May cause excitability especially in children. Do not take this product if you have asthma, glaucoma, difficulty in urination due to enlargement of prostate gland, high blood pressure, heart disease, diabetes, or thyroid disease except under advice and supervision of a physician. Do not exceed recommended dosage because at higher doses nervousness, dizziness, or sleeplessness may occur. If symptoms do not improve within seven days or are accompanied by a high fever, consult a physician before continuing use. This product contains aspirin. Do not take this product if you are allergic to aspirin.

Drug Interaction: Do not take this product if you are presently taking a prescription antihypertensive or antidepressant drug containing a monoamine oxidase inhibitor except under the advice and supervision of a physician.

Precaution: Do not give to children under six except under advice and supervision of physician. Avoid alcoholic beverages and driving a motor vehicle or operating heavy machinery while taking this product.

Dosage and Administration: Adults: Two capsules every four hours not to exceed 12 capsules in 24 hours. Children 6–12: One capsule every four hours not to exceed six capsules in 24 hours.

Professional Labeling: Same as those outlined under Indications.

How Supplied: Red/White capsules in bottles of 16, 36 and 75.

[*Shown in Product Identification Section*]

DRISTAN®
Decongestant/Antihistamine/ Analgesic Tablets

Active Ingredients: Each Dristan Tablet contains: Phenylephrine HCl 5 mg., Chlorpheniramine Maleate 2 mg., Aspirin 325 mg. and Caffeine 16.2 mg. to counteract possible drowsiness from the antihistamine.

Indications: Dristan Decongestant/ Antihistamine/Analgesic Tablets are indicated for temporary relief of concurrent symptoms of colds, sinusitis, hay fever, or other upper respiratory allergies: nasal congestion, sneezing, runny nose, fever, headache and minor aches and pains.

Actions: Each ingredient in Dristan Tablets is selected for temporary relief of symptoms of colds, sinusitis, hay fever, or other upper respiratory allergies. Each tablet contains aspirin as an analgesic and antipyretic, an oral nasal decongestant to reduce swollen mucosa of the upper respiratory tract, and an antihistamine as a rhinitis suppressant.

Aspirin is both analgesic and antipyretic. Therapeutic doses of aspirin will effectively reduce an elevated body tempera-

Continued on next page

Whitehall—Cont.

ture. Also aspirin is effective in reducing the discomfort of pain associated with headache.

Phenylephrine HCl is an oral nasal decongestant (Sympathomimetic Amine), effective as a vasoconstrictor to help reduce nasal/sinus congestion.

Chlorpheniramine Maleate is an antihistamine effective in the control of rhinorrhea, sneezing and lacrimation associated with elevated histamine levels in disorders of the respiratory tract.

Warnings: May cause drowsiness. May cause excitability, especially in children. Do not take this product if you have asthma, glaucoma, difficulty in urination due to enlargement of prostate gland, high blood pressure, heart disease, diabetes, or thyroid disease except under advice and supervision of a physician. Do not exceed recommended dosage because at higher doses nervousness, dizziness, or sleeplessness may occur. If symptoms do not improve within seven days or are accompanied by a high fever, consult a physician before continuing use. This product contains aspirin. Do not take this product if you are allergic to aspirin.

Drug Interaction: Do not take this product if you are presently taking a prescription antihypertensive or antidepressant drug containing a monoamine oxidase inhibitor except under the advice and supervision of a physician.

Precaution: Do not give to children under six except under advice and supervision of physician. Avoid alcoholic beverages and driving a motor vehicle or operating heavy machinery while taking this product.

Dosage and Administration: Adults: Two tablets every four hours not to exceed 12 tablets in 24 hours. Children 6–12: One tablet every four hours not to exceed six tablets in 24 hours.

Professional Labeling: Same as those outlined under Indications.

How Supplied: Yellow/White uncoated tablets in bottles of 24, 50 and 100.
[*Shown in Product Identification Section*]

DRISTAN-AF®
Decongestant/Antihistamine/Analgesic Tablets

Active Ingredients: Each Aspirin-Free Dristan-AF Tablet with Acetaminophen contains: Phenylephrine HCl 5 mg., Chlorpheniramine Maleate 2 mg., Acetaminophen 325 mg. and Caffeine 16.2 mg. to counteract possible drowsiness from the antihistamine.

Indications: Aspirin-Free Dristan-AF Decongestant/Antihistamine/Analgesic Tablets are indicated for temporary relief of concurrent symptoms of colds, sinusitis, hay fever, or other upper respiratory allergies: nasal congestion, sneezing, runny nose, fever, headache, and minor aches and pains.

Actions: Each ingredient in Aspirin-Free Dristan-AF Tablets is selected for temporary relief of symptoms of colds, sinusitis, hay fever, or other upper respiratory allergies. Each tablet contains Ac-

etaminophen as an analgesic and antipyretic, an oral nasal decongestant to reduce swollen mucosa of the upper respiratory tract, and an antihistamine as a rhinitis suppressant.

Acetaminophen is both an analgesic and antipyretic. It is as rapidly absorbed and effective as aspirin, but will cause little or no gastric irritation. Therapeutic doses of acetaminophen will effectively reduce an elevated body temperature, and is effective in reducing the discomfort of pain associated with headache.

Phenylephrine HCl is an oral nasal decongestant, (Sympathomimetic Amine), effective as a vasoconstrictor to help reduce nasal/sinus congestion.

Chlorpheniramine Maleate is an antihistamine effective in the control of rhinorrhea, sneezing and lacrimation associated with elevated histimine levels in disorders of the respiratory tract.

Warnings: May cause drowsiness. May cause excitability, especially in children. Do not take this product if you have asthma, glaucoma, difficulty in urination due to enlargement of prostate gland, high blood pressure, heart disease, diabetes, or thyroid disease except under advice and supervision of a physician. Do not exceed recommended dosage because at higher doses nervousness, dizziness or sleeplessness may occur. If symptoms do not improve within seven days or are accompanied by a high fever, consult a physician before continuing use.

Drug Interaction: Do not take this product if you are presently taking a prescription antihypertensive or antidepressant drug containing a monoamine oxidase inhibitor except under the advice and supervision of a physician.

Precaution: Do not give to children under six except under advice or supervision of a physician. Avoid alcoholic beverages and driving a motor vehicle or operating heavy machinery while taking this product.

Dosage and Administration: Adults: Two tablets every four hours not to exceed twelve tablets in 24 hours. Children 6–12: One tablet every four hours not to exceed six tablets in 24 hours.

Professional Labeling: Same as those outlined under Indications.

How Supplied: Blue-green/white uncoated tablets in tins of 12 and bottles of 24, 50, and 100 tablets.

DRISTAN®
Nasal Mist
DRISTAN®
Menthol Nasal Mist

Active Ingredients: Phenylephrine HCl 0.5%, Pheniramine Maleate 0.2%.

Other Ingredients: Dristan Nasal Mist: Benzalkonium Chloride 1:5000 in isotonic aqueous solution, Thimerosal preservative 0.002% (loss is unavoidable), Alcohol 0.4%.

Dristan Menthol Nasal Mist: Benzalkonium Chloride 1:5000 in isotonic aqueous solution, Thimerosal preservative 0.002% (loss is unavoidable) with aromatics (Menthol, Eucalyptol, Camphor, Methyl Salicylate).

Indications: For temporary relief of nasal congestion, due to the common cold, sinusitis, hay fever or other upper respiratory allergies.

Warnings: Do not exceed recommended dosage because symptoms may occur such as burning, stinging, sneezing, or increase of nasal discharge. Do not use this product for more than 3 days. If symptoms persist, consult a physician. The use of this dispenser by more than one person may spread infection. For adult use only. Do not give this product to children under 12 years except under the advice and supervision of a physician. Keep this and all medicines out of the reach of children. In case of accidental ingestion, seek professional assistance or contact a poison control center immediately.

Dosage and Administration: With head upright, insert nozzle in nostril. Spray quickly, firmly and sniff deeply. Adults: Spray 2 or 3 times into each nostril. Repeat every 4 hours as needed. Children under 12 years: As directed by a physician.

Professional Labeling: Same as those outlined under Indications.

How Supplied: 15 ml. and 30 ml. plastic squeeze bottles.
[*Shown in Product Identification Section*]

DRISTAN®
Long Lasting Nasal Mist
DRISTAN®
Long Lasting Menthol Nasal Mist

Active Ingredient: Oxymetazoline HCl 0.05%.

Other Ingredients: Dristan Long Lasting Nasal Mist: Benzalkonium Chloride 1:5000 in buffered isotonic aqueous solution, Thimerosal preservative 0.002% (loss is unavoidable).

Dristan Long Lasting Menthol Nasal Mist: Benzalkonium Chloride 1:5000 in buffered isotonic aqueous solution with aromatics (Menthol, Eucalyptol, Camphor), Thimerosal preservative 0.002% (loss is unavoidable).

Indications: Dristan Long Lasting Nasal Mist and Dristan Long Lasting Menthol Nasal Mist are indicated for temporary relief of nasal congestion due to the common cold, sinusitis, hay fever, or other upper respiratory allergies for up to 12 hours.

Actions: The sympathomimetic action of Dristan Long Lasting Nasal Mist and Dristan Long Lasting Menthol Nasal Mist constricts the smaller arterioles of the nasal passages, producing a prolonged, up to 12 hours, gentle and predictable decongesting effect.

Warnings: Do not exceed recommended dosage because symptoms may occur, such as burning, stinging, sneezing, or an increase of nasal discharge. Do not use this product for more than 3 days. If symptoms persist, consult a physician. The use of this dispenser by more than one person may spread infection. Keep this and all medicines out of the reach of children. In case of accidental ingestion, seek professional assistance or contact a poison control center immediately.

Dosage and Administration: With head upright, insert nozzle in nostril. Spray quickly, firmly and sniff deeply. Adults and children 6 years of age and over, spray 2 or 3 times into each nostril. Repeat twice daily—morning and evening. Not recommended for children under six.

Professional Labeling: Same as those outlined under Indications.

How Supplied: Dristan Long Lasting Nasal Mist: 15 ml. and 30 ml. plastic squeeze bottles.

Dristan Long Lasting Menthol Nasal Mist: 15 ml. plastic squeeze bottle.
[*Shown in Product Identification Section*]

DRY AND CLEAR®
Double Strength Cream
DRY AND CLEAR®
Acne Medication

Active Ingredients: Dry and Clear Double Strength Cream—10% Benzoyl Peroxide.

Dry and Clear Acne Medication Lotion—5% Benzoyl Peroxide.

Actions: Benzoyl Peroxide is a very effective antibacterial and drying agent. It speeds the flaking away of dead, blemished, upper skin layers, helps release trapped sebum and reveals a new skin layer underneath troubled skin. Also, the oxidizing action of Benzoyl Peroxide kills the acne-related bacteria P acnes.

Warnings: For external use only. Avoid contact with eyes, lips, and mouth. If undue skin irritation, excessive redness, peeling or any swelling occurs, discontinue use. If it persists, consult a physician. May bleach hair or dyed fabrics. Should not be used by patients with known sensitivity to Benzoyl Peroxide. Keep this and all medicines out of the reach of children.

Dosage and Administration: Clean affected areas thoroughly. Dry well.

Lotion or Cream: Apply to pimples, other blemishes and gently smooth into oily/acne-prone areas. Use one to three times daily, or as required. Shake lotion well before using.

How Supplied: Dry and Clear Double Strength Cream is available in a 1.0 oz. tube. Dry and Clear Acne Medication Lotion is a liquid dispersion available in 1.0 oz. and 2.0 oz. containers.

DRY AND CLEAR®
Medicated Acne Cleanser

Active Ingredients: Alcohol 50%, Salicylic Acid 0.5%, Benzoic Acid 0.5%, Benzethonium Chloride 0.1%.

Actions: Dry and Clear Medicated Acne Cleanser is specially formulated to combat the oil and dirt that attack a teenager's skin. Dry and Clear contains three effective germ killers which leave an invisible antibacterial barrier that works for hours. In addition, it has a special high concentration oil removing formula that penetrates surface oil, so that you can wipe away the oil and dirt that can cause problems to the skin.

Warnings: If skin becomes excessively dry, itchy or flaky, lessen the frequency of use. Avoid contact with eyes, lips and mouth. If severe skin irritation develops, discontinue use and consult a physician.

Dosage and Administration: Dry and Clear Medicated Cleanser should be used after washings to remove oil and dirt ordinary soap and water may leave behind. Moisten a cotton pad with cleanser and rub lightly over the entire face. Concentrate on oily areas, such as the forehead, cheeks and chin. Repeat the process if skin is excessively oily. Do not rinse after use. Dry and Clear leaves an invisible barrier of medication on the skin.

Professional Labeling: Same as those outlined above.

How Supplied: Dry and Clear Medicated Cleanser comes in a 4 oz. and 8 oz. bottle.

FREEZONE®
Solution

Active Ingredients: Zinc Chloride 2.18% w/w and Salicylic Acid 13.6% w/w in a collodion vehicle. Alcohol 20.5%, Ether 64.8% (some loss unavoidable).

Indications: For removal of corns and calluses.

Actions: Freezone penetrates corns and calluses painlessly, layer by layer, loosening and softening the corn or callus so that the whole corn or callus can be lifted off or peeled away in just a few days.

Warnings: Use only as directed. Do not use near fire or flame. Do not apply Freezone if corn or callus is infected. Diabetics and persons with impaired circulation should not use Freezone. For external use only. In case of accidental ingestion, contact a physician or a poison control center immediately. Keep all medication out of reach of children.

Precautions: Apply Freezone on corn or callus only. Avoid surrounding skin. In applying Freezone between the toes, hold toes apart until thoroughly dry.

Dosage and Administration: Using special glass applicator attached to cap, apply Freezone, drop by drop, directly onto the corn or callus. Avoid surrounding skin. Apply 2 coats daily. Repeat for 3 to 6 days. Then soak foot in warm water until corn or callus is easily removed. If condition persists, consult a physician. Replace cap securely.

Professional Labeling: Same as outlined under Indications.

How Supplied: Available in .31 Fl. Oz. glass bottle.

HEET®
Analgesic Liniment

Active Ingredients: Methyl Salicylate (15.0%), Camphor (3.6%), Oleoresin Capsicum (as Capsaicin 0.025%), Alcohol (70%).

Indications: For fast, temporary relief from minor aches and pains of arthritis, rheumatism, muscular low back pain, strains, muscle aches and pains, lumbago, neuralgia and neuritis.

Actions: Heet Liquid contains medications which penetrate into the skin and which act directly on nerves to replace pain arising from deep inside muscles with soothing warmth. The product increases blood flow to the affected area, thereby generating increased warmth to provide relief from minor pain and its stiffness. Helps tense aching muscles relax so mobility is increased.

Warnings: For external use only. Use Heet only as directed as it may be unsafe if directions are not followed. Do not use on irritated skin. Keep out of reach of children to avoid accidental poisoning. (If accidental ingestion occurs, contact a physician immediately.) If pain persists for more than 10 days or redness is present before Heet is applied or in conditions affecting children under 12 years of age, consult a physician immediately. Do not use near fire or flame. Do not get Heet in the eyes or on mucous membranes. If excessive irritation develops, discontinue use. If you have diabetes or impaired circulation, use Heet only upon the advice of a physician. Let Heet dry thoroughly before permitting contact with clothing.

Dosage and Administration: Using applicator attached to the bottle cap, brush Heet freely over and around sore areas. Do not bandage or apply external heat or hot water. If necessary, use Heet again in 15 minutes. When pain persists, Heet may be applied every two hours.

Professional Labeling: Same as stated under Indications.

How Supplied: Liquid: in 2.33 fl. oz. and 5 fl. oz. size bottles.

HEET®
Spray Analgesic

Active Ingredients: Methyl Salicylate (25%), Menthol (3.0%), Camphor (3.0%), Methyl Nicotinate (1.0%).

Indications: For fast, temporary relief from minor aches and pains of arthritis, rheumatism, muscular low back pain, strains, muscle aches and pains, lumbago, neuralgia and neuritis.

Actions: Heet Spray contains medications which penetrate into the skin and which act directly on nerves to replace pain arising from deep inside muscles with soothing warmth. The product increases blood flow to the affected area, thereby generating increased warmth to provide relief from minor pain and its stiffness. Helps tense aching muscles relax so mobility is increased.

Warnings: Avoid spraying in eyes. Contents under pressure. Do not puncture or incinerate. Keep away from fire or flame. Do not store at temperatures above 120°F. Keep out of reach of children. Use only as directed. Intentional misuse by deliberately concentrating and inhaling the contents can be harmful or fatal. For external use only. Do not use on broken or irritated skin. Keep out of reach of children to avoid accidental poisoning. (If swallowed accidentally, contact a physician immediately.) If pain persists for more than 10 days or redness is present before Heet is applied or in conditions affecting children under 12 years of age, consult a physician immediately. Do not get Heet in the eyes or on

Continued on next page

Whitehall—Cont.

mucous membranes. If excessive irritation develops, discontinue use. If you have diabetes or impaired circulation, use Heet only upon the advice of a physician.

Dosage and Administration: Spray affected area once from a distance of 6 to 8 inches. Let dry. Spray again. May be reapplied every 2–3 hours for temporary relief. No rubbing is necessary. Do not bandage or apply external heat or hot water.

Professional Labeling: Same as stated under Indications.

How Supplied: In 5 fl. oz. non-fluorocarbon aerosol spray cans.

INFRARUB®
Analgesic Cream

Description: InfraRub is a topical analgesic cream that is lightly and pleasantly scented.

Active Ingredients: Histamine Dihydrochloride 0.1% and Oleoresin Capsicum 0.4%.

Indications: An effective analgesic rub in a cream form for fast, soothing temporary relief of chronic minor pains of arthritis and rheumatism and the relief of muscular aches, minor aches and pains of lumbago, neuritis, neuralgia, sore joints and muscle strains.

Actions: InfraRub increases the flow of blood and produces an analgesic action at the affected area. This action provides soothing warmth and temporary relief of pain.

Warnings: Use only as directed. For external use only. If pain persists more than seven days or redness is present or in conditions affecting children under 12 years of age, consult a physician immediately. If rash appears, discontinue use. Avoid contact with mouth, eyes, nostrils, sensitive or irritated skin. Keep this and all medicines out of the reach of children.

Precautions: If patient has diabetes or impaired circulation, InfraRub should be used only upon the advice of a physician. Itching and hive-like elevations may develop in treated areas. These are temporary and should disappear quickly.

Dosage and Administration: Apply InfraRub freely to affected areas. Massage lightly until cream vanishes. Do not bandage or apply external heat or hot water. Repeat treatment 1–3 times daily and continue use as long as necessary. Wash hands after use. Do not apply to wounded or damaged skin. Allow to dry before putting on clothing.

Professional Labeling: Same as outlined under Indications.

How Supplied: Available in 1.5 oz. and 3.5 oz. tubes.

MOMENTUM®
Muscular Backache Formula

Active Ingredients: Each Momentum Tablet contains Salsalate (Salicylsalicylic Acid) 5 gr., Microfined Aspirin 2½ gr., and Phenyltoloxamine Citrate 12.5 mg.

Indications: Works in the back where inflamed muscles hurt. Helps relieve and relax tight knots of pain and, thus, its stiffness.

Actions: The action of the Microfined Aspirin starts to relieve pain of tense, knotted muscles in minutes. Relief is prolonged by the Salsalate with its longer duration of action. As pain subsides, muscles loosen and become less stiff, more relaxed and mobility is increased.

Warnings: Do not drive a car or operate machinery while taking this medication as this preparation may cause drowsiness in some persons. Keep this and all medicines out of children's reach. In case of accidental overdose, contact a physician immediately.

Dosage and Administration: Adults: Two tablets upon rising, then two tablets as needed at lunch, dinner, and bedtime. Dosage should not exceed 8 tablets in any 24-hour period. Not recommended for children.

Professional Labeling: Same as those outlined under Indications.

How Supplied: Bottles of 24 and 48 white, uncoated tablets.

OUTGRO®
Solution

Active Ingredients: Tannic Acid 25%, Chlorobutanol 5%, Isopropyl Alcohol 83% (by volume).

Indications: Provides fast, temporary relief of pain of ingrown toenails.

Actions: While Outgro temporarily decreases pain, reduces swelling and eases inflammation accompanying ingrown toenails, Outgro does not affect the growth, shape or position of the nail. Daily use of Outgro toughens tender skin—allowing the nail to be cut, and, thus preventing further pain and discomfort.

Warnings: Do not apply if toe is infected, but see a physician. Do not use if you are diabetic or have impaired circulation. Do not use near fire or flame. For external use only. In case of accidental ingestion, contact a physician or a poison control center immediately. Keep this and all medicines out of the reach of children.

Dosage and Administration: Use glass rod in bottle cap. Apply a few drops in the crevice where the nail grows into the flesh and along the entire margin of the nail. Work Outgro well under the nail. Let dry thoroughly. Don't rub off. Apply a few drops several times a day up to 10 days to toughen tender skin, allowing nail to be cut. If condition persists, consult a physician. Replace cap securely.

Professional Labeling: Same as those outlined under Indications.

How Supplied: Available in .31 Fl. Oz. glass bottles.

OXIPOR VHC®
Lotion for Psoriasis

Active Ingredients: Coal Tar Solution 48.5%, Salicylic Acid 1.0%, Benzocaine 2.0%, Alcohol 81% by volume.

Indications: Relieves itching, redness and helps dissolve and clear away the scales and crusts of psoriasis.

Actions: Coal tar solution helps control cell growth and therefore prevents formation of new scales. Salicylic acid has a keratolytic action which helps peel off and dissolve away scales. Benzocaine is a local anesthetic that gives prompt relief from pain and itching. Alcohol is the solvent vehicle.

Warnings: For external use only. Shake well before using. Avoid contact with eyes or mucous membranes and avoid unnecessary sunlight exposure after applying. Store at room temperature. Do not use near fire or flame and do not chill. Keep all medication out of the reach of children.

Precaution: Not for prolonged use. If condition persists or if a rash or irritation develops, discontinue use and consult a physician.

Dosage and Administration: SKIN: Wash affected area before applying to remove loose scales. With a small wad of cotton, apply twice daily. Allow to dry before contact with clothing.
SCALP: Apply to scalp with fingertips making sure to get down to the skin itself. Shampoo. Then remove all loose scales with a fine comb.

Professional Labeling: Same as those outlined under Indications.

How Supplied: Available in 1.9 oz. and 4.0 oz. glass bottles.

PREDICTOR®
In-Home Early Pregnancy Test

Ingredients: Human Chorionic Gonadotropin (HCG) on sheep red blood cells, HCG Antiserum (rabbit) and special buffer solution.

Indications: PREDICTOR is used to determine pregnancy by the detection of HCG in the urine.

Actions: If, after following directions, (see dosage and administration), dark brown doughnut shaped ring appears in the test tube, the patient can assume she is pregnant. If no brown ring occurs, she is probably not pregnant.
Clinical studies have determined the Predictor Method to be 98% accurate. The Predictor Method has been used in thousands of hospitals and in over thirteen million laboratory tests.

Warnings: The test is completely safe... only a urine specimen is required. For In-Vitro Diagnostic Use, not for internal use.

Drug Interaction: Test results may be interfered with if urine contains a large quantity of protein or patient is taking medication.

Dosage and Administration: Predictor can be used as early as the 9th day after missed menstruation. Add a measured amount of first morning urine and the buffered solution to the chemical pellets in the test tube. Shake vigorously for 10 seconds. Place test tube in test stand and leave undisturbed for 1 hour. Test results must be read between 1 and 2 hours after starting test. If a dark brown doughnut shaped ring is visible the patient can assume she is pregnant. If no brown ring occurs, she is probably not pregnant. If test proves negative and menstruation does not occur within another 7 days, the test should be repeated.

Professional Labeling: Same as those outlined under Indications.

How Supplied:

Regular Kit—A kit containing test tube of reagents, vial of special buffer solution with press fit cap, dropper, lid and test stand in carton with package insert.

Double Kit—A kit containing 2 test tubes of reagents, 2 vials of special buffer solution with press fit caps, 2 droppers, lid and test stand in a carton with package insert.

Refill Kit—A kit containing test tube of reagents, vial of special buffer solution with press fit cap, dropper, and package insert. (Note: Lid and test stand from regular or Double Predictor Test Kit required for use.)

PREPARATION H®
Hemorrhoidal Ointment
PREPARATION H®
Hemorrhoidal Suppositories

Active Ingredients: Live Yeast Cell Derivative, supplying 2,000 units skin respiratory factor per ounce of ointment or suppository base. Shark liver oil 3.0%; in a specially prepared base with Phenylmercuric Nitrate 1:10,000 (as a preservative).

Indications: To help shrink swelling of hemorrhoidal tissues caused by inflammation, and to give prompt, temporary relief in many cases from pain and itch in tissues.

Actions: Live Yeast Cell Derivative acts to: A) Increase the oxygen utilization of dermal tissue. B) Increases collagen formation. C) Increases the rate of wound healing. Shark liver oil has been incorporated to act as a protectant which softens and soothes the tissue. Preparation H also lubricates inflamed, irritated surfaces to help make bowel movements less painful.

Precaution: In case of bleeding, or if your condition persists, a physician should be consulted.

Dosage and Administration: Ointment: Apply freely night, morning, after each bowel movement and whenever symptoms occur. Lubricate applicator before each application and thoroughly cleanse after use.

Suppository: Insert one suppository night, morning, after each bowel movement and whenever symptoms occur. Store at controlled room temperature in cool place but not over 80° F.

Professional Labeling: Same as those outlined under Indications.

How Supplied: Ointment: Net wt. 1 oz. and 2 oz.

Suppository: 12's, 24's and 48's.

Reference: Goodson, W., Hohn, D., Hunt, T.K., Leung, D.Y.K.: Augmentation of Some Aspects of Wound Healing by a "Skin Respiratory Factor", J. Surg. Rsch. 21: 125-129, 1976.

[Shown in Product Identification Section]

PREPCORT™ CREAM
(0.5% Hydrocortisone)

Active Ingredient: Hydrocortisone 0.5%

Indications and Actions: For the temporary relief of anal itching. Prepcort Cream provides effective temporary relief from anal itching. It contains hydrocortisone, the most widely doctor-prescribed anal itch product for years, and until recently, only available by prescription. Now PREPCORT gives you this same relief in a soothing, lubricating cream.

Warning: For external use only. Avoid contact with the eyes. Discontinue use if condition worsens or if symptoms persist for more than 7 days and consult a physician. Do not use on children under 2 years of age except under the advice and supervision of a physician. Keep this and all drugs out of the reach of children. In case of accidental ingestion, seek professional assistance or contact a poison control center immediately.

Dosage and Administration: For adults and children 2 years of age and older, apply directly to affected area 3 to 4 times daily. For children under 2 years of age, consult a physician.

Professional Labeling: Same as those outlined under Indications.

How Supplied: Cream: net wt ½ oz. and 1 oz.

[Shown in Product Identification Section]

PRIMATENE®
Mist
(Epinephrine)

Active Ingredients: Each spray delivers approximately 0.2 mg. Epinephrine. A 0.5% w/w (= 5.5 mg./cc.) solution of U.S.P. Epinephrine containing Absorbic Acid as a preservative in an inert propellant. Alcohol 34%.

Indications: Provides temporary relief from acute paroxysms of bronchial asthma.

Warnings: For INHALATION ONLY. Contents under pressure. Do not puncture or throw container into incinerator. Using or storing near open flame or heating above 120° F may cause bursting.

Do not use unless a diagnosis of asthma has been established by a physician. Reduce dosage if bronchial irritation, nervousness, restlessness or sleeplessness occurs. Overdose may cause nervousness and rapid heartbeat. Use only on the advice of a physician if heart disease, high blood pressure, diabetes, or thyroid disease is present. If difficulty in breathing persists, or if relief does not occur within 20 minutes of inhalation, discontinue use and seek medical assistance immediately. Children under 6 years of age should use Primatene Mist only on the advice of a physician. KEEP THIS AND ALL MEDICINES OUT OF REACH OF CHILDREN.

Directions:

1. Take plastic cap off mouthpiece. (For refills, use mouthpiece from previous purchase).

2. Take plastic mouthpiece off bottle.

3. Place other end of mouthpiece on bottle.

4. Turn bottle upside down. Place thumb on bottom of mouthpiece over the words "Primatene Mist" and forefinger on top of vial. Empty the lungs as completely as possible by exhaling.

5. Place mouthpiece in mouth with lips closed around opening. Inhale deeply while squeezing mouthpiece and bottle together. Release immediately and remove unit from mouth, then complete taking the deep breath, drawing medication into your lungs, holding breath as long as comfortable.

6. Then exhale slowly keeping lips nearly closed. This distributes the medication in the lungs.

Dosage: Start with one inhalation by squeezing mouthpiece and bottle together. Release immediately and remove unit from mouth. Then wait at least one minute. If not relieved, use Primatene Mist once more; do not repeat treatment for at least 4 hours.

Professional Labeling: Same as stated under Indications.

How Supplied: ½ fl. oz. (15 cc) with mouthpiece.

½ fl. oz. (15 cc) refill

¾ fl. oz. (22.5 cc) refill

[Shown in Product Identification Section]

PRIMATENE®
Mist Suspension
(Epinephrine Bitartrate)

Active Ingredients: Each spray delivers 0.3 mg. Epinephrine Bitartrate equivalent to 0.16 mg. Epinephrine base. Contains Epinephrine Bitartrate 7.0 mg. per cc. in an inert propellant.

Indications: Provides temporary relief from acute paroxysms of bronchial asthma.

Warnings: For INHALATION ONLY. Contents under pressure. Do not puncture or throw container into incinerator. Using or storing near open flame or heating above 120° F may cause bursting.

Do not use unless a diagnosis of asthma has been established by a physician. Reduce dosage if bronchial irritation, nervousness, restlessness or sleeplessness occurs. Overdose may cause nervousness and rapid heartbeat. Use only on the advice of a physician if heart disease, high blood pressure, diabetes, or thyroid disease is present. If difficulty in breathing persists, or if relief does not occur within 20 minutes of inhalation, discontinue use and seek medical assistance immediately. Children under 6 years of age should use Primatene Mist only on the advice of a physician. KEEP THIS AND ALL MEDICINES OUT OF REACH OF CHILDREN.

Administration: Directions: 1. Shake well. 2. Hold inhaler with nozzle down while using. Empty the lungs as completely as possible by exhaling. 3. Purse the lips as in saying "o" and hold the nozzle up to the lips, keeping the tongue flat. As you start to take a deep breath, squeeze nozzle and can together, releas-

Continued on next page

Whitehall—Cont.

ing one full application. Complete taking deep breath, drawing medication into your lungs. 4. Hold breath for as long as comfortable. This distributes the medication in the lungs. Then exhale slowly, keeping the lips nearly closed. 5. Rinse nozzle daily with soap and hot water after removing from vial. Dry with clean cloth.

Dosage: Start with one inhalation—then wait at least one minute; if not relieved, use Primatene Mist Suspension once more; do not repeat treatment for at least 4 hours.

Professional Labeling: Same as stated under Indications.

How Supplied: ⅓ fl. oz. (10 cc.) pocket-size aerosol inhaler.

PRIMATENE®
Tablets

Available in two formulas, "M" or "P", depending on state. See details below in section on "How Supplied".

Active Ingredients: Theophylline 130 mg., Ephedrine Hydrochloride 24 mg., Phenobarbital 8 mg. (⅛ gr.) per tablet. In those states where Phenobarbital is ℞ only, Pyrilamine Maleate 16.6 mg. is substituted for the Phenobarbital.

Indications: For relief and control of attacks of bronchial asthma and associated hay fever.

Actions: Experimental results[1] indicate the following: in inhibiting the release of bronchoconstricting mediators (histamine and slow-reacting substance of anaphylaxis), which is produced by antigen-antibody (IgE) interaction on sensitive cells, a combination of a sympathomimetic and methylxanthine is more effective than either drug alone.

Warning: If symptoms persist, consult your physician. Some people are sensitive to ephedrine and, in such cases, temporary sleeplessness and nervousness may occur. These reactions will disappear if the use of the medication is discontinued. Do not exceed recommended dosage.

People who have heart disease, high blood pressure, diabetes or thyroid trouble should take this preparation only on the advice of a physician. "M" Formula may cause drowsiness. People taking the "M" Formula should not drive or operate machinery. "P" Formula may be habit forming.

Dosage and Administration: Adults —1 or 2 tablets initially and then one every 4 hours, as needed, not to exceed 6 tablets in 24 hours. Children (6-12) One half adult dose. For children under 6, consult a physician.

Professional Labeling: Same as stated under Indications.

How Supplied: Available in two forms coded "M" or "P". "M" formula, containing pyrilamine maleate, is available in

---

1. Kooperman, W.J., Orange, R. P. and Austen, K.F.: J. Immunol. 105: 1906, Nov., 1970.

---

those states where phenobarbital is ℞ only. "P" formula, containing phenobarbital, is available in all other states. Both "M" and "P" formulas are supplied in glass bottles of 24 and 60 tablets.
[*Shown in Product Identification Section*]

QUIET WORLD®
Analgesic/Sleeping Aid

Description: Occasionally people suffer from nighttime pain and have trouble falling asleep. Quiet World is specially formulated to provide relief of nighttime pain while it helps patients fall asleep.

Active Ingredients: Acetaminophen 2-½ gr. (162 mg.), Aspirin 3½ gr. (227 mg.), Pyrilamine Maleate (25 mg.) per tablet.

Indications: For occasional relief from nighttime pain while it helps one fall asleep.

Actions: Quiet World is for relief of occasional sleeplessness due to pain of headache, discomforts of colds or flu, sinus pain, muscle aches and menstrual discomfort.

Warnings: Keep this and all medicines out of children's reach. In case of accidental overdose, contact a physician immediately.

Precaution: Do not exceed 4 tablets in 24 hours. Do not drive a car or operate machinery after use. If pain persists for more than 10 days, or redness is present, or in conditions affecting children under 12 years of age, consult a physician immediately. Do not take without consulting a physician if under medical care.

Dosage and Administration: Take 2 tablets at bedtime to relieve pain and help fall asleep. If needed, may be repeated once after 4 hours.

Professional Labeling: Same as outlined under Indications.

How Supplied: Oblong Blue Tablets with "Q" imprinted. Tablets in bottles of 12's and 30's.

SEMICID®
Vaginal Contraceptive Suppositories

Description: Semicid is a contraceptive in vaginal suppository form.

Active Ingredient: Each slim, one-inch suppository contains 100 mg. of nonoxynol-9.

Actions: Semicid dissolves in the vagina and blends with natural vaginal lubrication to provide double birth control protection: a physical barrier, plus an effective sperm killing barrier that covers the cervical opening and adjoining vaginal walls. Each Semicid suppository contains the maximum allowable amount of nonoxynol-9, the most widely used non-prescription spermicide.

Semicid requires no applicator and has no unpleasant taste or odor. Nor does it drip or run like foams, creams and jellies. And it's not awkward to use like the diaphragm. As with all spermicides, some Semicid users experience irritation in using the product. However, since Semicid does not effervesce as some suppositories do, it is not as likely to cause a burning feeling.

Semicid is approximately as effective as vaginal foam contraceptives in actual

---

use, but is not as effective as the Pill or IUD.

Dosage and Administration: Insert one suppository into the vagina fifteen minutes before intercourse. Use the forefinger to position suppository as deeply as possible into the vagina. Proper positioning is key to Semicid's efficacy. If intercourse is delayed more than one hour, or repeated, another suppository must be inserted. Semicid can be used safely as frequently as needed and directions should be followed each time.

Precautions: If douching is desired, one should wait at least six hours after intercourse before douching.

If either partner experiences irritation, discontinue use. If irritation persists, consult a physician.

Do not insert in urethra.

Do not take orally.

If your doctor has told you that you should not become pregnant, ask your doctor if you can use Semicid.

If menstrual period is missed, a physician should be consulted.

Keep out of reach of children.

How Supplied: Package of 10, in a partitioned tray mold container. Also available in a Double Pack containing 2 tray molds. Semicid Vaginal Contraceptive Suppositories should be stored at a temperature below 86°F (30°C).

Semicid provides effective contraceptive protection when properly used. However, no contraceptive method or product can provide an absolute guarantee against becoming pregnant.

It is essential that Semicid be inserted at least 15 minutes before intercourse.

SLEEP–EZE®
Nighttime Sleep-aid Tablets

Active Ingredient: Pyrilamine Maleate—25 mg. per tablet.

Indications: For relief of occassional sleeplessness.

Warnings: Do not give to children under 12 years of age. If sleeplessness persists continuously for more than 2 weeks, consult your physician. Insomnia may be a symptom of serious underlying illness. Take this product with caution if alcohol has been consumed. If you are pregnant or nursing a baby, consult your physician before using. Do not take this product if you have asthma, glaucoma, or enlargement of the prostate gland except under the advice and supervision of a physician. Keep this and all medicines out of the reach of children. In case of accidental overdose or ingestion by a child, contact a physician or poison control center immediately.

Drug Interaction: Take this product with caution if alcohol has been consumed.

Precaution: This product contains an antihistamine drug.

Dosage and Administration: Two tablets with water 20 minutes before bedtime.

Professional Labeling: Same as outlined under Indications.

How Supplied: Bottles of 12's, 26's, 52's and 100's.

TRENDAR®
100% Aspirin-Free Premenstrual Tablets

Active Ingredients: Acetaminophen 325 mg. (5 gr.) and Pamabrom 25 mg. per tablet.

Description: Trendar is a 100% aspirin-free analgesic product with the added benefit of a diuretic to relieve water buildup.

Indications: Pre-period—for relief of puffiness and bloating due to water build-up, and symptoms of premenstrual discomfort such as headache, backache, pelvic discomfort, and painful breasts. During period—for relief of minor menstrual pain, cramps, headache, backache and other menstrual discomforts.

Warnings: Do not give to children under 12 or use for more than 10 days unless directed by a physician. Keep this and all medicines out of reach of children. In case of accidental overdose, contact a physician immediately.

Precautions: Do not take without consulting a physician if under medical care. Do not exceed recommended dosage because severe liver damage may occur.

Dosage and Administration: Start 4 to 7 days before period. Take 8 tablets daily—2 tablets after each meal, and at bedtime. Continue, if necessary, during period.

Professional Labeling: Same as those outlined under Indications.

How Supplied: Tablets in bottles of 24 and 50.

VIRO–MED®
Liquid

Active Ingredients: Each fluid ounce (2 tablespoonful) of Viro-Med Liquid contains Acetaminophen 650 mg., Pseudoephedrine HCl 30 mg., Dextromethorphan HBr 20 mg., Sodium Citrate 500 mg., and Alcohol 16.6%.

Indications: Viro-Med is indicated for the relief of all major virus cold and flu symptoms: Fever, nasal congestion, chills, headache, coughing, chest congestion, muscle aches, and scratchy throat.

Actions: The medications in this special Viro-Med formulation provide temporary relief of all major virus cold and flu symptoms.

Acetaminophen, both an analgesic and antipyretic, alleviates the pain and discomfort of headache and muscle aches, and reduces fever. It causes insignificant or no gastric irritation. And since acetaminophen is not a salicylate, Viro-Med Liquid can be taken by those who are sensitive to aspirin.

Pseudoephedrine HCl, a sympathomimetic amine, is an oral decongestant that vasoconstricts the nasopharyngeal mucosa thus reducing nasal/sinus congestion.

Dextromethorphan HBr, an antitussive, relieves or prevents cough.

Sodium Citrate provides an expectorant action that promotes the ejection of mucus from the bronchi, lungs, and trachea.

Warnings: Do not administer to children under 6 years of age or use for more than 10 days unless directed by a physi-

cian. If cough persists—which may indicate a serious condition—or in case of high fever—consult a physician. Individuals with high blood pressure, diabetes, heart or thyroid disease should use only as directed by physician. In case of accidental overdose, contact a physician immediately. Keep this and all medicines out of the reach of children. Use only as directed.

Dosage and Administration: Adults: 2 tablespoonful (1 fl. oz.) every 3 or 4 hours, not to exceed 8 tablespoonful in 24 hours.

Children (6–12 years): 1 tablespoonful (½ fl. oz.) every 3 or 4 hours, not to exceed 4 tablespoonsful in 24 hours. For children under six, consult a physician.

Professional Labeling: Same as outlined under Indications.

How Supplied: Viro-Med Liquid (dark amber) in 6 fl. oz. bottles.

VIRO–MED®
Tablets

Active Ingredients: Each Viro-Med Tablet contains Aspirin 5 gr., Chlorpheniramine Maleate 1 mg., Pseudoephedrine HCl 15 mg., Dextromethorphan HBr 7.5 mg., and Guaifenesin (Glyceral Guaiacolate) 50 mg.

Indications: Viro-Med is indicated for the relief of all major virus cold and flu symptoms: fever, nasal congestion, chills, headache, coughing, chest congestion, muscle aches, and scratchy throat.

Actions: The medications in this special Viro-Med formulation provide temporary relief of all major virus cold and flu symptoms.

Aspirin, both an analgesic and antipyretic, alleviates the pain and discomfort of headache and muscle aches, and reduces fever.

Chlorpheniramine Maleate, an antihistamine, acts to minimize tissue reaction to histamine. This relieves itching of the nasopharynx, eyes, and throat; sneezing; reduces nasal discharge; and shrinks and dries swollen membranes.

Pseudoephedrine HCl, a sympathomimetic amine, is an oral decongestant that vasoconstricts the nasopharyngeal mucosa thus reducing nasal/sinus congestion.

Dextromethorphan HBr, an antitussive, alleviates or prevents cough.

Guaifenesin is an expectorant that promotes the ejection of mucus from the lungs, bronchi, and trachea.

Precautions: If cough persists—which may indicate a serious condition—or in case of high fever—consult a physician. Do not drive or operate machinery while taking this medication as this preparation may cause drowsiness in some persons. If relief does not occur within 7 days, discontinue use and consult a physician.

Warning: May cause drowsiness. May cause excitability, especially in children. Individuals with asthma, glaucoma, difficulty in urination due to enlargement of the prostate gland, high blood pressure, diabetes, heart or thyroid disease should use only as directed by a physician. Keep this and all medicines out of the reach of

children. In case of accidental overdose, contact a physician immediately.

Dosage and Administration: Adults: 2 tablets every 4 hours. Do not exceed 12 tablets in 24 hours. Children (6–12): One half the adult dose. Do not give to children under 6 years of age or exceed the recommended dosage unless directed by a physician. Viro-Med Tablets contain no narcotics, barbiturates, or alcohol and may be taken day or night.

Professional Labeling: Same as outlined under Indications.

How Supplied: Orange/white uncoated tablets in bottles of 20 with a child-resistant safety closure, and bottles of 48 for households without young children.

The J. B. Williams Company, Inc.
767 FIFTH AVENUE
NEW YORK, NY 10153

ACU–TEST®
In-Home Pregnancy Test

Active Ingredient: hCG on sheep red blood cells, hCG antiserum from rabbits.

Indications: An *in vitro* pregnancy test for use in the home.

Actions: Indicates the presence of human chorionic gonadotropin, a hormone of pregnancy, in the urine.

Precautions: For use on or after the 9th day following the day when the menstrual period was due. The physician should be consulted if pregnancy is indicated.

Administration: Perform test exactly according to instructions, using the first morning urine.

How Supplied: Packages of one or two tests each with test tube, dropper and buffer solution.

DEEP–DOWN® Pain Relief Rub

Active Ingredients: Methyl salicylate 15%; menthol 5%; methyl nicotinate 0.7%; camphor 0.5%.

Indications: To relieve the pain of minor arthritis, sore joints, muscle aches and sprains, backache, lumbago.

Actions: Counterirritation: cutaneous stimulation for relief of pain in underlying structures.

Warnings: For external use only. Avoid getting in eyes or on mucous membranes, broken or irritated skin. Discontinue use if excessive skin irritation develops. If pain lasts more than 7 days, or redness is present, or in conditions affecting children under 12 years of age, consult a physician. Keep product out of children's reach. In case of accidental swallowing, call a physician or contact a poison control center immediately.

Dosage and Administration: Rub generously into painful area, then massage gently until ointment is absorbed and disappears. Reapply every 3 to 4 hours or as needed. Do not bandage.

How Supplied: Available in 1.25 and 3 oz collapsible tubes.

Continued on next page

Williams—Cont.

FEMIRON® Tablets

Active Ingredient: (Per Tablet) Iron (from ferrous fumarate) 20 mg.
Indications: For use as an iron supplement.
Actions: Supplements dietary iron intake; helps maintain iron stores.
Warnings: Keep out of reach of children.
Precaution: Alcoholics and individuals with chronic liver or pancreatic disease may have enhanced iron absorption with the potential for iron overload. NOTE: Unabsorbed iron may cause some darkening of the stool.
Drug Interaction Precaution: Taking with antacid or tetracycline may interfere with absorption.
Symptoms and Treatment of Oral Overdose: Toxicity and symptoms are primarily due to iron overdose. Abdominal pain, nausea, vomiting and diarrhea may occur, with possible subsequent acidosis and cardiovasular collapse with severe poisoning. **Treatment:** Induce vomiting immediately. Administer milk, eggs to reduce gastric irritation. Contact a physician immediately.
Dosage and Administration: Women: One tablet daily.
How Supplied: Bottles of 40 and 120 tablets.

FEMIRON® Multi-Vitamins and Iron

Active Ingredients: Iron (from ferrous fumarate) 20 mg; Vitamin A 5,000 I.U.; Vitamin D 400 I.U.; Thiamine (Vitamin B_1) 1.5 mg; Riboflavin (Vitamin B_2) 1.7 mg; Niacinamide 20 mg; Ascorbic Acid (Vitamin C) 60 mg; Pyridoxine (Vitamin B_6) 2 mg; Cyanocobalamin (Vitamin B_{12}) 6 mcg; Calcium Pantothenate 10 mg; Folic Acid .4 mg; and Tocopherol Acetate (Vitamin E) 15 I.U.
Indications: For use as an iron and vitamin supplement.
Actions: Helps insure adequate intake of iron and vitamins.
Warnings: Keep out of reach of children.
Precaution: Alcoholics and individuals with chronic liver or pancreatic disease may have enhanced iron absorption with the potential for iron overload. NOTE: Unabsorbed iron may cause some darkening of the stool.
Symptoms and Treatment of Oral Overdosage: Toxicity and symptoms are primarily due to iron overdose. Abdominal pain, nausea, vomiting and diarrhea may occur, with possible subsequent acidosis and cardiovascular collapse with severe poisoning. **Treatment:** Induce vomiting immediately. Administer milk, eggs to reduce gastric irritation. Contact a physician immediately.
Dosage and Administration: Women: One tablet daily.
How Supplied: Bottles of 35, 60, and 90 tablets.

GERITOL® Liquid
High Potency Iron & Vitamin Tonic

Active Ingredients: Per fluid ounce: Iron (from ferric ammonium citrate) 100 mg; Thiamine (B_1) 5 mg; Riboflavin (B_2) 5 mg; Niacinamide 100 mg; Panthenol 4 mg; Pyridoxine (B_6) 1 mg; Cyanocobalamin(B_{12}) 1.5 mcg; Methionine 50 mg; Choline Bitartrate 100 mg.
Indications: For iron or vitamin deficiency; for use as a dietary supplement.
Actions: Helps prevent deficiency in iron and specific vitamins.
Warnings: Keep out of reach of children.
Precaution: Alcohol accelerates absorption of ferric iron. Alcoholics and individuals with chronic liver or pancreatic disease may have enhanced iron absorption with the potential for iron overload. NOTE: Unabsorbed iron may cause some darkening of the stool.
Symptoms and Treatment of Oral Overdose: Toxicity and symptoms are primarily due to iron overdose. Abdominal pain, nausea, vomiting and diarrhea may occur, with possible subsequent acidosis and cardiovascular collapse with severe poisoning. **Treatment:** Induce vomiting immediately. Administer milk, eggs to reduce gastric irritation. Contact a physician immediately.
Dosage and Administration: For iron or vitamin deficiency, 3 tablespoonsful (1.5 fl. oz.) daily. As an iron and vitamin supplement, one tablespoon (0.5 fl. oz.) daily.
How Supplied: 4 ounce, 12 ounce, 24 ounce bottles.

GERITOL® Mega Vitamins

Active Ingredients: (per tablet) Vitamin A 10,000 I.U.; Vitamin C (Ascorbic Acid) 120 mg; Vitamin B_1 (Thiamine) 15 mg; Vitamin B_2 (Riboflavin) 15 mg; Vitamin B_6 (Pyridoxine) 10 mg; Vitamin B_{12} (Cyanocobalamin) 30 mcg; Niacin 100 mg; Calcium Pantothenate 20 mg; Iron (Ferrous Fumarate) 50 mg.
Indications: For use as a dietary supplement.
Actions: Supplements dietary intake of Vitamin A and C, the B-Complex Pantothenic acid, and iron.
Warnings: Keep out of reach of children.
Drug Interaction: Some interaction between therapeutic agents and micronutrients have been suggested. Individuals taking medications should consult the physician regarding vitamin supplementation.
Precaution: Alcoholics and individuals with chronic liver or pancreatic disease may have enhanced iron absorption with the potential for iron overload. NOTE: Unabsorbed iron may cause some darkening of the stool.
Symptoms and Treatment of Oral Overdose: Toxicity and symptoms are primarily due to iron overdose. Abdominal pain, nausea, vomiting and diarrhea may occur, with possible subsequent acidosis and cardiovascular collapse with severe poisoning. **Treatment:** Induce

vomiting immediately. Administer milk, eggs to reduce gastric irritation. Contact a physician immediately.
Dosage and Administration: As a dietary supplement: One tablet daily.
How Supplied: Bottles of 30, 60, and 100 tablets.

GERITOL® Tablets
High Potency Iron & Vitamin Tablets

Active Ingredients: (Per Tablet) Iron (as ferrous sulfate) 50 mg; Thiamine (Vitamin B_1) 5 mg; Riboflavin (Vitamin B_2) 5 mg; Vitamin C (as Sodium Ascorbate) 75 mg; Niacinamide 30 mg; Calcium Pantothenate 2 mg; Pyridoxine (Vitamin B_6) .5 mg; Cyanocobalamin (Vitamin B_{12}) 3 mcg
Indications: For iron or vitamin deficiency; for use as a dietary supplement.
Actions: Helps prevent deficiency in iron and specific vitamins.
Warnings: Keep out of reach of children.
Precaution: Alcoholics and individuals with chronic liver or pancreatic disease may have enhanced iron absorption with the potential for iron overload. NOTE: Unabsorbed iron may cause some darkening of the stool.
Symptoms and Treatment of Oral Overdose: Toxicity and symptoms are primarily due to iron overdose. Abdominal pain, nausea, vomiting and diarrhea may occur, with possible subsequent acidosis and cardiovascular collapse with severe poisoning. **Treatment:** Induce vomiting immediately. Administer milk, eggs to reduce gastric irritation. Contact a physician immediately.
Dosage and Administration: For iron or vitamin deficiency, 3 tablets daily or as directed by a physician. As a dietary supplement, 1 tablet daily.
How Supplied: Bottles of 14, 24, 40, 80, 100, 180 and 300.

SERUTAN® Concentrated Powder Laxative

Active Ingredient: Vegetable hemicellulose derived from Plantago Ovata 45%.
Indications: For aiding bowel regularity.
Actions: Softens stools, increases bulk volume and water content.
Warnings: Keep out of the reach of children.
Precaution: Patients with suspected intestinal disorders should consult a physician.
Dosage and Administration: Adults: Stir one heaping teaspoonful into a 6 oz. glass of water. Drink immediately. Take one to three times daily, preferably at mealtime.
How Supplied: 3½ oz, 7 oz, 14 oz, and 21 oz bottles.

SERUTAN® Concentrated Powder —Fruit Flavored Laxative

Active Ingredient: Vegetable hemicellulose derived from Plantago Ovata 45%.

Indications: For aiding bowel regularity.

Actions: Softens stools, increases bulk volume and water content.

Warnings: Keep out of the reach of children.

Precaution: Patients with suspected intestinal disorders should consult a physician.

Dosage and Administration: Adults: Stir one heaping teaspoonful into a 6 oz. glass of water. Drink immediately. Take one to three times daily, preferably at mealtime.

How Supplied: 3 oz, 6 oz, 12 oz, and 18 oz bottles.

SERUTAN® Toasted Granules Laxative

Active Ingredients: Vegetable hemicellulose derived from Plantago Ovata 39%.

Indications: For aiding bowel regularity.

Actions: Softens stools, increases bulk volume and water content.

Warnings: Keep out of the reach of children.

Precaution: Patients with suspected intestinal disorders should consult a physician. Not to be taken directly by spoon.

Dosage and Administration: Adults: Sprinkle one heaping teaspoonful on cereal or other food, one to three times daily.

How Supplied: Available in 3½, 7, and 18 oz. plastic bottles.

SOMINEX® Sleep Aid

Active Ingredient: Pyrilamine maleate, 25 mg per tablet.

Indications: To induce drowsiness and assist in falling asleep.

Actions: An antihistamine with anticholinergic and sedative effects.

Warnings: Do not give to children under 12 years of age. Do not exceed recommended dosage unless directed by physician. Consult physician if sleeplessness persists continuously for more than 2 weeks. Take product with caution if alcohol has been consumed. Do not take if suffering from asthma, glaucoma, or enlargement of the prostate gland except under the advice and supervision of a physician. Keep product out of the reach of children. In case of accidental overdose, seek professional assistance or contact a poison control center immediately.

Drug Interaction Precaution: The CNS depressant effect of Sominex (pyrilamine maleate) is heightened by alcohol and other CNS depressant drugs.

Symptoms and Treatment of Oral Overdosage: Overdose may result in nausea, vomiting, feverishness, excitability, mydriasis, hallucinations and convulsions. Coma and cardiorespiratory collapse may ensue in severe cases. Approaches to treatment include halting absorption of the drug, inducing emesis, controlling convulsions and assisting ventilation.

Dosage and Administration: Take 2 tablets with water at bedtime.

How Supplied: Available in bottles of 8, 16, 32, 72, 124 tablets, blister packs of 10 capsules.

VIVARIN® Stimulant Tablets

Active Ingredient: 200 mg caffeine alkaloid per tablet. Compounded in a formula containing dextrose.

Indications: For use as a quick stimulant to combat drowsiness.

Actions: Stimulates cerebrocortical areas involved with active mental processes.

Warnings: Keep out of reach of children. For adult use only. Do not take more than 1 tablet in any 4 hour period. Product should not be substituted for normal sleep.

Drug Interaction: Use of caffeine should be lowered or avoided if drugs are being used to treat cardiovascular ailments, psychological problems, or kidney trouble.

Precaution: Higher blood glucose levels may result from caffeine use.

Symptoms and Treatment of Oral Overdosage: Convulsions may occur if caffeine is consumed in doses larger than 10 g. Emesis should be induced to empty the stomach.

Dosage and Administration: Adults: 1 tablet every 4 hours, as needed.

How Supplied: Available in packages of 16, 40 and 80 tablets.

Winthrop Laboratories
Division of Sterling Drug Inc.
Consumer Products Division
90 PARK AVENUE
NEW YORK, NY 10016

BRONKAID® Mist

Description: BRONKAID Mist, brand of epinephrine, USP, 0.5%, contains ascorbic acid as preservative in an inert propellant. Alcohol 33% (w/w). Each activation of the measured dose valve delivers 0.27 mg epinephrine.

Action: Epinephrine is a sympathomimetic amine which relaxes bronchial muscle spasm, as occurs in attacks of bronchial asthma.

Indication: For temporary relief of acute paroxysms of bronchial asthma

Warnings: FOR ORAL INHALATION ONLY. Reduce dosage if nervousness, restlessness, sleeplessness, or bronchial irritation occurs. Do not use if high blood pressure, heart disease, diabetes, or thyroid disease is present, unless directed by a physician. If prompt relief is not obtained, consult your physician.

Avoid spraying in eyes. Contents under pressure. Do not break or incinerate. Do not store at temperature above 120 F. Keep out of reach of children.

Precaution: Children under 6 years of age should use BRONKAID Mist only on the advice of a physician. Avoid indiscriminate use of BRONKAID Mist as many people do with similar medications. Use only when actually needed for relief.

Dosage and Administration: Start with one inhalation, then wait at least one minute. If not relieved, use BRONKAID Mist once more. Do not repeat treatment for at least 4 hours. If difficulty in breathing persists, consult your physician.

Directions for Use:
1. Remove cap and mouthpiece from bottle.
2. Remove cap from mouthpiece.
3. Turn mouthpiece sideways and fit metal stem of nebulizer into hole in flattened end of mouthpiece.
4. Exhale, as completely as possible. Now, hold bottle **upside down** between thumb and forefinger and close lips loosely around end of mouthpiece.
5. Inhale deeply while pressing down firmly on bottle, once only.
6. Remove mouthpiece and hold your breath a moment to allow for maximum absorption of medication. Then exhale slowly through nearly closed lips.

After use, remove mouthpiece from bottle and replace cap. Slide mouthpiece over bottle for protection. When possible, rinse mouthpiece with tap water immediately after use. Soap and water will not hurt it. A clean mouthpiece always works better.

How Supplied: Bottles of ½ fl oz (15 ml) NDC 0024-4082-15 with actuator. Also available—refills (no mouthpiece) in 15 ml (½ fl oz) NDC 0024-4083-16 and 22.5 ml (¾ fl oz) NDC 0024-4083-22

BRONKAID® Mist Suspension

Active Ingredients: Each spray delivers 0.3 mg epinephrine bitartrate equivalent to 0.16 mg epinephrine base. Contains epinephrine bitartrate 7.0 mg per cc in an inert propellant.

Indication: Provides temporary relief from acute paroxysms of bronchial asthma.

Warnings: For INHALATION ONLY. Contents under pressure. Do not puncture or throw container into incinerator. Using or storing near open flame or heating above 120°F may cause bursting. Do not use unless a diagnosis of asthma has been established by a physician. Reduce dosage if bronchial irritation, nervousness, restlessness, or sleeplessness occurs. Overdose may cause nervousness and rapid heartbeat. Use only on the advice of a physician if heart disease, high blood pressure, diabetes, or thyroid disease is present. If difficulty in breathing persists, or if relief does not occur within 20 minutes of inhalation, discontinue use and seek medical assistance immediately. Children under 6 years of age

Continued on next page

This product information was effective as of January 1, 1982. On these and other products of Consumer Products Division, Winthrop Laboratories, detailed information may be obtained on a current basis by direct inquiry to 90 Park Avenue, New York, NY 10016 (212) 907-2520.

Winthrop—Cont.

should use BRONKAID Mist Suspension only on the advice of a physician. Keep this and all medicines out of reach of children.

Administration: (1) SHAKE WELL. (2) HOLD INHALER WITH NOZZLE DOWN WHILE USING. Empty the lungs as completely as possible by exhaling. (3) Purse the lips as in saying the letter "O" and hold the nozzle up to the lips, keeping the tongue flat. As you start to take a deep breath, squeeze nozzle and can together, releasing one full application. Complete taking deep breath, drawing medication into your lungs. (4) Hold breath for as long as comfortable. This distributes the medication in the lungs. Then exhale slowly keeping the lips nearly closed. (5) Rinse nozzle daily with soap and hot water after removing from vial. Dry with clean cloth.

Dosage: Start with one inhalation—then wait at least one minute; if not relieved, use BRONKAID Mist Suspension once more; do not repeat treatment for at least 4 hours.

Professional Labeling: Same as stated under Indication.

How Supplied: ⅓ fl oz (10 cc) pocket-size aerosol inhaler (NDC 0024-4082-10)

BRONKAID® Tablets

Description: Each tablet contains ephedrine sulfate 24 mg, guaifenesin (glyceryl guaiacolate) 100 mg, and theophylline 100 mg.

Actions: Theophylline and ephedrine both produce bronchodilation through relaxation of bronchial muscle spasm, as occurs in attacks of bronchial asthma, although they do so through different mechanisms. Guaifenesin produces an expectorant action by increasing the water content of bronchial mucus, probably by way of a vagal reflex.

Indication: For symptomatic control of bronchial asthma

Precautions: The recommended dosage of BRONKAID tablets is appropriate for home medication for the symptoms of bronchial congestion and bronchial asthma. If this dosage does not afford relief, and symptoms persist or worsen, it is an indication that the nature of your illness requires the attention of a physician. Under these conditions, or if fever is present, do not experiment with home medications. Consult your physician. Individuals with persistent coughs, high blood pressure, diabetes, heart or thyroid disease should use only as directed by a physician. If dryness of throat, nervousness, restlessness or sleeplessness occurs, discontinue the dosage and consult your physician. Occasionally, in certain individuals, this preparation may cause urinary retention and, if so, discontinue medication. Do not exceed recommended dosage unless directed by a physician.

Dosage and Administration: *Adult Dosage:* 1 tablet every three or four hours. Do not take more than 5 tablets in a 24-hour period. Swallow tablets whole with water.

Children (6 to 12): ½ tablet every three or four hours. Do not administer more than 5 times in a 24-hour period. Do not administer to children under 6 unless directed by a physician. Swallow whole with water.

Morning Dose: An early dose of 1 tablet (for adults) can relieve the coughing and wheezing caused by the night's accumulation of mucus, and can help you start the day with better breathing capacity.

Before an Attack: Many persons feel an attack of asthma coming on. One BRONKAID tablet beforehand may stop the attack before it starts.

During the Day: The precise dose of BRONKAID tablets can be varied to meet your individual needs as you gain experience with this product. It is advisable to take 1 tablet before going to bed, for nighttime relief. However, be sure not to exceed recommended daily dosage.

How Supplied:
Boxes of 24 (NDC 0024-4081-02)
Boxes of 60 (NDC 0024-4081-06)

CAMPHO–PHENIQUE® Liquid

Description: Contains phenol 4.7% (w/w) and camphor 10.8% (w/w) in an aromatic oily solution.

Actions: Pain-relieving antiseptic for sores, cuts, burns, insect bites, fever blisters, and cold sores.

Indications: For relief of pain and to combat infection from minor injuries and skin lesions.

Warnings: Not for prolonged use. Not to be used on large areas or in or near the eyes. In case of deep or puncture wounds, serious burns, or persisting redness, swelling or pain, discontinue use and consult physician. If rash or infection develops, discontinue use and consult physician. Do not bandage if applied to fingers or toes.

Keep this and all medicines out of children's reach. In case of accidental ingestion, seek professional assistance or contact a poison control center immediately.

Directions for Use: For external use. Apply with cotton three or four times daily.

How Supplied:
Bottles of   1 fl oz (NDC 0024-5150-01)
             2 fl oz (NDC 0024-5150-02)
             4 fl oz (NDC 0024-5150-04)
Also available—*Gel*-in tubes of .23 oz (6.5 g) (NDC 0024-0212-01) and .50 oz (14 g) (NDC 0024-0212-02)

HALEY'S M-O®

Description: An emulsion of Phillips'® Milk of Magnesia with 25 per cent pure mineral oil.

Action: Laxative and lubricant preparation; the mineral oil acting as a lubricant and the Milk of Magnesia as a mild saline cathartic.

Indications: For the relief of constipation especially in patients with hemorrhoids, obstetric and cardiac patients, and in geriatric patients where straining at stool is contraindicated.

Contraindications: Abdominal pain, nausea, vomiting, or other symptoms of appendicitis.

Warnings: Not to be used when abdominal pain, nausea, vomiting, or other symptoms of appendicitis are present. Habitual use of laxatives may result in dependency upon them. When used daily or with frequent regularity, do not take within two hours of a meal because mineral oil may interfere with the absorption of pro-Vitamin A.

Dosage and Administration: *Adults,* 2 tablespoons on arising and at bedtime. *Children 3 to 6 years*—1 to 2 teaspoons; *7 to 12 years,* 2 to 4 teaspoons. *Under 3 years,* as directed by physician.

How Supplied: Haley's M-O is available as Regular and Flavored (sugar-free) in bottles of:
Regular— 8 fl oz (NDC 0024-3130-08)
            16 fl oz (NDC 0024-3130-16)
            32 fl oz (NDC 0024-3130-32)
Flavored— 8 fl oz (NDC 0024-3230-08)
            16 fl oz (NDC 0024-3230-16)
            32 fl oz (NDC 0024-3230-32)

Long Acting NEO–SYNEPHRINE® II
xylometazoline hydrochloride
Nasal Spray 0.1%
Vapor Nasal Spray 0.1%
Nose Drops 0.1%
Children's Nose Drops 0.05%

Description: *Adult Strength Nasal Spray* and *Nose Drops* contain xylometazoline hydrochloride 0.1% with benzalkonium chloride and thimerosal 0.001% as preservatives. *Adult Strength Vapor Nasal Spray* contains xylometazoline hydrochloride 0.1% with aromatics (menthol, eucalyptol, camphor, methyl salicylate) and benzalkonium chloride and thimerosal 0.001% as preservatives. *Children's Nose Drops* contain xylometazoline hydrochloride 0.05% with benzalkonium chloride and thimerosal 0.001% as preservatives.

Action: Long-acting Nasal Decongestant

Indications: Provides long-lasting, 8 to 10 hour, temporary relief of nasal congestion due to common cold, sinusitis, hay fever, or other upper respiratory allergies, makes breathing through the nose easier, reduces swelling of nasal passages, and shrinks swollen membranes.

Warnings: Nasal Spray 0.1% and Nose Drops 0.1% should be administered only to adults. Do not give this product to children under 12 years. Children's Nose Drops 0.05% should be given only to children from 2 to 12 years of age. Do not give to children under 2 years of age unless under advice and supervision of a physician. Do not exceed recommended dosage because symptoms may occur such as burning, stinging, sneezing, or increase of nasal discharge. Do not use this product for more than three days. If symptoms persist, consult a physician. The use of this dispenser by more than one person may spread infection. Keep this and all drugs out of the reach of children. In case of accidental ingestion, seek professional assistance or contact a poison control center immediately. Do not use if allergic to xylometazoline.

Dosage and Administration: *Spray 0.1% for adults*—Always hold head upright to spray. Insert nosepiece into nostril pointing it slightly backward. To spray, squeeze bottle quickly and firmly. Spray two or three times into each nostril every 8 to 10 hours. Do not use more than three times daily.

Solution 0.1% for adults and children over 12—two or three drops in each nostril every 8 to 10 hours. Do not use more than three times daily.

Solution 0.05% for children 2 through 12 years of age—two or three drops in each nostril every 8 to 10 hours. Do not use more than 3 times daily.

How Supplied: *Nasal Spray Adult Strength*—plastic squeeze bottles of 15 ml (½ fl oz) NDC 0024-1338-01; *Vapor Nasal Spray Adult Strength*—squeeze bottles of 15 ml (½ fl oz) NDC 0024-1339-01.

Nose Drops Adult Strength—bottles of 30 ml (1 fl oz) with dropper NDC 0024-1336-02; *Children's Strength 0.05%*—bottles of 30 ml (1 fl oz) with dropper NDC 0024-1337-02.

NEO-SYNEPHRINE®
phenylephrine hydrochloride

Action: Rapid-acting nasal decongestant.

Indications: For temporary relief of nasal congestion due to common cold, hay fever or other upper respiratory allergies, or associated with sinusitis.

Precautions: Some hypersensitive individuals may experience a mild stinging sensation. This is usually transient and often disappears after a few applications. Do not exceed recommended dosage. Follow directions for use carefully. If symptoms are not relieved after several applications, a physician should be consulted. Frequent and continued usage of the higher concentrations (especially the 1% solution) occasionally may cause a rebound congestion of the nose. Therefore, long-term or frequent use of this solution is not recommended without the advice of a physician.

Prolonged exposure to air, metal, or strong light will cause oxidation and some loss of potency. Do not use if brown in color or contains a precipitate.

Adverse Reactions: Generally very well tolerated; systemic side effects such as tremor, insomnia, or palpitation rarely occur.

Dosage and Administration: *Topical*—dropper, spray, tampon, irrigation, or displacement. The *0.25% solution* is adequate in most cases *(0.125% for infants)*. In resistant cases, or if more powerful decongestion is desired, the *0.5 or 1% solution* should be used. Also used as *0.5% jelly.*

How Supplied: Nasal spray 0.25%—15 ml (for children and for adults who prefer a mild nasal spray)—NDC 0024-1348-03; nasal spray 0.5%—15 ml (for adults)—NDC 0024-1353-01; nasal solution 0.125% (for infants and small children), 1 fl oz bottles—NDC 0024-1345-02; nasal solution 0.25% (for children and adults who prefer a mild solution), 1 fl oz bottles—NDC 0024-1347-01 and 16 fl oz bottles—NDC 0024-1347-06; nasal solution 0.5% (for adults), 1 fl oz bottles

—NDC 0024-1351-01; nasal solution 1% (extra strength for adults), 1 fl oz bottles—NDC 0024-1355-01 and 16 fl oz bottles—NDC 0024-1355-06; and water soluble nasal jelly 0.5%, ⅝ oz tubes—NDC 0024-1367-01.

Also available — NEO-SYNEPHRINE Mentholated Nasal Spray 0.5% (for adults), ½ fl oz bottles—NDC 0024-1364-01.

NEO-SYNEPHRINE®
oxymetazoline HCl
12 HOUR

Nasal Spray 0.05%
Vapor Nasal Spray 0.05%
Nose Drops 0.05%
Children's Drops 0.025%

Description: *Adult Strength Nasal Spray* and *Nose Drops* contain oxymetazoline hydrochloride 0.05% with benzalkonium chloride and phenylmercuric acetate 0.002% as preservatives. *Adult Strength Vapor Nasal Spray* contains oxymetazoline hydrochloride 0.05% with aromatics (menthol, eucalyptol, camphor, methyl salicylate) with benzalkonium chloride and thimerosal as preservatives. *Children's Nose Drops* contain oxymetazoline hydrochloride 0.025% with benzalkonium chloride and phenylmercuric acetate 0.002% as preservatives.

Action: 12 HOUR Nasal Decongestant.

Indications: Provides temporary relief, for up to 12 HOURS, of nasal congestion due to colds, hay fever, sinusitis, or allergies. NEO-SYNEPHRINE 12-HOUR Nasal Sprays and Nose Drops contain oxymetazoline which provides the longest-lasting relief of nasal congestion available. It decongests nasal passages up to 12 HOURS, reduces swelling of nasal passages, and temporarily restores freer breathing through the nose.

Warnings: Do not exceed recommended dosage because symptoms may occur such as burning, stinging, sneezing, or increase of nasal discharge. (Nasal Spray 0.05%, Vapor Nasal Spray 0.05%, Nose Drops 0.05% not recommended for children under 6; Children's Drops 0.025% not recommended for children under 2.) Do not use these products for more than 3 days. If symptoms persist, consult a physician. The use of this dispenser by more than one person may spread infection.

Keep this and all medicines out of the reach of children. In case of accidental ingestion seek professional assistance or contact a poison control center immediately.

Dosage and Administration: *Adult Strength Nasal Spray*—For adults and children 6 years of age and over: With head upright, spray two or three times in each nostril twice daily—morning and evening. To spray, squeeze bottle quickly and firmly.

Adult Strength Nose Drops—For adults and children 6 years of age and over: two or three drops in each nostril twice daily—morning and evening.

Adult Strength Vapor Nasal Spray—For adults and children 6 years of age and

over: With head upright, spray two or three times in each nostril twice daily—morning and evening. To spray, squeeze bottle quickly and firmly. Contains cooling menthol vapors.

Children's Nose Drops—Specially formulated for children 2 through 5 years. Children 2 to under 6 years of age: two or three drops in each nostril twice daily—morning and evening.

How Supplied: *Nasal Spray Adult Strength*—plastic squeeze bottle of 15 ml (½ fl oz) NDC 0024-1390-03; *Vapor Nasal Spray Adult Strength*—squeeze bottles of 15 ml (½ fl oz) NDC 0024-1391-03; *Nose Drops Adult Strength*—bottles of 15 ml (½ fl oz) with dropper (NDC 0024-1392-01); *Children's Strength 0.025%*—bottles of 15 ml (½ fl oz) with dropper (NDC 0024-1393-01)

NEO-SYNEPHRINOL™
pseudoephedrine hydrochloride
120 mg
DAY RELIEF™ Capsules

Long-Acting Nasal Decongestant

Description: Neo-Synephrinol DAY RELIEF Capsules Long-Acting Nasal Decongestant contains pseudoephedrine hydrochloride, a decongestant in a special timed-release capsule.

Action: Long-acting Nasal Decongestant which provides up to 12 Hour temporary relief of nasal congestion—helps decongest sinus openings, sinus passages.

Indications: For temporary relief of nasal congestion due to the common cold, hay fever, or other upper respiratory allergies, and nasal congestion associated with sinusitis; promotes nasal and/or sinus drainage.

Warnings: Do not exceed recommended dosage because at higher doses nervousness, dizziness, or sleeplessness may occur. If symptoms do not improve within 7 days or are accompanied by high fever, consult a physician before continuing use. Do not take this product if you have high blood pressure, heart disease, diabetes, or thyroid disease, except under the advice and supervision of a physician. Keep this and all drugs out of the reach of children. In case of accidental overdose, seek professional assistance or contact a poison control center immediately.

Directions: Adults and Children 12 Years and Over—One capsule every 12 hours. Neo-Synephrinol is not recommended for children under 12 years of age.

Drug Interaction Precaution: Do not take this product if you are presently taking a prescription antihypertensive

Continued on next page

This product information was effective as of January 1, 1982. On these and other products of Consumer Products Division, Winthrop Laboratories, detailed information may be obtained on a current basis by direct inquiry to 90 Park Avenue, New York, NY 10016 (212) 907-2520.

Winthrop—Cont.

or antidepressant drug containing a monoamine oxidase inhibitor except under the advice and supervision of a physician.

How Supplied: Capsules-boxes of 10 (NDC 0024-1370-01)

NTZ® Solution

Description: Contains phenylephrine hydrochloride 0.5%, thenyldiamine hydrochloride 0.1%, and benzalkonium chloride 1:5000 in a buffered solution.
Action: Decongestant nose drops. The antiseptic preservative and wetting agent, benzalkonium chloride, promotes spread and penetration of solution.
Indications: For relief of nasal congestion in the common cold, allergic rhinitis including hay fever, vasomotor rhinitis, acute and chronic sinusitis.
Precautions: Some hypersensitive individuals may experience a mild stinging sensation. The stinging sensation often disappears if the spray or solution is used as recommended.
Do not exceed recommended dosage. Follow directions for use carefully. If symptoms are not relieved after several applications, a physician should be consulted. Frequent and continued usage of NTZ solution occasionally may cause a rebound congestion of the nose. Therefore, long-term or frequent use of this solution is not recommended without the advice of a physician.
Prolonged exposure to air, metal, or strong light will cause oxidation and some loss of potency. Do not use if brown in color or contains a precipitate.
Adverse Reactions: NTZ is well tolerated, with only occasional mild transient stinging on instillation.
Dosage and Administration: Intranasally by spray, dropper, or tampon.
How Supplied: Bottles of 30 ml (1 fl oz) with dropper (NDC 0024-1375-01)
Unbreakable plastic squeeze bottles of 22.5 ml (NDC 0024-1377-02)
Ample air space above the liquid in the spray bottle assures most efficient operation.

pHisoDerm®

Description: pHisoDerm, sudsing emollient skin cleanser, is a unique liquid emulsion containing Sodium Octoxynol-3 Sulfonate, White Petrolatum, Water, Petrolatum and Lanolin and Lanolin Alcohol, Sodium Benzoate, Octoxynol-1, Methylcellulose, and Lactic Acid. pHisoDerm contains no perfumes and irritating alkali. Its pH value, unlike that of soap, lies within the pH range of normal skin.
Actions: pHisoDerm is well tolerated and can be used frequently by those persons whose skin may be irritated by the use of soap or other alkaline cleansers, or by those who are sensitive to the fatty acids contained in soap. pHisoDerm contains an effective detergent for removing soil and acts as an active emulsifier of all types of oil—animal, vegetable, and min-

eral. It is a useful cleanser for the skin, hair, and scalp.
pHisoDerm produces suds when used with any kind of water—hard or soft, hot or cold (even cold sea water)—at any temperature and under acid, alkaline, or neutral conditions.
pHisoDerm deposits a fine film of lanolin cholesterols and petrolatum on the skin during the washing process and, thereby, helps protect against the dryness that soap can cause.
Indications: A sudsing emollient cleanser for use on skin, hair, and scalp of infants, children, and adults.
Useful for removal of ointments, cosmetics, and hair preparations from the skin and scalp.
Directions: For external use only.
HANDS. Squeeze a few drops of pHisoDerm into the palm, add a little water, and work up a lather. Rinse thoroughly.
FACE. After washing your hands, squeeze a small amount of pHisoDerm into the palm or onto a small sponge or washcloth, and work up a lather by adding a little water. Massage the suds onto the face for approximately one minute. Rinse thoroughly. Avoid getting suds into the eyes.
BATHING. First wet the body. Work a small amount of pHisoDerm into a lather with hands or a soft wet sponge, gradually adding small amounts of water to make more lather. When using a washcloth use more pHisoDerm. Spread the lather over all parts of the body. Rinse thoroughly.
SHAMPOOING. First wet the hair. Apply a small amount of pHisoDerm (depending on the amount and length of hair) for the initial shampoo, rubbing thoroughly. Avoid getting suds into the eyes. Copious suds may not be produced by this preliminary washing. Rinse thoroughly. Repeat the process, using the same amount or an even smaller amount of pHisoDerm. This second shampoo will produce copious suds. Rinse thoroughly and dry.
BABY BATHING. First wet the baby's body. Work a small amount of pHisoDerm into a lather with hands or a soft wet sponge, gradually adding small amounts of water to make more lather. Spread the lather over all parts of the baby's body, including the head. Avoid getting suds into the baby's eyes. Wash the diaper area last. Be sure to carefully cleanse all folds and creases. Rinse thoroughly. Pat the baby dry with a soft towel.
Caution: pHisoDerm suds that get into the eyes accidentally during washing should be rinsed out promptly with a sufficient amount of water.
pHisoDerm is intended for external use only. pHisoDerm should not be poured into measuring cups, medicine bottles, or similar containers since it may be mistaken for baby formula or medications. If swallowed, pHisoDerm may cause gastrointestinal irritation.
pHisoDerm should not be used on persons with sensitivity to any of its components.

How Supplied: pHisoDerm is supplied in three formulations for regular, dry, and oily skin. It is packaged in sanitary squeeze bottles of 5 ounces and 1 pint. The regular formula is also supplied in squeeze bottles of 9 ounces and plastic bottles of 1 gallon.
Dry Skin Formula: A high emolliency cleansing formulation that is especially suitable for people with dry skin. It can also help prevent dry skin chapping. This formula can be used for bathing babies, children, and adults to keep skin naturally soft and supple.
Oily Skin Formula: A low emolliency cleansing formulation designed for skin that is especially oily. This formulation is not recommended for use in bathing babies.
Also available—pHisoDerm–Fresh Scent in squeeze bottles of 5, 9, and 16 ounces.

WinGel®
Liquid and Tablets

Description: Each teaspoon (5 ml) of liquid and each tablet contain a specially processed, short polymer, hexitol stabilized aluminum-magnesium hydroxide equivalent to 180 mg of aluminum hydroxide and 160 mg of magnesium hydroxide. Mint flavored. Smooth, easy-to-chew tablets.
Action: Antacid.
Indications: An antacid for the relief of acid indigestion, heartburn, and sour stomach.
Warnings: *Adults and children over 6*—Patients should not take more than eight teaspoonfuls or eight tablets in a 24-hour period or use the maximum dosage of the product for more than 2 weeks, except under the advice and supervision of a physician.
Absorption of other drugs may be interfered with by the aluminum in the product.
Drug Interaction Precautions: This product should not be taken if the patient is presently taking a prescription antibiotic drug containing any form of tetracycline.
Dosage and Administration: *Adults and children over 6*—1 to 2 teaspoonfuls or 1 to 2 tablets up to four times daily, or as directed by a physician.
Professional Labeling: For the symptomatic relief of hyperacidity associated with the diagnosis of peptic ulcer, gastritis, peptic esophagitis, gastric hyperacidity, and hiatal hernia.
Acid Neutralization: WINGEL Liquid 23.2 mEq/2 teaspoons; WINGEL Tablets 24.6 mEq/2 tablets.
How Supplied: Liquid—bottles of 6 fl oz (NDC 0024-2247-03) and 12 fl oz (NDC 0024-2247-05).
Tablets—boxes of 50 (NDC 0024-2249-05) and 100 (NDC 0024-2249-06).

Products are cross-indexed by generic and chemical names in the
YELLOW SECTION

Wyeth Laboratories
Division of American Home
Products Corporation
P.O. BOX 8299
PHILADELPHIA, PA 19101

ALUDROX®
Antacid
(alumina and magnesia)
ORAL SUSPENSION • TABLETS

Composition: Nonconstipating, non-cathartic, effective and palatable antacid containing, in each 5 ml. teaspoonful of suspension, 307 mg. of aluminum hydroxide as a gel, and 103 mg. of magnesium hydroxide. Each tablet contains 233 mg. aluminum hydroxide as a dried gel and 83 mg. magnesium hydroxide. Sodium content is 0.07 mEq per tablet and 0.05 mEq per 5 ml suspension.

Indications: For the symptomatic relief of hyperacidity associated with the diagnosis of peptic ulcer, gastritis, peptic esophagitis, gastric hyperacidity, and hiatal hernia.

Dosage and Administration: Two tablets or 2 teaspoonfuls (10 ml.) of suspension every four hours, or as required. Suspension may be followed by a sip of water if desired. Tablets are designed to be chewed with or without water. Two ALUDROX tablets have the capacity to neutralize 23 mEq of acid; 10 ml. of ALUDROX suspension have the capacity to neutralize 28 mEq of acid.

Drug Interaction Precautions: This product must not be taken if the patient is presently taking a prescription antibiotic drug containing any form of tetracycline.

How Supplied: *Oral Suspension,* bottles of 12 fluidounces.
Tablets, boxes of 100; each tablet is sealed in cellophane so that a day's supply can be conveniently carried.

AMPHOJEL®
Antacid
(aluminum hydroxide gel)
SUSPENSION • TABLETS

Composition: *Suspension*—Each 5 ml. teaspoonful contains 320 mg. of aluminum hydroxide as a gel, and not more than 0.3 mEq of sodium. *Tablets* contain a dried gel. The 0.3 Gm. (5 grain) strength is equivalent to about 1 teaspoonful of the suspension and the 0.6 Gm. (10 grain) strength is equivalent to about 2 teaspoonfuls.

Indications: For the symptomatic relief of hyperacidity associated with the diagnosis of peptic ulcer, gastritis, peptic esophagitis, gastric hyperacidity, and hiatal hernia.

Dosage: *Suspension*—two teaspoonfuls followed by a sip of water if desired, five or six times daily, between meals and at bedtime. 2 teaspoonfuls have the capacity to neutralize 13 mEq of acid. *Tablets*—Two tablets of the 0.3 Gm. strength, or one tablet of the 0.6 Gm. strength, five or six times daily between meals and at bedtime. 2 tablets have the capacity to neutralize 18 mEq of acid.

Precaution: May cause constipation.
Drug Interaction Precautions: This product must not be taken if the patient is presently taking a prescription antibiotic drug containing any form of tetracycline.

How Supplied: *Suspension*—Peppermint flavored; without flavor—bottles of 12 fluidounces. *Tablets*—a convenient auxiliary dosage form—0.3 Gm. (5 gr.), bottles of 100; 0.6 Gm. (10 gr.), boxes of 100.

COLLYRIUM
with ephedrine
SOOTHING EYE DROPS

Description: A neutral solution of boric acid and borax, containing 0.4% antipyrine, 0.1% ephedrine and not more than 0.002% thimerosal (mercury derivative).

Indications: Soothes, cleanses and refreshes tired or irritated eyes; eyes smarting from wind, sun glare, smog and minor irritants; eyes irritated by prolonged reading or television viewing or by allergies such as hay fever.

Dosage and Administration: Two or three drops in each eye as required.

Warning: If irritation persists or increases, patients are advised to discontinue use and consult physician. Dropper tip should not be allowed to touch any surface since this may contaminate solution. Do not use in conjunction with a wetting solution for contact lens or other eye lotions containing polyvinyl alcohol. Container should be kept tightly closed and stored at room temperature, approx. 77°F (25°C).

How Supplied: Bottles of ½ fl. oz. with built-in eye dropper.

COLLYRIUM
a neutral borate
solution with antipyrine
SOOTHING EYE LOTION

Description: Containing 0.4% antipyrine, boric acid, borax and not more than 0.002% thimerosal (mercury derivative).

Indications: Soothes, cleanses and refreshes tired or irritated eyes resulting from long use, as in reading or close work or due to exposure to sun, strong light, irritation from dust, wind, etc.

Dosage and Administration: Patients are advised to rinse cup with clean water immediately before and after each use, and avoid contamination of rim and interior surface of cup. The half-filled cup should be pressed tightly to the eye to prevent the escape of the liquid, and the head tilted well backward. Eyelids should be opened wide and eyeball rotated to insure thorough bathing with the lotion.

Warning: If irritation persists or increases, patients are advised to discontinue use and consult physician. Do not use in conjunction with a wetting solution for contact lens or other eye lotions containing polyvinyl alcohol. Container should be kept tightly closed and kept at room temperature, approx. 77°F.

How Supplied: Bottles of 6 fl. oz. with eyecup.

SMA®
Iron fortified
infant formula
**READY–TO–FEED
CONCENTRATED LIQUID
POWDER**

Breast milk is the preferred feeding for newborns. Infant formula is intended to replace or supplement breast milk when breast-feeding is not possible or is inadequate, or when mothers elect not to breast-feed.

SMA® is unique among prepared formulas for its fat blend, whey-dominated protein composition, amino acid pattern and mineral content. SMA®, utilizing a hybridized safflower (oleic) oil, became the first infant formula offering fat and calcium absorption equal to that of human milk, with a physiologic level of linoleic acid. Thus, the fat blend in SMA® provides a ready source of energy, helps protect infants against neonatal tetany and produces a ratio of Vitamin E to polyunsaturated fatty acids (linoleic acid) more than adequate to prevent hemolytic anemia.

By combining demineralized whey with skimmed cow's milk, SMA® adjusts the protein content to within the range of human milk, reverses the whey-protein to casein ratio of cow's milk so that it is like that of human milk, and reduces the mineral content to a physiologic level. The resultant 60:40 whey-protein to casein ratio provides protein nutrition superior to a casein-dominated formula. In addition, the essential amino acids, including cystine, are present in amounts close to those of human milk. So the protein in SMA® is of high biologic value.

The physiologic mineral content makes possible a low renal solute load which helps protect the functionally immature infant kidney, increases expendable water reserves and helps protect against dehydration.

Use of lactose as the carbohydrate results in a physiologic stool flora and a low stool pH, decreasing the incidence of perianal dermatitis.

Ingredients: SMA® Concentrated Liquid or Ready-to-Feed. Water; nonfat milk; demineralized (electrodialyzed) whey; lactose; oleo, coconut, oleic (safflower), and soybean oils; soy lecithin, calcium carrageenan. *Minerals:* Potassium bicarbonate; calcium chloride and citrate; potassium chloride; sodium citrate; ferrous sulfate; sodium bicarbonate; zinc, cupric, and manganese sulfates. *Vitamins:* Ascorbic acid, dl-alpha tocopheryl acetate, niacinamide, vitamin A palmitate, calcium pantothenate, thiamine hydrochloride, riboflavin, pyridoxine hydrochloride, beta-carotene, folic acid, phytonadione, activated 7-dehydrocholesterol, biotin, cyanocobalamin.

SMA® Powder. Nonfat milk; demineralized (electrodialyzed) whey; lactose; oleo, coconut, oleic (safflower), and soybean oils; soy lecithin.
Minerals: Calcium chloride; sodium bicarbonate; calcium hydroxide; ferrous

Continued on next page

Wyeth—Cont.

sulfate; potassium hydroxide and bicarbonate; potassium chloride; zinc, cupric, and manganese sulfates. *Vitamins:* Ascorbic acid, dl-alpha tocopheryl acetate, niacinamide, vitamin A palmitate, calcium pantothenate, thiamine hydrochloride, riboflavin, pyridoxine hydrochloride, beta-carotene, folic acid, phytonadione, activated 7-dehydrocholesterol, biotin, cyanocobalamin.

PROXIMATE ANALYSIS
at 20 calories per fluidounce
READY-TO-FEED, POWDER, and CONCENTRATED LIQUID:

	(w/v)
Fat	3.6%
Carbohydrate	7.2%
Protein	1.5%
60% Lactalbumin (whey protein)	0.9%
40% Casein	0.6%
Ash	0.25%
Crude Fiber	None
Total Solids	12.6%
Calories/fl. oz.	20

Vitamins, Minerals: In normal dilution, each quart contains 2500 I.U. vitamin A, 400 I.U. vitamin D_3, 9 I.U. vitamin E, 55 mcg. vitamin K_1, 0.67 mg. vitamin B_1 (thiamine), 1 mg. vitamin B_2 (riboflavin), 55 mcg. vitamin C (ascorbic acid), 0.4 mg. vitamin B_6 (pyridoxine hydrochloride), 1 mcg. vitamin B_{12}, 9.5 mg. equivalents niacin, 2 mg. pantothenic acid, 50 mcg. folic acid, 14 mcg. biotin, 130 mg. choline, 420 mg. calcium, 312 mg. phosphorus, 50 mg. magnesium, 142 mg. sodium, 530 mg. potassium, 350 mg. chloride, 12 mg. iron, 0.45 mg. copper, 3.5 mg. zinc, 150 mcg. manganese, 65 mcg. iodine.

Preparation: *Ready-to-Feed* (8 and 32 fl. oz. cans of 20 calories per fluidounce formula)—shake can, open and pour into previously sterilized nursing bottle; attach nipple and feed. Cover opened can and immediately store in refrigerator. Use contents of can within 48 hours of opening.
Powder—For normal dilution supplying 20 calories per fluidounce, use 1 scoop (or 1 standard tablespoonful) of powder, packed and leveled, to 2 fluidounces of water. For larger amount of formula, use $\frac{1}{4}$ standard measuring cup of powder, packed and leveled, to 8 fluidounces (1 cup) of water. Three of these portions make 26 fluidounces of formula.
Concentrated Liquid—For normal dilution supplying 20 calories per fluidounce, use equal amounts of SMA® liquid and water.

How Supplied: *Ready-to-Feed*—presterilized and premixed, 32 fluidounce (1 quart) cans, cases of 6; 8 fluidounce cans, case of 24 (4 carriers of 6 cans). *Powder*—1 pound cans with measuring scoop, cases of 12. *Concentrated Liquid*—13 fluidounce cans, cases of 24.

Also Available: SMA® lo-iron. For those who appreciate the particular advantages of SMA®, the infant formula closest in composition to mother's milk, but who sometimes need or wish to recommend a formula that does not contain a high level of iron, now there is SMA® lo-iron with all the benefits of regular SMA® but with a reduced level of iron of 1.4 mg. per quart. Infants should receive supplemental dietary iron from an outside source to meet daily requirements. *Concentrated Liquid, 13 fl. oz. cans, cases of 24. Powder, 1 pound cans with measuring scoop, cases of 12. Ready-to-Feed, 32 fl. oz. cans, cases of 6.*
Preparation of the standard 20 calories per fluidounce formula of SMA® lo-iron is the same as SMA® iron fortified given above.

NURSOY® (soy protein formula), for infants with special feeding needs, soy protein replaces the cow's milk protein in the formula. Does *not* contain corn syrup solid derivatives. *Concentrated Liquid, 13 fl. oz. cans, cases of 24. Ready-to-Feed, 32 fl. oz. cans, cases of 6.*
Concentrated Liquid, 13 fl. oz. cans, cases of 24. Ready-to-Feed, 32 fl. oz. cans, cases of 6.
Preparation of the standard 20 calories per fluidounce formula of NURSOY Ready-to-Feed and Concentrated Liquid is the same as for SMA® Ready-to-Feed and Concentrated Liquid respectively given above.

SIMECO®
Antacid—Antiflatulent
(aluminum hydroxide gel, magnesium hydroxide, simethicone)
SUSPENSION

Composition: Each teaspoonful (5 ml) contains aluminum hydroxide gel equivalent to 365 mg of dried gel, USP, 300 mg of magnesium hydroxide and 30 mg of simethicone. Sodium content is 0.3 mEq-0.6 mEq per teaspoonful. High potency and low dose are provided by high concentration of antacid per teaspoonful.

Indications: For the symptomatic relief of hyperacidity associated with the diagnosis of peptic ulcer, gastritis, peptic esophagitis, gastric hyperacidity and hiatal hernia. To relieve the symptoms of gas.

Dosage and Administration: Usually: 1 or 2 teaspoonfuls undiluted or with a little water to be taken 3 or 4 times daily between meals and at bedtime. 5 ml SIMECO suspension neutralizes 22 mEq of acid.

Drug Interaction Precautions: Alumina-containing antacids should not be used concomitantly with any form of tetracycline therapy.

How Supplied: Suspension—Cool mint flavor, available in 12 fl. oz. plastic bottles.

WYANOIDS®
Hemorrhoidal Suppositories

Description: Each suppository contains 15 mg extract belladonna (0.19 mg equiv. total alkaloids), 3 mg ephedrine sulfate, zinc oxide, boric acid, bismuth oxyiodide, bismuth subcarbonate, and peruvian balsam in cocoa butter and beeswax. Wyeth Wyanoids have an unusual "torpedo" design which facilitates insertion and insures retention.

Indications: For the temporary relief of pain and itching of hemorrhoidal tissue in many cases.

Warning: Not to be used by persons having glaucoma or excessive pressure within the eye, by elderly persons (where undiagnosed glaucoma or excessive pressure within the eye occurs most frequently), or by children under 6 years of age, unless directed by a physician. Discontinue use if blurring of vision, rapid pulse, or dizziness occurs. Do not exceed recommended dosage. Not for frequent or prolonged use. If dryness of the mouth occurs, decrease dosage. If eye pain occurs, discontinue use and see your physician immediately as this may indicate undiagnosed glaucoma. In case of rectal bleeding, consult physician promptly.

Usual Dosage: One suppository twice daily for six days.

Directions: Remove wrapper of suppository and insert suppository rectally with gentle pressure, pointed end first. Use preferably upon arising and at bedtime.

How Supplied: Boxes of 12.

Also Available: Wyanoid® Hemorrhoidal Ointment.
The ointment contains zinc oxide, boric acid, ephedrine sulfate, benzocaine and peruvian balsam in a soothing emollient base. Tubes of 1 ounce with applicator.

W. F. Young, Inc.
111 LYMAN STREET
SPRINGFIELD, MA 01103

ABSORBINE JR.

Active Ingredient: Acetone, Menthol, Wormwood, Chloroxylenol and Thymol formulated with essential oils and tinctures.

Indications: For fast relief from sore, aching muscles due to overexertion.

Actions: Absorbine Jr. rubbed on the skin dilates peripheral blood vessels to speed fresh invigorating blood flow to the point of pain.

Warnings: Keep out of the reach of children. Extremely flammable. Keep away from fire, sparks and heated surfaces. For external use only.

Symptoms and Treatment of Oral Overdosage: In case of accidental ingestion contact a physician immediately.

Dosage and Administration: Apply Absorbine Jr. full strength and massage gently 3 or 4 times daily. For severe strains see your doctor.

How Supplied: Available in 1 oz., 2 oz., 4 oz. applicator bottles. Also available in 12 oz. non-applicator bottle.
[*Shown in Product Identification Section*]

Products are cross-indexed by

generic and chemical names

in the

YELLOW SECTION

Youngs Drug Products Corp.

P.O. BOX 385
865 CENTENNIAL AVENUE
PISCATAWAY, NJ 08854

Sole Distributors for products manufactured by HOLLAND-RANTOS COMPANY, INC.

KOROMEX® CONTRACEPTIVE FOAM

Description: KOROMEX CONTRACEPTIVE FOAM is a pure white delicately fragranced aerosol foam. It is highly spermicidal, non-staining, non-greasy.
Composition: Active ingredient is nonoxynol 9 12.5% in a base of water, propylene glycol, propellant 114, Isopropyl alcohol, Laureth-4, cetyl alcohol, propellant 12, PEG-50 stearate and fragrance.
Action: Spermicidal.
Indication: Contraception.
Side Effects: Should sensitivity to the ingredients or irritation of the vagina or penis develop, the patient should discontinue use and be instructed to consult a physician.
Warning: Contents under pressure. Do not puncture or incinerate container. Do not expose to heat or store at temperatures above 120° F. KEEP OUT OF REACH OF CHILDREN.
Dosage and Administration: One applicatorful of KOROMEX CONTRACEPTIVE FOAM should be inserted prior to each intercourse.
The patient may have intercourse any time up to one hour after the foam has been inserted. If intercourse is repeated, another applicatorful of the KOROMEX FOAM should be inserted.
When KOROMEX CONTRACEPTIVE FOAM is used, a cleansing douche is not essential. However, if a douche is recommended or desired, the patient should be instructed to wait at least 6 hours after intercourse.
How Supplied: KOROMEX CONTRACEPTIVE FOAM 22 gms. (0.78 oz.) can with applicator and purse for storage. Refills are available in 22 gm (0.78 oz.) and 55 gm (1.94 oz.).

KOROMEX^{II} CONTRACEPTIVE CREAM

Composition: KOROMEX^{II} CONTRACEPTIVE CREAM... Pearly-white in appearance... for those patients whose aesthetic preference is for a preparation with a lesser lubrication factor. Active ingredient is Octoxynol 3.0%—in a base of purified water, propylene glycol, stearic acid, sorbitan stearate, polysorbate 60, boric acid and fragrance. pH buffered and adjusted to 4.5.
Indications: Contraception and vaginal lubrication in conjunction with a vaginal diaphragm.
Warning: Keep this and all medication out of the reach of children.
Administration and Dosage: Approximately 1 to 2 teaspoonsful of KOROMEX^{II} CONTRACEPTIVE CREAM is placed on the dome surface of the diaphragm coming in direct contact with the cervix. The cream is then spread over the rubber and around the rim.
How Supplied: #20 KOROMEX^{II} C/C CREAM with measured dose applicator (2.65 oz.—75 grams), #25 KOROMEX^{II} C/C CREAM refill (2.65 oz.—75 grams), #225 KOROMEX^{II} C/C CREAM large refill (4.51 oz.—128 grams).

KOROMEX^{II} CONTRACEPTIVE JELLY

Composition: KOROMEX^{II} CONTRACEPTIVE JELLY contains the active ingredient Octoxynol 1.0%—in a base of purified water, propylene glycol, cellulose gum, boric acid, sorbitol, starch, simethicone and fragrance. pH buffered and adjusted to 4.5. Pleasantly scented to meet the patient's aesthetic requirements. Homogenized to help eliminate the primary patient complaint of messiness.
Indications: Contraception and vaginal lubrication in conjunction with a vaginal diaphragm.
Warning: Keep this and all medication out of the reach of children.
Administration and Dosage: Approximately 1 to 2 teaspoonsful of KOROMEX^{II} CONTRACEPTIVE JELLY is placed on the dome surface of the diaphragm coming in direct contact with the cervix. The jelly is then spread over the rubber and around the rim.
How Supplied: #10 KOROMEX^{II} C/C JELLY with measured dose applicator (2.85 oz.—81 grams), #15 KOROMEX^{II} C/C JELLY refill (2.85 oz.—81 grams), #115 KOROMEX^{II} C/C JELLY—large refill (4.76 oz.—135 grams).

KOROMEX^{II}-A CONTRACEPTIVE JELLY

Composition: Active ingredient Nonoxynol-9 2% in a base of propylene glycol, boric acid, sorbitol, cellulose gum, starch, simethicone, purified water, and fragrance. pH 4.5
Indications: Contraception and vaginal lubricant.
Action and Uses: KOROMEX^{II}-A CONTRACEPTIVE JELLY provides contraception immediately after insertion. It may, however, be introduced up to one hour before intercourse.
Side Effects: Should sensitivity to the ingredients or irritation of the vagina, or penis develop, discontinue use and consult your physician.
Warning: Keep this and all medication out of the reach of children.
Administration and Dosage: As directed by physician.
How Supplied: In 4.76 oz. (135 grams) tubes with applicator and 4.76 oz. (135 grams) refill tubes.

NYLMERATE^{II}® Solution Concentrate

Composition: SD alcohol 23A 50% v/v, purified water, acetic acid, boric acid, polysorbate 20, nonoxynol-9, sodium acetate, FD & C Blue #1, D & C Yellow #10.
Action and Uses: A cleansing acidified buffered vaginal irrigant. In recommended dilution pH is 4.5, thereby aiding in adjusting the vaginal pH. Helps relieve and combats offensive odors and pruritus by removing accumulated discharges.
Useful as an adjunct in specific vaginal therapy or routine vaginal cleansing.
Directions: One tablespoonful or ½ capful (filled to the top line inside of cap) to one quart of warm water. Do not add solution until the water is first added to the douche bag, then mix thoroughly.
Warning: Do not use more than twice weekly unless directed to do so by the physician. Do not use full strength. If irritation occurs, discontinue use.
How Supplied: 16 fluid oz. (473 ml) in a plastic bottle with measuring cap.

TRANSI-LUBE®
The Sexual Foaming Lubricant

Description: TRANSI-LUBE is a sexual lubricant that closely approximates the normal female transudate to enhance sexual pleasure. This medically oriented lubricant has the mild taste and aroma of strawberries. It is non-greasy, non-staining, non-irritating, maintains its lubricity for a long period of time, and is aesthetically acceptable to men and women. TRANSI-LUBE IS NOT A CONTRACEPTIVE.
Indications For Use: To enhance sexual pleasure. For improved sexual communication and response regardless of any physical or psychological disability.
Note: TRANSI-LUBE is not intended as a body lubricant. Genital play or sexual arousal is pleasantly enhanced when both partners use TRANSI-LUBE.
Contains: Purified water, isobutane propane, propylene glycol, sorbitol, PEG 14M, ceteth 10, methyl and propyl parabens, citric acid and flavor.
Side Effects: Should sensitivity to the ingredients or irritation of the vaginal area or penis develop, discontinue use. Due to the propellant, some coldness or irritation may be felt if placed directly on the penis or vagina. It is preferable to place the product on the hand, waiting 10 to 15 seconds before application.
Caution: Do not insert nozzle into the vagina or any body oriface for direct application.
Warning: FLAMMABLE—do not use near flame or while smoking. Contents under pressure. Do not puncture or incinerate. Do not store above 120° F. Keep out of reach of children. Use only as directed. Intentional misuse by deliberately concentrating and inhaling the contents can be harmful or fatal.
Packaging: Containers of 1.76 oz. (50 grams).

Products are cross-indexed by generic and chemical names in the
YELLOW SECTION

Educational Material

Part 1 contains a listing of books, booklets, brochures and other materials that can be obtained by contacting manufacturers listed in this edition.

Part 2 provides you with the names and addresses of organizations that can be contacted if you need help for a specific health problem.

Part 1—MANUFACTURERS' SERVICE MATERIAL

Beiersdorf, Inc.
Product Profile   Free
Information Sheets describing Eucerin, Aquaphor, Mediplast, Gelocast, Coverlet Eye Occlusor

Fleetwood Company
Wate-On's Guide to Successful Weight-Gaining   Free
Brochure describing methods of gaining weight

Health Care Industries   Free
Cosanyl and Cosanyl-DM   (maximum of 2)
Literature describing products

Hoechst-Roussel Pharmaceuticals Inc.
What You Should Know About Hemorrhoids and Fissures   Free
Pamphlet describing these conditions, with instructions on self-care and when to consult a physician
Hints on How to Avoid Constipation   Free
Pamphlet on ways to prevent and treat constipation

Johnson & Johnson Baby Products Company
Sun Hazards and Sun Sense Booklet   Free

Loma Linda Foods
Feeding Your New Baby During Infancy   Free
12 page booklet on Soyalac & i-Soyalac Infant Formula with baby's record chart
Here's New Information about an Old Solution for Sensitive Babies   Free
4 page brochure on Soyalac & i-Soyalac; comparative nutrients content chart

Optimox, Inc.

Optivite for Women   Free
Brochure containing information on the products: indications, mechanisms of action and complete
formula; fully referenced

Premenstrual Blues   Free
Booklet explaining the definition, classification, pathophysiology of premenstrual tension in lay terms
and its management by diet, exercise and nutritional supplements

Reed & Carnrick

Questions and Answers about Treating Pediculosis in the Patient's Environment   Free
How to eliminate lice from clothing, bedding and other household items

Questions and Answers about Head Lice   Free
How to recognize head lice; how they are spread; how to treat head lice

Requa Manufacturing Company, Inc.

Who Ever Heard of Charcoal for Intestinal Distress?   Free
Booklet

Effects of Orally Administered Activated Charcoal on Intestinal Gas   Free
Clinical study reprint from American Journal of Gastroenterology, March 1981, by Dr. Raymond Hall

Rowell Laboratories, Inc.

What Can You Do About a Common Problem: Pruritus Ani (Anal Itching)   Free
Booklet

The Medical Facts About Hemorrhoids (Piles)   Free
Booklet

Constipation: What you Should Know about It . . . and What You Can Do To Correct It   Free
Booklet

Living a Normal Lifestyle, Despite Ulcerative Colitis   Free
Booklet

Schering Corporation

The ABC's of Muscle-Joint Pain and Inflammation   Free
Pamphlet describing the types of inflammatory muscle-joint diseases and their general treatment

Athlete's Foot, Jock Itch   Free
Pamphlet describing the causes, symptoms and treatment of athlete's foot and jock itch

Choices on Birth Control   Free
Pamphlet describing the male and female reproductive systems and the major advantages and disadvantages of various methods of birth control; Available in English and Spanish

Facts About Allergy   Free
Pamphlet describing the causes, symptoms and treatment of allergy

Psoriasis   Free
Pamphlet answering commonly asked questions on psoriasis

SugarLo Company

Why LactAid - The Problem and the Answer   Free
Folder, pocket size, giving basic information about lactose intolerance and the use of LactAid to
alleviate problem

Thought Technology Ltd.

Relaxation, Stress Reduction, Biofeedback, etc.   Free
Books on their application in Athletics, Education, Medicine and personal well-being; pamphlet describing various books is free

Relaxation, Stress Reduction, Biofeedback, Autogenic Training, Progressive Relaxation, etc.   Free
Tapes describing their application in Athletics, Education, Medicine and personal well-being; pamphlet describing tapes is free

Learn Relaxation - Stress Reduction   Free
Pamphlet describes GSR 2 and GSR/TEMP 2 Biofeedback Relaxation/Education/Athletic Systems.

Part 2—HEALTH ASSOCIATIONS AND ORGANIZATIONS

**Alcohol and Drug Problems
Association of North America**
1101 15th Street, N.W.
Washington, DC 20005

Alcoholics Anonymous
P.O. Box 459 Grand Central Station
New York, NY 10163

**Alzheimer's Disease and
Related Disorders Association**
292 Madison Avenue, 8th floor
New York, NY 10017

American Anorexia Nervosa Assoc.
133 Cedar Lane
Teaneck, NJ 07666

**American Association of
Poison Control Centers**
University of California
225 Dickinson Street
San Diego, CA 92103

American Brittle Bone Society
1415 E. Marlton Pike
Cherry Hill, NJ 08077

American Cancer Society
777 Third Avenue
New York, NY 10017

**American Council
on Alcohol Problems**
6955 University Avenue
Des Moines, IA 50311

American Dental Association
211 E. Chicago Avenue
Chicago, IL 60611

American Diabetes Association
2 Park Avenue
New York, NY 10016

American Dietetic Association
430 North Michigan Avenue
Chicago, IL 60611

**American Foundation
for the Blind, Inc.**
15 W. 16th Street
New York, NY 10011

American Heart Association
7320 Greenville Avenue
Dallas, TX 75231

American Lung Association
1740 Broadway
New York, NY 10019

American Medical Association
535 North Dearborn Street
Chicago, IL 60610

American National Red Cross
17th and D Streets, N.W.
Washington, DC 20006

American Osteopathic Association
212 E. Ohio Street
Chicago, IL 60611

**American Osteopathic Hospital
Assoc.**
930 Busse Highway
Park Ridge, IL 60068

**American Physical Fitness
Research Institute**
824 Moraga Drive
Bel Air, CA 90049

American Physical Therapy Assoc.
1156 15th Street, N.W.
Washington, DC 20005

**American Society
of Internal Medicine**
2550 M Street, N.W., Suite 620
Washington, DC 20037

American Venereal Disease Assoc.
Box 22349
San Diego, CA 92122

Arthritis Foundation
3400 Peachtree Road, N.E.
Suite 1101
Atlanta, GA 30326

**Asthma and Allergy Foundation of
America**
19 W. 44 Street
New York, NY 10036

Center for Sickle Cell Disease
2121 Georgia Avenue, N.W.
Washington, DC 20059

Citizens Alliance for VD Awareness
222 W. Adams Street
Chicago, IL 60606

Corrective Eye Care Foundation
435 N. Michigan Ave., Suite 1717
Chicago, IL 60611

Cystic Fibrosis Foundation
6000 Executive Blvd., Suite 309
Rockville, MD 20852

**The Epilepsy Foundation
of America**
1828 L Street, N.W., Suite 406
Washington, DC 20036

Food and Drug Administration
Office of Public Affairs
5600 Fishers Lane
Rockville, MD 20857

Food and Nutrition Board
National Academy of Sciences
2101 Constitution Avenue, N.W.
Washington, DC 20418

Foundation for Child Development
345 E. 46th Street
New York, NY 10017

Institute of Rehabilitation Medicine
NYU Medical Center
400 East 34th Street
New York, NY 10016

Joslin Diabetes Center
1 Joslin Place
Boston, MA 02215

Juvenile Diabetes Foundation
23 East 26th Street
New York, NY 10010

Leukemia Society of America
800 Second Avenue
New York, NY 10017

**March of Dimes
Birth Defects Foundation**
1275 Mamaroneck Avenue
White Plains, NY 10605

**Medic Alert Foundation,
International**
1000 N. Palm
Turlock, CA 95380

Muscular Dystrophy Association
810 7th Avenue
New York, NY 10019

**National Association of Anorexia
Nervosa & Associated Disorders**
550 Frontage Road, Suite 2020
Northfield, IL 60093

National Association of the Deaf
814 Thayer Avenue
Silver Spring, MD 20910

**National Association
of Rehabilitation Facilities**
5530 Wisconsin Avenue, Suite 995
Washington, DC 20015

**National Association
for Sickle Cell Disease**
3460 Wilshire Blvd., Suite 1012
Los Angeles, CA 90010

National Council on Alcoholism
733 Third Avenue
New York, NY 10017

National Federation of the Blind
1800 Johnson Street
Baltimore, MD 21230

**National Foundation
for Ileitis and Colitis**
295 Madison Avenue
New York, NY 10017

National Health Council
70 W. 40th Street
New York, NY 10018

National Hemophilia Foundation
19 W. 34th Street
New York, NY 10001

**National Institute on Alcohol Abuse
and Alcoholism**
National Clearinghouse for
Alcohol Information
P.O. Box 2345
Rockville, MD 20852

National Institute on Drug Abuse
National Clearinghouse
for Drug Abuse Information
P.O. Box 416
Kensington, MD 20975

National Institutes of Health
9000 Rockville Pike
Bethesda, MD 20205
  National Cancer Institute
  National Eye Institute
  National Heart, Lung, and
    Blood Institute
  National Institute of Allergy and
    Infectious Diseases
  National Institute of Arthritis,
    Diabetes, Digestive and Kidney
    Diseases
  National Institute of Child Health
    and Human Development
  National Institute of Dental
    Research
  National Institute of·Environmental
    Health Sciences
  National Institute of General
    Medical Sciences
  National Institute of Neurological
    and Communicative Disorders
    and Strokes
  National Institute on Aging

**National Interagency Council
on Smoking and Health**
7320 Greenville Avenue
Dallas, TX 75231

National Kidney Foundation
2 Park Avenue
New York, NY 10016

National Mental Health Association
1800 N. Kent Street
Rosslyn, VA 22209

National Multiple Sclerosis Society
205 East 42nd Street
New York, NY 10017

National Parkinson Foundation
1501 N.W. 9th Avenue
Miami, FL 33136

National Rehabilitation Association
633 S. Washington Street
Alexandria, VA 22314

National Society for Autistic Children
1234 Massachusetts Avenue, N.W.
Suite 1017
Washington, DC 20005

**National Society to Prevent
Blindness**
79 Madison Avenue
New York, NY 10016

**National Spinal Cord Injury
Foundation**
369 Elliot Street
Newton Upper Falls, MA 02164

Nutrition Foundation, Inc.
489 Fifth Avenue
New York, NY 10017

Office on Smoking and Health
Technical Information Center
1-58 Park Building
Rockville, MD 20857

**Planned Parenthood Federation
of America, Inc.**
810 Seventh Avenue
New York, NY 10019

**United Cerebral Palsy Associations,
Inc.**
66 E. 34th Street
New York, NY 10016

United Ostomy Association
2001 W. Beverly Blvd.
Los Angeles, CA 90057

Venereal Disease Control Division
Centers for Disease Control
1600 Clifton Road
Building 1, Room 2000
Atlanta, GA 30333

**Wellness and Health Activation
Networks**
P.O. Box 923
Vienna, VA 22180

Common Health Problems

A Guide to Self-Treatment

Of the many afflictions that humans are subjected to, most of them are more an inconvenience than a threat to everyday functioning. The common cold, athlete's foot, and many other ills can usually be self-treated with products obtainable without a prescription. If you follow the instructions that accompany these products, most will probably relieve the symptoms and cause no harmful effects. And as the instructions say, if the condition is not helped by the product being used, you should see your doctor.

Acne

Acne is an inflammatory skin disease characterized by pimples, blackheads, and whiteheads. It is caused by increased activity of the sebaceous glands in the skin that normally produce the oils for the proper lubrication of the skin and hair. Teenagers are the most frequent victims of this condition because the large amounts of hormones their bodies produce during this period of growth cause an excess production of oils that become blocked in the pores.

Except in cases of severe acne, which should be treated by a dermatologist, most teenagers treat themselves with one or more of the many products available. These remedies include keratolytic drying and peeling preparations, plain skin cleansers, antibacterials, and vitamin A.

Allergy

The reason you feel so miserable when you have an allergy is that histamine is released in your body in response to the thing you are allergic to. The most common example of allergy is hay fever, which is usually not caused by hay at all, but by pollens from many plants. Dusts, molds, and foods may also contribute to the symptoms—itchy nose, mouth, and throat, watery nose, sneezing, sensitivity to light, headache, irritability, insomnia, and lack of appetite. These symptoms are treated with some of the same preparations used to treat the common cold—decongestants and antihistamines.

Some allergies are so severe that they require treatment by a doctor who specializes in allergies. The doctor builds up the patient's immunity to a particular allergy-causing substance by giving the patient a series of injections of small amounts of the substance.

Asthma, Bronchitis, and Emphysema

These three conditions are sometimes called wheeze diseases because of their effects on the lungs. They may be complicated by bacterial infection, but probably stem from more than one cause, including cigarette smoking and air pollution.

Bronchial asthma may have an allergic basis. The bronchial vessels in the lungs constrict when irritated and make breathing difficult. Bronchodilators, antihistamines, expectorants, and sedatives are some of the agents used to treat this condition.

Bronchitis is similar to asthma in that the bronchioles in the lungs are obstructed by mucus secretions and swollen membranes. Unlike asthma, however, bronchitis is not accompanied by spasm. The condition occurs mostly in middle-aged people, and it is characterized by a cough that brings up thick yellow mucus. Cough medicine containing a decongestant to dilate bronchial passages and an expectorant to loosen mucus can be used for self-treatment. Cough medicine containing a cough suppressant should generally be avoided because the cough is needed to bring up the mucus.

Emphysema is a lung condition in which the structures have deteriorated over the years, sometimes due to chronic bronchitis or bronchial asthma. It is often further aggravated by infections, air pollution, and cigarette smoking. Shortness of breath is the most common symptom. Cough medicine containing a decongestant and expectorant, but not a cough suppressant, helps expel mucus and phlegm from clogged bronchial passages. Bronchodilators may also be used.

Burns and Sunburn

A burn is the result of damage to the skin caused by heat from fire, electricity, chemicals, radioactivity, or friction. Sunburn results from overexposure to ultraviolet light either from a sunlamp or the sun itself. The seriousness of a burn depends on the depth of damage to the skin and the extent of the area involved. A first-degree burn is the least serious, resulting in pain and redness, but no blistering. A second-degree burn causes blisters. A third-degree burn is the most serious because it destroys skin and tissues and, depending on the size of the area of skin burned, may cause shock and other serious problems.

You should limit yourself to treating only first- and second-degree heat burns, and milder forms of sunburn. Some products contain only a local anesthetic to relieve pain, and others contain an antiseptic that is useful for preventing blisters from becoming infected.

The best way to avoid sunburn is to use sunscreen products containing chemicals that filter out the burning rays of the sun.

Take care to reapply them after swimming or if you have been perspiring heavily.

The Common Cold

The most widespread single human illness is the common cold (coryza). Over 100 different viruses can cause this upper respiratory infection, and for years scientists have been trying to find a vaccine to protect against it—to no avail.

The cold virus is spreading by coughing, sneezing, and direct contact. It is capable of living on inanimate objects such as handkerchiefs and eating utensils for hours. A cold usually lasts from two to seven days, but the symptoms—stuffy nose, sniffles, sneezing, and a general uncomfortable feeling—may make you want to seek some relief. There are many products on the market that will make these cold symptoms more tolerable—decongestants, antihistamines, pain relievers, and many others. Of course, if your cold is accompanied by fever, you will need rest and advice from your doctor.

Constipation

Constipation is an abnormally slow movement of feces through the colon, or large intestine. Most people are aware of what is abnormal for them, even though their habits may differ from another person's. Quite often constipation is caused by ignoring a natural urge to defecate because you are too busy doing something else like working or traveling. Any change in customary routine or diet, taking certain drugs, and stress or emotional upset can lead to constipation.

If you feel that your constipation must be treated, there are four basic types of laxatives to choose from: stimulants, salines, bulk formers, and lubricant-softeners. But remember—don't take a laxative if you have abdominal pain, nausea, or vomiting—symptoms that may indicate appendicitis. See your doctor.

Cough

Coughs frequently accompany colds because of congestion in the lungs and throat. The cough is a natural reflex of the body in its effort to get rid of phlegm from the air passages. Sometimes, however, coughing is dry and brings up no phlegm, which only irritates the air passages more.

Both dry and phlegm-producing coughs respond to preparations that contain two basic types of drugs—cough suppressants and expectorants.

Another way to ease a cough is to use a vaporizer or humidifier to raise the moisture content in the sick room; this helps soothe and lubricate dried breathing passages.

Coughs that hang on need the attention of a doctor.

Dandruff

Dandruff is a common problem that is a result of oversecretion of the sebaceous glands. The scaling is sometimes accompanied by itching and inflammation. Severe cases require treatment by a dermatologist.

Products for treatment of dandruff contain keratolytic agents, tars, zinc pyrithione, or selenium sulfide. One of the milder medicated shampoos may be used regularly to keep dandruff under control.

Diaper Rash and Prickly Heat

Diaper rash is an acute inflammation of an infant's buttocks and groin caused by bacteria that decompose urine into ammonia. The ammonia breaks down the natural protective skin oils and irritation results.

Prickly heat, or heat rash, is an acute irritation of the skin caused by blocked sweat ducts. This occurs mostly during hot, humid weather, or when too much clothing causes heavy sweating. This condition can occur in both infants and adults and is characterized by clusters of pinhead-size bumps that burn and itch.

These conditions are treated with one or more of the following agents: protectants that form a cover and/or absorb moisture, antiseptics to inhibit germ growth, healing agents, and antifungal agents.

Diarrhea

Diarrhea is the opposite of constipation. The symptoms include frequent passage of unformed and watery stools, sometimes accompanied by abdominal pain caused by the activity of the colon as it pushes waste matter along too fast. Diarrhea can be caused by bacterial or viral infection, eating spoiled food, or changes in the intestine caused by unfamiliar food and drink. Some drugs, such as antibiotics, can also cause diarrhea.

Most products used to treat diarrhea contain an adsorbant, which binds the bacteria or toxins causing the diarrhea and transports them through the intestines to be excreted. These products may also contain a substance that slows down the action of the intestine.

If diarrhea occurs in an on-again, off-again pattern over an extended period of time, it may be a sign that something is wrong and the help of a doctor is needed.

The Eyes

Redness, tearing or watering, stinging, itching, and swelling or congestion of the eyes when caused by allergy or minor irritation can often be treated with nonprescription products. However, if the condition lingers on, or you have any pain or blurring of vision, or an eye injury, you should promptly visit an eye doctor.

Eye preparations are of three basic types: decongestants (the only ones containing an active drug), artificial tears, and eye washes. People with glaucoma should avoid using any product containing a decongestant.

Feminine Hygiene

Deodorant sprays for application to the exterior vaginal area and various types of douches for internal vaginal use are available.

Fungal Infections: Athlete's Foot, Jock Itch, Ringworm

Athlete's foot infection occurs between the toes and on the sole and heel of the foot. The skin may split and crack, and the primary discomfort is intense itching, often accompanied by burning and stinging. The disease is probably spread from one person to another through the use of common shower or dressing facilities that harbor the fungus. Excessive perspiration, heat, and shoes that give poor ventilation allow the condition to fester.

Jock itch infection is confined to the groin area where an athletic supporter (jock strap) is worn. This causes intense itching and is aggravated by perspiration, heat, and poor ventilation.

Ringworm can occur anywhere on the body. It usually forms as a well-defined circular skin lesion about the skin of a quarter, and it burns and itches.

All three of these conditions are treated with the same products, which contain antifungal agents, drying agents, and keratolytic agents.

Hemorrhoids

Hemorrhoids are small veins in or just on the outside of the rectum that have become swollen and inflamed because the flow of blood through them has become partially obstructed. This can be the result of straining at stool because of constipation, irritation from diarrhea, prolonged standing or sitting, or abdominal pressure caused by pregnancy. Bleeding, itching, burning, and soreness often are the uncomfortable result of hemorrhoids. Many people seek relief with nonprescription products they can purchase; however, if you suspect that you have hemorrhoids, you should confirm this with your doctor.

The basic types of agents used to alleviate hemorrhoid symptoms are: anesthetics to relieve pain, astringents to constrict or draw together the swollen tissues, antiseptics to prevent infection, and lubricant-softeners for a soothing effect. Some products contain a combination of these agents, either in ointment or suppository form.

Indigestion

Everyone suffers from indigestion at one time or another. It can be caused by overindulgence in food or alcohol, poor chewing habits, swallowing air while eating, and certain drugs. Emotional upset can also cause indigestion, which complicates things even more.

The symptoms of indigestion include "heartburn," sour or acid stomach, cramps, nausea, and excessive gas. Fortunately, most of these symptoms are not long-lasting and easily respond to antacid products. Some products contain an extra ingredient to help with the gas problem.

If indigestion seems severe or occurs too frequently, it is advisable that you see a doctor.

Insomnia

Almost everyone experiences occasional sleeplessness. Lying awake and tossing and turning is unpleasant and can be harmful if too much sleep is lost. The principal ingredients used in nonprescription sleep aids are antihistamines because of their tendency to induce drowsiness.

If insomnia has become a constant problem for you, consult your doctor.

Liniments and Ointments for Arthritis and Muscle Pain

Besides the analgesics you take internally to treat arthritic and muscle pain, there are those that can be rubbed on the skin for relief of local pain. They are counterirritants that dilate the small blood vessels and bring blood closer to the skin's surface, producing increased circulation and warmth. Most of these compounds are "volatile oils" that have a familiar and pleasant odor. Oil of wintergreen, menthol, camphor, and turpentine oil are the most commonly used.

Some products contain ingredients that soothe pain and irritation by local anesthetic action.

You must be careful when using these products not to cover them with bandages, because this may cause the skin to blister.

Menstrual Problems

The most common symptoms experienced before and during menstruation are irritability, bloating of the abdomen, and increased tenderness of the breasts. Sometimes there is also sharp, cramping pain in the pelvic region and headache or upset stomach.

Most products used for this condition are pain relievers. Some have agents to decrease bloating, cramping, and tension.

Pain

Pain is nature's way of protecting you from the hazards of your environment. Without this warning signal, you wouldn't snatch your hand away from a hot stove, or know when you had torn a ligament in your ankle, or that you are developing an infection or disease. Fortunately, pain by its nature and severity will also tell you when to go to a doctor.

Sometimes pain comes from things that are not too serious, but are annoying. A headache, toothache, or minor arthritic or muscular ache will generally be temporarily relieved by an analgesic.

There are four basic analgesics available, either alone or in combination—aspirin, salicylamide, phenacetin, and acetamino-

phen. Some products also contain caffeine, which is not an analgesic. Caffeine is thought to be of value because it constricts dilated blood vessels that may be contributing to the pain.

Poison Ivy, Poison Oak, and Insect Bites and Stings

The reactions produced by contact with poison ivy, poison oak, poison sumac, and insect bites and stings are all the result of allergic reactions to substances foreign to the body. This results in inflammation and swelling of the skin, and intense itching. Treatment is needed to protect the injured skin, reduce itching, and reduce the chances of infection caused by scratching.

Some people are extremely sensitive to certain insect stings and may require emergency treatment at a hospital.

Five types of drugs are used to treat the symptoms of plant and insect-caused skin inflammation: local anesthetics, antihistamines, antiseptics, astringents, and hydrocortisone. Some products combine several of these drugs.

Psoriasis

Psoriasis is often confused with eczema, a term associated with many types of chronic skin disorders. Even dermatologists sometimes have difficulty differentiating between the two. Psoriasis is a chronic skin disease characterized by reddish patches covered with shiny, silvery scales. No one knows what causes it, and so far there is no certain cure. The lesions form, heal without scarring, and recur. They most commonly occur on the elbows and knees, the scalp, the back, and the buttocks. Psoriasis usually itches, but not as much as eczema.

The products used to treat psoriasis usually contain keratolytic agents or tars, or both.

Vitamins and Minerals

Vitamins are chemical compounds found in plants and animals that are necessary to maintain normal growth and metabolism of the body. Most vitamins cannot be manufactured by the body, so they have to be obtained from the food you eat or from vitamin supplements. The same is true for minerals.

Most experts agree that the best way to

get the proper vitamin and mineral intake is to eat a balanced diet. This is easier said than done, however. Some people do not or cannot plan and prepare a proper diet, either because they can't afford it, or they have developed poor eating habits. Foods that are cooked or processed often lose much of their vitamins. In addition, vitamin requirements increase during certain events in life such as pregnancy, illness, or dieting. However, when the diet is inadequate, necessary nutrients can be obtained from vitamin-mineral supplements.

Vitamins

Vitamin A is essential for healthy skin and hair, and necessary for adequate vision in dim light. It is found in milk, cream, butter, egg yolk, green leafy and yellow vegetables, and fish liver oils.

Vitamin B_1 (thiamine) is essential for normal digestion of food, because it helps digest carbohydrates into energy and fat. It is also essential for nerve cell and heart tissue function. It is found in dried yeast, fish, lean meat, liver, pork, poultry, milk, nuts, potatoes, and legumes (peas and beans).

Vitamin B_2 (riboflavin) helps maintain healthy skin and body tissues. Milk, cheese, liver, lean meat, eggs, and leafy green vegetables provide this vitamin.

Vitamin B_3 (niacin) helps keep the body tissues in healthy condition, and the central nervous system functioning. Dried yeast, liver, lean meat, fish, eggs, whole grains, and legumes provide vitamin B_3.

Vitamin B_5 (pantothenic acid) is involved in the metabolism of carbohydrates, fats, and proteins. It also aids energy production, keeps the nervous system and gastrointestinal tract in healthy condition, and plays a role in immunity. This vitamin is found in dried yeast, kidney, liver, eggs, nuts, and green leafy vegetables.

Vitamin B_6 (pyridoxine) aids the metabolism of proteins and fats, and is essential for proper cell function. It is found in dried yeast, liver, organ meat, fish, vegetables, whole-grain cereals, and legumes.

Vitamin B_{12} (cyanocobalamin) is needed to synthesize hemoglobin and the development of healthy red blood cells. It is also essential for nerve cell function and helps prevent certain forms of anemia. Sources are liver, kidney, lean meat, eggs, milk and

milk products, salt-water fish, oysters, and meats in general.

Folic acid (B_9) helps in the manufacture of red blood cells and metabolism of food to energy. It is found in organ meats, liver, dried yeast, leafy green vegetables, and fruits.

Vitamin C (ascorbic acid) is essential for normal teeth, bones, blood vessels, formation of collagen (a protein that helps support body structures), and wound healing; it is also an antioxidant that helps the body absorb and use iron from food. It is found in citrus fruits, tomatoes, potatoes, cantaloupe, berries, cabbage, green pepper, and green leafy vegetables.

Vitamin D (calciferol) promotes absorption of calcium and phosphorus to make strong bones and teeth. It is provided by fish liver oils, salmon, tuna, egg yolk, butter, and ultraviolent light.

Vitamin E (alpha-tocopherol) is an antioxidant that helps prevent oxygen from destroying other substances in the body and is needed for stability of muscle, red blood cell tissue, and membranes. Vegetable oils, whole-grain cereals, wheat germ, leafy vegetables, lettuce, egg yolk, and legumes contain this vitamin.

Vitamin K is essential for the formation of prothrombin, a substance necessary for normal blood clotting. This vitamin is available on prescription only for special conditions. It occurs naturally in leafy vegetables, pork liver, and vegetable oils. The body also makes its own.

Minerals

Minerals play an important role in fluid and electrolyte balance, acid-base regulation, enzyme activation, blood clotting, and other areas such as potassium and calcium function in extracellular body fluids to ensure normal muscle activity. A proper proportion of calcium to phosphorus is necessary for good bone development. Iron is an important component of blood hemoglobin, as zinc is to insulin, and iodine is to thyroxin. Copper, magnesium, fluorine, chromium, and selenium are the other essential minerals.

Dosage Recommendations

A term you see on vitamin and mineral product labels is RDA (Recommended Daily Dietary Allowances). The RDA was established by the National Research Council as a guide to the amounts of vitamins needed for maintenance of good nutrition. Vitamin and mineral amounts are expressed as milligrams (mg.), micorgrams (mcg.), or International Units (I.U.)

Vitamin and Mineral Interactions

- Iron absorption is decreased by antacids, and increased by vitamin C, when taken at the same time.
- Vitamin C effectiveness is reduced by aspirin.
- Vitamin A activity is increased by vitamin C and vitamin E.
- Vitamin E activity is increased by vitamin C and reduced by iron when they are taken together.
- The absorption of fat-soluble vitamins (A, D, E, and K) is diminished by mineral oil laxative.
- The minerals iron, calcium, and zinc interfere with absorption of tetracycline antibiotic, so they should not be taken within two hours of the time tetracycline is taken.

Warts and Corns

Warts and corns are both growths on the skin, but each has a different cause. Corns are caused by mechanical pressure and friction, usually from improperly fitted shoes or a foot deformity. Hard corns are found on the outer areas of the toes, while soft ones form between the toes. Warts are caused by a virus that can be passed by contact from one person to another. There are several different types of warts, but the common wart is sharply outlined, firm, rough, and light gray to grayish black in color. They grow most frequently on the back of the hands and fingers.

Keratolytic and caustic agents are used for treatment.

Weight Reduction

If you eat more food over an extended period of time than your body requires for producing energy, it will be stored as fat and you will become overweight. To curb the appetite or reduce the amount of food you eat, there are six different classes of products that can help. Bulk formers make you feel full and thus you eat less. Glucose preparations raise your blood glucose levels and make you feel like you don't need as much to eat. Phenylpropanolamine is a vasoconstrictor that acts as an appetite suppressant. Benzocaine acts as a local anesthetic in your mouth and numbs your taste buds. Dietary or low-calorie food substitutes eaten at one meal a day cut down total calorie intake. And artificial sweeteners give you that sweet taste without the calories of sugar.

Worm Infestations

Worms are parasites that must have a host, human or animal, to remain alive. It is estimated that about one-third of the world's population harbors worms, especially in areas where health and sanitation conditions are poor.

Worm eggs or larvae are transmitted by contaminated hands or food to the mouth and are swallowed. They live and grow as parasites in the intestines, and their eggs are expelled in the stool to start the cycle all over again.

Symptoms of worm infestation are vague and may go unnoticed until an adult worm is discovered in the stool. Pinworm infestations can cause intense itching in the anal region. Roundworms may cause only vague abdominal pain, but can grow to several inches and are capable of using up significant amounts of the host's food.

Medication for treatment is available by prescription from your doctor, and usually only a single dose is required to eradicate the worms.

Directory of Poison Control Centers

The Directory of Poison Control Centers has been compiled from information furnished by the National Clearinghouse for Poison Control Centers, Bureau of Drugs, 5600 Fishers Lane, Room 1347, Rockville, Md. 20857.
It includes those facilities which provide for the medical profession, on a 24-hour basis, information concerning the prevention and treatment of accidents involving ingestion of poisonous and potentially poisonous substances. Unless otherwise noted, inquiries should be addressed to: Poison Control Center

First Aid for Possible Poisoning

REMEMBER: ANY NON-FOOD SUBSTANCE MAY BE POISONOUS!

1. Keep all potential poisons—household products and medicines—out of the reach of small children.
2. Use "safety caps" (child-resistant containers) as intended to avoid accidents.
3. Have 1 oz. Syrup of Ipecac in your home and in your first aid kit for camping, travel, etc.
4. Keep your Poison Center's and your physician's phone number handy.

IF YOU THINK AN ACCIDENTAL INGESTION HAS OCCURRED:

1. Keep calm—do not wait for symptoms—call for help promptly!
2. Find out if the substance is toxic—Your Poison Control Center (listed by state and city on the following pages) or your physician can tell you if a risk exists and what you should do.
3. Have the product's container or label with you at the phone.

   A. IF A POISON IS ON THE SKIN:
   Immediately remove affected clothing.
   Flood involved parts of body with water, wash with soap or detergent and rinse thoroughly.

   B. IF A POISON IS IN THE EYE:
   Immediately flush the eye with water for 10 to 15 minutes.

   C. IF A POISON IS INHALED:
   Immediately get the person to fresh air. Give mouth to mouth resuscitation if necessary.

   D. IF A POISON IS SWALLOWED:
   Medicines: Do not give anything by mouth until calling for advice.
   Chemical or Household Product: Unless patient is unconscious, having convulsions, or cannot swallow give milk or water. Then call for professional advice as to whether you should induce vomiting.
   If Vomiting is recommended: Give one tablespoon of Ipecac syrup followed by a glass (8 oz.) of clear liquid (water, juices, or pop). If the patient doesn't vomit within 15 to 20 minutes, give another tablespoon of·Ipecac and more water. Do *not* use salt water. It can be dangerous.

NEVER INDUCE VOMITING IF:

1. The victim is in COMA (unconscious).
2. The victim is CONVULSING (having a fit or a seizure).
3. The victim has swallowed a CAUSTIC or CORROSIVE (e.g. LYE).

FOR REEMPHASIS:

1. Always call to be certain of possible toxicity before undertaking treatment.
2. Never induce vomiting until you are instructed to do so.
3. Do not rely on the label's antidote information—it may be out of date—call instead!
4. If you have to go to an Emergency Room, take the tablets, capsules, container, and/or label with you.
5. Don't hesitate to call your Poison Center or your doctor a second time if the victim seems to be getting worse.

Prepared by:
American Association of Poison Control Centers

ALABAMA

STATE COORDINATOR
Department of Public Health   (205) 832-3194
Montgomery 36117
Anniston
N.E. Alabama Regional Medical   235-5121
Center
400 E. 10th St. 36201
Birmingham
Children's Hospital   933-4050
1601 6th Ave., S. 35233   800/292-6678
Dothan
Southeast Alabama   793-8111
Medical Center
P.O. Drawer 6987,   36301

Gadsden
Baptist Memorial Hospital   492-8111
1007 Goodyear Avenue 35903
Mobile
University of So. Alabama   471-7100
Medical Center
2451 Fillingim St. 36617
Opelika
Lee County Hospital   749-3411
2000 Pepperill Parkway 36801   Ext. 258
Tuskegee
John A. Andrews Hospital   727-8488
Tuskegee Institute 36088

ALASKA

STATE COORDINATOR
Department of Health &   (907) 465-3100
Social Services
Juneau 99811
Anchorage
Providence Hospital   274-6535
3200 Providence Dr. 99504

ARIZONA

STATE COORDINATOR
College of Pharmacy   (602) 626-6016
University of Arizona   800/362-0101
Tucson 85724
Flagstaff
Flagstaff Hospital and   774-5233
Medical Center of Northern Arizona
1215 N. Beaver St. 86001
Phoenix
St. Luke's Hospital and   253-3334
Medical Center
525 N. 18th St. 85006
Tucson
Arizona Hlth. Sciences Ctr.   626-6016
University of Arizona 85724
Yuma
Yuma Regional Med. Center   344-2000
Avenue A and 24th St. 85364

ARKANSAS

STATE COORDINATOR
University of Arkansas   (501) 661-6161
Medical Science Campus
Little Rock 72201
El Dorado
Warner Brown Hospital   863-2266
460 West Oak St. 71730

Fort Smith
St. Edward's Mercy Medical Center   452-5100
7301 Rogers Avenue 72903   Ext. 2401
Sparks Regional Med. Center   441-5011
1311 S. Eye St. 72901
Harrison
Boone County Hospital   741-6141
620 N. Willow St. 72601   Ext. 275, 276
Helena
Helena Hospital   338-6411
Newman Drive 72342   Ext. 340
Little Rock
Univ. of Arkansas Medical Center   661-5544
4301 W. Markham St. 72201   800/482-8948
Osceola
Osceola Memorial Hospital   563-7180
611 Lee Ave. West 72370
Pine Bluff
Jefferson Hospital   535-6800
1515 W. 42nd Ave. 71601   Ext. 4706

CALIFORNIA

STATE COORDINATOR
Department of Health Services   (916) 322-4336
Sacramento 95814
Fresno
Central Valley Regional   445-1222
Poison Control Ctr.
Fresno Community Hospital and
Medical Center
Fresno & R Sts.
P.O. Box 1232   93715
Los Angeles
Thos. J. Fleming Memorial Ctr.   664-2121
Children's Hospital of Los Angeles
P.O. Box 54700
4650 Sunset Blvd. 90054
Oakland
Children's Hosp. Medical Center   428-3000
of Northern California
51st & Grove St. 94609
Orange
University of California   634-5988
Irvine Medical Center   634-6011
101 City Drive South 92688
Sacramento
Sacramento Medical Center   453-3692
Univ. of California, Davis   800/852-7221
2315 Stockton Blvd. 95817
San Diego
University Hospital   294-6000
225 W. Dickinson St. 92103
San Francisco
San Francisco General Hosp.   666-2845
1001 Potrerro Ave. 94102   800/792-0720
San Jose
Santa Clara Valley Medical Center   279-5112
751 S. Bascom Ave., 95128

COLORADO

STATE COORDINATOR
Department of Health;   (303) 320-8476
EMS Div
Denver 80220
Denver
Rocky Mountain Poison Center   629-1123
Denver General Hospital   800/332-3073
W. 8th Ave. & Cherokee St. 80204

CONNECTICUT

STATE COORDINATOR
University of Connecticut   (203) 674-3456
Health Center
Farmington 06032
Bridgeport
Bridgeport Hospital   384-3566
267 Grant St. 06602

St. Vincent's Hospital   576-5178
2820 Main St. 06602
Danbury
Danbury Hospital   797-7300
95 Locust Ave. 06810
Farmington
Connecticut Poison Center   674-3456
University of Connecticut   (800) 845-7633
Health Center 06032
Middletown
Middlesex Memorial Hospital   347-9471
28 Crescent St. 06457
New Haven
The Hosp. of St. Raphael   789-3469
1450 Chapel St. 06511

Dept. of Pediatrics
Yale-New Haven Hospital   436-1960
789 Howard Ave. 06504
Norwalk
Norwalk Hospital   852-2160
24 Stevens St. 06852
Waterbury
St. Mary's Hospital   574-6011
56 Franklin St. 06702

DELAWARE

STATE COORDINATOR
Wilmington Medical Center   (302) 655-3389
Delaware Division
Wilmington 19801
Wilmington
Wilmington Medical Center   655-3389
Delaware Division
501 W. 14th St. 19899

DISTRICT OF COLUMBIA

STATE COORDINATOR
Department of Human   (202) 673-6741
Services   (202) 673-6736
Washington, D.C. 20009
Washington, D.C.
Georgetown University Hospital   625-3333
3800 Reservoir Rd. 20007

FLORIDA

STATE COORDINATOR
Department of Health and   (904) 487-1566
Emergency Medical Services
Tallahassee 32301

Apalachicola
George E. Weems Memorial   653-8853
Hospital P.O. Box 610
Franklin Square 32320
Bradenton
Manatee Memorial Hospital   746-5111
206 2nd St. E. 33505   Ext. 466

Daytona Beach
Halifax Hospital   258-2002
Emergency Department
P.O. Box 1990   32014
Ft. Lauderdale
Broward General Medical Center   463-3131
1600 S. Andrews Ave. 33316   Ext. 1511
Fort Myers
Lee Memorial Hospital   332-1111
2776 Cleveland Ave.   Ext. 285
P.O. Drawer 2218   33902
Ft. Walton Beach
General Hospital of   392-1111
Ft. Walton Beach   Ext. 106
1000 Mar-Walt Drive 32548
Gainesville
Shands Teaching Hosp.   392-3740
and Clinics
University of Florida 32610
Inverness
Citrus Memorial Hosp.   726-2800
502 Highland Blvd. 32650
Jacksonville
St. Vincent's Medical Center   389-7751
Barrs St. & St. Johns Ave. 32204   Ext. 8315
Lakeland
Lakeland General Hospital   686-4913
Lakeland Hills Blvd.
P.O. Box 480   33802
Leesburg
Leesburg General Hospital   787-7222
600 E. Dixie 32748   Ext. 381
Melbourne
James E. Holmes Regional   727-7000
Medical Center   Ext. 675
1350 S. Hickory St. 32901
Miami
Jackson Memorial Hospital   325-6799
Attn: Pharmacy
1611 N.W. 12th Ave. 33136
Naples
Naples Community Hospital   262-7838
350 7th St. N. 33940
North Miami Beach
Parkway General Hosp., Inc.   653-3333
160 Northwest 170th St. 33169
Ocala
Munroe Memorial Hospital   732-1111
140 S.E. Orange St.   Ext. 187
P.O. Box 6000   32670
Orlando
Orlando Reg. Med. Ctr.   841-5222
Orange Memorial Hospital
1414 S. Kuhl Ave. 32806
Panama City
Bay Memorial Med. Ctr.   769-1511
600 N. MacArthur Ave. 32401   Ext. 415,416
Pensacola
Baptist Hospital   434-4611
1000 W. Moreno St. 32501   800/874-1555
Punta Gorda
Medical Center Hospital   637-2529
809 E. Marion Ave. 33950
Rockledge
Wuesthoff Memorial Hospital   636-2211
110 Longwood Ave. 32955   Ext. 168
St. Petersburg
Bay Front Medical Center, Inc.   821-5858
701 6th St., S. 33701
Sarasota
Memorial Hospital   953-1332
1901 Arlington Ave. 33579

Tallahassee
Tallahassee Regional 599-5411
Medical Center
1300 Miccouskee Road 32304
Tampa
Tampa General Hospital 251-6995
Davis Islands 33606
Titusville
Jess Parrish Mem. Hospital 268-6111
951 N. Washington Ave. 32780
West Palm Beach
Good Samaritan Hospital 655-5511
Flagler Dr. at Ext. 4230
Palm Beach Lakes Blvd. 33402
Winter Haven
Winter Haven Hospital, Inc. 299-9701
200 Avenue F., N.E. 33880

GEORGIA

STATE COORDINATOR
Department of Human (404) 894-5170
Resources
Atlanta 30308
Albany
Phoebe Putney Memorial Hosp. 883-1800
417 Third Avenue 31705 Ext. 4152
Athens
Athens General Hospital 543-5215
797 Cobb St. 30601
Atlanta
Grady Memorial Hospital 588-4400
80 Butler St., S.E. 30303 800 282-5846
(Deaf) 404 525-3323
Augusta
University Hospital 722-9011
1350 Walton Way 30902 Ext. 2440
Columbus
The Medical Center 324-4711
710 Center Street 31902 Ext. 6431
Macon
Medical Center of Central Georgia 742-1122
777 Hemlock St. 31201 Ext. 1146
Rome
Floyd Hospital 291-2196
P.O. Box 233 31061
Savannah
Savannah Reg. Poison Ctr. 355-5228
Depart. of Emergency Med.
Memorial Medical Center
P.O. Box 23089 31403
Thomasville
John D. Archbold 226-4121
Memorial Hospital Ext. 169
900 Gordon Ave. 31792
Valdosta
S. Georgia Medical Center 333-1110
P.O. Box 1727 31601
Waycross
Memorial Hospital 283-3030
410 Darling Ave. 31501

HAWAII

STATE COORDINATOR
Department of Health (808) 531-7776
Honolulu 96801
Honolulu
Kapiolani-Childrens Medical Center 941-4411
1319 Punahou St. 96826 1-800 362-3585

IDAHO

STATE COORDINATOR
Department of Health (208) 334-2241
and Welfare 1-800 632-800
Boise 83701
Boise
St. Alphonsus Hospital 376-1211
1055 N. Curtis Rd. 83704 Ext. 707
Idaho Falls
Idaho Falls Hospital 522-3600
Emergency Department
900 Memorial Dr. 83401
Pocatello
St. Anthony Hospital 232-2733
650 North 7th St. 83201 Ext. 244
1-800 632-9490

ILLINOIS

STATE COORDINATOR
Division of Emergency Medical (217) 785-2080
Services and Highway Safety
Springfield 62761
Chicago
Rush-Presbyterian-St. Lukes 942-5969
Medical Center 800 942-5969
1753 W. Congress Parkway 60612
Peoria
St. Francis Hospital & 672-2334
Medical Center 1-800 322-5330
530 N.E. Glen Oak Avenue 61637
Springfield
St. John's Hospital 753-3330
800 East Carpenter 62702 1-800 252-2022

INDIANA

STATE COORDINATOR
State Board of Health (317) 633-0332
Indianapolis 46206
Anderson
Community Hospital 646-5198
1515 N. Madison Ave. 46012

St. John's Hickey 646-8251
Memorial Hospital
2015 Jackson St. 46014
Angola
Cameron Memorial Hospital 665-2141
416 East Maumee St. 46703 Ext. 146
Columbus
Bartholomew County Hosp. 376-5277
2400 East 17th St., 47201
Crown Point
St. Anthony Medical Ctr. 738-2100
Main at Franciscan Rd. 46307
East Chicago
St. Catherine's Hospital 392-1700
4321 Fir Street 46312 392-7203
Elkhart
Elkhart General Hospital 294-2621
600 East Blvd. 46514 800 382-9697
Evansville
Deaconess Hospital 426-3405
600 Mary St. 47710

Welborn Memorial 426-8000
Baptist Hospital
401 S.E. 6th St. 47713

Fort Wayne

Lutheran Hospital	458-2211
3024 Fairfield Ave. 46807	
Parkview Memorial Hospital	484-6636
220 Randalia Dr. 46805	Ext. 6000
St. Joseph's Hospital	423-2614
700 Broadway 46802	

Frankfort

Clinton County Hospital	659-4731
1300 S. Jackson St. 46041	

Gary

Methodist Hospital of Gary, Inc.	886-4710
600 Grant St. 46402	

Goshen

Goshen General Hospital	533-2141
200 High Park Ave. 46526	

Hammond

St. Margaret's Hospital	932-2300
25 Douglas St. 46320	931-4477

Indianapolis

Methodist Hospital of Indiana, Inc.	924-3521
1604 N. Capitol Ave. 46202	
Indiana Poison Center	630-7351
1001 West 10th St. 46202	800 382-9097

Kendallville

McCray Memorial Hospital	347-1100
Hospital Drive 46755	

Kokomo

Howard Community Hospital	453-8444
3500 S. LaFountain St. 46901	

Lafayette

Lafayette Home Hospital	447-6811
2400 South Street 47902	
St. Elizabeth Hospital	423-6271
1501 Hartfort St. 47904	

LaGrange

LaGrange County Hospital	463-2144
Route #1 46761	

LaPorte

LaPorte Hospital, Inc.	362-1234
1007 Lincolnway 46350	

Lebanon

Witham Memorial Hospital	482-2700
1124 N. Lebanon St. 46052	Ext. 241

Madison

King's Daughter's Hospital	265-5211
112 Presbyterian Ave.	Ext. 109
P.O. Box 447 47250	

Marion

Marion General Hospital	662-4693
Wabash & Euclid Ave. 46952	

Muncie

Ball Memorial Hospital	747-3241
2401 University Ave. 47303	

Portland

Jay County Hospital	726-7131
505 W. Arch St. 47371	

Richmond

Reid Memorial Hospital	962-7010
1401 Chester Blvd. 47374	

Shelbyville

Wm. S. Major Hospital	392-3211
150 W. Washington St. 46176	Ext. 52

South Bend

St. Joseph's Hospital	237-7264
811 E. Madison St. 46622	

Terre Haute

Union Hospital, Inc.	238-7000
1606 N. 7th St. 47804	Ext. 7523

Valparaiso

Porter Memorial Hosp.	464-8611
814 LaPorte Ave. 46383	Ext. 232, 312, 334

Vincennes

The Good Samaritan	885-3348
Hospital	
520 S. 7th St. 47591	

IOWA

STATE COORDINATOR

Department of Health	(515) 281-4964
Des Moines 50319	

Des Moines
(Blank Mem. Hosp.)

Iowa Methodist Hospital	283-6254
1200 Pleasant St. 50308	1-800 362-2327

Dubuque

Mercy Medical Center	588-8050
Mercy Drive 52001	

Fort Dodge

Trinity Regional Hospital	573-7211
Poison Information Center	Night: 573-3101
Kenyon Rd. 50501	

Iowa City

Univ. of Iowa Hospital	356-2922
Poison Information	800 272-6477
Center 52240	

Waterloo

Allen Memorial Hospital	235-3893
1825 Logan Avenue 50703	

KANSAS

STATE COORDINATOR

Department of Health &	(913) 862-9360
Environment	Ext. 451
Topeka 66620	

Atchison

Atchison Hospital	367-2131
1301 N. 2nd St. 66002	

Dodge City

Dodge City Reg. Hosp.	225-9050
P.O. Box 1478	Ext. 381
Ross & Ave. "A" 67801	

Emporia

Newman Memorial Hospital	343-6800
12th & Chestnut Sts. 66801	Ext. 545

Fort Riley

Irwin Army Hospital 66442	239-7777
	239-7778

Fort Scott

Mercy Hospital	223-2200
821 Burke St. 66701	Night: 223-0476

Great Bend

Central Kansas Medical	792-2511
Center	Ext. 115
3515 Broadway 67530	

Hays

Hadley Regional Medical Center	628-8251
201 E. 7th St. 67601	

Kansas City

University of Kansas	588-6633
Medical Center	
39th & Rainbow Blvd. 66103	

Lawrence

Lawrence Memorial Hospital	843-3680
325 Maine St. 66044	Ext. 162, 163

Parsons

Labette County Medical	421-4880
Center	Ext. 320
S. 21st St. 67357	

Salina
St. John's Hospital   827-5591
139 N. Penn St. 67401   Ext. 112

Topeka
Stormont-Vail Regional Med. Ctr.   354-6100
10th & Washburn Sts. 66606

Wichita
Wesley Medical Center   688-2222
550 N. Hillside Ave. 67214

KENTUCKY

STATE COORDINATOR
Department For Human   (502) 564-3970
Resources
Frankfort 40601

Ashland
King's Daughters Hospital   324-2222
2201 Lexington Ave. 41101

Fort Thomas
St. Lukes Hospital   292-3216
85 N. Grand Ave. 41075   1-800 352-9900

Lexington
Central Baptist Hospital   278-3411
1740 S. Limestone St. 40503   Ext. 363

Drug Information Center   233-5320
University of Kentucky
Medical Center 40536

Louisville
Poison Control Center   589-8222
NKC, Inc.   1-800 722-5725
P.O. Box 35070   40232

Murray
Murray-Calloway County   753-7588
Hospital
803 Popular 42071

Owensboro
Owensboro-Daviess County   926-3030
Hospital   Ext. 180 or 186
811 Hospital Court 42301

Paducah
Western Baptist Hospital   444-5100
2501 Kentucky Ave. 42001   Ext. 105 or 180

Prestonsburg
Poison Control Center   886-8511
Highlands Reg. Med.   Ext. 132 or 160
Ctr. 41653

South Williamson
Appalachian Regional Hospitals   237-1010
Central Pharmaceutical Service
2000 Central Ave. 25661

LOUISIANA

STATE COORDINATOR
Emergency Medical Services   (504) 342-2600
of Louisiana
Baton Rouge 70801

Alexandria
Rapides General Hospital   487-8111
Emergency Dept.   Ext. 231
P.O. Box 7146   71301

Baton Rouge
Doctors Hospital   928-6558
2414 Bunker Hill Dr. 70808

Lafayette
Our Lady of Lourdes Hosp.   234-7381
P.O. Box 3827
611 St. Landry St. 70501

Lake Charles
Lake Charles Memorial Hosp.   478-6800
P.O. Drawer M 70601

Monroe
Northeast Louisiana University   342-3008
School of Pharmacy
700 University Ave. 71209

St. Francis Hospital   325-6454
P.O. Box 1901   71301

New Orleans
Charity Hospital   568-5222
1532 Tulane Ave. 70140

Shreveport
LSU Medical Center   425-1524
P.O. Box 33932   71130

MAINE

STATE COORDINATOR
Maine Poison Control Center   (207) 871-2950
Portland   04102

Portland
Maine Medical Center   871-2950
Emergency Division   1-800 442-6305
22 Bramhall St. 04102

MARYLAND

STATE CORODINATOR
Maryland Poison Information   (301) 528-7604
Center
University of Maryland School of
Pharmacy
Baltimore 21201

Baltimore
Maryland Poison Information Center   528-7701
University of Maryland   1-800 492-2414
School of Pharmacy
636 W. Lombard St. 21201

Cumberland
Sacred Heart Hospital   722-6677
900 Seton Drive 21502

MASSACHUSETTS

STATE COORDINATOR
Department of Public Health   (617) 727-2700
Boston 02111

Boston
Massachusetts Poison Control   232-2120
System   1-800 682-9211
300 Longwood Ave. 02115

MICHIGAN

STATE COORDINATOR
Department of Public Health   (517) 373-1406
Lansing 48909

Adrian
Emma L. Bixby Hospital   263-2412
818 Riverside Ave. 49221

Ann Arbor
University Hospital   764-5102
1405 E. Ann St. 48104

Battle Creek
Community Hospital   963-5521
183 West St. 49016

Bay City
Bay Medical Center   894-3131
100 15th St. 48706

Berrien Center
Berrien General Hospital   471-7761
Dean's Hill Rd. 49102

Coldwater
Community Health Center   279-7935
of Branch County
274 E. Chicago St. 49036
Detroit
Children's Hospital of Michigan   494-5711
Southeast Regional Poison Center   (800) 572-1655
3901 Beaubien 48201   (800) 462-6642

Mount Carmel Mercy Hosp.   927-7000
Pharmacy Dept.
6071 W. Outer Dr. 48235

Eloise
Wayne County General   Day: 722-3748
30712 Michigan Ave. 48132   Night: 724-3000

Flint
Hurley Hospital   766-0111
6th Ave & Begole 48502   (800) 572-5396
Grand Rapids
St. Mary's Hospital   774-6794
201 Lafayette, S.E. 49503

Western Michigan Regional   (800) 442-4571
Poison Center   (800) 632-2727
1840 Wealthy, S.E. 49506
Jackson
W.A. Foote Memorial Hosp.   788-4816
205 N. East St. 49201

Kalamazoo
Midwest Poison Center
Borgess Medical Center   383-7070
1521 Gull Rd. 49001   (1-800) 632-4177
Bronson Methodist Hospital   383-6409
252 E. Lovell St. 49006   (1-800) 442-4112

Lansing
St. Lawrence Hospital   372-5112
1210 W. Saginaw St. 48914   372-5113

Marquette
Marquette General Hospital   228-9440
420 W. Magnetic Dr. 49855   (1-800) 562-9781
Midland
Midland Hospital   631-8100
4005 Orchard 48640
Petoskey
Northern Michigan Hospitals, Inc.   347-0555
416 Connable 49770
Pontiac
St. Joseph Mercy Hospital   858-7373
900 S. Woodward Ave. 48053   858-7374
Port Huron
Port Huron Hospital   987-5555
1001 Kearney St. 48060   987-5000
Saginaw
Saginaw General Hospital   755-1111
1447 N. Harrison 48602
Traverse City
Munson Medical Center   947-6140
Sixth St. 49684

MINNESOTA

STATE COORDINATOR
State Department of Health   (612) 296-5281
Minneapolis 55404
Brainerd
St. Joseph's Hospital 56401   829-2861
                                 Ext. 211

Duluth
St. Luke's Hospital   727-6636
Emergency Department
915 E. First St. 55805
St. Mary's Hospital   726-4500
407 E. 3rd St. 55805
Edina
Fairview-Southdale Hospital   920-4400
6401 France Ave., S. 55435
Fergus Falls
Lake Region Hospital 56537   736-5475
Fridley
Unity Hospital   786-2200
550 Osborne Rd. 55432
Mankato
Immanual - St. Joseph's   625-4031
Hospital
325 Garden Blvd. 56001
Minneapolis
Fairview Hospital   371-6402
Outpatient Department
2312 S. 6th St. 55406
Hennepin Poison Ctr.   347-3141
Hennepin County Medical Center
701 Park Ave. 55415
Morris
Stevens County Memorial   589-1313
Hospital 56267
Rochester
Southeastern Minn. Poison   285-5123
Control Ctr.   Ext. 517
St. Mary's Hospital
1216 Second St., S.W. 55901
St. Cloud
St. Cloud Hospital   251-2700
1406 6th Avenue, N. 56301   Ext. 221
St. Paul
Bethesda Lutheran Hospital   221-2301
559 Capitol Blvd. 55103
St. John's Hospital   228-3132
403 Maria Ave. 55106
United Hospitals, Inc.   298-8402
300 Pleasant Ave. 55102
St. Paul-Ramsey Hospital   221-2113
640 Jackson St. 55101
Willmar
Rice Memorial Hospital   235-4543
402 W. 3rd St. 56201
Worthington
Worthington Regional Hosp.   372-2941
1016 6th Ave. 56187

MISSISSIPPI

STATE COORDINATOR
State Board of Health   (601) 354-6660
Jackson 39205
Biloxi
Gulf Coast Community Hospital   388-1919
4642 West Beach Blvd. 39531
USAF Hospital Keesler   377-6555
Keesler Air Force Base   377-6556
39534
Brandon
Rankin General Hospital   825-2811
350 Crossgates Blvd. 39042   Ext. 487
                                 Ext. 463

Columbia
Marion County General Hospital — 736-6303 Ext. 217
Sumrall Rd. 39429

Greenwood
Greenwood-LeFlore Hosp. — 453-9751 Ext. 2633
River Road 38930

Hattiesburg
Forrest County General Hosp — 264-4235
400 S. 28th Ave. 39401

Jackson
St. Dominic-Jackson Mem. Hosp — 982-0121 Ext. 2345
969 Lakeland Dr. 39216

State Board of Health — 354-6650
Bureau of Disease Control 39205

University Medical Center — 354-7660
2500 N. State St. 39216

Laurel
Jones County Community Hospital — 649-4000 Ext. 207, 218, 220, 248
Jefferson St. at 13th Ave. 39440

Meridian
Meridian Regional Hosp. — 433-6211
Highway 39, North 39301

Pascagoula
Singing River Hospital Emergency Room — 938-5162
2609 Denny Ave. East 39567

University
School of Pharmacy — 234-1522
University of Mississippi 38677

MISSOURI

STATE COORDINATOR
Missouri Division of Health — (314) 751-2713
Jefferson City 65102

Cape Girardeau
St. Francis Medical Ctr. — 651-6235
St. Francis Drive 63701

Columbia
University of Missouri Medical Center — 882-8091
807 Stadium Blvd. 65201

Hannibal
St. Elizabeth Hospital, Pharmacy Dept. — 221-0414 Ext. 101
109 Virginia St. 63401

Jefferson City
The Bureau of Emergency Medical Services — 635-7141 Ext. 173
Missouri Div. of Health P.O. Box 570 65102

Joplin
St. John's Medical Center — 781-2727 Ext. 2305
2727 McClelland Blvd. 64801

Kansas City
Children's Mercy Hospital — 234-3000
24th & Gillham Rd. 64108

Kirksville
Kirksville Osteopathic Health Center — 626-2121
Box 949
1 Osteopathy Ave. 63501

Poplar Bluff
Lucy Lee Hospital — 785-7721
2620 N. Westwood Blvd. 63901

Rolla
Phelps County Memorial Hosp. — 364-1322
1000 W. 10th St. 65401

St. Joseph
Methodist Medical Center — 271-7580 / 232-8481
Seventh to Ninth on Faraon Sts. 64501

St. Louis
Cardinal Glennon Memorial Hospital for Children — 772-5200 / (1-800) 392-9111
1465 S. Grand Ave. 63104

St. Louis Children's Hosp. — 367-2034
500 S. Kingshighway 63110

Springfield
Ozark Poison Center — 831-9746
Lester E. Cox Medical Center — 1-800-492-4824
1423 N. Jefferson St. 65802

St. John's Regional Health Center — 885-2115
1235 E. Cherokee 65802

West Plains
West Plains Memorial Hosp. — 256-9111 Ext. 258 or 259
1103 Alaska Ave. 65775

MONTANA

STATE COORDINATOR
Department of Health and Environmental Sciences — (406) 449-3895

Montana Poison Control System — 1-800-525-5042
Cogswell Bldg. Helena 59620

NEBRASKA

STATE COORDINATOR
Department of Health — (402) 471-2122
Lincoln 68502

Omaha
Nebraska Reg. Poison Center — 390-5400
Children's Memorial Hospital 8301 Dodge 68114
Nebraska (N.E. Residents) — 800-642-9999
Surrounding States — 800-228-9515

NEVADA

STATE COORDINATOR
Department of Human Resources — (702) 885-4750
Carson City 89710

Las Vegas
Southern Nevada Memorial Hosp. — 385-1277
1800 W. Charleston Blvd. 89102

Sunrise Hospital Med. Ctr. — 732-4989
3186 South Maryland Parkway 89109

Reno
St. Mary's Hospital — 789-3013
235 W. 6th 89503

Washoe Medical Center — 785-4129
77 Pringle Way 89502

NEW HAMPSHIRE

STATE COORDINATOR
Hanover
New Hampshire Poison Center — (603) 643-4000
May Hitchcock Hospital 03755

NEW JERSEY

STATE COORDINATOR
Department of Health   (609) 292-5666
Accident Prevention &
Poison Control Program
Trenton 08625
Atlantic City
Atlantic City Medical Center   344-4081
1925 Pacific Ave. 08401   Ext. 2359
Belleville
Clara Maass Memorial Hosp.   751-1000
1A Franklin Ave. 07109   Ext. 781, 782, 783
Boonton
Riverside Hospital   334-5000
Powerville Rd. 07055   Ext. 186, 187
Bridgeton
Bridgeton Hospital   451-6600
Irving Ave. 08302
Camden
West Jersey Hospital   795-5554
Evesham Ave. and
Voorhees Tnpk. 08104
Denville
St. Clare's Hospital   627-3000
Pocono Rd. 07834   Ext. 6063
East Orange
East Orange General   672-8400
Hospital   Ext. 223
300 Central Ave. 07019
Elizabeth
St. Elizabeth Hospital   527-5059
225 Williamson St. 07207
Englewood
Englewood Hospital   894-3440
350 Engle St. 07631
Flemington
Hunterdon Medical Center   782-2121
Route #31 08822   Ext. 369

Livingston
St. Barnabas Medical Center   992-5161
Old Short Hills Rd. 07039
Long Branch
Monmouth Medical Center   222-2210
Emergency Dept.
Dunbar & 2nd Ave. 07740

Montclair
Mountainside Hospital   746-6000
Bay & Highland Ave. 07042   Ext. 234
Mount Holly
Burlington County Memorial   267-7877
175 Madison Ave. 08060

Neptune
Jersey Shore Medical Center-   775-5500
Fitkin Hospital   (800) 822-9761 (NJ)
1945 Corlies Ave. 07753

Newark
Newark Beth Israel   926-7240
Medical Center   926-7241
201 Lyons Ave. 07112   926-7242
                                          926-7243

New Brunswick
Middlesex General Hospital   828-3000
180 Somerset St. 08903   Ext. 425, 308
St. Peter's Medical Center   745-8527
254 Easton Ave. 08903
Newton
Newton Memorial Hospital   383-2121
175 High St. 07860   Ext. 270, 271, 273

Orange
Hospital Center at Orange   266-2120
Emergency Dept.
188 S. Essex Ave. 07051
Passaic
St. Mary's Hospital   473-1000
211 Pennington Ave. 07055   Ext. 441
Perth Amboy
Perth Amboy General Hosp.   442-3700
530 New Brunswick Ave.   Ext. 2501
08861
Phillipsburg
Warren Hospital   859-1500
185 Roseberry St. 08865   Ext. 280
Point Pleasant
Point Pleasant Hospital   892-1100
Osborn Ave. & River Front   Ext. 385
08742
Princeton
Medical Center at Princeton   734-4554
253 Witherspoon St. 08540
Saddle Brook
Saddle Brook General Hosp.   368-6025
300 Market St. 07662
Somers Point
Shore Memorial Hospital   653-3515
Brighton & Sunny Aves. 08244
Somerville
Somerset Medical Center   725-4000
Rehill Ave. 08876   Ext. 431, 432, 433
Summit
Overlook Hospital   522-2232
193 Morris Ave. 07901
Teaneck
Holy Name Hospital   833-3000
718 Teaneck Rd. 07666
Trenton
Helene Fuld Med. Ctr.   396-1077
750 Brunswick Ave. 08638
Union
Memorial General Hospital   687-1900
1000 Galloping Hill Rd. 07083   Ext. 237
Wayne
Greater Paterson General   942-6900
Hospital   Ext. 224
224 Hamburg Tnpk. 07470   Ext. 225
                                          Ext. 226

NEW MEXICO

STATE COORDINATOR
N.M. Poison, Drug Inf. & Med.   (505) 843-2551
Crisis Center   1-800-432-6866
University of New Mexico
Albuquerque 87131

NEW YORK

STATE COORDINATOR
Department of Health   (518) 474-3785
Albany 12237
Binghamton
Southern Tier Poison Center
Binghamton General Hospital   723-8929
Mitchell Avenue 13903

Our Lady of Lourdes   798-5231
Memorial Hospital
169 Riverside Drive 13905
Buffalo
Western N.Y. Poison Control Center   878-7000
Children's Hospital   878-7654
219 Bryant St. 14222   878-7655

Dunkirk
Brooks Memorial Hospital 366-1111
10 West 6th St. 14048 Ext. 414
Ext. 415

East Meadow
Long Island Poison Center 542-2323
Nassau County Medical Ctr. 542-2324
2201 Hempstead Tpk. 11554 542-2325

Elmira
Arnot Ogden Memorial Hosp. 737-4100
Roe Ave. & Grove 14901

St. Joseph's Hospital 734-2662
Health Center
555 E. Market St. 14901

Endicott
Ideal Hospital 754-7171
600 High St. 13760

Glens Falls
Glens Falls Hospital 792-3151
100 Park St. 12801 Ext. 456

Jamestown
W.C.A. Hospital 487-0141
207 Foote Ave. 14701 484-8648

Johnson City
Wilson Memorial Hospital 773-6611
33-57 Harrison St. 14707

Kingston
Kingston Hospital 331-3131
396 Broadway 12401

New York
N.Y. City Poison Center 340-4494
Dept. of Health 764-7667
Bureau of Laboratories
455 First Ave. 10016

Nyack
Hudson Valley Poison Center 358-6200
Nyack Hospital (Pharmacy) Ext. 451, 452
North Midland Ave. 10960

Rochester
Finger Lakes Poison 275-5151
Control Center Life Line
Univ. of Rochester
Medical Center 14620

Schenectady
Ellis Hospital 382-4039
1101 Nott Street 12308 382-4121

Syracuse
Syracuse Poison Inf. Ctr. 476-7529
750 E. Adams St. 13210 473-5831

Troy
St. Mary's Hospital 272-5792
1300 Massachusetts Ave. 12180

Utica
St. Luke's Hospital Center 798-6200
P.O. Box 479   13502 798-6223

Watertown
House of the Good 788-8700
Samaritan Hospital
Corner Washington &
Pratt Sts. 13602

NORTH CAROLINA

STATE COORDINATOR
Duke University Medical Center (919)684-8111
Durham 27710

Asheville
Western N.C. Poison Control Center
Memorial Mission Hospital 255-4490
509 Biltmore Ave. 28801

Charlotte
Mercy Hospital 379-5827
2001 Vail Ave. 28207

Greensboro
Moses Cone Hospital 379-4105
1200 N. Elm St. 27420

Hendersonville
Margaret R. Pardee Memorial 693-6522
Hospital Ext. 555, 556
Fleming St. 28739

Hickory
Catawba Memorial Hospital 322-6649
Fairgrove-Church Rd. 28601

Jacksonville
Onslow Memorial Hospital 353-7610
Western Blvd. 28540

Wilmington
New Hanover Memorial Hosp. 343-7046
2131 S. 17th St. 28401

NORTH DAKOTA

STATE COORDINATOR
Department of Health (701) 224-2388
Bismarck 58505

Bismarck
Bismarck Hospital 223-4357
300 N. 7th St. 58501

Fargo
St. Luke's Hosptal 280-5575
Fifth St. at Mills Ave. 58122

Grand Forks
United Hospital 780-5000
1200 S. Columbia Rd. 58201

Minot
St. Joseph's Hospital 857-2553
Third St. & Fourth Ave., S.E. 58701

Williston
Mercy Hospital 572-7661
1301 15th Ave. W. 58801

OHIO

STATE COORDINATOR
Department of Health (614)466-5190
Columbus 43216

Akron
Children's Hospital 379-8562
281 Locust 44308 (1-800) 362-9922 (Ohio)

Canton
Aultman Hospital 452-9911
Emergency Room Ext. 203
2600 Sixth St., S.W. 44710

Cincinnati
Drug & Poison Inf. Ctr.
Bridge Bldg.
Univ. of Cincinnati 872-5111
Medcal Center, Rm. 7701
231 Bethesda Ave. 45267

Cleveland
Academy of Medicine 231-4455
11001 Cedar Ave. 44106

Columbus
Ohio Poison Center 228-1323
Children's Hospital
700 Children's Dr. 43205

Dayton
Children's Medical Center 222-2227
One Children's Plaza 45404

Lorain
Lorain Community Hospital 282-2220
3700 Kolbe Rd. 44053

Mansfield
Mansfield General Hospital 522-3411
335 Glessner Ave. 44903 Ext. 545
Springfield
Community Hospital 325-1255
2615 E. High St. 44505
Toledo
Poison Information Center 381-3897
Medical College Hospital
P.O. Box 6190   43679
Youngstown
Mahoning Valley Poison
Control Center
St. Elizabeth Hospital & Med Ctr. 746-2222
1044 Belmont Ave. 44501
Zanesville
Bethesda Hospital 454-4221
Poison Information Center
2951 Maple Ave. 43701

OKLAHOMA

STATE COORDINATOR
Oklahoma Poison Control Ctr (405) 271-5454
Oklahoma Children's 800-522-4611
Memorial Hospital
P.O. Box 26307
Oklahoma City 73126
Ada
Valley View Hospital 322-2323
1300 E. 6th St. 74820 Ext. 200
Ardmore
Memorial Hospital of 223-5400
Southern Oklahoma
1011-14th Ave. 73401
Lawton
Comanche County Memorial 355-8620
Hospital
3401 Gore Blvd. 73501
McAlester
McAlester General Hospital, West 426-1800
P.O. Box 669 74501 Ext. 240
Oklahoma City
Oklahoma Poison Control Center 271-5454
Oklahoma Children's 800-522-4611
Memorial Hospital
P.O. Box 26307
73126
Ponca City
St. Joseph Medical Center 765-3321
14th & Hartford 74601
Tulsa
Hillcrest Medical Center 584-1351
1653 East 12th 74104 Ext. 6165

OREGON

Portland
Oregon Poison Control and
Drug Info. Center
University of Oregon (503) 225-8968
Health Sciences Center 1-800-452-7165

PANAMA

U.S.A. Meddac Panama 52-7105
Gorgas U.S. Army Hospital
APO Miami 34004

PENNSYLVANIA

STATE COORDINATOR
Director, Division of Epidemiology
Department of Health (717) 787-2307
P.O. Box 90
Harrisburg 17108
Allentown
Lehigh Valley Poison Center 433-2311
17th & Chew St. 18102
Altoona
Altoona Region Poison Center 946-3711
Mercy Hospital
2500 Seventh Ave. 16603
Bloomsurg
The Bloomsburg Hospital 784-7121
549 E. Fair St. 17815
Bradford
Bradford Hospital 368-4143
Interstate Pkwy 16701
Bryn Mawr
The Bryn Mawr Hospital 896-3577
19010
Chester
Sacred Heart General Hosp. 494-0721
9th and Wilson St. 19013 Ext. 232
Clearfield
Clearfield Hospital 765-5341
809 Turnpike Ave. 16830
Coaldale
Coaldale State General 645-2131
Hospital 18218
Coudersport
Charles Cole Memorial 274-9300
Hospital
RD #3, Route 6   16915
Danville
Susquehanna Poison Center 275-6116
Geisinger Medical Center
North Academy Ave. 17821
Doylestown
Doylestown Hospital 345-2283
595 W. State St. 18901
East Stroudsburg
Pocono Hospital 421-4000
206 E. Brown St. 18301
Easton
Easton Hospital 258-6221
21st & Lehigh St. 18042
Erie
Doctors Osteopathic 454-2120
252 W. 11th St. 16501
Erie Osteopathic Hospital 864-4031
5515 Peach St. 16509
Hamot Medical Center 452-4242
201 State St. 16512
Northwest Poison Center 452-3232
St. Vincent Health Center
P.O. Box 740   16512
Gettysburg
Annie M. Warner Hospital 334-2121
S. Washington St. 17325
Greensburg
Westmoreland Hosp. Assn. 832-4000
532 W. Pittsburgh St. 15601
Hanover
Hanover General Hospital 637-3711
300 Highland Ave. 17331
Harrisburg
Harrisburg Hospital 782-3639
S. Front & Mulberry St. 17101

Polyclinic Hospital   782-4141
3rd & Polyclinic Ave. 17105   Ext. 4132

Hershey
Capital Area Poison Center   534-6111
Milton S. Hershey Medical   534-8955
Center
University Dr. 17033

Jeannete
Jeannete District Memorial   527-3551
Hospital
600 Jefferson Ave 15644

Jersey Shore
Jersey Shore Hospital   398-0100
Thompson St. 17740

Johnstown
Conemaugh Valley Memorial   535-5351
Hospital
1086 Franklin St. 15905

Cambria-Somerset Poison Center
Lee Hospital   535-5352
320 Main St. 15901

Mercy Hospital   535-5353
1020 Franklin St. 15905

Lancaster
Lancaster General Hospital   299-5511
555 North Duke St. 17604

St. Joseph's Hospital   299-4546
250 College Ave. 17604

Lansdale
North Penn Hospital   368-2100
7th & Broad St. 19446

Lebanon
Good Samaritan Hospital   272-7611
4th & Walnut Sts. 17042

Lehighton
Gnaden-Huetten Memorial   377-1300
Hospital
11th & Hamilton St. 18235

Lewiston
Lewiston Hospital   248-5411
Highland Ave. 17044

Muncy
Muncy Valley Hospital   546-8282
P.O. Box 340 17756

Nanticoke
Nanticoke State Hospital   735-5000
W. Washington St. 18634

Paoli
Paoli Memorial Hospital 19301   648-1043

Philadelphia
Philadelphia Poison   922-5523
Information   922-5524
321 University Ave. 19104

Philipsburg
Philipsburg State General   342-3320
Hospital 16866

Pittsburgh
Children's Hospital   681-6669
125 DeSoto St. 15213

Pittston
Pittston Hospital   654-3341
Oregon Heights 18640

Pottstown
Pottstown Memorial Medical   327-7000
Center
High St. & Firestone Blvd.
19464

Pottsville
Good Samaritan Hospital   622-3400
E. Norwegian and   Ext. 270
Tremont St. 17901

Reading
Community General Hospital   376-4881
145 N. 6th St. 19601   Ext. 267

Sayre
The Robert Packer Hospital   888-6666
Guthrie Square 18840

Sellersville
Grandview Hospital 18960   257-3611

Somerset
Somerset Community Hospital   443-2626
225 South Center Ave. 15501

State College
Centre Community Hospital   238-4351
16801

Titusville
Titusville Hospital   827-1851
406 W. Oak St. 16354
Tunkhannock Tyler
Memorial Hospital   836-2161
RD #1 18657

York
Memorial Osteopathic Hospital   843-8623
325 S. Belmont St. 17403

York Hospital   771-2311
1001 S. George St. 17405

PUERTO RICO

STATE COORDINATOR
University of Puerto Rico   (809) 765-4880
Rio Piedras   (809) 765-0615

Arecibo
District Hospital   878-6467
of Arecibo   (Info. Only)
00613

Fajardo
District Hospital   863-0939
of Fajardo   Ext. 202,
00649   203
Mayaguez
Mayaguez Medical Center   832-8686
Dept. of Health   Ext. 1224
P.O. Box 1868 00709

Ponce
District Hospital of   842-8364
Ponce 00731

Rio Piedras
Children's Hospital   754-8535
Center of Puerto   Ext. 8536
Rico   Ext. 8537
00936   Ext. 8538

San Juan
Pharmacy School   753-4849
Medical Sciences   (Info. Only)
Campus
00936

RHODE ISLAND

STATE COORDINATOR
Rhode Island Poison Control Center
Rhode Island Hospital   (401) 277-5727
593 Eddy St.
Providence 02902

SOUTH CAROLINA

STATE COORDINATOR
Department of Health   (803) 758-5654
Environmental Control
Columbia 29201
Charleston
National Pesticide
Telecommunications Network   792-4201
Medical University of   (800) 745-7633
South Carolina   (800) 922-0193
171 Ashley Ave. 29403
Columbia
Palmetto Poison Center   765-7359
College of Pharmacy   (1-800) 922-1117
University of S.C. 29208

SOUTH DAKOTA

STATE COORDINATOR
Department of Health   (605) 773-3361
Pierre 57501
Aberdeen
The Dakota Midland   225-1880
Poison Control   (1-800) 592-1889
Center 57401
Rapid City
Rapid City Regional   341-8222
Hospital Main   1-800-742-8925
353 Fairmont Blvd. 57701
Sioux Falls
McKennan Hospital Poison Center   336-3894
800 East 21st St. 57101   (1-800) 952-0123

TENNESSEE

STATE COORDINATOR
Department of Public Health   (615) 741-2407
Division of Emergency Serices
Nashville 37216
Chattanooga
T.C. Thompson Children's   755-6100
Hospital
910 Blackford St. 37403
Columbia
Maury County Hospital   381-4500
1224 Trotwood Ave.
38401
Cookeville
Cookeville General Hospital   526-4818
142 W. 5th St. 38501
Jackson
Madison General Hospital   424-0424
708 W. Forest 38301
Johnson City
Memorial Hospital   461-6111
Boone & Fairview Ave. 37601
Knoxville
Memorial Research Center   971-3261
and Hospital
1924 Alcoa Highway 37920
Memphis
Southern Poison Center   528-6048
University of Tennessee
College of Pharmacy
26 Dunlap St. 38163
Nashville
Vanderbilt University Hospital   322-3391
21st & Garland 37232

TEXAS

STATE COORDINATOR
Department of Health   (512) 458-7254
Div. of Occupational Health
Austin 78756
Abilene
Hendrick Hospital   677-7762
19th & Hickory Sts. 79601
Amarillo
Amarillo Hospital District   376-4292
Amarillo Emergency Receiving
Center
P.O. Box 1110
2103 W. 6th St. 79106
Austin
Brackenridge Hospital   478-4490
14th & Sabine Sts. 78701   476-6461
Beaumont
Baptist Hospital of   833-7409
Southeast Texas
P.O. Box 1591
College & 11th St. 77701
Corpus Christi
Memorial Medical Center   881-4559
P.O. Box 5280
2606 Hospital Blvd. 78405
El Paso
R.E. Thomason General   533-1244
Hospital
P.O Box 20009
4815 Alameda Ave. 79905
Fort Worth
W.I. Cook Children's   927-2007
Hospital
1212 W. Lancaster 76102
Galveston
Southeast Texas Poison   765-1420
Control Center
8th & Mechanic Sts. 77550
Harlingen
Valley Baptist Hospital   421-1860
P.O. Box 2588   421-1859
2101 S. Commerce St.
78550
Houston
Southeast Texas Poison   654-1701
Control Center
8th and Mechanic St.
Galveston, Tex. 77550
Laredo
Mercy Hospital   724-6247
1515 Logan St. 78040
Lubbock
Methodist Hospital   792-1011
Pharmacy
3615 19th St. 79410
Midland
Midland Memorial Hospital   685-1111
1908 W. Wall 79701
Odessa
Medical Center Hospital   333-7111
P.O. Box 633   79760
Plainview
Central Plains Regional Hospital   296-9601
2601 Dimmitt Rd. 79072
San Angelo
Shannon West Texas   653-6741
Memorial Hosphial   Ext. 210
P.O. Box 1879
9 S. Magdalen St. 76901

San Antonio
Department of Pediatrics   223-6361
Univ. of Texas Health Science   Ext. 295
Center at San Antonio
7703 Floyd Curl Dr. 78284
Tyler
Medical Center Hospital   597-0351
1000 S. Beckham St. 75701
Waco
Hillcrest Baptist Hosp.   756-8611
3000 Herring Ave. 76708
Wichita Falls
Wichita General Hospital   322-6771
Emergency Room
1600 8th St. 76301

UTAH

STATE COORDINATOR
Utah Department of Health   (801) 533-6161
Division Family Health Services
Salt Lake City 84113
Salt Lake City
Intermountain Regional   581-2151
Poison Control Center
50 N. Medical Drive 84132

VERMONT

STATE COORDINATOR
Department of Health   (802) 862-5701
Burlington 05401
Burlington
Vermont Poison Control   658-3456
Medical Center Hospital 05401

VIRGINIA

STATE COORDINATOR
Bureau of Emergency   (804) 786-5188
Medical Services
Richmond 23219
Alexandria
Alexandria Hospital   379-3070
4320 Seminary Rd. 22314
Arlington
Arlington Hospital   558-6161
5129 N. 16th St. 22205
Blacksburg
Montgomery County   951-1111
Community Hospital
Rt. 460, S. 24060
Charlottesville
Blue Ridge Poison Center   924-5543
Univ. of Virginia Hospital 22903
                 (1-800) 446-9876 (Deaf Out-of-State)
                 (1-800) 552-3723 (Deaf VA Only)
Danville
Danville Memorial Hospital   799-2100
142 S. Main St. 22201   Ext. 3869
Falls Church
Fairfax Hospital   698-3600
3300 Gallows Rd. 22046   698-3111
Hampton
Hampton General Hospital   727-1131
3120 Victoria Blvd. 23661
Harrisonburg
Rockingham Memorial Hospital   433-9706
738 S. Mason St. 22801

Lexington
Stonewall Jackson Hosp.   463-9141
22043
Lynchburg
Lynchburg Gen. Marshall   528-2066
Lodge Hosp., Inc.
Tate Springs Rd. 24504
Nassawadox
Northampton-Accomack   442-8700
Memorial Hospital 23413
Newport News
Riverside Hospital   599-2050
500 J. Clyde Morris Blvd. 23601
Norfolk
DePaul Hospital   489-5288
Granby St. at Kingsley
Lane 23505
Petersburg
Petersburg General Hospital   732-7220
Mt. Erin & Adams Sts. 23803
Portsmouth
U.S. Naval Hospital   398-5898
23708
Richmond
Central Virginia Poison Center   786-9123
Medical College of Virginia
Box 763 MCV Station 23298
Roanoke
Roanoke Memorial Hospital   981-7336
Belleview at Jefferson St.
P.O. Box 13367   24033
Staunton
King's Daughters' Hospital   885-6848
P.O. Box 2007   24401
Waynesboro
Waynesboro Community   942-4096
Hospital
501 Oak Ave. 22980
Williamsburg
Williamsburg Community Hosp.   253-6005
1238 Mt. Vernon Ave.
Drawer H 23185

VIRGIN ISLANDS

STATE COORDINATOR
Dept. of Health   (809) 774-1321
St. Thomas 00801   Ext. 275

ST. CROIX
Charles Harwood Memorial   773-1212
Hospital 00820   773-1311
                                                 Ext. 221

Ingeborg Nesbitt Clinic   772-0260
Fredericksted 00840   772-0212

ST. JOHN

Morris F. DeCastro Clinic   776-1469
Cruz Bay 00830

ST. THOMAS
Knud-Hansen Memorial   774-1321
Hospital   Ext. 224
00801   Ext. 225

WASHINGTON

STATE COORDINATOR
Department of Social &   (206) 522-7478
Health Services
Seattle 98115

Seattle
Children's Orthopedic   634-5252
Hosp. & Med. Center
4800 Sandpoint Way, N.E.
98105

Spokane
Deaconess Hospital   747-1077
W. 800 5th Ave. 99210   (1-800) 572-5842

Tacoma
Mary Bridge Children's   272-1281
Hospital   Ext. 259
S. L St. 98405

Yakima
Central Washington Poison Center   248-4400
Yakima Valley Memorial   (1-800) 572-9176
Hospital
2811 Tieton Dr. 98902

WEST VIRGINIA

STATE COORDINATOR
Department of Health   (304) 348-2971
Charleston 25305

Charleston
West Virginia Poison System   (1-800) 642-3625
3110 MacCorkle Ave. SE 29208   348-4211

WISCONSIN

STATE COORDINATOR
Department of Health & Social   (608) 267-7174
Services, Div. of Health
Madison 53701

Eau Claire
Luther Hospital   835-1515
1225 Whipple 54701

Green Bay
Green Bay Poison Control Center   433-8100
St. Vincent Hospital
835 S. Van Burean St. 54305

LaCrosse
St. Francis Hospital   784-3971
700 West Ave. N 54601

Madison
Madison Area Poison Center   262-3702
University Hospital and Clinic
600 Highland Ave. 53792

Milwaukee
Milwaukee Children's Hospital   931-4114
1700 W. Wisconsin 53233

WYOMING

STATE COORDINATOR
Office of Emergency Medical   (307) 777-7955
Services
Department of Health &
Social Services
Cheyenne 82001

Cheyenne
Wyoming Poison Center   635-9256
De Paul Hospital
2600 East 18th St. 82001

Glossary

Terms commonly used in the health field

by Charlotte Isler, Clinical Editor, RN Magazine

A

Abdominal aneurysm - usually due to dilatation of the aorta, the largest abdominal blood vessel, into a protruding sac caused by a weakening of its wall. May also occasionally occur in other abdominal blood vessels.

Abortion - the loss of the fetus in the course of pregnancy. Abortion may be spontaneous, induced, or done for therapeutic reasons.

Abrasion - removal of a portion of skin due to injury or a surgical procedure.

Abruptio placentae - the premature detachment of an otherwise normal placenta, the organ through which the developing fetus obtains nourishment and oxygen.

Abscess - localized collection of pus under the skin or in another part of the body, such as the ear, tooth, lung, brain or the liver; usually due to infection.

Acidosis - a condition in which the acid/base balance of body fluids is disturbed, thereby decreasing the alkaline content.

Aciduria - acid condition of the urine.

Acupuncture - ancient oriental treatment method using long fine needles in various areas of the body to reduce pain and alleviate various other disease conditions.

Acute - the quick, sharp onset of a condition such as pain, usually of limited duration.

Adenoma - a benign growth that is generally well circumscribed. It exerts pressure against surrounding tissue instead of infiltrating it as do other tumors.

Adrenal glands - two glands, each located near one of the kidneys, that secrete the hormones adrenaline and cortisone.

Adsorbent - a substance that can suck other substances to its surface, without requiring a chemical agent.

Agoraphobia - the fear of being in an open space.

Airway - the respiratory tract, or any part of the respiratory tract that acts as a passage for air during the process of breathing.

Airway obstruction - any foreign body, or physical process that occludes the respiratory tract or any of its parts, making breathing difficult or impossible.

Albumin - a body protein present in tissue and body fluids.

Alcohol dependency - the inability to manage life's functions and responsibilities without consuming a given quantity of alcohol, or experiencing withdrawal symptoms if alcohol consumption is stopped. Alcoholism.

Alcohol poisoning - the toxic effects of excessive alcohol intake.

Alkaloid - a type of chemical contained in many drugs that is made from plants or manufactured synthetically.

Allergy - an abnormal bodily reaction due to an acquired hypersensitivity on exposure to environmental substances such as dust, pollen, foods, bacteria or physical agents (heat, cold, light) that may be slight or severe. Symptoms appear in the form of respiratory symptoms (tearing, wheezing, coughing, sneezing); skin conditions (rashes, wheals or hives); or such digestive tract symptoms as belching, flatus, nausea, vomiting, abdominal pain or diarrhea.

Amblyopia - impaired vision, due to hereditary, structural or dietary deficiency.

Amebiasis - an infection caused by one-celled microorganisms (amebae) that mainly involves the intestine but may spread to other body organs, especially the liver.

Amenorrhea - the absence, or sudden cessation of the menstrual blood flow.

Amino acid - a substance formed during the digestive breakdown of proteins.

Amniocentesis - the withdrawal, under sterile conditions, of a sample of fluid (amniotic fluid) from a thin, tough, transparent membranous sac (the amniotic sac) that surrounds, cushions and protects the developing fetus. Done to determine possible defects, and sometimes the sex of the unborn child.

Amniotic fluid - the protective fluid that is present in the amniotic sac during pregnancy to cushion the growing fetus against injury.

Amyotrophic lateral sclerosis (ALS) - a progressive disease of unknown cause of the nerves and muscles. It affects certain portions of the spinal cord with the muscles gradually wasting away (atrophy), which causes increasing weakness and eventual paralysis, especially in the muscles of the arms, shoulders, legs and those that control breathing.

Anabolism - the process of using energy to turn food taken into the body into living tissues.

Anaerobe - a microorganism that grows only when there is little, or no oxygen present.

Anal - the lowest portion of the intestinal tract.

Analgesic - a medication used to relieve pain.

Anaphylaxis - a severe form of allergic (hypersensitive) reaction to a substance that can be fatal if not treated immediately.

Androsterone - a male sex hormone.

Anemia - an abnormal condition of the blood in which there is a deficiency of red blood cells, and/or a deficiency of hemoglobin, the substance which carries oxygen from the lungs to the tissues.

Aneurysm - a condition in which the wall of an artery weakens, balloons out and may burst, causing severe, possibly fatal bleeding.

Angina - a choking or suffocative type of spasmodic pain.

Angina pectoris - a severe, paroxysmal pain in the chest with a feeling of oppression or suffocation, due to an insufficient supply of blood oxygen to the heart muscle. These symptoms are usually precipitated by exertion or excitement.

Angioedema - swelling of body tissues, usually as part of an allergic reaction.

Anomaly - an abnormality or defect of a body organ or structure.

Anorectal - referring to the lowest portion of the intestinal tract, the anal canal and the rectum.

Anorexia - a loss of appetite due to illness, emotional disturbance or ingestion of certain drugs.

Anorexia nervosa - a psychological illness, mostly in adolescent girls, in which the patient eats little or no food, resulting in severe weight loss and possible death if not treated.

Anorexics - a category of drugs that suppresses the appetite, taken to enable a person to lose weight.

Antacid - an alkaline drug that neutralizes excessive stomach acids.

Anthelmintics - drugs given to destroy and expel intestinal worms.

Antibacterial - a drug that counteracts, inhibits, or destroys bacteria.

Antibody - a constituent of blood and body fluids that acts to protect the body against infection.

Anticaries agent - a drug that protects teeth or bones against decay or destruction.

Anticholinergics - drugs that suppress secretions from the stomach and other internal organs such as glands, dilate the pupils of the eyes, and decrease the actions of the respiratory, gastrointestinal and urinary systems.

Anticoagulant - a drug given to slow the clotting action of blood.

Antidiarrheal - an agent or substance, usually a drug, that counteracts the effects of diarrhea.

Antidote - an agent or substance, usually a drug, that counteracts a poison applied to the body externally or via ingestion, either by accident or by intention.

Antiemetic - an agent or substance, usually a drug, that counteracts nausea and/or vomiting.

Antiflatulent - an agent or substance, usually a drug, that counteracts excessive gas in the intestinal tract.

Antifungal - an agent or substance, usually a drug, that counteracts the effects of fungal organisms that cause infections of the skin, nails, hair, and of the mucous membranes.

Antigen - a substance which causes the production of antibodies when it is absorbed by the body through ingestion of food, inhalation, or application to the skin.

Antihistamine - a drug that counteracts the action of histamine, an organic compound that acts as a powerful dilator of small blood vessels. Antihistamine drugs are used to relieve symptoms of allergy and those of the common cold.

Antimicrobial (antibacterial) - an agent, usually a drug, that acts to destroy or inhibit the actions of disease-causing microorganisms, such as bacteria.

Antipruritic - an agent, usually a drug, that decreases, stops or prevents itching.

Antipyretic - an agent, usually a drug, that reduces fever.

Antiseptic - an agent, usually a drug, that inhibits the growth and development of microorganisms, such as bacteria.

Antiserum - a specially prepared liquid portion of blood that contains antibodies against a specific disease.

Antispasmodic - an agent, usually a drug, that reduces or relieves spasms in certain body tissues such as the sphincter (muscular opening) of the stomach, gallbladder or the rectum. An antispasmodic can also relieve spasms in blood vessels, or in such body parts as the bronchi.

Antitussive - an agent, usually a drug, that relieves or stops spasms of coughing.

Anxiety - a psychological condition that causes fear, apprehension and feelings of imminent danger, with accompanying physical symptoms such as difficulty in breathing, restlessness and an increase in the rate of heart beats.

Aorta - the main artery (largest blood vessel in the body), that arises from the heart, arches through the chest down into the abdomen and carries oxygenated blood from the heart to smaller arteries, bringing oxygen to nourish the organs and tissues throughout the body.

Aphasia - the inability to speak, write or communicate via appropriate signs, or to understand the writing or speaking of others, usually as a result of brain damage.

Apoplexy (stroke) - a condition caused by hemorrhage, or bleeding in the brain from a ruptured blood vessel, due to weakness in the blood vessel's wall, or blockage of the vessel from a local clot, or one that traveled from another site (embolus) in the arterial system or the heart.

Aqueous humor - fluid produced in the front portion of the eyeball. This fluid bathes the anterior structures of the eyeball. If its normal outflow is blocked, painful, dangerous pressure develops inside the eye, a condition known as glaucoma.

Arrhythmia - irregularity in the pattern of the heart beat.

Arteriography - X-ray study of part of the arterial system to diagnose disturbance of the blood supply to any body part or area.

Arteriosclerosis - hardening of one or more arteries.

Arteritis - inflammation of one or more arteries.

Arthritis - a condition in which body joints and their supporting structures are inflamed and painful.

Ascites - an abnormal collection of fluid in the abdominal area due to disease conditions of one or more organs such as the liver, the heart or the kidneys.

Ascorbic acid (vitamin C) - a nutritional substance essential to normal body function. Deficiency causes scurvy, a condition in which the affected person suffers from bleeding and inflammation of the gums, loose teeth, and bleeding in other body areas.

Aseptic - a substance that kills microorganisms, and sterilizes the area to which it is applied; sterile.

Asphyxia - state of suffocation due to some form of interference with normal breathing.

Aspirate - fluid or tissue removed from the body via suction.

Asthma - a breathing disorder caused by infection or allergy in the bronchi.

Astringent - a medication that contracts blood vessels and other tissues, thereby reducing swelling, bleeding or secretions.

Atelectasis - collapse of a portion of a lung.

Athlete's foot - an infection of the foot caused by a fungal microorganism.

Atopic - a type of allergy that occurs only in humans.

Atrium - the upper, thin, muscular walled chamber of the right and left heart. The right atrium receives deoxygenated blood from the large veins before it courses through the lower right heart chamber (right ventricle) on its way to the lungs to be oxygenated. The left atrium receives oxygenated blood from lung vessels which then flows down into the lower left heart chamber (left ventricle), to be pumped out into the aorta and the arterial system to provide oxygen to the body tissues.

Atrophy - the wasting of tissue, muscles or any other body part or organ.

Auscultation - listening to various sounds, such as those produced by the heart or the lungs, with the ear or through a stethoscope.

Autism - a psychological disorder of children and some adults in which the person escapes real life by living in a world of fantasy, unable and unwilling to respond to ordinary human contact.

Autoantibody - an antibody produced by the body in reaction to its own tissues.

Autoantigen - a substance present in the body to which an individual is allergic.

Autogenous vaccine - a vaccine prepared from material taken from the body of a person who will subsequently receive the vaccine.

Autoimmune disease - a condition caused when the body produces antibodies against its own tissues.

Autoinfection - a condition in which a person becomes reinfected by microorganisms that had caused an earlier infection.

Autosomal inheritance - inherited traits passed on by genes located in 22 pairs of autosomes, which carry all characteristics other than those of sex.

Avitaminosis - a deficiency of essential vitamins.

B

Bacillary - referring to a bacillus, a rod-shaped type of microorganism occurring in some forms that are harmless, and in others that cause disease.

Bacteremia - blood poisoning caused by the presence of bacteria in the blood.

Barium enema - a diagnostic X-ray procedure done to examine the lower intestinal tract. Barium is given in the form of an enema to make the bowel visible on the X-ray film.

Beriberi - a disease involving the heart and the nervous system, caused by a deficiency of vitamin B_1 (thiamine).

Biliary - referring to the gallbladder or any portion of the gallbladder tract.

Biliary calculus - a stone in the gallbladder or in any part of the gallbladder tract.

Biopsy - the removal of a small portion of tissue from the body for diagnostic purposes.

Blackhead - fatty material that has hardened into a plug inside a skin pore.

Blepharitis - an inflammation of the eyelids.

Blister - a collection of fluid formed inside a sac on or in the skin, caused by irritation, fever, or one of various skin or infectious diseases.

Blood - the fluid that circulates through the arteries, veins and smaller blood vessels to bring nourishment to the tissues and remove wastes.

Blood brain barrier - a mechanism that prevents many substances that circulate in the blood, such as certain drugs, from getting into the circulation of the brain.

Blood component - any constituent of blood, such as red blood cells, white blood cells, platelets and others.

Blood gases - gases, such as oxygen and carbon dioxide that are dissolved in the blood.

Blood groups - also called blood types. There are four main blood groups (types) A, B, AB and O. There are also many sub-groups. Persons who have one type of blood can only receive a blood transfusion from another person who has the same blood type. The same is true for a blood donor, who can donate his blood only to a person of the same type. The exceptions are a donor of type O blood (universal donor), whose blood can be administered to any other person regardless of the other's blood type, and a person with type AB blood (universal recipient), who can receive blood from any other person, whatever his blood type. But the AB type donor can give blood only to another AB type recipient.

Blood pressure - the pressure exerted by the circulating blood against the walls of the blood vessels through which it flows.

Blood volume - the amount (volume) of blood in the body at any time, generally considered normal at 8 - 9% of body weight.

Boil - an area of skin filled with pus due to an infection.

Bone marrow - tissues that are contained in the cavities of bones. Red bone marrow contains developing red blood cells, white blood cells and platelets, while yellow bone marrow consists of a fatty substance.

Bowel - another term for the intestine, which consists of two parts: the small intestine and the large intestine (small bowel and large bowel).

Bowel incontinence - inability to retain or control bowel movements.

Bradycardia - a very slow heart beat, usually considered to be less than 60 beats per minute.

Breech presentation - a birth process in which the baby's buttocks present first in the mother's birth canal, in contrast to the more common head-first presentation. A breech birth process is more prone to complications, and more likely to require instrumentation or surgery during delivery than a normal, head-first presentation.

Bronchiectasis - a disease in which the bronchi (hollow tubular structures that carry inhaled air from the windpipe (trachea) to the lungs), and/or their smaller subdivisions (bronchioles) are widened due to repeated bouts of infection in the lungs. This disease is marked by foul-smelling breath and coughing spells, accompanied by spitting, and coughing up of mucous, pus-filled material from the bronchi.

Bronchitis - inflammation of the lining of the bronchi.

Bronchodilator - a drug given to dilate the bronchial tubes when they are shut down by spasms, such as occur in asthma.

Bronchogenic - any disease or other condition that arises in the bronchi.

Bronchopneumonia - inflammation, usually due to infection, of the lower portions of the bronchi (bronchioles) and the lungs.

Bronchoscopy - visualization of the windpipe (trachea) and the bronchial structures via an endoscope, a lighted instrument passed into these passages, for examination or treatment.

Bruxism - clenching or grinding of the teeth, usually done during sleep.

Bunion - a condition, usually due to wearing improperly fitting shoes, which causes a painful deformity of the big toe.

Bursitis - inflammation of a bursa, a sac-like cavity filled with a thick fluid that lubricates areas otherwise likely to sustain damage through friction; mainly affects bursae near joints, or those underneath the tendons that move the joints.

C

Calciferol (vitamin D) - an essential nutritional substance that affects the development of bone. With insufficient intake of this vitamin bone disease may occur.

Calcium - a vital element essential to the healthy composition of bones and teeth. Insufficient intake of calcium via foods may produce bone and teeth problems.

Callus - a hardened portion of skin, usually found on the palms of the hands or the soles, due to continual pressure and friction on these areas.

Caloric value - the measurement of heat produced by a food when it is burned (metabolized) in the body.

Calorie - a unit of heat content or energy.

Candida - a common type of yeastlike fungus. In man, Candida fungus is frequently found on the skin, in the throat, vagina, and in feces. Infection caused by this type of fungus is called candidiasis or moniliasis.

Canker sore - a small, usually ulcerated sore on the inside of the mouth, due to illness, irritation, or vitamin deficiency.

Capillary - relates to a tiny blood or lymph vessel.

Carbuncle - a skin condition caused by an infection, in which an area is filled with pus, enclosed by a hard covering that has a number of openings through which the pus may be discharged. It is bigger, and reaches down into the skin further than a boil.

Carcinogen - any substance in the environment or in food, or in some other agent, that may contribute to the development of cancer.

Cardiac - relating to the heart.

Cardiac arrest - a sudden stopping of the pumping of the heart that is fatal if not reversed within a few minutes.

Cardiac catheterization - the passing of a very fine tube into the chambers of the heart for diagnostic purposes.

Cardiovascular - relating to the heart or to the blood vessels.

Carditis - inflammation of the heart.

Caries - a condition that indicates decay of teeth or bones.

Cartilage - whitish, tough, flexible tissue situated around joints, in the spinal column, the ears, windpipe, voice box (larynx) and the tip of the nose.

Catabolism - the breakdown process of food during digestion into less complex substances.

Cataract - a condition in which the lens of the eye becomes cloudy, impairing vision. This process may be due to aging, disease, trauma, or may sometimes be found at birth as a congenital condition.

Catarrh - an inflammation of mucous membranes usually accompanied by a discharge. When it occurs only in the nose (as in the common cold), it is called rhinitis. If it affects both the nose and the throat, it is also called nasopharyngitis.

Catecholamines - chemical substances in the body that affect the actions of the involuntary nervous system.

Cathartic - a drug that speeds up the emptying action of the bowel.

Catheterization - a process in which a tube is passed into a body organ to empty it, as in urinary catheterization, or for diagnostic or treatment purposes.

CAT scan - a complex new X-ray procedure, whose full name is computerized axial tomography. It produces a reconstructed image of a transverse section of the body part being examined. It allows in-depth, accurate visualization that is helpful in diagnosing disease or injury, without the need to cut, or otherwise physically invade the body part.

Cat-scratch disease - a relatively mild infection believed to be transmitted via a virus that lives in cats, when a person is scratched by an otherwise healthy cat. Symptoms involve headache, fever and swelling of some lymph glands.

Cellulitis - inflammation of cellular or connective tissue in various parts of the body.

Centigrade - a measurement of heat used throughout the world based on a scale that is divided into 100 degrees. Normal body temperature on this scale is 37°C, which corresponds to the Fahrenheit scale at 98.6°F.

Central nervous system - that part of the nervous system that includes the brain and the spinal cord.

Cerebral hemorrhage - bleeding from an artery or other blood vessel in the brain, caused by weakness, injury, congenital abnormality or a disease such as high blood pressure.

Cerebral palsy - a condition of weakness, poor muscular coordination and spasm caused by damage to the brain that may occur before, during, or shortly after birth.

Cerebrospinal fluid - the fluid that bathes the brain and the spinal cord.

Cerebrovascular accident (CVA) - bleeding in the brain, the brain's coverings, or the formation of a blood clot that deprives a portion of the brain of oxygen which its tissues need to survive.

Cerumen - the wax in the ears.

Cerumenolytics - agents or drugs that dissolve ear wax.

Cervix - the neck of the womb, an important part of a woman's birth canal.

Cesarean section (C-section) - the surgical delivery of a baby through the abdomen, done when the baby is in distress during labor, when the mother is ill and not considered strong enough to cope with a normal vaginal delivery, or if the mother's birth canal is malformed, so that the baby cannot pass through safely.

Chalazion - a usually painless, slow-growing localized swelling in the margin of the eyelid due to a blockage of a small gland that is chronically inflamed.

Chancre - a symptom of syphilis, a venereal disease caused by spirochetal bacteria called treponema pallidum. The chancre is a hard skin lesion that occurs during the first stage of the disease, at the site where the spirochetes entered the body.

Chemotherapy - chemical agents or drugs used to treat various diseases, or to prevent them.

Chilblains - the swelling, reddening and itching of body parts such as the hands, fingers, nose and ears following prolonged exposure to cold.

Chloasma - brown pigmented spots or patches on the skin of the face and other parts of the body that occur with pregnancy, the menopause, or with the use of oral contraceptives.

Cholecystitis - inflammation of the gallbladder.

Cholecystokinetics - drugs that promote and affect the functioning of the gallbladder.

Cholera - an acute intestinal infection caused by bacteria that spread the disease via polluted water, food, insects and excrement.

Cholesterol - a white, crystalline substance that dissolves in fat and is present in all body tissues. It is a steroid made by the liver and the adrenal glands, and it is thought to contribute to the hardening of the arteries.

Cholinergics - drugs that act on the involuntary nervous system to increase the activity of internal organs such as the gastrointestinal tract, the heart, the lungs and produce expansion of the blood vessels.

Chorea - twitching, involuntary and irregular movement of the muscles that occurs in a number of nervous system diseases.

Chromosomes - the carriers of the genes that determine the sex and physical characteristics of each person.

Chronic - a state, or disease condition that lasts for a long period of time, without any appreciable change.

Ciliary body - a structure in the eye that holds and supports the iris (round colored portion of the eye) in place.

Circumcision - the removal of some or all of the foreskin (prepuce) of the penis, done in many infants shortly after birth, but also performed later in life if the foreskin interferes with normal function.

Cirrhosis - a degenerative disease of the liver in which liver cells are destroyed and replaced by useless fatty or fibrous tissue.

Citric acid - the acid found in citrus fruits. Useful as a scurvy preventive.

Claudication (intermittent) - lameness, limping and leg pain (chiefly in the calf muscles) on exertion. This happens when arteries narrowed by disease provide an insufficient blood supply to the muscles, often limiting the affected person to walking only a short distance at a time.

Claw toes - a deformity of the toes due to poorly fitting shoes.

Cleft lip (harelip) - a birth defect in which a baby is born with a split in the tissues below the nose extending down through the upper lip, or the lip may be absent entirely. This condition often occurs together with a cleft palate, causing feeding problems. Both conditions can be repaired by surgery.

Coagulation - the clotting of blood or other fluid into a gel or solid.

Coagulation time - a test to determine whether there is a deficiency in the blood that delays its ability to clot within a short time when it is exposed to air. The test is also done in persons who are taking certain drugs to lengthen the clotting time of the blood.

Cobalamin (vitamin B_{12}) - an essential nutritive substance required for the adequate development of the red blood cells, for normal functions of the nervous system, and for various other cellular functions.

Cobalt - an essential substance which is a component of vitamin B$_{12}$, normally present in green, leafy vegetables. Inadequate amounts in the diet may produce anemia in children.

Coitus - the act of sexual intercourse.

Colic - abdominal pain usually caused by cramps in the intestine or stomach.

Colitis - inflammation of the lower portion of the bowel called the colon.

Collagen - the predominant protein of the white fibers in connective tissue, cartilage and bone.

Colles fracture - a break in the wrist bone that causes the hand to be displaced backward and outward.

Colonoscopy - the visualization of the inside of the colon with a lighted tube called a colonoscope that is passed into the colon through the rectum.

Colostomy - an opening into the colon, created by abdominal surgery, to relieve an intestinal obstruction or other disease of the colon. This allows the discharge of feces through the opening instead of through the rectum.

Colostrum - the fluid expressed from a new mother's breast before her milk is formed in the breast glands, a process completed about three days after the baby's birth.

Colposcopy - an examination of the vagina and cervix with an instrument called a colposcope, that permits visualization of the internal portions of these body parts.

Coma - a level of unconsciousness from which a person cannot be aroused. Coma may be due to disease, drug abuse, other forms of poisoning or injury.

Comedone - blackhead.

Comminuted fracture - a break that occurs in such a way that the bone is broken into several pieces.

Communicable disease - a contagious disease that can be spread to other persons in a variety of ways.

Complete blood count - a laboratory examination done to determine whether a person has the normal quantity and appearance of blood constituents.

Compound fracture - a break in which the broken portion of the bone has penetrated the skin and created an open wound.

Compression fracture - a fracture in which one bony surface is driven towards another bony surface. Commonly found in fractures of the spine involving the bony segments of the spinal column.

Compulsive behavior - a psychological disturbance in which a person feels forced to behave in certain, often inappropriate ways.

Congenital - a condition, deformity or disease present at the time of birth.

Congestive heart failure - a condition in which the heart fails to provide sufficient pumping action to circulate blood adequately, resulting in congestion of the lungs and other vital organs due to the accumulation of blood.

Conjunctivitis - inflammation of the mucous membrane that lines the eye balls and the inner parts of the eyelids.

Contact dermatitis - irritation of the skin due to exposure to an irritating, or sensitizing substance such as poison ivy.

Contact lens - a very small lens made either of glass or plastic that is worn directly on the eye instead of eye glasses. It may also be worn by a person after a cataract operation, in which case the contact lens replaces the lens removed during surgery. A contact lens provides better vision for a person whose cataract has been removed because it permits peripheral vision, which eye glasses don't provide.

Contusion - a bruise; the swelling and discoloration that appear on the skin after an injury, or pressure has been applied to that area.

Convalescent serum - serum obtained from a person who has recovered from an infectious disease. It may be given to another person who is susceptible, to immunize him against the disease, or to modify its severity, if he develops it.

Conversion reaction - a psychiatric response to a stressful situation in which the affected individual suddenly cannot see, or becomes unable to walk, even though there is no physical basis for these symptoms.

Convulsion - seizure; the contraction of muscles in the entire body, or a body part, with resulting contortion of the affected parts. This condition may occur due to disturbances of the nervous system, as a symptom of epilepsy, during periods when an individual has a very high temperature, and in various other disease states.

Copper - an essential nutritive element present in such foods as organ meat, oysters, nuts and whole grain cereals. Its deficiency can cause anemia in children.

Corn - a thickened, often painful area on or between the toes. Usually caused by poorly fitting shoes.

Cornea - the clear, transparent portion of the eye that permits the entry of light, refracts light rays and helps focus the eye.

Coronary artery - the principal artery providing the blood supply to the heart via its right and left branches.

Coronary occlusion - the blockage or obstruction of the heart's blood flow; occurs as a result of heart disease in which the arteries of the heart narrow due to deposits that form on their walls, allowing formation of blood clots that cause the obstruction.

Corpus luteum - a small glandular structure in the egg-forming body (ovary) of a woman's reproductive tract, which secretes estrogen and progesterone hormones and plays an important part during pregnancy.

Coryza - nasal discharge and inflammation of the upper respiratory tract, as occurs during a cold, or in persons who have hay fever.

Counterirritant - a substance or medication applied to the skin to irritate and mildly inflame it, in order to produce a feeling of warmth and comfort; helpful when applied to painful muscle areas during a cold, or after exertion.

Cradle cap - a fatty type of skin condition in small infants who develop yellow scaly areas and skin cracks behind the ears, crusts on the scalp, and red pimples on the face. This condition is often worse during the winter than during other seasons.

Cranium - the bony structure of the skull that contains the brain.

Crepitus - a creaking, crackling or rattling noise heard and/or felt over broken bones or joints that are subject to wear and tear. The term is also used to describe a noisy discharge of gas from the intestine.

Crohn's disease - an inflammatory condition of a part of the intestine called the ileum. It may also affect the colon, and sometimes still other parts of the gastrointestinal tract. Also known as regional ileitis.

Croup - a respiratory condition in young children, often due to infection, featured by a harsh, brassy cough and crowing, difficult breathing. Commonly occurs at night. If unrelieved by exposure to a warm, moist environment produced by a steam inhalator, or bathroom filled with moisture by a hot, running shower, emergency treatment must be provided, preferably in a hospital.

Culture - a process in which microorganisms in a specimen such as blood, urine or a throat swab are placed in a nutrient broth and allowed to grow, so that they can be identified, and appropriate treatment given.

Cutaneous - pertaining to the skin.

Cyst - a sac of tissue anywhere in the body that contains fluid, gas, fatty or other matter.

Cystitis - inflammation of the urinary bladder, usually due to irritation or infection.

Cystoscopy - examination of the urinary bladder and the lower portion of the urinary tract with a lighted instrument called a cystoscope.

Cytology - the examination and study of cells.

Cytotoxic - any substance, drug, or other matter that is harmful to cells.

D

Debridement - removal of diseased, dirty or foreign matter from a wound.

Decongestant - a drug that relieves the discomfort and swelling caused by such conditions as hay fever or a cold, by shrinking the mucous membranes of the nose.

Decubitus (bed sore) - a condition caused by being bedfast, disabled, or having to lie in one position for a long time, allowing pressure on the area to break down the skin, and the underlying structures. It can be prevented by frequent change of position, exercise, good skin care and good nutrition.

Dehydration - great loss of body fluid due to vomiting, diarrhea, loss of blood and other disease conditions.

Delirium - a condition of confusion and restlessness, due to psychological or other causes, such as a high fever.

Delirium tremens - also known as the DT's; a condition of confusion and disorientation commonly associated with chronic alcoholism.

Delusion - a psychological disturbance in which a person has a false impression, belief or concept which he is convinced is true; reasonable discussion or argument will not change his belief.

Dementia - impairment of the mind; generally appears together with emotional and behavioral disturbances.

Demulcent - a substance or drug that soothes and relieves irritations of such body surfaces as the skin and mucous membranes. Internal mucous membranes, such as those lining the intestinal tract, are also relieved by demulcents when affected by certain irritating conditions.

Dengue - also known as dengue fever; an infectious disease that occurs commonly in the tropics, but may also be found in the southern U.S. It is a viral disease with symptoms that include joint pains, fever, rash, headache and weakness.

Depressant - a substance or drug that slows down excessive mental or physical activity. A tranquilizing drug, for instance, can be used to depress (reduce) excited behavior.

Depression - a state of mind in which a person feels low, has little or no hope, and may consider himself worthless. Counseling and/or treatment with an appropriate drug may relieve the condition.

Dermatitis - a skin condition caused by infection, irritation, or other disease.

Dermatologic - referring to skin, or the treatment of a skin condition.

Diabetes insipidus - a condition caused by a malfunctioning pituitary gland, which controls body fluids. Pituitary hormone replacement in the form of pituitary extract, or a synthetic substitute controls the disease.

Diabetes mellitus - a disease that can be inherited, in which the pancreas doesn't secrete sufficient insulin to properly utilize body carbohydrates. In milder, adult forms of the disease weight reduction, diet or oral medication may be sufficient for treatment. In more severe cases, and in the juvenile onset form of the disease, insulin must be injected at regular intervals, and a special diet followed to control the disease and to prevent complications.

Diabetic coma - a state of unconsciousness that results when blood sugar rises to a very high level and no effort is made to reduce it with an appropriate amount of insulin. When the blood sugar level is out of control, other metabolic disturbances follow that affect the nervous system and the level of consciousness. When this happens, treatment must be given immediately or death may result.

Diagnostic findings - findings that result from a careful physical examination, including the patient's history, laboratory tests and other special studies done to identify a condition or disease so that appropriate treatment may be started, if needed.

Diagnostic radiology - X-ray studies performed to study a complaint in order to contribute to the accurate identification of a condition or disease.

Diaper rash - reddened, irritated or sore skin in the diaper region. May be caused by insufficient exposure to air, infrequent diaper changes, the composition of the baby's urine, and other factors. Frequent diaper changes, skin exposure to air, careful rinsing of diapers during laundry to remove all traces of soap or bleach help to prevent this condition.

Diaphoresis - perspiration or sweat that is visible or perceptible.

Diaphoretic - a substance, drug or measure used to increase sweating.

Diarrhea - a condition in which a person has frequent watery bowel movements, with or without abdominal cramps, that may be caused as a result of eating certain foods, by intestinal infection or by a disease process.

Diastolic phase of blood pressure (diastole) - the lowest level noted during blood pressure measurement. It reflects the pressure within the artery and the heart's chambers as the heart muscles relax and the chambers fill with blood to prepare for the next contraction.

Dislocation - displacement of one or more bones of a joint, or other body part, from its original position. Commonly occurs during a traumatic event such as a fall.

Disorientation - a mental state in which a person is confused, may not recognize other persons he knows well, or know the time or place, or other facts he's normally well familiar with. May be due to a disease process, or to toxic states such as alcohol or drug abuse.

Diuretic - a substance or drug that causes increased urination.

Diverticulitis - a condition in which pouches (diverticula) in the colon (lower bowel) become filled with feces and other waste material, which in turn causes inflammation and frequently infection. Often accompanied by abdominal pain.

Diverticulum - one of a number of small pouches that develop inside the colon.

Dominant inheritance - some inherited traits are dominant over others. When a fetus receives two genetic traits, and one is stronger genetically than the other, he will be born exhibiting the dominant characteristic.

Dosage - the exact quantity of a drug that has been prescribed for a given time period.

Dropsy - a condition in which one or more body parts show swelling, usually due to a chronic disease; also called edema.

Dry socket - a condition that may follow tooth extraction. The blood clot formed after the extraction disintegrates prematurely, leaving the tooth socket empty and prone to infection. Generally occurs within two to three days after the extraction, and may last, causing considerable pain, for several weeks.

Ductus arteriosus - an opening between the artery that carries blood to the lungs (pulmonary artery) and the aorta, that closes shortly after birth under normal conditions.

Dumping syndrome - a condition that sometimes follows gastrointestinal surgery, particularly after removal, or partial removal of the stomach. Symptoms include sweating, dizziness, nausea, vomiting and palpitations (increased heart rate) after meals.

Duodenum - the first portion of the small intestine.

Duodenal ulcer - a lesion in the duodenum that results in the loss of tissue due to inflammation. The ulcer may penetrate the wall of the duodenum causing hemorrhage and other complications. It is caused by excessive secretion of stomach acid, intake of certain drugs, foods, or stress.

Dwarfism - a condition in which a person remains abnormally small.

Dysentery - a severe intestinal infection that produces diarrhea; it may be caused by a variety of microorganisms.

Dyskinesia - a condition in which a person has difficulty in carrying out voluntary movements.

Dysmenorrhea - pain during menstrual periods.

Dyspareunia - pain during sexual intercourse.

Dysphagia - difficulty in swallowing.

Dysphasia - difficulty in speaking, and in expressing oneself understandably to others, usually due to brain damage.

Dyspnea - difficulty in breathing; shortness of breath, usually due to disease of the heart or lungs.

Dystrophy, muscular - a disease of unknown origin in which muscles do not function normally, and eventually deteriorate.

Dysuria - difficulty or pain during urination.

E

Ecchymosis - an area of purplish discoloration on the skin, due to bleeding underneath that area.

Eclampsia - a condition in which a pregnant woman develops convulsions (seizures) shortly before, or during labor, as a result of having high blood pressure during the pregnancy, associated with kidney problems.

Ectopic pregnancy - a pregnancy which develops in one of the fallopian tubes (the tubes that conduct the fertilized egg from the ovary to the womb) instead of in the womb.

Eczematous - an acute or chronic inflammatory condition of the skin, due to allergy or other causes.

Edema - swelling in body tissues or in a body part, such as the legs.

Edentia - state of not having any teeth.

Electrocardiogram (ECG, EKG) - a record made by a machine called the electrocardiograph that traces the electrical activity of the heart, and indicates abnormalities if any are present.

Electroencephalogram (EEG) - a record made by a machine called an electroencephalograph that traces the electrical activity of the brain (brain waves).

Electrolyte - a substance capable of conducting an electric current when it is in solution.

Electromyogram (EMG) - a record made with a machine called an electromyograph that traces the electrical activity of muscles. It is used to diagnose muscle diseases.

Embolism - an obstruction in a blood vessel by a traveling blood clot or various other substances.

Emesis - the act of vomiting.

Emetic - a drug used to induce vomiting.

Emollient - a substance or drug that smoothes and softens irritated skin or mucous membranes.

Emphysema - a condition in which the lungs have enlarged air sacs which cause difficulty in breathing.

Empyema - the formation of pus in one of the body cavities, frequently the lung.

Encephalitis - inflammatory condition of the brain, usually due to infection.

Endocrine - refers to a gland, such as the pituitary, which secretes a hormone directly into the blood stream.

Endogenous - refers to a body process that begins, or is produced, in the body or in one of its parts.

Endometrium - the mucous membrane that lines the womb (uterus).

Endometriosis - a condition in which cells that normally line the walls of the womb begin to grow on the surfaces of other organs within the pelvic structure, and sometimes also in distant areas of the body.

Endotoxin - a toxic (poisonous) substance released by certain microorganisms inside the body when their cell walls are injured.

Enterocolitis - inflammation of the small and large intestines.

Enterovirus - a virus that lives in the intestinal tract.

Entropion - turning in of the eyelid toward the eye.

Enuresis - bedwetting during the night, a condition that occurs primarily in children. It is involuntary.

Enzyme - a body substance that reduces complex compounds such as food into simpler compounds so they can be absorbed by the body.

Epidemic - a contagious disease that spreads through a large area of a community, a country, and sometimes an entire continent.

Epidermis - the outermost portion of the skin.

Epididymitis - inflammation of the sperm duct in the testicles.

Epiglottis - a piece of cartilage behind and below the tongue that closes the top of the windpipe (trachea) when a person is about to swallow, so that the food will go down the gullet (esophagus) and not the windpipe.

Epilepsy - a disease of the nervous system in which the victim has convulsions (seizures) and lapses of unconsciousness at different intervals. Newer medications help to control this disorder.

Epiphysis - the end portion of long bone.

Epistaxis - nosebleed.

Erb's palsy - injury of the baby's upper arm muscles during birth which produces paralysis of the arm.

Eructation - the act of belching.

Erysipelas - a painful infection of the skin caused by streptococcus bacteria.

Erythema - a reddened condition of the skin, due to irritation or infection.

Erythema multiforme - a skin disease due to a variety of causes, which presents in the form of tiny elevations and small blisters.

Erythroblastosis fetalis - a blood disease of newborn infants caused by the interaction of blood factors between an Rh negative mother and a Rh positive father.

Erythrocyte - red blood cell.

Erythrocyte sedimentation rate (ESR) - a laboratory test that determines the presence of infection in the body.

Esophageal - referring to the esophagus (gullet).

Esophagoscopy - examination of the inside of the esophagus (gullet) with a lighted tube called an esophagoscope.

Essential fatty acids - fats ingested in foods that are broken down by the body into simpler fat compounds and absorbed.

Etiology - the study of the causes of disease.

Euphoria - a feeling of happiness and well being, not necessarily based on reality, that may be caused by a drug or illness.

Exocrine - a glandular secretion delivered directly, or through a duct to the linings of body parts or to the skin.

Exophthalmos - a condition in which the eyeballs protrude, present in certain diseases.

Exotoxin - toxic substances released by bacteria or other microorganisms in the body.

Expectorant - a medication that helps in getting rid of mucus and phlegm that has accumulated in the respiratory tract.

Extremity - an arm or a leg.

F

Fahrenheit - a scale for measuring temperature in which the freezing point is 32°F, normal body temperature is 98.6°F, and the boiling point is 212°F.

Fallopian tubes - the tubes that carry the egg from the ovary to the womb.

Fecal incontinence - inability to control bowel movements.

Feces - stool, bowel movement.

Fetal - pertaining to an unborn child in the mother's womb.

Fiberoptics - a process based on newer optical instruments that allows the visualization of many internal parts of the body.

Fibrillation - fast, purposeless twitching of muscles. An extremely dangerous condition when it happens to the heart muscle, and fatal if not reversed quickly.

Fibrin - a body protein essential in the clotting of blood when blood is exposed to air, such as during an injury.

Fibrosis - scar tissue that is formed after injury or surgery.

Fibrositis - an inflammation of fibrous tissue.

Fissure - a crack or fold in skin or underlying tissue.

Fistula - a passage or channel that is formed between two internal body parts, or between an interior part of the body and the surface.

Flatus - discharge of intestinal gas.

Fluorine - an element that helps to protect teeth when it is compounded with other substances and added to drinking water, or applied directly to teeth via toothpaste or a dental treatment.

Folacin (folic acid) - an essential nutritive substance required for the proper development of red blood cells. Deficiency causes various forms of anemia.

Foreign body - any substance or material embedded in a part of the body where it doesn't belong and where it may cause injury.

Foreskin - a fold of skin that covers the tip of the penis. Also known as the prepuce.

Fowler's position - a position in which a patient's head is elevated 18-20" and the knees are raised somewhat with a pillow or other support. Helpful in case of respiratory difficulties and various other conditions.

Fracture - a break in a bone, or other body part.

Fremitus - a thrill or noise perceived through vibrations when the hand is placed on a person's chest.

Frostbite - damage done to the skin and underlying tissues when exposed to cold.

Fumigation - disinfection of a contaminated area by means of antiseptic fumes.

Furuncle - same as a boil; an infected area of skin filled with pus.

G

Gallbladder series - X-ray examination of the gallbladder to determine whether it contains gallstones, or whether there are any other abnormalities in the gallbladder or related areas.

Gamma globulin - a body protein that contains antibodies against various infections. It may be injected into a person at danger of developing an infection, to confer temporary immunity.

Gangrene - tissue death that occurs if tissues freeze, are deprived of nourishment, after sustaining injury or with a severe infection.

Gastrectomy - the removal of the stomach by surgery.

Gastric aspiration - using suction to draw food or fluid from the stomach. Done for diagnostic purposes, after surgery of the abdomen, or in drug poisoning situations.

Gastric fluid - fluid secreted by, and present in the stomach. The stomach secretes several fluids, one of which is hydrochloric acid, which prevents the growth of bacteria and promotes digestion of food as it passes through.

Gastric lavage - a process of washing out the stomach, needed when a toxic substance has been ingested that must be removed as part of the treatment that helps the victim to survive. Lavage may also be done when a person is bleeding into the stomach. Iced fluid is injected via a tube into the stomach, removed, and new fluid is injected. The process is continued until the bleeding stops, or until a different treatment method is started.

Gastritis - inflammation of the stomach.

Gastrointestinal - refers to the stomach and the intestines.

Gastroscopy - an examination with a lighted tube called a gastroscope that enables the physician to inspect the inside of the stomach for any abnormalities or disease conditions.

Genetic disorder - a disease or abnormality that is passed on to a member of the next generation via heredity.

Genital wart - also known as venereal wart; caused by a virus, this type of wart is usually transmitted via sexual contact, and thrives in the warm moist areas of the genital and anal regions.

Genitourinary - refers to the genital and urinary tract areas.

Geriatric - refers to the elderly.

Germicide - any substance or drug that can kill germs.

Gestation - pregnancy.

Giardiasis - an intestinal infection caused by the organism Giardia lamblia.

Gigantism - a condition in which a person has an unusually large body, or body parts.

Gingivitis - inflammation of the gums. Symptoms include bleeding and discomfort. If untreated, infection and loss of teeth may result.

Glaucoma - an eye disease in which the fluid pressure within the eye rises, with or without accompanying pain. If the condition is not recognized, damage to eye structures and loss of vision may result.

Glucagon - a body hormone that activates sugar stored in the liver; it also affects various other body functions.

Glucose - body sugar.

Glycogen - the form in which glucose is stored in the liver.

Gonad - the sex gland; ovary in the female, and testicle in the male.

Gonococcus - the microorganism that causes gonorrhea.

Gout - a disease due to an unusually high amount of uric acid in the blood. Uric acid is deposited in the tissues, since the kidneys can't excrete the increased amount rapidly enough. Gout affects joints such as the big toe, which becomes inflamed, hot and painful.

Grand mal - the severe seizure of epilepsy.

Granulocyte - a white blood cell.

Granuloma - a nodular inflammatory lesion that contains areas of granulation. When found around the groin and genitals it is generally granuloma inguinale, a venereal dsease that requires specific medical treatment.

Gravid - pregnant.

Greenstick fracture - incomplete fracture of a long bone, usually seen in children, in which the bone is bent, but splintered only on its convex side.

Grippe - also called influenza. An acute infectious disease, caused by one of the various influenza viruses. Symptoms include chills, fever, elevated temperature, aches and pains all over the body, headache, weakness, loss of appetite and inflammation of the respiratory tract.

Growth retardation - a condition also known as "failure to thrive." It occurs as a result of genetic predisposition, certain diseases, endocrine disturbances, malnutrition and in cases where the infant does not receive enough attention and love.

Gynecologic - refers to any condition of the female, including the female anatomy and reproductive system.

H

Hallucinogen - a substance or drug that produces unrealistic perceptions in the individual who takes it.

Hammer toe - a congenital deformity, usually of the fourth or fifth toe at the joint that connects the toe to the foot bones (metatarsals).

Heimlich maneuver - a method used to quickly remove a chunk of food that has accidentally slipped into the respiratory tract of a person who will choke to death if the food is not recovered within a few minutes.

Hematemesis - vomiting blood.

Hematinic - an agent or drug that increases the number of red blood cells in the blood, as well as the concentration of hemoglobin.

Hematologic - referring to blood, or the study of blood.

Hematoma - a collection of blood, or of clotted blood somewhere in the body, usually caused by injury or following surgery.

Hematopoietic - the development of blood cells and other constituents.

Hematuria - blood in the urine.

Hemianopia - partial blindness, usually due to brain damage.

Hemiplegia - paralysis of one side of the body, frequently due to a stroke.

Hemodialysis - a process of removing impurities and waste from the blood with a machine when a person's kidneys are unable to perform this essential function.

Hemoglobin - the pigment in blood that carries oxygen to the tissues, carbon dioxide (a waste product) to the lungs, and colors the blood red.

Hemolysis - destruction of red blood cells; occurs in infection, due to a toxic substance or drug, or in the laboratory after freezing, thawing, or other activities or studies involving red blood cells.

Hemophilia - an inherited disorder in which the affected individual bleeds easily and may develop serious hemorrhage even after very minor injury, due to the presence of a clotting factor deficiency.

Hemoptysis - spitting up of blood that comes from a hemorrhage in the lungs, usually due to a disease such as tuberculosis.

Hemorrhage - severe bleeding in, or from any part of the body.

Hemorrhoid - an enlarged vein, or group of veins that develop this condition as a result of pressure, continual irritation or disease. Most frequently occurs in the veins of the rectum, but appears in other parts of the body as well.

Hemostasis - the process of stopping bleeding, either with drugs, or mechanically, with an instrument.

Hepatic - refers to the liver.

Hepatitis - inflammation of the liver, usually due to infection, or following ingestion of a toxic substance.

Hepatosplenomegaly - enlargement of the liver and spleen.

Hernia - a condition in which an organ inside one of the body's cavities protrudes from the cavity, usually due to a weakness of the muscles that surround it, or following disease or surgery.

Herpes simplex - a skin infection caused by the herpes simplex virus that may be triggered by many different events, such as exposure to sunlight, stress, pregnancy, or other infections. The virus appears in two forms: herpes simplex type I generally affects the face (mouth or lips); herpes simplex type II usually infects the genital area and is spread primarily through sexual contact.

Herpes zoster (shingles) - a viral infection whose configuration follows the pathways of certain nerves. It consists of crops of blisters that break and form crusted lesions. These may be preceded, accompanied, or followed by severe pain along the course of the affected nerve segment. The condition may be particularly serious and disabling in elderly and/or debilitated persons.

Hirsutism - a condition characterized by the growth of hair in unusual places and/or excessive amounts, especially in women.

Histoplasmosis - a fungus infection caused by an organism called Histoplasma capsulatum, found in the soil and in the excrement of a number of animals in various parts of the country. The infection affects the lungs when tiny particles of the fungus are inhaled.

Homeostasis - a balance within the body of its chemical and other functions and constituents, necessary for continued health.

Hormone - one of many body substances secreted by various glands, essential for normal body functioning.

Hospice - an institution which provides professional care to patients with chronic, irreversible or terminal diseases.

Humectant - an agent or substance that helps to preserve moisture in specific body areas such as the skin; or in a room, or in an oxygen tent.

Hydrocephalus - a condition which may be congenital or acquired, in which the head becomes abnormally large and there is increased pressure in the brain, due to excessive secretion and accumulation of cerebrospinal fluid in the ventricles (chambers in the brain).

Hyperalimentation - a process of providing food for a malnourished or debilitated person, or one unable to eat normally by infusing nourishing fluids directly into the bloodstream through a central vein.

Hyperglycemia - excessive amount of sugar in the blood, as happens in uncontrolled diabetes mellitus.

Hyperkalemia - excessive amount of potassium present in the blood.

Hyperplasia - an increase in tissue, or size of an organ.

Hyperpyrexia - excessively high fever.

Hypersensitivity - excessive sensitivity to an agent or stimulus, as happens when a person is allergic.

Hypersomnia - a condition in which a person sleeps excessively at intervals, but is normal during waking periods, in contrast to being inclined to sleep continuously, as happens during periods of somnolence.

Hyperthermia - an abnormally high body temperature that may be due to a heat stroke, or is brought on by the injection of foreign protein for treatment purposes, or by other physical agents, substances or equipment.

Hyperthyroidism - a condition in which the thyroid gland, situated at the front of the neck, is enlarged, swollen and produces an excessive amount of a thyroid hormone called thyroxine. This produces weight loss, nervousness, an increased heart beat and other symptoms. Treatment is aimed at counteracting the effects of the hormone.

Hypertonic - refers to a concentration of salt (sodium chloride) greater than that present in blood.

Hypertriglyceridemia - excessive amount of fatty substances in the blood.

Hypertrophic - excessive growth of an organ or body part.

Hyperventilation - overbreathing; an increase in the depth and/or rate of breathing that may cause dizziness and occasional fainting.

Hypervitaminosis - excessive intake of vitamins, with possible toxic reactions.

Hypnotic - an agent or drug given to induce sleep.

Hypocalcemia - an insufficient amount of calcium in the blood.

Hypoglycemia - an abnormally low blood sugar level.

Hypogonadism - inadequate functioning of the sex glands.

Hypokalemia - insufficient amount of potassium in the blood.

Hypotension - abnormally low blood pressure.

Hypothermia - abnormally low body temperature, due to accidental exposure to cold, immersion in cold water, or intentionally induced as a treatment, or during surgery by using an electrically controlled hypothermia mattress.

Hypotonic - refers to a concentration of salt lower than that present in blood.

Hypoventilation - reduced ventilation of the air sacs of the lungs (alveoli), due to inadequate breathing or blockage of the airways (bronchi). Prolonged hypoventilation may lead to respiratory depression and coma.

Hypovolemic shock - a state of shock caused by a greatly reduced volume of blood, generally due to hemorrhage.

Hypoxemia - inadequate oxygenation of blood.

Hysterectomy - the removal of the womb by surgery.

Hysteria - a psychological disturbance evidenced by inappropriate, excessively emotional behavior.

I

Iatrogenic - an effect upon the patient that results from the suggestions, treatment or prescribed activity by a doctor.

Icterus - jaundice; the yellow discoloration of the skin, due to an excess of bile in blood.

Idiopathic thrombocytopenic purpura (ITP) - a blood disease of unknown origin whose chief symptom is platelet destruction, which leaves the victim prone to bleed.

Idiosyncrasy (to drugs) - unusual sensitivity to certain drugs by some individuals.

Ileitis - inflammation of the part of the small intestine called the ileum.

Ileostomy - an opening created by surgery in the abdomen and the ileum (section of small intestine) to allow discharge of fecal material.

Ileus - acute intestinal obstruction due to various causes, accompanied by severe, colicky pain, vomiting and dehydration; a serious, potentially fatal condition, if not relieved by prompt, effective treatment.

Immune globulin - a pooled blood fraction that contains antibodies present in a large number of adults. When injected in an individual, it may confer temporary immunity against a number of infectious diseases.

Immunity, active - a person who has developed his own antibodies against a particular infectious disease is actively immune against that disease.

Immunity, passive - a person injected with immune globulin or some other type of inoculation is said to be passively (and usually only temporarily) immune against a particular infectious disease.

Immunization - the process of developing one's own antibodies against an infectious disease, or being inoculated with inactivated or killed microorganisms that cause a particular infectious disease, in order to develop antibodies and acquire protection against the infection.

Immunodeficient - every healthy individual has the capacity to fight infection with certain blood factors that fend off invading microorganisms, and prevent them from multiplying. Illness, disability and other factors may decrease a person's capacity to fend off harmful organisms, or the development of foreign cells, such as cancer cells, for instance. When that happens, the person is immunodeficient.

Immunodiffusion - a laboratory test in which the interactions of specific antigens and antibodies are observed.

Immunoglobulins - body proteins that function as antibodies to ward off infection.

Immunosuppression - suppression of the body's rejection mechanism by means of certain drugs.

Immunotherapy - treating the body in such a way as to bolster its capacity to ward off infection, or the invasion of harmful foreign cells such as cancer cells.

Impacted cerumen (ear wax) - ear wax that has hardened inside the ear, requiring special methods, such as softening and irrigation in order to remove it without damaging the delicate structures inside the ear.

Impacted feces - feces that have become too hard to leave the intestine in the process of normal elimination. Special softening agents or manual removal are required to remove the feces and prevent injury to the bowel.

Impaired consciousness - a state that occurs when a person is not fully alert, due to injury, drug abuse or for other reasons. He may be semiconscious, stuporous, or in coma.

Impetigo - an infection of the skin often seen in children, usually due to the staphylococcus bacterium. It is very contagious, and may spread all over the surface of the skin.

Impotence - the inability to complete the sex act.

Inadequate personality - a person who indicates by his behavior that he cannot cope with others, and with ordinary life responsibilities has an inadequate personality.

Inanition - a state of exhaustion due to lack of food, or the inability to assimilate (utilize) food properly.

Incontinence - the inability to control urination or the elimination of feces.

Incubation period - the period of time that elapses between exposure to an infectious disease, and showing symptoms of the disease.

Induced abortion - an abortion that is brought about by the use of drugs or other methods.

Infarction - tissue death due to deprivation of oxygen.

Infection - a disease process caused by the invasion and damaging action of microorganisms, such as bacteria or viruses.

Infectious mononucleosis - an infectious disease caused by a virus that is relatively mild and occurs mostly in young adults. Symptoms include headache, fever, sore throat, enlargd lymph glands and spleen. Also known as the "kissing disease."

Infertility - inability of an individual or a couple to have a child.

Infiltration - to pass, or inject fluid or any other material into the tissues.

Inflammation - the irritation, swelling and other harmful changes of tissue as a result of trauma, pressure, or other physical interference in some part of the body. May also be caused by illness, infection or drugs.

Influenza - an infectious disease caused by a variety of influenza viruses, some of which cause more severe illness than others. Symptoms include headache, fever, joint pains and cough.

Inguinal hernia - protrusion of a portion of intestine through a weakened muscular wall in the groin (inguinal region).

Injection - using a needle, attached to a syringe or other sterile container, to infuse liquid material into the skin, muscles or veins to administer drugs, feed, or hydrate an individual.

Inoculation - injection of a small quantity of inactivated or killed microorganisms, or toxin produced by the organisms, to challenge an individual's body to develop antibodies against these organisms.

Input and output (I & O) - measuring the amount of liquid a person consumes within a given period, such as 24 hours, against the amount of liquid (urine, wound drainage, vomitus, etc.) the person loses within that same time period. Done to determine whether the person receives enough liquid, and to calculate the amount of additional liquid that may need to be given to meet that person's fluid requirements.

Insomnia - inability to fall asleep, or to sleep long enough to meet the body's requirements for rest.

Insulin - a hormone produced by cell groups inside the pancreas (a gland lying across and behind the stomach) called the islets of Langerhans. Insulin converts blood sugar into body energy. When a person produces too little insulin, he develops diabetes mellitus.

Insulinoma - a tumor (growth) of the cell groups called islets of Langerhans in the pancreas, which may produce excessive amounts of insulin.

Insulin shock - a condition that results if a diabetic person takes too much insulin, if his body cannot utilize the amount of insulin injected, or if he doesn't eat enough food to balance the amount of insulin injected. Symptoms include a lowered blood sugar level, tremors, cold sweat, weakness, dizziness and coma, if the condition is not reversed quickly by eating or drinking carbohydrate-containing food such as a few pieces of sugar, or a glass of orange juice. If a person develops insulin coma, he must be given glucose by injection.

Intercurrent infection - a second infectious process that occurs in a person who already has an infectious disease.

Interferon - a natural body substance formed in response to infection that defends the body against further attack by the foreign cells, organisms or viruses.

Intermittent positive pressure breathing (IPPB) - artificial respiration via a breathing machine that intermittently inflates the lungs with air or oxygen under pressure in cases where a person is unwilling, as in a case of postoperative pain, or unable to breathe normally.

Interstitial - relating to a space between cells, or inside a body organ.

Intra-articular - inside a joint.

Intra-cranial - inside the skull.

Intramuscular injection - an injection of fluid or a drug into muscular tissue.

Intrauterine device (IUD) - a device inserted in the womb to prevent pregnancy.

Intravenous infusion - introducing fluid, nutritive substances or drugs into a vein with a sterile needle and syringe, or other sterile apparatus.

Intravenous pyelogram (IVP) - a diagnostic procedure in which the patient is given an intravenous injection of contrast agent, allowing diagnostic X-ray studies to be done of the kidneys and the urinary tract.

Intubation - insertion of a tube into a body opening or passage.

Iodine - a trace element essential to health in minute (trace) quantity. Also used externally as an antiseptic.

Iron - a trace element essential to certain body functions, such as the proper and adequate formation of hemoglobin. Iron deficiency results in anemia, "spoon nails," bowel disease and other symptoms.

Irrigation - bathing a body part or cavity with fluids or medicated fluids for cleansing, healing or antiseptic purposes.

Irritant - a drug or agent that irritates the skin or other body part, either accidentally or with intent to produce tissue stimulation.

Ischemic - a body part or area that has insufficient, or no blood supply.

Isolation - placement of a patient who has an infectious disease into a separate room or area, and using various other precautions to prevent the spread of the disease to others.

J

Jaundice - yellow discoloration of the skin and the whites of the eyes caused by the presence of too much bile in the blood, usually due to liver or gallbladder disease.

Jejunum - a portion of the small intestine.

K

Karyotype - a pattern of chromosomes, lettered and numbered in pairs to perform genetic study of an individual's hereditary characteristics.

Keratitis - inflammation of the cornea, the transparent structure located at the front of the eye.

Keratoconus - a condition of unknown origin in which the cornea becomes cone-shaped, which interferes with normal vision.

Keratolytic - refers to a drug or agent that loosens or separates the horny layer of skin.

Keratomalacia - a disease of the cornea (the transparent structure at the front of the eye) in which it becomes dry, ulcerated and may perforate. The cause is malnutrition or debilitating disease.

Kernicterus - a serious illness of the newborn in which the baby develops jaundice in certain portions of the brain.

Ketoacidosis - a state which results from the accumulation of incompletely metabolized fatty acids in the blood, upsetting the body's metabolic balance.

Kidney machine - a machine used to remove impurities and waste products from the blood of a person whose kidneys are unable to perform this vital function.

Knee-chest position - the patient is positioned by the doctor or an assistant so that he rests on his chest and knees, in order to facilitate certain examinations.

Koplik's spots - tiny blue-and-white spots surrounded by red rings that appear inside the mouth at the points where the upper and lower teeth meet. The spots appear during the first two or three days of the onset of measles, before the rash can be seen.

Korsakoff's psychosis - a condition in which a person's memory is impaired, and he is disoriented as to time and place. He may invent facts to cover up his inability to remember certain events. Usually caused by alcoholism.

Kwashiorkor - a condition of extreme malnutrition, especially of proteins. Occurs in children who live in poor countries, or in areas of deprivation. They develop anemia, swelling of body tissues, a pot belly and other physical characteristics.

L

Labyrinthitis - inflammation of the structures of the inner ear.

Laceration - a break or tear of skin or other body tissues, usually caused by injury.

Lacrimal apparatus - the tear glands, sacs, and ducts that produce tears, and carry them down through the eyes and into the nose.

Lactation - the process following childbirth during which milk is formed in the mother's breasts to enable her to nourish her infant through suckling.

Lactic dehydrogenase (LDH) - an enzyme in the blood that rises to higher levels within several days after a person has had a heart attack. Laboratory determination of this and other enzymes helps to make a diagnosis of heart attack, and to distinguish this condition from various other diagnoses.

Lactose - milk sugar.

Laparoscopy (abdominoscopy; peritoneoscopy; ventioscopy) - a surgical procedure in which an electrically lighted tubular instrument is passed through the abdominal wall to visualize the internal organs and structures for diagnostic or treatment purposes.

Laryngitis - inflammation of the voice box.

Laryngotracheobronchitis - a respiratory disease that occurs mostly in children as a result of infection of the respiratory tract.

Larynx - the voice box, which enables a person to speak.

Lavage - the washing out of an organ or body cavity, such as the stomach.

Legionnaire's disease - a pneumonia-like disease caused by the organism Legionella pneumophila, which infects persons who have been exposed to it in areas where the organisms live and have become activated.

Leprosy - an infectious disease, also known as Hansen's disease, caused by a mycobacterium that appears in various forms and affects nerves, the face, eyes or the extremities, depending on which type of the disease the patient has contracted. It may lead to destruction of tissue, causing various deformities in the affected body parts.

Leukapheresis - a process in which a certain amount of blood is removed from a donor, so that the white blood cells can be removed. The remaining blood is then returned to the donor. The separated white blood cells may be used to treat another person, or for various other purposes.

Leukemia - also known as cancer of the blood, leukemia is a disease of the blood-forming organs, which produces a large number of abnormal white blood cells. The disease occurs in acute and chronic form.

Leukocyte - a white blood cell.

Leukoplakia - small whitish, sometimes leathery patches on the skin that occur due to various causes.

Leukorrhea - a whitish vaginal discharge.

Levin tube - a tube that is passed into the stomach to aspirate fluid for examination, to drain fluid from the stomach postoperatively, or to perform certain treatments.

Lichen planus - a skin condition that may occur in many body areas, depending on the particular form of the disease affecting the patient.

Limbic system - that part of the nervous system that affects primarily the internal organs of the body.

Lipids - a collective term that includes body substances such as fatty acids, glycerides, and various others.

Lipoma - a benign growth composed of fatty tissues.

Lipoproteins - body compounds that contain both proteins and fatty substances.

Lithotomy position - a position in which the patient is placed on the back, with legs and knees raised for examination or treatment.

Lockjaw - a dangerous infectious disease caused by Clostridium tetani, an anaerobic bacterial organism. The disease is acquired when the organism invades the body through a dirty wound such as a nail puncture. The patient must be treated at once to prevent the disease, which produces spasms of all the voluntary muscles, including the jaw, which is clamped shut. Tetanus immunization, repeated at intervals, helps to protect people against this disease which may be fatal if treatment is delayed.

Lues - syphilis.

Lumbago - a general term for backache in the lower part of the spine: mid-or lower back, or the lumbar and/or lumbosacral area.

Lumbar puncture - the insertion of a sterile needle into the spinal canal to withdraw spinal fluid for examination, to administer spinal anesthesia during surgery, to instill medication and for various other purposes.

Lymph - a colorless fluid in the body that runs through the lymphatic channels and eventually joins the venous circulation. It consists of white blood cells and tissue fluid.

Lymphadenitis - inflammation of the lymph nodes, which are located throughout the body along the lymphatic channels.

Lymphangitis - inflammation of the lymphatic channels.

Lymphocyte - white blood cell made in lymph nodes.

M

Magnesium - an element present in the body that aids in muscle contraction, bone and tooth formation, nerve conduction and various other functions. Deficiency may produce irritability of muscles and nerves.

Malaise - a term that describes a general feeling of illness, headache, muscular, joint, and other pains that occur when a person has the flu or other febrile illness.

Malaria - an infectious, febrile disease transmitted (spread) through the bite of a mosquito that earlier sucked blood from another person infected by one of the several types of Plasmodium organisms that are capable of causing the disease.

Malignant - any condition that is resistant to treatment, is very severe, and may lead to death.

Mammography - X-ray examination of the breast.

Mania - a form of hyperactive behavior in which an individual becomes hyperexcitable; may be a phase of the mental disorder called manic-depressive psychosis.

Manic-depressive illness - a mental disease characterized by mood swings, in which the victim becomes alternately deeply depressed and highly excited.

Mantoux Test (PPD) - a test in which a small amount of a purified protein derivative (PPD) of tuberculin (the fluid containing the tubercle bacillus that causes tuberculosis) is injected into the skin, raising a small wheal. The area is inspected two days later to determine whether or not the person is susceptible to the disease.

Marasmus - extreme form of malnutrition.

Masochism - a psychologic condition in which a person derives sexual gratification while being abused or hurt.

Mastectomy - surgical removal of the breast.

Mastitis - inflammation of the breast.

Mastoiditis - inflammation of the mastoid, a bone located behind the ear.

Meconium - fecal material passed through the birth canal by the fetus if it is in distress, and by the newborn infant during the first few days of life. The stool is colored dark green, and its consistency is pasty.

Megacolon - a condition present at birth in some babies in which the nerves essential to elimination from the lower bowel are absent. This produces an accumulation of feces, and distention of the bowel and abdomen which requires surgical correction.

Melanoma - a tumor that appears on the skin. If malignant, it may spread to other parts of the body. The lesion is dark brown due to the pigment melanin.

Melasma (chloasma) - a patchy discoloration of the skin, often seen in pregnant women.

Melena - bowel movement that has a black, tar-like appearance, caused by bleeding somewhere in the intestinal tract. When such bowel movements are discovered, the individual should be promptly examined by a physician.

Menadione - a synthetic preparation of vitamin K, an essential nutrient which aids in the normal clotting process of blood. Deficiency may produce bleeding.

Menarche - the onset of the first menstrual period.

Meningitis - inflammation of the meninges, the covering membranes of the spinal cord and the brain.

Meningocele - a body defect in which a portion of the spinal cord membrane protrudes through the bones of the spinal column.

Menorrhagia - excessive bleeding during the menstrual period.

Metrorrhagia - irregular menses.

Micturition - urination.

Migraine - a severe headache that may appear on only one side of the head and cause other symptoms such as nausea, vomiting, and a special sensitivity to light and noise.

Miliary tuberculosis - a form of tuberculosis that spreads throughout the body into all tissues and organs.

Minimal brain dysfunction (MBD) - a developmental or learning disorder in children, more often in boys than in girls, for which no physical basis is found, although some have slight neurological symptoms. Among the symptoms these children show are hyperactivity, poor coordination of the muscles, impulsiveness and difficulty in perception. A child with such symptoms should be carefully examined by experts to help him overcome his problems.

Mitral valve - the valve that separates the upper left chamber of the heart from the lower left chamber.

Mononucleosis - same as infectious mononucleosis, or "kissing" disease; an infectious disease caused by a virus that occurs primarily in young adults, with symptoms such as fever, sore throat, enlarged lymph nodes and spleen, and an initial decrease of white blood cells that changes to an increase as the disease runs its course.

Morbidity - state of disease, or calculated ratio of a disease state to the normal state.

Moxibustion - a popular therapeutic process first used in the Orient that produces counter-irritation on some part of the skin; done by placing a cone-shaped container filled with cotton or similar material on the skin and setting the material on fire.

Mucosa - the smooth membranous lining of the interior organs of the body. It is present in the gastrointestinal tract, the respiratory tract, the urinary tract and the genitourinary tract of men and women.

Mucus - the material secreted by the mucous membranes.

Multipara - a woman who has given birth to two or more children.

Multiple sclerosis (MS) - a degenerative disease of portions of the nervous system that results in progressive disability of muscle functions. The affected person develops difficulty in walking, using his hands, or with his vision. The disease may show signs of improvement, then become worse again. It may progress to complete paralysis, or leave the victim partially disabled for many years without further progression of symptoms.

Munchausen's syndrome - describes the illness of a person who has the abnormal urge to manufacture signs of illness, such as an artificially elevated temperature, apparent blood in the urine or other body part or cavity where it is not normally found, and other symptoms or signs that have no physical basis. Psychiatric treatment must be obtained to discover the reasons for the person's need for forging the illness. Such persons often move from hospital to hospital to avoid being recognized, to gain admission and treatment for their often ingeniously produced "symptoms."

Muscular atrophy - weakness and wasting of muscles due to lack of use, illness that forces a person to remain in bed for long periods, and other conditions that result in the loss of muscle mass.

Muscular dystrophy - a disease that often starts during childhood, in which muscles begin to waste away and gradually become totally useless. The cause of this disease is not yet known; heredity appears to be a factor.

Musculoskeletal - refers to the muscles and the bones of the skeleton.

Myalgia - muscular pain.

Myasthenia gravis - a disease in which muscles are chronically weak and unable to function normally. The cause of this disease is not known. It occurs more frequently in women between the ages of 20-40, and requires symptomatic, supportive treatment.

Myeloma - a cancerous, progressive disease that involves the bloodforming organs of the bone marrow, causing plasma cell tumors, weakened bone structures, anemia and kidney damage.

Myocardial infarction - the sudden loss of blood supply to the heart muscle due to a dangerous narrowing of one of the blood vessels such as the coronary artery, or an obstruction such as a blood clot. Commonly called a heart attack.

Myoclonus - continuous rhythmic spasms of a muscle or a group of muscles.

Myoma - excessive growth of muscular tissue into a tumor.

Myositis - inflammation of a muscle, or a group of muscles.

Myringitis - inflammation of the ear drum.

Myxedema - a disease caused by insufficient secretion of the hormone thyroxine by the thyroid gland.

N

Narcotic - a medication given to relieve pain, that often also makes a patient sleepy or stuporous, or has still other side effects. Most of these drugs can lead to addiction if they are taken indiscriminately, or for long periods of time.

Narcotic antagonist - a drug that counteracts effects of a narcotic medication.

Nasal septum - the bone that separates the two sides of the nose.

Necrosis - death of cells, tissues or organs due to lack of oxygen, infection, injury, exposure to cold or burn.

Necrotizing enterocolitis - an extremely grave disease of the bowel that occurs in adults following certain types of abdominal surgery, and some other illnesses. It can also occur in newborns. The disease causes tissue death, abdominal pain, nausea, high fever and diarrhea that may be bloody. Treatment involves fluid replacement, relief of pain and antibiotics.

Neonatal - concerns the newborn period, generally the first four weeks after birth.

Neoplastic - refers to any abnormal growth in the body.

Nephritis - inflammation of the kidneys.

Nephropathy - disease state affecting the kidneys.

Neuralgia - pain that travels along peripheral nerve tracts.

Neuritis - inflammation of one or more nerves.

Neurologic - refers to an examination or study of the nervous system.

Neuroma - a tumor that arises from cells somewhere in the nervous system.

Neurosis - a behavioral disturbance with many symptoms; the most frequently apparent symptom is anxiety.

Neurosyphilis - the third stage of syphilis which includes involvement of the nervous system.

Nevus - a mole or birthmark.

Niacin (nicotinic acid, niacinamide) - an essential nutritive substance that aids metabolic functions. Deficiency causes pellagra, a disease that causes blisters, reddened areas and swelling of the skin, of the gastrointestinal system and the mucous membranes of the mouth; also affects the nervous system; alcoholics may have these symptoms because they frequently suffer from severe malnutrition and vitamin deficiencies.

Nightblindness - inability to see in the dark, or in poor light, due to vitamin A deficiency.

Nits - the eggs of a louse, found in the hair of persons with louse infestation.

Nocturia - frequent urination during the night, due to excessive fluid intake before going to bed at night, or to illness.

Nodule - a small swelling.

Nosocomial - refers to an infection, or other disorder picked up by a patient while he is hospitalized.

Nulliparous - refers to a woman who has never given birth.

Nystagmus - involuntary regular movements of the eyes, that may be due to congenital weakness or certain diseases.

O

Obstetric - refers to the care of the pregnant woman, including the prenatal period, labor, delivery and the period immediately following the delivery, as well as care in between pregnancies.

Occult blood - blood present in such small quantities and often altered in color or consistency that it can be detected only by chemical tests, or via microscopic or spectroscopic examination of the suspected material.

Ocular - refers to the eye.

Oligomenorrhea - abnormally infrequent or scanty menstruation.

Oligospermia - a low concentration of sperm in a man's ejaculate.

Oliguria - a small amount of urinary output in a given period of time.

Oncology - the study of cancerous diseases.

Ophthalmic - refers to the eye.

Opportunistic infection - an infection that occurs because an individual has lost his natural capacity to fight it, due to weakness and incompetence of his immune system, as a result of illness, malnutrition and other causes.

Optometry - a profession whose practitioners examine eyes, determine if a person has any eye problems or disease, and prescribe, and produce corrective lenses and other optical aids.

Oral cavity - the mouth.

Orthopedics - a medical specialty whose practitioners are experts in problems or diseases of bones, joints and related structures. Orthopedic surgeons are experts in setting fractured bones, performing bone and joint surgery, and in prescribing rehabilitative treatment for people who have bone and joint diseases, trauma, or deformities that require correction for adequate or improved functioning.

Orthopnea - inability to breathe except while sitting up.

Osmosis - a process in which fluid flows from one area where the liquid is of a lower concentration across a semi-permeable membrane to an area in which liquid is of a higher concentration.

Osteoarthritis - a degenerative disease that affects the joints, and often occurs as a person ages, or following injury.

Osteogenic sarcoma - a malignant bone tumor that most often occurs in the young, at ages 10-20.

Osteomalacia - a bone disease in which the bones soften and bend, with varying degrees of pain. May occur in pregnancy, metabolic disease or in vitamin D deficiency.

Osteomyelitis - inflammatory disease of the bone marrow, the surrounding bone and the end portions of bone (epiphyseal areas).

Osteoporosis - increasing weakness and fragility of the bones. Most frequently occurs in elderly, postmenopausal women and in elderly men.

OTC (over the counter, or nonprescription) drug - medicine that is available in the pharmacy or in other stores without a doctor's prescription. An OTC medication is safe and effective if the instructions on its label or box are carefully followed.

Otic - refers to the ear.

Otitis media - inflammation of the middle ear.

Otorhinolaryngologic - refers to the ear, nose and throat.

Ovary - the female sex gland, present on each side in a woman's lower abdomen. Inside, egg cells (ova) are formed. It also secretes sex hormones that help the development, growth and regulation of the female reproductive system.

Oxytocic - a drug or agent that speeds up the onset of strong uterine contractions during labor. It may also be given after delivery to cause the uterus to contract and prevent uterine bleeding.

P

Pacemaker - a built in mechanism that controls the heart's activity. When its mechanism doesn't function adequately, a mechanical pacemaker may be used, either temporarily or permanently. An artificial pacemaker may be external, or it may be inserted under the patient's skin. The latter technique is commonly used when the patient requires a permanent pacemaker.

Paget's disease - There are two unrelated diseases, both called by this name. One is a chronic bone disease, also known as osteitis deformans, the other is an unusual form of breast cancer.

Palpation - using the hands to touch, feel or lightly press a certain body area to determine if any abnormality is present.

Palpitation - a very rapid heart beat caused by exertion such as running, by excitement, nervousness, certain drugs and various disease conditions.

Pancreas - a glandular organ that lies across and behind the stomach. It produces pancreatic juice that aids in the digestion of food in the upper intestine. It also produces insulin.

Papanicolaou (Pap) smear - a reliable and simple test done on various body cells to determine abnormalities and detect the presence of cancer.

Papilledema - swelling inside the brain or nearby areas that affects the optic nerve and may compromise vision.

Paracentesis - a puncture of a body cavity for the purpose of removing fluid.

Paralysis - inability to move the extremities or a body part due to loss of muscular function.

Paranoid - a condition in which a person is abnormally suspicious of others, with feelings of delusion and of being persecuted by hostile people or forces.

Paraplegic - a condition in which both legs, and usually the lower portion of the trunk are paralyzed. This may happen after a stroke, an injury, and under certain other circumstances.

Parasite - an organism that lives on, and obtains its nourishment from, another organism called the host.

Parenteral drug administration - a method of administering a drug in some way other than through the gastrointestinal tract.

Parkinsonism - a disease in which the victim gradually loses control of his voluntary muscles. Also known as shaking palsy and paralysis agitans.

Paronychia - inflammation or infection in the tissue surrounding a finger or a toenail.

Parturition - childbirth.

Passive immunity - immunity temporarily conferred against a certain infectious disease by inoculating a person with a substance that contains antibodies against that disease.

Patch test - a skin test done to detect sensitivity of a person to certain substances to which he may be allergic, or to certain infections.

Pathogen - a disease-causing microorganism.

Pathologic - refers to disease, or to the study of disease.

Pediatric - refers to the medical specialty concerned with the care of children.

Pediculosis - infestation with lice.

Pellagra - a vitamin deficiency disease that occurs when a person doesn't eat enough foods containing niacin (nicotinic acid, nicotinamide). The vitamin is present in yeast, liver, meat and whole grain enriched cereals. Pellagra symptoms include blisters, reddened areas and swelling of the skin, the gastrointestinal system and the mucous membranes of the mouth. The nervous system may also be affected.

Peptic ulcer - an inflammatory injury in the lining of the stomach or the adjacent portion of small intestine, called the duodenum. Peptic ulcer is a disease that tends to occur in people who suffer from tension and anxiety. It is treated with drugs, diet, counseling, and may require blood replacement or surgery if the ulcer penetrates the wall of the stomach or intestine, causing hemorrhage and other complications.

Peristalsis - wavelike movements of the gastrointestinal tract to move its contents from one end to the other.

Peritonitis - inflammation of the lining of the abdominal cavity and its organs.

Pernicious anemia - a type of anemia that occurs mostly in elderly people when their bloodforming organs fail to develop red blood cells normally. The condition is treated by giving injections of vitamin B_{12}, a treatment that must be continued for the remainder of the person's life.

Pertussis - whooping cough.

Petit mal - a minor seizure in which the affected person may seem to be absent-minded, daydreaming, or twitching slightly for a few seconds, then return to his normal state.

Phenylketonuria (PKU) - inherited metabolic abnormality in which the affected individual is unable to process a certain constituent of protein foods called phenylalanine. A toxic side product is formed that accumulates first in the blood and urine, and subsequently affects the brain and nervous system, producing mental retardation if not recognized and treated early. The condition can be diagnosed in a newborn baby's urine or blood, and corrected by providing a diet free of foods containing phenylalanine. In many parts of the country a test for this condition is required by law, so that corrective action can be taken before symptoms appear.

Pheochromocytoma - a tumor in the adrenal gland that may cause high blood pressure and related symptoms, which disappear if the tumor is diagnosed and removed by surgery.

Phimosis - a condition in which the foreskin of the penis is narrowed so that it cannot be retracted over its tip.

Phlebitis - inflammation of a vein.

Phosphorus - an essential body element that aids in the formation of bones and teeth, the conduction of nervous impulses, in contraction of muscles and in enzyme activity.

Pituitary - an important endocrine gland, also called hypophysis, that is located at the base of the brain. It secretes a number of important hormones. These include an adrenal-stimulating hormone called ACTH, a growth-stimulating hormone, a thyroid-stimulating hormone, a gonadotropic hormone which stimulates the production of sex hormones in the ovaries and testicles, a hormone that stimulates milk production in mothers who are nursing, and a hormone that stimulates the production of the pigment called melanin.

Placenta - a structure that develops in the womb of a pregnant woman, which is attached to the umbilical cord, the organ through which the growing fetus obtains its food, oxygen, and discharges its wastes. The placenta also produces sex hormones that affect the course of pregnancy. After the birth of the baby, the placenta separates from its place of attachment in the womb, and is expelled a short while later.

Placenta previa - the premature separation of the placenta from the womb prior to the baby's birth, a serious complication of late pregnancy.

Plasma - the liquid portion of blood.

Plasmapheresis - a procedure in which blood is withdrawn from a donor, the red blood cells are removed, and are then retransfused into the donor; the remaining blood constituents are then separated and prepared for administration to patients who need the various blood fractions or plasma.

Platelets - tiny discs in the blood stream that aid in the clotting process also known as thrombocytes.

Pleural - refers to a thin membrane that covers the lungs and lines the inside of the chest wall.

Pleurisy - inflammation of the membrane covering the lungs and the inside of the chest wall. It usually causes pain on breathing and the development of fluid in the pleural cavity (space between the two layers of pleura).

Pneumoencephalogram (PEG) - X-ray studies of the brain following the injection of air or gas to make these structures visible.

Pneumonia - inflammation of the lungs.

Pneumothorax - a condition that occurs when air or gas gets into the pleural cavity and exerts pressure on the lung, causing it to collapse. When this happens as a result of trauma or rupture of a lung air sac, breathing problems develop requiring prompt treatment.

Polydipsia - increased amount of fluid intake due to excessive thirst.

Polyuria - excessive urination.

Porphyria - a metabolic defect that involves a group of body pigments called porphyrins. Depending on the type of illness, the affected person may have abdominal pain, the nervous system may be involved, and urine may turn dark brown on standing.

Postpartum - referring to the period that follows childbirth.

Postprandial - after a meal.

Potassium - an essential body element that aids in the contractions of muscles, in the transmission of nerve impulses, and in water, and acid-/base balance in the blood and tissues. Deficiency may produce disturbances of heart functions and interfere with other vital body activities.

Presbyopia - decreased elasticity of the lens of the eye that occurs in the elderly and impairs accommodation, thus interfering with accurate vision.

Preventive health care - a concept which provides for health examinations given at regular intervals to detect any beginning signs of illness, so that treatment can be provided to stop the illness before it can progress. Health counseling is also given, to help retain good health through appropriate diet, rest, exercise and other factors that promote a healthy lifestyle.

Primigravida - a woman who is pregnant for the first time.

Proctitis - inflammation of the rectum.

Proctoscopy - examination of the rectal structures with a tubular instrument.

Prophylaxis - preventive treatment or health care.

Prostate - a gland present in men that surrounds the urethra (the passage through which urine flows from the bladder) at the point where it joins the urinary bladder.

Prostration - physical or mental exhaustion that may follow psychological stress, great physical exertion, exposure to very hot environmental temperatures, or severe illness.

Pruritus - itching.

Psoriasis - a skin disease that produces itchy reddened patches and scales. It is not a contagious disease, but tends to run in families.

Psychiatric - refers to an abnormal mental or emotional state.

Psychosis - severe emotional disturbance in which a person behaves irrationally, unpredictably, and may harm himself or others.

Pterygium - a disease of the eye in which a triangular piece of tissue grows out of the lining of the eyelid at its inner aspect (next to the nose) and extends toward the pupil of the eye.

Puerperium - the period of time between childbirth and the return of the womb to its normal, pre-pregnant size and shape.

Pulmonary - refers to the lungs.

Purpura - bleeding into the skin, as a result of injury or a blood disorder.

Pus - a thick, yellowish liquid produced by inflammation or infection. It consists of fluid (serum) and germ-destroying cells, other microorganisms and dead tissue.

Pyelonephritis - inflammation of the kidneys.

Pyloric stenosis - a narrowing of the muscular valve at the far end of the stomach called the pylorus.

Pyogenic - refers to an agent or organism that causes the formation of pus.

Pyorrhea - inflammation of the gums in the periodontal spaces (where the gums join the teeth), often accompanied by pus formation, and the loosening of teeth.

Pyridoxine (vitamin B_6) - an essential vitamin that aids the functions of body cells and the metabolism of amino and fatty acids. Deficiency of this vitamin may produce anemia, nervous system problems, skin lesions and seizures in small infants.

Pyuria - pus in the urine.

Q

Q fever - an infection caused by rickettsial microorganisms that occurs mainly on farms, and in slaughterhouse workers. It is acquired from animals such as goats and cows through contact with their urine and feces. Symptoms include headache, chills, fever and cough.

Quinsy - a sore throat, followed by an abscess in the tissues that surround the tonsils. This condition may occur together with tonsillitis. If the abscess becomes very large, it may need to be opened and drained.

R

Rabies - a virus infection transferred to man by an infected animal through a bite. The symptoms of the disease involve muscle spasms, paralysis, convulsions, excitement and rage, alternating with periods of calm. The virus moves along nerve channels and eventually enters the brain. Or, it may pass from an open skin surface into the body. Since the disease is potentially fatal, immunization must be provided when a person has been bitten by a rabid animal, or one suspected of having the disease.

Radiation therapy - the use of radioactive substances to treat a person for a variety of diseases, but especially those which produce large numbers of abnormal cells that have a destructive effect on human tissues, such as cancer. The effect of radiation therapy is to destroy the cancer cells. Measures are taken to protect healthy tissues.

Radionuclide - a radioactive substance that is used to perform diagnostic and treatment procedures in a field called nuclear medicine.

Refraction - an examination of the eyes by an eye doctor or an optometrist to determine the presence of nearsightedness, farsightedness or other vision abnormalities, prior to prescribing corrective lenses.

Regurgitation - vomiting.

Remission - a chronic disease whose symptoms have temporarily disappeared.

Renal failure - inability of the kidneys to perform their essential functions of removing waste products from the blood and excreting them in the urine.

Respiratory arrest - the sudden cessation of breathing.

Respiratory tract - the organs and passages concerned with breathing: the nose, pharynx, larynx, epiglottis, trachea, bronchi and the lungs.

Resuscitation - emergency procedures used to restart respiratory and heart functions that have stopped due to illness, trauma or for other reasons, to allow the victim to survive.

Retina - the light-sensitive inner layer of the eye that transmits nerve impulses to the optic nerve.

Retinol (vitamin A) - an essential vitamin that aids vision and certain cellular functions. Deficiency produces nightblindness, dry eyes and other eye problems.

Retrolental fibroplasia (RLF) - a disease of premature infants in which there is an abnormal growth of fibrous tissue behind the lens of the eye, causing blindness. The condition is caused by the excessive administration of oxygen after the birth of the premature infant, which is toxic to his eye structures.

Reverse isolation - isolation precautions used for the protection of the patient whose immune system is weak, so that he will not be exposed to any infectious organisms carried by people in his environment.

Reye's syndrome - a virus disease usually found in children that may follow an upper respiratory infection or other virus disease. It is a dangerous disease that affects the brain and nervous system, and produces fatty accumulations in various body organs. Special treatment procedures are now available in various medical centers to help victims to survive this illness.

Rheumatoid arthritis - an inflammatory disease of the joints of the fingers, wrists or feet, but it may also affect other joints. It produces pain and swelling, destroys surrounding cartilage and decreases motion in the affected joints. Rheumatoid arthritis is a chronic disease that may cripple the affected individual. Treatment includes heat, exercise, medication and rest, under the supervision of an experienced physician. The cause of the disease is not known. It may affect children as well as adults.

Riboflavin (vitamin B_2) - an essential vitamin that aids in protein metabolism, maintains healthy mucous membranes and helps the body convert food into energy. Deficiency may cause soreness and fissures of the lips.

Rickets - a disease of children caused by a deficiency of vitamin D, which prevents calcification (hardening) of the bones. As a result, the child develops bowlegs.

Roentgen - an international unit of X- and gamma radiation.

Rubefacient - a counterirritant which reddens the skin when applied.

Rubella - German measles.

Rubeola - measles.

S

Sadism - sexual gratification obtained by inflicting pain on another individual.

Salmonella infection - food poisoning caused by eating food contaminated by salmonella bacteria.

Salpingitis - inflammation of the fallopian tubes.

Scabies - a skin infection caused by a mite that burrows into the skin.

Scarlatina - also called scarlet fever. A skin disease that is highly contagious, caused by a streptococcal organism; symptoms include fever and a bright red rash over the body, followed later by peeling of the affected skin areas.

Scurvy - a disease caused by a deficiency of vitamin C; symptoms include a tendency to bleed into the gums, inflammation of the gums, and loose teeth.

Sedative - a drug given to reduce nervousness, abnormally great excitement or irritability.

Seminal fluid - the fluid that carries semen.

Sepsis - infection.

Septic abortion - an abortion performed under unsanitary conditions, with the result that the woman having the abortion develops an infection of her reproductive organs that may progress to blood poisoning.

Septicemia - blood poisoning. The presence of harmful organisms or their toxins in the blood stream.

Serum - the liquid portion of blood that is left after the clotting components have been removed.

Shock - a group of symptoms that occur when a person's circulatory system collapses. This may happen in a severe allergic response, when a person hemorrhages, after major surgery, serious burns, or following trauma.

Sigmoidoscopy - examination of the portion of colon (sigmoid colon) just above the rectum with a lighted tube.

Sims position - lying semi-prone.

Sinus - a small, hollow channel or passage inside the body, that may contain fluid or air.

Sodium - an essential element in the body that aids fluid and acid/base balance, nervous impulse transmission and muscle contractility. Deficiency may produce swelling of the tissues and other symptoms of fluid imbalance.

Staphylococcus - a bacterial organism that may cause different types of infections.

Stenosis - the narrowing of a channel, duct or passage in the body.

Sterile - an area that is free of germs.

Stimulant - a drug or other substance that increases mental or physical activity.

Stoma - an opening; a term used to describe an artificial opening made by a surgeon in a body part, such as a colostomy, an opening into the colon made through the abdominal wall.

Strabismus - an eye condition which makes it impossible for a person to focus both eyes on the same place. Treatment may include eye glasses, exercises, medication and surgery.

Streptococcus - a bacterial organism that causes a variety of infectious diseases.

Stroke - injury to the brain as a result of bleeding, or a blocked artery somewhere in the brain. Stroke may cause paralysis of one side of the body if the brain is damaged in an area that controls body movements. It is usually caused by chronic high blood pressure or hardening of the arteries (arteriosclerosis). Stroke is also called cerebral hemorrhage, or apoplexy. Expert rehabilitative treatment may restore most or all functions lost when the stroke first occurs.

Subcutaneous injection - an injection that is given under the skin.

Superinfection - a new infection of the same type a patient already has.

Supraventricular tachycardia - an increase in the heart rate caused by an electrical impulse in the heart that originates somewhere above the region of the ventricles (lower chambers of the heart).

Surfactant antiseptic - a specially prepared fluid that inactivates or kills certain bacteria, fungi and viruses when applied to the skin.

Sustained release dosage - a term that indicates that a drug has been manufactured so that tiny portions of each tablet or capsule are released over a period of hours at carefully calculated intervals.

Swimmer's ear - infection of the external ear caused by moisture, allergy, a disease-causing organism or a chemical irritant. More common during the summer season.

Symptom - some change in a body part, organ or function that indicates illness or a developing disorder.

Syncope - fainting.

Syndrome - a group of symptoms that occur together, suggesting the presence of a disorder or illness known to include this group of symptoms.

Synovial fluid - the fluid found in joints.

Synovitis - inflammation of the lining of a joint (synovial membrane).

Syringomyelia - a progressive disease that affects the nervous system by producing small cavities filled with fluid at the back of the spinal cord. Pain, weakness and loss of sensation occur in the victim's hand or arm, and the legs may become spastic.

Systemic - relating to the body as a whole.

Systemic lupus erythematosus - a disease that affects connective tissue (bone, tendons, cartilage) as well as other organs such as the heart, lungs and kidneys. The patient has pain in the muscles, joints, and in his abdomen. Various drugs are used to control the disease.

Systolic phase of blood pressure (systole) - the highest level noted during blood pressure measurement. It reflects the pressure within the artery and the heart's chambers as the heart muscles go into systole (contract), forcing blood to be pumped out of the heart, back into the arterial circulation.

T

Tachycardia - an abnormally fast heart rate.

Tachypnea - very rapid breathing.

Talipes - clubfoot; a congenital foot deformity in which the foot is twisted inward, outward or in several other abnormal positions so that normal use of the foot for standing and walking is not possible. May be corrected, or greatly improved by surgery.

Tamponade - compression of a body part as a result of an accumulation of fluid in a surrounding body area.

Tapeworm - one of a group of long worms that lives in the intestines of man as well as in animals; may grow as long as 30 feet.

Tendinitis - inflammation of a tendon, a tough and strong band of connective tissue that connects muscles to bones.

Tennis elbow - a condition in which there is pain either on the outer or inner portion of the elbow due to an inflammation in the surrounding structures. The outer (lateral epicondylitis) form is more common than the inner (medial epicondylitis). Pain is aggravated when the hand tries to grip or grasp an object.

Teratogen - any agent that may cause a growing fetus to be born with an abnormality.

Tetanus - lock jaw.

Tetany - a disorder caused by a calcium deficiency in the blood. Inadequate calcium levels produce irritability of the nerves, muscular cramps or spasms, and sometimes convulsions. There are several possible causes for the disease. Depending on the cause, treatment consists of calcium, vitamin D, or parathyroid hormone.

Tetrahydrocannabinol (THC) - marijuana.

Thalassemia - a particular type of anemia that occurs in areas that border on the Mediterranean, and in Southeast Asia.

Therapeutic abortion - an abortion performed on a woman likely to develop a serious mental or physical illness if she carries the pregnancy to term and gives birth to a child.

Therapeutic dosage - the quantity of a drug calculated to improve the condition for which it is being prescribed.

Thermography - a diagnostic device that uses the temperatures in various body parts to determine the presence of abnormal conditions in these areas.

Thiamine (vitamin B_1) - an essential vitamin that aids carbohydrate metabolism, and heart and nervous functions. Deficiency causes symptoms in the circulatory and nervous systems. Deficiency disease is called beriberi.

Thoracentesis - withdrawal of fluid from the pleural cavity (the cavity created by the membranes that line the lungs and the chest wall), to relieve pressure on the lungs.

Threatened abortion - signs and symptoms, such as spotting or vaginal bleeding, that are warning signals for a pregnant woman that she may not be able to continue to carry the pregnancy.

Thrombocytopenia - an abnormally small number of platelets in the blood.

Thrombophlebitis - inflammation of a vein, generally in the leg, that occurs along with the presence of thrombosis in that area.

Thrombosis - the presence of a blood clot inside a blood vessel, blocking the vessel.

Thrush - a fungal infection of the mouth.

Thyroidectomy - removal of the thyroid gland by surgery.

Thyroiditis - inflammation of the thyroid gland.

Tic douloureux - a condition that irritates the trigeminal nerve which branches out through the face, causing severe facial pain. Medication, dental therapy and neurosurgery can provide relief.

Tinnitus - a condition in which a person hears noises or ringing in his ears. May be caused by a problem of certain nerves, by inflammation and by certain drugs.

Tocopherol (vitamin E) - a vitamin that is believed to aid healing, and contribute to the stability of biologic membranes. Deficiency can produce destruction of red blood cells.

Topical anesthetic - an anesthetic agent directly applied to the area where pain relief is needed.

Topical medication - a medication directly applied to the area where it is needed, rather than being taken by mouth or in some other way.

Torticollis - a contraction, often occurring in spasms, of the muscles of the neck, which causes the head to be drawn to one side. May be a congenital condition, or acquired after birth.

Toxicologic - refers to the study of poisonous agents and how they affect the body.

Toxin - a poisonous substance. It may be a chemical agent, or a harmful substance secreted by a microorganism.

Trachea - the windpipe.

Tracheostomy - an incision made into the windpipe when a person is unable to breathe normally.

Transfusion - any fluid introduced into a vein, but generally refers to blood given as replacement for blood lost in hemorrhage due to injury, during surgery, or to increase an inadequate blood supply due to a blood disease.

Transient ischemic attack (TIA) - brief period during which an elderly person may be confused, feel dizzy, unable to remember certain events, experience weakness of the legs, tingling or burning of the arms or legs, or have slurred speech. This occurs because of a temporary spasm in one of the blood vessels of the brain that is narrowed by hardening of the arteries, or because of a temporary blockage in a blood vessel. Such attacks may be the warning signals of an impending stroke.

Transplant - the transfer of tissue or an organ from one body area to another, or from one person to another, to replace a missing, diseased, or non-functioning body part or organ.

Tremor - a state of trembling of one or more body parts, such as the hands or the head, due to illness or weakness.

Trendelenburg position - a position in which the patient's head is at an angle of 45° below his pelvis, while he is lying on the operating table, or in bed, if he is being treated for shock.

Trichinosis - a disease caused by a roundworm called Trichinella spiralis, that lives in pigs and is transmitted when a person eats infected pork that has not been adequately cooked. When the worms' larvae enter the bloodstream, they travel to all body tissues, where they cause an inflammatory response. As cysts they can survive in muscle fibers for years. Symptoms include fever, nausea, vomiting, diarrhea and abdominal pain in the first few weeks after infection. Muscle pains and swelling in the affected areas follow the initial symptoms.

Tube feeding - also known as gavage, this procedure is performed when a person is unable to take nourishment by eating and drinking normally. A tube is inserted through the nose or mouth and passed down into the stomach. It is anchored with adhesive tape so that it cannot move, and liquids or blended foods can then be given at prescribed intervals.

Tuberculosis - an infectious disease caused by the Mycobacterium tuberculosis. It affects primarily the lungs, but may also affect other organs, such as the stomach, skin, bones or lymph glands. A particularly severe type of the disease, called miliary tuberculosis, affects most body parts, including the brain. Infected sputum droplets passed through the air by coughing or sneezing transmit the disease to others. Treatment includes medication, adequate nourishment and sufficient rest.

Tularemia - an infectious disease acquired through bites from certain wild animals.

Turista - travelers' diarrhea; an intestinal infection caused by bacteria, viruses, and the toxins they secrete. It is acquired by eating contaminated food, or drinking contaminated water, usually while traveling in foreign areas.

Tympanic membrane - the eardrum; a structure that transmits sounds received from the outer ear by vibrating as the sound waves hit the membrane.

Type and crossmatch - a laboratory test done prior to giving a blood transfusion to make sure the donor's blood type and other blood characteristics match those of the recipient. If this is not done, the recipient may develop a serious, and possibly fatal reaction to the donor's blood.

Typhoid fever - an infectious disease caused by a salmonella bacillus. The disease is transmitted through food, water or milk contaminated by the organism. People who have the disease may continue to act as carriers after they recover by harboring the organisms in their urine and feces. Symptoms include headache, high fever, chills, and a rash on the chest and abdomen. Antibiotics, supportive measures and urine and stool precautions are used in the treatment.

U

Ultrasonography - a diagnostic technique that utilizes the reflection and transmission of ultrasonic waves to determine abnormality or disease of internal body structures.

Uremia - the presence of an abnormally high level of urea and other nitrogenous waste substances in the blood, caused by poorly or non-functioning kidneys.

Ureters - two tubes, each connecting a kidney to the bladder. Urine flows from the kidneys through the ureters into the bladder.

Ureteritis - inflammation of the ureters.

Urethra - the passageway through which urine flows from the bladder out of the body.

Urinary calculus - a stone in the urinary bladder; a hard, solid mass of varying size, formed somewhere in the urinary tract through an accumulation of body chemicals, that is lodged in the bladder. It may be very painful, and produce spasms and other urinary tract problems. A high fluid intake may help to pass the stone, and prevent future occurrences. Diet modifications may be prescribed.

Urinary incontinence - inability to retain or control urination.

Urinary urgency - frequency; a frequent urge to urinate; occurs with enlargement of the prostate that causes pressure on the bladder, with irritation, inflammation and infection of the bladder and the urethra.

Urine culture - a laboratory technique done to determine the presence and type of harmful microorganisms in the urinary tract, so that appropriate treatment can be prescribed.

Urolithiasis - the presence of a stone in the urinary tract.

Urologic - refers to the urinary tract.

Urticaria - hives; a rash usually due to an allergic reaction against food, a psychological event, a drug or some other environmental irritant.

Uterus - the womb.

V

Vaccine - a preparation that contains infectious organisms that are alive, or that have been inactivated or killed. When given to an individual in carefully prescribed amounts, his system is challenged to develop antibodies against these microorganisms and the disease they cause, so that he develops immunity against it.

Varices - varicose veins; a condition in which certain veins become dilated, knotted and weakened due to stress or disease.

Varicocele - enlarged scrotum due to a varicose enlargement of the veins of the spermatic duct, located inside the scrotum.

Varicose ulcer - an open, sore area on a varicose vein caused by erosion of the surface of the vein, or by infection.

Vascular - referring to the circulatory system.

Vascular fragility - a tendency of blood vessels to disintegrate due to brittleness, weakness, infection or disease.

Vasectomy - the process of cutting the vas deferens, which normally carries sperm from the testicles to the penis, for contraceptive purposes.

Vasoconstrictor - an agent or drug that causes blood vessels to constrict or narrow.

Vasodilator - an agent or drug that dilates blood vessels.

Venereal - refers to a disease, infection or other event affecting the genital area.

Ventricle - one of the two lower chambers of the heart. The left ventricle pumps oxygenated blood through the body to nourish the tissues; the right ventricle pumps blood to the lungs to be reoxygenated.

Ventricular failure - failure of the ventricles to pump blood adequately, due to injury, weakness or disease.

Vertigo - severe dizziness.

Vesicle - a bladder, or bladder-like structure, as in the case of a blister or sac-like cavity; caused by friction, inflammation or infection.

Virus - a small particle considered borderline between living and non-living matter. Viruses consist of molecules that are composed of proteins and nucleic acids. When they gain access to a living cell, they can change the cell's usual functions and reproductive capacity. Some viruses are useful, others cause disease.

Vitamin toxicity - a form of poisoning that occurs when a person ingests excessive amounts of vitamins.

Vitreous humor - the semifluid substance contained in the eyeball behind the lens.

Void - the process of urinating.

Vulva - the external female genitalia.

W

Wart - a benign hard growth on the skin caused by a virus; also known as verruca. May occur anywhere on the body, but appears most frequently on the sole of the foot, where it is called a plantar wart.

Wet lung - lung filled with fluid.

White blood cell- leukocyte; a constituent of blood, formed in the bone marrow and the lymph glands. White blood cells defend the body against infection.

Wound culture - a laboratory procedure done to determine whether a wound is infected, and to identify the microorganism that causes the infection.

X

X-chromosome - a sex chromosome; if a fetus has two X-chromosomes in its genetic make-up, it will develop as a female.

Xeroderma - a skin condition which produces excessively dry skin.

Y

Y-chromosome - a sex chromosome; if a fetus has a Y-chromosome in its genetic makeup, it will develop as a male.

Yellow fever - an infectious disease that is transmitted by various species of mosquitoes that carry the causative organism. High fever and jaundice are the main symptoms.

Z

Zinc - a trace element that aids wound healing, and acts as a component of several body enzymes.

Zoonosis - an infection or infestation present in animals as well as in man.

PERSONAL HEALTH DIARY

Doctor's appointments

Date	Doctor	Checkup or Complaint	Treatment given or advice

Dental care

Date	Dentist	Checkup or Complaint	Cleaning, Prophylaxis Treatment given

Prescriptions filled

Drug dose; how often	Doctor who ordered it	Reason for taking it	Date of purchase or refill

Nonprescription drugs

Drug	Reason for purchase (complaint)	Date purchased	Effect

Prescriptions filled

Drug dose; how often	Doctor who ordered it	Reason for taking it	Date of purchase or refill

Nonprescription drugs

Drug	Reason for purchase (complaint)	Date purchased	Effect

Weight Record

Check weight each month

Month	Weight

Blood Pressure Record

Take blood pressure as instructed by your doctor

Date	Blood Pressure	Date	Blood Pressure

Health aids record

Aid or equipment	date purchased	due for checkup or maintenance problems
Eye glasses		
Contact lenses		
Arch supports		
Ace bandage or Elastic stockings		
Hearing aid		
Blood pressure equipment (self-testing)		